FOR THE INSTRUCTOR

- Want an easy way to test your students prior to an exam that *doesn't* create more work for you?

- Want to access your supplements *without* having to bring them all to class?

- Want to integrate current happenings into your lectures *without* all the searching and extra work?

- Want an *easy* way to get your course on-line?

- Want to *free up more time* in your day to get more done?

Of course you do!

Then check out your
Online Learning Centre!

- Downloadable Supplements
- PageOut
- Online Resources

McGraw-Hill Ryerson

Higher Learning. Forward Thinking.™

K. Van Dongen

A Child's World

Infancy Through Adolescence

First Canadian Edition

Diane E. Papalia

Sally Wendkos Olds

Ruth Duskin Feldman

Richard Kruk
University of Manitoba

McGraw-Hill Ryerson

Toronto   Montréal   Burr Ridge, IL   Dubuque, IA   Madison, WI   New York
San Francisco   St. Louis   Bangkok   Bogotá   Caracas   Kuala Lumpur   Lisbon
London   Madrid   Mexico City   Milan   New Delhi   Santiago   Seoul   Singapore
Sydney   Taipei

A Child's World
Infancy Through Adolescence
First Canadian Edition

Statistics Canada information is used with the permission of the Minister of Industry, as Minister responsible for Statistics Canada. Information on the availability of the wide range of data from Statistics Canada can be obtained from Statistics Canada's Regional Offices, its World Wide Web site at http://www.statcan.ca, and its toll-free access number 1-800-263-1136.

ISBN: 0-07-090567-3

1 2 3 4 5 6 7 8 9 10 TCP 0 9 8 7 6 5 4

Printed and bound in Canada

Care has been taken to trace ownership of copyright material contained in this text; however, the publisher will welcome any information that enables them to rectify any reference or credit for subsequent editions.

Vice President, Editorial and Media Technology: Patrick Ferrier
Sponsoring Editor: James Buchanan
Senior Developmental Editor: Jennifer DiDomenico
Marketing Manager: Kim Verhaeghe
Copy Editor: Ian MacKenzie
Production Coordinator: Andrée Davis
Page Layout: First Folio
Cover Design: Dianna Little
Interior Design: © Jim Cummins/Taxi
Printer: Transcontinental Printing Group

National Library of Canada Cataloguing in Publication

A child's world : infancy through adolescence / Diane E. Papalia ... [et al.]. — Canadian ed.

Includes bibliographical references and index.
ISBN 0-07-090567-3

1. Child development. 2. Child psychology. 3. Adolescence. I. Papalia, Diane E.

HQ767.9.C4438 2003   **305.231**   **C2002-906084-2**

To our parents,
Madeline and Edward Papalia,
Leah and Samuel Wendkos,
Boris and Rita Duskin,
and Walerian and Zofia Kruk
for their unfailing love, nurturance, and
confidence in us, and for their abiding conviction
that childhood is a wondrous time of life.

And to our children,
Anna Victoria,
Nancy, Jennifer, and Dorri,
Steven, Laurie, and Heidi,
Ian Benjamin Austin,
and our grandchildren,
Stefan, Maika, Anna, Lisa, and Nina,
Daniel, Emmett, Rita, Carol, Eve, and Isaac,
who have helped us revisit childhood
and see its wonders and challenges
with new eyes.

About the Authors

As a professor, **Diane E. Papalia** taught thousands of undergraduates at the University of Wisconsin-Madison. She received her bachelor's degree, majoring in psychology, from Vassar College and both her master's degree in child development and family relations and her Ph.D. in lifespan developmental psychology from West Virginia University. She has published numerous articles in such professional journals as *Human Development, International Journal of Aging and Human Development, Sex Roles, Journal of Experimental Child Psychology,* and *Journal of Gerontology.* Most of these papers have dealt with her major research focus, cognitive development from childhood through old age. She is especially interested in intellectual development and factors that contribute to the maintenance of intellectual functioning. She is a Fellow in the Gerontological Society of America. She is the co-author, with Sally Wendkos Olds and Ruth Duskin Feldman, of *Human Development,* now in its eighth edition, and of *Adult Development and Aging,* with Harvey L. Sterns, Ruth Duskin Feldman, and Cameron J. Camp, now entering its second edition.

Sally Wendkos Olds is an award-winning professional writer who has written more than 200 articles in leading magazines and is the author or co-author of six books addressed to general readers, in addition to the three textbooks she has co-authored with Diane E. Papalia. Her book *The Complete Book of Breastfeeding,* a classic since its publication in 1972, was reissued in 1999 in a completely updated and expanded edition; more than 2 million copies are in print. She is also the author of *The Working Parents' Survival Guide* and *The Eternal Garden: Seasons of Our Sexuality* and the co-author of *Raising a Hyperactive Child* (winner of the Family Service Association of America National Media Award) and *Helping Your Child Find Values to Live By.* She has spoken widely on the topics of her books and articles to both professional and lay audiences, in person and on television and radio. She received her bachelor's degree from the University of Pennsylvania, where she majored in English literature and minored in psychology. She was elected to Phi Beta Kappa and graduated summa cum laude.

About the Authors

Ruth Duskin Feldman is an award-winning writer and educator. With Diane E. Papalia and Sally Wendkos Olds, she co-authored the fourth, seventh, and eighth editions of *Human Development* and the eighth edition of *A Child's World*. She also is co-author, with Dr. Papalia, Cameron J. Camp, and Harvey Sterns, of *Adult Development and Aging*. A former teacher, she has developed educational materials for all levels from elementary school through university and has prepared ancillaries to accompany the Papalia-Olds books. She is author or co-author of four books addressed to general readers, including *Whatever Happened to the Quiz Kids? Perils and Profits of Growing up Gifted* (republished in 2000 as an Authors Guild Backinprint edition of iuniverse.com). She has written for numerous newspapers and magazines and has lectured extensively and made national and local media appearances throughout the United States on education and gifted children. She received her bachelor's degree from Northwestern University, where she graduated with highest distinction and was elected to Phi Beta Kappa.

Richard Kruk has taught undergraduate and graduate students at universities and colleges, in Quebec, Ontario, Manitoba, and Saskatchewan, and is currently a member of the faculty at the Department of Psychology of the University of Manitoba. He received his bachelor's degree, specializing in psychology, from the University of Toronto, and both his master's degree and Ph.D. from the Ontario Institute for Studies in Education of the University of Toronto, where he focused on reading difficulty, perceptual development, and applied linguistics. He continued his research training in an SSHRC-sponsored post-doctoral fellowship in Australia, examining the relationships between perceptual development and cognitive skills related to reading. He has published articles in such professional journals as *Cognitive Neuropsychology*, *Journal of Learning Disability*, and *Human Factors*, written book chapters on reading processes, and co-edited, with Dale Willows and Evelyn Corcos, *Visual Processes in Reading and Reading Disability*, published by Lawrence Erlbaum Associates. Most of his published work has dealt with his major research focus: perceptual and neurological factors related to reading skill development and to difficulties children face in learning to read.

Dana Gross, chief consultant to the U.S. Ninth Edition, received her Ph.D. in child psychology from the Institute of Child Development at the University of Minnesota. Since 1988 she has been at St. Olaf College, where she is an associate professor of psychology, director of Linguistic Studies, and an affiliate faculty member of the Asian Studies department. Her broad teaching and research interests include perception, language, cognition, and social cognition, as well as cross-cultural child development. She has published in several professional journals, has presented her work at numerous conferences, and co-authored a chapter in *Developing Theories of Mind,* edited by Astington, Harris, and Olson. Dr. Gross has prepared instructors' manuals and test banks for several McGraw-Hill textbooks and served as chief consultant on the eighth edition of *A Child's World,* and on Papalia, Olds, and Feldman's recent publication of *Human Development,* Eighth Edition.

Brief Contents

Contents

Part 3 Infancy and Toddlerhood

Part 4 Early Childhood

Part 5   Middle Childhood

Part 6   Adolescence

Preface

Writing the First Canadian Edition of *A Child's World* has been both a delight and a challenge. It has been a delight to co-author a text designed specifically to meet the needs of Canadian child-development students and instructors and to contribute to the benefits that Canadian students reap when they are provided with information that is relevant to their own experiences. At the same time, it has been a rewarding challenge to identify exactly what it means to study child development in a Canadian context and from a Canadian point of view, and to choose from the wealth of recent high-quality Canadian research on child development.

Before I began writing, I reflected on my own experiences growing up as an immigrant in a country in which identity is not understood in a simple way. I encountered this issue as a young adolescent embarking on my first secondary school debating exercise, arguing valiantly for the perspective that Canada was not a "branch plant" of the United States. If I had known then what I now know of Canada's cultural values, triumphs, and difficulties, and our own place within a global culture, I am sure I would have made more of an impact on my debating opponents.

With my school debating experience in mind, I have striven to make *A Child's World*, First Canadian Edition, relevant to Canadian students and instructors with excellent Canadian research and statistics and continual attention to the fact that Canada is a unique country with two official languages and a multitude of cultures. The First Canadian Edition is based on our values: We celebrate our diversity as a population and are welcoming of the differences in views, attitudes, and ideas that exist among us. Each chapter has been reconceived to discuss Canadian developmental contexts and values with a seamless and organic incorporation of Canadian and international research. Over 400 new Canadian references have been added to this edition.

Aims of the First Canadian Edition

The primary aims of this First Canadian Edition are both different from and similar to those of the first nine American editions of *A Child's World*. The specifically Canadian aims are to emphasize research, issues, and values that are uniquely Canadian and to highlight excellence in Canadian research and policy aimed at improving our understanding of children and promoting healthy development. This text shares the aims of previous editions of *A Child's World* in its emphasis on the continuity of development from conception to adolescence, highlighting of interrelationships among the physical, cognitive, and psychosocial realms of development, and integration of theoretical, research-related, and practical concerns.

Retained Features

The First Canadian Edition retains the proven, student-driven pedagogical features of the previous American editions and adapts them for Canadian students and instructors:

- A **chronological approach** provides a sense of the multi-faceted sweep of human development, as we get to know first the developing person-to-be in the uterus, then the infant and toddler, then the young child, the schoolchild, and the adolescent on the brink of adulthood.
- A **personal, dynamic writing style** appeals to students of all ages and backgrounds. Complex issues and topics in human development are clearly explained and illustrated throughout the text.
- A **comprehensive learning system** helps students build upon their knowledge as they move through each chapter and test their mastery of the content. A coordinated set of marginal features, including *Guideposts*, *Checkpoints*, and *What's Your View?* questions, guides student learning. Please see the visual walk-through on pages xxi-xxii to preview the learning system in detail.
- Four types of **thematic boxes** allow students to explore high-interest topics in depth and forge links between child-development theory and practice: *The Research World, Around the World, The Everyday World*, and *The Social World*. Please see the visual walk-through on pages xxiii-xxv to preview these boxed features.

Content Changes: What's New in the First Canadian Edition?

In this adaptation, we have taken special pains to draw on the most recent information available from Canadian and international sources. In line with the growing recognition of child development as a rigorous scientific enterprise, we have broadened the research base of each chapter even more extensively than before and have updated throughout, using the most current available statistics. We have striven to make our coverage as concise and readable as possible, while still doing justice to the vast scope and significance of current theoretical and research work.

This edition continues to expand on cultural coverage, reflecting the diversity of the population in Canada and in other countries around the world. Our photo illustrations show our commitment to depicting the diversity of the Canadian cultural mosaic. The text provides new or enhanced discussions of such topics as cultural differences in temperament, parenting styles, and goals of preschool education; the role of culture in cognitive development; and cultural influences on aggression and school achievement.

This edition also has expanded coverage of historical influences. In addition to our treatment in chapter 1 of the history of the study of child development in Canada, discussions in other parts of the book place issues ranging from infant feeding to homework in a historical context.

Among the other important topics given new or greatly revised coverage are the following:

Chapter 1: Studying a Child's World

- The Social World Box: The Residential School Experience of Aboriginal Children
- History of Canadian child-development research
- Highlights of Canadian immigration and family history
- Description of the Aboriginal Canadian context
- Highlights from the Canadian National Longitudinal Survey of Children and Youth (NLSCY)

Chapter 2: A Child's World: How We Discover It

- Miller's relational model of development
- Canadian cross-cultural research on friendship

- Expanded discussion of the importance of variance in correlational research
- Description of NLSCY results on risk and protective factors
- Example of Siegler's microgenetic method
- The Tri-Council Policy Statement on ethics

Chapter 3: Forming a New Life: Conception, Heredity, and Environment

- Canadian birth statistics
- Canadian government policies on assisted reproductive technologies
- Human Genome Project at the Hospital for Sick Children
- Canadian legal information added to The Everyday World box on Alternative Ways to Parenthood
- Policies on genetic testing in Canada
- Rise in cases of autism and autism-related conditions

Chapter 4: Pregnancy and Prenatal Development

- Focus vignette on Canadian FAS success story
- The Social World box: Fetal Welfare and Mothers' Rights with Canadian perspectives
- Canadian research and policy initiatives on prenatal and postnatal health

Chapter 5: Birth and the Newborn Baby

- History of Canadian childbirth practices
- Current policies and statistics in Canadian childbirth practices
- Canadian statistics on high-risk birth events including perinatal conditions and low birth weight
- Canadian research on effects of extremely low birth weight

Chapter 6: Physical Development and Health During the First Three Years

- Research and recommendations on early feeding, from Canadian sources
- Added information on Romanian adoptive children
- Recent research on visual and neurological development
- Canadian statistics and policy statements on infant health

Chapter 7: Cognitive Development during the First Three Years

- Discussion of the use of U.S.-based intelligence tests in Canada
- Influence of early years experiences on neurological development
- Canadian research on language development in infancy

Chapter 8: Psychosocial Development during the First Three Years

- Canadian perspectives on infant pain and crying
- Parental employment and child care statistics in Canada
- Immigrant experience and parenting
- NLSCY data on risk factors in emotional disorders, patterns of attachment, and impact of stability of child-care arrangements
- Canadian research on social referencing, birth order, and social development

Chapter 9: Physical Development and Health in Early Childhood

- Growth norms reflect new CDC charts
- Policy from Canada's Food Guide to Healthy Eating
- Canadian statistics on children's diets and food-bank use
- Dietary concerns in remote and Aboriginal communities
- Oral health
- Canadian mortality statistics for toddlers
- Hospitalization rates and causes for Canadian children
- Statistics Canada's Low Income Cut-off, and effects of poverty in Canada
- The Social World box on How Poverty Affects Children in Canada
- Exposure to environmental tobacco smoke
- Childhood maltreatment in Canada
- Neighbourhood cohesion in Canadian child development

Chapter 10: Cognitive Development in Early Childhood

- Canadian research on false beliefs and childhood eyewitness testimony
- Additional Canadian perspectives on theory of mind
- Canadian studies on literacy and academic development in childhood
- Aboriginal perspectives on early childhood education
- Aboriginal Head Start initiatives
- Age-of-entry to kindergarten effects

Chapter 11: Psychosocial Development in Early Childhood

- Focus vignette on Buffy Sainte-Marie
- Canadian perspectives and research on corporal punishment
- Positive parenting; Aboriginal and immigrant approaches to parenting
- Canadian research on altruism and aggression in children

Chapter 12: Physical Development and Health in Middle Childhood

- Focus vignette on Terry Fox
- Growth rates of Aboriginal children
- Nutritional problems of Canadian children, especially in remote communities
- Obesity in Canadian children
- Sports participation and fitness of children in Canada
- Activity limitations, children with special needs
- Visual problems, asthma in Canadian children
- HIV incidence in pregnant Canadians
- Non-insulin-dependent diabeties
- Injury statistics for Canadian children

Chapter 13: Cognitive Development in Middle Childhood

- Canadian research on problem solving and mathematics skill development
- Moral development in Canadian children
- Problems in use of U.S. intelligence tests with Canadian school-aged children, particularly immigrant and Aboriginal children
- Dynamic cognitive assessment approach
- Literacy learning, and balanced literacy approach
- French immersion in Canada
- Academic achievement indicators in Canadian children
- Canadian children with special needs
- Internet use by Canadian children

Chapter 14: Psychosocial Development in Middle Childhood

- Diversity of parenting practices in Canadian ethnic groups
- Developmental trends in parental employment
- Canadian trends in childhood poverty, risk and protective factors
- Changes in family structures in Canada
- Canadian research on sibling and peer relations
- NLSCY data on childhood aggression
- Canadian research on bullying and conduct disorder in children
- Patterns of depression in Aboriginal and non-Aboriginal children
- Mental health status of immigrant children

Chapter 15: Physical Development and Health in Adolescence

- Canadian statistics on health status and health-care use by youth
- Physical activity statistics for Canadian adolescents
- Nutrition and obesity in Canadian youth
- Body image, self-perception, and body-esteem in young Canadians
- Research and prevalence statistics on drug, alcohol, and tobacco use by Canadian youth
- Canadian initiatives for drug problems
- STDs in Canadian adolescents
- Maltreatment of Canadian youth
- Adolescent risk behaviours
- Suicide prevalence in Canadian Aboriginal and non-Aboriginal youth

Chapter 16: Cognitive Development in Adolescence

- Moral development and parenting practices
- Academic achievement in Canadian youth, immigrant populations, and comparisons with other countries
- Drop-out statistics for Canadian adolescents
- Transition to the workplace in Canada
- Culturally sensitive career counselling for Aboriginal youth

Chapter 17: Psychosocial Development in Adolescence

- Focus vignette on David Suzuki
- Ethnic factors in identity formation
- Canadian multiculturalism
- Adaptation and identity of immigrant youth
- Sexual behaviour of Canadian youth, sex-education practices
- Adolescent pregnancy and regional differences
- Adolescent–parent relationships and "connectedness"
- Friendship and loneliness in Canadian youth
- The Social World box: An Epidemic of Youth Violence with a focus on Taber, Alberta
- Conduct disorder in Canadian adolescent women
- Youth crime and intervention in Canada

Supplementary Materials

Instructor Resources

i-Learning Sales Specialist

Your *Integrated Learning sales specialist* is a McGraw-Hill Ryerson representative who has the experience, product knowledge, training, and support to help you assess and integrate any of the below-noted products, technology, and services into your course for optimum teaching and learning performance. Whether it's how to use our test bank software, to help your students improve their grades, or to put your entire course on-line, your *i*-Learning sales specialist is there to help. Contact your local *i*-Learning sales specialist today to learn how to maximize all McGraw-Hill Ryerson resources!

eServices

McGraw-Hill Ryerson offers a unique services package designed for Canadian faculty. Our mission is to equip providers of higher education with superior tools and resources required for excellence in teaching. For additional information visit www.mcgrawhill.ca/highereducation/eservices/

Instructor's Manual

The Instructor's Manual, fully adapted for a Canadian audience, provides a variety of tools for both seasoned instructors and those new to the child development course. An innovative annotated outline called the Total Teaching Package has been added to each chapter. Building on a traditional chapter outline, all the resources available to the instructor have been correlated to the main concepts in each chapter. The learning objectives, key terms, discussion and lecture topics, and the Take a Stand feature, which presents controversial issues in a debate format, have all been fully adapted to accord with the First Canadian Edition.

Test Bank

This comprehensive test bank has been fully adapted for Canada and includes a wide range of multiple-choice, fill-in-the-blank, critical thinking, and essay questions from which instructors can create their test material. Each item is designated as factual, conceptual, or applied, as defined by Benjamin Bloom's Taxonomy of Educational Objectives, and is also linked explicitly to specific learning objectives.

Computerized Test Bank

This test bank on CD-ROM works on both Macintosh and Windows platforms and contains all the questions in the print version with editing and selection capabilities.

Online Learning Centre

This extensive website, designed specifically to accompany *A Child's World,* First Canadian Edition, offers an array of resources for both instructor and student. A password-protected downloadable Instructor's Manual, Microsoft® PowerPoint® Presentations, author-selected images from the database, Web links, and more resources can be found by logging on to the OLC at **www.mcgrawhill.ca/college/papalia**.

PowerWeb

This unique online tool provides premium content such as current articles, curriculum-based materials, weekly updates with assessment, informative and timely world news, refereed Web links, research tools, interactive exercises, and more. A PowerWeb access card is packaged for *free* with each new copy of the text! Visit **www.dushkin.com/powerweb** for a tour!

Annual Editions—Child Growth and Development

Published by Dushkin.McGraw-Hill, this is a collection of articles on topics related to the latest research and thinking in child growth and development.

PageOut—Build Your Own Course Website in Less Than an Hour

You don't have to be a computer whiz to create a website, especially with an exclusive McGraw-Hill product called PageOut™. It requires no prior knowledge of HTML. No long hours of coding. And no design skills on your part. Check out **www.pageout.ne**t.

For the Student

Study Guide

Closely correlated to the First Canadian Edition of the text and its innovative learning system, this revised Study Guide includes learning objectives, a chapter outline and brief overview, and a wide variety of quizzing tools such as multiple-choice, fill-in-the-blank, and true or false questions complete with answer keys. Recommendations for further readings are also included, as well as critical thinking exercises that can be used as study group tools.

PowerWeb

This unique online tool provides premium content such as current articles, curriculum-based materials, weekly updates with assessment, informative and timely world news, refereed Web links, research tools, interactive exercises, and more. A PowerWeb access card is packaged for *free* with each new copy of the text! Visit **www.dushkin.com/powerweb** for a tour!

Multimedia Courseware for Child Development

This interactive set of two CD-ROMs brings the central concepts and classic experiments in child development to life with video footage and other integrated digital media. To preview the courseware, please visit **www.mhhe.com/socscience/devel/patterson/index.html**.

Making the Grade CD-ROM

User-friendly, this CD-ROM gives students an opportunity to test their comprehension of the course material. It contains a Learning Assessment questionnaire that help students determine what type of learner they are. It offers interactive multiple-choice questions (approximately 25 questions per chapter) with feedback on each answer chosen so that a student not only realizes an answer is correct/incorrect but understands why this is so.

Online Learning Centre

The official website for the text contains chapter outlines, practice quizzes that can be e-mailed to the instructor, links to relevant websites, and other interactive activities such as crosswords and flashcards. Visit **www.mcgrawhill.ca/college/papalia**.

Acknowledgments

I am grateful to the many friends and colleagues who, through their work and interest, helped clarify my thinking about child development in the Canadian context. I am especially grateful for the valuable help given by those who reviewed the Ninth American Edition of *A Child's World* and the manuscript drafts of this First Canadian Edition. Their evaluations and suggestions helped immensely in identifying areas, issues, and topics that Canadian students of child development would find relevant, useful, and interesting. Not only did the reviewers identify research on issues that are important to include in a Canadian child-development text, but they also made interesting suggestions for adding information that is timely. These reviewers are as follows:

Scott Adler, York University
Gary Anderson, Camosun College
Pearl Arden, Camosun College
Anna Baas-Anderson, Sheridan College
Gordon Beckett, Sheridan College
Christine Chambers, University of British Columbia
Maple Melder Crozier, University College of the Fraser Valley
Nukte Edguer, Brandon University
Valerie Gonzales, University of Victoria
Mary Knight, Durham College
Bev Lenihan, Camosun College

David Lockwood, Humber College
Carole Massing, Grant MacEwan College
Nicki Monahan, George Brown College
R. Ronald Niemi, University of Manitoba
Cheryl Park, Cambrian College
Linda Pipe, Loyalist College
Marilyn Quinn, Niagara College
Colleen Thomas, George Brown College

I also extend thanks to the many reviewers who contributed to the U.S. Ninth Edition text: Frank Belcastro, Dubuque University; Kathleen Bey, Palm Beach Community College; Raimee Robeson Cooney, Creighton University; Rebecca Eaton, University of Alabama in Huntsville; Diane Feibel, Raymond Walters College-University of Cincinnati; Karla Gingerich, Colorado State University; Earl Wade Gladdin, Bob Jones University; Bernard Gorman, Nassau Community College; Alec Gross, Brandeis University; Susan Harris, Northern Arizona University; Yolanda Jackson, University of Kansas; Lesley Lambright, Macomb Community College; Lorraine Martin, Grossmont College; Pamela A. Meinert, Kent State University; Wendy Micham, Victor Valley College; Ligaya P. Paguio, University of Georgia; Sandra Portko, Grand Valley State University; Joe Price, San Diego State University; Norma Ritchey, Morton College; Mary Rogers, Inver Hills Community College; Irvin Schonfeld, City College of the City University of New York; Lansdale Shaffmaster, Keystone College; Peggy Skinner, South Plains College; Mary Helen Spear, Prince George's Community College; Colleen Stevenson, Muskingum College; Vetta Thompson, University of Missouri; and Alida Westman, Eastern Michigan University.

I appreciate the strong support I have from McGraw-Hill Ryerson. My special thanks go to Veronica Visentin, who first approached me with the opportunity to write this adaptation; James Buchanan, sponsoring editor; Kelly Dickson, manager, Editorial Services; Andrée Davis, production coordinator; Dianna Little, cover designer; and Ian MacKenzie, copy editor at n2n Publishing. Of special note is Jennifer DiDomenico, senior developmental editor at McGraw-Hill Ryerson, who saw me through every stage of writing this adaptation. Jennifer's support in listening to my concerns and worries, suggesting alternative approaches, and encouraging me to meet the challenges of writing this adaptation creatively and rigorously, contributed immeasurably to the excellence of this project.

I also thank the authors of the Ninth American Edition of *A Child's World*, Diane Papalia, Sally Wendkos Olds, and Ruth Duskin Feldman, for producing the excellent text upon which this edition is based. As well, I thank Dana Gross Ph.D., who contributed to the research and conceptual development of the Ninth American Edition.

Thanks also go to my friends and colleagues in the Department of Psychology at the University of Manitoba. My many discussions with them about issues in Canadian developmental psychology and the process of writing a Canadian adaptation, and the spirit of collegiality that pervades the department, were great sources of inspiration to me. As well, I had the privilege of working with an excellent graduate student in developmental psychology, Heather Tiede. Heather identified much of the current Canadian research used in the text, offered useful and interesting insights on issues included in the adaptation, and worked overtime in helping me keep to my appointed timeline for the changes to the book. Finally, I wish to acknowledge the tangible and intangible support that my family provided me in completing this project. My partner, Brenda Austin-Smith, gave love, support, insight, criticism, and immense patience in living with what she affectionately referred to as the "fourth member of the family." To Ian, I offer thanks for making sure, in his own way, that I know exactly what it is to live in a child's world—he is the ultimate inspiration.

As the co-author of the First Canadian Edition, I welcome and appreciate comments from readers. These will help improve the Canadian adaptation of *A Child's World*.

Richard Kruk

Visual Walk-Through

A comprehensive, unified **Learning System** in the First Canadian Edition will help students focus their reading and review and retain what they learn. It forms the conceptual framework for each chapter, is carried across all text supplements, and contains four parts:

Checkpoint ✔

Can you . . .

✔ Trace highlights in the evolution of the study of child development?

✔ Name some pioneers in that study and summarize their most important contributions?

✔ Give examples of practical applications of research on child development?

Checkpoints

These detailed marginal questions, placed at the end of major sections of text, enable students to test their understanding of what they have read. Students should be encouraged to stop and review any section for which they cannot answer one or more Checkpoints.

Guideposts for Study

These topical questions, similar to Learning Objectives, are first posed near the beginning of each chapter to capture students' interest and motivate them to look for answers as they read. The questions are broad enough to form a coherent outline of each chapter's content, but specific enough to invite careful study. Each Guidepost is repeated in the margin at the beginning of the section that deals with the topic in question and is repeated in the Chapter Summary to facilitate study.

Guideposts for Study

1. What is child development, and how has its study evolved?

2. What are six fundamental points on which consensus has emerged?

3. What do developmental scientists study?

4. What are the three major aspects and five periods of child development?

5. What kinds of influences make one child different from another?

What's Your View?

These periodic marginal questions challenge students to interpret, apply, or critically evaluate information presented in the text.

What's your view **?**

- Why do you think various societies divide the periods of development differently?

Chapter Summaries

The Chapter Summaries are organized by the major topics in the chapter, with Guidepost questions appearing under the appropriate major topics. Each Guidepost is followed by a series of brief statements restating the most important points that fall under it, thus creating a self-testing question-answer format. Students should be encouraged to try to answer each Guidepost question before reading the summary material that follows. Key terms are listed for review under relevant Summary topics, in the order in which they first appear, and are cross-referenced to pages where they are defined.

Summary and Key Terms

The Study of Child Development: Then and Now

Guidepost 1 What is child development, and how has its study evolved?

- Child development is the scientific study of processes of change and stability.

- The scientific study of child development began toward the end of the nineteenth century. Adolescence was not considered a separate phase of development until the twentieth century. The field of child development is now part of the study of the entire lifespan, or human development.

- Ways of studying child development are still evolving, making use of advanced technologies.

- The distinction between basic and applied research has become less meaningful.

Guidepost 2 What are six fundamental points on which consensus has emerged?

- Consensus has emerged on several important points: (1) the interrelationship of domains of development, (2) the existence of a wide range of individual differences, (3) bidirectionality of influence, (4) the importance of history and culture, (5) children's potential for resilience, and (6) continuity of development throughout life.

  child development (5)

Child Development Today: An Introduction to the Field

Guidepost 3 What do developmental scientists study?

- Developmental scientists study developmental change, both quantitative, and qualitative, as well as stability of personality and behaviour.

  quantitative change (8)   qualitative change (8)

Guidepost 4 What are three major aspects and five periods of child development?

- The three major domains, or aspects, of development are physical, cognitive, and psychosocial. Each affects the others.

- The concept of periods of development is a social construction. In this book, child development is divided into five periods: the prenatal period, infancy and toddlerhood, early childhood, middle childhood, and adolescence. In each period, children have characteristic developmental needs and tasks.

  social construction (9)

Influences on Development

Guidepost 5 What kinds of influences make one child different from another?

- Influences on development come from both heredity and environment. Many typical changes during childhood are related to maturation. Individual differences increase with age.

  **individual differences (9)   heredity (10)   environment (10)
  maturation (10)**

- In some societies, the nuclear family predominates; in others, the extended family.

- Socio-economic status (SES) affects developmental processes and outcomes through the quality of home and neighbourhood environments, of nutrition, medical care, supervision, and schooling. The most powerful neighbourhood influences seem to be neighbourhood income and human capital. Multiple risk factors increase the likelihood of poor outcomes.

- Important environmental influences stem from ethnicity, culture, and the historical context. In large, multiethnic societies, immigrant groups often acculturate to the majority culture while preserving aspects of their own.

  **nuclear family (10)   extended family (10)
  socio-economic status (SES) (12)   risk factors (12)   culture (13)
  ethnic group (13)**

Other Special Features in This Edition

The First Canadian Edition includes four different types of boxed material. Each box contains a critical-thinking *What's Your View?* question, as well as *Check It Out!*, which directs students to the Online Learning Centre.

"The Research World" Boxes

These boxes report on exciting new developments or current controversies in the field of child development. These include treatments of such contemporary topics as whether there is a critical period for language acquisition; whether early temperament can predict adult personality; the case against corporal punishment; and the home-work debate.

The Research World

Box 1-2 *Is There a Critical Period for Language Acquisition?*

In 1970, a 13½-year-old girl named Genie (not her real name) was discovered in a suburb of Los Angeles (Curtiss, 1977; Fromkin, Krashen, Curtiss, Rigler, & Rigler, 1974; Pines, 1981; Rymer, 1993). The victim of an abusive father, she had been confined for nearly 12 years to a small room in her parents' home, tied to a potty chair and cut off from normal human contact. She weighed only 59 pounds, could not straighten her arms or legs, could not chew, had no bladder or bowel control, and did not speak. She recognized only her own name and the word *sorry.*

Only three years before, Eric Lenneberg (1967, 1969) had proposed that there is a critical period for language acquisition, beginning in early infancy and ending around puberty. Lenneberg argued that it would be difficult, if not impossible, for a child who had not yet acquired language to do so after that age.

The discovery of Genie offered the opportunity for a test of Lenneberg's hypothesis. Could Genie be taught to speak, or was it too late? The U.S. National Institutes of Mental Health (NIMH) funded a study, and a series of researchers took over Genie's care and gave her intensive testing and language training.

Genie's progress during the next few years (before the NIMH withdrew funding and her mother regained custody) both challenges and supports the idea of a critical period for language acquisition. Genie did learn some simple words and could string them together into primitive, but rule-governed, sentences. She also learned the fundamentals of sign language. But she never used language normally, and "her speech remained, for the most part, like a somewhat garbled telegram" (Pines, 1981, p. 29). When her mother became unable to manage Genie's challenging behaviour, welfare offices placed Genie into a series of poorly supervised foster homes, where she regressed into total silence.

What explains Genie's initial progress and her inability to sustain it? The fact that she was just beginning to show signs of puberty at age 13½ may indicate that she was still in the critical period, though near its end. The fact that she apparently had learned a few words before being locked up at the age of 20 months may mean that her language-learning mechanisms may have been triggered early in the critical period, allowing later learning to occur. On the other hand, the fact that she was so abused and neglected may have retarded her so much—

emotionally, socially, and cognitively—that, like Victor, she cannot be considered a true test of the critical period (Curtiss, 1977).

Case studies like those of Genie and Victor dramatize the difficulty of acquiring language after the early years of life, but they do not permit conclusive judgments because there are too many complicating factors. Researchers seeking study participants who lack early exposure to language, but whose environment and development are otherwise normal, have therefore turned to deaf persons for whom American Sign Language (ASL) is the primary language. In one cross-sectional study, the older a person had been when first exposed to ASL, the more likely that person was to sign ungrammatically and inconsistently (Newport, 1991).

A cross-sectional study of Chinese and Korean immigrants supports a critical period for second-language learning as well. The later their age of arrival, up to late adolescence, the worse their mastery of English, which held steady at a low level among those who had arrived as adults (Newport, 1991).

If a critical period for language learning exists, what explains it? Do the brain's mechanisms for acquiring language decay as the brain matures? That would seem strange, since other cognitive abilities improve. An alternative hypothesis is that this very increase in cognitive sophistication interferes with an adolescent's or adult's ability to learn a language. Young children acquire language in small chunks that can be readily digested. Older learners, when they first begin learning a language, tend to absorb a great deal at once and then may have trouble analyzing and interpreting it (Newport, 1991).

What's your view

Do you see any ethical problems in the studies of Genie and Victor? Is the knowledge gained from such studies worth any possible damage to the individuals involved? (Keep this question, and your answer, in mind when you read the section on ethics of research in chapter 2.)

Check it out

For more information on this topic, go to **www.mcgrawhill.ca/college/papalia.**

Box 8-2 *Fatherhood in Three Cultures*

Fatherhood has different meanings in different cultures. In some societies, fathers are more involved in their young children's lives—economically, emotionally, and in time spent—than in other cultures. In many parts of the world, what it means to be a father has changed—and is changing (Engle & Breaux, 1998.)*

These changes can be accelerated when families immigrate to Canada (Howell, 1996). The great diversity among immigrants coming to Canada means that some groups experience changes more than others. However, children often can have untraditional relationships with their parents, when world language skills in English or French are better than those of their parents. The differences in values between those of the country of origin and of Canada can become a cause of concern, with the influences of school, peer groups, television, and other sources of socialization that can lead to differences in values between the parents and their children (Howell, 1996).

Urbanization in West Africa and Inner Mongolia
In Cameroon and other rural areas of West Africa (Nsamenang, 1987, 1992a, 1992b), men often have more than one wife, and children grow up in large extended families linked to kinship-based clans. Although children guarantee the perpetuation of a man's family line, they belong to the kinship group, not just to the parents. After weaning, they may have multiple caregivers or may even be given to other members of the group to raise.

The father has the dominant position in the family and gives his children their connection with the clan. The mother is literally the breadwinner, responsible for providing her children's food, but the father controls his wives and their earnings; and wives compete for their husbands' favour. Fathers are primarily disciplinarians and advisers. They have little contact with infants but serve as guides, companions, and models for older children.

With the coming of urbanization and the values of industrialized societies, these traditional patterns are breaking up. Many men are pursuing financial goals and are spending almost no time with their children. With the vanishing of traditional folkways, these men no longer know how to be fathers. They can no longer tell folk tales to young children around the fire or teach their sons how to do a man's work.

Similarly, among the Huhot of Inner Mongolia, a province of China, fathers traditionally are responsible for discipline and mothers for nurturing; but fathers also provide economic support (Jankowiak, 1992). Children have strong bonds with mothers, who live in the homes of their mothers-in-law and have no economic power. Fathers are stern and aloof, and their children respect and

fear them. Men almost never hold infants; they are believed to be incapable of it. Fathers interact more with toddlers but perform child-care duties reluctantly, and only if the mother is absent.

Here, as in Cameroon, urbanization is changing these attitudes—but in the opposite direction. Families now live in very small quarters, and women work outside the home. Fathers—especially college-educated ones—now seek more intimate relationships with children, especially sons. China's official one-child policy has accentuated this change, leading both parents to be more deeply involved with their only child (Engle & Breaux, 1998).

The Aka People
The Aka are hunter-gatherers in the tropical forests of central Africa who move frequently from camp to camp in small, tightly knit groups and are highly protective of young children. In contrast with fathers in the other two cultures just described, Aka fathers are just as nurturing and emotionally supportive as Aka mothers. In fact, "Aka fathers provide more direct infant care than fathers in any other known society" (Hewlett, 1992, p. 169). They hold their babies frequently and hug, kiss, clean, and play gently with them (Hewlett, 1987).

This behaviour is in line with *family systems theory,* which predicts that fathers will be more involved in the care of young children in cultures in which husbands and wives frequently cooperate in subsistence tasks and other activities (Hewlett, 1992). Among the Aka and other societies with high paternal involvement in infant care, the key is not just that both parents participate in such activities, but that they do it together. The father's role in child care is part of his role in the family.

How do you think your relationship with your father might have been different if you had grown up in Cameroon? Among the Huhot of Inner Mongolia? Among the Aka people?

For more information on this topic, go to **www.mcgrawhill.ca/ college/papalia** for a link to a discussion of the varieties of fatherhood and a review of research on the influence of fathers on their children's development.

*Unless otherwise referenced, this box is based on Engle & Breaux, 1998.

"Around the World" Boxes

This boxed feature offers windows on child development in societies other than our own (in addition to the cultural coverage in the main body of text). Topics include cross-cultural comparisons of fatherhood, healthcare, and popularity.

"The Everyday World" Boxes

These boxes highlight practical applications of research findings. Subjects include imaginary companions, the math wars, and whether parents should stay together for the sake of the children.

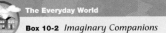

Box 10-2 *Imaginary Companions*

At 3½, Anna had 23 "sisters" with such names as Och, Elmo, Zeni, Aggie, and Ankie. She often talked to them on the telephone, since they lived about 100 miles away, in the town where her family used to live. During the next year, most of the sisters disappeared, but Och continued to visit, especially for birthday parties. Och had a cat and a dog (which Anna had begged for in vain), and whenever Anna was denied something she saw advertised on television, she announced that she already had one at her sister's house. But when a live friend came over and Anna's mother happened to mention one of her imaginary companions, Anna quickly changed the subject.

All 23 sisters—and some "boys" and "girls" who had followed them—lived only in Anna's imagination, as she well knew. Like an estimated 25 to 65 per cent of children between ages 3 and 10 (Woolley, 1997), she created imaginary companions, with whom she talked and played. This normal phenomenon of childhood is seen most often in first-born and only children, who lack the close company of siblings. Like Anna, most children who create imaginary companions have many of them (Gleason, Sebanc, & Hartup, 2000). Girls are more likely than boys to have imaginary "friends" (or at least to acknowledge them). Girls' imaginary playmates are usually other children, whereas boys' are more often animals (D. G. Singer & Singer, 1990).

Children who have imaginary companions can distinguish fantasy from reality, but in free-play sessions they are more likely to engage in pretend play than are children without imaginary companions (M. Taylor, Cartwright, & Carlson, 1993). They play more happily and more imaginatively than other children and are more cooperative with other children and adults (D. G. Singer & Singer, 1990; J. L. Singer & Singer, 1981); and they do

not lack for friends at preschool (Gleason et al., 2000). They are more fluent with language, watch less television, and show more curiosity, excitement, and persistence during play. In one study, 4-year-olds—regardless of verbal intelligence—who reported having imaginary companions did better on theory-of-mind tasks (such as differentiating between appearance and reality and recognizing false beliefs) than children who did not create such companions (M. Taylor & Carlson, 1997).

Children's relationships with imaginary companions are like peer relationships; they are usually sociable and friendly, in contrast with the nurturing way in which children treat personified objects, such as stuffed animals and dolls (Gleason et al., 2000). Imaginary playmates are good company for an only child like Anna. They provide wish-fulfillment mechanisms ("There was a monster in my room, but Elmo scared it off with magic dust"), scapegoats ("I didn't eat those cookies—Och must have done it!"), displacement agents for the child's own fears ("Aggie is afraid she's going to be washed down the drain"), and support in difficult situations. (One 6-year-old "took" her imaginary companion with her to see a scary movie.)

How should parents respond to children's talk about imaginary companions?

For more information on this topic, go to the Online Learning Centre: **www.mcgrawhill.ca/college/papalia,** which provides a link to a Web page about children's imaginary companions.

"The Social World" Boxes

This box series takes an in-depth view of topics pertaining to different stages of development. Topics include the experience of First Nations children in residential schools, fetal welfare versus mother's rights, and how poverty affects Canadian children.

The Social World

Box 1-1 *The Residential School Experience of First Nations Children*

The importance of looking at the life course in its social and historical context is exemplified by the experience of Aboriginal youth in Canada from the 1920s to the 1970s. Before that time, Aboriginal communities gave children the freedom to explore their environment and to develop independence, without the use of corporal punishment (Johnson & Cremo, 1995). Aboriginal languages and traditional spirituality and customs flourished. The established European majority saw the typical child-rearing practice of Aboriginal communities as permissive and neglectful. Drawing upon public opinion and an emphasis on assimilation to the majority culture, the federal government in the 1920s followed a policy of removing Aboriginal children from their families and placing them in government-sponsored residential schools (Sinclair, Phillips, & Bala, 1991) typically run by church missionaries (Miller, 1996). The era of residential schools, which ended in the 1970s, exacted a huge toll in human suffering of members of Aboriginal communities. The residential school authorities did not permit the children to use their heritage languages, and as a consequence of their experiences the children lost touch with their cultures and traditional

ways (Grant, 1996). In some cases, evidence of physical, psychological, and sexual abuse along with human rights violations emerged. The impact of this experience on the cohort of Aboriginal youth from the early 1920s to the 1970s involved feelings of inferiority, apathy, unwillingness to work, confusion over values, and anti-religious attitudes (Grant, 1996). Today, the effects of the residential school era are beginning to be addressed. Part of this process involves recognizing the practice as a form of cultural genocide (Miller, 1996), and emphasizing healing, and renewing of language and cultural traditions for future generations of Aboriginal people by promoting distinct Aboriginal people's educational programs. This healing is beginning to be seen in increasing numbers of Aboriginal people celebrating the diversity of their cultures through annual celebrations and gatherings, in individual communities and nationally. Aboriginal groups are emerging as a political force changing the social and cultural landscape through the work of the Assembly of First Nations, post-secondary educational institutions like the Saskatchewan Indian Federated College, and the establishment of popular cultural outlets like the Aboriginal People's Television Network.

As the history of the residential school cohort of Aboriginal youth has emerged, their life experiences—as documented by interviews with former students and school and government officials, archival data, and photographs—give researchers a window into the processes of development and their links with socio-historical change. The longer-term effects of the residential school era are being documented particularly with children of survivors, and changes in the roles of elders and Aboriginal education.

What's your view

Can you think of a major cultural event within your lifetime that shaped the lives of families and children? How would you go about studying such effects?

Check it out

For more information on this topic, go to **www.mcgrawhill.ca/college/papalia.**

Aboriginal children during residential school internment. The experience of growing up in a Church-run residential school shows how a government policy can affect children's current and future development.

Studying A Child's World

There is nothing permanent except change.

—Heraclitus, fragment (sixth century B.C.E)

Focus *Victor, the Wild Boy of Aveyron**

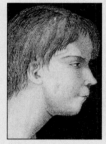

Victor

On January 8, 1800, a naked boy, his face and neck heavily scarred, appeared on the outskirts of the village of Saint-Sernin in the sparsely populated province of Aveyron in south central France. The boy, who was only four and a half feet tall but looked about 12 years old, had been spotted several times during the previous two and a half years, climbing trees, running on all fours, drinking from streams, and foraging for acorns and roots.

When the dark-eyed boy came to Saint-Sernin, he neither spoke nor responded to speech. Like an animal accustomed to living in the wild, he spurned prepared foods and tore off the clothing people tried to put on him. It seemed clear that he had either lost his parents or been abandoned by them, but how long ago this had occurred was impossible to tell.

The boy appeared during a time of intellectual and social ferment, when a new, scientific outlook was beginning to replace mystical speculation. Philosophers debated questions about the nature of human beings—questions that would become central to the study of child development. Are the qualities, behaviour, and ideas that define what it means to be human inborn or acquired, or both? How important is social contact during the formative years? Can its lack be overcome? A study of a child who had grown up in isolation might provide evidence of the relative impact of "nature" (inborn characteristics) and "nurture" (upbringing, schooling, and other societal influences).

After initial observation, the boy, who came to be called Victor, was sent to a school for deaf-mutes in Paris. There, he was turned over to Jean-Marc-Gaspard Itard, an ambitious 26-year-old practitioner of the emerging science of "mental medicine," or psychiatry. Itard believed that Victor's development had been limited by isolation and that he simply needed to be taught the skills that children in civilized society normally acquire.

Itard took Victor into his home and, during the next five years, gradually "tamed" him. Itard first awakened his pupil's ability to discriminate sensory experience through hot baths and dry rubs. He then moved on to painstaking, step-by-step training of emotional responses and instruction in moral and social behaviour, language, and thought. The methods Itard used—based on principles of imitation, conditioning, and behavioural modification, all of which we discuss in chapter 2—were far ahead of their time, and he invented many teaching devices used today.

But the education of Victor (which was dramatized in Francois Truffaut's film *The Wild Child*) was not an unqualified success. The boy did make remarkable progress: He learned the names of many objects and could read and write simple sentences; he could express desires, obey commands, and exchange ideas. He showed affection, especially for Itard's housekeeper, Madame Guérin, as well as such emotions as pride, shame, remorse, and the desire to please. However, aside from uttering some vowel and consonant sounds, he never learned to speak. Furthermore, he remained totally focused on his own wants and needs and never seemed to

*Sources of information about Victor were Frith (1989) and Lane (1976).

lose his yearning "for the freedom of the open country and his indifference to most of the pleasures of social life" (Lane, 1976, p. 160). When the study ended, Victor—no longer able to fend for himself, as he had done in the wild—went to live with Madame Guérin until his death in his early forties in 1828.

• • •

Why did Victor fail to fulfill Itard's hopes for him? The boy may have been a victim of brain damage, autism (a brain disorder involving lack of social responsiveness), or severe early maltreatment. Itard's instructional methods, advanced as they were, may have been inadequate. Itard himself came to believe that the effects of long isolation could not be fully overcome, and that Victor may have been too old, especially for language learning.

Although Victor's story does not yield definitive answers to the questions Itard set out to explore, it is important because it was one of the first systematic attempts to study child development. Since Victor's time, we have learned much about how children develop, but developmental scientists are still investigating such fundamental questions as the relative importance of nature and nurture and how they work together. Victor's story dramatizes the challenges and complexities of the scientific study of child development—the study on which you are about to embark.

In this chapter, we describe how the field of child development has itself developed as scientists have learned more about infants, children, and adolescents. We present the goals and basic concepts of the field today. We identify aspects of development and show how they interrelate. We summarize major developments during each period of a child's life. We look at influences on development and the contexts in which it occurs.

After you have read and studied this chapter, you should be able to answer each of the Guidepost questions that appear at the top of the next page. Look for them again in the margins, where they point to important concepts throughout the chapter. To check your understanding of these Guideposts, review the end-of-chapter summary. Checkpoints located at periodic spots throughout the chapter will help you verify your understanding of what you have read.

Guideposts for Study

1. What is child development, and how has its study evolved?

2. What are six fundamental points on which consensus has emerged?

3. What do developmental scientists study?

4. What are the three major aspects and five periods of child development?

5. What kinds of influences make one child different from another?

The Study of Child Development: Then and Now

From the moment of conception, human beings undergo processes of development. The field of **child development** is the scientific study of those processes. Developmental scientists—people engaged in the professional study of child development—look at ways in which children change from conception through adolescence, as well as at characteristics that remain fairly stable.

Child development has, of course, been going on as long as children have existed, but its formal scientific study is relatively new. Looking back, we can see dramatic changes in the ways of investigating the world of childhood.

child development Scientific study of processes of change and stability from conception through adolescence

Early Approaches

Early forerunners of the scientific study of child development were *baby biographies,* journals kept to record the early development of a single child. One early journal, published in 1787 in Germany, contained Dietrich Tiedemann's (1897/1787) observations of his son's sensory, motor, language, and cognitive behaviour during the first 2½ years. Typical of the speculative nature of such observations was Tiedemann's conclusion, after watching the infant suck more continuously on a cloth tied around something sweet than on a nurse's finger, that sucking appeared to be "not instinctive, but acquired" (Murchison & Langer, 1927, p. 206).

It was Charles Darwin, originator of the theory of evolution, who first emphasized the *developmental* nature of infant behaviour. In 1877, in the belief that human beings could be better understood by studying their origins—both as a species and as individuals—Darwin published an abstract of his notes on his son's sensory, cognitive, and emotional development during the first 12 months (see Focus vignette at the beginning of chapter 7). Darwin's journal gave "baby biographies" scientific respectability; about 30 more were published during the next three decades (Dennis, 1936).

By the end of the nineteenth century, several important trends were preparing the way for the scientific study of child development. Scientists had unlocked the mystery of conception and (as in the case of Victor) were arguing about the relative importance of "nature" and "nurture" (inborn characteristics and external influences). The discovery of germs and immunization made it possible for many more children to survive infancy. Because of an abundance of cheap labour, children were less needed as workers. Laws protecting them from long workdays let them spend more time in school, and parents and teachers became more concerned with identifying and meeting children's developmental needs. The new science of psychology taught that people could understand themselves by learning what had influenced them as children.

Still, this new discipline had far to go. Adolescence was not considered a separate period of development until the early twentieth century, when G. Stanley Hall, a pioneer in child study, published a popular (though unscientific) book called *Adolescence* (1904/1916).

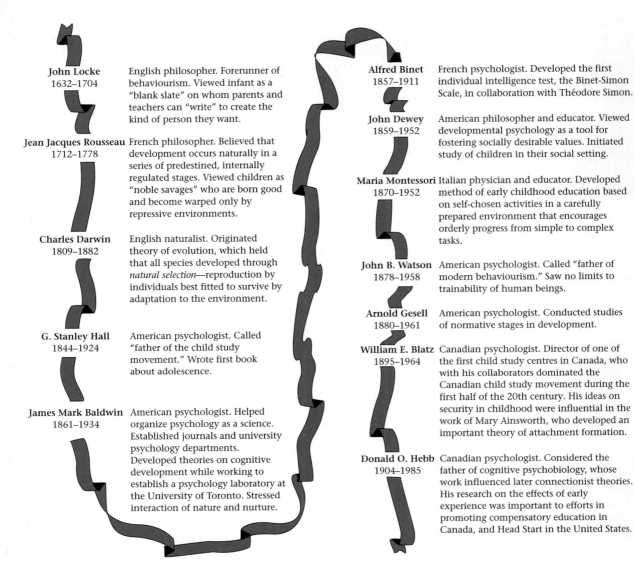

John Locke
1632–1704

English philosopher. Forerunner of behaviourism. Viewed infant as a "blank slate" on whom parents and teachers can "write" to create the kind of person they want.

Jean Jacques Rousseau
1712–1778

French philosopher. Believed that development occurs naturally in a series of predestined, internally regulated stages. Viewed children as "noble savages" who are born good and become warped only by repressive environments.

Charles Darwin
1809–1882

English naturalist. Originated theory of evolution, which held that all species developed through *natural selection*—reproduction by individuals best fitted to survive by adaptation to the environment.

G. Stanley Hall
1844–1924

American psychologist. Called "father of the child study movement." Wrote first book about adolescence.

James Mark Baldwin
1861–1934

American psychologist. Helped organize psychology as a science. Established journals and university psychology departments. Developed theories on cognitive development while working to establish a psychology laboratory at the University of Toronto. Stressed interaction of nature and nurture.

Alfred Binet
1857–1911

French psychologist. Developed the first individual intelligence test, the Binet-Simon Scale, in collaboration with Théodore Simon.

John Dewey
1859–1952

American philosopher and educator. Viewed developmental psychology as a tool for fostering socially desirable values. Initiated study of children in their social setting.

Maria Montessori
1870–1952

Italian physician and educator. Developed method of early childhood education based on self-chosen activities in a carefully prepared environment that encourages orderly progress from simple to complex tasks.

John B. Watson
1878–1958

American psychologist. Called "father of modern behaviourism." Saw no limits to trainability of human beings.

Arnold Gesell
1880–1961

American psychologist. Conducted studies of normative stages in development.

William E. Blatz
1895–1964

Canadian psychologist. Director of one of the first child study centres in Canada, who with his collaborators dominated the Canadian child study movement during the first half of the 20th century. His ideas on security in childhood were influential in the work of Mary Ainsworth, who developed an important theory of attachment formation.

Donald O. Hebb
1904–1985

Canadian psychologist. Considered the father of cognitive psychobiology, whose work influenced later connectionist theories. His research on the effects of early experience was important to efforts in promoting compensatory education in Canada, and Head Start in the United States.

Figure 1-1

Some pioneers in the study of a child's world: A timeline

In Canada, early research in child development began with James Baldwin and his students, including Frederick Tracy, in the late 1800s, who focused on mental development in childhood. With the emerging interest in "mental hygiene" in the 1920s and '30s, institutes of child study were established in Montreal and Toronto, directed by Katharine Banham and William Blatz (Wright, 2002). Since that time, Canadian researchers across the country have made significant contributions to our understanding of child development (Wright, 1999). Figure 1-1 presents summaries, in historical order, of the ideas and contributions of Darwin, Hall, and other early pioneers in the study of child development.

Studying the Lifespan

Full lifespan studies in Canada and the United States grew out of programs designed to follow children through to adulthood. William E. Blatz, founder of St. George's School for Child Study at the University of Toronto, Department of Psychology in the 1920s, carried out a longitudinal project at Regal Road Public School in Toronto studying behavioural difficulties and adjustment of 1400 children from the school years through adolescence and into adulthood (Raymond, 1991). Blatz was also instrumental in developing the laboratory school for the Dionne Quintuplets, the first known set of identical quintuplets, in the 1930s; however, the ethics of the quintuplets' lack of privacy and freedom to withdraw have been questioned (Proncher & Doyon, 1997). The Stanford Studies of Gifted Children (begun in 1921 under the direction of Lewis M. Terman) continue to trace the development of people (now in old age) who were identified as unusually intelligent in childhood. Other major studies that began around 1930—the Fels Research Institute Study, the Berkeley Growth and Guidance Studies, and the Oakland (Adolescent) Growth Study—have given us much information on long-term development.

Today the study of child development is part of the broader study of *human development,* which covers the entire lifespan from conception to death. Although growth and development are most obvious in childhood, they occur throughout life. Students of child development draw on a wide range of disciplines, including psychology, psychiatry, sociology, anthropology, biology, genetics (the study of inherited characteristics), family science (the interdisciplinary study of family relations), education, history, philosophy, and medicine. This book includes findings from research in all these fields.

New Frontiers

Although children have been the focus of scientific study for more than one hundred years, this exploration is an ever-evolving endeavour. The questions that developmentalists seek to answer, the methods they use, and the explanations they propose are more sophisticated than they were even 25 years ago. These shifts reflect progress in understanding, as new investigations build on or challenge those that went before. They also reflect the changing cultural and technological context.

Sensitive instruments that measure eye movements are turning up intriguing connections between infant visual attentiveness and childhood intelligence. Cameras, videocassette recorders, and computers allow investigators to scan infants' facial expressions for early signs of emotions and to analyze how mothers and babies communicate. Advances in brain imaging make it possible to probe the mysteries of temperament and to pinpoint the sources of logical thought.

The classic distinction between *basic research,* the kind undertaken purely in a spirit of intellectual inquiry, and *applied research,* which addresses a practical problem, is becoming less meaningful. Increasingly, research findings have direct application to child rearing, education, health, and social policy. For example, research into preschool children's understanding of death can enable adults to help a child deal with bereavement; research on children's memory can help determine the weight to be given children's courtroom testimony; and research on factors that increase the risks of low birth weight, antisocial behaviour, and teenage suicide can suggest ways to prevent these ills.

An Emerging Consensus

As the study of children has matured, a consensus has emerged on several fundamental points.

1. *All domains of development are interrelated.* Although developmental scientists often look separately at various *domains,* or aspects, of development, each affects the others. For example, increasing physical mobility helps a baby learn about the world. The hormonal and physical changes of puberty affect emotional development.
2. *Normal development includes a wide range of individual differences.* Each child, from the start, is unlike anyone else in the world. One is outgoing, another shy. One is agile, another awkward. How do those differences, and a multitude of others, come about? Some of the influences on individual development are inborn; others come from experience, or, most often, from a combination of the two. Family characteristics, the effects of gender, social class, and ethnicity, and the presence or absence of physical, mental, or emotional disability all affect the way a child develops.
3. *Children help shape their own development and influence others' responses to them.* Right from the start, through the responses they evoke in others, infants mould their environment and then respond to the environment they have helped create. Influence is *bidirectional:* When babies babble and coo, adults tend to talk to them, and babies then "talk" more.

Checkpoint ✔

Can you . . .

✔ Trace highlights in the evolution of the study of child development?

✔ Name some pioneers in that study and summarize their most important contributions?

✔ Give examples of practical applications of research on child development?

Guidepost 2

What are six fundamental points on which consensus has emerged?

4. *Historical and cultural contexts strongly influence development.* Each child develops within a specific environment, bounded by time and place. A child born in Canada today is likely to have experiences very different from those of a child born in colonial Canada, and also from a child born in Morocco or Greenland.

5. *Early experience is important, but children can be remarkably resilient.* A traumatic incident or a severely deprived childhood may well have grave emotional consequences, but the life histories of countless people show that often the effects of risks to healthy development, such as growing up in low-income families, can be overcome, particularly in the presence of protective factors such as a supportive family environment.

6. *Development in childhood is connected to development throughout the rest of life.* At one time, it was believed that growth and development end, as this book does, with adolescence. Today most developmental scientists agree that development goes on throughout life. As long as people live, they have the potential to change.

Checkpoint ✔

Can you . . .

✔ Summarize six fundamental points of agreement that have emerged from the study of child development?

Guidepost 3

What do developmental scientists study?

The Study of Child Development: Basic Concepts

The processes of change and stability that developmental scientists study occur in all aspects of development and throughout all periods of the lifespan.

Developmental Processes: Change and Stability

Developmental scientists study two kinds of change: *quantitative* and *qualitative.* **Quantitative change** is a change in number or amount, such as growth in height, weight, vocabulary, or frequency of communication. **Qualitative change** is a change in kind, structure, or organization. It is marked by the emergence of new phenomena that cannot easily be anticipated on the basis of earlier functioning, such as the change from a nonverbal child to one who understands words and can communicate verbally.

Despite these changes, most people show an underlying *stability,* or constancy, of personality and behaviour. For example, about 10 to 15 per cent of children are consistently shy, and another 10 to 15 per cent are very bold. Although various influences can modify these traits somewhat, they seem to persist to a moderate degree, especially in children at one extreme or the other (see chapter 3).

Which of a child's characteristics are most likely to endure? Which are likely to change, and why? These are among the questions that developmental scientists seek to answer.

quantitative change Change in number or amount, such as in height, weight, or size of vocabulary

qualitative change Change in kind, structure, or organization, such as the change from nonverbal to verbal communication

Guidepost 4

What are three major aspects and five periods of child development?

Domains of Development

The study of child development is complicated by the fact that change and stability occur in various aspects of the self. To simplify discussion, developmental scientists talk separately about *physical development, cognitive development,* and *psychosocial development.* Actually, though, these domains of development are interrelated. Throughout life, each affects the others.

Growth of the body and brain, sensory capacities, motor skills, and health are part of *physical development* and may influence other aspects of development. For example, a child with frequent ear infections may develop language more slowly than a child without this problem. During puberty, dramatic physiological and hormonal changes affect the developing sense of self.

Change and stability in mental abilities, such as learning, memory, language, thinking, moral reasoning, and creativity constitute *cognitive development.* They are closely related to physical and emotional growth. The ability to speak depends on the physical development of the mouth and brain. A child who has difficulty with words may evoke negative reactions in others, influencing the child's popularity and sense of self-worth.

Change and stability in personality, emotional life, and social relationships together constitute *psychosocial development,* and this can affect cognitive and physical functioning. Anxiety about taking a test can impair performance. Social support can help children cope with the potentially negative effects of stress on physical and mental health. Conversely, physical and cognitive capacities can affect psychosocial development. They contribute greatly to self-esteem and can affect social acceptance.

Although we will be looking separately at physical, cognitive, and psychosocial development, a child is more than a bundle of isolated parts. Development is a unified process. Throughout the text, we will highlight links among the three major domains of development.

Periods of Development

The concept of periods of development is a **social construction** that is generally accepted in European and North American society: an idea about the nature of reality accepted by members of a particular society at a particular time on the basis of shared subjective perceptions or assumptions. Although developmental theories often refer to stages of development and divide development into periods marked by specific milestones like a child's first step, or first word, there is no single, objectively definable moment when a child becomes an adolescent, or an adolescent becomes an adult. Indeed, the concept of childhood itself can be viewed as a social construction. Some evidence indicates, though it has been disputed, that children in earlier times were regarded and treated much like small adults (Ariès, 1962; Elkind, 1986; Pollock, 1983). Even now, in some developing countries, children labour alongside their elders, doing the same kinds of work for equally long hours.

In industrial societies, as we have mentioned, the concept of adolescence as a period of development is quite recent. In some nonindustrial societies, it does not exist. The Chippewa, for example, have only two periods of childhood: from birth until the child walks, and from walking to puberty. What we call adolescence is, for them, part of adulthood (Broude, 1995), as was true in societies before industrialization.

In this book, we follow a sequence of five periods generally accepted in North American and European industrial societies. After describing the crucial changes that occur in the first period, before birth, we trace all three aspects of development through infancy and toddlerhood, early childhood, middle childhood, and adolescence (see Table 1-1). These age divisions are approximate and somewhat arbitrary. Individual differences exist in the way children deal with the characteristic events and issues of each period. One toddler may be toilet trained by 18 months; another, not until 3 years. Despite these differences, however, developmental scientists believe that certain basic developmental needs must be met and certain developmental tasks must be mastered during each period for normal development to occur.

Infants are dependent on adults to meet their basic needs for food, clothing, and shelter, as well as for human contact and affection. They form attachments to parents or caregivers, who also become attached to them. With the development of speech and self-locomotion, toddlers become more self-reliant; they need to assert their autonomy but also need parents to help them keep their impulses in check. During early childhood, children develop more self-control and more interest in other children. During middle childhood, control over behaviour gradually shifts from parent to child, and the peer group becomes increasingly important. A main task of adolescence is the search for identity—personal, sexual, and occupational. As adolescents become physically mature, they deal with sometimes conflicting needs and emotions as they prepare to separate from the parental nest.

Influences on Development

Students of development are interested in processes of development that affect every normal child, but they also want to know about **individual differences,** both in influences on development and in its outcome. Children differ in sex, height, weight, and body build; in constitutional factors such as health and energy level; in intelligence; and in personality

characteristics and emotional reactions. The contexts of their lives and lifestyles differ, too: the homes, communities, and societies they live in, the relationships they have, the kinds of schools they go to (or whether they go to a formal school at all), and how they spend their free time.

All these differences, and more, may help explain why one child turns out unlike another. Because development is complex, and the factors that affect it cannot always be measured precisely, scientists cannot answer that question fully. However, they have learned much about what children need to develop normally, how they react to the many influences upon and within them, and how they can best fulfill their potential.

Heredity, Environment, and Maturation

heredity Inborn influences or traits inherited from biological parents

environment Totality of nonhereditary, or experiential, influences on development

maturation Unfolding of a natural sequence of physical and behavioural changes, including readiness to master new abilities

Some influences on development originate primarily with **heredity:** the inborn genetic endowment from the biological parents. Others come largely from the inner and outer **environment:** the experiences that impinge on a person, beginning in the womb. Individual differences increase as children grow older. Many typical changes of infancy and early childhood seem to be tied to **maturation** of the body and brain—the unfolding of a natural sequence of physical changes and behaviour patterns, including readiness to master new abilities such as walking and talking. As children grow into adolescents and then into adults, differences in innate (inborn) characteristics and life experience play a greater role as children adapt to, or deal with, the internal and external conditions in which they find themselves.

Even in processes that all children go through, rates and timing of development vary. Throughout this book, we talk about average ages for the occurrence of certain behaviours: the first word, the first step, the first menstruation or "wet dream," the development of logical thought. But these ages are merely *averages*. Only when deviation from the average is extreme should we consider development exceptionally advanced or delayed.

In trying to understand the similarities and differences in development, then, we need to look at the *inherited* characteristics that give each person a special start in life. We also need to consider the many *environmental* factors that affect people, especially such major contexts as family, neighbourhood, socio-economic status, ethnicity, and culture. We need to see how heredity and environment interact. We need to look at influences that affect many or most children at a certain age or a certain time in history, and also at those that affect only certain individuals. Finally, we need to look at how timing can affect the impact of certain influences.

Major Contextual Influences

Human beings are social beings. Right from the start, they develop within a social and historical context. For an infant, the immediate context is normally the family; and the family in turn is subject to the wider and ever-changing influences of neighbourhood, community, and society.

Family

nuclear family Kinship and household unit made up of parents and their natural or adopted children

extended family Kinship network of parents, children, and other relatives, sometimes living together in an *extended-family household*

Family may mean something different in different times and places. The dominant family unit in North American and European societies, dating back to pre-industrial times, is the **nuclear family**, a two-generational kinship, economic, and household unit consisting of two parents and their natural or adopted children (Hareven, 1986).

In many other societies, such as those of Asia and Latin America, the **extended family**—a multi-generational kinship network of grandparents, aunts, uncles, cousins, and more distant relatives—is the traditional pattern of societal organization, and many or most people live in *extended-family households,* where they have daily contact with kin. However, that pattern is now eroding in developing countries, due to industrialization and migration to urban centres (N. M. Brown, 1990; Gorman, 1993).

In Canada, it is not uncommon for extended families to be spread through all regions of the country, with family members moving for work or education. However, among many Canadian ethnic groups, particularly Aboriginal Canadians—including First Nations, Inuit, and Metis—the extended family is an integral part of children's experiences (Ward, 1998).

Age Period	Physical Developments	Cognitive Developments	Psychosocial Developments
Prenatal Period (conception to birth)	Conception occurs The genetic endowment interacts with environmental influences from the start. Basic body structures and organs form. Brain growth spurt begins. Physical growth is the most rapid in the lifespan. Vulnerability to environmental influences is great.	Abilities to learn and remember and to respond to sensory stimuli are developing.	
Infancy and Toddlerhood (birth to age 3)	All senses and body systems operate at birth to varying degrees. The brain grows in complexity and is highly sensitive to environmental influence. Physical growth and development of motor skills are rapid.	Abilities to learn and remember are present, even in early weeks. Use of symbols and ability to solve problems develop by end of second year. Comprehension and use of language develop rapidly.	Attachments to parents and others form. Self-awareness develops. Shift from dependence to autonomy occurs. Interest in other children increases.
Early Childhood (3 to 6 years)	Growth is steady; appearance becomes more slender and proportions more adultlike. Appetite diminishes, and sleep problems are common. Handedness appears; fine and gross motor skills and strength improve.	Thinking is somewhat egocentric, but understanding of other people's perspectives grows. Cognitive immaturity leads to some illogical ideas about the world. Memory and language improve. Intelligence becomes more predictable.	Self-concept and understanding of emotions become more complex; self-esteem is global. Independence, initiative, self-control, and self-care increase. Gender identity develops. Play becomes more imaginative, more elaborate, and more social. Altruism, aggression, and fearfulness are common. Family is still focus of social life, but other children become more important. Attending preschool is common.
Middle Childhood (6 to 11 years)	Growth slows. Strength and athletic skills improve. Respiratory illnesses are common, but health is generally better than at any other time in lifespan.	Egocentrism diminishes. Children begin to think logically but concretely. Memory and language skills increase. Cognitive gains permit children to benefit from formal schooling. Some children show special educational needs and strengths.	Self-concept becomes more complex, affecting self-esteem. Coregulation reflects gradual shift in control from parents to child. Peers assume central importance.
Adolescence (11 to about 20 years)	Physical growth and other changes are rapid and profound. Reproductive maturity occurs. Major health risks arise from behavioural issues, such as eating disorders and drug abuse.	Ability to think abstractly and use scientific reasoning develops. Immature thinking persists in some attitudes and behaviours. Education focuses on preparation for university or vocation.	Search for identity, including sexual identity, becomes central. Relationships with parents are generally good. Peer groups help develop and test self-concept but also may exert an antisocial influence.

Grandparents traditionally assumed a major role in raising children in Aboriginal communities, and despite the practices of the mainstream culture that undermined this strength of Aboriginal families (see Box 1-1), the traditional roles are beginning to return (Parler, 2001).

Recent immigrant families from Asia, Africa, the Caribbean, and Europe also involve the extended family in child rearing (Baker, 2001). Close extended family ties provide strong support systems, and extended-family households are common. Social roles tend to be flexible: Adults often share breadwinning, and children are given responsibility for younger brothers and sisters (Harrison, Wilson, Pine, Chan, & Buriel, 1990; Levitt, Guacci-Franco, & Levitt, 1993).

The role of the community in bringing up children is also significant among religious-based settlements, such as Mennonites in Manitoba and Ontario, and Hutterites in Alberta, who live apart from mainstream Canadian society (Dreidger, 2000; Peter, 1983).

Socio-economic Status and Neighbourhood

socio-economic status (SES)
Combination of economic and social factors describing an individual or family, including income, education, and occupation

risk factors Conditions that increase the likelihood of a negative developmental outcome

Socio-economic status (SES) combines several related factors, including income, education, and occupation. Throughout this book, we describe many studies that relate SES to developmental processes (such as differences in mothers' verbal interaction with their children) and to developmental outcomes and other **risk factors** (such as health and family environment; see Table 1-2). It is generally not SES itself that affects these outcomes, but factors associated with SES, such as the kinds of homes and neighbourhoods children live in and the quality of nutrition, supervision, schooling, and other opportunities available to them. The National Longitudinal Survey of Children and Youth (NLSCY), begun in 1994, is tracking 35,000 children from all regions of Canada every two years from birth. Results from this survey have already shown that although coming from a disadvantaged neighbourhood is related to emotional and behaviour problems in childhood, the most powerful factor that predicts future behaviour problems is family socio-economic status (Boyle & Lipman, 1998). In addition, living in more affluent and cohesive neighbourhoods is associated with higher levels of school readiness, and school performance (Brooks-Gunn, Britto, & Brady, 1998; Brooks-Gunn & Duncan, 1997; Duncan & Brooks-Gunn, 1997; Kohen, Hertzman, & Brooks-Gunn, 1998; McLoyd, 1998). The harm done by poverty may be indirect, through its impact on parents' emotional state and parenting practices and on the home environment they create. The challenges of poverty can strain relationships and drain time and energy from parenting. (In chapter 14 we'll look more closely at indirect effects of poverty.)

SES limits a family's choice of where to live. Researchers have begun to study how the composition of a neighbourhood affects the way children turn out. So far, the most powerful factors seem to be average neighbourhood *income* and *human capital*—the presence of educated, employed adults who can build the community's economic base and provide models of what a child can hope to achieve (Brooks-Gunn et al., 1997; Leventhal & Brooks-Gunn, 2000). Threats to children's well-being multiply if several risk factors—conditions that increase the likelihood of a negative outcome—coexist. Living in a poor neighbourhood with large numbers of people who are unemployed and on welfare makes it less likely that effective social support will be available (Black & Krishnakumar, 1998). As well, liv-

Table 1-2	Higher Risk for Low-income Children
Outcome	**Low-income Children's Higher Risk Relative to More Affluent Children**
Mental Health	
Emotional Problems	1.3 times more likely
Behavioural Problems	1.3 times more likely
Family Environment	
Single Parent	5.5 times more likely
Ineffective Parenting	1.04 times more likely
Parental Depression	1.8 times more likely
Family Dysfunction	1.3 times more likely

Source: Adapted from Beiser, Hou, Hyman, & Tousignant, 2002, p. 222.

ing in persistent poverty is associated with larger risk of negative outcomes. About one in eight Canadian children aged 12 years or younger experience a severe period of poverty (four or more consecutive years of family income below the poverty line) (Canadian Council on Social Development, 2001).

Culture and Ethnicity

Culture refers to a society's or group's total way of life, including customs, traditions, beliefs, values, language, and physical products, from tools to artworks—all the learned behaviour passed on from parents to children. Culture is constantly changing, often through contact with other cultures. After immigrant groups live in Canada for more than a generation, some of their parenting practices shift from a pattern typically used in the country of origin to one more commonly used by parents in mainstream Canadian families.

Some cultures have variant *subcultures,* associated with certain groups, usually ethnic groups, within a society. An **ethnic group** consists of people united by ancestry, race, religion, language, and/or national origins, which contribute to a sense of shared identity and shared attitudes, beliefs, and values. Most ethnic groups trace their roots to a country of origin, where they or their forebears had a common culture that continues to influence their way of life.

Canada has always been a nation of immigrants and ethnic groups. The two founding groups, English and French, live alongside a third group of more recent immigrants who consist of many distinct ethnic groups—who come from all regions of the world. About 28 per cent of the Canadian population identifies itself as having origins other than British, French, or Canadian, with visible minorities constituting over 11 per cent of the population (Health Canada, 1999). The majority of recent immigrants—about 75 per cent of all new immigrants—have arrived from Asia, Africa, the Middle East, and Latin America (Beiser, Dion, Gotowiec, Hyman, & Nhi, 1995). There is also diversity within ethnic groups. Québécois, Franco-Ontarians, Franco-Manitobans, and Acadians—all French Canadians—have different histories and cultures and socio-economic status. Similarly, African-Canadian descendants of immigrants from the United States differ from those of Caribbean ancestry. Asian-Canadians, too, come from a variety of countries with distinct cultures and linguistic groups. Aboriginal peoples constitute the original inhabitants of Canada and are made up of many linguistic and ethnic groups: First Nations, Inuit, and Metis populations represent a diverse group of about one million people in Canada. With 11 language groups and 58 dialects across 596 bands, living in 2284 reserves, and in small and large urban centres, there is a large amount of cultural and linguistic diversity along with differences in values both between and within Aboriginal communities (Kirmayer, Brass, & Tait, 2000).

In large, multi-ethnic societies such as Canada, immigrant or minority groups *acculturate,* or adapt, to the majority culture by learning the language and customs needed to get along in the dominant culture while trying to preserve some of their own cultural practices and values. (Acculturation is not the same as cultural *assimilation,* in which the minority simply adopts the ways of the majority.) Children often grow up in neighbourhoods with other members of their own ethnic group, reinforcing shared cultural patterns. These cultural patterns may influence the composition of the household, its economic and social resources, the way its members act toward one another, the foods they eat, the games children play, the way they learn, and how well they do in school. To recognize the diversity of the Canadian cultural mosaic, communities across the country celebrate Canada's multicultural heritage in annual festivals. The federal government, through the Heritage Canada ministry, works to promote the cultural diversity of the Canadian population.

The Historical Context

At one time developmental scientists paid little attention to the historical context—the time in which children grow up. Then, as the early longitudinal studies of childhood extended into the adult years, investigators began to focus on how particular experiences, tied to time and place, affect the course of children's lives. The Regal Road study sample would have lived through the Great Depression and reached adulthood during the Second World War. What did it mean to be a child in these periods? To be an adolescent? To become an adult? The answers differ in important ways (Modell, 1989).

culture A society's or group's total way of life, including customs, traditions, beliefs, values, language, and physical products—all learned behaviour passed on from parents to children

ethnic group Group united by ancestry, race, religion, language, and/or national origins, which contribute to a sense of shared identity

Checkpoint ✔

Can you . . .

✔ Explain why individual differences tend to increase with age?

✔ Give examples of the influences of family and neighbourhood composition, socioeconomic status, culture, ethnicity, and historical context?

Children of European settlers at Confederation often worked from an early age, and networks of kinship with neighbours gave a secure social base where few social institutions existed (Parr, 1982). Children were often institutionalized until the family could use them as labour, or until a widowed father remarried. As Canada developed as an industrial nation in the late 1800s and early 1900s, a new perspective on child care emerged aiming to protect children's health, ensure access to quality education, and place victims of abuse and neglect into individual homes rather than large institutions (Sutherland, 2000). In Canada today, in a more culturally diverse country, children are brought up in ways that are substantially changed from those of past generations because of ideas, customs, and practices that evolved over the past 50 years (Sutherland, 2000). The perspective has progressed from children being regarded as family property during Canada's colonial period, to being viewed as dependent on the protection of the state during the first half of the 20th century, to being recognized as having inherent rights after the Second World War, particularly with the 1982 Canadian Charter of Rights and Freedoms (Howe, 1995). However, despite being a party to the UN Convention on the Rights of the Child, the Canadian government has not yet recognized the right of children to protection from poverty (Howe, 1995).

Today, as we'll discuss in the next section, the historical context is part of the study of development.

Normative and Non-Normative Influences

To understand similarities and differences in development, we must look at influences that impinge on many or most people and at those that touch only certain individuals. We also need to consider influences of time and place (Baltes, Reese, & Lipsitt, 1980).

A **normative** event is experienced in a similar way by most people in a group. *Normative age-graded influences* are highly similar for people in a particular age group. They include biological events (such as puberty) and social events (such as entry into formal education). The timing of biological events is fixed, within a normal range. (Children don't experience puberty at age 3.) The timing of social events is more flexible and varies in different times and places, within maturational limits. Children in North American and European industrial societies generally begin formal education around age 5 or 6; but in some developing countries, schooling begins much later, if at all.

Normative history-graded influences are common to a particular **cohort**: a group of people who share a similar experience, in this case growing up at the same time in the same place, such as living in Canada during the Great Depression. Depending on when and where they live, entire generations of children may feel the impact of wars, famines, or nuclear explosions. In North American and European countries, medical advances, as well as improvements in nutrition and sanitation, have dramatically reduced infant and child mortality. As children grow up, they are likely to be influenced by computers, digital television, the Internet, and other technological developments. Social changes, such as the increase in numbers of employed mothers, have greatly altered family life. These changes are occurring more slowly in developing countries.

Non-normative influences are unusual events that have a major impact on individual lives and may cause stress because they are unexpected. They are either typical events that happen at an atypical time of life (such as marriage in the early teens, or the death of a parent when a child is young) or atypical events (such as having a birth defect or being in an automobile crash). They can also, of course, be happy events (such as winning a scholarship). Young people may help create their own non-normative life events—say, by driving after drinking or by applying for a scholarship—and thus participate actively in their own development.

Timing of Influences: Critical or Sensitive Periods

A **critical period** is a specific time when a given event, or its absence, has the greatest impact on development. For example, if a woman receives X-rays, takes certain drugs, or contracts certain diseases at certain times during pregnancy, the fetus may show specific ill effects. The amount and kind of damage will vary, depending on the nature of the "shock" and on its timing.

normative Characteristic of an event that occurs in a similar way for most people in a group

cohort Group of people who share a similar experience, such as growing up at the same time and in the same place

non-normative Characteristic of an unusual event that happens to a particular person, or a typical event that happens at an unusual time of life

What's your view

• How might you be different if you had grown up in a culture other than your own?

critical period Specific time when a given event, or its absence, has the greatest impact on development

Box 1-1 *The Residential School Experience of Aboriginal Children*

The importance of looking at the life course in its social and historical context is exemplified by the experience of Aboriginal youth in Canada from the 1920s to the 1970s. Before that time, Aboriginal communities gave children the freedom to explore their environment and to develop independence, without the use of corporal punishment (Johnson & Cremo, 1995). Aboriginal languages and traditional spirituality and customs flourished. The established European majority saw the typical child-rearing practice of Aboriginal communities as permissive and neglectful. Drawing upon public opinion and an emphasis on assimilation to the majority culture, the federal government in the 1920s followed a policy of removing Aboriginal children from their families and placing them in government-sponsored residential schools (Sinclair, Phillips, & Bala, 1991) typically run by church missionaries (Miller, 1996). The era of residential schools, which ended in the 1970s, exacted a huge toll in human suffering of members of Aboriginal communities. The residential school authorities did not permit the children to use their heritage languages, and as a consequence of their experiences the children lost touch with their cultures and traditional

ways (Grant, 1996). In some cases, evidence of physical, psychological, and sexual abuse along with human rights violations emerged. The impact of this experience on the cohort of Aboriginal youth from the early 1920s to the 1970s involved feelings of inferiority, apathy, unwillingness to work, confusion over values, and anti-religious attitudes (Grant, 1996). Today, the effects of the residential school era are beginning to be addressed. Part of this process involves recognizing the practice as a form of cultural genocide (Miller, 1996), and emphasizing healing, and renewing of language and cultural traditions for future generations of Aboriginal people by promoting distinct Aboriginal people's educational programs. This healing is beginning to be seen in increasing numbers of Aboriginal people celebrating the diversity of their cultures through annual celebrations and gatherings, in individual communities and nationally. Aboriginal groups are emerging as a political force changing the social and cultural landscape through the work of the Assembly of First Nations, post-secondary educational institutions like the Saskatchewan Indian Federated College, and the establishment of popular cultural outlets like the Aboriginal People's Television Network.

As the history of the residential school cohort of Aboriginal youth has emerged, their life experiences—as documented by interviews with former students and school and government officials, archival data, and photographs—give researchers a window into the processes of development and their links with socio-historical change. The longer-term effects of the residential school era are being documented particularly with children of survivors, and changes in the roles of elders and Aboriginal education.

What's your view ?

Can you think of a major cultural event within your lifetime that shaped the lives of families and children? How would you go about studying such effects?

Check it out !

For more information on this topic, go to **www.mcgrawhill.ca/college/papalia.**

Aboriginal children during residential school internment. The experience of growing up in a Church-run residential school shows how a government policy can affect children's current and future development.

A child deprived of certain kinds of experience during a critical period is likely to have permanently stunted physical development. For example, if a muscle problem interfering with the ability to focus both eyes on the same object is not corrected early in life, the brain mechanisms necessary for binocular depth perception will not develop (Bushnell & Boudreau, 1993).

The concept of critical periods is more controversial when applied to cognitive and psychosocial development. Ethological psychologists believe that there is a critical period for infants to bond with a caregiver as Konrad Lorenz found in his studies of newborn goslings who imprinted on him during a critical period, mistaking Lorenz for their mother (Miller, 2002). In these domains there seems to be greater **plasticity,** or modifiability of performance. Although the human organism may be particularly *sensitive* to certain psychological experiences at certain times of life, later events can often reverse the effects of early ones. One investigator (Lenneberg, 1967, 1969) did propose a critical period for language development, before puberty, and this concept has been advanced as one explanation for Victor's limited progress in learning to talk (Lane, 1976; see Box 1-2).

Newer research suggests, however, that the capacity for language acquisition may be fairly resilient. Even if the parts of the brain best suited to language processing are

plasticity Modifiability of performance

What's your view ?

• In view of the critical effect of undernourishment on infants' brain development, does society have a responsibility to prevent it?

Box 1-2 *Is There a Critical Period for Language Acquisition?*

In 1970, a 13½-year-old girl named Genie (not her real name) was discovered in a suburb of Los Angeles (Curtiss, 1977; Fromkin, Krashen, Curtiss, Rigler, & Rigler, 1974; Pines, 1981; Rymer, 1993). The victim of an abusive father, she had been confined for nearly 12 years to a small room in her parents' home, tied to a potty chair and cut off from normal human contact. She weighed only 59 pounds, could not straighten her arms or legs, could not chew, had no bladder or bowel control, and did not speak. She recognized only her own name and the word *sorry*.

Only three years before, Eric Lenneberg (1967, 1969) had proposed that there is a critical period for language acquisition, beginning in early infancy and ending around puberty. Lenneberg argued that it would be difficult, if not impossible, for a child who had not yet acquired language to do so after that age.

The discovery of Genie offered the opportunity for a test of Lenneberg's hypothesis. Could Genie be taught to speak, or was it too late? The U.S. National Institutes of Mental Health (NIMH) funded a study, and a series of researchers took over Genie's care and gave her intensive testing and language training.

Genie's progress during the next few years (before the NIMH withdrew funding and her mother regained custody) both challenges and supports the idea of a critical period for language acquisition. Genie did learn some simple words and could string them together into primitive, but rule-governed, sentences. She also learned the fundamentals of sign language. But she never used language normally, and "her speech remained, for the most part, like a somewhat garbled telegram" (Pines, 1981, p. 29). When her mother became unable to manage Genie's challenging behaviour, welfare offices placed Genie into a series of poorly supervised foster homes, where she regressed into total silence.

What explains Genie's initial progress and her inability to sustain it? The fact that she was just beginning to show signs of puberty at age 13½ may indicate that she was still in the critical period, though near its end. The fact that she apparently had learned a few words before being locked up at the age of 20 months may mean that her language-learning mechanisms may have been triggered early in the critical period, allowing later learning to occur. On the other hand, the fact that she was so abused and neglected may have retarded her so much—

emotionally, socially, and cognitively—that, like Victor, she cannot be considered a true test of the critical period (Curtiss, 1977).

Case studies like those of Genie and Victor dramatize the difficulty of acquiring language after the early years of life, but they do not permit conclusive judgments because there are too many complicating factors. Researchers seeking study participants who lack early exposure to language, but whose environment and development are otherwise normal, have therefore turned to deaf persons for whom American Sign Language (ASL) is the primary language. In one cross-sectional study, the older a person had been when first exposed to ASL, the more likely that person was to sign ungrammatically and inconsistently (Newport, 1991).

A cross-sectional study of Chinese and Korean immigrants supports a critical period for second-language learning as well. The later their age of arrival, up to late adolescence, the worse their mastery of English, which held steady at a low level among those who had arrived as adults (Newport, 1991).

If a critical period for language learning exists, what explains it? Do the brain's mechanisms for acquiring language decay as the brain matures? That would seem strange, since other cognitive abilities improve. An alternative hypothesis is that this very increase in cognitive sophistication interferes with an adolescent's or adult's ability to learn a language. Young children acquire language in small chunks that can be readily digested. Older learners, when they first begin learning a language, tend to absorb a great deal at once and then may have trouble analyzing and interpreting it (Newport, 1991).

What's your view ?

Do you see any ethical problems in the studies of Genie and Victor? Is the knowledge gained from such studies worth any possible damage to the individuals involved? (Keep this question, and your answer, in mind when you read the section on ethics of research in chapter 2.)

Check it out !

For more information on this topic, go to **www.mcgrawhill.ca/college/papalia.**

Checkpoint ✓

Can you . . .

✔ Give examples of normative age-graded, normative history-graded, and non-normative influences? (Include some normative history-graded influences that affected different generations.)

✔ Explain the concept of "critical" periods and give examples?

damaged, nearly normal language development can occur—though the child may have to keep playing catch-up with normal children at each new stage of language development (M. H. Johnson, 1998). Further research may help delineate which aspects of development are decisively formed during critical periods and which aspects remain modifiable.

Now that you have had a brief introduction to the field of child development and some of its basic concepts, it's time to look more closely at the issues developmental scientists think about and how they do their work. In chapter 2, we discuss some influential theories of how development takes place and the methods investigators commonly use to study it.

Summary and Key Terms

The Study of Child Development: Then and Now

Guidepost 1 What is child development, and how has its study evolved?

- Child development is the scientific study of processes of change and stability.
- The scientific study of child development began toward the end of the nineteenth century. Adolescence was not considered a separate phase of development until the twentieth century. The field of child development is now part of the study of the entire lifespan, or human development.
- Ways of studying child development are still evolving, making use of advanced technologies.
- The distinction between basic and applied research has become less meaningful.

Guidepost 2 What are six fundamental points on which consensus has emerged?

- Consensus has emerged on several important points: (1) the interrelationship of domains of development, (2) the existence of a wide range of individual differences, (3) bidirectionality of influence, (4) the importance of history and culture, (5) children's potential for resilience, and (6) continuity of development throughout life.

  child development (5)

Child Development Today: An Introduction to the Field

Guidepost 3 What do developmental scientists study?

- Developmental scientists study developmental change, both quantitative, and qualitative, as well as stability of personality and behaviour.

  quantitative change (8)   qualitative change (8)

Guidepost 4 What are three major aspects and five periods of child development?

- The three major domains, or aspects, of development are physical, cognitive, and psychosocial. Each affects the others.
- The concept of periods of development is a social construction. In this book, child development is divided into five periods: the prenatal period, infancy and toddlerhood, early childhood, middle childhood, and adolescence. In each period, children have characteristic developmental needs and tasks.

  social construction (9)

Influences on Development

Guidepost 5 What kinds of influences make one child different from another?

- Influences on development come from both heredity and environment. Many typical changes during childhood are related to maturation. Individual differences increase with age.

  **individual differences (9)   heredity (10)   environment (10)
  maturation (10)**

- In some societies, the nuclear family predominates; in others, the extended family.
- Socio-economic status (SES) affects developmental processes and outcomes through the quality of home and neighbourhood environments, of nutrition, medical care, supervision, and schooling. The most powerful neighbourhood influences seem to be neighbourhood income and human capital. Multiple risk factors increase the likelihood of poor outcomes.
- Important environmental influences stem from ethnicity, culture, and the historical context. In large, multiethnic societies, immigrant groups often acculturate to the majority culture while preserving aspects of their own.

  **nuclear family (10)   extended family (10)
  socio-economic status (SES) (12)   risk factors (12)   culture (13)
  ethnic group (13)**

- Influences may be normative (age-graded or history-graded) or non-normative.
- There is strong evidence of critical periods for certain kinds of early development.

  **normative (13)   cohort (13) non-normative (13)
  critical period (13)   plasticity (15)**

OLC Preview

Chapter 1

The Online Learning Centre for *A Child's World,* First Canadian Edition, offers links to additional information on language acquisition, historic views of childhood, and the residential school exprience of First Nations children. Check out **www.mcgrawhill.ca/ college/papalia.**

A Child's World: How We Discover It

There is one thing even more vital to science than intelligent methods: and that is, the sincere desire to find out the truth, whatever it may be.

—Charles Sanders Peirce, *Collected Papers*, vol. 5, 1934

Focus *Margaret Mead, Pioneer in Cross-cultural Research*

Margaret Mead

Margaret Mead (1901–1978) was a world-famous American anthropologist. In the 1920s, at a time when it was rare for a woman to expose herself to the rigours of field work with remote, preliterate peoples, Mead spent nine months on the South Pacific island of Samoa, studying girls' adjustment to adolescence. Her best-selling first book, *Coming of Age in Samoa* (1928), challenged accepted views about the inevitability of adolescent rebellion.

An itinerant childhood built around her parents' academic pursuits prepared Mead for a life of roving research. In New Jersey, her mother, who was working on her doctoral thesis in sociology, took Margaret along on interviews with recent Italian immigrants—the child's first exposure to fieldwork. Her father, a professor at the University of Pennsylvania's Wharton business school, taught her respect for facts and "the importance of thinking clearly" (Mead, 1972, p. 40). He stressed the link between theory and application—as Margaret did when, years later, she applied her theories of child rearing to her daughter. Margaret's grandmother, a former schoolteacher, sent her out in the woods to collect and analyze mint specimens. "I was not well drilled in geography or spelling," Mead wrote in her memoir *Blackberry Winter* (1972, p. 47). "But I learned to observe the world around me and to note what I saw."

Margaret took copious notes on the development of her younger brother and two younger sisters. Her curiosity about why one child in a family behaved so differently from another led to her later interest in temperamental variations within a culture.

How cultures define male and female roles was another research focus. Margaret saw her mother and her grandmother as educated women who had managed to have husbands, children, and professional careers; and she expected to do the same. She was dismayed when, at the outset of her career, the distinguished anthropologist Edward Sapir told her she "would do better to stay at home and have children than to go off to the South Seas to study adolescent girls" (Mead, 1972, p. 11).

Margaret's choice of anthropology as a career was consistent with her homebred respect for the value of all human beings and their cultures. Recalling her father's insistence that the only thing worth doing is to add to the store of knowledge, she saw an urgent need to document once-isolated cultures now "vanishing before the onslaught of modern civilization" (Mead, 1972, p. 137).

"I went to Samoa—as, later, I went to the other societies on which I have worked—to find out more about human beings, human beings like ourselves in everything except their culture," she wrote. "Through the accidents of history, these cultures had developed so differently from ours that knowledge of them could shed a kind of light upon us, upon our potentialities and our limitations" (Mead, 1972, p. 293). The ongoing quest to illuminate those "potentialities and limitations" is the business of theorists and researchers in human development.

● ● ●

Margaret Mead's life was all of a piece. The young girl who filled notebooks with observations about her siblings became the scientist who travelled to distant lands and studied cultures very different from her own.

Mead's story underlines several important points about the study of child development. First, the study of children is not dry, abstract, or esoteric. It deals with the substance of real life.

Second, a cross-cultural perspective can reveal which patterns of behaviour, if any, are universal and which are not. Most studies of child development have been done in North American and European societies, using white, middle-class participants. Today developmental scientists are increasingly conscious of the need to expand the research base, as Mead and her colleagues sought to do.

Third, theory and research are two sides of the same coin. As Mead reflected on her own experiences and observed the behaviour of others, she constantly formed tentative explanations to be tested by later research.

Fourth, although the goal of science is to obtain verifiable knowledge through open-minded, impartial investigation, observations about human behaviour are products of very human individuals whose inquiries and interpretations may be influenced by their own background, values, and experiences. As Mead's daughter, Mary Catherine Bateson (1984), herself an anthropologist, noted in response to methodological criticism of Mead's early work in Samoa, a scientific observer is like a lens, which may introduce some distortion into what is observed. This is why scientists have others check their results. In striving for greater objectivity, investigators must scrutinize how they and their colleagues conduct their work, the assumptions on which it is based, and how they arrive at their conclusions. And in studying the results of research, it is important to keep these potential biases in mind.

In the first part of this chapter, we present major issues and theoretical perspectives that underlie much research in child development. In the remainder of the chapter, we look at how researchers gather and assess information, so that you will be better able to judge whether their conclusions rest on solid ground.

After you have read and studied this chapter, you should be able to answer each of the Guidepost questions that appear at the top of the next page. Look for them again in the margins, where they point to important concepts throughout the chapter. To check your understanding of these Guideposts, review the end-of-chapter summary. Checkpoints located throughout the chapter will help you verify your understanding of what you have read.

Guideposts for Study

1. What purposes do theories serve?

2. What are three basic theoretical issues on which developmental scientists differ?

3. What are five theoretical perspectives on child development, and what are some theories representative of each?

4. How do developmental scientists study children, and what are some advantages and disadvantages of each research method?

5. What ethical problems may arise in research on children?

Basic Theoretical Issues

Developmental scientists have come up with many theories about how children develop. A **theory** is a set of logically related concepts or statements, which seeks to describe and explain development and to predict what kinds of behaviour might occur under certain conditions. Theories organize data, the information gathered by research, and are a rich source of **hypotheses**—tentative explanations or predictions that can be tested by further research.

Theories change to incorporate new findings. Sometimes research supports a hypothesis and the theory on which it was based. At other times, as with Mead's findings challenging the inevitability of adolescent rebellion, scientists must modify their theories to account for unexpected data. Research findings often suggest additional questions and hypotheses to be examined and provide direction for dealing with practical issues.

The way theorists explain development depends in part on the way they view three basic issues: (1) the relative weight given to heredity and environment, with a view to understanding the interactions between the two; (2) whether children are active or passive in their own development, focusing on the circumstances under which children tend to be active or passive; and (3) whether development is continuous or occurs in stages. These three basic issues give us a context for understanding how researchers have characterized development. In all aspects of development, the most accurate perspective on each issue lies between the two extremes.

Issue 1: Which Is More Important—Heredity or Environment?

Which has more impact on development: heredity or environment? This issue has aroused intense debate. Theorists have differed in the relative importance they give to *nature* (the inborn traits and characteristics inherited from the biological parents) and *nurture* (environmental influences, both before and after birth, including influences of family, peers, schools, neighbourhoods, society, and culture).

How much is inherited? How much is environmentally influenced? These questions matter. If parents believe that intelligence can be strongly influenced by experience, they may make special efforts to talk to and read to their children and offer them toys that help them learn. If parents believe that intelligence is inborn and unchangeable, they may be less likely to make such efforts.

Today, scientists have found ways to measure more precisely the roles of heredity and environment in the development of specific traits within a population (Neisser et al., 1996). When we look at a particular child, however, research on almost all characteristics points to a blend of inheritance and experience. Thus, even though intelligence has a strong hereditary component, parental stimulation, education, peer influence, and other variables make a difference. While there is still considerable dispute about the relative importance of nature and nurture, many contemporary theorists and researchers are more interested in finding ways to explain how they work together.

Guidepost 1

What purposes do theories serve?

theory Coherent set of logically related concepts that seeks to organize, explain, and predict data

hypotheses Possible explanations for phenomena, used to predict the outcome of research

Guidepost 2

What are three basic theoretical issues on which developmental scientists differ?

Issue 2: Are Children Active or Passive in Their Development?

Are children active or passive in their own development? This controversy goes back to the eighteenth century (refer back to Figure 1-1), when the English philosopher John Locke held that a young child is a *tabula rasa*—a "blank slate"—on which society "writes." In contrast, the French philosopher Jean Jacques Rousseau believed that children are born "noble savages" who would develop according to their own positive natural tendencies unless corrupted by a repressive society. We now know that both views are too simplistic. Children have their own internal drives and needs, as well as hereditary endowments, that influence development; but children also are social animals, who cannot achieve optimal development in isolation.

The debate over Locke's and Rousseau's philosophies led to two contrasting models, or images, of development: *mechanistic* and *organismic*. Locke's view was the forerunner of the **mechanistic model** of development. In this model, people are like machines that react to environmental input (Pepper, 1942). Fill a car with gas, turn the ignition key, press the accelerator, and the vehicle will move. In the mechanistic view, human behaviour is much the same. If we know enough about how the human "machine" is put together and about the internal and external forces impinging on it, we can predict what the person will do. Mechanistic research seeks to identify and isolate the factors that make people behave—or react—as they do.

Rousseau was the precursor of the **organismic model** of development. This model sees people as active, growing organisms that set their own development in motion (Pepper, 1942). They initiate events; they do not just react. The impetus for change is internal. Environmental influences do not cause development, though they can speed or slow it. Human behaviour is an organic whole; it cannot be predicted by breaking it down into simple responses to environmental stimulation, as the mechanistic model suggests.

mechanistic model Model that views development as a passive, predictable response to stimuli

organismic model Model that views development as internally initiated by an active organism and as occurring in a sequence of qualitatively different stages

Issue 3: Is Development Continuous, or Does It Occur in Stages?

The mechanistic and organismic models also differ on the third issue: Is development continuous, or does it occur in stages?

Mechanistic theorists see development as continuous, like walking or crawling up a ramp (see Figure 2-1). These theorists describe development as always governed by the same processes, allowing prediction of earlier behaviours from later ones. These theorists focus on *quantitative* change: for example, changes in the frequency with which a response is made, rather than changes in the kind of response.

Figure 2-1

A major difference among developmental theories is *(a)* whether development occurs in distinct stages, as Piaget, Freud, and Erikson maintained or *(b)* whether it proceeds continuously, as learning theorists and information-processing theorists propose

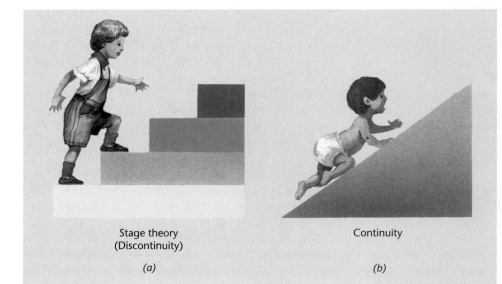

Stage theory
(Discontinuity)

(a)

Continuity

(b)

Organismic theorists emphasize *qualitative* change (Looft, 1973). They see development as occurring in a series of distinct stages, like stair steps. At each stage, people cope with different kinds of problems and develop different kinds of abilities. Each stage builds on the previous one and prepares the way for the next.

An Emerging Consensus

As the study of human development has evolved, the mechanistic and organismic models have shifted in influence and support (Parke, Ornstein, Rieser, & Zahn-Waxler, 1994). Most of the early pioneers in the field, such as Hall, Alfred Binet, and Arnold Gesell (refer back to Figure 1-1), favoured organismic or stage approaches. So did Sigmund Freud, Erik Erikson, and Jean Piaget. However, the mechanistic view gained support during the 1960s with the popularity of learning theories derived from the work of John B. Watson. (We discuss all these theorists in the next section.)

Today the pendulum has swung back part way. Quasi-organismic approaches centred on the biological bases of behaviour are on the rise; but instead of looking for broad stages, there is an effort to discover what specific kinds of behaviour show continuity or lack of continuity and what processes are involved in each.

Just as a consensus is emerging about how heredity and environment work together, many developmentalists are coming to a more balanced view of active versus passive development. There is wide agreement that influence is bidirectional: Children change their world even as it changes them. A baby girl born with a cheerful disposition is likely to get positive responses from adults, which strengthen her trust that her smiles will be rewarded and motivate her to smile more. As children grow older, their natural tendencies lead them to choose or initiate activities, such as studying a musical instrument, that further develop those tendencies.

Checkpoint ✔

Can you . . .

✔ State three basic issues regarding the nature of child development?

✔ Contrast the mechanistic and organismic models of development?

Theoretical Perspectives

Despite the growing consensus on the basic issues just discussed, many investigators view development from differing theoretical perspectives. Theories generally fall within these broad perspectives, each of which emphasizes different kinds of developmental processes. These perspectives influence the questions researchers ask, the methods they use, and the ways they interpret data. Therefore, to evaluate and interpret research, it is important to recognize the theoretical perspective on which it is based. It is also important to recognize that these theories have their roots in European and North American culture, and do not necessarily reflect perspectives on child development for all cultures, particularly eastern cultures.

Five major perspectives (summarized in Table 2-1) underlie much influential theory and research on child development: (1) *psychoanalytic* (which focuses on unconscious emotions and drives); (2) *learning* (which studies observable behaviour); (3) *cognitive* (which analyzes thought processes); (4) *ethological* (which considers evolutionary underpinnings of behaviour); and (5) *contextual* (which emphasizes the impact of the historical, social, and cultural context).

Perspective 1: Psychoanalytic

The **psychoanalytic perspective** views development as shaped by unconscious forces that motivate human behaviour. Sigmund Freud (1856–1939), a Viennese physician, developed *psychoanalysis,* a therapeutic approach aimed at giving patients insight into unconscious emotional conflicts. Other theorists and practitioners, including Erik H. Erikson, have expanded and modified the psychoanalytic perspective.

Sigmund Freud: Psychosexual Development

Freud (1953, 1964a, 1964b) believed that people are born with biological drives that must be redirected to make it possible to live in society. By asking his patients questions designed to summon up long-buried memories, Freud concluded that the source of emotional

Guidepost 3

What are five theoretical perspectives on child development, and what are some theories representative of each?

psychoanalytic perspective
View of development as shaped by unconscious forces

The Viennese physician Sigmund Freud developed an influential but controversial theory of childhood emotional development.

Table 2-1   Five Perspectives on Human Development

Perspective	Important Theories	Basic Beliefs
Psychoanalytic	Freud's psychosexual theory	Behaviour is controlled by powerful unconscious urges.
	Erikson's psychosocial theory	Personality is influenced by society and develops through a series of crises.
Learning	Behaviourism, or traditional learning theory (Pavlov, Skinner, Watson)	People are responders; the environment controls behaviour.
	Social-learning (social-cognitive) theory (Bandura)	Children learn in a social context by observing and imitating models; person is an active contributor to learning.
Cognitive	Piaget's cognitive-stage theory	Qualitative changes in thought occur between infancy and adolescence. Person is active initiator of development.
	Information-processing theory	Human beings are processors of symbols.
Ethological	Bowlby's and Ainsworth's attachment theory	Human beings have the adaptive mechanisms to survive; critical or sensitive periods are stressed; biological and evolutionary bases for behaviour and predisposition toward learning are important.
Contextual	Bronfenbrenner's bio-ecological theory	Development occurs through interaction between a developing person and five surrounding, interlocking contextual systems of influences, from microsystem to chronosystem.
	Vygotsky's socio-cultural theory	Socio-cultural context is central to development.

psychosexual development
In Freudian theory, an unvarying sequence of stages of personality development during infancy, childhood, and adolescence, in which gratification shifts from the mouth to the anus and then to the genitals

The psychoanalyst Erik H. Erikson departed from Freudian theory in emphasizing societal, rather than chiefly biological, influences on personality.

disturbances lay in repressed traumatic experiences of early childhood. He proposed that personality is formed in childhood, as children deal with unconscious conflicts between these inborn urges and the requirements of civilized life. These conflicts occur in an unvarying sequence of five maturationally based stages of **psychosexual development** (see Table 2-2), in which pleasure shifts from one body zone to another—from the mouth to the anus and then to the genitals. At each stage, the behaviour that is the chief source of gratification (or frustration) changes—from feeding to elimination and eventually to sexual activity.

Freud considered the first three stages—those of the first few years of life—crucial. He suggested that if children receive too little or too much gratification in any of these stages, they are at risk of *fixation*—an arrest in development that can show up in adult personality. For example, babies whose needs are not met during the *oral stage*, when feeding is the main source of sensual pleasure, may grow up to become nail-biters or develop "bitingly" critical personalities.

Freud proposed three hypothetical parts of the personality: the *id*, the *ego*, and the *superego*. Newborns are governed by the *id*, which seeks immediate satisfaction under the *pleasure principle*. When gratification is delayed, as it is when infants have to wait to be fed, they begin to see themselves as separate from the outside world. The *ego*, which represents reason, develops gradually during the first year or so of life and operates under the *reality principle*. The ego's aim is to find realistic ways to gratify the id that are acceptable to the *superego*, which develops at about age 5 or 6. The *superego* includes the conscience and incorporates socially approved "shoulds" and "should nots" into the child's own value system. The superego is highly demanding; if its demands are not met, a child may feel guilty and anxious.

According to Freud, a key event in psychosexual development occurs in early childhood. Boys develop sexual attachment to their mothers and girls to their fathers, and they have aggressive urges toward the same-sex parent, whom they regard as a rival. Children eventually resolve their anxiety over these feelings by identifying with the same-sex parent and move into the *latency stage* of middle childhood. They become socialized, develop skills, and learn about themselves and society. The *genital stage*, the final one, lasts throughout adulthood. The sexual urges repressed during latency now resurface to flow in socially approved channels, which Freud defined as heterosexual relations with persons outside the family of origin.

Technique Used	Stage-Oriented	Causal Emphasis	Active or Passive Individual
Clinical observation	Yes	Innate factors modified by experience	Passive
Clinical observation	Yes	Interaction of innate and experiential factors	Active
Rigorous scientific (experimental) procedures	No	Experience	Passive
Rigorous scientific (experimental) procedures	No	Experienced modified by innate factors	Active and passive
Flexible interviews; meticulous observation	Yes	Interaction of innate and experiential factors	Active
Laboratory research; technological monitoring of physiologic responses	No	Interaction of innate and experiential factors	Active and passive
Naturalistic and laboratory observation	No	Interaction of innate and experiential factors	Active or passive (theorists vary)
Naturalistic observation and analysis	No	Interaction of innate and experiential factors	Active
Cross-cultural research; observation of child interacting with more competent person	No	Experience	Active

Freud described a number of *defence mechanisms,* or ways in which people deal with childhood experiences that cause anxiety, such as the birth of a sibling or entrance into school. A person may *repress* these early experiences, or the feelings they arouse, that is, block them from consciousness and memory. Or a child dealing with a worrisome event may *regress*—revert to earlier behaviour, such as sucking a thumb or wetting the bed.

Freud's theory made historic contributions, and several of his central themes have been validated by research, though others have not (Emde, 1992; Westen, 1998). Freud made us aware of the importance of unconscious thoughts, feelings, and motivations; the role of childhood experiences in forming personality; the ambivalence of emotional responses, especially to parents; and ways in which early relationships affect later ones. Freud also opened our eyes to the presence from birth of sexual urges. Although many psychoanalysts today reject his narrow emphasis on sexual and aggressive drives, his psychoanalytic method greatly influenced modern-day psychotherapy.

We need to remember that Freud's theory grew out of his place in history and in society. Freud based his theories about normal development, not on a population of average children, but on a clientele of upper-middle-class adults, mostly women, in therapy. His concentration on biological and maturational factors and on early experience does not take into account other, and later, influences on personality—including the influences of society and culture, which many heirs to the Freudian tradition, notably Erikson, stress.

Erik Erikson: Psychosocial Development

Erik Erikson (1902–1994), a German-born psychoanalyst who originally was part of Freud's circle in Vienna, modified and extended Freudian theory by emphasizing the influence of society on the developing personality. Whereas Freud maintained that early childhood experiences permanently shape personality, Erikson contended that ego development is lifelong.

Erikson's (1950, 1982; Erikson, Erikson, & Kivnick, 1986) theory of **psychosocial development** covers eight stages across the lifespan (refer to Table 2-2), which we will discuss in the appropriate chapters. Each stage involves a "crisis" in personality—a major developmental issue that is particularly important at that time and will remain an issue to some degree throughout the rest of life. The crises, which emerge according to a maturational timetable, must be satisfactorily resolved for healthy ego development.

Checkpoint

Can you . . .

✔ Identify the chief focus of the psychoanalytic perspective?

✔ Name Freud's five stages of development and three parts of the personality?

psychosocial development In Erikson's eight-stage theory, the socially and culturally influenced process of development of the ego, or self

Table 2-2	Developmental Stages According to Various Theories	
Psychosexual Stages (Freud)	**Psychosocial Stages (Erikson)**	**Cognitive Stages (Piaget)**
Oral (birth to 12–18 months). Baby's chief source of pleasure involves mouth-oriented activities (sucking and feeding).	*Basic trust versus mistrust (birth to 12–18 months).* Baby develops sense of whether world is a good and safe place. Virtue: hope.	*Sensorimotor (birth to 2 years).* Infant gradually becomes able to organize activities in relation to the environment through sensory and motor activity.
Anal (12–18 months to 3 years). Child derives sensual gratification from withholding and expelling feces. Zone of gratification is anal region, and toilet training is important activity.	*Autonomy versus shame and doubt (12–18 months to 3 years).* Child develops a balance of independence and self-sufficiency over shame and doubt. Virtue: will.	*Pre-operational (2 to 7 years).* Child develops a representational system and uses symbols to represent people, places, and events. Language and imaginative play are important manifestations of this stage. Thinking is still not logical.
Phallic (3 to 6 years). Child becomes attached to parent of the other sex and later identifies with same-sex parent. Superego develops. Zone of gratification shifts to genital region.	*Initiative versus guilt (3 to 6 years).* Child develops initiative when trying out new activities and is not overwhelmed by guilt. Virtue: purpose.	
Latency (6 years to puberty). Time of relative calm between more turbulent stages.	*Industry versus inferiority (6 years to puberty).* Child must learn skills of the culture or face feelings of incompetence. Virtue: skill.	*Concrete operations (7 to 11 years).* Child can solve problems logically if they are focused on the here and now, but cannot think abstractly.
Genital (puberty through adulthood). Re-emergence of sexual impulses of phallic stage, channelled into mature adult sexuality.	*Identity versus identity confusion (puberty to young adulthood).* Adolescent must determine own sense of self ("Who am I?") or experience confusion about roles. Virtue: fidelity.	*Formal operations (11 years through adulthood).* Person can think abstractly, deal with hypothetical situations, and think about possibilities.
	Intimacy versus isolation (young adulthood). Person seeks to make commitments to others; if unsuccessful, may suffer from isolation and self-absorption. Virtue: love.	
	Generativity versus stagnation (middle adulthood). Mature adult is concerned with establishing and guiding the next generation or else feels personal impoverishment. Virtue: care.	
	Integrity versus despair (late adulthood). Elderly person achieves acceptance of own life, allowing acceptance of death, or else despairs over inability to relive life. Virtue: wisdom.	

Note: All ages are approximate.

Checkpoint ✓

Can you . . .

✔ Tell two ways in which Erikson's theory differs from Freud's?

✔ Explain Erikson's concept of crises in development?

Successful resolution of each of the eight crises requires the balancing of a positive trait and a corresponding negative one. Although the positive quality should predominate, some degree of the negative is needed as well. The crisis of infancy, for example, is *basic trust versus basic mistrust*. People need to trust the world and the people in it, but they also need to learn some mistrust to protect themselves from danger. The successful outcome of each crisis is the development of a particular "virtue" or strength—in this first crisis, the virtue of *hope*.

Erikson's theory has held up better than Freud's, especially in its emphasis on social and cultural influences and on development beyond adolescence. However, some of Erikson's concepts (like Freud's) are difficult to test.

A recent psychoanalytic perspective by Jean Baker Miller emphasizes the importance of relationships as a source of psychological growth and health in women. According to Miller's Relational Model of women's development, interactions through relationships lead to healthy development through empathic listening in day-to-day interactions. These interactions create moments of connection that foster healthy psychological growth (Miller & Stiver, 1997). Miller's perspective has contributed to our understanding of development that is specific to women, but it has been criticized for assuming that traditional gender roles and distinctions are universal, and that other characteristics might not be as important in fostering healthy psychological growth.

Perspective 2: Learning

The **learning perspective** maintains that development results from learning, a long-lasting change in behaviour based on experience, or adaptation to the environment. Learning theorists are concerned with finding out the objective laws that govern changes in observable behaviour. They see development as continuous (not in stages) and emphasize quantitative change.

Learning theorists have helped to make the study of human development more scientific. Their terms are defined precisely, and their theories can be tested in the laboratory. By stressing environmental influences, they help explain cultural differences in behaviour.

Two important learning theories are *behaviourism* and *social learning theory*.

Learning Theory 1: Behaviourism

Behaviourism is a mechanistic theory, which describes observed behaviour as a predictable response to experience. Although biology sets limits on what people do, behaviourists view the environment as much more influential. They hold that human beings at all ages learn about the world the same way other organisms do: by reacting to conditions, or aspects of their environment, that they find pleasing, painful, or threatening. Behaviourists look for events that determine whether or not a particular behaviour will be repeated. Behavioural research focuses on *associative learning,* in which a mental link is formed between two events. Two kinds of associative learning are *classical conditioning* and *operant conditioning.*

Classical Conditioning The Russian physiologist Ivan Pavlov (1849–1936) devised experiments in which dogs learned to salivate at the sound of a bell that rang at feeding time. These experiments were the foundation for **classical conditioning**, in which a response (salivation) to a stimulus (the bell) is evoked after repeated association with a stimulus that normally elicits it (food).

The American behaviourist John B. Watson (1878–1958) applied stimulus–response theories to children, claiming that he could mould any infant in any way he chose. In one of the earliest and most famous demonstrations of classical conditioning in human beings (Watson & Rayner, 1920), he taught an 11-month-old baby known as "Little Albert" to fear furry white objects.

In this study, Albert was exposed to a loud noise just as he was about to stroke a furry white rat. The noise frightened him, and he began to cry. After repeated pairings of the rat with the loud noise, Albert whimpered with fear whenever he saw the rat. Although such research would be considered unethical today, the study did show that a baby could be conditioned to fear things he had not been afraid of before.

Critics of such methods sometimes associate conditioning with thought control and manipulation. Actually, as we will discuss in chapter 7, classical conditioning is a natural form of learning that occurs even without intervention. By learning what events go together, children can anticipate what is going to happen, and this knowledge makes their world a more orderly, predictable place.

Operant Conditioning Baby Terrell is eating breakfast happily in his high chair. Suddenly, he throws his spoon full of Pablum onto the floor, and his parents stop talking and turn to the baby in surprise. His father returns the spoon, after brushing some cereal from his trousers, and the parents resume their breakfast conversation. Minutes later, the spoon hits the floor again, as Terrell's parents turn to him again in surprise. As this sequence is repeated, Terrell learns that something he does (throwing down the spoon) can produce something he likes (his parents' attention); and so he keeps throwing the spoon to attract his parents' attention.

This kind of learning is called **operant conditioning** because the individual learns from the consequences of "operating" on the environment. Unlike classical conditioning, operant conditioning involves voluntary behaviour, such as Terrell's spoon tossing.

The American psychologist B. F. Skinner (1904–1990), who formulated the principles of operant conditioning, worked primarily with rats and pigeons, but Skinner (1938) maintained

---

learning perspective View of development that holds that changes in behaviour result from experience, or adaptation to the environment

behaviourism Learning theory that emphasizes the predictable role of environment in causing observable behaviour

classical conditioning Learning based on associating a stimulus that does not ordinarily elicit a particular response with another stimulus that ordinarily does elicit the response

What's your view ?

- In an experiment with classical conditioning, what standards would you suggest to safeguard participants' rights?

operant conditioning Learning based on reinforcement or punishment

reinforcement In operant conditioning, a stimulus that encourages repetition of a desired behaviour

punishment In operant conditioning, a stimulus that discourages repetition of a behaviour

The American psychologist B. F. Skinner formulated the principles of operant conditioning.

social learning theory Theory that behaviours are learned by observing and imitating models; also called *social cognitive theory*

observational learning Learning through watching the behaviour of others

Checkpoint ✔

Can you . . .

✔ Identify the chief concerns, strengths, and weaknesses of the learning perspective?

✔ Tell how classical conditioning and operant conditioning differ?

✔ Distinguish among positive reinforcement, negative reinforcement, and punishment?

✔ Compare behaviourism and social learning (social cognitive) theory?

that the same principles apply to human beings. He found that an organism will tend to repeat a response that has been reinforced and will suppress a response that has been punished. **Reinforcement** is a consequence of behaviour that increases the likelihood that the behaviour will be repeated; in Terrell's case, his parents' attention reinforces his spoon throwing. **Punishment** is a consequence of behaviour that *decreases* the likelihood of repetition. If Terrell's parents ignored him when he threw the spoon, he would be less likely to throw the spoon again. Whether a consequence is reinforcing or punishing depends on the person. What is reinforcing for one person may be punishing for another. For example, for a child who likes being alone, being sent to his or her room could be reinforcing rather than punishing.

Reinforcement can be either positive or negative. *Positive reinforcement* consists of *giving* a reward, such as food, gold stars, money, or praise—or playing with a baby. *Negative reinforcement* consists of *taking away* something the individual does not like (known as an *aversive event*), such as a loud noise. Negative reinforcement is sometimes confused with punishment. However, they are different. Punishment *suppresses* a behaviour by *bringing on* an aversive event (such as spanking a child or giving an electric shock to an animal), or by *withdrawing* a positive event (such as watching television). Negative reinforcement *encourages* repetition of a behaviour by *removing* an aversive event. When an older baby signals a wet diaper, the removal of the diaper may encourage the child to signal again the next time a diaper is wet.

Reinforcement is most effective when it immediately follows a behaviour. If a response is no longer reinforced, it will eventually be *extinguished,* that is, return to its original (baseline) level. If, after a while, no one reacts to Terrell when he throws a spoon, he may not stop spoon throwing but will do so far less than if his throwing still brought reinforcement.

Behaviour modification, or behaviour therapy, is a form of operant conditioning used to eliminate undesirable behaviour or to instill positive behaviour. Behaviour modification is particularly effective among children with special needs, such as youngsters with mental or emotional disabilities.

Learning Theory 2: Social Learning (Social Cognitive) Theory

Social learning theory maintains that children learn social behaviours by observing and imitating models. The Canadian-born psychologist Albert Bandura (b. 1925) developed many of the principles of social learning theory, also known as *social cognitive theory,* which today is more influential than behaviourism.

Whereas behaviourists see the environment as moulding the person, social learning theorists (Bandura, 1977, 1989) believe that the person also *acts upon* the environment— in fact, *creates* the environment to some extent. People learn in a social context, and human learning is more complex than simple conditioning. Social learning theorists see cognitive responses to perceptions, rather than largely automatic responses to reinforcement or punishment, as central to development.

In social learning theory people acquire new abilities through **observational learning**— by watching other people. Children actively advance their own social learning by choosing *models* to imitate—say, a parent or a popular sports hero. According to social learning theory, imitation of models is the most important element in how children learn a language, deal with aggression, develop a moral sense, and learn gender-appropriate behaviours. However, observational learning can occur even if the child does not imitate the observed behaviour.

The specific behaviour children imitate depends on what they perceive as valued in their culture. If all the teachers in Carl's school are women, he probably will not copy their behaviour, which he may consider contrary to his idea of himself as male. However, if he meets a male teacher he likes, he may change his mind about the value of teachers as models.

Cognitive processes are at work as people observe models, learn "chunks" of behaviour, and mentally put the chunks together into complex new behaviour patterns. Rita, for example, imitates the toes-out walk of her dance teacher but models her dance steps after those of Danielle, a slightly more advanced student. Even so, she develops her own style of dancing by putting her observations together into a new pattern. Children's developing ability to use mental symbols to stand for a model's behaviour enables them to form standards for judging their own behaviour.

Perspective 3: Cognitive

The **cognitive perspective** focuses on thought processes and the behaviour that reflects those processes. This perspective encompasses both organismic and mechanistically influenced theories. It includes the cognitive-stage theory of Piaget, the newer information-processing approach, and neo-Piagetian theories, which combine elements of both. It also includes contemporary efforts to apply findings of brain research to the understanding of cognitive processes.

cognitive perspective View that thought processes are central to development

Jean Piaget's Cognitive-Stage Theory

Much of what we know about how children think is due to the Swiss theoretician Jean Piaget (1896–1980). Piaget's theory was the forerunner of today's "cognitive revolution" with its emphasis on mental processes. Piaget viewed children organismically, as active, growing beings with their own internal impulses and patterns of development. He saw cognitive development as the product of children's efforts to understand and act on their world.

As a young man studying in Paris, Piaget set out to standardize the tests Alfred Binet had developed to assess the intelligence of French schoolchildren (see chapter 7). Piaget became intrigued by the children's wrong answers, finding in them clues to their thought processes. Piaget's *clinical method* combined observation with flexible questioning. To find out how children think, Piaget followed up their answers with more questions. In this way he discovered that a typical 4-year-old believed that pennies or flowers were more numerous when arranged in a line than when heaped or piled up. From his observations of his own and other children, Piaget created a comprehensive theory of cognitive development.

The Swiss psychologist Jean Piaget studied children's cognitive development by observing and talking with his own youngsters and others.

Piaget believed that cognitive development begins with an inborn ability to adapt to the environment. As they encounter new experiences, children modify their view of the world and act accordingly. By rooting for a nipple, feeling a pebble, or exploring the boundaries of a room, young children develop a more accurate picture of their surroundings and greater competence in dealing with them.

Piaget described cognitive development as occurring in a series of qualitatively different stages (listed in Table 2-2 and discussed in detail in later chapters). At each stage a child's mind develops a new way of operating. From infancy through adolescence, mental operations evolve from learning based on simple sensory and motor activity to logical, abstract thought. This gradual development occurs through three interrelated principles: *organization, adaptation,* and *equilibration.*

Organization is the tendency to create increasingly complex cognitive structures: systems of knowledge or ways of thinking that incorporate more and more accurate images of reality. These structures, called **schemes,** are organized patterns of behaviour that a person uses to think about and act in a situation. As children acquire more information, their schemes become more and more complex. An infant has a simple scheme for sucking, but soon develops varied schemes for how to suck at the breast, a bottle, or a thumb.

Adaptation is Piaget's term for how a child handles new information that seems to conflict with what the child already knows. Adaptation may involve two processes: (1) **assimilation,** taking in information and incorporating it into existing cognitive structures, and (2) **accommodation,** changing one's cognitive structures to include the new knowledge.

Equilibration—a constant striving for a stable balance, or equilibrium—dictates a shift from assimilation to accommodation. When children cannot handle new experiences within their existing structures, they organize new mental patterns that integrate the new experience, thus restoring equilibrium. A breast- or bottle-fed baby who begins to suck on the spout of a "sippy" cup is showing assimilation—using an old scheme to deal with a new object or situation. When the infant discovers that sipping from a cup requires tongue and mouth movements somewhat different from those used to suck on a breast or bottle, she accommodates by modifying the old scheme. She has adapted her original sucking scheme to deal with a new experience: the cup. Thus, assimilation and accommodation work together to produce equilibrium and cognitive growth.

Piaget's careful observations have yielded a wealth of information, including some surprising insights. Who, for example, would have thought that not until about age 7 do children realize that when a ball of clay is rolled into a "worm" before their eyes, it still contains the same amount of clay? Or that an infant might think that a person who has

organization Piaget's term for integration of knowledge into systems

schemes Piaget's term for organized patterns of behaviour used in different situations

adaptation Piaget's term for adjustment to new information about the environment

assimilation Piaget's term for incorporation of new information into an existing cognitive structure

accommodation Piaget's term for changes in a cognitive structure to include new information

equilibration Piaget's term for the tendency to seek a stable balance among cognitive elements

moved out of sight may no longer exist? Piaget has shown us that children's minds are not miniature adult minds. Understanding how children think makes it easier for parents and teachers to teach them.

Yet, as we discuss in chapters 7 and 10, Piaget seriously underestimated the abilities of infants and young children, and he paid little attention to individual differences. Some contemporary psychologists question his clearly demarcated stages; they point to evidence that cognitive development is more gradual and continuous (Flavell, 1992). Furthermore, as we will see, research beginning in the late 1960s has challenged Piaget's basic idea that children's thinking develops in a single, universal progression leading to formal thought. Instead, children's cognitive processes seem closely tied to specific content (what they are thinking *about*), as well as to the particular context of a problem and the kinds of information and thought a culture considers important (Case & Okamoto, 1996).

The Information-Processing Approach

information-processing approach Approach to the study of cognitive development by observing and analyzing the mental processes involved in perceiving and handling information

The newer **information-processing approach**, although not originally a developmental model, has been useful to developmentalists who attempt to explain cognitive development by observing and analyzing the mental processes involved in perceiving and handling information. The information-processing approach is a framework, or set of assumptions, that underlies a wide range of theories and research that focus on different types of cognitive processes.

Information-processing theorists compare the brain to a computer. Sensory impressions go in; behaviour comes out. But what happens in between? How does the brain take sensation and perception, say, of an unfamiliar face, and use it to recognize that face again?

Information-processing researchers *infer* what goes on between a stimulus and a response. For example, they may ask a child to recall a list of words and then observe any difference in performance if the child repeats the list over and over before being asked to recall the words. Through such studies, some information-processing researchers have developed *computational models* or flow charts analyzing the specific steps children go through in gathering, storing, retrieving, and using information.

Despite the use of the "passive" computer model, information-processing theorists see people as active thinkers about their world. Unlike Piaget, they generally do not propose stages of development, but they do note age-related increases in the speed, complexity, and efficiency of mental processing and in the amount and variety of material that can be stored in memory.

The information-processing approach has practical applications for child development. It enables researchers to estimate an infant's later intelligence from the efficiency of sensory perception and processing. It enables parents and teachers to help children learn by making them more aware of their own mental processes, and of strategies to enhance them. And psychologists can use information-processing models to test, diagnose, and treat learning problems. By pinpointing weaknesses in the information-processing system, they can tell whether a child's difficulty is with vision or hearing, attentiveness, or getting information into memory (R. M. Thomas, 1996).

Neo-Piagetian Theories

During the 1980s, in response to challenges to Piaget's theory, neo-Piagetian developmental psychologists began to integrate some elements of his theory with the information-processing approach. Instead of describing a single, general system of increasingly logical mental operations, neo-Piagetians focus on *specific* concepts, strategies, and skills. They believe that children develop cognitively by becoming more efficient at processing information. According to the Canadian developmentalist Robbie Case (1944–2000), there is a limit to the amount of information a child can keep in mind (Case 1985, 1992). For example, a 6-year-old who is sounding out letters may not be able to think about the meaning of what he is reading at the same time. By practising, the child can become faster and more proficient, freeing mental "space" for additional information and more complex problem solving. Maturation of neurological processes also expands available memory capacity.

Case (Case & Okamoto, 1996) tested a model (further discussed in chapter 13) that modified Piaget's idea of cognitive structures. Unlike Piaget's *operational* structures, such as concrete and formal operations, which apply to any domain of thought, Case proposed *conceptual*

Checkpoint ✔

Can you ...

✔ Contrast Piaget's assumptions and methods with those of classical learning theory and of the information-processing approach?

✔ List three interrelated principles that bring about cognitive growth, according to Piaget, and give an example of each?

✔ Describe what information-processing researchers do?

structures within specific domains such as number, story understanding, and spatial relations. As children acquire knowledge, they go through stages in which their conceptual structures become more complex, better coordinated, and multidimensional. For example, a child's understanding of spatial concepts begins by recognizing the shapes of objects, moves on to a sense of their relative size and location, and then to an understanding of perspective.

The neo-Piagetian approach is a promising effort to explain the processes by which changes in cognition occur. Because of its emphasis on efficiency of processing, it helps account for individual differences in cognitive ability and for uneven development in various domains. Currently the work of a number of French and Swiss researchers is exploring the multiple processes and individual pathways of development that Piaget, for the most part, treated merely as variations on a general pattern (Larivée, Normandeau, & Parent, 2000).

The Cognitive Neuroscience Approach

For most of the history of psychology, theorists and researchers studied cognitive processes apart from the physical structures in which these processes occur. Now that sophisticated instruments make it possible to see the brain in action, adherents of the **cognitive neuroscience approach** argue that an accurate understanding of cognitive functioning must be linked to what happens in the brain.

Brain research supports important aspects of information-processing models, such as the existence of separate physical structures to handle conscious and unconscious memory. Neurological research also may be able to shed light on such issues as whether intelligence is general or specialized and what influences a young child's readiness for formal learning (Byrnes & Fox, 1998). It is assumed that experiences in early childhood can affect healthy neurological development, which in turn affects the outcome of all later development (McCain & Mustard, 1999).

cognitive neuroscience approach Approach to the study of cognitive development that links brain processes with cognitive ones

Checkpoint ✔

Can you . . .

✔ Tell how Case's theory draws from both Piaget and the information-processing approach?

✔ Explain how brain research contributes to the understanding of cognitive processes?

Perspective 4: Ethological

The **ethological perspective** focuses on biological and evolutionary bases of behaviour. It looks beyond the immediate adaptive value of behaviour for an individual to its function in promoting the survival of the group or species.

The scientific discipline of *ethology* is the study of the behaviour of species of animals by observing them, usually in their natural surroundings. In the 1950s, the British psychologist John Bowlby extended ethological principles to human development.

Ethologists believe that, for each species, a number of innate behaviours have evolved to increase its odds of survival. They do comparative research to identify which behaviours are universal and which are specific to a particular species or are modified by culture. They also identify behaviours that are adaptive at different parts of the lifespan; for example, an infant needs to stay close to the mother, but for an older child, more independent exploration is important.

So far, the ethological method—careful, detached observation of children in their natural settings—has been applied chiefly to a few specific developmental issues, such as parent–child attachment, dominance and aggression among peers, and everyday problem-solving skills. Its methods can fruitfully be combined with other techniques, such as verbal questioning (P. H. Miller, 1993).

ethological perspective View of development that focuses on biological and evolutionary bases of behaviour

Checkpoint ✔

Can you . . .

✔ Identify the chief focus of the ethological perspective?

✔ Tell what kinds of topics ethological researchers study, and think of some potential uses of their methods?

Perspective 5: Contextual

From the **contextual perspective**, development can be understood only in its social context. Contextualists see the individual, not as a separate entity interacting with the environment, but as an inseparable part of it.

contextual perspective View of development that sees the individual as inseparable from the social context

Urie Bronfenbrenner's Bioecological Theory

The American psychologist Urie Bronfenbrenner's (1979, 1986, 1994; Bronfenbrenner & Morris, 1998) currently influential **bioecological theory** describes the range of interacting influences that affect a developing child. Every biological organism develops within ecological systems that support or stifle its growth. Just as we need to understand the

bioecological theory Bronfenbrenner's approach to understanding processes and contexts of development

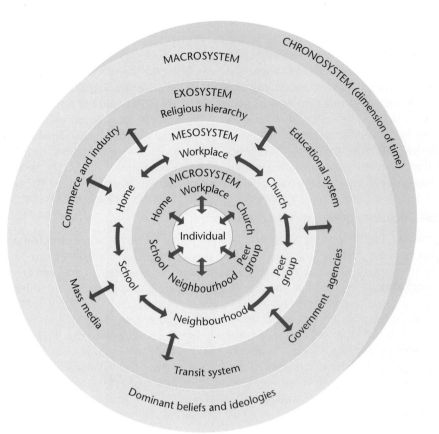

Figure 2-2

Bronfenbrenner's bioecological theory. Concentric circles show five levels of environmental influence, from the most intimate environment (innermost circle) to the broadest—all within the dimension of time. The circles form a set of nested influences, like egg-shaped containers that fit inside one another, encasing the developing person. The figure shows what we would see if we sliced the nested "containers" across the middle and looked inside. Keep in mind that the boundaries are fluid, and the containers are interconnected.

Source: Adapted from Cole & Cole, 1989

ecology of the ocean or the forest if we wish to understand the development of a fish or a tree, we need to understand the ecology of the human environment if we wish to understand how children develop.

According to Bronfenbrenner, development occurs through increasingly complex regular, active, two-way interaction between a developing child and the immediate, everyday environment—processes that are affected by more remote contexts of which the child may not even be aware. To understand these processes, we must study the multiple contexts in which they occur. These begin with the home, classroom, and neighbourhood; connect outward to societal institutions, such as educational and transportation systems; and finally encompass cultural and historical patterns that affect the family, the school, and virtually everything else in a person's life. By highlighting the interrelated contexts of, and influences on, development, Bronfenbrenner's theory provides a key to understanding the processes that underlie such diverse phenomena as antisocial behaviour and academic achievement.

Bronfenbrenner identifies five interlocking contextual systems, from the most intimate to the broadest: the *microsystem, mesosystem, exosystem, macrosystem,* and *chronosystem* (see Figure 2-2). Although we separate the various levels of influence for purposes of illustration, in reality they continually interact.

A **microsystem** is a pattern of activities, roles, and relationships within a setting, such as the home, school, workplace, or neighbourhood, in which a person interacts with others every day, face to face. It is through the microsystem that more distant influences, such as social institutions and cultural values, reach the developing child.

microsystem Bronfenbrenner's term for a setting in which a child interacts with others every day, face to face

A microsystem involves personal, face-to-face relationships, and bidirectional influences flow back and forth. How, for example, does a new baby affect the parents' lives? How do their feelings and attitudes affect the baby?

A **mesosystem** is the interaction of two or more microsystems that contain the developing child. It may include linkages between home and school (such as parent–teacher conferences) or between the family and the peer group. Attention to mesosystems can alert us to differences in the ways the same person acts in different settings. For example, a child who can satisfactorily complete a school assignment at home may become tongue-tied when asked a question about the assignment in class.

An **exosystem**, like a mesosystem, consists of linkages between two or more settings; but in an exosystem, unlike a mesosystem, at least one of these settings—such as parents' workplaces and parents' social networks—does *not* contain the developing child and thus affects the child only indirectly. A woman whose employer encourages breast-feeding by providing pumping and milk-storage facilities may be more likely to continue nursing her baby.

The **macrosystem** consists of overall cultural patterns, like those Margaret Mead studied: dominant values, beliefs, customs, and economic and social systems of a culture or subculture, which filter down in countless ways to individuals' daily lives. For example, whether a child grows up in a nuclear or extended-family household is strongly influenced by a culture's macrosystem.

The **chronosystem** adds the dimension of time: the degree of stability or change in a child's world. This can include changes in family composition, place of residence, or parents' employment, as well as larger events such as wars, economic cycles, and waves of migration. Changes in family patterns (such as the increase in numbers of working mothers in industrial societies and the decline of the extended-family household in developing countries) are chronosystem factors.

According to Bronfenbrenner, a person is not merely an outcome of development, but a shaper of it. People affect their own development through their biological and psychological characteristics, talents and skills, disabilities, and temperament.

Lev Vygotsky's Socio-cultural Theory

The Russian psychologist Lev Semenovich Vygotsky (1896–1934) was a prominent proponent of the contextual perspective, particularly as it applies to children's cognitive development. In contrast with Bronfenbrenner, who sees contextual systems as centred on the individual person, Vygotsky's focus is the social, cultural, and historical complex of which a child is a part. To understand cognitive development, he maintained, one must look to the social processes from which a child's thinking is derived.

Vygotsky's (1978) **socio-cultural theory,** like Piaget's theory of cognitive development, stresses children's active engagement with their environment. But whereas Piaget described the solo mind taking in and interpreting information about the world, Vygotsky saw cognitive growth as a *collaborative* process. Children, said Vygotsky, learn through social interaction. They acquire cognitive skills as part of their induction into a way of life. Shared activities help children to internalize their society's ways of thinking and behaving and to make those ways their own.

According to Vygotsky, adults (or more advanced peers) must help direct and organize a child's learning before the child can master and internalize it. This guidance is most effective in helping children cross the **zone of proximal development (ZPD),** the gap between what they are already able to do and what they are not quite ready to accomplish by themselves. (*Proximal* means "nearby.") Children in the ZPD for a particular task can almost, but not quite, perform the task on their own. With the right kind of guidance, however, they can do it successfully. Responsibility for directing and monitoring learning gradually shifts from the adult to the child.

When an adult teaches a child to float, the adult first supports the child in the water and then lets go gradually as the child's body relaxes into a horizontal position. When the child seems ready, the adult withdraws all but one finger and finally lets the child float freely. Some followers of Vygotsky (Wood, 1980; Wood, Bruner, & Ross, 1976) have applied the metaphor of scaffolds—the temporary platforms on which construction workers stand—to

mesosystem Bronfenbrenner's term for linkages of two or more microsystems

exosystem Bronfenbrenner's term for linkages between two or more settings, one of which does not contain the child

macrosystem Bronfenbrenner's term for overall cultural patterns

chronosystem Bronfenbrenner's term for effects of time on other developmental systems

According to the Russian psychologist Lev Semenovich Vygotsky, children learn through social interaction.

socio-cultural theory Vygotsky's theory of how contextual factors affect children's development

zone of proximal development (ZPD) Vygotsky's term for the difference between what a child can do alone and with help

scaffolding Temporary support to help a child master a task

Checkpoint ✓

Can you . . .

✔ Identify the chief assumptions of the contextual perspective?

✔ Name Bronfenbrenner's five systems of contextual influence?

✔ Explain how Vygotsky's focus differs from Bronfenbrenner's and Piaget's?

✔ Tell how Vygotsky's theory applies to educational teaching and testing?

What's your view ?

• Which theoretical perspective would be most useful for (a) a parent trying to get a child to say "please," (b) a teacher interested in stimulating critical thinking, (c) a researcher studying siblings' imitation of one another?

Guidepost 4

How do developmental scientists study children, and what are the advantages and disadvantages of each research method?

scientific method System of established principles and processes of scientific inquiry

this way of teaching. **Scaffolding** is the temporary support that parents, teachers, or others give a child to do a task until the child can do it alone.

Vygotsky's theory has important implications for education and for cognitive testing. Tests based on the ZPD, which focus on a child's potential, provide a valuable alternative to standard intelligence tests that assess what the child has already learned; and many children may benefit from the sort of expert guidance Vygotsky prescribes.

A major contribution of the contextual perspective has been its emphasis on the social component in development. Research attention has shifted from the individual to larger, interactional units—parent and child, sibling and sibling, the entire family, the neighbourhood, and broader societal institutions. The contextual perspective also reminds us that the development of children in one culture or one group within a culture (such as white, middle-class Canadians) may not be an appropriate norm for children in other societies or cultural groups.

How Theory and Research Work Together

No one theory of human development is universally accepted, and no single theoretical perspective explains all facets of development. Lacking a widely accepted "grand" theory (such as those of Freud and Piaget), the trend today is toward smaller, more limited "minitheories" aimed at explaining specific phenomena, such as how poverty influences family relations. At the same time, as you will see throughout this book, there is increasing theoretical and research exploration of the interplay among the physical, cognitive, and psychosocial domains. There also is growing awareness of the importance of historical change and of the need to explore cultural diversity in a rigorous, disciplined way.

Theories of child development often grow out of, and are tested by, research. Thus research questions and methods tend to reflect the theoretical orientation of the researcher. For example, in trying to understand how a child develops a sense of right and wrong, a behaviourist would examine the way parents have responded to the child's behaviour in the past, that is, what kinds of behaviour they have punished or praised; a social learning theorist would focus on imitation of moral examples, possibly in stories children read or in movies; and an information-processing researcher might do a task analysis to identify the steps a child goes through in determining the range of moral options available and then in deciding which option to pursue.

With this in mind, let's look at the methods developmental researchers use.

Research Methods

While researchers coming from various theoretical perspectives use a variety of methods to study children in a variety of settings, the **scientific method** refers to an overall process that characterizes scientific inquiry in any field. Following the scientific method enables researchers to come to sound conclusions about child development. The steps in the method are

• *Identifying a problem* to be studied, often on the basis of a theory or of previous research
• *Formulating hypotheses* to be tested by research
• *Collecting data*
• *Analyzing the data* to determine whether or not they support the hypothesis
• *Disseminating findings* so that other observers can check, learn from, analyze, repeat, and build on the results

Two key issues at the outset of any investigation are how the participants will be chosen and how the data will be collected. These decisions often depend on what questions the researcher wants to answer. All these issues play a part in a research design, or plan.

Sampling

How can we be sure that the results of research are true generally, and not just for specific participants? First, we need to determine who gets into the study. Because studying an entire *population* (a group to which we want to apply the findings) is usually too costly and time-consuming, investigators select a **sample**, a smaller group within the population. The sample should adequately represent the population under study—that is, it should show relevant characteristics in the same proportions as in the entire population. Otherwise the results cannot properly be *generalized,* or applied to the population as a whole. To judge how generalizable the findings are likely to be, we need to carefully compare the characteristics of the people in the sample with the population as a whole.

Often researchers seek to achieve representativeness through *random selection,* in which each person in a population has an equal and independent chance of being chosen. If we wanted to study the effects of a pilot educational program, one way to select a random sample would be to put all the names of participating children into a large bowl, stir it, and then draw out a certain number of names. A random sample, especially a large one, is likely to represent the population well.

A random sample of a large population is often difficult to obtain. Instead, many studies use samples selected for convenience or accessibility (for example, children born in a particular hospital or attending a particular daycare centre). The findings of such studies may not apply to the population as a whole. Only repeated studies of the same phenomenon showing similar results would allow for some generalization.

sample Group of participants chosen to represent the entire population under study

Forms of Data Collection

Common ways of gathering data (see Table 2-3) include self-reports (verbal reports by study participants), tests and other behavioural measures, and observation. Depending in part on time and financial constraints, researchers may use one or more of these data collection techniques in any research design. Currently there is a trend toward increased use of self-reports and observation in combination with more objective measures.

Self-Reports: Diaries, Interviews, Questionnaires

The simplest form of self-report is a *diary* or log. Adolescents may be asked, for example, to record what they eat each day, or the times when they feel depressed. In studying young children, *parental self-reports*—diaries, journals, interviews, or questionnaires—are commonly used, often together with other methods, such as videotaping or recording. Parents may be videotaped playing with their babies and then may be shown the tapes and asked to explain why they reacted as they did.

Table 2-3	Characteristics of Major Methods of Data Collection		
Type	**Main Characteristics**	**Advantages**	**Disadvantages**
Self-report: diary, interview, or questionnaire	Participants are asked about some aspect of their lives; questioning may be highly structured or more flexible	Can provide firsthand information about a person's life, attitudes, or opinions.	Participants may not remember information accurately or may distort responses in a socially desirable way; how question is asked or by whom may affect answer.
Behavioural measures	Participants are tested on abilities, skills, knowledge, competencies, or physical responses.	Provides objectively measurable information; avoids subjective distortions.	Cannot measure attitudes or other non-behavioural phenomena; results may be affected by extraneous factors.
Naturalistic observation	People are observed in their normal setting, with no attempt to manipulate behaviour.	Provides good description of behaviour; does not subject people to unnatural settings that may distort behaviour.	Lack of control; observer bias.
Laboratory observation	Participants are observed in the laboratory, with no attempt to manipulate behaviour.	Provides good descriptions; greater control than naturalistic observation, since all participants are observed under same conditions.	Observer bias; controlled situation can be artificial.

In a face-to-face or telephone *interview,* researchers ask questions about attitudes, opinions, or behaviour. Interviews may cover such topics as parent–child relationships, sexual activities, and occupational goals. In a *structured* interview, each participant is asked the same set of questions. An *open-ended* interview is more flexible; as in Piaget's clinical method, the interviewer can vary the topics and order of questions and can ask follow-up questions based on the responses. To reach more people and protect their privacy, researchers sometimes distribute a printed *questionnaire,* which participants fill out and return.

By questioning a large number of people, investigators get a broad picture—at least of what the respondents *say* they believe or do or did. However, people willing to participate in interviews or fill out questionnaires tend to be an unrepresentative sample. Furthermore, heavy reliance on self-reports may be unwise, since people may not have thought about what they feel and think, or they honestly may not know. Some people forget when and how events actually took place, and others consciously or unconsciously distort their replies to fit what is considered socially desirable.

How a question is asked, and by whom, can affect the answer. When researchers at the U.S. National Institute on Drug Abuse reworded a question about alcohol use to indicate that a "drink" meant "more than a few sips," the percentage of teenagers who reported drinking alcohol dropped significantly (National [U.S.] Institute on Drug Abuse, 1996). When questioned about risky or socially disapproved behaviour, such as sexual habits and drug use, respondents may be more candid in responding to a computerized survey than to a paper-and-pencil one (Turner et al., 1998).

Behavioural and Performance Measures

For many kinds of research, investigators use more objective measures instead of, or in addition to, self-reports. A behavioural or performance measure *shows* something about a child rather than asking the child or someone else, such as a parent, to *tell* about it. Tests and other behavioural and neuropsychological measures, including mechanical and electronic devices, may be used to assess abilities, skills, knowledge, competencies, or physiological responses, such as heart rate and brain activity. Although these measures are less subjective than self-reports, results can be affected by such factors as fatigue and self-confidence.

Some tests, such as intelligence tests, compare performance with that of other test-takers. Tests can be meaningful and useful only if they are both *valid* (that is, the tests measure the abilities they claim to measure) and *reliable* (that is, the results are reasonably consistent from one time to another). To avoid bias, intelligence tests must be *standardized,* that is, given and scored by the same methods and criteria for all test-takers.

When measuring a characteristic such as intelligence, it is important to define exactly what is to be measured in a way that other researchers will understand and can comment about the results. For this purpose, research scientists use **operational definitions**— definitions stated solely in terms of the operations or procedures used to produce or measure a phenomenon. Intelligence, for example, can be defined as the ability to achieve a certain score on a test covering logical relationships, memory, and vocabulary recognition. Some people may not agree with this definition, but no one can claim that it is not clear. (Intelligence testing is further discussed in chapters 10 and 12.)

Naturalistic and Laboratory Observation

Observation can take two forms: *naturalistic observation* and *laboratory observation.* In **naturalistic observation**, researchers look at children in real-life settings. The researchers do not try to alter behaviour or the environment; they simply record what they see. In **laboratory observation,** researchers observe and record behaviour in a controlled situation, such as a laboratory. By observing all participants under the same conditions, investigators can more clearly identify any differences in behaviour not attributable to the environment.

Both kinds of observation can provide valuable descriptions of behaviour, but they have limitations. For one, they do not explain *why* children behave as they do, though they may suggest interpretations. Then, too, an observer's presence can alter behaviour. When children know they are being watched, they may act differently. Finally, there is a risk of

operational definitions
Definitions stated in terms of operations or procedures used to produce or measure a phenomenon

naturalistic observation
Research method in which behaviour is studied in natural settings without intervention or manipulation

laboratory observation
Research method in which all participants are observed in the same situation, under controlled conditions

observer bias: the researcher's tendency to interpret data to fit expectations, or to emphasize some aspects and minimize others.

During the 1960s, laboratory observation was most commonly used so as to achieve more rigorous control. Currently, a growing use of naturalistic observation is supplemented by such technological devices as portable videotape recorders and computers, which increase objectivity and enable researchers to analyze moment-by-moment changes in facial expressions or other behaviour.

Basic Research Designs

A research design is a plan for conducting a scientific investigation: what questions are to be answered, how participants are to be selected, how data are to be collected and interpreted, and how valid conclusions can be drawn. Four of the basic designs used in developmental research are case studies, ethnographic studies, correlational studies, and experiments. Each design has advantages and drawbacks, and each is appropriate for certain kinds of research problems (see Table 2-4).

Case Studies

A **case study** is a study of a single case or individual, such as Victor (discussed in the Focus of chapter 1). A number of theories, notably Freud's, have grown out of clinical case studies, which include careful observation and interpretation of what patients say and do. Case studies also may use behavioural or neuropsychological measures and biographical, autobiographical, or documentary materials.

Case studies offer useful, in-depth information. They can explore sources of behaviour and can test treatments. They also can suggest a need for other research. Another important advantage is flexibility: the researcher is free to explore avenues of inquiry that arise during the course of the study. However, case studies have shortcomings. From studying Victor, for instance, we learn much about the development of a single child, but not how the information applies to children in general. Furthermore, case studies cannot explain behaviour with certainty, because there is no way to test their conclusions. Even though it seems reasonable that Victor's severely deprived environment caused or contributed to his language deficiency, it is impossible to know whether he would have developed normally with a normal upbringing.

Checkpoint ✔

Can you . . .

✔ Summarize the five steps in the scientific method and tell why each is important?

✔ Explain the purpose of random selection and tell how it can be achieved?

✔ Compare the advantages and disadvantages of various forms of data collection?

case study Study covering a single case or life

Table 2-4	Basic Research Designs		
Type	**Main Characteristics**	**Advantages**	**Disadvantages**
Case study	Study of single individual in depth.	Flexibility; provides detailed picture of one person's behaviour and development; can generate hypotheses.	May not generalize to others; conclusions not directly testable; cannot establish cause and effect.
Ethnographic study	In-depth study of a culture or subculture.	Can help overcome culturally based biases in theory and research; can test universality of developmental phenomena.	Subject to observer bias.
Correlational study	Attempt to find positive or negative relationship between variables.	Allows prediction of one variable on basis of another; can suggest hypotheses about causal relationships.	Cannot establish cause and effect.
Experiment	Controlled procedure in which an experimenter controls the independent variable to determine its effect on the dependent variable; may be conducted in the laboratory or field.	Establishes cause-and-effect relationships; highly controlled procedure that can be repeated by another investigator. Degree of control is greatest in the laboratory experiment.	Findings, especially when derived from laboratory experiments, may not generalize to situations outside the laboratory.

Box 2-1 *Purposes of Cross-cultural Research*

When David, an American child, was asked to identify the missing detail in a picture of a face with no mouth, he said, "The mouth." But Ari, an Asian immigrant child of the same age in Israel, said that the *body* was missing. Since art in his culture does not present a head as a complete picture, he thought the absence of a body was more important than the omission of "a mere detail like the mouth" (Anastasi, 1988, p. 360).

By looking at children from different cultural groups, researchers can learn in what ways development is universal (and thus intrinsic to the human condition) and in what ways it is culturally determined. For example, children everywhere learn to speak in the same sequence, advancing from cooing and babbling to single words and then to simple combinations of words. The words vary from culture to culture, but around the world toddlers put them together to form sentences similar in structure. Such findings suggest that the capacity for learning language is universal and inborn.

On the other hand, culture can exert a surprisingly large influence on early motor development. African babies, whose parents often prop them in a sitting position and bounce them on their feet, tend to sit and walk earlier than U.S. babies (Rogoff & Morelli, 1989).

The society in which children grow up influences the skills they learn and the kinds of friendships they form. In Canada, where the majority culture tends to maintain a more individualist orientation, the long-term stability of friendships is similar to that of more collectivist cultures like Taiwan, although there is typically greater conflict and less agreement among friends in Canadian than in Taiwanese contexts (Benjamin, Schneider, Greenman, & Hum, 2001).

One important reason to conduct research among different cultural groups is to recognize biases in traditional North American and European theories and research that often go unquestioned until they are shown to be a product of cultural influences. "Working with people from a quite different background can make one aware of aspects of human activity that are not noticeable until they are missing or differently arranged, as with the fish who reputedly is unaware of water until removed from it" (Rogoff & Morelli, 1989, p. 343).

Since so much research in child development has focused on industrialized societies, many people have defined typical development in these societies as the norm, or standard of behaviour. Measuring against this "norm" leads to narrow—and often, wrong—ideas about development. Pushed to its extreme, this belief can cause the development of children in other ethnic and cultural groups to be seen as deviant (Rogoff & Morelli, 1989).

In this book we discuss several influential theories developed from research in societies that do not hold up when tested on people from other cultures—theories about gender roles, abstract thinking, moral reasoning, and other aspects of human development. Throughout this book, we consistently look at children in cultures and subcultures other than the dominant one in Canada to show how closely development is tied to society and culture and to add to our understanding of normal development in many settings.

What's your view ?

Can you think of a situation in which you made an incorrect assumption about a person because you were unfamiliar with her or his cultural background?

Check it out !

For more information on this topic, go to **www.mcgrawhill.ca/ college/papalia.**

Ethnographic Studies

ethnographic study In-depth study of a culture, which uses a combination of methods including participant observation

participant observation Research method in which the observer lives with the people or participates in the activity being observed

An **ethnographic study** seeks to describe the pattern of relationships, customs, beliefs, technology, arts, and traditions that make up a society's way of life. Ethnographic research can be qualitative, quantitative, or both. It uses a combination of methods, including **participant observation.** Participant observation is a form of naturalistic observation in which researchers live or participate in the societies or groups they observe, as Margaret Mead (1928, 1930, 1935) did, often for long periods of time; thus their findings are especially open to observer bias.

Despite later disputes over Mead's sampling methods and her findings on adolescence (D. Freeman, 1983; L. D. Holmes, 1987), the anthropologist Robert LeVine wrote, "Mead's basic message to the child development field remains as valid today as in 1930: To understand how children grow up under varied environmental conditions, one must be willing to go to where those conditions already exist, to examine them with respect and in detail, and to change one's assumptions in the face of new observations" (LeVine et al., 1994, p. 9).

Ethnographic research can help overcome cultural biases in theory and research (see Box 2-1). Ethnography demonstrates the error of assuming that principles developed from research in one culture are universally applicable.

Correlational Studies

A **correlational study** is an attempt to find a *correlation,* or statistical relationship, between *variables,* phenomena that change or vary among people or can be varied for purposes of research. Correlations are expressed in terms of direction (positive or negative) and magnitude (degree). Two variables that are related *positively* increase or decrease together. A positive, or direct, correlation between televised violence and aggressiveness would exist if children who watched more violent television hit, bit, or kicked more than children who watched less violent television. Two variables have a *negative,* or inverse, correlation if, as one increases, the other decreases. Studies show a negative correlation between amount of schooling in youth and the risk of developing dementia (mental deterioration) due to Alzheimer's disease in old age. In other words, the less education, the more dementia (Katzman, 1993).

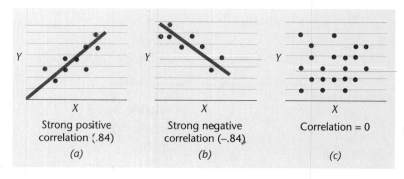

Figure 2-3

Correlational studies may find positive or negative correlations or no correlation. In a positive, or direct, correlation (a), data plotted on a graph cluster around a line showing that one variable (X) increases as the other variable (Y) increases. In a negative, or inverse, correlation (b), one variable (X) increases as the other variable (Y) decreases. No correlation, or a zero correlation (c), exists when increases and decreases in two variables show no consistent relationship (that is, data plotted on a graph show no pattern).

Correlations are reported as numbers ranging from –1.0 (a perfect negative relationship) to +1.0 (a perfect positive relationship). Perfect correlations are rare. The closer a correlation comes to –1.0 or +1.0, the stronger the relationship, either positive or negative. A correlation of zero means that the variables have no relationship (see Figure 2-3).

Correlations allow us to predict one variable on the basis of another. If, for example, we found a positive correlation between watching televised violence and fighting, we would predict that children who watch violent shows are more likely to get into fights. The greater the magnitude of the correlation between two variables, the greater the ability to predict one from the other. Variance reflects the spread of scores measured on a variable. Large variance indicates widely distributed scores. If two variables are strongly correlated, then we can say that a significant percentage of the variance in one measure, like the time spent watching televised violence, is accounted for by the variance in the other measure, like incidence of fighting. In psychology, a variable that is strongly correlated with another could typically account for up to 25 per cent or more of the variance in another variable.

Although strong correlations may suggest possible causes, these possible cause-and-effect relations need to be examined very critically. We cannot be sure from a positive correlation between televised violence and aggressiveness that watching televised violence *causes* aggressive play; we can conclude only that the two variables are related. It is possible that the causation goes the other way: aggressive play may lead children to watch more violent programs. Or a third variable—perhaps an inborn predisposition toward aggressiveness, or living in a more violent environment—may cause a child both to watch violent programs and to act aggressively. Similarly, we cannot be sure that schooling protects against dementia; it may be that another variable, such as socio-economic status, might explain both lower levels of schooling and higher levels of dementia. The only way to show with certainty that one variable causes another is through a controlled experiment—something that, in studying human beings, is not always possible for practical or ethical reasons.

Experiments

An **experiment** is a controlled procedure in which the experimenter manipulates variables to learn how one affects another. Scientific experiments must be conducted and reported in such a way that another experimenter can *replicate* them, that is, repeat them in exactly the same way with different participants to verify the results and conclusions. Figure 2-4 shows how an experiment might be designed.

Groups and Variables At the outset, the experimenter may divide the participants into two kinds of groups. An **experimental group** is composed of people who are to be exposed to the experimental manipulation or *treatment*—the phenomenon the researcher wants to

correlational study Research design intended to discover whether a statistical relationship between variables exists

experiment Rigorously controlled, replicable procedure in which the researcher manipulates variables to assess the effect of one on the other

experimental group In an experiment, the group receiving the treatment under study

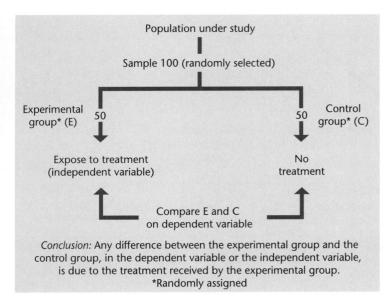

Population under study

Sample 100 (randomly selected)

Experimental group* (E) 50   50 Control group* (C)

Expose to treatment (independent variable)   No treatment

Compare E and C on dependent variable

Conclusion: Any difference between the experimental group and the control group, in the dependent variable or the independent variable, is due to the treatment received by the experimental group.
*Randomly assigned

Figure 2-4

Design for an experiment. This experiment takes a random sample from the larger population being studied, randomly assigns participants to either the experimental (E) or control (C) group, and exposes the experimental group to a treatment that is not given to the control group. By comparing the two groups after the experimental group has received the treatment, the researcher can conclude that any difference between them is due to the experimental treatment.

control group In an experiment, a group of people similar to the people in the experimental group who do not receive the treatment whose effects are to be measured

independent variable In an experiment, the condition over which the experimenter has direct control

dependent variable In an experiment, the condition that may or may not change as a result of changes in the independent variable

study. Afterward, the effect of the treatment will be measured one or more times to find out what changes, if any, it caused. A **control group** is composed of people who are similar to the experimental group but do not receive the treatment, or receive a different treatment. An experiment may include one or more of each type of group. Or, if the experimenter wants to compare the effects of different treatments (say, of two methods of teaching), the overall sample may be divided into *treatment groups,* each of which receives one of the treatments under study.

One team of researchers (Whitehurst, et al., 1988) wanted to find out what effect *dialogic reading,* a special method of reading picture books to very young children, might have on their language and vocabulary skills. The researchers compared two groups of middle-class children ages 21 to 35 months. In the *experimental group,* the parents adopted the new read-aloud method (the treatment), which consisted of encouraging children's active participation and giving frequent, age-based feedback. In the *control group,* parents simply read aloud as they usually did. After 1 month, the children in the experimental group were 8.5 months ahead of the control group in level of speech and 6 months ahead in vocabulary; 9 months later, the experimental group was still 6 months ahead of the controls. It is fair to conclude, then, that this read-aloud method improved the children's language and vocabulary skills.

In this experiment, the type of reading approach was the *independent variable,* and the children's language skills were the *dependent variable.* An **independent variable** is something over which the experimenter has direct control. A **dependent variable** is something that may or may not change as a result of changes in the independent variable; in other words, it *depends* on the independent variable. In an experiment, a researcher manipulates the independent variable to see how changes in it will affect the dependent variable.

If an experiment finds a significant difference in the performance of the experimental and control groups, how do we know that the cause was the independent variable, in other words that the conclusion is valid? For example, in the read-aloud experiment, how can we be sure that the reading method and not some other factor (such as intelligence) caused the difference in language development of the two groups? The best way to control for effects of such extraneous factors is *random assignment:* assigning the participants to groups in such a way that each person has an equal chance of being placed in any group.

If assignment is random and the sample is large enough, differences in such factors as age, sex, race, IQ, and socio-economic status will be evenly distributed so that the groups initially are as alike as possible in every respect except for the variable to be tested. Otherwise, unintended differences between the groups might *confound,* or contaminate, the results, and any conclusions drawn from the experiment would have to be viewed with great suspicion. Also, during the course of the experiment, the experimenter must make sure that everything except the independent variable is held constant. For example, in the read-aloud study, parents of the experimental and control groups must spend the same amount of time reading to their children. In that way, the experimenter can be sure that any differences between the reading skills of the two groups are due to the reading method, and not some other factor.

When participants in an experiment are randomly selected and randomly assigned to treatment groups, the experimenter can be fairly confident that a causal relationship has (or has not) been established. However, random assignment of some variables, such as age, gender, and race, is not often possible: we cannot assign Terry to be 5 years old and Brett to be 10, or one to be a boy and the other a girl, or one to be black and the other white. Still,

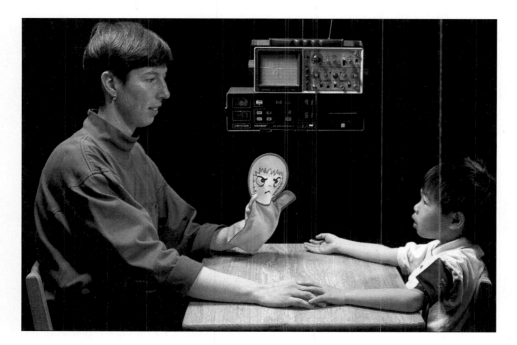

Experiments use strictly controlled procedures that manipulate variables to determine how one affects another. To study emotional resiliency, this research project monitors the heart rate and blood pressure of young children as they explain their feelings in response to a hand puppet's happy or angry face.

when studying such a variable—for example, whether boys or girls are stronger in certain abilities—researchers can strengthen the validity of their conclusions by randomly selecting participants and by trying to make sure that they are statistically equivalent in other ways that might make a difference in the study.

Laboratory, Field, and Natural Experiments The control necessary for establishing cause and effect is most easily achieved in *laboratory experiments*. In a laboratory experiment the participants are brought to a special place where they experience conditions manipulated by the experimenter. The experimenter records the participants' reactions to these conditions, perhaps comparing them with their own or other participants' behaviour under different conditions.

However, not all experiments can be readily done in the laboratory. A *field experiment* is a controlled study conducted in a setting that is part of everyday life, such as a child's home or school. The experiment in which parents tried out a new way of reading aloud was a field experiment.

Laboratory and field experiments differ in two important respects. One is the *degree of control* exerted by the experimenter; the other is the degree to which findings can be *generalized* beyond the study situation. Laboratory experiments can be more rigidly controlled and thus easier to replicate. However, the results may be less generalizable to real life; because of the artificiality of the situation, participants may not act as they normally would. For example, if children who watch violent television shows in the laboratory become more aggressive in that setting, we cannot be sure that children who watch a lot of violent shows at home hit their little brothers or sisters more often than children who watch fewer such programs.

When, for practical or ethical reasons, it is impossible to conduct a true experiment, a *natural experiment* may provide a way of studying certain events. A natural experiment compares people who have been accidentally "assigned" to separate groups by circumstances of life—one group of children who were exposed, say, to famine or AIDS or a birth defect or superior education, and another group who were not. A natural experiment, despite its name, is actually a correlational study, since controlled manipulation of variables and random assignment to treatment groups are not possible.

Experiments have important advantages over other research designs: the ability to establish cause-and-effect relationships and to permit replication. However, experiments can be too artificial and too narrowly focused. In recent decades, therefore, many researchers have concentrated less on laboratory experimentation or have supplemented it with a wider array of methods.

Checkpoint ✔

Can you . . .

✔ Compare the uses and drawbacks of case studies, ethnographic studies, correlational studies, and experiments?

✔ Explain why only a controlled experiment can establish causal relationships?

✔ Distinguish among laboratory, field, and natural experiments, and tell what kinds of research seem most suitable to each setting?

Developmental Research Designs

The two most common research strategies used to study child development are *longitudinal* and *cross-sectional* studies (see Figure 2-5). Longitudinal studies reveal how children change or stay the same as they grow older; cross-sectional studies show similarities and differences among age groups. Because each of these designs has drawbacks, researchers also have devised *sequential* designs. To directly observe change, *microgenetic studies* can be used.

Longitudinal, Cross-Sectional, and Sequential Studies

longitudinal study Study design to assess changes in a sample over time

cross-sectional study Study design in which people of different ages are assessed on one occasion

In a **longitudinal study**, researchers study the same child or children more than once, sometimes years apart. They may measure a single characteristic, such as vocabulary size, height, or aggressiveness, or they may look at several aspects of development to find relationships among them. The National Longitudinal Survey of Children and Youth, designed to assess behavioural and emotional development from birth to young adulthood, measures children on a variety of characteristics every two years. The study has shown that a child's family socio-economic status (SES) has a large influence on school achievement (Ryan & Adams, 1998). SES accounts for much of the variability in vulnerability to behaviour problems in children in lone-parent families (Ross, Roberts, & Scott, 1998), but that the presence of protective factors like having close affectionate relationships can reduce the likelihood that a child will develop difficult behaviours (Jenkins & Keating, 1999).

In a **cross-sectional study**, children of different ages are assessed at one time. In one cross-sectional study, researchers asked 3-, 4-, 6-, and 7-year-olds about what a pensive-looking woman was doing, or about the state of someone's mind. There was a striking increase with age in children's awareness of mental activity (J. H. Flavell, Green, & Flavell, 1995). These findings strongly suggest that as children become older, their understanding of mental processes improves. However, we cannot draw such a conclusion with certainty. We don't know whether the 7-year-olds' awareness of mental activity when they were 3 years old was the same as that of the current 3-year-olds in the study. The only way to see whether change occurs with age is to conduct a longitudinal study of a particular person or group.

Both cross-sectional and longitudinal designs have strengths and weaknesses (see Table 2-5). Longitudinal research, by repeatedly studying the same people, can track individual patterns of continuity and change. It avoids confounding developmental effects with effects of cohort membership (the differing experiences of children born, for example, before and after the advent of the Internet). However, a longitudinal study done on one cohort may not apply to another. (The results of a study of children born in the 1920s may not apply to children born in the 1990s.) Furthermore, longitudinal studies generally are more time-consuming and expensive than cross-sectional studies; it is hard to keep track of a large group of participants over the years, to keep records, and to keep the study going despite turnover in research personnel. Then there is the problem of attrition: participants may die, move away, or drop out. Another likely difficulty is bias in the sample: People who volunteer for such studies, and especially those who stay with them, tend to be above average in intelligence and socio-economic status. Also, results can be affected by repeated testing: Participants may do better in later tests because of familiarity with test materials and procedures.

Advantages of cross-sectional research include speed and economy; data can be gathered fairly quickly from large numbers of people. And, since participants are assessed only once, there is no problem of attrition or repeated testing. A drawback of cross-sectional studies is that they may overlook individual differences by focusing on group averages. Their major disadvantage, however, is that the results may be affected by cohort differences.

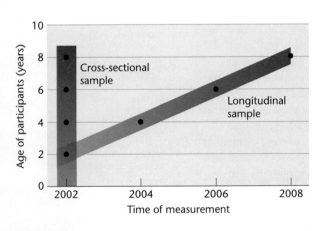

Figure 2-5

Common developmental designs. In this *cross-sectional* study, 2-, 4-, 6-, and 8-year-olds were tested in 2002 to obtain data about age differences. In the *longitudinal* study, participants were measured in 2002, when they were 2 years old; follow-up testing is done when the children are 4, 6, and 8 to measure age-related changes. (*Note:* Dots indicate times of measurement.)

Table 2-5	Longitudinal, Cross-Sectional, and Sequential Research: Pros and Cons		
Type of Study	**Procedure**	**Advantages**	**Disadvantages**
Longitudinal	Data are collected on same person or persons over a period of time	Can show age-related change or continuity; avoids confounding age with cohort effects	Time-consuming, expensive; problems of attrition, bias in sample, and effects of repeated testing; results may be valid only for cohort tested or sample studied
Cross-sectional	Data are collected on people of different ages at the same time	Can show similarities and differences among age groups; speedy, economical; no problem of attrition or repeated testing	Cannot establish age effects; masks individual differences; can be confounded by cohort effects
Sequential	Data are collected on successive cross-sectional or longitudinal samples	Can avoid drawbacks of both cross-sectional and longitudinal designs	Requires large amount of time and effort and the analysis of very complex data

Cross-sectional studies are sometimes interpreted as yielding information about developmental changes in groups or individuals, but such information is often misleading. Thus, although cross-sectional studies still dominate the field—no doubt because they are so much easier to do—the proportion of research devoted to longitudinal studies, especially short-term ones, is increasing (Parke et al., 1994).

The **sequential study**—a sequence of cross-sectional and/or longitudinal studies—is a complex strategy designed to overcome the drawbacks of longitudinal and cross-sectional research (again see Table 2-5). Researchers may assess a cross-sectional sample on two or more occasions (that is, in sequence) to find out how members of each age cohort have changed. This procedure permits researchers to separate age-related changes from cohort effects. Another sequential design consists of a sequence of longitudinal studies, running concurrently but starting one after another. This design allows researchers to compare individual differences in the course of developmental change. A combination of cross-sectional and longitudinal sequences (as shown in Figure 2-6) can provide a more complete picture of development than would be possible with longitudinal or cross-sectional research alone.

The major drawbacks of sequential studies involve time, effort, and complexity. Sequential designs require large numbers of participants and the collection and analysis of huge amounts of data over a period of years. Interpreting their findings and conclusions can demand a high degree of sophistication.

sequential study Study design that combines cross-sectional and longitudinal techniques

Microgenetic Studies

Developmentalists can rarely observe change directly in everyday life because it usually happens so slowly. But what if the process could be compressed into a very short time? A **microgenetic study** does just that, by repeatedly exposing participants to a stimulus for change, or opportunity for learning, over a short time, enabling researchers to see and analyze the processes by which change occurs.

In an experiment examining number conservation, measuring children's abilities to identify which of two rows of buttons contained the greater amount, 5-year-old children who had not yet mastered number conservation were given four training sessions in one of three different conditions: receiving feedback on performance, feedback with request to explain their reasoning, or feedback with request to explain the experimenter's reasoning (Siegler, 1995). Each training session involved 12 trials, during which it was possible to track the progress children made in learning. Children who were asked to explain the experimenter's reasoning did better than the other two groups. The method allowed Siegler to identify the kinds of reasoning that children were using, and to track what children who successfully learned had realized about the task; namely, that the length of the row did not predict the number of buttons in the row, and that the manner in which the row length and number of buttons were manipulated did predict the number of buttons.

microgenetic study Study design that allows researchers to directly observe change by repeated testing over a short time

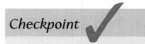

Checkpoint

Can you . . .

✔ List advantages and disadvantages of longitudinal, cross-sectional, and sequential research?

✔ Explain how microgenetic studies are done and what kinds of data they can reveal?

Figure 2-6

A sequential design. Two successive cross-sectional groups of 2-, 4-, 6-, and 8-year-olds were tested in 2002 and 2004. Also, a longitudinal study of children first measured in 2002, when they were 2 years old, will be followed by a similar longitudinal study of children who were 2 years old in 2004.

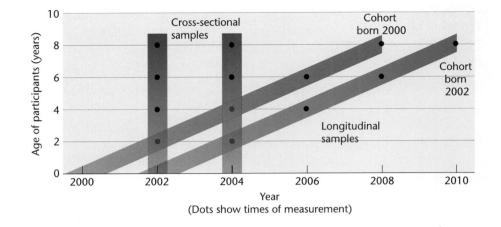

Ethics of Research

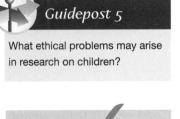

Guidepost 5

What ethical problems may arise in research on children?

Checkpoint ✔

Can you . . .

✔ Name three principles that govern inclusion of participants in research?

✔ Name five rights of research participants?

Should research that might harm its participants ever be undertaken? How can we balance the possible benefits against the risk of mental, emotional, or physical injury to individuals?

In resolving such ethical dilemmas, researchers are supposed to be guided by three principles: (1) *beneficence:* the obligation to maximize potential benefits to participants and minimize possible harm; (2) *respect* for participants' autonomy and protection of those who are unable to exercise their own judgment; and (3) *justice:* inclusion of diverse groups while being sensitive to any special impact the research situation may have on them. They should also consider children's developmental needs (Thompson, 1990), as well as rights of participants. These rights include informed consent and avoidance of deception, protection from harm and loss of dignity, and guarantees of privacy and confidentiality. Participants must also have the right to decline or withdraw at any time, and investigators must be responsible for correcting any undesirable effects. Three Canadian government research funding bodies—SSHRC, NSERC, and CIHR—have developed a recent policy on ethical conduct for research involving humans, called the Tri-Council Policy Statement: Ethical Conduct for Research Involving Humans (Adair, 2001; NSERC, 2000), which has been adopted by universities across Canada. The policy is based on principles of ethics that include, in addition to those listed above, protection of vulnerable persons. Information about this policy is available online at **www.nserc.ca**.

Our final word in these introductory chapters is that this entire book is far from the final word. Although we have tried to incorporate the most important and the most up-to-date information about how children develop, developmental scientists are constantly learning more. As you read this book, you are certain to come up with your own questions. By thinking about them, and perhaps eventually conducting research to find answers, it is possible that you, now just embarking on the study of child development, will someday add to our knowledge about the interesting species to which we all belong.

Summary and Key Terms

Basic Theoretical Issues

Guidepost 1 What purposes do theories serve?

- A theory is used to explain data and generate hypotheses that can be tested by research.

  theory (21)   hypotheses (21)

Guidepost 2 What are three basic theoretical issues on which developmental scientists differ?

- Developmental theories differ on three basic issues: the relative importance of heredity and environment, the active or passive character of development, and the existence of stages of development.

- Some theorists subscribe to a mechanistic model of development; others to an organismic model.

  mechanistic model (22)   organismic model (22)

Theoretical Perspectives

Guidepost 3 What are five theoretical perspectives on human development, and what are some theories representative of each?

- The psychoanalytic perspective sees development as motivated by unconscious emotional drives or conflicts. Leading examples are Freud's and Erikson's theories.

  psychoanalytic perspective (23) **psychosexual development (24)** **psychosocial development (25)**

- The learning perspective views development as a result of learning based on experience. Leading examples are Watson's and Skinner's behaviourism and Bandura's social learning theory.

  learning perspective (27) **behaviourism (27)** **classical conditioning (27)** **operant conditioning (27)** **reinforcement (28)** **punishment (28)** **social learning theory (28)** **observational learning (28)**

- The cognitive perspective is concerned with thought processes. Leading examples are Piaget's cognitive-stage theory, the information-processing approach, and the cognitive neuroscience approach, based on brain research.

  cognitive perspective (29) **organization (29)** **schemes (29)** **adaptation (29)** **assimilation (29)** **accommodation (29)** **equilibration (29)** **information-processing approach (30)** **cognitive neuroscience approach (31)**

- The ethological perspective, represented by Bowlby and Ainsworth, describes adaptive behaviours that promote group survival.

  ethological perspective (31)

- The contextual perspective focuses on interaction between the individual and the social context. Leading examples are Bronfenbrenner's and Vygotsky's theories.

  contextual perspective (31) **bioecological theory (31)** **microsystem (32)** **mesosystem (33)** **exosystem (33)** **macrosystem (33)** **chronosystem (33)** **socio-cultural theory (33)** **zone of proximal development (ZPD) (33)** **scaffolding (34)**

Research Methods

Guidepost 4 How do developmental scientists study children, and what are some advantages and disadvantages of each research method?

- To arrive at sound conclusions, researchers use the scientific method.

- Random selection of a research sample can ensure generalizability.

  scientific method (34) **sample (35)**

- Three forms of data collection are self-reports (diaries, interviews, and questionnaires); behavioural and performance measures; and observation.

  operational definitions (36) **naturalistic observation (36)** **laboratory observation (36)**

- Four basic designs used in developmental research are the case study, ethnographic study, correlational study, and experiment. Only experiments can firmly establish causal relationships. Cross-cultural research can indicate whether certain aspects of development are universal or culturally influenced.

  case study (37) **ethnographic study (38)** **participant observation (38)** **correlational study (39)** **experiment (39)**

- Experiments must be rigorously controlled in order to be valid and replicable. Random assignment of participants can ensure validity.

- Laboratory experiments are easiest to control and replicate, but findings of field experiments may be more generalizable beyond the study situation. Natural experiments may be useful in situations in which true experiments would be impractical or unethical.

  experimental group (39) **control group (40)** **independent variable (40)** **dependent variable (40)**

- The two most common designs used to study age-related development are longitudinal and cross-sectional. Cross-sectional studies compare age groups; longitudinal studies describe continuity or change in the same participants. The sequential study is intended to overcome the weaknesses of the other two designs. A microgenetic study allows direct observation of change over a short period of time.

  longitudinal study (42) **cross-sectional study (42)** **sequential study (43)** **microgenetic study (43)**

Guidepost 5 What ethical problems may arise in research on children?

- Researchers seek to resolve ethical issues on the basis of principles of beneficence, respect, and justice.

- Ethical issues in research on child development involve the rights of participants to informed consent and avoidance of deception, protection from harm and loss of dignity, and guarantees of privacy and confidentiality.

OLC Preview

The Online Learning Centre for *A Child's World,* First Canadian edition, offers links to fascinating further reading on such topics as the adaptive value of immaturity, research ethics, and cross-cultural research. Check out **www.mcgrawhill.ca/college/papalia.**

Forming a New Life: Conception, Heredity, and Environment

Of the cell, the wondrous seed
Becoming plant and animal and mind
Unerringly forever after its kind . . .

—William Ellery Leonard, *Two Lives,* 1923

Focus *Louise Brown, the First "Test-tube Baby"*[*]

Louise Brown

The writer Aldous Huxley foresaw it in 1932: human life created in the laboratory. As Huxley described it in *Brave New World,* the feat would be accomplished by immersing female *ova* (egg cells), which had been incubated in test tubes, in a dish of free-swimming male sperm. Huxley envisioned his "brave new world" as 600 years off; yet it took only 46 years before a birth through *in vitro fertilization,* or fertilization outside the mother's body, became a reality.

Louise Brown, the world's first documented "test-tube baby," was born July 25, 1978, at a four-story red brick hospital in the old textile mill town of Oldham in northwest England. She had been conceived, not in a test tube, but by placing a ripe ovum from her 30-year-old mother, Lesley Brown, in a shallow glass dish with fluid containing sperm from her 38-year-old father, John Brown. After 2 days, during which the resulting single-celled organism multiplied to eight cells, the embryo had been implanted in Lesley's womb.

Until this precedent-shattering event, Lesley and her husband, a truck driver for the British Railway Network, were—by their own description—an ordinary couple who lived in a low-rent row house in Bristol. Although they were raising John's 17-year-old daughter from a previous marriage, they desperately wanted to have a baby together. After 7 years of failure to conceive, they turned to the then-experimental *in vitro* method. The fulfillment of the Browns' wish was the culmination of more than a decade of painstaking preparatory research by Patrick Steptoe, a gynecologist, and Robert Edwards, a physiologist at Cambridge University. The outcome was far more than a single baby. Steptoe's and Edwards's work gave birth to a new branch of medicine: *assisted reproductive technology.*

Questions were in the air as Lesley and John Brown awaited the birth of what was to be called, in banner headlines, the "Miracle Baby" and "Baby of the Century." Despite strenuous efforts by the couple and their doctors to keep the birth secret, the news leaked out. Hordes of newspaper and television reporters from around the world hovered outside the hospital and, later, camped on the Browns' front lawn.

The story launched a debate about the moral implications of tampering with nature—and, down the road, the possibility of mass baby farms and reproductive engineering, which could alter or custom design the "products" of reproduction. More immediately, what about the risks to mother and baby? What if the baby were born grossly deformed? Could *any* baby conceived in a laboratory dish have a normal life?

Lesley was checked and monitored more frequently than most expectant mothers are, and, as a precaution, spent the last three months of her pregnancy in the hospital. The birth

[*]Sources of information about Louise Brown were Barthel (1982); Faltermayer et al. (1996); Lawson (1993); "Louise Brown" (1984); "Louise Brown" (1994); "Test-Tube Baby" (1978); "The First Test-Tube Baby" (1978); and Van Dyck (1995).

took place about two weeks before the due date, by Caesarean delivery, because Lesley had developed toxemia (blood poisoning) and the fetus did not seem to be gaining weight. The delivery went smoothly without further complications.

The blond, blue-eyed, 2600 g baby was, from all accounts, a beautiful, normal infant, who emerged crying lustily. "There's no difference between her and any other little girl," her father maintained. "We just helped nature a bit" ("Louise Brown," p. 82).

By the time Louise celebrated her fourth birthday, she had a "test-tube" sister, Natalie, born June 14, 1982. Lesley and John used part of the nest egg obtained from interview, book, and film rights to buy a modest house; the rest remained in trust for the children. At last report, on her twentieth birthday, Louise Brown was working at a daycare centre in Bristol, England, and said she loved looking after children. She also liked swimming, pub-crawling, and playing darts and said she was no different from others her age (Channel 3000 News, 1998).

● ● ●

What made Louise Brown the person she is? Like any other child, she began with a hereditary endowment from her mother and father. For example, she has her father's stocky build, wide forehead, and chubby cheeks and her mother's tilted nose and curved mouth—as well as her mother's sudden temper. Louise also has been affected by a host of environmental influences, from that famous laboratory dish to the tremendous public interest in her story. As a preschooler, she was mentally precocious, mischievous, and (by her parents' admission) "spoiled." As a teenager, like many of her classmates, she liked to swim and ride horses, wore two gold studs in each ear, watched music videos, and had a crush on the actor Tom Cruise.

Most children do not become famous, especially at birth; but every child is the product of a unique combination of hereditary and environmental influences set in motion by the parents' decision to form a new life. We begin this chapter by describing how a life is conceived, either through normal reproduction or through alternative technologies, some of them developed since Louise Brown's birth. We examine the mechanisms and patterns of heredity—the inherited factors that affect development—and how genetic counselling can help couples weigh the decision to become parents. We look at how heredity and environment work together and how their effects on development can be studied.

After you have read and studied this chapter, you should be able to answer each of the Guidepost questions that appear at the top of the next page. Look for them again in the margins, where they point to important concepts throughout the chapter. To check your understanding of these Guideposts, review the end-of-chapter summary. Checkpoints located throughout the chapter will help you verify your understanding of what you have read.

Guideposts for Study

1. How does conception normally occur, and how have beliefs about conception changed?

2. What causes multiple births?

3. What causes infertility, and what are alternative ways of becoming parents?

4. What genetic mechanisms determine sex, physical appearance, and other characteristics?

5. How are birth defects and disorders transmitted?

6. How do scientists study the relative influences of heredity and environment, and how do heredity and environment work together?

7. What roles do heredity and environment play in physical health, intelligence, and personality?

Becoming Parents

The choice, timing, and circumstances of parenthood can have vast consequences for a child. Whether a birth was planned or accidental, whether the pregnancy was welcomed or unwanted, whether it came about through normal or extraordinary means, whether the parents were married or unmarried, and how old the parents were when a child was conceived or adopted are all factors in the *microsystem* identified in Bronfenbrenner's bioecological approach (refer back to chapter 2). Whether the culture encourages large or small families, whether it values one sex over the other, and how much it supports families with children are *macrosystem* issues likely to influence that child's development.

We'll be bringing up such contextual issues throughout this book. For now, let's look at the act of conception and then at options for couples unable to conceive in the normal way.

Conception

We are approaching a point at which scientists will be able to **clone** (make a genetic copy of) a human being, and this has created a great deal of controversy in ensuring that research in the area is based on firm ethical principles (see Box 3-1). Until then, every person's biological beginning will continue to be a split-second event when a single spermatozoon (usually called *sperm*), one of millions of sperm cells from the biological father, joins an ovum, one of the several hundred thousand ova (plural of *ovum*) produced by the biological mother's body. As we will see, which sperm meets which ovum has tremendous implications for the new person.

Changing Ideas about Conception*

Most adults, and even most children in industrialized countries have a reasonably accurate idea of where babies come from. Yet only a generation or two ago, many parents told their children that a stork had brought them. The folk belief that children came from wells, springs, or rocks was common in north and central Europe as late as the beginning of the twentieth century. Conception was believed to be influenced by cosmic forces; just as the lunar cycle governed the sowing and harvesting of crops, it also determined the sex of a child. A baby conceived under a new moon would be a boy; during the moon's last quarter, a girl (Gélis, 1991).

*Unless otherwise referenced, this discussion is based on Eccles, 1982, and Fontanel & d'Harcourt, 1997.

Guidepost 1

How does conception normally occur, and how have beliefs about conception changed?

clone *(verb)* To make a genetic copy of an individual; *(noun)* a genetic copy of an individual

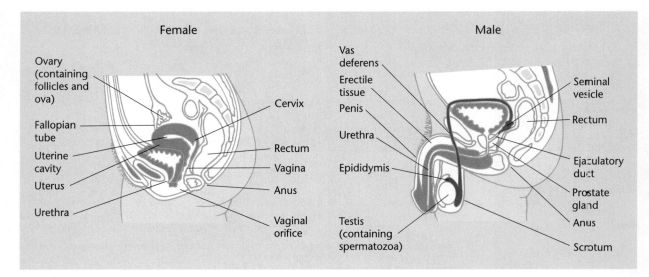

Figure 3-1

Human reproductive systems

Theories about conception go back to ancient times. The Greek physician Hippocrates, known as the father of European medicine, held that a fetus results from the joining of male and female seeds. The philosopher Aristotle had a contrary view: that "the woman functions only as a receptacle, the child being formed exclusively by means of the sperm" (Fontanel & d'Harcourt, 1997, p. 10). According to Aristotle, the production of male babies was in the natural order of things; a female came about only if development was disturbed.

Hippocrates' *two-seed theory* remained influential in sixteenth- and seventeenth-century England. Obstetrics textbooks reflected the ancient belief that there was virtually no significant anatomical difference between men and women, except that women's genitals were located inside the body and men's on the outside. Then, with the invention of the microscope, scientists obtained an increasingly detailed picture of male and female anatomy. It became hard to sustain the idea of a correspondence between male and female reproductive parts, and the two-seed theory lost ground.

For a while, a debate raged between two schools of biological thought. Harking back to Aristotle, the *animalculists* (so named because the sperm were then called *animalcules*) claimed that fully formed "little people" were contained in the heads of sperm, ready to grow when deposited in the nurturing environment of the womb. The *ovists,* inspired by the influential work of the English physician William Harvey, held an opposite but equally incorrect view: that a female's ovaries contained tiny, already formed humans whose growth was activated by the male's sperm. Finally, in the late eighteenth century, the German-born anatomist Kaspar Friedrich Wolff demonstrated that embryos are not preformed in either parent and that both contribute equally to the formation of a new being.

How Fertilization Takes Place

fertilization Union of sperm and ovum fuse to produce a zygote; also called *conception*

zygote One-celled organism resulting from fertilization

Fertilization, or conception, is the process by which sperm and ovum—the male and female *gametes,* or sex cells—combine to create a single cell called a **zygote,** which then duplicates itself again and again by cell division to become a baby. At birth, a girl has all the ova she will ever have—about 400,000. At birth, these immature ova are in her two ovaries (see Figure 3-1), each ovum in its own small sac, or *follicle.* In a sexually mature woman, *ovulation*—rupture of a mature follicle in either ovary and expulsion of its ovum—occurs about once every 28 days until menopause. The ovum is swept along through the Fallopian tube by tiny hair cells, called *cilia,* toward the uterus. Fertilization normally occurs during the brief time the ovum is passing through the Fallopian tube.

Sperm are produced in the testicles (testes), or reproductive glands, of a mature male (refer back to Figure 3-1) at a rate of several hundred million a day and are ejaculated in the semen at sexual climax. They enter the vagina and try to swim through the *cervix* (the opening of the uterus) and into the Fallopian tubes, but only a tiny fraction make it that far.

Fertilization is most likely if intercourse occurs on the day of ovulation or during the five days before (Wilcox, Weinberg, & Baird, 1995). If fertilization does not occur, the ovum and any sperm cells in the woman's body die. The sperm are absorbed by the woman's white blood cells, and the ovum passes through the uterus and exits through the vagina.

What Causes Multiple Births?

Multiple births may occur in two ways. Most commonly, the mother's body releases two ova within a short time (or sometimes, perhaps, a single unfertilized ovum splits) and then both are fertilized. The resulting babies are **dizygotic (two-egg) twins,** commonly called *fraternal twins.* The second way is for a single *fertilized* ovum to split into two. The babies that result from this cell division are **monozygotic (one-egg) twins,** commonly called *identical twins.* Triplets, quadruplets, and other multiple births can result from either of these processes or a combination of both.

Monozygotic twins have the same hereditary makeup and are the same sex, but—in part because of differences in prenatal as well as postnatal experience—they differ in some respects. They may not be identical in **temperament** (disposition, or style of approaching and reacting to situations). In some physical characteristics, such as hair whorls, dental patterns, and handedness, they may be mirror images of each other; one may be left-handed and the other right-handed. Dizygotic twins, who are created from different sperm cells and usually from different ova, are no more alike in hereditary makeup than any other siblings and may be the same sex or different sexes.

Monozygotic twins—about one-third of all twins—seem to be the result of an "accident" of prenatal development; their incidence is about the same in all ethnic groups. Dizygotic twins are most common among people of African descent or people from northern Europe or India, and are least common among people from Asian countries other than India (Behrman, 1992). These differences may be due to hormonal tendencies that may make women of some ethnic groups more likely to release more than one ovum at the same time.

The incidence of multiple births in Canada has grown rapidly. Between 1974 and 1990, live twin births increased by 35 per cent, and the incidence of triplet and higher-order births increased by 250 per cent (Millar, Wadhera, & Nimrod, 1992; Society of Obstetricians and Gynecologists of Canada, 2000). Because of the increased chance of premature delivery—about 50 per cent of multiple births are premature (Health Canada, 2000)—the higher incidence of multiple births now accounts for 20 per cent of the cost of caring for premature babies.

The rise in multiple births is due in part to a trend toward delayed childbearing, since such births are more common among older women. The percentage of all live births in Canada in 1995 to women 35 years of age and above was 12.2; in 1980 the percentage was 4.4 (Health Canada, 2000).

A more important factor in the multiple birth rate is the increased use of fertility drugs, which spur ovulation, and of such techniques as in vitro fertilization. This is of concern, since multiple births are more likely to lead to disability or death in infancy (Martin & Park, 1999).

Infertility

About 7 per cent of Canadian couples experience infertility—the inability to conceive a baby after 12 to 18 months of trying (ISLAT Working Group, 1998; Mosher & Pratt, 1991)—during their reproductive years (Federal, Provincial, and Territorial Advisory Committee on Population Health, 1996).

Infertility is far from a new concern. To enhance fertility, doctors in ancient times advised men to eat fennel, and women to drink the saliva of lambs and wear necklaces of

Guidepost 2

What causes multiple births?

dizygotic (two-egg) twins Twins conceived by the union of two different ova (or a single ovum that has split) with two different sperm cells; also called *fraternal twins*

monozygotic (one-egg) twins Twins resulting from the division of a single zygote after fertilization; also called *identical twins*

temperament Characteristic disposition, or style of approaching and reacting to situations

These 2-year-old monozygotic twins look so much alike that they could be mistaken for one child sitting by a mirror.

Guidepost 3

What causes infertility, and what are alternative ways of becoming parents?

infertility Inability to conceive after 12 to 18 months of trying

earthworms. After intercourse, the woman was supposed to lie flat with her legs crossed and "avoid becoming angry" (Fontanel & d'Harcourt, 1997, p. 10). By the late Middle Ages, the list of foods recommended to spur conception had expanded to include leeks, carrots, asparagus, and several kinds of nuts; by the Renaissance, squabs, sparrows, cockscombs and testicles, bull's genitals, truffles, mint, parsley, rice cooked in cow's milk, and various spices. In the early seventeenth century, Louise Bourgeois, midwife to Marie de Médicis, the queen of France, advocated bathing the vagina with camomile, mallow, marjoram, and catnip boiled in white wine.

Today we know that the most common cause of infertility in men is production of too few sperm. Although only one sperm is needed to fertilize an ovum, a sperm count lower than 60 to 200 million per ejaculation makes conception unlikely. Sometimes an ejaculatory duct is blocked, preventing the exit of sperm; or sperm may be unable to "swim" well enough to reach the cervix. Some cases of male infertility seem to have a genetic basis (King, 1996; Phillips, 1998; Reijo, Alagappan, Patrizio, & Page, 1996).

If the problem is with the woman, she may not be producing ova; the ova may be abnormal; mucus in the cervix may prevent sperm from penetrating it; or a disease of the uterine lining may prevent implantation of the fertilized ovum. A major cause of declining fertility in women after age 30 is deterioration in the quality of their ova. However, the most common female cause is the problem Lesley Brown had: blockage of the Fallopian tubes, preventing ova from reaching the uterus. In about half of these cases, the tubes are blocked by scar tissue from sexually transmitted diseases (King, 1996).

Infertility burdens a marriage emotionally. Partners may become frustrated and angry with themselves and each other and may feel empty, worthless, and depressed (Abbey, Andrews, & Halman, 1992; Jones & Toner, 1993). Their sexual relationship may suffer as sex becomes a matter of "making babies, not love." Such couples may benefit from professional counselling or support from other infertile couples.

About 50 per cent of infertile couples eventually conceive, with or without artificial help, and some adopt children (see chapter 14). An increasing proportion get medical treatment (Jones & Toner, 1993). Hormone treatment may raise a man's sperm count or increase a woman's ovulation. Sometimes drug therapy or surgery can correct the problem. However, fertility drugs increase the likelihood of multiple, and often premature, births (King, 1996). Also, men undergoing fertility treatment are at increased risk of producing sperm with chromosomal abnormalities (Levron et al., 1998).

Since human beings seldom abandon their desires simply because they run into obstacles, it is no surprise that many infertile adults who want children, like Lesley and John Brown, eagerly embrace techniques that bypass ordinary biological processes (see Box 3-1). However, recent research on birth defects and assisted reproductive technology shows that artificially conceived infants have twice the risk of developing birth defects like heart problems, and are twice as likely to have low birth weight as naturally conceived infants (Hansen, Kurinczuk, Bower, & Webb, 2002; Mitchell, 2002). Others choose the more traditional route of adoption (see chapter 14).

Checkpoint ✔

Can you . . .

✔ Explain how and when fertilization normally takes place?

✔ Distinguish between monozygotic and dizygotic twins, and tell how each comes about?

✔ Identify several causes of male and female infertility?

✔ Describe four means of assisted reproduction, and mention several issues they raise?

Guidepost 4

What genetic mechanisms determine sex, physical appearance, and other characteristics?

Mechanisms of Heredity

The science of genetics is the study of *heredity*—the inborn factors, inherited from the biological parents, that affect development. When ovum and sperm unite—whether by normal fertilization or by assisted reproduction, as with Louise Brown—they endow the baby-to-be with a genetic makeup that influences a wide range of characteristics from colour of eyes and hair to health, intellect, and personality.

The Genetic Code

deoxyribonucleic acid (DNA)
Chemical that carries inherited instructions for the formation and function of body cells

The basis of heredity is a chemical called **deoxyribonucleic acid (DNA),** which contains all the inherited material passed from biological parents to children. DNA carries the biochemical instructions that direct the formation of each cell in the body and tell the cells how to make the proteins that enable them to carry out specific body functions.

Box 3-1 *Alternative Ways to Parenthood*

Many couples yearn to have children who carry on their hereditary legacy. Technology now enables many people to have children who are genetically at least half their own.

Artificial insemination—injection of sperm into a woman's cervix—can be done when a man has a low sperm count. Sperm from several ejaculations can be combined for one injection. Thus, with help, a couple can produce their own biological offspring. If the man is infertile, a couple may choose *artificial insemination by a donor (AID)*. The donor may be matched with the prospective father for physical characteristics. If the woman has no explicable cause of infertility, the chances of success can be greatly increased by stimulating her ovaries to produce excess ova and injecting semen directly in the uterus (Guzick et al., 1999).

Since the birth of Louise Brown, more than 250,000 babies worldwide have been given their start through *in vitro fertilization (IVF)*, fertilization outside the mother's body. First, fertility drugs are given to increase production of ova. Then a mature ovum is surgically removed, fertilized in a laboratory dish, and implanted in the mother's uterus. Many of the women, like Lesley Brown, who have conceived in this way have Fallopian tubes blocked or scarred beyond surgical repair. This method also can address male infertility, since a single sperm can be injected into the ovum.

In spite of the great expense and effort involved, IVF has a low success rate; estimates range from 12 to 20 per cent. Two newer techniques with higher success rates are *gamete intrafallopian transfer (GIFT)* and *zygote intrafallopian transfer (ZIFT)*, in which the egg and sperm or the fertilized egg are inserted in the Fallopian tube (Society for Assisted Reproductive Technology, 1993).

A woman who is producing poor-quality ova or who has had her ovaries removed may try ovum transfer. In this procedure (the female counterpart of AID), an ovum, or *donor egg*—provided, usually anonymously, by a fertile young woman—is fertilized in the laboratory and implanted in the prospective mother's uterus. Alternatively, the ovum can be fertilized in the donor's body by artificial insemination. The donor's uterus is flushed out a few days later, and the embryo is retrieved and inserted into the recipient's uterus.

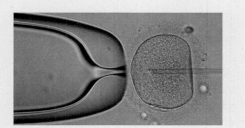

In *in vitro fertilization,* a microscopically tiny needle *(right)* injects the DNA from a man's sperm into a ripe ovum *(centre)*, which has been surgically removed from a woman's body. A flat-nosed pipette *(left)* is used to hold the ovum steady during the insertion. After cell division, the fertilized ovum is implanted in the womb. This technique is one of several forms of assisted reproduction that are helping some infertile couples to reproduce.

In surrogate motherhood, a fertile woman is impregnated by the prospective father, usually by artificial insemination. She carries the baby to term and gives the child to the father and his mate. Surrogate motherhood is in legal limbo, and the Canadian government has introduced legislation, Bill C-56, placing strict conditions on the practice, including a ban on payment to the surrogate mother. The Royal Commission on New Reproductive Technologies (1993) identified the need for legislation on reproductive and genetic technologies, which includes not only surrogacy but also sex selection, buying and selling of ova and sperm, human embryo cloning, and the use of human stem cells for research.

Perhaps the most objectionable aspect of surrogacy, aside from the possibility of forcing the surrogate to relinquish the baby, is the payment of money. The creation of a "breeder class" of poor and disadvantaged women who carry the babies of the well-to-do strikes many people as wrong. Similar concerns have been raised about payment for donor eggs. Exploitation of the would-be parents is an issue, too. Some observers worry about the rapid growth of fertility clinics driven by profit that may prey on desperate couples through misleading claims (Gabriel, 1996).

New and unorthodox means of conception raise serious questions. Must people who use fertility clinics be infertile, or should people be free to make such arrangements simply for convenience? Should single people and cohabiting and homosexual couples have access to these methods? What about older people, who may become frail or die before the child grows up? Should the children know about their parentage? Should genetic tests be performed on prospective donors and surrogates, to identify potential abnormalities or susceptibility to certain diseases or disorders? What about routine screening for existing disease? Should there be legal limits on the number of embryos implanted? Should fertility clinics be required to disclose risks, options, and success rates? What happens if a couple who have contracted with a surrogate divorce before the birth? When a couple chooses in vitro fertilization, what should be done with any unused embryos? (In more than one court case, a couple who had arranged for the freezing of excess embryos later divorced. The woman then wanted to be able to use the embryos to conceive; the man wanted them destroyed.)

One thing seems certain: As long as there are people who want children but are unable to conceive or bear them, human ingenuity and technology will come up with ways to satisfy their need.

What's your view ?

If you or your partner were infertile, would you seriously consider or undertake one of the methods of assisted reproduction described here? Why or why not?

Check it out !

For more information on this topic, go to **www.mcgrawhill.ca/ college/papalia.**

The structure of DNA resembles a long, spiraling ladder made of four chemical units called *bases* (see Figure 3-2). The bases—adenine, thymine, cytosine, and guanine—are known by their initials: *A, T, C,* and *G*. They pair up in four combinations—AT, TA, CG, and GC—and coil around each other. The sequence of 3 billion base pairs constitutes the **genetic code,** which determines all inherited characteristics.

Within each cell nucleus are **chromosomes,** coils of DNA that contain smaller segments called **genes,** the functional units of heredity. A typical gene contains thousands of base pairs; each base pair is part of a three-pair grouping called a codon, giving instructions for building proteins. Each cell in the human body is now believed to contain about 30,000 genes (Venter et al. 2001). Each gene is a small unit of DNA, located in a definite position on its chromosome, and each gene contains the "instructions" for building a specific protein. The complete sequence of genes in the human body constitutes the **human genome.** The genome specifies the order in which genes are expressed, or activated.

Every cell except the sex cells has 23 pairs of chromosomes—46 in all. Through a complex process of cell division called *meiosis,* each sex cell, or gamete (sperm or ovum) ends up with only 23 chromosomes—one from each pair. Thus, when sperm and ovum fuse at conception, they produce a zygote with 46 chromosomes, half from the father and half from the mother.

Three-quarters of the genes every child receives are identical to those received by every other child; they are called *monomorphic genes.* The other one-quarter of a child's genes are *polymorphic genes,* which define each person as an individual. Since many of these come in several variations, and since meiotic division is random, it is virtually impossible for any two children (other than monozygotic twins) to receive exactly the same combination of genes.

At conception, then, the single-celled zygote has all the biological information needed to guide its development into a human baby. This happens through *mitosis,* a process by which the cells divide in half over and over again. When a cell divides, the DNA spirals replicate themselves, so that each newly formed cell has the same DNA structure as all the others. Thus, each cell division creates a duplicate of the original cell, with the same hereditary information. When development is normal, each cell (except the gametes) continues to have 46 chromosomes identical to those in the original zygote. As the cells divide and the child grows and develops, the cells differentiate, specializing in a variety of complex bodily functions.

Genes do not do their work automatically. They spring into action when conditions call for the information they can provide. Genetic action that triggers growth of body and brain is often regulated by hormonal levels, which are affected by such environmental conditions as nutrition and stress. Thus, from the start, heredity and environment are interrelated (Brown, 1999).

What Determines Sex?

In many villages in Nepal, it is common for a man whose wife has borne no male babies to take a second wife. In some societies, a woman's failure to produce sons is justification for divorce. The irony in these customs is that it is the father's sperm that determines a child's sex.

At the moment of conception, the 23 chromosomes from the sperm and the 23 from the mother's ovum form 23 pairs. Twenty-two pairs are **autosomes,** chromosomes that are not related to sexual expression. The twenty-third pair are **sex chromosomes**—one from the father and one from the mother—which govern the baby's sex.

Sex chromosomes are either *X chromosomes* or *Y chromosomes.* The sex chromosome of every ovum is an X chromosome, but the sperm may contain either an X or a Y chromosome. The Y chromosome contains the gene for maleness, called the SRY gene. When an ovum (X) is fertilized by an X-carrying sperm, the zygote formed is XX, a female. When an ovum (X) is fertilized by a Y-carrying sperm, the resulting zygote is XY, a male (see Figure 3-3).

---

genetic code Sequence of base pairs within DNA, which determine inherited characteristics

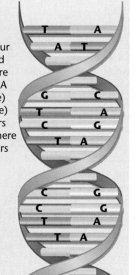

DNA is the genetic material in all living cells. It consists of four chemical units, called bases. These bases are the letters of the DNA alphabet. A (adenine) pairs with T (thymine) and C (cytosine) pairs with G (guanine). There are 3 billion base pairs in human DNA.

Letters of the DNA alphabet

T = Thymine
A = Adenine
G = Guanine
C = Cytosine

Figure 3-2

DNA: The genetic code

Source: Ritter, 1999.

chromosomes Coils of DNA that carry the genes

genes Small segments of DNA located in specific positions on particular chromosomes

human genome Complete sequence or mapping of genes in the human body and their locations

autosomes The 22 pairs of chromosomes not related to sexual expression

sex chromosomes Pair of chromosomes that determines sex: XX in the normal female, XY in the normal male

Initially, the embryo's rudimentary reproductive system is identical in males and females. About 6 to 8 weeks after conception, male embryos normally start producing the male hormone testosterone. Exposure to steady, high levels of testosterone results in the development of a male body with male sexual organs.

Until recently, then, it was assumed that femaleness is a genetic "default setting," which will be operative unless a gene for maleness and a resulting exposure to male hormones overrides it. Now, however, it appears that the development of female characteristics is controlled by a signalling molecule called *Wnt-4,* a mutation of which can "masculinize" a genetically female fetus (Vainio, Heikkiia, Kispert, Chin, & McMahon, 1999). Thus, sexual differentiation appears to be a more complex process than was previously thought.

Patterns of Genetic Transmission

During the 1860s, Gregor Mendel, an Austrian monk, laid the foundation for our understanding of patterns of inheritance. He crossbred pea plants that produced only yellow seeds with pea plants that produced only green seeds. The resulting hybrid plants produced only yellow seeds, meaning, he said, that yellow was *dominant* over green. Yet when he bred the yellow-seeded hybrids with each other, only 75 per cent of their offspring had yellow seeds, and the other 25 per cent had green seeds. This showed, Mendel said, that a hereditary characteristic (in this case, the colour green) can be *recessive,* that is, carried by an organism that does not express, or show, it.

Mendel also tried breeding for two traits at once. Crossing pea plants that produced round yellow seeds with plants that produced wrinkled green seeds, he found that colour and shape were independent of each other. Mendel thus showed that hereditary traits are transmitted separately.

Today we know that the genetic picture in humans is far more complex than Mendel imagined. Most human traits fall along a continuous spectrum (for example, from light skin to dark). It is hard to find a single normal trait that people inherit through simple dominant transmission other than the ability to curl the tongue lengthwise. Let's look at various forms of inheritance.

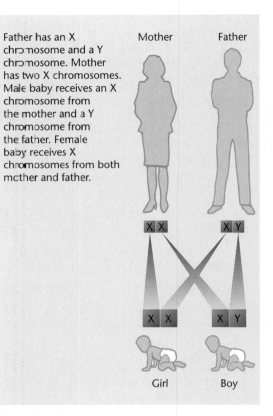

Father has an X chromosome and a Y chromosome. Mother has two X chromosomes. Male baby receives an X chromosome from the mother and a Y chromosome from the father. Female baby receives X chromosomes from both mother and father.

Figure 3-3

Determination of sex. Since all babies receive an X chromosome from the mother, sex is determined by whether an X or Y chromosome is received from the father.

Dominant and Recessive Inheritance

Can you curl your tongue? If so, you inherited this ability through *dominant inheritance.* If your parents can curl their tongues but you cannot, *recessive inheritance* occurred. How do these two types of inheritance work?

Genes that can produce alternative expressions of a characteristic (such as ability or inability to curl the tongue) are called **alleles.** Every person receives a pair of alleles for a given characteristic, one from each biological parent. When both alleles are the same, the person is **homozygous** for the characteristic; when they are different, the person is **heterozygous.** In **dominant inheritance,** when a person is heterozygous for a particular trait, the dominant allele governs. In other words, when an offspring receives contradictory alleles for a trait, only one of them, the dominant one, will be expressed. **Recessive inheritance,** the expression of a recessive trait, occurs only when a person receives the recessive allele from both parents.

If you inherited one allele for tongue-curling ability from each parent (see Figure 3-4), you are homozygous for tongue curling and can curl your tongue. If, say, your mother passed on an allele for the ability and your father passed on an allele lacking it, you are heterozygous. Since the ability is dominant (D) and its lack is recessive (d), you, again, can curl your tongue. But if you received the recessive allele from both parents, you would not be a tongue-curler.

alleles Paired genes (alike or different) that affect a trait

homozygous Possessing two identical alleles for a trait

heterozygous Possessing differing alleles for a trait

dominant inheritance Pattern of inheritance in which, when a child receives contradictory alleles, only the dominant one is expressed

recessive inheritance Pattern of inheritance in which a child receives identical recessive alleles, resulting in expression of a nondominant trait

Figure 3-4

Figure 3-4

Dominant and recessive inheritance. Because of dominant inheritance, the same observable phenotype (in this case, the ability to curl the tongue lengthwise) can result from two different genotypes (DD and Dd). A phenotype expressing a recessive characteristic (such as inability to curl the tongue) must have a homozygous genotype (dd).

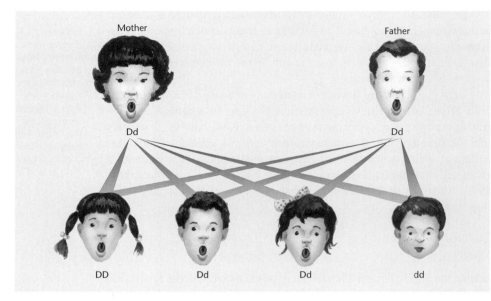

quantitative trait loci (QTL)
Interaction of multiple genes, each with effects of varying size, to produce a complex trait

multifactorial transmission
Combination of genetic and environmental factors to produce certain complex traits

phenotype Observable characteristics of a person

genotype Genetic makeup of a person, containing both expressed and unexpressed characteristics

Checkpoint ✔

Can you . . .

✔ Explain why no two people, other than monozygotic twins, have the same genetic heritage?

✔ Explain why it is the sperm that determines a baby's sex?

✔ Tell how dominant inheritance and recessive inheritance work, and why most normal traits are not the products of simple dominant or recessive transmission?

Most traits seem to be transmitted by the interaction of several genes with effects of varying sizes, or **quantitative trait loci (QTL).** QTL is one reason that simple dominance and recessiveness cannot explain the inheritance of such complex human traits as intelligence, which may be affected by 50 or more genes. Indeed, whereas there are more than 1,000 rare genes that individually determine abnormal traits, there is no known single gene that, by itself, significantly accounts for individual differences in any complex normal behaviour. Instead, such behaviours are likely to be influenced by many genes with small but sometimes identifiable effects (Plomin, 1995; Plomin & DeFries, 1999). In addition, **multifactorial transmission,** a combination of genetic and environmental factors, plays a role in the expression of most traits. Let's see how.

Genotypes and Phenotypes: Multifactorial Transmission

If you can curl your tongue, that ability is part of your **phenotype,** the array of observable characteristics through which your **genotype,** or underlying genetic makeup, is expressed. Except for monozygotic twins, no two people have the same genotype. The phenotype is the product of the genotype and any relevant environmental influences.

As Figure 3-4 shows, the same phenotypical characteristic may arise from different genotypes: either a homozygous combination of two dominant alleles or a heterozygous combination of one dominant allele and one recessive allele. If you are heterozygous for tongue curling and you and a mate who is also heterozygous for the trait have four children, the statistical probability is that one child will be homozygous for the ability, one will be homozygous lacking it, and the other two will be heterozygous. Thus, three of your children will have phenotypes that include tongue curling (they will be able to curl their tongues), but this ability will arise from two different genotypical patterns (homozygous and heterozygous).

Tongue curling has a strong genetic base; but for most traits, experience modifies the expression of the genotype. Let's say that Steven has inherited musical talent. If he takes music lessons and practises regularly, he may delight his family with his performances. If his family likes and encourages classical music, he may play Bach preludes; if the other children on his block influence him to prefer popular music, he may eventually form a rock group. However, if from early childhood he is not encouraged and not motivated to play music, and if he has no access to a musical instrument or to music lessons, his genotype for musical ability may not be expressed (or may be expressed to a lesser extent) in his phenotype. Some physical characteristics (including height and weight) and most psychological characteristics (such as intelligence and personality traits, as well as musical ability) are products of multifactorial transmission.

The difference between genotype and phenotype helps explain why even a clone can never be an exact duplicate of another human being. Later in this chapter we discuss in more detail how environmental influences work together with the genetic endowment to influence development.

Genetic and Chromosomal Abnormalities

One of John and Lesley Brown's chief worries before Louise's birth—whether or not she would be a "normal" baby—is shared by every prospective biological parent. Babies born with serious birth defects are at high risk of dying at or shortly after birth or during infancy or childhood (Skjaerven, Wilcox, & Lie, 1999). Birth disorders accounted for 27 per cent of infant deaths in 1997 (CICH, 2000). Most of the serious malformations involve the circulatory or central nervous systems (see Table 3-1).

Because many defects are hereditary, affected people risk passing them on to their children. This may be one reason that women with birth defects are less likely than other women to have children (Skjaerven et al, 1999).

It is in genetic defects and diseases that we see most clearly the operation of dominant and recessive transmission in humans, and also of a variation, *sex-linked inheritance*. Some defects are due to abnormalities in genes or chromosomes, which may result from **mutations:** permanent alterations in genetic material that may produce harmful characteristics. Mutations can occur spontaneously or can be induced by environmental hazards, such as radiation. It has been estimated that the human species undergoes at least 1.6 harmful mutations per person in each generation. Eventually, mutations may be eliminated from the human genome by **natural selection,** the failure of affected individuals to survive and reproduce (Crow, 1999; Eyre-Walker & Keightley, 1999).

Many disorders arise when an inherited predisposition interacts with an environmental factor, either before or after birth. Spina bifida (incomplete closure of the vertebral canal) and cleft palate (a fissure in the roof of the mouth) probably result from multifactorial transmission (Botto, Moore, Khoury, & Erickson, 1999). Attention deficit hyperactivity disorder is one of a number of behavioural disorders thought to be transmitted multifactorially.

Not all genetic or chromosomal abnormalities show up at birth. Symptoms of Tay-Sachs disease (a fatal degenerative disease of the central nervous system that at one time occurred mostly among Jews of eastern European ancestry) and sickle-cell anemia (a blood disorder most common among people of African descent) may not appear until at least 6 months of age; cystic fibrosis (a condition, especially common in children of northern European descent, in which excess mucus accumulates in the lungs and digestive tract), not until age 4; and glaucoma (a disease in which fluid pressure builds up in the eye) and Huntington's disease (a progressive degeneration of the nervous system) usually not until middle age.

Defects Transmitted by Dominant or Recessive Inheritance

As Mendel discovered, characteristics can be passed on from parent to child by dominant or recessive inheritance. Most of the time, normal genes are dominant over those carrying abnormal traits, but sometimes the gene for an abnormal trait is dominant. When one parent has a dominant abnormal gene and one recessive normal gene and the other parent has two recessive normal genes, each of their children has a 50:50 chance of inheriting the abnormal gene. Among the 1,800 disorders known to be transmitted by dominant inheritance are achondroplasia (a type of dwarfism) and Huntington's disease.

Recessive defects are expressed only if a child receives the same recessive gene from each biological parent. Some defects transmitted recessively, such as Tay-Sachs disease and sickle-cell anemia, are more common among certain ethnic groups, which, through inbreeding (marriage and reproduction within the group) have passed down recessive characteristics (see Table 3-2).

Defects transmitted by recessive inheritance are more likely to be lethal at an early age than those transmitted by dominant inheritance. If a dominantly transmitted defect killed before the age of reproduction, it could not be passed on to the next generation and therefore would soon disappear. A recessive defect can be transmitted by carriers who do not have the disorder and thus may live to reproduce.

Guidepost 5

How are birth defects and disorders transmitted?

mutations Permanent alterations in genes or chromosomes that may produce harmful characteristics

natural selection According to Darwin's theory of evolution, process by which characteristics that promote survival of a species are reproduced in successive generations, and characteristics that do not promote survival die out

| Table 3-1 | Some Birth Defects |

Condition	Characteristics of Condition	Who Is at Risk	What Can Be Done
Alpha₁ antitrypsin deficiency	Enzyme deficiency that can lead to cirrhosis of the liver in early infancy and emphysema and degenerative lung disease in middle age.	1 in 1,000 white births	No treatment
Alpha thalassemia	Severe anemia that reduces ability of the blood to carry oxygen; nearly all affected infants are stillborn or die soon after birth.	Primarily families of Malaysian, African, and Southeast Asian descent	Frequent blood transfusions
Beta thalassemia (Cooley's anemia)	Severe anemia resulting in weakness, fatigue, and frequent illness; usually fatal in adolescence or young adulthood.	Primarily families of Mediterranean descent	Frequent blood transfusions
Cystic fibrosis	Body makes too much mucus, which collects in the lung and digestive tract; children do not grow normally and usually do not live beyond age 30; the most common inherited *lethal* defect among white people.	1 in 2,000 white births	Daily physical therapy to loosen mucus; antibiotics for lung infections; enzymes to improve digestion; gene therapy (in experimental stage)
Duchenne's muscular dystrophy	Fatal disease usually found in males, marked by muscle weakness; minor mental retardation not uncommon; respiratory failure and death usually occur in young adulthood.	1 in 3,000 to 5,000 male births	No treatment
Hemophilia	Excessive bleeding, usually affecting males rather than females; in its most severe form, can lead to crippling arthritis in adulthood.	1 in 10,000 families with a history of hemophilia	Frequent transfusions of blood with clotting factors
Neural-tube defects:			
Anencephaly	Absence of brain tissues; infants are stillborn or die soon after birth.	1 in 1,000	No treatment
Spina bifida	Incompletely closed spinal canal, resulting in muscle weakness or paralysis and loss of bladder and bowel control; often accompanied by hydrocephalus, an accumulation of spinal fluid in the brain, which can lead to mental retardation.	1 in 1,000	Surgery to close spinal canal may prevent further injury; shunt placed in brain drains excess fluid and prevents mental retardation
Phenylketonuria (PKU)	Metabolic disorder resulting in mental retardation.	1 in 10,000 to 25,000 births	Special diet begun in first few weeks of life can offset mental retardation
Polycystic kidney disease	*Infantile form:* enlarged kidneys, leading to respiratory problems and congestive heart failure. *Adult form:* kidney pain, kidney stones, and hypertension resulting in chronic kidney failure.	1 in 1,000	Kidney transplants
Sickle-cell anemia	Deformed, fragile red blood cells that can clog the blood vessels, depriving the body of oxygen; symptoms include severe pain, stunted growth, frequent infections, leg ulcers, gallstones, susceptibility to pneumonia, and stroke.	1 in 500 people of African descent	Painkillers, transfusions for anemia, and to prevent stroke, antibiotics for infections
Tay-Sachs disease	Degenerative disease of the brain and nerve cells, resulting in death before age 5.	1 in 3,000 people of eastern European Jewish descent, rarer in other groups	No treatment

Source: Adapted from AAP Committee on Genetics, 1996; Tisdale, 1988, pp 68–69.

Table 3-2

Table 3-2	Chances of Genetic Disorders for Various Ethnic Groups	
If You Are	**The Chance Is About**	**That**
African descent	1 in 12	You are a carrier of sickle-cell anemia.
	7 in 10	You will have milk intolerance as an adult.
African descent male	1 in 10	You have a hereditary predisposition to develop hemolytic anemia after taking sulfa or other drugs.
African descent female	1 in 50	You have a hereditary predisposition to develop hemolytic anemia after taking sulfa or other drugs.
White	1 in 25	You are a carrier of cystic fibrosis.
	1 in 80	You are a carrier of phenylketonuria (PKU).
Jewish (Ashkenazic) descent	1 in 100	You are a carrier of familial dysautonomia.
Italian descent Greek descent	1 in 10	You are a carrier of beta thalassemia.
Armenian or Jewish (Sephardic) descent	1 in 45	You are a carrier of familial Mediterranean fever.
Afrikaner (white South African) descent	1 in 330	You have porphyria.
Asian descent	almost 100%	You will have milk intolerance as an adult.

Source: Adapted from Milunsky, 1992, p. 122.

Defects Transmitted by Sex-Linked Inheritance

In **sex-linked inheritance** (see Figure 3-5) certain recessive disorders linked to genes on the sex chromosomes show up differently in male and female children. Red-green colour-blindness is one of these sex-linked conditions. Another is hemophilia, a disorder in which blood does not clot when it should.

Sex-linked recessive traits are carried on one of the X chromosomes of an unaffected mother. Sex-linked disorders almost always appear only in male children; in females, a normal dominant gene on the X chromosome from the father overrides the defective gene on the X chromosome from the mother. Boys are more vulnerable to these disorders because there is no opposite dominant gene on the shorter Y chromosome from the father to override a defect on the X chromosome from the mother.

Occasionally, a female does inherit a sex-linked condition. For example, if her father is a hemophiliac and her mother happens to be a carrier for the disorder, the daughter has a 50 per cent chance of receiving the abnormal X chromosome from each parent and having the disease.

Genome Imprinting

Through *genome imprinting,* some genes seem to be temporarily imprinted, or chemically altered, in either the mother or the father. These genes, when transmitted to offspring, have effects different from comparable genes from the other parent. A particularly dramatic example of genome imprinting appeared among 80 girls and young women with Turner syndrome (discussed in the next section), in which an X chromosome is missing. Those who had received their single X chromosome from their fathers were better adjusted socially and had stronger verbal and cognitive skills than those who had received the X chromosome from their mothers. This suggests that social competence is influenced by an imprinted gene or genes on the X chromosome, which is "turned off" when that chromosome comes from the mother (Skuse et al., 1997).

sex-linked inheritance Pattern of inheritance in which certain characteristics carried on the X chromosome inherited from the mother are transmitted differently to her male and female offspring

Checkpoint

Can you . . .

✔ Compare the operation of dominant inheritance, recessive inheritance, sex-linked inheritance, and genome imprinting in transmission of birth defects?

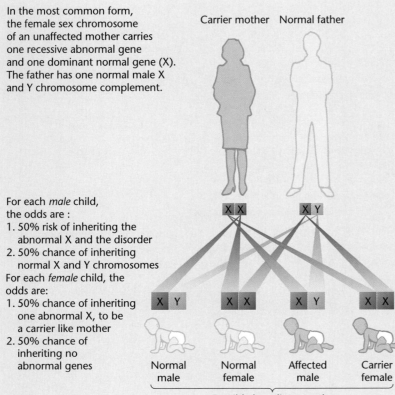

In the most common form, the female sex chromosome of an unaffected mother carries one recessive abnormal gene and one dominant normal gene (X). The father has one normal male X and Y chromosome complement.

Carrier mother   Normal father

For each *male* child, the odds are :
1. 50% risk of inheriting the abnormal X and the disorder
2. 50% chance of inheriting normal X and Y chromosomes

For each *female* child, the odds are:
1. 50% chance of inheriting one abnormal X, to be a carrier like mother
2. 50% chance of inheriting no abnormal genes

Normal male   Normal female   Affected male   Carrier female

Possible hereditary results

Figure 3-5

Sex-linked inheritance of a birth defect

Down syndrome Chromosomal disorder characterized by moderate-to-severe mental retardation

genetic counselling Clinical service that advises couples of their probable risk of having children with hereditary defects

Chromosomal Abnormalities

About 1 in every 156 children born in industrialized countries is estimated to have a chromosomal abnormality (Milunsky, 1992). Some of these abnormalities are inherited; others result from accidents during prenatal development and are not likely to recur in the same family.

Some chromosomal disorders, such as Klinefelter syndrome, are caused by an extra sex chromosome (shown by the pattern XXY). Others, such as Turner syndrome, result from a missing sex chromosome (XO). Characteristics of the most common sex chromosome disorders are shown in Table 3-3.

Other chromosomal abnormalities occur in the autosomes. **Down syndrome,** the most common of these, is responsible for about one-third of all cases of near-normal/mild-to-severe mental retardation. The condition is also called *trisomy-21,* because it is usually caused by an extra twenty-first chromosome or the translocation of part of the twenty-first chromosome onto another chromosome. Down syndrome involves a combination of about 50 symptoms, and any given child with Down syndrome could have 20 to 30 of these.

About 1 in every 1000 Canadian babies born alive has Down syndrome (Lia, 1996). The risk is greatest with older parents and teenagers, although in general more children with Down syndrome are born to younger women, given that younger women give birth to more children than older women. When the mother is under age 35, the disorder is more likely to be hereditary. The extra chromosome seems to come from the mother's ovum in 95 per cent of cases (Antonarakis & Down Syndrome Collaborative Group, 1991); the other 5 per cent of cases seem to be related to the father.

The prognosis for children with Down syndrome is brighter than was once thought. As adults, many live in small group homes and support themselves; they tend to do well in structured job situations. More than 70 per cent of people with Down syndrome live into their sixties, but they are at special risk of developing Alzheimer's disease (Hayes & Batshaw, 1993). Men are particularly at risk (Schupf, Kapell, Nightingale, Rodriguez, Tycko, Mayeux, 1998).

Genetic Counselling

Genetic counselling can help prospective parents assess their risk of bearing children with genetic or chromosomal defects. People who have already had a child with a genetic defect, who have a family history of hereditary illness, who suffer from conditions known or suspected to be inherited, or who come from ethnic groups at higher-than-average risk of passing on genes for certain diseases can get information about their likelihood of producing affected children.

A genetic counsellor may be a pediatrician, an obstetrician, a family doctor, a nurse, or a genetic specialist. She or he takes a family history and gives the prospective parents and any biological children physical examinations. Laboratory investigations of blood, skin, urine, or fingerprints may be performed. Chromosomes from body tissues may be analyzed and photographed, and the photographs enlarged and arranged according to size and structure on a chart called a *karyotype.* This chart can show chromosomal abnormalities and can indicate whether a person who appears normal might transmit genetic defects to a child (see Figure

Table 3-3	Sex Chromosome Abnormalities		
Pattern/Name	**Characteristic***	**Incidence**	**Treatment**
XYY	Male; tall stature; tendency to low IQ, especially verbal.	1 in 1,000 male births	No special treatment
XXX (triple X)	Female, normal appearance, menstrual irregularities, learning disorders, mental retardation.	1 in 1,000 female births	Special education
XXY (Kleinfelter)	Male, sterility, underdeveloped secondary sex characteristics, small testes, learning disorders.	1 in 1,000 male births	Hormone therapy, special education
XO (Turner)	Female, short stature, webbed neck, impaired spatial abilities, no menstruation, infertility, underdeveloped sex organs, incomplete development of secondary sex characteristics.	1 in 1,500 to 2,500 female births	Hormone therapy, special education
Fragile X	Minor-to-severe mental retardation; symptoms, which are more severe in males, include delayed speech and motor development, speech impairments, and hyperactivity; the most common *inherited* form of mental retardation.	1 in 1,200 male births; 1 in 2,000 female births	Educational and behavioural therapies when needed

*Not every affected person has every characteristic.

3–6). The counsellor tries to help clients understand the mathematical risk of a particular condition, explains its implications, and presents information about alternative courses of action.

Geneticists have made great contributions to avoidance of birth defects. For example, since so many Jewish couples have been tested for Tay-Sachs genes, far fewer Jewish babies have been born with the disease; in fact, it is now far more likely to affect non-Jewish babies (Kaback et al., 1993). Similarly, screening and counselling of women of childbearing age from Mediterranean countries, where beta thalassemia (refer back to Table 3-1) is common, has brought a decline in births of affected babies and greater knowledge of the risks of being a carrier (Cao, Saba, Galanello, & Rosatelli, 1997).

Today, researchers are rapidly identifying genes that contribute to many serious diseases and disorders, as well as those that influence normal traits. Their work is likely to lead to widespread **genetic testing** to reveal genetic profiles—a prospect that involves dangers as well as benefits (see Box 3-2).

Nature and Nurture: Influences of Heredity and Environment

How do nature and nurture influence development? That question was a major issue among early psychologists and the general public (refer back to chapters 1 and 2). Today it has become clear that, while certain rare physical disorders are virtually 100 per cent inherited, phenotypes for most complex normal traits, such as those having to do with health, intelligence, and personality, are subject to a complex array of hereditary and environmental forces. Let's see how scientists study and explain the influences of heredity and environment and how these two forces work together.

Studying the Relative Influences of Heredity and Environment

One approach to the study of heredity and environment is quantitative: it seeks to measure *how much* heredity and environment influence particular traits. This is the traditional goal of the science of **behavioural genetics.**

Checkpoint ✓

Can you . . .

✔ Tell three ways in which chromosomal disorders occur?

✔ Explain the purposes of genetic counselling?

genetic testing Procedure for ascertaining genetic makeup to identify predispositions to herditary diseases or disorders

Guidepost 6

How do scientists study the relative influences of heredity and environment, and how do heredity and environment work together?

behavioural genetics Quantitative study of relative hereditary and environmental influences

Figure 3-6

A karyotype is a photograph that shows the chromosomes when they are separated and aligned for cell division. We know that this is a karyotype of a person with Down syndrome, because there are three chromosomes instead of the usual two on chromosome 21. Since pair 23 consists of two X's, we know that this is the karyotype of a female.
Source: Babu & Hirschhorn, 1992; March of Dimes, 1987.

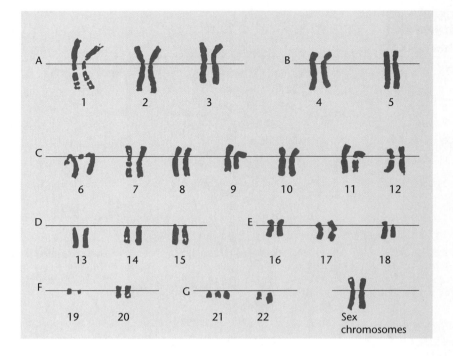

heritability Statistical estimate of contribution of heredity to individual differences in a specific trait within a given population

Measuring Heritability

Heritability is a statistical estimate of how great a contribution heredity makes toward individual differences in a specific trait at a certain time *within a given population*. Heritability does *not* refer to the relative influence of heredity and environment in a particular individual; those influences may be virtually impossible to separate. Nor does heritability tell us how traits develop. It merely indicates the statistical extent to which genes contribute to a trait.

Heritability is expressed as a percentage ranging from zero to 100 per cent; the greater the percentage, the greater the heritability of a trait. Since heritability cannot be measured directly, researchers in behavioural genetics rely chiefly on three types of correlational research: family, adoption, and twin studies.

Such studies are based on the assumption that immediate family members are more genetically similar than more distant relatives, monozygotic twins are more genetically similar than dizygotic twins, and adopted children are genetically more like their biological families than their adoptive families. Thus, if heredity is an important influence on a particular trait, siblings should be more alike than cousins with regard to that trait, monozygotic twins should be more alike than dizygotic twins, and adopted children should be more like their biological parents than their adoptive parents. By the same token, if a shared environment exerts an important influence on a trait, persons who live together should be more similar than persons who do *not* live together.

Family studies go beyond noting similarities in traits among family members, as we did for Louise Brown and her mother and father. Researchers measure the *degree* to which biological relatives share certain traits and whether the closeness of the familial relationship is associated with the degree of similarity. If the correlation is strong, the researchers infer a genetic influence. However, family studies cannot rule out environmental influences on a trait. A family study alone cannot tell us whether obese children of obese parents inherited the tendency or whether they are fat because their diet is like that of their parents. For that reason, researchers do adoption studies, which can separate the effects of heredity from those of a shared environment.

Adoption studies look at similarities between adopted children and their adoptive families and also between adopted children and their biological families. When adopted children are more like their biological parents and siblings in a particular trait (say, obesity), we see the influence of heredity. When they resemble their adoptive families more, we see the influence of environment.

Box 3-2 *Genetic Testing and Genetic Engineering*

What are your chances of developing colon, breast, or prostate cancer or Alzheimer's disease, or another genetically influenced condition? Genetic testing is becoming more common as scientists find ways to identify people genetically at risk to develop a variety of diseases and disorders.

The Human Genome Project, under the joint leadership of the National Institutes of Health and the U.S. Department of Energy, in cooperation with Celera Genomics, a private firm in Rockville, Maryland, has now mapped the order of DNA base pairs in all the genes in the human body. Detailed genetic mapping of human chromosome 7, which accounts for 5 per cent of the human genome, is being conducted at the Hospital for Sick Children in Toronto, as part of the human genome project. In addition, this work will provide a basis for studying diseases, including many cancer conditions, that are associated with anomalies in chromosome 7, and will give us some indication of how genetic material is expressed in human biology during child development and during old age. As part of the project, researchers will develop new genetic mapping techniques that will benefit work on the human genome. The project will enable scientists to more readily identify genes that cause or trigger particular disorders.

The genetic information gained from such research could increase our ability to predict, control, treat, and cure disease. Already, genetic screening of newborns is saving lives and preventing complications associated with disorders, such as premature death, by permitting identification and treatment of infants with sickle-cell anemia or phenylketonuria (Holtzman, Murphy, Watson, & Barr, 1997). Genetic information can help people decide whether to have children and with whom, and it can help people with family histories of a disease to know the worst that is likely to happen (Post, 1994; Wiggins et al., 1992).

Gene therapy (repairing or replacing abnormal genes) is already an option for some rare genetic disorders and has been tried experimentally *in utero* (Flake et al., 1996). In 2000, French researchers reversed severe combined immunodeficiency, a serious immune disease, in three babies from 1 to 11 months old by taking bone marrow cells from the babies, genetically altering the cells, and then injecting them into the babies. The patients remained healthy as much as a year later (Cavazanna-Calvo et al., 2000).

However, human gene transfer experiments raise ethical concerns about safety, benefit to participants, and the difficulty of obtaining meaningful informed consent (Sugarman, 1999). Gene therapy carries serious risks: an 18-year-old died after researchers at the University of Pennsylvania gave him an experimental infusion of gene-altered viruses intended to treat a liver disorder (Stolberg, 2000). A group of scientists, ethicists, lawyers, and theologians, under auspices of the American Association for the Advancement of Science, concluded that gene therapy can inadvertently damage reproductive cells and that it cannot yet be safely and responsibly performed on human beings (Chapman & Frankel, 2000).

Genetic testing itself involves ethical issues. For one thing, predictions are imperfect; a false positive result may cause needless anxiety, while a false negative result may delude a person into complacency. And what if a genetic condition is incurable? Is there any point in knowing you have the gene for a potentially debilitating condition if you cannot do anything about it? A panel of experts has recommended against genetic testing for diseases for which there is no known cure (Institute of Medicine [IOM], 1993).

What about privacy? Although medical data are supposed to be confidential, it is almost impossible to keep such information private. And do parents, children, or siblings have a legitimate claim to information about a patient that may affect them (Plomin & Rutter, 1998; Rennie, 1994)? In Canada, it is recommended that people undergoing genetic testing be made aware of its consequences and limitations. The consequences include the potential for discrimination, negative impact on the family, and potential loss of some types of support services such as life insurance, especially for those likely to have genetically based late-onset diseases (Jamieson, 2001).

A major concern is *genetic determinism:* the misconception that a person with a gene for a disease is bound to get the disease. All genetic testing can tell us is the *likelihood* that a person will get a disease. Most diseases involve a complex combination of genes or depend in part on lifestyle or other environmental factors (Plomin & Rutter, 1998). Job and insurance discrimination on the basis of genetic information has already occurred—even though tests may be imprecise and unreliable and people deemed at risk of a disease may never develop it (Lapham, Kozma, & Weiss, 1996). This could lead, according to a policy report issued to the Canadian government, to a new socially stigmatized group of the "not-yet-ill" (Shrecker, Somerville, Hoffmaster, & Wellington, 2001, p. 189).

Specific issues have to do with testing of children. Whose decision should it be to have a child tested—the parent's or the child's? Should a child be tested to benefit a sibling or someone else? How will a child be affected by learning that he or she is likely to develop a disease 20, 30, or 50 years later? If testing shows that a presumed biological father is not really the father of the child, should that information be disclosed?

Particularly chilling is the prospect that genetic testing could be misused to justify sterilization of people with "undesirable" genes, or abortion of a normal fetus with the "wrong" genetic makeup (Plomin & Rutter, 1998). Gene therapy has the potential for similar abuse. Should it be used to make a short child taller, or a chubby child thinner? To improve an unborn baby's appearance or intelligence? The path from therapeutic correction of defects to genetic engineering for cosmetic or functional purposes may well be a slippery slope (Anderson, 1998), leading to a society in which some parents could afford to provide the "best" genes for their children while others could not (Rifkin, 1998).

Within the next 15 years, genetic testing and gene therapy "will almost certainly revolutionize the practice of medicine" (Anderson, 1998, p. 30). It is not yet clear whether the benefits of these new biotechnologies will outweigh the risks.

What's your view ?

Would you want to know that you had a gene predisposing you to lung cancer? To Alzheimer's disease? Would you want your child to be tested for these genes?

Check it out !

For more information on this topic, go to **www.mcgrawhill.ca/college/papalia.**

Studies of twins compare pairs of monozygotic twins and same-sex dizygotic twins. (Same-sex twins are used so as to avoid any confounding effects of gender.) Monozygotic twins are twice as genetically similar, on average, as dizygotic twins, who are no more genetically similar than other same-sex siblings. When monozygotic twins are more **concordant** (that is, have a statistically greater tendency to show the same trait) than dizygotic twins, we see the likely effects of heredity. Concordance rates, which may range from zero to 100 per cent, tell what percentage of pairs of twins in a sample are concordant, or similar.

When monozygotic twins show higher concordance for a trait than do dizygotic twins, the likelihood of a genetic factor can be studied further through adoption studies. Studies of monozygotic twins separated in infancy and reared apart have found strong resemblances between the twins. Such findings support a hereditary basis for many physical and psychological characteristics.

Still, the effects of genetic influences, especially on behavioural traits, are rarely inevitable: even in a trait strongly influenced by heredity, the environment can have substantial impact, as much as 50 per cent. In fact, environmental interventions sometimes can overcome genetically "determined" conditions. A special diet soon after birth can often prevent mental retardation in children with the genetic disease phenylketonuria (PKU) (Plomin & DeFries, 1999; refer back to Table 3-1). As we'll see in the next section, current studies based in part on behavioural genetics are throwing more light on the complex relationship between heredity and environment.

Critics of behavioural genetics claim that its assumptions and methods tend to maximize the importance of hereditary effects and minimize environmental ones. Furthermore, there are great variations in the findings, depending on the source of the data. For example, twin studies generally come up with higher heritability estimates than adoption studies do. This wide variability, critics say, "means that no firm conclusions can be drawn about the relative strength of these influences on development" (Collins, Maccoby, Steinberg, Hetherington, & Bornstein, 2000, p. 221).

Effects of the Prenatal Environment

Two newer types of twin studies—*co-twin control* and *chorion control* studies—allow researchers to look at the nature and timing of non-genetic influences in the womb (Phelps, Davis, & Schartz, 1997). *Co-twin control studies* compare the prenatal (or postnatal) development and experiences of one monozygotic twin with those of the other, who serves as a one-person "control group." *Chorion control studies* focus on prenatal influences by comparing two types of monozygotic twins: (1) *monochorionic* twins, who developed within the same fluid-filled sac and thus had a similar prenatal environment, and (2) *dichorionic* twins, who grew within separate sacs, as about one-third of monozygotic twins, like all dizygotic twins, do.

Monochorionic twins normally share blood and have similar hormonal levels, which affect brain development. They also share exposure to any infectious agents that come from the mother's body. Because dichorionic twins are attached to different parts of the uterine wall, one twin may be better nourished than the other and better protected against infection. Twin studies that do not take account of these factors may either underestimate or overestimate genetic influences. Monochorionic twins tend to be more concordant than dichorionic twins in IQ, certain personality patterns, and cholesterol levels.

How Heredity and Environment Work Together

Today, as research in cognitive neuroscience and molecular biology increasingly underlines the complexity of development, many developmental scientists have come to regard a solely quantitative approach to the study of heredity and environment as simplistic (Collins et al., 2000). They see these two forces as fundamentally intertwined and inseparable. Instead of looking at genes and experience as operating directly on an organism, they see both as part of a complex *developmental system* (Gottlieb, 1991). From conception on, throughout life, a combination of constitutional factors (related to biological and psychological makeup), and social, economic, and cultural factors help shape development. The

Checkpoint ✔

Can you . . .

✔ State the basic assumption underlying studies of behavioural genetics and how it applies to family studies, twin studies, and adoption studies?

✔ Cite criticisms of the behavioural genetics approach?

✔ Identify two types of twin studies that focus on environmental influences in the womb?

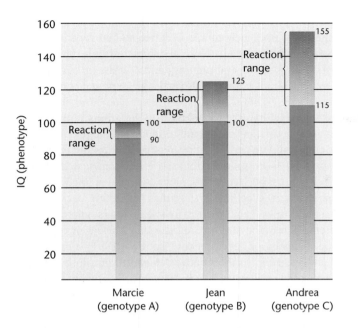

Figure 3-7

Intelligence and reaction range. Children with different genotypes for intelligence will show varying reaction ranges when exposed to a restricted (blue portion of bar) or enriched (entire bar) environment.

more advantageous these circumstances and the experiences to which they give rise, the greater is the likelihood of optimum development (Horowitz, 2000).

Let's consider several ways in which inheritance and experience work together.

Reaction Range and Canalization

Many characteristics vary, within limits, under varying hereditary or environmental conditions. The concepts of *reaction range* and *canalization* can help us visualize how this happens.

Reaction range is the conventional term for a range of potential expressions of a hereditary trait. Body size, for example, depends largely on biological processes, which are genetically regulated. Even so, a range of sizes is possible, depending on environmental opportunities and constraints and a person's own behaviour. In societies in which nutrition has dramatically improved, an entire generation has grown up to tower over the generation before. The better-fed children share their parents' genes but have responded to a healthier world. Once a society's average diet becomes adequate for more than one generation, however, children tend to grow to heights similar to their parents'. Ultimately, height has genetic limits: we don't see people who are only a foot tall, or any who are 10 feet tall.

Heredity can influence whether a reaction range is wide or narrow. For example, a child born with a defect producing mild retardation is more able to respond to a favourable environment than a child born with more severe limitations. A child of normal native intelligence is likely to have a higher IQ if raised in an enriched home and school environment than if raised in a more restrictive environment; but a child with more native ability will probably have a much wider reaction range (see Figure 3-7).

Instead of talking about a reaction range, advocates of a developmental system model prefer the term *norm of reaction*. While recognizing that heredity does set some limits, they argue that, because development is so complex, these limits are unknowable and their effects unpredictable (Gottlieb, 1991).

The metaphor of **canalization** illustrates how heredity restricts the range of development for some traits. After a heavy storm, the rainwater that has fallen on a pavement has to go somewhere. If the street has potholes, the water will fill them. If deep canals have been dug along the edges of the street, the water will flow into the canals instead. Some human characteristics, such as eye colour, are so strongly programmed by the genes that they are said to be highly canalized: there is little opportunity for variance in their expression.

reaction range Potential variability, depending on environmental conditions, in the expression of a hereditary trait

canalization Limitation on variance of expression of certain inherited characteristics

Certain behaviours also develop along genetically "dug" channels; it takes an extreme change in environment to alter their course. Behaviours that depend largely on maturation seem to appear when a child is ready. Normal babies follow a typical sequence of motor development: crawling, walking, and running, in that order, at certain approximate ages. Still, this development is not completely canalized; experience can affect its pace and timing.

Cognition and personality are more subject to variations in experience: the kinds of families children grow up in, the schools they attend, and the people they encounter. Consider language. Before children can talk, they must reach a certain level of neurological and muscular maturation. No 6-month-old could speak this sentence, no matter how enriched the infant's home life might be. Yet environment does play a large part in language development. If parents encourage babies' first sounds by talking back to them, children are likely to start to speak earlier than if their early vocalizing is ignored.

Recently scientists have begun to recognize that a usual or typical experience, too, can dig canals, or channels for development (Gottlieb, 1991). For example, infants who hear only the sounds peculiar to their native language soon lose the ability to perceive sounds characteristic of other languages (see chapter 7). Throughout this book you will find many examples of how socio-economic status, neighbourhood conditions, and educational opportunity can powerfully shape developmental outcomes, from the pace and complexity of language development to the likelihood of early sexual activity and antisocial behaviour.

Genotype–Environment Interaction

genotype–environment interaction The portion of phenotypic variation that results from the reactions of genetically different individuals to similar environmental conditions

Genotype–environment interaction usually refers to the effects of similar environmental conditions on genetically different individuals. To take a familiar example, many people are exposed to pollen and dust, but people with a genetic predisposition are more likely to develop allergic reactions. Some researchers point out that interactions can work the other way as well: Genetically similar children often develop differently, depending on their home environment (Collins et al., 2000). As we discuss in chapter 8, a child born with a "difficult" temperament may develop adjustment problems in one family and thrive in another, depending largely on parental handling. Thus it may take the interaction of hereditary and environmental factors, not just one or the other, to produce certain conditions.

Genotype–Environment Correlation

genotype–environment correlation Tendency of certain genetic and environmental influences to reinforce each other; may be passive, reactive (evocative), or active; also called *genotype–environment covariance*

The environment often reflects or reinforces genetic differences. That is, certain genetic and environmental influences tend to act in the same direction. This is called **genotype–environment correlation,** or *genotype–environment covariance,* and it works in three ways to strengthen the phenotypic expression of a genotypic tendency (Bergeman & Plomin, 1989; Scarr, 1992; Scarr & McCartney, 1983):

- *Passive correlations:* Generally parents, who provide the genes that predispose a child toward a trait, also provide an environment that encourages the development of that trait. For example, a musical parent is likely to create a home environment in which music is heard regularly, to give a child music lessons, and to take the child to musical events. If the child inherited the parent's musical talent, the child's musicality will reflect a combination of genetic and environmental influences. This type of correlation is called *passive* because the child does not control it; it is most applicable to young children, whose parents, the source of their genetic legacy, also have a great deal of control over their early experiences.
- *Reactive, or evocative, correlations:* Children with differing genetic makeups evoke different responses from adults. Parents who are *not* musically inclined may make a special effort to provide musical experiences to a child who shows interest and ability in music. This response, in turn, strengthens the child's genetic inclination toward music.
- *Active correlations:* As children get older and have more freedom to choose their own activities and environments, they actively select or create experiences consistent with their genetic tendencies. A child with a talent for music will probably seek out

musical friends, take music classes, and go to concerts if such opportunities are available. A shy child is likely to spend more time in solitary pursuits than an outgoing youngster. This tendency to seek out environments compatible with one's genotype is called **niche-picking;** it helps explain why identical twins reared apart tend to be quite similar.

What Makes Siblings So Different? The Non-shared Environment

Although two children in the same family may bear a striking physical resemblance to each other, siblings tend to be more different than alike in intellect and especially in personality (Plomin, 1989). One reason, of course, may be genetic differences, which lead children to need different kinds of stimulation or to respond differently to a similar home environment. A child with a high IQ may be more stimulated by a roomful of books and puzzles than a child with a markedly lower IQ—an example of genotype–environment interaction. Surprisingly, though, studies in behavioural genetics suggest that the environment itself may make siblings more different—as different, in fact, as any two unrelated children! According to this research, the experiences that strongly affect development are not those that are similar for all children in a family, but those that are different (Plomin & Daniels, 1987; Plomin & DeFries, 1999).

These **non-shared environmental effects** result from the unique environment in which each child in a family grows up. What factors contribute to this non-shared environment? One is family composition—the differences between boys' and girls' experiences, or between those of firstborns and laterborns. Another is the way parents and siblings treat each child. Certain events, such as illnesses and accidents, and experiences outside the home (for example, with teachers and peers) affect one child and not another. Behavioural geneticists conclude that, while heredity accounts for most of the similarity between siblings, the non-shared environment accounts for most of the difference. Indeed, a great deal of research across the lifespan suggests that most of the variability in behavioural traits in the population as a whole is environmental, but of the non-shared type (McClearn et al., 1997; Plomin, 1996; Plomin & Daniels, 1987; Plomin & DeFries, 1999; Plomin, Owen, & McGuffin, 1994).

Genotype–environment correlations may play an important role in the non-shared environment. Children's genetic differences may lead parents and siblings to react to them differently and treat them differently; and genes may influence how children perceive and respond to that treatment, and what its outcome will be. Children also mould their own environments by the choices they make—what they do and with whom—and their genetic makeup influences these choices. In other words, "genes drive experience" (Scarr & McCartney, 1983, p. 425). A child who has inherited artistic talent may spend a great deal of time creating "masterpieces" in solitude, while a sibling who is athletically inclined spends more time playing ball with others. Thus, not only will the children's abilities (in, say, painting or soccer) develop differently, but their social lives will be different as well. These differences tend to be accentuated as children grow older and have more experiences outside the family (Bergeman & Plomin, 1989; Bouchard, 1994; Plomin, 1990, 1996; Plomin et al., 1994; Scarr, 1992; Scarr & McCartney, 1983).

Critics of behavioural genetics research say that these studies give short shrift to the influence of parenting. These critics point to the narrow range of families sampled in some studies and to a lack of direct observation of family life. Instead, they look to longitudinal studies of effects of parenting practices and direct interventions that seem to foster effective parenting. Such studies offer evidence that parental influence contributes greatly to developmental outcomes, independent of hereditary effects or bi-directional processes. At the same time, this research points to "the interrelated effects of parenting, non-familial influences, and the role of the broader context in which families live" (Collins et al., 2000, p. 228).

The old nature–nurture puzzle is far from resolved, but we do know now that the problem is far more complex than previously thought. A variety of research designs can continue to augment and refine our understanding of the forces affecting development.

What's your view ?

- In what ways are you more like your mother and in what ways like your father? How are you similar and dissimilar to your siblings? Which differences would you guess come chiefly from heredity and which from environment? Can you see possible effects of both?

Checkpoint ✔

Can you . . .

✔ Explain and give at least one example of reaction range, canalization, genotype–environment interaction, and genotype–environment correlation?

✔ List three kinds of influences that contribute to non-shared environmental effects?

✔ Explain the meaning of "genes drive experience"?

✔ List three types of studies that highlight effects of parenting?

Some Characteristics Influenced by Heredity and Environment

Keeping in mind the complexity of unravelling the influences of heredity and environment, let's look at what is known about their roles in producing certain characteristics.

Physical and Physiological Traits

Not only do monozygotic twins generally look alike; they are also more concordant than dizygotic twins in their risk for such medical disorders as hypertension (high blood pressure), heart disease, stroke, rheumatoid arthritis, peptic ulcers, and epilepsy (Brass, Isaacsohn, Merikangas, & Robinette, 1992; Plomin et al., 1994).

obesity Extreme overweight in relation to age, sex, height, and body type; sometimes defined as having a body mass index (weight-for-height) at or above the 85th or 95th percentile of growth curves for children of the same age and sex

Obesity—extreme overweight, variously defined in childhood as having a body mass index (comparison of weight to height) at or above the 85th or 95th percentile for age and sex—is a multifactorial condition. Twin studies, adoption studies, and other research suggest that as much as 80 per cent of the risk of obesity is genetic (Leibel, 1997). In genetic mapping, as many as 200 genes and other genetic markers have been linked with obesity so far (Pérusse, Chagnon, Weisnagel, & Bouchard, 1999). However, the kind and amount of food eaten in a particular home or in a particular social or ethnic group, and the amount of exercise that is encouraged, can increase or decrease the likelihood that a person will become obese. The rapid rise in the prevalence of obesity in industrialized countries seems to result from the interaction of a genetic predisposition with inadequate exercise (Leibel, 1997; see chapters 9, 12, and 15).

Our longevity seems to be greatly affected by our genes. In one study, adopted children whose biological parents had died before age 50 were twice as likely to have died young themselves as adopted children whose biological parents had lived past 49 (Sorensen, Nielsen, Andersen, & Teasdale, 1988). Still, sound health and fitness practices can increase longevity by tempering predispositions toward certain illnesses, such as cancer and heart disease.

Intelligence and School Achievement

Heredity seems to exert a strong influence on general intelligence and also on specific abilities (McClearn et al., 1997; Plomin et al., 1994; Plomin & DeFries, 1999). Still, experience counts, too; an enriched or impoverished environment can substantially affect the development and expression of innate ability (Neisser et al., 1996; see chapter 13). This seems to be a case of QTL: Many genes, each with its own small effect, combine to establish a range of possible reactions to a range of possible experiences (Scarr, 1997a; Weinberg, 1989; refer back to Figure 3-7).

Evidence of the role of heredity in intelligence has emerged from adoption and twin studies. Adopted children's IQs are consistently closer to the IQs of their biological mothers than to those of their adoptive parents and siblings, and monozygotic (identical) twins are more alike in intelligence than dizygotic (fraternal) twins. The studies yield a consistent estimate of heritability: 50 to 60 per cent for verbal abilities and 50 per cent for spatial abilities, meaning that genetic differences explain at least half of the observed variation among members of a population. The close correlation between verbal and spatial abilities suggests a genetic link among the components of intelligence (Plomin & DeFries, 1999).

Furthermore, the measured genetic influence increases with age. The family environment seems to have more influence on younger children, whereas adolescents are more apt to find their own niche by actively selecting environments compatible with their hereditary abilities and related interests (McClearn et al., 1997; McGue, 1997; McGue, Bouchard, Iacono, & Lykken, 1993; Plomin & DeFries, 1999).

The main environmental influences on intelligence, then, seem to occur early in life (McGue, 1997). In fact, an analysis of 212 studies (Devlin, Daniels, & Roeder, 1997) points to the impact of the earliest environment: the uterus. According to this analysis, the prenatal environment may account for 20 per cent of the similarity in IQ between twins and 5 per cent of the similarity in non-twin siblings (who occupy the same womb at different times), bringing heritability of IQ below 50 per cent. Thus the influence of genes on intelligence may be weaker, and the influence of the prenatal environment stronger, than was previously thought, underlining the importance of a healthy prenatal environment (see chapter 4). The possibility that prenatal intervention could raise the average IQ of the population is a fascinating one. However, just what aspects of the prenatal environment are most influential is as yet unclear.

Personality

Certain aspects of personality appear to be inherited, at least in part. Analyses of five major groupings of traits—extraversion, neuroticism (a group of traits involving anxiety), conscientiousness, agreeableness, and openness to experience—suggest a heritability of about 40 per cent. Setting aside variances attributable to measurement error brings heritability closer to 66 per cent for these trait groupings (Bouchard, 1994).

Temperament (discussed in detail in chapter 8) appears to be largely inborn and is often consistent over the years, though it may respond to special experiences or parental handling (A. Thomas & Chess, 1984; A. Thomas, Chess, & Birch, 1968). An observational study of 100 pairs of 7-year-old siblings (half of them adoptive siblings and half siblings by birth) found significant genetic influences on activity, sociability, and emotionality (Schmitz, Saudino, Plomin, Fulker, & DeFries, 1996). A large body of research (also discussed in chapter 8) strongly suggests that shyness and its opposite, boldness, are largely inborn and tend to stay with a person throughout life.

Although the research discussed so far provides strong evidence of genetic influences on personality, this evidence is indirect. Now scientists have begun to identify genes directly linked with specific personality traits. One of these genes has been found to play a part in neuroticism, which may contribute to depression. An estimated 10 to 15 other genes also may be involved in anxiety (Lesch et al., 1996).

Psychopathology

There is evidence for a strong hereditary influence on schizophrenia and autism, among other disorders. Both tend to run in families and to show greater concordance between monozygotic twins than between dizygotic twins. However, heredity alone does not produce such disorders; an inherited tendency can be triggered by environmental factors.

Schizophrenia, a disorder marked by loss of contact with reality and by such symptoms as hallucinations and delusions, seems to have a strong genetic component. The risk of schizophrenia is 10 times as great among siblings and offspring of schizophrenics as among the general population; and twin and adoption studies suggest that this increased risk comes from shared genes, not shared environments. The estimated genetic contribution is between 63 and 85 per cent (McGuffin, Owen, & Farmer, 1995).

However, since not all monozygotic twins are concordant for the illness, its cause cannot be purely genetic. Co-twin studies suggest that a prenatal viral infection, carried in the blood shared by monochorionic twins, may play a part (Phelps et al., 1997). In a study of the incidence of schizophrenia among all persons born in Denmark between 1935 and 1978, people born in urban areas were more likely to be schizophrenic than those born in rural areas, perhaps because of greater likelihood of birth complications and of exposure to infections during pregnancy and childhood (Mortenson et al., 1999).

A postmortem examination of the brains of schizophrenics suggests that the disorder may originate in a lack of a chemical called *reelin,* which is present in the regions of the adult brain that handle higher mental functions, such as language and problem solving. Reelin helps to correctly position and align nerve cells in the developing brain (Impagnatiello et al., 1998). A defective gene for reelin may result in misplacement of nerve cells, and this may create a predisposition, or vulnerability, to schizophrenia. Reelin normally goes into action again in late adolescence or early adulthood, when unnecessary, inefficient nerve connections need to be pruned out. This is the time when schizophrenia typically appears.

What's your view ?

• What practical difference does it make whether a trait such as obesity, intelligence, or shyness is influenced more by heredity or by environment, since heritability can be measured only for a population, not for an individual?

schizophrenia Mental disorder marked by loss of contact with reality; symptoms include hallucinations and delusions

autism Pervasive developmental disorder of the brain, characterized by lack of normal social interaction, impaired communication and imagination, and repetitive, obsessive behaviours

Autism is a disorder of brain functioning. It is one of a group of severe *pervasive developmental disorders* and is characterized by lack of normal social interaction, impaired communication and imagination, and a highly restricted range of activities and interests. Autism or related disorders affect an estimated 16 of every 10,000 people. It usually appears within the first 3 years, mostly in boys, and it continues to varying degrees throughout life (National [U.S] Institute of Neurological Disorders and Stroke [NINDS], 1999; Rapin, 1997; Rodier, 2000). There has been a dramatic rise in the number of reported cases of autism, and autism-related disorders like Asperger's, Rett's, and Pervasive Developmental Disorder, likely due to an increase in awareness of the disorders, and a broadening of the diagnostic criteria used to identify them (Infectious Diseases and Immunization Committee, Canadian Paediatric Society, 2001).

An autistic baby may fail to notice the emotional signals of others (Sigman, Kasari, Kwon, & Yirmiya, 1992) and may refuse to cuddle or make eye contact. An autistic child may speak in a singsong voice, paying little or no attention to the listener. Severely autistic children often show repetitive behaviours, such as spinning, rocking, hand-flapping, and head-banging, and are obsessed with certain subjects, rituals, or routines (NINDS, 1999). About three out of four autistic children are mentally retarded (American Psychiatric Association, 1994), but they often do well on tests of manipulative or visual–spatial skill and may perform unusual mental feats, such as memorizing entire train schedules.

Autism has no single cause but runs in families and seems to have a strong genetic basis (Bailey, Le Couteur, Gottesman, & Bolton, 1995; NINDS, 1999; Szatmari, 1999; Trottier, Srivastava, & Walker, 1999, Rodier, 2000). Several different genes may be involved in cases of varying symptoms and severity (Cook et al., 1997; Szatmari, 1999). One likely candidate is a variant of a gene called HOXA1, which is involved in the development of the brain stem, the most primitive part of the brain (Rodier, 2000). This fits in with findings of brain abnormalities in people with autism, which point to an early prenatal injury to the developing brain. Various other environmental factors, such as exposure to certain viruses or chemicals, also may play a part. It seems likely, then, that autism results from a genetic predisposition combined with an environmental assault (NINDS, 1999; Trottier et al., 1999; Rodier, 2000).

Autism has no known cure, but improvement, sometimes substantial, can occur. Some autistic children can be taught to speak, read, and write. Behaviour therapy (see chapter 2) can help autistic children learn such basic social skills as paying attention, sustaining eye contact, and feeding and dressing themselves, and can help control problem behaviours. Drugs may help to manage specific symptoms, but their usefulness is limited. Only about 5 to 10 per cent of autistic children grow up to live independently; most need some degree of care throughout life ("Autism–Part II," 1997; Rapin, 1997).

In this chapter we have looked at some ways in which heredity and environment act to make children what they are. A child's first environment is the world within the uterus, which we discuss in chapter 4.

Checkpoint ✔

Can you . . .

✔ Assess the evidence for genetic and environmental influences on obesity, intelligence, and temperament?

✔ Name and describe two mental disorders that show a strong genetic influence?

Summary and Key Terms

Becoming Parents

Guidepost 1 How does conception normally occur, and how have beliefs about conception changed?

- Early beliefs about conception reflected incorrect beliefs about nature and about male and female anatomy.

- Fertilization, the union of an ovum and a sperm, results in the formation of a one-celled zygote, which then duplicates itself by cell division.

  clone (49)   fertilization (50)   zygote (50)

Guidepost 2 What causes multiple births?

- Multiple births can occur either by the fertilization of two ova (or one ovum that has split) or by the splitting of one fertilized ovum. Larger multiple births result from either one of these processes or a combination of the two.

- Dizygotic (fraternal) twins have different genetic makeups and may be of different sexes; monozygotic (identical) twins have the same genetic makeup. Because of differences in prenatal and postnatal experience, "identical" twins may differ in temperament and other respects.

  dizygotic (two-egg) twins (51)   monozygotic (one-egg) twins (51)
  temperament (51)

Guidepost 3 What causes infertility, and what are alternative ways of becoming parents?

- The most common cause of infertility in men is a low sperm count; the most common cause in women is blockage of the Fallopian tubes. Infertile couples now have several options for assisted reproduction, but these techniques may involve thorny ethical and practical issues.

  infertility (51)

Mechanisms of Heredity

Guidepost 4 What genetic mechanisms determine sex, physical appearance, and other characteristics?

- The basic functional units of heredity are the genes, which are made of deoxyribonucleic acid (DNA). DNA carries the biochemical instructions, or genetic code, that governs bodily functions and determines inherited characteristics. Each gene seems to be located by function in a definite position on a particular chromosome. The complete sequence of genes in the human body is the human genome.

  deoxyribonucleic acid (DNA) (52)   genetic code (54)
  chromosomes (54)   genes (54)   human genome (54)

- At conception, each normal human being receives 23 chromosomes from the mother and 23 from the father. These form 23 pairs of chromosomes—22 pairs of autosomes and 1 pair of sex chromosomes. A child who receives an X chromosome from each parent will be a female. If the child receives a Y chromosome from the father, a male will be conceived.

- The simplest patterns of genetic transmission are dominant and recessive inheritance. When a pair of alleles are the same, a person is homozygous for the trait; when they are different, the person is heterozygous.

  autosomes (54)   sex chromosomes (54)   alleles (55)
  homozygous (55)   heterozygous (55)   dominant inheritance (55)
  recessive inheritance (55)

- Most normal human characteristics are the result of quantitative trait loci (QTL) effects or multifactorial transmission. Except for monozygotic twins, each child inherits a unique genotype. Dominant inheritance and multifactorial transmission explain why a person's phenotype does not always express the underlying genotype.

  quantitative trait loci (QTL) (56)   multifactorial transmission (56)
  phenotype (56)   genotype (56)

Guidepost 5 How are birth defects and disorders transmitted?

- Birth defects and diseases may result from simple dominant, recessive, or sex-linked inheritance, from mutations, or from genome imprinting. Chromosomal abnormalities also can cause birth defects.

- Through genetic counselling, prospective parents can receive information about the mathematical odds of bearing children with certain defects.

- Genetic testing involves risks as well as benefits.

  mutations (57)   natural selection (57)
  sex-linked inheritance (59)   Down syndrome (60)
  genetic counselling (60)   genetic testing (61)

Nature and Nurture: Influences of Heredity and Environment

Guidepost 6 How do scientists study the relative influences of heredity and environment, and how do heredity and environment work together?

- Research in behavioural genetics is based on the assumption that the relative influences of heredity and environment can be measured statistically. If heredity is an important influence on a trait, genetically closer persons will be more similar in that trait. Family studies, adoption studies, and studies of twins enable researchers to measure the heritability of specific traits.

- Critics claim that traditional behavioural genetics is too simplistic. Instead, they study complex developmental systems, reflecting a confluence of constitutional, economic, social, and biological influences.

- The concepts of reaction range, canalization, genotype–environment interaction, genotype–environment correlation (or covariance), and niche-picking describe ways in which heredity and environment work together.

- Siblings tend to be more different than alike in intelligence and personality. According to behaviour genetics research, heredity accounts for most of the similarity, and non-shared environmental effects account for most of the difference. Critics claim that this research, for methodological reasons, minimizes the role of the shared family environment.

  behavioural genetics (61)   heritability (62)   concordant (64)
  reaction range (65)   canalization (65)
  genotype–environment interaction (66)
  genotype–environment correlation (66)   niche-picking (67)
  non-shared environmental effects (67)

Guidepost 7 What roles do heredity and environment play in physical health, intelligence, and personality?

- Obesity, longevity, intelligence, and temperament are influenced by both heredity and environment. The relative influences of heredity and environment may vary across the lifespan.

- Schizophrenia and autism are psychopathological disorders influenced by both heredity and environment.

  obesity (68)   schizophrenia (69)   autism (70)

OLC Preview

The Online Learning Centre for *A Child's World,* First Canadian Edition, contains additional information on reproduction, assisted reproduction technology, human cloning and its implications, and the Human Genome Project with links to the National Institute of Child Health and Human Development, the Hospital for Sick Children, and the Human Genome website. Check out **www.mcgrawhill.ca/college/papalia.**

Pregnancy and Prenatal Development

If I could have watched you grow
as a magical mother might,
if I could have seen through my magical transparent belly,
there would have been such ripening within. . . .

—Anne Sexton, *Live or Let Die*, 1966

Focus *Karen Lutke and Fetal Alcohol Syndrome*

Fetal alcohol syndrome (FAS) and fetal alcohol effects (FAS/E) are clusters of abnormalities shown by children whose mothers drank during pregnancy, and are leading causes of mental retardation. But in the late 1970s, when Jan Lutke adopted the first of her eight adopted children diagnosed with FAS/E, the facts about FAS were not widely publicized or scientifically investigated, though the syndrome had been observed for centuries.

The child, a girl named Karen, was diagnosed at age 3 with FAS. She was removed from her birth mother soon after she was born and was placed in a succession of family and foster-care homes for the first 3 years of her life. Her disruptive behaviour and hyperactivity made it difficult for caregivers to cope, and she was ultimately placed in a resource facility before being adopted by Lutke.

Seventeen years later, as Lutke relates in *Works in Progress: The Meaning of Success for Individuals with FAS/E* (Lutke, 2000), Karen is typical of young Canadian adults with FAS. She is a self-assured young woman, who works as a dog-groomer, and she gives public talks on FAS. Despite her successes, she has had to overcome the challenges of a lower-than-average IQ, immature social and emotional functioning, and susceptibility to perseveration, repeating stereotyped behaviour. Throughout her life, in particular during her adolescence, a key factor in her successful development was unobtrusive supervision by peer mentors, older unaffected siblings, adult friends, and social services staff. This supervision worked to protect her from poor decisions that could have led to dangerous situations. With an emphasis on her strengths, Karen has acquired skills needed for active and independent living, while at the same time developing techniques for overcoming the challenges of potentially difficult behaviour, particularly that associated with perseveration.

Fetal alcohol syndrome had been identified during the 1970s, while Karen was growing up. Once alcohol enters a fetus's bloodstream, it remains there in high concentrations for long periods of time, causing brain damage and harming other body organs. There is no cure. As one medical expert wrote, "for the fetus the hangover may last a lifetime" (Enloe, 1980, p. 15).

• • •

For students of child development, the story of Karen Lutke is a hopeful note on the successes that are possible with a supportive home environment, but also a reminder of the responsibility prospective biological parents have for the crucial development that occurs before birth. The uterus is the developing child's first environment, and its impact on the child is immense. In addition to what the mother does and what happens to her, there are other environmental influences, from those that affect the father's sperm to the technological, social, and cultural environment, which may affect the kind of prenatal care a woman gets.

In this chapter we begin by looking at the experience of pregnancy and how prospective parents prepare for a birth. We trace how the fertilized ovum becomes an embryo and then a fetus, already with a personality of its own. Then we discuss environmental factors that can affect the developing person-to-be, describe techniques for determining whether development is proceeding normally, and explain the importance of prenatal care.

After you have read and studied this chapter, you should be able to answer each of the Guidepost questions that appear at the top of the next page. Look for them again in the margins, where they point to important concepts throughout the chapter. To check your understanding of these Guideposts, review the end-of-chapter summary. Checkpoints located at periodic spots throughout the chapter will help you verify your understanding of what you have read.

Prenatal Development: Three Stages

If you had been born in China, you would probably celebrate your birthday on your estimated date of conception rather than your date of birth. This Chinese custom recognizes the importance of *gestation,* the approximately 9-month (or 266-day) period of development between conception and birth. Scientists, too, date *gestational age* from conception.

What turns a fertilized ovum, or *zygote,* into a creature with a specific shape and pattern? Research suggests that an identifiable group of genes is responsible for this transformation in vertebrates, presumably including human beings. These genes produce molecules called *morphogens,* which are switched on after fertilization and begin sculpting arms, hands, fingers, vertebrae, ribs, a brain, and other body parts (Echeland et al., 1993; Kraus, Concordet, & Ingham, 1993; Riddle, Johnson, Laufer, & Tabin, 1993). Scientists are also learning about the environment inside the womb and how it affects the developing person.

Prenatal development takes place in three stages: *germinal, embryonic,* and *fetal.* (Table 4-1 gives a month-by-month description.) During these three stages of gestation, the original single-celled zygote grows into an *embryo* and then a *fetus.* Both before and after birth, development proceeds according to two fundamental principles. Growth and motor development occur from top down and from the centre of the body outward.

The **cephalocaudal principle** (from Latin, meaning "head to tail") dictates that development proceeds from the head to the lower part of the trunk. An embryo's head, brain, and eyes develop earliest and are disproportionately large until the other parts catch up. At 2 months of gestation, the embryo's head is half the length of the body. By the time of birth, the head is only one-fourth the length of the body but is still disproportionately large. According to the **proximodistal principle** (from Latin, "near to far"), development proceeds from parts near the centre of the body to outer ones. The embryo's head and trunk develop before the limbs, and the arms and legs before the fingers and toes.

Germinal Stage (Fertilization to 2 Weeks)

During the **germinal stage,** from fertilization to about 2 weeks of gestational age, the zygote divides, becomes more complex, and is implanted in the wall of the uterus (see Figure 4-1).

Within 36 hours after fertilization, the zygote enters a period of rapid cell division and duplication, or *mitosis* (refer back to chapter 3). Seventy-two hours after fertilization, it has divided into 16 to 32 cells; a day later it has 64 cells. This division continues until the original single cell has developed into the 800 billion or more specialized cells that make up the human body.

While the fertilized ovum is dividing, it is also making its way down the Fallopian tube to the uterus, a journey of 3 or 4 days. Its form changes into a fluid-filled sphere, a *blastocyst,* which floats freely in the uterus for a day or two and then begins to implant itself in the uterine wall. As cell differentiation begins, some cells around the edge of the blastocyst cluster on one side to form the *embryonic disk,* a thickened cell mass from which the embryo begins to develop. This mass is already differentiating into two layers. The upper layer, the *ectoderm,* will become the outer layer of skin, the nails, hair, teeth, sensory organs, and the nervous system, including the brain and spinal cord. The lower layer, the *endoderm,* will become the digestive system, liver, pancreas, salivary glands, and respiratory

cephalocaudal principle Principle that development proceeds in a head-to-tail direction; that is, upper parts of the body develop before lower parts

proximodistal principle Principle that development proceeds from within to without; that is, parts of the body near the centre develop before the extremities

germinal stage First 2 weeks of prenatal development, characterized by rapid cell division, increasing complexity and differentiation, and implantation in the wall of the uterus

Table 4-1   Prenatal Development

Month	Description

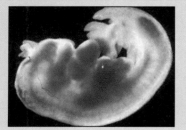

1 month

During the first month, growth is more rapid than at any other time during prenatal or postnatal life: The embryo reaches a size 10,000 times greater than the zygote. By the end of the first month, it measures about 1.5 cm in length. Blood flows through its veins and arteries, which are very small. It has a minuscule heart, beating 65 times a minute. It already has the beginnings of a brain, kidneys, liver, and digestive tract. The umbilical cord, its lifeline to the mother, is working. By looking very closely through a microscope, it is possible to see the swellings on the head that will eventually become eyes, ears, mouth, and nose. Its sex cannot yet be determined.

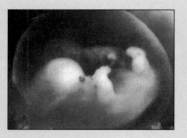

2 months

By the end of the second month, the organism is less than 2.5 cm long and weighs only 2.2 g. Its head is half its total body length. Facial parts are clearly developed, with tongue and teeth buds. The arms have hands, fingers, and thumbs, and the legs have knees, ankles, and toes. It has a thin covering of skin and can make handprints and footprints. Bone cells appear at about 8 weeks. Brain impulses coordinate the function of the organ system. Sex organs are developing; the heartbeat is steady. The stomach produces digestive juices; the liver, blood cells. The kidneys remove uric acid from the blood. The skin is now sensitive enough to react to tactile stimulation. If an aborted 8-week-old fetus is stroked, it reacts by flexing its trunk, extending its head, and moving back its arms.

3 months

By the end of the third month, the fetus weighs about 30 g, and measures about 7.5 cm in length. It has fingernails, toenails, eyelids (still closed), vocal cords, lips, and a prominent nose. Its head is still large—about one-third its total length—and its forehead is high. Sex can easily be determined. The organ systems are functioning, and so the fetus may now breathe, swallow amniotic fluid into the lungs and expel it, and occasionally urinate. Its ribs and vertebrae have turned into cartilage. The fetus can now make a variety of specialized responses: It can move its legs, feet, thumbs, and head; its mouth can open and close and swallow. If its eyelids are touched, it squints; if its palm is touched, it makes a partial fist; if its lip is touched, it will suck; and if the sole of the foot is stroked, the toes will fan out. These reflexes will be present at birth but most will be less easily elicited during the first months of life because brain development will permit voluntary control.

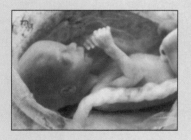

4 months

The body is catching up to the head, which is now only one-fourth the total body length, the same proportion it will be at birth. The fetus now measures 20 to 25 cm and weighs about 175 g. The umbilical cord is as long as the fetus and will continue to grow with it. The placenta is now fully developed. The mother may be able to feel the fetus kicking, a movement known as *quickening,* which some societies and religious groups consider the beginning of human life. The reflex activities that appeared in the third month are now brisker because of increased muscular development.

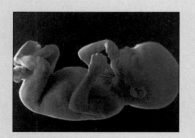

5 months

The fetus, now weighing about 350 to 450 g and measuring about 30 cm, begins to show signs of an individual personality. It has definite sleep–wake patterns, has a favourite position in the uterus (called its *lie*), and becomes more active—kicking, stretching, squirming, and even hiccupping. By putting an ear to the mother's abdomen, it is possible to hear the fetal heartbeat. The sweat and sebaceous glands are functioning. The respiratory system is not yet adequate to sustain life outside the womb; a baby born at this time does not usually survive. Coarse hair has begun to grow for eyebrows and eyelashes, fine hair is on the head, and a woolly hair called *lanugo* covers the body.

Table 4-1 Prenatal Development (*Continued*)

Month	Description
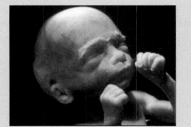 6 months	The rate of fetal growth has slowed down a little—by the end of the sixth month, the fetus is about 35 cm long and weighs 575 g. It has fat pads under the skin; the eyes are complete, opening, closing, and looking in all directions. It can hear, and it can make a fist with a strong grip. A fetus born during the sixth month still has only a slight chance of survival, because the breathing apparatus has not matured. However, some fetuses of this age do survive outside the womb.
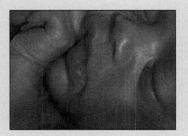 7 months	By the end of the seventh month, the fetus, about 40 cm long and weighing 1.5 to 2.5 kg, now has fully developed reflex patterns. It cries, breathes, swallows, and may suck its thumb. The lanugo may disappear at about this time, or it may remain until shortly after birth. Head hair may continue to grow. The chances that a fetus weighing at least 1.5 kg will survive are fairly good, provided it receives intensive medical attention. It will probably need to be kept in an incubator until a weight of 2.5 kg is attained.
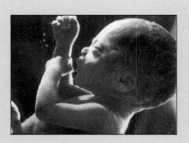 8 months	The 8-month-old fetus is 45 to 50 cm long and weighs between 2 and 3 kg. Its living quarters are becoming cramped, and so its movements are curtailed. During this month and the next, a layer of fat is developing over the fetus's entire body, which will enable it to adjust to varying temperatures outside the womb.
 9 months–newborn	About a week before birth, the fetus stops growing, having reached an average weight of about 3.5 kg and a length of about 50 cm, with boys tending to be a little longer and heavier than girls. Fat pads continue to form, the organ systems are operating more efficiently, the heart rate increases, and more wastes are expelled through the umbilical cord. The reddish colour of the skin is fading. At birth, the fetus will have been in the womb for about 266 days, although gestational age is usually estimated at 280 days, since most doctors date the pregnancy from the mother's last menstrual period.

Note: Even in these early stages, individuals differ. The figures and descriptions given here represent averages.

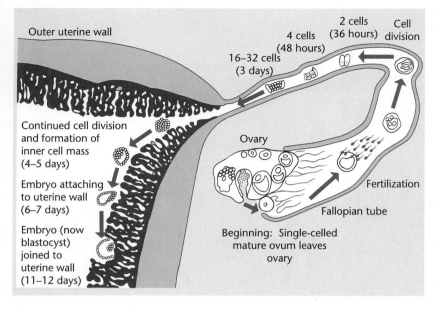

Figure 4-1

Early development of a human embryo. This simplified diagram shows the progress of the ovum as it leaves the ovary, is fertilized in the Fallopian tube, and then divides while travelling to the lining of the uterus. Now a blastocyst, it is implanted in the uterus, where it will grow larger and more complex until it is ready to be born.

system. Later a middle layer, the *mesoderm,* will develop and differentiate into the inner layer of skin, muscles, skeleton, and excretory and circulatory systems.

Other parts of the blastocyst begin to develop into organs that will nurture and protect the unborn child: the *placenta,* the *umbilical cord,* and the *amniotic sac* with its outermost membrane, the *chorion.* The *placenta,* which has several important functions, will be connected to the embryo by the *umbilical cord.* Through this cord the placenta delivers oxygen and nourishment to the developing baby and removes its body wastes. The placenta also helps to combat internal infection and gives the unborn child immunity to various diseases. It produces the hormones that support pregnancy, prepares the mother's breasts for lactation, and eventually stimulates the uterine contractions that will expel the baby from the mother's body. The *amniotic sac* is a fluid-filled membrane that encases the developing baby, protecting it and giving it room to move. The *trophoblast,* the outer cell layer of the blastocyst (which becomes part of the placenta), produces tiny threadlike structures that penetrate the lining of the uterine wall and enable the developing organism to cling there until it is fully implanted in the uterine lining.

Only about 10 to 20 per cent of fertilized eggs complete the task of implantation and continue to develop. Researchers have identified a gene called *Hoxa10,* which appears to affect whether an embryo will be successfully implanted in the uterine wall (Taylor, Arici, Olive, & Igarashi, 1998). Timing appears to be important; implantation more than 8 to 10 days after ovulation increases the risk of pregnancy loss (Wilcox, Baird, & Weinberg, 1999).

Embryonic Stage (2 to 8 Weeks)

embryonic stage Second stage of gestation (2 to 8 weeks), characterized by rapid growth and development of major body systems and organs

During the **embryonic stage,** the second stage of gestation, from about 2 to 8 weeks, the organs and major body systems—respiratory, digestive, and nervous—develop rapidly. This is a critical period, when the embryo is most vulnerable to destructive influences in the prenatal environment (see Figure 4-2). An organ system or structure that is still developing at the time of exposure is most likely to be affected. Defects that occur later in pregnancy are likely to be less serious.

The most severely defective embryos seldom survive beyond the first *trimester,* or 3-month period, of pregnancy. A **spontaneous abortion,** commonly called a *miscarriage,* is the expulsion from the uterus of an embryo or fetus that is unable to survive outside the womb. Most miscarriages result from abnormal pregnancies; about 50 to 70 per cent involve chromosomal abnormalities.

spontaneous abortion Natural expulsion from the uterus of an embryo or fetus that cannot survive outside the womb; also called *miscarriage*

Males are more likely than females to be spontaneously aborted or *stillborn* (dead at birth). Thus, although about 125 males are conceived for every 100 females—a fact that has been attributed to the greater mobility of sperm carrying the smaller Y chromosome—only 105 boys are born for every 100 girls. Males' greater vulnerability continues after birth: More of them die early in life (Statistics Canada, 1997), and at every age they are more susceptible to many disorders. Furthermore, the proportion of male births appears to be falling in Canada, the United States, and several European countries, while the incidence of birth defects among males is rising, perhaps reflecting effects of environmental pollutants (Davis, Gottlieb, & Stampnitzky, 1998).

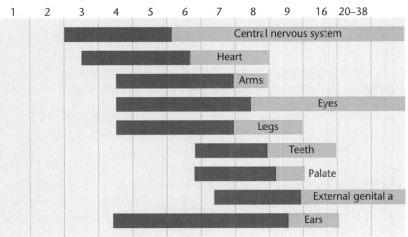

Weeks after conception:

Central nervous system
Heart
Arms
Eyes
Legs
Teeth
Palate
External genital a
Ears

Figure 4-2

When birth defects occur. Body parts and systems are most vulnerable to damage when they are developing most rapidly *(dark areas),* generally within the first trimester of pregnancy.

Note: Intervals of time are not all equal.

Source: J. E. Brody, 1995; data from March of Dimes

Fetal Stage (8 Weeks to Birth)

The appearance of the first bone cells at about 8 weeks signals the **fetal stage,** the final stage of gestation. During this period, the fetus grows rapidly to about 20 times its previous length, and organs and body systems become more complex. Right up to birth, "finishing touches" such as fingernails, toenails, and eyelids develop.

Fetuses are not passive passengers in their mothers' wombs. They breathe, kick, turn, flex their bodies, do somersaults, squint, swallow, make fists, hiccup, and suck their thumbs. The flexible membranes of the uterine walls and amniotic sac, which surround the protective buffer of amniotic fluid, permit and stimulate limited movement.

Scientists can observe fetal movement through **ultrasound,** using high-frequency sound waves to detect the outline of the fetus. Other instruments can monitor heart rate, changes in activity level, states of sleep and wakefulness, and cardiac reactivity. In one study, fetuses monitored from 20 weeks of gestation until term had decreasing but more variable heart rates—possibly in response to the increasing stress of the mother's pregnancy—and greater cardiac response to stimulation. They also showed less, but more vigorous, activity—perhaps a result of the increasing difficulty of movement for a growing fetus in a constricted environment, as well as of maturation of the nervous system. A significant "jump" in all these aspects of fetal development seems to occur between 28 and 32 weeks; it may help explain why infants born prematurely at this time are more likely to survive and flourish than those born earlier (DiPietro et al., 1996).

The movements and activity level of fetuses show marked individual differences, and their heart rates vary in regularity and speed. There also are differences between males and females. Male fetuses, regardless of size, are more active and tend to move more vigorously than female fetuses throughout gestation. Thus infant boys' tendency to be more active than girls may be at least partly inborn (DiPietro et al., 1996).

Apparent differences in temperament appear as early as 24 weeks of gestation and remain stable throughout the prenatal period and beyond. Three to 6 months after birth, infants who had moved around more in the womb tended to be more difficult, unpredictable, and active and less adaptable, according to their mothers, than infants whose fetal activity had been calmer (DiPietro, Hodgson, Costigan, & Johnson, 1996). It is possible, however, that the mothers' reports about their infants' temperament were influenced by perceptions formed during pregnancy.

Beginning at about week 12 of gestation, the fetus swallows and inhales some of the amniotic fluid in which it floats. The amniotic fluid contains substances that cross the placenta from the mother's bloodstream and enter the fetus's own bloodstream. Taking in these substances may stimulate the budding senses of taste and smell and may contribute to the

Guidepost 2

What can fetuses do?

fetal stage Final stage of gestation (from 8 weeks to birth), characterized by increased detail of body parts and greatly enlarged body size

ultrasound Prenatal medical procedure using high-frequency sound waves to detect the outline of a fetus and its movements, in order to determine whether a pregnancy is progressing normally

development of organs needed for breathing and digestion (Mennella & Beauchamp, 1996a; Ronca & Alberts, 1995; Smotherman & Robinson, 1995, 1996). Mature taste cells appear at about 14 weeks of gestation. The olfactory system, which controls the sense of smell, is also well developed before birth (Bartoshuk & Beauchamp, 1994; Mennella & Beauchamp, 1996a).

Fetuses also respond to the mother's voice and heartbeat and the vibrations of her body, suggesting that they can hear and feel. Familiarity with the mother's voice may have a basic survival function: to help newborns locate the source of food. Hungry infants, no matter on which side they are held, turn toward the breast in the direction from which they hear the mother's voice (Noirot & Algeria, 1983, cited in Rovee-Collier, 1996). Responses to sound and vibration seem to begin at 26 weeks of gestation, rise, and then reach a plateau at about 32 weeks (Kisilevsky, Muir, & Low, 1992).

Fetuses seem to learn and remember. In one experiment, 3-day-old infants sucked more on a nipple that activated a recording of a story their mother had frequently read aloud during the last 6 weeks of pregnancy than they did on nipples that activated recordings of two other stories. Apparently, the infants recognized the pattern of sound they had heard in the womb. A control group, whose mothers had not recited a story before birth, responded equally to all three recordings (DeCasper & Spence, 1986). Similar experiments have found that newborns 2 to 4 days old prefer musical and speech sequences heard before birth. They also prefer their mother's voice to those of other women, female voices to male voices, and their mother's native language to another language (DeCasper & Fifer, 1980; DeCasper & Spence, 1986; Moon, Cooper, & Fifer, 1993; Fifer & Moon, 1995; Lecanuet, Granier-Deferre, & Busnel, 1995).

How do we know that these preferences develop before rather than after birth? Newborns were given the choice of sucking to turn on a recording of the mother's voice or a "filtered" version of her voice as it might sound in the womb. The newborns sucked more often to turn on the filtered version, suggesting that fetuses develop a preference for the kinds of sounds they hear before birth (Fifer & Moon, 1995; Moon & Fifer, 1990).

Prenatal Development: Environmental Influences

The pervasive influence of the prenatal environment underlines the importance of providing an unborn child with the best possible start in life. Only recently have scientists become aware of some of the myriad environmental influences that can negatively affect the developing organism. The role of the father used to be virtually ignored; today we know that various environmental factors can affect a man's sperm and the children he fathers. Although the mother's role has been recognized far longer, researchers are still discovering environmental hazards that can affect her fetus. Some of these findings have led to ethical debate over a woman's responsibility for avoiding activities that may harm her unborn child (see Box 4-1).

Maternal Factors

Since the prenatal environment is the mother's body, virtually everything that impinges on her well-being, from her diet to her moods, may alter her unborn child's environment and affect its growth.

Not all environmental hazards are equally risky for all fetuses. Some factors that are **teratogenic** (birth defect–producing) in some cases have little or no effect in others. The timing of exposure to a teratogen, its intensity, and its interaction with other factors may be important (refer back to Figure 4-2).

Vulnerability may depend on a gene in either the fetus or the mother. For example, fetuses with a particular variant of a growth gene, called *transforming growth factor alpha,* have six times more risk than other fetuses of developing a cleft palate if the mother

Checkpoint ✔

Can you . . .

✔ Identify two principles that govern physical development and give examples of their application during the prenatal period?

✔ Describe how a zygote becomes an embryo?

✔ Explain why defects and miscarriages are most likely to occur during the embryonic stage?

✔ Describe findings about fetal activity, sensory development, and memory?

Guidepost 3

What environmental influences can affect prenatal development?

teratogenic Capable of causing birth defects

A Winnipeg woman is apprehended by Child and Family Services for inhaling solvents while pregnant. A court orders her to enter a treatment program after finding her mentally incompetent, despite contrary evidence in a psychiatric report. A year later, the decision is overturned by the Manitoba Court of Appeal, and by the Supreme Court of Canada, arguing that there is no legal basis to order addicted pregnant women to seek treatment to protect the developing fetus (Kuxhaus, 1997).

In this case, the issue is the conflict between protection of a fetus and a woman's right to privacy or to make her own decisions about her body. It is tempting to require a pregnant woman to adopt practices that will ensure her baby's health, or to stop or punish her if she doesn't. But what about her personal freedom? Can civil rights be abrogated for the protection of the unborn?

The argument about the right to choose abortion, which rests on similar grounds, is far from settled. But the example just given deals with a different aspect of the problem. What can or should society do about a woman who does *not* choose abortion, but instead goes on carrying her baby while engaging in behaviour destructive to it, or refuses tests or treatment that medical providers consider essential to its welfare?

Should a woman be forced to submit to intrusive procedures that pose a risk to her, such as a surgical delivery or intrauterine transfusions, when doctors say such procedures are essential to the delivery of a healthy baby? Should a woman from a fundamentalist sect that rejects modern medical care be taken into custody until she gives birth? Such measures have been invoked and have been defended as protecting the rights of the unborn. But women's rights advocates claim that they reflect a view of women as mere vehicles for carrying offspring, and not as persons in their own right (Greenhouse, 2000b).

Medical professionals warn that such measures also may have important practical drawbacks. Legal coercion could jeopardize the doctor–patient relationship. Coercion could also open the door to go further into pregnant women's lives—demanding prenatal screening and fetal surgery or restricting their diet, work, and athletic and sexual activity (Kolder, Gallagher, & Parsons, 1987). For these reasons, the overwhelming attitude of medical, legal, and social critics is that the state should intervene only in circumstances in which there is a high risk of serious disease or a high degree of accuracy in the test for a defect, strong evidence that the proposed treatment will be effective, danger that deferring treatment until after birth will cause serious damage, minimal risk to the mother and modest interference with her privacy, and persistent but unsuccessful efforts to educate her and obtain her informed consent.

Does a woman have the right to knowingly ingest a substance, such as alcohol or another drug, that can permanently damage her unborn child? Some advocates for fetal rights think it should be against the law for pregnant women to smoke or use alcohol, even though these activities are legal for other adults. Other experts argue that incarceration for substance abuse is unworkable and self-defeating. They say that expectant mothers who have a drinking or drug problem need education and treatment, not prosecution (Marwick, 1997, 1998). If failure to follow medical advice can bring forced surgery, confinement, or criminal charges, some women may avoid doctors altogether and thus deprive their fetuses of needed prenatal care (Nelson & Marshall, 1998).

There has been no successful prosecution of a Canadian woman for abusing dangerous substances while pregnant. An alternative, and likely more effective, way to help ensure that pregnant women avoid ingesting harmful substances is public education. As an example, across Canada provincial liquor boards and commissions now employ advertising campaigns to alert pregnant women to the dangers of alcohol consumption during pregnancy.

What's your view?

Does society's interest in protecting an unborn child justify coercive measures against pregnant women who ingest harmful substances or refuse medically indicated treatment? Should pregnant women who refuse to stop drinking or get treatment be incarcerated until they give birth? Should mothers who repeatedly give birth to children with FAS be sterilized? Should liquor companies be held liable if adequate warnings are not on their products? Would your answers be the same regarding smoking or use of cocaine or other potentially harmful substances?

Check it out!

For more information on this topic, go to **www.mcgrawhill.ca/college/papalia**.

smokes while pregnant, and almost nine times more risk if she smokes more than 10 cigarettes a day (Hwang et al., 1995). Women without the abnormal allele who smoke at least 20 cigarettes a day are at heightened risk of having babies with cleft palates, but their risk is even greater if the abnormal gene is present (Shaw, Wasserman, et al., 1996).

Nutrition

Women need to eat more than usual when pregnant: typically, 300 to 500 more calories a day, including extra protein. Pregnant women who gain between 10 and 20 kg are less likely to miscarry or to bear babies who are stillborn or whose weight at birth is dangerously low (Abrams & Parker, 1990; Ventura, Martin, Curtin, & Mathews, 1999).

Malnutrition during fetal growth may have long-range effects. In rural Gambia, in western Africa, people born during the "hungry" season, when foods from the previous harvest are badly depleted, are 10 times more likely to die in early adulthood than people born during other parts of the year (Moore et al., 1997). Psychiatric examinations of Dutch military recruits whose mothers had been exposed to wartime famine during pregnancy suggest that severe prenatal nutritional deficiencies in the first or second trimesters affect the developing brain, increasing the risk of antisocial personality disorders at age 18 (Neugebauer, Hoek, & Susser, 1999).

Malnourished women who take dietary supplements while pregnant tend to have bigger, healthier, more active, and more visually alert infants (J. L. Brown, 1987; Vuori et al., 1979); and women with low zinc levels who take daily zinc supplements are less likely to have babies with low birth weight and small head circumference (Goldenberg et al., 1995). However, certain vitamins (including A, B_6, C, D, and K) can be harmful in excessive amounts. Iodine deficiency, unless corrected before the third trimester of pregnancy, can cause cretinism, which may involve severe neurological abnormalities or thyroid problems (Cao et al., 1994; Hetzel, 1994).

Only recently have we learned of the critical importance of folic acid, or folate (a B vitamin) in a pregnant woman's diet. For some time, scientists have known that China has the highest incidence in the world of babies born with the neural-tube defects anencephaly and spina bifida (refer back to Table 3-1), but it was not until the 1980s that researchers linked that fact with the timing of the babies' conception. Traditionally, Chinese couples marry in January or February and try to conceive as soon as possible. That means pregnancies often begin in the winter, when rural women have little access to fresh fruits and vegetables, important sources of folic acid.

After medical detective work established the lack of folic acid as a cause of neural-tube defects, China embarked on a massive program to give folic acid supplements to prospective mothers, which resulted in a large reduction in the prevalence of these defects (Berry et al., 1999). In Canada, women of childbearing age are now urged to include this vitamin in their diets by eating plenty of fresh fruits and vegetables, or taking vitamin supplements, even before becoming pregnant, since damage from folic acid deficiency can occur during the early weeks of gestation (Society of Obstetricians and Gynaecologists of Canada [SOGC], 1993). Increasing women's folic acid consumption by just 0.4 mg each day would reduce the incidence of neural-tube defects by at least half (AAP Committee on Genetics, 1999; Centers for Disease Control and Prevention, 1999b; Daly, Kirke, Molloy, Weir, & Scott, 1995). Canadian initiatives designed to promote healthy prenatal development, like the Healthy Babies, Healthy Children program in Ontario, and the Building Better Babies Pregnancy Outreach Program, operated by the Tillicum Haus Native Friendship Centre in British Columbia, provide education and material support like food and vitamin supplements to pregnant women.

Obese women also risk having children with neural-tube defects. Women who, before pregnancy, weigh more than 80 kg or have an elevated body mass index (weight compared with height) are more likely to produce babies with such defects, regardless of folate intake.

Obesity also increases the risk of other complications of pregnancy, including miscarriage, stillbirth, and *neonatal death* (death during the first month of life) (Cnattingius, Bergstrom, Lipworth, & Kramer, 1998; Goldenberg & Tamura, 1996; G. M. Shaw, Velie, & Schaffer, 1996; Werler, Louik, Shapiro, & Mitchell, 1996). Either overweight or underweight can be risky: Among women having their first babies, those who were overweight before pregnancy had the most risk of stillbirth or of losing their babies during the first week of life. On the other hand, underweight women are more likely to have dangerously small babies (Cnattingius et al., 1998).

Physical Activity

Moderate exercise does not seem to endanger the fetuses of healthy women (Carpenter et al., 1988). Regular exercise prevents constipation and improves respiration, circulation, muscle tone, and skin elasticity, all of which contribute to a more comfortable pregnancy and an easier, safer delivery.

Employment during pregnancy generally entails no special hazards. However, strenuous working conditions, occupational fatigue, and long working hours may be associated with a greater risk of premature birth (Luke et al., 1995).

The Society of Obstetricians and Gynaecologists of Canada (2000) recommends that women in low-risk pregnancies be guided by their own abilities and stamina. The safest course seems to be for pregnant women to exercise moderately, not pushing themselves and not raising their heart rate above 150, and, as with any exercise, tapering off at the end of each session rather than stopping abruptly.

Checkpoint ✓

Can you . . .

✔ Summarize recommendations concerning an expectant mother's diet and physical activity?

Drug Intake

Practically everything an expectant mother takes in makes its way to the uterus. Drugs may cross the placenta, just as oxygen, carbon dioxide, and water do. Vulnerability is greatest in the first few months of gestation, when development is most rapid. Some problems resulting from prenatal exposure to drugs can be treated if the presence of a drug can be detected early.

What are the effects of the use of specific drugs during pregnancy? Let's look first at medical drugs; then at alcohol, nicotine, and caffeine; and finally at some illegal drugs: marijuana, opiates, and cocaine.

Medical Drugs It was once thought that the placenta protected the fetus against drugs the mother took during pregnancy—until the early 1960s, when a tranquilizer called *thalidomide* was banned after it was found to have caused stunted or missing limbs, severe facial deformities, and defective organs in some 12,000 babies worldwide, with about 120 survivors living in Canada today. The thalidomide disaster sensitized medical professionals and the public to the potential dangers of taking drugs while pregnant. Today, nearly 30 drugs have been found to be teratogenic in clinically recommended doses (Koren, Pastuszak, & Ito, 1998). Among them are the antibiotic tetracycline; certain barbiturates, opiates, and other central nervous system depressants; several hormones, including diethylstilbestrol (DES) and androgens; certain anti-cancer drugs, such as methotrexate; Accutane, a drug often prescribed for severe acne; and Aspirin and other nonsteroidal anti-inflammatory drugs, which should be avoided during the third trimester.

Effects may be far-reaching and long-lasting. In one study, Danish men in their thirties whose mothers had taken phenobarbital during pregnancy (especially during the last trimester) had significantly lower verbal intelligence scores than a control group. Coming from a lower socio-economic background or having been the product of an unwanted pregnancy tended to magnify the negative outcome, showing an interaction of environmental factors before and after birth (Reinisch, Sanders, Mortensen, Psych, & Rubin, 1995).

The effects of taking a drug during pregnancy do not always show up immediately. In the late 1940s and early 1950s, the synthetic hormone diethylstilbestrol (DES) was widely prescribed (ineffectually, as it turned out) to prevent miscarriage. Not until years later, when the daughters of women who had taken DES during pregnancy reached puberty, did about 1 in 1,000 develop a rare form of vaginal or cervical cancer (Melnick, Cole, Anderson, & Herbst, 1987). So far, "DES daughters" have shown no unusual risk of other cancers (Hatch et al., 1998). However, they have had more trouble bearing their own children than other women do, with higher risks of miscarriage or premature delivery (A. Barnes et al., 1980). In studies with mice, researchers have found that DES inhibits the activity of a gene called *Writ-7a,* which plays an important role in the development of the reproductive tract (Miller, Degenhart, & Sassoon, 1998).

Using prescription medication while breast-feeding is a cause for concern, given that medications could pass into breast milk, affecting the nursing child. The Motherisk program at Toronto's Hospital for Sick Children reports that most prescription drugs do not pose a risk to the breast-fed infant; the major exceptions being medications for cancer therapy and anticonvulsants (Moretti, Lee, & Ito, 2000). Drugs of abuse, like alcohol, cocaine, and amphetamines, should be avoided as they have been found to pass through to breast milk. Pregnant women should not take over-the-counter drugs without consulting a doctor (Koren et al., 1998); about one in four Canadian women reports using medication during pregnancy (Human Resources Development Canada, 1996).

fetal alcohol syndrome (FAS)
Combination of mental, motor, and developmental abnormalities affecting the offspring of some women who drink heavily during pregnancy

What's your view

- Thousands of adults now alive suffered gross abnormalities because, during the 1950s, their mothers took the tranquilizer thalidomide during pregnancy. As a result, the use of thalidomide was banned in Canada and some other countries. Now thalidomide has been found to be effective in treating or controlling many illnesses, from mouth ulcers to brain cancer. Should its use for these purposes be permitted even though there is a risk that pregnant women might take it? If so, what safeguards should be required?

Alcohol Like Karen Lutke, about 1 infant in 750 suffers from **fetal alcohol syndrome (FAS),** a combination of slow prenatal and postnatal growth, facial and bodily malformations, and disorders of the central nervous system. Problems related to the central nervous system in infancy, can include poor sucking response, brain-wave abnormalities, and sleep disturbances; and, throughout childhood, slow information processing, short attention span, restlessness, irritability, hyperactivity, learning disabilities, retarded growth, and motor impairments. Prebirth exposure to alcohol seems to affect a portion of the *corpus callosum,* which coordinates signals between the two hemispheres of the brain. In macaques (and, presumably, in humans as well) the affected portion, toward the front of the head, is involved in initiating voluntary movement and other higher-order processing (Miller, Astley, & Clarren, 1999).

For every child with FAS, as many as 10 others may be born with *fetal alcohol effects.* This less severe condition can include mental retardation, retardation of intrauterine growth, and minor congenital abnormalities.

Even moderate drinking may harm a fetus, and the more the mother drinks, the greater the effect. According to research with rats, even a single drinking binge of 4 hours or more can do tremendous damage to the developing brain (Ikonomidou et al., 2000). Moderate or heavy drinking during pregnancy seems to alter the character of a newborn's cry, an index of neurobehavioural status. (So does moderate smoking during pregnancy.) Disturbed neurological and behavioural functioning may, in turn, affect early social interaction with the mother, which is vital to emotional development (Nugent, Lester, Greene, Wieczorek-Deering, & O'Mahony, 1996).

Some FAS problems recede after birth; but others, such as retardation, behavioural and learning problems, and hyperactivity, tend to persist. Unfortunately, enriching these children's education or general environment does not seem to enhance their cognitive development (Kerns, Don, Mateer, & Streissguth, 1997; Spohr, Willms, & Steinhausen, 1993; Streissguth et al., 1991; Strömland & Hellström, 1996). Because there is no known safe level of drinking during pregnancy, it is best to avoid alcohol from the time a woman begins *thinking* about becoming pregnant until she stops breast-feeding (AAP Committee on Substance Abuse and Committee on Children with Disabilities, 1993).

Nicotine About a quarter of Canadian women report smoking during pregnancy (Human Resources Development Canada, 1996), with 84 per cent of smokers continuing throughout pregnancy, and 90 per cent doing so during the first trimester (CICH, 2000). Tobacco use by pregnant women early in pregnancy can cause miscarriage, neonatal death, low birth weight, and need for intensive care for infants (DiFranza & Lew, 1995).

Since women who smoke during pregnancy also tend to smoke after giving birth, it is hard to separate the effects of prenatal and postnatal exposure. One study did this by examining 500 newborns about 48 hours after birth, while they were still in the hospital's non-smoking maternity ward and thus had not been exposed to smoking outside the womb. Newborns whose mothers had smoked during pregnancy were shorter and lighter and had poorer respiratory functioning than babies of non-smoking mothers (Stick, Burton, Gurrin, Sly, & LeSouëf, 1996). A mother's smoking during pregnancy may also increase her child's risk of cancer (Lackmann et al., 1999).

Smoking during pregnancy seems to have some of the same effects on children when they reach school age as drinking during pregnancy: poor attention span, hyperactivity, anxiety, learning and behaviour problems, perceptual-motor and linguistic problems, poor IQ scores, low grade placement, and neurological problems (Landesman-Dwyer & Emanuel, 1979; Milberger, Biederman, Faraone, Chen, & Jones, 1996; Naeye & Peters, 1984; D. Olds, Henderson, & Tatelbaum, 1994a, 1994b; Streissguth et al., 1984; Wakschlag et al., 1997; Weitzman, Gortmaker, & Sobol, 1992; Wright et al., 1983). A 10-year longitudinal study of 6- to 23-year-old offspring of women who reported having smoked heavily during pregnancy found a fourfold increase in risk of conduct disorder in boys, beginning before puberty, and a fivefold increased risk of drug dependence in girls, beginning in adolescence, in comparison with young people whose mothers had not smoked during pregnancy (Weissman, Warner, Wickramaratne, & Kandel, 1999). An 18-year Ottawa study found both short-term and long-term effects: lowered birth weight, nicotine withdrawal tremors in the first days after birth, delays in learning to use language sounds leading to delayed speech development, impulsiveness and hyperactivity, and a slightly lower IQ (Fried, James, & Watkinson, 2001; Fried & Watkinson, 2001). These effects were lessened if mothers reduced or stopped smoking during pregnancy. A more recent concern involves maternal and infant exposure to environmental tobacco smoke (ETS), or second-hand smoke. About 13 per cent of pregnant non-smokers in Canada report living with a partner who smokes (Health Canada, 1999). ETS exposure appears to have the same effects on prenatal and postnatal development as does smoking by pregnant women (Cornelius & Day, 2000), and in addition increases the risk of sudden infant death syndrome (SIDS) and inner ear infection in infancy (Helgason & Lund, 2001).

A woman who drinks and smokes while pregnant is taking grave risks with her future child's health.

Caffeine Can the caffeine a pregnant woman swallows in coffee, tea, cola, or chocolate cause trouble for her fetus? For the most part, the answer is uncertain. It does seem clear that caffeine is not a teratogen for human babies (Hinds, West, Knight, & Harland, 1996). A controlled study of 1,205 new mothers and their babies showed no effect of reported caffeine use on low birth weight, premature birth, or retarded fetal growth (Santos, Victora, Huttly, & Carvalhal, 1998). On the other hand, four or more cups of coffee a day may dramatically increase the risk of sudden death in infancy (Ford et al., 1998; see chapter 6).

In some research, caffeine consumption has been associated with spontaneous abortion (Dlugosz et al., 1996; Infante-Rivard, Fernández, Gauthier, David, & Rivard, 1993), with risk of first-trimester spontaneous abortion increasing with amount of caffeine consumed (Cnattingius, Signorello et al., 2000). Other studies suggest that moderate caffeine use—five cups a day or less—does not increase the risk of miscarriage (Klebanov, Levine, DerSimonian, Clemens, & Wilkins, 1999; Mills et al., 1993).

Marijuana, Opiates, and Cocaine Although findings about marijuana use by pregnant women are mixed (Dreher, Nugent, & Hudgins, 1994; Lester & Dreher, 1989), some evidence suggests that heavy use can lead to birth defects. A Canadian study found temporary neurological disturbances, such as tremors and startles, as well as higher rates of low birth weight in the infants of marijuana smokers (Fried, Watkinson, & Willan, 1984). An analysis of blood samples from the umbilical cords of 34 newborns found a greater prevalence of cancer-causing mutations in the infants of mothers who smoked marijuana. These women did not use tobacco, cocaine, or opiates, suggesting that marijuana use alone can increase cancer risk (Ammenheuser, Berenson, Babiak, Singleton, & Whorton, 1998).

Women addicted to morphine, heroin, and codeine are likely to bear premature, addicted babies who will be addicted to the same drugs and will suffer the effects until at least age 6 (Hulse, O'Neill, Pereira, & Brewer, 2001). Prenatally exposed newborns are restless and irritable and often have tremors, convulsions, fever, vomiting, and breathing difficulties (Henly & Fitch, 1966; Ostrea & Chavez, 1979). Those who survive cry often, are less alert and less responsive than other babies (Strauss, Lessen-Firestone, Starr, & Ostrea, 1975) and tend to show acute withdrawal symptoms during the neonatal period, requiring prompt treatment (Wagner, Katikaneni, Cox, & Ryan, 1998). Although methadone is the standard medical treatment for heroin addiction in pregnancy, because it can reduce some harmful effects of heroin, like low birth weight (Kandall, Doberczak, Jantunen, & Stein, 1999), there are concerns about its safety in cases of women who continue using heroin while taking methadone. This combination results in greater risk of neonatal mortality than if no methadone were taken (Hulse & O'Neill, 2001) and lower birth weight than would be expected if only methadone were used (Hulse, Milne, English, & Holman, 1997). Moreover, methodone use in pregnancy results in abnormal non-stress tests of neonatal heart rate, indicating changes in neural responsiveness in the fetus (Anyaegbunam, Tran, Jadali, Randolph, & Mikhail, 1997). Alternatives to methadone are being investigated, but with uncertain efficacy compared to methadone (Annitto, 2000; Marquet, Chevrel, Lavignasse, Merle, & Lachatre, 1997).

At 1 year, these infants are likely to show somewhat slowed psychomotor development (Bunikowski et al., 1998). In early childhood they weigh less, are shorter, are less well adjusted, and score lower on tests of perceptual and learning abilities (Wilson, McCreary, Kean, & Baxter, 1979). These children tend not to do well in school, to be unusually anxious in social situations, and to have trouble making friends (Householder, Hatcher, Burns, & Chasnoff, 1982).

A pregnant woman's use of cocaine is associated with a higher risk of spontaneous abortion, prematurity, low birth weight, and small head size. "Cocaine babies" are generally not as alert as other babies and not as responsive, either emotionally or cognitively; or they may be more excitable, more irritable, and less able to regulate their sleep–wake patterns (Alessandri, Sullivan, Imaizumi, & Lewis, 1993; Kliegman, Madura, Kiwi, Eisenberg, & Yamashita, 1994; Napiorkowski et al., 1996; Ness et al., 1999; Phillips, Sharma, Premachandra, Vaughn, & Reyes-Lee, 1996; Singer et al., 1994; Tronick, Frank, Cabral, Mirochnick, & Zuckerman, 1996).

These infants may show impaired motor activity (Fetters & Tronick, 1996) or excessive activity, as well as extreme muscular tension, jerky movements, startles, tremors, and other signs of neurological stress (Napiorkowski et al., 1996). They tend to have trouble regulating attention (Mayes, Granger, Frank, Schottenfeld, & Bornstein, 1993) and emotional arousal. When interrupted, frustrated, or upset, it is hard for them to "regroup," recover, and move on (Bendersky, Alessandri, & Lewis, 1996; Bendersky & Lewis, 1998). Electroencephalographic (EEG) measurements of sleep patterns indicate subtle impairments in neurological development at birth and at 1 year (Scher, Richardson, & Day, 2000). The more cocaine a woman takes while pregnant, the greater the odds of impaired fetal growth and neurological functioning (Chiriboga, Brust, Bateman, & Hauser, 1999).

A cocaine baby's inactivity, lethargy, irritability, or unresponsiveness may frustrate the mother and prevent her from forming a close, caring relationship with her infant. On the other hand, it may be that cocaine-exposed infants do not learn to regulate and express their emotions because their cocaine-using mothers are less sensitive and responsive than other mothers (Alessandri, Sullivan, Bendersky, & Lewis, 1995; Bendersky et al., 1996; Bendersky & Lewis, 1998; Phillips et al., 1996).

Physically, some cocaine-exposed infants do recover. Especially if they had good prenatal care, they often catch up in weight, length, and head circumference by 1 year of age (Racine, Joyce, & Anderson, 1993; Weathers, Crane, Sauvain, & Blackhurst, 1993). However, deficiencies in motor control, especially hand use and eye–hand coordination, have been found at age 2 (Arendt, Angelopoulos, Salvator, & Singer, 1999). Psychosocial effects tend to last longer; cocaine-exposed children show a tendency toward such behavioural problems as aggressiveness and anxiety, especially when under stress (Azar, 1997). Exposure to *low* levels of cocaine seems to have little long-term effect on cognition, but exposure to *high* levels may lead to difficulties, especially in learning complex skills (Alessandri, Bendersky, & Lewis, 1998).

Sexually Transmitted Diseases and Other Maternal Illnesses

acquired immune deficiency syndrome (AIDS) Viral disease that undermines effective functioning of the immune system

Acquired immune deficiency syndrome (AIDS) is a disease caused by the human immunodeficiency virus (HIV), which undermines functioning of the immune system. If an expectant mother has the virus in her blood, it may cross over to the fetus's bloodstream through the placenta. After birth, the virus can be transmitted through breast milk.

Important advances have been made in the prevention, detection, and treatment of HIV infection in infants. These include the successful use of the drug zidovudine (formerly azidothymidine), commonly called AZT, to curtail transmission; the recommendation that women with HIV should not breast-feed; and the availability of new drugs to treat AIDS-related pneumonia. Between 1992 and 1997, when zidovudine therapy became widespread, the number of babies who got AIDS from their mothers dropped by about two-thirds, raising the hope that mother-to-child transmission of the virus can be virtually eliminated (Lindegren et al., 1999). The risk of transmission also can be reduced by choosing Caesarean delivery (International Perinatal HIV Group, 1999).

Prospects for children born with HIV infection have improved. The progress of the disease, at least in some children, seems slower than was previously thought. While some develop full-blown AIDS by their first or second birthday, others live for years with little apparent effect if any at all (European Collaborative Study, 1994; Grubman et al., 1995; Nielsen et al., 1997; Nozyce et al., 1994).

Syphilis can cause problems in fetal development, and gonorrhea and genital herpes can have harmful effects on the baby at the time of delivery. The incidence of genital herpes simplex virus (HSV) has increased among newborns, who may acquire the disease from the mother or father either at or soon after birth (Sullivan-Bolyai, Hull, Wilson, & Corey, 1983), causing blindness, other abnormalities, or death. Again, Caesarean delivery may help avoid infection.

Other maternal illnesses can lead to health problems in the child. A diabetic mother's metabolic regulation, especially during the second and third trimesters of pregnancy, unless carefully managed, may affect her child's long-range neurobehavioural development and cognitive performance (Rizzo, Metzger, Dooley, & Cho, 1997). Risks of diabetic pregnancies can be greatly reduced by screening pregnant women for diabetes, followed by careful monitoring and a controlled diet (Kjos & Buchanan, 1999).

Both prospective parents should try to prevent all infections—common colds, flu, urinary tract and vaginal infections, as well as sexually transmitted diseases. If the mother does contract an infection, she should have it treated promptly. Pregnant women also should be screened for thyroid deficiency, which can affect their children's future cognitive performance (Haddow et al., 1999).

Rubella (German measles), if contracted by a woman before her 11th week of pregnancy, is almost certain to cause deafness and heart defects in her baby. Chances of catching rubella during pregnancy have been greatly reduced in Canada since the late 1960s, when a vaccine was developed that is now routinely administered to infants and children (CICH, 2000). However, rubella is still a serious problem in non-industialized countries where inoculations are not routine (Plotkin, Katz, & Cordero, 1999).

Maternal Age

Women today typically start having children later in life than was true 15 or 20 years ago, often because they spend their early adult years getting advanced education and establishing careers (Canadian Institute of Child Health [CICH], 2000; Mathews & Ventura, 1997; Ventura et al., 1999). About a third of all Canadian babies are born to women over the age of 30 (Canadian Institute of Child Health, 2000).

How does delayed childbearing affect the risks to mother and baby? Pregnant women who are older are more likely to suffer complications due to diabetes, high blood pressure, or severe bleeding. Most risks to the infant's health are not much greater than for babies born to younger mothers. Still, after age 35 there is more chance of miscarriage or stillbirth, and more likelihood of premature delivery, retarded fetal growth, other birth-related complications, or birth defects, such as Down syndrome (refer back to chapter 3). However, due to widespread screening for fetal defects among older expectant mothers, fewer babies with prenatally identified defects are born nowadays (Berkowitz, Skovron, Lapinski, & Berkowitz, 1990; P. Brown, 1993; Cunningham & Leveno, 1995).

Women age 40 and over are at increased risk of needing operative deliveries (Caesarean or by forceps or vacuum extraction—see chapter 5). Risks of all birth complications are increased, and the infants are more likely to be born prematurely and underweight (Gilbert, Nesbitt, & Danielsen, 1999).

Adolescents also tend to have premature or underweight babies—perhaps because a young girl's still-growing body consumes vital nutrients the fetus needs (Fraser, Brockert, & Ward, 1995). These newborns are at heightened risk of death in the first month, disabilities, or health problems. If teenage mothers are unwed, they are likely to suffer great financial hardship and may drop out of school, narrowing their future vocational choices. And, try as they may to do their best at mothering, their lack of parenting skills may put their babies at a disadvantage (AAP Committee on Adolescence, 1999; Alan Guttmacher Institute, 1999a; Children's Defense Fund, 1998). Risks of teenage pregnancy are discussed further in chapter 17.

Outside Environmental Hazards

Chemicals, radiation, extremes of heat and humidity, and other hazards of modern life can affect prenatal development. Women who work with chemicals used in manufacturing semiconductor chips have about twice the rate of miscarriage as other female workers (Markoff, 1992). Infants exposed prenatally to high levels of lead score lower on tests of cognitive abilities than those exposed to low or moderate levels (Bellinger, Leviton, Watermaux,

Checkpoint ✔

Can you . . .

✔ Describe the short-term and long-term effects on the developing fetus of a mother's use of medical drugs, alcohol, tobacco, caffeine, marijuana, opiates, and cocaine during pregnancy?

✔ Summarize the risks of maternal illnesses, delayed childbearing, and exposure to chemicals and radiation?

Needleman, & Rabinowitz, 1987; Needleman & Gatsonis, 1990). Children exposed prenatally to heavy metals have higher rates of childhood illness and lower measured intelligence than children not exposed to these metals (Lewis, Worobey, Ramsay, & McCormack, 1992).

Radiation can cause genetic mutations. Nuclear radiation affected Japanese infants after the atomic bomb explosions in Hiroshima and Nagasaki (Yamazaki & Schull, 1990) and infants as far away as Germany after the spill-out at the nuclear power plant at Chernobyl in the Soviet Union (West Berlin Human Genetics Institute, 1987). In utero exposure to radiation has been linked to greater risk of mental retardation, small head size, chromosomal malformations, Down syndrome, seizures, and poor performance on IQ tests and in school. The critical period seems to be 8 through 15 weeks after fertilization (Yamazaki & Schull, 1990).

Paternal Factors

The father, too, can transmit environmentally caused defects. A man's exposure to lead, marijuana or tobacco smoke, large amounts of alcohol or radiation, DES, or certain pesticides may result in abnormal sperm. Offspring of male workers at a British nuclear processing plant were found to have an elevated risk of being born dead (Parker, Pearce, Dickinson, Aitkin, & Craft, 1999). Also, babies whose fathers had diagnostic X-rays within the year prior to conception tend to have low birth weight and slowed fetal growth (Shea, Little, & the ALSPAC Study Team, 1997). And fathers whose diet is low in vitamin C are more likely to have children with birth defects and certain types of cancer (Fraga et al., 1991). A study of 2000 farm couples showed that preconception exposure to herbicides by fathers resulted in an increased risk of early miscarriage (Arbuckle, Savitz, Mery, & Curtis, 1999). Pesticide residues have been found in samples of semen of farmers, which could account for the increased risk of early miscarriage (Arbuckle, Schrader, Cole, Hall, Bancej, Turner, & Claman, 1999).

A man's use of cocaine can cause birth defects in his children. The cocaine seems to attach itself to his sperm, and this cocaine-bearing sperm then enters the ovum at conception. Other toxins, such as lead and mercury, may "hitchhike" onto sperm in the same way (Yazigi, Odem, & Polakoski, 1991).

Older fathers may be a significant source of birth defects (Crow, 1993, 1995). A later paternal age (averaging in the late thirties) is associated with increases in the risk of several rare conditions, including Marfan's syndrome (deformities of the head and limbs) and dwarfism (G. Evans, 1976). Advanced age of the father may also be a factor in about 5 per cent of cases of Down syndrome (Antonarakis & Down Syndrome Collaborative Group, 1991). More male cells than female ones undergo mutations, and mutations may increase with paternal age.

A father's smoking is a harmful environmental influence, which has been linked with low birth weight and cancer in childhood and adulthood ((Ji et al., 1997; D. H. Rubin, Krasilnikoff, Leventhal, Weile, & Berget, 1986; Sandler, Everson, Wilcox, & Browder, 1985). Paternal smoking brings increased risk of infant respiratory infections and sudden infant death, whether or not the mother also smokes (Wakefield, Reid, Roberts, Mullins, & Gillies, 1998).

What's your view

- Since cocaine, marijuana, tobacco, and other substances can produce genetic abnormalities in a man's sperm, should fertile men be forced to abstain from them? How could such a prohibition be enforced?

Checkpoint ✔

Can you . . .

✔ Identify at least three ways in which environmentally caused defects can be influenced by the father?

Guidepost 4

What techniques can assess a fetus's health and well-being, and what is the importance of prenatal care?

Monitoring Prenatal Development

Not long ago, almost the only decision parents had to make about their babies before birth was the decision to conceive; most of what happened in the intervening months was beyond their control. Now we have an array of tools to assess an unborn baby's progress and well-being (see Box 4-2), and even to intervene to correct some abnormal conditions. In line with these developments is a growing emphasis on the importance of early prenatal care.

Conditions detected by prenatal assessment can be corrected before birth in three ways: administration of medicine, blood transfusion, and surgery. Fetuses can swallow and absorb medicines, nutrients, vitamins, and hormones that are injected into the amniotic fluid, and drugs that might not pass through the placenta can be injected through the umbilical cord. Blood can be transfused through the cord as early as the 18th week of gesta-

Box 4-2 *Prenatal Assessment Techniques*

Normal prenatal development is overwhelmingly the rule. Still, we need to be aware of the many ways development can go awry and how best to avoid problems. Techniques for monitoring fetal development, coupled with increased knowledge of ways to improve the child's prenatal world, make pregnancy much less a cause for concern than in earlier times. Access to prenatal diagnosis of birth defects, coupled with the legal availability of abortion and the possibility of fetal therapy, have encouraged many couples with troubling medical histories to take a chance on conception.

Ultrasound and Amniocentesis

Some parents see their baby for the first time in a *sonogram,* a picture of the uterus, fetus, and placenta created by *ultrasound* directed into the mother's abdomen. Ultrasound is used to measure fetal growth, to judge gestational age, to detect multiple pregnancies, to evaluate uterine abnormalities, to detect major structural abnormalities in the fetus, and to determine whether a fetus has died, as well as to guide other procedures, such as amniocentesis.

A newer technique called *sonoembryology,* which involves high-frequency transvaginal probes and digital image processing, has made possible earlier detection of unusual defects during the embryonic stage. Sonoembryology reportedly can detect 60 per cent of all malformations during the first trimester of pregnancy and, in combination with ultrasound, more than 80 per cent during the second trimester (Kurjak, Kupesic, Matijevic, Kos, & Marton, 1999).

In *amniocentesis,* a sample of the amniotic fluid, which contains fetal cells, is withdrawn and analyzed to detect the presence of certain genetic or multifactorial defects and all recognizable chromosomal disorders. Only 3.2 per cent of mothers who had live births used amniocentesis in 1996, as compared with 64 per cent who had ultrasound (Ventura, Martin, Curtin, & Mathews, 1998). Amniocentesis is recommended for pregnant women aged 35 and over. It is also recommended if the woman and her partner are both known carriers of such diseases as Tay-Sachs and sickle-cell anemia, or if they have a family history of such conditions as Down syndrome, spina bifida, Rh disease, and muscular dystrophy.

Amniocentesis is usually done between the 15th and 18th weeks of pregnancy. Women who have the test earlier may greatly increase their risk of miscarriage, which is more common during the first trimester. A randomized Canadian study found a 7.6 per cent rate of fetal loss when amniocentesis was done between the 11th and 12th weeks of gestation, as compared with 5.9 per cent between the 15th and 16th weeks (Canadian Early and Mid-Trimester Amniocentesis Trial [CEMAT] Group, 1998).

Both amniocentesis and ultrasound can reveal the sex of the fetus, which may help in diagnosing sex-linked disorders. In some Asian countries in which sons are preferred, both procedures have been used (in some places, illegally) for "sex-screening" of unborn babies, with the result that in these populations males now predominate (Burns, 1994; Kristof, 1993; WuDunn, 1997). Such early sex-screening is not supported in Canada except in the case of possible sex-linked disorders. In the recently introduced Act Respecting Assisted Human Reproduction, identifying the sex of an embryo that was created using assisted reproductive technology is prohibited except for medical reasons.

Other Assessment Methods

In *chorionic villus sampling (CVS),* tissue from the ends of villi—hairlike projections of the chorion, the membrane surrounding the fetus, which are made up of fetal cells—are tested for the presence of birth defects and disorders. This procedure can be performed between 8 and 13 weeks of pregnancy (earlier than amniocentesis), and it yields results within about a week. However, there is almost a 5 per cent greater chance of miscarriage or neonatal death after CVS than after amniocentesis (D'Alton & DeCherney, 1993).

Embryoscopy, insertion of a tiny viewing scope into a pregnant woman's abdomen, can provide a clear look at embryos as young as 6 weeks. The procedure is promising for early diagnosis and treatment of embryonic and fetal abnormalities (Quintero, Abuhamad, Hobbins, & Mahoney, 1993).

Preimplantation genetic diagnosis can identify some genetic defects in embryos of four to eight cells, which were conceived by in vitro fertilization and have not yet been implanted in the mother's uterus. Defective embryos are not implanted.

By inserting a needle into tiny blood vessels of the umbilical cord under the guidance of ultrasound, doctors can take samples of a fetus's blood. This procedure, called *umbilical cord sampling* or *fetal blood sampling,* can test for infection, anemia, heart failure, and certain metabolic disorders and immunodeficiencies and seems to offer promise for identifying other conditions. However, the technique is associated with miscarriage, bleeding from the umbilical cord, early labour, and infection (Chervenak, Isaacson, & Mahoney, 1986; D'Alton & DeCherney, 1993; Kolata, 1988).

A blood sample taken from the mother between the 16th and 18th weeks of pregnancy can be tested for the amount of alpha fetoprotein (AFP) it contains. This *maternal blood test* is appropriate for women at risk of bearing children with defects in the formation of the brain or spinal cord, such as anencephaly or spina bifida, which may be detected by high AFP levels. To confirm or refute the presence of suspected conditions, ultrasound or amniocentesis, or both, may be performed. Blood tests of samples taken between the 15th and 20th weeks of gestation can predict about 60 per cent of cases of Down syndrome. This blood test is particularly important for women under 35, who bear 80 per cent of all Down syndrome babies but usually are not targeted to receive amniocentesis because their personal risk is lower (Haddow et al., 1992).

The discovery that fetal cells that "leak" into the mother's blood early in pregnancy can be isolated and analyzed (Simpson & Elias, 1993) will make it possible to detect genetic as well as chromosomal disorders from a maternal blood test without using riskier procedures, such as amniocentesis, chorionic villus sampling, and fetal blood sampling. Already researchers have succeeded in screening fetal blood cells for single genes for sickle-cell anemia and thalassemia (Cheung, Goldberg, & Kan, 1996).

What's your view?

In Canada, women who undergo ultrasound or amniocentesis often are given the choice of whether or not they will be told their unborn babies' sex. Suppose it became known that substantial numbers of Canadian women were aborting their fetuses for reasons of sex preference, as has happened in some East Asian countries. In that case, would you favour a law forbidding use of a prenatal diagnostic procedure to reveal the sex of a fetus?

Check it out

For more information on this topic, go to **www.mcgrawhill.ca/college/papalia**.

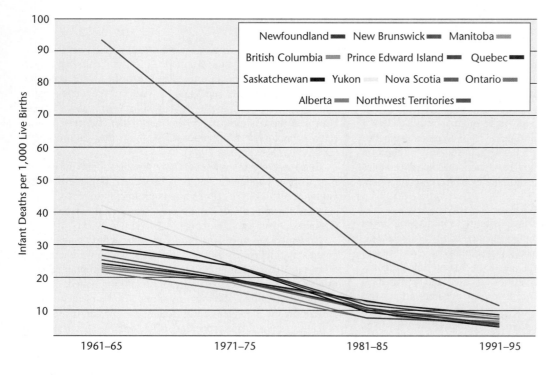

Figure 4-3

Infant mortality rates in Canadian provinces and territories 1961–65 to 1991–95.

Source: Dzakpasu, S. et al. The Matthew Effect: Infant Mortality in Canada and Internationally, *Pediatrics 106* p. 2

tion. In 1996, surgeons successfully performed a bone marrow transplant in the womb to prevent the development of a rare sex-linked genetic disorder, severe combined immuno-deficiency, in a fetus identified by chorionic villus sampling as having the mutant gene for it. The baby was born healthy by Caesarean delivery and showed no sign of the disorder throughout infancy (Flake et al., 1996). Eventually transplantation procedures, in the form of gene therapy, may be used to treat other congenital diseases in utero.

Screening for treatable defects and diseases is only one reason for the importance of prenatal care. Early, high-quality prenatal care, which includes educational, social, and nutritional services, can help prevent maternal and infant death and other complications of birth. It can provide first-time mothers with information about pregnancy, childbirth, and infant care. Poor women who get prenatal care benefit by being put in touch with other needed services, and they are more likely to get medical care for their infants after birth (Shiono & Behrman, 1995).

In Canada prenatal care is widespread, but despite universal health insurance, socio-economic status affects the quality of prenatal care provided to pregnant women (Canadian Perinatal Surveillance System, 2000). As an indicator of different effectiveness of prenatal care, low-income groups experience over 150 per cent the infant mortality rate of higher-income groups. However, the disparity in infant mortality rates between income groups and between regions in Canada is decreasing (Dzakpasu, Joseph, Kramer, & Allen, 2000; see Figure 4-3).

Even as usage of prenatal care has increased, rates of low birthweight and premature birth have worsened (Kogan et al., 1998; Ventura et al., 1999). Why?

One answer is the increasing number of multiple births, which require especially close prenatal attention. Twin pregnancies often end, for precautionary reasons, in early births, either induced or by Caesarean delivery. Intensive prenatal care may allow early detection of problems requiring immediate delivery, as, for example, when one or both fetuses are not

What's your view

- Can you suggest ways to induce more pregnant women to seek early prenatal care?

thriving. This may explain why a Canadian study of twin births between 1986 and 1997 found parallel upward trends in use of prenatal care and rates of preterm birth—along with a decline in mortality of twin infants (Joseph, Marcoux, Ohlsson, Liu, Allen, Kramer, & Wen, 2001).

Another possible explanation for these parallel trends is that the benefits of prenatal care are not evenly distributed, particularly in Northern and remote communities. Merely increasing the quantity of prenatal care does not address the *content* of care (Misra & Guyer, 1998). Most prenatal care programs in Canada focus on screening for major complications and are not designed to attack the causes of low birth weight. A U.S. national panel has recommended that prenatal care be restructured to provide more visits early in the pregnancy and fewer in the last trimester. In fact, care should begin *before* pregnancy. Prepregnancy counselling could make more women aware, for example, of the importance of getting enough folic acid in their diet and making sure that they are immune to rubella. In addition, care needs to be made more accessible to poor and minority women (Shiono & Behrman, 1995).

Good prenatal care can give every child the best possible chance for entering the world in good condition to meet the challenges of life outside the uterus—challenges we discuss in the next three chapters.

> ### Checkpoint ✔
>
> Can you . . .
>
> ✔ Describe seven techniques for identifying defects or disorders prenatally?
>
> ✔ Tell why early, high-quality prenatal care is important, and how it could be improved?

Summary and Key Terms

Prenatal Development: Three Stages

Guidepost 1 What are the three stages of prenatal development, and what happens during each stage?

- Prenatal development occurs in three stages of gestation: the germinal, embryonic, and fetal stages.
- Growth and development both before and after birth follow the cephalocaudal principle (head to tail) and the proximodistal principle (centre outward).
- About one-third of all conceptions end in spontaneous abortion, usually in the first trimester of pregnancy.

  cephalocaudal principle (75)   proximodistal principle (75)
  germinal stage (75)   embryonic stage (78)
  spontaneous abortion (78)   fetal stage (79)

Guidepost 2 What can fetuses do?

- As fetuses grow, they move less, but more vigorously. Swallowing amniotic fluid, which contains substances from the mother's body, stimulates taste and smell. Fetuses seem able to hear, exercise sensory discrimination, learn, and remember.

  ultrasound (79)

Prenatal Development: Environmental Influences

Guidepost 3 What environmental influences can affect prenatal development?

- The developing organism can be greatly affected by its prenatal environment. The likelihood of a birth defect may depend on the timing and intensity of an environmental event and its interaction with genetic factors.
- Important environmental influences involving the mother include nutrition, physical activity, smoking, intake of alcohol or other drugs, transmission of maternal illnesses or infections, maternal age, incompatibility of blood type, and external environmental hazards, such as chemicals and radiation. External influences may also affect the father's sperm.

  teratogenic (80)   fetal alcohol syndrome (FAS) (83)
  acquired immune deficiency syndrome (AIDS) (86)

Monitoring Prenatal Development

Guidepost 4 What techniques can assess a fetus's health and well-being, and what is the importance of prenatal care?

- Ultrasound, amniocentesis, chorionic villus sampling, embryoscopy, preimplantation genetic diagnosis, umbilical cord sampling, and maternal blood tests can be used to determine whether an unborn baby is developing normally. Some abnormal conditions can be corrected through fetal therapy.
- Early, high-quality prenatal care is essential for healthy development. It can lead to detection of defects and disorders and, especially if begun early and targeted to the needs of at-risk women, may help reduce maternal and infant death, low birth weight, and other birth complications.

OLC Preview

The Online Learning Centre for *A Child's World*, First Canadian Edition, offers information on traditional cultures and new technology and on pregnancy in the 21st century, as well as links to recommended websites on fetal welfare versus mothers' rights and prenatal assessment techniques. Check out **www.mcgrawhill.ca/college/papalia.**

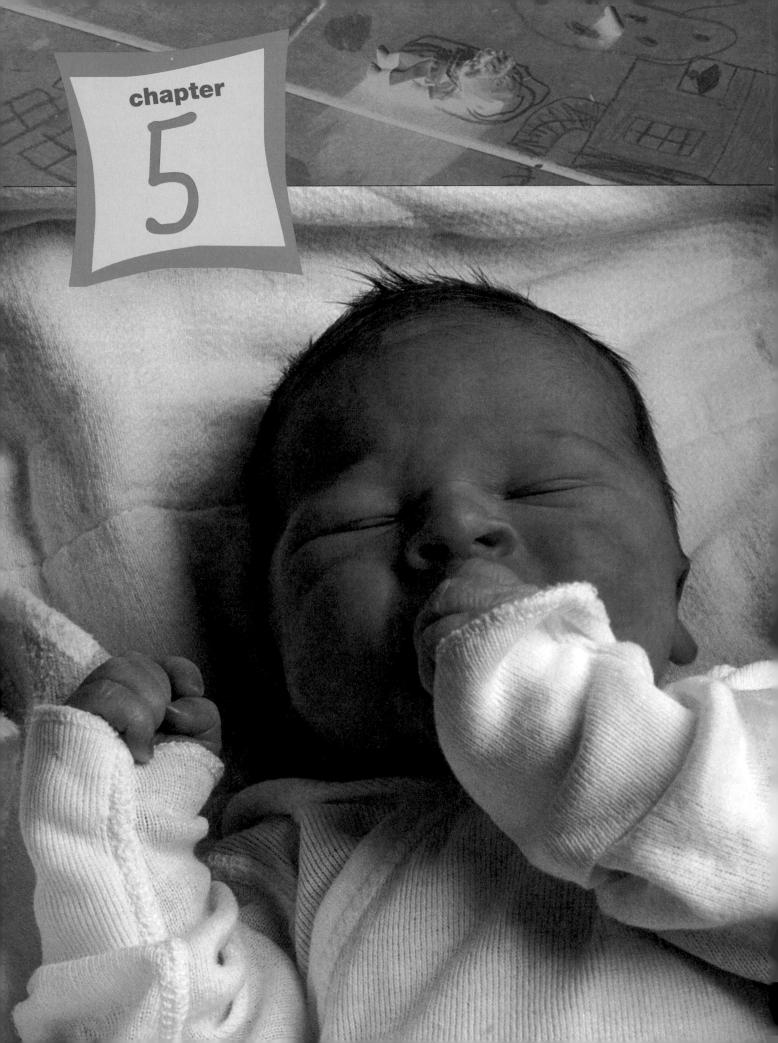

Birth and the Newborn Baby

A newborn baby is an extraordinary event; and I have never seen two babies who looked exactly alike. Here is the breathing miracle who could not live an instant without you, with a skull more fragile than an egg, a miracle of eyes, legs, toenails, and lungs.

—James Baldwin, *No Name in the Street*, 1972

Focus *The Birth of Elvis Presley*[*]

Elvis Presley

Elvis Presley (1935–1977) was born in a 30- by 15-foot cottage in East Tupelo, Mississippi. Today, the modest birthplace of the now-legendary "king" of rock music is painted sparkling white, the walls are papered with primroses, and dainty curtains hang at the windows—among the many homey touches added for the benefit of tourists. But, like many of the popular myths about Elvis's early life, this "cute little doll house" (Goldman, 1981, p. 60) bears only slight resemblance to the reality: a bare board shack with no indoor plumbing or electricity, set in a dirt-poor hamlet that wasn't much more than "a wide spot in the road" (Clayton & Heard, 1994, p. 8).

During the Great Depression, Elvis's near-illiterate father, Vernon Presley, sometimes did odd jobs for a farmer named Orville Bean, who owned much of the town. Elvis's mother, Gladys, was vivacious and high-spirited, as talkative as Vernon was taciturn. She, like Vernon, came from a family of sharecroppers and migrant workers. She had moved to East Tupelo to be close to the garment factory where she worked.

Gladys first noticed handsome Vernon on the street and then, soon after, met him in church. They eloped on June 17, 1933. Vernon was 17 and Gladys, 21. They borrowed the three dollars for the marriage licence.

At first the young couple lived with friends and family. When Gladys became pregnant, Vernon borrowed $180 from his employer, Bean, to buy lumber and nails and, with the help of his father and older brother, built a two-room cabin next to his parents' house on Old Saltillo Road. Bean, who owned the land, was to hold title to the house until the loan was paid off.

Vernon and Gladys moved into their new home in December 1934, about a month before she gave birth. Her pregnancy was a difficult one; her legs swelled, and she finally quit her job at the garment factory, where she had to stand on her feet all day pushing a heavy steam iron.

When Vernon got up for work in the wee hours of January 8, a bitterly cold morning, Gladys was hemorrhaging. The midwife told Vernon to get the doctor, Will Hunt. (His $15 fee was paid by welfare.) At about 4 o'clock in the morning, Dr. Hunt delivered a stillborn baby boy, Jesse Garon. The second twin, Elvis Aron, was born about 35 minutes later. Gladys—extremely weak and losing blood—was taken to the hospital charity ward with baby Elvis. They stayed there for more than 3 weeks.

Baby Jesse remained an important part of the family's life. Gladys frequently talked to Elvis about his brother. "When one twin died, the one that lived got the strength of both," she

[*] Sources of information about Elvis Presley's birth were Clayton & Heard (1994); Dundy (1985); Goldman (1981); Guralnick (1994); and Marling (1996).

would say (Guralnick, 1994, p. 13). Elvis took his mother's words to heart. Throughout his life, his twin's imagined voice and presence were constantly with him.

As for Elvis's birthplace, he lived there only until the age of 3. Vernon, who sold a pig to Bean for $4, was accused of altering the check to $40. He was sent to prison, and when the payment on the house loan came due, Bean evicted Gladys and her son, who had to move in with family members. In later years, Elvis would drive back to East Tupelo (now Tupelo's suburban Presley Heights). He would sit in his car in the dark, looking at the cottage on what is now called Elvis Presley Drive and "thinking about the course his life had taken" (Marling, 1996, p. 20).

● ● ●

Elvis Presley is just one of many well-known people born at home. At one time, medical care during pregnancy was rare, and the prevalence of birth complications, stillbirth, and maternal mortality was higher than it is today. A rising standard of living, together with medical advances, has eased childbirth and reduced its risks. Today, the overwhelming majority of births in Canada (but a smaller proportion in some European countries) occur in hospitals. However, there is a small but growing movement back to home birth, as is still the custom in many less industrialized countries.

In this chapter, we describe how babies come into the world: the stages, methods, joys, and complications of birth. We describe how newborn infants look and how their body systems work. We discuss ways to assess their health, and how birth complications can affect development. We also consider how the birth of a baby affects the people most vital to the infant's well-being: the parents.

After you have read and studied this chapter, you should be able to answer each of the Guidepost questions that appear at the top of the next page. Look for them again in the margins, where they point to important concepts throughout the chapter. To check your understanding of these Guideposts, review the end-of-chapter summary. Checkpoints located throughout the chapter will help you verify your understanding of what you have read.

Guideposts for Study

1. How have customs surrounding birth changed?

2. How does labour begin, and what happens during each of the four stages of childbirth?

3. What alternative methods and settings of delivery are available today?

4. How do newborn infants adjust to life outside the womb?

5. How can we tell whether a new baby is healthy and is developing normally?

6. What complications of childbirth can endanger newborn babies, and what can be done to improve the chances of a positive outcome?

7. How do parents bond with their baby and respond to the baby's patterns of sleep and activity?

8. How does parenthood change the parents' relationship with one another?

How Childbirth Has Changed[*]

Guidepost 1

How have customs surrounding birth changed?

In many pre-contact Aboriginal communities, childbirth was assisted by a midwife, who administered traditional herbs and medicines, and whose role included transmitting values from one generation to the next (Carroll & Benoit, 2001). Among the Carrier people in B.C., the reproductive role was a source of social status, and women who raised families successfully were influential in their communities, with the wisdom of elderly women recognized in the esteem in which grandmothers were held (Carroll et al., 2001).

For centuries, childbirth in Europe, and later in colonial Canada, followed a familiar pattern, much as in some developing countries today (see Box 5-1). Birth was a female social ritual. The woman, surrounded by female relatives and neighbours, sat up in her own bed, modestly draped in a sheet; if she wished, she might stand, walk around, or squat over a birth stool. Chinks in the walls, doors, and windows were stuffed with cloth to keep out chills and evil spirits.

The midwife who presided over the event had no formal training; she offered "advice, massages, potions, irrigations, and talismans." Salves made of fat of viper, gall of eel, powdered hoof of donkey, tongue of chameleon, or skin of snake or hare might be rubbed on the prospective mother's abdomen to ease her pain or hasten her labour; but "the cries of the mother during labor were considered to be as natural as those of the baby at birth" (Fontanel & d'Harcourt, 1997, p. 28).

The prospective father was nowhere to be seen; he may have been out gathering firewood. Nor, until the 15th century, was a doctor present, and then only for wealthy women if complications arose.

After the baby emerged, the midwife cut and tied the umbilical cord and cleaned and examined the newborn, testing the reflexes and joints. The other women helped the new mother wash and dress, made her bed with clean sheets, and served her food to rebuild her strength. Within a few hours or days, a peasant mother would be back at work in the fields; a more affluent or noble woman could "lie in" and rest for several weeks.

Childbirth in those times was "a struggle with death" (Fontanel & d'Harcourt, 1997, p. 34) for both mother and baby. In 17th- and 18th-century France, a woman had a 1 in 10 chance of dying while, or shortly after, giving birth. Thousands of babies were stillborn, and 1 out of 4 who were born alive died during its first year.

The development of the science of obstetrics early in the 19th century professionalized childbirth, especially in urban settings. Even though most deliveries still occurred at home

[*]This discussion is based largely on Eccles, 1982; Fontanel & d'Harcourt, 1997; Gelis, 1991; and Scholten, 1985

Box 5-1 *Having a Baby in the Himalayas*

Between 1993 and 1995, Sally Olds, one of the authors of this book, made four visits to Badel, a remote hill village in the small Asian country of Nepal, where she stayed with local families. The following account from her journal describes a visit that she, the friend she travelled with, and their guide, Buddi, made to the village midwife.

Sabut Maya Mathani Rai has been helping childbearing mothers for almost 50 of her 75 years. Only three days ago she attended the birth of a baby girl.

When Sabut Maya attends a woman about to give birth, she says, "First I feel on the outside of the woman's belly. I look to see where is the head and the other organs. I help the mother push down when her time comes."

She does not use forceps. "I don't have any instruments," she says. "I just use my hands. If the baby is upside down, I turn it from the outside."

Nepali hill women usually give birth right after, or in the middle of, working in house or fields. The delivery may occur inside or outside of the house, depending on when the woman goes into labour. Women usually give birth on their knees. This kneeling position allows the mother to use her strong thigh and abdominal muscles to push the baby out. If the mother has other children, they usually watch, no matter how small they are. But the husbands don't want to watch and the women don't want them there.

Most women are not attended by a midwife; they handle the delivery and dispose of the placenta and umbilical cord themselves. Buddi's mother once gave birth on the path as she was walking back from working in the fields, and then asked for her husband's knife to cut the cord.

"If the baby is not coming fast, I use special medicine," the midwife says. "I put grasses on the mother's body and I massage her with oil from a special plant. I don't give the mother any herbs or anything like that to eat or drink, only hot water or tea."

In a complicated birth—if, say, the baby is not emerging or the mother gets sick—the midwife calls the *shaman* (spiritual healer). Inevitably, some babies and some mothers die. In most cases, however, all goes well, and most deliveries are easy and quick.

How is the newborn cared for? "After the baby is born I wash the baby," says the midwife. "I leave this much of the cord on the

baby [indicating about half an inch] and I tie it up with very good cotton. Then I wrap a piece of cotton cloth around the baby's tummy. This stays on for a few days until the cord falls off." Sometimes a small piece of the umbilical cord is saved and inserted into a metal bead that will be given to the child to wear on a string around the neck, to ward off evil spirits. A family member flings the placenta high up on a tree near the house to dry out; eventually it is thrown away.

No one but the mother—not even the father—is allowed to hold the baby at first. This may help to protect both mother and baby from infection and disease when they are most vulnerable. Then, at three days of age for a girl or seven days for a boy (girls are thought to mature earlier), a purification rite and naming ceremony takes place.

My friend and I tell how in our culture women lie on their backs, a position unknown in most traditional societies, and how the doctor sometimes breaks the woman's water. We also describe how a doctor sometimes puts on surgical gloves and reaches inside the woman to turn a baby in a breech or other position. "We don't have gloves and we don't have instruments," the midwife repeats. "We don't do any of those things. I'm just a helper." Sabut Maya really is a combination of midwife and doula (described in this chapter)—a kind of helper now seen with growing frequency in delivery rooms of Europe and North America. It seems ironic that it has taken the industrialized world so long to rediscover some of the wisdom that "primitive" societies have known for centuries.

What's your view?

What aspects of traditional ways of delivering babies might enhance childbearing practices without giving up medical techniques that save lives? Could advanced medical techniques be introduced into traditional societies without invalidating practices that seem to serve women in those societies well?

Check it out!

For more information on this topic, go to **www.mcgrawhill.ca/college/papalia**.

Source: (c) Sally Wendkos Olds, in press

and women were on hand to help and offer emotional support, a (male) physician was usually in charge, with surgical instruments ready in case of trouble. Midwives were now given training, and obstetrics manuals were widely disseminated.

After the turn of the 20th century, maternity hospitals, where conditions were antiseptic and medical management was easier, became the birth setting of choice for those who could afford them (though not for many country women, like Gladys Presley), and anaesthesia for pain relief became standard practice. In 1926, the first year national statistics were taken, 18 per cent of Canadian deliveries took place in hospitals; by 1960 the rate was 95 per cent, and by 1983 the rate was over 99 per cent (Leacy, 1983). A similar trend took place in the United States and Europe.

The safety of childbirth has continued to improve. At the end of the 19th century, in England and Wales, an expectant mother was almost 50 times as likely to die in childbirth as today (Saunders, 1997). The dramatic reductions in risks surrounding pregnancy and childbirth, particularly during the past 50 years, are largely due to the availability of antibiotics, blood transfusions, safe anaesthesia, improved hygiene, and drugs for inducing labour when necessary. In addition, improvements in prenatal assessment and care make it far more likely that a baby will be born healthy.

Yet the medicalization of childbirth has had its costs. "To many, a hospital birth has become a surgical act in which the woman is hooked up to a monitor and stretched out on a table under glaring lights and the stares of two or three strangers, her feet in stirrups" (Fontanel & d'Harcourt, 1997, p. 57). Today some women in industrialized countries are opting for the emotionally satisfying experience of home birth, usually attended by a trained nurse-midwife, and with the resources of medical science close at hand in case of need. About a third of Canadian women indicate preferences for birthing centres rather than hospitals, while 80 per cent indicate a willingness to be cared for by a nurse or midwife after birth (Wen et al., 1999); however, attitudes towards home birth are mixed (Tyson, 1991). Hospitals, too, are finding ways to "humanize" childbirth: in Canada hospitals are adopting a family-centred approach, emphasizing the importance of a warm, comforting, one-room environment for labour, birth, and recovery together with family members (Health Canada, 2000). Labour and delivery may take place in a quiet, homelike birthing room, under soft lights, with the father present as a "coach." The woman is given local anaesthesia if she wants and needs it, but she can see and participate in the birth and can hold her newborn on her belly immediately afterward. By "demedicalizing the experience, some hospitals and birthing centers are seeking to establish—or reestablish—around childbirth an environment in which tenderness, security, and emotion carry as much weight as medical techniques" (Fontanel & d'Harcourt, 1997, p. 57). In many provinces in Canada, such as British Columbia, Aboriginal midwifery, which incorporates traditional and contemporary Aboriginal practices, is slowly becoming recognized and supported by mainstream health authorities (Carroll et al., 2001; Revised Statutes of British Columbia, 1996).

The Birth Process

Birth is both a beginning and an end: the climax of all that has happened from the moment of fertilization. *Labour* is an apt term. Birth is hard work for both mother and baby—but work that yields a rich reward.

Parturition—the process of uterine, cervical, and other changes that brings on labour, or normal vaginal childbirth—typically begins about two weeks before delivery, when the balance between progesterone and estrogen shifts. During most of gestation, progesterone keeps the uterine muscles relaxed and the cervix firm. During parturition, sharply rising estrogen levels stimulate the uterus to contract and the cervix to become more flexible. The timing of parturition seems to be determined by the rate at which the placenta produces a protein called *corticotropin-releasing hormone (CRH)*, which also promotes maturation of the fetal lungs to ready them for life outside the womb. The rate of CRH production as early as the fifth month of pregnancy may predict whether a baby will be born early, "on time," or late (Smith, 1999).

The uterine contractions that expel the fetus begin—typically, 266 days after conception—as mild tightenings of the uterus. A woman may have felt similar contractions at times during the final months of pregnancy, but she may recognize birth contractions as the "real thing" because of their greater regularity and intensity.

Stages of Childbirth

Labour takes place in four overlapping stages (see Figure 5-1). The *first stage,* the longest, typically lasts 12 hours or more for a woman having her first child. In later births the first stage tends to be shorter. During this stage, regular and increasingly frequent uterine contractions cause the cervix to dilate, or widen.

The *second stage* typically lasts about 1½ hours or less. It begins when the baby's head begins to move through the cervix into the vaginal canal, and it ends when the baby emerges completely from the mother's body. If this stage lasts longer than 2 hours, signaling that the baby needs more help, a doctor may grasp the baby's head with forceps or, more often, use vacuum extraction with a suction cup to pull it out of the mother's body (Curtin & Park, 1999). At the end of this stage, the baby is born; but it is still attached to the placenta in the mother's body by the umbilical cord, which must be cut and clamped.

Checkpoint ✓

Can you . . .

✔ Identify at least three ways in which childbirth has changed in Europe and North America?

✔ Give reasons for the reduction in risks of pregnancy and childbirth?

Guidepost 2

How does labour begin, and what happens during each of the four stages of childbirth?

parturition Process of uterine, cervical, and other changes, usually lasting about two weeks, preceding childbirth

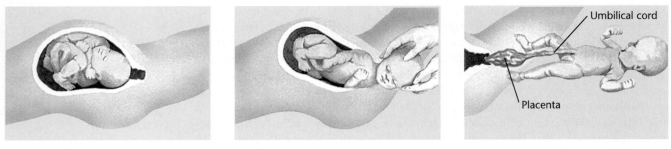

(a) First stage   *(b)* Second stage   *(c)* Third stage

Figure 5-1

The first three stages of childbirth. *(a)* During the first stage of labour, a series of stronger and stronger contractions dilates the cervix, the opening to the mother's womb. *(b)* During the second stage, the baby's head moves down the birth canal and emerges from the vagina. *(c)* During the brief third stage, the placenta and umbilical cord are expelled from the womb. Then the cord is cut. During the fourth stage, recovery from delivery (not shown), the mother's uterus contracts.

Source: Adapted from Lagercrantz & Slotkin, 1986.

electronic fetal monitoring
Mechanical monitoring of fetal heartbeat during labour and delivery

During the *third stage,* which lasts about 5 to 30 minutes, the placenta and the remainder of the umbilical cord are expelled from the mother. The couple of hours after delivery constitute the *fourth stage,* when the mother rests in bed while her recovery is monitored.

Electronic fetal monitoring is often used to track the fetus's heartbeat during labour and delivery. The procedure is intended to detect a lack of oxygen, which may lead to brain damage. It can provide valuable information in high-risk deliveries, including those in which the fetus is very small or seems to be in distress. Yet monitoring has drawbacks when used routinely in low-risk pregnancies. It is costly; it restricts the mother's movements during labour; and, most important, it has an extremely high "false positive" rate, suggesting that fetuses are in trouble when they are not. Such warnings may prompt doctors to deliver by the riskier Caesarean method (described in the next section) rather than vaginally (Nelson, Dambrosia, Ting, & Grether, 1996).

Guidepost 3

What alternative methods and settings of delivery are available today?

Caesarean delivery Delivery of a baby by surgical removal from the uterus

Methods of Delivery

The primary concern in choosing a method for delivering a baby is the safety of both mother and baby. Second is the mother's comfort.

Vaginal versus Caesarean Delivery

The normal method of childbirth, described above, is vaginal delivery. **Caesarean delivery** is a surgical procedure to remove the baby from the uterus by cutting through the abdomen. In 1997–1998, 19 per cent of Canadian births occurred this way, as compared with only 5 per cent in the late 1960s (Canadian Perinatal Surveillance System, 2000; Guyer et al., 1999).

The operation is commonly performed when labour progresses too slowly, when the fetus seems to be in trouble, or when the mother is bleeding vaginally. Often a Caesarean is needed when the fetus is in the breech position (feet first) or in the transverse position (lying crosswise in the uterus), or when its head is too big to pass through the mother's pelvis. Surgical deliveries are more likely when the birth involves a first baby, a large baby, or an older mother. Mothers aged 40 and older are more than twice as likely to have Caesarean deliveries as teenage mothers. Thus the increase in Caesarean rates since 1970 is in part a reflection of a proportional increase in first births, a rise in average birth weight, and a trend toward later childbirth (Guyer et al., 1999; Parrish, Holt, Easterling, Connell, & LeGerfo, 1994). Other suggested explanations include increased used of electronic fetal monitoring, physicians' fear of malpractice litigation, and the desire to avoid a difficult labour (Sachs, Kobelin, Castro, & Frigoletto, 1999).

Caesarean birthrates in Canada are among the highest in the world, but rising rates in European countries during the past decade have narrowed the gap (Notzon, 1990; Sachs et al., 1999). Despite efforts to decrease the rate of Caesarean birth, has remained steady over the past 15 years, as has the percentage of vaginal births after a previous Caesarean

(Canadian Perinatal Surveillance System, 2000). There is growing belief that the Caesarean delivery is unnecessary or harmful in many cases (Curtin & Park, 1999). About 4 percent of Caesareans result in serious complications, such as bleeding and infections (Nelson et al., 1996). For the baby, there may be an important risk in bypassing the struggle to be born, which apparently stimulates the production of stress hormones that may aid in the adjustment to life outside the womb (Lagercrantz & Slotkin, 1986).

Still, some physicians argue that efforts to push for a further reduction in Caesarean deliveries—through greater reliance on operative vaginal deliveries (use of forceps or suction) and encouragement of vaginal delivery for women who have had previous Caesarean deliveries—may be misguided. Although these procedures are fairly safe, they do carry risks, which must be weighed against the risks of Caesarean delivery (Sachs et al., 1999). The greatest risk is to women whose labour is unsuccessful and who therefore must undergo a Caesarean after all (McMahon, Luther, Bowes, & Olshan, 1996). The chances of brain hemorrhage, for example, are higher either in an operative vaginal delivery or in a Caesarean undertaken after labour has begun than in a normal vaginal delivery or a Caesarean done before labour, suggesting that the risk is from abnormal labour (Towner, Castro, Eby-Wilkens, & Gilbert, 1999). Perhaps these considerations figure in the 8 per cent increase since 1994 in Caesarean births after previous Caesarean delivery (Canadian Perinatal Surveillance System, 2000).

Medicated versus Unmedicated Delivery

In the mid-19th century, Queen Victoria became the first woman in history to be put to sleep during delivery, that of her eighth child. Sedation with ether or chloroform became common practice as more births took place in hospitals (Fontanel & d'Harcourt, 1997).

In North America, the use of pain relief was controversial at first. Some of the arguments had to do with its safety for mother and baby. More commonly, doctors argued that pain in childbirth was "part of the curse of Eve, and mere mortals should not try to eliminate it" or that it "strengthened the love of a mother for her child" (Scholten, 1985, p. 104). Early forms of relief included the use of hyoscine, or "twilight sleep," which erased the memory of the delivery rather than relieve pain, and general anaesthetic (Arnup, 1994).

Today general anaesthesia, which renders the woman completely unconscious, is rarely used, even in Caesarean births. The woman is given local anaesthesia if she wants and needs it, but she can see and participate in the birth and can hold her newborn immediately afterward. Regional (local) anaesthesia blocks the nerve pathways that would carry the sensation of pain to the brain, or the mother can receive a relaxing analgesic (pain killer). All these drugs pass through the placenta to enter the fetal blood supply and tissues, and thus may pose dangers to the baby.

Alternative methods of childbirth were developed to minimize the use of drugs while maximizing both parents' active involvement. In 1914 a British physician, Grantly Dick-Read, suggested that pain in childbirth was caused mostly by fear. To eliminate fear, he advocated **natural childbirth:** educating women about the physiology of reproduction and training them in physical fitness and in breathing and relaxation during labour and delivery. By mid-century, Dr. Fernand Lamaze was using the **prepared childbirth** method. This technique substitutes voluntary, or learned, physical responses to the sensations of uterine contractions for the old responses of fear and pain.

In the Lamaze method, a woman learns about the anatomy and physiology of childbirth. She is trained to pant or breathe rapidly "in sync" with the contractions and to concentrate on other sensations. She learns to relax her muscles as a conditioned response to the voice of her "coach" (usually the father or a friend), who attends classes with her, takes part in the delivery, and helps with the exercises.

Advocates of natural methods argue that use of drugs poses risks for babies and deprives mothers of what can be an empowering and transforming experience. In some early studies, infants appeared to show immediate ill effects of obstetric medication in poorer motor and physiologic responses (A. D. Murray, Dolby, Nation, & Thomas, 1981) and, through the first year, in slower motor development (Brackbill & Broman, 1979). However, later research suggested that medicated delivery may *not* do measurable harm. When babies born to medicated and non-medicated mothers were compared on strength, tactile

natural childbirth Method of childbirth that seeks to prevent pain by eliminating the mother's fear through education about the physiology of reproduction and training in breathing and relaxation during delivery

prepared childbirth Method of childbirth that uses instruction, breathing exercises, and social support to induce controlled physical responses to uterine contractions and reduce fear and pain

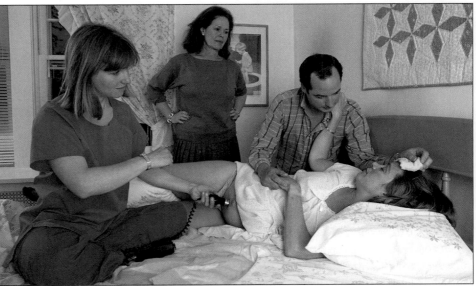

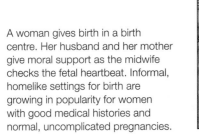

A woman gives birth in a birth centre. Her husband and her mother give moral support as the midwife checks the fetal heartbeat. Informal, homelike settings for birth are growing in popularity for women with good medical histories and normal, uncomplicated pregnancies.

sensitivity, activity, irritability, and sleep patterns, no evidence of any drug effect appeared (Kraemer, Korner, Anders, Jacklin, & Dimiceli, 1985).

Improvements in medicated delivery during the past two decades have led more mothers to choose pain relief. Spinal or epidural injections have become increasingly common as physicians have found effective ways to relieve pain with smaller doses of medication (Hawkins, 1999). "Walking epidurals" enable a woman to feel sensations, move her legs, and fully participate in the birth. In a recent analysis of 10 studies involving 2,369 births in Europe, the United States, and Canada, women who had regional injections (epidurals) enjoyed more effective pain relief—but longer labour—than women who had narcotic injections, and their babies tended to arrive in healthier condition (Halpern, Leighton, Ohlsson, Barrett, & Rice, 1998).

Settings and Attendants for Childbirth

Settings and attendants for childbirth tend to reflect the overall cultural system. A Mayan woman in Yucatan gives birth in the hammock in which she sleeps every night; the father-to-be is expected to be present, along with the midwife. To evade evil spirits, mother and child remain at home for a week (Jordan, 1993). By contrast, among the Ngoni in East Africa, men are excluded from the event. In rural Thailand, a new mother generally resumes normal activity within a few hours after giving birth (Broude, 1995; Gardiner, Mutter, & Kosmitzki, 1998).

In Canada, about 99 per cent of babies are born in hospitals; 96 per cent are attended by physicians and 4 per cent by midwives. Most midwives are registered nurses with special training in midwifery; some have been trained by apprenticeship. A midwife may or may not work under a doctor's direction. In Canada during the 1990s, midwives attained legal status in Ontario, Alberta, British Columbia, Quebec, and Manitoba. However, their status in provincial health care plans varies from province to province. The trend is moving towards provincially funded independent midwives working in all settings—a significant shift from earlier decades in which midwives had no legal status in Canada. In traditional Aboriginal practices, the midwife played a prominent role.

Women using nurse-midwives rather than doctors for low-risk hospital births tend to have equally good outcomes with less anaesthesia. They are less likely to need episiotomies (incisions to enlarge the vaginal opening before birth), to have labour induced, or to have Caesarean deliveries (Rosenblatt et al., 1997). Of course, these results may not be due to something the midwives did or did not do; rather, women who choose midwives may be more likely to take care of themselves during pregnancy, increasing their chances of normal delivery.

As safety in childbirth has become more assured, some women are opting for the more intimate, personal experience of home birth, which can involve the whole family. A home

What's your view

- If you or your partner were expecting a baby, and the pregnancy seemed to be going smoothly, would you prefer (a) medicated or non-medicated delivery, (b) hospital, birth centre, or home birth, and (c) attendance by a physician or midwife? Give reasons. If you are a man, would you choose to be present at the birth? If you are a woman, would you want your partner present?

birth is usually attended by a nurse-midwife, with the resources of medical science close at hand. Studies suggest that home births can be at least as safe as—and much less expensive than—hospital births in low-risk deliveries attended by skilled practitioners (Anderson & Anderson, 1999; Durand, 1992; Korte & Scaer, 1984).

In recent years, many hospitals have sought to humanize childbirth by establishing homelike birth centres, where labour and delivery can take place under soft lights while the father or other companion stays with the mother. Many hospitals also have rooming-in policies, which allow babies to stay in the mother's room much or all of the time. The average length of stay in the hospital in Canada decreased from 5 days in 1984 to 3 days in 1994 (Wen, Liu, Marcoux, & Fowlwer, 1998).

Freestanding birth centres generally offer prenatal care and are staffed principally by nurse-midwives, with one or more physicians and nurse-assistants. Designed for low-risk births with return home the same day, they appear to be a safe alternative to hospital delivery (Guyer, Strobino, Ventura, & Singh, 1995). A study of attitudes by Canadian women to alternative birthplaces showed that 53 per cent of expectant mothers prefer the traditional hospital caseroom, 29 per cent preferring a hospital birthing room, 15 per cent a birth centre, and 3 per cent a home birth (Soderstrom, Stewart, Kaitell, & Chamberlain, 1990).

In many traditional cultures, childbearing women are attended by a *doula* (a word derived from Ancient Greek for the most important female servant). Today, a doula can furnish emotional support and, unlike a doctor, can stay at a woman's bedside throughout labour. In Canada, doulas (who often take special training) attend only 1 per cent of births; they are, however, gaining wider acceptance (Gilbert, 1998).

In 11 randomized, controlled studies, women attended by doulas had shorter labour, less anaesthesia, and fewer forceps and Caesarean deliveries than mothers who had not had doulas. The benefits of the father's presence during labour and delivery were not as great. In one such study, 6 weeks after giving birth, mothers who had had doulas were more likely to be breast-feeding and reported higher self-esteem, less depression, and a more positive view of their babies and their own caregiving abilities (Klaus & Kennell, 1997). Perhaps, having had easier births, the doula-attended women recovered more quickly and felt more able to cope with mothering; or the emotional nurturing provided by the doulas may have served as a model for them. These findings remind us that social and psychological factors can have profound effects even on such a basic biological process as childbirth.

Checkpoint ✔

Can you . . .

✔ Describe the four stages of vaginal childbirth?

✔ Discuss the uses and disadvantages of Caesarean births and electronic fetal monitoring?

✔ Compare medicated delivery, natural childbirth, and prepared childbirth?

✔ Weigh the comparative advantages of various types of settings and attendants for childbirth?

The Newborn Baby

A newborn baby, or **neonate,** is, in an extreme sense, a survivor. After struggling through a difficult passage, the newcomer is faced with many more challenges. A baby must start to breathe, eat, adapt to the climate, and respond to confusing surroundings—a mighty challenge for someone who weighs but a few kilograms and whose organ systems are not fully mature. As we'll see, most infants arrive with systems ready to meet that challenge.

The first 4 weeks of life, the **neonatal period,** is a time of transition from the uterus, where a fetus is supported entirely by the mother, to an independent existence. What are the physical characteristics of newborn babies, and how are they equipped for this crucial transition?

Size and Appearance

An average newborn in Canada is about 50 cm long and weighs about 3.5 kg. At birth, 92 per cent of full-term babies weigh between 2.5 and 5 kg and are between 45 and 55 cm long. Boys tend to be slightly longer and heavier than girls, and a firstborn child is likely to weigh less at birth than laterborns.

In their first few days, neonates lose as much as 10 per cent of their body weight, primarily because of a loss of fluids. They begin to gain weight again at about the fifth day and are generally back to birth weight by the 10th to the 14th day.

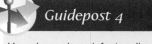
Guidepost 4

How do newborn infants adjust to life outside the womb?

neonate Newborn baby, up to 4 weeks old

neonatal period First 4 weeks of life, a time of transition from intrauterine dependency to independent existence

Table 5-1	A Comparison of Prenatal and Postnatal Life	
Characteristic	**Prenatal Life**	**Postnatal Life**
Environment	Amniotic fluid	Air
Temperature	Relatively constant	Fluctuates with atmosphere
Stimulation	Minimal	All senses stimulated
Nutrition	Dependent on mother's blood	Dependent on external food and functioning of digestive system
Oxygen supply	Passed from maternal bloodstream through the placenta	Passed from neonate's lungs to pulmonary blood vessels
Metabolic elimination	Passed into maternal bloodstream through the placenta	Discharged by skin, kidneys, lungs, and gastrointestinal tract

Source: Timiras, 1972, p. 174.

New babies have distinctive features, including a large head (a quarter of the body length) and a receding chin (which makes it easier to nurse). At first, a neonate's head may be long and misshapen because of the "moulding" that eased its passage through the mother's pelvis. This temporary shaping was possible because an infant's skull bones are not yet fused; they will not be completely joined for 18 months. The places on the head where the bones have not yet grown together—the soft spots, or **fontanels**—are covered by a tough membrane; they will close over within the first month of life. Since the cartilage in the baby's nose also is malleable, the trip through the birth canal may leave the nose looking misshapen for a few days.

Many newborns have a pinkish cast; their skin is so thin that it barely covers the capillaries through which blood flows. During the first few days, some neonates are very hairy because some of the **lanugo,** a fuzzy prenatal hair, has not yet fallen off. All new babies are covered with **vernix caseosa** ("cheesy varnish"), an oily protection against infection that dries within the first few days.

Body Systems

The newborn's need to survive puts a host of new demands on the body systems. Before birth, blood circulation, breathing, nourishment, elimination of waste, and temperature regulation were accomplished through the mother's body. After birth, babies must do all of this themselves (see Table 5-1).

The fetus and mother have separate circulatory systems and separate heartbeats; the fetus's blood is cleansed through the umbilical cord, which carries "used" blood to the placenta and returns a fresh supply. After birth, the baby's circulatory system must operate on its own. A neonate's heartbeat is fast and irregular, and blood pressure does not stabilize until about the 10th day of life.

The fetus gets oxygen through the umbilical cord, which also carries away carbon dioxide. A newborn needs much more oxygen than before and must now get it alone. Most babies start to breathe as soon as they are exposed to air. If breathing has not begun within about 5 minutes, the baby may suffer permanent brain injury caused by **anoxia,** lack of oxygen. Because infants' lungs have only one-tenth as many air sacs as adults' do, infants (especially those born prematurely) are susceptible to respiratory problems.

In the uterus, the fetus relies on the umbilical cord to bring food from the mother and to carry fetal body wastes away. At birth, babies have a strong sucking reflex to take in milk, and their own gastrointestinal secretions to digest it. During the first few days infants secrete **meconium,** a stringy, greenish-black waste matter formed in the fetal intestinal tract. When the bowels and bladder are full, the sphincter muscles open automatically; a baby will not be able to control these muscles for many months.

Three or four days after birth, about half of all babies (and a larger proportion of babies born prematurely) develop **neonatal jaundice:** their skin and eyeballs look yellow. This kind of jaundice is caused by the immaturity of the liver. Usually it is not serious, does not need treatment, and has no long-term effects. More severe jaundice is treated by putting the baby under fluorescent lights and sometimes by exchange transfusion of the

fontanels Soft spots on head of young infant

lanugo Fuzzy prenatal body hair, which drops off within a few days after birth

vernix caseosa Oily substance on a neonate's skin that protects against infection

anoxia Lack of oxygen, which may cause brain damage

meconium Fetal waste, excreted during the first few days after birth

neonatal jaundice Condition, in many newborn babies, caused by immaturity of liver and evidenced by yellowish appearance; can cause brain damage if not treated promptly

Table 5-2	Apgar Scale		
Sign*	0	1	2
Appearance (colour)	Blue, pale	Body pink, extremities blue	Entirely pink
Pulse (heart rate)	Absent	Slow (below 100)	Rapid (over 100)
Grimace (reflex irritability)	No response	Grimace	Coughing, sneezing, crying
Activity (muscle tone)	Limp	Weak, inactive	Strong, active
Respiration (breathing)	Absent	Irregular, slow	Good, crying

*Each sign is rated in terms of absence or presence from 0 to 2; highest overall score is 10.

Source: Adapted from V. Apgar, 1953.

baby's blood. Severe jaundice that is not monitored and treated promptly may result in brain damage.

The layers of fat that develop during the last two months of fetal life enable healthy full-term infants to keep their body temperature constant after birth despite changes in air temperature. Newborn babies also maintain body temperature by increasing their activity when air temperature drops.

Is the Baby Healthy?

Although the great majority of births result in normal, healthy babies, some do not. How can we tell whether a newborn is at risk? What complications of birth can cause damage, and what are the long-term prospects for babies with complicated births?

Medical and Behavioural Assessment

The first few minutes, days, and weeks after birth are crucial for development. It is important to know as soon as possible whether a baby has any problem that needs special care.

The Apgar Scale

One minute after delivery, and then again 5 minutes after birth, most babies are assessed using the **Apgar scale** (see Table 5-2). Its name, after its developer, Virginia Apgar (1953), helps us remember its five subtests: *a*ppearance (colour), *p*ulse (heart rate), *g*rimace (reflex irritability), *a*ctivity (muscle tone), and *r*espiration (breathing). The newborn is rated 0, 1, or 2 on each measure, for a maximum score of 10. A 5-minute score of 7 to 10 indicates that the baby is in good to excellent condition (Ventura et al., 1998). A score below 7 means the baby needs help to establish breathing; a score below 4 means the baby needs immediate lifesaving treatment. If resuscitation is successful, bringing the baby's score to 4 or more, no long-term damage is likely to result (AAP Committee on Fetus and Newborn and American College of Obstetricians and Gynecologists [ACOG] Committee on Obstetric Practice, 1996; Society of Obstetricians and Gynaecologists of Canada [SOGC], 1998; 1996a).

An infant's score may be affected by the amount of medication the mother received; or neurological or cardiorespiratory conditions may interfere with one or more vital signs. Premature infants (those born before 37 weeks of gestation) may score low because of physiological immaturity. Scores of 0 to 3 at 10, 15, and 20 minutes after birth are increasingly associated with cerebral palsy (muscular impairment due to brain damage before or during birth) or other future neurological problems; such conditions may or may not be caused by oxygen deprivation (ACOG, 1996; SOGC, 1998; 1996). Low Apgar scores are also more likely with repeated Caesarean section deliveries (Burt, Vaughan, & Daling, 1988).

Checkpoint ✔

Can you . . .

✔ Describe the normal size and appearance of a newborn and name several changes that occur within the first few days?

✔ Compare four fetal and neonatal body systems?

✔ Identify two dangerous conditions that can appear soon after birth?

Guidepost 5

How can we tell whether a new baby is healthy and is developing normally?

Apgar scale Standard measurement of a newborn's condition; it assesses appearance, *p*ulse, *g*rimace, *a*ctivity, and *r*espiration

Assessing Neurological Status: The Brazelton Scale

The **Brazelton Neonatal Behavioural Assessment Scale (NBAS)** is used to assess neonates' responsiveness to their physical and social environment, to identify problems in neurological functioning, and to predict future development. The test is named for its designer, T. Berry Brazelton (1973, 1984; Brazelton & Nugent, 1995). It assesses *motor organization* as shown by such behaviours as activity level and the ability to bring a hand to the mouth; *reflexes; state changes,* such as irritability, excitability, and ability to quiet down after being upset; *attention and interactive capacities,* as shown by general alertness and response to visual and auditory stimuli; and indications of *central nervous system instability,* such as tremors and changes in skin colour. The NBAS takes about 30 minutes, and scores are based on a baby's best performance.

Neonatal Screening for Medical Conditions

Children who inherit the enzyme disorder phenylketonuria, or PKU (refer back to Table 3-1), will become mentally retarded unless they are fed a special diet beginning in the first 3 to 6 weeks of life. Screening tests that can be administered soon after birth can often discover such correctable defects.

Routine screening of all newborn babies for such rare conditions as PKU (1 case in 10,000 to 25,000 births), congenital hypothyroidism (1 in 3,600 to 5,000), galactosemia (1 in 60,000 to 80,000), and other, even rarer disorders is expensive. Yet the cost of testing thousands of newborns to detect one case of a rare disease may be less than the cost of caring for one mentally retarded person for a lifetime. All provinces require routine screening for PKU and congenital hypothyroidism; provinces vary on requirements for other screening tests (Society of Obstetricians and Gynaecologists of Canada, 1996b). However, there is some risk in doing these tests. They can generate false-positive results, suggesting that there is a problem when there is not, and triggering anxiety and costly, unnecessary treatment.

Complications of Childbirth

For a small minority of babies, the passage through the birth canal is a particularly harrowing journey. About 2 newborns in 1,000 are injured in the process (Wegman, 1994). **Birth trauma** (injury sustained at the time of birth) may be caused by anoxia (oxygen deprivation), diseases or infections, or physical injury. Sometimes the trauma leaves permanent brain damage, causing mental retardation, behaviour problems, or even death. A larger proportion of infants are born very small or remain in the womb too long—complications that can impair their chances of survival and well-being.

Low Birth Weight

In 1999, 5.6 per cent of babies born in Canada had **low birth weight**—they weighed less than 2,500 g at birth. Very-low-birth weight babies, who weigh less than 1,500 g, accounted for 1.1 per cent of births in 1998. Low birth weight, which has been trending downward slightly since the late 1980s (Canadian Perinatal Health Report, 2000; Canadian Institute of Child Health [CICH], 2000), contributes to perinatal illnesses, the leading cause of infant death in Canada. The next leading cause of death in Canadian infants is birth defects (CICH, 2000). Preventing and treating low birth weight can increase the number of babies who survive the first year of life.

Low–birth weight babies fall into two categories: *preterm* and *small for gestational age.* Babies born before completing the 37th week of gestation are called **preterm (premature) infants;** they may or may not be the appropriate size for their gestational age. The increase in preterm births may in part reflect the rise in multiple births from the use of new reproductive technology, in Caesarean deliveries, induced labour, and births to older women, ages 35 and up (Kramer et al., 1998). **Small-for-gestational age infants,** who may or may not be preterm, weigh less than 90 per cent of all babies of the same gestational age. Their small size is generally the result of inadequate prenatal nutrition, which slows fetal growth. Much of the increased prevalence of low birth weight is attributed to the rise in multiple births.

Who Is Likely to Have a Low–Birth Weight Baby? Factors increasing the likelihood that a woman will have an underweight baby include: (1) *demographic and socio-economic factors,* such as being under age 17 or over 40, poor, unmarried, or undereducated; (2) *medical factors predating the pregnancy,* such as having no children or more than four, being short or thin, having had previous low–birth weight infants or multiple miscarriages, having had low birth weight herself, or having genital or urinary abnormalities or chronic hypertension; (3) *prenatal behavioural and environmental factors,* such as poor nutrition, inadequate prenatal care, smoking, use of alcohol or other drugs, or exposure to stress, abuse, high altitude, or toxic substances; and (4) *medical conditions associated with the pregnancy,* such as vaginal bleeding, infections, high or low blood pressure, anemia, too little weight gain, and having last given birth less than 6 months or 10 or more years before conception (S. S. Brown, 1985; Chomitz, Cheung, & Lieberman, 1995; Murphy, Schei, Myhr, & Du Mort, 2001; Nathanielsz, 1995; Shiono & Behrman, 1995; Wegman, 1992; Zhu, Rolfs, Nangle, & Horan, 1999). The safest interval between pregnancies is 18 to 23 months (Zhu et al., 1999).

Many of these factors are interrelated, and socio-economic status cuts across many of them. Teenagers' higher risk of having low–birth weight babies may stem more from malnutrition and inadequate prenatal care than from age, since teenagers who become pregnant are likely to be poor. Federal and provincial programs are designed to prevent low birth weight by providing prenatal care and nutrition for pregnant women who are in risk groups such as low socio-economic status (CICH, 2000). At least one-fifth of all low birth weights are attributed to smoking. Even before they become pregnant, women can reduce their chances of having a low–birth weight baby by eating well, not smoking or using drugs, drinking little or no alcohol, and getting good medical care (Chomitz et al., 1995; Shiono & Behrman, 1995).

Although Canada is more successful than most countries in *saving* low–birth weight babies, the rate of such births to Canadian women is higher than in many European nations, but not as high as in the United States or the United Kingdom (CICH, 2000; UNICEF, 1996). One of the factors thought to contribute to the incidence of low–birth weight children is the dramatic increase in multiple births in Canada, associated with the use of new reproductive technologies like fertility drugs and in vitro fertilization. In 1976 the multiple birth rate in Canada was 936 per 100,000 births; by 1996, the number climbed to 2469. About half of multiple births are preterm compared to 6 per cent of singleton births (CICH, 2000).

Definitions for low and high birth weight might be inappropriate for some ethnic groups in Canada. A study of first-year growth rates of Canadian children of Chinese descent indicated that although their length growth was similar to the national average, their weight was below average, despite diets consistent with Canadian Paediatric Society guidelines (Sit, Yeung, He, & Anderson, 2001). On the other hand, the birth weights of Aboriginal Canadian infants are higher than the national average, which might reflect a genetic predisposition to having heavier babies (CICH, 2000).

A number of measures, such as enhanced prenatal care, nutritional interventions, and administration of drugs, bed rest, and hydration for women who go into early labour, have been tried, without success, to stem the growing tide of premature births. As many as 80 per cent of these births are associated with uterine infection, which does not seem to respond to antibiotics once labour has begun. However, early antibiotic treatment of women with urinary or vaginal infections may be a promising approach (Goldenberg & Rouse, 1998).

Immediate Treatment and Outcomes The most pressing fear for very small babies is that they will die in infancy. Because their immune systems are not fully developed, they are especially vulnerable to infection. Their nervous systems may not be mature enough for them to perform functions basic to survival, such as sucking, and they may need to be fed intravenously (through the veins). Because they do not have enough fat to insulate them and to generate heat, it is hard for them to stay warm. Respiratory distress syndrome, also called *hyaline membrane disease,* is common. Low Apgar scores in preterm newborns are a strong indication of heightened risk and of the need for intensive care (Weinberger et al., 2000).

Many very small preterm babies lack surfactant, an essential lung-coating substance that keeps air sacs from collapsing; they may breathe irregularly or stop breathing altogether. Administering surfactant to high-risk preterm newborns, along with other medical interventions, has dramatically increased the survival rate of infants who weigh as little as 500 g, enabling four out of five in this lowest-weight group to survive (Corbet et al., 1995; Goldenberg & Rouse, 1998; Horbar et al., 1993). However, these infants are likely to be in poor health and to have neurological deficits—at 20 months, a 20 per cent rate of mental retardation and 10 per cent likelihood of cerebral palsy (Hack, Friedman, & Fanaroff, 1996).

A low–birth weight baby is placed in an *incubator* (an antiseptic, temperature-controlled crib) and fed through tubes. To counteract the sensory impoverishment of life in an incubator, hospital workers and parents are encouraged to give these small babies special handling. Gentle massage seems to foster growth, weight gain, motor activity, alertness, and behavioural organization, as assessed by the Brazelton NBAS (T. M. Field, 1986, 1998b; Schanberg & Field, 1987). A combination of massage and lullabies can shorten the hospital stay (Standley, 1998).

Long-term Outcomes Even if low–birth weight babies survive the dangerous early days, as more and more are doing today, there is concern about their development. Small-for-gestational age infants are more likely to be neurologically and cognitively impaired than equally premature infants whose weight was appropriate for their gestational age (McCarton, Wallace, Divon, & Vaughan, 1996). A longitudinal study of 1,064 full-term British infants who were small-for-gestational-age found small but significant deficits in academic achievement at ages 5, 10, and 16 as compared with children born during the same week with normal birth weight. At age 26, this group had lower incomes and professional attainments than the control group and were physically shorter. Still, they were just as likely to have completed their education and to be employed, married, and satisfied with life (Strauss, 2000).

Babies of *very* low birth weight have a less promising prognosis. At school age, those who weighed the least at birth have the most behavioural, social, attention, and language problems (Klebanov, Brooks-Gunn, & McCormick, 1994). Jakobson, Frisk, Knight, Downie, & White (2001) found neurological differences, in very low birth weight children compared to children who had average birth weight, that were related to underdeveloped fine motor skills and reading difficulties. As teenagers, the less they weighed at birth, the lower their IQs and achievement test scores and the more likely they are to require special education or to repeat a grade (Saigal, Hoult, Streiner, Stoskopf, & Rosenbaum, 2000).

Birth weight alone does not necessarily determine the outcome. Boys are more likely than girls to have childhood problems that interfere with everyday activities, and to need special education or other special help (Verloove-Vanhorick et al., 1994). Gender and other factors, such as family income and the mother's educational level and marital status, seem to play a major role in whether or not a low–birth weight child will be emotionally handicapped or will suffer a speech and language impairment. Demographic factors also play some part in the prevalence of specific learning disabilities and in mild mental handicaps. Only the most severe educational disabilities are affected solely or primarily by birth complications; milder educational problems are more likely to be influenced by socio-demographic factors (Resnick et al., 1998).

Canadian research on long-term effects found that a large percentage of extremely low–birth weight (ELBW) children experience developmental coordination disorder (DCD) by middle childhood (51 per cent of their sample, compared to up to 9 per cent of the normal birth weight population) (Holsti, Grunau, & Whitfield, 2002). These children experienced impaired motor coordination, lower academic achievement, particularly mathematics, and lower intelligence scores on measures involving motor coordination, compared with ELBW children who did not develop DCD. ELBW children also tend to score lower-than-normal birth weight chidren on language measures (Grunau, Kearney, & Whitfield, 1990). Grunau and colleagues also examined long-term effects of ELBW on pain perception in childhood. They found that ELBW children's parents, when asked to rate their child's pain sensitivity at 18 months, reported lower pain sensitivity than did parents of normal birth weight children. They found that the child's temperament affected rated pain sensitivity only in full birth-weight children, and that parental style did not affect the ratings of pain sensitivity (Grunau, Whitfield, & Petrie, 1994).

What's your view ?

- In view of the long-term outlook for babies of very low birth weight and the expense involved in helping them survive, how much of society's resources should be put into rescuing these babies?

Postmaturity

Close to 9 per cent of pregnant women have not gone into labour 2 weeks after the due date, or 42 weeks after the last menstrual period (Ventura et al., 1998). At that point, a baby is considered **postmature.** Postmature babies tend to be long and thin, because they have kept growing in the womb but have had an insufficient blood supply toward the end of gestation. Possibly because the placenta has aged and become less efficient, it may provide less oxygen. The baby's greater size also complicates labour: The mother has to deliver a baby the size of a normal 1-month-old.

Since postmature fetuses are at risk of brain damage or even death, doctors sometimes induce labour with drugs or perform Caesarean deliveries. However, if the due date has been miscalculated, a baby who is actually premature may be delivered. To help make the decision, doctors monitor the baby's status with ultrasound to see whether the heart rate speeds up when the fetus moves; if not, the baby may be short of oxygen. Another test involves examining the volume of amniotic fluid; a low level may mean the baby is not getting enough food.

Stillbirth

A stillbirth is a tragic union of opposites—birth and death. Sometimes fetal death is diagnosed prenatally; in other cases, as with Elvis Presley's twin brother, the baby's death is discovered during labour or delivery.

The number of third-trimester stillbirths in Canada has been substantially reduced during the past two decades. This improvement may be due to electronic fetal monitoring, ultrasound, and other measures to identify fetuses at risk for pre-eclampsia (a toxic condition) or restricted growth. Fetuses believed to have these problems can then be delivered prematurely (Goldenberg & Rouse, 1998).

How do parents cope with the loss of a child they never, or barely, got to know? Fathers and mothers tend to react somewhat differently. Men tend to worry, ignore the situation, or seek social support, whereas women are more likely to engage in wishful thinking, turn to spiritual support, or seek out others who have had a similar loss (McGreal, Evans, & Burrows, 1997). One study followed 127 young adults who had lost an infant through stillbirth, neonatal death, or sudden infant death syndrome (SIDS) for 15 months. Those whose adjustment was most positive tended to be better educated, and the women tended to have more friends in whom they could confide (Murray & Terry, 1999).

Checkpoint ✔

Can you . . .

✔ Discuss the risk factors, treatment, and outcomes for low–birth weight babies?

✔ Explain the risks of postmaturity?

✔ Discuss the coping responses of parents who have experienced stillbirth?

Can a Supportive Environment Overcome Effects of Birth Complications?

A child's prospects for overcoming the early disadvantage of low birth weight depend on several interacting factors. One is the family's socio-economic circumstances (Aylward, Pfeiffer, Wright, & Verhulst, 1989; McGauhey, Starfield, Alexander, & Ensminger, 1991; Ross, Lipper, & Auld, 1991). Another is the quality of the early environment.

The Infant Health and Development Studies

The socio-cultural context in which babies are born can determine the type of health care they receive. In a cross-national study of low–birth weight infant survivability in Canada, the United States, Australia, and the United Kingdom, results showed that although the United States puts more resources into neonatal intensive care units, it does not have any better mortality rates for low–birth weight children than the other countries, which emphasize prevention of low birth weight through prenatal care (Thompson, Goodman, & Little, 2002).

A large-scale study (Infant Health & Development Program [IHDP], 1990) followed 985 preterm, low–birth weight babies in eight parts of the United States—most of them from poor inner-city families—from birth to age 3. One-third of the heavier (but still low–birth weight) babies and one-third of the lighter ones were randomly assigned to "intervention" groups and the remaining two-thirds in each weight category to "follow-up" groups. The parents of the intervention groups received home visits that provided

Thanks to their own resilience, fully a third of the at-risk children studied by Emmy Werner and her colleagues developed into self-confident, successful adults.

counselling, information about children's health and development, and instruction in children's games and activities; at 1 year, these babies entered an educational daycare program. The children in all four groups received pediatric follow-up services.

When the program stopped, the 3-year-olds in both the lower– and higher–birth weight intervention groups were doing better on cognitive and social measures, were much less likely to show mental retardation, and had fewer behavioural problems than the groups that had received only follow-up (Brooks-Gunn, Klebanov, Liaw, & Spiker, 1993). However, 2 years later, at age 5, the children in the lower–birth weight intervention group no longer held a cognitive edge over the comparison group. Furthermore, having been in the intervention program made no difference in health or behaviour (Brooks-Gunn et al., 1994). By age 8, the cognitive superiority of children in the higher–birth weight intervention group over their counterparts in the follow-up group had dwindled to 4 IQ points; and all four groups had substantially below-average IQs and vocabulary scores (McCarton et al., 1997; McCormick, McCarton, Brooks-Gunn, Belt, & Gross, 1998). It seems, then, that for such an intervention to have lasting effects, it needs to continue beyond age 3.

Studies of the full IHDP sample underline the importance of what goes on in the home. Children who got little parental attention and care were more likely to be undersized and to do poorly on cognitive tests than children from more favourable home environments (Kelleher et al., 1993; McCormick et al., 1998). Those whose cognitive performance stayed high had mothers who scored high themselves on cognitive tests and who were responsive and stimulating. Babies who had more than one risk factor (such as poor neonatal health combined with having a mother who did not receive counselling or was less educated or less responsive) fared the worst (Liaw & Brooks-Gunn, 1993).

The Kauai Study

A longer-term study shows how a favourable environment can counteract effects of low birth weight, birth injuries, and other birth complications. For more than 4 decades, Emmy E. Werner (1987, 1995) and a research team of pediatricians, psychologists, public health workers, and social workers have followed 698 children born in 1955 on the Hawaiian island of Kauai—from the prenatal period through birth, and then into young adulthood. The researchers interviewed the mothers; recorded their personal, family, and reproductive histories; monitored the course of their pregnancies; and interviewed them again when the children were 1, 2, and 10 years old. They also observed the children interacting with their parents at home and gave them aptitude, achievement, and personality tests in elementary and high school. The children's teachers reported on their progress and their behaviour. The young people themselves were interviewed at ages 18 and 30.

Among the children who had suffered problems at or before birth, physical and psychological development was seriously impaired *only* when they grew up in persistently poor environmental circumstances. From toddlerhood on, unless the early damage was so serious as to require institutionalization, those children who had a stable and enriching environment did well (E. E. Werner, 1985, 1987). In fact, they had fewer language, perceptual, emotional, and school problems than children who had *not* experienced unusual stress at birth but who had received little intellectual stimulation or emotional support at home (E. E. Werner, 1989; E. E. Werner et al., 1968). The children who had been exposed to *both* birth-related problems and later stressful experiences showed the worst health problems and the most retarded development (E. E. Werner, 1987).

Given a supportive environment, then, many children can overcome a poor start in life. Even more remarkable is the resilience of children who escape damage despite *multiple* sources of stress. Even when birth complications were combined with such environmental risks as chronic poverty, family discord, divorce, or parents who were mentally ill, many children came through relatively unscathed. Of the 276 children who at age 2 had been identified as having four or more risk factors, two-thirds developed serious learning or behaviour problems by the age of 10 or, by age 18, had become pregnant, gotten in trouble with the law, or become emotionally troubled. Yet by age 30, one-third of these highly at-risk children had managed to become "competent, confident, and caring adults" (E. E. Werner, 1995, p. 82).

Protective factors, which tended to reduce the impact of early stress, fell into three categories: (1) individual attributes that may be largely genetic, such as energy, sociability, and intelligence; (2) affectionate ties with at least one supportive family member, and (3) rewards at school, work, or place of worship that provide a sense of meaning and control over one's life (E. E. Werner, 1987). While the home environment seemed to have the most marked effect in childhood, in adulthood the individuals' own qualities made a greater difference (E. E. Werner, 1995).

These studies underline the need to look at child development in context. They show how biological and environmental influences interact, making resiliency possible even in babies born with serious complications. (Characteristics of resilient children are further discussed in chapter 14.)

Newborns and Their Parents

Birth is a major transition, not only for the baby, but for the parents as well. The mother's body systems have undergone massive physical change. For both mother and father, especially with a first birth, the newcomer in their lives brings insistent demands that challenge their ability to cope and force adjustments in their relationship. Meanwhile, parents (and, perhaps, siblings) are getting acquainted with this newcomer—developing emotional bonds and becoming familiar with the infant's patterns of sleeping, waking, feeding, and activity.

Childbirth and Bonding

How and when does the **caregiver–infant bond**—the close, caring connection between caregiver and newborn—develop? Some researchers studying this topic have followed the ethological approach (introduced in chapter 2), which considers behaviour in human beings, as in animals, to be biologically determined and emphasizes critical, or sensitive, periods for development of certain behaviours.

In one well-known study, Konrad Lorenz (1957) waddled, honked, and flapped his arms—and got newborn ducklings to follow him as they would the mother duck. Lorenz showed that newly hatched ducklings will follow the first moving object they see, whether or not it is a member of their own species. This phenomenon is called **imprinting,** and Lorenz believed that it is automatic and irreversible. Usually, this first attachment is to the mother; but if the natural course of events is disturbed, other attachments (like the one to Lorenz)—or none at all—can form. Imprinting, said Lorenz, is the result of a *predisposition toward learning:* the readiness of an organism's nervous system to acquire certain information during a brief critical period in early life.

Does something similar to imprinting happen between human newborns and their mothers? Apparently not. Research has concluded that, unlike the animals Lorenz studied, a critical period for bonding does *not* exist for human beings (Chess & Thomas, 1982; Klaus & Kennell, 1982; M. E. Lamb, 1983). This finding has relieved the worry and guilt sometimes felt by adoptive parents and parents who had to be separated from their infants after birth.

Fathers, like mothers, form close bonds with their babies soon after birth. The babies contribute simply by doing the things normal babies do: opening their eyes, grasping their fathers' fingers, or moving in their fathers' arms. Fathers who are present at the birth of a child often see the event as a "peak emotional experience" (May & Perrin, 1985), but a man can become emotionally committed to his newborn whether or not he attended the birth (Palkovitz, 1985).

Getting to Know the Baby: States of Arousal and Activity Levels

The bond between parents and infant helps them get to know their baby's needs. Newborns show their individuality, as well as their neurological maturation, through their patterns of sleeping and waking and of activity when awake. Parents show their love for the baby through their sensitivity and responsiveness to these patterns.

protective factors Influences that reduce the impact of early stress and tend to predict positive outcomes

Checkpoint ✔

Can you . . .

✔ Discuss the effectiveness of the home environment and of intervention programs in overcoming effects of low birthweight and other birth complications?

✔ Name three protective factors identified by the Kauai study?

Guidepost 7

How do parents bond with their baby and respond to the baby's patterns of sleep and activity?

caregiver–infant bond The caregiver's feeling of close, caring connection with his or her newborn

imprinting Instinctive form of learning in which, during a critical period in early development, a young animal forms an attachment to the first moving object it sees, usually the mother

Table 5-3	States of Arousal in Infancy			
State	**Eyes**	**Breathing**	**Movements**	**Responsiveness**
Regular sleep	Closed; no eye movement	Regular and slow	None, except for sudden, generalized startles	Cannot be aroused by mild stimuli
Irregular sleep	Closed; occasional rapid eye movements	Irregular	Muscles twitch, but no major movements	Sounds or light bring smiles or grimaces in sleep
Drowsiness	Open or closed	Irregular	Somewhat active	May smile, startle, suck, or have erections in response to stimuli
Alert inactivity	Open	Even	Quiet; may move head, limbs, and trunk while looking around	An interesting environment (with people or things to watch) may initiate or maintain this state.
Waking activity and crying	Open	Irregular	Much activity	External stimuli (such as hunger, cold, pain, being restrained, or being put down) bring about more activity, perhaps starting with soft whimpering and gentle movements and turning into a rhythmic crescendo of crying or kicking, or perhaps beginning and enduring as uncoordinated thrashing and spasmodic screeching.

Source: Adapted from information in Prechtl & Beintema, 1964; P. H. Wolff, 1966.

state of arousal An infant's physiological and behavioural status at a given moment in the periodic daily cycle of wakefulness, sleep, and activity

Babies have an internal "clock," which regulates their daily cycles of eating, sleeping, and elimination, and perhaps even their moods. These periodic cycles of wakefulness, sleep, and activity, which govern an infant's **state of arousal,** or degree of alertness (see Table 5-3), seem to be inborn and highly individual. Newborn babies average about 16 hours of sleep a day, but one may sleep only 11 hours while another sleeps 21 hours (Parmelee, Wenner, & Schulz, 1964). Changes in state are coordinated by multiple areas of the brain and are accompanied by changes in the functioning of virtually all body systems: heart rate and blood flow, breathing, temperature regulation, cerebral metabolism, and the workings of the kidneys, glands, and digestive system (Ingersoll & Thoman, 1999).

Not many adults would want to "sleep like a baby." Most new babies wake up every 2 to 3 hours, day and night. Short stretches of sleep alternate with shorter periods of consciousness, which are devoted mainly to feeding. Newborns have about six to eight sleep periods, which vary between quiet and active sleep. Active sleep is probably the equivalent of rapid eye movement (REM) sleep, which in adults is associated with dreaming. Active sleep appears rhythmically in cycles of about 1 hour and accounts for 50 to 80 per cent of a newborn's total sleep time.

Premature infants tend to be uneven in their state development compared with full-term infants the same age. They are more alert and wakeful, have longer stretches of quiet sleep, and show more REMs in active sleep. On the other hand, their sleep is more fragmented and they have more transitions between sleeping and waking (Ingersoll & Thoman, 1999).

At about 3 months, babies grow more wakeful in the late afternoon and early evening and start to sleep through the night. By 6 months, more than half their sleep occurs at night. By this time, active sleep accounts for only 30 per cent of sleep time, and the length of the cycle becomes more consistent (Coons & Guilleminault, 1982). The amount of REM sleep continues to decrease steadily throughout life.

Cultural variations in feeding practices may affect sleep patterns. Many Canadian parents time the evening feeding so as to encourage nighttime sleep. Mothers in rural Kenya allow their babies to nurse as they please, and their 4-month-olds continue to sleep only 4 hours at a stretch (Broude, 1995).

Parents and caregivers spend a great deal of time and energy trying to change babies' states—mostly by soothing a fussy infant to sleep. Although crying is usually more dis-

Box 5-2 *Comforting a Crying Baby*

All babies cry. It is their only way to let us know they are hungry, uncomfortable, lonely, or unhappy. And since few sounds are as distressing as a baby's cry, parents or other caregivers usually rush to feed or pick up a crying infant. As babies quiet down and fall asleep or gaze about in alert contentment, they may show that their problem has been solved. At other times, the caregiver cannot figure out what the baby wants. The baby keeps crying. It is worth trying to find ways to help: Babies whose cries bring relief seem to become more self-confident, seeing that they can affect their own lives.

In Chapter 7 we discuss several kinds of crying and what the crying may mean. Unusual, persistent crying patterns may be early signs of trouble. For healthy babies who just seem unhappy, the following may help (Eiger & Olds, 1999).

- Hold the baby, perhaps laying the baby on his or her stomach on your chest, to feel your heartbeat and breathing. Or sit with the baby in a comfortable rocking chair.
- Put the baby in a carrier next to your chest and walk around.
- If you are upset, ask someone else to hold the baby; infants sometimes sense and respond to their caregivers' moods.
- Pat or rub the baby's back, in case a bubble of air is causing discomfort.
- Wrap the baby snugly in a small blanket; some infants feel more secure when firmly swaddled from neck to toes, with arms held close to the sides.

- Make the baby warmer or cooler; put on or take off clothing or change the room temperature.
- Give the baby a massage or a warm bath.
- Sing or talk to the baby. Or provide a continuous or rhythmic sound, such as music from the radio, a simulated heartbeat, or background noise from a whirring fan, vacuum cleaner, or other appliance.
- Take the baby out for a ride in a stroller or car seat—at any hour of the day or night. In bad weather, some parents walk around in an enclosed mall; the distraction helps them as well as the baby.
- If someone other than a parent is taking care of the baby, it sometimes helps if the caregiver puts on a robe or a sweater that the mother or father has recently worn so the baby can sense the familiar smell.
- Pick up on the baby's signals.

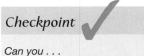

Have you ever tried to soothe a crying baby? What techniques seemed to work best?

Check it out!

For more information on this topic, go to **www.mcgrawhill.ca/college/papalia**.

---

tressing than serious, it is particularly important to quiet low–birth weight babies, because quiet babies maintain their weight better. Steady stimulation is the time-proven way to soothe crying babies: by rocking or walking them, wrapping them snugly, or letting them hear rhythmic sounds (see Box 5-2).

Some new babies are more active than others. These activity levels reflect temperamental differences that continue throughout childhood, and often throughout life. Neonates' unique behaviour patterns elicit varying responses from their caregivers. Adults react very differently to a placid baby and to an excitable one; to an infant they can quiet easily and one who is often inconsolable; to a baby who is often alert and to one who seems uninterested in the surroundings. Babies, in turn, respond to the way their caregivers treat them. This bi-directional influence can have far-reaching effects on what kind of person a baby turns out to be. From the start, children affect their own lives by moulding the environment in which they grow. Babies are also affected by how mothers and fathers feel about being parents, and these feelings in turn may affect and be affected by the marital relationship.

Checkpoint ✔

Can you . . .

✔ Summarize research on bonding between parents and infants?

✔ Describe patterns of sleep, arousal, and activity during the first few months?

How Parenthood Affects a Marriage

Along with excitement, wonder, and awe, most new parents feel some anxiety about the responsibility of caring for a child and the commitment of time and energy it entails and about the feeling of permanence that parenthood imposes on their marriages. Pregnancy and the recovery from childbirth can affect a couple's future sexual relationship, sometimes making it more intimate, sometimes creating barriers.

Marital satisfaction typically declines during the childraising years. In a 10-year longitudinal study of predominantly white couples who married in their late 20s, both husbands and wives reported a sharp decline in satisfaction during the first four years, followed by a plateau and then another decline (Kurdek, 1999).

Guidepost 8

How does parenthood change the parents' relationship with one another?

Of course, this statistical pattern is an average; it is not necessarily true of all couples. One research team followed 128 middle- and working-class couples in their late 20s from the first pregnancy until the child's third birthday. Some marriages got stronger, while others deteriorated, especially in the eyes of the wives. Many spouses loved each other less, became more ambivalent about their relationship, argued more, and communicated less. In these marriages, the partners tended to be younger and less well educated, to earn less money, and to have been married a shorter time. One or both partners tended to have low self-esteem, and husbands were likely to be less sensitive. The mothers who had the hardest time were those whose babies had difficult temperaments. Couples who were most romantic "prebaby" had more problems "postbaby," perhaps because they had unrealistic expectations. Also, women who had planned their pregnancies were unhappier, possibly because they had expected life with a baby to be better than it turned out to be (Belsky & Rovine, 1990).

One problem involves the division of household tasks. If a couple shared these tasks fairly equally before becoming parents, and then, after the birth, the burden shifts to the wife, marital happiness tends to decline, especially for non-traditional wives (Belsky, Lang, & Huston, 1986). Among young Israeli first-time parents, fathers who saw themselves as caring, nurturing, and protecting experienced less decline in marital satisfaction than other fathers and felt better about parenthood. Men who were less involved with their babies, and whose wives were more involved, tended to be more dissatisfied. The mothers who became most dissatisfied with their marriages were those who saw themselves as disorganized and unable to cope with the demands of motherhood (Levy-Shiff, 1994).

Are adoptive parents' experiences different from those of biological parents? Researchers in Israel looked at 104 couples before they became parents, and then again when their babies—half adopted, half biological offspring—were 4 months old (Levy-Shiff, Goldschmidt, & Har-Even, 1991). The adoptive parents reported more positive expectations and more satisfying parenting experiences than did the others. The adoptive parents, who tended to be older and married longer, may have been more mature and resourceful, or they may have appreciated parenthood more when it finally came. Or they may have felt the need to speak positively about parenthood, since they had gone to special lengths to achieve it.

Many elements go into the family relationships that exert a strong influence on a baby's development; and infants themselves exert a strong influence on the people who play the biggest role in their lives. We will see further examples of bi-directional influence in part 3, as we examine physical, cognitive, and psychosocial development in infancy and toddlerhood.

Checkpoint ✔

Can you . . .

✔ Cite at least three factors that can influence a new baby's effect on the parents' marriage?

Summary and Key Terms

How Childbirth Has Changed

Guidepost 1   How have customs surrounding birth changed?

- In Europe, Canada, and the United States, childbirth before the 19th century took place in a manner much like that in some developing countries today. Birth was a female ritual, which occurred at home and was attended by a midwife. Pain relief was minimal, and risks for mother and baby were high.

- The development of the science of obstetrics professionalized childbirth. Births took place in hospitals, attended by physicians. Medical advances dramatically improved safety.

- Today some women again are choosing the "demedicalized" experience of home birth, but with the resources of medical science close at hand.

The Birth Process

Guidepost 2   How does labour begin, and what happens during each of the four stages of childbirth?

- Birth normally occurs after a preparatory period of parturition and consists of four stages: (1) dilation of the cervix; (2) descent and emergence of the baby; (3) expulsion of the umbilical cord and the placenta; (4) contraction of the uterus and recovery of the mother.

- Electronic fetal monitoring is widely used (and may be overused) during labour and delivery. It is intended to detect signs of fetal distress, especially in high-risk births.

parturition (97)   electronic fetal monitoring (98)

Guidepost 3 What alternative methods and settings of delivery are available today?

- Nineteen per cent of births in Canada are by Caesarean delivery—an unnecessarily high rate, according to critics.

- Natural or prepared childbirth can minimize the need for pain-killing drugs and maximize parents' active involvement. Modern epidurals can give effective pain relief with smaller doses of medication than in the past.

- Delivery at home or in birth centres, and attendance by midwives, are alternatives to physician-attended hospital delivery for women with normal, low-risk pregnancies who want to involve family members and make the experience more intimate and personal. The presence of a doula can provide physical benefits as well as emotional support.

  **Caesarean delivery (98)   natural childbirth (99)
  prepared childbirth (99)**

The Newborn Baby

Guidepost 4 How do newborn infants adjust to life outside the womb?

- The neonatal period is a time of transition from intrauterine to extrauterine life. During the first few days, the neonate loses weight and then regains it; the lanugo (prenatal hair) falls off and the protective coating of vernix caseosa dries up. The fontanels (soft spots) in the skull close within the first 18 months.

- At birth, the circulatory, respiratory, gastrointestinal, and temperature regulation systems become independent of the mother's. If a newborn cannot start breathing within about 5 minutes, brain injury may occur.

- Newborns have a strong sucking reflex and secrete meconium from the intestinal tract. They are commonly subject to neonatal jaundice, due to immaturity of the liver.

  **neonate (101)   neonatal period (101)   fontanels (102)
  lanugo (102)   vernix caseosa (102)   anoxia (102)
  meconium (102)   neonatal jaundice (102)**

Is the Baby Healthy?

Guidepost 5 How can we tell whether a new baby is healthy and is developing normally?

- At 1 minute and 5 minutes after birth, a neonate's Apgar score can indicate how well he or she is adjusting to extrauterine life. The Brazelton Neonatal Behavioural Assessment Scale can assess responses to the environment and predict future development.

- Neonatal screening is done for certain rare conditions, such as PKU and congenital hypothyroidism.

  **Apgar scale (103)
  Brazelton Neonatal Behavioural Assessment Scale (NBAS) (104)**

Guidepost 6 What complications of childbirth can endanger newborn babies, and what can be done to improve the chances of a positive outcome?

- A small minority of infants suffer lasting effects of birth trauma. Other complications include low birth weight and postmature birth.

- Low–birth weight babies may be either preterm (premature) or small-for-gestational age. Low birth weight is a major factor in infant mortality and can cause long-term physical and cognitive problems. Very low–birth weight babies have a less promising prognosis than those who weigh more.

- A supportive postnatal environment and other protective factors can often improve the outcome for babies suffering from birth complications.

  **birth trauma (104)   low birth weight (104)   perinatal (104)
  preterm (premature) infants (104)
  small-for-gestational age infants (104)   postmature (107)
  protective factors (109)**

Newborns and Their Parents

Guidepost 7 How do parents bond with their baby and respond to the baby's patterns of sleep and activity?

- Researchers following the ethological approach have suggested that there is a critical period for the formation of the mother–infant bond. However, research has not confirmed this hypothesis. Fathers typically bond with their babies whether or not they are present at the birth.

- A newborn's state of arousal is governed by periodic cycles of wakefulness, sleep, and activity, which seem to be inborn. Sleep takes up the major, but a diminishing, amount of a neonate's time. Newborns' activity levels show stability and may be early indicators of temperament. Parents' responsiveness to babies' states and activity levels is an important influence on development.

  **caregiver–infant bond (109)   imprinting (109)
  state of arousal (110)**

Guidepost 8 How does parenthood change the parents' relationship with one another?

- Marital satisfaction typically declines during the childraising years. Expectations and sharing of tasks can contribute to a marriage's deterioration or improvement.

OLC Preview

The Online Learning Centre for *A Child's World,* First Canadian Edition, supplements the boxed material in the chapter on "Having a Baby in the Himalayas" and "Comforting a Baby" and provides links to recommended parenting websites. Check out **www.mcgrawhill.ca/college/papalia.**

Physical Development and Health During the First Three Years

There he lay upon his back
The yearling creature, warm and moist with life
To the bottom of his dimples,—to the ends
Of the lovely tumbled curls about his face.

—Elizabeth Barrett Browning, *Aurora Leigh*, 1857

Focus *Helen Keller and the World of the Senses**

Helen Keller

"What we have once enjoyed we can never lose," the author Helen Keller (1880–1968) once wrote. "A sunset, a mountain bathed in moonlight, the ocean in calm and in storm—we see these, love their beauty, hold the vision to our hearts. All that we love deeply becomes a part of us" (Keller, 1929, p. 2).

This quotation is especially remarkable—and especially poignant—in view of the fact that Helen Keller never saw a sunset, or a mountain, or moonlight, or an ocean, or anything else after the age of 19 months. It was then that she contracted a mysterious fever, which left her deaf and with inexorably ebbing sight.

Before her illness, Helen had been a normal, healthy baby—lively, friendly, and affectionate. Now she became expressionless and unresponsive. At 1 year, she had begun to walk; now she clung to her mother's skirts or sat in her lap. She had also begun to talk; one of her first words was *water.* After her illness, she continued to say "wah-wah," but not much else.

Her distraught parents first took her to a mineral spa and then to medical specialists, but there was no hope for a cure. At a time when physical and cognitive development normally enter a major growth spurt, the sensory gateways to the exploration of Helen's world had slammed shut—but not entirely. Deprived of two senses, she leaned more heavily on the other three, especially smell and touch. She later explained that she could tell a doctor from a carpenter by the odours of ether or wood that came from them. She used her ever-active fingertips to trace the "delicate tremble of a butterfly's wings . . . , the soft petals of violets . . . , the clear, firm outline of face and limb, the smooth arch of a horse's neck and the velvety touch of his nose" (Keller, 1920, pp. 6–7). Memories of the daylight world she had once inhabited helped her make sense of the unrelieved night in which she now found herself.

Helen realized that she was not like other people, but at first she had no clear sense of who or what she was. "I lived in a world that was a no-world. . . . I did not know that I knew [anything], or that I lived or acted or desired" (1920, p. 113). Sometimes, when family members were talking to each other, she would stand between them and touch their lips, and then frantically move her own—but nothing happened. Her frustration found its outlet in violent, inconsolable tantrums; she would kick and scream until she was exhausted.

Out of pity, her parents indulged her whims. Finally, more in desperation than in hope, they engaged a teacher for her: a young woman named Anne Sullivan, who herself had limited vision and who had been trained in a school for the blind. Arriving at the Keller home, Sullivan

*Sources of information about Helen Keller included Keller (1905, 1920) and Lash (1980).

found 6-year-old Helen to be "wild, wilful, and destructive" (Lash, 1980, p. 348). Once, after figuring out how to use a key, Helen locked her mother in the pantry. Another time, frustrated by her teacher's attempts to spell the word *doll* into her palm, she hurled her new doll to the floor, smashing it to bits.

Yet, that same day, the little girl made her first linguistic breakthrough. As she and her teacher walked in the garden, they stopped to get a drink at the pump. Sullivan placed Helen's hand under the spout, at the same time spelling "w-a-t-e-r" over and over into her other hand. "I stood still," Keller later wrote, "my whole attention fixed upon the motions of her fingers. Suddenly I felt a misty consciousness as of something forgotten—a thrill of returning thought; and somehow the mystery of language was revealed to me. I knew then that 'w-a-t-e-r' meant the wonderful cool something that was flowing over my hand. That living word awakened my soul, gave it light, hope, joy, set it free!" (Keller, 1905, p. 35).

● ● ●

The story of how Anne Sullivan tamed this unruly child and brought her into the light of language and thought is a familiar and inspiring one. One lesson we can draw from the story of Helen Keller's early development is the central importance of the senses—the windows to a baby's world—and their connection with all other aspects of development. Had Helen Keller not lost her vision and hearing, or had she been born without one or the other, or both, her physical, cognitive, and psychosocial development undoubtedly would have been quite different.

In this chapter, we show how sensory perception goes hand in hand with an infant's growing motor skills and shapes the astoundingly rapid development of the brain. We describe typical growth patterns of body and brain, and we see how a nourishing environment can stimulate both. We see how infants, who spend most of their time sleeping and eating, become busy, active toddlers and how parents and other caregivers can foster healthy growth and development. We discuss threats to infant life and health and how to ward them off.

After you have read and studied this chapter, you should be able to answer each of the Guidepost questions that appear at the top of the next page. Look for them again in the margins, where they point to important concepts throughout the chapter. To check your understanding of these Guideposts, review the end-of-chapter summary. Checkpoints located throughout the chapter will help you verify your understanding of what you have read.

1. How do babies grow, and what influences their growth?

2. How and what should babies be fed?

3. How does the brain develop, and how do environmental factors affect its early growth?

4. How do the senses develop during infancy?

5. What are some early milestones in motor development, and what are some influences on it?

6. How can we enhance babies' chances of survival and health?

Growth and Nutrition

Patterns of Growth

Children grow faster during the first 3 years, especially during the first few months, than they ever will again (see Figure 6-1). At 5 months, the average baby boy's birth weight has doubled to 7 kg, and, by 1 year, has nearly tripled to 10 kg. This rapid growth rate tapers off during the second and third years; a boy typically gains about 2 kg by his second birthday and 1.5 kg by his third, when he tips the scales at about 14 kg. A boy's height typically increases by 25 cm during the first year (making the typical 1-year-old boy about 75 cm tall), by almost 13 cm during the second year (so that the average 2-year-old boy is approaching 90 cm tall); and by a little more than 8 cm during the third year to top 95 cm. Girls follow a parallel pattern but are slightly smaller; at 3, the average girl weighs 500 g less and is 1 cm shorter than the average boy (Kuczmarski et al., 2000).

Teething usually begins around 3 or 4 months, when infants begin grabbing almost everything in sight to put into their mouths; but the first tooth may not actually arrive until sometime between 5 and 9 months of age, or even later. By the first birthday, babies generally have 6 to 8 teeth; by age 2½, they have a mouthful of 20.

As a baby grows, body shape and proportions change too; a 3-year-old is typically slender compared with a chubby, potbellied 1-year-old. Physical growth and development follow the maturational principles introduced in chapter 3: the *cephalocaudal principle* and *proximodistal principle.* According to the cephalocaudal principle, growth occurs from top down. Because the brain grows so rapidly before birth, a newborn baby's head is disproportionately large. By 1 year, the brain is 70 per cent of its adult weight, but the rest of the body is only about 10 to 20 per cent of adult weight. The head becomes proportionately smaller as the child grows in height and the lower parts of the body develop (see Figure 6-2). As we'll see later in this chapter, sensory and motor development proceed according to the same principle: infants learn to use the upper parts of the body before the lower parts. They see objects before they can control their trunk, and they learn to do many things with their hands long before they can crawl or walk. According to the proximodistal principle (inner to outer), growth and motor development proceed from the centre of the body outward. In the womb, the head and trunk develop before the arms and legs, then the hands and feet,

Guidepost 1

How do babies grow, and what influences their growth?

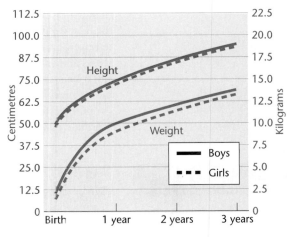

Figure 6-1

Growth in height and weight during infancy and toddlerhood. Babies grow most rapidly in both height and weight during the first few months of life, then taper off somewhat by age 3. Baby boys are slightly larger, on average, than baby girls. *Note:* Curves shown are for the 50th percentiles for each sex.

Source: Kuczmarski et al., 2000

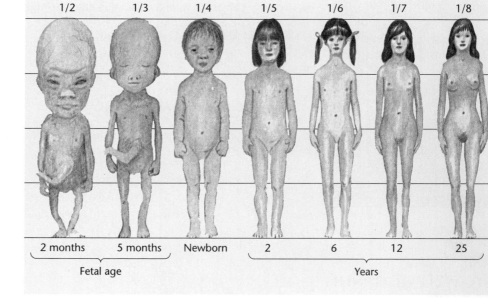

| 1/2 | 1/3 | 1/4 | 1/5 | 1/6 | 1/7 | 1/8 |

| 2 months | 5 months | Newborn | 2 | 6 | 12 | 25 |

Fetal age Years

Figure 6-2

Changes in proportions of the human body during growth. The most striking change is that the head becomes smaller relative to the rest of the body. The fractions indicate head size as a proportion of total body length at several ages. More subtle is the stability of the trunk proportions (from neck to crotch). The increasing leg proportion is almost exactly the reverse of the decreasing head proportion.

and then the fingers and toes. During infancy and early childhood, the limbs continue to grow faster than the hands and feet. Similarly, babies first develop the ability to use their upper arms and upper legs (which are closest to the centre of the body), then the forearms and forelegs, then hands and feet, and finally, fingers and toes.

Influences on Growth

The genes an infant inherits have a strong influence on whether the child will be tall or short, thin or stocky, or somewhere in between. This genetic influence interacts with such environmental influences as nutrition and living conditions, which also affect general health and well-being. For example, Japanese American children are taller and weigh more than children the same age in Japan, probably because of dietary differences (Broude, 1995).

Well-fed, well-cared-for children grow taller and heavier than less nourished and nurtured children. They also mature sexually and attain maximum height earlier, and their teeth erupt sooner. Today, children in many industrialized countries are growing taller and maturing sexually at an earlier age than a century ago (see chapter 15), probably because of better nutrition, improved sanitation, and the decrease in child labour. Better medical care, especially immunization and antibiotics, also plays a part; heart disease, kidney disease, and some infectious illnesses can have grave effects on growth. Children who are ill for a long time may never achieve their genetically programmed stature because they may never make up for the loss of growth time while they were sick. Malnutrition, even apart from the effects of such related factors as low birth weight and illness, can interfere with normal cognitive growth (Rose, 1994).

Nourishment

Guidepost 2

How and what should babies be fed?

Babies can grow normally and stay healthy under a variety of feeding regimens. Still, some feeding practices are more beneficial than others.

Early Feeding: Past and Present

From the beginnings of human history, babies were breast-fed.* A woman who was either unable or unwilling to nurse her baby usually found another woman, a "wet nurse," to do it. At first a prerogative of upper-class women too busy with social rounds to nurse their

*Unless otherwise referenced, the historical material in this section is based on Eccles (1982) and Fontanel & d'Harcourt (1997).

babies, the custom of wet nursing spread by the Middle Ages to the working class in cities and villages, and it persisted in some places until the early 20th century.

Ironically, the babies of peasant women, who could not afford wet nurses, often thrived better than the children of the rich. The greater mortality rates among high-born, wet-nursed infants may have been due in part to the stress of separation, as well as to the lack of built-in immunity from the mother's *colostrum,* an antibody-rich fluid produced in the first few days after childbirth.

If a mother or wet nurse produced too little milk, became ill, or died, the baby might be suckled by a goat or cow, or fed from bottles. During the Middle Ages, some babies were given cows' or goats' milk in "bottles" made from animal horns partially stopped up with canvas, cork, leather, or sponges.

Between the 16th and 18th centuries, in an effort to bring down the high rate of infant deaths, doctors and clergy in Europe and the New World colonies urged mothers to nurse their own babies. Wet nursing, it was said, was "against nature" and could cause great harm, not only to the baby but to the mother, whose unconsumed milk could back up into her system and make her ill (Fontanel & d'Harcourt, 1997, p. 99). Babies fed non-human milk were even more likely to fall ill and die, and by the 19th century doctors were warning mothers to avoid the "poisonous bottle" at all costs (Fontanel & d'Harcourt, 1997, p. 121). Not only were the bottles and nipples unsanitary, but the milk itself was often given raw, diluted with water to make it go farther, mixed with a variety of flavourings, and thickened with whitewash, plaster, white clay, or starch. Not until the first decade of the 20th century, some 20 years after the discovery of germs in 1878, did the medical establishment agree on the need to boil animal milk fed to infants.

Breast milk can be called the "ultimate health food" because it offers so many benefits to babies—physical, cognitive, and emotional.

By this time, thanks in part to the writings of Rousseau, who extolled the virtues of pastoral family life, maternal breast-feeding had come back in vogue. Diarrhea was the main cause of infant deaths, and artificially fed infants died of it at much higher rates than breast-fed babies (Brosco, 1999). Then, with the advent of dependable refrigeration, pasteurization, and sterilization, manufacturers began to develop formulas to modify and enrich cow's milk for infant consumption. With improvements in the design of bottles, bottle-feeding became safe, nutritious, and popular.

During the next half-century, formula feeding became the norm in Canada and some other industrialized countries despite medical recommendations for breast-feeding. By 1971, only 25 per cent of Canadian mothers even tried to nurse. Since then, recognition of the benefits of breast milk has brought about a reversal of this trend, so that today about 77 per cent of new mothers in Canada breast-feed. However, only about 46 per cent are still breast-feeding at 4 months, and many of these supplement breast milk with formula (Canadian Perinatal Surveillance System, 2000; Ryan, 2000). In comparison with the national rate of breast-feeding, younger women, women from non-white ancestries, low socioeconomic status, or from Eastern Canada tend to have lower rates of breast-feeding, the majority of whom cite concern for the baby's nutrition as the reason to formula-feed (Williams, Innis, Vogel, & Stephen, 1999).

In some developing countries, where bottle-feeding has been promoted as the more modern method, some poor mothers dilute formula or use unclean water to make it, unwittingly endangering their babies' health and lives. Even in highly developed countries, as we'll see, breast-fed babies are healthier than formula-fed infants (AAP Work Group on Breastfeeding, 1997).

Breast or Bottle?

Breast milk is almost always the best food for newborns and is recommended for at least the first 12 months. The only acceptable alternative is an iron-fortified formula based on either cow's milk or soy protein and containing supplemental vitamins and minerals. Breast milk is more digestible and more nutritious than formula and is less likely to produce allergic reactions (Canadian Paediatric Society, Dietitians of Canada and Health Canada, 1998; Eiger & Olds, 1999). Human milk is a complete source of nutrients for at least the first 6 months; during this time breast-fed babies normally do not need any other food other than a vitamin D supplement (Canadian Paediatric Society, Dietitians of Canada and Health Canada, 1998).

The health advantages of breast-feeding are striking during the first 2 years and even later in life (A. S. Cunningham, Jelliffe, & Jelliffe, 1991; J. Newman, 1995; A. L. Wright, Holberg, Taussig, & Martinez, 1995). Among the illnesses prevented or minimized by breast-feeding are diarrhea, respiratory infections (such as pneumonia and bronchitis), otitis media (an infection of the middle ear), and staphylococcal, bacterial, and urinary tract infections (Canadian Paediatric Society, Dietitians of Canada and Health Canada, 1998; A. S. Cunningham et al., 1991; Dewey, Heinig, & Nommsen-Rivers, 1995; J. Newman, 1995; Scariati, Grummer-Strawn, & Fein, 1997a). Resistance to some illnesses (influenza, diphtheria, and diarrhea) can be enhanced in bottle-fed babies by fortifying their formula with nucleotides, components of human milk that stimulate the immune system; but babies breast-fed more than 6 months do better over all (Pickering et al., 1998). Breast-feeding may reduce the risk of sudden infant death syndrome, discussed later in this chapter (CPS Joint Statement, 1999; National Institute of Child Health and Human Development [NICHD], 1997, updated 2000). And breast-feeding may also help prevent obesity (von Kries et al., 1999). Breast-feeding seems to have benefits for visual acuity (Makrides, Neumann, Simmer, Pater, & Gibson, 1995), neurological development (Lanting, Fidler, Huisman, Touwen, & Boersma, 1994), and cognitive development (Canadian Paediatric Society, Dietitians of Canada and Health Canada, 1998; Horwood & Fergusson, 1998; Jacobson, Chiodo, & Jacobson, 1999). Fortified breast milk or formula designed for premature infants is recommended as the preferred food for premature infants (Nutrition Committee, Canadian Paediatric Society, 1995). There is considerable variation in breast-feeding support in hospitals across Canada (Levitt, Kaczorowski, Hanvey, Avard, & Chance, 1996). The Baby-Friendly Health Initiative (BFHI) was introduced in 1991 as a national campaign to encourage breast-feeding, including providing support and information on breast-feeding practices, in maternity hospitals across Canada (Martens, Phillips, Cheang, Rosolowich, & Breastfeeding Promotion Steering Committee of Manitoba, 2000). Adopting BFHI practices appears to reduce the likelihood of early weaning (Martens et al., 2000).

Nursing mothers need to be as careful as pregnant women about what they take into their bodies. Breast-feeding is inadvisable for a mother infected with the AIDS virus, which can be transmitted through her milk—but only if the mother has access to a safe alternative feeding method. Likewise, breast-feeding is discouraged if the mother has another infectious illness; if she has untreated active tuberculosis; or if she is taking any drug that would not be safe for the baby (Canadian Paediatric Society, Dietitians of Canada and Health Canada, 1998; Eiger & Olds, 1999; Miotti et al., 1999; Nduati et al., 2000; WHO/UNICEF Constitution on HIV Transmission and Breastfeeding, 1992).

Feeding a baby is an emotional as well as a physical act. Warm contact with the mother's body fosters emotional linkage between mother and baby. Such bonding can take place through either breast- or bottle-feeding and through many other caregiving activities, most of which can be performed by fathers as well as mothers. The quality of the relationship between parent and child and the provision of abundant affection and cuddling may be more important than the feeding method.

Cow's Milk, Solid Foods, and Juice

Iron-deficiency anemia is the world's most common nutritional disorder, affecting as many as one fourth of all 6- to 24-month-old babies in Canada. Infants with iron-deficiency anemia do more poorly on cognitive tests than other infants. They also tend to be less independent, joyful, attentive, and playful, and more wary, hesitant, and easily tired (Lozoff et al., 1998). Because infants fed plain cow's milk in the early months of life may suffer from iron deficiency, the Canadian Paediatric Society (Canadian Paediatric Society, Dietitians of Canada and Health Canada, 1998) recommends that babies receive breast milk or, alternatively, iron-fortified formula for at least the first year.

Iron-enriched solid foods—usually beginning with single-grain cereals—should be gradually introduced during the second half of the first year as a precaution against allergic reactions (Canadian Paediatric Society, Dietitians of Canada and Health Canada, 1998). At

What's your view ?

• "Every mother who is physically able should breast-feed." Do you agree or disagree? Give reasons.

this time, too, fruit juice may be introduced. A study based on mothers' reports of toddlers' diets (Skinner, Carruth, Moran, Houck, & Coletta, 1999) did not support earlier findings that large amounts of fruit juice interfere with growth (M. M. Smith & Lifshitz, 1994).

At 1 year, babies can switch from breast (or bottle) to cow's milk if they are getting a balanced diet of supplementary solid foods that provide one third of their caloric intake (Canadian Paediatric Society, Dietitians of Canada and Health Canada, 1998). To promote proper growth, the milk should be homogenized whole milk fortified with vitamin D, not skim milk or reduced-fat (1 or 2 per cent) milk (Canadian Paediatric Society, Dietitians of Canada and Health Canada, 1998).

Is obesity a problem in infancy? Not necessarily. Two factors seem to most strongly influence the chances that an obese child will become an obese adult: whether or not the child has an obese parent and the age of the child.

In a 40-year follow-up of Swedish children, whether obese infants became obese adults depended on obesity in the family, especially in the mother. If she was obese, her child was likely to remain obese, even if the child ate a recommended diet (Mossberg, 1989). In a more recent study in Washington State, obese children under age 3 who did not have an obese parent were unlikely to grow up to be obese, but among children above that age, obesity in childhood was an increasingly important predictor of adult obesity (Whitaker, Wright, Pepe, Seidel, & Dietz, 1997). Thus a 1- or 2-year-old who has an obese parent—or especially two obese parents—may be a candidate for prevention efforts, if it can be determined what factors, such as a too-rich diet or too little exercise, are contributing to the problem.

Another concern is a potential buildup of *cholesterol,* a waxy substance found in human and animal tissue. High levels of one type of cholesterol (LDL, or "bad" cholesterol) can dangerously narrow blood vessels, leading to heart disease. This condition is called *atherosclerosis.* Since atherosclerosis begins in childhood, so should heart disease prevention. In a controlled longitudinal study in Finland, a low-saturated fat, low-cholesterol diet beginning in the eighth month of infancy resulted in significant reductions in fat and cholesterol intake by age 5, with no effect on growth or neurological development (Rask-Nissilä et al., 2000).

All in all, the best ways parents can avoid obesity and cardiac problems in themselves and in their children is to adopt a more active lifestyle for the entire family—and to breast-feed their babies.

Checkpoint ✔

Can you . . .

✔ Summarize typical patterns of growth during the first 3 years?

✔ Mention several factors that affect growth?

✔ Summarize pediatric recommendations on early feeding and the introduction of cow's milk, solid foods, and fruit juices?

✔ Cite factors that contribute to obesity and cardiac problems in later life?

The Brain and Reflex Behaviour

Guidepost 3

How does the brain develop, and how do environmental factors affect its early growth?

What makes newborns respond to a nipple? What tells them to start the sucking movements that allow them to control their intake of fluids? These are functions of the **central nervous system**—the brain and *spinal cord* (a bundle of nerves running through the backbone)—and of a growing peripheral network of nerves extending to every part of the body. Through this network, sensory messages travel to the brain, and motor commands travel back.

central nervous system Brain and spinal cord

Building the Brain

The growth of the brain both before birth and during the childhood years is fundamental to future physical, cognitive, and emotional development. Through various brain-imaging tools, researchers are gaining a clearer picture of how that growth occurs (Behrman, 1992; Casaer, 1993; Gabbard, 1996).* For example, from positron emission tomography (PET) scans showing patterns of glucose metabolism, which are indicators of changes in functional activity, we have learned that the brain's maturation takes much longer than was previously thought (Chugani, 1998).

The brain at birth weighs only about 25 per cent of its eventual adult weight of 1.5 kg. It reaches nearly 90 per cent of that weight by age 3. By age 6, it is almost adult size; but

---

*Unless otherwise referenced, the discussion in this section is largely based on Gabbard (1996).

Figure 6-3

Fetal brain development from 25 days of gestation through birth. The *brain stem,* which controls basic biological functions such as breathing, develops first. As the brain grows, the front part expands greatly to form the *cerebrum* (the large, convoluted upper mass). Specific areas of the grey matter (the outer covering of the brain) have specific functions, such as sensory and motor activity; but large areas are "uncommitted" and thus are free for higher cognitive activity, such as thinking, remembering, and problem solving. The brain stem and other structures below the cortical layer handle reflex behaviour and other lower-level functions. The *cerebellum,* which maintains balance and motor coordination, grows most rapidly during the first year of life.

Source: Casaer, 1993; Restak, 1984.

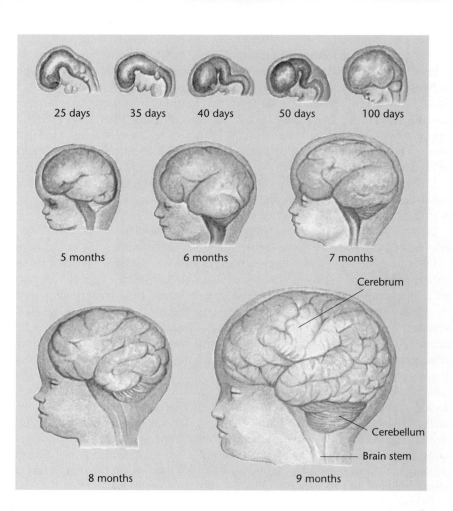

25 days   35 days   40 days   50 days   100 days

5 months   6 months   7 months

Cerebrum

Cerebellum

Brain stem

8 months   9 months

growth and functional development of specific parts of the brain continue into adulthood. Increases in brain weight and volume can be measured before birth by ultrasound and after birth by the circumference of the baby's head. These measurements provide a check on whether the brain is growing normally.

The brain's growth during the first 3 years is not smooth and steady; it occurs in fits and starts. **Brain growth spurts,** periods of rapid growth and development, coincide with changes in cognitive behaviour (Fischer & Rose, 1994, 1995; Segalowitz, 1995). Different parts of the brain grow more rapidly at different times, and brain growth depends very much on the child's early experiences. Some events are called experience-expectant, such as language exposure, which give the brain signals to begin growing, and others are experience-dependent, like the specific language a child first learns, which help to shape the way the brain is growing (Segalowitz, 1995).

brain growth spurts Periods of rapid brain growth and development

Major Parts of the Brain

Beginning about two weeks after conception, the brain gradually develops from a long hollow tube into a spherical mass of cells (see Figure 6-3). By birth, the growth spurt of the spinal cord and *brain stem* (the part of the brain responsible for such basic bodily functions as breathing, heart rate, body temperature, and the sleep–wake cycle) has almost run its course. The *cerebellum* (the part of the brain that maintains balance and motor coordination) grows fastest during the first year of life (Casaer, 1993).

The *cerebrum,* the largest part of the brain, is divided into right and left halves, or hemispheres, each with specialized functions. This specialization of the hemispheres is called **lateralization.** The left hemisphere is mainly concerned with language and logical thinking, the right hemisphere with visual and spatial functions such as map reading and drawing. The two hemispheres are joined by a tough band of tissue called the *corpus callosum,* which

lateralization Tendency of each of the brain's hemispheres to have specialized functions

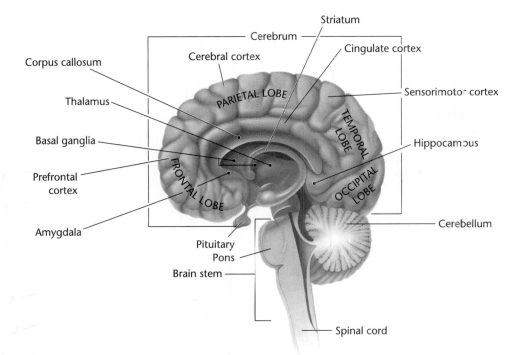

Figure 6-4

Parts of the brain, side view. The brain consists of three main parts: the brain stem, the cerebellum, and, above those, the large cerebrum. The brain stem, an extension of the spinal cord, is one of the regions of the brain most completely developed at birth. It controls such basic bodily functions as breathing, circulation, and reflexes. The cerebellum, at birth, begins to control balance and muscle tone; later it coordinates sensory and motor activity. The cerebrum constitutes almost 70 per cent of the weight of the nervous system and handles thought, memory, language, and emotion. It is divided into two halves, or hemispheres, each of which has four sections, or lobes *(right to left)* *(a)* The occipital lobe processes visual information. *(b)* The temporal lobe helps with hearing and language. *(c)* The parietal lobe allows an infant to receive touch sensations and spatial information, which facilitates eye–hand coordination. *(d)* The frontal lobe develops gradually during the first year, permitting such higher-level functions as speech and reasoning. The cerebral cortex, the outer surface of the cerebrum, consists of grey matter; it is the seat of thought processes and mental activity. Parts of the cerebral cortex—the sensorimotor cortex and cingulate cortex—as well as several structures deep within the cerebrum, the thalamus, hippocampus, and basal ganglia, all of which control basic movements and functions, are largely developed at birth.

allows them to share information and coordinate commands. The corpus callosum grows dramatically during childhood, reaching adult size by about age 10.

Each cerebral hemisphere has four lobes, or sections: the *occipital, parietal, temporal,* and *frontal* lobes, which control different functions (see Figure 6-4) and develop at different rates. The regions of the *cerebral cortex* (the outer surface of the cerebrum) that govern vision and hearing are mature by 6 months of age, but the areas of the frontal lobe responsible for making mental associations, remembering, and producing deliberate motor responses remain immature for several years.

Brain Cells

The brain is composed of *neurons* and *glial cells.* **Neurons,** or nerve cells, send and receive information. *Glial cells* support and protect the neurons.

Beginning in the second month of gestation, an estimated 250,000 immature neurons are produced every minute through cell division (mitosis). At birth, most of the more than 100 billion neurons in a mature brain are already formed but are not yet fully developed. The number of neurons increases most rapidly between the 25th week of gestation and the first few months after birth. This cell proliferation is accompanied by a dramatic growth in cell size.

Originally the neurons are simply cell bodies with a nucleus, or centre, composed of deoxyribonucleic acid (DNA), which contains the cell's genetic programming. As the brain grows, these rudimentary cells migrate to various parts of it. There they sprout *axons* and

neurons Nerve cells

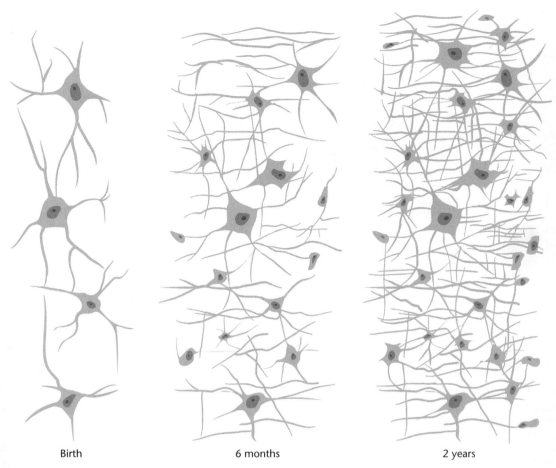

| Birth | 6 months | 2 years |

Figure 6-5

Growth of neural connections during first 2 years of life. The rapid increase in the brain's density and weight is due largely to the formation of dendrites, extension of nerve cell bodies, and the synapses that link them. This mushrooming communications network sprouts in response to environmental stimulation and makes possible impressive growth in every domain of development.

Source: Conel, 1959.

dendrites—narrow, branching extensions. Axons send signals to other neurons, and dendrites receive incoming messages from them, through *synapses,* the nervous system's communication links. The synapses are tiny gaps, which are bridged with the help of chemicals called *neurotransmitters.* Eventually a particular neuron may have anywhere from 5,000 to 100,000 synaptic connections to and from the body's sensory receptors, its muscles, and other neurons within the central nervous system.

The multiplication of dendrites and synaptic connections, especially during the last 2½ months of gestation and the first 6 months to 2 years of life (see Figure 6-5), accounts for much of the brain's growth in weight and permits the emergence of new perceptual, cognitive, and motor abilities. Most of the neurons in the cortex, which is responsible for complex, high-level functioning, are in place by 20 weeks of gestation, and its structure becomes fairly well defined during the next 12 weeks. Only after birth, however, do the cells begin to form connections that allow communication to take place.

As the neurons multiply, migrate to their assigned locations, and develop connections, they undergo the complementary processes of *integration* and *differentiation.* Through **integration,** the neurons that control various groups of muscles coordinate their activities. Through **differentiation,** each neuron takes on a specific, specialized structure and function.

At first the brain produces more neurons and synapses than it needs. Those that are not used or do not function well die out. This process of **cell death,** or pruning of excess cells

integration Process by which neurons coordinate the activities of muscle groups

differentiation Process by which neurons acquire specialized structure and function

cell death Elimination of excess brain cells to achieve more efficient functioning

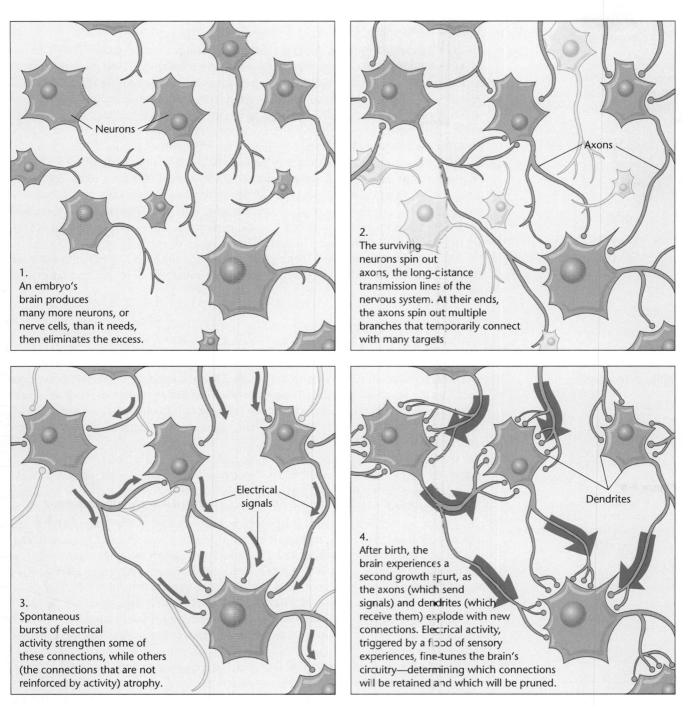

Figure 6-6

Wiring the brain: Development of neural connections before and after birth

Source: Nash, 1997, p. 51.

and synapses, begins during the prenatal period and continues after birth (see Figure 6-6), helping to create an efficient nervous system. The number of synapses seems to peak at about age 2, and their elimination continues well into adolescence. Even as some neurons die out, new research suggests, others may continue to form during adult life (Eriksson et al., 1998; Gould, Reeves, Graziano, & Gross, 1999). Connections among cortical cells continue to improve into adulthood, allowing more flexible and more advanced motor and cognitive functioning.

Myelination

Much of the credit for improvement in efficiency of communication goes to the glial cells, which coat the neural pathways with a fatty substance called *myelin.* This process of **myelination** enables signals to travel faster and more smoothly, permitting the achievement of mature functioning. Myelination begins about halfway through gestation in some parts of the brain and continues into adulthood in others. The pathways related to the sense of touch—the first sense to develop—are myelinated by birth. Myelination of visual pathways, which are slower to mature, begins at birth and continues during the first 5 months of life. Pathways related to hearing may begin to be myelinated as early as the 5th month of gestation, but the process is not complete until about age 4. The parts of the cortex that control attention and memory, which are slower to develop, are not fully myelinated until young adulthood. Myelination in an information relay zone of the *hippocampus,* a structure deep in the temporal lobe that plays a key role in memory, and related formations continues to increase until at least age 70 (Benes, Turtle, Khan, & Farol, 1994).

Myelination of sensory and motor pathways, first in the fetus's spinal cord and later, after birth, in the cerebral cortex, may account for the initially evident, and later not evident early reflexes.

Early Reflexes

When you blink at a bright light, your eyelids are acting involuntarily. Such an automatic, innate response to stimulation is called a **reflex behaviour.** Reflex behaviours are controlled by the lower brain centres that govern other involuntary processes, such as breathing and heart rate. These are the parts of the brain most fully myelinated at birth. Reflex behaviours play an important part in stimulating the early development of the central nervous system and muscles.

Human infants have an estimated 27 major reflexes, many of which are present at birth or soon after (Gabbard, 1996; see Table 6-1 for examples). *Primitive reflexes,* such as sucking, rooting for the nipple, and the Moro reflex (a response to being startled or beginning to fall), are related to instinctive needs for survival and protection. Some primitive reflexes may be part of humanity's evolutionary legacy. One example is the grasping reflex, by which infant monkeys hold on to the hair of their mothers' bodies. As the higher brain centres become active, during the first 2 to 4 months, infants begin to show *postural reflexes:* reactions to changes in position or balance. For example, infants who are tilted downward extend their arms in the parachute reflex, an instinctive attempt to break a fall.

Locomotor reflexes, such as the walking and swimming reflexes, resemble voluntary movements that do not appear until months after the reflexes have disappeared. As we'll see, there is debate about whether or not locomotor reflexes prepare the way for their later, voluntary counterparts.

Most of the early reflexes become less evident during the first 6 to 12 months. Reflexes that continue to serve protective functions—such as blinking, yawning, coughing, gagging, sneezing, shivering, and the pupillary reflex (dilation of the pupils in the dark)—remain. Disappearance of unneeded reflexes on schedule is a sign that motor pathways in the cortex have been partially myelinated, enabling a shift to voluntary behaviour. Thus we can evaluate a baby's neurological development by seeing whether certain reflexes are present or absent.

What is normal, however, seems to vary somewhat from culture to culture (D. G. Freedman, 1979). For example, differences show up in the Moro reflex. To elicit this reflex, the baby's body is lifted, supporting the head. Then the head support is released, and the head is allowed to drop slightly. Caucasian newborns reflexively extend both arms and legs, cry persistently, and move about agitatedly. Navajo babies do not extend their limbs in the same way, rarely cry, and almost immediately stop any agitated motion. Since these reflexive differences are displayed soon after birth, they may reflect innate variability among ethnic groups.

Table 6-1   Early Human Reflexes

Reflex	Stimulation	Baby's Behaviour	Typical Age of Appearance	Typical Age of Disappearance
Moro	Baby is dropped or hears loud noise.	Extends legs, arms, and fingers, arches back, draws back head	7th month of gestation	3 months
Darwinian (grasping)	Palm of baby's hand is stroked.	Makes strong fist; can be raised to standing position if both fists are closed around a stick.	7th month of gestation	4 months
Tonic neck	Baby is laid down on back.	Turns head to one side, assumes "fencer" position, extends arms and legs on preferred side, flexes opposite limbs.	7th month of gestation	5 months
Babkin	Both of baby's palms are stroked at once.	Mouth opens, eyes close, neck flexes, head tilts forward.	Birth	3 months
Babinski	Sole of baby's foot is stroked.	Toes fan out; foot twists in.	Birth	4 months
Rooting	Baby's cheek or lower lip is stroked with finger or nipple.	Head turns; mouth opens; sucking movements begin.	Birth	9 months
Walking	Baby is held under arms, with bare feet touching flat surface.	Makes steplike motions that look like well-coordinated walking.	1 month	4 months
Swimming	Baby is put into water face down.	Makes well-coordinated swimming movements.	1 month	4 months

Darwinian reflex

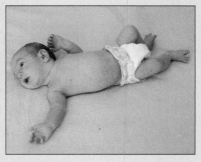

Tonic neck reflex

Rooting reflex

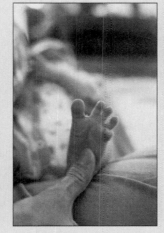

Babinski reflex

Walking reflex

Moro reflex

Source: Adapted in part from Gabbard, 1996.

Moulding the Brain: The Role of Experience

The brain growth spurt that begins at about the third trimester of gestation and continues until at least the fourth year of life is important to the development of neurological functioning. Smiling, babbling, crawling, walking, and talking—all the major sensory, motor, and cognitive milestones of infancy and toddlerhood—are made possible by the rapid development of the brain, particularly the cerebral cortex.

Until the middle of the 20th century, scientists believed that the brain grew in an unchangeable, genetically determined pattern. This does seem to be largely true before birth. But it is now widely believed, largely on the basis of animal studies, that the postnatal brain is "moulded" by experience. This is so especially during the early months of life, when the cortex is still growing rapidly and organizing itself (J. E. Black, 1998). The technical term for this malleability, or modifiability, of the brain is **plasticity.** Early synaptic connections, some of which depend on sensory stimulation, refine and stabilize the brain's genetically designed "wiring." Thus early experience can have lasting effects on the capacity of the central nervous system to learn and store information (J. E. Black, 1998; Chugani, 1998; Greenough, Black, & Wallace, 1987; McCain & Mustard, 1999; Pally, 1997; Wittrock, 1980).

In one series of experiments, rats were raised in cages with wheels to run on, rocks to climb on, levers to manipulate, or other animals to interact with. These animals were then compared with littermates raised in standard cages or in isolation. The "enriched" animals had heavier brains with thicker cortical layers, more cells in the visual cortex, more complex cells, and higher levels of neurochemical activity, making it easier to form synaptic connections (Rosenzweig, 1984; Rosenzweig & Bennett, 1976).

By the same token, early abuse or sensory impoverishment may leave an imprint on the brain (J. E. Black, 1998). In one experiment, kittens fitted with goggles that allowed them to see only vertical lines grew up unable to see horizontal lines and bumped into horizontal boards in front of them. Other kittens, whose goggles allowed them to see only horizontal lines, grew up blind to vertical columns (Hirsch & Spinelli, 1970). This did not happen when the same procedure was carried out with adult cats. Apparently, neurons in the visual cortex became programmed to respond only to lines running in the direction the kittens were permitted to see. Thus, if certain cortical connections are not made early in life, these circuits may "shut down" forever.

Early emotional development, too, may depend on experience. Infants whose mothers are severely depressed show less activity in the left frontal lobe, the part of the brain that is involved in positive emotions such as happiness and joy, and more activity in the right frontal lobe, which is associated with negative emotions (Dawson, Frey, Panagiotides, Osterling, & Hessl, 1997; Dawson, Klinger, Panagiotides, Hill, & Spieker, 1992).

Sometimes corrective experience can make up for past deprivation (J. E. Black, 1998). Plasticity continues throughout life as neurons change in size and shape in response to environmental experience (M. C. Diamond, 1988; Pally, 1997). Brain-damaged rats, when raised in an enriched setting, grow more dendritic connections (M. C. Diamond, 1988). Such findings have sparked successful efforts to stimulate the physical and mental development of children with Down syndrome and to help infants and children who have experienced brain damage recover function.

Ethical constraints prevent controlled experiments on the effects of environmental deprivation on human infants. However, the discovery of thousands of infants and young children who had spent virtually their entire lives in overcrowded Romanian orphanages offered an opportunity for a natural experiment (Ames, 1997). Discovered after the fall of the dictator Nicolae Ceausescu in December 1989, these abandoned children appeared to be starving, passive, and emotionless. They had spent much of their time lying quietly in their cribs or beds, with nothing to look at. They had had little contact with one another or with their caregivers and had heard little conversation or even noise. Most of the 2- and 3-year-olds did not walk or talk, and the older children played aimlessly. PET scans of their brains showed extreme inactivity in the temporal lobes, which regulate emotion and receive sensory input.

Many of these children were adopted by Canadian families. At the time of adoption, all the children showed delayed motor, language, or psychosocial development, and nearly 8 out of 10 were behind in all these areas. Three years later, when compared with children

plasticity Modifiability, or "moulding," of the brain through experience

What's your view **?**

- In view of what is now known about the plasticity of the infant brain, should society make sure that every baby has access to an appropriately stimulating environment? If so, how can this be done?

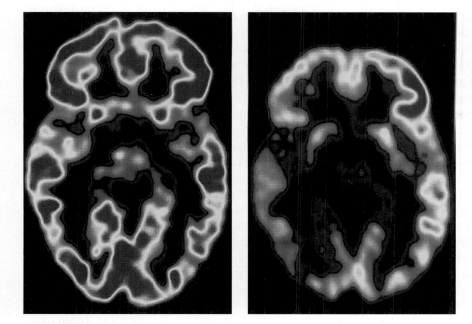

Extreme environmental deprivation in infancy can affect the structure of the brain, resulting in cognitive and emotional problems. A PET scan of a normal child's brain *(left)* shows regions of high *(red)* and low *(blue and black)* activity. A PET scan of the brain of a Romanian orphan institutionalized after birth *(right)* shows little activity.

left behind in the Romanian institutions, they showed remarkable progress. Even when compared with Canadian children reared in their own homes from birth, about one third had no serious problems and were doing well—in a few cases, better than the average home-raised child. Another third—generally those who had been in institutions the longest—still had serious developmental problems. The rest were moving toward average performance and behaviour (Ames, 1997; Morison, Ames, & Chisholm, 1995).

However, another study suggests that age of adoption makes a difference. Among 111 Romanian children adopted in England before age 2, those adopted before age 6 months had largely caught up physically and had made a complete cognitive recovery by age 4, as compared with a control group of English adopted children. However, 85 per cent of the English adoptees were more cognitively advanced than the average Romanian child adopted *after* 6 months of age (Rutter & the English and Romanian Adoptees [ERA] Study Team, 1998). A further study of Romanian children adopted by Canadians showed that those who spent 8 months or more in Romanian orphanages scored lower than non-adopted Canadian-born children in cognitive development, and lower than Romanian children who spent less than 4 months in orphanages before being adopted by Canadians. However, the early adoptees scored lower than Canadian-born children, indicating that prenatal and peri-natal environments, genetic factors, and the experience of adoption can influence cognitive development. Better quality adoptive home environments and less time spent in the orphanages were associated with better development (Morison & Ellwood, 2000). Apparently, then, it may take very early environmental stimulation to overcome the effects of extreme deprivation.

Checkpoint ✔

Can you . . .

✔ Describe important features of early brain development?

✔ Explain the functions of reflex behaviours and why some drop out during the early months?

✔ Discuss how early experience affects brain development?

Early Sensory Capacities

Guidepost 4

How do the senses develop during infancy?

"The baby, assailed by eyes, ears, nose, skin, and entrails at once, feels that all is one great blooming, buzzing confusion," wrote the psychologist William James in 1890. We now know that this is far from true. The developing brain enables newborn infants to make fairly good sense of what they touch, see, smell, taste, and hear; and their senses develop rapidly in the early months of life.

Touch and Pain

Touch seems to be the first sense to develop, and for the first several months it is the most mature sensory system. When a newborn's cheek is stroked near the mouth, the baby responds by trying to find a nipple. Early signs of this rooting reflex (refer back to Table

6-1) show up in the womb, 2 months after conception. By 32 weeks of gestation, all body parts are sensitive to touch, and this sensitivity increases during the first 5 days of life (Haith, 1986).

Often physicians performing surgery on newborn babies have used no anaesthesia because of a mistaken belief that neonates cannot feel pain, or feel it only briefly. Actually, even on the first day of life, babies can and do feel pain; and they become more sensitive to it during the next few days. Furthermore, pain experienced during the neonatal period may sensitize an infant to later pain, perhaps by affecting the neural pathways that process painful stimuli. Circumcised 4- and 6-month-olds have stronger reactions to the pain of vaccination than uncircumcised infants; the reaction is muted among infants who are treated with a painkilling cream before being circumcised (Taddio, Katz, Ilersich, & Koren, 1997). The Canadian Paediatric Society (2000) now maintains that prolonged or severe pain can do long-term harm to newborns, and that pain relief is essential. Although hospitals in Canada routinely use anaesthetic during major surgery for infants, they have used anaesthetic less frequently in minor surgery and in easing post-operative and disease-related pain (Fernandez & Rees, 1994).

Smell and Taste

The senses of smell and taste also begin to develop in the womb. The flavours and odours of foods an expectant mother consumes may be transmitted to the fetus through the amniotic fluid. After birth, a similar transmission occurs through breast milk (Mennella & Beauchamp, 1996b).

A preference for pleasant odours seems to be learned in utero and during the first few days after birth, and the odours transmitted through the mother's breast milk may further contribute to this learning (Bartoshuk & Beauchamp, 1994). Six-day-old breast-fed infants prefer the odour of their mother's breast pad over that of another nursing mother, but 2-day-olds do not, suggesting that babies need a few days' experience to learn how their mothers smell (Macfarlane, 1975). Bottle-fed babies do not make such a distinction (Cernoch & Porter, 1985). This preference for the fragrance of the mother's breast may be a survival mechanism.

Certain taste preferences seem to be largely innate (Bartoshuk & Beauchamp, 1994). Newborns prefer sweet tastes to sour or bitter ones. The sweeter the fluid, the harder they suck and the more they drink (Haith, 1986). Sweetened water calms crying newborns, whether full-term or 2 to 3 weeks premature—evidence that not only the taste buds themselves (which seem to be fairly well developed by 20 weeks of gestation), but the mechanisms that produce this calming effect are functional before normal term (B. A. Smith & Blass, 1996). An inborn "sweet tooth" may help a baby adapt to life outside the womb, since breast milk is quite sweet. Newborns' rejection of bitter tastes is probably another survival mechanism, since many bitter substances are toxic (Bartoshuk & Beauchamp, 1994).

Hearing

Hearing, too, is functional before birth; fetuses respond to sounds and seem to learn to recognize them. As we reported in chapter 4, babies less than 3 days old respond to a story heard while in the womb differently from the way they respond to other stories; can distinguish their mother's voice from a stranger's; and prefer their native language to a foreign tongue (DeCasper & Fifer, 1980; DeCasper & Spence, 1986; C. Moon, Cooper, & Fifer, 1993). Early recognition of voices and language heard in the womb may lay the foundation for the relationship between parents and child.

Auditory discrimination develops rapidly after birth. Three-day-old infants can distinguish new speech sounds from those they have heard before (L. R. Brody, Zelazo, & Chaika, 1984). At 1 month, babies can distinguish sounds as close as "ba" and "pa" (Eimas, Siqueland, Jusczyk, & Vigorito, 1971).

Because hearing is a key to language development, hearing impairments should be identified as early as possible. Although there is support for universally testing hearing in newborns (Hyde & Riko, 2000), only 10 per cent of Canadian hospitals report having programs for screening newborn hearing (Canadian Working Group on Childhood Hearing, 2001). Among 10,372 infants born in Honolulu during a 5-year period, hearing screening

Checkpoint ✔

Can you . . .

✔ Give evidence for the early development of the senses?

✔ Tell how breast-feeding plays a part in the development of touch and taste?

✔ Tell how auditory discrimination in newborns is related to fetal hearing?

✔ List at least three ways in which newborns' vision is underdeveloped?

within the first 3 days followed by hearing aids and aural therapy before age 6 months for those found to have hearing problems, enabled them to achieve normal speech and language development (Mason & Herrmann, 1998).

Sight

Vision is the least developed sense at birth. Some visual capabilities are present at birth and others require time and experience to mature. A great deal of visual development takes place during the first year, but different visual functions mature at different rates (Gwiazda & Birch, 2001). Newborns are capable of attending to objects in the environment, looking at edges, contours, and curves, and showing preference for the human face. This preference, and their abilities to recognize faces after short delays (Pascalis & deSchoner, 1994) has led some researchers to speculate that newborns have an innate sensitivity to the human face (Slater, 2000).

The eyes of newborns are smaller than those of adults, the retinal structures are incomplete, and the optic nerve is underdeveloped. Newborns blink at bright lights. Their peripheral vision is very narrow; it more than doubles between 2 and 10 weeks of age (E. Tronick, 1972). Visual information moves from the eye, along the optic nerve, to several brain structures. The information travels along several pathways responsible for different perceptual jobs. The pathway that is mature at birth takes care of vision in a rudimentary way, involving a primitive brain structure (Atkinson, 1995). Within the first several months after birth, other pathways that process visual information in the cortex develop rapidly—beginning with the pathway that is responsible for colour and patterns, followed by the pathway that is responsible for detecting motion, which allows the infant to track moving objects (Atkinson, 1995). These two pathways continue to mature for several years. By about 2 months, babies can tell red from green; by about 3 months, they can distinguish blue (Haith, 1986). Four-month-old babies can discriminate among red, green, blue, and yellow. Like most adults, they prefer red and blue (M. Bornstein, Kessen, & Weiskopf, 1976; Teller & Bornstein, 1987).

Vision becomes more acute during the first year, reaching the 20/20 level by about the sixth month (Aslin, 1987). (This measure of vision means that a person can read letters on a specified line on a standard eye chart from 20 feet away.) *Binocular vision*—the use of both eyes to focus, allowing perception of depth and distance—does not usually develop until 4 or 5 months (Bushnell & Boudreau, 1993). Another feature of visual development involves the coordination of visual skills and motor movement. Evidence of the beginnings of eye–hand coordination has been found in neonates as young as 3 to 5 days after birth, whose hand movements towards a ball were influenced by visual contact with the ball (Ennouri & Bloch, 1996). Likewise, the direction of movement of eyes and head begins to become coordinated as early as 2 weeks (Bloch & Carchon, 1992).

Motor Development

Babies do not have to be taught such basic motor skills as grasping, crawling, and walking. They just need room to move and freedom to see what they can do. When the central nervous system, muscles, and bones are ready and the environment offers the right opportunities for exploration and practice, babies keep surprising the adults around them with their new abilities.

Milestones of Motor Development

Motor development is marked by a series of "milestones": achievements a child masters before going on to more difficult ones. These milestones are not isolated achievements; they develop systematically, each newly mastered ability preparing a baby to tackle the next. Babies first learn simple skills and then combine them into increasingly complex **systems of action,** which permit a wider or more precise range of movement and more effective control of the environment. In developing the precision grip, for example, an infant first tries to pick things up with the whole hand, fingers closing against the palm. Later the baby masters the *pincer grasp,* in which thumb and index finger meet at the tips to form

Guidepost 5

What are some early milestones in motor development, and what are some influences on it?

systems of action Increasingly complex combinations of skills, which permit a wider or more precise range of movement and more control of the environment

a circle, making it possible to pick up tiny objects. In learning to walk, an infant first gains control of separate movements of the arms, legs, and feet before putting these movements together to take that momentous first step.

A number of clinical screening tests, like the Gesell Developmental Schedules (Knobloch, Stevens, & Malone, 1980), have been developed to chart the progress of motor development in children from birth to 3 years. This test, used in Canada, determines whether children are developing normally, and it is sensitive to individual differences, giving information on adaptive, gross motor, fine motor, language, and personal/social areas of development. The Denver Developmental Screening Test (Frankenburg, Dodds, Fandal, Kazuk, & Cohrs, 1975), is another test that measures **gross motor skills** (those using large muscles), such as rolling over and catching a ball, and **fine motor skills** (using small muscles), such as grasping a rattle and copying a circle. The Denver test has been criticized largely because of its weaknesses in standardization and norms, which do not reflect the cultural diversity of Canada's population.

As we trace typical progress in head control, hand control, and locomotion, notice how these developments follow the *cephalocaudal* (head to tail) and *proximodistal* (inner to outer) principles outlined earlier.

gross motor skills Physical skills that involve the large muscles

fine motor skills Physical skills that involve the small muscles and eye–hand coordination

Head Control

At birth, most infants can turn their heads from side to side while lying on their backs. While lying chest down, many can lift their heads enough to turn them. Within the first 2 to 3 months, they lift their heads higher and higher—sometimes to the point where they lose their balance and roll over on their backs. By 4 months of age, almost all infants can keep their heads erect while being held or supported in a sitting position.

Hand Control

Babies are born with a grasping reflex. If the palm of an infant's hand is stroked, the hand closes tightly. At about 3½ months, most infants can grasp an object of moderate size, such as a rattle, but have trouble holding a small object. Next they begin to grasp objects with one hand and transfer them to the other, and then to hold (but not pick up) small objects. Some time between 7 and 11 months, their hands become coordinated enough to pick up a tiny object, such as a pea, using the pincer grasp. After that, hand control becomes increasingly precise. By 15 months, the average baby can build a tower of two cubes. A few months after the third birthday, the average toddler can copy a circle fairly well.

Locomotion

By about 3 months, the average infant is experiencing accidental rolling as a result of reflex behaviour. Over the next two months deliberate rolling, first from front to back and then from back to front, becomes more under the control of the infant's intentions. The average baby can sit without support by 6 months and can assume a sitting position without help about 2½ months later.

Between 6 and 10 months, most babies begin to get around under their own power by means of various forms of creeping or crawling. This new achievement of self-locomotion has striking cognitive and psychosocial ramifications (see Box 6-1).

By holding onto a helping hand or a piece of furniture, the average baby can stand at a little past 7 months of age. A little more than 4 months later, most babies let go and stand alone. The average baby can stand well about 2 weeks or so before the first birthday.

All these developments are milestones along the way to the major motor achievement of infancy: walking. Humans begin to walk later than other species, possibly because babies' heavy heads and short legs make balance difficult. For some months before they can stand without support, babies practise "cruising" while holding onto furniture. Soon after they can stand alone well. At about 11½ months, most infants take their first unaided steps. Within a few weeks, soon after the first birthday, the child is walking well and thus achieves the status of toddler.

During the second year, children begin to climb stairs one at a time, putting one foot after another on each step; later they will alternate feet. Walking down stairs comes later. In

Box 6-1 *The Far-reaching Implications of Crawling*

Between 7 and 9 months, babies change greatly in many ways. They show an understanding of such concepts as "near" and "far." They imitate more complex behaviours, and they show new fears; but they also show a new sense of security around their parents and other caregivers. Since these changes involve so many different psychological functions and processes and occur during such a short time span, some observers tie them all in with a reorganization of brain function. This neurological development may be set in motion by a skill that emerges at this time: the ability to crawl, which makes it possible to get around independently. Crawling (a term we use here to refer to all forms of self-locomotion) has been called a "setting event" because it sets the stage for other changes in the infant and his or her relationships with the environment and the people in it (Bertenthal & Campos, 1987; Bertenthal, Campos, & Barrett, 1984; Bertenthal, Campos, & Kermoian, 1994).

Crawling exerts a powerful influence on babies' cognitive development by giving them a new view of the world. Infants become more sensitive to where objects are, how big they are, whether they can be moved, and how they look. Crawling helps babies learn to judge distances and perceive depth. As they move about, they see that people and objects look different close up and far away. Crawling babies, for example, can differentiate similar forms that are unlike in colour, size, or location (J. Campos, Bertenthal, & Benson, 1980). Babies are more successful in finding a toy hidden in a box when they move around the box themselves than when they are carried around it (Benson & Uzgiris, 1985).

The ability to crawl gets babies into new situations. As they become more mobile, they begin to hear such warnings as "Come back!" and "Don't touch!" They receive loving help as adult hands pick them up and turn them in a safer direction. They learn to look to caregivers for clues about whether a situation is secure or frightening—a skill known as social referencing (see chapter 8). Crawling babies do more social referencing than babies who have not yet begun to crawl (J. B. Garland, 1982). Crawling babies also may develop fear of heights; they learn to be afraid of places from which they might fall.

The ability to move from one place to another has other emotional and social implications: Crawling babies are no longer "prisoners" of place. If Ashley wants to be close to her mother and far away from a strange dog, she can move toward the one and away from the other. This is an important step in developing a sense of mastery, enhancing self-confidence and self-esteem.

Thus the physical milestone of crawling has far-reaching effects in helping babies see and respond to their world in new ways.

What's your view?

Which do you think has more important overall effects on development: crawling or walking? Why? Would you consider walking to be a setting event? Can you think of any other milestones that might be considered setting events?

Check it out!

For more information on this topic, go to **www.mcgrawhill.ca/college/papalia**.

---

their second year, toddlers run and jump. By age 3½, most children can balance briefly on one foot and begin to hop.

How Motor Development Occurs: Maturation in Context

The sequence just described was traditionally thought to be genetically programmed—a largely automatic, preordained series of steps directed by the maturing brain. Today, many developmentalists consider this view too simplistic. Instead, according to Esther Thelen (1995), motor development is a continuous interaction between baby and environment.

Thelen points to the *walking reflex:* stepping movements a neonate makes when held upright with the feet touching a surface. This behaviour usually disappears by the fourth month. Not until the latter part of the first year, when a baby is getting ready to walk, do such movements appear again. The usual explanation is a shift to cortical control: thus, an older baby's deliberate walking is a new skill masterminded by the developing brain. But, Thelen observes, a newborn's stepping involves the same kinds of movements the neonate makes while lying down and kicking. Why would stepping stop, only to reappear months later, whereas kicking continues? The answer, she suggests, may be that babies' legs become thicker and heavier during the early months, but not yet strong enough to carry the increased weight (Thelen & Fisher, 1982, 1983). In fact, when young infants are held in warm water, which helps support their legs, stepping reappears. Their ability to produce the movement has not changed—only the physical and environmental conditions that inhibit or promote it.

Maturation alone cannot explain such observations, says Thelen. Infant and environment form an interconnected system, and development has interacting causes. One is the infant's motivation to do something (say, pick up a toy or get to the other side of the room). The infant's physical characteristics and position in a particular setting (for example, lying in a crib or being held upright in a pool) offer opportunities and constraints that affect whether and how the baby can achieve the goal. Ultimately, a solution emerges as the baby tries out behaviours and retains those that most efficiently reach the goal. Rather than being solely in charge of this process, the maturing brain is only one part of it.

According to Thelen, normal babies develop the same skills in the same order because they are built approximately the same way and have similar physical challenges and needs. Thus they eventually discover that walking is more efficient than crawling in most situations. However, this discovery arises from each particular baby's experience in a particular context, and this may help explain why some babies learn to walk earlier than others.

Motor Development and Perception

Thelen's work builds in part on earlier studies by Eleanor and James Gibson, which point to a bi-directional connection between perception and motion. Infants' sensory perceptions help them learn about their environment so they can navigate in it. Motor experience sharpens and modifies their perceptions of what will happen if they move in a certain way.

How do crawling babies decide whether to try to cross a muddy patch or climb a hill? Crawling and, later, walking require infants to continually perceive the "fit," or *affordance,* between their own changing physical abilities and the characteristics of a variety of terrains—smooth or rough, flat or sloping (J. J. Gibson, 1979).

When and how do infants become aware of affordances? In a classic experiment (Walk & Gibson, 1961), researchers put babies on a Plexiglass tabletop over a checkerboard pattern that created the illusion of a vertical drop in the centre of the table—a **visual cliff.** Would infants perceive the illusion of depth and sense danger?

Six-month-old babies did see a difference between the "ledge," which seemed to afford them safe passage, and the "drop," which did not. They crawled freely on the "ledge" but avoided the "drop," even when they saw their mothers beckoning on the far side of the table. When even younger infants, ages 2 and 3 months, were placed face down over the visual cliff, their hearts slowed down, suggesting that **depth perception,** the ability to perceive objects and surfaces three-dimensionally, is either innate or learned very early (Campos, Langer, & Krowitz, 1970). However, a slowed heart rate, which indicates interest, does not mean that the younger infants were afraid of falling; fear would be indicated by a *faster* heart rate. Not until babies can get around by themselves do they learn from experience, or from a caregiver's warnings, that a steep drop-off can be dangerous (Bertenthal et al., 1994).

Motor experience sensitizes infants and toddlers to the affordances of slopes of varying steepness. When crawling and walking babies (average ages 8½ and 14 months) were placed on a walkway with an adjustable slope, neither the crawlers nor the walkers hesitated to climb uphill, a task that posed little danger. Going downhill was a different story. The inexperienced crawlers plunged down even the steepest slopes. The older and more experienced walkers walked down a shallow slope but slid down a steep one or avoided it altogether (Eppler, Adolph, & Weiner, 1996).

In a companion longitudinal study, infants were tested on various surfaces every 3 weeks from the time they began to crawl until a few weeks after they began to walk. The goal was to get a microgenetic picture (at short, frequent intervals) of how the infants adapted their perceptions of affordance to their changing motor abilities. As crawling

visual cliff Apparatus designed to give an illusion of depth and used to assess depth perception in infants

depth perception Ability to perceive objects and surfaces three-dimensionally

No matter how enticing a mother's arms are, this baby is staying away from them. As young as she is, she can perceive depth and wants to avoid falling off what looks like a cliff.

infants became more experienced, their judgments seemed to become more accurate and their explorations more efficient. However, this learning did not generalize to a new type of movement: When they began to walk, they had to learn to cope with slopes all over again (Adolph, 1997).

Cultural Influences on Motor Development

Although motor development follows a virtually universal sequence, its pace does seem to respond to certain contextual factors. When children are well fed and well cared for and have physical freedom and the chance to explore their surroundings, their motor development is likely to be normal. However, what is normal in one culture may not be in another.

African babies tend to be more advanced than U.S. and European infants in sitting, walking, and running. In Uganda, for example, babies typically walk at 10 months, as compared with 15 months in Canada and 12 months in the United States (Canadian Paediatric Society, 1999; Gardiner et al., 1998). Asian babies tend to develop these skills more slowly. Such differences may in part be related to ethnic differences in temperament (H. Kaplan & Dove, 1987; see chapter 8) or may reflect a culture's child-rearing practices (Gardiner et al., 1998).

Some cultures actively encourage early development of motor skills. In many African and West Indian cultures with advanced infant motor development, adults use special "handling routines," such as bouncing and stepping exercises, to strengthen babies' muscles (Hopkins & Westra, 1988). In one study, Jamaican infants, whose mothers used such handling routines daily, sat, crawled, and walked earlier than English infants, whose mothers gave them no such special handling (Hopkins & Westra, 1990).

On the other hand, some cultures discourage early motor development. Children of the Ache in eastern Paraguay do not begin to walk until 18 to 20 months of age—about 5 months later than Canadian babies (H. Kaplan & Dove, 1987). Ache mothers pull their babies back to their laps when the infants begin to crawl away. The Ache mothers closely supervise their babies to protect them from the hazards of nomadic life, and also because the women's primary responsibility is child-raising rather than subsistence labour. Yet, as 8- to 10-year-olds, Ache children climb tall trees, chop branches, and play in ways that enhance their motor skills (H. Kaplan & Dove, 1987). Normal development, then, need not follow the same timetable to reach the same destination.

Training Motor Skills Experimentally

Can systematic training speed up motor development? For many years, developmental scientists thought the answer was no. In a famous experiment, Arnold Gesell (1929) trained one monozygotic twin, but not the other, in stair-climbing, block-building, and hand coordination. As the children got older, the untrained twin became just as expert as the trained one, showing, said Gesell, "the powerful influence of maturation." Gesell concluded that children perform certain activities when they are ready, and training gives no advantage.

Yet culturally induced differences in rates of motor development (discussed in the preceding section) seem to challenge Gesell's view; and more recent experimental findings indicate that early training *can* influence walking. In one study, infants trained in stepping at 8 weeks walked at an average of 10 months, while those in an untrained control group did not begin walking until an average of 12½ months (P. R. Zelazo, Zelazo, & Kolb, 1972). Why did this happen? Perhaps there is a critical period during which the newborn's repetitive walking response can be translated into a specific later voluntary action. Then again, practice in one such behaviour pattern might promote maturation of the brain's ability to control related activities. Another possibility, in line with Thelen's view, is that training strengthened the infants' legs, allowing them to resume stepping at an earlier-than-usual age.

Such findings do not indicate whether changes in the brain or in muscle strength, or both, are involved; but they do seem to rule out a view of early motor development as purely biologically determined and suggest that learning plays a greater role than has generally been believed.

Checkpoint ✔

Can you . . .

✔ Trace a typical infant's progress in head control, hand control, and locomotion?

✔ Discuss how maturation, perception, environmental influence, and training relate to early motor development?

What's your view

- Is it advisable to try to teach babies skills such as walking before they develop them on their own?

Guidepost 6

How can we enhance babies' chances of survival and health?

Many Canadian parents put their babies in mobile walkers in the belief that the babies will learn to walk earlier. Actually, by restricting babies' motor exploration, and sometimes their view of their own movements, walkers may *delay* motor skill development. In one study, infants who used walkers sat, crawled, and walked later than babies who did not use walkers, and they also scored lower on tests of cognitive development (Siegel & Burton, 1999). Furthermore, walkers can be dangerous. The Canadian Paediatric Society has therefore recommended against their use (CPS Injury Prevention Committee, 1985; reaffirmed 2000).

Health

Infancy and toddlerhood are risky times of life, though far less so than they used to be. How many babies die during the first year, and why? What can be done to prevent dangerous or debilitating childhood diseases? How can we ensure that infants and toddlers will live, grow, and develop as they should?

Reducing Infant Mortality

One of the most tragic losses is the death of an infant. Great strides have been made in protecting the lives of new babies, but these improvements are not evenly distributed throughout the population. Too many babies still die—some of them without warning and for no apparent reason.

Trends in Infant Mortality

In recent decades, prospects for surviving the early years of life have improved in all regions of the world. The improvement is especially dramatic in Africa, the Middle East, and Southeast Asia, where the threat of early death from such causes as birth complications, neonatal disorders, diarrhea, respiratory disease, and vaccine-preventable disease remains the greatest (Wegman, 1999). Worldwide, in 1998 an estimated 7.7 million children were expected to die before their first birthday, accounting for about 14 per cent of all deaths. But while infant deaths represent as many as 25 per cent of all deaths in non-industrialized countries, they account for only 1 per cent of deaths in the industrialized world (U.S. Bureau of the Census, 1999).

infant mortality rate Proportion of babies born alive who die within the first year

In Canada, the **infant mortality rate**—the proportion of babies who die within the first year—is the lowest ever. In 1995 there were 7 deaths in the first year for every 1,000 live male births and 6 for every 1,000 live female births, compared with 15 per 1,000 for males and 12 per 1,000 for females in 1975 (Canadian Institute of Child Health [CICH], 2000). The overall infant mortality rate in Aboriginal communities is higher than the Canadian average. In 1995, the rate was 15 deaths for every 1,000 live births (CICH, 2000). Two-thirds of infant deaths take place during the neonatal period (Guyer et al., 1999; Mathews et al., 2000; NCHS, 1999). Most likely to die in infancy are babies whose mothers were teenagers, did not finish high school, were unmarried, smoked during pregnancy, had no prenatal care, or had multiple births; and those who were born preterm or of low birth weight (Mathews et al., 2000).

The continuing improvement in infant mortality rates during the 1990s, even at a time when more babies are born perilously small, has been due in part to effective treatment for respiratory distress and to prevention of sudden infant death syndrome (SIDS) (discussed in the next section), as well as to medical advances in keeping very small babies alive and treating sick newborns. Still, in 1997, 1,927 infants died during their first year. Canadian babies, not including Aboriginal infants, have a better chance of reaching their first birthday than babies in many other industrialized countries (see Figure 6-7). This comparison, particularly in comparison with the United States, provides an interesting illustration of socio-cultural influences on child health. Despite maintaining one of the most technologically advanced medical systems in the world, the United States ranks quite poorly in the world on infant mortality. The higher survival rates of infants in Canada and other industrialized countries compared to the United States may be attributable to free and accessible pre- and postnatal health care (Gardiner et al., 1998).

Perinatal conditions (including low birth weight) were the leading cause of infant deaths in Canada in 1997. Second was birth defects (congenital abnormalities), and third was SIDS; these causes together accounted for 80 per cent of all infant deaths. Other significant causes were injury (poisonings and self-inflicted injuries), and nervous system and circulatory problems. SIDS is the greatest cause of death in Aboriginal infants, accounting for 27 per cent of total deaths, followed by perinatal conditions (24 per cent) and congenital anomalies (19 per cent) (CICH, 2000).

For example, there is an increasing prevalence of diabetes in Aboriginal communities in Canada, but the standards of care for this condition among Aboriginal groups do not meet recommended guidelines (Indian and Inuit Health Committee, Canadian Paediatric Society [CPS], 1994). The higher prevalence of high–birth weight babies in Aboriginal communities, compared to non-Aboriginal babies in Canada, might be related to this difficulty (CICH, 2000; CPS, 1994; see Figure 6-8). Furthermore, Aboriginal babies are more than twice as likely to die in their first year as the national rate—15 as compared with 6 per 1,000 live births in 1995 (CICH, 2000). However, mortality rates in the neonatal period are becoming comparable between Aboriginal and non-Aboriginal populations in Canada (CICH, 2000; see Figure 6-9).

Although infant mortality has declined for all ethnic groups since 1980, largely as a result of improvements in treatment and care of low–birth weight newborns, disparities have increased—perhaps because such measures have disproportionately benefited white infants (Alexander, Tompkins, Allen, & Hulsey, 2000; CICH, 2000).

Sudden Infant Death Syndrome (SIDS)

Sudden infant death syndrome (SIDS), sometimes called "crib death," is the sudden death of an infant under 1 year of age in which the cause of death remains unexplained after a thorough investigation that includes an autopsy. In 1998, 154 Canadian babies died as a result of SIDS (CICH, 2000). Although there has been no change in the number of SIDS deaths in Aboriginal populations, there has been a drop in SIDS deaths in the non-Aboriginal population (CICH, 2000).

A number of risk factors, such as being male, and premature or of low birth weight, are associated with SIDS. Often SIDS mothers are young, have received late or no prenatal care, and smoked during pregnancy (Canadian Foundation for the Study of Infant Deaths, the Canadian Institute of Child Health, the Canadian Paediatric Society and Health Canada, 1999, reaffirmed 2000; CICH 2000; USDHHS, 1990). The risk of SIDS may be worsened by poor socio-economic circumstances, but SIDS also strikes infants in advantaged families.

What causes SIDS? Mounting evidence points to brain abnormalities (NICHD, 1997, updated 2000). Researchers in Italy have found a strong correlation between some cases of SIDS or near-SIDS and an unusual abnormality in the heartbeat, which may be genetic (Schwartz, Stramba-Badiale, et al., 1998; Schwartz et al., 2000).

It seems likely that SIDS most often results from a combination of factors. An underlying biological defect may make some infants vulnerable, during a critical period in their development, to certain contributing or triggering experiences, such as exposure to smoke, prenatal exposure to caffeine, or sleeping on the stomach (Canadian Foundation for the Study of Infant Deaths, the Canadian Institute of Child Health, the Canadian Paediatric

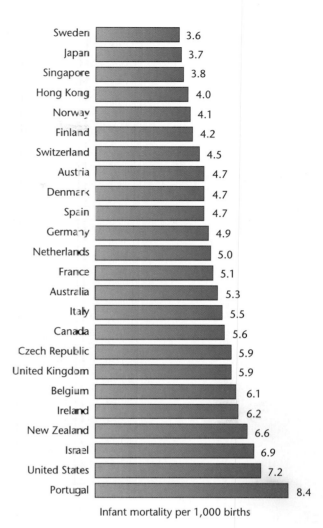

Infant mortality per 1,000 births

Figure 6-7

Infant mortality rates in industrialized countries, 1997. In recent years most nations, including Canada, have shown dramatic improvement.

Note: Rates for Finland, Denmark, and Portugal are for 1998; rates for Canada and Spain are for 1996. Rates for Japan, Finland, United Kingdom, France, Spain, Greece, and Portugal are based on preliminary data.

Source: Guyer et al., 1999, Table 11, p. 1241, based on data from United Nations 1997 Demographic Yearbook, United Nations Personnel, and country profiles

sudden infant death syndrome
Sudden and unexplained death of an apparently healthy infant

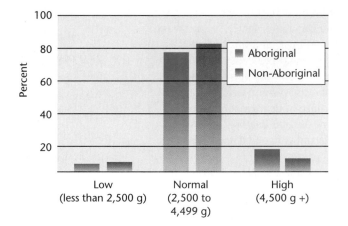

Figure 6-8

Birth Weight Distribution by Ethnic Group in Canada (1997)

Source: Adapted from CICH, 2000, p. 156.

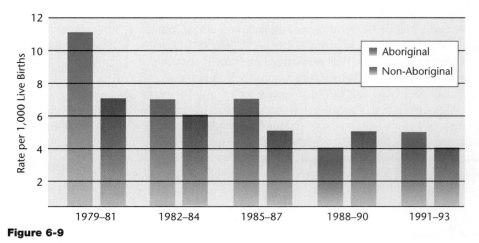

Figure 6-9

Neonatal Mortality Rates in Canada, 1979 to 1993

Source: Adapted from CICH, 2000, p. 173.

Society and Health Canada, 1999, reaffirmed 2000; Cutz, Perrin, Hackman, & Czegledy-Nagy, 1996; R. P. Ford et al., 1998).

An important clue to what often happens in SIDS has emerged from the discovery of defects in chemical receptors, or nerve endings, in the brain stem, which receive and send messages that regulate breathing, heart beat, body temperature, and arousal. These defects, which may originate early in fetal life, may prevent SIDS babies from awakening when they are breathing too much stale air containing carbon dioxide trapped under their blankets (Kinney et al., 1995; Panigrahy et al., 2000). This may be especially likely to happen when the baby is sleeping face down. Many SIDS babies may be deficient in a protective mechanism that allows an infant to become aroused enough to turn the head when breathing is restricted (Canadian Foundation for the Study of Infant Deaths, the Canadian Institute of Child Health, the Canadian Paediatric Society and Health Canada, 1999, reaffirmed 2000; Waters, Gonzalez, Jean, Morielli, & Brouillette, 1996). Even in normal, healthy infants, "tummy" sleeping inhibits the swallowing reflex, which protects the airways from choking on an infusion of nasal and digestive fluids (Jeffery, Megevand, & Page, 1999).

Research strongly supports a relationship between SIDS and sleeping on the stomach. Side-sleeping is not safe either, because infants put to bed on their sides often turn onto their stomachs (Canadian Foundation for the Study of Infant Deaths, the Canadian Institute of Child Health, the Canadian Paediatric Society and Health Canada, 1999, reaffirmed 2000; Skadberg, Morild, & Markestad, 1998; J. A. Taylor et al., 1996). SIDS rates fell by as much as 70 per cent in some countries following recommendations that healthy babies be put to sleep on their backs (Dwyer, Ponsonby, Blizzard, Newman, & Cochrane, 1995; C. E. Hunt, 1996; Skadberg et al., 1998; Willinger, Hoffman, & Hartford, 1994). Infants should not sleep on soft surfaces, such as pillows, quilts, or sheepskin, or under loose covers, which, especially when the infant is face down, may increase the risk of overheating or rebreathing (breathing the infant's own waste products) (Canadian Foundation for the Study of Infant Deaths, the Canadian Institute of Child Health, the Canadian Paediatric Society and Health Canada, 1999, reaffirmed 2000).

As many as 1 in 5 SIDS deaths occurs in a child-care setting, where infants often sleep on their stomachs (Moon, Patel, & Shaefer, 2000).

Sleeping on the back does tend to result in a slight temporary delay in the development of motor skills requiring upper-body strength, such as rolling over, sitting, crawling, and standing. However, these milestones are still attained within the normal age range (Davis, Moon, Sachs, & Ottolini, 1998), and no difference is detectable by 18 months. It is important for infants to have plenty of "tummy time" while awake and supervised, for development of shoulder strength.

Sharing a bed with the mother is a common practice in some cultures; its possible role in preventing or promoting SIDS has been controversial (see Box 6-2).

This Kergez infant in China—securely placed face up in a hammock-like rope cradle—is being protected against sudden infant death syndrome (SIDS).

Death from Injuries

Accidents and injuries are the fourth leading cause of death in infancy in Canada, following SIDS, birth defects, and perinatal conditions. In 1997, 3 per cent of infant deaths in the general Canadian population were caused by injury (CICH, 2000). In a 3-year study of injury deaths of infants, based on Canadian national data collected between 1994 and 1997, the greatest cause of injury death was surgery, accounting for 11 deaths per 100,000, followed by falls, at 9 per 100,000 deaths (CICH, 2000). Among the rest, the leading causes of death were from intentional injuries (we discuss child abuse and related fatalities in chapter 9) medical misadventure, being struck, and drug side effects. In Aboriginal communities, 7 per cent of infant deaths between 1989 and 1993 resulted from injury (CICH, 2000).

Immunization for Better Health

Such once-familiar and sometimes fatal childhood illnesses as measles, pertussis (whooping cough), and infantile paralysis (polio) are now largely preventable, thanks to the development of vaccines that mobilize the body's natural defences. Unfortunately, many children still are inadequately protected. In the non-industrialized world, 18 per cent of deaths of children under age 5 are from vaccine-preventable diseases: measles, neonatal tetanus, pertussis, and tuberculosis (Wegman, 1999).

Since the development of the Canadian Immunization Guide (Health Canada, 1998), vaccination rates have jumped and the prevalence of vaccine-preventable illnesses has dropped sharply. By 1997, immunization rates for 19- to 35-month-olds had reached 87 per cent. Still, many children lack one or more of the required shots, and there is substantial variation in coverage (National Advisory Committee on Immunization (NACI), 1999).

One reason some parents hesitate to immunize their children is fear that vaccines (especially pertussis vaccine) may cause brain damage. However, the association between pertussis vaccine and neurologic illness appears very small (Gale et al., 1994). The potential damage from the diseases that this vaccine prevents is far greater than the risks of the vaccine.

New and improved vaccines are being devised. A new vaccine for chicken pox is recommended for all children over 1 year of age and for adolescents and adults who have not had the disease ([U.S.] Centers for Disease Control and Prevention, 1999a). Although sometimes considered a mild disease, chicken pox is the leading cause of vaccine-preventable deaths of children in the United States; and the vaccine is more than 95 per cent effective in preventing severe cases (Jefferson, 1999). Recently or soon to be approved are new vaccines against pneumonia, meningitis, influenza, gastric ulcers, cervical cancer caused by human papilloma virus, and rheumatic heart disease that follows a type of streptococcal infection. A vaccine against the AIDS virus is being tested ([U.S.] Centers for Disease Control and Prevention, 1999a).

Checkpoint ✔

Can you . . .

✔ Summarize trends in infant mortality?

✔ Discuss risk factors, causes, and prevention of sudden infant death syndrome?

✔ Explain why full immunization of all infants and preschoolers is important?

What's your view

• Who should be primarily responsible for ensuring that children are immunized: parents, community agencies, or government?

There is considerable cultural variation in newborns' sleeping arrangements. In many cultures, including many Canadian Aboriginal and immigrant groups, infants sleep in the same room as their mothers for the first few years of life, and frequently in the same bed, making it easier to nurse at night (Broude, 1995). In Canada, many households have a separate bed and a separate room for the infant, reflecting the recommendations of some child-care experts.

Some experts find benefits in the shared sleeping pattern. One research team that has been monitoring sleep patterns of mothers and their 3-month-old infants found that those who sleep together tend to wake each other up during the night and suggested that this may prevent the baby from sleeping too long and too deeply and having long breathing pauses that might be fatal (McKenna & Mosko, 1993). However, the American Academy of Pediatrics Task Force on Infant Positioning and SIDS (1997) did not find this evidence persuasive; instead, the Task Force found that, under some conditions, such as the use of soft bedding, or maternal smoking or drug use, bed-sharing can increase the risk of SIDS. Indeed, in a review of medical examiners' investigations of deaths in the St. Louis area between 1994 and 1997, a shared sleep surface was the site of death in nearly half (47.1 per cent) of the cases investigated (Kemp et al., 2000).

This is far from a new concern: Medieval church authorities forbade parents to sleep next to their newborns for fear of suffocation (Nakajima & Mayor, 1996). Adult beds are not designed to meet safety standards for infants, as cribs are (Health Canada, 2000). Yet modern-day Japan, where mothers and infants commonly sleep in the same bed, has one of the lowest SIDS rates in the world (Hoffman & Hillman, 1992).

One thing is clear: Bed-sharing promotes breast-feeding. Infants who sleep with their mothers breast-feed about three times longer during the night than infants who sleep in separate beds (McKenna, Mosko, & Richard, 1997). By snuggling up together, mother and baby stay oriented toward each other's subtle bodily signals. Mothers can respond more quickly and easily to an infant's first whimpers of hunger, rather than having to wait until the baby's cries are loud enough to be heard from the next room.

Societal values influence parents' attitudes and behaviours. Throughout this book we will see many ways in which such culturally determined attitudes and behaviours affect children.

What's your view?

In view of preliminary medical evidence that bed-sharing between mother and infant may contribute to SIDS, should mothers from cultures in which sharing a bed is customary be discouraged from doing so?

Check it out

For more information on this topic, go to **www.mcgrawhill.ca/ college/papalia**.

Summary and Key Terms

Growth and Nutrition

Guidepost 1 How do babies grow, and what influences their growth?

- Normal physical growth and sensory and motor development proceed according to the cephalocaudal and proximodistal principles.

- A child's body grows most dramatically during the first year of life; growth proceeds at a rapid but diminishing rate throughout the first 3 years.

Guidepost 2 How and what should babies be fed?

- Historic shifts in feeding practices reflected efforts to improve infant survival and health.

- Breast-feeding offers many health advantages and sensory and cognitive benefits. However, the quality of the relationship between parents and infant may be more important than the feeding method.

- Babies should not start solid foods and fruit juices until 6 months of age and should not get cow's milk until 1 year.

- Obese babies are *not* at special risk of becoming obese adults, unless they have obese parents. However, too much fat and cholesterol intake may lead to eventual cardiac problems.

The Brain and Reflex Behaviour

Guidepost 3 How does the brain develop, and how do environmental factors affect its early growth?

- The central nervous system controls sensorimotor functioning. Brain growth spurts coincide with changes in cognitive behaviour. Lateralization enables each hemisphere of the brain to specialize in different functions.

- The brain grows most rapidly during the months before and immediately after birth as neurons migrate to their assigned locations, form synaptic connections, and undergo integration and differentiation. Cell death and myelination improve the efficiency of the nervous system.

- Reflex behaviours—primitive, locomotor, and postural—are indications of neurological status. Most early reflexes drop out during the first year as voluntary, cortical control develops.

- Especially during the early period of rapid growth, environmental experience can influence brain development positively or negatively.

  central nervous system (121)   brain growth spurts (122) lateralization (122)   neurons (123)   integration (124) differentiation (124)   cell death (124)   myelination (126) reflex behaviours (126)   plasticity (128)

Early Sensory Capacities

Guidepost 4   How do the senses develop during infancy?

- Sensory capacities, present from birth and even in the womb, develop rapidly in the first months of life. Very young infants can discriminate between stimuli.

- Touch seems to be the first sense to develop and mature. Newborns are sensitive to pain. Smell, taste, and hearing also begin to develop in the womb.

- Vision is the least developed sense at birth but sharpens within the first 6 months.

Motor Development

Guidepost 5   What are some early milestones in motor development, and what are some influences on it?

- Motor skills develop in a certain sequence, which may depend largely on maturation but also on context, experience, and motivation. Simple skills combine into increasingly complex systems.

- Self-locomotion seems to be a "setting event," bringing about changes in all domains of development.

- Depth perception is present at a very early age and is related to motor development.

- Environmental factors, including cultural practices, may affect the pace of early motor development.

- Training or practice can accelerate acquisition of specific motor skills.

  systems of action (131)   gross motor skills (132) fine motor skills (132)   visual cliff (134)   depth perception (134)

Health

Guidepost 6   How can we enhance babies' chances of survival and health?

- Although infant mortality has diminished, it is still disturbingly high for Aboriginal babies. Perinatal conditions and birth defects are the leading causes of death in the first year; for Aboriginal infants, SIDS is the leading cause.

- Sudden infant death syndrome (SIDS) is the third leading cause of death in infants in Canada. Major risk factors are exposure to smoke and, prenatally, to caffeine, and sleeping in the prone position.

- Injuries are the fourth leading cause of death.

- Vaccine-preventable diseases have declined as rates of immunization have improved, but many preschoolers are not fully protected.

  infant mortality rate (136) sudden infant death syndrome (SIDS) (137)

OLC Preview

The Online Learning Centre for *A Child's World,* First Canadian Edition, offers additional information and links to recommended websites on topics such as the implications of crawling and sleep customs and the developmental and relational issues surrounding infant sleep. Check out **www.mcgrawhill.ca/college/papalia.**

Cognitive Development During the First Three Years

So runs my dream; but what am I?
An infant crying in the night;
An infant crying for the light,
And with no language but a cry.

—Alfred, Lord Tennyson, *In Memoriam*, Canto 54 1850

Focus *William Erasmus Darwin, Naturalist's Son*

Charles and
"Doddy" Darwin

On December 27, 1839, when the naturalist Charles Darwin was 30 years old, his first baby, William Erasmus Darwin, affectionately known as Doddy, was born. That day—20 years before the publication of Charles Darwin's *Origin of Species,* which outlined his theory of evolution based on natural selection—the proud father began keeping a diary of observations of his newborn son. It was these notes, published in 1877,[*] that first called scientific attention to the developmental nature of infant behaviour.

What abilities are babies born with? How do they learn about their world? How do they communicate, first non-verbally and then through language? These were among the questions Darwin set out to answer—questions still central to the study of cognitive development.

Darwin's keen observation illuminates how coordination of physical and mental activity helps an infant adapt to the world—as in this entry written when Doddy was 4 months old:

> Took my finger to his mouth & as usual could not get it in, on account of his own hand being in the way; then he slipped his own back & so got my finger in.—This was not chance & therefore a kind of reasoning. (Diary, p. 12; quoted in Keegan & Gruber, 1985, p. 135)

In Darwin's notes, we can see Doddy developing new cognitive skills through interaction not only with his father's finger, but with other objects as well. The diary depicts a series of encounters with reflected images. In these episodes Doddy gains knowledge, not in sudden bursts or jumps, but through gradual integration of new experience with existing patterns of behaviour. In Darwin's view—as, later, in Piaget's—this was not merely a matter of piling new knowledge upon old; it involved an actual transformation of the way the mind is organized.

When Doddy, at 4½ months, saw his likeness and his father's in a mirror, Darwin noted that the baby "seemed surprised at my voice coming from behind him, my image being in front" (Diary, p. 18; quoted in Keegan & Gruber, 1985, p. 135). Two months later, Doddy apparently had solved the mystery: Now, when his father, standing behind him, made a funny face in the mirror, the infant "was aware that the image . . . was not real & therefore . . . turned round to look" (Diary, pp. 21–22; quoted in Keegan & Gruber, 1985, pp. 135–136).

At first, this newfound understanding did not generalize to other reflective materials. Two weeks later, Doddy seemed puzzled to see his father's reflection in a window. By 9 months, however, the boy realized that "the shadow of a hand, made by a candle, was to be looked for behind, in [the] same manner as in [a] looking glass" (Diary, p. 23; quoted in Keegan

---

[*]The source for analysis of Darwin's diary was Keegan and Gruber (1985).

& Gruber, 1985, p. 136). His recognition that reflections could emanate from objects behind him now extended to shadows, another kind of two-dimensional image.

Darwin was particularly interested in documenting his son's progress in communication. He believed that language acquisition is a natural process, akin to earlier physical expressions of feelings. Through smiling, crying, laughing, facial expressions, and sounds of pleasure or pain, Doddy managed to communicate quite well with his parents even before uttering his first word. One of his first meaningful verbal expressions was "Ah!"—uttered when he recognized an image in a glass.

● ● ●

Darwin made these observations more than 160 years ago, at a time when infants' cognitive abilities were widely underestimated. We now know—as Darwin inferred from his observations of Doddy—that normal, healthy infants are born with the ability to learn and remember and with a capacity for acquiring and using speech. They use their growing sensory and cognitive capacities to exert control over their behaviour and their world.

In this chapter we look at infants' and toddlers' cognitive abilities from three classic perspectives—behaviourist, psychometric, and Piagetian—and then from three newer perspectives: information processing, cognitive neuroscientific, and social-contextual. We trace the early development of language and discuss how it comes about. Finally, we see how adults help infants and toddlers become more competent with language.

After you have read and studied this chapter, you should be able to answer each of the Guidepost questions that appear at the top of the next page. Look for them again in the margins, where they point to important concepts throughout the chapter. To check your understanding of these Guideposts, review the end-of-chapter summary. Checkpoints located throughout the chapter will help you verify your understanding of what you have read.

1. How do infants learn, and how long can they remember?

2. Can infants' and toddlers' intelligence be measured, and how can it be improved?

3. How did Piaget describe infants' and toddlers' cognitive development, and how have his claims stood up?

4. How can we measure infants' ability to process information, and how does this ability relate to future intelligence?

5. When do babies begin to think about characteristics of the physical world?

6. What can brain research reveal about the development of cognitive skills?

7. How does social interaction with adults advance cognitive competence?

8. How do babies develop language?

9. What influences contribute to linguistic progress?

Studying Cognitive Development: Classic Approaches

When Doddy Darwin, at 4 months, figured out how to get his father's finger into his mouth by moving his own hand out of the way, he showed **intelligent behaviour.** Intelligent behaviour is *goal-oriented* and *adaptive:* directed at adjusting to the circumstances and conditions of life. Intelligence is influenced by both inheritance and experience (refer back to chapter 3). Intelligence enables people to acquire, remember, and use knowledge; to understand concepts and relationships; and to solve everyday problems.

intelligent behaviour Behaviour that is goal-oriented and adaptive to circumstances and conditions of life

How and when do babies learn to solve problems? How and when does memory develop? What accounts for individual differences in cognitive abilities? Can we measure a baby's intelligence? Can we predict how smart that baby will be in the future? Many investigators have taken one of three classic approaches to the study of such questions:

- The **behaviourist approach** studies the basic *mechanics* of learning. It is concerned with how behaviour changes in response to experience.
- The **psychometric approach** seeks to measure individual differences in *quantity* of intelligence by using intelligence tests. The higher a child scores, the more intelligent she or he is presumed to be.
- The **Piagetian approach** looks at changes, or stages, in the *quality* of cognitive functioning. It is concerned with how the mind structures its activities and adapts to the environment.

behaviourist approach Approach to the study of cognitive development that is concerned with basic mechanics of learning

psychometric approach Approach to the study of cognitive development that seeks to measure the quantity of intelligence a person possesses

Piagetian approach Approach to the study of cognitive development that describes qualitative stages in cognitive functioning

All three approaches, as well as the three newer ones we discuss in the following section—the information-processing, cognitive-neuroscience, and social-contextual approaches—help us understand intelligent behaviour. Let's see what each of the three classic approaches can tell us about the cognitive development of infants and toddlers.

Behaviourist Approach: Basic Mechanics of Learning

Babies are born with the ability to learn from what they see, hear, smell, taste, and touch, and they have at least some ability to remember what they learn. Of course, maturation is essential to this process. But while learning theorists recognize maturation as a limiting factor, their main interest is in mechanisms of learning.

Let's look first at two simple learning processes (introduced in chapter 2) that behaviourists study: *classical conditioning* and *operant conditioning.* Later we will consider *habituation,* another simple form of learning, which information-processing researchers study.

Guidepost 1

How do infants learn, and how long can they remember?

Figure 7-1

Three Steps in Classical Conditioning

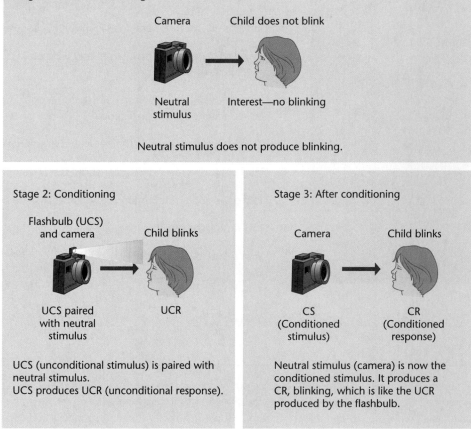

Stage 1: Before conditioning

Camera Child does not blink

Neutral Interest—no blinking
stimulus

Neutral stimulus does not produce blinking.

Stage 2: Conditioning

Flashbulb (UCS) Child blinks
and camera

UCS paired UCR
with neutral
stimulus

UCS (unconditional stimulus) is paired with
neutral stimulus.
UCS produces UCR (unconditional response).

Stage 3: After conditioning

Camera Child blinks

CS CR
(Conditioned (Conditioned
stimulus) response)

Neutral stimulus (camera) is now the
conditioned stimulus. It produces a
CR, blinking, which is like the UCR
produced by the flashbulb.

Classical and Operant Conditioning

Eager to capture Anna's memorable moments on film, her father took pictures of the infant smiling, crawling, and showing off her other achievements. Whenever the flash went off, Anna blinked. One evening when Anna was 11 months old, she saw her father hold the camera up to his eye—and she blinked *before* the flash. She had learned to associate the camera with the bright light, so that the sight of the camera alone activated her blinking reflex.

Anna's blinking is an example of **classical conditioning,** in which a person or animal learns to make a reflex (involuntary) response (in this case, blinking) to a stimulus (the camera) that did not originally provoke the response. As Figure 7-1 shows, the camera was initially a neutral stimulus; It did not make Anna blink. The flash was an unconditioned stimulus (UCS); Anna's blinking when she saw it go off was an unconditioned response (UCR). After Anna learned to connect the camera with the flash, the camera became a conditioned stimulus (CS); Anna's blinking before the flash was a conditioned response (CR).

Classical conditioning enables infants to anticipate an event before it happens by forming associations between stimuli (such as the camera and the flash) that regularly occur together. Classically conditioned learning will fade, or become *extinct,* if it is not reinforced. Thus, if Anna frequently saw the camera without the flash, she would eventually stop blinking.

In classical conditioning, the learner is passive, absorbing and automatically reacting to stimuli. By contrast, in **operant conditioning**—as when a baby learns that smiling brings loving attention—the learner acts, or operates, on the environment. The infant learns to make a certain response to an environmental stimulus (smiling at sight of the parents) in order to produce a particular effect (parental attention).

Infant Memory

Can you remember anything that happened to you before you were 3 years old? The chances are you can't. This inability to remember early events is called *infantile amnesia.*

classical conditioning Learning based on associating a stimulus that does not ordinarily elicit a particular response with another stimulus that ordinarily does elicit the response

operant conditioning Learning based on reinforcement or punishment

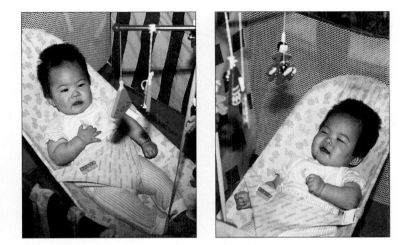

Babies 2 to 6 months old can remember, after a hiatus of 2 days to 2 weeks, that they were able to activate a mobile by kicking; they show this by kicking as soon as they see the mobile.

One explanation, supported by Piaget (1969) and others, is that early events are not stored in memory because the brain is not yet developed enough. Other researchers suggest that children cannot store events in memory until they can talk about them.

Now, research using operant conditioning with non-verbal, age-appropriate tasks suggests that infants' memory processes may not be fundamentally different from those of older children and adults. These studies have found that babies will repeat an action days or weeks later—*if* they are periodically reminded of the situation in which they learned it (Rovee-Collier, 1999).

In a series of experiments by Carolyn Rovee-Collier and her associates, infants have been operantly conditioned to kick to activate a mobile attached to one ankle by a ribbon. Babies 2 to 6 months old, when again shown the mobiles days or weeks later, repeat the kicking, even though their legs are no longer attached to the mobiles. When the infants see the mobiles, they kick more than before the conditioning, showing that recognition of the mobiles triggers a memory of their initial experience with them (Rovee-Collier, 1996, 1999). In a similar task designed for older infants and toddlers, the child is conditioned to press a lever to make a miniature train go around a track. The length of time a conditioned response can be retained increases with age, from 2 days for 2-month-olds to 13 weeks for 18-month-olds (Hartshorn et al., 1998; Rovee-Collier, 1996, 1999; see Figure 7-2).

Young infants' memory of a behaviour seems to be specifically linked to the original cue. Two- to 6-month-olds will repeat a learned behaviour only when they see the original mobile or train. However, older infants, between 9 and 12 months, will "try out" the behaviour on a different train, if no more than 2 weeks have gone by since the training (Rovee-Collier, 1999).

Context can affect recollection when a memory has weakened. Three-, 9-, and 12-month-olds can initially recognize the mobile or train in a setting different from the one in which they were trained, but not after long delays. Periodic non-verbal reminders through brief exposure to the original stimulus can sustain a memory from early infancy through 1½ to 2 years of age (Rovee-Collier, 1999).

Since infants can remember, why don't their early memories last? It may be because the crucial match between the situation in which something is learned and the situation in which it can be recalled is lost after a long period of time—a period in which the child begins to rely more on verbal than on non-verbal cues (Rovee-Collier, 1999).

Psychometric Approach: Developmental and Intelligence Testing

The precise nature of intelligence has been debated for many years, as has the best way to measure it. Beginning in the 19th century, there were attempts to measure intelligence by such characteristics as head size and reaction time, and then by tests that scored strength of hand squeeze, pain sensitivity, weight discrimination, judgment of time, and rote recall. However, these tests had little predictive value.

Checkpoint ✔

Can you . . .

✔ Distinguish the goals of the behaviourist, psychometric, and Piagetian approaches to the study of cognitive development?

✔ Identify conditions under which newborns can be classically or operantly conditioned?

✔ Summarize what studies of operant conditioning have shown about infant memory?

Figure 7-2

Maximum number of weeks that infants of varying ages can retain knowledge of how to operate either a mobile or a miniature train. Regardless of the task, retention improves with age.

Source: Rovee-Collier, 1999, Fig. 4, p. 83.

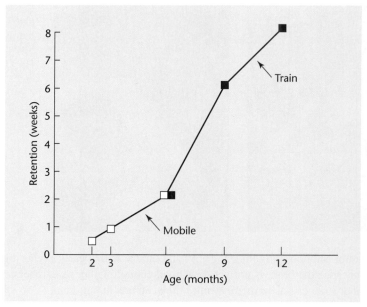

Guidepost 2

Can infants' and toddlers' intelligence be measured, and how can it be improved?

Then, at the beginning of the 20th century, school administrators in Paris asked the psychologist Alfred Binet to devise a way to identify children who could not handle academic work and who should be removed from regular classes and given special training. The test that Binet and his colleague Theodore Simon developed was the forerunner of psychometric tests, used for children of all levels of ability, which score intelligence by numbers. One is the Stanford-Binet Intelligence Scale, an American version of the traditional Binet-Simon tests (see chapter 10), and another is the Wechsler Preschool and Primary Scales of Intelligence, third edition (WPPSI–III). Although American tests, like the Stanford-Binet and the WPPSI–III, are used in Canada, their use for Canadian children may not be appropriate. The test norms used to compare individual children's performance do not reflect the make-up of the Canadian population (French, French, & Rutherford, 1999), and the tests could be biased against some ethnic groups in Canada. New Canadians and Aboriginal children could obtain lower scores than they would have achieved if the tests were appropriate to their language backgrounds, cultural experiences, and upbringing (Dolan, 1999; Saklofske & Schwean, 1995). Newer editions, like the Weschler Intelligence Scale for Children–III, are distributed in Canada with Canadian-based norms (Wechsler, 1996).

The goals of psychometric testing are to quantitatively measure the factors that are thought to make up intelligence (such as comprehension and reasoning), and, from the results of that measurement, to predict future performance (such as school achievement). **IQ (intelligence quotient) tests** consist of questions or tasks that are supposed to show how much of the measured abilities a person has, by comparing that person's performance with that of other test-takers.

For school-age children, intelligence test scores can predict school performance fairly accurately and reliably. Testing infants and toddlers is another matter.

Testing Infants and Toddlers

Measuring infants' intelligence is virtually impossible. Since babies cannot tell us what they know and how they think, the most obvious way to gauge their intelligence is by assessing what they can do. But if they do not grasp a rattle, it is hard to tell whether they do not know how, do not feel like doing it, do not realize what is expected of them, or have simply lost interest.

Still, sometimes there are reasons to test an infant's cognitive development. Developmental testing may reassure worried parents that their child's development is normal—or may alert them to a problem.

The **Bayley Scales of Infant Development** (Bayley II, 1993; see Table 7-1) are designed to assess the developmental status of children from 1 month to 3½ years. The

IQ (intelligence quotient) tests Psychometric tests that seek to measure intelligence by comparing a test-taker's performance with standardized norms

Bayley Scales of Infant Development Standardized test of infants' mental and motor development

Table 7-1	Sample Tasks in the Bayley Scales of Infant Development	
Age (in months)	**Mental Scale***	**Motor Scale***
1	Eyes follow moving person	Lifts head when held at shoulder
3	Reaches for suspended ring	Turns from back to side
6	Manipulates bell, showing interest in detail	Turns from back to stomach
9	Jabbers expressively	Raises self to standing position
12	Pats toy in imitation	Walks alone
14–16	Uses two different words appropriately	Walks up stairs with help
20–22	Names three objects	Jumps off floor with both feet
26–28	Matches four colours	Imitates hand movements
32–34	Uses past tense	Walks up stairs, alternating feet
38–42	Counts	Walks down stairs, alternating feet

*Task most children this age can do

Source: Bayley, 1993.

Bayley–II has three sections: a *mental scale,* which measures such abilities as perception, memory, learning, and vocalization; a *motor scale,* which measures motor skills, such as sitting, standing, grasping, and sensory-motor coordination; and a *behaviour rating scale* completed by the examiner. Separate scores, called *developmental quotients (DQs),* are calculated for each scale. DQs are most useful for early detection of emotional disturbances, learning problems, and sensory, neurological, and environmental deficits.

Although these scores give a reasonably accurate picture of a child's *current* developmental status, they are not IQs and are poor predictors of future functioning (Anastasi & Urbina, 1997). Environmental influences such as socio-economic status and family and neighbourhood characteristics seem to affect cognitive development more strongly as children approach age 3 (Klebanov, Brooks-Gunn, McCarton, & McCormick, 1998). Also, the developmental tests traditionally used for babies measure mostly sensory and motor abilities, whereas intelligence tests for older children place more emphasis on verbal abilities (Bornstein & Sigman, 1986; Colombo, 1993; McCall & Carriger, 1993). Not until at least the third year of life, when children may be tested with the Stanford-Binet or the WPPSI–III, do a child's IQ scores, along with such factors as the parents' IQ and educational level, usually help to predict later test scores (Kopp & Kaler, 1989; Kopp & McCall, 1982; McCall & Carriger, 1993).

Socio-economic Status, Parenting Practices, and IQ

The correlation between socio-economic status and IQ is well documented (Neisser et al., 1996). As an ecological analysis suggests, poverty can curb children's cognitive growth by limiting parents' ability to provide educational resources and by exerting a negative psychological effect on the parents and their parenting practices (McLoyd, 1990, 1998; see chapter 14). Even in well-functioning families, specific aspects of parenting associated with socio-economic status can influence cognitive development. A longitudinal study suggests how (B. Hart & Risley, 1992, 1996).

Once a month for more than 2 years, until the participating children turned 3, researchers visited the homes of 40 families and observed parent–child interactions. Parents in higher-income families spent more time with their children, talked more with them, and showed more interest in what they had to say. Children whose parents did these things tended to do well on IQ tests 6 years later. They also did better in school and on language and achievement tests. Much more of the talk of the lower-income parents included such negative words as "stop," "quit," and "don't"; and the children of parents who talked that way had lower IQs and achievement (B. Hart & Risley, 1989, 1992, 1996; D. Walker, Greenwood, Hart, & Carta, 1994). This study pinpoints early parenting practices that *may* help account for differences in future IQ and school performance of children from higher-

and lower-income families. We say "may" because, as we discuss in the next section, parenting practices may reflect parental intelligence, which itself predicts children's IQs.

Assessing the Impact of the Home Environment

How do researchers measure the characteristics of the early home environment that influence intelligence? Using the **Home Observation for Measurement of the Environment (HOME)** (R. H. Bradley, 1989; Caldwell & Bradley, 1984), trained observers rate the resources and atmosphere in a child's home and interview the parents.

One important factor in HOME is parental responsiveness. HOME gives credit to the parent of an infant or toddler for caressing or kissing the child during an examiner's visit, to the parent of a preschooler for spontaneously praising the child, and to the parent of an older child for answering the child's questions. A longitudinal study found positive correlations between parents' responsiveness to their 6-month-olds and the children's IQ, achievement test scores, and teacher-rated classroom behaviour at age 10 (R. Bradley & Caldwell, 1982; R. Bradley, Caldwell, & Rock, 1988).

HOME also assesses the number of books in the home, the presence of playthings that encourage the development of concepts, and parents' involvement in children's play. High scores on all these factors are fairly reliable in predicting children's IQ. In one study, the single most important factor in predicting high intelligence was the mother's ability to create and structure an environment that fostered learning (Stevens & Bakeman, 1985).

Of course, we cannot be sure on the basis of HOME and correlational findings that parental responsiveness or an enriched home environment actually increases a child's intelligence. All we can say is that these factors are associated with high intelligence. Intelligent, well-educated parents may be more likely to provide a positive, stimulating home environment; and since they also pass their genes on to their children, there may be a genetic influence as well. (This is an example of a *passive genotype–environment correlation,* described in chapter 3.) Adoption studies support a genetic influence (Braungart, Fulker, & Plomin, 1992; Coon, Fulker, DeFries, & Plomin, 1990). However, studies of Romanian orphans adopted by Canadian families indicated that orphans' developmental status, including IQ, improved when placed with Canadian adoptive families, particularly in environments rated high on the HOME scale (Morison & Ellwood, 2000).

Early Intervention

In other research, six **developmental priming mechanisms**—aspects of the home environment that pave the way for normal cognitive and psychosocial development and help make children ready for school—have repeatedly been associated with positive outcomes. The six mechanisms are (1) encouragement to explore; (2) mentoring in basic cognitive and social skills, such as labelling, sequencing, sorting, and comparing; (3) celebration of accomplishments; (4) guidance in practising and expanding skills; (5) protection from inappropriate punishment, teasing, or disapproval for mistakes or unintended consequences of exploring and trying out skills; and (6) stimulation of language and other symbolic communication. The consistent presence of all six of these conditions early in life may be essential to normal brain development (C. T. Ramey & S. L. Ramey, 1998a, 1998b; S. L. Ramey & C. T. Ramey, 1992). Table 7-2 lists suggestions for helping babies develop both cognitive and social competence.

What can be done to help children who do not get such developmental support? **Early intervention** is a systematic provision of therapeutic and educational services to families that need help in meeting young children's developmental needs. One of the first home-based intervention programs in Canada was started in B.C. in the 1970s, and subsequently spread throughout Canada (Mitchell, Brynelsen, & Holm, 1988).

In Ontario the *Early Years* report, which makes public policy recommendations about early years support for children, demonstrates how intervention in the first 3 years can influence developmental gains more than at any other time in the lifespan (McCain & Mustard, 1999). As illustrated in Figure 7-3, more public support is needed for programs devoted to learning, behaviour problems, and health for children in the early years to ensure healthy development when brain growth is most rapid.

Home Observation for Measurement of the Environment (HOME) Instrument to measure the influence of the home environment on children's cognitive growth

---

Checkpoint ✓

Can you . . .

✔ Tell why developmental tests are sometimes given to infants and toddlers and describe one such widely used test?

✔ Explain why tests of infants and toddlers are unreliable in predicting later IQ?

✔ Discuss the relationship between socio-economic status, parenting practices, and cognitive development?

✔ Identify specific aspects of the home environment that may influence measured intelligence, and explain why such influence is hard to show?

---

developmental priming mechanisms Aspects of the home environment that seem necessary for normal cognitive and psychosocial development

early intervention Systematic provision of therapeutic and educational services to families to help meet young children's developmental needs

Findings from the Harvard Preschool Project, from studies using the HOME scales, and from neurological studies and other research suggest the following guidelines for fostering infants' and toddlers' cognitive development:

1. In the early months, *provide sensory stimulation*, but avoid overstimulation and distracting noises.

2. As babies grow older, *create an environment that fosters learning*—one that includes books, interesting objects (which do not have to be expensive toys), and a place to play.

3. *Respond to babies' signals.* This establishes a sense of trust that the world is a friendly place and gives babies a sense of control over their lives.

4. *Give babies the power to make changes,* through toys that can be shaken, moulded, or moved. Help a baby discover that turning a doorknob opens a door, flicking a light switch turns on a light, and opening a faucet produces running water for a bath.

5. *Give babies freedom to explore.* Do not confine them regularly during the day in a crib, jump seat, or small room, and keep them only for short periods in a playpen. Baby-proof the environment and let them go!

6. *Talk to babies.* They will not pick up language from listening to the radio or television; they need interaction with adults.

7. In talking to or playing with babies, *enter into whatever they are interested in* at the moment instead of trying to redirect their attention to something else.

8. *Arrange opportunities to learn basic skills,* such as labelling, comparing, and sorting objects (say, by size or colour), putting items in sequence, and observing the consequences of actions.

9. *Applaud new skills, and help babies practise and expand them.* Stay nearby but do not hover.

10. *Read to babies in a warm, caring atmosphere from an early age.* Reading aloud and talking about the stories develop preliteracy skills.

11. *Use punishment sparingly.* Do not punish or ridicule results of normal trial-and-error exploration.

Sources: R. R. Bradley & Caldwell, 1982; R. R. Bradley, Caldwell, & Rock, 1988; R. H. Bradley et al., 1989; C. T. Ramey & Ramey, 1998a, 1998b; S. L. Ramey & Ramey, 1992; Staso, quoted in Blakeslee, 1997; J. H. Stevens & Bakeman, 1985; B. L. White, 1971; B. L. White, Kaban, & Attanucci, 1979.

What's your view ?

- On the basis of the six developmental priming mechanisms listed in the text, can you suggest specific ways to help infants and toddlers get ready for schooling?

Studies like the Abecedarian Project (C. T. Ramey & Campbell, 1991) demonstrate how effective early intervention can be. The project involved 174 babies in at-risk homes, from 6 weeks of age until kindergarten. The program group was enrolled in a full-day, year-round early childhood education program, with low child–teacher ratio and learning games to foster cognitive, linguistic, perceptual-motor, and social-skill growth. The control group received pediatric and social services, formula, and home visits, as the experimental group did, but was not enrolled in the program.

The program group experienced more growth than the control group in developmental test scores in the first 18 months. By age 3, program children's average IQ was 101, consistent with the general population, but the control children's average IQ was only 84 (C. T. Ramey & S. L. Ramey, 1998).

However, these early gains were not fully maintained. Between the ages of 3 and 8, IQs dropped. Still, scores were higher and more stable among program children than control children, indicating that early intervention can moderate the negative effects of low socio-economic status (Burchinal, Campbell, Bryant, Wasik, & Ramey, 1997). At age 15, the program children continued to outdo the control children on IQ, on reading and math achievement, and were less likely to repeat a school grade (C. T. Ramey et al., 2000).

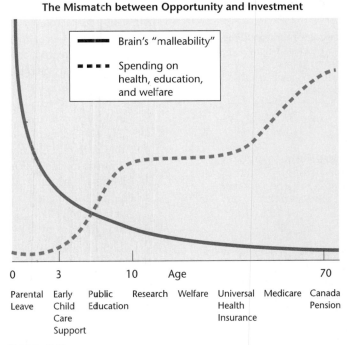

The Mismatch between Opportunity and Investment

— Brain's "malleability"

---- Spending on health, education, and welfare

0	3	10	Age	70
Parental Leave	Early Child Care Support	Public Education	Research Welfare	Universal Health Insurance Medicare Canada Pension

Figure 7-3

The relationship between public expenditures on programs fostering healthy development throughout the life cycle and public expenditures aimed at the critical years of rapid brain development.

Source: Adapted from B. Perry, 2002.

Checkpoint

Can you . . .

✔ Identify six developmental priming mechanisms?

✔ Summarize findings about the value of early intervention?

Guidepost 3

How did Piaget describe infants' and toddlers' cognitive development, and how have his claims stood up?

sensorimotor stage In Piaget's theory, the first stage in cognitive development, during which infants learn through sensory and motor activity

schemes Piaget's term for organized patterns of behaviour used in particular situations

circular reactions Piaget's term for processes by which an infant learns to reproduce desired occurrences originally discovered by chance

These findings suggest that early educational intervention can boost cognitive development. The most effective early interventions are those that (1) start early and continue throughout the preschool years; (2) are highly time-intensive (i.e., occupy more hours in a day, or more days in a week, month, or year); (3) provide direct educational experiences, not just parental training; (4) take a comprehensive approach, including health, family counselling, and social services; and (5) are tailored to individual differences and needs (McCain & Mustard, 1999). Studies using IQ are limited because they assume that intelligence involves abilities that are useful in school. Other perspectives on intelligence, such as Howard Gardner's theory of multiple intelligences, propose that there are other important aspects of intelligent behaviour, such as social skills, creativity, and self-knowledge (chapter 13). Another perspective, that of Jean Piaget, introduced in chapter 2, examines universal principles underlying the development of intelligence.

Piagetian Approach: The Sensorimotor Stage

Piaget's theory has inspired much research on cognition in infancy and early childhood. Some of this research, as we will see, has shown that—as important as Piaget's contributions were—he underestimated young children's abilities. For now, let's look at how Piaget described early cognitive development.

The Sensorimotor Stage

The first of Piaget's four stages of cognitive development (refer back to Table 2-2 in chapter 2) is the **sensorimotor stage.** During this stage (birth to approximately age 2), infants learn about themselves and their world—as Doddy Darwin seemed to do—through their developing sensory and motor activity. Babies change from creatures who respond primarily through reflexes and random behaviour into goal-oriented toddlers.

The sensorimotor stage consists of six substages (see Table 7-4), which flow from one to another as a baby's **schemes,** organized patterns of behaviour, become more elaborate. During the first five substages, babies learn to coordinate input from their senses and organize their activities in relation to their environment. During the sixth and last substage, they progress from trial-and-error learning to the use of symbols and concepts to solve simple problems.

Much of this early cognitive growth comes about through **circular reactions,** in which an infant learns to reproduce pleasurable or interesting events originally discovered by chance. Initially, an activity produces a sensation so enjoyable that the baby wants to repeat it. The repetition then feeds on itself in a continuous cycle in which cause and effect keep reversing (see Figure 7-4). The originally chance behaviour has been consolidated into a new scheme.

In the *first substage* (birth to about 1 month), as neonates exercise their inborn reflexes, they gain some control over them. They begin to engage in a behaviour even when the stimulus that normally elicits it is not present. For example, newborns suck reflexively when their lips are touched. They soon learn to find the nipple even when they are not touched, and they suck at times when they are not hungry. Thus infants modify and extend the scheme for sucking as they begin to initiate activity.

In the *second substage* (about 1 to 4 months), babies learn to repeat a pleasant bodily sensation first achieved by chance (say, sucking their thumbs, as in the first part of Figure 7-4). Piaget called this a *primary circular reaction.* They begin to turn toward sounds, showing the ability to coordinate different kinds of sensory information (vision and hearing).

The *third substage* (about 4 to 8 months) coincides with a new interest in manipulating objects and learning about their properties. Babies engage in *secondary circular reactions:* intentional actions repeated not merely for their own sake, as in the second substage, but to get results *beyond the infant's own body.* For example, a baby this age will repeatedly shake a rattle to hear its noise, or (as in the second part of Figure 7-4) coo when a friendly face appears, to make the face stay longer.

By the time infants reach the *fourth substage, coordination of secondary schemes* (about 8 to 12 months), they have built on the few schemes they were born with. They have learned to generalize from past experience to solve new problems and to distinguish means

Table 7-3		Six Substages of Piaget's Sensorimotor Stage of Cognitive Development*	
Substage	**Ages**	**Description**	**Behaviour**
Use of reflexes	birth to 1 month	Infants exercise their inborn reflexes and gain some control over them. They do not coordinate information from their senses. They do not grasp an object they are looking at.	Dorri begins sucking when her mother's breast is in her mouth.
Primary circular reactions	1 to 4 months	Infants repeat pleasurable behaviours that first occur by chance (such as thumb-sucking). Activities focus on infant's body rather than the effects of the behaviour on the environment. Infants make first acquired adaptations; that is, they suck different objects differently. They begin to coordinate sensory information and grasp objects.	When given a bottle, Jesse, who is usually breast-fed, is able to adjust his sucking to the rubber nipple.
Secondary circular reactions	4 to 8 months	Infants become more interested in the environment; they repeat actions that bring interesting results (such as shaking a rattle) and prolong interesting experiences. Actions are intentional but not initially goal-directed.	Benjamin's spoon makes a funny sound when he strikes it against his plate. He keeps hitting the plate with his spoon to hear the sound again and again.
Coordination of secondary schemes	8 to 12 months	Behaviour is more deliberate and purposeful (intentional) as infants coordinate previously learned schemes (such as looking at and grasping a rattle) and use previously learned behaviours to attain their goals (such as crawling across the room to get a desired toy). They can anticipate events.	Nancy pushes the button on her musical nursery rhyme book and "Twinkle, Twinkle, Little Star" plays. She pushes this button over and over again, choosing it instead of the buttons for the other songs.
Tertiary circular reactions	12 to 18 months	Toddlers show curiosity and experimentation; they purposefully vary their actions to see results (for example, by shaking different rattles to hear their sounds). They actively explore their world to determine what is novel about an object, event, or situation. They try out new activities and use trial and error in solving problems.	When Tony's big sister holds his favourite board book up to his crib bars, he reaches for it. His first efforts to bring the book into his crib fail because the book is too wide. Soon, Tony turns the book sideways and hugs it, delighted with his success.
Mental combinations	18 to 24 months	Since toddlers can mentally represent events, they are no longer confined to trial and error to solve problems. Symbolic thought allows toddlers to begin to think about events and anticipate their consequences without always resorting to action. Toddlers begin to demonstrate insight. They can use symbols, such as gestures and words, and can pretend.	Jenny plays with her shape box, searching carefully for the right hole for each shape before trying—and succeeding.

*Note: Infants show enormous cognitive growth during Piaget's sensorimotor stage, as they learn about the world through their senses and their motor activities. Note their progress in problem solving and the coordination of sensory information. All ages are approximate.

from ends. They will crawl to get something they want, grab it, or push away a barrier to it (such as someone else's hand). They try out, modify, and coordinate previous schemes, to find one that works. Thus this substage marks the beginning of *intentional* behaviour.

In the *fifth substage* (about 12 to 18 months), babies begin to experiment with new behaviour to see what will happen. Once they begin to walk, they can more easily explore their environment. They now engage in *tertiary circular reactions, varying* an action to get a similar result, rather than merely *repeating* pleasing behaviour they have accidentally discovered. For example, a toddler may squeeze a rubber duck that squeaked when stepped on, to see whether it will squeak again (as in the third part of Figure 7-4). For the first time, children show originality in problem solving. By trial and error, they try out behaviours until they find the best way to attain a goal.

The *sixth substage, mental combinations* (about 18 months to 2 years) is a transition into the preoperational stage of early childhood. **Representational ability**—the ability to mentally represent objects and actions in memory, largely through symbols such as words, numbers, and mental pictures—blossoms. The ability to manipulate symbols frees children from immediate experience. They can now engage in **deferred imitation,** imitating actions they no longer see

representational ability Piaget's term for capacity to mentally represent objects and experiences, largely through the use of symbols

deferred imitation Piaget's term for reproduction of an observed behaviour after the passage of time by calling up a stored symbol of it

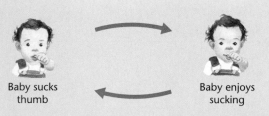

(a) Primary circular reaction: Action and response both involve infant's own body (1 to 4 months).

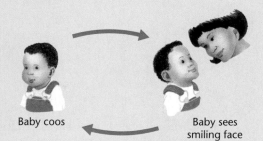

Baby coos — Baby sees smiling face

(b) Secondary circular reaction: Action gets a response from another person or object, leading to baby's repeating original action (4 to 8 months).

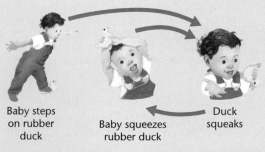

Baby steps on rubber duck — Baby squeezes rubber duck — Duck squeaks

(c) Tertiary circular reaction: Action gets one pleasing result, leading baby to perform similar actions to get similar results (12 to 18 months).

Figure 7-4

Primary, secondary, and tertiary circular reactions.

object permanence Piaget's term for the understanding that a person or object still exists when out of sight

A, not-B error Tendency, noted by Piaget, for 8- to 12-month-old infants to search for a hidden object in a place where they previously found it, rather than in the place where they most recently saw it being hidden

in front of them. They can pretend. They can *think* about actions before taking them. They no longer have to go through laborious trial and error to solve problems. Piaget's daughter Lucienne seemed to show representational ability when, in figuring out how to pry open a partially closed matchbox to remove a watch chain, she opened her mouth wider to represent her idea of widening the slit in the box (Piaget, 1936/1952).

Development of Knowledge about Objects and Space

The *object concept*—the idea that objects have their own independent existence, characteristics, and location in space—is fundamental to an orderly view of physical reality. The object concept is the basis for children's awareness that they themselves exist apart from objects and other people. It is essential to understanding a world full of objects and events. Doddy Darwin's struggle to understand the existence and location of reflective images was part of his development of an object concept.

One aspect of the object concept is **object permanence,** the realization that an object or person continues to exist when out of sight. This realization allows a child whose parent has left the room to feel secure in the knowledge that the parent still exists and will return. The development of this concept in many cultures can be seen in the game of peekaboo (see Box 7-1).

According to Piaget, object permanence develops gradually during the sensorimotor stage. At first, infants have no such concept. By the third substage, from about 4 to 8 months, they will look for something they have dropped, but if they cannot see it, they act as if it no longer exists. In the fourth substage, about 8 to 12 months, they will look for an object in a place where they first found it after seeing it hidden, even if they later saw it being moved to another place. (Piaget called this the **A, not-B error.**) In the fifth substage, 12 to 18 months, they no longer make this error; they will search for an object in the *last* place they saw it hidden. However, they will *not* search for it in a place where they did *not* see it hidden. By the sixth substage, 18 to 24 months, object permanence is fully achieved; toddlers will look for an object even if they did not see it hidden.

Piaget (1954) observed the A, not-B error when his son, Laurent, was 9½ months old. Piaget placed Laurent on a sofa, with a "coverlet" (A)—perhaps a small blanket—on his right and a wool garment (B) on his left. As the baby watched, Piaget hid his watch under the coverlet. Laurent lifted the coverlet and retrieved the watch. After repeating this game several times, Piaget placed the watch under the garment instead of under the coverlet. Laurent watched intently, then again lifted the coverlet and searched for the watch there. Two analyses of later research verified the prevalence of the A, not-B error (Marcovitch & Zelazo, 1999; Wellman, Cross, & Bartsch, 1986).

Piaget saw the A, not-B error as a sign of incomplete understanding of the object concept, together with an egocentric (self-centred) view of spatial relations. He reasoned that the infant must believe that the object's existence is linked to a particular location (the one where it was first found) and to the infant's own action in retrieving it from that location. A more recent explanation is that infants—and even toddlers and preschoolers—may simply find it hard to restrain the impulse to repeat behaviour that was previously reinforced by success (Diamond, Cruttenden, & Neiderman, 1994; Zelazo, Reznick, & Spinazzola, 1998).

With their emerging representational abilities, children between 2 and 3 years of age enter into the second major stage of cognitive development, the preoperational stage, which characterizes thinking in early childhood (chapter 10). Children now experience a growing understanding of space, causality, identity, categorization, and number, which builds upon the milestones that emerged at the end of the sensorimotor stage.

What Abilities May Develop Earlier than Piaget Thought?

According to Piaget, the journey from reflex behaviour to the beginnings of thought is a long, slow one. For a year and a half or so, babies learn only from their senses and movements; not until the last half of the second year do they make the breakthrough to conceptual thought. Today there is growing evidence that some of the limitations Piaget saw in infants' early cognitive abilities may instead have reflected immature linguistic and motor skills. Researchers using simplified tasks and modern research tools have built an impressive case for babies' cognitive strengths.

Object Permanence Piaget may have underestimated young infants' grasp of object permanence because of his testing methods. Babies may fail to search for hidden objects because they cannot yet carry out a two-step sequence of actions, such as moving a cushion or lifting the cover of a box before grasping the object. When object permanence is tested with a more age-appropriate procedure, in which the object is hidden only by darkness and thus can be retrieved in one motion, infants in the third substage (4 to 8 months) perform surprisingly well. In one study, 6½-month-olds saw a ball drop down a chute and land in one of two spots, each identifiable by a distinctive sound. When the light was turned off, and the procedure was repeated, the babies reached for the ball in the appropriate location, guided only by the sound (Goubet & Clifton, 1998). This showed that they knew the ball continued to exist and could tell where it had gone.

According to Piaget, deferred imitation and pretend play—both indications of representational ability—do not occur until about 18 months, but research has found that both abilities occur earlier. Here 16-month-old Olivia gives her stuffed pet a drink, as she has seen her parents do for her.

Methods based only on what infants look at, and for how long, eliminate the need for *any* motor activity and thus can be used at even earlier ages. As we report later in this chapter, studies since the late 1970s, using information-processing methodology, suggest that very young infants may form mental representations—images or memories of objects not physically present—an ability Piaget said does not emerge before 18 months. According to this research (the interpretation of which is in dispute) infants as young as 3 or 4 months old not only seem to have a sense of object permanence, but also know certain principles about the physical world, understand categorization and causality, and have a rudimentary concept of number. Other research deals with infants' and toddlers' ability to remember and imitate what they see. (Table 7-4 compares these findings with Piaget's views; refer back to this table as you read on.)

Imitation Piaget maintained that **invisible imitation**—imitation using parts of the body that a baby cannot see, such as the mouth—develops at about 9 months, after **visible imitation**—the use of hands or feet, for example, which babies can see. Yet in a series of studies by Andrew Meltzoff and M. Keith Moore (1983, 1989), babies less than 72 hours old appeared to imitate adults by opening their mouths and sticking out their tongues, as well as by duplicating adults' head movements.

However, a review of Meltzoff and Moore's work, and of attempts to replicate it, found clear, consistent evidence of only one apparently imitative movement—sticking out the tongue (Anisfeld, 1996)—and that response disappears by about 2 months of age. Since it seems unlikely that an early and short-lived imitative capacity would be limited to one gesture, some researchers have instead suggested that the tongue thrust may serve other purposes—perhaps as an early attempt to interact with the mother, or simply as exploratory behaviour aroused by the intriguing sight of an adult tongue (Bjorklund, 1997; S. S. Jones, 1996). Pending further research, then, the age when invisible imitation begins will remain in doubt.

Piaget also held that children under 18 months cannot engage in *deferred imitation* of an act they saw some time before. Yet babies as young as 6 *weeks* have imitated an adult's facial movements after a 24-hour delay, in the presence of the same adult, who this time was expressionless. This suggests that very young babies can retain a mental representation of an event (Meltzoff & Moore, 1994, 1998).

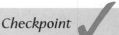

Checkpoint

Can you . . .

✔ Summarize major developments during Piaget's sensorimotor stage?

✔ Explain how primary, secondary, and tertiary circular reactions work?

✔ Tell why representational ability is important?

✔ Summarize Piaget's views on the development of object permanence and spatial knowledge?

invisible imitation Imitation with parts of one's body that one cannot see

visible imitation Imitation with parts of one's body that one can see

In rural South Africa, a Bantu mother smiles at her 9-month-old son, covers her eyes with her hands, and asks, *"Uphi?"* (Where?) After 3 seconds, the mother says, "Here!" and uncovers her eyes to the baby's delight. In Tokyo, a Japanese mother plays the same game with her 12-month-old daughter, who shows the same joyous response. In suburban Connecticut, a 15-month-old boy who sees his grandfather for the first time in two months raises his shirt to cover his eyes—as Grandpa did on his previous visit.

Peekaboo is played across diverse cultures, using similar routines (Fernald & O'Neill, 1993). In all cultures in which the game is played,* the moment when the mother or other caregiver reappears is exhilarating. It is marked by exaggerated gestures and voice tones. Infants' pleasure from the immediate sensory stimulation of the game is heightened by their fascination with faces and voices, especially the high-pitched tones the adult usually uses.

The game serves several important purposes. Psychoanalysts say that it helps babies master anxiety when their mother disappears. Cognitive psychologists see it as a way babies play with developing ideas about object permanence. It may also be a social routine that helps babies learn rules that govern conversation, such as taking turns. It may provide practice in paying attention, a prerequisite for learning.

As babies develop the cognitive competency to predict future events, the game takes on new dimensions. Between 3 and 5 months, the baby's smiles and laughter as the adult's face moves in and out of view signal the infant's developing expectation of what will happen next. At 5 to 8 months, the baby shows anticipation by looking and smiling as the adult's voice alerts the infant to the adult's imminent reappearance. By 1 year, babies are no longer merely observers but usually initiate the game, actively engaging adults in play. Now it is the adult who generally responds to the baby's physical or vocal cues, which can become quite insistent if the adult doesn't feel like playing.

To help infants who are learning peekaboo or other games, parents often use *scaffolding* (see chapter 2). In an 18-month longitudinal study at the University of Montreal, 25 mothers were videotaped playing peekaboo with their babies, using a doll as a prop (Rome-Flanders, Cronk, & Gourde, 1995). The amount and type of scaffolding varied with the infant's age and skill. Mothers frequently tried to attract a 6-month-old's attention to begin the game; this became less and less necessary as time went on. Modelling (performing the peekaboo sequence to encourage a baby to imitate it) also was most frequent at 6 months and decreased significantly by 12 months, when there was an increase in direct verbal instruction ("Cover the doll") as babies became more able to understand spoken language. Indirect verbal instruction ("Where is the doll?"), used to focus attention on the next step in the game, remained constant throughout the entire age range. Reinforcement (showing satisfaction with the infant's performance, for example, by saying "Peekaboo!" when the infant uncovered the doll) was fairly constant from 9 months on. The overall amount of scaffolding dropped substantially at 24 months, by which time most babies have fully mastered the game.

What's your view?

Have you ever played peekaboo periodically with the same infant? If so, did you notice changes with age in the child's participation, as described in this box?

Check it out!

For more information on this topic, go to **www.mcgrawhill.ca/college/papalia.**

*The cultures included in this report are found in Malaysia, Greece, India, Iran, Russia, Brazil, Indonesia, Korea, and South Africa.

Six- to 9-month-olds have shown deferred imitation of a complex sequence of actions they observed but did not immediately have an opportunity to try (Meltzoff & Moore, 1998). In one experiment in New Zealand, infants of various ages watched a researcher pull a mitten off a puppet, jingle a bell inside the mitten three times, and then put the mitten back on the puppet. Infants as young as 9 months mimicked these actions 24 hours later, if the context was the same—that is, if they saw the same puppet in the same place and with the same people. Even 6-month-olds, if given extra time for demonstration sessions, repeated part of the sequence the next day, but less accurately than the older infants did (Barr, Dowden, & Hayne, 1996).

During a child's second year, specific contextual links between the training and test situations become less critical (Barnat, Klein, & Meltzoff, 1996; Hayne, MacDonald, & Barr, 1997). In one study, 14- to 18-month-olds who watched other children play with objects (for example, putting beads in a cup or sounding a buzzer), either in a laboratory or in a daycare centre, repeated the behaviour when given the same objects at home *2 days* later—evidence that toddlers are capable of deferred imitation in a totally different context (Hanna & Meltzoff, 1993).

Thus the findings on deferred imitation agree with those on operant conditioning (Rovee-Collier, 1999): Infants and toddlers do seem capable of remembering over fairly long periods of time.

Table 7-4

Table 7-4	Key Developments of the Sensorimotor Stage	
Concept or Skill	**Piaget's View**	**More Recent Findings**
Object permanence	Develops gradually between third and sixth substage. Infants in fourth substage (8–12 months) make A, not-B error.	Infants as young as 3½ months (second substage) seem to show object knowledge, though interpretation of findings is in dispute. A, not-B error may persist into second year or longer.
Spatial knowledge	Development of object concept and spatial knowledge is linked to self-locomotion and coordination of visual and motor information.	Research supports Piaget's timetable and relationship of spatial judgments to decline of egocentrism. Link to motor development is less clear.
Causality	Develops slowly between 4 and 12 months, based on infant's discovery, first of effects of own actions and then of effects of outside forces.	Some evidence suggests early awareness of specific causal events in the physical world, but general understanding of causality may be slower to develop.
Number	Depends on use of symbols, which begins in sixth substage (18–24 months).	Infants as young as 5 months may recognize and mentally manipulate small numbers, but interpretation of findings is in dispute.
Categorization	Depends on representational thinking, which develops during sixth substage (18–24 months).	Infants as young as 3 months seem to recognize perceptual categories.
Imitation	Invisible imitation develops around 9 months, deferred imitation after development of mental representations in sixth substage (18–24 months).	Controversial studies have found invisible imitation of facial expressions in newborns and deferred imitation as early as 6 weeks. Deferred imitation of complex activities seems to exist as early as 6 months.

Overall, infants and toddlers seem to be far more cognitively competent than Piaget imagined and show earlier signs of conceptual thought. This does not mean that infants come into the world with minds fully formed. As Piaget observed, immature forms of cognition seem to give way to more mature forms. We can see this, for example, in the errors young infants make in searching for hidden objects. But Piaget may have been wrong in his emphasis on motor experience as the primary "engine" of cognitive growth. Infants' perceptions are far ahead of their motor abilities, and today's methods allow researchers to make observations and inferences about those perceptions. How perception relates to cognition is a major area of investigation, as we will see in the next section.

Studying Cognitive Development: Newer Approaches

During the past few decades, researchers have turned to three new approaches to add to our knowledge about infants' and toddlers' cognitive development:

- The **information-processing approach** focuses on the processes involved in perception, learning, memory, and problem solving. It seeks to discover what children do with information from the time they encounter it until they use it.

What's your view ?

- What comments might Piaget have made about Darwin's diary entries on his son's early cognitive development?

- On the basis of observations by Piaget and the research they inspired, what factors would you consider in designing or purchasing a toy or book for an infant or toddler?

Checkpoint ✔

Can you . . .

✔ Explain why Piaget may have underestimated some of infants' cognitive abilities, and discuss the implications of research on imitation in infants and toddlers?

information-processing approach Approach to the study of cognitive development by observing and analyzing the mental processes involved in perceiving and handling information

cognitive neuroscience approach Approach to the study of cognitive development that links brain processes with cognitive ones

social-contextual approach Approach to the study of cognitive development focusing on environmental influences, particularly of parents and other caregivers

How can we measure infants' ability to process information, and how does this ability relate to future intelligence?

- The **cognitive neuroscience approach** examines the "hardware" of the central nervous system. It seeks to identify what brain structures are involved in specific aspects of cognition.
- The **social-contextual approach** examines environmental aspects of the learning process, particularly the role of parents and other caregivers.

Information-Processing Approach: Perceptions and Representations

Like the psychometric approach, information-processing theory is concerned with individual differences in intelligent behaviour. Unlike the psychometric approach, it aims to describe the mental processes involved in acquiring and remembering information or solving problems, rather than merely inferring differences in mental functioning from answers given or problems solved. Information-processing research uses new methods to test ideas about cognitive development that sprang from the psychometric and Piagetian approaches. For example, information-processing researchers analyze the separate parts of a complex task, such as Piaget's object search tasks, to figure out what abilities are necessary for each part of the task and at what age these abilities develop. Information-processing researchers also measure, and draw inferences from, what infants pay attention to, and for how long.

Habituation

At about 6 weeks, Stefan lies peacefully in his crib near a window, sucking a pacifier. It is a cloudy day, but suddenly the sun breaks through, and a shaft of light appears on the end of the crib. Stefan stops sucking for a few moments, staring at the pattern of light and shade. Then he looks away and starts sucking again.

We don't know what was going on in Stefan's mind when he saw the shaft of light, but we can tell by his sucking and looking behaviour at what point he began paying attention and when he stopped. These simple behaviours can be indicators of sensory perception and discrimination and even of future intelligence.

Much information-processing research with infants is based on **habituation,** a type of learning in which repeated or continuous exposure to a stimulus (such as the shaft of light) reduces attention to that stimulus. In other words, familiarity breeds loss of interest. As infants habituate, they transform the novel into the familiar, the unknown into the known (Rheingold, 1985).

habituation Simple type of learning in which familiarity with a stimulus reduces, slows, or stops a response; compare *dishabituation*

Researchers study habituation in newborns by repeatedly presenting a stimulus (usually a sound or visual pattern) and then monitoring such responses as heart rate, sucking, eye movements, and brain activity. A baby who has been sucking typically stops when the stimulus is first presented and does not start again until after it has ended. After the same sound or sight has been presented again and again, it loses its novelty and no longer causes the baby to stop sucking. Resumption of uninterrupted sucking shows that the infant has habituated to the stimulus. A new sight or sound, however, will capture the baby's attention and the baby will again stop sucking. This increased response to a new stimulus is called **dishabituation.**

dishabituation Increase in responsiveness after presentation of a new stimulus; compare *habituation*

Researchers gauge the efficiency of infants' information processing by measuring how quickly babies habituate to familiar stimuli, how fast their attention recovers when they are exposed to new stimuli, and how much time they spend looking at the new and the old. Efficiency of habituation correlates with later signs of cognitive development, such as a preference for complexity, rapid exploration of the environment, sophisticated play, quick problem solving, and the ability to match pictures. In fact, as we will see, speed of habituation and other information-processing abilities show promise as predictors of intelligence (Bornstein & Sigman, 1986; Colombo, 1993; McCall & Carriger, 1993).

Habituation has been used to study topics ranging from infants' ability to detect differences between visual patterns to the ability to categorize people, objects, and events—abilities that would seem to require mental representations. For example, 3-month-olds who have been looking at a picture of a dog will look longer at a picture of a cat than at another picture of a dog, showing that they know the difference between cats and dogs (Quinn, Eimas, &

Rosenkrantz, 1993). However, it is important not to overstate the results of such research. The fact that an infant pays closer attention to a new shape or pattern than to a familiar one shows that the infant can see a difference between the two but does not reveal what *cognitive* meaning, if any, the infant attaches to that difference (Haith & Benson, 1998).

Early Perceptual and Processing Abilities

The amount of time a baby spends looking at different sights is a measure of **visual preference,** which is based on the ability to make visual distinctions. Classic research by Robert Fantz and his colleagues revealed that babies less than 2 days old prefer curved lines to straight lines, complex patterns to simple patterns, three-dimensional objects to two-dimensional objects, pictures of faces to pictures of other things, and new sights to familiar ones (Fantz, 1963, 1964, 1965; Fantz, Fagen, & Miranda, 1975; Fantz & Nevis, 1967).

Can this baby tell the difference between Raggedy Ann and Raggedy Andy? This researcher may find out by seeing whether the baby has habituated—become used to—one face and then stops sucking on the nipple when a new face appears, showing recognition of the difference.

visual preference Tendency of infants to spend more time looking at one sight than another

If infants pay more attention to new stimuli than to familiar ones—a phenomenon called *novelty preference*—they are showing that they can tell the new from the old. Therefore, say information-processing theorists, they must be able to remember the old. Their ability to compare new information with information they already have suggests that they can form mental representations (P. R. Zelazo, Kearsley, & Stack, 1995). The efficiency of information processing depends on the speed with which they form and refer to such images.

Contrary to Piaget's view, habituation and novelty preference studies suggest that this ability exists at birth or very soon after, and it quickly becomes more efficient. Newborns can tell sounds they have already heard from those they have not. In one study, infants who heard a certain speech sound 1 day after birth appeared to remember that sound 24 hours later, as shown by a reduced tendency to turn their heads toward the sound and even a tendency to turn away (Swain, Zelazo, & Clifton, 1993). Indeed, as we reported in chapter 4, newborns seem to remember sounds they heard in the womb.

Piaget believed that the senses are unconnected at birth and are only gradually integrated through experience. If so, this integration begins very early. The fact that newborns will look at a source of sound shows that they associate hearing and sight. A more sophisticated ability is **cross-modal transfer,** the ability to use information gained from one sense to guide another—as when a person negotiates a dark room by feeling for the location of familiar objects, or identifies objects by sight after feeling them with eyes closed. In one study, 1-month-old infants showed that they could transfer information gained from sucking (touch) to vision. When the infants saw a rigid object (a hard plastic cylinder) and a flexible one (a wet sponge) being manipulated by a pair of hands, the infants looked longer at the object they had just sucked (Gibson & Walker, 1984). The use of cross-modal transfer to judge some other properties of objects, such as shape, does not seem to develop until a few months later (Maurer, Stager, & Mondloch, 1999). Visually guided reaching involves combining information from one sense with voluntary motor behaviour in reaching and grasping. By using visual contact with an object to guide hand movements (Ennouri et al., 1996), infants 4 to 7 months of age become more sophisticated in their abilities to reach for objects, demonstrating a clear hand preference for grasping (Morange & Bloch, 1996).

cross-modal transfer Ability to use information gained by one sense to guide another

Speed of processing increases rapidly during the first year of life. It continues to increase during the second and third years, when interference from previously processed information comes under better control (P. R. Zelazo et al., 1995).

Information Processing as a Predictor of Intelligence

Because of the weak correlation between infants' scores on developmental tests and their later IQ, many psychologists believed that the cognitive functioning of infants had little in common with that of older children and adults—in other words, that there was a discontinuity in cognitive development (Kopp & McCall, 1982). Piaget believed this, too. However, when researchers assess how infants and toddlers process information, some aspects of mental development seem to be fairly continuous from birth (McCall & Carriger, 1993). Children who, from the start, were efficient at taking in and interpreting sensory information score well on intelligence tests.

In many longitudinal studies, habituation and attention-recovery abilities during the first 6 months to 1 year of life were moderately useful in predicting childhood IQ. So was **visual recognition memory**—the ability to distinguish familiar sights from unfamiliar ones when shown both at the same time, as measured by the tendency to look longer at the new (Bornstein & Sigman, 1986; Colombo, 1993; McCall & Carriger, 1993). In one study, a combination of visual recognition memory at 7 months and cross-modal transfer at 1 year predicted IQ at age 11 and also showed a modest (but nonetheless remarkable after 10 years!) relationship to processing speed and memory at that age (Rose & Feldman, 1995, 1997).

Visual reaction time and *visual anticipation* can be measured by the *visual expectation paradigm.* A series of computer-generated pictures briefly appears, some on the right and some on the left sides of an infant's peripheral visual field. The same sequence of pictures is repeated several times. The infant's eye movements are measured to see how quickly his or her gaze shifts to a picture that has just appeared (reaction time) or to the place where the infant expects the next picture to appear (anticipation). These measurements are thought to indicate attentiveness and processing speed, as well as the tendency to form expectations on the basis of experience. In a longitudinal study, visual reaction time and visual anticipation at 3½ months correlated with IQ at age 4 (Dougherty & Haith, 1997).

All in all, there is much evidence that the abilities infants use to process sensory information are related to the cognitive abilities intelligence tests measure. Still, we need to be cautious in interpreting these findings. Most of the studies used small samples. Also, the predictability of childhood IQ from measures of habituation and recognition memory is only modest. It is no higher than the predictability from parental education and socio-economic status, and not as high as the predictability from some other infant behaviours, such as early vocalization. Predictions based on information-processing measures alone do not take into account the influence of environmental factors (Colombo & Janowsky, 1998; Laucht, Esser, & Schmidt, 1994; McCall & Carriger, 1993). For example, maternal responsiveness in early infancy seems to play a part in the link between early attentional abilities and cognitive abilities later in childhood (Bornstein & Tamis-LeMonda, 1994) and even at age 18 (Sigman, Cohen, & Beckwith, 1997).

Violation of Expectations and the Development of Thought

According to **violation-of-expectations** research, infants begin to think and reason about the physical world much earlier than Piaget believed. In the violation-of-expectations method, infants are first habituated to seeing an event happen as it normally would. Then the event is changed in a way that conflicts with (violates) normal expectations. An infant's tendency to look longer at the changed event (dishabituation) is interpreted as evidence that the infant recognizes it as surprising.

Researchers using this method claim that some of the concepts Piaget described as developing toward the end of the sensorimotor stage, such as object permanence, number, and causality—all of which depend on formation of mental representations—actually arise much earlier (refer back to Table 7-3). It has been proposed that infants may be born with reasoning abilities—*innate learning mechanisms* that help them make sense of the information they encounter—or may acquire these abilities very early (Baillargeon, 1994). Some investigators go further, suggesting that infants at birth may already have intuitive *knowledge* about basic physical principles—knowledge that then develops further with experience (Spelke, 1994, 1998). As we will see, these interpretations and conclusions are highly controversial.

---

visual-recognition memory
Ability to distinguish a familiar visual stimulus from an unfamiliar one when shown both at the same time

---

Guidepost 5

When do babies begin to think about characteristics of the physical world?

---

violation-of-expectations
Research method in which dishabituation to a stimulus that conflicts with previous experience is taken as evidence that an infant recognizes the new stimulus as surprising

---

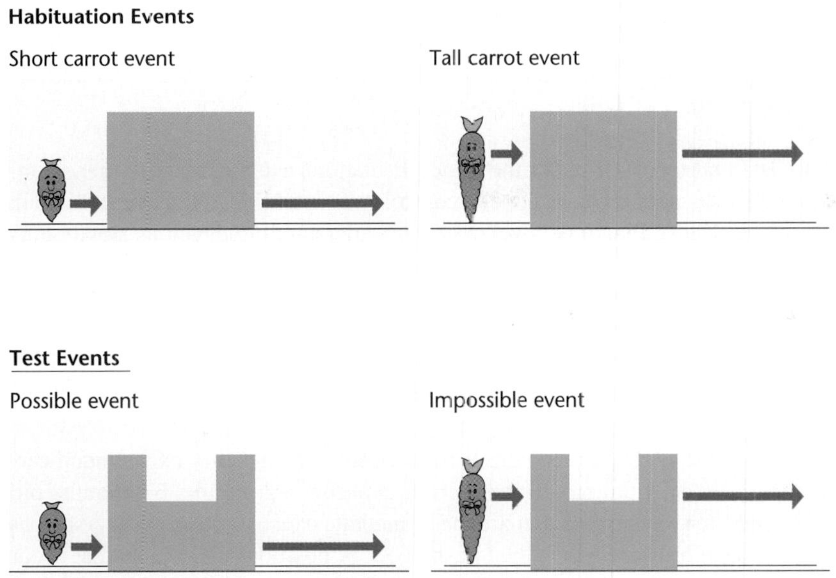

Habituation Events

Short carrot event

Tall carrot event

Test Events

Possible event

Impossible event

Figure 7-5

How early do infants show object permanence? In this experiment, 3½-month-olds watched a short carrot and then a tall carrot slide along a track, disappear behind a screen, and then reappear. After they became accustomed to seeing these events, the opaque screen was replaced by a screen with a large notch at the top. The short carrot did not appear in the notch when passing behind the screen; the tall carrot, which should have appeared in the notch, also did not. The babies looked longer at the tall than at the short carrot event, suggesting that they were surprised that the tall carrot did not reappear.

Source: Baillargeon & DeVos, 1991.

Object Permanence Using the violation-of-expectations method, Renée Baillargeon and her colleagues claim to have found evidence of object permanence in infants as young as 3½ months. The babies appeared surprised by the failure of a tall carrot that slid behind a screen of the same height to show up in a large notch in the upper part of the screen before appearing again on the other side (Baillargeon & DeVos, 1991; see Figure 7-5). Of course, since this task is so different from Piaget's, it may not assess precisely the same ability. Recognition that an object that disappeared on one side of a screen is the same as the object that reappears on the other side need not imply knowledge that the object should have continued to exist behind the screen (Meltzoff & Moore, 1998). Still, this experiment raises the possibility that at least a rudimentary form of object permanence may be present in the early months of life.

Critics offer two challenges to the early emergence of object permanence (Haith & Benson, 1998). If infants as young as 3½ months have such a concept, then why is it not until several months after they can grasp objects that they begin to search for something they saw hidden? And why do they make errors in their searches? One proposed answer is that a rudimentary form of object knowledge may exist in early infancy and may become more sophisticated as infants gain experience in reaching for and handling objects (Spelke, 1998).

Number Violation-of-expectations research suggests that an understanding of number may begin long before Piaget's sixth substage, when he claimed children first begin to use symbols. In a series of experiments, Karen Wynn (1992) tested whether 5-month-old babies can add and subtract small numbers of objects. The infants watched as Mickey Mouse dolls were placed behind a screen, and a doll was either added or taken away. The screen then was lifted to reveal either the expected number or a different number of dolls. In all the experiments, the babies looked longer at surprising "wrong" answers than at expected "right" ones, suggesting (according to Wynn) that they had mentally "computed" the right answers. Other researchers who replicated these experiments got similar results, even when one of the dolls was replaced with a different doll, indicating that it was the *number* of dolls, and not their physical appearance or identity, to which the infants were responding (Simon, Hespos, & Rochat, 1995).

According to Wynn, this research raises the possibility that numerical concepts are inborn—that when parents teach their babies numbers, they may only be teaching them the names ("one, two, three") for concepts the babies already know. However, the idea of an innate ability is only speculation, since the infants in these studies were already 5 and 6 months old. Furthermore, simple sensory memory may explain the findings. Infants may simply be responding to the puzzling presence of a doll they saw removed from behind the screen, or the absence of a doll they saw placed there (Haith, 1998; Haith & Benson, 1998). A more recent experiment suggests that infants discriminate between small sets of objects on the basis of other visible characteristics, such as collective mass, rather than number (Clearfield & Mix, 1999).

Causality An understanding of *causality,* the principle that one event causes another, is important because it "allows people to predict and control their world" (L. B. Cohen, Rundell, Spellman, & Cashon, 1999). Piaget believed that this understanding develops slowly during the first year of life. At about 4 to 6 months, as infants become able to grasp objects, they begin to recognize that they can act on their environment. Thus the concept of causality is rooted in a dawning awareness of the power of their own intentions. However, according to Piaget, infants do not yet know that causes must come before effects; and not until close to 1 year do they realize that forces outside of themselves can make things happen.

Some research suggests that a mechanism for recognizing causality exists much earlier (Mandler, 1998). In habituation–dishabituation experiments, infants 6½ months old have seen a difference between events that are the immediate cause of other events (such as a brick striking a second brick, which is then pushed out of position) and events that occur with no apparent cause (such as a brick moving away from another brick without having been struck by it). Thus, at an early age, infants seem aware of continuity of relationships in time and space—perhaps a first step toward understanding causality (L. B. Cohen & Amsel, 1998; Leslie, 1982, 1984).

Such research has been interpreted to suggest that very young infants may have a special built-in brain "module" that acts as a causal-motion detector, directing attention to causally linked events (Leslie, 1988, 1994; Leslie & Keeble, 1987). However, the infants in these studies may be responding simply to differences in the positions of objects in space and time, not to what caused those changes (Cohen & Amsel, 1998; Leslie, 1994).

Investigators who support Piaget's slower timetable for the development of causal understanding attribute this understanding to a gradual development in information-processing skills. By 7 months, infants may make causal interpretations about a particular set of objects and simple events, but not until between 10 and 15 months do they perceive causality in more complex circumstances involving a chain of several events. As infants accumulate more information about how objects behave, they are better able to see causality as a general principle operating in a variety of situations (L. B. Cohen & Amsel, 1998; L. B. Cohen & Oakes, 1993; L. B. Cohen et al., 1999; Oakes, 1994).

Evaluating Violation-of-Expectations Research There is some skepticism about what violation-of-expectations studies show. Does the infant's reaction reveal a conceptual understanding of the way things work, or merely a perceptual awareness that something novel or unusual has happened? The fact that an infant looks longer at one scene than at another may show only that the infant can see a difference between the two. It does not show what the infant knows about the difference, or that the infant is actually surprised. The "mental representation" the infant refers to may be no more than a brief sensory memory of something just seen. It's also possible that an infant, in becoming accustomed to the habituation event, develops the expectations that are then violated by the "surprising" event, and did not have such knowledge or expectations before (Goubet & Clifton, 1998; Haith, 1998; Haith & Benson, 1998; Mandler, 1998; Munakata, 2001; Munakata, McClelland, Johnson, & Siegler, 1997).

Defenders of the new research insist that a conceptual interpretation best accounts for the evidence (Baillargeon, 1999; Spelke, 1998), but a variation on one of Baillargeon's experiments suggests otherwise. In her original research, Baillargeon (1994) showed infants of various ages a "drawbridge" rotating 180 degrees. When the infants became habituated to the rotation, a barrier was introduced in the form of a box. At 4½ months, infants seemed to show (by longer looking) that they realized the drawbridge could not move through the entire box (see Figure 7-6). Later investigators replicated the experiment but eliminated the box. Five-month-olds still looked longer at the 180-degree rotation than at a lesser degree

Checkpoint ✓

Can you . . .

✔ Describe the violation-of-expectations method, tell how and why it is used, and list some criticisms of it?

✔ Discuss three areas in which violation-of-expectations research seems to contradict Piaget's account of development?

of rotation, even though no barrier was present—suggesting that the explanation might simply be a preference for greater movement (Rivera, Wakeley, & Langer, 1999).

Further research is needed to clarify these issues. In the meantime, developmental scientists must be cautious about inferring the existence of adult-like cognitive abilities that are not conclusively established, when the data may have simpler explanations or may represent only partial achievement of mature abilities (Haith, 1998).

Cognitive Neuroscience Approach: The Brain's Cognitive Structures

Piaget's belief that neurological maturation is a major factor in cognitive development was merely a supposition. Today research in cognitive neuroscience, the study of the brain structures that govern thinking and memory, bears him out.

We are learning about infant neurological development by studying monkeys, rabbits, and other animals, and by using instruments that measure human brain activity. Studies of infant brain functioning have made use of behaviourist principles and Piagetian tasks. Other studies have recorded brainwave changes associated with information processing and have determined which brain structures affect which aspects of memory.

Studies of normal and brain-damaged adults point to two separate long-term memory systems—*explicit* and *implicit*—which acquire and store different kinds of information. Brain scans provide direct physical evidence of the location of these systems (Squire, 1992; Vargha-Khadem et al., 1997). **Explicit memory** is conscious or intentional recollection, usually of facts, names, events, or other things that people can state or declare. **Implicit memory** refers to remembering that occurs without effort or even conscious awareness; it generally pertains to habits and skills, such as knowing how to throw a ball or ride a bicycle.

Implicit memory seems to develop earlier and mature faster. Two kinds of implicit memory are present during the first few months of life: memory for procedures (such as a sequence of lights), which seems to be centred in the *striatum;* and conditioning, which appears to depend on the *cerebellum* and parts of the *brain stem.* A reflex-like precursor of explicit memory is chiefly dependent on the *hippocampus,* a sea horse–shaped structure deep in the central portion of the brain. This pre-explicit memory system permits infants to remember specific sights or sounds for a few seconds—long enough to show simple novelty preferences (Nelson, 1995; refer back to Figure 6-4 in chapter 6 for locations of brain structures).

Sometime between 6 and 12 months, or perhaps earlier (Rovee-Collier, 1999), a more sophisticated form of explicit memory modifies or replaces the pre-explicit form. It draws upon cortical structures, which are the primary site of general knowledge *(semantic memory),* as well as structures associated with the hippocampus, which govern memory of specific experiences *(episodic memory)* (Nelson, 1995; Vargha-Khadem et al., 1997). This advance is responsible for the emergence of complex forms of cross-modal transfer.

The *prefrontal cortex* (the large portion of the frontal lobe directly behind the forehead) is believed to control many aspects of cognition. This part of the brain develops more slowly than any other (M. H. Johnson, 1998). During the second half of the first year, the prefrontal cortex and associated circuitry develop the capacity for **working memory**—short-term storage of information the brain is actively processing, or working on. It is in working memory that mental representations are prepared for, or recalled from, storage.

The relatively late appearance of working memory may be largely responsible for the slow development of object permanence, which seems to be seated in a rearward area of the prefrontal cortex (Nelson, 1995). By 12 months, this region may be developed enough to permit an infant to avoid the A, not-B, error by controlling the impulse to search in a place where the object was previously found (Diamond, 1991). Electroencephalogram (EEG) studies show a link between prefrontal cortex functioning and success in a delayed search (Bell & Fox, 1992). Maturation of the hippocampus may explain the abrupt transition at 21 to 22 months to the use of landmarks as reminders of where an object was hidden (Mangan, Franklin, Tignor, Bolling, & Nadel, 1994; Newcombe, Huttenlocher, Drummey, & Wiley, 1998).

Guidepost 6

What can brain research reveal about the development of cognitive skills?

explicit memory Memory that is intentional and conscious

implicit memory Unconscious recall, generally of habits and skills, sometimes called *procedural memory*

working memory Short-term storage of information being actively processed

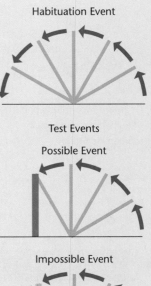

Habituation Event

Test Events

Possible Event

Impossible Event

Figure 7-6

Test for infants' understanding of how a barrier works.

Source: Adapted from Baillargeon, 1994.

Checkpoint ✔

Can you . . .

✔ Identify the brain structures apparently involved in implicit, pre-explicit, explicit, and working memory and mention a task made possible by each?

✔ Tell how brain research helps explain Piagetian developments and information-processing skills?

Guidepost 7

How does social interaction with adults advance cognitive competence?

guided participation
Participation of an adult in a child's activity in a manner that helps to structure the activity and to bring the child's understanding of it closer to that of the adult

Checkpoint ✔

Can you . . .

✔ Compare two cultural patterns of guided participation in toddlers' learning?

Guidepost 8

How do babies develop language?

language Communication system based on words and grammar

Although explicit memory and working memory continue to develop beyond infancy, the early emergence of the brain's memory structures underlines the importance of environmental stimulation during the first months of life. Social-contextual theorists and researchers pay particular attention to the impact of environmental influences.

Social-Contextual Approach: Learning from Interactions with Caregivers

Researchers influenced by Vygotsky's socio-cultural theory study how the cultural context affects early social interactions that may promote cognitive competence.

The concept of **guided participation** (Rogoff, 1990, 1998; Rogoff, Mistry, Göncü, & Mosier, 1993) was inspired by Vygotsky's zone of proximal development (refer back to chapter 2) and his view of learning as a collaborative process. Guided participation refers to interactions with adults that help structure children's activities and bridge the gap between the child's understanding and the adult's. Guided participation often occurs in shared play and in ordinary, everyday activities in which children informally learn the skills, knowledge, and values important in their culture.

In one cross-cultural study (Rogoff et al., 1993), researchers visited the homes of 14 1- to 2-year-olds in each of four places: a Mayan town in Guatemala, a tribal village in India, and middle-class urban neighbourhoods in the United States and Turkey. The investigators interviewed caregivers about their child-rearing practices and watched them help the toddlers learn to dress themselves and to play with unfamiliar toys.

Cultural differences affected the types of guided participation the researchers observed. In the Guatemalan town, where toddlers normally saw their mothers sewing and weaving at home to help support the family, and in the Indian village, where they accompanied their mothers at work in the fields, the children customarily played alone or with older siblings while the mother worked nearby. After initial demonstration and instruction, mostly non-verbal, the children took the lead in their own learning, while a parent or other caregiver remained available to help.

The U.S. toddlers, who had full-time homemaker mothers or were in daycare, interacted with their parents in the context of child's play rather than in the parents' work or social worlds. Caregivers spoke with the children as peers and managed and motivated their learning with praise and mock excitement. Turkish families, who were in transition from a rural to an urban way of life, showed a pattern somewhere between the other two.

The cultural context, then, influences the way caregivers contribute to cognitive development. These researchers suggest that direct adult involvement in children's play and learning may be less adaptive in a rural community in non-industrialized country, in which children frequently observe and participate in adult activities, than in a middle-class urban community, in which homemaker mothers have more time, greater verbal skills, and possibly more interest in children's play and learning. The ways adults involve themselves in children's learning in one culture may be no better or worse than in another—just different.

Language Development

Doddy Darwin's use of the word "Ah!" to express his first recognition of his image in a glass is a striking example of the connection between **language,** a communication system based on words and grammar, and cognitive development. Once children know words, they can use them to represent objects and actions. They can reflect on people, places, and things; and they can communicate their needs, feelings, and ideas in order to exert control over their lives.

The growth of language illustrates the interaction of all aspects of development. As the physical structures needed to produce sounds mature, and the neuronal connections necessary to associate sound and meaning become activated, social interaction with adults introduces babies to the communicative nature of speech. Let's look at the typical sequence of language development (see Table 7-5), at some characteristics of early speech, at how babies acquire language and make progress in using it, and at how parents and other caregivers help toddlers prepare for **literacy,** the ability to read and write.

literacy Ability to read and write

Sequence of Early Language Development

Before babies can use words, they make their needs and feelings known—as Doddy Darwin did—through sounds that progress from crying to cooing and babbling, then to accidental imitation, and then deliberate imitation. These sounds are known as **prelinguistic speech.** Infants also grow in the ability to recognize and understand speech sounds and to use meaningful gestures. Babies typically say their first word around the end of the first year, and toddlers begin speaking in sentences about 8 months to a year later.

prelinguistic speech Forerunner of linguistic speech; utterance of sounds that are not words; includes crying, cooing, babbling, and accidental and deliberate imitation of sounds without understanding their meaning

Early Vocalization

Crying is a newborn's only means of communication. Different pitches, patterns, and intensities signal hunger, sleepiness, or anger (Lester & Boukydis, 1985).

Between 6 weeks and 3 months, babies start *cooing* when they are happy—squealing, gurgling, and making vowel sounds like "ahhh." At about 3 to 6 months, babies begin to play with speech sounds, matching the sounds they hear from people around them.

Babbling—repeating consonant-vowel strings, such as "ma-ma-ma-ma"—occurs between 6 and 10 months of age and is often mistaken for a baby's first word. Babbling is not real language, since it does not hold meaning for the baby, but it becomes more word-like. This form of language begins as a result of biological maturation and does not require exposure to language sounds to emerge. It is present in deaf infants, and, although it becomes more complex when reinforced in hearing children during the first year it drops

Table 7-5	Language Milestones from Birth to 3 Years
Age in Months	**Development**
Birth	Can perceive speech, cry, make some response to sound
1½–3	Coos and laughs
3	Plays with speech sounds
5–6	Makes consonant sounds, trying to match what she or he hears
6–10	Babbles in strings of consonants and vowels
9	Uses gestures to communicate and plays gesture games
9–10	Begins to understand words (usually "no" and baby's own name); imitates sounds
10–12	Can no longer discriminate sounds not in own language
9–12	Uses a few social gestures
10–14	Says first word (usually a label for something)
10–18	Says single words
13	Understands symbolic function of naming
13	Uses more elaborate gestures
14	Uses symbolic gesturing
16–24	Learns many new words, expanding vocabulary rapidly, going from about 50 words to up to 400; uses verbs and adjectives
18–24	Says first sentence (two words)
20	Uses fewer gestures; names more things
20–22	Has comprehension spurt
24	Uses many two-word phrases; no longer babbles; wants to talk
30	Learns new words almost every day; speaks in combinations of three or more words; understands very well; makes grammatical mistakes
36	Says up to 1,000 words, 80 per cent intelligible; makes some mistakes in syntax

Source: Bates, O'Connell, & Shore, 1987; Capute, Shapiro, & Palmer, 1987; Lalonde & Werker, 1995; Lenneberg, 1969.

away in deaf children only to be replaced by manual babbling as they acquire sign language (Meer & Willerman, 1995; Petitto & Marentette, 1991).

Language development continues with accidental *imitation of language sounds* that babies hear and then imitation of themselves making these sounds. At about 9 to 10 months, infants deliberately imitate sounds without understanding them. Once they have a repertoire of sounds, they string them together in patterns that sound like language but seem to have no meaning.

Recognizing Language Sounds

The ability to perceive differences between sounds is essential to language development. As we have seen, this ability is present from or even before birth, and it becomes more refined during the first year of life. In getting ready to understand and use speech, infants first become familiar with the sounds of words and phrases and later attach meanings to them (Jusczyk & Hohne, 1997).

The process apparently begins in the womb. In one experiment, two groups of Parisian women in their 35th week of pregnancy each recited a different nursery rhyme, saying it three times a day for 4 weeks. At the end of that time, researchers played recordings of both rhymes close to the women's abdomens. The fetuses' heart rates slowed when the rhyme the mother had spoken was played, but not for the other rhyme. Since the voice on the tape was not that of the mother, the fetuses apparently were responding to the linguistic sounds they had heard the mother use. This suggests that hearing the "mother tongue" before birth may "pretune" an infant's ears to pick up its sounds (DeCasper, Lecanuet, Busnel, Granier-Deferre, & Maugeais, 1994). In a classic study of basic language sound perception, infants as young as 1 month were able to discriminate between the basic sounds, or phonemes, used in their parents' languages, despite minimal prior exposure to language sounds (Eimas, Siqueland, Jusczyk, & Vigorito, 1971).

By 6 months of age, babies have learned to recognize phonemes of their native language, and to adjust to slight differences in the way different speakers form those sounds. In one study, 6-month-old Swedish and U.S. babies routinely ignored variations in sounds common in their own language but noticed variations in an unfamiliar language (Kuhl, Williams, Lacerda, Stevens, & Lindblom, 1992).

Before infants can connect sounds to meanings, they seem to recognize sound patterns they hear frequently, such as their own names. Four-and-a-half-month-olds listen longer to their own names than to other names, even names with stress patterns similar to theirs (Mandel, Jusczyk, & Pisoni, 1995). Six-month-olds look longer at a video of their mothers when they hear the word *mommy* and of their fathers when they hear *daddy,* suggesting that they are beginning to associate sound with meaning—at least with regard to special people (Tincoff & Jusczyk, 1999).

Infants have an uncanny ability to break down a stream of spoken words into individual words, based on the relationship between speech sounds in neighbouring words. Studies of 8-month-old infants demonstrated word-segmentation ability based on as little as 2 minutes of exposure to a segment of fluent speech, indicating that infants have access to a powerful learning mechanism that allows them to extract information about sound relationships between words very early in development (Aslin, Saffran, & Newport, 1998; Saffran, Aslin, & Newport, 1996).

By about 10 months, babies lose their earlier sensitivity to sounds that are not part of the language they hear spoken. For example, Japanese infants no longer make a distinction between "ra" and "la," a distinction that does not exist in the Japanese language. Although the ability to perceive nonnative sounds is not entirely lost—it can be revived, with effort, in adulthood—the brain no longer routinely discriminates them (Bates, O'Connell, & Shore, 1987; Lalonde & Werker, 1995; Werker, 1989).

Meanwhile, during the second half of the first year, as babies become increasingly familiar with the sounds of their language, they begin to become aware of its phonological rules—how sounds are arranged in speech. In one series of experiments (Marcus, Vijayan, Rao, & Vishton, 1999), 7-month-olds listened longer to "sentences" containing a different order of nonsense sounds (such as "wo fe wo," or ABA) from the order to which the infants had been habituated (such as "ga ti ti," or ABB). The sounds used in the test were different from those used in the habituation phase, so the infants' discrimination must have been based on the patterns of repetition alone. This finding suggests that infants may have a mechanism for discerning abstract rules of sentence structure.

Gestures

At 9 months Maika *pointed* to an object, sometimes making a noise to show that she wanted it. Between 9 and 12 months, she learned some *conventional social gestures:* waving bye-bye, nodding her head to mean "yes," and shaking her head to signify "no." By about 13 months, she used more elaborate *representational gestures;* for example, she would hold an empty cup to her mouth to show that she wanted a drink or hold up her arms to show that she wanted to be picked up.

Symbolic gestures, such as blowing to mean "hot," or sniffing to mean "flower," often emerge around the same time as babies say their first words, and they function much like words. By using them, children show an understanding that symbols can refer to specific objects, events, desires, and conditions. Gestures usually appear before children have a vocabulary of 25 words and drop out when children learn the word for the idea they were gesturing and can say it instead (Lock, Young, Service, & Chandler, 1990).

Learning gestures seems to help babies learn to talk. In one experiment (Goodwyn & Acredolo, 1998), 11-month-olds learned gestures by watching their parents perform them and say the corresponding words. Between 15 and 36 months, when tested on vocal language development, these children outperformed two other groups—one whose parents had only said words and another who had received neither vocal nor gestural training. Gestures, then, can be a valuable alternative or supplement to words, especially during the period of early vocabulary formation.

First Words

Doddy Darwin, at 11 months, said his first word—"ouchy"—which he attached to a number of objects. Doddy's development was typical in this respect. The average baby says a first word sometime between 10 and 14 months, initiating **linguistic speech**—verbal expression that conveys meaning. Before long, the baby will use many words and will show some understanding of grammar, pronunciation, intonation, and rhythm. For now, an infant's total verbal repertoire is likely to be "mama" or "dada." Or it may be a simple syllable that has more than one meaning depending on the context in which the child utters it. "Da" may mean "I want that," "I want to go out," or "Where's Daddy?" A word like this, which expresses a complete thought, is called a **holophrase.**

Babies understand many words before they can use them. The first words most babies understand are the ones they are likely to hear most often: their own names and the word *no,* as well as words with special meaning for them.

By 13 months, most children understand that a word stands for a specific thing or event, and they can quickly learn the meaning of a new word (Woodward, Markman, & Fitzsimmons, 1994). In a further study, Janet Werker at the University of British Columbia demonstrated in well-controlled studies that 14-month-old infants can learn to associate words with objects with minimal exposure and no social or contextual support (Werker, Cohen, Lloyd, Casasola, & Stager, 1998). Werker and colleagues suggest that as infants get better at perceiving phonemes in their native languages, and later at learning to associate words and objects, they experience a "functional reorganization" of their language abilities. This reorganization involves dropping their knowledge of details as they move on to increasingly complex language tasks (Werker & Tees, 1999). This is evident in the loss of phonemes that infants are sensitive to by the end of the first year, and in the remarkable abilities of 14-month-olds to associate words and objects. Although 14-month-olds were able to make the associations between pairs of words and objects when the words sounded distinctly different, the infants had difficulty making the associations when the words were phonetically similar (Werker et al. 1998). This inattention to phonetic detail, which made it difficult for the infants to carry out the association task, represents a dropping off of detailed language knowledge as a new kind of ability emerges. As children move on to learning more words, the access to phonetic details likely returns to distinguish between words that sound similar (Werker et al., 1999). The same kind of functional reorganization seems to occur when infants learn to produce words, when they fail

linguistic speech Verbal expression designed to convey meaning

holophrase Single word that conveys a complete thought

to pronounce words correctly or consistently, at one point pronouncing "dog" as "gog," and later using the initial "d" sound to mispronounce "truck" as "duck." It is as though infants temporarily lose their capacity to use their established language knowledge when a new language ability begins to emerge. Addition of new words to their *expressive* (spoken) vocabulary is slower at first. As children come to rely more on words than on gestures to express themselves, the sounds and rhythms of speech grow more elaborate.

Vocabulary continues to grow throughout the single-word stage, which generally lasts until about 18 months of age. Sometime between 16 and 24 months a "naming explosion" occurs. Within a few weeks, a toddler may go from saying about 50 words to saying about 400 (Bates, Bretherton, & Snyder, 1988). These rapid gains in spoken vocabulary reflect a steady increase in the speed and accuracy of word recognition during the second year of life (Fernald, Pinto, Swingley, Weinberg, & McRoberts, 1998).

The most common early spoken words in English are *names* of things (nouns), either general ("bow-wow" for *dog*) or specific ("Unga" for one particular dog). Others are *action* words ("bye-bye"), *modifiers* ("hot"), words that arise out of *personal feelings or social relationships* (the ever-popular "no"), and a few *functional* words ("for") (Nelson, 1973, 1981). After the first 100 words, this pattern shifts, and the proportion of verbs to nouns begins to increase (Owens, 1996). Toddlers in Beijing, China, were observed to use more verbs than nouns—not surprising, since word order in their Mandarin language (subject-object-verb) makes verbs especially prominent (Tardif, 1996).

First Sentences

The next important linguistic breakthrough comes when a toddler puts two words together to express one idea ("Dolly fall"). Generally, children do this between 18 and 24 months, about 8 to 12 months after they say their first word. However, this age range varies greatly. Although prelinguistic speech is fairly closely tied to chronological age, linguistic speech is not. Most children who begin talking fairly late catch up eventually—and many make up for lost time by talking nonstop to anyone who will listen! (True delayed language development is further discussed in chapter 10.)

A child's first sentences typically deal with everyday events, things, people, or activities (Braine, 1976; Rice, 1989; Slobin, 1973). Darwin noted instances in which Doddy expressed his developing moral sense in words. At 27 months the boy gave his sister the last bit of his gingerbread, exclaiming, "Oh, kind Doddy, kind Doddy!"

telegraphic speech Early form of sentence consisting of only a few essential words

At first children typically use **telegraphic speech,** consisting of only a few essential words. When Rita says, "Damma deep," she seems to mean "Grandma is sweeping the floor." Children's use of telegraphic speech, and the form it takes, varies, depending on the language being learned (Braine, 1976; Slobin, 1983). Word order generally conforms to what a child hears; Rita does not say "Deep Damma" when she sees her grandmother pushing a broom.

Does the omission of functional words such as *is* and *the* mean that a child does not know these words? Not necessarily; the child may merely find them hard to reproduce. Even during the first year, infants are sensitive to the presence of functional words; at 10½ months, they can tell a normal passage from one in which the functional words have been replaced by similar-sounding nonsense words (Jusczyk, in press).

syntax Rules for forming sentences in a particular language

Sometime between 20 and 30 months, children show increasing competence in **syntax,** the rules for putting sentences together in their language. They become somewhat more comfortable with articles *(a, the),* prepositions *(in, on),* conjunctions *(and, but),* plurals, verb endings, past tense, and forms of the verb *to be (am, are, is).* They also become increasingly aware of the communicative purpose of speech and of whether their words are being understood (Shwe & Markman, 1997)—a sign of growing sensitivity to the mental lives of others (see Box 7-2). By age 3, speech is fluent, longer, and more complex; although children often omit parts of speech, they get their meaning across well.

Characteristics of Early Speech

Early speech has a character all its own—no matter what language a child is speaking (Slobin, 1971).

At what age can babies begin to "read" what is on other people's minds? Twelve-month-olds will give an object to a person who points to it and asks for it. But does the baby realize that the request reflects an inner desire, or is the child merely responding to observable behaviour (pointing)? Eighteen-month-olds will offer a toy to a crying child. But do they realize that their comforting may change the other child's mental state, or are they merely trying to change an overt behaviour (crying)? And, since they usually offer a toy they themselves would find comforting, are they capable of distinguishing another person's state of mind from their own?

Since most toddlers can't talk well enough to tell us what they are thinking, one research team (Repacholi & Gopnik, 1997) designed a non-verbal experiment to test their ability to discern another person's food preferences.

Each of 159 children—about half of them 14 months and the other half 18 months old—took part in an individual free-play session. During the session, the child and an experimenter were offered two bowls of snacks: one that young children typically like (goldfish crackers) and one that they typically do not like (raw broccoli flowerets). First the child tasted the snacks, and then the experimenter did. As expected, more than 9 out of 10 children preferred the crackers.

Equal numbers of boys and girls of each age were randomly assigned to two testing conditions: one in which the experimenter's apparent food preference matched the child's expected preference and one in which it did not. In the "matched" condition, the experimenter showed pleasure after tasting the cracker ("Mmm!") and disgust after tasting the broccoli ("Eww"). In the "mismatched" condition, the experimenter acted as if she preferred the broccoli.

Next, the experimenter asked the child to give her some food. The child also had another opportunity to taste the snacks. This was done to see whether the children's food preferences had been influenced by the experimenter's preferences. Only 6 children (4 per cent) changed their apparent preference.

What did the children do when the experimenter asked for food? Nearly 7 out of 10 of the 14-month-olds did not respond.

About 1 in 3 "teased" the experimenter by offering the crackers and then pulling back. Most of the 14-month-olds who did respond offered crackers, regardless of which food the experimenter seemed to prefer. By contrast, only 3 out of 10 of the 18-month-olds failed to respond to the request; and, of those who did, 3 out of 4 gave the experimenter the food she had shown a liking for, whether or not it was the one they themselves liked.

Thus 18-month-olds, but not 14-month-olds, seem able to use another person's emotional cues to figure out what that person likes and wants, even when that person's desire is different from their own, and then to apply the information in a different situation in which there are no visible cues to the other person's preference. This suggests a rather sophisticated understanding of mental states: an awareness that two people can have opposite feelings about the same thing.

In a similar vein, a Queen's University study showed that children as young as 2 years of age were able to "read minds" by using other people's gazes as non-verbal clues about what people desire (Lee, Eskritt, Symons, & Muir, 1998). When shown pictures of faces looking at one of several surrounding objects, the children were able to use gazing information to work out the correct internal state of the person in the picture and correctly answer questions about the internal state.

Young children who can interpret another person's desire are on their way to developing a *theory of mind,* a topic we discuss in chapter 10.

What's your view

Have you ever been in a conversation with a toddler who seemed aware of your mental state? How could you tell?

Check it out!

For more information on this topic, go to **www.mcgrawhill.ca/college/papalia.**

As we have seen, children *simplify.* They use telegraphic speech to say just enough to get their meaning across ("No drink milk!").

Children *understand grammatical relationships they cannot yet express.* At first, Nina may understand that a dog is chasing a cat, but she cannot string together enough words to express the complete action. Her sentence comes out as "Puppy chase" rather than "Puppy chase kitty."

Children *underextend word meanings.* Lisa's uncle gave her a toy car, which the 13-month-old called her "koo-ka." Then her father came home with a gift, saying, "Look, Lisa, here's a little car for you." Lisa shook her head. "Koo-ka," she said and ran and got the one from her uncle. To her, *that* car—and *only* that car—was a little car, and it took some time before she called any other toy cars by the same name. Lisa was underextending the word *car* by restricting it to a single object.

Children also *overextend word meanings.* At 14 months, Eddie jumped in excitement at the sight of a grey-haired man on the television screen and shouted, "Gampa!" Eddie was overgeneralizing, or *overextending,* a word; he thought that because his grandfather had grey hair, all grey-haired men could be called "Grandpa." As children develop a larger vocabulary and get feedback from adults on the appropriateness of what they say, they overextend less. ("No, Honey, that man looks a little like Grandpa, but he's somebody else's grandpa, not yours.")

Checkpoint ✔

Can you . . .

✔ Trace the typical sequence of milestones in early language development, pointing out the influence of the language babies hear around them?

✔ Describe five ways in which early speech differs from adult speech?

Almost all children, like this Japanese baby, learn their native language, mastering the basics in the same age-related sequence without formal teaching. Nativists say this shows that all human beings are born with the capacity to acquire language.

nativism Theory that human beings have an inborn capacity for language acquisition

language acquisition device (LAD) In Chomsky's terminology, an inborn mechanism that enables children to infer linguistic rules from the language they hear

Children *overregularize rules:* They apply them rigidly, not knowing that some rules have exceptions. When John says "mouses" instead of "mice" or Megan says "I thinked" rather than "I thought," this represents progress. Both children initially used the correct forms of these irregular words, but merely in imitation of what they heard. Once children learn the rules for plurals and past tense (a crucial step in learning language), they apply them universally. The next step is to learn the exceptions to the rules, which they generally do by early school age.

Classic Theories of Language Acquisition: The Nature–Nurture Debate

How do children gain access to the secrets of verbal communication? Is linguistic ability learned or inborn? In the 1950s, a debate raged between two schools of thought: one led by B. F. Skinner, the foremost proponent of learning theory, the other by the linguist Noam Chomsky.

Skinner (1957) maintained that language learning, like other learning, is based on experience. According to classic learning theory, children learn language through operant conditioning. At first, babies utter sounds at random. Caregivers reinforce the sounds that happen to resemble adult speech with smiles, attention, and praise. Infants then repeat these reinforced sounds. Sounds that are not part of the native language are not reinforced, and the child gradually stops making them. According to social learning theory, babies imitate the sounds they hear adults make and, again, are reinforced for doing so. Word learning depends on selective reinforcement; the word *kitty* is reinforced only when the family cat appears. As this process continues, children are reinforced for speech that is more and more adult-like. Sentence formation is a more complex process: The child learns a basic word order (subject-verb-object—"I want ice cream") and then learns that other words can be substituted in each category ("Daddy eats meat").

Observation, imitation, and reinforcement probably do contribute to language development, but, as Chomsky (1957) persuasively argued, they cannot fully explain it (Flavell, Miller, & Miller, 1993; Owens, 1996). For one thing, word combinations and nuances are so many and so complex that they cannot all be acquired by specific imitation and reinforcement. Then, caregivers often reinforce utterances that are not strictly grammatical, as long as they make sense. ("Gampa go bye-bye.") Adult speech itself is an unreliable model to imitate, as it is often ungrammatical, containing false starts, unfinished sentences, and slips of the tongue. Also, learning theory does not account for children's imaginative ways of saying things they have never heard—as when 2-year-old Anna described a sprained ankle as a "sprangle" and said she didn't want to go to sleep yet because she wasn't "yawny."

Chomsky's own view is called **nativism.** Unlike Skinner's learning theory, nativism emphasizes the active role of the learner. Since language is universal among human beings, Chomsky (1957, 1972) proposed that the human brain has an innate capacity for acquiring language; babies learn to talk as naturally as they learn to walk. He suggested that an inborn **language acquisition device (LAD)** programs children's brains to analyze the language they hear and to figure out its rules. More recently, Chomsky (1995) has sought to identify a simple set of universal principles that underlie all languages, and a single multi-purpose mechanism for connecting sound to meaning.

Support for the nativist position comes from newborns' ability to differentiate similar sounds, suggesting that they are "born with perceptual mechanisms that are tuned to the properties of speech" (Eimas, 1985, p. 49). Nativists point out that almost all children master their native language in the same age-related sequence without formal teaching. Furthermore, the brains of human beings, the only animals with fully developed language, contain a structure that is larger on one side than on the other, suggesting that an inborn mechanism for language may be localized in the larger hemisphere—the left for most people. A similar imbalance in the size of this brain structure, the *planum temporale,* has been discovered in chimpanzees, which also show some ability to learn language (Gannon, Holloway, Broadfield, & Braun, 1998). Still, the nativist approach does not explain precisely how such a mechanism operates. It does not tell us why some children acquire language

Figure 7-7

Example of hand-babbling by a non-hearing baby who had been exposed to sign language. The baby repeated this series of hand movements over and over again in sequence. Each motion is comparable to a syllable in a sequence of vocal babbling.

Source: Petitto & Marentette, 1991.

more rapidly and efficiently than others, why children differ in linguistic skill and fluency, or why (as we'll see) speech development appears to depend on having someone to talk with, not merely on hearing spoken language.

Aspects of both learning theory and nativism have been used to explain how deaf babies learn sign language, which is structured much like spoken language and is acquired in the same sequence. Deaf babies of deaf parents seem to copy the sign language they see their parents using, just as hearing babies copy vocal utterances. Using hand motions more systematic and deliberate than those of hearing babies, deaf babies first string together meaningless motions and repeat them over and over in what has been called *hand-babbling* (Petitto & Marentette, 1991; see Figure 7-7). As parents reinforce these gestures, the babies attach meaning to them.

However, some deaf children make up their own sign language when they do not have models to follow—evidence that environmental influences alone cannot explain the emergence of linguistic expression (Goldin-Meadow & Mylander, 1998). Furthermore, learning theory does not explain the correspondence between the ages at which linguistic advances in both hearing and non-hearing babies typically occur (Padden, 1996). Deaf babies begin hand-babbling before 10 months of age, about the age when hearing infants begin voice-babbling (Petitto & Marentette, 1991). Deaf babies also begin to use sentences in sign language at about the same time that hearing babies begin to speak in sentences (Meier, 1991; Newport & Meier, 1985). This suggests that an inborn language capacity may underlie the acquisition of both spoken and signed language and that advances in both kinds of language are tied to brain maturation.

Most developmentalists today believe that language acquisition, like most other aspects of development, depends on an intertwining of nature and nurture. Children, whether hearing or deaf, probably have an inborn capacity to acquire language, which may be activated or constrained by experience.

Influences on Language Development

What determines how quickly and how well children learn to understand and use language? Research has focused on influences both within and outside the child.

Maturation of the Brain

The tremendous brain growth and reorganization during the early months and years is closely linked with language development. Which brain structures control which language functions, and when do these structures develop and mature? Scientists have two basic methods of finding out. The first is to study specific language deficiencies in people who have suffered damage to particular regions of the brain. The second is to observe brain activity in normal people as they engage in particular language functions. The development of modern techniques that produce images of what is going on in the brain has aided both approaches.

The brain's linguistic processes are extremely complex and may involve different components in different people (Caplan, 1992). These processes seem to arise from the coordination of a variety of brain structures (Owens, 1996).

Cortical regions associated with language do not fully mature until at least the late preschool years or beyond—some, not even until adulthood. A newborn's cries are controlled by the *brain stem* and *pons,* the most primitive parts of the brain and the earliest to develop (refer back to Figure 6-4). Repetitive babbling may emerge with the maturation of parts of the *motor cortex,* which control movements of the face and larynx. Not until early in the second year, when most children begin to talk, do the pathways that link auditory and motor activity mature (Owens, 1996).

Checkpoint ✓

Can you . . .

✔ Summarize how learning theory and nativism seek to explain language acquisition, and point out strengths and weaknesses of each?

Guidepost 9

What influences contribute to linguistic progress?

How linguistic processes come to be organized in the brain may depend heavily on experience. In about 98 per cent of people, the left hemisphere is dominant for language, though the right hemisphere participates as well. This lateralization may be genetically determined, but it also seems to be environmentally influenced. Studies of brain-damaged children suggest that a sensitive period exists before lateralization of language is firmly fixed. The plasticity of the infant brain seems to allow functions to be transferred from damaged areas to other regions. Thus, whereas an adult whose left hemisphere is removed or injured will be severely language-impaired, a young child who undergoes this procedure may eventually have nearly normal speech and comprehension (Nobre & Plunkett, 1997; Owens, 1996).

Brains of normal infants also show plasticity. In one study, researchers measured brain activity at various places on the scalp as babies listened to a series of words, some of which they did not understand. Between ages 13 and 20 months, a period of marked vocabulary growth, the infants showed increasing lateralization and localization of comprehension (Mills, Cofley-Corina, & Neville, 1997). Other evidence of neural plasticity comes from findings that the upper regions of the temporal lobe, which are involved in hearing and understanding speech, can be activated by a born-deaf person's use of sign language (Nishimura et al., 1999). Such findings suggest that the assignment of language functions to brain structures may be a gradual process linked to verbal experience and cognitive development (Nobre & Plunkett, 1997).

Social Interaction: The Role of Parents and Caregivers

As the story of Victor (refer back to chapter 1 Focus) shows, language is a social act. Parents or other caregivers play an important role at each stage of language development.

Prelinguistic Period At the babbling stage, adults help an infant advance toward true speech by repeating the sounds the baby makes; the baby soon joins in the game and repeats the sounds back. Parents' imitation of babies' sounds affects the pace of language learning (Hardy-Brown & Plomin, 1985; Hardy-Brown, Plomin, & DeFries, 1981). It also helps babies experience the social aspect of speech, the sense that a conversation consists of taking turns, an idea most babies seem to grasp at about 7½ to 8 months of age. Even as young as 4 months, babies in a game of peekaboo show sensitivity to the structure of social exchange with an adult (Rochat, Querido, & Striano, 1999; refer back to Box 7-1).

Caregivers may help babies understand spoken words by, for example, pointing to a doll and saying, "Please give me Kermit." If the baby doesn't respond, the adult may pick up the doll and say, "Kermit." In one naturalistic observational study, researchers videotaped 40 mothers playing with their 9-month-old infants at home and rated the mothers' verbal sensitivity. The mother's verbal sensitivity, for example, naming a toy in response to a baby's interest, turned out to be an important predictor of the baby's language comprehension (as reported by the mother) 4 months later (Baumwell, Tamis-LeMonda, & Bornstein, 1997).

Vocabulary Development When babies begin to talk, parents or caregivers often help them by repeating their first words and pronouncing them correctly. Vocabulary gets a boost when an adult seizes an appropriate opportunity to teach a child a new word. If Jordan's mother says, "This is a ball," when Jordan is looking at the ball, he is more likely to remember the word than if he were playing with something else and she tried to divert his attention to the ball (Dunham, Dunham & Curwin, 1993). Adults help a toddler who has begun to put words together by expanding on what the child says. If Christina says, "Mommy sock," her mother may reply, "Yes, that is Mommy's sock."

Babies learn by listening to what adults say. A strong relationship has appeared between the frequency of various words in mothers' speech and the order in which children learn these words (Huttenlocher, Haight, Bryk, Seltzer, & Lyons, 1991), as well as between mothers' talkativeness and the size of toddlers' vocabularies (Huttenlocher, 1998).

However, sensitivity and responsiveness to a child's level of development count more than the number of words a mother uses. In one longitudinal study, in which toddlers were observed interacting with their mothers at 13 and 20 months, the mothers increased their vocabulary use to match their children's growing language abilities; and the children with

Checkpoint ✔

Can you . . .

✔ Name two important areas of the brain involved in use of language, and tell the function of each?

✔ Give evidence for plasticity in the brain's linguistic areas?

the biggest vocabularies had mothers who were most responsive (Bornstein Tamis-LeMonda, & Haynes, 1999).

In households where two languages are spoken, babies often use elements of both languages at first, sometimes in the same utterance—a phenomenon called **code mixing.** Still, as we have seen, even young infants do learn to discriminate between languages. A naturalistic observation in Montreal (Genesee, Nicoladis, & Paradis, 1995) suggests that children as young as 2 in dual-language households differentiate between the two languages, using French, for example, with a predominantly French-speaking father and English with a predominantly English-speaking mother. This ability to shift from one language to another is called **code switching.** (Chapter 13 discusses second-language learning.)

Influence of Socio-economic Status Socio-economic status seems to affect the amount and quality of verbal interaction between parents and children, and also the children's long-range language and cognitive development. In a longitudinal study of 7-month-old children, those in lower-income families heard less varied language and had less opportunity to talk, and their spoken vocabulary was more limited (Hart & Risley, 1989, 1992, 1996)—disadvantages later reflected in linguistic and academic performance between ages 5 and 10 (Walker et al., 1994). However, further analysis showed that the parents in more crowded homes were less verbally responsive to their infants and toddlers, suggesting that it is household size, not poverty itself, that may produce impoverished speech (Evans, Maxwell, & Hart, 1999).

Child-Directed Speech

You do not have to be a parent to speak "parentese." If, when you talk to an infant or toddler, you speak slowly in a high-pitched voice with exaggerated ups and downs, simplify your speech, exaggerate vowel sounds, and use short words and sentences and much repetition, you are using **child-directed speech (CDS).** Most adults, and even children, do it naturally. Such "baby talk" may well be universal; it has been documented in many languages and cultures (Kuhl et al., 1997). Apparently this kind of linguistic input helps infants hear the distinguishing features of speech sounds. At 20 weeks, the babies' babbling contained distinct vowels that reflected the phonetic differences to which their mothers' speech had alerted them (Kuhl et al., 1997).

CDS may teach babies how to carry on a conversation: how to introduce a topic, comment on and add to it, and take turns talking. It teaches them how to use new words, structure phrases, and put ideas into language. Because CDS is confined to simple, down-to-earth topics, infants and toddlers can use their own knowledge of familiar things to help them work out the meanings of the words they hear. CDS also helps babies develop a relationship with adults and enables them to respond to emotional cues (Fernald, 1984; Fernald & Simon, 1984). Likewise, babies also influence the degree of CDS they receive. In a study of French-speaking mothers in Quebec, mothers were found to adjust their use of CDS based on their children's interest and degree of engagement (Brousseau, Malcuit, Pomerleau, & Feider, 1996).

Some investigators challenge the value of CDS. They contend that babies speak sooner and better if they hear and can respond to more complex adult speech. In fact, some researchers say, children discover the rules of language faster when they hear complex sentences that use these rules more often and in more ways (Gleitman, Newport, & Gleitman, 1984; Oshima-Takane, Goodz, & Derevensky, 1996).

Nonetheless, infants themselves prefer simplified speech. This preference is clear before 1 month of age, and it does not seem to depend on any specific experience (Cooper & Aslin, 1990; Kuhl et al., 1997; McLeod & Watt, 1995; Werker, Pegg, & McLeod, 1994). Two-day-old infants of both English-speaking and Japanese-speaking parents prefer infant-directed to adult-directed singing (Masataka, 1999). In fact, a McMaster University team found that by 6 months of age infants were able to distinguish between and alter their behaviour in response to lullabies and songs intended for play. This shows that parents may use singing to communicate with and regulate their children's internal states between sleep-oriented and play-oriented emotions (Rock, Trainor, & Addison, 1999).

The preference for CDS is not limited to spoken language. In an observational study in Japan, deaf mothers were videotaped reciting everyday sentences in sign language, first to

code mixing Use of elements of two languages, sometimes in the same utterance, by young children in households where both languages are spoken

code switching Process of changing one's speech to match the situation, as in people who are bilingual

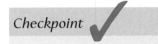

Checkpoint

Can you . . .

✔ Explain the importance of social interaction and give at least three examples of how parents or caregivers help babies learn to talk?

✔ Tell how socioeconomic status and other family characteristics may influence language development?

child-directed speech (CDS) Form of speech often used in talking to babies or toddlers; includes slow, simplified speech, a high-pitched tone, exaggerated vowel sounds, short words and sentences, and much repetition; also called *parentese*

By reading aloud to his 2-year-old son and asking questions about the pictures in the book, this father is helping the boy build language skills and prepare to become a good reader.

their deaf 6-month-old infants and then to deaf adult friends. The mothers signed more slowly and with more repetition and exaggerated movements when directing the sentences to the infants, and other infants the same age paid more attention and appeared more responsive when shown these tapes (Masataka, 1996). What's more, 6-month-old *hearing* infants who had never been exposed to sign language also showed a preference for infant-directed sign (Masataka, 1998). This is powerful evidence that infants, whether hearing or deaf, are universally attracted to child-directed communication.

Preparing for Literacy: The Benefits of Reading Aloud

Most babies love to be read to, and the frequency with which parents or caregivers read to them, as well as the way they do it, can influence how well children speak and eventually how well and how soon they read. Children who learn to read early are generally those whose parents read to them very frequently when they were very young.

Reading to an infant or toddler offers opportunities for emotional intimacy and fosters parent–child communication. Adults help a child's language development when they paraphrase what the child says, expand on it, talk about what interests the child, remain quiet long enough to give the child a chance to respond, and ask specific questions (Rice, 1989). Read-aloud sessions offer a perfect opportunity for this kind of interaction.

A child will get more out of such sessions if adults ask challenging, open-ended questions rather than those calling for a simple yes or no ("What is the cat doing?" instead of "Is the cat asleep?"). In one study, 21- to 35-month-olds whose parents did this—and who added to the child's answers, corrected wrong ones, gave alternative possibilities, encouraged the child to tell the story, and bestowed praise—scored 6 months higher in vocabulary and expressive language skills than did a control group whose parents did not use these practices in reading to the children. The experimental group also got a boost in *preliteracy skills,* the competencies helpful in learning to read, such as learning how letters look and sound (Arnold & Whitehurst, 1994; Whitehurst et al., 1988). Children who are read to often, especially in this way, when they are 1 to 3 years old show better language skills at ages 2½, 4½, and 5 and better reading comprehension at age 7 (Crain-Thoreson & Dale, 1992; Wells, 1985). A study at the University of Guelph found that children whose parents involved them in letter activities at home are more likely to do well on letter-name and letter-sound learning in kindergarten (Evans, Shaw, & Bell, 2000).

Social interaction in reading aloud, play, and other daily activities is a key to much of childhood development. Children elicit responses from the people around them and, in turn, react to those responses. In chapter 8, we look more closely at these bi-directional influences as we explore early psychosocial development.

Checkpoint ✔

Can you . . .

✔ Assess the arguments for and against the value of child-directed speech (CDS)?

✔ Tell why reading aloud to children at an early age is beneficial?

✔ Describe an effective way of reading aloud to infants and toddlers?

Summary and Key Terms

Studying Cognitive Development: Classic Approaches

Guidepost 1 How do infants learn, and how long can they remember?

- Two simple types of learning that behaviourists study are classical conditioning and operant conditioning.

- Rovee-Collier's research suggests that infants' memory processes are much like those of adults, but their memories fade quickly without periodic reminders.

  **intelligent behaviour (145)   behaviourist approach (145)
  classical conditioning (146)   operant conditioning (146)**

Guidepost 2 Can infants' and toddlers' intelligence be measured, and how can it be improved?

- Psychometric tests measure presumed factors in intelligence.

  psychometric approach (145)   IQ (intelligence quotient) tests (148)

- Developmental tests, such as the Bayley Scales of Infant Development, can indicate current functioning but are generally poor predictors of later intelligence.

- Socio-economic status, parenting practices, and the home environment may affect measured intelligence.

- If the developmental priming mechanisms are not present, early intervention may be needed.

  **Bayley Scales of Infant Development (148)   Home Observation for Measurement of the Environment (HOME) (150)
  developmental priming mechanisms (150)   early intervention (150)**

Guidepost 3 How did Piaget describe infants' and toddlers' cognitive development, and how have his claims stood up?

- During Piaget's sensorimotor stage, infants' schemes become more elaborate. They progress from primary to secondary to tertiary circular reactions and finally to the development of representational ability, which makes possible deferred imitation, pretending, and problem solving.

  Piagetian approach (145)   sensorimotor stage (152) schemes (152)   circular reactions (152)   representational ability (153)   deferred imitation (153)

- Object permanence develops gradually throughout the sensorimotor stage. Piaget saw the A, not-B, error as a sign of incomplete object knowledge and the persistence of egocentric thought.

- Research suggests that a number of abilities develop earlier than Piaget described. For example, he may have underestimated young infants' grasp of object permanence and their imitative abilities.

  object permanence (154)   A, not-B, error (154) invisible imitation (155)   visible imitation (155)

Studying Cognitive Development: Newer Approaches

Guidepost 4   How can we measure infants' ability to process information, and how does this ability relate to future intelligence?

- Information-processing researchers measure mental processes through habituation and other signs of visual and perceptual abilities. Contrary to Piaget, such research suggests that representational ability is present virtually from birth.

- Indicators of the efficiency of infants' information processing, such as speed of habituation, tend to predict later intelligence.

  information-processing approach (157)   habituation (158) dishabituation (158)   visual preference (159)   cross-modal transfer (159)   visual recognition memory (160)

Guidepost 5   When do babies begin to think about characteristics of the physical world?

- Violation-of-expectations research suggests that infants as young as 3½ to 5 months may have a rudimentary grasp of object permanence, a sense of number, the beginning of an understanding of causality, and an ability to reason about other characteristics of the physical world. Some researchers suggest that infants may have innate learning mechanisms for acquiring such knowledge. However, the meaning of these findings is in dispute.

  violation-of-expectations (160)

Guidepost 6   What can brain research reveal about the development of cognitive skills?

- Brain studies have found that some forms of implicit memory and a primitive form of preexplicit memory develop during the first few months of life. Explicit memory and working memory emerge between 6 and 12 months of age. Neurological developments help explain the emergence of Piagetian skills and information-processing abilities.

cognitive neuroscience approach (158)   explicit memory (163) implicit memory (163)   working memory (163)

Guidepost 7   How does social interaction with adults advance cognitive competence?

- Social interactions with adults contribute to cognitive competence through shared activities that help children learn skills, knowledge, and values important in their culture.

  social-contextual approach (158)   guided participation (164)

Language Development

Guidepost 8   How do babies develop language?

- The acquisition of language is an important aspect of cognitive development.

- Prelinguistic speech includes crying, cooing, babbling, and imitating language sounds. By 6 months, babies have learned the basic sounds of their language and begin to become aware of its phonological rules and to link sound with meaning.

- Before they say their first word, babies use gestures.

  language (164)   literacy (165)   prelinguistic speech (165) linguistic speech (167)

- The first word typically comes sometime between 10 and 14 months, initiating linguistic speech. A "naming explosion" typically occurs sometime between 16 and 24 months of age.

  holophrase (167)

- The first brief sentences generally come between 18 and 24 months. By age 3, syntax and communicative abilities are fairly well developed.

  telegraphic speech (168)   syntax (168)

- Early speech is characterized by simplification, underextending and overextending word meanings, and overregularizing rules.

- Two classic theoretical views about how children acquire language are learning theory and nativism. Today, most developmentalists hold that an inborn capacity to learn language may be activated or constrained by experience.

  nativism (170)   language acquisition device (LAD) (170)

Guidepost 9   What influences contribute to linguistic progress?

- Influences on language development include brain maturation and social interaction.

- Family characteristics, such as socio-economic status and household size, may affect language learning.

- Child-directed speech (CDS) seems to have cognitive, emotional, and social benefits, and infants show a preference for it. However, some researchers dispute its value.

- Reading aloud to a child from an early age helps pave the way for literacy.

  code mixing (173)   code switching (173) child-directed speech (CDS) (173)

OLC Preview

As well as offering information on topics such as dynamic play therapy, the Online Learning Centre for *A Child's World*, First Canadian Edition, provides a link to more information on "Can Toddlers 'Read' Others' Wishes?" Check out **www.mcgrawhill.ca/college/papalia.**

Psychosocial Development During the First Three Years

I'm like a child
trying to do everything
say everything
and be everything
all at once

—John Hartford, "Life Prayer," 1971

Focus *Mary Catherine Bateson, Anthropologist**

Mary Catherine Bateson

Mary Catherine Bateson (b. 1939) is an anthropologist, the daughter of two famous anthropologists: Margaret Mead (refer back to chapter 2, Focus) and Gregory Bateson, Mead's third husband and research partner. Hers was probably one of the most documented infancies on record—her mother taking notes, her father behind the camera. Margaret Mead's memoir, *Blackberry Winter* (1972), and Mary Catherine Bateson's *With a Daughter's Eye* (1984) together provide a rare and fascinating dual perspective on a child's first 3 years of life.

Cathy—Mead's only child—was born when her mother was 38 years old. Her parents divorced when she was 11. Their work during World War II often necessitated long absences and separations. But during her infancy and toddlerhood, when they were still together, Cathy was the focus of their love and wholehearted attention. Her early recollections include sitting with her parents on a blanket outdoors, being read to on her mother's lap; and watching the two of them hold up their breakfast spoons to reflect the morning light, making a pair of "birds" flash across the walls for her amusement.

To avoid subjecting her to frustration, her parents tried to respond quickly to her needs. Mead arranged her professional commitments around breast-feeding and nursed "on demand," like the mothers in the island cultures she had studied.

Like their friend Erik Erikson, Mead and Bateson placed great importance on the development of trust. They never left Cathy in a strange place with a strange person; she always met a new caregiver in a familiar place. "Her warm responsiveness, her trustingness, and her outgoing interest in people and things . . . set the stage for her expectation that the world was a friendly place" (Mead, 1972, p. 266). As an adult, Catherine observed that, during difficult periods in her life, she often found "resources of faith and strength, a foundation that must have been built in those [first] two years" (Bateson, 1984, p. 35). Yet, as Mead wrote, "How much was temperament? How much was felicitous accident? How much could be attributed to upbringing? We may never know" (1972, p. 268).

Mead tried to avoid overprotectiveness and to let Cathy be herself. Catherine remembers her father pushing her swing so high that he could run under it. Later he taught her to climb tall pine trees, testing every branch for firmness and making sure that she could find her way back down, while her mother, watching, tried not to show her fear.

*Sources of biographical information about Mary Catherine Bateson are Bateson (1984) and Mead (1972).

When Cathy was 2 and her parents' wartime travel increased, they merged their household with that of a friend and colleague, Lawrence Frank. The decision fit in with Mead's belief, gleaned from her studies, that children benefit from having multiple caregivers and learning to adapt to different situations.

The ménage in Frank's brownstone in Greenwich Village included his infant son, Colin, and five older children. "Thus," Catherine writes, "I did not grow up in a nuclear family or as an only child, but as a member of a flexible and welcoming extended family . . . , in which five or six pairs of hands could be mobilized to shell peas or dry dishes." Her summertime memories are of a lakeside retreat in New Hampshire, where "each child was cared for by enough adults so that there need be no jealousy, where the garden bloomed and the evenings ended in song. . . . I was rich beyond other children . . . and yet there were all those partings. There were all those beloved people, yet often the people I wanted most were absent" (Bateson, 1984, pp. 38–39).

● ● ●

I n Margaret Mead's and Mary Catherine Bateson's complementary memoirs, we can see how Mead put into practice the beliefs she had developed about child rearing, in part from memories of her own childhood and in part from observations of distant cultures. We see her seeking solutions to a problem that has become increasingly common: child care for children of working parents. And we see a bi-directional influence: how early experiences with parents help shape a child's development, and how a child's needs can shape parents' lives.

This chapter is about the shift from the dependence of infancy to the independence of childhood. We first examine foundations of psychosocial development: emotions, temperament, and early experiences with parents. We consider Erikson's views about the development of trust and autonomy. We look at relationships with caregivers, at the emerging sense of self, and at the foundations of conscience. We explore relationships with siblings and other children and with grandparents. Finally, we consider the increasingly widespread impact of early day care.

After you have read and studied this chapter, you should be able to answer each of the Guidepost questions that appear at the top of the next page. Look for them again in the margins, where they point to important concepts throughout the chapter. To check your understanding of these Guideposts, review the end-of-chapter summary. Checkpoints located throughout the chapter will help you verify your understanding of what you have read.

Guideposts for Study

1. When and how do emotions develop, and how do babies show them?

2. How do infants show temperamental differences, and how enduring are those differences?

3. What roles do mothers and fathers play in early personality development?

4. How do infants gain trust in their world and form attachments?

5. How do infants and caregivers "read" each other's non-verbal signals?

6. When does the sense of self arise, and what are three steps in its development?

7. How do toddlers develop autonomy and standards for socially acceptable behaviour?

8. How do infants and toddlers interact with siblings and other children?

9. How do parental employment and early child care affect infants' and toddlers' development?

Foundations of Psychosocial Development

While babies share common patterns of development, they also—from the start—show distinct personalities, which reflect both inborn and environmental influences. From infancy on, personality development is intertwined with social relationships (see Table 8-1).

Emotions

Emotions, such as sadness, joy, and fear, are subjective reactions to experience that are associated with physiological and behavioural changes. All normal human beings have the

emotions Subjective reactions to experience that are associated with physiological and behavioural changes

Table 8-1	Highlights of Infants' and Toddlers' Psychosocial Development, Birth to 36 Months
Approximate Age, Months	**Characteristics**
0–3	Infants are open to stimulation. They begin to show interest and curiosity, and they smile readily at people.
3–6	Infants can anticipate what is about to happen and experience disappointment when it does not. They show this by becoming angry or acting warily. They smile, coo, and laugh often. This is a time of social awakening and early reciprocal exchanges between the baby and the caregiver.
6–9	Infants play "social games" and try to get responses from people. They "talk" to, touch, and cajole other babies to get them to respond. They express more differentiated emotions, showing joy, fear, anger, and surprise.
9–12	Infants are intensely preoccupied with their principal caregiver, may become afraid of strangers, and act subdued in new situations. By 1 year, they communicate emotions more clearly, showing moods, ambivalence, and gradations of feeling.
12–18	Toddlers explore their environment, using the people they are most attached to as a secure base. As they master the environment, they become more confident and more eager to assert themselves.
18–36	Toddlers sometimes become anxious because they now realize how much they are separating from their caregiver. They work out their awareness of their limitations in fantasy and in play and by identifying with adults.

Source: Adapted from Sroufe, 1979.

Guidepost 1

When and how do emotions develop, and how do babies show them?

same range of emotions, but people differ in how often they feel a particular emotion, in the kinds of events that may produce it, in the physical manifestations they show (such as heart-rate changes), and in how they act as a result. A person's characteristic pattern of emotional reactions begins to develop during infancy and is a basic element of personality.

From an ethological perspective, emotions serve several functions important to human survival and well-being. One is to communicate a person's inner condition to others and elicit a response. This communicative function is crucial for infants, who must depend on caring adults to meet their basic needs. A second function is to guide and regulate behaviour—a function that, during toddlerhood, begins to shift from the caregiver to the child. Eemotions such as fear and surprise mobilize action in emergencies. Other emotions, such as interest and excitement, promote exploration of the environment, which leads to learning that can protect or sustain life.

Human emotions are flexible and modifiable. Cognitive development plays an important role in emotion as infants learn to appraise the meaning of a situation or event in its context and to gauge what is happening against expectations based on past experience. Eight-month-old Melissa's fear of a stranger who tries to pick her up involves memory for faces, the ability to compare the stranger's appearance with her parent's, and perhaps the recollection of situations in which she has been left with a stranger. If Melissa is allowed to get used to the stranger gradually in a familiar setting, she may react more positively (Lewis, 1997; Sroufe, 1997).

Early Signs of Emotion

Newborns plainly show when they are unhappy. They let out piercing cries, flail their arms and legs, and stiffen their bodies. It is harder to tell when they are happy. During the first month, they become quiet at the sound of a human voice or when they are picked up, and they may smile when their hands are moved together to play pat-a-cake. As time goes by, infants respond more to people—smiling, cooing, reaching out, and eventually going to them.

These early signals or clues to babies' feelings are important steps in development. When babies want or need something, they cry; when they feel sociable, they smile or laugh. When their messages bring a response, their sense of connection with other people grows. Their sense of control over their world grows, too, as they see that their cries bring help and comfort and that their smiles and laughter elicit smiles and laughter in return. They become more able to actively participate in regulating their states of arousal and their emotional life.

As time goes by, the meaning of babies' emotional signals changes. At first, crying signifies physical discomfort; later, it more often expresses psychological distress. An early smile comes spontaneously as an expression of well-being; around 3 to 6 weeks, a smile may show pleasure in social contact. As babies get older, smiles and laughter at novel or incongruous situations reflect increasing cognitive awareness and growing ability to handle excitation (Sroufe, 1997).

Crying Crying is the most powerful way—and sometimes the only way—infants can communicate their needs. Almost all adults around the world respond quickly to a crying infant (Broude, 1995).

Some research has distinguished four patterns of crying (Wolff, 1969): the basic *hunger cry* (a rhythmic cry, which is not always associated with hunger); the *angry cry* (a variation of the rhythmic cry, in which excess air is forced through the vocal cords); the *pain cry* (a sudden onset of loud crying without preliminary moaning, sometimes followed by holding the breath); and the *frustration cry* (two or three drawn-out cries, with no prolonged breath-holding). Current perspectives, particularly among Canadian researchers, on the nature of infant crying, focus on the role of crying as a *sign,* an objective indicator of the child's physical state, such as hunger, fatigue, or pain, or as a *symptom,* or evidence of a medical condition, such as too much or too little crying in potential disabilities. From a developmental perspective, crying can play a third role as a *signal* of the child's developmental status. As a signal, crying functions as a response to—or a form of—communication with a caregiver in a particular context, such as indicating pain (Barr, Hopkins, & Green, 2000). As a way of communicating pain, crying is very adaptive and indicates to caregivers the severity of pain and the effectiveness of pain relief. For example, Taddio, Nulman, Goldbach, Ipp, & Koren (1994) found that an infant's first cry in response to pain typically occurs immediately, whereas after a topical anaesthetic is applied there is a delay between the stimulus and the first cry. Other indicators of pain intensity include the duration of the cry and the pitch of the cry, with more intense pain associated with cries of longer duration and higher pitch (Craig, Gilbert-MacLeod, & Lilley, 2000). A parent's success in interpreting and responding to the infant's cries is important to gaining confidence in parenting and to the infant's development (Leavitt, 1998).

Some parents worry that they will spoil a child by picking up a crying baby. Delays in responding to fussing may help babies learn to deal with minor irritations on their own (Hubbard & van IJzendoorn, 1991). But if parents wait until cries of distress escalate to shrieks of rage, it may become more difficult to soothe the baby; and such a pattern, if experienced repeatedly, may interfere with infants' developing the ability to regulate, or manage, their own emotional state (R. A. Thompson, 1991).

Smiling and Laughing The earliest faint smiles occur spontaneously soon after birth, apparently as a result of subcortical nervous system activity. These involuntary smiles frequently appear during periods of REM sleep (refer back to chapter 5). They become less frequent during the first 3 months as the cortex matures (Sroufe, 1997).

The earliest *waking* smiles may be elicited by mild sensations, such as gentle jiggling or blowing on the infant's skin. In the second week, a baby may smile drowsily after a feeding. By the third week, most infants begin to smile when they are alert and paying attention to a caregiver's nodding head and voice. At about 1 month, smiles generally become more frequent and more social. During the second month, as visual recognition develops, babies smile more at visual stimuli, such as faces they know (Sroufe, 1997; Wolff, 1963). By 4 months, a spontaneous smile can be elicited by the infant at the sight of a parent, an early indication of cognitive development in the child.

At about the fourth month, infants start to laugh out loud when kissed on the stomach or tickled. As babies grow older, they become more actively engaged in mirthful exchanges. A 6-month-old may giggle in response to the mother making unusual sounds or appearing with a towel over her face; a 10-month-old may laughingly try to put the towel back on her face. This change reflects cognitive development: By laughing at the unexpected, babies show that they know what to expect. By turning the tables, they show a dawning awareness that they can cause things to happen, engage the world around them, and play an active role in beginning interactions with others. Laughter also helps babies discharge tension, such as fear of a threatening object (Sroufe, 1997).

When Do Various Emotions Develop?

At what age do sadness, joy, fear, and other emotions develop? To answer that question, we need first to determine that an infant of a certain age is *showing* a particular emotion. Identifying infants' emotions is a challenge because babies cannot tell us what they feel. Still, parents, caregivers, and researchers learn to recognize clues. For example, Carroll Izard and his colleagues have videotaped infants' facial expressions and have interpreted them as showing joy, sadness, interest, and fear, and to a lesser degree anger, surprise, and disgust (Izard, Huebner, Resser, McGinness, & Dougherty, 1980). Of course, we do not know that these babies actually had the feelings they were credited with, but their facial expressions were remarkably similar to adults' expressions when experiencing these emotions.

Facial expressions are not the only, or necessarily the best, index of infants' emotions; motor activity, body language, and physiological changes are also important indicators. An infant can be fearful without showing a "fear face"; the baby may show fear by turning away or averting the gaze, or by a faster heartbeat, and these signs do not necessarily accompany each other. Different criteria may point to different conclusions about the timing of emergence of specific emotions. In addition, this timetable shows a good deal of individual variation (Sroufe, 1997).

Nevertheless, the process of emotional development is an orderly one. Emotions do not arise full-blown. Just as the spontaneous neonatal smile is a forerunner of smiles of pleasure in response to people or events, complex emotions build on earlier, simpler ones (Sroufe, 1997). According to one model (Lewis, 1997; see Figure 8-1), soon after birth babies

Figure 8-1

Differentiation of emotions during the first 3 years. The primary, or basic, emotions emerge during the first 6 months or so; the self-conscious emotions develop beginning in the second half of the second year, as a result of the emergence of self-awareness (consciousness of self) together with accumulation of knowledge about societal standards and rules.

Note: There are two kinds of embarrassment. The earlier form does not involve evaluation of behaviour and may simply be a response to being singled out as the object of attention. The second kind, evaluative embarrassment, which emerges during the third year, is a mild form of shame.

Source: Adapted from Lewis, 1997, Figure 1, p. 120.

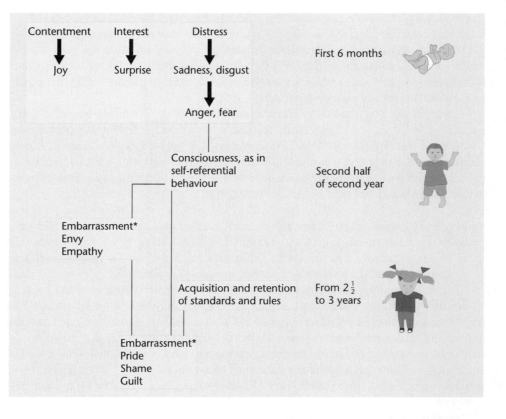

self-awareness Realization that one's existence and functioning are separate from those of other people and things

show signs of contentment, interest, and distress. These are diffuse, reflexive, mostly physiological responses to sensory stimulation or internal processes. During the next 6 months or so, these early emotional states differentiate into true emotions: joy, surprise, sadness, disgust, and last, anger and fear—reactions to events that have meaning for the infant. As we'll discuss in the next section, the emergence of these basic, or primary, emotions is related to the biological "clock" of neurological maturation.

Although the repertoire of basic emotions seems to be universal, there are cultural variations in their expression. In laboratory observations, videotaped faces of 11-month-old Chinese infants whose arms were briefly restrained, or who were approached by a growling gorilla head, were less expressive of emotion than those of American and Japanese infants who underwent the same treatments (Camras et al., 1998). It is unclear whether these findings reflect cultural attitudes or innate differences in emotional reactivity.

Self-conscious emotions, such as embarrassment, empathy, and envy, arise only after children have developed **self-awareness:** the cognitive understanding that they are functioning beings, separate from the rest of their world. Consciousness of self seems to emerge between 15 and 24 months, when (according to Piaget) infants become able to make mental representations—of themselves as well as other people and things. Self-awareness is necessary before children can be aware of being the focus of attention, identify with what other "selves" are feeling, or wish they had what someone else has. During the third year, having acquired a good deal of knowledge about their society's accepted standards, rules, and goals—largely from parental attitudes and parental reactions to their behaviour—children develop *self-evaluative* emotions, such as pride, shame, and guilt. They now can evaluate their own thoughts, plans, desires, and behaviour against what is considered socially appropriate (Lewis, 1995, 1997, 1998).

Brain Growth and Emotional Development

The growth of the brain after birth is closely connected with changes in emotional life. This is a bi-directional process: Social and emotional experience are not only affected by brain development but can have long-lasting effects on the structure of the brain (Mlot, 1998; Sroufe, 1997).

Separate but interacting regions of the brain (refer back to Figure 6-4 in chapter 6) may be responsible for various emotional states. For example, fear seems to be seated in the *amygdala,* an almond-shaped structure in the centre of the brain, but the left side of the prefrontal cortex can modulate its activity (LeDoux, 1989; Mlot, 1998). The hypothalamus and parts of the brain stem are thought to be involved in frustration and rage, and parts of the prefrontal cortex in effortful control (Rothbart, Ahadi, & Evans, 2000).

There appear to be four major shifts in brain organization, which roughly correspond to changes in emotions (Schore, 1994; Sroufe, 1997). During the first 3 months, differentiation of basic emotions begins as the *cerebral cortex* becomes functional, bringing cognitive perceptions into play. REM sleep and reflexive behaviour, including the spontaneous neonatal smile, diminish. The social smile reflects a growing desire to seek and maintain contact with outside stimuli.

The second shift occurs around 9 or 10 months, when the *frontal lobes* mature and limbic structures such as the *hippocampus* become larger and more adult-like. Connections between the frontal cortex and the *hypothalamus* and limbic system, which process sensory information, may facilitate the relationship between the cognitive and emotional spheres. As these connections become denser and more elaborate, an infant can experience and interpret emotions at the same time. The development of recognition and recall, object permanence, and other cognitive advances makes it possible to coordinate past and present events and future expectations. A baby this age may become upset when a ball rolls under a couch and may smile or laugh when it is retrieved. Fear of strangers often develops at this time.

The third shift takes place during the second year, when infants develop self-awareness, self-conscious emotions, and a greater capacity for regulating their own emotions and activities. These changes, which coincide with greater physical mobility and exploratory behaviour, may be related to myelination of the frontal lobes.

The emergence of evaluative emotions around age 3 may be connected with hormonal changes in the autonomic nervous system. Underlying the development of such emotions as shame may be a shift away from dominance by the *sympathetic system,* which prepares the body for action, and the maturation of the *parasympathetic system,* which is involved in excretion and sexual excitation. The experience of shame may, in turn, activate the inhibitory circuits of the limbic system and deactivate the excitatory circuits, eventually bringing the two circuits into balance.

Neurological factors also may play a part in temperamental differences (Mlot, 1998), the topic we turn to next.

Checkpoint ✓

Can you . . .

✔ Cite two important functions of emotions?

✔ Explain the significance of patterns of crying, smiling, and laughing?

✔ Trace a typical sequence of emergence of the basic, self-conscious, and evaluative emotions, and explain its connection with cognitive and neurological development?

Temperament

Temperament—sometimes defined as a person's characteristic, biologically based way of approaching and reacting to people and situations—has been described as the *how* of behaviour: not *what* people do, but how they go about doing it (Thomas & Chess, 1977). Two toddlers, for example, may be equally able to dress themselves and may be equally motivated, but one may do it more quickly than the other, be more willing to put on a new outfit, and be less distracted if the cat jumps on the bed.

Some researchers look at temperament more broadly. A child may not act the same way in all situations. And temperament may affect not only the way children approach and react to the outside world, but the way they regulate their own mental, emotional, and behavioural functioning (Rothbart et al., 2000).

Temperament has an emotional basis; but while emotions such as fear, excitement, and boredom come and go, temperament is relatively consistent and enduring. Individual differences in temperament, which are thought to derive from a person's basic biological makeup, form the core of a developing personality (Eisenberg, Fabes, Guthrie, & Reiser, 2000).

Guidepost 2

How do infants show temperamental differences, and how enduring are those differences?

temperament Characteristic disposition, or style of approaching and reacting to situations

Aspects and Patterns of Temperament: New York Longitudinal Study

The New York Longitudinal Study (NYLS), begun in 1956 by Alexander T. Thomas, Stella C. Chess, and Herbert B. Birch, is considered the pioneering study on temperament. These

Table 8-2	Three Temperamental Patterns (according to the New York Longitudinal Study)	
"Easy" Child	**"Difficult" Child**	**"Slow-to-Warm-Up" Child**
Has moods of mild to moderate intensity, usually positive	Displays intense and frequently negative moods; cries often and loudly; also laughs loudly	Has mildly intense reactions, both positive and negative
Responds well to novelty and change	Responds poorly to novelty and change	Responds slowly to novelty and change
Quickly develops regular sleep and feeding schedules	Sleeps and eats irregularly	Sleeps and eats more regularly than difficult child, less regularly than easy child
Takes to new foods easily	Accepts new foods slowly	Shows mildly negative initial response to new stimuli (a first encounter with a new person, place, or situation)
Smiles at strangers	Is suspicious of strangers	
Adapts easily to new situations	Adapts slowly to new situations	
Accepts most frustrations with little fuss	Reacts to frustration with tantrums	
Adapts quickly to new routines and rules of new games	Adjusts slowly to new routines	Gradually develops liking for new stimuli after repeated, unpressured exposures

Source: Adapted from A. Thomas & Chess, 1984.

researchers followed 133 infants into adulthood, interviewing, testing, and observing them and interviewing their parents and teachers.

The researchers looked at how active the children were; how regular they were in hunger, sleep, and bowel habits; how readily they accepted new people and situations; how they adapted to changes in routine; how sensitive they were to noise, bright lights, and other sensory stimuli; how intensely they responded; whether their mood tended to be pleasant, joyful, and friendly or unpleasant, unhappy, and unfriendly; and whether they persisted at tasks or were easily distracted (A. Thomas, Chess, & Birch, 1968). The children differed in all these characteristics, almost from birth, and the differences tended to continue. However, many children changed their behavioural style, apparently reacting to special experiences or parental handling (Lerner & Galambos, 1985; A. Thomas & Chess, 1984).

Almost two-thirds of the children in the NYLS fell into one of three categories (see Table 8-2). Forty per cent were **"easy" children:** generally happy, rhythmic in biological functioning, and accepting of new experiences. Ten per cent were what the researchers called **"difficult" children:** more irritable and harder to please, irregular in biological rhythms, and more intense in expressing emotion. Fifteen per cent were **"slow-to-warm-up" children:** mild but slow to adapt to new people and situations (A. Thomas & Chess, 1977, 1984).

Many children (including 35 per cent of the NYLS sample) do not fit neatly into any of these three groups. A baby may eat and sleep regularly but be afraid of strangers. A child may be easy most of the time, but not always. Another child may warm up slowly to new foods but adapt quickly to new babysitters (A. Thomas & Chess, 1984). A child may laugh intensely but not show intense frustration, and a child with rhythmic toilet habits may show irregular sleeping patterns (Rothbart et al., 2000). All these variations are normal.

"easy" children Children with a generally happy temperament, regular biological rhythms, and a readiness to accept new experiences

"difficult" children Children with irritable temperament, irregular biological rhythms, and intense emotional responses

"slow-to-warm-up" children Children whose temperament is generally mild but who are hesitant about accepting new experiences

Effects of Temperament on Adjustment: "Goodness of Fit"

goodness of fit Appropriateness of environmental demands and constraints to a child's temperament

According to the NYLS, the key to healthy adjustment is **goodness of fit**—the match between a child's temperament and the environmental demands and constraints the child must deal with. If a very active child is expected to sit still for long periods, if a slow-to-warm-up child is constantly pushed into new situations, or if a persistent child is constantly taken away from absorbing projects, trouble may occur.

When parents recognize that a child acts in a certain way, not out of willfulness, laziness, or stupidity, but largely because of inborn temperament, they are less likely to feel guilty, anxious, or hostile or to be rigid or impatient. Rather than seeing a child's temperament as an impediment, they can anticipate the child's reactions and help the child adapt.

How Is Temperament Measured?

Many researchers have found the complex interviewing and scoring procedures used in the NYLS too cumbersome and have resorted to short-form questionnaires. Now a parental self-report instrument—the Rothbart Infant Behavior Questionnaire (IBQ)—has been validated in part by home and laboratory observations (Rothbart et al., 2000). The IBQ focuses on several dimensions of infant temperament similar to those in the NYLS: fear, frustration, positive emotion, soothability, and duration of orienting (a combination of distractibility and attention span). These researchers also developed a Children's Behavior Questionnaire (CBQ), which covers three clusters of personality characteristics: (1) *extraversion* (impulsiveness, intense pleasure, high activity level, boldness, risk taking, comfort in new social situations), (2) *negative affect* (sadness, discomfort, anger, frustration, fear, high reactivity), and (3) *effortful control* (inhibitory control, low-intensity pleasure, ability to focus attention, perceptual sensitivity).

How Stable Is Temperament?

Temperament appears to be largely inborn and probably hereditary (Braungart, Plomin, DeFries, & Fulker, 1992; Emde et al., 1992; Schmitz et al., 1996; A. Thomas & Chess, 1977, 1984). It also tends to be fairly stable. Newborn babies show different patterns of sleeping, fussing, and activity, and these differences tend to persist (Korner, 1996; Korner et al., 1985).

That does not mean temperament is fully formed at birth. Temperament develops as various emotions and self-regulatory capacities appear (Rothbart et al., 2000). And temperament can change during the early months in response to parental attitudes and treatment (Belsky, Fish, & Isabella, 1991; Lerner & Galambos, 1985).

Still, studies using the IBQ during infancy and the CBQ at age 7 found strong links between infant temperament and childhood personality (Rothbart et al., 2000). Research using the IBQ also found links between temperament and language development: 13-month-olds who were easily soothed, smiled and laughed a lot, and had long attention spans were most likely at 20 to 21 months to use multi-noun utterances, suggesting that their emotional stability left them freer to learn new words (Dixon & Shore, 1997).

Other researchers using temperamental types similar to those of the NYLS have studied the extent to which temperament at age 3 predicts adult personality (see Box 8-1).

Biological Bases of Temperament

Temperament, like emotion, seems to have a biological basis. In longitudinal research with about 400 children starting in infancy, Jerome Kagan and his colleagues have studied an aspect of temperament called *inhibition to the unfamiliar,* or shyness, which has to do with how sociable a child is with strange children and how boldly or cautiously the child approaches unfamiliar objects and situations. This characteristic is associated with differences in physical features and brain functioning, which are reflected in physiological signs such as heart rate, blood pressure, and pupil dilation. The shyest children (about 15 per cent of the sample) tended to have blue eyes and thin faces and to be subject to allergies, constipation, and unusual fears. When asked to solve problems or learn new information, they showed higher and less variable heart rates than bolder children, and the pupils of their eyes dilated more. The boldest children (about 10 to 15 per cent) tended to be energetic and spontaneous and to have very low heart rates (Arcus & Kagan, 1995).

Four-month-olds who are highly reactive—that is, who show much motor activity and distress, or who fret or cry readily in response to new stimuli—are likely to show the inhibited pattern at 14 and 21 months. Babies who are highly inhibited or uninhibited seem to maintain these patterns to some degree during childhood and adolescence (Kagan, 1997; Kagan & Snidman, 1991a, 1991b).

Experience can moderate or accentuate early tendencies. Male toddlers who were inclined to be fearful and shy were more likely to remain so at age 3 if their parents were highly accepting of the child's reactions. But if parents encouraged their sons to venture into new situations, the boys tended to become less inhibited (Park, Belsky, Putnam, & Crnic, 1997).

Checkpoint ✔

Can you . . .

✔ List and describe nine aspects and three patterns of temperament identified by the New York Longitudinal Study?

✔ Assess evidence for the stability of temperament?

✔ Discuss how temperament can affect social adjustment, and explain the importance of "goodness of fit"?

What's your view ❓

- In Canada, many people consider shyness undesirable. How should a parent handle a shy child? Do you think it is best to accept the child's temperament or try to change it?

Box 8-1 *Does Early Temperament Predict Adult Personality?*

Do temperamental differences persist into adult life? The answer is yes, according to a longitudinal study of 1,037 3-year-olds born in a single year in Dunedin, New Zealand.

Examiners tested the children on cognitive and motor skills and then rated them on a checklist of behavioural characteristics. Five personality types emerged, three of them much like the temperamental types identified by Thomas and Chess in the New York Longitudinal Study.

Well-adjusted children (about 40 per cent of the sample, as in the NYLS) were similar to the "easy" type. They were reasonably self-confident, capable of self-control when it was demanded of them, and comfortable with new people and situations. *Undercontrolled* children (10 per cent of the sample) resembled the "difficult" type. They were impulsive, restless, negative, distractible, and volatile. *Inhibited* children (again, about 10 per cent) were somewhat like the "slow-to-warm-up" type. They were shy, fearful, and socially ill-at-ease. These three types uncovered in the Dunedin study have been validated using a variety of methods in a number of countries, including Iceland, Netherlands, Germany, and the United States. The researchers also identified two additional types—*confident* and *reserved*—which may be variations on the other categories.

When the participants were restudied at ages 18 (through self-report personality questionnaires) and 21 (through descriptions of people who knew them well), their early temperamental patterns proved remarkably predictive. Those who had been well adjusted as children—the bulk of the sample—remained so; they grew up to be normal, average adults.

By contrast, those who had been undercontrolled at age 3 were likely to be aggressive, socially alienated, and low on constraint—reckless, careless, and thrill-seeking. They tended to have problems at school and at work and to have conflicted personal and romantic relationships. They were prone to risky or antisocial behaviour: dangerous driving, unsafe sex, alcohol dependence, violent crime, and suicide attempts. Friends described them as unreliable and untrustworthy.

Inhibited children showed a different pattern: they often grew up to be cautious, overcontrolled, unassertive, and subject to depression. They had few friends and companions, and those who knew them described them as low in affection, confidence, and vitality. They were less likely to get involved in antisocial behaviour than the undercontrolled group, perhaps because they were more likely to be afraid of getting caught; but they, too, were prone to suicidal behaviour.

What accounts for this remarkable stability of personality? A proposed explanation points to the frequent similarity in temperament between parents and children. Warm, accepting parents tend to have easygoing children; parents who discipline harshly or inconsistently tend to have difficult children. This is an example of genotype–environment correlation (refer back to chapter 3), in which the environment that parents create reinforces the genetic tendencies they have passed on to their children. It is also an example of bi-directional influence, since difficult children tend to elicit harsh or inconsistent discipline from their parents. As children grow up, they continue to seek out environments that strengthen their natural tendencies. It is not surprising, then, that temperamental patterns, both healthy and unhealthy, tend to persist.

This does not mean that nothing can be done about a "difficult" temperament. Although continuity is more likely than change, it is not inevitable. As the New York Longitudinal Study found, temperament can change, especially during infancy. Goodness of fit between parent and child is a key to healthy adjustment. By the age of 3, however, the patterns undergirding future personality development may be largely set.

Sources: Caspi, 2000; Caspi & Silva, 1995; Newman, Caspi, Moffitt, & Silva, 1997.

Seven-month-old Daniel's ready smile and willingness to try a new food are signs of an easy temperament.

What's your view❓

Ask your parents what you were like as an infant and as a toddler. What do they remember about you at ages 1, 2, and 3? How similar or different are the qualities you showed at those ages compared with the way you are today?

Check it out❗

For more information on this topic, go to **www.mcgrawhill.ca/college/papalia** for links to theoretical and empirical information about temperamental traits from birth to 3 years.

Cross-cultural Differences

Temperament may be affected by culturally influenced child-raising practices. Infants in Malaysia, an island group in Southeast Asia, tended to be less adaptable, more wary of new experiences, and more readily responsive to stimuli than a comparison group of U.S. babies. This may be because Malay parents do not often expose young children to situations that require adaptability, and they encourage children to be acutely aware of sensations, especially uncomfortable ones such as the need for a diaper change (Banks, 1989).

In a cross-cultural study of Chinese and Canadian 2-year-olds, Canadian mothers of inhibited children tended to be punitive or overprotective, whereas Chinese mothers of such children were warm and accepting and encouraged them to achieve. The Chinese toddlers were significantly more inhibited than the Canadian ones; but because this was a correlational study, we don't know whether the children's temperament was a consequence or a cause of their mothers' treatment, or perhaps a bi-directional effect. In Canada, shy, inhibited children tend to be seen as incompetent, immature, and unlikely to accomplish much. Their mothers may show disappointment by emotionally rejecting them or may think they need special guidance and protection. In China, shyness and inhibition are socially approved. Thus a naturally inhibited Chinese child may be less motivated to come out of his or her shell than a Canadian one, or less subject to parental prodding to do so (Chen et al., 1998).

Checkpoint

Can you . . .

✔ Give evidence of cultural differences in temperament and discuss ways of interpreting it?

Earliest Social Experiences: The Infant in the Family

Guidepost 3

What roles do mothers and fathers play in early personality development?

In the past, research on infant psychosocial development focused almost exclusively on mothers and babies, but now researchers are studying relationships between infants and their fathers, siblings, and other caregivers, as well as characteristics of the family as a whole, such as socio-economic status. By looking at the family as a functioning unit, we get a fuller picture of the network of relationships among all its members.

Child-raising practices and patterns of social interaction vary greatly around the world. In some societies, as Margaret Mead found in the South Seas, infants have multiple caregivers. Among the Efe people of the African country of Zaire, infants typically receive care from five or more people in a given hour and are routinely breast-fed by other women as well as by their mothers, even though the mother is the major caregiver. At age 3, they spend about 70 per cent of their time with people other than their mothers (Tronick, Morelli, & Ivey, 1992). Unlike Canadian babies, who spend more time alone or with just one or two family members and may learn to amuse themselves earlier than Efe babies, the Efe may learn to be more sociable at an earlier age.

Among the Gusii in western Kenya, where infant mortality is high, parents are more likely than those in industrial societies to keep their infants close to them, respond quickly when they cry, and feed them on demand (LeVine, 1974, 1989, 1994). The same is true of Aka foragers (hunter-gatherers) in central Africa, who move around frequently in small, tightly knit groups marked by extensive sharing, cooperation, and concern about danger. However, Ngandu farmers in the same region, who tend to live farther apart and to stay in one place for long periods of time, are more likely to leave their infants alone and to let them fuss or cry, smile, vocalize, or play (Hewlett, Lamb, Shannon, Leyendecker, & Schölmerich, 1998).

All cultures recognize the fathering role; but, beyond the initial act of insemination, it is essentially a social construction (Doherty, Kouneski, & Erickson, 1998; refer back to chapter 1). The role may be taken or shared by someone other than the biological father: the mother's brother, as in Botswana (where young mothers remain with their own childhood family until their partners are in their forties), or a grandfather, as in Vietnam (Engle & Breaux, 1998; Richardson, 1995; Townsend, 1997). Sometimes the father is not even present; 12 per cent of families in Canada are headed by women (mostly single mothers), and even higher rates are reported in the United States, Norway, and in some African and Caribbean countries. This is a growing trend in non-industrialized countries, reflecting urbanization, employment of women, and a decline in male employment (CICH, 2000; Engle & Breaux, 1998).

We need to remember, then, that patterns of psychological development we take for granted may be culture-based. With that caution in mind, let's look first at the roles of the mother and father—how they care for and play with their babies, and how their influence begins to shape personality differences between boys and girls—and then at the changing roles of grandparents. Later in this chapter, we look more deeply at relationships with parents and, finally, at interactions with siblings.

The Mother's Role

In a series of pioneering experiments by Harry Harlow and his colleagues, rhesus monkeys were separated from their mothers 6 to 12 hours after birth and raised in a laboratory. The

In a series of classic experiments, Harry Harlow and Margaret Harlow showed that food is not the most important way to a baby's heart. When infant rhesus monkeys could choose whether to go to a wire surrogate "mother" or a warm, soft terry-cloth "mother," they spent more time clinging to the cloth mother, even if they were being fed by bottles connected to the wire mother.

infant monkeys were put into cages with one of two kinds of surrogate "mothers": a plain cylindrical wire-mesh form or a form covered with terry cloth. Some monkeys were fed from bottles connected to the wire "mothers"; others were "nursed" by the warm, cuddly cloth ones. When the monkeys were allowed to spend time with either kind of "mother," they all spent more time clinging to the cloth surrogates, even if they were being fed only by the wire ones. In an unfamiliar room, the babies "raised" by cloth surrogates showed more natural interest in exploring than those "raised" by wire surrogates, even when the appropriate "mothers" were there.

Apparently, the monkeys also remembered the cloth surrogates better. After a year's separation, the "cloth-raised" monkeys eagerly ran to embrace the terry-cloth forms, whereas the "wire-raised" monkeys showed no interest in the wire forms (Harlow & Zimmerman, 1959). None of the monkeys in either group grew up normally, however (Harlow & Harlow, 1962), and none were able to nurture their own offspring (Suomi & Harlow, 1972).

It is hardly surprising that a dummy mother would not provide the same kinds of stimulation and opportunities for development as a live mother. These experiments show that feeding is not the most important thing babies get from their mothers. Mothering includes the comfort of close bodily contact and, in monkeys, the satisfaction of an innate need to cling. Human infants also have needs that must be satisfied if they are to grow up normally. A major task of developmental research is to find out what those needs are.

The Father's Role

The father's role, like the mother's, entails emotional commitments, and often direct involvement in the care and upbringing of children (Engle & Breaux, 1998). Still, in most cultures, while fathers' roles vary greatly (see Box 8-2), women are children's primary caregivers.

What conditions promote "responsible fathering"—a biological father's active involvement in meeting his child's financial, physical, and emotional needs? A father's involvement may depend on many factors, including his motivation, his confidence in his parenting skills, his success as a breadwinner, his relationship with the mother, and the extent to which she encourages his involvement (Doherty et al., 1998; Lamb, Pleck, Charnov, & Levine, 1985; Pleck, 1997).

A recent study of Canadian mothers' and fathers' relations with their children showed that although the mothers' past childhood experiences had little relation to the quality of their interactions with their children, the same was not true of fathers. Fathers who reported negative childhood experiences but who had support from their spouses were more likely to have positive interactions with their own children than the fathers who had less support from their spouses (Onyskiw, Harrison, Magill-Evans, 1997).

Parents in most Canadian families work outside the home (Symons & Carr, 1995). Along with the assumption that both parents share financial responsibility for the household income, there is an expectation that each parent shares in the responsibility of raising children (Silver, 2000). Although employed mothers tend to spend more time with young children than fathers—six and a half compared to four hours a day—as children get older the gap narrows, closing by the time children reach adolescence, with both parents spending almost three hours per day with their children.

The most time-consuming activity that is shared by parents with young children is personal care, followed by playing. As children grow older, the time spent on personal care decreases, and time spent in other types of child care like teaching, reading, and travelling increase. Mothers also tend to spend a greater proportion of their leisure time with their children, compared to fathers (Silver, 2000).

A highly physical style of play, characteristic of many fathers in Canada, is not typical of fathers in all cultures. Swedish and German fathers do not usually play with their babies this way (Lamb, Frodi, Frodi, & Hwang, 1982; Parke, Grossman, & Tinsley, 1981). African Aka fathers (Hewlett, 1987) and those in New Delhi, India, also tend to play gently with small children (Roopnarine, Hooper, Ahmeduzzaman, & Pollack, 1993; Roopnarine, Talokder, Jain, Josh, & Srivastav, 1992). Such cross-cultural variations suggest that rough play is *not* a function of male biology, but instead is culturally influenced.

Research has found a relationship between a father's close involvement with his baby and the baby's development. In an observational study of 54 African-American 1- to 3-year-olds, those whose fathers showed sensitivity during free play (for example, by letting

Box 8-2 *Fatherhood in Three Cultures*

Fatherhood has different meanings in different cultures. In some societies, fathers are more involved in their young children's lives—economically, emotionally, and in time spent—than in other cultures. In many parts of the world, what it means to be a father has changed—and is changing (Engle & Breaux, 1998.)*

These changes can be accelerated when families immigrate to Canada (Howell, 1996). The great diversity among immigrants coming to Canada means that some groups experience changes more than others. However, children often can have untraditional relationships with their parents, when their language skills in English or French are better than those of their parents. The differences in values between those of the country of origin and of Canada can become a cause of concern, with the influences of school, peer groups, television, and other sources of socialization that can lead to differences in values between the parents and their children (Howell, 1996).

Urbanization in West Africa and Inner Mongolia

In Cameroon and other rural areas of West Africa (Nsamenang, 1987, 1992a, 1992b), men often have more than one wife, and children grow up in large extended families linked to kinship-based clans. Although children guarantee the perpetuation of a man's family line, they belong to the kinship group, not just to the parents. After weaning, they may have multiple caregivers or may even be given to other members of the group to raise.

The father has the dominant position in the family and gives his children their connection with the clan. The mother is literally the breadwinner, responsible for providing her children's food, but the father controls his wives and their earnings; and wives compete for their husbands' favour. Fathers are primarily disciplinarians and advisers. They have little contact with infants but serve as guides, companions, and models for older children.

With the coming of urbanization and the values of industrialized societies, these traditional patterns are breaking up. Many men are pursuing financial goals and are spending almost no time with their children. With the vanishing of traditional folkways, these men no longer know how to be fathers. They can no longer tell folk tales to young children around the fire or teach their sons how to do a man's work.

Similarly, among the Huhot of Inner Mongolia, a province of China, fathers traditionally are responsible for discipline and mothers for nurturing; but fathers also provide economic support (Jankowiak, 1992). Children have strong bonds with mothers, who live in the homes of their mothers-in-law and have no economic power. Fathers are stern and aloof, and their children respect and fear them. Men almost never hold infants; they are believed to be incapable of it. Fathers interact more with toddlers but perform child-care duties reluctantly, and only if the mother is absent.

Here, as in Cameroon, urbanization is changing these attitudes—but in the opposite direction. Families now live in very small quarters, and women work outside the home. Fathers—especially college-educated ones—now seek more intimate relationships with children, especially sons. China's official one-child policy has accentuated this change, leading both parents to be more deeply involved with their only child (Engle & Breaux, 1998).

The Aka People

The Aka are hunter-gatherers in the tropical forests of central Africa who move frequently from camp to camp in small, tightly knit groups and are highly protective of young children. In contrast with fathers in the other two cultures just described, Aka fathers are just as nurturing and emotionally supportive as Aka mothers. In fact, "Aka fathers provide more direct infant care than fathers in any other known society" (Hewlett, 1992, p. 169). They hold their babies frequently and hug, kiss, clean, and play gently with them (Hewlett, 1987).

This behaviour is in line with *family systems theory,* which predicts that fathers will be more involved in the care of young children in cultures in which husbands and wives frequently cooperate in subsistence tasks and other activities (Hewlett, 1992). Among the Aka and other societies with high paternal involvement in infant care, the key is not just that both parents participate in such activities, but that they do it together. The father's role in child care is part of his role in the family.

What's your view?

How do you think your relationship with your father might have been different if you had grown up in Cameroon? Among the Huhot of Inner Mongolia? Among the Aka people?

Check it out!

For more information on this topic, go to **www.mcgrawhill.ca/college/papalia** for a link to a discussion of the varieties of fatherhood and a review of research on the influence of fathers on their children's development.

*Unless otherwise referenced, this box is based on Engle & Breaux, 1998.

---

the child set the pace and control the choice of activities tended to have better self-help and motor skills than the other children. Toddlers whose fathers valued strictness and obedience tended to have less advanced cognitive and social development. Here again, children influence the adults around them; toddlers with more advanced skills may elicit more sensitivity from their fathers (Kelley, Smith, Green, Berndt, & Rogers, 1998).

How Parents Shape Gender Differences

Being male or female affects how people look, how they move their bodies, and how they work, play, and dress. It influences what they think about themselves and what others think of them. All those characteristics—and more—are included in the word *gender:* what it means to be male or female.

gender Significance of being male or female

In Japan, grandmothers like this one traditionally wear red as a sign of their noble status. Grandparenthood is an important milestone in industrialized societies as well.

gender-typing Socialization process by which children learn appropriate gender roles

Measurable differences between baby boys and girls are few. Males are physically more vulnerable than females from conception on. On the other hand, baby boys are a bit longer and heavier than baby girls and may be slightly stronger. Newborn boys and girls react differently to stress, possibly suggesting genetic, hormonal, or temperamental differences (Davis & Emory, 1995). An analysis of a large number of studies found baby boys more active than baby girls, though this difference is not consistently documented (Eaton & Enns, 1986). The two sexes are equally sensitive to touch and tend to teethe, sit up, and walk at about the same ages (Maccoby, 1980).

Parental shaping of boys' and girls' personalities appears to begin very early. Fathers, especially, promote **gender-typing,** the process by which children learn behaviour that their culture considers appropriate for each sex (Bronstein, 1988). Fathers treat boys and girls more differently than mothers do, even during the first year (M. E. Snow, Jacklin, & Maccoby, 1983). During the second year, fathers talk more and spend more time with sons than with daughters (Lamb, 1981). Mothers talk more, and more supportively, to daughters than to sons. Overall, fathers are less talkative and supportive—but also less negative—in their speech than mothers are. These differences are especially pronounced with toddlers, whose mothers typically spend much more time with them than fathers do (Leaper, Anderson, & Sanders, 1998). Fathers of toddlers play more roughly with sons and show more sensitivity to daughters (Kelley et al., 1998). Home observations of 12-month-old, 18-month-old, and 5-year-old children found the biggest gender differences at 18 months, when both mothers and fathers tended to foster gender-typed play (Fagot & Hagan, 1991).

We discuss gender-typing and gender differences in more depth in chapter 11.

Grandparents' Roles

In traditional societies and in some minority communities in Canada that are characterized by large, multi-generational *extended-family households,* grandparents who live with the family play an integral role in child raising and family decisions. But most Canadian children grow up in *nuclear families* limited to parents and siblings, and many grandparents live far away or are busy with careers or other interests. Over 90 per cent of 10-year-old children have at least one living grandparent (Rosenthal & Gladstone, 2000).

A major study of an American nationally representative three-generation sample found that "grandparents play a limited but important role in family dynamics," and many have strong emotional ties to their grandchildren (Cherlin & Furstenberg, 1986a, p. 26). Most grandparents (55 per cent) fall into a *companionate* pattern; they do not intervene directly in the children's upbringing but are frequent, casual companions. Grandparents tend to be more *involved*—giving advice, helping out, providing care and nurturing, and discussing the child's problems with the parents—during the earliest years or in a time of family crisis (Cherlin & Furstenberg, 1986a, 1986b). In 1993, nearly 17 per cent of preschool children of employed mothers were under a grandparent's daytime care (Casper, 1996). Unpaid help in child care is provided by about 36 per cent of Canadian women aged 45 to 54, by 42 per cent of those aged 55 to 64, and by 22 percent of those aged 65 years and over. In comparison, a far smaller percentage of men in the comparable age groups provide unpaid childcare (Rosenthal & Gladstone, 2000). The extent of a grandparent's involvement with the grandchild depends on a variety of factors, including geographic proximity—living closer increases contact (Rosenthal et al., 2000)—with greater contact with a maternal grandchild rather than a paternal grandchild (Sherer Smith, 1991), and age and timing of grandparenthood—with very young and very old grandparents having less positive atti-

What's your view ?

• Should parents try to treat male and female infants and toddlers alike?

• On the basis of your own early memories or of what family members have told you, what was your grandparents' impact on your development and on your family, especially during your first 3 years of life?

tudes about their grandparenthood than individuals at intermediate ages on first becoming grandparents (Rosenthal et al., 2000).

Because ties with grandparents can be important to children's development, grandparents can, with special permission of the Court, ask for custody or access. However, cases of grandparent custody requests are very rare, granted typically when a parent abandons or maltreats a child.

Another current trend is the increasing number of grandparents serving as "parents by default" for children whose parents are unable to care for them—often the result of teenage pregnancy or substance abuse (Casper & Bryson, 1998; Chalfie, 1994; Minkler & Roe, 1996). In 1997, nearly 7 per cent of U.S. households with children under 18 were maintained by grandparents, and about one-third of these households had no parent present (Casper & Bryson, 1998). In some low-income urban areas, an estimated 30 to 50 per cent of children are in *kinship care,* living in homes of grandparents or other relatives without their parents (Minkler & Roe, 1996). In Canada, about 21 per cent of children under 12 years, who are under non-parental care, are cared for by a relative (CICH, 2000).

Checkpoint ✔

Can you . . .

✔ Discuss the implications of research on monkeys "raised" by inanimate "mothers"?

✔ Compare the roles of fathers and mothers and their influences on gender-typing?

✔ Discuss the changing roles of grandparents?

Developmental Issues in Infancy

Guidepost 4

How do infants gain trust in their world and form attachments?

How does a dependent newborn, with a limited emotional repertoire and pressing physical needs, become a 3-year-old with complex feelings, a strong will, and the beginnings of a conscience? Much of this development revolves around issues regarding the self in relation to others. In this section, we look at the development of trust and attachment in infancy and at emotional communication between infants and caregivers—developments that pave the way for the very different issues of toddlerhood. We also look at three phenomena widely believed to be common during late infancy: stranger anxiety, separation anxiety, and social referencing.

Developing Trust

For a far longer period than the young of other mammals, human babies are dependent on other people for food, for protection, and for their very lives. How do they come to trust that their needs will be met? According to Erikson (1950), early experiences are the key.

The first of the eight crises, or critical developmental stages, Erikson identified (refer back to Table 2-2 in chapter 2) is **basic trust versus basic mistrust.** This stage begins in infancy and continues until about 18 months. In these early months, babies develop a sense of the reliability of the people and objects in their world. They need to develop a balance between trust (which lets them form intimate relationships) and mistrust (which enables them to protect themselves). If trust predominates, as it should, children develop the "virtue" of *hope:* the belief that they can fulfill their needs and obtain their desires (Erikson, 1982). If mistrust predominates, children will view the world as unfriendly and unpredictable and will have trouble forming relationships.

The critical element in developing trust is sensitive, responsive, consistent caregiving. Erikson saw feeding time as the setting for establishing the right mix of trust and mistrust. Can the

basic trust versus basic mistrust Erikson's first crisis in psychosocial development, in which infants develop a sense of the reliability of people and objects in their world

Diane's sensitivity to Anna's needs contributes to the development of Anna's sense of basic trust—her ability to rely on the people and things in her world. Trust is necessary, according to Erikson, for children to form intimate relationships.

Checkpoint

Can you . . .

✔ Explain the importance of basic trust and identify the critical element in its development?

attachment Reciprocal, enduring tie between infant and caregiver, each of whom contributes to the quality of the relationship

Strange Situation Laboratory technique used to study attachment

secure attachment Pattern in which an infant cries or protests when the primary caregiver leaves and actively seeks out the caregiver upon his or her return

avoidant attachment Pattern in which an infant rarely cries when separated from the primary caregiver and avoids contact upon his or her return

ambivalent (resistant) attachment Pattern in which an infant becomes anxious before the primary caregiver leaves, is extremely upset during his or her absence, and both seeks and resists contact on his or her return

disorganized-disoriented attachment Pattern in which an infant, after being separated from the primary caregiver, shows contradictory behaviours upon his or her return

baby count on being fed when hungry, and can the baby therefore trust the mother as a representative of the world? Trust enables an infant to let the mother out of sight "because she has become an inner certainty as well as an outer predictability" (Erikson, 1950, p. 247).

Developing Attachments

Attachment is a reciprocal, enduring emotional tie between an infant and a caregiver, each of whom contributes to the quality of the relationship. Attachments have adaptive value for babies, ensuring that their psychosocial as well as physical needs will be met. According to ethological theory (see chapter 2), infants and parents are biologically predisposed to become attached to each other, and attachment promotes a baby's survival.

Studying Patterns of Attachment

Mary Ainsworth first studied attachment in the early 1950s with John Bowlby after completing her graduate studies at the University of Toronto. Bowlby (1951), on the basis of ethological studies of bonding in animals and observation of disturbed children in a London psychoanalytic clinic, was convinced of the importance of the mother–baby bond; he warned against separating mother and baby without providing good substitute caregiving. Ainsworth, after studying attachment in African babies in Uganda through naturalistic observation in their homes (Ainsworth, 1967), devised the **Strange Situation,** a now-classic laboratory-based technique designed to assess attachment patterns between an infant and an adult. Typically, the adult is the mother (though other adults have taken part as well), and the infant is 10 to 24 months old.

The Strange Situation consists of a sequence of eight episodes, which takes less than half an hour. During that time, the mother twice leaves the baby in an unfamiliar room, the first time with a stranger. The second time she leaves the baby alone, and the stranger comes back before the mother does. The mother then encourages the baby to explore and play again and gives comfort if the baby seems to need it (Ainsworth, Blehar, Waters, & Wall, 1978). Of particular concern is the baby's response each time the mother returns.

When Ainsworth and her colleagues observed 1-year-olds in the Strange Situation and at home, they found three main patterns of attachment: *secure* (the most common category, into which 66 per cent of babies fell) and two forms of anxious, or insecure, attachment: *avoidant* (20 per cent of babies) and *ambivalent, or resistant* (12 per cent).

Babies with **secure attachment** cry or protest when the mother leaves and greet her happily when she returns. They use her as a secure base, leaving her to go off and explore but returning occasionally for reassurance. They are usually cooperative and relatively free of anger. Babies with **avoidant attachment** rarely cry when the mother leaves, and they avoid her on her return. They tend to be angry and do not reach out in time of need. They dislike being held but dislike being put down even more. Babies with **ambivalent (resistant) attachment** become anxious even before the mother leaves and are very upset when she goes out. When she returns, they show their ambivalence by seeking contact with her while at the same time resisting it by kicking or squirming. Resistant babies do little exploration and are hard to comfort. These three attachment patterns are universal in all cultures in which they have been studied—cultures as different as those in Africa, China, and Israel—though the percentage of infants in each category varies (van IJzendoorn & Kroonenberg, 1988; van IJzendoorn & Sagi, 1999).

Later research (Main & Solomon, 1986) has identified a fourth pattern, **disorganized-disoriented attachment.** Babies with the disorganized pattern often show inconsistent, contradictory behaviours. They greet the mother brightly when she returns but then turn away or approach without looking at her. They seem confused and afraid. This may be the least secure pattern. It is most likely to occur in babies whose mothers are insensitive, intrusive, or abusive (Carlson, 1998). (Table 8-3 describes how babies with each of the four patterns of attachment react to the Strange Situation.)

Table 8-3	Attachment Behaviours in Strange Situation
Attachment Classification	**Behaviour**
Secure	Gloria plays and explores freely when her mother is nearby. She responds enthusiastically when her mother returns.
Insecure-Avoidant	When Sam's mother returns, Sam does not make eye contact or greet her. It is almost as if he has not noticed her return.
Insecure-Resistant	James hovers close to his mother during much of the Strange Situation, but he does not greet her positively or enthusiastically during the reunion episode. Instead, he is angry and upset.
Disorganized/Disoriented	Erica responds to the Strange Situation with inconsistent, contradictory behaviour. She seems to fall apart, overwhelmed by the stress.

Based on Thompson, 1998, pp. 37–39.

Although much research on attachment has been based on the Strange Situation, some investigators have questioned its validity. The Strange Situation *is* strange; it is also artificial. It asks mothers not to initiate interaction, exposes babies to repeated comings and goings of adults, and expects the infants to pay attention to them. Since attachment influences a wider range of behaviours than are seen in the Strange Situation, some researchers have called for a more comprehensive, sensitive method to measure it, one that would show how mother and infant interact during natural, unstressful situations (T. M. Field, 1987).

It has been suggested that the Strange Situation may be especially inappropriate for studying attachment in children of employed mothers, since these children are used to routine separations from their mothers and the presence of other caregivers. However, a comparison of 1,153 randomly sampled 15-month-olds born in ten U.S. cities, who had received varying amounts, types, and quality of day care starting at various ages, found "no evidence … that the Strange Situation was less valid for children with extensive child-care experience than for those without" (NICHD Early Child Care Research Network, 1997a, p. 867).

The Strange Situation may be less valid in some non-industrialized cultures, which have different expectations for babies' interaction with their mothers and in which mothers may encourage different kinds of attachment-related behaviour. Research on Japanese infants, who are less commonly separated from their mothers than Canadian or U.S. babies, showed high rates of resistant attachment, which may reflect the extreme stressfulness of the Strange Situation for these babies (Miyake, Chen, & Campos, 1985).

Some researchers have begun to supplement the Strange Situation with methods that allow children to be studied in their natural settings. Using a Q-sort technique, observers sort a set of descriptive words or phrases ("cries a lot"; "tends to cling") into categories ranging from most to least characteristic of the child. The Waters and Deane (1985) Attachment Q-set (AQS) has mothers or other observers compare descriptions of children's everyday behaviour with expert descriptions of the "hypothetical most secure child." The Preschool Assessment of Attachment (PAA) (Crittenden, 1993), an instrument for measuring attachment after 20 months of age, takes into account older preschoolers' more complex relationships and language abilities.

In a cross-cultural study using the AQS, mothers in China, Colombia, Germany, Israel, Japan, Norway, and the United States described their children as behaving more like than unlike the "most secure child." Furthermore, the mothers' descriptions of "secure-base" behaviour were about as similar across cultures as within a culture. These findings suggest that the tendency to use the mother as a secure base is universal, though it may take somewhat varied forms (Posada et al., 1995).

How Attachment Is Established

Both mothers and babies contribute to security of attachment by the way they respond to each other. Virtually any activity on a baby's part that leads to a response from an adult can be an

This baby, like most infants, is developing a strong attachment to his mother. Both mother and baby contribute to the security of attachment by their personalities and behaviour and their responsiveness to each other.

attachment-seeking behaviour: sucking, crying, smiling, clinging, or looking into the caregiver's eyes. As early as the eighth week of life, babies direct some of these behaviours more to their mothers than to anyone else. These overtures are successful when the mother responds warmly, expresses delight, and gives the baby frequent physical contact and freedom to explore (Ainsworth, 1969).

Attachment behaviours vary across cultures. Among the Gusii, for example, infants are greeted with handshakes, and Gusii infants reach out for a parent's hand much as Canadian infants cuddle up for a hug (van IJzendoorn & Sagi, 1999).

On the basis of a baby's interactions with the mother, said Bowlby, the baby builds a "working model" of what can be expected from her (Bretherton, 1997). The various patterns of emotional attachment represent different cognitive representations that result in different expectations. As long as the mother continues to act the same way, the model holds up. If her behaviour changes—not just once or twice but consistently—the baby may revise the model, and security of attachment may change.

A baby's working model of attachment is related to Erikson's concept of basic trust. Secure attachment evolves from trust; insecure attachment reflects mistrust. Securely attached babies have learned to trust not only their caregivers but their own ability to get what they need. Thus babies who cry a lot and whose mothers respond by soothing them tend to be securely attached (Del Carmen, Pedersen, Huffman, & Bryan, 1993).

Mothers of securely attached infants and toddlers tend to be sensitive and responsive (Ainsworth et al., 1978; De Wolff & van IJzendoorn, 1997; Isabella, 1993; NICHD Early Child Care Research Network, 1997a), although the mother's own cognitive representations about the quality of attachment account for only a small part of the relationship between sensitivity and secure attachment (Pederson, Gleason, Moran, & Bento, 1998). Equally important are mutual interaction, stimulation, a positive attitude, warmth and acceptance, and emotional support (De Wolff & van IJzendoorn, 1997).

Contextual factors may influence attachment (De Wolff & van IJzendoorn, 1997). One such factor is a mother's employment and her attitude toward the separation it causes. In one study, if employed mothers were highly anxious about being away from home, their babies tended to develop avoidant attachments, as measured at 18 months by the Strange Situation (Stifter, Coulehan, & Fish, 1993).

Contrary to Ainsworth's original findings, babies seem to develop attachments to both parents at about the same time, and security of attachment to father and mother is usually quite similar (Fox, Kimmerly, & Schafer, 1991). If not, a secure attachment to the father can sometimes offset an insecure attachment to the mother (Engle & Breaux, 1998).

The Role of Temperament

How much influence does temperament exert on attachment, and in what ways? Findings vary (Susman-Stillman, Kalkoske, Egeland, & Waldman, 1996; Vaughn et al., 1992). In a study of 6- to 12-month-olds and their families (which used frequent home observations, maternal reports, and Q-sorts in addition to the Strange Situation), both a mother's sensitivity and her baby's temperament influenced attachment patterns (Seifer, Schiller, Sameroff, Resnick, & Riordan, 1996). Some studies have identified frustration levels, amounts of crying, and irritability as predictors of attachment (Calkins & Fox, 1992; Izard, Porges, Simons, Haynes, & Cohen, 1991). Neurological or physiological conditions may underlie temperamental differences in attachment. For example, variability in heart rate is associated with irritability, and heart rate seems to vary more in insecurely attached infants (Izard, Porges, et al., 1991).

A baby's temperament may have not only a direct impact on attachment but also an indirect impact through its effect on the parents. In a series of studies in the Netherlands (van den Boom, 1989, 1994), 15-day-old infants classified as irritable were much more likely than non-irritable infants to be insecurely (usually avoidantly) attached at 1 year. However, irritable infants whose mostly low-SES mothers received home visits, with instruction on how to soothe their babies, were as likely to be rated as securely attached as the non-irritable infants. Thus infant irritability may prevent the development of secure attachment unless the mother has the skills to cope with the baby's temperament (Rothbart et al., 2000). "Goodness of fit" between parent and child may well be a key to understanding security of attachment.

Intergenerational Transmission of Attachment Patterns

The way a mother remembers her attachment to her parents seems to predict the way her children will be attached to *her*. The *Adult Attachment Interview (AAI)* (George, Kaplan, & Main, 1985; Main, 1995; Main, Kaplan, & Cassidy, 1985) is a semi-structured interview that asks adults to recall and interpret feelings and experiences related to their childhood attachments. An analysis of 18 studies using the AAI found that the clarity, coherence, and consistency of responses reliably predicts the security with which the respondent's own child will be attached to him or her (van IJzendoorn, 1995).

Apparently, the way adults recall early experiences with parents or caregivers affects the way they respond to their own children (Slade, Belsky, Aber, & Phelps, 1999). A mother who was securely attached to *her* mother, or who understands why she was insecurely attached, can accurately recognize the baby's attachment behaviours, respond encouragingly, and help the baby form a secure attachment to her (Bretherton, 1990). In a study of 124 mothers of first-born sons, mothers rated as autonomous, or secure, on the AAI were most likely to describe their relationship with their children coherently, in ways expressing joy or pleasure; and these mothers were observed, when their sons were 15 and 21 months old, to engage in more positive mothering (Slade et al., 1999).

The important thing is not the way a mother *actually* was attached as a child, but the way she *remembers* her attachment. Adults' perceptions of their own early attachments may be influenced by later experiences, such as physical or sexual abuse, serious illness, or the death of a parent. Adults who have experienced such events tend to be preoccupied with their early attachment relationships (Beckwith, Cohen, & Hamilton, 1999).

Stranger Anxiety and Separation Anxiety

Sophie used to be a friendly baby, smiling at strangers and going to them, continuing to coo happily as long as someone—anyone—was around. Now, at 8 months, she turns away when a new person approaches and howls when her parents try to leave her with a baby-sitter. Sophie is experiencing both **stranger anxiety,** wariness of a person she does not know, and **separation anxiety,** distress when a familiar caregiver leaves her.

Separation anxiety and stranger anxiety used to be considered emotional and cognitive milestones of the second half of infancy, reflecting attachment to the mother. However, newer research suggests that although stranger anxiety and separation anxiety are fairly typical, they are not universal. Whether a baby cries when a parent leaves or when someone new approaches may say more about the baby's temperament or life circumstances than about security of attachment (R. J. Davidson & Fox, 1989).

Babies rarely react negatively to strangers before 6 months of age, commonly do so by 8 or 9 months, and do so more and more throughout the rest of the first year (Sroufe, 1997). Even then, however, a baby may react positively to a new person, especially if the mother speaks positively about the stranger (Feinman & Lewis, 1983) or if the person waits a little while and then approaches the baby gradually, gently, and playfully (Sroufe, 1997).

Separation anxiety may be due, not so much to the separation itself, as to the quality of substitute care. When substitute caregivers are warm and responsive and play with 9-month-olds *before* they cry, the babies cry less than when they are with less responsive caregivers (Gunnar, Larson, Hertsgaard, Harris, & Brodersen, 1992). Babies as young as 4 months are capable of distinguishing between adults who have been responsive to them in the past and those who have not been responsive, even if the amount of prior contact has been brief (Bigelow & Birch, 2000).

Stability of care is important. Pioneering work by René Spitz (1945, 1946) on institutionalized children emphasizes the need for substitute care to be as close as possible to good mothering. Research has underlined the value of continuity and consistency in caregiving, so children can form early emotional bonds with their caregivers.

Today, neither intense fear of strangers nor intense protest when the mother leaves is considered to be a sign of secure attachment. Researchers measure attachment more by what happens when the mother returns than by how many tears the baby sheds at her departure.

stranger anxiety Wariness of strange people and places, shown by some infants during the second half of the first year

separation anxiety Distress shown by an infant when a familiar caregiver leaves

Long-term Effects of Attachment

As attachment theory proposes, security of attachment seems to affect emotional, social, and cognitive competence (van IJzendoorn & Sagi, 1997). The more secure a child's attachment to a nurturing adult, the easier it is for the child to eventually become independent of that adult and to develop good relationships with others. The link between attachment in infancy and characteristics observed years later underscores the continuity of development and the interrelationships of its various aspects.

Securely attached toddlers have larger, more varied vocabularies than those who are insecurely attached (Meins, 1998). They also are more sociable (Elicker, Englund, & Sroufe, 1992; Main, 1983). They have more positive interactions with peers, and their friendly overtures are more likely to be accepted (Fagot, 1997).

From ages 3 to 5, securely attached children are more curious, competent, empathic, resilient, and self-confident, get along better with other children, and are more likely to form close friendships (Arend, Gove, & Sroufe, 1979; Elicker et al., 1992; J. L. Jacobson & Wille, 1986; Waters, Wippman, & Sroufe, 1979; Youngblade & Belsky, 1992). They interact more positively with parents, preschool teachers, and peers and are better able to resolve conflicts (Elicker et al., 1992). They tend to have a more positive self-image (Elicker et al., 1992; Verschueren, Marcoen, & Schoefs, 1996).

Their advantages continue into middle childhood and adolescence. When 10- and 11-year-olds were observed in summer day camp, those with histories of secure attachment were better at making and keeping friends and functioning in a group than children who had been classified as avoidant or resistant. They were also more self-reliant, self-assured, and adaptable and better physically coordinated. In a reunion of 15-year-olds who had gone to camp together, the adolescents who had been securely attached in infancy were rated higher on emotional health, self-esteem, ego resiliency, and peer competence by their counsellors and peers and by the researchers who observed them (Sroufe, Carlson, & Shulman, 1993).

If, on the basis of early experience, children have positive expectations about their ability to get along with others and engage in social give-and-take, and if they think well of themselves, they may set up social situations that tend to reinforce these beliefs and the gratifying interactions that result from them (Elicker et al., 1992; Sroufe et al., 1993). And if children, as infants, had a secure base and could count on parents' or caregivers' responsiveness, they are likely to feel confident enough to be actively engaged in their world (Jacobsen & Hofmann, 1997).

Insecurely attached infants, by contrast, often have later problems: inhibitions at age 2, hostility toward other children at age 5, and dependency during the school years (Calkins & Fox, 1992; Lyons-Ruth, Alpern, & Repacholi, 1993; Sroufe et al., 1993). Those with disorganized attachment tend to have behaviour problems at all levels of schooling and psychiatric disorders at age 17 (Carlson, 1998). However, it may be that the correlations between attachment in infancy and later development stem, not from attachment itself, but from personality characteristics that affect both attachment and parent–child interactions *after* infancy (Lamb, 1987).

Checkpoint ✔

Can you . . .

✔ Describe four patterns of attachment?

✔ Discuss how attachment is established, including the roles of mothers and fathers and of the baby's temperament?

✔ Discuss factors affecting stranger anxiety and separation anxiety?

✔ Describe long-term behavioural differences influenced by attachment patterns?

Guidepost 5

How do infants and caregivers "read" each other's non-verbal signals?

mutual regulation Process by which infant and caregiver communicate emotional states to each other and respond appropriately

Emotional Communication with Caregivers: Mutual Regulation

Interactions that influence the quality of attachment depend on the ability of both infant and caregiver to respond appropriately to signals about each other's emotional states. Infants take an active part in this process by influencing the way caregivers behave toward them.

In this process of **mutual regulation,** healthy interaction occurs when a caregiver "reads" a baby's signals accurately and responds appropriately. When a baby's goals are met, the baby is joyful, or at least interested (E. Z. Tronick, 1989). If a caregiver ignores an invitation to play or insists on playing when the baby has signalled "I don't feel like it," the baby may feel frustrated or sad. When babies do not achieve desired results, they keep on sending signals to repair the interaction. Normally, interaction moves back and forth between well-regulated and poorly regulated states, and babies learn from these shifts how to send signals and what to do when their initial signals do not result in a comfortable emotional balance. Mutual regulation helps babies learn to "read" others' behaviour and to develop expectations about it. Even very young infants can perceive emotions expressed by others and can adjust their own behaviour accordingly (Lelwica & Haviland, 1983; Termine & Izard, 1988).

The **"still-face" paradigm** is a research method used to measure mutual regulation in infants from 2 to 9 months old. In the *still-face* episode, which follows a normal face-to-face interaction, the mother suddenly becomes stony-faced, silent, and unresponsive. Then, a few minutes later, she resumes normal interaction (the *reunion* episode). During the still-face episode, infants tend to stop smiling and looking at the mother. They may make faces, sounds, or gestures or may touch themselves, their clothing, or a chair, apparently to comfort themselves or to relieve the emotional stress created by the mother's unexpected behaviour (Cohn & Tronick, 1983; E. Z. Tronick, 1980; 1989; Weinberg & Tronick, 1996).

How do infants react during the reunion episode? One study combined a microanalysis of 6-month-olds' facial expressions during this episode with measures of heart rate and nervous system reactivity. The infants' reactions were mixed. On the one hand, they showed even more positive behaviour—joyous expressions and utterances, and gazes and gestures directed toward the mother—than before the still-face episode. On the other hand, the persistence of sad or angry facial expressions, "pick-me-up" gestures, distancing, and indications of stress, as well as an increased tendency to fuss and cry, suggested that while infants welcome the resumption of interaction with the mother, the negative feelings stirred by a breakdown in mutual regulation are not readily eased (Weinberg & Tronick, 1996).

Gender differences in mutual regulation have been found as early as 6 months of age. In a laboratory observation, 6-month-old boys seemed to have a harder time than girls in regulating their own emotions during the still-face episode. They made their needs known to their mothers through a wider variety of expressive behaviour—both positive and negative—than girls did. In *normal* face-to-face interaction, sons maintained better coordination of emotional signals with their mothers than daughters did, but also took longer to repair mismatches (Weinberg, Tronick, Cohn, & Olson, 1999).

Apparently the still-face reaction is universal and is not limited to interactions with mothers. A laboratory observation of 94 four-month-olds found that fathers are equally sensitive to their infants' signals, and infants react similarly to fathers and mothers (Braungart-Rieker, Garwood, Powers, & Notaro, 1998). In cross-cultural experiments, both Chinese and Canadian infants responded similarly to mothers and fathers—and also to strangers—in comparison with control groups that did not experience the still-face episode (Kisilevsky et al., 1998).

What's your view ?

- Do you see any ethical problems with the still-face paradigm or the Strange Situation?
- Do you think the benefits of these kinds of research are worth the risks?

How a Mother's Depression Affects Mutual Regulation

Reading emotional signals lets mothers assess and meet babies' needs; and it lets babies influence or respond to the mother's behaviour toward them. What happens, then, if that communication system seriously breaks down, and what can be done about it?

Temporary postpartum depression, which affects 10 to 40 per cent of new mothers (Kendall-Tackett, 1997), may have little or no impact on the way a mother interacts with her baby, but severe or chronic depression lasting 6 months or more (which is far less common) can have serious effects (Campbell, Cohn, & Meyers, 1995; Teti, Gelfand, Messinger, & Isabella, 1995).

Chronically depressed mothers tend to be either withdrawn or intrusive (T. Field, 1998a, 1998c). They are less sensitive and less engaged with their infants than nondepressed mothers, and their interactions with their babies are less positive (NICHD Early Child Care Research Network, 1999b). Depressed mothers are less able to interpret and respond to an infant's cries (Donovan, Leavitt, & Walsh, 1998). Babies of depressed mothers may give up on sending emotional signals and try to comfort themselves by sucking or rocking. If this defensive reaction becomes habitual, babies learn that they have no power to draw responses from other people, that their mothers are unreliable, and that the world is untrustworthy. They also tend to become depressed themselves (Gelfand & Teti, 1995; Teti et al., 1995).

We cannot be sure, however, that such infants become depressed through a failure of mutual regulation. They may inherit a predisposition to depression, or acquire it prenatally through exposure to hormonal or other biochemical influences. Newborns of mothers with depressive symptoms are less expressive, less active and robust, more excitable, and less oriented to sensory stimuli than other newborns, suggesting an inborn tendency (Lundy, Field, & Pickens, 1996).

Infants of depressed mothers tend to show unusual patterns of brain activity, similar to the mothers' own patterns. Within 24 hours after birth, they show relatively less activity in the left frontal region of the brain, which seems to be specialized for "approach" emotions such as joy and anger, and more activity in the right frontal region, which controls "withdrawal" emotions, such as distress and disgust (G. Dawson et al., 1992, 1999; T. Field, 1998a, 1998c; T. Field, Fox, Pickens, Nawrocki, & Soutollo, 1995; N. A. Jones, Field, Fox, Lundy, & Davalos, 1997). Newborns of depressed mothers also have lower scores on the Brazelton Neonatal Behavior Assessment Scale and lower vagal tone, which is associated with attention and learning (T. Field, 1998a, 1998c; N. A. Jones et al., 1998). In a study of 63 pregnant women, depressed expectant mothers had higher levels of stress hormones (cortisol and norepinephrine) and lower levels of dopamine—and so did their newborns, who also had low Brazelton scores (Lundy et al., 1999). These findings suggest that a mother's depression during pregnancy may contribute to her newborn's neurological and behavioural functioning.

It may well be that a combination of genetic, prenatal, and environmental factors puts infants of depressed mothers at risk of becoming depressed. It is likely that a bi-directional influence is at work; an infant who does not respond normally may further depress the mother, and her unresponsiveness may in turn increase the infant's depression (T. Field, 1995, 1998a, 1998c; Lundy et al., 1999). Interactions with a non-depressed adult—the father or a child-care worker or nursery-school teacher—can help infants compensate for the effects of depressed mothering (T. Field, 1995, 1998a, 1998c).

Both as infants and as preschoolers, children with severely or chronically depressed mothers tend to be insecurely attached to them (Gelfand & Teti, 1995; Teti et al., 1995). They are less motivated to explore and more apt to prefer relatively unchallenging tasks (Hart, Field, del Valle, & Pelaez-Nogueras, 1998; Redding, Harmon, & Morgan, 1990).

As toddlers these children tend to have trouble suppressing frustration and tension (Cole, Barrett, & Zahn-Waxler, 1992; Seiner & Gelfand, 1995). They are likely to grow poorly, to perform poorly on cognitive and linguistic measures, and to have behaviour problems (T. Field, 1998a, 1998c; T. M. Field et al., 1985; Gelfand & Teti, 1995; NICHD Early Child Care Research Network, 1999b; B. S. Zuckerman & Beardslee, 1987). The National Longitudinal Study of Children and Youth (NLSCY), showed an increased likelihood of an emotional disorder in Canadian children aged 2 to 3 years whose primary caregiver was depressed. Parental depression was associated with a higher likelihood of emotional disorder, conduct disorder, hyperactivity, and relationship problems in children between 4 and 11 years of age (Landy & Tam, 1998).

Techniques that may help improve a depressed mother's mood include listening to music, visual imagery, aerobics, yoga, relaxation, and massage therapy (T. Field, 1995, 1998a, 1998b, 1998c). Massage also can help depressed babies (T. Field, 1998a, 1998b; T. Field et al., 1996), possibly through effects on neurological activity (N. A. Jones et al., 1997). In one study, mood-brightening measures plus social, educational, and vocational rehabilitation for the mother and day care for the infant improved their interaction. The infants showed faster growth and had fewer pediatric problems, more normal biochemical values, and better developmental test scores than a control group (T. Field, 1998a, 1998b).

Social Referencing

If, at a formal dinner party, you have ever cast a sidelong glance to see which fork the person next to you was using, you have read another person's non-verbal signals to get information on how to act. Through **social referencing,** one person forms an understanding of how to act in an ambiguous, confusing, or unfamiliar situation by seeking out and interpreting another person's perception of it. Babies seem to use social referencing when they look at their caregivers upon encountering a new person or toy. This pattern of behaviour may emerge some time after 6 months of age, when infants begin to judge the possible con-

social referencing
Understanding an ambiguous situation by seeking out another person's perception of it

sequences of events, imitate complex behaviours, and distinguish among and react to various emotional expressions.

A longitudinal study of 25 infants from age 6 to 12 months in Montreal showed that the use of social referencing as a way of understanding the causes of unfamiliar events grows. Children as young as 6 months used social referencing with their mothers when an object was placed in an unusual place. Social referencing, as a way of getting information about an ambiguous situation, occurred if the infant looked to the mother and back to the object with a puzzled or surprised expression; by the end of the study most of the infants were regularly engaging in this behaviour (Desrochers, Ricard, Decarie, & Allard, 1994).

In a study using the visual cliff (a measure of depth perception described in chapter 6), when the drop looked very shallow or very deep, 1-year-olds did not look to their mothers; they were able to judge for themselves whether or not to cross over. When they were uncertain about the depth of the "cliff," however, they paused at the "edge," looked down, and then looked up at their mothers. Most of the babies whose mothers showed joy or interest crossed the "drop," but very few whose mothers looked angry or afraid crossed it (Sorce, Emde, Campos, & Klinnert, 1985).

However, the idea that infants engage in social referencing has been challenged. When infants as young as 8 months old spontaneously look at caregivers in ambiguous situations, it is not clear that they are looking for information; they may be seeking comfort, attention, sharing of feelings, or simply reassurance of the caregiver's presence—typical attachment behaviours (Baldwin & Moses, 1996).

Developmental Issues in Toddlerhood

About halfway between their first and second birthdays, babies become toddlers. This transformation can be seen not only in such physical and cognitive skills as walking and talking, but in the ways children express their personalities and interact with others. Let's look at three psychological issues that toddlers—and their caregivers—have to deal with: the emerging *sense of self;* the growth of *autonomy,* or self-determination; and the *internalization of behavioural standards.*

The Emerging Sense of Self

Before children can take responsibility for their own activities, they must have a cognitive sense of themselves as physically distinct persons separate from the rest of the world, whose characteristics and behaviour can be described and evaluated. Self-awareness is the first step toward developing standards of behaviour; it lets children understand that a parent's response to something they have done is directed at *them* and not just at the act itself.

How does the **self-concept,** or sense of self, begin to develop? After interviewing the mothers of 123 children 14 to 40 months old, a team of researchers (Stipek, Gralinski, & Kopp, 1990) identified a three-step sequence.

The first step is *physical self-recognition and self-awareness.* Toddlers recognize themselves in mirrors or pictures by 18 to 24 months, showing awareness of themselves as physically distinct beings. In a classic line of research, investigators dabbed rouge on the noses of 6- to 24-month-olds and sat them in front of a mirror. Three-fourths of 18-month-olds and all 24-month-olds touched their red noses more often than before, whereas babies younger than 15 months never did. This behaviour suggests that the older babies knew they didn't normally have red noses and that they recognized the image in the mirror as their own (Lewis, 1997; Lewis & Brooks, 1974). By 20 to 24 months, toddlers begin to use first-person pronouns, another sign of self-awareness (Lewis, 1997).

Next comes *self-description and self-evaluation.* Once they have a concept of themselves as distinct beings, children begin to apply descriptive terms (*big* or *little; straight hair* or *curly hair*) and evaluative ones (*good, pretty,* or *strong*) to themselves. This normally occurs sometime between 19 and 30 months, as representational ability and vocabulary expand.

In the third stage, *emotional response to wrongdoing,* children show that they are upset by a parent's disapproval and will stop doing something they are not supposed to do—

Checkpoint ✓

Can you . . .

✔ Describe how mutual regulation works?

✔ Discuss how a mother's depression can affect her baby?

✔ Tell what social referencing is, and give examples of how infants seem to use it?

Guidepost 6

When does the sense of self arise, and what are three steps in its development?

self-concept Sense of self; descriptive and evaluative mental picture of one's abilities and traits

What's your view

• How would you expect each of the three early stages in self-concept development to affect the parent–child relationship?

Guidepost 7

How do toddlers develop autonomy and standards for socially acceptable behaviour?

at least while they are being watched. This stage lays the foundation for moral understanding and the development of conscience.

Developing Autonomy

As children mature—physically, cognitively, and emotionally—they are driven to seek independence from the very adults to whom they are attached. Erikson (1950) identified the period from about 18 months to 3 years as the second "crisis" in personality development, **autonomy versus shame and doubt,** which is marked by a shift from external control to self-control. Having come through infancy with a sense of basic trust in the world and an awakening self-awareness, toddlers begin to substitute their own judgment for their caregivers'. The "virtue" that emerges during this stage is *will*. Toilet training is an important step toward autonomy and self-control. So is language; as children are better able to make their wishes understood, they become more powerful and independent.

Since unlimited freedom is neither safe nor healthy, said Erikson, shame and doubt have a necessary place. As in all of Erikson's crises, an appropriate balance is crucial. Toddlers need adults to set appropriate limits, and shame and doubt help them recognize the need for those limits.

The "terrible twos" are a normal manifestation of the drive for autonomy. Toddlers have to test the new notion that they are individuals, that they have some control over their world, and that they have new, exciting powers. They are driven to try out their own ideas, exercise their own preferences, and make their own decisions. This drive typically shows itself in the form of *negativism,* the tendency to shout "No!" just for the sake of resisting authority. Almost all children show negativism to some degree; it usually begins before 2 years of age, tends to peak at about 3½ to 4, and declines by age 6. Parents and other caregivers who view children's expressions of self-will as a normal, healthy striving for independence, not as stubbornness, can help them learn self-control, contribute to their sense of competence, and avoid excessive conflict. (Table 8-4 gives specific, research-based suggestions for dealing with the "terrible twos.")

Socialization and Internalization: Developing a Conscience

Socialization is the process by which children develop habits, skills, values, and motives that make them responsible, productive members of society. Compliance with parental expectations can be seen as a first step toward compliance with societal standards. Socialization rests on **internalization** of these standards. Children who are successfully socialized no longer merely obey rules or commands to get rewards or avoid punishment; they have made society's standards their own (Grusec & Goodnow, 1994; Kochanska & Aksan, 1995; Kochanska, Tjebkes, & Forman, 1998).

Developing Self-Regulation

Katy, age 2, is about to poke her finger into an electric outlet. In her "child-proofed" apartment, the sockets are covered, but not here in her grandmother's home. When Katy hears her father shout "No!" the toddler pulls her arm back. The next time she goes near an outlet, she starts to point her finger, hesitates, and then says "No." She has stopped herself from doing something she remembers she is not supposed to do. She is beginning to show **self-regulation:** control of her own behaviour to conform to a caregiver's demands or expectations, even when the caregiver is not present.

Self-regulation is the foundation of socialization, and it links all domains of development—physical, cognitive, social, and emotional. Until Katy was physically able to get around on her own, electric outlets posed no hazard. To stop herself from poking her finger into an outlet requires that she consciously understand and remember what her father told her. Cognitive awareness, however, is not enough; restraining herself also requires emotional control. Differences in self-regulation in infants are related to both cognitive performance and emotional responses (Lewis, Koroshegyi, Douglas, & Kampe, 1997).

By "reading" their parents' emotional responses to their behaviour, children continually absorb information about what conduct their parents approve of. As children process,

Table 8-4	Dealing with the "Terrible Twos"

The following research-based guidelines can help parents of toddlers discourage negativism and encourage socially acceptable behaviour:

- *Be flexible.* Learn the child's natural rhythms and special likes and dislikes.
- *Think of yourself as a safe harbour,* with safe limits, from which a child can set out and discover the world—and keep coming back for support.
- *Make your home "child-friendly."* Fill it with unbreakable objects that are safe to explore.
- *Avoid physical punishment.* It is often ineffective and may even lead a toddler to do more damage.
- *Offer a choice*—even a limited one—to give the child some control. ("Would you like to have your bath now, or after we read a book?")
- *Be consistent* in enforcing necessary requests.
- *Don't interrupt an activity unless absolutely necessary.* Try to wait until the child's attention has shifted.
- *If you must interrupt, give warning.* ("We have to leave the playground soon.")
- *Suggest alternative activities* when behaviour becomes objectionable. (When Ashley is throwing sand in Keiko's face, say, "Oh, look! Nobody's on the swings now. Let's go over and I'll give you a good push!")
- *Suggest; don't command.* Accompany requests with smiles or hugs, not criticism, threats, or physical restraint.
- *Link requests with pleasurable activities.* ("It's time to stop playing, so that you can go to the store with me.")
- *Remind the child of what you expect:* ("When we go to this playground, we *never* go outside the gate.")
- *Wait a few moments before repeating a request* when a child doesn't immediately comply.
- *Use "time out"* to end conflicts. In a non-punitive way, remove either yourself or the child from a situation.
- *Expect less self-control during times of stress* (illness, divorce, the birth of a sibling, or a move to a new home).
- *Expect it to be harder for toddlers to comply with "do's" than with "don'ts."* "Clean up your room" takes more effort than "Don't write on the furniture."
- *Keep the atmosphere as positive as possible.* Make your child *want* to cooperate.

Source: Haswell, Hock, & Wenar, 1981; Kochanska & Aksan, 1995; Kopp, 1982; Kuczynski & Kochanska, 1995; Power & Chapieski, 1986.

store, and act upon this information, their strong desire to please their parents leads them to do as they know their parents want them to, whether or not the parents are there to see. Mutual regulation of emotional states during infancy contributes to the development of self-control, especially in temperamentally "difficult" children, who may need extra help in achieving it (R. Feldman, Greenbaum, & Yirmiya, 1999).

The growth of self-regulation parallels the development of the self-conscious and evaluative emotions, such as empathy, shame, and guilt (Lewis, 1995, 1997, 1998). It requires flexibility and the ability to wait for gratification. When young children want very badly to do something, however, they easily forget the rules; they may run into the street after a ball or take a forbidden cookie. In most children, the full development of self-regulation takes at least 3 years (Kopp, 1982).

Origins of Conscience: Committed Compliance

Before children can develop **conscience,** which includes both emotional discomfort about doing something wrong and the ability to refrain from doing it, they need to have internalized standards. Conscience depends on willingness to do the right thing because a child believes it is right, not (as in self-regulation) just because someone else said so. *Inhibitory control*—conscious, or effortful, control of behaviour, a mechanism of self-regulation that emerges during toddlerhood—may contribute to the underpinnings of conscience by first enabling the child to comply with parental do's and don'ts (Kochanska, Murray, & Coy, 1997).

Grazyna Kochanska (1993, 1995, 1997a, 1997b) and her colleagues have sought the origins of conscience in a longitudinal study of a group of toddlers and mothers in Iowa.

Checkpoint ✔

Can you . . .

✔ Tell when and how self-regulation develops and how it contributes to socialization?

conscience Internal standards of behaviour, which usually control one's conduct and produce emotional discomfort when violated

Researchers videotaped 103 children ages 26 to 41 months and their mothers playing together with toys for 2 to 3 hours, both at home and in a homelike laboratory setting (Kochanska & Aksan, 1995). After a free-play period, the mother gave the child 15 minutes to put the toys away. The laboratory had a special shelf with other, unusually attractive toys, such as a bubble gum machine, a walkie-talkie, and a music box. The child had been told not to touch anything on the shelf. After about an hour, the experimenter asked the mother to go into an adjoining room, leaving the child alone with the toys. A few minutes later, a woman entered, played with several of the forbidden toys, and then left the child alone again for 8 minutes.

Children were judged to show **committed compliance** if they willingly followed the orders to clean up and not to touch the toys, without reminders or lapses. Children showed **situational compliance** if they needed prompting to obey; their compliance depended on ongoing parental control.

Committed compliance, which seems to be an early form of conscience, is strongly related to internalization of parental values and rules. Children whose mothers rated them as having internalized household rules refrained from touching the forbidden toys even when left alone with them, whereas children whose compliance was only situational tended to yield to temptation when their mothers were out of sight.

Committed compliance and situational compliance seem to be distinct patterns of behaviour. The two kinds of compliance can be distinguished in children as young as 13 months, but their roots go back to infancy. Committed compliers, who are more likely to be girls than boys, tend to be those who, at 8 to 10 months, could refrain from touching when told "No!" Committed compliance increases with age, while situational compliance decreases (Kochanska et al., 1998).

Factors in the Success of Socialization

Some children internalize societal standards more readily than others. The way parents go about their job, together with a child's temperament and the quality of the parent–child relationship, may help predict how hard or easy it will be to socialize a particular child (Kochanska, 1993, 1995, 1997a, 1997b). Factors in the success of socialization may include security of attachment, observational learning of parents' behaviour, and the mutual responsiveness of parent and child (Maccoby, 1992). All these, as well as socio-economic and cultural factors (Harwood, Schoelmerich, Ventura-Cook, Schulze, & Wilson, 1996), may play a part in motivation to comply.

Eleanor Maccoby (1992; Maccoby & Martin, 1983) describes socialization as a process of initiating a child into a system of **reciprocity**—of mutually binding, mutually responsive relationships—which begins with the parents and then extends to the community. Kochanska's longitudinal findings support this model.

A warm, mutually responsive relationship seems to foster committed compliance. Mothers of committed compliers, as contrasted with mothers of situational compliers, tend to rely on gentle guidance rather than force, threats, or other forms of negative control (Kochanska & Aksan, 1995). Children may more readily comply with parental demands when the parent has repeatedly affirmed the child's autonomy—for example, by following the child's lead during play. Mothers who can readily see a child's point of view seem to be most successful in doing this (Kochanska, 1997b).

Gentle guidance seems particularly suited to temperamentally fearful or anxious children, who tend to become upset when they misbehave. Such a child will readily internalize parental messages with a minimum of prodding; displays of power would merely make the child more anxious. Something more is needed with bolder children, but they too are likely to respond better to appeals to cooperate than to threats, and they are more likely to comply if they are securely attached (Kochanska, 1995, 1997a).

Contact with Other Children

Although parents exert a major influence on children's lives, relationships with other children—both in the home and out of it—are important, too, from infancy on.

committed compliance
Wholehearted obedience to a parent's orders without reminders or lapses

situational compliance
Obedience to parent's orders only in the presence of prompting or other signs of ongoing parental control

What's your view ?

- In view of Kochanska's research on the roots of conscience, what questions would you ask about the early socialization of anti-social adolescents and adults?

reciprocity System of mutually binding, mutually responsive relationships into which a child is socialized

Checkpoint ✓

Can you . . .

✔ Distinguish between committed and situational compliance?

✔ Discuss how temperament and parenting practices affect socialization?

Siblings

Guidepost 8

How do infants and toddlers interact with siblings and other children?

If you have brothers or sisters, your relationships with them are likely to be the longest-lasting you'll ever have. They share your roots; they "knew you when," they accepted or rejected the same parental values, and they probably deal with you more candidly than almost anyone else you know.

The Arrival of a New Baby

Children react in various ways to the arrival of a sibling. To bid for the mother's attention, some suck their thumbs, wet their pants, or use baby talk. Others withdraw. Some suggest taking the baby back to the hospital or flushing it down the toilet. Some take pride in being the "big ones," who can dress themselves, use the potty, and help care for the baby.

Much of the variation in children's adjustment to a new baby may have to do with such factors as the older child's age, the quality of his or her relationship with the mother, and the family atmosphere. A Montreal study of effects on a first-born child of a sibling's birth indicated that younger children show more distress after the birth than older ones. The level of support provided by the mother before and after the birth of a sibling, and degree of support by the father after birth are related to the child's level of distress after the birth (Gottlieb & Mendelson, 1990). Not surprisingly, attachment to the mother often becomes temporarily less secure (Teti, Sakin, Kucera, Corns, & Eiden, 1996).

The birth of a younger sibling may change the way a mother acts toward an older child, at least until the newcomer "settles in." The mother is likely to play less with the older child, to be less sensitive to her or his interests, to give more orders, to have more confrontations, to use physical punishment, and to initiate fewer conversations and games that help develop skills. An older boy, especially, may show temporary behaviour problems (Baydar, Greek, & Brooks-Gunn, 1997; Baydar, Hyle, & Brooks-Gunn, 1997; Dunn, 1985; Dunn & Kendrick, 1982).

If the mother has been working outside the home and does not return to work, the arrival of a new baby may mean that the mother can spend more, rather than less, time with the older child. However, with less family income and another mouth to feed, fewer resources for learning (such as play materials and outings) may be available to the older child. Also, financial worries may affect the mother's emotional well-being, contributing to negative maternal interactions with the older sibling. On the positive side, the arrival of a baby tends to enhance the older child's language development, perhaps because the child talks more than before with the father and other family members (Baydar, Greek, & Brooks-Gunn, 1997; Baydar, Hyle, & Brooks-Gunn, 1997).

How Siblings Interact

Young children usually become attached to their older brothers and sisters. Although rivalry is often present, so is affection. The more securely attached siblings are to their parents, the better they get along with each other (Teti & Ablard, 1989).

Nevertheless, as babies begin to move around and become more assertive, they inevitably come into conflict with siblings. Sibling conflict increases dramatically after the younger child reaches 18 months of age (Vandell & Bailey, 1992). During the next few months, younger siblings begin to participate more fully in family interactions and become more involved in family disputes. As they do, they become more aware of others' intentions and feelings. They are beginning to recognize what kind of behaviour will upset or annoy an older brother or sister and what behaviour is considered "naughty" or "good" (Dunn & Munn, 1985).

As this cognitive and social understanding grows, sibling conflict tends to become more constructive, and the younger sibling participates in attempts to reconcile. Constructive conflict helps children recognize each other's needs, wishes, and point of view, and it helps them learn how to fight, disagree, and compromise within a safe, stable relationship (Vandell & Bailey, 1992).

Parents walk a fine line in deciding when and how to intervene in children's quarrels. In constructive conflicts, it is usually best for parents to let children work

Babies and toddlers become closely attached to their older brothers and sisters, especially when, as with these Chinese children, the older siblings assume a large measure of care for the younger ones.

things out on their own. However, when anger is intense or someone is being victimized or abused, action is called for. Parents can often defuse the conflict by calmly acknowledging each child's feelings and point of view, describing the problem, and then leaving the room so the children can resolve it. To reduce the frequency of sibling struggles, parents should avoid comparing their children, show pride in each child's achievements, and spend time alone with each (Vandell & Bailey, 1992).

Sociability with Non-siblings

Although the family is the centre of a baby's social world, infants and—even more so—toddlers show interest in people outside the home, particularly people their own size. During the first few months, they show interest in other babies by looking, smiling, and cooing (T. M. Field, 1978). During the last half of the first year, they increasingly smile at, touch, and babble to another baby, especially when they are not distracted by the presence of adults or toys (Hay, Pedersen, & Nash, 1982).

At about 1 year, when the biggest items on their agenda are learning to walk and to manipulate objects, babies pay more attention to toys and less to other people (T. M. Field & Roopnarine, 1982). This stage does not last long, though; from about 1½ years of age to almost 3, they show more interest in what other children do and increasing understanding of how to deal with them. This insight seems to accompany awareness of themselves as separate individuals. A 10-month-old who holds out a toy to another baby pays no attention to whether the other's back is turned, but an 18-month-old knows when the offer has the best chance of being accepted and how to respond to another child's overtures (Eckerman, Davis, & Didow, 1989; Eckerman & Stein, 1982).

Toddlers learn by imitating one another. Games such as follow-the-leader help toddlers connect with other children and pave the way for more complex games during the preschool years (Eckerman et al., 1989). Imitation of each other's actions leads to more frequent verbal communication (such as "You go in playhouse," "Don't do it!" or "Look at me") which helps peers coordinate joint activity (Eckerman & Didow, 1996).

As with siblings, conflict, too, can have a purpose: helping children learn how to negotiate and resolve disputes. In one study, groups of three toddlers who had not known one another before were observed playing with toys. Two-year-olds got into more conflicts than 1-year-olds but also resolved them more often—for example, by sharing toys when there were not enough to go around (Caplan, Vespo, Pedersen, & Hay, 1991).

Some children, of course, are more sociable than others, reflecting such temperamental traits as their usual mood, readiness to accept new people, and ability to adapt to change. Sociability is also influenced by experience; babies who spend time with other babies, as in child care, become sociable earlier than those who spend all their time at home alone. They also engage in increasingly complex play with peers. However, this depends on the quality of caregiving and the security of the child's attachment (Howes, 1997).

Children of Working Parents

Over the last two decades, the rate of maternal employment has increased by over 40 per cent, with most of the increase occurring during the 1980s, and continuing into the 1990s. In 1999, almost 80 per cent of mothers with school-aged children, 72 per cent of mothers with children aged 3 to 5 years, and 65 per cent of women with children younger than 3 years of age were employed (Canadian Council on Social Development, 2001). This change, coupled with an increase in the percentage of Canadian children living with lone parents has increased the demand for child care (Connor & Brink, 1999). Early non-parental child care is now a way of life for most Canadian families, and its impact is the subject of much debate, particularly for government policy-making. In Canada, there is significant government support offered to families for maternal and parental leave, as well as licensing of and financial support for non-parental care (Symons & Carr, 1995). In response to concerns about the importance of parental involvement in child care in the first year, the Canadian government instituted a new Employment Insurance policy, which began in January 2001. The policy grants up to 1 year of

Checkpoint ✔

Can you . . .

✔ Discuss factors affecting adjustment to a new baby?

✔ Describe changes in sibling interaction and sibling conflict during toddlerhood?

✔ Trace changes in sociability during the first 3 years, and state two influences on it?

Guidepost 9

How do parental employment and early child care affect infants' and toddlers' development?

financial support to new parents to stay at home, to be shared between the mother and the father. In addition, Quebec offers substantial support to offset the cost of licensed daycare for children (Canadian Council on Social Development, 2001).

Effects of Parental Employment

What are the short-term and long-term consequences of a mother's going to work during the first 3 years of her child's life? Hardly any, according to recent research.

The National Longitudinal Survey of Children and Youth (NLSCY) showed no relationship between non-parental care and likelihood of learning difficulties in Canadian children. A weak positive relationship was found between number of weeks in the labour force and children's vocabulary: Mothers who were more committed to their careers tended to spend as much time reading to their children, and the combination of the educational benefits of being read to by the parent and being in a higher-income family was related to improved vocabulary in children (Lefebvre & Merigan, 1998). In fact, a Nova Scotia study found that children whose mothers returned to work 6 months after birth were more securely attached than children whose mothers did not work in the first 2 years after birth (Symons, 1998). In addition, the Canadian Transition to Child Care Study found that children of employed mothers who preferred to work and who showed higher levels of sensitivity tended to be more securely attached than children whose mothers preferred to stay at home and who were less sensitive. However, the provision of high quality out-of-home child care tended to reduce the negative outcomes of reduced maternal sensitivity (McKim, Cramer, Stuart, & O'Connor, 1999).

However, a mother's *feelings* about her work situation may make a difference. In a study of 55 white, educated, married mothers of 4- to 6-month-olds, feelings of conflict about going to work (or staying home) reduced mothers' ability to discriminate among different types of cries—an indication of lessened sensitivity and responsiveness to a baby's signals (Donovan et al., 1998).

How does a mother's employment affect the father's relationship with the baby? In an 8-month study of 63 predominantly white, middle-class, employed fathers, the child's tendency to distress and the father's marital satisfaction and involvement in caregiving were more important predictors of men's responsiveness to their infants than whether or not the mother worked outside the home (Grych & Clark, 1999).

In a longitudinal study of 17 infants raised primarily by fathers, the men developed growing confidence in their caregiving skills and responsiveness to the babies' needs. Standardized tests showed the children's emotional, social, and cognitive development to be strong in infancy and beyond. As infants, their social skills were relatively advanced, and they seemed unusually curious and open to stimulation from adults other than their parents (Pruett, 1998).

The Impact of Early Child Care

One way parents' working affects children is through substitute child care. When we look for effects of early child care, we need to consider variations in type, quality, amount, and stability of care, as well as the age at which children start receiving it.

In 1996–97, almost 2 million Canadian children younger than 12 years received non-parental child care, exclusive of kindergarten and school. About 25 per cent of infants, 46 per cent of children between 1 and 5 years, and 44 per cent of children aged 6 to 11 years were involved in regular non-parental child care. Most preschoolers (55 per cent) aged 1 to 5 years were cared for in a home other than their own, 25 per cent received care in their own home, and almost 20 per cent attended a child-care centre. Relatives took care of 24 per cent of children between 0 and 5 years of age (Johnson, Lero, & Rooney, 2001). In home settings, where most Canadian babies stay during the first year of life, quality of care is related to family income; the higher the income, the better the care.

These children in a high-quality group daycare program are likely to do at least as well cognitively and socially as children cared for full time at home. The most important element of infant daycare is the caregiver or teacher, who exerts a strong influence on the children in her care.

Table 8-5	Checklist for Choosing a Good Child-Care Facility

- Is the facility licensed? Does it meet minimum provincial standards for health, fire, and safety? (Many centres and home-care facilities are not licensed or regulated.)
- Is the facility clean and safe? Does it have adequate indoor and outdoor space?
- Does the facility have small groups, a high adult-to-child ratio, and a stable, competent, highly involved staff?
- Are caregivers trained in child development?
- Are caregivers warm, affectionate, accepting, responsive, and sensitive? Are they authoritative but not too restrictive, and neither too controlling nor merely custodial?
- Does the program promote good health habits?
- Does it provide a balance between structured activities and free play? Are activities age-appropriate?
- Do the children have access to educational toys and materials, which stimulate mastery of cognitive and communicative skills at a child's own pace?
- Does the program nurture self-confidence, curiosity, creativity, and self-discipline?
- Does it encourage children to ask questions, solve problems, express feelings and opinions, and make decisions?
- Does it foster self-esteem, respect for others, and social skills?
- Does it help parents improve their child-rearing skills?
- Does it promote cooperation with public and private schools and the community?

Sources: American Academy of Pediatrics [AAP], 1986; Belsky, 1984; K. A. Clarke-Stewart, 1987; NICHD Early Child Care Research Network, 1996; Norris, Brink, and Mosher, 1999; S. W. Olds, 1989; Scarr, 1998.

Despite the high demand for quality child care in Canada, child-care arrangements do not always meet the needs of Canadian families (Health Canada, 1999). In 1994, 34 per cent of children under 12 years were cared for by individuals other than relatives in unregulated child-care arrangements. About 42 per cent of regulated daycare spaces were subsidized for low-income families (Health Canada, 1999). These subsidies have been reduced in many provinces, with some provincial governments lowering standards for child-care centres, and cutting back on monitoring and enforcement of regulations (Health Canada, 1999). These trends indicate that parents need to be particularly careful in choosing daycare facilities for their children. Table 8-5 lists guidelines for judging quality of care.

The most important element in the quality of care is the caregiver; stimulating interactions with responsive adults are crucial to early cognitive, linguistic, and psychosocial development (Burchinal, Roberts, Nabors, & Bryant, 1996). Low staff turnover is critical; infants need consistent caregiving in order to develop trust and secure attachments. In one longitudinal study, 4-year-olds who had formed secure attachments to child-care providers tended to be more sociable, sensitive, empathic, and better liked than those who were insecurely attached (Howes, Matheson, & Hamilton, 1994).

Data from the NLSCY show that stability of child-care arrangements seems to have an impact on healthy development. Infants and toddlers who experience changes in child-care arrangements (representing about 23 per cent of children in the survey who were in non-parental child care) were more likely to be described by their mothers as having poorer mental health and more difficult temperaments than those who did not experience change. As children enter preschool age, those who experience change in child-care arrangements are more likely to have lower vocabulary scores than those who did not experience change. By school age, children who experience child-care change were more likely to have behavioural problems than those who did not experience change (Kohen, Hertzman, & Wiens, 1998). In addition, children from low-income families who experience non-parental daycare outside of the home are more likely to score higher on measures of vocabulary than children from low-income families who are cared for at home (Connor & Brink, 1999).

A study of the impact of quality of daycare carried out in Montreal showed that any potential negative effects related to early age of entry into daycare can be offset by the beneficial effects of quality daycare conditions. Long stays at low-quality daycare centres

Table 8-6	Aspects of Development Affected by Characteristics of Early Child Care[*]					
	Attachment	Parent–Child Relationships	Cooperation	Problem Behaviours	Cognitive Development and School Readiness	Language Development
Quality	•	•		−	+	+
Amount	•	•		•		
Type			•	•	+	+
Stability	•					

*Results after taking into account all family and child variables.

Source: Peth-Pierce, 1998, summary table of findings, p. 15.

+ Consistent effects

• Effects under some conditions

increased the likelihood that children showed anger and defiance in group situations, whereas attendance at high-quality daycare facilities was associated with high levels of interest and positive interactions in groups (Hausfather, Toharia, LaRoche, & Engelsmann, 1997).

A U.S. study conducted by the National Institute of Child Health and Human Development (NICHD) also showed that the quantity and quality of care children receive, as well as the type and stability of care, influence specific aspects of development (Peth-Pierce, 1998; see Table 8-6).

Sometimes family and child-care characteristics work together. For example, the U.S. study found that child care itself has no direct effect on attachment (as measured at 15 months by the Strange Situation), no matter how early infants enter care or how many hours they spend in it. Nor do the stability or quality of care matter, in themselves. However, when unstable, poor quality, or more-than-minimal amounts of child care (10 or more hours a week) are added to the impact of insensitive, unresponsive parenting, insecure attachment is more likely. On the other hand, high-quality care may help to offset insensitive parenting (NICHD Early Child Care Research Network, 1997a).

Quality of care contributes to cognitive and psychosocial development. Children in child-care centres with low child–staff ratios, small group sizes, and trained, sensitive, responsive caregivers who provide positive interactions and language stimulation score higher on tests of language comprehension, cognition, and readiness for school; and their mothers report fewer behaviour problems (NICHD Early Child Care Research Network, 1997c, 1999a, 2000). In Canada family income, the home environment, and the amount of mental stimulation the parent provides are even more influential (Lefebvre & Merrigan, 1998; Ryan & Adams, 1998).

It should not be surprising that what on the surface appear to be effects of child care often may be effects of family characteristics. After all, stable families with high incomes and educational backgrounds and favourable home environments are more likely to place their children in high-quality care. It will be illuminating to follow the long-term progress of the NLSCY sample; in some earlier longitudinal studies, apparent early effects of child care faded out during the school years, while family characteristics continued to be important (Lefebvre & Merrigan, 1998; Ryan & Adams, 1998; Scarr, 1997b).

Even if child care may have little long-term effect on most children, those from low-income families or stressful homes do seem to benefit from care that supplies emotional support and cognitive stimulation, which may otherwise be lacking in their lives (Scarr, 1997b). Disadvantaged children in good child-care programs tend not to show the declines in IQ often seen when such children reach school age, and they may be more motivated to learn (AAP, 1986; Belsky, 1984; Bronfenbrenner, Belsky, & Steinberg, 1977; McCain & Mustard, 1999).

However infants and toddlers are cared for, the experiences of the first 3 years lay the foundation for future development. In Part 4, we'll see how young children build on that foundation.

Checkpoint ✔

Can you . . .

✔ List at least five criteria for good child care?

✔ Compare the impact of child care and of family characteristics on emotional, social, and cognitive development?

What's your view ?

• In the light of findings about effects of early child care, what advice would you give a new mother about the timing of her return to work and the selection of child care?

Summary and Key Terms

Foundations of Psychosocial Development

Guidepost 1 When and how do emotions develop, and how do babies show them?

- The development and expression of emotions seem to be tied to brain maturation and cognitive development.
- Crying, smiling, and laughing are early signs of emotion. Other indices include facial expressions, motor activity, body language, and physiological changes.
- The repertoire of basic emotions seems to be universal, but there are cultural variations in their expression.
- Complex emotions seem to develop from earlier, simpler ones. Self-conscious and evaluative emotions arise after the development of self-awareness.
- Separate but interacting regions of the brain may be responsible for various emotional states.

emotions (179)   self-awareness (182)

Guidepost 2 How do infants show temperamental differences, and how enduring are those differences?

- Many children seem to fall into three categories of temperament: "easy," "difficult," and "slow-to-warm-up." Temperamental patterns appear to be largely inborn and to have a biological basis. They are generally stable but can be modified by experience.
- Goodness of fit between a child's temperament and environmental demands aids adjustment.
- Cross-cultural differences in temperament may reflect child-raising practices.

temperament (183)   "easy" children (184)
"difficult" children (184)   "slow-to-warm-up" children (184)
goodness of fit (184)

Guidepost 3 What roles do mothers and fathers play in early personality development?

- Child-raising practices and caregiving roles vary around the world.
- Infants have strong needs for maternal closeness and warmth as well as physical care.
- In most cultures, mothers provide more infant care than fathers. Mothers and fathers in some cultures have different styles of play with babies.
- Although significant gender differences typically do not appear until after infancy, parents begin gender-typing boys and girls almost from birth.
- Distance or divorce may diminish the connection with grandparents; but many grandparents are heavily involved in grandchildren's lives.

gender (189)   gender-typing (190)

Developmental Issues in Infancy

Guidepost 4 How do infants gain trust in their world and form attachments?

- According to Erikson, infants in the first 18 months experience the first crisis in personality development, basic trust versus basic mistrust. Sensitive, responsive, consistent caregiving is the key to successful resolution of this crisis.
- Research based on the Strange Situation has found four patterns of attachment: secure, avoidant, ambivalent (resistant), and disorganized-disoriented.
- Newer instruments measure attachment in natural settings and in cross-cultural research.
- Attachment patterns may depend on a baby's temperament, as well as on the quality of parenting, and may have long-term implications for development. A parent's memories of childhood attachment can influence his or her own child's attachment.
- Separation anxiety and stranger anxiety may arise during the second half of the first year and appear to be related to temperament and circumstances.

basic trust versus basic mistrust (191)   attachment (192)
Strange Situation (192)   secure attachment (192)
avoidant attachment (192)
ambivalent (resistant) attachment (192)
disorganized-disoriented attachment (192)
stranger anxiety (195)   separation anxiety (195)

Guidepost 5 How do infants and caregivers "read" each other's non-verbal signals?

- Mutual regulation enables babies to play an active part in regulating their emotional states.
- A mother's depression, especially if severe or chronic, may have serious consequences for her infant's development.
- The belief that babies, after about 6 months of age, display social referencing is in dispute.

mutual regulation (196)   "still-face" paradigm (197)
social referencing (198)

Developmental Issues in Toddlerhood

Guidepost 6 When does the sense of self arise, and what are three steps in its development?

- The self-concept begins to emerge in the following sequence, beginning at about 18 months: (1) physical self-recognition and self-awareness, (2) self-description and self-evaluation, and (3) emotional response to wrongdoing.

self-concept (199)

Guidepost 7 How do toddlers develop autonomy and standards for socially acceptable behaviour?

- Erikson's second crisis concerns autonomy versus shame and doubt. Negativism is a normal manifestation of the shift from external control to self-control.

- Socialization, which rests on internalization of societally approved standards, begins with the development of self-regulation.

- A precursor of conscience is committed compliance with a caregiver's demands; toddlers who show committed compliance tend to internalize adult rules more readily than those who show situational compliance.

- Parenting practices, a child's temperament, the quality of the parent–child relationship, and cultural and class standards may be factors in the ease and success of socialization.

  **autonomy versus shame and doubt (200)   socialization (200)
  internalization (200)   self-regulation (200)   conscience (201)
  committed compliance (202)   situational compliance (202)
  reciprocity (202)**

Contact with Other Children

Guidepost 8 How do infants and toddlers interact with siblings and other children?

- Siblings influence each other from an early age. Parents' actions and attitudes affect sibling relationships.

- Contact with other children, especially during toddlerhood, affects cognitive and psychosocial development. Sociability increases with contact.

Children of Working Parents

Guidepost 9 How do parental employment and early child care affect infants' and toddlers' development?

- Mothers' workforce participation during a child's first 3 years seems to have little impact on development.

- Substitute child care varies widely in type and quality. The most important element in quality of care is the caregiver.

- Although quality, quantity, stability, and type of care have some influence on psychosocial and cognitive development, the influence of family characteristics seems greater.

- Low-income children, especially, benefit from good child care.

OLC Preview

The official website for *A Child's World,* First Canadian Edition, offers additional information and links to recommended sites on topics such as temperamental traits, varieties of fatherhood, and the influence of fathers on their children's development. Check out **www.mcgrawhill.ca/college/papalia.**

chapter

9

Physical Development and Health in Early Childhood

Children's playings are not sports and should be deemed as their most serious actions.

—Michel de Montaigne, *Essays*, 1575

Focus *Wang Yani, Self-taught Artist**

Wang Yani

Wang Yani (b. 1975) is a gifted young Chinese artist. Now in her 20s, she had her first exhibit in Shanghai at the age of 4 and produced four thousand paintings by the time she turned 6. Since she was 10 her work has been shown throughout Asia and in Europe and the United States.

Yani (her given name)** began painting at 2½. Her father, Wang Shiqiang, was a professional artist and educator. Her father gave her big brushes and large sheets of paper to permit bold strokes. Rather than teach her, he let her learn by doing, in her own way, and always praised her work. In contrast with traditional Chinese art education, which emphasizes conformity and imitation, he allowed his daughter's imagination free rein.

Yani went through the usual stages in preschoolers' drawing, but far more quickly than usual. Her early paintings after the scribble stage were made up of dots, circles, and apparently meaningless lines, which stood for people, birds, or fruit. By the age of 3, she painted recognizable but highly original forms.

Yani's father encouraged her to paint what she saw outdoors near their home in the scenic riverside town of Gongcheng. Like traditional Chinese artists, she did not paint from life but constructed her brightly coloured compositions from mental images of what she had seen. Her visual memory has been called astounding. When she was only 4, her father taught her Chinese characters (letters) of as many as 25 strokes by "writing" them in the air with his finger. Yani immediately put them down on paper.

Her father helped develop her powers of observation and imagery by carrying her on his shoulders as he hiked in the fields and mountains or lying with her in the grass and telling stories about the passing clouds. The pebbles along the riverbank reminded her of the monkeys at the zoo, which she painted over and over between the ages of 3 and 6. Yani made up stories about the monkeys she portrayed. They often represented Yani herself—eating a snack, refereeing an argument among friends, or trying to conquer her fear of her first shot at the doctor's office. Painting, to Yani, was not an objective representation of reality; it was a mirror of her mind, a way to transform her sensory impressions into simple but powerful semi-abstract images onto which she projected her thoughts, feelings, and dreams.

Because of her short arms, Yani's brush strokes at first were short. Her father trained her to hold her brush tightly, by trying to grab it from behind when she was not looking. She learned to paint with her whole arm, twisting her wrist to produce the effect she wanted. As her physical dexterity and experience grew, her strokes became more forceful, varied, and precise: broad, wet strokes to define an animal's shape; fuzzy, nearly dry ones to suggest feathers, fur,

---

*Sources of biographical information about Wang Yani were Bond (1989), Costello (1990), Ho (1989), Stuart (1991), and Zhensun & Low (1991).

**In Chinese custom, the given name follows the family name.

or tree bark. The materials she used—bamboo brushes, ink sticks, and rice paper—were traditional, but her style—popularly called *xieyi,* "idea writing"—was not. It was, and remains, playful, free, and spontaneous.

With quick reflexes, a fertile imagination, remarkable visual abilities, strong motivation, and her father's sensitive guidance, Yani's artistic progress has been swift. As a young adult, she is considered an artist of great promise. Yet she herself finds painting very simple: "You just paint what you think about. You don't have to follow any instruction. Everybody can paint" (Zhensun & Low, 1991, p. 9).

• • •

Although Wang Yani's artistic growth has been unusual, it rested on typical developments of early childhood: rapid improvement in muscular control and eye–hand coordination. Youngsters in this age group grow more slowly than before, but still at a fast pace; and they make so much progress in muscle development and coordination that they can do much more. Like other children, Yani's gain in fine motor skills was accompanied by a growing cognitive understanding of the world around her—an understanding guided by her powers of observation and memory and her interactions with her father. Together these physical, cognitive, and social influences helped her express her thoughts and emotions through art.

In this chapter, as we look at physical development during the years from 3 to 6, we will see other examples of its interconnection with cognitive and psychosocial development. Nutrition and handedness are influenced by cultural attitudes, and sleep patterns by emotional experiences. Environmental influences, including the parents' life circumstances, affect health and safety. The link between developmental realms is especially evident in the tragic results of child abuse and neglect, poverty, and homelessness; although the most obvious effects may be physical, these conditions affect other aspects of a child's development as well.

After you have read and studied this chapter, you should be able to answer each of the Guidepost questions that appear at the top of the next page. Look for them again in the margins, where they point to important concepts throughout the chapter. To check your understanding of these Guideposts, review the end-of-chapter summary. Checkpoints located throughout the chapter will help you verify your understanding of what you have read.

Guideposts for Study

1. How do children's bodies change between ages 3 and 6, and what are their nutritional and dental needs?

2. What sleep patterns and problems tend to develop during early childhood?

3. What are the main motor achievements of early childhood, and how does children's artwork show their physical and cognitive maturation?

4. What are the major health and safety risks for children?

5. What are the causes and consequences of child abuse and neglect, and what can be done about it?

Aspects of Physiological Development

Guidepost 1

How do children's bodies change between ages 3 and 6, and what are their nutritional and dental needs?

In early childhood, children slim down and shoot up. They need less sleep than before and are more likely to develop sleep problems. They improve in running, hopping, skipping, jumping, and throwing balls. They also become better at tying shoelaces (in bows instead of knots), drawing with crayons (on paper rather than on walls), and pouring cereal (into the bowl, not onto the floor); and they begin to show a preference for either the right or left hand.

Bodily Growth and Change

At about age 3, children begin to take on the slender, athletic appearance of childhood. As abdominal muscles develop, the toddler potbelly tightens. The trunk, arms, and legs grow longer. The head is still relatively large, but the other parts of the body continue to catch up as body proportions steadily become more adult-like.

The pencil mark on the wall that shows Eve's height at 3 years is 95 cm from the floor, and she now weighs about 13 kg. Her twin brother Isaac, like most boys this age, is a little taller and heavier and has more muscle per kilogram of body weight, whereas Eve, like most girls, has more fatty tissue. Both boys and girls typically grow 5 to 8 cm a year during early childhood and gain 2 to 3 kg annually (see Figure 9-1). Boys' slight edge in height and weight continues until the growth spurt of puberty.

These changes in appearance reflect developments inside the body. Muscular and skeletal growth progresses, making children stronger. Cartilage turns to bone at a faster rate than before, and bones become harder, giving the child a firmer shape and protecting the internal organs. These changes, coordinated by the maturing brain and nervous system, promote the development of a wide range of motor skills. The increased capacities of the respiratory and circulatory systems build physical stamina and, along with the developing immune system, keep children healthier.

As in infancy and toddlerhood, proper growth and health depend on good nutrition and adequate sleep (see Box 9-1). However, preschoolers' dietary and sleep needs are quite different from those of infants or toddlers. They are more likely to become overweight, especially if they are not very active, and many develop sleep-related problems.

Nutrition

Preschoolers eat less in proportion to their size than infants do; as growth slows, they need fewer calories per kilogram of body weight. Preschoolers who are allowed to eat when they are hungry and are not pressured to eat everything given to them are more likely to regulate their own caloric intake than are children fed on schedule (S. L. Johnson & Birch, 1994). In one study of self-regulated feeding, 15 children ages 2 to 5 took in roughly the same

Box 9-1 *Helping Children Eat and Sleep Well*

One child refuses to eat anything but peanut butter and jelly sandwiches. Another seems to live on bananas. Mealtimes seem more like art class, as preschoolers make snowmen out of mashed potatoes or lakes out of applesauce, and food remains uneaten on the plate.

Although a diminished appetite in early childhood is normal, many parents make the mistake of insisting that children eat more than they want, setting in motion a contest of wills. Bedtime, too, often becomes an issue ("Daddy, leave the light on! … I want a drink of water … What's that noise by the window? … I'm cold"). When a child delays or has trouble going to sleep or wakes often during the night, parents tend to become irritated, and the entire family feels the strain.

The following research-based suggestions can help make mealtimes and bedtimes pleasanter and children healthier (American Academy of Child and Adolescent Psychiatry [AACAP], 1997; American Academy of Pediatrics [AAP], 1992b; Adams & Rickert, 1989; Canadian Paediatric Society [CPS], 1999; Graziano & Mooney, 1982; Rolls, Engell, & Birch, 2000; Williams & Caliendo, 1984):

Encouraging Healthy Eating Habits

- Keep a record of what a child eats. The child may in fact be eating enough.
- Serve simple, easily identifiable foods. Preschoolers often balk at mixed dishes like casseroles.
- Serve finger foods as often as possible.
- Introduce only one new food at a time, along with a familiar one the child likes.
- Offer small servings, especially of new or disliked foods; give second helpings if wanted.
- Don't pressure the child to clean the plate.
- After a reasonable time, remove the food and do not serve more until the next meal. A healthy child will not suffer from missing a meal, and children need to learn that certain times are appropriate for eating.
- Give the child a choice of foods containing similar nutrients: rye or whole wheat bread, a peach or an apple, yogourt or milk.
- Encourage a child to help prepare food by making sandwiches or mixing and spooning out cookie dough.
- Have nutritious snacks handy and allow the child to select favourites.
- Turn childish delights to advantage. Serve food in appealing dishes; dress it up with garnishes or little toys; make a "party" out of a meal.
- Don't fight "rituals," in which a child eats foods one at a time, in a certain order.
- Make mealtimes pleasant with conversation on interesting topics, keeping talk about eating itself to a minimum.
- Serve healthy, well-balanced meals offering a wide variety of tastes and textures that children find enjoyable. Prepare foods in a variety of ways.
- Use nutritional information and Canada's Food Guide to Healthy Eating (see Figure 9-2) to help in introducing new foods and working out average amounts.

- Encourage an interest in food by having older children help with shopping.
- Never use food as a reward or punishment.

Helping Children Go to Sleep

- Establish a regular, unrushed bedtime routine—about 20 minutes of quiet activities, such as reading a story, singing lullabies, or having quiet conversation.
- Allow no scary or loud television shows.
- Avoid highly stimulating, active play before bedtime.
- Keep a small night light on if it makes the child feel more comfortable.
- Don't feed or rock a child at bedtime.
- Stay calm but don't yield to requests for "just one more" story, one more drink of water, or one more bathroom trip.
- If you're trying to break a child's habit, offer rewards for good bedtime behaviour, such as stickers on a chart, or simple praise.
- Try putting your child to sleep a little later. Sending a child to bed too early is a common reason for sleep problems.
- If a child's fears about the dark or going to sleep have persisted for a long time, look for a program to help the child learn how to relax, how to substitute pleasant thoughts for frightening ones, and how to cope with stressful situations.

Helping Children Go Back to Sleep

- If a child gets up during the night, take him or her back to bed. Speak calmly, pat the child gently on the back, but be pleasantly firm and consistent.
- After a nightmare, reassure a frightened child and occasionally check in on the child. If frightening dreams persist for more than 6 weeks, consult your doctor.
- After night terrors, do not wake the child. If the child wakes, don't ask any questions. Just let the child go back to sleep.
- Help your child get enough sleep on a regular schedule; overtired or stressed children are more prone to night terrors.
- Walk or carry a sleepwalking child back to bed. Child-proof your home with gates at the top of stairs and at windows and with bells on the child's bedroom door, so you'll know when she or he is out of bed.

What's your view?

Have you ever tried to get a young child to eat properly or go to sleep at bedtime? If so, did you find any of the tactics suggested in this box helpful?

Check it out!

For more information on this topic, go to **www.mcgrawhill.ca/college/papalia** for a link to a parent resource with many useful articles by experts in pediatric sleep disorders and nutrition. Select a topic from the list, search for articles using keywords, or choose one of the experts listed at the website.

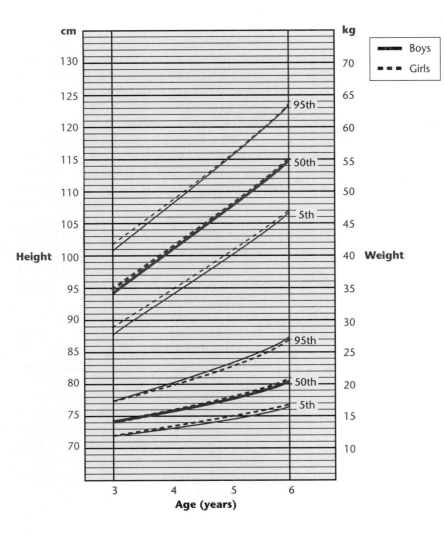

Figure 9-1

Boys' and girls' physical growth in height and weight during early childhood. Note: Curves shown are for the 50th percentile for each sex, with additional curves for 95th and 5th percentiles.

Source: National Center for Health Statistics, 2000a; 2000b

number of calories every day for 6 days, even though they often ate very little at one meal and a great deal at another (Birch, Johnson, Andersen, Peters, & Schulte, 1991).

What children eat is a different matter. According to the Canadian Paediatric Society, a quarter of Canadian children are obese, and the major contributing factors are poor diet and lack of exercise (Healthy Active Living Committee, Canadian Paediatric Society, 2002). Young people of all ages eat too much fat and sugar and too few servings of fruits, vegetables, grains, and dairy products. Diets of poor and minority children are especially deficient (Muñoz, Krebs-Smith, Ballard-Barbash, & Cleveland, 1997). Another potential consequence of a poor diet is iron deficiency and iron-deficiency anemia, which affects over 10 per cent of children 18 months of age (Nutrition Committee, Canadian Paediatric Society, 1991). To prevent iron deficiency in infants and young children, the Canadian Paediatric Society recommends iron-fortified cereals, formula, and other iron-rich foods for infants after 6 months of age.

To avoid excessive weight and prevent cardiac problems, young children should get only about 30 per cent of their total calories from fat, and less than 10 per cent of the total from saturated fat. Canadian children's diets include about 35 per cent intake from fat, and 13 per cent saturated fat (Gibson, MacDonald, & Smit Vanderkooy, 1993). However, current trends in children's dietary habits indicate that their fat consumption is decreasing to the recommended levels (CPS, 2001). Lean meat and dairy foods should remain in the diet to provide protein, iron, and calcium. Milk and other dairy products can now be skim or low-fat (AAP Committee on Nutrition, 1992a). Studies have found no negative effects on height, weight, body mass, or neurological development from a moderately low-fat diet (Rask-Nissilä et al., 2000; Shea et al., 1993).

What's your view ?

- Much television advertising aimed at young children fosters poor nutrition by promoting fats and sugars rather than proteins and vitamins. How might parents counteract these pressures?

CANADA'S

Food Guide

TO HEALTHY EATING
FOR PEOPLE FOUR YEARS
AND OVER

Enjoy a variety
of foods from each
group every day.

Choose lower-
fat foods
more often.

Grain Products
Choose whole grain
and enriched
products more often.

Vegetables and Fruit
Choose dark green and
orange vegetables and
orange fruit more often.

Milk Products
Choose lower-fat milk
products more often.

Meat and Alternatives
Choose leaner meats,
poultry and fish, as well
as dried peas, beans,
and lentils more often.

Figure 9-2

Canada's Food Guide to Healthy Eating, Health Canada.

Obesity today is more common among preschoolers (especially girls, who tend to be less active than boys) than 20 years ago. Between 1981 and 1996, the prevalence of childhood obesity in Canada tripled (Tremblay & Willms, 2000).

Overweight children, especially those who have overweight parents, tend to become overweight adults (CPS, 2002; Whitaker, et al., 1997), and excess body mass can be a threat to health. A tendency to obesity is partly hereditary, but it also depends on fat intake and exercise (Jackson et al., 1997; Klesges, Klesges, Eck, & Shelton, 1995; Leibel, 1997; Ogden et al., 1997). Early to middle childhood is a good time to treat obesity, when a child's diet is still subject to parental influence or control (Whitaker et al., 1997).

At the other extreme, food-bank use in Canada is on the increase. Forty per cent of food-bank users in Canada are children under 18 years of age, yet they make up only a quarter of the population (Wilson & Steinman, 2000; Wilson & Tsoa, 2001; see Box 9-2).

As children move through the preschool period, their eating patterns become environmentally influenced, like those of adults. Whereas 3-year-olds will eat only until they are full, 5-year-olds tend to eat more when a larger portion is put in front of them. Thus a key to preventing obesity may be to make sure older preschoolers are served appropriate portions—and not to admonish them to clean their plates (Rolls et al., 2000). Over 75 per cent of Canadian children in Grade 6 report eating fruit and vegetables daily, although this falls to 70 per cent by the time they reach Grade 10 (King, Boyce, & King, 1999). When it comes to less nutritious and fatty foods like french fries, hamburgers, and potato chips, which can be harmful to physical development and contribute to becoming overweight, more Grade 6 boys than girls report eating such food daily (ranging from 10 per cent eating hamburgers daily, to 22 per cent eating french fries daily). Just over half the number of girls as boys report eating less nutritious foods. People in remote northern communities, particularly Aboriginal people, who are serviced by food mail, are at risk of health problems related to inadequate nutrition, including obesity, respiratory illness, and non–insulin dependent diabetes. The diet in remote communities often consists of convenience foods that are less nutritious than fresh fruit and vegetables that are readily available in less remote centres (CICH, 2000). Obesity is discussed further in chapters 12 and 15.

To help parents to maintain healthy diets for their children, Health Canada has developed a food guide that lists recommended types and quantities of food for children (Figure 9-2).

Oral Health

By age 3, all the primary, or deciduous, teeth are in place. The permanent teeth, which will begin to appear at about age 6, are developing.

Use of fluoride and improved dental care have dramatically reduced the incidence of tooth decay since the 1970s (Brown, Wall, & Lazar, 2000). The Canadian Paediatric Society recommends parents use fluoride supplements for children 6 months of age and older in areas that do not fluoridate the water supply, but also to limit the amount of toothpaste used in order to avoid fluorosis. Fluorosis results in pitting and brown staining of the teeth, particularly in the first 6 months (Nutrition Committee, Canadian Paediatric Society, 1996). Tooth decay in early childhood often stems from over-consumption of sweetened milk and juices in infancy, together with lack of regular dental care. A common source of early childhood tooth decay is going to bed with a bottle of milk, juice, or formula—a practice that the Canadian Dental Association recommends that parents avoid (Canadian Dental Association, 2002). The pain resulting from oral infection may contribute to slowed growth by interfering with normal eating and sleep. In one study of 300 three-year-olds, nearly 14 per cent of those with serious tooth decay weighed less than 80 per cent of their ideal weight. After a year and a half of dental rehabilitation, these children caught up in weight with a comparison group who had had relatively healthy teeth and normal weight (Acs, Shulman, Ng, & Chussid, 1999).

Parents can usually safely ignore the normal and common habit of thumb-sucking in children under 4 years of age. However, the permanent teeth, which begin to develop long before they appear at about age 6, may be affected if thumb-sucking does not stop after age 4. If children stop sucking thumbs or fingers by then, their teeth are not likely to be permanently affected (Herrmann & Roberts, 1987; Umberger & Van Reenen, 1995).

Sleep Patterns and Problems

Sleep patterns change throughout the growing-up years (see Figure 9-3), and early childhood has its own distinct rhythms. Young children usually sleep more deeply at night than they will later in life, but most Canadian children still need a daytime nap or quiet rest until about age 5.

Children in different cultures may get the same amount of sleep each day, but its timing may vary. In many traditional cultures, such as the Gusii of Kenya, the Javanese in Indonesia, and the Zuni in New Mexico, young children have no regular bedtime and are allowed to stay up watching adult activities until they are sleepy. Among the Canadian Hare-Chipewyan, 3-year-olds do not take naps but are put to sleep right after dinner and are allowed to sleep as long as they wish in the morning (Broude, 1995).

Young children may develop elaborate routines to put off retiring, and it may take them longer than before to fall asleep. Bedtime may bring on a form of separation anxiety, and the child may do all she or he can to avoid it. Regular, consistent sleep routines can help minimize this common problem. It is recommended that children past infancy not be put to sleep by feeding or rocking, as this may make it hard for them to fall asleep on their own (American Academy of Child and Adolescent Psychiatry (AACAP), 1997).

Children are likely to want a light left on and to sleep with a favourite toy or blanket (Beltramini & Hertzig, 1983). Such *transitional objects,* used repeatedly as bedtime companions, help a child shift from the dependence of infancy to the independence of later childhood. Parents sometimes worry if their child cannot fall asleep without a tattered blanket or stuffed animal, but such worry seems unfounded. In one longitudinal study, 11-year-olds who at age 4 had insisted on taking cuddly objects to bed were now outgoing, sociable with adults, and self-confident; they enjoyed playing by themselves and tended not to be worriers. At age 16, they were just as well adjusted as children who had not used transitional objects (Newson, Newson, & Mahalski, 1982).

Sleep Disturbances and Disorders

About 20 to 30 per cent of children in their first 4 years engage in *bedtime struggles* lasting more than an hour and wake their parents frequently at night. Five experiences tend to distinguish children with these problems. One is sleeping in the same bed with parents; it is simply more tempting and easier to wake someone in the same bed than in the next room. The other four conditions signal family stress. The family is likely to have experienced a stressful accident or illness; or the mother is likely to be depressed, to have mixed feelings about the child, or to have recently changed her schedule so as to be away for most of the day (Lozoff, Wolf, & Davis, 1985).

Checkpoint ✔

Can you . . .

✔ Describe typical physiological changes around the age of 3?

✔ Summarize preschoolers' dietary needs and explain why obesity and tooth decay can become concerns at this age?

✔ Discuss how and when thumb-sucking should be treated?

Guidepost 2

What sleep patterns and problems tend to develop during early childhood?

Figure 9-3

Typical sleep requirements in childhood. Unlike infants, who sleep about as long day and night, preschoolers get all or almost all their sleep in one long nighttime period. The number of hours of sleep steadily decreases throughout childhood, but individual children may need more or fewer hours than shown here.

Source: Ferber, 1985.

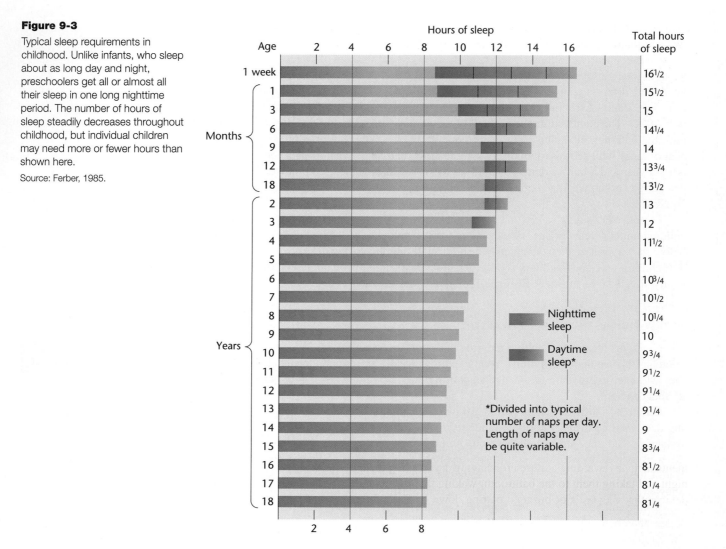

Walking and talking during sleep are fairly common in early childhood. Although sleep-walking itself is harmless, sleepwalkers may be in danger of hurting themselves (AACAP, 1997; Vgontzas & Kales, 1999). This and such other sleep disturbances as nightmares and sleep terrors, are caused by accidental activation of the brain's motor control system (Hobson & Silvestri, 1999). They are mostly occasional and usually outgrown. However, persistent sleep problems may indicate an emotional condition that needs to be examined.

A *nightmare* is a frightening dream, often brought on by staying up too late, eating a heavy meal close to bedtime, or overexcitement—for example, from watching an over-stimulating television program, seeing a terrifying movie, or hearing a frightening bedtime story (Vgontzas & Kales, 1999). Nightmares usually come toward morning and are often vividly recalled. They are quite common, especially among girls (AACAP, 1997); half of 3- to 6-year-olds experience them (Hobson & Silvestri, 1999). An occasional bad dream is no cause for alarm, but frequent or persistent nightmares, especially those that make a child fearful or anxious during waking hours, may signal excessive stress. A repeated theme may point to a specific problem the child cannot solve while awake.

A child who experiences a *sleep terror* awakens abruptly from a deep sleep in a state of panic. The child may scream and sit up in bed, breathing rapidly and staring. Yet he is not re-ally awake, quiets down quickly, and the next morning remembers nothing about the episode. Unlike nightmares, night terrors tend to occur within an hour after falling asleep. They typically begin between ages 4 and 12. Like sleepwalking, they are most common among boys and run in families (AACAP, 1997; Hobson & Silvestri, 1999). Night terrors alarm parents more than they do children and may simply be an effect of very deep sleep; they rarely signify a serious emotional problem and usually go away by age 6. While the first concern is to protect the child from injury, it is best not to interrupt sleepwalking or night terrors; interruptions may confuse and further frighten the child (Vgontzas & Kales, 1999).

Bedwetting

Most children stay dry, day and night, by 3 to 5 years of age; but **enuresis,** repeated urination in clothing or in bed, is common, especially at night. About 7 per cent of 5-year-old boys and 3 per cent of girls wet the bed regularly, while 5 per cent of boys and less than 1 per cent of girls wet nightly. Most outgrow the condition without special help (American Psychiatric Association [APA], 1994; Schmitt, 1997).

Children this age normally recognize the sensation of a full bladder while asleep and awaken to empty it in the toilet. Children who wet the bed do not have this awareness. Fewer than 1 per cent of bedwetters have a physical disorder, though they may have a small bladder capacity. Nor is persistent enuresis primarily an emotional, mental, or behavioural problem—though such problems can develop because of the way bedwetters are treated by playmates and family (National [U.S.] Enuresis Society, 1995; Schmitt, 1997).

Enuresis runs in families. About 75 per cent of bedwetters have a close relative who also wets the bed, and identical twins are more concordant for the condition than fraternal twins (APA, 1994; Fergusson, Horwood, & Shannon, 1986). The discovery of the approximate site of a gene linked to enuresis (Eiberg, 1995; Eiberg, Berendt, & Mohr, 1995) points to heredity as a major factor, possibly in combination with such other factors as slow motor maturation, allergies, and poor behavioural control (Goleman, 1995b). The gene does not appear to account for occasional bedwetting. Many children who wet the bed are lacking in an anti-diuretic hormone, which concentrates urine during sleep. As a result, they produce more urine than their bladders can hold (National [U.S.] Enuresis Society, 1995).

Children and their parents need to be reassured that enuresis is common and not serious. The child is not to blame and should not be punished. Generally parents need not do anything unless children themselves see bedwetting as a problem. The most effective treatments include rewarding children for staying dry; waking them periodically throughout the night and taking them to the bathroom; waking them when they begin to urinate by using devices that ring bells or buzzers; cutting down on fluids before bedtime; hypnosis; and teaching children to practise controlling the sphincter muscles and to stretch the bladder (Canadian Paediatric Society, 1997, 1999; National [U.S.] Enuresis Society, 1995; Rappaport, 1993). As a last resort, hormones or antidepressant drugs may be given for a short time, but moisture alarms have the best long-term cure rates and the lowest relapse rates (Canadian Paediatric Society, 1997; National [U.S.] Enuresis Society, 1995; Schmitt, 1997).

Motor Development

Children ages 3 to 6 make great advances in motor skills—both **gross motor skills,** which involve the large muscles, such as running and jumping (see Table 9-1), and **fine motor skills,** manipulative skills involving eye–hand and small-muscle coordination, such as buttoning and drawing. They also begin to show a preference for either the right or left hand.

Gross Motor Skills

At 3, David could walk a straight line and jump a short distance. At 4, he could hop a few steps on one foot. On his fifth birthday, he could jump nearly a metre and hop for 5 metres and was learning to roller skate.

Motor skills such as these do not develop in isolation. The skills that emerge in early childhood build on the achievements of infancy and toddlerhood. As children's bodies change, permitting them to do more, they integrate their new and previously acquired skills into *systems of action,* producing ever more complex capabilities.

In early childhood, development of the sensory and motor areas of the cortex permits better coordination between what children want to do and what they can do. Their bones and muscles are stronger, and their lung capacity is greater, making it possible to run, jump, and climb farther, faster, and better.

enuresis Repeated urination in clothing or in bed

Checkpoint ✔

Can you . . .

✔ Identify four common sleep problems and give recommendations for handling them?

Guidepost 3

What are the main motor achievements of early childhood, and how does children's artwork show their physical and cognitive maturation?

gross motor skills Physical skills that involve the large muscles

fine motor skills Physical skills that involve the small muscles and eye–hand coordination

Table 9-1	Gross Motor Skills in Early Childhood		
3-Year-Olds	**4-Year-Olds**	**5-Year-Olds**
Cannot turn or stop suddenly or quickly	Have more effective control of stopping, starting, and turning	Can start, turn, and stop effectively in games
Can jump a distance of 40 to to 60 cm	Can jump a distance of 60 to 80 cm	Can make a running jump of 70 to 90 cm
Can ascend a stairway unaided, alternating feet	Can descend a long stairway alternating feet, if supported	Can descend a long stairway unaided, alternating feet
Can hop, using largely an irregular series of jumps with some variations added	Can hop four to six steps on one foot	Can easily hop a distance of 5 m

Source: Corbin, 1973.

At about 2½, children begin to jump with both feet, a skill they have not been able to master before this time, probably because their leg muscles were not yet strong enough to propel their body weight upward. Hopping is hard to master until about 4 years of age.

Going upstairs is easier than going down; by 3½, most children comfortably alternate feet going up, but not until about 5 do they easily descend that way. Children begin to gallop at about 4, do fairly well by 5, and are quite skilful by 6½. Skipping is harder; although some 4-year-olds can skip, most children cannot do it until age 6 (Corbin, 1973). Of course, children vary in aptitude, depending on their genetic endowment and their opportunities to learn and practise motor skills.

The gross motor skills developed during early childhood are the basis for sports, dancing, and other activities that begin during middle childhood and may continue for a lifetime. There seems to be virtually no limit to the number and kind of motor acts children can learn, at least to some degree, by the age of 6. However, those under 6 are rarely ready to take part in any organized sport. Only 20 per cent of 4-year-olds can throw a ball well, and only 30 per cent can catch well (AAP Committee on Sports Medicine and Fitness, 1992).

Young children develop best physically when they can be active at an appropriate maturational level in unstructured free play. Parents and teachers can help by offering young children the opportunity to climb and jump on safe, properly sized equipment, by providing balls and other toys small enough to be easily grasped and soft enough not to be harmful, and by offering gentle coaching when a child seems to need help.

Fine Motor Skills and Artistic Development

Gains in *fine motor skills,* such as tying shoelaces and cutting with scissors, allow young children to take more responsibility for their personal care. At 3, Winnie can pour milk into her cereal bowl, eat with silverware, and use the toilet alone. She can also draw a circle and a rudimentary person—without arms. At 4, Nelson can dress himself with help. He can cut along a line, draw a fairly complete person, make designs and crude letters, and fold paper into a double triangle. At 5, Jean can dress himself without much help, copy a square or triangle, and draw a more elaborate person than before.

Most 3- to 5-year-olds may not be as accomplished artists as Wang Yani, but with progress in fine motor coordination, they too can use their growing cognitive powers and express themselves emotionally through art.

In pioneering research, Rhoda Kellogg (1970) examined more than 1 million drawings by children, half of them under age 6. Since she found drawings by young children similar in different cultures, she concluded that stages in early drawing (see Figure 9-4) reflect maturation of the brain as well as of the muscles.

Two-year-olds *scribble,* and their scribbles are not random. Kellogg identified 20 basic scribbles, such as vertical and zigzag lines, and 17 patterns of placement of scribbles on paper, which appear by age 2.

By age 3, the *shape* stage appears. Now a child draws diagrams in six basic shapes: circles, squares or rectangles, triangles, crosses, Xs, and odd forms. Next, children quickly

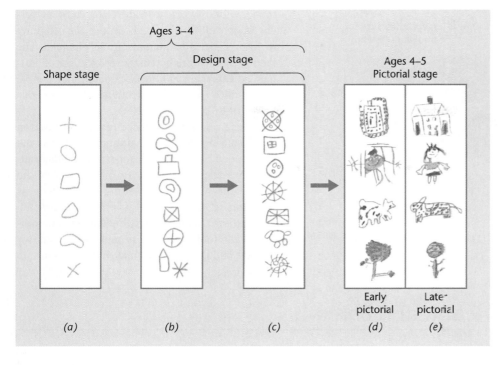

Figure 9-4

Artistic development in early childhood. There is a great difference between the very simple shapes shown in (a) and the detailed pictorial drawings in (e). The challenge for adults is to encourage children's creativity while acknowledging their growing facility in drawing.

Source: Kellogg, 1970.

Ages 3–4

Design stage

Shape stage

Ages 4–5
Pictorial stage

Early pictorial

Late pictorial

(a)   (b)   (c)   (d)   (e)

move on to the *design* stage, in which they combine two basic shapes into a more complex abstract pattern.

Most children enter the *pictorial* stage between ages 4 and 5, though Wang Yani reached it at 3. Early drawings at this stage suggest real-life objects or people; later drawings are better defined. Although most adults see the later drawings as a sign of progress, Kellogg views the switch from abstraction to representation as a fundamental change in the purpose of children's drawing—a move away from a concern with form and design, the primary elements of art—often under the "guidance" of adults who encourage children to portray reality (Kellogg, 1970).

Kellogg quotes artist Pablo Picasso: "Adults should not teach children to draw but should learn from them" (1970, p. 36). Like Wang Yani's father, adults can sustain children's early creativity by letting them draw what they like without imposing suggestions or standards.

Handedness

Handedness, the preference for using one hand over the other, is usually evident by 3 years of age. Since the left hemisphere of the brain, which controls the right side of the body, is usually dominant, most people favour their right side. In people whose brains are more symmetrical, the right hemisphere tends to dominate, making them left-handed. Handedness is not always clear-cut; not everybody prefers one hand for every task. Boys are more likely to be left-handed than girls.

The incidence of left-handedness in a population depends in part on cultural attitudes. Many cultures discourage left-handedness, sometimes by forcing left-handed children to use the right hand (as was true in Canada at the beginning of the 20th century) or even by binding the left hand with tape. In the most restrictive societies, only 1.8 per cent of the population are left-handed, as compared with 10.4 per cent in more permissive societies (Hardyck & Petrinovich, 1977).

Is handedness genetic or learned? That question has been controversial. A new theory proposes the existence of a single gene for right-handedness. According to this theory, people who inherit this gene from either or both parents—about 82 per cent of the population—are right-handed. Those who do not inherit the gene still have a 50:50 chance of being right-handed; otherwise they will be left-handed or ambidextrous. Random determination of handedness among those who do not receive the gene could explain why some

What's your view

- Drawings from children's early pictorial stage show energy and freedom; those from the later pictorial stage show care and accuracy. Why do you think these changes occur? How would you evaluate them?

handedness Preference for using a particular hand

Checkpoint

Can you . . .

✔ List at least three gross motor skills and three fine motor skills, and tell when they typically develop?

✔ Identify four stages in young children's drawing?

✔ Tell how brain functioning is related to physical skills and handedness?

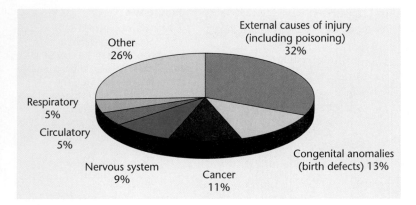

Figure 9-5

Leading causes of death for children aged 1–4 years in Canada, 1997. Total deaths: 455.

Source: Statistics Canada, 1999.

monozygotic twins have differing hand preferences, as well as why 8 per cent of the offspring of two right-handed parents are left-handed. The theory closely predicted the proportion of left-handed offspring in a three-generational sample of families recruited through advertisements (Klar, 1996).

Since scientific evidence provides no reason for favouring "righties," prejudice against the left-handed has largely disappeared in industrialized countries. However, in other parts of the world superstitions surrounding left-handedness continue. If handedness is primarily genetic, such beliefs may eventually die out, and environments and tools designed to make life easier for the left-handed minority may become common (Klar, 1996).

Health and Safety

Guidepost 4

What are the major health and safety risks for children?

What used to be a very vulnerable time of life is much safer now. Because of widespread immunization, many of the major diseases of childhood are now fairly rare in industrialized countries. In the non-industrialized world, however, such vaccine-preventable diseases as measles, pertussis (whooping cough), and tuberculosis still take a large toll. Diarrheal infections account for nearly one-fifth of the 11.2 million deaths of children under age 5 in these regions each year (Wegman, 1999).

In Canada, children's death rates from all causes have come down in recent years. Deaths in childhood are relatively few compared with deaths in adulthood, and most are caused by injury rather than illness, particularly during adolescence (see Figure 9-5). Still, environmental influences make this a less healthy time for some children than for others.

Minor Illnesses

Coughs, sniffles, stomach aches, and runny noses are a part of early childhood. These minor illnesses typically last a few days and are seldom serious enough to need a doctor's attention. Because the lungs are not fully developed, respiratory problems are common, though less so than in infancy. Three- to 5-year-olds catch an average of seven to eight colds and other respiratory illnesses a year. It's a good thing they do, since these illnesses help build natural immunity (resistance to disease). During middle childhood, when the respiratory system is more fully developed, children average fewer than six such illnesses a year (Denny & Clyde, 1983). Minor illnesses may have emotional and cognitive benefits as well. Repeated experience with illness helps children learn to cope with physical distress and understand its causes, increasing their sense of competence (Parmelee, 1986).

Accidental Injuries

Because young children are naturally venturesome and often unaware of danger, it is hard for caregivers to protect them from harm without *over*protecting them. By far the most common cause of injury in early childhood is falls, accounting for over 60 per cent of all injuries in this age group, based on NLSCY data, and injuries outside the home are becoming more common (Kohen, Soubhi, & Raina, 1999). Although most cuts, bumps, and scrapes are "kissed away" and quickly forgotten, some accidental injuries result in lasting damage or death. Indeed, accidents and poisonings are the leading cause of death throughout childhood and adolescence in Canada (CICH, 2000). Most of these deaths are from motor vehicle injuries, particularly during adolescence (Health Canada, 1998; Rivara, 1999). Deaths from pedestrian injuries have fallen by 65 per cent since the late 1970s, but the risk of serious brain damage and lifelong disability from head injuries remains high (Rivara, 1999). Post-traumatic stress disorder is a common, but frequently overlooked, consequence of pedestrian accidents (de Vries et al., 1999).

Hospitalization for injury from motor vehicle traffic accidents and other road injuries become more common in childhood. In 1996–1997, 42 out of every 100,000 children aged 5 to 9 years were hospitalized as a result of a traffic accident, and 38 out of every 100,000 children of the same age range were hospitalized after other road injuries (CICH, 2000). All 10 provinces and three territories require young children in cars to be in specially designed seats or to wear standard seat belts. Four-year-olds who "graduate" from car seats to lap and shoulder belts may need booster seats until they grow bigger. Airbags designed to inflate rapidly so as to protect adults riding in the front seat of a car in high-impact collisions *increase* the risk of fatal injury to children under age 13 by as much as 34 per cent (Rivara, 1999). It is safer, therefore, for young children always to ride in the back seat.

The cost to the health-care system of unintentional injury can be staggering. Injuries due to falls account for over half of the costs of caring for accidents, according to the British Columbia Injury Research and Prevention Unit (Cloutier & Albert, 2001). The cost of caring for children needing hospitalization due to falls in B.C. is estimated at $108 million per year (Cloutier et al., 2001). Faced with such a situation, health authorities throughout the country are stressing prevention as a way of reducing the monetary and personal costs associated with injuries, including use of bicycle helmets, child safety seats, road safety improvements, smoke alarms, and poison control services (Cloutier et al., 2001).

The ingestion of toxic substances by children under 5 accounts for about one-third of hospital cases. Most poisonings occur in the home. The most common substances reported to Canadian Poison Control centres to have been ingested by children under 5 are acetaminophen, cold medication, multivitamins without iron, rubbing alcohol, nail polish remover, iron, multivitamins with iron, acetylsalicylic acid, camphor, and essential oils (Health Canada, 1998). Because these substances are so commonplace, parents do not often perceive them as highly dangerous (Health Canada, 1998). Medications are responsible for more than half (52 per cent) of deaths from poisoning. However, the greatest risks are from swallowing anticonvulsant and antidepressant drugs and iron supplements. Safe storage could prevent many of these deaths (Litovitz et al., 1999; Shannon, 2000).

Laws requiring "childproof" caps on medicine bottles and other dangerous household products, regulation of product safety, mandatory helmets for bicycle riders, and safe storage of firearms have improved child safety. About 23 per cent of Canadian households owns a gun. In 1992, 153 children under 19 years died of firearm injuries. Twenty-three of these deaths were in the 1–14 year age group. The majority of the injuries in this group were unintentional, or were homicides. Since federal gun-control legislation was introduced in 1978, the number of gun-related injuries, particularly suicide, declined (Canadian Paediatric Society, 1996). Recommended changes to gun-control legislation would increase standards for storage of firearms, given that the most common reason given by children for using guns was their accessibility. Making playgrounds safer would be another valuable child-safety measure. An estimated 3 per cent of children in daycare are hurt badly enough each year to need medical attention, and about half of accidents at child-care centres occur on playgrounds. Nearly 1 in 5 are from falls, often resulting in skull injury and brain damage (Briss, Sacks, Addiss, Kresnow, & O'Neil, 1994).

Children are less likely to be injured in daycare, however, than in and around the home (Thacker, Addiss, Goodman, Holloway, & Spencer, 1992), where most fatal non-vehicular accidents occur. Children drown in bathtubs, pools, and buckets containing liquids (as well as in lakes, rivers, and oceans); are burned by scalding or in fires or explosions; fall from heights; drink or eat poisonous substances; get caught in mechanical contrivances; and suffocate in traps, such as abandoned refrigerators. Another dangerous place is the supermarket shopping cart (U.S. Consumer Product Safety Commission, 1991). Almost 250 hospitalizations of children under the age of 5 occurring annually in Canada are the result of the child falling off the cart (Canadian Hospitals Injury Reporting and Prevention Program [CHIRPP], 1999).

Temperament may make some children injury-prone. In a longitudinal study of 59 children, those who were more extraverted and had less inhibitory control as toddlers and preschoolers tended to overestimate their physical abilities at age 6, and they also had had considerably more injuries requiring medical treatment. Such risk-prone children need special attention to teaching about safety precautions. Still, protective measures, such as gates at railroad crossings, are imperative (Schwebel & Plumert, 1999).

Also at special risk are children whose primary caregivers are young, uneducated, and overburdened. In a study of all children born in Tennessee between 1985 and 1994, children born to mothers under 20 years old, with less than a high school education and three or more other children, were 15 times as likely to die of injuries before the age of 5 as children whose mothers were college educated, more than 30 years old, and had fewer than three other children. If the mortality rate for all children could be reduced to that of this lowest-risk group, injury-related deaths might be reduced by more than 75 per cent (Scholer, Mitchel, & Ray, 1997). Home visitation programs to teach parents to use car restraints and smoke detectors, lower water-heater thermostats to avoid scalding, and undertake other safety measures can substantially reduce injuries (Roberts, Kramer, & Suissa, 1996). (Table 9-2 summarizes suggestions for reducing accident risks in various settings.)

Health in Context: Environmental Influences

Why do some children have more illnesses or injuries than others? The genetic heritage contributes: Some children seem predisposed toward some medical conditions. But the environment children live in—indeed, the air they breathe—makes a tremendous difference.

Checkpoint

Can you . . .

✔ Identify two benefits of minor illnesses?

✔ Tell where and how young children are most likely to be injured, and list ways in which injuries can be avoided?

Table 9-2	Reducing Accident Risks for Children
Activity	**Precautions**
Bicycling	Helmets reduce risk of head injury by 85 per cent and brain injury by 88 per cent.
Skateboarding and rollerblading	Children should wear helmets and protective padding on knees, elbows, and wrists.
Using fireworks	Families should not purchase fireworks for home use.
Lawn mowing	Children under 12 should not operate walk-behind mowers; those under 14 should not operate ride-on mowers; small children should not be close to a moving mower.
Swimming	Swimming pools should not be installed in backyards of homes with children under 5; pools already in place need a high fence around all four sides, with gates having high, out-of-reach, self-closing latches. Adults need to watch children very closely near pools, lakes, and other bodies of water.
Playing on a playground	A safe surface under swings, slides, and other equipment can be 10-inch-deep sand, 12-inch-deep wood chips, or rubber outdoor mats; separate areas should be maintained for active play and quiet play, for older and younger children.
Using firearms	Guns should be kept unloaded and locked up, with bullets locked in separate place; children should not have access to keys; adults should talk with children about the risks of gun injury.
Eating	To prevent choking, young children should not eat hard candies, nuts, grapes, and hot dogs (unless sliced lengthwise, then across); food should be cut into small pieces; children should not eat while talking, running, jumping, or lying down.
Ingesting toxic substances	Only drugs and toxic household products with safety caps should be used; toxic products should be stored out of children's reach. Suspected poisoning should be reported immediately to the nearest poison control centre.
Motor vehicles	Young children should sit in approved car seats, in the back seat. Adults should observe traffic laws and avoid aggressive drivers.

Source: Adapted in part from American Academy of Pediatrics (AAP) Committee on Injury and Poison Prevention, 1995a; AAP and Center to Prevent Handgun Violence, 1994; Rivara, 1999; Shannon, 2000.

Exposure to Illness

Preschoolers in daycare centres are 2 to 4 times more likely to pick up mild infectious diseases (such as colds, flu, and diarrhea) than are children raised at home. They also have a higher risk of contracting otitis media (middle ear infection), gastrointestinal diseases, and hepatitis A (Nafstad, Hagen, Oie, Magnus, & Jaakkola, 1999; Thacker et al., 1992). However, early mild infections may protect against more serious respiratory illness. In an American longitudinal study of 1,035 Tucson, Arizona, children followed from birth, those who were exposed to older siblings at home or who were in daycare during the first 6 months of life were less likely to develop asthma or frequent wheezing later in childhood (Ball et al., 2000).

Exposure to Smoking

Parental smoking is an important preventable cause of childhood illness and death. About 2.8 million Canadian children under the age of 15 live with smokers and are exposed to secondhand smoke in the home (Government of Saskatchewan, 2000). Secondhand smoke is responsible for 400,000 illnesses in Canadian children every year (Canadian Health Network, 2001). Passive exposure increases the risk of contracting a number of medical problems, including bronchitis, serious infectious illnesses, otitis media, burns, and asthma (Allergy Section, Canadian Paediatric Society [CPS], 1986). It also may lead to cancer in adulthood (Aligne & Stoddard, 1997; AAP Committee on Environmental Health, 1997; U.S. Environmental Protection Agency, 1994). The Canadian Paediatric Society recommends that children be raised in a smoke-free environment (CPS Psychosocial Paediatrics Committee, 2001).

Poverty

Poverty is stressful, unhealthy, and dangerous. Low income is the *chief* factor associated with poor health of children and adolescents, over and above race and family structure (Montgomery, Kiely, & Pappas, 1996; refer back to Table 1-2 in chapter 1). A commonly used "poverty line" measure is Statistics Canada's low-income cut-off (LICO), which is an income level required for basic needs, adjusted for family size and size of the community in which a family resides. A higher income is typically needed to meet the needs of larger families living in larger urban centres, compared with rural communities. Although social assistance is provided to families in need across Canada, it does not provide families with adequate means to meet their needs. For example, the level of assistance available to a lone-parent family with one child ranges from a low of 50 per cent of the LICO in Alberta to a high of 69 per cent of the LICO in Newfoundland and Labrador (CICH, 2000).

A growing proportion of children in Canada are poor: In 1997 about 1,400,000 Canadian children under the age of 18 years lived in poverty, almost double the 1981 number of 763,000 children (CICH, 2000). This increase occurred despite a 1989 House of Commons resolution to eradicate child poverty in Canada by the year 2000. Although poverty strikes all parts of the population, it besets young families—including working families—and minorities disproportionately.

In all regions of Canada, about 22 per cent of children 14 years or younger live in poverty. About half of all immigrant children live in poverty at some time during their early years in Canada, although these children experience fewer emotional and behavioural problems than non-immigrant Canadian children who live in poverty (Beiser, Hou, Hyman, & Tousignant, 2002). This likely reflects the readjustment of the family to a new country, which often involves a temporary period of low poverty followed by improved family income (Beiser, Hou, Hyman, & Tousignant, 1998; Smith & Jackson, 2002). About half of Aboriginal children live in poverty, as do 43 per cent of visible minorities (CICH, 2000). Children with lone parents are also more likely to be in low-income families. The developmental outcomes for these children are typically no different from those of other children in low-income families, other than the effects of a higher probability of experiencing hostile parenting. This is likely a reflection of the unique stresses faced by lone parents and is associated with an increased prevalence of emotional and behavioural problems (Lipman,

Box 9-2 *How Poverty Affects Children*

Low income can introduce risks to healthy child development, either directly in limiting the kinds of resources a parent can provide to create an enriched environment for the child, or indirectly through increased stresses that parents experience, which can have detrimental effects on children by reducing the capacity of parents to provide supportive and consistent parenting, and by increasing the likelihood of hostile parenting and parental depression (Lipman, Boyle, Dooley, & Offord, 1998; Ryan & Adams, 1998). Social and governmental initiatives, like the National Child Tax Benefit, which are aimed at reducing the negative effects of low-income, often have limited effectiveness, due to clawbacks of benefits offered to low-income families by provincial governments (Lipman et al., 1998).

One reflection of the growing problem of childhood poverty in Canada is the increase in use of food banks across the country. About 41 per cent of food bank recipients are children, representing 2 per cent of the population, or 57,000 families (McIntyre & Connor, 2000; Wilson & Tsoa, 2001). This is an indication that food insecurity—inconsistent access to adequate, safe, and nutritionally sound food—is becoming a fact of life for many

Families with children are the fastest growing part of the homeless population. Homeless children tend to have more health problems than children with homes.

Canadian children who live in families of limited income facing rising housing costs. Children who experience the physical and psychological stresses of food insecurity often do poorly in school, experience attention problems, and are at risk of developing psychosocial functioning problems (Doherty, 1997).

Typically, parents go hungry to prevent their children from missing meals, but often are forced to divert funds from food budgets to meet the costs of maintaining adequate housing (Wilson et al., 2001). The income difference between Canadian families who experience frequent hunger and those who experience occasional hunger is $5,000 (McIntyre, Connor, & Warren, 1998). The majority of families using food banks spend more than 30 per cent of their incomes on housing, representing those in "core housing need," who are at risk of becoming homeless. The number of homeless families with children is growing across Canada (CICH, 2000). In Toronto alone, it is estimated that 19 per cent of homeless people, or 5,300, are children (Golden, Currie, Greaves, & Latimer, 1999).

The prevalence of low-income families in urban neighbourhoods has been linked to poor developmental outcomes in children. In a Vancouver study, entire sections of the city have been shown to include higher proportions of children experiencing higher risks of developing multiple problems in physical health, social competence, emotional maturity, and communication skills (Hertzman, 2002). Typically, less affluent neighbourhoods that have declining median incomes, and increases in low-income families, single-parent families, and proportion of income spent on rent were associated with higher numbers of developmental risks. Part of the problem has to do with the lower availability of social supports, like child-care facilities and neighbourhood recreation centres in less affluent neighbourhoods.

To combat homelessness, a number of communities and community development groups are building low-income housing units and reclaiming neighbourhoods with the help of federal, provincial, local, foundation, and private financing (CDF, 1998).

What's your view?

What strategies to deal with childhood poverty and hunger do you think would be most effective?

Check it out!

For more information on this topic, go to **www.mcgrawhill.ca/college/papalia** to link to the website for the Government of Canada's National Homelessness Initiative.

Boyle, Dooley, & Offord, 1998). Living in poverty has been shown to put the developing child at risk in many ways (see Box 9-2).

The health problems of poor children often begin before birth. Many poor mothers do not eat well and do not receive adequate prenatal care; their babies are more likely than babies of more affluent mothers to be of low birth weight or to die in infancy. Poor children who do not eat properly do not grow properly, and thus are weak and susceptible to disease. Many poor families live in crowded, unsanitary housing, and the children may lack adequate supervision, especially when the parents are at work. They are more likely than other children to suffer lead poisoning, hearing and vision loss, and iron-deficiency anemia, as well as such stress-related conditions as asthma, headaches, insomnia, and irritable bowel. They also tend to have more behaviour problems, psychological disturbances, and learning disabilities (J. L. Brown, 1987; Egbuono & Starfield, 1982; Santer & Stocking, 1991; Starfield, 1991).

The Canada Health Act is designed to ensure universal access to medically necessary health services for all Canadians. However, despite the principles of the act, there is evidence that accessibility to health services is not necessarily consistent in all regions. Canadians in remote and northern areas are concerned about limited health services in their communities (Health Canada, 2000). In response, the federal government has started a number of health programs for people living in remote areas. These include the Innovations in Rural and Community Health Initiative, which is designed to improve access to health care and prescription drugs in rural and remote areas, telehealth to improve the delivery of health care, and incentives to attract physicians and other health-care workers to rural communities (Health Canada, 2000).

In addition to the concerns of people living in remote and northern communities, there is evidence that equality of access is not always guaranteed in urban communities. For example, although residents of Winnipeg's poorest neighbourhoods were more likely to see family doctors than were residents of middle- and upper-income neighbourhoods, people in the poor neighbourhoods were less likely to be referred to specialists. In Ontario, people living in lower- and middle-income neighbourhoods were less likely to receive cardiac surgery and more likely to die after being hospitalized with a heart attack, in comparison to residents of wealthier areas (Canadian Institute for Health Information and Statistics Canada, 2000).

Exposure to Lead

Lead poisoning has been called the greatest hazard to the health of children under age 6 (Tesman & Hills, 1994). The proportion of children in Ontario with lead levels above the acceptable maximum was about 50 per cent in 1984 (The Learning Disabilities Association of Canada, 2001), 2 years after leaded gas had been banned in Canada. However, very few cases of lead poisoning occur in Canada in any year. Children can get lead in the bloodstream from lead-contaminated food or water, from putting contaminated fingers in their mouths, or from inhaling dust in homes or schools where there is lead-based paint. Lead poisoning can seriously interfere with cognitive development and can bring on a variety of neurological and behavioural problems (AAP Committee on Environmental Health, 1998; Needleman, Riess, Tobin, Biesecker, & Greenhouse, 1996; Tesman & Hills, 1994). Yet it can be completely prevented by removing sources of lead from children's environment (Tesman & Hills, 1994).

Lead exposure and high blood lead-levels have been associated with sensorimotor deficits, lower IQ, and poorer academic achievement. (Which specific areas of cognition are affected is still unclear and may depend on the age of exposure and on socio-economic status.) Lead is strongly linked to such behavioural problems as hyperactivity (see chapter 13), impulsiveness, irritability, distractibility, and a short attention span (Tesman & Hills, 1994). It is associated with antisocial and delinquent behaviour (Needleman et al., 1996) and can lead to seizures, mental retardation, or death (AAP Committee on Environmental Health, 1993).

There is no safe level of exposure to lead. However, the degree of toxicity depends on the dose, how long a child is exposed, and the child's developmental and nutritional vulnerability (AAP Committee on Environmental Health, 1998). Even low levels of exposure may have detrimental behavioural effects in very young preschoolers, particularly those who have other risk factors, such as poverty and maternal depression (Mendelsohn et al., 1998). Moderate lead poisoning can be treated (Ruff, Bijur, Markowitz, Ma, & Rosen, 1993), but reduced exposure may only partially reverse the cognitive effects (Tong, Baghurst, Sawyer, Burns, & McMichael, 1998).

Laws mandating removal of lead from gasoline, paints, and soldered food cans have helped prevention, but dust and soil in many places are still contaminated (Pirkle et al., 1994; Tesman & Hills, 1994). The [U.S.] Centers for Disease Control and Prevention (1997) calls for universal screening of residential areas with at least 27 per cent of housing built before 1950 and in populations in which the percentage of 1- and 2-year-olds with

Checkpoint ✔

Can you . . .

✔ Discuss several environmental influences that endanger children's health and development?

What's your view ?

- Who should be responsible for children's well-being when parents cannot provide adequate food, clothing, shelter, and health care: government, religious and community institutions, the private sector, or a combination of these?

elevated blood lead levels is 12 per cent or more. Parents need to learn how to reduce lead exposure (AAP Committee on Environmental Health, 1998). Washing hands before meals and before bed, keeping fingernails clipped, and eating a well-balanced diet can help. Chipping or peeling paint should be removed carefully, and barriers can be put up to keep children away from areas that contain lead (Kimbrough, LeVois, & Webb, 1994).

Guidepost 5

What are the causes and consequences of child abuse and neglect, and what can be done about them?

physical abuse Action taken to endanger a child involving potential bodily injury

neglect Failure to meet a child's basic needs

sexual abuse Sexual activity involving a child and an older person

emotional maltreatment Action or inaction that may cause behavioural, cognitive, emotional, or mental disorders

Maltreatment: Abuse and Neglect

Although most parents are loving and nurturing, some cannot or will not take proper care of their children, and some deliberately hurt or kill them. *Maltreatment,* whether perpetrated by parents or others, is deliberate or avoidable endangerment of a child. Maltreatment takes several forms (U.S. Department of Health and Human Services [USDHHS], 1999a; Trocmé & Wolfe, 2001); any one form is likely to be accompanied by one or more of the others (Belsky, 1993).

In general, *abuse* refers to action that inflicts harm; *neglect* refers to inaction that leads to harm. **Physical abuse** involves injury to the body through punching, beating, kicking, or burning. **Neglect** is failure to meet a child's basic needs, such as food, clothing, medical care, protection, and supervision. **Sexual abuse** is sexual activity involving a child and another person. **Emotional maltreatment** includes acts of abuse or neglect that may cause behavioural, cognitive, emotional, or mental disorders. It may include rejection, terrorization, isolation, exploitation, degradation, ridicule, or failure to provide emotional support, love, and affection. Emotional maltreatment is hard to identify; its effects may not surface immediately and may be difficult to distinguish from signs of emotional disturbance and other developmental problems (USDHHS, 1999a; Trocmé et al., 2001).

Maltreatment: Facts and Figures

The incidence of maltreatment is uncertain. Although Canada has not kept national statistics on child maltreatment, the Canadian Incidence Study of Reported Child Abuse and Neglect (CIS) (Trocmé & Wolfe, 2001) is the first examination of the incidence of child maltreatment in Canada. In the United States, statistics on child maltreatment gathered since 1976 have shown a steep rise in reported cases and serious injuries, which may reflect an increase in maltreatment, better recognition and reporting of abuse and neglect, or (more likely) both.

The reported number of abused and neglected children in the United States has declined since its peak in 1993. Still, the number of cases investigated and confirmed by state child protective services agencies in 1998 was more than 900,000, and the actual number may well have been considerably higher (USDHHS, 2000). Many, if not most, cases are never reported to protective agencies, and many of those reported are not investigated (USDHHS, 1999a).

In 1998, 40 per cent of investigations of maltreatment in Canada involved neglect, particularly failure to supervise leading to physical harm, and almost a third (31 per cent) involved physical abuse, with inappropriate punishment being most common. Nearly 10 per cent of victims were sexually abused, the most common form being inappropriate touching and fondling, and 19 per cent of investigations were of cases of emotional maltreatment, with exposure to family violence being the most prevalent type (Trocmé & Wolfe, 2001).

The prevalence of child maltreatment is dramatically lower in Canada (21 cases for every 1,000 children) than in the United States (43 cases per 1,000 children). Higher rates of neglect in the United States account for most of the difference, which may reflect higher poverty rates and more limited access to social, medical, and educational services for many American families (Health Canada, 2001). Although boys and girls are equally likely to be victims of maltreatment (Trainor & Mihorean, 2001), an Ontario survey indicates that physical abuse is more prevalent in males (31 per cent) than in females (21 per cent). However, females are over three times more likely to have been the victims of sexual abuse (13 per cent compared to 4 per cent for males) (MacMillan, Fleming, Trocmé et al., 1997).

About 80 per cent of adult offenders are the child's parents. However, almost half of sexually abused children were abused by someone other than the child's parent. Other types of abuse are most commonly perpetrated by a parent: 90 per cent of cases of neglect are committed by the mother or mother-figure; 90 per cent of sexual abuse cases are committed by a male—half of these cases involving the child's father (Health Canada, 2001).

Rates of child homicide and spousal violence in Canada have been dropping over the last decade. However, the rate of spousal abuse is higher in Aboriginal families than in non-Aboriginal families (Trainor & Mihorean, 2001). Although the number of children admitted to shelters has been declining in Canada, the proportion of children who have been abused has grown from 86 percent in 1998 to 91 percent in 2000. Most of these children were under 5 years of age (Trainor & Mihorean, 2001).

Maltreatment has become a major cause of death among young children, and, again, the full incidence of such deaths is unknown. Estimates based on a review of all deaths of children under 11 years old in North Carolina between 1985 and 1994 are that more than 3 times as many child deaths nationally are due to abuse than are officially reported (9,467 as opposed to 2,973). In 63 per cent of the North Carolina cases, biological parents were responsible (Herman-Giddens et al., 1999).

Contributing Factors: An Ecological View

Maltreatment by parents is a symptom of extreme disturbance in child rearing, usually aggravated by other family problems, such as poverty, alcoholism, or antisocial behaviour. A disproportionate number of abused and neglected children are in large, poor, or single-parent families, which tend to be under stress and to have trouble meeting children's needs (Sedlak & Broadhurst, 1996). Yet, what pushes one parent over the edge, another may take in stride. Although most neglect occurs in very poor families, most low-income parents do not neglect their children. Abuse and neglect reflect the interplay of many contributing factors involving the family, the community, and the larger society (Health Canada, 2001; USDHHS, 1999a).

Characteristics of Abusive Parents

Many abusers are lonely, unhappy, anxious, depressed, angry, or aggressive. They tend to have low self-esteem and poor impulse control and coping skills. About one-third of abusing parents were abused themselves as children (National Research Council [NRC], 1993b; Schmitt & Kempe, 1983; USDHHS, 1999a; Wolfe, 1985). Substance abuse is a factor in at least one-third of substantiated cases of abuse and neglect (USDHHS, 1999a).

Unlike neglectful parents, who tend to be apathetic, incompetent, irresponsible, or emotionally withdrawn (Wolfe, 1985), abusive parents are overly involved with the child. Often deprived of good parenting themselves, they are greatly upset by behaviour that most parents accept as normal (Reid, Patterson, & Loeber, 1982; Wolfe, 1985). Abuse may begin when a parent who is already anxious, depressed, or hostile tries to control a child physically but loses self-control and ends up shaking or beating the child (USDHHS, 1999a). When parents who had troubled childhoods think poorly of themselves and find negative emotions hard to handle have children who are particularly needy or demanding, who cry a lot, or who are unresponsive, the likelihood of maltreatment increases. These children's greater needs may stem from poor health, "difficult" personalities, or physical disabilities. They are more likely than non-abused children to have been preterm or low–birth weight babies; to be hyperactive, mentally challenged, or physically challenged; or to show behavioural abnormalities (NRC, 1993b; Reid et al., 1982; USDHHS, 1999a).

Abusive parents tend to have marital problems and to fight physically. Their households tend to be disorganized, and they experience more stressful events than other families (Reid et al., 1982; Sedlak & Broadhurst, 1996). Many abusive parents cut themselves off from others, leaving them with no one to turn to in times of stress and no one to see what is happening.

Neighbourhood and Social Support

The outside world can create a climate for family violence. Poverty, unemployment, job dissatisfaction, social isolation, and lack of assistance for the primary caregiver are closely correlated with child and spouse abuse. None of these, however, are determining factors.

What makes one low-income neighbourhood a place where children are highly likely to be maltreated, while another, matched for ethnic population and income levels, is safer?

According to NLSCY data, neighbourhood cohesion is an important protective factor in reducing the risk of childhood injury in Canada, while neighbourhood problems like low neighbourhood income, education, and occupation tended to put children at risk of injury. These risk factors interact with child behaviour to increase the likelihood of aggression and oppositional behaviour in children (Soubhi, Raina, & Kohen, 2001). This result is echoed by the outcome of the Vancouver neighbourhood study mentioned above, describing the risks to development in less affluent neighbourhoods (Hertzman, 2002). In one inner-city Chicago neighbourhood, the proportion of children who died from maltreatment (1 death for every 2,541 children) was about twice the proportion in another inner-city neighbourhood. Researchers who interviewed community leaders found a depressed atmosphere in the high-abuse community. Criminal activity was rampant, and facilities for community programs were dark and dreary. This was an environment with "an ecological conspiracy against children" (Garbarino & Kostelny, 1993, p. 213). In the low-abuse neighbourhood, people described their community as a poor but decent place to live. They painted a picture of a neighbourhood with robust social support networks, well-known community services, and strong political leadership. In a community like this, maltreatment is less likely to occur.

Cultural Values and Patterns

Two cultural factors associated with child abuse are societal violence and physical punishment of children. In countries where violent crime is infrequent and children are rarely spanked, such as Japan, China, and Tahiti, child abuse is rare (Celis, 1990).

Section 43 of the Canadian criminal code states that "every schoolteacher, parent or person standing in the place of a parent is justified in using force by way of correction toward a pupil or child, as the case may be, who is under his care, if the force does not exceed what is reasonable under the circumstances." Although there have been efforts to change this law, Canadian culture is more accepting of physical punishment than other cultures. Canadian mothers report being more likely to use physical punishment in disciplining their children than Swedish mothers, who live in a culture that does not condone physical punishment (Durrant, Broberg, & Rose-Krasnor, 1999).

Effects of Maltreatment

Maltreatment can produce grave consequences—not only physical, but emotional, cognitive, and social. The emotional harm that is related to maltreatment includes changes in behaviour (regression and withdrawal from social interactions), sleep and hygiene patterns, and emotions (clinging, crying, and anxiety). In 34 per cent of cases of maltreatment in Canada, according to CIS data, evidence of emotional harm was identified, and 21 per cent were considered severe enough to warrant treatment (Trocmé et al., 2001). Emotional harm occurs most often in cases of sexual abuse and is also present in many cases of physical abuse, neglect, and emotional maltreatment.

Maltreated children often start speaking late (Coster, Gersten, Beeghly, & Cicchetti, 1989). They are more likely to repeat a grade, to do poorly on cognitive tests, and to have behaviour problems in school (Eckenrode, Laird, & Doris, 1993). They often have disorganized-disoriented attachments to their parents (refer back to chapter 8) and negative, distorted self-concepts. Deprived of early positive social interactions, they do not develop social skills and have difficulty making friends (Price, 1996). Chronic neglect during early childhood has especially negative effects on later school performance, social relationships, adaptability, and problem solving (NRC, 1993b).

Almost a third of special-needs children in an Alberta study were found to have confirmed histories of maltreatment. Whether the maltreatment is part of the cause of special needs, or a correlate with special needs, it is clear that maltreatment contributes to poor school achievement and is related to behaviour problems in children (Sobsey, 2002).

Maltreated children may become either overly aggressive or withdrawn (USDHHS, 1999a). Physically abused youngsters tend to be fearful, uncooperative, less able to respond appropriately to friendly overtures, and, consequently, less well liked than other children (Coie & Dodge, 1998; Haskett & Kistner, 1991; Salzinger, Feldman, Hammer, & Rosario, 1993).

Table 9-3	Developmentally Related Reactions to Sexual Abuse
Age	**Most Common Symptoms**
Preschoolers	Anxiety
	Nightmares
	Inappropriate sexual behaviour
School-age children	Fear
	Mental illness
	Aggression
	Nightmares
	School problems
	Hyperactivity
	Regressive behaviour
Adolescents	Depression
	Withdrawn, suicidal, or self-injurious behaviours
	Physical complaints
	Illegal acts
	Running away
	Substance abuse

Source: Adapted from Kendall-Tackett, Williams, & Finkelhor, 1993.

Although few abused children become delinquent, criminal, or mentally ill, abuse makes it likelier that they will (Dodge, Bates, & Pettit, 1990; NRC, 1993b; Widom, 1989). Teenagers who were abused when they were younger may react by running away, which may be self-protective, or may abuse drugs, which is not (NRC, 1993b).

Consequences of sexual abuse vary with age (see Table 9-3). In a study that followed 68 sexually abused children for 5 years, the abused children showed more disturbed behaviour, had lower self-esteem, and were more depressed, anxious, or unhappy than a control group matched for age and sex. The abused children were also more likely to injure themselves or commit suicide (Swanston, Tebbutt, O'Toole, & Oates, 1997). Sexually abused children may become sexually active at an early age. Among 1,026 African-American first-time mothers, sexual abuse during childhood (but not physical or emotional abuse) was predictive of younger ages of first intercourse and first pregnancy (Fiscella, Kitzman, Cole, Sidora, & Olds, 1998).

Fearfulness and low self-esteem often continue into adulthood. Adults who were sexually abused as children tend to be anxious, depressed, angry, or hostile; to mistrust people; to feel isolated and stigmatized; to be sexually maladjusted (Browne & Finkelhor, 1986); and to abuse alcohol or drugs (NRC, 1993b; USDHHS, 1999a).

Emotional maltreatment is more subtle than physical maltreatment, and its effects may be harder to pin down. It has been linked to lying, stealing, low self-esteem, emotional maladjustment, dependency, underachievement, depression, aggression, learning disorders, homicide, and suicide, as well as to psychological distress later in life (S. N. Hart & Brassard, 1987).

Still, many maltreated children show remarkable resilience, especially if they have been able to form an attachment to a supportive person (Egeland & Sroufe, 1981, Jenkins & Keating, 1998). Above-average intelligence, advanced cognitive abilities, and high self-esteem seem to help. Also important is the child's interpretation of the abuse or neglect. Children who see it as coming from a parent's weaknesses or frustrations seem to cope better than those who take it as parental rejection (Garmezy, Masten, & Tellegen, 1984; Zimrin, 1986).

Few abused children grow up to abuse their own children (Kaufman & Zigler, 1987; USDHHS, 1999a). Abused children who grow up to be *non*abusing parents are likely to have had someone to whom they could turn for help, to have received therapy, and to have good marital or love relationships. They are likely to have been abused by only one parent and to have had a loving, supportive relationship with the other (Egeland, Jacobvitz, & Sroufe, 1988; Kaufman & Zigler, 1987; NRC, 1993b).

Helping Families in Trouble or at Risk

Since maltreatment is a multifactorial problem, it needs many-pronged solutions. Effective community prevention and intervention should be comprehensive, neighbourhood-based, centred on protecting children, and aimed at strengthening families if possible and removing children if necessary (USDHHS, 1999a).

Some abuse-prevention programs teach basic parenting skills (USDHHS, 1999a; Wolfe, Edwards, Manion, & Koverola, 1988). Other programs offer subsidized daycare, volunteer homemakers, home visitors, and temporary "respite homes" or "relief parents" to take over occasionally. In one program in a semi-rural New York community, first-time unmarried expectant teenage mothers were visited by nurses once a month during pregnancy and then during the child's first 2 years. At the end of that period, there were 80 per cent fewer verified cases of abuse and neglect among the nurse-visited children than in a control group; and 15 years later, their mothers were only about half as likely to have been reported as abusers or neglecters (D. L. Olds, Eckenrode, et al., 1997; D. L. Olds, Henderson, et al., 1999).

Provincial and local child protective services agencies investigate reports of child maltreatment; determine what steps, if any, need to be taken; and marshal community resources to help. This may involve helping the family resolve their problems or arranging for alternative care for children who cannot safely remain at home (Larner, Stevenson, & Behrman, 1998; Minister of Public Works and Government Services Canada, 2001; Trocmé, MacLaurin, et al., 2001). One way to stop maltreatment is to treat abusers as criminal offenders; people arrested for family violence are less likely to repeat the offence (Bouza, 1990; Sherman & Berk, 1984). Services for abused children and adults include shelters, education in parenting skills, and therapy. Parents Anonymous and other organizations offer free, confidential support groups. Abused children may receive play or art therapy and daycare in a therapeutic environment. In communities where abuse or neglect is widespread, school-based programs can be effective (Trocmé, MacLaurin, et al., 2001).

When authorities remove children from their homes, the usual alternative is foster care, which has increased markedly since the 1980s. Foster care removes a child from immediate danger, but it is often unstable, may also turn out to be an abusive situation, and further alienates the child from the family. It is intended as a temporary emergency measure; but in some cities the average stay is 5 years, often with a series of placements in different homes (NRC, 1993b). However, the growing number of children placed in kinship foster care (31 per cent), due in part to a scarcity of traditional foster care homes and an increasing caseload (Berrick, 1998), may make a difference.

The plight of abused and neglected children is one for which society needs to find more effective remedies. Without help, maltreated children often grow up with serious problems, at great cost to themselves and to society, and may continue the cycle of maltreatment when they have children of their own.

Fortunately, few children are maltreated. Preschool children who are in good health and whose basic physical needs are met are able to make major advances in cognitive development, as we'll see in chapter 10.

Checkpoint ✔

Can you . . .

✔ Define four types of child abuse and neglect?

✔ Discuss the incidence of maltreatment and explain why it is hard to measure?

✔ Identify contributing factors having to do with the child, the family, the neighbourhood, and the wider society?

✔ Give examples of effects of child abuse and neglect?

✔ Describe ways to prevent or stop maltreatment and help its victims?

Summary and Key Terms

Aspects of Physiological Development

Guidepost 1 How do children's bodies change between ages 3 and 6, and what are their nutritional and dental needs?

• Physical growth increases during the years from 3 to 6, but more slowly than during infancy and toddlerhood. Boys are on average slightly taller, heavier, and more muscular than girls. Internal body systems are maturing, and all primary teeth are present.

• Preschool children generally eat less for their weight than before—and need less—but the prevalence of obesity has increased.

• Tooth decay has decreased since the 1970s but remains a problem among disadvantaged children.

• Thumb-sucking can safely be ignored unless it continues beyond age 4, when permanent teeth begin to develop.

Guidepost 2 What sleep patterns and problems tend to develop during early childhood?

- Sleep patterns change during early childhood, as throughout life, and are affected by cultural expectations.
- It is normal for preschool children to develop bedtime rituals that delay going to sleep. Prolonged bedtime struggles or persistent sleep terrors or nightmares may indicate emotional disturbances that need attention.
- Bed-wetting is common and is usually outgrown without special help.

    enuresis (219)

Motor Development

Guidepost 3   What are the main motor achievements of early childhood and how does children's artwork show their physical and cognitive maturation?

- Children progress rapidly in gross and fine motor skills and eye–hand coordination, developing more complex systems of action.
- Handedness is usually evident by age 3, reflecting dominance by one hemisphere of the brain.
- Stages of art production, which appear to reflect brain development and fine motor coordination, are the scribbling stage, shape stage, design stage, and pictorial stage.

    **gross motor skills (219)   fine motor skills (219)
    handedness (221)**

Health and Safety

Guidepost 4   What are the major health and safety risks for children?

- Although major contagious illnesses are rare today in industrialized countries as a result of widespread immunization, preventable disease continues to be a major problem in the non-industrialized world.
- Minor illnesses, such as colds and other respiratory illnesses, are common during early childhood and help build immunity to disease.
- Accidents, most commonly motor vehicle injuries, are the leading cause of death in childhood in Canada. Most fatal non-vehicular accidents occur at home.
- Environmental factors such as exposure to illness, smoking, poverty, and homelessness increase the risks of illness or injury. Lead poisoning can have serious physical, cognitive, and behavioural effects.

Maltreatment: Abuse and Neglect

Guidepost 5   What are the causes and consequences of child abuse and neglect and what can be done about it?

- The incidence of reported maltreatment of children has increased greatly.
- Forms of maltreatment are physical abuse, neglect, sexual abuse, and emotional maltreatment.
- Characteristics of the abuser or neglecter, the victim, the family, the community, and the larger culture all contribute to child abuse and neglect.
- Maltreatment can interfere with physical, cognitive, emotional, and social development, and its effects can continue into adulthood. Still, many maltreated children show remarkable resilience.
- Preventing or stopping maltreatment may require multi-faceted, coordinated community efforts.

    **physical abuse (228)   neglect (228)   sexual abuse (228)
    emotional maltreatment (228)**

OLC Preview

The official website for *A Child's World,* First Canadian edition, supplements the chapter's boxed material on "Helping Children Eat and Sleep Well" and "How Homelessness Affects Children" and provides links to such recommended websites as Government of Canada's National Homelessness Initiative. Check out **www.mcgrawhill.ca/college/papalia.**

Cognitive Development in Early Childhood

Childhood is a world of miracle and wonder: as if creation rose, bathed in light, out of darkness, utterly new and fresh and astonishing. The end of childhood is when things cease to astonish us. When the world seems familiar, when one has got used to existence, one has become an adult.

—Eugene Ionesco, *Fragments of a Journal* 1976

Focus *Albert Einstein, Nuclear Physicist**

In the public mind, the name Albert Einstein (1879–1955) is synonymous with "genius." His general theory of relativity ("the greatest revolution in thought since Newton"), his discovery of the fundamental principle of quantum physics, and his other contributions to the reshaping of our knowledge of the universe cause him to be considered "one of the greatest physicists of all time" (Whitrow, 1967, p. 1).

Albert Einstein

Yet the young Einstein hardly seemed destined for intellectual stardom. Born in the German town of Ulm, he was slow in learning to walk and did not begin talking until at least his third year. His parents feared he might be mentally retarded. Einstein himself always insisted that he did not *try* to speak until after the age of 3, skipping babbling and going directly into sentences. Actually, his sentences may have come a bit earlier. When his sister, Maja, was born 4 months before Albert's third birthday, Albert (who had been promised a new baby to play with and apparently thought it would be a toy) reportedly asked in disappointment, "Where are the wheels?"

Regardless of the exact timing, "Albert was certainly a late and reluctant talker" (Brian, 1996, p. 1). The reasons may have had more to do with personality than with cognitive development; he was a shy, taciturn child, whom adults thought backward and other children considered dull. He would not play marbles or soldiers or other games with his peers, but he would crouch for hours, observing an ant colony.

When he started school, he did poorly in most subjects; the headmaster predicted he would never amount to anything. Albert hated the regimentation and rote learning stressed in German schools; he did not have a retentive memory and could not give clear answers to his teachers' questions. He was a daydreamer, his questioning mind occupied with its own speculations. He would not even try to learn anything unless he was interested in it—and then his concentration was intense.

His wonder about the workings of the universe was awakened at the age of 4 or 5, when he was sick in bed and his father gave him a magnetic pocket compass to keep him amused. The boy was astonished: No matter which way he turned the compass, the needle pointed to N (for "north"). What controlled its motion? He pestered his Uncle Jacob, who had studied engineering, with questions. His uncle told him about the earth's north and south poles and about magnetic fields, but Albert still was not satisfied. He believed there must be some mysterious force in what appeared to be the empty space around the needle. He carried the compass

*Sources of biographical information about Albert Einstein are Bernstein (1973); Brian (1996); French (1979); Goldsmith, Mackay, & Woudhuysen (1980); Michelmore (1962); Quasha (1980); Schilpp (1970); and Whitrow (1967).

around for weeks, trying to figure out its secret. Years later, at the age of 67, he wrote, ". . . this experience made a deep and lasting impression upon me. Something deeply hidden had to be behind things" (Schilpp, 1970, p. 9).

That sense of wonder was reawakened several years later, when Uncle Jacob, noticing that Albert showed an interest in arithmetic, introduced him to algebra and geometry. Albert solved every problem in the books his uncle brought him and then went searching for more. It was that same insatiable curiosity and persistence—what Einstein himself called "a furious impulse to understand" (Michelmore, 1962, p. 24)—that underlay his lifetime quest for scientific knowledge.

• • •

Albert Einstein's story touches on several themes of cognitive development in early childhood. One is the variation in normal language development. Second, Einstein's reaction to the compass may have been unusually intense, but it was characteristic of young children's understanding of the physical world—their growing recognition that natural phenomena have causes, but also their tendency to confuse appearance and reality. Einstein's lifelong memory of that incident may shed light on why some kinds of early memories last while others do not. Finally, the underestimation of Einstein's cognitive abilities by his parents and teachers raises issues about how intelligence can best be assessed.

In this chapter, we examine all these aspects of cognitive development in early childhood, as revealed by recent research as well as by such earlier theorists as Piaget and Vygotsky. We see how preschool children's thinking has advanced since toddlerhood and in what ways it is still immature—particularly in understanding of their own mental processes. We look at children's increasing fluency with language and what impact this has on other aspects of cognition, as well as on psychosocial development. We examine memory, drawing on the information-processing and social-contextual approaches; and we compare psychometric intelligence tests with assessments based on Vygotsky's theories. Finally, we look at the widening world of preschool and kindergarten.

After you have read and studied this chapter, you should be able to answer each of the Guidepost questions that appear at the top of the next page. Look for them again in the margins, where they point to important concepts throughout the chapter. To check your understanding of these Guideposts, review the end-of-chapter summary. Checkpoints located throughout the chapter will help you verify your understanding of what you have read.

Guideposts for Study

1. What are typical cognitive advances and immature aspects of preschool children's thinking?

2. How does language improve, and what happens when its development is delayed?

3. What memory abilities expand in early childhood?

4. How is preschoolers' intelligence measured, and what are some influences on it?

5. What purposes does early childhood education serve, and how do children make the transition to kindergarten?

Piagetian Approach: The Pre-operational Child

Jean Piaget named early childhood the **pre-operational stage.** The characteristic development in this second major stage of cognitive development, which lasts from approximately ages 2 to 7, is a great expansion in the use of symbolic thought, or representational ability, which first emerges at the end of the sensorimotor stage (refer back to chapter 7). However, according to Piaget, children cannot think logically until the stage of concrete operations in middle childhood (chapter 13).

Let's look at some advances and immature aspects of pre-operational thought (see Tables 10-1 and 10-2), and at recent research findings, some of which challenge Piaget's conclusions.

Advances of Pre-operational Thought

Advances in symbolic thought are accompanied by a growing understanding of space, causality, identities, categorization, and number. Some of these understandings have roots in infancy and toddlerhood; others begin to develop in early childhood but are not fully achieved until middle childhood. Piaget identified two substages in the pre-operational period: *pre-conceptual*, lasting from 2 to 4 years, and *intuitive*, lasting from about 5 to 7 years. During the *pre-conceptual* substage, children are developing their abilities to use symbols to represent objects through their rapidly developing language skills, imaginative play, and deferred imitation. As they progress through the *intuitive* substage, children begin to show evidence of further developing thought processes, seen in their new-found understandings of relationships between objects, identities and categorization, and number. However, despite having these new abilities, children cannot understand the principles behind these mental operations.

The Symbolic Function

"I want ice cream!" announces Kerstin, age 4, trudging indoors from the hot, dusty backyard. She has not seen anything that triggered this desire—no open freezer door, no television commercial. She no longer needs this kind of sensory cue to think about something. She remembers ice cream, its coldness and taste, and she purposefully seeks it out. This absence of sensory or motor cues characterizes the **symbolic function:** the ability to use symbols, or mental representations—words, numbers, or images to which a person has attached meaning. Having symbols for things helps children to remember and think about them without having them physically present.

Preschool children show the symbolic function through deferred imitation, pretend play, and language. *Deferred imitation,* which appears to begin in infancy (refer back to chapter 7), is based on having kept a mental representation of an observed action—as when 3-year-old Bart scolds his little sister, using the same words he heard his father say to the delivery boy who was late in bringing the pizza. In *pretend play* (also called *symbolic play, fantasy play, dramatic play,* or *imaginative play*), which we discuss in chapter 11, children

Guidepost 1

What are typical cognitive advances and immature aspects of preschool children's thinking?

pre-operational stage In Piaget's theory, the second major stage of cognitive development, in which children become more sophisticated in their use of symbolic thought but are not yet able to use logic

symbolic function In Piaget's terminology, ability to use mental representations (words, numbers, or images) to which a child has attached meaning

Table 10-1 Cognitive Advances During Early Childhood

Advance	Significance	Example
Use of symbols	Children do not need to be in sensorimotor contact with an object, person, or event in order to think about it.	Simon asks his mother about the elephants they saw on their trip to the circus several months earlier.
	Children can imagine that objects or people have properties other than those they actually have.	Rolf pretends that a slice of apple is a vacuum cleaner "vrooming" across the kitchen table.
Understanding of identities	Children are aware that superficial alterations do not change the nature of things.	Jeffrey knows that his teacher is dressed up as a pirate but is still his teacher underneath the costume.
Understanding of cause and effect	Children realize that events have causes.	Seeing a ball roll from behind a wall, Marie looks behind the wall for the person who kicked the ball.
Ability to classify	Children organize objects, people, and events into meaningful categories.	Emily sorts the pine cones she collected on a nature walk into two piles according to their size: "big" and "little."
Understanding of number	Children can count and deal with quantities.	Lindsay shares some candy with her friends, counting to make sure that each girl gets the same amount.
Empathy	Children become more able to imagine how others might feel.	James tries to comfort his friend when he sees that his friend is upset.
Theory of mind	Children become more aware of mental activity and the functioning of the mind.	Jennifer wants to save some cookies for herself, so she hides them from her brother in a pasta box. She knows her cookies will be safe there because her brother will not look in a place where he doesn't expect to find cookies.

make an object stand for (symbolize) something else; for example, a doll may represent a child. *Language,* discussed later in this chapter, involves the use of a common system of symbols (words) to communicate.

Early Symbolic Development and Spatial Thinking

The use of symbols is a universal mark of human culture. Without symbols, people could not communicate verbally, make change, read maps, or treasure photos of distant loved ones. Yet an understanding of symbolism comes only gradually. Until about age 3 or later, most children do not reliably grasp the relationships between pictures, maps, or scale models and the objects or spaces they represent (DeLoache, Miller, & Pierroutsakos, 1998).

In studies of early development of the "picture concept" in the United States and Africa's Ivory Coast, infants used their hands to explore pictures as objects—feeling, rubbing, patting, or grasping them. Not until about 19 months—according to Piaget, the dawn of representational thought—did they show by pointing and other behaviour a glimmer of understanding that a picture is a representation of something else (DeLoache, Pierroutsakos, Uttal, Rosengren, & Gottlieb, 1998).

Very young children often spend a good deal of time watching television, but how clearly do they realize that what they are seeing is a representation of reality? In one experiment, 2-year-olds who watched through a window as an object was being hidden found it easily. So did 2½-year-olds who watched on a video monitor, but 2-year-olds did not—perhaps because the 2-year-olds had had less experience with images on screen (Troseth & DeLoache, 1998). Even 3-year-olds sometimes become confused between a screen image and what it depicts. When shown a television image of a bowl of popcorn and asked whether the popcorn would spill if the television set were turned upside down, a significant number of 3-year-olds said yes (Flavell, Flavell, Green, & Korfmacher, 1990).

The growth of representational thinking enables children to make more accurate judgments about spatial relationships. In another experiment, 2½-year-olds who were told that a "shrinking machine" had shrunk a room to the size of a miniature model were more successful in finding a toy hidden in the room on the basis of its position in the model than were children the same age who were told that the "little room" was just like the "big room." According to the **dual representation hypothesis,** what makes the second task

dual representation hypothesis
Proposal that children under the age of 3 have difficulty grasping spatial relationships because of the need to keep more than one mental representation in mind at the same time

Table 10-2   Limitations of Pre-operational Thought (according to Piaget)

Limitation	Description	Example
Centration: inability to decentre	Children focus on one aspect of a situation and neglect others.	Timothy teases his younger sister that he has more juice than she does because his juice box has been poured into a tall, skinny glass, but hers has been poured into a short, wide glass.
Irreversibility	Children fail to understand that some operations or actions can be reversed, restoring the original situation.	Timothy does not realize that the juice in each glass can be poured back into the juice box from which it came, contradicting his claim that he has more than his sister.
Focus on states rather than transformations	Children fail to understand the significance of the transformation between states.	In the conservation task, Timothy does not understand that transforming the shape of a liquid (pouring it from one container into another) does not change the amount.
Transductive reasoning	Children do not use deductive or inductive reasoning; instead they jump from one particular to another and see cause where none exists.	Sarah was mean to her brother. Then her brother got sick. Sarah concludes that she made her brother sick.
Egocentrism	Children assume everyone else thinks, perceives, and feels as they do.	Kara doesn't realize that she needs to turn a book around so that her father can see the picture she is asking him to explain to her. Instead, she holds the book directly in front of her, where only she can see it.
Animism	Children attribute life to objects not alive.	Amanda says that spring is trying to come but winter is saying, "I won't go! I won't go!"
Inability to distinguish appearance from reality	Children confuse what is real with outward appearance.	Courtney is confused by a sponge made to look like a rock. She states that it looks like a rock and it really is a rock.

harder is that it requires a child to mentally represent both the symbol (the "little room") and its relationship to the thing it stands for (the "big room") at the same time. With the "shrinking machine," children do not have to perform this dual operation, because they are told that the room and the model are one and the same. Three-year-olds do not seem to have this problem with models (DeLoache, Miller, & Rosengren, 1997).

Older preschoolers can use simple maps, and they can transfer the spatial understanding gained from working with models to maps and vice versa (DeLoache, Miller, & Pierroutsakos, 1998). In one experiment, 4-year-olds and most 3-year-olds were able to use a rectangle with a dot inside to find the corresponding location of a small black disk in a similarly shaped (but much larger) sandbox (Huttenlocher, Newcombe, & Vasilyeva, 1999).

The dual representation hypothesis has practical implications. It means that preschool teachers should not assume that children will understand when they use concrete objects, such as blocks of varying sizes, to stand for abstract concepts, such as numerical relationships. It also calls into question the use of anatomically correct dolls to ask children about possible abuse, since the children are required to regard the doll's body as a model of their own (DeLoache, et al., 1997—see Box 10-1).

Causality

Although Piaget recognized that toddlers have some understanding of a connection between actions and reactions, he believed that pre-operational children cannot yet reason logically about cause and effect. Instead, he said, they reason by **transduction.** They view one situation as the basis for another situation, often one occurring at about the same time, whether or not there is logically a causal relationship. For example, they may think that their "bad" thoughts or behaviour caused their own or another child's illness or their parents' divorce. Yet when tested on situations they can understand, young children do accurately link cause and effect.

In one study, preschoolers were shown a row of blocks touching each other. When a rod was pushed against the first block, the entire row tumbled like dominos. Even 3-year-olds could predict that removing some of the centre blocks would prevent the ones on the far end from falling (Bullock, Gelman, & Baillargeon, 1982). Apparently, then, young children's understanding of familiar events in the physical world enables them to think logically about causation (Wellman & Gelman, 1998).

transduction Piaget's term for a pre-operational child's tendency to mentally link particular experiences, whether or not there is logically a causal relationship

Child abuse is a crime that often can be proved only by the testimony of a preschool child. If a child's testimony is inaccurate, an innocent adult may be unfairly punished.

Children responding to adults' suggestions have been known to "remember" events that never occurred. For 11 consecutive weeks, an interviewer told a 4-year-old, "You went to the hospital because your finger got caught in a mousetrap. Did this ever happen to you?" At first the boy said, "No, I've never been to the hospital." In the second interview he said, "Yes, I cried." By the 11th interview, he gave a detailed recital of the event and the trip to the hospital, which he now said had happened the day before (Ceci, in Goleman, 1993).

On the other hand, among 96 two- to twelve-year-olds in Newfoundland who had been hospitalized with serious injuries, children as young as 3 volunteered memories of the injuries and the hospital stays as much as two years later. This study suggests that young children can accurately describe events that are important to them after long periods of time—*if* they are questioned neutrally (Peterson, 1999).

Preschoolers tend to be more suggestible than older children. This difference may be due to younger children's weaker memory for specific events and their greater vulnerability to bribes, threats, and adult expectations (Bruck, Ceci, & Hembrooke, 1998; Ceci & Bruck, 1993; Leichtman & Ceci, 1995). Suggestibility seems to diminish after age 4½ (Portwood & Repucci, 1996). However, some children, regardless of age, are more suggestible than others (Bruck & Ceci, 1997).

Young children may not know whether they "remember" something from experience or from imagining or being told or asked about it (Woolley & Bruell, 1996). In one experiment, researchers had a man called "Sam Stone" drop in at a child-care centre for a few minutes (Leichtman & Ceci, 1995). The visitor commented on a story that was being read, strolled around the room, and then waved good-bye and left. Some of the children who witnessed the event had repeatedly been told stories about "Sam Stone" before his visit, depicting him as a well-meaning bumbler, and/or were given false suggestions afterward that he had ripped a book and dirtied a teddy bear.

After four weekly interviews, nearly half of the 3- and 4-year-olds and 30 per cent of 5- and 6-year-olds who had received *both* the stereotyped advance preparation and the misleading questioning spontaneously reported the book-ripping and teddy bear–dirtying to a new interviewer; and when asked probing questions, nearly three out of four of the younger children said the visitor had done one or the other, or both. Lesser proportions of children who had received *only* advance preparation or suggestive questioning gave false reports. By contrast, *none* of the children in a control group, which had received neither advance preparation nor suggestive questioning, made false reports, showing that young children's testimony *can* be accurate when elicited neutrally.

Reports are likely to be more reliable if children are interviewed only once, soon after the event, by people who do not have an opinion about what took place; if the interviewers do not ask leading questions, ask open-ended rather than yes/no questions, and do not repeatedly ask the same questions; if they are patient and non-judgmental; and if they do not selectively reward or reinforce responses or convey veiled threats or accusations

(Bruck & Ceci, 1997; Bruck et al., 1998; Leichtman & Ceci, 1995; Steward & Steward, 1996).

Often young children are given anatomically correct dolls to point out where they were touched. According to some research, many children will insert fingers or sticks into a doll's vagina or anus, reporting that someone did that to them, even when it did not happen (Bruck & Ceci, 1997; Ceci & Bruck, 1993). In interviews with 72 children, ages 2½ to 4, the children gave more accurate information about where they had been touched by an experimenter when asked directly or told to point to the place on their own bodies than when asked to show it by using a doll (DeLoache, 1994). In other studies, however, use of dolls to jog memory did *not* increase false reports but rather produced more complete reports (Steward & Steward, 1996).

Young children are apt to err in recalling precise details of an event that varies with repetition (Powell & Thomson, 1996). They tend to confuse what happened during a particular episode with what happened during other, similar episodes; all may blur together in memory into a generic "script." Thus a child may have trouble answering questions about a *specific instance* of abuse, even though the child accurately remembers a *pattern* of abuse.

Often young children's testimony is excluded because they cannot demonstrate a clear understanding of the difference between truth and falsehood and of the morality and consequences of telling a lie. Often they do not understand such questions the way they are asked or cannot explain the concepts involved. Furthermore, abused children often have seriously delayed language skills. The Lyon-Saywitz Oath-Taking Competency Picture Task avoids these problems by simply asking a prospective young witness whether a child in a story is telling the truth about a pictured event and what would happen if the child told a lie. Among 192 maltreated 4- to 7-year-olds awaiting court appearances, a majority of 5-year-olds successfully performed this task, and even 4-year-olds did better than chance would predict (Lyon & Saywitz, 1999).

Issues concerning the reliability of young children's testimony are still being sorted out, but it appears that children *can* give reliable testimony if care is taken to avoid biased interviewing techniques. Researchers are trying to develop and validate "model" interview techniques that will expose adults who harm children, while protecting those who may be falsely accused (Bruck, et al., 1998). A promising technique called Source-Monitor Training helps children distinguish between events they witnessed from events they heard about, and has successfully reduced the likelihood of false reports by 7- and 8-year-old children, but not by younger children (Poole & Lindsay, 2002).

What's your view ❓

What information would you seek and what factors would you consider in deciding whether to believe a preschooler's testimony in a child abuse case?

Check it out ❗

For more information on this topic, go to the World Wide Web: **www.mcgrawhill.ca/college/papalia** for relevant website links.

Some research even suggests that preschoolers can see analogies involving familiar items—an ability that, according to Piaget, does not develop until the stage of formal operations in adolescence. This may have been because the verbal analogies he tested them on were too difficult for young children. When shown a picture of a chocolate bar paired with a picture of melted chocolate, even some 3-year-olds realize that the analogous pair for a picture of a snowman is a melted snowman, and not a melted crayon, a dirty snowman, a scarecrow, or a sled (Goswami & Brown, 1989).

Preschoolers' unrealistic views about causes of illness may reflect a belief that all causal relationships are equally and absolutely predictable. In one series of experiments, 3- to 5-year-olds, unlike adults, were just as sure that a person who does not wash hands before eating will get sick as they were that a person who jumps up will come down (Kalish, 1998).

Understanding of Identities and Categorization

The world becomes more orderly and predictable as preschool children develop a better understanding of *identities:* the concept that people and many things are basically the same even if they change in form, size, or appearance. This understanding underlies the emerging self-concept.

Categorization, or classification, requires a child to identify similarities and differences. By age 4, many children can classify by two criteria, such as colour and shape. Children use this ability to order many aspects of their lives, categorizing people as "good," "bad," "friend," "non-friend," and so forth. Thus categorization is a cognitive ability that has emotional and social implications.

What characteristics distinguish living from non-living things? When Piaget asked young children whether the wind and the clouds were alive, their answers led him to think they were confused about what is alive and what is not. (The tendency to attribute life to objects that are not alive is called **animism.**) But when later researchers questioned 3- and 4-year-olds about something more familiar to them—differences between a rock, a person, and a doll—the children showed they understood that people are alive and rocks and dolls are not (Gelman, Spelke, & Meck, 1983). They did not attribute thoughts or emotions to rocks, and they cited the fact that dolls cannot move on their own as evidence that dolls are not alive.

Of course, plants do not move on their own either, nor do they utter sounds, as most animals do. Yet preschoolers know that both plants and animals can grow and decay and, when injured, can heal themselves (Rosengren, Gelman, Kalish, & McCormick, 1991; Wellman & Gelman, 1998).

Culture can affect such beliefs. In a cross-cultural study, 5- to 9-year-old Israeli children, whose tradition views plants primarily in terms of their usefulness as food, were less likely than U.S. and Japanese children to attribute to plants the qualities of living things, such as respiration, growth, and death. On the other hand, Japanese children were more likely to attribute such qualities to inanimate objects, such as a stone and a chair, which, in their culture, are sometimes viewed as if they were alive and had feelings (Hatano et al., 1993).

animism Tendency to attribute life to objects that are not alive

Number

By age 3 or 4, children have words for comparing quantities. They can say one tree is *bigger* than another, or one cup holds *more* juice than another. They know that if they have one cookie and then get another cookie, they have more cookies than they had before, and that if they give one cookie to another child, they have fewer cookies. Such quantitative knowledge appears to be universal, though it develops at different rates, depending on how important counting is in a particular family or culture (Resnick, 1989; Saxe, Guberman, & Gearhart, 1987).

By age 5, most children can count to 20 or more and know the relative sizes of the numbers 1 through 10. Some can do simple, single-digit addition and subtraction (Siegler, 1998). Children intuitively devise strategies for adding, by counting on their fingers or by using other objects.

Sometime in early childhood, children come to recognize five principles of counting (Gelman & Gallistel, 1978; Sophian, 1988):

1. The *1-to-1 principle:* Say only one number-name for each item being counted ("One…two…three…").
2. The *stable-order principle:* Say number-names in a set order ("One, two, three…" rather than "Three, one, two…").
3. The *order-irrelevance principle:* Start counting with any item, and the total count will be the same.
4. The *cardinality principle:* The last number-name used is the total number of items being counted. (If there are five items, the last number-name will be 5.)
5. The *abstraction principle:* The principles above apply to any kind of object. (Seven buttons are equal in number to seven birds.)

There is debate about whether children need to understand these principles before they can learn to count (Gelman & Gallistel, 1978) or whether they deduce the principles from experience with counting (Ho & Fuson, 1998; Siegler, 1998).

How quickly children learn to count depends in part on the number system of their culture. At age 3, when most number learning is focused on counting from 1 through 10, U.S. and Chinese children perform about equally well. At ages 4 and 5, when U.S. youngsters are still counting by ones between 11 and 20, Chinese youngsters learn their culture's more efficient system based on tens and ones (10 + 1, 10 + 2, and so forth). It's not surprising, then, that U.S. children's performance begins to lag (Miller, Smith, Zhu, & Zhang, 1995).

Checkpoint ✔

Can you . . .

✔ Summarize findings about preschool children's understanding of symbols, space, causality, identities, categories, and number?

Immature Aspects of Pre-operational Thought

According to Piaget, one of the main characteristics of pre-operational thought is **centration:** the tendency to focus on one aspect of a situation and neglect others. He said preschoolers come to illogical conclusions because they cannot **decentre**—think about several aspects of a situation at one time. Centration can limit young children's thinking about both physical and social relationships.

Conservation

centration In Piaget's theory, tendency of pre-operational children to focus on one aspect of a situation and neglect others

decentre In Piaget's terminology, to think simultaneously about several aspects of a situation

A classic example is the failure to understand **conservation,** the fact that two things that are equal remain so if their appearance is altered, so long as nothing is added or taken away. Piaget found that children do not fully grasp this principle until the stage of concrete operations and that they develop different kinds of conservation at different ages. Table 10-3 shows how various dimensions of conservation have been tested.

conservation Piaget's term for awareness that two objects that are equal according to a certain measure remain equal in the face of perceptual alteration so long as nothing has been added to or taken away from either object

In one type of conservation task, conservation of liquid, 5-year-old Jeffrey is shown two identical clear glasses, each one short and wide and each holding the same amount of water. Jeffrey is asked, "Is the amount of water in the two glasses equal?" When he agrees, the researcher pours the water in one glass into a third glass, a tall, thin one. Jeffrey is now asked, "Do both glasses contain the same amount of water? Or does one contain more? Why?" In early childhood—even after watching the water being poured out of one of the short, fat glasses into a tall, thin glass or even after pouring it himself—Jeffrey will say that either the taller glass or the wider one contains more water. When asked why, he says, "This one is bigger this way," stretching his arms to show the height or width. Pre-operational children cannot consider height *and* width at the same time. Since they centre on one aspect, they cannot think logically, said Piaget.

irreversibility Piaget's term for a pre-operational child's failure to understand that an operation can go in two or more directions

The ability to conserve is also limited by **irreversibility:** failure to understand that an operation or action can go two or more ways. Once Jeffrey can imagine restoring the original state of the water by pouring it back into the other glass, he will realize that the amount of water in both glasses is the same.

Pre-operational children commonly think as if they were watching a filmstrip with a series of static frames: They *focus on successive states,* said Piaget, and do not recognize the transformation from one state to another. In the conservation experiment, they focus on the water as it stands in each glass rather than on the water being poured from one glass to another, and so they fail to realize that the amount of water is the same.

Table 10-3   Tests of Various Kinds of Conservation

Conservation Task	Show Child (and Have Child Acknowledge) that Both Items Are Equal	Perform Transformation	Ask Child	Pre-operational Child Usually Answers
Number	Two equal, parallel rows of candies	Space the candies in one row farther apart.	"Are there the same number of candies in each row or does one row have more?"	"The longer one has more."
Length	Two parallel sticks of the the same length	Move one stick to the right.	"Are both sticks the same size or is one longer?"	"The one on the right (or left) is longer."
Liquid	Two identical glasses holding equal amounts of liquid	Pour liquid from one glass into a taller, narrower glass.	"Do both glasses have the same amount of liquid or does one have more?"	"The taller one has more."
Matter (mass)	Two balls of clay of the same size	Roll one ball into a sausage shape.	"Do both pieces have the same amount of clay or does one have more?"	"The sausage has more."
Weight	Two balls of clay of the same weight	Roll one ball into a sausage shape.	"Do both weigh the same or does one weigh more?"	"The sausage weighs more."
Area	Two toy rabbits, two pieces of cardboard (representing grassy fields), with blocks or toys (representing barns on the fields); same number of "barns" on each board	Rearrange the blocks on one piece of board.	"Does each rabbit have the same amount of grass to eat or does one have more?"	"The one with the blocks close together has more to eat."
Volume	Two glasses of water with two equal-sized balls of clay in them	Roll one ball into a sausage shape.	"If we put the sausage back in the glass, will the water be the same height in each glass, or will one be higher?"	"The water in the glass with the sausage will be higher."

Egocentrism

Egocentrism is a form of centration. According to Piaget, young children centre so much on their own point of view that they cannot take in another's. Three-year-olds are not as egocentric as newborn babies; but, said Piaget, they still think the universe centres on them. Egocentrism may help explain why young children (as we will see) sometimes have trouble separating reality from what goes on inside their own heads and why they may show confusion about what causes what. When Jeffrey believes that his "bad thoughts" have made his sister sick, or that he caused his parents' marital troubles, he is thinking egocentrically.

To study egocentrism, Piaget designed the *three-mountain task* (see Figure 10-1). A child sits facing a table that holds three large mounds. A doll is placed on a chair at the opposite side of the table. The investigator asks the child how the "mountains" would look to the doll. Piaget found that young children usually could not answer the question correctly; instead, they described the "mountains" from their own perspective. Piaget saw this as evidence that pre-operational children cannot imagine a different point of view (Piaget & Inhelder, 1967).

However, another experimenter who posed a similar problem in a different way got different results (Hughes, 1975). A child sat in front of a square board divided by "walls" into four sections. A toy police officer stood at the edge of the board; a doll was moved from one section to another. After each move the child was asked, "Can the police officer see the doll?" Then another toy police officer was brought into the action, and the child was told to hide the doll from both officers. Thirty children between ages 3½ and 5 were correct 9 out of 10 times.

Why were these children able to take another person's point of view (the police officer's) when those doing the mountain task were not? It may be because the "police officer" task calls for thinking in more familiar, less abstract ways. Most children do not look at mountains and do not think about what other people might see when looking at one, but most 3-year-olds know about dolls and police officers and hiding. Thus young children may show egocentrism primarily in situations beyond their immediate experience.

egocentrism Piaget's term for inability to consider another person's point of view

Checkpoint ✔

Can you . . .

✔ Tell how centration limits preoperational thought?

✔ Give several reasons why preoperational children have difficulty with conservation?

✔ Discuss research that challenges Piaget's views on egocentrism in early childhood?

Figure 10-1

Piaget's three-mountain task. A pre-operational child is unable to describe the "mountains" from the doll's point of view—an indication of egocentrism, according to Piaget.

Do Young Children Have Theories of Mind?

theory of mind Awareness and understanding of mental processes

Piaget (1929) was the first scholar to investigate children's **theory of mind,** their emerging awareness of their own mental processes and those of other people. He asked children such questions as "Where do dreams come from?" and "What do you think with?" On the basis of the answers, he concluded that children younger than 6 cannot distinguish between thoughts or dreams and real physical entities and have no theory of mind. However, more recent research indicates that between ages 2 and 5, children's knowledge about mental processes—their own and others'—grows dramatically (Astington, 1993; Bower, 1993; Flavell, et al., 1995).

Again, methodology seems to have made the difference. Piaget's questions were abstract, and he expected children to be able to put their understanding into words. Contemporary researchers use vocabulary and objects children are familiar with. Instead of talking in generalities, they observe children in everyday activities or give them concrete examples. In this way, we have learned, for example, that 3-year-olds can tell the difference between a boy who has a cookie and a boy who is thinking about a cookie; they know which boy can touch, share, and eat it (Astington, 1993).

Let's look at several aspects of theory of mind.

Knowledge about Thinking

Between ages 3 and 5, children come to understand that thinking goes on inside the mind; that it can deal with either real or imaginary things; that someone can be thinking of one thing while doing or looking at something else; that a person whose eyes and ears are covered can think about objects; that someone who looks pensive is probably thinking; and that thinking is different from seeing, talking, touching, and knowing (Flavell et al., 1995).

However, preschoolers generally believe that mental activity starts and stops. Not until middle childhood do children know that the mind is continuously active (Flavell, 1993; Flavell et al., 1995). Preschoolers also have little or no awareness that they or other people think in words, or "talk to themselves in their heads," or that they think while they are looking, listening, reading, or talking (Flavell, Green, Flavell, & Grossman, 1997). At the same time, not until age 7 or 8 do most children realize that people who are asleep do *not* engage in conscious mental activity, such as thinking, deciding, and even knowing they are asleep (Flavell, Green, Flavell, & Lin, 1999).

Social Cognition

social cognition Ability to understand that others have mental states and to judge their feelings and intentions

Human beings have what seems to be the unique ability to understand that others have mental states. This ability, sometimes called **social cognition,** is fundamental to the maintenance of social relationships. Learning to gauge the feelings and intentions of others enables us to function as members of a family and a society (Lillard & Curenton, 1999).

empathy Ability to put oneself in another person's place and feel what that person feels

Piaget believed that egocentrism delays the development of **empathy,** the ability to imagine being in another person's mental state, until the concrete operational stage. But new research has shown that empathy begins so early that it may be "an innate potential, like the ability to learn language" (Lillard & Curenton, 1999, p. 52). Even 10- to 12-month-old babies cry when they see another child crying; by 13 or 14 months, they pat or hug a crying child; by 18 months they may hold out a new toy to replace a broken one or give a bandage to someone with a cut finger (Yarrow, 1978).

In one experiment (Carpenter, Akhtar, & Tomasello, 1998), 14- to 18-month-olds watched an adult do such things as pulling a ring that made a small toy pop out of a bird feeder. Sometimes the adult said, "There!" indicating that the result had been intended; sometimes the adult said, "Woops!" indicating that it was accidental. The toddlers were twice as likely to imitate the adult's "intentional" actions as "accidental" ones, showing some ability to infer the intentions of another person from vocal expressions.

By age 3, children's understanding of others' emotional and mental states is becoming more sophisticated. They realize that a person who does not immediately find what she wants will keep looking. They know that if someone gets what he wants he will be happy, and if not, he will be sad (Wellman & Woolley, 1990).

Four-year-olds begin to understand that people have differing beliefs about the world, and that these beliefs—true or mistaken—affect their actions.

The young girl on the right is old enough to know that her cousin needs consoling. Empathy, the ability to understand another person's feelings, begins at an early age.

False Beliefs and Deception

A researcher shows 5-year-old Mariella a candy box and asks what is in it. "Candy," she says. But when Mariella opens the box, she finds crayons, not candy. "What will a child who hasn't opened the box think is in it?" the researcher asks. "Candy!" shouts Mariella, grinning at the joke. When the researcher repeats the same procedure with 3-year-old Bobby, he too answers the first question with "Candy." But after seeing the crayons in the box, when asked what another child would think was in the box, he says, "Crayons." And then he says that he himself originally thought crayons would be in the box (Flavell, 1993; Flavell et al., 1995).

The understanding that people can hold false beliefs flows from the realization that people hold mental representations of reality, which can sometimes be wrong. Three-year-olds, at least in some studies, appear to lack such an understanding (Flavell et al., 1995). However, other researchers claim that 3-year-olds have at least a rudimentary understanding of false beliefs but may not show it when presented with complicated situations (Hala & Chandler, 1996).

Three-year-olds' failure to recognize false beliefs may stem from egocentric thinking. At that age, children tend to believe that everyone else knows what they know and believes what they do. A child who falls down in the playground at preschool may think his mother knows all about the incident, because he himself does. Three-year-olds also have trouble understanding that their own beliefs can be false (Lillard & Curenton, 1999). In fact, when actually presented with video evidence of their false beliefs, it is interesting that 3-year-old children fail to report what they had once claimed. For example, they continue to hold on to the belief that they had previously thought a candy box contained string, despite seeing a video of themselves claiming that the box contained candy (Zelazo & Boseovski, 2001).

Older preschoolers' more advanced understanding of mental representations seems to be related to a decline in egocentrism. Four-year-olds understand that people who see or hear different versions of the same event may come away with different beliefs. Not until about age 6, however, do children realize that two people who see or hear the *same* thing may interpret it differently (Pillow & Henrichon, 1996).

Deception is an effort to plant a false belief in someone else's mind, and it requires a child to suppress the impulse to be truthful. In other words, lying represents cognitive development! Some studies have found that children become capable of deception as early as age 2 or 3, others, at 4 or 5. Children as young as 3 are capable of telling "white lies" to be polite (Talwar & Lee, 2002). The difference may have to do with the means of deception children are expected to use. In a series of experiments, 3-year-olds were asked whether they would like to play a trick on an experimenter by giving a false clue about which of two boxes a ball was hidden in. The children were better able to carry out the deception when asked to put a picture of the ball on the wrong box, or to point to that box with an arrow, than when they pointed with their fingers, which children this age are accustomed to doing truthfully (Carlson, Moses, & Hix, 1998). There seems to be a difference between knowing about pretending and deceiving. Three-year-olds are able to understand the pretending in fairy tales, but when it comes to the victims of deception by a character in a fairy tale,

3-year-olds are unable to correctly identify the tricked victim's false beliefs. This difficulty might reflect an inability to understand another person's beliefs, when the beliefs conflict with those of the child (Peskin, 1996). This difficulty usually disappears by the age of 4.

Piaget maintained that young children regard all falsehoods—intentional or not—as lies. However, when 3- to 6-year-olds were told a story about a subject close to their experience—the danger of eating contaminated food—and were given a choice between interpreting a character's action as a lie or a mistake, about three-fourths of the children in all age groups characterized it accurately (Siegal & Peterson, 1998). Apparently, then, even 3-year-olds have some understanding of the role of intent in deception. However, understanding that other people can intentionally ignore facts in order to deceive themselves doesn't emerge until 9 years (Johnson, 1997).

Distinguishing between Appearance and Reality

Related to awareness of false beliefs is the ability to distinguish between appearance and reality: Both require a child to refer to two conflicting mental representations at the same time. According to Piaget, not until about age 5 or 6 do children understand the distinction between what *seems* to be and what *is*. Much research bears him out, though some studies have found this ability beginning to emerge before age 4 (Friend & Davis, 1993; C. Rice, Koinis, Sullivan, Tager-Flusberg, & Winner, 1997).

In one series of experiments (Flavell, Green, & Flavell, 1986), 3-year-olds apparently confused appearance and reality in a variety of tests. For example, the experimenters showed preschoolers a red car and then covered it with a filter that made it look black. When the children were asked what colour the car really was, they said, "Black." When the children put on special sunglasses that made milk look green, they said the milk *was* green, even though they had just seen white milk. When an experimenter put on a Halloween mask in front of the children, they thought the experimenter was someone else.

However, when 3-year-olds were shown a sponge that looked like a rock and were asked to help trick someone else into thinking it was a rock, the children were able to make the distinction between the way the sponge looked (like a rock) and what it actually was (a sponge). Apparently, putting the task in the context of a deception helped the children realize that an object can be perceived as other than what it actually is (Rice et al., 1997).

Three-year-olds' difficulty distinguishing appearance from reality may itself be more apparent than real. When children were asked questions about the uses of such objects as a candle wrapped like a crayon, only 3 out of 10 answered correctly. But when asked to respond with actions rather than words ("I want a candle to put on a birthday cake"), 9 out of 10 handed the experimenter the crayon-like candle (Sapp, Lee, & Muir, 2000).

Distinguishing between Fantasy and Reality

Sometime between 18 months and 3 years, children learn to distinguish between real and imagined events. Three-year-olds know the difference between a real dog and a dog in a dream, and between something invisible (such as air) and something imaginary. They can pretend and can tell when someone else is pretending (Flavell et al., 1995).

Still, the line between fantasy and reality may seem to blur at times. It is difficult to know, when questioning children about "pretend" objects, whether children are giving "serious" answers or are keeping up the pretense (M. Taylor, 1997). In one study (Harris, Brown, Marriott, Whittall, & Harmer, 1991), 40 four- to six-year-olds were shown two cardboard boxes. They were asked to pretend that there was a monster in one box and a bunny in the other. Each box had a small hole in it, and the children were asked whether they wanted to put a finger or a stick in the holes. The experimenter then left the room, and some of the children did touch the boxes. Even though most of the children claimed they were just pretending about both the bunny and the monster, most preferred to touch the box holding the imaginary bunny, and more put their fingers in that box and put the stick in the monster box.

This research suggests that even though young children understand the distinction between fantasy and reality, they sometimes act as if the creatures of their imagination could exist. On the other hand, the children may simply have been carrying on the unfinished pretend game in the experimenter's absence. That was the conclusion of a partial replication

---

What's your view ?

- Is it better to let children who are slow in developing such concepts as the distinction between appearance and reality develop these concepts at their own pace, or is it better to teach them?

Box 10-2 Imaginary Companions

At 3½, Anna had 23 "sisters" with such names as Och, Elmo, Zeni, Aggie, and Ankie. She often talked to them on the telephone, since they lived about 100 miles away, in the town where her family used to live. During the next year, most of the sisters disappeared, but Och continued to visit, especially for birthday parties. Och had a cat and a dog (which Anna had begged for in vain), and whenever Anna was denied something she saw advertised on television, she announced that she already had one at her sister's house. But when a live friend came over and Anna's mother happened to mention one of her imaginary companions, Anna quickly changed the subject.

All 23 sisters—and some "boys" and "girls" who had followed them—lived only in Anna's imagination, as she well knew. Like an estimated 25 to 65 per cent of children between ages 3 and 10 (Woolley, 1997), she created imaginary companions, with whom she talked and played. This normal phenomenon of childhood is seen most often in first-born and only children, who lack the close company of siblings. Like Anna, most children who create imaginary companions have many of them (Gleason, Sebanc, & Hartup, 2000). Girls are more likely than boys to have imaginary "friends" (or at least to acknowledge them). Girls' imaginary playmates are usually other children, whereas boys' are more often animals (D. G. Singer & Singer, 1990).

Children who have imaginary companions can distinguish fantasy from reality, but in free-play sessions they are more likely to engage in pretend play than are children without imaginary companions (M. Taylor, Cartwright, & Carlson, 1993). They play more happily and more imaginatively than other children and are more cooperative with other children and adults (D. G. Singer & Singer, 1990; J. L. Singer & Singer, 1981); and they do not lack for friends at preschool (Gleason et al., 2000). They are more fluent with language, watch less television, and show more curiosity, excitement, and persistence during play. In one study, 4-year-olds—regardless of verbal intelligence—who reported having imaginary companions did better on theory-of-mind tasks (such as differentiating between appearance and reality and recognizing false beliefs) than children who did not create such companions (M. Taylor & Carlson, 1997).

Children's relationships with imaginary companions are like peer relationships; they are usually sociable and friendly, in contrast with the nurturing way in which children treat personified objects, such as stuffed animals and dolls (Gleason et al., 2000). Imaginary playmates are good company for an only child like Anna. They provide wish-fulfillment mechanisms ("There was a monster in my room, but Elmo scared it off with magic dust"), scapegoats ("I didn't eat those cookies—Och must have done it!"), displacement agents for the child's own fears ("Aggie is afraid she's going to be washed down the drain"), and support in difficult situations. (One 6-year-old "took" her imaginary companion with her to see a scary movie.)

What's your view?

How should parents respond to children's talk about imaginary companions?

Check it out

For more information on this topic, go to the Online Learning Centre: **www.mcgrawhill.ca/college/papalia,** which provides a link to a Web page about children's imaginary companions.

of the study, in which the experimenter remained in the room and clearly ended the pretense. Only about 10 per cent of the children touched or looked in the boxes, and when questioned, almost all showed a clear understanding that the creatures were imaginary (Golomb & Galasso, 1995). It's possible, of course, that if the experimenter had left the room after ending the pretense, the children might have felt more free to act on their fantasies (Woolley, 1997).

The belief that "wishing will make it so" may be linked more to a belief in magic than to preschoolers' otherwise realistic understanding of how causality works in the real world. Both of these beliefs tend to decrease near the end of the preschool period (Woolley, Phelps, Davis, & Mandell, 1999). A review of the literature suggests that magical or wishful thinking in children age 3 and older does *not* stem from confusion between fantasy and reality. Often magical thinking is a way to explain events that do not seem to have obvious realistic explanations (usually because children lack knowledge about them, as young Einstein did about the workings of the compass), or simply to indulge in the pleasures of pretending—as with the belief in imaginary companions (see Box 10-2). Children, like adults, generally are aware of the magical nature of such fantasy figures but are more willing to entertain the possibility that they may be real (Woolley, 1997).

Influences on Theory-of-Mind Development

Some children develop theory-of-mind abilities earlier than others. This development reflects brain maturation and improvements in cognition. Hereditary and environmental influences play a large part.

Difficulties in social interaction associated with Turner's syndrome, and typical delays in autistic children's understanding of false beliefs, support a strong genetic influence on social cognition, since both of these disorders have genetic origins. Brain imaging shows increased activity in the left frontal lobe (a brain region in which autistic persons show abnormalities) during theory-of-mind tasks (Sabbagh & Taylor, 2000). A study of 119 same-sex 3-year-old twins found a heritability of 67 per cent in understanding of false beliefs and deception (Hughes & Cutting, 1999).

Children whose teachers rate them high on social skills are better able to recognize false beliefs (Watson, Nixon, Wilson, & Capage, 1999). So are children with several siblings (Hughes & Cutting, 1999) and children with advanced language development, who are better able to take part in family discussions about such matters (Astington & Jenkins, 1999; Cutting & Dunn, 1999). The quality of relationship between mother and child is related to performance on theory-of-mind tasks. High maternal sensitivity toward their children, reflecting availability for interaction and social exchanges, and higher levels of maternal emotional distress, with more rumination about what they and others are thinking, when children were 2 years of age predicted better performance at 5 years of age on a theory-of-mind task that involved caregiver location (Symons & Clark, 2000).

Talking with children about mental states, and about how the characters in a story feel, helps them develop social understanding (Lillard & Curenton, 1999). Empathy usually arises earlier in children whose families talk a lot about feelings and causality (Dunn, 1991; Dunn, Brown, Slomkowski, Tesla, & Youngblade, 1991). Younger siblings, who have older siblings to talk to, understand false beliefs earlier than older siblings do. Families that encourage pretend play stimulate the development of theory-of-mind skills. As children play roles, they try to assume others' perspectives. When children pretend together, they must deal with other children's views of their imaginary world (Lillard & Curenton, 1999). The presence of siblings in the family might compensate for poorer theory-of-mind development in children who experience difficulties in their language development (Jenkins & Astington, 1996).

Socio-economic status may make a difference. Most research on theory of mind has been done among middle- to upper-middle-class children with educated parents. In one study of working-class and middle-class urban preschoolers of various ethnic backgrounds, the middle-class children and those with better language skills did better on theory-of-mind tasks involving false beliefs and understanding others' emotions (Cutting & Dunn, 1999).

Different cultures have different ways of looking at the mind, and these cultural attitudes influence children (Lillard, 1998). For example, middle-class Northern Europeans and North Americans pay a lot of attention to how mental states affect behaviour, whereas Asians focus on how situations call for certain behaviours. Japanese parents and teachers frequently talk to children about how their behaviour affects other people's feelings (Azuma, 1994). A Japanese child who refuses to finish a meal may be told that the farmer who worked hard to grow the food will be hurt if the child doesn't eat it.

Language Development

Preschoolers are full of questions: "How many sleeps until tomorrow?" "Who filled the river with water?" "Do babies have muscles?" "Do smells come from inside my nose?" Young children's growing facility with language helps them express their own unique view of the world.

Preschoolers also make rapid advances in vocabulary, grammar, and syntax. The child who, at 3, describes how Daddy "hatches" wood (chops with a hatchet), or asks Mommy to "piece" her food (cut it into little pieces) may, by the age of 5, tell her mother, "Don't be ridiculous!" or proudly point to her toys and say, "See how I organized everything?"

Vocabulary

At 3 the average child can use 900 to 1,000 different words and uses about 12,000 each day. By the age of 6, a child typically has a spoken vocabulary of 2,600 words and understands more than 20,000 (Owens, 1996), having learned an average of 9 new words a day since about 1½ years of age (M. L. Rice, 1982). With the help of formal schooling, a youngster's passive, or receptive, vocabulary (words she can understand) will grow four times as large—to 80,000 words—by the time of entry into high school (Owens, 1996).

How do children expand their vocabularies so quickly? Apparently they do it by **fast mapping,** which allows them to absorb the meaning of a new word after hearing it only once or twice in conversation. From the context, children seem to form a quick hypothesis about the meaning of the word and store it in memory. Linguists are not sure how fast mapping works, but it seems likely that children draw on what they know about the rules for forming words, about similar words, about the immediate context, and about the subject under discussion.

Names of objects (nouns) seem to be easier to fast map than names of actions (verbs), which are less concrete. Yet one experiment showed that children just under 3 years old can fast map a new verb and apply it to another situation in which the same action is being performed (Golinkoff, Jacquet, Hirsh-Pasek, & Nandakumar, 1996).

Many 3- and 4-year-olds seem able to tell when two words refer to the same object or action (Savage & Au, 1996). They know that a single object cannot have two proper names (a dog cannot be both Spot and Fido). They also know that more than one adjective can apply to the same noun ("Fido is spotted and furry") and that an adjective can be combined with a proper name ("smart Fido!") (Hall & Graham, 1999).

Theory of mind can have an effect on vocabulary learning, allowing children to understand whether a source of word information is valid and worthy of attention. When 3- and 4-year-old children were taught a new word, only words taught by an adult who appeared certain were learned by children. However, when adults who hesitated but were able to demonstrate expert knowledge of a word, the 4-year-olds successfully learned the word while the 3-year-olds did not. With greater sophistication in theory of mind, children are able to distinguish a speaker's hesitancy from a speaker's knowledge about a word and successfully acquire new vocabulary. Younger children focused on hesitancy information, regardless of whether it was relevant to the speaker's knowledge (Sabbagh & Baldwin, 2001).

The use of *metaphor,* a figure of speech in which a word or phrase that usually designates one thing is applied to another, becomes increasingly common during these years (Vosniadou, 1987). Once Joanne, upset by her parents' quarrelling, exclaimed, "Why are you two being such grumpy old bears?" Joanne's use of metaphor reflected her growing ability to see similarities between (in this case) parents and bears, and thus was related to her ability to classify. The use of metaphors shows an ability to use knowledge about one type of thing to better understand another, an ability needed for acquiring many kinds of knowledge.

Grammar and Syntax

The ways in which children combine syllables into words and words into sentences grow increasingly sophisticated during early childhood (Owens, 1996). At 3, children typically begin to use plurals, possessives, and past tense and know the difference between *I, you,* and *we.* However, they still make errors of over-regularization because they have not yet learned exceptions to rules (refer back to chapter 7). Their sentences are generally short and simple, often leaving out small words such as *a* and *the,* but including some pronouns, adjectives, and prepositions. Most of their sentences are declarative ("Kitty wants milk"), but they can ask—and answer—*what* and *where* questions. (*Why* and *how* are harder to grasp.)

Between ages 4 and 5, sentences average four to five words and may be declarative, negative ("I'm not hungry"), interrogative ("Why can't I go outside?"), or imperative ("Catch the ball!"). Four-year-olds use complex, multi-clause sentences ("I'm eating because I'm hungry") more frequently if their parents often use such sentences (Huttenlocher, Vasilyeva, Cymerman, & Levine, in preparation). Children this age tend to string sentences together in long run-on stories (". . . And then . . . And then . . ."). In some respects, comprehension may be immature. For example, 4-year-old Noah can carry out a command that includes more than one step ("Pick up your toys and put them in the cupboard"). However, if his mother tells him "You may watch TV after you pick up your toys," he may process the words in the order in which he hears them and think he can first watch television and then pick up his toys.

By ages 5 to 7, children's speech has become quite adult-like. They speak in longer and more complicated sentences. They use more conjunctions, prepositions, and articles. They use compound and complex sentences and can handle all parts of speech.

fast mapping Process by which a child absorbs the meaning of a new word after hearing it once or twice in conversation

This preschool boy can use his growing vocabulary and knowledge of grammar and syntax to communicate more effectively. He has learned how to ask his father for things, to carry on a conversation, and to tell a story, perhaps about what happened at preschool.

Still, while children this age speak fluently, comprehensibly, and fairly grammatically, they have yet to master many fine points of language. They rarely use the passive voice ("I was dressed by Grandpa"), conditional sentences ("If I were big, I could drive the bus"), or the auxiliary verb *have* ("I have seen that lady before") (C. S. Chomsky, 1969). They often make errors because they have not yet learned exceptions to rules. Saying "holded" instead of "held" or "eated" instead of "ate" is a normal sign of linguistic progress. When young children discover a rule, such as adding *-ed* to a verb for past tense, they tend to over-generalize—to use it even with words that do not conform to the rule. Eventually, they notice that *-ed* is not always used to form the past tense of a verb. Children are more likely to overgeneralize the use of transitive or intransitive verbs in constructions that call for the other type of verb ("He disappeared it" or "He's hitting") if the verb they are using is not very familiar to them (Brooks, Tomasello, Dodson, & Lewis, 1999).

Pragmatics and Social Speech

As children learn vocabulary, grammar, and syntax, they become more competent in **pragmatics**—the practical knowledge of how to use language to communicate. This includes knowing how to ask for things, how to tell a story or joke, how to begin and continue a conversation, and how to adjust comments to the listener's perspective (M. L. Rice, 1982). These are all aspects of **social speech:** speech intended to be understood by a listener.

Children use both gestures and speech communicatively from an early age. By age 2, they engage in conversation, trying to make their own speech relevant to what someone else has said. However, children this age have trouble keeping a conversation going without changing the subject (Owens, 1996).

With improved pronunciation and grammar, it becomes easier for others to understand what children say. Most 3-year-olds are quite talkative, and they pay attention to the effect of their speech on others. If people cannot understand them, they try to explain themselves more clearly. Four-year-olds, especially girls, use "parentese" when speaking to 2-year-olds (Owens, 1996; Shatz & Gelman, 1973; refer back to chapter 7).

Most 5-year-olds can adapt what they say to what the listener knows. They can now use words to resolve disputes, and they use more polite language and fewer direct commands in talking to adults than to other children. Almost half of all 5-year-olds can stick to a conversational topic for about a dozen turns—if they are comfortable with their partner and if the topic is one they know and care about (Owens, 1996).

Private Speech

Anna, age 4, was alone in her room painting. When she finished, she was overheard saying aloud, "Now I have to put the pictures somewhere to dry. I'll put them by the window. They need to get dry now. I'll paint some more dinosaurs."

Private speech—talking aloud to oneself with no intent to communicate with others—is normal and common in childhood, accounting for 20 to 50 per cent of what 4- to 10-year-old children say (Berk, 1986a). Two- to 3-year-olds playfully repeat rhythmic sounds; older children "think out loud" or mutter in barely audible tones (see Table 10-4).

Piaget (1962/1923) saw private speech as egocentric, a sign of cognitive immaturity. Unable to communicate meaningfully or to recognize others' viewpoints, young children simply vocalize whatever is on their own minds. Another reason young children talk while they do things, said Piaget, is that the symbolic function is not fully developed: they do not yet distinguish between words and the actions the words stand for. By the end of the pre-operational stage, with cognitive maturation and social experience, children become less egocentric and more capable of symbolic thought, and so discard private speech.

Like Piaget, Vygotsky (1962/1934) believed that private speech helps young children to integrate language with thought, and to organize and regulate thinking. However, Vygotsky did not look upon private speech as egocentric. He saw it as a special form of communication: conversation with the self. As such, he said, it serves a very important function in the transition between early social speech (often experienced in the form of adult commands) and inner speech (thinking in words)—a transition toward the internalization of socially

Table 10-4

Type	Child's Activity	Examples
Wordplay, repetition	Repeating words and sounds, often in playful, rhythmic recitation	Jean wanders around the room, repeating in a singsong, "Put the mushroom on your head, put the mushroom in your pocket, put the mushroom on your nose."
Solitary fantasy play and speech addressed to non-human objects	Talking to objects, playing roles, producing sound effects for objects	Darryl says, "Ka-powee ka-powee," aiming his finger like a gun. Ashley says in a high-pitched voice while playing in the doll corner, "I'll be better after the doctor gives me a shot. Ow!" she remarks as she pokes herself with her finger (an imaginary needle).
Emotional release and expression	Expressing emotions or feelings directed inward rather than to a listener	Keiko is given a new box of crayons and says to no one in particular, "Wow! Neat!" Rachel is sitting at her desk with an anxious expression on her face, repeating to herself, "My mom's sick, my mom's sick."
Egocentric communication	Communicating with another person, but expressing the information so incompletely or peculiarly that it can't be understood	David and Mark are seated next to one another on the rug. David says to Mark, "It broke," without explaining what or when. Susan says to Ann at the art table, "Where are the paste-ons?" Ann says, "What paste-ons?" Susan shrugs and walks off.
Describing or guiding one's own activity	Narrating one's actions, thinking out loud	Omar sits down at the art table and says to himself, "I want to draw something. Let's see, I need a big piece of paper. I want to draw my cat." Working in her arithmetic workbook, Cathy says to no one in particular, "Six." Then, counting on her fingers, she continues, "Seven, eight, nine, ten. It's ten, it's ten. The answer's ten."
Reading aloud, sounding out words	Reading aloud or sounding out words while reading	While reading a book, Tom begins to sound out a difficult word. "Sher-lock Holm-lock," he says slowly and quietly. Then he tries again, "Sher-lock-Holm-lock, Sherlock Holme," he says, leaving off the final *s* in his most successful attempt.
Inaudible muttering	Speaking so quietly that the words cannot be understood by an observer	Tony's lips move as he works a math problem.

Source: Adapted from Berk & Garvin, 1984.

derived control of behaviour ("Now I have to put the pictures somewhere to dry"). Vygotsky suggested that private speech follows an inverted U-shaped curve: It increases during the preschool years as children use it for self-regulation and then fades away during the early elementary school years as they become more able to guide and master their actions.

Research generally supports Vygotsky on the functions of private speech. In an observational study of 93 low- to middle-income 3- to 5-year-olds, 86 per cent of the children's remarks were *not* egocentric (Berk, 1986a). The most sociable children, and those who engage in the most social speech, tend to use the most private speech as well, apparently supporting Vygotsky's view that private speech is stimulated by social experience (Berk, 1986a, 1986b, 1992; Berk & Garvin, 1984; Kohlberg, Yaeger, & Hjertholm, 1968).

There is also evidence for the role of private speech in self-regulation (Berk & Garvin, 1984; Furrow, 1984). Private speech tends to increase when children are trying to do difficult tasks, especially without adult supervision (Berk, 1992; Berk & Garvin, 1984). Private speech serves other functions for younger children. Two-year-olds often engage in "crib talk," playing with sounds and words. For 4- and 5-year-olds, private speech may be a way to express fantasies and emotions (Berk, 1992; Small, 1990).

According to one ranking (Bivens & Berk, 1988), children progress through at least three levels of private speech: (1) speech that is purely self-expressive (wordplay, repetition of syllables, expression of feelings, or talking to dolls or imaginary playmates); (2) vocal statements relevant to a task at hand (commenting on what one is doing or needs to do or has done, asking and then answering one's own questions, or sounding out words); and (3) external signs of task-directed inner speech (inaudible muttering or lip and tongue movements). Preschool girls, who tend to be more verbally advanced than preschool boys, use more mature forms of private speech; and middle-income children use more mature forms than low-income children (Berk, 1986a).

How much do children engage in private speech? The pattern now appears more complex than Vygotsky's U-shaped curve. Some studies have reported no age changes in

Checkpoint ✔

Can you . . .

✔ Trace normal progress in 3- to 6-year-olds' vocabulary, grammar, syntax, and conversational abilities?

✔ Give reasons why children of various ages use private speech?

overall use of private speech; others have found variations in the timing of its decline. The brightest children tend to use it earliest. Whereas Vygotsky considered the need for private speech a universal stage of cognitive development, studies have found a wide range of individual differences, with some children using it very little or not at all (Berk, 1992).

Understanding the significance of private speech has practical implications, especially in school (Berk, 1986a). Talking to oneself or muttering should not be considered misbehaviour; a child may be struggling with a problem and may need to think out loud.

Delayed Language Development

The fact that Albert Einstein did not start to speak until he was close to 3 years old may encourage parents of other children whose speech develops later than usual. About 3 per cent of preschool-age children show language delays, though their intelligence is usually average or better (M. L. Rice, 1989). Boys are more likely than girls to be late talkers (Plomin et al., 1998).

It is unclear why some children speak late. They do not necessarily lack linguistic input at home. These children may have a cognitive limitation that makes it hard for them to learn the rules of language (Scarborough, 1990). Some late speakers have a history of otitis media (an inflammation of the middle ear) between 12 and 18 months of age; these children improve in language ability when the infection, with its related hearing loss, clears up (Lonigan, Fischel, Whitehurst, Arnold, & Valdez-Menchaca, 1992).

Some current investigations focus on problems in fast mapping. Children with delayed language skills may need to hear a new word more often than other children do before they can incorporate it into their vocabularies (M. L. Rice, 1989; M. Rice, Oetting, Marquis, Bode, & Pae, 1994). Heredity seems to play a role in the most severe cases of language delay. Among 3,039 pairs of 2-year-old twins, if one monozygotic twin fell in the bottom 5 per cent in vocabulary knowledge, the other twin had an 80 per cent chance of being equally delayed. With dizygotic twins, the chances of equivalent delays were only 42 per cent (Plomin et al., 1998).

Many children who speak late—especially those whose comprehension is normal—eventually catch up (Thal, Tobias, & Morrison, 1991). Still, delayed language development can have far-reaching cognitive, social, and emotional consequences. Children who often mispronounce words at age 2, who have poor vocabulary at age 3, or who have trouble naming objects at age 5 are apt to have reading disabilities later on (M. Rice et al., 1994; Scarborough, 1990). Children who do not speak or understand as well as their peers tend to be judged negatively by adults and other children (M. L. Rice, Hadley, & Alexander, 1993) and to have trouble finding playmates or friends (Gertner, Rice, & Hadley, 1994). Children viewed as unintelligent or immature may "live down" to these expectations, and their self-image may suffer.

Speech and language therapy may include therapy that focuses on specific language forms, a specialized preschool program targeting language skills, and follow-up programs either in or out of school during the elementary school years (M. L. Rice, 1989). In a promising technique called *dialogic reading* (mentioned in chapter 2), reading picture books becomes a vehicle for parent–child dialogue about the story. Three- to 6-year-olds with mild-to-moderate language delays whose mothers were trained in dialogic reading improved more than a comparison group whose mothers had been trained to use similar principles in talking with their children, but not about books (Dale, Crain-Thoreson, Notari-Syverson, & Cole, 1996).

Why is shared reading more effective than just talking with a child? Shared reading affords a natural opportunity for giving information and increasing vocabulary. It provides a focus for attention and for asking and responding to questions. In addition, it is enjoyable for both children and adults; it fosters emotional bonding while enhancing cognitive development.

emergent literacy Preschoolers' development of skills, knowledge, and attitudes that underlie reading and writing

Social Interaction and Preparation for Literacy

Emergent literacy is the development of skills, knowledge, and attitudes that underlie reading and writing. These include such specific skills as the realization that words are composed of distinct sounds, or *phonemes,* and the ability to link phonemes with the corresponding alphabetic letters or combinations of letters (Whitehurst & Lonigan, 1998).

As children learn the skills they will need to translate the written word into speech, they also learn that writing can express ideas, thoughts, and feelings. Preschool children pretend to write by scribbling, lining up their marks from left to right (Brenneman, Massey, Machado, & Gelman, 1996). Later they begin using letters, numbers, and letter-like shapes to represent words, syllables, or phonemes. Often their spelling is so inventive that they may not be able to read it themselves (Whitehurst & Lonigan, 1998)!

Social interaction can promote emergent literacy. Children are more likely to become good readers and writers if, during the preschool years, parents provide conversational challenges the children are ready for—if they use a rich vocabulary and centre dinner-table talk on the day's activities or on questions about why people do things and how things work (Snow, 1990, 1993).

In a longitudinal study of 24 white, middle-class two-parent families (Reese, 1995), the quality of mother–child conversation at ages 3 and 4—particularly about past events—was a strong predictor of literacy skills prior to entering Grade 1. Most influential was mothers' use of questions and comments that helped children elaborate on events or link them with other incidents.

Reading to children is one of the most effective paths to literacy. Children who are read to from an early age learn that reading and writing move from left to right and from top to bottom and that words are separated by spaces (Siegler, 1998; Whitehurst & Lonigan, 1998). They also are motivated to learn to read. A study of Canadian parents' contributions to literacy skills of children in kindergarten through Grade 2 showed a relationship between reading support and children's scores on reading-related tasks. Children whose parents provided coaching in sounding out words, frequent trips to the local library, and explicit instruction about letters tended to perform better on early reading achievement, letter naming and sounding, and phonological awareness than did children without higher levels of reading support (Evans, 1998).

Too much time spent watching television can rob children of such interactive language opportunities, but moderate exposure to educational television can help prepare children for literacy, especially if parents talk with children about what they see. In one study, the more time 3- to 5-year-olds spent watching *Sesame Street,* the more their vocabulary improved (M. L. Rice, Huston, Truglio, & Wright, 1990).

What's your view ?

- Suppose you wanted to set up a program to encourage preliteracy development in high-risk children. What elements would you include in your program? How would you judge its success?

Checkpoint ✔

Can you . . .

✔ Discuss possible causes, consequences, and treatment of delayed language development?

✔ Identify factors in preparation for literacy?

Information-Processing Approach: Memory Development

Guidepost 3

What memory abilities expand in early childhood?

When Anna was 3, she went on an apple-picking trip. Months later, she talked about riding on the bus, visiting a farm, picking apples, bringing them home, and eating them. She had a vivid memory of the event and enjoyed talking about it.

During early childhood, children show significant improvement in attention and in the speed and efficiency with which they process information; and they begin to form long-lasting memories.

Recognition and Recall

Recognition is the ability to identify something encountered before (for example, to pick out a missing mitten from a lost-and-found box). **Recall** is the ability to reproduce knowledge from memory (for example, to describe the mitten to someone). Preschool children, like all age groups, do better on recognition than on recall, but both abilities improve with age (Lange, MacKinnon, & Nida, 1989; Myers & Perlmutter, 1978). The more familiar children are with an item, the better they can recall it.

Recall depends both on motivation to master skills and on the way a child approaches a task. In one observational study (Lange et al., 1989), 3- and 4-year-olds handled two assortments of toys in succession and then tried to name them from memory. The best predictor of success was *mastery motivation:* the tendency to be independent, self-directed,

recognition Ability to identify a previously encountered stimulus

recall Ability to reproduce material from memory

and generally resourceful, as rated by the child's teacher. The only other relevant factor was what the child did while studying the toys. The more children named or grouped the toys, or spent time thinking about or repeating their names (in other words, used strategies to help them remember), the better their recall.

Forming Childhood Memories

As we mentioned in chapter 7, *infantile amnesia* is the inability of most people to remember early events in their lives. This phenomenon is puzzling, since even infants and very young children do seem to remember things that happened to them for surprisingly long periods of time. Children younger than 2 can talk about events that occurred a month before, and 4-year-olds recall trips they took at age 2 (Nelson, 1992). Why, then, don't these early memories last? And how do children begin to form permanent memories?

Some investigators have distinguished three types of childhood memory: *generic, episodic,* and *autobiographical* (Nelson, 1993b). **Generic memory,** which begins at about age 2, produces a **script,** or general outline of a familiar, repeated event without details of time or place. The script contains routines for situations that come up again and again; it helps a child know what to expect and how to act. For example, a child may have scripts for riding the bus to preschool or having lunch at Grandma's house.

Episodic memory is the awareness of having experienced a particular incident that occurred at a specific time and place. Young children more clearly remember events that are unique or new, like Anna's apple-picking excursion. Three-year-olds may recall details about a trip to the circus for a year or longer (Fivush, Hudson, & Nelson, 1983), whereas generic memories of frequent events (such as going to the park) tend to blur together.

Given a young child's limited memory capacity, episodic memories are temporary. Unless they recur several times (in which case they are transferred to generic memory), they last for a few weeks or months and then fade. The reliability of children's episodic memory has become an important issue in lawsuits involving charges of child abuse (refer back to Box 10-1).

Autobiographical memory refers to memories that form a person's life history. These memories are specific and long-lasting. Although autobiographical memory is a type of episodic memory, not everything in episodic memory becomes part of it—only those memories that have special meaning to the child. Autobiographical memory begins for most people around age 4, and rarely before age 3. It increases slowly between ages 5 and 8; memories from then on may be recalled for 20, 40, or more years (Nelson, 1992).

One suggested explanation for the relatively late arrival of autobiographical memory (Howe & Courage, 1993, 1997) is that children cannot store in memory events about their own lives until they develop a concept of self around which to organize those memories. In a longitudinal study of 58 nineteen-month-olds in Dunedin, New Zealand, those who already recognized themselves in a mirror proved at age 2½ to have better independent memory of earlier events than those whose self-recognition had come later (Harley & Reese, 1999).

The advent of autobiographical memory also may be linked with the development of language, which, as we have seen, advances rapidly at this time. A child may not need to talk about an event to remember it, but verbal skills may affect whether and how the memory is carried into later life (Fivush & Schwarzmueller, 1998).

According to the **social interaction model,** based on Vygotsky's socio-cultural theory, children collaboratively construct autobiographical memories as they talk with parents or other adults about shared events (Nelson, 1993a). Parents initiate and guide these conversations, which enable children to learn how memories are organized in narrative form in their culture (Welch-Ross, 1997). When parents prompt 2- and 3-year-olds with frequent questions about context ("When did you find the pine cone?" "Where did you find it?" "Who was with you?"), children soon learn to include this information (Peterson & McCabe, 1994). When parents of 3-year-olds comment on subjective reactions ("You *wanted* to go on the slide," "It was a *huge* bowl," "Mommy was *wrong*"), the children at 5½ are more likely to weave such comments into their reminiscences (Haden, Haine, & Fivush, 1997).

It is important to keep in mind that most research on memory has focused on middle-class Canadian, American, or western European children, most of whom have been talking since at least age 2. We are only beginning to learn about the relationship between memory and language among children who begin to speak later because of different social and cul-

generic memory Memory that produces scripts of familiar routines to guide behaviour

script General remembered outline of a familiar, repeated event, used to guide behaviour

episodic memory Long-term memory of specific experiences or events, linked to time and place

autobiographical memory Memory of specific events in one's own life

social interaction model Model, based on Vygotsky's socio-cultural theory, which proposes that children construct autobiographical memories through conversation with adults about shared events

tural practices, and among deaf children of hearing parents who cannot as easily converse with them (Nelson, 1993b).

Influences on Autobiographical Memory

Why do some early memories, like Einstein's memory of the compass, last longer than others? One factor is the uniqueness of the event. A second factor is children's active participation, either in the event itself or in its retelling or re-enactment. A third factor is parents' way of talking with children about past events.

Preschoolers tend to remember things they *did* better than things they merely *saw*. Researchers in New Zealand (Murachver, Pipe, Gordon, Owens, & Fivush, 1996) measured 5- and 6-year-olds' recall of a novel event (visiting a "pirate") that they either observed, heard a story about, or experienced directly. A few days later, the children recalled details (such as trying on pirate clothes, steering the ship, making a treasure map, and finding the treasure) more completely, more accurately, and in a more organized way when they themselves had participated (Murachver et al., 1996).

The way adults talk with a child about a shared experience can influence how well the child will remember it (Haden & Fivush, 1996; Reese & Fivush, 1993). When a child becomed stuck, adults with a *repetitive* conversational style tend to repeat their own previous statements or questions. Adults with an *elaborative* style are more likely to move on to a new aspect of the event or add more information. A repetitive-style parent might ask, "Do you remember how we travelled to P.E.I.?" and then, receiving no answer, ask, "How did we get there? We went in the _____ ." An elaborative-style parent might instead follow up the first question by saying, "Did we go by car or by plane?" Elaborative parents seem more focused on having a mutually rewarding conversation and affirming the child's responses, whereas repetitive parents are more focused on checking the child's memory performance. Three-year-olds of elaborative-style parents take part in longer conversations about events and remember more details, and they tend to remember the events better at ages 5 and 6 (Reese, Haden, & Fivush, 1993). Even as early as 19 to 32 months, a mother's elaborative reminiscing predicts children's ability to repeat and elaborate on shared memories (Harley & Reese, 1999).

Implicit Memory

Some memories—the kinds we have been discussing—are conscious (explicit); others are preserved in unconscious (implicit) form (Lie & Newcombe, 1999; Newcombe & Fox, 1994). In one study, 9- and 10-year-olds were shown photos of preschool classmates they had not seen for 5 years, along with photos of children they had never known. Only one in five children recognized the former classmates. Researchers measured the children's *skin conductance* (movement of electrical impulses through the skin) as they viewed the pictures. In a small but significant number of cases, positive responses appeared when the children saw pictures of their former classmates, even when they did not consciously recognize the faces (Newcombe & Fox, 1994). Similarly, when 8-year-olds were tested on implicit memory by asking them to match front views of children's faces with side views showing only partial features, the children made fewer errors with faces of former classmates than with faces of unknown children (Lie & Newcombe, 1999). These findings suggest that people may retain early memories of which they are not aware, and which may affect behaviour.

Intelligence: Psychometric and Vygotskian Approaches

One factor that may affect how early children develop both language and memory is intelligence. Let's look at two ways intelligence is measured—through traditional psychometric tests and through newer tests of cognitive potential—and at influences on children's performance.

What's your view ?

- Since an elaborative conversational style seems most effective in jogging young children's memory, would you favour training mothers to use it? Why or why not? What difficulties or objections would you anticipate?

Checkpoint ✓

Can you . . .

✔ Compare preschoolers' recognition and recall ability?

✔ Explain how language development may contribute to the onset of autobiographical memory?

✔ Identify factors that affect how well a preschool child will remember an event?

Guidepost 4

How is preschoolers' intelligence measured, and what are some influences on it?

Traditional Psychometric Measures

Because 3-, 4-, and 5-year-olds are more proficient with language than younger children, intelligence tests can now include more verbal items; and these tests produce more reliable results than the largely non-verbal tests used in infancy. As children approach age 5, there is a higher correlation between their scores on intelligence tests and the scores they will achieve later (Bornstein & Sigman, 1986). IQ tests given near the end of kindergarten are among the best predictors of future school success (Tramontana, et al., 1988).

Although preschool children are easier to test than infants and toddlers, they still need to be tested individually. The two most commonly used individual tests for preschoolers are the Stanford-Binet Intelligence Scale and the Wechsler Preschool and Primary Scale of Intelligence.

The **Stanford-Binet Intelligence Scale** takes 30 to 40 minutes. The child is asked to define words, string beads, build with blocks, identify the missing parts of a picture, trace mazes, and show an understanding of numbers. The child's score is supposed to measure memory, spatial orientation, and practical judgment in real-life situations. The fourth edition, revised in 1985, includes an equal balance of verbal and non-verbal, quantitative, and memory items. Instead of providing the IQ as a single overall measure of intelligence, the revised version assesses patterns and levels of cognitive development.

The **Wechsler Preschool and Primary Scale of Intelligence (WPPSI–III),** an hour-long individual test used with children ages 3 to 7, yields separate verbal and performance scores as well as a combined score. Its separate scales are similar to those in the Wechsler Intelligence Scale for Children (WISC–III), discussed in chapter 13. Verbal tasks involve activities such as answering general-information questions about the world and arithmetic problems, while performance tasks involve activities like recreating geometric patterns using blocks, and identifying missing parts of pictures. The 2002 revision includes new subtests and new picture items. The WPPSI–III has been restandardized on a sample of children representing the population of preschool-age children in Canada.

Influences on Measured Intelligence

Many people believe that IQ scores represent a fixed quantity of intelligence a person is born with. That is not so: The score is simply a measure of how well a child can do certain tasks in comparison with others of the same age. Test scores of children in industrialized countries have risen steadily since testing began, forcing test developers to raise standardized norms. This is called the *Flynn effect* (Flynn, 1984, 1987). The reasons for this upward trend are in dispute; it may in part reflect exposure to educational television, preschools, better-educated parents, and a wider variety of experiences, as well as changes in the tests themselves.

How well a particular child does on intelligence tests may be influenced by many factors. These include temperament, the match between cognitive style and the tasks posed, social and emotional maturity, ease in the testing situation, preliteracy or literacy skills, socio-economic status, and ethnic background. (We will examine several of these factors in chapter 13.)

Temperament and Parent–Child Interaction

Children's temperament—or at least, the way parents perceive it—may contribute to the way parents treat them, and both of these factors may affect children's cognitive potential. In one longitudinal study (Fagot & Gauvain, 1997), researchers asked 93 mothers to rate their 18-month-olds' temperament. They also observed how mother and child interacted during play at home. A year later, at 2½, the children did two problem-solving tasks with their mothers in the laboratory. Finally, at age 5, the children did two independent laboratory problem-solving tasks and took an intelligence test (the WPSSI), and their kindergarten teachers reported on whether the children had any learning problems.

Mothers who considered their children "difficult" tended to give them more assistance and instruction or to be more critical and coercive; and their children failed to develop independent problem-solving skills. They were likely to give up, make errors, and develop learning problems. Children whose mothers, when the children were 2½, gave them

Stanford-Binet Intelligence Scale Individual intelligence test used to measure memory, spatial orientation, and practical judgment

Wechsler Preschool and Primary Scale of Intelligence (WPPSI–III) Individual intelligence test for children ages 3 to 7, which yields verbal and performance scores as well as a combined score

suggestions for solving problems or showed them effective strategies did better on the arithmetic and vocabulary subtests of the WPPSI at age 5, whereas children whose mothers had given *either* more approval *or* disapproval or had told them what to do did worse (Fagot & Gauvain, 1997).

The Family Environment

At one time it was believed that the family environment played a major role in cognitive development. Now the extent of that influence is in question. We don't know how much of parents' influence on intelligence comes from their genetic contribution, and how much from the fact that they provide a child's earliest environment for learning.

Twin and adoption studies suggest that family life has its strongest influence in early childhood, and this influence diminishes greatly by adolescence (McGue, 1997; Neisser et al., 1996). However, these studies have been done largely with white, middle-class samples; their results may not apply to low-income and non-white families (Neisser et al., 1996).

In two longitudinal studies of low-income African-American children, although the influence of the home environment did diminish between infancy and middle childhood, it remained substantial—at least as strong as the influence of the mother's IQ (Burchinal et al., 1997). In a study of 175 African-American 3-year-olds, a father's satisfaction with his parenting role was associated with his child's IQ, and paternal involvement and nurturance were associated with language skills and other aspects of well-being (Black et al., 1999).

Family economic circumstances can exert a powerful influence, not so much in themselves as in the way they affect parenting practices and the atmosphere in the home. Results from the NLSCY show that among Canadian families, SES has a substantial influence on school achievement in children. Low SES has been shown to be related to lower levels of social support in children, and increased parental depression, higher levels of parental hostility, family dysfunction, and fewer academic skills in children, all of which have significant impacts on children's achievement in school (Ryan & Adams, 1998). But socio-economic status is only one of several social and family risk factors. Assessments of 152 children at ages 4 and 13 revealed no single pattern of risk. Instead, a child's IQ was related to *the total number* of such risk factors as the mother's behaviour, mental health, anxiety level, education, and beliefs about children's development; family size and social support; stressful life events; parental occupations; and disadvantaged status. The more risk factors there were, the lower the child's IQ score (Sameroff, Seifer, Baldwin, & Baldwin, 1993).

Giving suggestions and strategies for solving a puzzle or problem—without showing strong approval or disapproval—can foster cognitive growth.

Testing and Teaching Based on Vygotsky's Theory

According to Vygotsky, children learn by internalizing the results of their interactions with adults. Adults direct children's learning most effectively in the *zone of proximal development (ZPD),* that is, in tasks children are almost ready to accomplish on their own.

Tests based on Vygotsky's approach emphasize potential rather than present achievement. These tests contain items up to two years above a child's current level of competence. The items a child can answer with help determine the ZPD, or potential level of development. Vygotsky (1956) gives an example of two children, each with a mental age of 7 years (based on ability to do various cognitive tasks). With the help of leading questions, examples, and demonstrations, Natasha can easily solve problems geared to a mental age of 9, 2 years beyond her mental age; but Ivan, with the same kind of help, can do tasks at only a 7½-year-old level. If we measure these children by what they can do on their own (as traditional IQ tests do), their intelligence seems about the same; but if we measure them by their immediate potential development (their ZPD), they are quite different.

The ZPD, in combination with the related concept of *scaffolding* (refer back to chapter 2), can help parents and teachers efficiently guide children's cognitive progress. The less able a child is to do a task, the more direction an adult must give. As the child can do more and more, the adult helps less and less. When the child can do the job alone, the adult takes away the "scaffold" that is no longer needed.

What's your view ❓

- If you were a preschool or kindergarten teacher, how helpful do you think it would be to know a child's IQ? the child's ZPD?

Checkpoint ✔

Can you . . .

✔ Describe two commonly used individual intelligence tests for preschoolers?

✔ Discuss several influences on measured intelligence?

✔ Explain why an intelligence test score using the ZPD might be significantly different from a traditional psychometric test score?

In one study, 3- and 4-year-olds were asked to give their parents directions for finding a hidden mouse in a dollhouse. The parents gave the children feedback when their directions needed clarifying. The parents proved to be highly sensitive to the children's scaffolding needs; they gave more directive prompts to 3-year-olds, whose directions tended to be less clear than those of 4-year-olds. The parents used fewer directive prompts as the children gained experience in giving clear directions (Plumert & Nichols-Whitehead, 1996).

Early Childhood Education

Guidepost 5

What purposes does early childhood education serve, and how do children make the transition to kindergarten?

Going to preschool is an important step, widening a child's physical, cognitive, and social environment. Today more 4-year-olds than ever, and even many 3-year-olds, are enrolled in early childhood education. The transition to kindergarten, the beginning of "real school," is another momentous step.

Goals and Types of Preschools: A Cross-cultural View

In some countries, such as China, preschools are expected to provide academic preparation for schooling. In contrast, most preschools in Canada and many other industrialized countries traditionally have followed a "child-centred" philosophy stressing social and emotional growth in line with young children's developmental needs—though some, such as those based on the theories of Piaget or the Italian educator Maria Montessori (refer back to chapter 1), have a stronger cognitive emphasis.

As part of a debate over how to improve education, pressures have built to offer instruction in basic academic skills in Canadian preschools. Defenders of the traditional developmental approach maintain that academically oriented programs neglect young children's need for exploration and free play and that, although children in such programs may learn more at first, too much teacher-centred instruction may stifle their interest and interfere with self-initiated learning (Elkind, 1986; Zigler, 1987).

Interviews with parents from three First Nations communities in Ontario showed that parents valued play as an appropriate way of learning in early childhood, and had positive attitudes towards play-oriented daycare centres, which they saw as consistent with their cultural values. The parents also stressed the importance of teaching First Nations culture and language in early child education, respect for elders, enhanced parental communication, the need for qualified daycare providers, and the continuation of teaching of culture and language in elementary and secondary schools (Gillis, 1992).

A variety of models or perspectives on preschool teaching have emerged since the traditional teacher-centred approach was dominant. One perspective involves a society-centred approach, which emphasizes skills and attitudes that promote group harmony. Two other types of preschool perspectives are child-centred and role-centred.

Child-centred preschools are more individualized, and follow the North American approach that emphasizes self-expression, free choice, and individual interaction with teachers. Role-centred preschools, which are popular in Japanese private preschools (Holloway, 1999), concentrate on preparing children for roles in society, and include in addition to basic subjects, English, art, gymnastics, swordsmanship, tea ceremonies, and Japanese dance.

Checkpoint ✔

Can you . . .

✔ Compare goals of varying types of preschool programs in Canada and Japan?

✔ Summarize findings on the short-term and long-term effects of academic and child-centred preschool programs?

What type of preschool is best for children? Studies in Canada and the United States support a child-centred, developmental approach. One field study (Marcon, 1999) compared 721 randomly selected, predominantly low-income and African-American 4- and 5-year-olds from three types of preschool classrooms in Washington, D.C.: *child-initiated, academically directed,* and *middle-of-the-road* (a blend of the other two approaches). Children from child-initiated programs, in which they actively directed their own learning experiences, excelled in basic academic skills in all subject areas. They also had more advanced motor skills than the other two groups and scored higher than the middle-of-the-road group in behavioural and communicative skills. These findings suggest that a single, coherent philosophy of education may work better than an attempt to blend diverse approaches and that a child-centred approach seems more effective than an academically oriented one.

Compensatory Preschool Programs

Children from deprived socio-economic backgrounds often enter school at a considerable disadvantage. They may make as much progress as more advantaged classmates, but because they start out behind, they remain behind (Stipek & Ryan, 1997). It has been estimated that more than two-thirds of children in poor urban areas enter school poorly prepared to learn (Zigler, 1998). Since the 1960s, large-scale programs have been developed to help such children compensate for what they have missed and to prepare them for school.

Compensatory preschool education, such as the Aboriginal Head Start program these children are enrolled in, often yields long-lasting gains. Some positive effects of Head Start have held up through high school.

The best-known compensatory preschool program for 3- and 4-year-old children of low-income families in the United States is Project Head Start, a federally funded program launched in 1965. The goals were to improve physical health, enhance cognitive skills, and foster self-confidence, relationships with others, social responsibility, and a sense of dignity and self-worth for the child and the family.

Head Start is effective in improving school readiness (Ripple et al., 1999), and the most successful Head Start programs have been those with the most parental participation, the best-trained teachers, the lowest staff-to-child ratios, the longest school days and weeks, and the most extensive services. Outcomes are best when the programs last at least 2 years (S. Ramey, 1999).

However, it is not clear that benefits last (Ripple et al., 1999). Although Head Start children do better on intelligence tests than other children from comparable backgrounds, this advantage disappears after the children start school. Nor have Head Start children equalled the average middle-class child in school achievement or on standardized tests (Collins & Deloria, 1983; Zigler & Styfco, 1993, 1994). Still, children from Head Start and other such programs are less likely to be placed in special education or to repeat a grade and are more likely to finish high school than low-income children who did not attend compensatory preschool programs (Neisser et al., 1996).

The Aboriginal Head Start Program (AHS) is an intervention started in 1995 to meet the social and cultural needs of First Nations, Metis, and Inuit children in urban and northern communities across Canada. Funded by Health Canada under the Aboriginal Head Start Initiative, about 100 programs in eight provinces and three northern territories involve 3,000 to 4,000 children from 2½ to 5 years, with the aim of preparing children for elementary school and building understanding and pride in their native culture (Dunning, 2000). The programs are operated as high-quality child care centres, emphasizing social and cognitive skill development, and include cultural elements with formal involvement of the family and Aboriginal community to promote the retention and growth of Aboriginal cultures and languages. The family and community are integral parts of the AHS; parents work as aids in the classroom, as curriculum planners, kitchen helpers, and custodians, among other roles. All aspects of the children's experiences, including curriculum activities and materials, daily snacks, parent education, and resources, are designed to reflect their traditional culture whenever possible. The key is to develop a connection between Aboriginal language and culture and the educational experiences of the children. Community elders, who are active daily in the AHS centres, maintain a special role in promoting language and culture. Programs like the Waabinong Head Start Family Resource Centre in Sault Ste. Marie (Dunning, 2000), and the Tungasuvvingat Inuit Head Start in Ottawa (Reynolds, 1998), are examples of positive school environments that give parents opportunities to be involved in the decision making of their children's education, and become exposed to their own cultural heritage. For many of the parents, this experience is the first contact with their own language and culture, given their past in the traditional school system. Often parents are beginning to learn their language alongside their children. The AHS programs offer a unique opportunity for Aboriginal youth to develop self-awareness and pride in their own culture and language.

Advocates of compensatory programs say the results point to a need for earlier and longer-lasting intervention (Reynolds & Temple, 1998; Zigler & Styfco, 1993, 1994). They say that many economically disadvantaged children need more time and a continuous, predictable learning environment to fully absorb the benefits; and that the transition to formal

What's your view ?

• Is publicly funded
compensatory education the
best way to help poor children
catch up?

schooling is a sensitive or critical period, when children need extra support and stability (McCain & Mustard, 1999; Reynolds & Temple, 1998). The Early Years Study showed that more government support was needed to promote development in the first 6 years (McCain & Mustard, 1999). In response to the report's recommendations, the Ontario government has funded community-based Ontario Early Years Centres to provide parents with support and resources to ensure that all children in Ontario have access to enriched environments that support healthy growth (Ministry of Community, Family and Children's Services, 2002).

Some positive effects of compensatory preschool programs have persisted through elementary or high school or even beyond (Darlington, 1991; Haskins, 1989). A major benefit is a lesser likelihood of juvenile delinquency (see chapter 17). Poor African-American children who participated in the Perry Preschool Program of the High/Scope Educational Research Foundation (which predated Head Start) have been followed to age 27. They were much more likely than a comparison group who lacked preschool experience to finish high school, to enrol in university, college, or vocational training, and to be employed. They also were less likely to have been arrested, and the women were less likely to have become pregnant in their teens (Berrueta-Clement, Schweinhart, Barnett, Epstein, & Weikart, 1985; Schweinhart, Barnes, & Weikart, 1993). It seems, then, that early childhood education can help compensate for deprivation and that well-planned programs produce long-term personal and societal benefits that far exceed the original cost (Haskins, 1989; Schweinhart et al., 1993).

The Transition to Kindergarten

Once a year of transition between the relative freedom of home or preschool and the structure of "real school," kindergarten is now more like Grade 1. Children spend less time on self-chosen activities and more time on worksheets and preparing to read. Possibly for the first time, they receive critical evaluation of their abilities. Partly because of pressures for academic achievement and partly to meet the needs of working parents, many kindergartners now spend a full day in school rather than the traditional half day. And, as academic and emotional pressures mount, many parents hold children back a year so that they now start kindergarten at age 6.

How do children adjust to kindergarten? The answer may depend on both the child's characteristics—age, gender, cognitive and social competencies, and coping skills—and the support or stress generated by the home, school, and neighbourhood. Children with extensive preschool experience tend to adjust more easily than those who spent little or no time in preschool. Children who start kindergarten with peers they know and like, or who have a "secure base" of ongoing neighbourhood friendships, generally do better (Ladd, 1996; see Chapter 11).

A study of 200 children in Alberta examined the effects of age of kindergarten entry on academic performance in Grades 1, 3, 6, and 9. Children who were younger when they started kindergarten tended to have higher IQs than the older group, but the children in the younger group were more likely to repeat a school year or need remedial education at some point in their academic careers (Wilgosh, Meyer, & Mueller, 1996).

Some researchers have explored a link between the home environment and a child's adaptation to kindergarten. In a 6-year longitudinal study of 72 couples, beginning in late pregnancy, those who had had happy childhoods, were happily married in the child's early years, and had an authoritative parenting style (see chapter 11) had children who did better in kindergarten, both socially and academically (P. A. Cowan, Cowan, Schulz, & Heming, 1994).

A child's relationship with the kindergarten teacher greatly affects that child's success. Children who are close to their teachers tend to do well academically and to be highly involved in classroom activities. Children who are either overdependent on, or antagonistic toward, the teacher tend to do poorly, to dislike school, and to be less involved (Birch & Ladd, 1997).

One pair of studies, which followed 399 full-day kindergarten students throughout the year, found a number of interlocking factors that play a part in cognitive achievement and social adjustment. Pre-existing risk and protective factors having to do with the child and the home environment, such as those already mentioned, interact with features of the classroom environment, such as the child's developing relationships with teacher and peers; and the effects become intensified as time goes on. Children who show pro-social behaviour during the early weeks become more well liked, whereas children who initially show anti-social behaviour become more disliked. They tend to get into conflicts with teachers, to participate less, and to be lower achievers. Children who are more cognitively mature tend to participate more, and those who participate more achieve better. A supportive family background also influences achievement. However, negative, or stressful factors seem to be more influential than positive, or supportive ones (Ladd, Birch, & Buhs, 1999).

Psychometric tests, along with other measures, are used to predict how well a child will do in school. IQ is among the best predictors; children's ability to understand and to express themselves with language predicts reading competence; and visual–motor and visual–perceptual measures predict reading, math, and general achievement, at least through Grade 1. The most important behavioural measure is attentiveness (Tramontana et al., 1988).

The burgeoning physical and cognitive skills of early childhood have psychosocial implications, as we'll see in chapter 11.

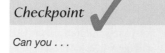

Checkpoint ✔

Can you . . .

✔ Discuss factors that affect adjustment to kindergarten?

Summary and Key Terms

Piagetian Approach: The Pre-operational Child

Guidepost 1 What are typical cognitive advances and immature aspects of preschool children's thinking?

- Children in the pre-operational stage show several important advances, as well as some immature aspects of thought.

- The symbolic function enables children to reflect upon people, objects, and events that are not physically present. It is shown in deferred imitation, pretend play, and language.

- Early symbolic development helps pre-operational children make more accurate judgments of spatial relationships. They can understand the concept of identity, link cause and effect, categorize living and non-living things, and understand principles of counting.

- Centration keeps pre-operational children from understanding principles of conservation. Their logic also is limited by irreversibility and a focus on states rather than transformations.

- Pre-operational children appear to be less egocentric than Piaget thought; they (and even younger children) are capable of empathy.

- The theory of mind, which develops markedly between the ages of 3 and 5, includes awareness of a child's own thought processes, social cognition, understanding that people can hold false beliefs, ability to deceive, ability to distinguish appearance from reality, and ability to distinguish fantasy from reality. Hereditary and environmental influences affect individual differences in theory-of-mind development.

  pre-operational stage (237)   symbolic function (237)
  dual representation hypothesis (238)   transduction (239)
  animism (241)   centration (242)   decentre (242)
  conservation (242)   irreversibility (242)   egocentrism (243)
  theory of mind (244)   social cognition (244)   empathy (244)

Language Development

Guidepost 2 How does language improve, and what happens when its development is delayed?

- During early childhood, vocabulary increases greatly, and grammar and syntax become fairly sophisticated. Children become more competent in pragmatics.

- Private speech is normal and common; it may aid in the shift to self-regulation and usually disappears by age 10.

- Causes of delayed language development are unclear. If untreated, it may have serious cognitive, social, and emotional consequences.

- Interaction with adults can promote emergent literacy.

  fast mapping (249)   pragmatics (250)   social speech (250)
  private speech (250)   emergent literacy (252)

Information-Processing Approach: Memory and Other Processing Skills

Guidepost 3 What memory abilities expand in early childhood?

- At all ages, recognition is better than recall, but both increase during early childhood.

- Early episodic memory is only temporary; it fades or is transferred to generic memory. Autobiographical memory begins at about age 3 or 4 and may be related to early self-recognition ability and language development. According to the social interaction model, children and adults co-construct autobiographical memories by talking about shared experiences.

- Children are more likely to remember unusual activities that they actively participate in. The way adults talk with children about events influences memory formation.

- Implicit memories may unconsciously affect behaviour.

  recognition (253)   **recall (253)**   **generic memory (254)**
  script (254)   **episodic memory (254)**
  autobiographical memory (254)   **social interaction model (254)**

Intelligence: Psychometric and Vygotskian Approaches

Guidepost 4   How is preschoolers' intelligence measured, and what are some influences on it?

- The two most commonly used psychometric intelligence tests for young children are the Stanford-Binet Intelligence Scale and the Wechsler Preschool and Primary Scale of Intelligence (WPPSI–III).

- Intelligence test scores may be influenced by social and emotional functioning, as well as by parent–child interaction and socio-economic factors.

- Newer tests based on Vygotsky's concept of the zone of proximal development (ZPD) indicate immediate potential for achievement. Such tests, when combined with scaffolding, can help parents and teachers guide children's progress.

  Stanford-Binet Intelligence Scale (256)   **Wechsler Preschool and Primary Scale of Intelligence (WPPSI–III) (256)**

Early Childhood Education

Guidepost 5   What purposes does early childhood education serve, and how do children make the transition to kindergarten?

- Goals of preschool education vary in different cultures. Since the 1970s the academic content of early childhood education programs in Canada has increased. A similar trend has occurred in some Japanese preschools. For low-income children in the United States, academically oriented programs seem less effective than child-centred ones.

- Compensatory preschool programs have had positive outcomes, but participants generally have not equalled the performance of middle-class children. Compensatory programs that extend into the primary grades have better long-term results.

- Adjustment to kindergarten may depend on interaction among the child's characteristics and those of the home, school, and neighbourhood environments.

OLC Preview

The official website for *A Child's World,* First Canadian Edition, supplements the chapter's boxed material and offers additional information and hot links to recommended websites on topics such as the criminal justice system's response to child victims and witnesses, and imaginary companions. Check out **www.mcgrawhill.ca/college/papalia**.

Psychosocial Development in Early Childhood

Children's playings are not sports and should be deemed as their most serious actions.

—Michele de Montaigne, *Essays*, 1575

Focus *Buffy Sainte-Marie, Artist and Educator**

Buffy Sainte-Marie

Buffy Sainte-Marie has made a major impact on Canadian culture and on the lives of countless Aboriginal children throughout North America. Born at the Piapot (Cree) reserve in the Qu'Appelle Valley in Saskatchewan, and raised by adoptive parents (who were themselves part Mi'kmaq) in Maine and Massachusetts, she distinguished herself throughout her life, earning a Ph.D. in fine art, and degrees in oriental philosophy and education.

As a student in the 1960s, she became a highly popular singer and songwriter of folk and protest songs, many of which reflected her experiences as an Aboriginal woman growing up in a mainstream culture that had very inaccurate and misguided understandings of Aboriginal culture, the contributions of Aboriginal peoples to North American society, and the dire need for support for Aboriginal children and youth.

Her hit songs, like "Until It's Time for You to Go," and "Universal Soldier," were focal songs of the 1960s, bringing her great fame and fortune, and were recorded by over 200 artists in 16 languages. In the 1960s, she sought to combine her very successful singing career with contact with Aboriginal communities, striving to find a way to bridge the gap between mainstream and Aboriginal cultures. Thanks to her concerts throughout the world, she had the opportunity to meet with indigenous people in many countries, recognizing many common difficulties that Aboriginal people everywhere face when marginalized by a majority culture. She used her wealth to make a difference in the lives of Aboriginal children in Canada and the United States. She established the Nihewan (a Cree word meaning "talk Cree," or "be your culture") Foundation in 1969, an educational organization dedicated to Aboriginal youth, to prepare children for success in school, and to promote a more accurate understanding of Aboriginal peoples internationally and in their own communities.

In 1976, with the birth of her son, she stopped recording, but later began appearing in television episodes of *Sesame Street*, in which she presented material on Aboriginal culture in North America, reaching young people in Canada, the United States, and around the world with the message that Aboriginal people are an important part of Canadian and American society.

The Nihewan Foundation has expanded to focus on Aboriginal curriculum for elementary school children, with the Cradleboard Teaching Project, which is dedicated to developing teaching materials on North American Aboriginal cultures. The purpose of the project is to encourage the development of a healthy sense of self-esteem, identity, and pride in Aboriginal children, and to improve relations between indigenous and colonial populations. The project combines traditional Aboriginal culture with high-tech innovations, connecting classrooms of children from Aboriginal and non-Aboriginal communities. In 1993 she helped establish a

* Sources of biographical information on Buffy Sainte-Marie were Hunter (1999), King (2000), Sainte-Marie (1996), and Wilson (1996).

Juno award category for Aboriginal Canadian music. In recognition of her impact on North American culture she has won many awards and distinctions, including the Order of Canada, and a Lifetime Achievement Award by the American Indian College Fund. She has continued with her love of teaching, teaching digital art as an adjunct professor of fine arts at Saskatchewan Indian Federated College in Regina, and at York University in Toronto, and combines her concert career with her work with the Cradleboard Teaching Project.

● ● ●

Buffy Sainte-Marie's life as an Aboriginal Canadian growing up in mainstream American society made her recognize the innaccurate perceptions non-Aboriginal people had of the cultures and traditions of Aboriginal peoples throughout North America. She became determined to change those perceptions and is working to ensure that young children in Aboriginal communities have positive educational experiences at a critical point in their development.

The years from ages 3 to 6 are pivotal ones in children's psychosocial development. As children's self-concept grows stronger, they learn what sex they are and begin to act accordingly. Their behaviour also becomes more socially directed.

In this chapter we discuss preschool children's understanding of themselves and their feelings. We see how their identification of themselves as male or female arises and how it affects their behaviour. We describe the activity on which children typically spend most of their time: play. We consider the influence, for good or ill, of what parents do. Finally, we discuss relationships with siblings and other children.

After you have read and studied this chapter, you should be able to answer each of the Guidepost questions that appear at the top of the next page. Look for them again in the margins, where they point to important concepts throughout the chapter. To check your understanding of these Guideposts, review the end-of-chapter summary. Checkpoints throughout the chapter will help you verify your understanding of what you have read.

Guideposts for Study

1. How does the self-concept develop during early childhood, and how do children advance in understanding their emotions?

2. How do young children develop initiative and self-esteem?

3. How do boys and girls become aware of the meaning of gender, and what explains differences in behaviour between the sexes?

4. How do preschoolers play, and how does play contribute to and reflect development?

5. How do parenting practices influence development?

6. Why do young children help or hurt others, and why do they develop fears?

7. How do young children get along with (or without) siblings?

8. How do young children choose playmates and friends, and why are some children more popular than others?

The Developing Self

"Who in the world am I? Ah, *that's* the great puzzle," said Alice in Wonderland, after her size had abruptly changed—again. Solving Alice's "puzzle" is a lifelong process of getting to know one's self.

The Self-concept and Cognitive Development

The **self-concept** is our image of ourselves. It is what we believe about who we are—our total picture of our abilities and traits. It is "a *cognitive construction, . . .* a system of descriptive and evaluative representations about the self," which determines how we feel about ourselves and guides our actions (Harter, 1996, p. 207). The sense of self also has a social aspect: Like Buffy Sainte-Marie, who had to deal with the misperceptions about Aboriginal cultures throughout her life, children incorporate into their self-image their growing understanding of how others see them.

The picture of the self comes into focus in toddlerhood, as children develop self-awareness (refer back to chapter 8). The self-concept becomes clearer and more compelling as a person gains in cognitive abilities and deals with the developmental tasks of childhood, of adolescence, and then of adulthood.

Early Self-concept Development: The Continuous Self

How does the self-concept change in early childhood? A shift in self-awareness may occur near the age of 4, as autobiographical memory and a more sophisticated theory of mind develop. When 3½- and 4-year-olds were shown a videotape or photograph, taken a few minutes earlier, of a researcher placing a large sticker on their heads—an act of which they had been unaware—the children instantly reached up to feel and remove the sticker. Two-year-olds and younger 3-year-olds did not do that. Yet when shown the same thing happening in a mirror, the younger children did seem aware that a sticker was on their heads.

Does this mean that these children recognized themselves in a mirror but not in a photograph or videotape? That does not seem likely. Nor does it seem likely that they did not remember participating in a photograph session a few minutes earlier. A likelier explanation is that because younger children's memories are generic rather than autobiographical, they may not have thought of the events in the videotape or photograph as having happened to *them* (Povinelli, Landau, & Perilloux, 1996).

Guidepost 1

How does the self-concept develop during early childhood, and how do children advance in understanding their emotions?

self-concept Sense of self; descriptive and evaluative mental picture of one's abilities and traits

Self-Definition: A Neo-Piagetian View

self-definition Cluster of characteristics used to describe oneself

By age 4, Jason's attempts at **self-definition** are becoming more comprehensive as he begins to identify a cluster of characteristics to describe himself:

> My name is Jason and I live in a big house with my mother and father and sister, Lisa. I have a kitty that's orange and a television set in my own room. . . . I like pizza and I have a nice teacher. I can count up to 100, want to hear me? I love my dog, Skipper. I can climb to the top of the jungle gym, I'm not scared! Just happy. You can't be happy *and* scared, no way! I have brown hair, and I go to preschool. I'm really strong. I can lift this chair, watch me! (Harter, 1996, p. 208)

The way Jason describes himself is typical of children his age. He talks mostly about concrete, observable behaviours; external characteristics, such as physical features; preferences; possessions; and members of his household. He mentions particular skills (running and climbing) rather than general abilities (being athletic). His self-descriptions are unrealistically positive, and they frequently spill over into demonstrations; what he *thinks* about himself is almost inseparable from what he *does*. Not until middle childhood (around age 7) will he describe himself in terms of generalized traits, such as *popular, smart,* or *dumb;* recognize that he can have conflicting emotions; and be self-critical while holding a positive overall self-concept.

During the past 25 years, researchers have become interested in pinpointing the intermediate changes that make up this "age 5 to 7 shift." An analysis based on neo-Piagetian theory (Case, 1985, 1992; Fischer, 1980) describes the 5 to 7 shift as occurring in three steps, which actually form a continuous progression.* At 4, Jason is at the first step: His statements about himself are **single representations**—isolated, one-dimensional items. His thinking jumps from particular to particular, without logical connections. At this stage he cannot imagine having two emotions at once ("You can't be happy *and* scared"). He cannot decentre, in part because of his limited working memory capacity, and so he cannot consider different aspects of himself at the same time. His thinking is all-or-nothing. He cannot acknowledge that his **real self**, the person he actually is, is not the same as his **ideal self**, the person he would like to be. So he describes himself as a paragon of virtue and ability.

single representations In neo-Piagetian terminology, first stage in development of self-definition, in which children describe themselves in terms of individual, unconnected characteristics and in all-or-nothing terms

real self The self one actually is

ideal self The self one would like to be

At about age 5 or 6, Jason moves up to the second step, as he begins to link one aspect of himself to another: "I can run fast, and I can climb high. I'm also strong. I can throw a ball real far, I'm going to be on a team some day!" (Harter, 1996, p. 215) However, these **representational mappings**—logical connections between parts of his image of himself— are still expressed in completely positive, all-or-nothing terms. Since good and bad are opposites, he cannot see how he might be good at some things and not at others.

representational mappings In neo-Piagetian terminology, the second stage in development of self-definition, in which a child makes logical connections between aspects of the self but still sees these characteristics in all-or-nothing terms

The third step, *representational systems,* takes place in middle childhood (see chapter 14), when children begin to integrate specific features of the self into a general, multidimensional concept. As all-or-nothing thinking declines, Jason's self-descriptions will become more balanced ("I'm good at hockey but bad at arithmetic").

Understanding Emotions

"I hate you!" Maya, age 5, shouts to her mother. "You're a mean mommy!" Angry because her mother sent her to her room for pinching her baby brother, Maya cannot imagine ever loving her mother again. "Aren't you ashamed of yourself for making the baby cry?" her father asks Maya a little later. Maya nods, but only because she knows what response he wants. In truth, she feels a jumble of emotions—not the least of which is feeling sorry for herself.

Understanding their own emotions helps children to guide their behaviour in social situations and to talk about feelings (Laible & Thompson, 1998). It enables them to control the way they show their feelings and to be sensitive to how others feel (Garner & Power, 1996). Much of this development occurs during the preschool years.

---

* This discussion of children's developing understanding of themselves from age 4 on, including their understanding of their emotions, is indebted to Susan Harter (1990, 1993, 1996, 1998).

Because early emotional experience occurs within the context of the family, it should not be surprising that family relationships affect the development of emotional understanding. A study of 41 preschoolers found a relationship between security of attachment to the mother and a child's understanding of negative emotions observed in others, such as fear, anger, and sadness—both as observed among their peers, and as inferred from stories enacted by puppets. Securely attached children apparently feel more comfortable discussing sensitive issues involving these emotions with their mothers (Laible & Thompson, 1998).

Preschoolers can talk about their feelings and often can discern the feelings of others, and they understand that emotions are connected with experiences and desires (Saarni, Mumme, & Campos, 1998). However, they still lack a full understanding of such self-directed emotions as shame and pride, and they have trouble reconciling conflicting emotions, such as being happy about getting a new bicycle but disappointed because it's the wrong colour (Kestenbaum & Gelman, 1995).

Emotions Directed toward the Self

Emotions directed toward the self, such as shame and pride, develop during the third year, after children gain self-awareness. These emotions depend on internalization of parental standards of behaviour. But even children a few years older often lack the cognitive sophistication to recognize such emotions and what brings them on.

In one study (Harter, 1993), 4- to 8-year-olds were told two stories. In the first story, a child takes a few coins from a jar after being told not to do so; in the second story, a child performs a difficult gymnastic feat—a flip on the bars. Each story was presented in two versions: one in which a parent sees the child doing the act, and another in which no one sees the child. The children were asked how they and the parent would feel in each circumstance.

The answers revealed a gradual progression in understanding of feelings about the self (Harter, 1996). At ages 4 to 5, children did not say that either they or their parents would feel pride or shame. Instead they used such terms as "worried" or "scared" (for the money jar incident) and "excited" or "happy" (about the gymnastic accomplishment). At 5 to 6, children said their parents would be ashamed or proud of them but did not acknowledge feeling these emotions themselves. At 6 to 7, children said they would feel proud or ashamed, but only if they were observed. At 7 to 8, children acknowledged that even if no one saw them, they would feel ashamed or proud of themselves. By this age, the standards that produce pride and shame appear to be fully internalized. Until that happens, children need the prod of parental observation—a sort of emotional "scaffolding."

Simultaneous Emotions

Part of the confusion in young children's understanding of their feelings is inability to recognize that they can experience different emotional reactions at the same time. Children gradually acquire an understanding of simultaneous emotions between ages 4 and 12 (Harter, 1996):

- *Level 0:* At first children do not understand that *any* two feelings can coexist. A child at the stage of *single representations* may say, "You can't have two feelings at the same time because you only have one mind!" The child cannot even acknowledge feeling two *similar* emotions at once (such as happy and glad).
- *Level 1:* Children are developing separate categories for positive and negative emotions—and can differentiate between emotions within each category, such as "happy" and "glad," or "mad" and "sad." They can now be aware of two emotions at the same time, but only if both are either positive or negative and are directed toward the same target ("If my brother hit me, I would be mad and sad").
- *Level 2:* Children capable of *representational mappings* can recognize having two feelings of the same kind directed toward different targets ("I was excited about going to Mexico and glad to see my grandparents"). However, they cannot acknowledge holding contradictory feelings ("I couldn't feel happy and scared at the same time; I would have to be two people at once!").

- *Level 3:* Children who have developed *representational systems* can integrate their sets of positive and negative emotions. They can understand having contrary feelings at the same time, but only if they are directed toward different targets. Ashley can express a negative feeling toward her baby brother ("I was mad at Tony, so I pinched him") and a positive feeling toward her father ("I was happy my father didn't spank me"), but she cannot recognize that she has positive and negative feelings (anger and love) toward both.
- *Level 4:* Older children can describe conflicting feelings toward the same target ("I'm excited about going to my new school, but I'm a little scared too").

In this study, not until children were 10 or 11 did they seem to understand conflicting emotions (Level 4). In later research, kindergartners, especially girls, showed this understanding (J. R. Brown & Dunn, 1996). The different findings may reflect differences in methodology. In the earlier study, the children were asked to tell their own stories involving mixed feelings; thus, narrative skills as well as understanding of emotions were involved. In the later study, only 1 in 4 kindergartners was able to recount such a story from personal experience. However, when *told* a story about, for example, a child receiving a present but not being allowed to open it, or riding a two-wheeled bicycle for the first time, 1 in 3 could identify conflicting emotions, and most could explain the emotions when told what they were.

Individual differences in understanding conflicting emotions seem to go back at least to age 3. Three-year-olds who could identify whether a face looked happy or sad and could tell how a puppet felt when enacting a situation involving happiness, sadness, anger, or fear were better able at the end of kindergarten to explain a story character's conflicting emotions. These children tended to come from families that often discussed why people behave as they do (J. R. Brown & Dunn, 1996).

Checkpoint

Can you . . .

✔ Trace self-concept development between ages 3 and 6?

✔ Describe the typical progression in understanding of (1) emotions directed toward the self and (2) simultaneous emotions?

Guidepost 2

How do young children develop initiative and self-esteem?

initiative versus guilt Erikson's third crisis in psychosocial development, in which children balance the urge to pursue goals with moral reservations that may prevent carrying them out

Erikson: Initiative versus Guilt

The need to deal with conflicting feelings about the self is at the heart of the third crisis of personality development identified by Erik Erikson (1950): **initiative versus guilt.** The conflict arises from the growing sense of purpose, which lets a child plan and carry out activities, and the growing pangs of conscience the child may have about such plans.

Preschool children can do—and want to do—more and more. At the same time, they are learning that some of the things they want to do meet social approval, while others do not. How do they reconcile their desire to *do* with their desire for approval?

This conflict marks a split between two parts of the personality: the part that remains a child, full of exuberance and a desire to try new things and test new powers, and the part that is becoming an adult, constantly examining the propriety of motives and actions. Children who learn how to regulate these opposing drives develop the "virtue" of *purpose,* the courage to envision and pursue goals without being unduly inhibited by guilt or fear of punishment (Erikson, 1982).

If this crisis is not resolved adequately, said Erikson, a child may turn into an adult who is constantly striving for success or showing off, or who is inhibited and unspontaneous or self-righteous and intolerant, or who suffers from impotence or psychosomatic illness. With ample opportunities to do things on their own—but under guidance and consistent limits—children can attain a healthy balance between the tendency to overdo competition and achievement and the tendency to be repressed and guilt-ridden.

Self-esteem

self-esteem The judgment a person makes about his or her self-worth

Children cannot articulate a concept of self-worth until about age 8, but they show by their behaviour that they have one (Harter, 1990, 1993, 1996). Young children's **self-esteem—** the judgment they make about their worth—is not based on a realistic appraisal of abilities or personality traits. In fact, young children usually overrate their abilities. Although they can make judgments about their competence at various activities, they are not yet able to rank them in importance; and they tend to accept the judgments of adults, who often give positive, uncritical feedback (Harter, 1990, 1996, 1998).

Self-esteem in early childhood tends to be global—"I am good" or "I am bad" (Harter, 1996, 1998). Parents' supportive behaviours—listening to a child, reading stories, making snacks, kissing away tears—are major contributors to self-esteem (Haltiwanger & Harter, 1988). Not until middle childhood do personal evaluations of competence and adequacy (based on internalization of parental and societal standards) normally become critical in shaping and maintaining a sense of self-worth (Harter, 1990, 1996, 1998).

When self-esteem is high, a child is motivated to achieve. However, if self-esteem is *contingent* on success, children may view failure or criticism as an indictment of their worth and may feel helpless to do better. About one-third to one-half of preschoolers, kindergartners, and first-graders show elements of this "helpless" pattern: self-denigration or self-blame, negative emotion, lack of persistence, and lowered expectations for themselves (Burhans & Dweck, 1995; Ruble & Dweck, 1995). Instead of trying a different way to complete a puzzle, as a child with unconditional self-esteem might do, "helpless" children feel ashamed and give up, or go back to an easier puzzle they have already done. They do not expect to succeed, and so they do not try. Whereas older children who fail may conclude that they are dumb, preschoolers interpet poor performance as a sign of being "bad." Furthermore, they believe that "badness" is permanent. This sense of being a bad person may persist into adulthood. To avoid fostering the "helpless" pattern, parents and teachers can give children specific, focused feedback rather than criticizing the child as a person ("Look, the tag on your shirt is showing in front," not "Can't you see your shirt is on backwards? When are you going to learn to dress yourself?").

Gender

Gender identity, awareness of one's femaleness or maleness and all it implies in a particular society, is an important aspect of the developing self-concept. How different are young boys and girls? What causes those differences? How do children develop gender identity, and how does it affect their attitudes and behaviour?

Gender Differences

Gender differences are psychological or behavioural differences between the sexes. Here girls seem to have a biological advantage; they are less vulnerable than boys, develop faster, are less reactive to stress, and are more likely to survive infancy (Keenan & Shaw, 1997). One of the earliest *behavioural* differences, appearing as early as age 2, is in the choice of toys and play activities and of playmates of the same sex (Turner & Gervai, 1995).

Still, while some gender differences become more pronounced after age 3, boys and girls on average remain more alike than different. A landmark review of more than 2,000 studies found few significant gender differences (Maccoby & Jacklin, 1974). The clearest difference is that boys, from preschool age on, act more aggressively than girls, both physically and verbally (Coie & Dodge, 1998; Turner & Gervai, 1995). Most studies find that girls are more empathic and prosocial (Keenan & Shaw, 1997), and some find that girls are more compliant, and cooperative with parents and seek adult approval more than boys do (N. Eisenberg, Fabes, Schaller, & Miller, 1989; M. L. Hoffman, 1977; Maccoby, 1980; Turner & Gervai, 1995).

Overall, intelligence test scores show no gender differences (Keenan & Shaw, 1997). This is not surprising, since the most widely used tests are designed to eliminate gender bias (Neisser et al., 1996). Females tend to do better at verbal tasks (but not analogies), at mathematical computation, and at tasks requiring fine motor and perceptual skills, while males excel in most spatial abilities and in abstract mathematical and scientific reasoning (Halpern, 1997).

Some of these cognitive differences, which seem to exist across cultures, begin quite early in life. Girls' superiority in perceptual speed and verbal fluency appears during infancy and toddlerhood, and boys' greater ability to mentally manipulate figures and shapes and solve mazes becomes evident early in the preschool years. Other differences do not become apparent in children of average ability until pre-adolescence or beyond (Halpern, 1997; Levine, Huttenlocher, Taylor, & Langrock, 1999).

What's your view ?

- Looking back, can you think of ways in which your parents or other adults helped you develop self-esteem?

Checkpoint ✔

Can you . . .

✔ Explain the significance of Erikson's third crisis of personality development?

✔ Tell how young children's self-esteem differs from that of school-age children?

Guidepost 3

How do boys and girls become aware of the meaning of gender, and what explains differences in behaviour between the sexes?

gender identity Awareness, developed in early childhood, that one is male or female

As toddlers, boys and girls are equally likely to hit, bite, and throw temper tantrums, and they are just as likely to show "difficult" temperament. Around age 4, however, problem behaviour diminishes in girls, whereas boys tend to get in trouble or "act up." This absence of problem behaviour among girls persists until adolescence, when they become more prone to anxiety and depression (Keenan & Shaw, 1997).

Possible reasons for this divergence may lie in the biological and cognitive differences reported above. Lower reactivity to stress may enable girls to deal with frustration or anger in a more controlled way, and girls' greater facility with language may enable them to communicate their feelings in healthier ways. Another reason may be a difference in the way boys and girls are socialized. Girls, more than boys, are taught to control themselves, to share toys, and to think about how their actions affect others; and their greater empathic ability may help them internalize social standards (Keenan & Shaw, 1997).

We need to remember, of course, that gender differences are valid for large groups of boys and girls but not necessarily for individuals. By knowing a child's sex, we cannot predict whether that *particular* boy or girl will be faster, stronger, smarter, more compliant, or more assertive than another child.

Perspectives on Gender Development: Nature and Nurture

What accounts for gender differences, and why do some of them emerge with age? The most influential explanations, until recently, centred on the differing experiences and social expectations that boys and girls meet almost from birth (Halpern, 1997; Neisser et al., 1996). These experiences and expectations concern three related aspects of gender identity: *gender roles, gender-typing,* and *gender stereotypes.*

Gender roles are the behaviours, interests, attitudes, skills, and personality traits that a culture considers appropriate for males or females. All societies have gender roles. Historically, in most cultures, women have been expected to devote most of their time to caring for the household and children, while men were providers and protectors. Women were expected to be compliant and nurturant; men, to be active, aggressive, and competitive. Today, gender roles in North American and European cultures have become more diverse and more flexible. **Gender-typing** (refer back to chapter 8), the acquisition of a gender role, takes place early in childhood; but children vary in the degree to which they take on gender roles.

Gender stereotypes are preconceived generalizations about male or female behaviour ("All females are passive and dependent; all males are aggressive and independent"). Gender stereotypes pervade many cultures. They are seen to some degree in children as young as 2½ or 3, increase during the preschool years, and reach a peak at age 5 (Haugh, Hoffman, & Cowan, 1980; Ruble & Martin, 1998; J. E. Williams & Best, 1982). As we might expect from our discussion of self-concept, younger preschoolers often attribute positive qualities to their own sex and negative qualities to the other sex. Still, at this early age *both* boys and girls call boys strong, fast, and cruel, and girls fearful and helpless (Ruble & Martin, 1998).

How do young children acquire gender roles, and why do they adopt gender stereotypes? Are these purely social constructs, or do they reflect underlying biological differences between males and females? Do social and cultural influences create gender differences, or merely accentuate them?

Today investigators are uncovering evidence of biological explanations for gender differences: genetic, hormonal, and neurological. These explanations are not either–or. Both nature and nurture probably play important parts in what it means to be male or female. Biological influences are not necessarily universal, inevitable, or unchangeable; nor are social and cultural influences easily overcome.

Let's look, then, at four perspectives on gender development (summarized in Table 11-1): *biological, psychoanalytic, cognitive,* and *socialization-based* approaches. Each of these perspectives can contribute to our understanding; none fully explains why boys and girls turn out differently in some respects and not in others.

Checkpoint ✔

Can you . . .

✔ Summarize the main behavioural and cognitive differences between boys and girls?

gender roles Behaviours, interests, attitudes, skills, and traits that a culture considers appropriate for males or for females

gender-typing Socialization process by which children learn appropriate gender roles

gender stereotypes Preconceived generalizations about male or female role behaviour

Table 11-1	Four Perspectives on Gender Development		
Theories	**Major Theorists**	**Key Processes**	**Basic Beliefs**
Biological Approach		Genetic, neurological, and hormonal activity	Many or most behavioural differences between the sexes can be traced to biological differences.
Psychoanalytic Approach			
Psychosexual theory	Sigmund Freud	Resolution of unconscious emotional conflict	Gender identity occurs when child identifies with same-sex parent.
Cognitive Approach			
Cognitive-developmental theory	Lawrence Kohlberg	Self-categorization	Once a child learns she is a girl or he is a boy, child sorts information about behaviour by gender and acts accordingly.
Gender-schema theory	Sandra Bern, Carol Lynn Martin, & Charles F. Halverson	Self-categorization based on processing of cultural information	Child organizes information about what is considered appropriate for a boy or a girl on the basis of what a particular culture dictates, and behaves accordingly. Child sorts by gender because the culture dictates that gender is an important schema.
Socialization Approach			
Social cognitive theory	Albert Bandura	Modelling, reinforcement, and teaching	Gender-typing is a result of interpretation, evaluation, and internalization of socially transmitted standards.

Biological Approach

The existence of similar gender roles in many cultures suggests that some gender differences, at least, may be biologically based. Indeed, there is some evidence of biological differences that may affect behaviour.

By age 5, when the brain reaches approximate adult size, boys' brains are about 10 per cent larger than girls' brains, mostly because boys have more grey matter in the cerebral cortex, whereas girls have greater neuronal density. What these findings may tell us about brain organization and functioning is unknown (Reiss, Abrams, Singer, Ross, & Denckla, 1996).

We do have evidence that size differences in the *corpus callosum*, the band of tissue joining the right and left hemispheres, are correlated with verbal fluency (Hines, Chiu, McAdams, Bentler, & Lipcamon, 1992). Since girls have a larger corpus callosum, better coordination between the two hemispheres may help explain girls' superior verbal abilities (Halpern, 1997).

Hormones in the bloodstream before or about the time of birth may affect the developing brain and influence gender differences. The male hormone testosterone, along with low levels of the neurotransmitter serotonin, seems related to aggressiveness, competitiveness, and dominance, perhaps through action on certain brain structures, such as the hypothalamus and amygdala (Bernhardt, 1997). Attempts also have been made to link prenatal hormonal activity with other aspects of brain functioning, such as those involved in spatial and verbal skills (Neisser et al., 1996), but this research is controversial (Ruble & Martin, 1998).

Other research focuses on children with unusual hormonal histories. Girls with a disorder called *congenital adrenal hyperplasia (CAH)* have high prenatal levels of *androgens* (male sex hormones). Although raised as girls, they tend to develop into "tomboys," showing preferences for "boys' toys," rough play, and male playmates, as well as strong spatial skills (Berenbaum & Snyder, 1995). *Estrogens* (female sex hormones), on the other hand, seem to have less influence on boys' gender-typed behaviour. Since these studies are natural experiments, they cannot establish cause and effect; other factors besides hormonal differences, such as early interactions with parents, may play a role. Also, hormonal differences may themselves be affected by environmental or other factors. In any case, such atypical patterns of behaviour have not been found in children with normal hormonal variations (Ruble & Martin, 1998).

All in all, the lack of strong evidence of biological bases of behaviour—together with the fact that psychological and behavioural differences among individuals of the same sex are much larger than the differences between the sexes—suggests that the role of biology in gender differences is limited.

Checkpoint ✓

Can you . . .

✔ Assess evidence for biological explanations of gender differences?

Psychoanalytic Approach

"Dad, where will you live when I grow up and marry Mommy?" asks Timmy, age 4. From the psychoanalytic perspective, Timmy's question is part of his acquisition of gender identity. That process, according to Freud, is one of **identification,** the adoption of characteristics, beliefs, attitudes, values, and behaviours of the parent of the same sex. Freud and other classical psychoanalytic theorists considered identification an important personality development of early childhood; some social learning theorists also have used the term.

According to Freud, identification will occur for Timmy when he represses or gives up the wish to possess the parent of the other sex (his mother) and identifies with the parent of the same sex (his father). Although this explanation for gender development has been influential, it has been difficult to test. Despite some evidence that preschoolers tend to act more affectionately toward the opposite-sex parent and more aggressively toward the same-sex parent (Westen, 1998), the theory has little research support (Maccoby, 1992). Most developmental psychologists today favour other explanations.

identification In Freudian theory, the process by which a young child adopts characteristics, beliefs, attitudes, values, and behaviours of the parent of the same sex

Cognitive Approach

Sarah figures out she is a girl because people call her a girl. She discovers that she will always be a girl. She comes to understand gender the same way she comes to understand everything else: by actively thinking about and constructing her own gender-typing. This is the heart of Lawrence Kohlberg's (1966) cognitive-developmental theory.

According to Kohlberg, children classify themselves as male or female and then organize their behaviour around that classification. They do this by adopting behaviours they perceive as consistent with their gender. Thus, Sarah prefers dolls to trucks because she views playing with dolls as consistent with her idea of herself as a girl. According to Kohlberg, **gender constancy,** more recently called *sex-category constancy*—a child's realization that his or her sex will always be the same—leads to the acquisition of gender roles. Once children realize they are permanently male or female, they adopt what they see as gender-appropriate behaviours.

When does gender constancy emerge? Answers vary from ages 3 to 7. This wide range in findings may be due to the kinds of questions asked, to differing criteria, to differences in children's reasoning at different ages, or to methodological differences (Ruble & Martin, 1998; Szkrybalo & Ruble, 1999).

Gender constancy does not appear all at once. Instead, it seems to occur in three stages (Ruble & Martin, 1998; Szkrybalo & Ruble, 1999). First, between 2 and 3, children become aware of their own gender and that of others. Next, a girl realizes that she will grow up to be a woman, and a boy that he will grow up to be a man—in other words, that gender remains the same across time. Children at this stage may base judgments about gender on superficial external appearances and stereotyped behaviours. Finally comes the realization that a girl remains a girl even if she has a short haircut and wears pants, and a boy remains a boy even if he has long hair and earrings.

There is little evidence for Kohlberg's view that gender constancy is the key to gender-typing. Long before children attain the final stage of gender constancy, they show gender-typed preferences (Bussey & Bandura, 1992; Ruble & Martin, 1998). They categorize activities and objects by gender, know a lot about what males and females do, and often acquire gender-appropriate behaviours (G. D. Levy & Carter, 1989; Luecke-Aleksa,

gender constancy Awareness that one will always be male or female; also called *sex-category constancy*

Anderson, Collins, & Schmitt, 1995). Even at 2½, girls show more interest in dolls and boys in cars, and both begin to prefer being with children of their own sex (Ruble & Martin, 1998).

It is possible that gender constancy, once achieved, may further sensitize children to gender-related information (Ruble & Martin, 1998). Five-year-old boys who have reached or are on the brink of gender constancy pay more attention to male characters on television and watch more sports and action programs than other boys their age (Luecke-Aleksa et al., 1995). Later, children develop more complex beliefs about gender and become more flexible in their views about gender roles (Ruble & Martin, 1998; M. G. Taylor, 1996)

A second cognitive approach, which combines elements of cognitive-developmental and social learning theory, is **gender-schema theory.** Among its leading proponents is Sandra Bem (1983, 1985, 1993); others are Carol Lynn Martin and Charles F. Halverson (1981).

A *schema* is a mentally organized network of information that influences a particular category of behaviour. According to gender-schema theory, children begin (very likely in infancy) to categorize events and people, organizing their observations around the schema, or category, of gender. They organize information on this basis because they see that their society classifies people that way: Males and females wear different clothes, play with different toys, and use separate bathrooms. Once children know what sex they are, they take on gender roles by developing a concept of what it means to be male or female in their culture. Children then match their own behaviour to their culture's gender schema—what boys and girls are "supposed" to be and do.

According to this theory, gender schemas promote gender stereotypes by influencing judgments about behaviour. When a new boy his age moves in next door, 4-year-old Brandon knocks on his door, carrying a toy truck. He assumes that the new boy will like the same toys he likes: "boys' toys." Children are quick to accept gender labels; when told that an unfamiliar toy is for the other sex, they will drop it like a hot potato, and they expect others to do the same (C. L. Martin, Eisenbud, & Rose, 1995; Ruble & Martin, 1998). However, it is not clear that gender schemas are at the root of this behaviour. Nor does gender-schema theory explain why some children show less stereotyped behaviour than others (Bussey & Bandura, 1992, 1999; Ruble & Martin, 1998).

Another problem with both gender-schema theory and Kohlberg's theory is that gender-typing does not necessarily become stronger with increased gender knowledge; in fact, the opposite is often true (Bussey & Bandura, 1999). One explanation, which has some research support, is that while children are constructing and then consolidating their gender schemas (around ages 4 to 6), they notice and remember only information consistent with them. Later, around age 8, schemas become more complex as children begin to take in and integrate contradictory information, such as the fact that many girls wear pants (Ruble & Martin, 1998; Welch-Ross & Schmidt, 1996).

Cognitive approaches to gender development have made an important contribution by exploring how children think about gender and what they know about it at various ages. However, these approaches do not fully explain the link between knowledge and conduct. What prompts children to act out gender roles, and why do some children become more strongly gender-typed than others? Some investigators point to socialization (Bussey & Bandura, 1992).

Socialization-Based Approach

Anna, at age 5, insisted on dressing in a new way. She wanted to wear leggings with a skirt over them, and boots—indoors and out. When her mother asked her why, Anna replied, "Because Katie dresses like this—and Katie's the king of the girls!"

According to Albert Bandura's (1986; Bussey & Bandura, 1999) **social cognitive theory,** an expanded version of social learning theory, children learn gender roles through socialization. Bandura sees gender identity as the outcome of a complex array of interacting influences, personal and social. The way a child interprets experiences with parents, teachers, peers, and cultural institutions plays a central part.

As in traditional social learning theory, children initially acquire gender roles by observing models. Children generally pick models they see as powerful or nurturing. Typically, one model is a parent, often of the same sex, but children also pattern their behaviour after other adults or (as Anna did) after peers. Behavioural feedback, together with direct teaching

Anna's enjoyment of her truck shows that she is not restricted in her play by gender stereotypes. According to Bem's gender-schema theory, parents can help their children avoid such stereotypes by encouraging them to pursue their own interests, even when these interests are unconventional for their sex.

gender-schema theory Theory, proposed by Bem, that children socialize themselves in their gender roles by developing a mentally organized network of information about what it means to be male or female in a particular culture

social cognitive theory Albert Bandura's expansion of social learning theory; holds that children learn gender roles through socialization

by parents and other adults, reinforces gender-typing. A boy who models his behaviour after his father or male peers is commended for acting "like a boy." A girl receives compliments on a pretty dress or hairstyle.

Socialization begins in infancy, long before a conscious understanding of gender begins to form. Gradually, as children begin to regulate their own activities, standards of gender-related behaviour become internalized. A child no longer needs praise, rebukes, or a model's presence to act in socially appropriate ways. Children feel good about themselves when they live up to their internal standards and feel bad if they don't. A substantial part of this shift from socially guided control to self-regulation of gender preferences may take place between ages 3 and 4 (Bussey & Bandura, 1992).

Early childhood, then, is a prime period for socialization. Let's look more closely at how parents, peers, and the media influence gender development.

Parental Influences It is not clear how much effect parental influences actually have (Ruble & Martin, 1998). Some studies have found that parental treatment affects children's gender *knowledge* more than their *behaviour* (Fagot & Leinbach, 1995; Turner & Gervai, 1995). A girl may know that baseball bats are "supposed" to be for boys but may want to use one anyway.

One reason for discrepancies in findings may be that researchers study different kinds of gender-related behaviour and use different measuring instruments (Turner & Gervai, 1995). Gender-typing has many facets, and the particular combination of "masculine" and "feminine" traits and behaviours that a child acquires is an individual matter. Also, today many parents' own gender roles are less stereotyped than they once were.

In general, boys are more strongly gender-socialized in play preferences than girls. Parents, especially fathers, tend to show more discomfort if a boy plays with a doll than if a girl plays with a truck (Lytton & Romney, 1991). Girls have more freedom than boys in their clothes, games, and choice of playmates (Miedzian, 1991).

In egalitarian households, the father's role in gender socialization seems especially important (Fagot & Leinbach, 1995). In an observational study of 4-year-olds in Cambridge, England, and Budapest, Hungary, boys and girls whose fathers did more housework and child care were less aware of gender stereotypes and engaged in less gender-typed play (Turner & Gervai, 1995). Gender-role socialization also tends to be untraditional in single-parent families headed by mothers or fathers who must play both the customary masculine and feminine roles (Leve & Fagot, 1997).

Peer Influences Even in early childhood, the peer group is a major influence on gender-typing (Turner & Gervai, 1995). Peers begin to reinforce gender-typed behaviour by age 3, and their influence increases with age. Children show more disapproval of boys who act "like girls" than of girls who are tomboys (Ruble & Martin, 1998). Although both 3- and 4-year-olds know what behaviours peers consider gender-appropriate, 4-year-olds more consistently apply these judgments to themselves (Bussey & Bandura, 1992). In a Toronto study of stated preferences for descriptions of fictitious boys and girls, children as young as 5 years preferred fictitious boys or girls whose behaviour was more in keeping with the stereotyped behaviour of the children's own sex. Boys preferred masculine boys and girls, while girls preferred feminine boys and girls (Zucker, Wilson-Smith, Kurita, & Stern, 1995).

In the study of British and Hungarian 4-year-olds' play preferences (Turner & Gervai, 1995), these preferences seemed less affected by the parents' gender-typing than were other aspects of their behaviour; at this age, such choices may be more strongly influenced by peers and the media than by the models children see at home. Generally, however, peer and parental attitudes reinforce each other. Social cognitive theory sees peers, not as an independent influence for socialization but as part of a complex cultural system that encompasses parents and other socializing agents as well (Bussey & Bandura, 1999).

Cultural Influences The Russian psychologist Lev Vygotsky analyzed how cultural practices affect development. When, for example, a Hindu girl in a village in Nepal touched the plow that her brother was using, she was severely rebuked. In this way she learned that as a female she was restricted from acts her brother was expected to perform (Skinner, 1989).

What's your view ?

- Where would you place your own views on the continuum between the following extremes? Explain.

1. Family A thinks girls should wear only ruffly dresses and boys should never wash dishes or cry.

2. Family Z treats sons and daughters exactly alike, without making any references to the children's sex.

A major channel for the transmission of cultural attitudes toward gender is television. Although women in television programs and commercials are now more likely to be working outside the home and men are sometimes shown caring for children or doing the marketing, for the most part life as portrayed on television continues to be more stereotyped than life in the real world (Coltrane & Adams, 1997; Ruble & Martin, 1998).

Social cognitive theory predicts that children who watch a lot of television will become more gender-typed by imitating the models they see on the screen. Dramatic supporting evidence emerged from a natural experiment in several western Canadian towns, one of which, dubbed "Notel" to protect the anonymity of the participants, obtained access to television transmission for the first time in 1973. Children who had had relatively unstereotyped attitudes in Notel showed marked increases in traditional views 2 years later (Kimball, 1986). In another study, children who watched a series of non-traditional episodes, such as a father and son cooking together, had less stereotyped views than children who had not seen the series (J. Johnston & Ettema, 1982).

Children's books have long been a source of gender stereotypes. Today, friendship between boys and girls is portrayed more often, and girls are braver and more resourceful. Still, male characters predominate, females are more likely to need help, and males are more likely to give it (Beal, 1994; Evans, 1998). So pervasive is the influence of these stereotypes that when children are exposed to an alternative, non-sexist version of a fairy tale, they expect it to follow the usual stereotyped patterns and may even be indignant when it does not (Evans, 1998).

Major strengths of the socialization approach include the breadth and multiplicity of processes it examines and the scope for individual differences it reveals. But this very complexity makes it difficult to establish clear causal connections between the way children are raised and the way they think and act. Just what aspects of the home environment and the peer culture promote gender-typing? Underlying this question is a chicken-and-egg problem: Do parents and peers treat boys and girls differently because they *are* different, or because the culture says they *should be* different? Does differential treatment *produce* or *reflect* gender differences? Perhaps, as social cognitive theory suggests, there is a bi-directional relationship. Further research may help to show how socializing agents mesh with children's own tendencies in gender-related attitudes and behaviour.

Checkpoint ✔

Can you . . .

✔ Distinguish among four basic approaches to the study of gender development?

✔ Compare how various theories explain the acquisition of gender roles, and assess the support for each theory?

Play: The Business of Early Childhood

Guidepost 4

How do preschoolers play, and how does play contribute to and reflect development?

Carmen, age 3, pretends that the pieces of cereal floating in her bowl are "fishies" swimming in the milk, and she "fishes," spoonful by spoonful. After breakfast, she puts on her mother's hat, picks up a briefcase, and is a "mommy" going to work. She rides her tricycle through the puddles, comes in for an imaginary telephone conversation, turns a wooden block into a truck and says, "Vroom, vroom!" Carmen's day is one round of play after another.

It would be a mistake to dismiss Carmen's activities as no more than "having fun." Play is the work of the young, and it contributes to all domains of development. Through play, children stimulate the senses, learn how to use their muscles, coordinate sight with movement, gain mastery over their bodies, and acquire new skills. Through pretending, they try out roles, cope with uncomfortable emotions, gain understanding of other people's viewpoints, and construct an image of the social world. They develop problem-solving skills, experience the joy of creativity, and become more proficient with language (Bodrova & Leong, 1998; J. I. F. Davidson, 1998; Furth & Kane, 1992; J. E. Johnson, 1998; Nourot, 1998; Singer & Singer, 1990). By making "tickets" for an imaginary train trip or "reading" eye charts in a "doctor's office," they build emergent literacy (Christie, 1991, 1998). As they sort blocks of different shapes, count how many they can pile on each other, or announce that "my tower is bigger than yours," they lay the foundation for mathematical concepts (Jarrell, 1998). As they play with computers, they learn new ways of thinking (Silvern, 1998).

Preschoolers engage in different types of play at different ages. Particular children have different styles of play, and they play at different things. Researchers categorize children's play by its *content* (what children do when they play) and its *social dimension* (whether they play alone or with others). What can we learn about children by seeing how they play?

Types of Play

Carol, at 3, "talked for" a doll, using a deeper voice than her own. Michael, at 4, wore a kitchen towel as a cape and "flew" around as Batman. These children were engaged in pretend play involving make-believe people or situations.

Pretend play is one of four categories of play identified by Piaget and others as showing increasing levels of cognitive complexity (Piaget, 1951; Smilansky, 1968). The simplest form, which begins during infancy, is active **functional play** involving repetitive muscular movements (such as rolling or bouncing a ball). As gross motor skills improve, preschoolers run, jump, skip, hop, throw, and aim.

The second level of cognitive complexity is seen in toddlers' and preschoolers' **constructive play** (using objects or materials to make something, such as a house of blocks or a crayon drawing). Four-year-olds in preschools or daycare centres may spend more than half their time in this kind of play, which becomes more elaborate by ages 5 and 6 (J. E. Johnson, 1998).

The third level, **pretend play,** also called *fantasy play, dramatic play,* or *imaginative play,* rests on the symbolic function, which emerges near the end of the sensorimotor stage (Piaget, 1962). Pretend play typically begins during the last part of the second year, increases during the preschool years, and then declines as school-age children become more involved in the fourth cognitive level of play, *formal games with rules,* such as hopscotch and marbles.

An estimated 10 to 17 per cent of preschoolers' play and 33 per cent of kindergartners' is pretend play, often using dolls and real or imaginary props (Bretherton, 1984; Garner, 1998; J. E. Johnson, 1998; K. H. Rubin, Fein, & Vandenberg, 1983). Children who often play imaginatively tend to cooperate more with other children and to be more popular and more joyful than those who don't (Singer & Singer, 1990). Children who watch a great deal of television tend to play less imaginatively, perhaps because they are accustomed to passively absorbing images rather than generating their own (Howes & Matheson, 1992). Television also seems to have influenced the kinds of roles preschoolers choose to play. Instead of modelling their dramatic play after real people, they more often pretend to be television adventure heroes (French & Pena, 1991).

Toward the end of this period and into middle childhood, *rough-and-tumble play* involving wrestling, kicking, and sometimes chasing, becomes more common (Pellegrini, 1998).

The Social Dimension of Play

In the 1920s, Mildred B. Parten (1932) identified six types of early play, ranging from the least to the most social (see Table 11-2). She found that as children get older, their play tends to become more interactive and more cooperative. At first they play alone, then alongside other children, and finally, together.

Is solitary play less mature than social play? Parten thought so. She and some other observers suggest that young children who play alone may be at risk of developing social, psychological, and educational problems. However, most researchers now view Parten's characterization of children's play development as too simplistic. Non-social play does not necessarily diminish through the years, to be replaced by social play; instead, children of all ages engage in all of Parten's categories of play. Although solitary active play becomes less common between ages 3 and 6, solitary constructive play does not. Furthermore, playing near other children and watching what they do is often a prelude to joining in their play (K. H. Rubin, Bukowski, & Parker, 1998).

Much non-social play consists of activities that foster cognitive, physical, and social development. In one study of 4-year-olds, some kinds of non-social play, such as *parallel constructive play* (for example, working on puzzles near another child) were most common among children who were good problem solvers, were popular with other children, and were seen by teachers as socially skilled (K. Rubin, 1982). Such play may reflect independence and maturity, not poor social adjustment. Children need some time alone to concentrate on tasks and problems, and some simply enjoy individual activities more than group activities. We need to look, then, at what children *do* when they play, not just at whether they play

---

functional play In Piaget's and Smilansky's terminology, the lowest cognitive level of play, involving repetitive muscular movements

constructive play In Piaget's and Smilansky's terminology, the second cognitive level of play, involving use of objects or materials to make something

pretend play In Piaget's and Smilansky's terminology, the third cognitive level of play, involving imaginary people or situations; also called *fantasy play, dramatic play,* or *imaginative play*

What's your view

- How do you think use of computers might affect preschool children's cognitive and social development?

Table 11-2	Parten's Categories of Social and Non-social Play

Category	Description
Unoccupied behaviour	The child does not seem to be playing, but watches anything of momentary interest.
Onlooker behaviour	The child spends most of the time watching other children play. She talks to them, asking questions or making suggestions, but does not enter into the play. She is definitely observing particular groups of children rather than anything that happens to be exciting
Solitary independent play	The child plays alone with toys that are different from those used by nearby children and makes no effort to get close to them.
Parallel play	The child plays independently, but among the other children, playing with toys like those used by the other children, but not necessarily playing with them in the same way. Playing *beside* rather than *with* the others, the parallel player does not try to influence the other children's play.
Associative play	The child plays with other children. They talk about their play, borrow and lend toys, follow one another, and try to control who may play in the group. All the children play similarly if not identically; there is no division of labour and no organization around any goal. Each child acts as she or he wishes and is interested more in being with the other children than in the activity itself.
Cooperative or organized supplementary play	The child plays in a group organized for some goal—to make something, play a formal game, or dramatize a situation. One or two children control who belongs to the group and direct activities. By a division of labour, children take on different roles and supplement each other's efforts.

Source: Adapted from Parten, 1932, pp. 249–251.

alone or with someone else (K. H. Rubin et al., 1998). Some investigators have modified Parten's system to more realistically gauge developmental and individual differences in play by assessing both its cognitive and social dimensions (Cheah, Nelson, & Rubin, 2001; Coplan & Rubin, 1998).

One kind of play that does become more social during the preschool years is imaginative play, which shifts from solitary pretending to dramatic play involving other children (K. H. Rubin et al., 1998; Singer & Singer, 1990). Young children follow unspoken rules in organizing dramatic play, staking out territory ("I'm the daddy; you're the mommy"), negotiating ("Okay, I'll be the daddy tomorrow"), or setting the scene ("Watch out—there's a train coming!"). As imaginative play becomes increasingly collaborative, storylines become more complex and more innovative. Dramatic play offers rich opportunities to practise interpersonal and language skills and to explore social roles and conventions (Bodrova & Leong, 1998; Christie, 1991; J. E. Johnson, 1998; Nourot, 1998).

How Gender Influences Play

A tendency toward sex segregation in play seems to be universal. It is common among preschoolers as young as 3 and becomes even more common in middle childhood (Maccoby, 1988, 1990, 1994; Ramsey & Lasquade, 1996; Snyder, West, Stockemer, Gibbons, & Almquist-Parks, 1996).

Boys and girls play differently (Serbin, Moller, Gulko, Powlishta, & Colburne, 1994). Most boys like rough-and-tumble play in fairly large groups; girls are inclined to quieter play with one playmate (Benenson, 1993). The difference is not just based on liking different kinds of activities. Even when boys and girls play with the same toys, they play more socially with others of the same sex (Neppl & Murray, 1997). Boys play more boisterously; girls play more cooperatively, taking turns to avoid clashes (Maccoby, 1980).

Children's developing gender concepts seem to influence dramatic play. Whereas boys' stories often involve danger and discord (such as mock battles), girls' plots generally

Checkpoint ✔

Can you . . .

✔ Describe four cognitive levels of play, according to Piaget and others, and six categories of social and non-social play, according to Parten?

✔ Explain the connection between the cognitive and social dimensions of play?

focus on maintaining or restoring orderly social relationships (playing house) (Fagot & Leve, 1998; Nourot, 1998).

From an evolutionary viewpoint, gender differences in children's play provide practice for adult behaviours important for reproduction and survival. Boys' rough-and-tumble play mirrors adult males' competition for dominance and status, and for fertile mates. Girls' play parenting prepares them to care for the young (Geary, 1999).

How Culture Influences Play

The amount of time spent in play varies around the world. In non-literate societies, children spend less time playing, and girls spend more time on household chores (Larson & Verma, 1999). The frequency of specific forms of play differs across cultures and is influenced by the play environments adults set up for children, which in turn reflect cultural values (Bodrova & Leong, 1998).

One observational study compared 48 middle-class Korean-American and 48 middle-class Anglo-American children in separate preschools (Farver, Kim, & Lee, 1995). The Anglo-American preschools, in keeping with typical American values, encouraged independent thinking, problem solving, and active involvement in learning by letting children select from a wide range of activities. The Korean-American preschool, in keeping with traditional Korean values, emphasized developing academic skills and completing tasks. The Anglo-American preschools encouraged social interchange among children and collaborative activities with teachers. In the Korean-American preschool, children were allowed to talk and play only during outdoor recess.

Not surprisingly, the Anglo-American children engaged in more social play, whereas the Korean-Americans engaged in more unoccupied or parallel play. Korean-American children played more cooperatively, often offering toys to other children—very likely a reflection of their culture's emphasis on group harmony. Anglo-American children were more aggressive and often responded negatively to other children's suggestions, reflecting the competitiveness of American culture.

An ethnographic study compared pretend play among 2½- to 4-year-olds in five Irish-American families in the United States and nine Chinese families in Taiwan. Play was primarily social in both cultures, but Irish-American children were more likely to pretend with other children and Chinese children with caregivers, who often used the play as a vehicle to teach proper conduct. Children in both cultures used objects (such as toy soldiers) in play, though this was more typical of Irish-American children, whose play tended to centre on fantasy or movie themes (Haight, Wang, Fung, Williams, & Mintz, 1999).

Parenting

As children gradually become their own persons, their upbringing can be a complex challenge. Parents must deal with small people who have minds and wills of their own, but who still have a lot to learn about what kinds of behaviour work well in a civilized society. How do parents discipline children and teach them self-discipline? Are some ways of parenting more effective than others?

Forms of Discipline

Discipline refers to methods of teaching children character, self-control, and acceptable behaviour. It can be a powerful tool for socialization. What forms of discipline work best? Researchers have looked at a wide range of techniques. Although discipline involves imparting knowledge and skill, it is often confused with punishment and control (Psychosocial Paediatrics Committee, Canadian Paediatric Society [CPS], 1997). There are other ways of disciplining children that are more effective than using punishment.

Reinforcement and Punishment

"What are we going to do with that child?" Noel's mother says. "The more we punish him, the more he misbehaves!"

Parents sometimes punish children to stop undesirable behaviour, but children usually learn more from being reinforced for good behaviour. *External* reinforcements may be tan-

Checkpoint ✔

Can you . . .

✔ Tell how gender and culture influence the way children play, and give examples?

Guidepost 5

How do parenting practices influence development?

discipline Methods of moulding children's character and of teaching them self-control and acceptable behaviour

gible (candy, money, toys, or gold stars) or intangible (a smile, a word of praise, a hug, extra attention, or a special privilege). Whatever the reinforcement, the child must see it as rewarding and must receive it fairly consistently after showing the desired behaviour. Eventually, the behaviour should provide its own *internal* reward: a sense of pleasure or accomplishment. In Noel's case, his parents often ignore him when he behaves well but scold or spank him when he acts up. In other words, they unwittingly reinforce his *mis*behaviour by giving him attention when he does what they do *not* want him to do.

Still, at times punishment is commonly used. Children may have to be prevented from running out into traffic or hitting another child. Sometimes a child is wilfully defiant. In such situations, punishment, if consistent, immediate, and clearly tied to the offence, may be effective. It should be administered calmly, in private, and aimed at eliciting compliance, not guilt. It is most effective when accompanied by a short, simple explanation (Baumrind, 1996a, 1996b; CPS, 1997). However, the Canadian Paediatric Society recommends against corporal punishment, like disciplinary spanking, and recommends alternatives like time-out and away-from-the-moment reasoning (CPS, 1997).

Imprudent punishment can be counterproductive. Children who are punished harshly and frequently may have trouble interpreting other people's actions and words; they may attribute hostile intentions where none exist (B. Weiss, Dodge, Bates, & Pettit, 1992). Young children who have been punished harshly may later act aggressively, even though the punishment is intended to stop what a parent sees as purposely aggressive behaviour (Nix et al., 1999). Or such children may become passive because they feel helpless. Children may become frightened if parents lose control and may eventually try to avoid a punitive parent, undermining the parent's ability to influence behaviour (Grusec & Goodnow, 1994).

Corporal punishment has been defined as "the use of physical force with the intention of causing a child to experience pain, but not injury, to correct or control the child's behaviour" (Straus, 1994a, p. 4). It can include spanking, hitting, slapping, pinching, shaking (which can be fatal to infants), and other physical acts. Its use is extremely common in Canada and the United States—so much so that it is as a pervasive part of the socialization of many children. Corporal punishment is popularly believed to be more effective than other remedies and to be harmless if done in moderation by loving parents. However, a growing body of evidence suggests that these beliefs are untrue, that corporal punishment can have serious negative consequences, and that it should not be used (MacMillan et al., 1999; Straus, 1999; Straus & Stewart, 1999; see Box 11-1). Outside of the family and despite Section 43 of the Canadian Criminal Code, provincial laws like Ontario's Day Nurseries Act prohibit the use of corporal punishment, harsh or degrading measures, or the deprivation of basic needs in disciplining children by daycare workers (Revised Regulations of Ontario, 1990).

corporal punishment Use of physical force with the intention of causing pain, but not injury, to correct or control behaviour

Power Assertion, Induction, and Withdrawal of Love

Reinforcement and punishment are not the only ways to influence behaviour. Contemporary research has focused on three broader categories of discipline: *power assertion, induction,* and *temporary withdrawal of love.*

Power assertion is intended to stop or discourage undesirable behaviour through physical or verbal enforcement of parental control; it includes demands, threats, withdrawal of privileges, and spanking. **Inductive techniques** are designed to induce desirable behaviour (or discourage undesirable behaviour) by reasoning with a child; they include setting limits, demonstrating logical consequences of an action, explaining, discussing, and getting ideas from the child about what is fair. **Withdrawal of love** may take the form of ignoring, isolating, or showing dislike for a child. The choice and effectiveness of a disciplinary strategy may depend on the personality of the parent, the personality and age of the child, and the quality of their relationship, as well as on culturally based customs and expectations (Grusec & Goodnow, 1994).

Most parents call upon more than one strategy, depending on the situation. Parents tend to use reasoning to get a child to show concern for others. They use power assertion to stop play that becomes too rough, and they use both power assertion and reasoning to deal with lying and stealing (Grusec & Goodnow, 1994).

power assertion Disciplinary strategy to discourage undesirable behaviour through physical or verbal enforcement of parental control

inductive techniques Disciplinary techniques to induce desirable behaviour by appealing to a child's sense of reason and fairness

withdrawal of love Disciplinary strategy that may involve ignoring, isolating, or showing dislike for a child

Box 11-1 *The Case Against Corporal Punishment*

Recent court challenges of Section 43 of the Canadian Criminal Code, which was ultimately upheld, have made corporal punishment a live issue today. While some professionals view corporal punishment as verging on child abuse (Straus, 1994b), others defend it as necessary or desirable in moderation, when prudently administered by loving parents (Baumrind, 1996a, 1996b).

Corporal punishment has diminished in many European countries since the passage of laws against it in Sweden in 1979, followed by Austria, Cyprus, Denmark, Finland, Italy, Norway, Croatia, and Latvia; and a number of other countries are considering such laws. Yet in Canada, considered to be a society that is tolerant of physical punishment (Durrant, 1995), an estimated 70 to 90 per cent of parents spank their children, and one-third of those report doing so at least once a week (Durrant, Broberg, & Rose-Krasnor, 1999). Canadian mothers are more likely than Swedish mothers to spank their children, and the likelihood of spanking is higher if mothers have a positive attitude towards spanking and believe that their children's behaviours are changeable (Durrant et al., 1999). In fact, 80 per cent of respondents in a retrospective study of non-abused adults in Ontario reported having experienced some form of corporal punishment as children (MacMillan et al., 1999).

Some form of corporal, or bodily, punishment is widely used on infants, and it is virtually universal among parents of toddlers. In interviews with a nationally representative sample of 991 parents in 1995, 35 per cent reported using corporal punishment—usually hand slapping—on infants during the previous year, and fully 94 per cent on 3- and 4-year-olds. About half of the parents were still hitting children by age 12, one-third at age 14, and 13 per cent at age 17 (Straus & Stewart, 1999).[*]

Opponents of corporal punishment are not against disciplining children, but they maintain there are more effective, less risky or harmful ways to do it. A large body of research has consistently found negative outcomes from its use. Apart from the risk of injury to the child, these outcomes include increased physical aggression in childhood and anxiety disorders, depression, alcohol problems, antisocial behaviour, or partner abuse later in life (MacMillan et al., 1999; Strassberg, Dodge, Pettit, & Bates, 1994).

Most of this research was cross-sectional or retrospective, and the few longitudinal studies did not consider that the spanked children may have been aggressive in the first place, and that their aggressive behaviour might have led their parents to spank them. Since 1997 several large, American, nationally representative landmark studies (Brezina, 1999; Gunnoe & Mariner, 1997; Simons, Lin, & Gordon, 1998; Straus, Sugarman, & Giles-Sims, 1997; and Straus & Paschall, 1999) have overcome this defect by taking account of the child's own behaviour at the time of first measurement.

These studies, which included youngsters ranging from age 3 through adolescence, found that corporal punishment is counterproductive: the more a child receives, the more aggressive or antisocial the child's behaviour becomes, and the more likely that child is to show antisocial or other maladaptive behaviour as a child and as an adult (Straus & Stewart, 1999).

Why is this so? One answer is that physical punishment stimulates aggressive behaviour by leading children to imitate the punisher and to consider infliction of pain an acceptable response to problems. Furthermore, as with any punishment, the effectiveness of spanking diminishes with repeated use; children may feel free to misbehave if they are willing to take the consequences. Reliance on physical punishment may weaken parents' authority when children become teenagers and most parents recognize that spanking becomes inappropriate—if not impractical (AAP Committee on Psychosocial Aspects of Child and Family Health, 1998; McCord, 1996; Psychosocial Paediatrics Committee of the Canadian Paediatric Society, 1997).

Spanking may even inhibit cognitive development, according to data on 2- to 4-year-olds and 5- to 9-year-olds from the U.S. National Longitudinal Study of Youth. Children whose mothers used little or no corporal punishment (such as spanking or hand-slapping) during a 2-week period showed greater cognitive gains than children who received corporal punishment (Straus & Paschall, 1999).

The CPS Psychosocial Paediatrics Committee urges parents to avoid spanking. Instead, the committee suggests such inductive methods as helping children learn to use words to express feelings, giving children choices and helping them evaluate the consequences, and modelling orderly behaviour and collaborative conflict resolution. The committee recommends positive reinforcement to encourage desired behaviours, and verbal reprimands, "time-outs," or removal of privileges to discourage undesired behaviours—all within a positive, supportive, loving parent–child relationship.

What's your view?

Did your parents ever spank you? If so, how often and in what kinds of situations? Would you spank, or have you ever spanked, your own child? Why or why not?

Check it out!

For more information and relevant links on this topic, go to the Online Learning Centre: **www.mcgrawhill.ca/college/papalia.**

[*]Unless otherwise referenced, the material and viewpoint in this box are based on Straus (1999) and Straus & Stewart (1999).

The strategy parents choose may depend not only on their belief in its effectiveness but on their confidence that they can carry it out. In one observational study of parental handling of sibling conflicts, mothers were more likely to use inductive techniques, while fathers were more likely to use power-assertive strategies. Still, what both mothers and fathers did most often was not to intervene at all (Perozynski & Kramer, 1999).

An important goal of socialization is to help a child internalize parental teachings in the form of self-discipline. Induction is usually the most effective method, and power assertion the least effective, of getting children to accept parental standards (M. L. Hoffman, 1970a,

1970b). Kindergartners whose mothers reported using reasoning were more likely to see the moral wrongness of behaviour that hurts other people (as opposed to merely breaking rules) than children whose mothers took away privileges (Jagers, Bingham, & Hans, 1996). This may be because removal of privileges encourages children to focus on themselves and their own feelings rather than on the way their behaviour affects others (McCord, 1996).

The effectiveness of parental discipline may hinge on how well the child understands and accepts the parent's message, both cognitively and emotionally (Grusec & Goodnow, 1994). For the child to accept the message, the child has to recognize it as appropriate; so parents need to be fair and accurate, and clear and consistent about their expectations. They need to fit their actions to the misdeed and to the child's temperament and cognitive and emotional level. A child may be more motivated to accept the message if the parents are normally warm and responsive, if they arouse the child's empathy for someone harmed by the misdeed, and if they make the child feel less secure in their affections as a result of the misbehaviour (Grusec & Goodnow, 1994).

One point on which experts agree is that a child interprets and responds to discipline in the context of an ongoing relationship with a parent. Some researchers therefore have looked beyond specific parental practices to overall styles, or patterns, of parenting.

Parenting Styles

Why does Stacy hit and bite the nearest person when she cannot finish a jigsaw puzzle? What makes David sit and sulk when he cannot finish the puzzle, even though his teacher offers to help him? Why does François work on the puzzle for 20 minutes and then shrug and try another? Why are children so different in their responses to the same situation? Temperament is a major factor, of course; but some research suggests that styles of parenting may affect children's competence in dealing with their world.

Baumrind's Model

In her pioneering research, Diana Baumrind (1971, 1996b; Baumrind & Black, 1967) studied 103 preschool children from 95 families. Through interviews, testing, and home studies, she measured how children were functioning, identified three parenting styles, and described typical behaviour patterns of children raised according to each.

Authoritarian parents, according to Baumrind, value control and unquestioning obedience. They try to make children conform to a set standard of conduct and punish them arbitrarily and forcefully for violating it. They are more detached and less warm than other parents. Their children tend to be more discontented, withdrawn, and distrustful.

Permissive parents value self-expression and self-regulation. They make few demands and allow children to monitor their own activities as much as possible. When they do have to make rules, they explain the reasons for them. They consult with children about policy decisions and rarely punish. They are warm, non-controlling, and undemanding. Their preschool children tend to be immature—the least self-controlled and the least exploratory.

Authoritative parents value a child's individuality but also stress social constraints. They have confidence in their ability to guide children, but they also respect children's independent decisions, interests, opinions, and personalities. They are loving and accepting, but also demand good behaviour, are firm in maintaining standards, and are willing to impose limited, judicious punishment when necessary, within the context of a warm, supportive relationship. They explain the reasoning behind their stands and encourage verbal give-and-take. Their children apparently feel secure in knowing both that they are loved and what is expected of them. These preschoolers tend to be the most self-reliant, self-controlled, self-assertive, exploratory, and content.

Eleanor Maccoby and John Martin (1983) added a fourth parenting style—**neglectful, or uninvolved**—to describe parents who, sometimes because of stress or depression, focus on their own needs rather than on those of the child. Neglectful parenting, discussed in chapter 9, has been linked with a variety of behavioural disorders in childhood and adolescence (Baumrind, 1991; Parke & Buriel, 1998; R. A. Thompson, 1998).

Why does authoritative parenting seem to enhance children's competence? It may be because authoritative parents set sensible expectations and realistic standards. By making clear, consistent rules, they let children know what is expected of them. In authoritarian

Checkpoint ✔

Can you . . .

✔ Compare various forms of discipline and identify factors that influence their effectiveness?

What's your view ?

- As a parent, what forms of discipline would you favour in what situations? Give specific examples, and tell why.

authoritarian Baumrind's term for parenting style emphasizing control and obedience

permissive Baumrind's term for parenting style emphasizing self-expression and self-regulation

authoritative Baumrind's term for parenting style blending respect for a child's individuality with an effort to instill social values

neglectful/uninvolved Maccoby and Martin's term for parents who focus on their own needs rather than on those of the child

homes, children are so strictly controlled that often they cannot make independent choices about their own behaviour. In permissive homes, children receive so little guidance that they may become uncertain and anxious about whether they are doing the right thing. In authoritative homes, children know when they are meeting expectations and can decide whether it is worth risking parental displeasure to pursue a goal. These children are expected to perform well, fulfill commitments, and participate actively in family duties as well as family fun. They know the satisfaction of meeting responsibilities and achieving success. Parents who make reasonable demands show that they believe their children can meet them—and that the parents care enough to insist that they do.

The question of how much freedom children should be allowed is a major source of conflict between parents and children in mainstream Canadian culture. Most Canadian parents believe that even preschoolers are entitled to their own opinions and should have control over some aspects of their lives so as to promote competence and self-esteem. However, the precise boundaries where a child's area of autonomy ends and the area of parental control begins are matters of negotiation and may vary among ethnic and socio-economic groups (Nucci & Smetana, 1996). When conflict arises, an authoritative parent can teach the child positive ways to communicate his or her own point of view and negotiate acceptable alternatives. ("If you don't want to throw away those smelly clam shells you found, where do you think we should keep them?") Internalization of this broader set of skills, not just of specific behavioural demands, may well be a key to the success of authoritative parenting (Grusec & Goodnow, 1994).

What's your view ?

- To what extent would you like your children to adopt your values and behavioural standards? Can you give examples?

Support and Criticisms of Baumrind's Model

Baumrind's work has inspired much research, and the superiority of authoritative parenting (or similar conceptions of parenting style) has repeatedly been supported (Baumrind, 1989; Darling & Steinberg, 1993). For example, a longitudinal study of 585 ethnically and socio-economically diverse families in Tennessee and Indiana from pre-kindergarten through Grade 6 found that four aspects of early supportive parenting—warmth, use of inductive discipline, interest and involvement in children's contacts with peers, and proactive teaching of social skills—predicted children's later behavioural, social, and academic outcomes (Pettit, Bates, & Dodge, 1997).

Similar principles apply to teachers and other caregivers. In a low-income daycare centre for 3- to 6-year-olds at risk for developing disruptive behaviour, teachers' laxity (similar to permissive parenting) tended to elicit misbehaviour; and children's misbehaviour, in turn, elicited either laxity or overreactivity (similar in some ways to authoritarian parenting) from the teachers. The results suggest that teachers, like parents, need to learn how to set and enforce firm, consistent, and appropriate rules (Arnold, McWilliams, & Arnold, 1998).

Still, because Baumrind's model seems to suggest that there is one "right" way to raise children well, it has provoked some controversy. Since Baumrind's findings were correlational, they merely establish associations between each parenting style and a particular set of child behaviours. They do not show that different styles of child rearing *cause* children to be more or less competent. Sandra Scarr (1992, 1993), for example, argues that heredity normally exerts a much greater influence than parenting practices.

It is also impossible to know whether the children Baumrind studied were, in fact, raised in a particular style. It may be that some of the better-adjusted children were raised inconsistently, but by the time of the study their parents had adopted the authoritative pattern. Furthermore, parents often behave differently in different situations (Holden & Miller, 1999).

In addition, Baumrind did not consider innate factors, such as temperament, that might have affected children's competence and exerted an influence on the parents. Parents of "easy" children may be more likely to respond to the child in a permissive or authoritative manner, while parents of "difficult" children may become more authoritarian.

Cultural Differences in Parenting Styles

Baumrind's categories reflect the dominant North American view of child development and may be misleading when applied to some cultures or socio-economic groups. Among Chinese parents, for example, obedience and strictness—rather than being associated with harshness and domination—have more to do with caring, concern, and involvement and with maintaining family harmony. Traditional Chinese culture, with its emphasis on respect for elders, stresses adults' responsibility to maintain the social order by teaching children socially proper behaviour. This obligation is carried out through firm and just control and governance of the child. Although Asian parenting is frequently described as authoritarian, the warmth and supportiveness that characterize Chinese family relationships more closely resemble Baumrind's authoritative parenting. Authoritarian parenting in China is associated with aggression and low acceptance by peers, whereas authoritative parenting in China is associated with high levels of social and academic adjustment (Chen, Dong, & Zhou, 1997).

In general, Canadian parents adopt a positive parenting style, characterized by offering support and encouragement to children (Landy & Tam, 1996). Positive parenting approaches are associated with good developmental outcomes in social development and helping behaviour. However, children are particularly vulnerable to poor developmental outcomes if their family situations contain more than several risk factors including family dysfunction, low social support, being in a single-parent family, having a teenage parent, and living in poverty. The impact of these factors on child development is typically diminished by positive parenting practices (Landy & Tam, 1996).

The traditional Aboriginal parenting style in Canada is much like Baumrind's permissive style. However, as is the case with the preferred parenting style in families of Asian background, there is no detrimental influence on Aboriginal children's development (Johnson & Cremo, 1995). Among Canadian immigrant groups, there are differences in parenting style, which may reflect differences in social values in the countries of origin. Egyptian Canadians, for example, were found to score higher on measures of authoritarianism and collectivism than were Anglo-Canadians (Rudy & Grusec, 2001). The best predictor of authoritarian parenting style in Egyptian Canadian parents was high levels of collectivism, in comparison to individualism, whereas in Anglo-Canadians the best predictor of authoritarian parenting was a combination of collectivism and lack of warmth (Rudy et al., 2001). It may be misleading, then, to consider parenting styles without looking at the goals parents are trying to achieve and the constraints their life circumstances present.

Promoting Altruism and Dealing with Aggression and Fearfulness

Three specific issues of especial concern to parents, caregivers, and teachers of preschool children are how to promote altruism, curb aggression, and deal with fears that often arise at this age.

Pro-social Behaviour

Alex, at 3½, responded to two fellow preschoolers' complaints that they did not have enough modelling clay, his favourite plaything, by giving them half of his. Alex was showing **altruism**—acting out of concern for another person with no expectation of reward. Altruistic acts like Alex's often entail cost, self-sacrifice, or risk. Altruism is the heart of **pro-social behaviour,** voluntary activity intended to benefit another.

Even before the second birthday, children often help others, share belongings and food, and offer comfort. Such behaviours may reflect a growing ability to imagine how another person might feel (Zahn-Waxler, Radke-Yarrow, Wagner, & Chapman, 1992). An analysis of 179 studies found increasing evidence of concern for others from infancy throughout childhood and adolescence (Fabes & Eisenberg, 1996). Although girls tend to be more pro-social than boys, the differences are small (Eisenberg & Fabes, 1998).

In a study of pro-social behaviour in children, a team of researchers in Nova Scotia gave children opportunities to share stickers with others, either at no cost to themselves (choosing stickers for themselves and for another person), or at a cost (choosing between taking two stickers or taking one for themselves and giving one to another person). In both cases, 3- and 4-year old children shared, but much more sharing took place in the no-cost condition. When given the choice between immediately receiving a sticker, or waiting awhile to be given a sticker for themselves as well as for another person, older children tended to delay their gratification in order to share, while 3-year-olds tended to choose being given a sticker immediately (Moore, Barresi, & Thompson, 1998).

Checkpoint ✔

Can you . . .

✔ Describe and evaluate Baumrind's model of parenting styles?

✔ Discuss how parents' way of resolving conflicts with young children can contribute to the success of authoritative child rearing?

Guidepost 6

Why do young children help or hurt others, and why do they develop fears?

altruism Behaviour intended to help others out of inner concern and without expectation of external reward

pro-social behaviour Any voluntary behaviour intended to help others

The family is important as a model and as a source of explicit standards of behaviour (Eisenberg & Fabes, 1998). Parents of pro-social children are typically pro-social themselves. They point out models of pro-social behaviour and steer children toward stories, films, and television programs that depict cooperation, sharing, and empathy and encourage sympathy, generosity, and helpfulness (Singer & Singer, 1998). Relationships with siblings (discussed later in this chapter) provide an important "laboratory" for trying out caring behaviour and learning to see another person's point of view. Peers and teachers also can model and reinforce pro-social behaviour (Eisenberg, 1992; Eisenberg & Fabes, 1998).

Parents encourage pro-social behaviour when they use inductive disciplinary methods instead of power-assertive techniques (Eisenberg & Fabes, 1998). When Sara took candy from a store, her father did not lecture her on honesty, spank her, or tell her what a bad girl she had been. Instead, he explained how the owner of the store would be harmed by her failure to pay for the candy, and he took her back to the store to return it. When such incidents occur, Sara's parents ask, "How do you think Mr. Jones feels?" or, "How would you feel if you were Mr. Jones?"

Motives for pro-social behaviour may change as children grow older and develop more mature moral reasoning (see chapters 13 and 16). Preschoolers tend to show egocentric motives; they want to earn praise and avoid disapproval. They weigh costs and benefits and consider how they would like others to act toward them. As children grow older, their motives become less self-centred. They adopt societal standards of "being good," which eventually become internalized as principles and values (Eisenberg & Fabes, 1998).

Cultures vary in the degree to which they foster pro-social behaviour. Traditional cultures in which people live in extended family groups and share work seem to foster pro-social values more than cultures that stress individual achievement (Eisenberg & Fabes, 1998).

Aggression

When Peter roughly snatches a ball away from Tommy, he is interested only in getting the ball, not in hurting or dominating Tommy. This is **instrumental aggression,** or aggression used as an instrument to reach a goal—the most common type of aggression in early childhood. Between ages 2½ and 5, children commonly struggle over toys and control of space. Aggression surfaces mostly during social play; children who fight the most also tend to be the most sociable and competent. In fact, the ability to show some instrumental aggression may be a necessary step in social development.

Between ages 2 and 4, as children develop more self-control and become better able to express themselves verbally and to wait for what they want, they typically shift from showing aggression with blows to doing it with words (Coie & Dodge, 1998). However, individual differences remain; children who more frequently hit or grab toys from other children at age 2 are likely to be more physically aggressive at age 5 (Cummings, Iannotti, & Zahn-Waxler, 1989). After age 6 or 7, most children become less aggressive as they become more cooperative, less egocentric, more empathic, and better able to communicate. They can now put themselves in someone else's place, can understand why the other person may be acting in a certain way, and can develop more positive ways of dealing with that person.

As aggression declines overall, **hostile aggression**—action intended to hurt another person—proportionately increases (see chapter 14). Some children do not learn to control aggression; they continue to be destructive and anti-social throughout life (Coie & Dodge, 1998).

Are boys more aggressive than girls? Many studies say yes. Indeed, it has been suggested that the male hormone testosterone may underlie aggressive behaviour. From infancy, boys are more likely to grab things from others. As children learn to talk, girls are more likely to rely on words to protest and to work out conflicts (Coie & Dodge, 1998).

However, girls may be more aggressive than they seem; they just show aggressiveness differently (McNeilly-Choque, Hart, Robinson, Nelson, & Olsen, 1996). Boys engage in more **overt aggression,** either instrumental or hostile. Overt aggression, either physical or verbal, is openly directed against its target. Girls tend to practise **relational aggression** (also called *covert, indirect,* or *psychological aggression*). This more subtle kind of aggression consists of damaging or interfering with relationships, reputation, or psychological well-being. It may involve spreading rumours, name-calling, withholding friend-

What's your view ?

- In a society in which "good Samaritans" are sometimes reviled for "butting into other people's business" and sometimes attacked by the very persons they try to help, is it wise to encourage children to offer help to strangers?

instrumental aggression
Aggressive behaviour used as a means of achieving a goal

hostile aggression Aggressive behaviour intended to hurt another person

overt aggression Aggression openly directed at its target

relational aggression Aggression aimed at damaging or interfering with another person's relationships, reputation, or psychological well-being; also called *covert, indirect,* or *psychological aggression*

ship, or excluding someone from a group. NLSCY data indicate that aggressive girls in Canada experience more difficulty than non-agressive girls in their family and peer relations, and come from homes with higher levels of ineffective parenting, family violence, and difficulties in relations with parents and with siblings. The types of problems they experience, including emotional, self-concept, and behavioural difficulties, are similar to those of aggressive boys (Pepler & Sedighdeilami, 1998).

Sources and Triggers of Aggression What sets off aggression? Why are some children more aggressive than others?

Biology may play a part. So may temperament: Children who are intensely emotional and low in self-control tend to express anger aggressively (Eisenberg, Fabes, Nyman, Bernzweig, & Pinuelas, 1994). Family relations are also important, particularly for children from lower socio-economic levels: Children from the same family show more similarity in aggression levels than do children from different families (Tremblay et al., 1996).

A negative early relationship with the mother is an important factor, which may interact with other risk factors, such as low socio-economic status and single parenthood. In longitudinal studies, insecure attachment and lack of maternal warmth and affection in infancy have predicted aggressiveness in early childhood (Coie & Dodge, 1998). Furthermore, negative parent–child relationships may set the stage for prolonged, destructive sibling conflicts, in which children imitate their parents' hostile behaviour. These coercive family processes (Patterson, 1984) may foster aggressive tendencies. Among 180 low-income 5-year-olds with close-in-age siblings, a combination of rejecting parents (by age 2) and high levels of destructive sibling conflict predicted aggressive or anti-social conduct at home and at school at age 6 (Garcia, Shaw, Winslow, & Yaggi, 2000).

Parents of children who become anti-social often fail to reinforce good behaviour and are harsh or inconsistent, or both, in stopping or punishing misbehaviour (Coie & Dodge, 1998). Parents who back down when confronted with a preschooler's coercive demands (such as whining or shouting when scolded for not going to bed) may reinforce repetition of the undesirable behaviour (G. R. Patterson, 1995). On the other hand, harsh punishment, especially spanking, can backfire; children who are spanked not only suffer frustration, pain, and humiliation (which can be spurs to aggression) but also see aggressive behaviour in an adult model.

Exposure to real or televised violence can trigger aggression (see chapter 14). In a classic social learning experiment (Bandura, Ross, & Ross, 1961), 3- to 6-year-olds individually watched adult models play with toys. Children in one experimental group saw the adult play quietly. The model for a second experimental group began to assemble Tinkertoys, but then spent the rest of the 10-minute session punching, throwing, and kicking a life-size inflated doll. A control group did not see any model. After the sessions, the children, who were mildly frustrated by seeing toys they were not allowed to play with, went into another playroom. The children who had seen the aggressive model acted much more aggressively than those in the other groups, imitating many of the same things they had seen the model say and do. The children who had been with the quiet model were less aggressive than the control group. This finding suggests that parents may be able to moderate the effects of frustration by showing non-aggressive behaviour to their children.

Influence of Culture How much influence does culture have on aggressive behaviour? One research team asked closely matched samples of 30 Japanese and 30 U.S. middle- to upper-middle-class preschoolers to choose pictured solutions to hypothetical conflicts or stressful situations (such as having one's block tower knocked down, having to stop playing and go to bed, being hit, hearing parents argue, or fighting on a jungle gym). The children also were asked to act out and complete such situations using dolls and props. The U.S. children showed more anger, more aggressive behaviour and language, and less control of emotions than the Japanese children (Zahn-Waxler, Friedman, Cole, Mizuta, & Hiruma, 1996).

These results are consistent with child-rearing values in the two cultures. In Japan, anger and aggression are seen as clashing with the emphasis on harmonious relationships. Japanese mothers are more likely than U.S. mothers to use reasoning and induce guilt, pointing out how aggressive behaviour hurts others. Japanese mothers also show strong disappointment when children fail to meet their behavioural standards. However, the cross-cultural difference in children's anger and aggressiveness was significant even apart from mothers' behaviour, suggesting that temperamental differences also may be at work (Zahn-Waxler et al., 1996).

On the other hand, a correlational study of 207 Russian 3- to 6-year-olds, based on parental questionnaires and nursery-school teachers' ratings of children's behaviour, identified much the same family influences on aggression as have studies in North American and European cultures: parental coercion and lack of responsiveness. Coercive (power-assertive) discipline by either parent was linked with overt aggression in both boys and girls (C. H. Hart, Nelson, Robinson, Olsen, & McNeilly-Choque, 1998).

Fearfulness

Passing fears are common in early childhood. Many 2- to 4-year-olds are afraid of animals, especially dogs. By 6 years, children are more likely to be afraid of the dark. Other common fears are of thunderstorms, doctors, and imaginary creatures (DuPont, 1983; Stevenson-Hinde & Shouldice, 1996). Most of these disappear as children grow older and lose their sense of powerlessness.

Young children's fears stem largely from their intense fantasy life and their tendency to confuse appearance with reality. Sometimes their imaginations become carried away, making them worry about being attacked by a lion or being abandoned. Young children are more likely to be frightened by something that looks scary, such as a cartoon monster, than by something capable of doing great harm, such as a nuclear explosion (Cantor, 1994). For the most part, older children's fears are more realistic and self-evaluative (for example, fear of failing a test), since they know they are being evaluated by others (Stevenson-Hinde & Shouldice, 1996; see Table 11-3).

Fears may come from personal experience or from hearing about other people's experiences (Muris, Merckelbach, & Collaris, 1997). A preschooler whose mother is sick in bed may become upset by a story about a mother's death, even if it is an animal mother. Often fears come from appraisals of danger, such as the likelihood of being bitten by a dog, or are triggered by events, as when a child who was hit by a car becomes afraid to cross the street. Children who have lived through an earthquake, a kidnapping, or some other frightening event may fear that it will happen again (Kolbert, 1994).

Parents can help prevent children's fears by instilling a sense of trust and normal caution without being too protective, and also by overcoming their own unrealistic fears. They can help a fearful child by reassurance and by encouraging open expression of feelings. Ridicule ("Don't be such a baby!"), coercion ("Pat the nice doggie—it won't hurt you"), and logical persuasion ("The closest bear is 20 miles away, locked in a zoo!") are not helpful. Not until elementary school can children tell themselves that what they fear is not real (Cantor, 1994).

Children can also be helped to overcome fears by *systematic desensitization*, a therapeutic technique involving gradual exposure to a feared object or situation. This technique has been used successfully to help children overcome fears ranging from those of snakes to elevators (Murphy & Bootzin, 1973; Sturges & Sturges, 1998).

What's your view ?

- Are there situations in which a child should be encouraged to be aggressive?

Checkpoint ✓

Can you . . .

✔ Discuss how parental and other influences contribute to altruism, aggression, and fearfulness?

Guidepost 7

How do young children get along with (or without) siblings?

self-efficacy Sense of capability to master challenges and achieve goals

Relationships with Other Children

Although the most important people in young children's world are the adults who take care of them, relationships with siblings and playmates become more important in early childhood. Virtually every characteristic activity and personality issue of this age, from gender development to pro-social or aggressive behaviour, involves other children. Sibling and peer relationships provide a measuring stick for **self-efficacy,** children's growing sense of capability to master challenges and achieve their goals. By competing with and comparing themselves with other children, they can gauge their physical, social, cognitive, and linguistic competencies and gain a more realistic sense of self (Bandura, 1994).

Table 11-3	Childhood Fears
Age	**Fears**
0–6 months	Loss of support, loud noises
7–12 months	Strangers; heights; sudden, unexpected, and looming objects
1 year	Separation from parent, toilet, injury, strangers
2 years	Many stimuli, including loud noises (vacuum cleaners, sirens and alarms, trucks, and thunder), animals, dark rooms, separation from parent, large objects or machines, changes in personal environment, unfamiliar peers
3 years	Masks, dark, animals, separation from parent
4 years	Separation from parent, animals, dark, noises (including noises at night)
5 years	Animals, "bad" people, dark, separation from parent, bodily harm
6 years	Supernatural beings (e.g., ghost, witches), bodily injury, thunder and lightning, dark, sleeping or staying alone, separation from parent
7–8 years	Supernatural beings, dark, media events (e.g., news reports on the threat of nuclear war or child kidnapping), staying alone, bodily injury
9–12 years	Tests and examinations in school, school performances, bodily injury, physical appearance, thunder and lightning, death, dark

Source: Adapted from Morris & Kratochwill, 1983; Stevenson-Hinde & Shouldice, 1996.

Siblings—or Their Absence

Ties between brothers and sisters often set the stage for later relationships. Let's look at sibling relationships, and then at children who grow up with no siblings.

Brothers and Sisters

"It's mine!"

"No, it's mine!"

"Well, I was playing with it first!"

The earliest, most frequent, and most intense disputes among siblings are over property rights—who owns a toy or who is entitled to play with it. Although exasperated adults may not always see it that way, sibling disputes and their settlement can be viewed as socialization opportunities, in which children learn to stand up for moral principles. Studies of sibling interactions in Canada have shown that conflict and aggression is common, with conflict around property and possession of objects being the most typical (Perlman & Ross, 1997).

Among 40 pairs of 2- and 4-year-old siblings, property disputes arose, on average, about every 15 minutes during a 9-hour observation period. Even children as young as 2½ argued on the basis of clear principles: the owner's right to a toy should take precedence over who was currently using it, but when the toy belonged to both children (as was true in about half the disputes), the current user should have exclusive rights. Parents did not clearly favour claims based on either ownership or possession but were more inclined to stress sharing and avoiding damage, or to suggest alternate playthings (Ross, 1996).

Should parents step into sibling disputes? A home observation of 88 three- to five-year-olds and their older siblings suggests that younger children are more likely to benefit from parental intervention than older ones. When parents stayed out of sibling conflicts, both older and younger pairs, but especially younger ones, tended to behave more antagonistically in later conflicts. However, older pairs developed less positive, close sibling relationships if their mothers intervened (Kramer, Perozynski, & Chung, 1999).

Despite the frequency of conflict, sibling rivalry is *not* the main pattern between brothers and sisters early in life. While some rivalry exists, so do affection, interest, companionship, and influence. Observations spanning 3½ years, which began when younger siblings were about 1½ years old and the older ones ranged from 3 to 4½, found pro-social and play-oriented behaviours to be more common than rivalry, hostility, and competition (Abramovitch, Corter, & Lando, 1979; Abramovitch, Corter, Pepler, & Stanhope, 1986; Abramovitch, Pepler, & Corter, 1982). Older siblings initiated more behaviour, both friendly and unfriendly; younger siblings tended to imitate the older ones. Siblings got

Box 11-2 *A Nation of Only Children*

In 1979, to control an exploding population, the People's Republic of China established an official policy of limiting families to one child each. In addition to propaganda campaigns and incentives (housing, money, child care, health care, and preference in school placement) to induce voluntary compliance, millions of involuntary abortions and sterilizations have taken place. People who have had children without first getting a permit faced fines and loss of jobs. By 1985, at least 8 out of 10 young urban couples and half of those in rural areas had only one child (Yang, Ollendick, Dong, Xia, & Lin, 1995), and by 1997, the country's estimated population growth was holding steady at a little more than 1 per cent.

Today the one-child policy is unevenly enforced. Economic growth is exerting a natural check on family size and also making it easier for families who want a second child to pay the fine (Faison, 1997). The State Family Planning Commission has now prohibited forced sterilizations and abortions and has begun to switch to a system stressing education, contraceptive choice, and heavy taxation for families with more than one child. In a small but growing number of counties, fixed quotas and permit requirements have been eliminated (Rosenthal, 1998).

Still, in many Chinese cities, kindergartens and primary classrooms are almost completely filled with children who have no brothers or sisters. This situation marks a great change in Chinese society, in which newlyweds were traditionally congratulated with the wish, "May you have a hundred sons and a thousand grandsons."

Since 1979 the People's Republic of China has officially limited families to one child each. The implications of this policy for children growing up without siblings, cousins, or aunts and uncles are hotly debated by educators, researchers, and politicians.

What kind of future population are the Chinese raising? Among 4,000 third- and sixth-graders, personality differences between only children and those with siblings—as rated by parents, teachers, peers, and the children themselves—were few. In academic achievement and physical growth, only children did about the same as, or better than, those with siblings (Falbo & Poston, 1993). A review of the literature found no significant differences in behaviour problems; the small number of severe problems that did appear in only children were attributed to parental overindulgence and overprotection (Tao, 1998).

Indeed, only children seem to be at a distinct psychological advantage in China. When questionnaires were administered to 731 urban children and adolescents, children with siblings reported higher levels of fear, anxiety, and depression than only children, regardless of sex or age. Apparently children with siblings are less well adjusted in a society that favours and rewards the only child (Yang et al., 1995).

Only children seem to do better cognitively, too. A randomized study in Beijing schools (Jiao, Ji, & Jing, 1996) found that only children outperformed Grade 1 classmates with siblings in memory, language, and mathematics skills. This finding may reflect the greater attention, stimulation, hopes, and expectations that parents shower on a baby they know will be their first and last. Grade 5 only children, who were born before the one-child policy was strongly enforced—and whose parents may have originally planned for a larger family—did not show a pronounced cognitive edge.

Both of these studies used urban samples. Further research may reveal whether the findings hold up in rural areas and small towns, where children with siblings are more numerous, and whether only children maintain their cognitive superiority as they move through school.

China's population policy has wider implications. If it succeeds, most Chinese will eventually lack aunts, uncles, nephews, nieces, and cousins, as well as siblings. How this will affect individuals, families, and the social fabric is incalculable.

A more sinister question is this: What happened to the girls? A 1990 census suggests that 5 per cent of all infant girls born in China (some half a million infants born alive each year) are unaccounted for. Suspicions are that many parents, being permitted only one child, had their baby girls killed or let them die of neglect to allow the parents the chance to bear and raise more highly valued sons. A more benign explanation is that these girls were hidden and raised secretly to evade the one-child policy (Kristof, 1991, 1993). In either case, China's one-child policy appears to be having ramifications its developers may not have considered, and concern about these unforeseen effects may be one factor in the current relaxation of enforcement.

What's your view ?

Governmental control of reproduction may seem like the ultimate in totalitarianism, but what course of action would you propose for a country that cannot support an exploding population?

Check it out !

For more information on this topic, go to **www.mcgrawhill.ca/ college/papalia,** where you will be directed to the website from the Public Broadcasting Corporation about China and reproductive issues.

along better when their mother was not with them. (Squabbling can be a bid for parental attention.) As the younger children reached their fifth birthday, the siblings became less physical and more verbal, both in showing aggression (through commands, insults, threats, tattling, put-downs, bribes, and teasing) and in showing care and affection (by compliments and comforting rather than hugs and kisses).

At least one finding of this research has been replicated in many studies: same-sex siblings, particularly girls, are closer and play together more peaceably than boy-girl pairs (Kier & Lewis, 1998). The quality of relationships with brothers and sisters often carries over to relationships with other children; a child who is aggressive with siblings is likely to be aggressive with friends as well. However, a child who is dominated by an older sibling may be able to take a dominant role with a playmate (Abramovitch et al., 1986).

The Only Child

People often think of only children as spoiled, selfish, lonely, or maladjusted, but research does not bear out this stereotype. According to an analysis of 115 studies, "onlies" do comparatively well (Falbo & Polit, 1986; Polit & Falbo, 1987). In occupational and educational achievement and intelligence, they surpass children with siblings. Only children also tend to be more mature and motivated to achieve and to have higher self-esteem. They do not differ, however, in overall adjustment or sociability. Perhaps these children do better because their parents spend more time with them and focus more attention on them, talk to them more, do more with them, and expect more of them.

Research in China, which mandates one-child families, has produced encouraging findings about only children (see Box 11-2).

Playmates and Friends

Friendships develop as people develop. Toddlers play alongside or near each other, but not until about age 3 do children begin to have friends. Through friendships and interactions with casual playmates, young children learn how to get along with others. They learn that being a friend is the way to have a friend. They learn how to solve problems in relationships, they learn how to put themselves in another person's place, and they see models of various kinds of behaviour. They learn moral values and gender-role norms, and they practise adult roles.

Choosing Playmates and Friends

Preschoolers usually like to play with children of their own age and sex. In preschool, they tend to spend most of their time with a few other children with whom they have had positive experiences and whose behaviour is like their own. Children who have frequent positive experiences with each other are most likely to become friends (Rubin et al., 1998; Snyder et al., 1996). About 3 out of 4 preschoolers have such mutual friendships (Hartup & Stevens, 1999).

The traits that young children look for in a playmate are similar to the traits they look for in a friend (C. H. Hart, DeWolf, Wozniak, & Burts, 1992). In one study, 4- to 7-year-olds rated the most important features of friendships as doing things together, liking and caring for each other, sharing and helping one another, and to a lesser degree, living nearby or going to the same school. Younger children rated physical traits, such as appearance and size, higher than did older ones and rated affection and support lower (Furman & Bierman, 1983). Preschool children prefer pro-social playmates (C. H. Hart et al., 1992). They reject disruptive, demanding, intrusive, or aggressive children and ignore those who are shy, withdrawn, or tentative (Ramsey & Lasquade, 1996; Roopnarine & Honig, 1985).

Well-liked preschoolers and kindergartners, and those who are rated by parents and teachers as socially competent, generally cope well with anger. They respond directly, in ways that minimize further conflict and keep relationships going. They avoid insults and threats. Unpopular children tend to hit back or tattle (Fabes & Eisenberg, 1992).

Not all children without playmates have poor social adjustment, however. Among 567 kindergartners, almost 2 out of 3 socially withdrawn children were rated (through direct observation, teacher questionnaires, and interviews with classmates) as socially and cognitively competent; they simply preferred to play alone (Harrist, Zain, Bates, Dodge, & Pettit, 1997).

Checkpoint

Can you . . .

✔ Explain how the resolution of sibling disputes contributes to socialization?

✔ Tell how birth order and gender affect typical patterns of sibling interaction?

Checkpoint

Can you . . .

✔ Compare development of only children with that of children with siblings?

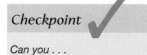

Guidepost 8

How do young children choose playmates and friends, and why are some children more popular than others?

Characteristics and Effects of Friendships

Preschoolers act differently with their friends and with other children. They have more positive, pro-social interactions, but also more quarrels and fights (Rubin et al., 1998). Children may become just as angry with a friend as with someone they dislike, but they are more likely to control their anger and express it constructively (Fabes, Eisenberg, Smith, & Murphy, 1996).

Friendships are more satisfying—and more likely to last—when children see them as relatively harmonious and as validating their self-worth. Being able to confide in friends and get help from them is less important at this age than when children are older (Ladd, Kochenderfer, & Coleman, 1996).

Children with friends enjoy school more (Ladd & Hart, 1992). Among 125 kindergartners, those who had friends in their class when they entered in August liked school better 2 months later, and those who kept up these friendships continued to like school better the following May. Children whose friendships are a source of help and self-validation are happier, have more positive attitudes toward school, and feel they can look to classmates for support (Ladd et al., 1996).

Parenting and Popularity

Parenting styles and practices can influence peer relationships. Popular children generally have warm, positive relationships with both mother and father. The parents are likely to be authoritative, and the children to be both assertive and cooperative (Isley, O'Neil, & Parke, 1996; Kochanska, 1992; Roopnarine & Honig, 1985). Children who are insecurely attached or whose parents are harsh, neglectful, or depressed or have troubled marriages are at risk of developing unattractive social and emotional patterns and of being rejected by peers (Rubin et al., 1998).

Children whose parents rely on power-assertive discipline tend to use coercive tactics in peer relations; children whose parents engage in give-and-take reasoning are more likely to resolve conflicts with peers that way (Crockenberg & Lourie, 1996). Children whose parents clearly communicate disapproval rather than anger, as well as strong positive feelings, are more pro-social, less aggressive, and better liked (Boyum & Parke, 1995). Children whose physical play with their fathers is characterized—on both sides—by pouting, whining, anger, teasing, mocking, or boredom tend to share less than other children, to be more verbally and physically aggressive, and to avoid social contact (Carson & Parke, 1996).

Helping Children with Peer Relations

Adults can help young children's relationships with peers by getting them together with other children, monitoring their play, and suggesting strategies to use in approaching other children.

Children whose parents arrange play dates for them have more playmates, see them more often, and initiate more get-togethers themselves (Ladd & Colter, 1988; Ladd & Hart, 1992). They also tend to be more outgoing and cooperative in kindergarten. In arranging and supervising play dates, parents promote pro-social behaviour as well as sociability by prompting children to think about the needs and wishes of their guests. Since children who behave pro-socially tend to be more popular, such guidance can have long-lasting consequences (Ladd & Hart, 1992).

Other helpful strategies include making a special effort to find a play group for young children who do not often have the opportunity to be with other youngsters; encouraging "loners" to play with another lone child or a small group of two or three children, or just to play side by side with other children at first; praising signs of empathy and responsiveness; and teaching friendship skills indirectly through puppetry, role-playing, and books about animals and children who learn to make friends (Ramsey & Lasquade, 1996; Roopnarine & Honig, 1985).

Peer relationships become even more important during middle childhood, which we examine in chapters 12, 13, and 14.

Checkpoint

Can you . . .

✔ Explain how preschoolers choose playmates and friends, how they behave with friends, and how they benefit from friendships?

✔ Discuss how relationships at home can influence relationships with peers?

Summary and Key Terms

The Developing Self

Guidepost 1 How does the self-concept develop during early childhood, and how do children advance in understanding their emotions?

- The self-concept undergoes major change in early childhood. According to neo-Piagetians, self-definition shifts from single representations to representational mappings. Young children do not see the difference between the real self and the ideal self.

- Understanding of emotions directed toward the self and of simultaneous emotions develops gradually.

  self-concept (267) **self-definition (268)**
  single representations (268) **real self (268)**
  ideal self (268) **representational mappings (268)**

Guidepost 2 How do young children develop initiative and self-esteem?

- According to Erikson, the chief developmental crisis of early childhood is initiative versus guilt. Successful resolution of this conflict results in the "virtue" of *purpose*.

- Self-esteem in early childhood tends to be global and unrealistic, reflecting adult approval. If self-esteem is contingent on success, children may develop a "helpless" pattern of thought and behaviour.

  initiative versus guilt (270) **self-esteem (270)**

Gender

Guidepost 3 How do boys and girls become aware of the meaning of gender, and what explains differences in behaviour between the sexes?

- Gender identity is an important aspect of the developing self-concept.

- The main gender difference in early childhood is boys' greater aggressiveness. Girls tend to be more empathic and pro-social and less prone to problem behaviour. Some cognitive differences appear early, others not until pre-adolescence or later.

- Children learn gender roles at an early age through gender-typing. Gender stereotypes peak during the preschool years.

- Four major perspectives on gender development are the biological, psychoanalytic, cognitive, and socialization-based approaches.

- Evidence of differences in brain size and prenatal hormonal activity suggests that some gender differences may be biologically based.

- In Freudian theory, a child identifies with the same-sex parent after giving up the wish to possess the other parent.

- Cognitive-developmental theory maintains that gender identity develops from thinking about one's gender. According to Kohlberg, gender constancy leads to acquisition of gender roles. Gender-schema theory holds that children

categorize gender-related information by observing what males and females do in their culture.

- According to social cognitive theory, children learn gender roles through socialization: observation of models, reinforcement of gender-appropriate behaviour, and internalization of standards. Parents, peers, and the media influence gender-typing.

  gender identity (271) **gender roles (272)** **gender-typing (272)**
  gender stereotypes (272) **identification (274)**
  gender constancy (274) **gender-schema theory (275)**
  social cognitive theory (275)

Play

Guidepost 4 How do preschoolers play, and how does play contribute to and reflect development?

- Play has physical, cognitive, and psychosocial benefits. Changes in the types of play children engage in reflect cognitive and social development.

- According to Piaget and Smilansky, children progress cognitively from functional play to constructive play, pretend play, and then formal games with rules. Pretend play becomes increasingly common during early childhood and helps children develop social and cognitive skills. Rough-and-tumble play also begins during early childhood.

- According to Parten, play becomes more social during early childhood. However, later research has found that non-social play is not necessarily immature, depending on what children do when they play.

- Children prefer to play with (and play more socially with) others of their sex.

- Both the cognitive and social aspects of play are influenced by the culturally approved environments adults create for children.

  functional play (278) **constructive play (278)**
  pretend play (278)

Parenting

Guidepost 5 How do parenting practices influence development?

- Discipline can be a powerful tool for socialization.

- Both positive reinforcement and prudently administered punishment can be appropriate tools of discipline within the context of a positive parent–child relationship.

- Power assertion, inductive techniques, and withdrawal of love can each be effective in certain situations. Reasoning is generally the most effective and power assertion the least effective in promoting internalization of parental standards. Spanking and other forms of corporal punishment can have negative consequences.

- Baumrind identified three child-rearing styles: authoritarian, permissive, and authoritative. A fourth style, neglectful or uninvolved, was identified later. According to much research, authoritative parents tend to raise more competent children. However, Baumrind's findings may be misleading when applied to some cultures or socio-economic groups.

- Family conflict can help children learn standards of behaviour and negotiating skills.

discipline (280) corporal punishment (281)
power assertion (281) inductive techniques (281)
withdrawal of love (281) authoritarian (283)
permissive (283) authoritative (283)
neglectful/uninvolved (283)

Guidepost 6 Why do young children help or hurt others, and why do they develop fears?

- The roots of altruism and pro-social behaviour appear early. This may be an inborn disposition, which can be cultivated by parental modelling and encouragement.

- Instrumental aggression—first physical, then verbal—is most common in early childhood.

- Most children become less aggressive after age 6 or 7, but the proportion of hostile aggression increases. Boys tend to practise overt aggression, whereas girls engage in relational aggression. Aggression may be influenced by the home and culture.

- Preschool children show temporary fears of real and imaginary objects and events; older children's fears tend to be more realistic. Some fears can be overcome by systematic desensitization.

altruism (285) pro-social behaviour (285)
instrumental aggression (286) hostile aggression (286)
overt aggression (286) relational aggression (286)

Relationships with Other Children

Guidepost 7 How do young children get along with (or without) siblings?

- Sibling and peer relationships contribute to self-efficacy.

- Most sibling interactions are positive. Older siblings tend to initiate activities, and younger ones to imitate. Same-sex siblings, especially girls, get along best.

- Siblings tend to resolve disputes on the basis of moral principles. Parental intervention in sibling conflict, especially among younger siblings, may prevent worse conflict later.

- The kind of relationship children have with siblings often carries over into other peer relationships.

- Only children seem to develop at least as well as children with siblings.

self-efficacy (288)

Guidepost 8 How do young children choose playmates and friends, and why are some children more popular than others?

- Preschoolers choose playmates and friends who are like them. Aggressive children are less popular than pro-social children.

- Friends have more positive and negative interactions than other playmates.

- Parenting can affect children's social competence with peers.

OLC Preview

As well as offering additional information on such topics as corporal punishment and discipline, the official website for *A Child's World,* First Canadian Edition, provides a direct link to a website about China and its stance on reproductive issues. Check out **www.mcgrawhill.ca/college/papalia**.

Physical Development and Health in Middle Childhood

The healthy human child will keep
Away from home, except to sleep.
Were it not for the common cold,
Our young we never would behold.

—Ogden Nash, *You Can't Get There from Here,* 1957

Focus *Terry Fox, Canadian Hero**

Terry Fox

Terry Fox (1958–1981) was a true Canadian success. Born in Winnipeg and raised in Port Coquitlam, B.C., Terry remembered his childhood as filled with the warmth and closeness of a loving family. His father was a switchman for the Canadian National Railway, and his mother managed a card shop. He had two brothers and a sister.

Terry's intense determination that brought him success in the Marathon of Hope was evident in his childhood. Full of resolution and tenaciousness as a toddler, he would work ceaselessly at projects like stacking blocks until they stayed in place. His patience, evident in his love of long-lasting games and sports in childhood, was an essential quality that he used as a young adult in his struggle to run across Canada to raise funds for cancer research.

Although he was not considered an outstanding student, he ended high school with an A average, having made the school basketball team. In 1977, in his first year at Simon Fraser University, he was diagnosed with a rare form of bone cancer that resulted in the amputation of a leg.

Describing himself as ordinary, he embarked on an extraordinary mission: to run across Canada in an effort to raise money for cancer research. Sponsored by the Canadian Cancer Society, he embarked on his Marathon of Hope in April 1980, dipping his artificial leg in the Atlantic Ocean in St. John's. His prosthesis was rudimentary, causing him discomfort as he ran. He persevered nevertheless. Along the way, his marathon gained momentum in attracting attention across Canada and around the world. Tragically, his cancer reappeared in Thunder Bay, where his run came to an abrupt end in September 1980. His cause was taken up by celebrities who organized a telethon that raised many millions of dollars; he lived long enough to see his dream of a dollar raised for every Canadian for cancer research. His remarkable accomplishment, not only in his run but also in his spirit of determination in raising awareness of the need to support cancer research was recognized by the many awards he was given: He was made a Companion of the Order of Canada and was awarded the highest honour of the American Cancer Society, the Sword of Hope. He was inducted posthumously into the Sports Hall of Fame and was named Athlete of the Decade by The Sports Network.

He has become a symbol of hope to people around the world, who commemorate his efforts through annual Terry Fox runs for cancer research.

*Sources of biographical information about Terry Fox were Brown & Harvey, 1980, Zola, 1984, and Scrivener, 2000.

Terry Fox was able to overcome his physical disability and accomplish a remarkable physical feat. His exceptional determination and selflessness, evident from early childhood, allowed him to respond to his physical disability by helping others. In his childhood, his physical competence had cognitive and psycho-social ramifications as well.

Although motor abilities improve less dramatically in middle childhood than before, these years are an important time for the development of the strength, stamina, endurance, and motor proficiency needed for active sports. Despite frequent colds and sore throats, this is a healthy time for most children. Some, however, are not as healthy or fit as they should be, and some have eating problems that can lead to malnutrition or obesity.

In this chapter we will look at normal growth, which depends on proper nutrition and good health. As we explore health concerns, we examine children's understanding of health and illness, which links physical, cognitive, and emotional issues. As children do more, their risk of accidents increases; we examine some ways to lower the risks.

After you have read and studied this chapter, you should be able to answer each of the Guidepost questions that appear at the top of the next page. Look for them again in the margins, where they point to important concepts throughout the chapter. To check your understanding of these Guideposts, review the end-of-chapter summary. Checkpoints located throughout the chapter will help you verify your understanding of what you have read.

1. What are normal growth patterns during middle childhood, and how can abnormal growth be treated?

2. What are some nutritional and oral health concerns for school-age children?

3. What gains in motor skills typically occur at this age, and what kinds of play do boys and girls engage in?

4. What are the principal health and fitness concerns in middle childhood, and what can adults do to make the school years healthier and safer?

Growth and Physiological Development

If we were to walk by a typical elementary school just after the 3 o'clock bell, we would see a virtual explosion of children of all shapes and sizes. Tall ones, short ones, husky ones, and skinny ones would be bursting out of the school doors into the open air. We would see that school-age children look very different from children a few years younger. They are taller, and most are fairly wiry; but more are likely to be overweight than in past decades, and some may be malnourished.

Guidepost 1

What are normal growth patterns during middle childhood, and how can abnormal growth be treated?

Height and Weight

Compared with its rapid pace in early childhood, growth in height and weight during middle childhood slows considerably. Still, although day-by-day changes may not be obvious, they add up to a startling difference between 6-year-olds, who are still small children, and 11-year-olds, many of whom are now beginning to resemble adults.

School-age children grow about 2 to 7 cm each year and gain about 2 to 4 kg or more, doubling their average body weight (see Figure 12-1). Girls retain somewhat more fatty tissue than boys, a characteristic that will persist through adulthood. Of course, these figures are just averages. Individual children vary widely—so widely that a child of average height at age 7 who did not grow at all for 2 years would still be within the normal limits of height at age 9.

Aboriginal children tend to be heavier at birth and grow heavier at a faster rate than non-Aboriginal children. However, heights of Aboriginal children change at about the same rate as in non-Aboriginal children (Indian and Inuit Health Committee, CPS, 1987). Because of the great diversity in growth patterns in Aboriginal communities, there are no standard growth charts available, and doctors are recommended to use charts like ones in Figure 12-1 to track growth in Aboriginal children (Indian and Inuit Health Committee, CPS, 1987).

Implicit in these variations in growth is a warning. When judging health or screening for abnormalities, observers often rely on measures of a child's physical growth and development. In the face of evidence that children from diverse ethnic groups develop differently, it would be useful to establish separate growth standards for different populations, as is already done for boys and girls.

Although most children grow normally, some do not. One type of growth disorder arises from the body's failure to produce enough growth hormone—or sometimes any growth hormone at all. Administration of synthetic growth hormone in such cases can result in rapid growth in height, especially during the first 2 years (Albanese & Stanhope, 1993; Vance & Mauras, 1999). However, synthetic growth hormone is also being used for children who are much shorter than other children their age, but whose bodies *are* producing normal quantities of the hormone. Its use for this purpose is highly controversial (Vance & Mauras, 1999).

Figure 12-1

Boys' and girls' physical growth in height and weight during middle childhood. Note: Curves shown are for the 50th percentile for each sex, with additional curves for 95th and 5th percentiles.

Source: National Center for Health Statistics, 2000a; 2000b

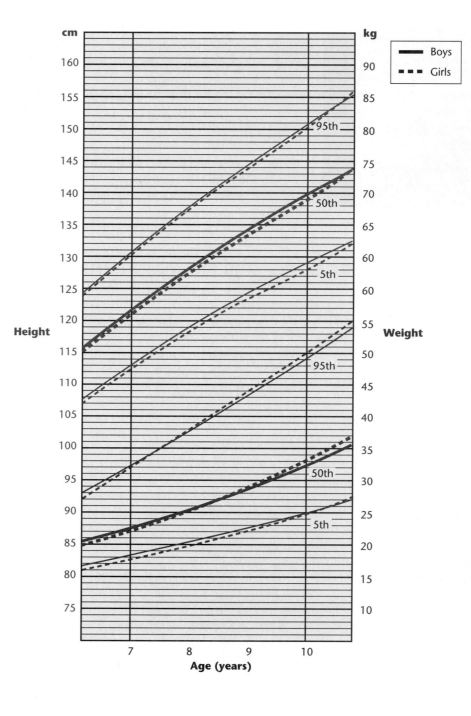

Checkpoint ✓

Can you . . .

✔ Summarize typical growth patterns of boys and girls in middle childhood and give reasons for variations?

✔ Discuss the advisability of administering synthetic growth hormone to short children?

The procedure has risks. It has been used for only about a dozen years, and we do not know what the long-term effects may be. The treatment is costly and lengthy, and although it often brings short-term gains, there is mixed evidence on whether it makes children who are normally short any taller as adults (Hintz, Attie, Baptista, & Roche for the Genentech Collaborative Group, 1999; Vance & Mauras, 1999). If unsuccessful, the therapy may do psychological harm by creating unfulfilled expectations or by giving short children the feeling that something is wrong with them. The American Academy of Pediatrics Committee on Drugs and Committee on Bioethics (1997) and other medical experts recommend extreme caution in prescribing growth hormone except as a replacement for natural hormone.

Nutrition and Oral Health

Guidepost 2

What are some nutritional and oral health concerns for school-age children?

Most schoolchildren have good appetites and eat far more than younger children. To support their steady growth and constant exertion, children need, on average, 2,400 calories every day—more for older children and less for younger ones. Breakfast should supply about one-fourth of total calories. Nutritionists recommend a varied diet including plenty of grains, fruits, and vegetables, which are high in natural nutrients, with no more than 30 per cent as fat, and 10 per cent as saturated fat (CPS and Health Canada, 1994/2001). Canadian children of all ages eat too much fat and sugar and artificially fortified or low-nutrient food (Muñoz et al., 1997; Subar, Krebs-Smith, Cook, & Kahle, 1998).

It used to be thought that sugar makes children hyperactive, interferes with learning, or has other negative effects on behaviour or mood. However, although sweets are less desirable than nutritious foods in anyone's diet because they generally provide non-nutritive or "empty" calories, recent research suggests that neither sugar nor the artificial sweetener aspartame significantly affects most children's behaviour, cognitive functioning, or mood (Kinsbourne, 1994; B. A. Shaywitz et al., 1994; Wolraich et al., 1994; Wolraich, Wilson, & White, 1995).

Tooth Development and Dental Care

Most of the adult teeth arrive early in middle childhood. The primary teeth begin to fall out at about age 6 and are replaced by permanent teeth at a rate of about four teeth per year for the next 5 years.

Between 1971–74 and 1988–94, the number of children aged 6 to 18 with untreated cavities dropped nearly 80 per cent. Improvements cut across ethnic and socio-economic lines (Brown, Wall, & Lazar, 1999). Much of the improvement in children's dental health is attributed to use of adhesive sealants on the rough, chewing surfaces (L. J. Brown, Kaste, Selwitz, & Furman, 1996).

Malnutrition

More than half of young children in south Asia, 30 per cent of those in sub-Saharan Africa, and 10 per cent in the western hemisphere are believed to suffer from malnutrition (World Health Organization [WHO], 1996). In Canada, an estimated 3.9 per cent of children each year do not get enough to eat. Aboriginal children are four times more likely to experience hunger than non-Aboriginal children (McIntyre, Connor, & Warren, 1998).

These girls proudly show off a childhood milestone—the normal loss of baby teeth, which will be replaced by permanent ones. Canadian children today have fewer dental cavities than those in the early 1970s, probably owing to better nutrition, widespread use of fluoride, and better dental care.

Checkpoint ✔

Can you . . .

✔ Discuss nutritional needs of school-age children?

✔ Give a reason why health of permanent teeth has improved?

✔ Describe effects of malnutrition and identify factors that may influence the long-term outcome?

What's your view ?

- In view of childhood malnutrition's long-term effects on physical, social, and cognitive development, what can and should various sectors of society—government agencies, community groups, and private organizations—do to combat it?

Obesity often results from an inherited tendency. A child with two obese parents, like this boy, is likely to become obese—unless he eats a carefully planned diet and gets plenty of exercise.

Because undernourished children usually live in poverty and suffer other kinds of environmental deprivation, the specific effects of malnutrition may be hard to isolate. However, taken together, these deprivations may negatively affect not only growth and physical well-being but cognitive and psychosocial development as well. One study of 328 low-income parents of school-age children did attempt to isolate hunger as a factor. In families that, by parents' reports, lacked enough food on more than one occasion, the children more often showed behavioural, emotional, and academic problems on a standardized measure of social dysfunction than children from the same communities whose families did not report multiple experiences of hunger (Kleinman et al., 1998).

Schooling can make a difference. One longitudinal study followed about 1,400 Guatemalan children in impoverished rural villages, many of whom had stunted growth due to malnutrition and who lived in unsanitary, infection-causing conditions. Those who completed at least 4 years of school did better on tests of cognition during adolescence than those who dropped out earlier (Gorman & Pollitt, 1996).

Effects of malnutrition early in life can be largely reversed with improved diet (Lewit & Kerrebrock, 1997b). In Massachusetts, when low-income students in Grades 3 to 6 took part in a school breakfast program, their achievement test scores rose (Meyers, Sampson, Weitzman, Rogers, & Kayne, 1989).

Since malnutrition affects all aspects of development, its treatment may need to go beyond physical care. One longitudinal study (Grantham-McGregor, Powell, Walker, Chang, & Fletcher, 1994) followed two groups of Jamaican children with low developmental levels who were hospitalized for severe malnourishment in infancy or toddlerhood. The children came from extremely poor and often unstable homes. Health-care paraprofessionals played with an experimental group in the hospital and, after discharge, visited them at home every week for 3 years, showing the mothers how to use homemade toys and encouraging them to interact with their children. A control group received only standard medical care.

Three years after the program stopped, the experimental group's IQs were well above those of the control group (though not as high as those of a third, well-nourished group); and their IQs remained significantly higher 7, 8, 9, and 14 years after leaving the hospital. The continuity of the program was important; not only did it last 3 years, but the mothers in the experimental group enrolled their children in preschools at earlier ages than in the control group.

Obesity and Body Image

Obesity in children has become a major health issue in Canada. The proportion of children ages 7 to 13 who are obese more than tripled between 1981 and 1996—from 5 per cent to nearly 17 per cent for boys and 15 per cent for girls (Tremblay & Willms, 2000). A child whose *body mass index,* or *BMI* (weight in comparison with height) was in the 95th percentile (that is, higher than that of 95 per cent of children of the same age and sex in a standardized sample) was considered obese. Furthermore, standards have become more lenient, obscuring the full extent of the problem.

Causes of Obesity

People become overweight when they consume more calories than they expend. But when two people eat the same number of calories, why does only one get fat? And what makes some people eat more than they need?

As we reported in chapter 3, obesity often results from an *inherited tendency,* aggravated by too little exercise and too much, or the wrong kinds of, food. Researchers have identified several genes that seem to be involved in obesity (Clément et al., 1998; Jackson et al., 1997; Montague et al., 1997; Ristow, Muller-Wieland, Pfeiffer, Krone, & Kahn, 1998). One of these genes governs production of a brain protein called *leptin,* which seems to help regulate body fat. A defect in this gene, originally found in mice, can disrupt appetite control (Campfield, Smith, Guisez, Devos, & Burn, 1995; Friedman & Halaas, 1998; Halaas et al., 1995; Kristensen et al., 1998; Pelleymounter et al., 1995; Zhang et al., 1994). A mutation in the human gene for leptin has been found in two young cousins who had been extremely obese from an early age and whose leptin level was very low (Montague et al., 1997). Other researchers have found a natural hormone that stimulates the production of fat cells (Forman et al., 1995; Kliewer et al., 1995). Such research may lead to identification and treatment of children predisposed to obesity.

Environment is also influential, since children tend to eat the same kinds of foods and develop the same kinds of habits as the people around them. Although children of all ages eat too much fat and sugar and too few healthful foods, diets of poor and minority children are especially unbalanced (Muñoz et al., 1997). Aboriginal people living in remote northern communities are at risk of obesity and related health problems, particularly diabetes, because of lack of access to nutritious food. The food needs of these communities are supplemented by a food mail service, but the typical diet tends to be high in fat, sugar, and salt, which contributes to the prevalence of obesity (CIHC, 2000). Children living in families of low socio-economic status are also at higher risk for childhood obesity (Canadian Task Force on the Periodic Health Examination, 1994).

Inactivity may be a major factor in the sharp rise in obesity (Freedman et al., 1997; Harrell, Gansky, Bradley, & McMurray, 1997). There is a negative correlation between *activity level* and weight. But are heavier children less active because they are fat, or do they become fat because they are less active? Since people in general claim to be eating no more than in the past, the second explanation seems likely. Children who watch 4 or more hours of television each day have more body fat and a higher BMI than those who watch less than 2 hours a day (Andersen, Crespo, Bartlett, Cheskin, & Pratt, 1998).

Why Treat Childhood Obesity?

Obese children often suffer emotionally because of taunts from peers, and they may compensate by indulging themselves with treats, making their physical and social problems even worse. They also tend to become overweight adults, at risk of high blood pressure, heart disease, orthopedic problems, and diabetes. Childhood obesity may be a stronger predictor of some diseases than adult obesity (Must, Jacques, Dallal, Bajema, & Dietz, 1992). In the Bogalusa Heart Study, overweight schoolchildren were two and a half to three times as likely to have high LDL and total cholesterol as children of normal weight. They also tended to have higher blood pressure and insulin levels (Freedman, Dietz, Srinivasan, & Berenson, 1999). While the rate of increase in body fat was faster in childhood than in adulthood, the yearly rate of increase in body fat was related to increases in blood pressure, cholesterol, and insulin levels, regardless of original body fat level (Srinivasan, Myers, & Berenson, 2001).

For all these reasons, a panel of American pediatric-obesity experts recommends that all children with a BMI in the 95th percentile or higher be screened for possible treatment. So should those in the 85th percentile or higher who are massively obese, are younger than 2, or show such complications as hypertension (high blood pressure) and orthopedic or sleep disorders. Treatment should begin early, involve the family, and aim for permanent changes in lifestyle through gradual, targeted increases in activity and reductions in high-fat, high-calorie foods (Barlow & Dietz, 1998). Despite the potential health benefits, Canadian health authorities do not recommend special measures to screen for childhood obesity, or special low-calorie diets for obese children, but doctors are urged to keep records of height and weight changes during childhood (Canadian Task Force on the Periodic Health Examination, 1994).

Body Image and Eating Disorders

Unfortunately, children who try to lose weight are not always the ones who need to do so. Concern with **body image**—how one believes one looks—begins to be important toward the end of middle childhood, especially for girls, and may develop into eating disorders that become more common in adolescence (see chapter 15). As pre-adolescent girls begin to fill out and add body fat, some—perhaps influenced by the ultrathin models in the media—see this normal development as undesirable. In one study, about 40 per cent of 9- and 10-year-old girls were trying to lose weight (Schreiber et al., 1996).

What's your view

- If obesity "runs in families," either because of heredity or lifestyle, how can parents who have not been able to control their own weight help their children?

Checkpoint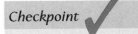

Can you . . .

✔ Discuss why childhood obesity has increased, how it can affect adult health, and how it can be treated?

body image Descriptive and evaluative beliefs about one's appearance.

Motor Development and Physical Play

Guidepost 3

What gains in motor skills typically occur at this age, and what kinds of play do boys and girls engage in?

During the middle years, children's motor abilities continue to improve (see Table 12-1). Children keep getting stronger, faster, and better coordinated—and they derive great pleasure from testing their bodies and learning new skills.

In non-literate societies, children spend less time playing than in industrial societies, and more time on household chores. By middle childhood, children in most non-literate and transitional societies go to work, and this along with increased household responsibilities, especially for girls, leaves them little time and freedom to play (Larson & Verma, 1999). In North America, children's lives today are more tightly organized than they were a generation ago. They spend less time in free, unstructured activities, such as rough-and-tumble play and informal games, and more time in organized sports (Hofferth & Sandberg, 1998).

Rough-and-Tumble Play

rough-and-tumble play
Vigorous play involving wrestling, hitting, and chasing, often accompanied by laughing and screaming

Should you come across a couple of schoolboys tumbling over each other, you may hardly be able to tell whether they are fighting or playing except by the expressions on their faces. About 10 per cent of schoolchildren's free play at recess in the early grades consists of **rough-and-tumble play,** vigorous play that involves wrestling, kicking, tumbling, grappling, and sometimes chasing, often accompanied by laughing and screaming. This kind of play peaks in middle childhood; the proportion typically drops to about 5 per cent at age 11, about the same as in early childhood (Pellegrini, 1998; Pellegrini & Smith, 1998).

This kind of play reminds us of our evolutionary heritage; unlike symbolic play, which is distinctly human, rough-and-tumble play was first described in monkeys. It also seems to be universal, since it takes place from early childhood through adolescence in such diverse places as India, Mexico, Okinawa, the Kalahari in Africa, the Philippines, Great Britain, and the United States (Humphreys & Smith, 1984).

Anthropologists suggest that rough-and-tumble play evolved to provide practice in skills for fighting and hunting (Symons, 1978). Today it serves other purposes, aside from physical exercise. Rough-and-tumble play helps children jockey for dominance in the peer group by assessing their own and each other's strength. Boys around the world engage in rough-and-tumble play more than girls do, a fact generally attributed to a combination of hormonal differences and socialization (Pellegrini, 1998; Pellegrini & Smith, 1998).

Table 12-1	Motor Development in Middle Childhood
Age	**Selected Behaviours**
6	Girls are superior in movement accuracy; boys are superior in forceful, less complex acts. Skipping is possible. Can throw with proper weight shift and step.
7	One-footed balancing without looking becomes possible. Can walk 5 cm-wide balance beams. Can hop and jump accurately into small squares. Can execute accurate jumping-jack exercise
8	Have 5.4-kg pressure on grip strength. Number of games participated in by both sexes is greatest at this age. Can engage in alternate rhythmic hopping in a 2-2, 2-3, or 3-3 pattern. Girls can throw a small ball 12 m.
9	Boys can run 5 m per second. Boys can throw a small ball 21 m.
10	Can judge and intercept pathways of small balls thrown from a distance. Girls can run 5 m per second.
11	Standing broad jump of 1.5 m is possible for boys; 15 cm less for girls.

Source: Adapted from Cratty, 1986.

Box 12-1 *Children's Understanding of Health and Illness*

When Angela was sick, she overheard her doctor refer to *edema* (an accumulation of fluid, which causes swelling), and she thought her problem was "a demon." Being sick is frightening at any age. For young children, who do not understand what is happening, it can be especially distressing and confusing.

From a Piagetian perspective, children's understanding of health and illness is tied to cognitive development. As they mature, their explanations for disease change. Before middle childhood, children are egocentric; they tend to believe that illness is magically produced by human actions, often their own ("I was a bad boy, so now I feel bad"). Later they explain all diseases— only a little less magically—as the doing of all-powerful germs; the only "protection" is a variety of superstitious behaviours to ward them off. "Watch out for germs," a child may say. As children approach adolescence, they see that there can be multiple causes of disease, that contact with germs does not automatically lead to illness, and that people can do much to keep healthy.

Children's understanding of AIDS increases with age, like their understanding of colds and of cancer, but they understand the cause of colds earlier than they do the causes of the other two illnesses, probably because they are more familiar with colds (Kistner et al., 1997; Schonfeld, Johnson, Perrin, O'Hare, & Cicchetti, 1993). Although most 6- and 7-year-olds have heard of HIV/AIDS, misconceptions about its causes and symptoms persist. Among 231 African-American children, ages 6 through 11, those whose mothers were infected showed fewer misconceptions than their peers (Armistead et al., 1999). Misconceptions about the disease can be harmful, because children who harbour them are likely to avoid contact with classmates with AIDS (Kistner et al., 1997).

Interviews with 361 children in kindergarten through Grade 6 (Schonfeld et al., 1993) found that children often give superficially correct explanations but lack real understanding of the processes involved in AIDS. For example, although 96 children mentioned drug use as a cause, most did not seem to realize that the disease is spread through blood adhering to a needle shared by drug users. One Grade 2 student gave this version of how someone gets AIDS: "Well, by doing drugs and something like that . . . by going by a drug dealer who has AIDS. . . . Well, you go by a person who's a drug dealer and you might catch the AIDS from 'em by standing near 'em" (Schonfeld et al., 1993, p. 393).

From a young child's point of view, such a statement may be a logical extension of the belief that germs cause disease. The child may wrongly assume that AIDS can be caught, as colds are, from sharing cups and utensils, from being near someone who is coughing or sneezing, or from hugging and kissing. One

AIDS education program (Sigelman et al., 1996) sought to replace such intuitive "theories" with scientifically grounded ones and to test Piaget's idea that if children have not mastered a concept, they are probably not yet ready to do so. The developers of the program hypothesized that what young children lack is knowledge about disease, not the ability to think about it.

A carefully scripted program was tried on 306 students in Grades 3, 5, and 7. Trained health instructors conducted two 50-minute sessions consisting of lectures, video clips, drawings, and discussion, and using vocabulary appropriate for Grade 3 students. Content included an introduction to contagious and non-contagious diseases; specific information about HIV, the AIDS virus; an overview of the immune system; the meaning of the letters in *AIDS;* differences between transmission of colds and of AIDS; misconceptions about how the AIDS virus is transmitted; risk factors for AIDS; how the disease develops; and how it can be prevented. The curriculum emphasized that there are only a few ways to get AIDS and that normal contact with infected people is not one of them. Flip charts summarized key points.

Experimental and control groups were tested before the program began and again about 2 weeks afterward. Students who had received instruction knew more about AIDS and its causes than those who had not, were no more (and no less) worried about it than before, and were more willing to be with people with AIDS. Almost a year later, the gains generally were retained. Grade 3 students gained about as much from the program as those in Grade 7. It was somewhat less effective with fifth-graders, perhaps because children that age already know more about AIDS than younger children but find it less relevant to their own lives than older ones do. The success of this program shows that, contrary to Piaget, even relatively young children can grasp complex scientific concepts about disease if teaching is geared to their level of understanding.

What's your view?

How old do you think children should be before being taught about AIDS?

Check it out

For more information on this topic, go to **www.mcgrawhill.ca/ college/papalia,** which will direct you to websites dedicated to the dissemination of on-line information for those interested in child health.

Organized Sports

When children outgrow rough-and-tumble play and begin playing games with rules, many concentrate on organized, adult-led sports. About 53 per cent of 6- to 8-year-olds report participating in supervised sports at least once a month, and this number increases to almost 57 per cent for children between 9 and 11 years of age. Activity in unsupervised sports is much higher, with 83 per cent of the younger group and 85 per cent of the older group taking part at least once a month (Offord, Lipman, & Duku, 1998). Too often, parents and coaches pressure children to practise long hours, focus on winning rather than playing the game, criticize children's skills, or offer bribes to make them do well (Wolff,

Checkpoint ✔

Can you . . .

✔ Explain the significance of rough-and-tumble play?

✔ Describe changes in the types of physical play children engage in as they grow older?

✔ Give reasons why fewer girls than boys participate in organized sports?

1993). All these tactics discourage rather than encourage participation. To help children improve their motor skills, organized athletic programs should offer the chance to try a variety of sports, should gear coaching to building skills rather than winning games, and should include as many children as possible rather than concentrating on a few star athletes (American Academy of Pediatrics Committee on Sports Medicine and Committee on School Health, 1989).

Participation in organized sports has risen among both sexes. However, more boys than girls take part in both supervised and unsupervised sports. In Canada, about 71 per cent of boys take part in supervised sports, and 88 per cent participate in unsupervised sports. Girls' participation is 58 per cent in supervised sports and 80 per cent in unsupervised sports (Offord et al., 1998). Even though athletic programs are more open to girls than in the past, opportunities and standards often are not the same as for boys (Butterfield & Loovis, 1993), and many girls lack the confidence or motivation to participate (Trost et al., 1996). The disparity in time boys and girls spend in sports increases as children grow older (Hofferth & Sandberg, 1998). Socio-economic status is also related to participation in sports: Children from low-income families are less likely to participate in sports than children from higher-income families (Offord et al., 1998).

Guidepost 4

What are the principal health and fitness concerns in middle childhood, and what can adults do to make the school years healthier and safer?

Health and Safety

The development of vaccines for major childhood illnesses has made middle childhood a relatively safe time of life. Since immunizations are required for school admission, children this age are likely to be protected. The death rate in these years is the lowest in the lifespan. Still, many children get too little exercise to maintain physical fitness; some suffer from acute or chronic medical conditions; and some are injured in accidents. As children's experience with illness increases, so does their cognitive understanding of the causes of health and illness and of how people can promote their own health (see Box 12-1).

Maintaining Health and Fitness

Although it is well established that exercise promotes health and fitness, less than half of Canadian children are active enough to ensure healthy growth (Craig, Cameron, Russell, & Beaulieu, 2001). About 44 per cent of girls and 53 per cent of boys are considered active enough for optimal health benefits. On average, Canadian children spend 16.5 hours a week in physical activity, with bicycling, swimming, and using playground swings as the top three physical activities (Craig et al., 2001).

Unfortunately, most physical activities, in and out of school, are team and competitive sports and games. These activities will usually be dropped after leaving school and typically are aimed at the fittest and most athletic children. In a multi-ethnic sample of 2,410 Grade 3 students in four American states, the most active children were those who were good at sports and were encouraged to participate. Again, boys were more active than girls—a finding echoed in a number of studies (Simons-Morton et al., 1997).

A sound physical education program for *all* children should emphasize skill mastery based on realistic goals, rather than winning or losing. It should include a variety of competitive and recreational sports that can be part of a lifetime fitness regimen, such as tennis, bowling, running, swimming, golf, and skating—but not boxing, which involves direct blows to the head (American Academy of Pediatrics [AAP] Committee on Sports Medicine and Committee on School Health, 1989; AAP Committee on Sports Medicine and Fitness, 1997). Unfortunately, over half of Canadian parents report that their children spend less than the minimum recommended time in physical education classes (Craig et al., 2001), and only 37 per cent of Canadian schools offer daily physical education classes (Sullivan, 1994). Three out of four children engage in sedentary activities like watching television, reading, and playing computer or video games after school.

Checkpoint ✔

Can you . . .

✔ Explain the importance of adequate exercise and give some recommendations for parents?

Box 12-2 *How Cultural Attitudes Affect Health Care*

One morning Buddi Kumar Rai, a university-educated resident of Badel, a remote hill village in Nepal, carried his 2½-year-old daughter, Kusum, to the shaman, the local "medicine man." Kusum's little face was sober, her usually golden complexion pale, and her almond-shaped eyes droopy from the upper-respiratory infection she had been suffering the past week, complete with fever and a hacking cough.

Two days before, Kusum had been in her father's arms when he had slipped and fallen backwards off a veranda to the ground about a metre below, still tightly holding his little daughter. Neither was hurt, but little Kusum had screamed in fright.

Now the shaman told Buddi that Kusum's illness was due to that fright. He prescribed incantations and put a mark, a charcoal smudge the size of a loonie, on the child's forehead to drive away the evil spirit that had entered her body when she had her scare.

Two months before this incident, Buddi himself had gone to one of the 10 shamans in Badel. "We have no doctors here, no medicine," he explains with a shrug. "One time I put on those stupid army boots my uncle gave me, and I walk with my wife to my father-in-law's house in Rakha, maybe 2 hours. And when I come home, my ankle hurt me so bad I can't walk on that foot. So I call the shaman, and he say my ankle hurts because I crossed the river without praying to the river god. So the shaman chanted over the ankle and told me to go back down to the river and pray, and after a couple of days my foot feels better."

Such adherence to ancient beliefs about illness is common in many parts of the industrialized world, where many people cling to beliefs that are at odds with mainstream scientific and medical thinking. To provide better medical care to members of various ethnic minorities, policy-makers need to understand the cultural beliefs and attitudes that influence what people do, what decisions they make, and how they interact with the broader society.

Many cultures see illness and disability as a form of punishment inflicted upon someone who has transgressed (as did Buddi in failing to pray to the river god), has done something wrong in a previous life, or is paying for an ancestor's sin. People with such beliefs tend to distance themselves from, and often to be unsympathetic to, the afflicted person. Another belief, common in Latin America and Southeast Asia, is that an imbalance of elements in the body causes illness and the patient has to re-establish his or her own equilibrium.

In many societies people believe that a severely disabled child will not survive. Since there is no hope, they do not expend time, effort, or money on the child—which often creates a self-fulfilling prophecy. Such a belief makes it nearly impossible for parents to plan realistically for the child's future. In some religious households, parents hold out hope for a miracle and refuse surgery or other treatment.

Of course, standard medical practice in Canada is also governed by a cultural belief system. Here, parents are asked to make decisions about their child without consulting members of the extended family, as would be done in many other cultures. To foster independence and self-sufficiency, parents are discouraged from "babying" a disabled child. People from other cultures may not respond well to mainstream Canadian values: Parents may feel a need to consult their own parents about medical decisions and may not consider it important, for example, for a disabled daughter to become self-supporting.

Professionals need to explain clearly, whenever possible in the family's language, what course of treatment they recommend, why they favour it, and what they expect to happen.

This Peruvian healer treats a child by traditional methods, such as herbs and incantations. In many Latin American cultures, such practices are believed to cure illness by restoring the natural balance of elements in the body.

Sources: S. W. Olds in press; Groce & Zola, 1993.

What's your view?

How would Piaget interpret the belief in some cultures that illness and disabilities are punishments for human actions? Does such a belief suggest that Piaget's theory is limited in its applicability to non-industrialized cultures?

Check it out!

For more information on this topic, go to **www.mcgrawhill.ca/college/papalia.**

Just changing everyday behaviour can bring about improvement. Parents can make exercise a family activity, by hiking or playing ball together, building strength on playground equipment, walking whenever possible, using stairs instead of elevators, and limiting television.

Medical Problems

acute medical conditions
Illnesses that last a short time

activity limitations
Chronic conditions that continually restrict everyday behaviours

chronic medical conditions
Illnesses or impairments that persist for at least 3 months

Illness in middle childhood tends to be brief. **Acute medical conditions**—occasional, short-term conditions, such as infections, allergies, and warts—are common. Six or seven bouts a year with colds, flu, or viruses are typical at this age, as germs pass among children at school or at play (Behrman, 1992). Upper-respiratory illnesses, sore throats, strep throats, and ear infections decrease with age; but acne, headaches, and transitory emotional disturbances increase as children approach puberty (Starfield et al., 1984).

According to the National Population Health Survey (CIHC, 2000), 7.7 per cent of Canadians between birth and age 19 years have **activity limitations** and **chronic medical conditions:** physical, developmental, behavioural, and/or emotional conditions requiring special health services. Children with special health needs spend three times as many days sick in bed and miss school three times as often as other children (Newacheck et al., 1998).

Socio-economic status plays an important part in children's health. Poor children (living in families below the low-income cut-off (Statistics Canada, 1994)) and those living with a single parent are more likely than other children to have chronic conditions (Newacheck et al., 1998). These disadvantaged children tend to be in fair or poor health, to have been hospitalized, and to have health-related limitations on activities. Why is this so? Parents with higher socio-economic status tend to know more about good health habits and have better access to preventive health care, and two-parent families tend to have higher incomes and more wholesome diets than single-parent families (Collins & LeClere, 1997). Also, parents of children with special needs experience difficulty finding adequate care for them, which would permit the parents to find full- or part-time work (CIHC, 2000; Irwin & Lero, 1997). Another factor in variations in health care is differing beliefs and attitudes about health and healing among cultural and ethnic groups (see Box 12-2).

Children with chronic conditions tend to be remarkably resilient. Few show problems in mental health, behaviour, or schooling (AAP Committee on Children with Disabilities and Committee on Psychosocial Aspects of Child and Family Health, 1993). However, by adolescence, some mental-health indicators like history of abuse, emotional distress, and low self-esteem are more likely to be found in children with chronic illness than in children without health problems (CIHC, 2000). Still, certain conditions—such as vision and hearing problems, stuttering, asthma, and AIDS—can greatly affect everyday living.

Vision and Hearing Problems

Most children in middle childhood have keener vision than when they were younger. Children under 6 years old tend to be far-sighted. By age 6, vision is typically more acute; and because the two eyes are better coordinated, they can focus better.

About 10 to 15 per cent of Canadian preschool children experience some visual problem, with up to 5 per cent experiencing amblyopia, and 5 per cent experiencing strebismus. About 15 per cent of Canadian preschoolers experience short-term hearing problems, and 3 per cent experience persistent hearing difficulties (Feightner, 1994). Current screening guidelines may miss many children with very high frequency impairments. This is of concern, since even slight hearing loss can affect communication, behaviour, and social relationships (Niskar et al., 1998).

Stuttering

stuttering Involuntary, frequent repetition or prolongation of sounds or syllables

Stuttering—involuntary, frequent repetition or prolongation of sounds or syllables—interferes with social functioning. As stutterers become frustrated and anxious about ordinary conversation, their self-esteem plummets.

What causes stuttering? Various theories point to faulty training in articulation and breathing; problems with brain functioning, including defective feedback about one's own speech; parental pressures to speak properly; and deep-seated emotional conflicts. The condition runs in families, suggesting a genetic component, and is three times more common in boys than in girls. In 98 per cent of cases, it begins before age 10; it is more prevalent among young children than older ones. Typically, stuttering starts gradually. About 10 per cent of prepubertal children stutter; of these, 80 per cent recover, usually before age 16.

Sixty per cent do so spontaneously, the other 20 per cent in response to treatment (American Psychiatric Association [APA], 1994).

Asthma

Asthma, a chronic respiratory disease, is the primary cause of childhood disability, affecting an estimated 845,000 Canadian children. Its prevalence has increased from 2 per cent of individuals younger than 19 years in 1978 to 12 per cent in 1996 (CICH, 2000). Apparently allergy-based, it is characterized by sudden attacks of coughing, wheezing, and difficulty in breathing; and it can be fatal. Although fewer than 10 Canadian children die from asthma per year, this rate is unacceptable given that asthma is a fully treatable disease; however, the asthma mortality rate has been decreasing since 1987 (Health Canada, 2001). The cause of the asthma explosion is unknown, but some experts point to more tightly insulated houses that permit less air circulation and early exposure to environmental toxins and allergens (Habbick, Pizzichini, Taylor, Rennie, Senthilselvan, & Sears, 1999; Health Canada, 2001; Nugent, 1999; Sly, 2000; Stapleton, 1998).

Poor, minority children, especially boys, are most likely to be affected, as are children in single-parent families (Newacheck & Halfon, 2000; Stapleton, 1998). Twenty-two per cent of children with asthma report limited activity for 1 to 5 days per year, and 13 percent report 6 or more days of restricted activity (Health Canada, 2001). A 1999 survey found asthma accounting for 20 per cent absenteeism from school (Glaxo Wellcome, 2000)—almost twice as often as children with other chronic ailments (Newacheck & Halfon, 2000). Some of this sickness may be avoidable; most children with moderate to severe asthma—especially young children from poor families—do not get adequate treatment (Glaxo Wellcome, 2000; Halterman, Aligne, Auinger, McBride, & Szilagyi, 2000).

HIV and AIDS

Children infected with the human immunodeficiency virus (HIV) are at a high risk to develop AIDS (acquired immune deficiency syndrome). Seventy-eight per cent of these children acquired the AIDS virus from their mothers, almost all of them in the uterus, during delivery, or through breast milk (Bureau of HIV/AIDS, STD and TB, Centre for Infectious Disease Prevention and Control [CIDPC], 2001; refer back to chapter 4). However, treatment has greatly reduced the likelihood of mother–child transmission, so that even though the number of children born to HIV-positive mothers has increased since 1989, the number of newborns infected with HIV has remained constant (CIDPC, 2001). About three to four pregnant women in 10,000 are found to be HIV-positive each year in Canada. Since December 1998, as reported by the CPS in 2000, 924 Canadian babies were born to HIV-infected women, 325 were HIV positive, and 107 have died of AIDS (Infectious Diseases and Immunization Committee, Canadian Paediatric Society, 2000).

Most children infected with HIV who reach school age function normally, just like other children. Those with symptoms of AIDS may develop central nervous system dysfunction that can interfere with their ability to learn, but antiretroviral therapy can improve their functioning (AAP Committee on Pediatric AIDS, 2000).

Since there is virtually no risk of infecting classmates (refer back to Box 12-1), children who carry the AIDS virus do not need to be isolated, either for their own health or for that of other children. They should be encouraged to participate in all school activities, including athletics, to the extent they are able (AAP Committee on Pediatric AIDS, 2000; AAP Committee on Sports Medicine and Fitness, 1999).

Diabetes

About 6 per cent of Canadians are affected by diabetes (Montour, MacAulay, & Adelson, 1989). However, there has been a dramatic increase in non-insulin-dependent diabetes among Aboriginal children in some communities, which concerns pediatricians and Aboriginal groups (Evers, 1987; Montour et al., 1989). Until 1940, diabetes was a rare condition among Aboriginal children, but its prevalence has grown since that time (Dean, Mundy, & Moffatt, 1992; Indian and Inuit Health Committee, CPS, 1994). An important factor involved in the outset of the disease is obesity, and programs are under way to

asthma A chronic respiratory disease characterized by sudden attacks of coughing, wheezing, and difficulty in breathing

What's your view **?**

- Medical evidence shows virtually no evidence that children with HIV infection who are symptom-free can transmit the virus to others except through bodily fluids. Yet many parents are afraid to have their children go to school with a child who is HIV-positive. Can you suggest ways to deal with this problem?

Many accidental injuries occur on school playgrounds. By wearing protective helmets when bicycling or roller skating, these children are dramatically reducing their risk of head injury.

increase public awareness to promote physical fitness in Aboriginal children in communities across Canada. Unfortunately, the needed medical care is often not provided because of the lack of trained health-care educators and practitioners who are members of Aboriginal communities (Indian and Inuit Health Committee, CPS, 1994).

Accidental Injuries

Injuries increase between ages 5 and 14, as children take part in more physical activities and are supervised less. As in early childhood, accidental injuries are the leading cause of death (CICH, 2000; National Center for Health Statistics [NCHS], 1999).

Parents tend to overestimate the safety skills of young children. Many kindergartners and Grade 1 students walk alone to school, often crossing busy streets without traffic lights, although they do not have the skills to do this safely. Many accidents could be prevented by providing school buses or more crossing guards (Dunne, Asher, & Rivara, 1992; Rivara, Bergman, & Drake, 1989).

Children, too, often overestimate their physical abilities. In one study, 6-year-olds whose estimation of their abilities was the most inaccurate were the most vulnerable to accidental injury. Eight-year-olds, with the benefit of more experience, were better judges of what they could safely do (Plumert, 1995).

The hospitalization rate due to injury is about 700 per 100,000 children under 5 years of age. This rate drops to about 560 for children 5 to 9 years of age, and 660 for children aged 10 to 14 years. Injury is the leading cause of death for all children (CIHC, 2000). Injury-related deaths in Aboriginal children are three times the national average (Health Canada, 1999). The most common type of injury requiring hospitalization involves falls (CIHC, 2000). An important aspect of determining severity of accidental injury is measuring the pain associated with the injury. Great strides in this area have been made by Canadian researchers, who have identified effective ways of uncovering fine-grained measures, but are hampered by habituation to chronic pain over time (McGrath, 1996).

The dangers of riding a bicycle can be reduced dramatically by using helmets (D. C. Thompson, Rivara, & Thompson, 1996). Slightly more than half of all children aged 12 and younger regularly wear bicycle helmets while riding bicycles or tricycles, though the rate varies across Canada due to variations in provincial regulations on helmet use (CIHC, 2000). Protective headgear is also vital for football, roller skating, roller blading, skateboarding, scooter riding, horseback riding, hockey, speed sledding, and tobogganing. For soccer, protective goggles and mouth guards may help reduce head and facial injuries. "Heading" the ball should be minimized because of the danger of brain injury, and aggressive or violent infractions of rules should be dealt with strongly (AAP Committee on Sports Medicine and Fitness, 2000).

There is a relationship between income and injury for boys. Male children in low-income families tend to be more susceptible to injury than males in high-income families (CIHC, 2000). This may be due to unsafe housing conditions and neighbourhoods that lack the facilities to provide safe playgrounds and recreational activities (CIHC, 2000).

Most injuries experienced by children younger than 5 years took place in the home, while playing. The same is true of children 5 to 9 years of age, but now a substantial proportion of injuries occur in the school. By the time children reach 10 to 14 years of age, most injuries take place in school, followed by the home, and sports and recreational environments. Although most injuries continue to occur while children are playing, a large percentage now occur while they are engaged in organized sports activities. This indicates that children, parents, and coaches need to be better informed about safety equipment, safe play, and sporting behaviours (CIHC, 2000).

Unfortunately, the media do not encourage safety consciousness. In the 25 most popular G- and PG-rated non-animated movies between 1995 and 1997, most characters did not wear automobile safety belts, look both ways when crossing streets, use crosswalks, wear helmets when bicycling, or wear flotation devices while boating (Pelletier et al., 2000).

One reason for some accidents is children's immaturity, both cognitive (preventing them from being aware of some dangers) and emotional (leading them to take dangerous risks). We discuss cognitive development in middle childhood in chapter 13 and emotional and social development in chapter 14.

Checkpoint ✔

Can you . . .

✔ Distinguish between acute and chronic medical conditions, and discuss how chronic conditions can affect everyday life?

✔ Identify factors that increase the risks of accidental injury?

Summary and Key Terms

Growth and Physiological Development

Guidepost 1 What are normal growth patterns during middle childhood, and how can abnormal growth be treated?

- Physical development is less rapid in middle childhood than in earlier years. Wide differences in height and weight exist.

- Children with retarded growth due to growth-hormone deficiency may be given synthetic growth hormone. Although the hormone is sometimes prescribed for short children who do *not* have hormone deficiency, extreme caution is advised in such cases.

Guidepost 2 What are some nutritional and oral health concerns for school-age children?

- Proper nutrition is essential for normal growth and health.

- The permanent teeth arrive in middle childhood. Dental heath has improved, in part because of use of sealants on chewing surfaces.

- Malnutrition can affect all aspects of development.

- Obesity, which is increasingly common among Canadian children, entails health risks. It is influenced by genetic and environmental factors and can be treated.

- Concern with body image, especially among girls, may lead to eating disorders.

  body image (303)

Motor Development and Physical Play

Guidepost 3 What gains in motor skills typically occur at this age, and what kinds of play do boys and girls engage in?

- Because of improved motor development, boys and girls in middle childhood can engage in a wide range of motor activities.

- About 10 per cent of schoolchildren's play, especially among boys, is rough-and-tumble play.

- Many children, mostly boys, go on to organized, competitive sports, which are geared to the most athletic children. A sound physical education program should aim at skill development for all children.

  rough-and-tumble play (304)

Health and Safety

Guidepost 4 What are the principal health and fitness concerns in middle childhood, and what can adults do to make the school years healthier and safer?

- Middle childhood is a relatively healthy period; most children are immunized against major illnesses, and the death rate is the lowest in the lifespan. However, many children, especially girls, do not meet fitness standards.

- Respiratory infections and other acute medical conditions are common. Chronic conditions such as asthma are most prevalent among poor children.

- Children's understanding of health and illness is related to their cognitive level. Cultural beliefs affect expectations of health care.

- Vision becomes keener during middle childhood, but a minority of children have defective vision or hearing. Stuttering is fairly common.

- Most children who are HIV-positive function normally in school and should not be excluded from any activities of which they are physically capable.

- Accidents are the leading cause of death in middle childhood. Use of helmets and other protective devices and educating children, parents, and coaches about safe equipment and practices during play and sports can greatly reduce injuries.

  acute medical conditions (308)   activity limitations (308)
  chronic medical conditions (308)   stuttering (308)   asthma (309)

OLC Preview

The official website for *A Child's World*, First Canadian Edition, offers additional information on child health care and safety issues with links to the "World Health Report 2000, Health Systems: Improving Performance," published by the World Health Organization. Check out **www.mcgrawhill.ca/college/papalia**.

Cognitive Development in Middle Childhood

What we must remember above all in the education of our children is that their love of life should never weaken.

—Natalia Ginzburg, *The Little Virtues*, 1985

Focus *Akira Kurosawa, Master Filmmaker**

Akira Kurosawa

The Japanese filmmaker Akira Kurosawa (1910–1998), who wrote and directed such classics as the Academy Award–winning *Rashomon* (1951) and *Seven Samurai* (1954), has been called a cinematographic genius. Kurosawa uses the screen as if it were a canvas. Artistic intelligence—an unerring sense of composition, form, colour, and texture—pervades his scenes.

In his mid-20s, as an apprentice to the great film director Kajiro Yamamoto, he was a quick study. Assigned to write scenarios, the talented novice came up with idea after idea. "He is completely creative," Yamamoto said of him (Richie, 1984, p. 12).

Yet, as a child, during his first 2 years at a Westernized school in Tokyo, Kurosawa remembers being a slow learner. Because he had trouble following the lessons, he just sat quietly, trying to amuse himself. Finally his teacher moved Akira's desk and chair away from the other students and frequently aroused snickers with such comments as "Akira probably won't understand this, but . . ." (Kurosawa, 1983, p. 8).

That initial school experience left an indelible mark on Kirosawa. He felt isolated and miserable. Then, toward the end of his second year of school, his family moved to another part of the city, and he was transferred to a traditional Japanese school. His new classmates, with their close-shaved heads, duck-cloth trousers, and wooden clogs, made fun of Akira's long hair and European-style clothing. The youngest of seven children, Akira had been a crybaby; now he became a laughingstock.

It was in Grade 3 that he came out of his intellectual and emotional fog. The strongest catalyst for this change was his teacher, a man named Tachikawa. In art class, instead of having all the students copy a picture and giving the top grade to the closest imitation, as was the custom, he let the children draw whatever they liked. Akira became so carried away that he pressed on his coloured pencils until they broke, and then he licked his fingertips and smeared the colours all over the paper. When Mr. Tachikawa held up Akira's drawing, the class laughed boisterously. But the teacher lavished it with praise and gave it the highest grade.

"From that time on," Kurosawa later wrote, ". . . I somehow found myself hurrying to school in anticipation on the days when we had art classes. . . . I became really good at drawing. At the same time my marks in other subjects suddenly began to improve. By the time Mr. Tachikawa left . . . , I was the president of my class, wearing a little gold badge with a purple ribbon on my chest" (1983, p. 13).

Academically, his performance was uneven: the best in his class in the subjects he liked, he did barely passable work in science and math. Still, he graduated as valedictorian. According to former classmate Uekusa Keinosuke, who became a scriptwriting colleague, "He

*Sources of biographical information about Akira Kurosawa are Goodwin (1994), Kurosawa (1983), and Richie (1984).

certainly was not the little-genius type who merely gets good grades" but a "commanding" figure who became popular seemingly without effort (Richie, 1984, p. 10).

It was Mr. Tachikawa who introduced Akira to the fine arts and to film. Akira's father and his older brother Heigo discussed great literature with him and took him to Japanese vaudeville and Western movies.

Even after Mr. Tachikawa left the school, Akira and his friend Uekusa would go to the teacher's home and sit around talking for hours. So strong was Akira's spirit by this time that when Mr. Tachikawa's conservative successor lambasted one of his paintings, the boy simply made up his mind to "work so hard that this teacher would never be able to criticize me again" (Kurosawa, 1983, p. 25).

• • •

We can learn several lessons from Akira Kurosawa's school experience. First, children—even highly gifted ones—develop at different rates. A late bloomer should not be expected to progress as fast as a more precocious child. Second, Kurosawa's story illustrates the strong impact a teacher can have and how the influences of home and school interact. Finally, we see once again the tie-in between cognitive and psychosocial development. The flowering of Kurosawa's cognitive and social competence followed closely upon Mr. Tachikawa's move to boost his self-esteem. As Kurosawa later wrote, "When someone is told over and over again that he's no good at something, he loses more and more confidence and eventually does become poor at it. Conversely, if he's told he's good at something, his confidence builds and he actually becomes better at it" (1983, p. 40).

School is a major formative experience in middle childhood, impinging on every aspect of development. Even today, when many children go to preschool and most go to kindergarten, the start of Grade 1 is a milestone—a sign that a child has entered a new stage of development. During the next few years, children typically gain in self-confidence as they read, think, talk, play, and imagine in ways that were well beyond them only a few years before.

In this chapter we examine cognitive advances during the first 5 or 6 years of formal schooling, from about ages 6 to 11. Entry into Piaget's stage of concrete operations enables children to think logically and to make more mature moral judgments. As children improve in memory and problem solving, intelligence tests become more accurate in predicting school performance. The abilities to read and write open the door to a wider world. We describe all these changes, and we examine the controversies over IQ testing, homework, mathematics instruction, and bilingual education. Finally, we examine influences on school achievement and how schools try to meet special educational needs.

After you have read and studied this chapter, you should be able to answer each of the Guidepost questions that appear at the top of the next page. Look for them again in the margins, where they point to important concepts throughout the chapter. To check your understanding of these Guideposts, review the end-of-chapter summary. Checkpoints located throughout the chapter will help you verify your understanding of what you have read.

**Guideposts
for Study**

1. How do school-age children's thinking and moral reasoning differ from those of younger children?

2. What advances in memory and other information-processing skills occur during middle childhood?

3. How accurately can schoolchildren's intelligence be measured?

4. How do communicative abilities expand during middle childhood?

5. What influences school achievement?

6 How do schools meet the needs of non-English-speaking children and those with learning problems?

7. How is giftedness assessed and nurtured?

Piagetian Approach: The Concrete Operational Child

Guidepost 1

How do school-age children's thinking and moral reasoning differ from those of younger children?

At about age 7, according to Piaget, children enter the stage of **concrete operations,** when they can use mental operations to solve concrete (actual) problems. Children now can think logically because they can take multiple aspects of a situation into account. However, children are still limited to thinking about real situations in the here and now.

concrete operations Third stage of Piagetian cognitive development (approximately from ages 7 to 12), during which children develop logical but not abstract thinking

Cognitive Advances

Children in the stage of concrete operations can perform many tasks at a much higher level than they could in the pre-operational stage (see Table 13-1). They have a better understanding of spatial concepts, of causality, of categorization, of conservation, and of number.

Space

Why can many 6- or 7-year-olds find their way to and from school, whereas most younger children cannot? One reason is that children in the stage of concrete operations can better understand spatial relationships. They have a clearer idea of how far it is from one place to another and how long it will take to get there, and they can more easily remember the route and the landmarks along the way. Experience plays a role in this development: A child who walks to school becomes more familiar with the neighbourhood outside the home.

Both the ability to use maps and models and the ability to communicate spatial information improve with age (Gauvain, 1993). Although 6-year-olds can search for and find hidden objects, they usually do not give well-organized directions for finding the same objects—perhaps because they lack the appropriate vocabulary or do not realize what information the other person needs (Plumert, Pick, Marks, Kintsch, & Wegesin, 1994).

Schooling—especially learning measurement skills—may contribute to the development of spatial thinking. However, it is unclear whether schooling develops spatial awareness or whether the development of spatial awareness makes children ready to learn about measurement in school (Gauvain, 1993).

Causality

Judgments about cause and effect improve during middle childhood. When 5- to 12-year-olds were asked to predict how levers and balance scales would perform under varying conditions, the older children gave more correct answers than the younger children.

Table 13-1	Advances in Selected Cognitive Abilities During Middle Childhood
Ability	**Example**
Spatial thinking	Danielle can use a map or model to help her search for a hidden object and can give someone else directions for finding the object. She can find her way to and from school, can estimate distances, and can judge how long it will take her to go from one place to another.
Cause and effect	Douglas knows which physical attributes of objects on each side of a balance scale will affect the result (i.e., number of objects matters but colour does not). He does not yet know which spatial factors, such as position and placement of the objects, make a difference.
Classification	Elena can sort objects into categories, such as shape, colour, or both. She knows that a subclass (roses) has fewer members than the class of which it is a part (flowers).
Seriation and transitive inference	Catherine can arrange a group of sticks in order, from the shortest to the longest, and can insert an intermediate-size stick into the proper place. She knows that if one stick is longer than a second stick, and the second stick is longer than a third, then the first stick is longer than the third.
Inductive and deductive reasoning	Dara can solve both inductive and deductive problems and knows that inductive conclusions (based on particular premises) are less certain than deductive ones (based on general premises).
Conservation	Stacy, at age 7, knows that if a clay ball is rolled into a sausage, it still contains the same amount of clay (conservation of substance). At age 9, she knows that the ball and the sausage weigh the same. Not until early adolescence will she understand that they displace the same amount of liquid if dropped in a glass of water.
Number and mathematics	Kevin can count in his head, can add by counting up from the smaller number, and can do simple story problems.

Children understood the influence of physical attributes (the number of objects on each side of a scale) earlier than they recognized the influence of spatial factors (the distance of objects from the centre of the scale) (Amsel, Goodman, Savoie, & Clark, 1996).

Categorization

Categorization now includes such sophisticated abilities as *seriation, transitive inference,* and *class inclusion.* Children show that they understand **seriation** when they can arrange objects in a series according to one or more dimensions, such as weight (lightest to heaviest) or colour (lightest to darkest). By 7 or 8, children can grasp the relationships among a group of sticks on sight and arrange them in order of size (Piaget, 1952).

Transitive inference is the ability to recognize a relationship between two objects by knowing the relationship between each of them and a third object. Catherine is shown three sticks: a yellow one, a green one, and a blue one. She is shown that the yellow stick is longer than the green one, and the green one is longer than the blue. Without physically comparing the yellow and blue sticks, she knows that the yellow one is longer than the blue one (Chapman & Lindenberger, 1988; Piaget & Inhelder, 1967).

Class inclusion is the ability to see the relationship between a whole and its parts. If pre-operational children are shown a bunch of 10 flowers—seven roses and three carnations—and are asked whether there are more roses or more flowers, they are likely to say there are more roses, because they are comparing the roses with the carnations rather than with the whole bunch. Not until the stage of concrete operations do children come to realize that roses are a subclass of flowers and that, therefore, there cannot be more roses than flowers (Flavell, 1963).

The ability to categorize helps children think logically. According to Piaget, children in the stage of concrete operations use **inductive reasoning.** Starting with observations about particular members of a class of people, animals, objects, or events, they then draw general conclusions about the class as a whole. ("My dog barks. So does Terry's dog and

seriation Ability to order items along a dimension

transitive inference Understanding of the relationship between two objects by knowing the relationship of each to a third object

class inclusion Understanding of the relationship between a whole and its parts

inductive reasoning Type of logical reasoning that moves from particular observations about members of a class to a general conclusion about that class

Melissa's dog. So it looks as if all dogs bark.") Inductive conclusions must be tentative because it is always possible to come across new information (a dog that does not bark) that does not support the conclusion.

Deductive reasoning, which Piaget believed does not develop until adolescence, starts with a general statement (premise) about a class and applies it to particular members of the class. If the premise is true of the whole class, and the reasoning is sound, then the conclusion must be true: "All dogs bark. Spot is a dog. Spot barks."

Researchers gave 16 inductive and deductive problems to 16 kindergartners, 17 students in Grade 2, 16 in Grade 4, and 17 in Grade 6. The problems were designed so as *not* to call upon knowledge of the real world. For example, one deductive problem was, "All poggops wear blue boots. Tombor is a poggop. Does Tombor wear blue boots?" The corresponding inductive problem was, "Tombor is a poggop. Tombor wears blue boots. Do all poggops wear blue boots?" Contrary to Piagetian theory, students in Grade 2 (but not kindergartners) were able to correctly answer both kinds of problems, to see the difference between them, and to explain their responses, and they (appropriately) expressed more confidence in their deductive answers than in their inductive ones (Galotti, Komatsu, & Voelz, 1997).

Conservation

In solving various types of conservation problems, children in the stage of concrete operations can work out the answers in their heads; they do not have to measure or weigh the objects.

If one of two identical clay balls is rolled or kneaded into a different shape—say, a long, thin "sausage,"—Felipe, who is in the stage of concrete operations, will say that the ball and the "sausage" still contain the same amount of clay. Stacy, who is in the pre-operational stage, is deceived by appearances. She says the long, thin roll contains more clay because it looks longer.

Felipe, unlike Stacy, understands the principle of *identity:* he knows the clay is still the same clay, even though it has a different shape. He also understands the principle of *reversibility:* he knows he can change the sausage back into a ball. And he can *decentre:* he can focus on both length and width. He recognizes that although the ball is shorter than the "sausage," it is also thicker. Stacy centres on one dimension (length) while excluding the other (thickness).

Typically, children can solve problems involving conservation of substance, like this one, by about age 7 or 8. However, in tasks involving conservation of weight—in which they are asked, for example, whether the ball and the "sausage" weigh the same—children typically do not give correct answers until about age 9 or 10. In tasks involving conservation of volume—in which children must judge whether the "sausage" and the ball displace an equal amount of liquid when placed in a glass of water—correct answers are rare before age 12.

Piaget's term for this inconsistency in the development of different types of conservation is **horizontal décalage.** Children's thinking at this stage is so concrete, so closely tied to a particular situation, that they cannot readily transfer what they have learned about one type of conservation to another type, even though the underlying principles are the same.

Number and Mathematics

Children intuitively devise strategies for adding, by counting on their fingers or by using other objects. By age 6 or 7, many children can count in their heads. They also learn to *count on:* to add 5 and 3, they start counting at 5 and then go on to 6, 7, and 8 to add the 3. It may take 2 or 3 more years for them to perform a comparable operation for subtraction, but by age 9 most children can either count up from the smaller number or down from the larger number to get the answer (Resnick, 1989).

Children also become more adept at solving simple story problems, such as: "Peter went to the store with $5 and spent $2 on candy. How much

deductive reasoning Type of logical reasoning that moves from a general premise about a class to a conclusion about a particular member or members of the class

What's your view **?**

• How can parents and teachers help children improve their reasoning ability?

horizontal décalage Piaget's term for inability to transfer learning about one type of conservation to other types, which causes a child to master different types of conservation tasks at different ages

Are there more red checkers or black checkers? This girl counting the checkers is solving a Piagetian conservation task. Because the red checkers are more spread out, a pre-operational child would say there are more of them. A child in the stage of concrete operations will count, as this girl is doing, and say there are equal numbers of each colour.

did he have left?" When the original amount is unknown ("Peter went to the store, spent $2 and had $3 left. How much did he start out with?"), the problem is harder because the operation needed to solve it (addition) is not as clearly indicated. Few children can solve this kind of problem before age 8 or 9 (Resnick, 1989).

Research with minimally schooled people in non-industrialized countries suggests that the ability to add develops nearly universally and often intuitively, through concrete experience in a cultural context (Guberman, 1996; Resnick, 1989). These intuitive procedures are different from those taught in school. In a study of Brazilian street vendors ages 9 to 15, a researcher acting as a customer says, "I'll take two coconuts." Each one costs 40 cruzeiros; she pays with a 500-cruzeiros bill and asks, "What do I get back?" The child counts up from 80: "Eighty, 90, 100 . . . " and gives the customer 420 cruzeiros. However, when this same child is given a similar problem in the classroom ("What is 500 minus 80?"), he arrives at the wrong answer by incorrectly using a series of steps learned in school (Carraher, Schliemann, & Carraher, 1988). This suggests that teaching math through concrete applications, not only through abstract rules, may be more effective. The style of teaching might have an influence on how effectively children learn basic mathematical skills. When tutoring is contingent on the child's performance on a task like long division, Grade 4 and 5 children tend to learn more effectively than when tutoring is not determined by a child's performance (Pratt & Savoy-Levine, 1998).

Some intuitive understanding of fractions seems to exist by age 4 (Mix, Levine, & Huttenlocher, 1999), as children show when they deal a deck of cards or distribute portions of pizza (Frydman & Bryant, 1988; Sophian, Garyantes, & Chang, 1997). However, children tend not to think about the quantity a fraction represents; instead, they focus on the numerals that make it up. Thus they may say that ½ plus ⅓ equals ⅖. Also difficult for many children to grasp at first is the fact that ½ is bigger than ¼—that the smaller fraction (¼) has the larger denominator (Siegler, 1998; Sophian & Wood, 1997). Seven-year-olds are more consistent than 5-year-olds in recognizing that the more people among whom a pizza is divided, the smaller each person's share (Sophian et al., 1997). Nevertheless, in comparison with younger children, 5-year-olds are able to identify displays of the largest amount of cookies when asked to choose between two options, while younger children choose the one with the largest individual cookie, regardless of the number that are present in the other display (Sophian, 2000).

Influences of Neurological Development and Culture

Cross-cultural studies support a progression from the rigid, illogical thinking of younger children to the flexible, logical thinking of older ones (Broude, 1995; Gardiner et al., 1998). Piaget maintained that this shift depends on neurological maturation and adaptation to the environment and is not tied to cultural experience.

Support for a neurological basis of conservation of volume comes from scalp measurements of brain activity during a conservation task. Children who had achieved conservation of volume showed brainwave patterns different from those of children who had not yet achieved it, suggesting that they were using different brain regions for the task (Stauder, Molenaar, & Van der Molen, 1993).

Abilities such as conservation may depend in part on familiarity with the materials being manipulated. Children can think more logically about things they know something about. Mexican children who make pottery understand that a clay ball that has been rolled into a coil still has the same amount of clay sooner than they understand other types of conservation (Broude, 1995); and these children show signs of conservation of substance earlier than children who do not make pottery (Price-Williams, Gordon, & Ramirez, 1969). Thus, understanding of conservation may come not only from new patterns of mental organization, but also from culturally defined personal experience with the physical world.

Moral Reasoning

To draw out children's moral thinking, Piaget (1932) would tell them a story about two little boys: "One day Augustus noticed that his father's inkpot was empty and decided to help his father by filling it. While he was opening the bottle, he spilled a lot of ink on the table-

Checkpoint ✓

Can you . . .

✔ Identify five kinds of cognitive abilities that emerge or strengthen during middle childhood, and explain how?

✔ Name three principles that help school-aged children understand conservation, and explain why children master different kinds of conservation at different ages?

✔ Weigh the evidence for influences of neurological development and cultural experience on Piagetian tasks?

Table 13-2 Piaget's Two Stages of Moral Development

	Stage I: Morality of Constraint	Stage II: Morality of Cooperation
Point of view	Children cannot put themselves in place of others. They view an act as either totally right or totally wrong and think everyone sees it the same way.	Children put themselves in place of others. They are not absolutist in judgments but see that more than one point of view is possible.
Intention	Child judges acts in terms of actual physical consequences, not the motivation behind them.	Child judges acts by intentions, not consequences.
Rules	Child obeys rules because they are sacred and unalterable.	Child recognizes that rules are made by people and can be changed by people. Children consider themselves just as capable of changing rules as anyone else.
Respect for authority	Unilateral respect leads to feeling of obligation to conform to adult standards and obey adult rules.	Mutual respect for authority and peers allows children to value their own opinions and abilities and to judge other people realistically.
Punishment	Child favours severe punishment. Child feels that punishment itself defines the wrongness of an act; an act is bad if it will elicit punishment.	Child favours milder punishment that compensates the victim and helps the culprit recognize why an act is wrong, thus leading to reform.
Concept of justice	Child confuses moral law with physical law and believes that any physical accident or misfortune that occurs after a misdeed is a punishment willed by God or some other supernatural force.	Child does not confuse natural misfortune with punishment.

Source: Adapted partly from M. L. Hoffman, 1970b; Kohlberg, in M. L. Hoffman & Hoffman, 1964.

cloth. The other boy, Julian, played with his father's inkpot and spilled a little ink on the cloth." Then Piaget would ask, "Which boy was naughtier, and why?"

Children younger than 7 usually considered Augustus naughtier, since he made the bigger stain. Older children recognized that Augustus meant well and made the large stain by accident, whereas Julian made a small stain while doing something he should not have been doing. Immature moral judgments, Piaget concluded, centre only on the degree of offense; more mature judgments consider intent.

According to Piaget, moral development is linked to cognitive growth. Piaget maintained that children make sounder moral judgments when they can look at things from more than one perspective. He proposed that moral reasoning develops in two stages (summarized in Table 13-2). Children may go through these stages at varying ages, but the sequence is the same.

In the first stage, **morality of constraint** (up to about age 7, corresponding with the pre-operational stage), the young child thinks rigidly about moral concepts. In this stage children are quite egocentric; they cannot imagine more than one way of looking at a moral issue. They believe that rules cannot be bent or changed, that behaviour is right or wrong, and that any offense (like Augustus's) deserves punishment, regardless of intent (unless they themselves are the offenders!).

The second stage, **morality of cooperation** (ages 7 up, corresponding with the stages of concrete operations and formal operations) is characterized by flexibility. As children mature, they interact with more people and come into contact with a wider range of viewpoints. They discard the idea that there is a single, absolute standard of right and wrong, and they begin to formulate their own moral code. Because they can consider more than one aspect of a situation, they can make more subtle moral judgments, such as taking into consideration the intent behind Augustus's and Julian's behaviour.

Not until children enter the stage of morality of cooperation (usually beginning at age 7 or 8), Piaget observed, do they see the need for mutual agreement on rules and on the consequences of breaking them. Beginning at ages 11 or 12, children codify their own complex sets of rules to cover all foreseeable situations. If disagreements arise, the children find ways to work them out. Rules are no longer externally imposed, but a result of mutual self-regulation (DeVries, 1998; DeVries, Hildebrandt, & Zan, 2000).

Current perspectives are beginning to challenge the traditional view that children pass through universal stages of moral development. Instead, children as young as 6 years of age

What's your view

- Do you agree that intent is an important factor in morality? How does the criminal justice system reflect this view?

morality of constraint First of Piaget's two stages of moral development, characterized by rigid, egocentric judgments

morality of cooperation Second of Piaget's two stages of moral development, characterized by flexible judgments and formation of one's own moral code

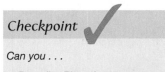

Checkpoint

Can you . . .

✔ Describe Piaget's two stages of moral development and explain their link to cognitive maturation?

have been shown to be sensitive to the context and domain of moral issues. In a study of 72 Canadian children, Helwig and Jasiobedzka (2001) found that using simple tasks that did not require responses to open-ended questions, 6-year-old children were as capable as 8- and 10-year-old children in evaluating fairness of just and unjust laws, and reasoning about the consequences of violating socially unjust laws. In fact children as young as 3 years are capable of understanding the nature of psychological harm in making moral judgments, though they tend to focus on the outcome of the act rather than the intention of the act, which older children tend to do (Helwig, Zelazo, & Wilson, 2001). Earlier research on moral reasoning might reflect children's developing abilities to articulate abstract moral principles, rather than their basic moral reasoning abilities (Helwig et al., 2001).

Lawrence Kohlberg's influential theory of moral development, which builds on Piaget's, is discussed in chapter 16.

Guidepost 2

What advances in memory and other information-processing skills occur during middle childhood?

Information-Processing Approach: Memory and Other Processing Skills

Unlike Piaget, who described broad changes in the way school-age children's minds operate, information-processing researchers focus on improvements in the *efficiency* of mental operations: how much information children can handle at a given time and how quickly and accurately they can process it. More efficient processing makes it easier for children to learn and remember. Differences in efficiency of processing may help account for the range of scores on psychometric intelligence tests, which now become more reliable predictors of school performance.

As children move through the school years, they make steady progress in their abilities to process and retain information. They understand more about how memory works, and this knowledge enables them to use strategies, or deliberate plans, to help them remember. In addition, as their knowledge expands, they become more aware of what kinds of information are important to pay attention to and remember.

Basic Processes and Capacities

Information-processing theorists think of memory as a filing system that has three steps, or processes: *encoding, storage,* and *retrieval.* **Encoding** is like putting information in a folder to be filed in memory; it attaches a "code" or "label" to the information to prepare it for storage, so that it will be easier to find when needed. Events are encoded along with information about the context in which they were encountered. Children between ages 5 and 7 become increasingly able to recall such details as when and where an event occurred (Janowsky & Carper, 1996). **Storage** is putting the folder away in the filing cabinet. The last step, **retrieval,** occurs when the information is needed; the child then searches for the file and takes it out. Retrieval may involve either recognition or recall. Difficulties in any of these processes can interfere with efficiency.

Information-processing models depict the mind as containing three "storehouses": *sensory memory, working memory,* and *long-term memory.* **Sensory memory** is a temporary "holding tank" for information that comes in through vision, hearing, or other senses. Without processing (encoding), sensory memories fade quickly. Sensory memory shows little change with age; a 5-year-old's immediate recall is about as good as that of an adult (Siegler, 1998).

Information that is being encoded or retrieved is kept in **working memory,** a short-term "storehouse" for information a person is actively working on (trying to understand or remember). Researchers may assess the capacity of working memory by asking children to recall a series of spoken digits in reverse order (for example, "2-8-3-7-5-1" if they heard "1-5-7-3-8-2"). The capacity of working memory increases rapidly in middle childhood (Cowan, Nugent, Elliott, Ponomarev, & Saults, 1999). At ages 5 to 6, children usually remember only two digits; the typical adolescent remembers six.

According to a widely used model, a **central executive** controls the processing of information in working memory (Baddeley, 1981, 1986). The central executive orders infor-

encoding Process by which information is prepared for long-term storage and later retrieval

storage Retention of memories for future use

retrieval Process by which information is accessed or recalled from memory storage

sensory memory Initial, brief, temporary storage of sensory information

working memory Short-term storage of information being actively processed

central executive In Baddeley's model, element of working memory that controls the processing of information

mation encoded for transfer to **long-term memory,** a "storehouse" of virtually unlimited capacity that holds information for long periods of time. The central executive also retrieves information from long-term memory for processing in working memory. The central executive can temporarily expand the capacity of working memory by moving information into two separate subsidiary systems. One of these keeps verbal information, and the other, visual and spatial images, "on hold" while the central executive is occupied with other tasks.

The central executive seems to mature sometime between ages 8 and 10. Ten-year-olds are less likely than younger children to become confused when given a visual task (identifying the colours of numbers flashed on a computer screen) while trying to do a verbal task (committing the numbers to memory). This suggests that the visual and verbal components of working memory have become independent of each other (Hale, Bronik, & Fry, 1997). Similarly, when children were asked to recall lists of numbers they heard while paying attention to a computer game in which they had to match up pictures with rhyming names, Grade 1 students recalled fewer numbers than adults did under the same conditions, but students in Grade 4 recalled just as many as the adults (Cowan et al., 1999).

During middle childhood, reaction time improves, and processing speed for such tasks as matching pictures, adding numbers in one's head, and recalling spatial information increases rapidly as unneeded synapses, or neural connections in the brain, are pruned away (Hale et al., 1997; Janowsky & Carper, 1996; Kail, 1991, 1997; Kail & Park, 1994). Faster, more efficient processing increases the amount of information a child can keep in working memory, making possible better recall and more complex, higher-level thinking (Flavell et al., 1993).

Completing a science fair project and displaying the results, as this student is doing, promotes the use of higher-level thinking.

long-term memory Storage of virtually unlimited capacity, which holds information for very long periods

Metamemory: Understanding Memory

Between ages 5 and 7, the brain's frontal lobes may undergo significant development and reorganization, making improved recall and **metamemory,** knowledge about the processes of memory, possible (Janowsky & Carper, 1996). From kindergarten through Grade 5, children advance steadily in understanding of memory (Flavell et al., 1993; Kreutzer, Leonard, & Flavell, 1975). Kindergartners and first-graders know that people remember better if they study longer, that people forget things with time, and that relearning something is easier than learning it for the first time. By Grade 3, children know that some people remember better than others and that some things are easier to remember than others.

One pair of experiments looked at beliefs of preschoolers and students in Grades 1 and 3 about what influences remembering and forgetting. Most children in all three age groups believed that important events in a story about a birthday party (such as a guest falling into the cake) were more likely to be retained than minor details (such as a guest bringing a ball as a present). Most Grade 1 and Grade 3 students, but not most preschoolers, believed that a later experience (playing with a friend who was not at the party) might distort a child's recollection of who was at the party. Not until Grade 3 did most children recognize that memory can be distorted by suggestions from others—say, a parent who suggests that the friend was at the party (O'Sullivan, Howe, & Marche, 1996).

metamemory Understanding of processes of memory

mnemonic strategies Techniques to aid memory

external memory aids Mnemonic strategies using something outside the person

Mnemonics: Strategies for Remembering

Devices to aid memory are called **mnemonic strategies.** The most common mnemonic strategy among both children and adults is use of *external memory aids.* Other common mnemonic strategies include *rehearsal, organization,* and *elaboration* (see Table 13-3).

Writing down a telephone number, making a list, setting a timer, and putting a library book by the front door are examples of **external memory aids:** prompting by something outside the person. Saying a telephone number over and over after looking it up, so as not to forget it before dialing, is a form of **rehearsal,** or conscious repetition. **Organization** is mentally placing information into categories (such as animals, furniture, vehicles, and

rehearsal Mnemonic strategy to keep an item in working memory through conscious repetition

organization Mnemonic strategy of categorizing material to be remembered

Table 13-3	Four Common Memory Strategies		
Strategy	**Definition**	**Development in Middle Childhood**	**Example**
External memory aids	Prompting by something outside the person	5- and 6-year-olds can do this, but 8-year-olds are more likely to think of it.	Dana makes a list of the things she has to do today.
Rehearsal	Conscious repetition	6-year-olds can be taught to do this; 7-year-olds do it spontaneously.	Tim says the letters in his spelling words over and over until he knows them.
Organization	Grouping by categories	Most children do not do this until at least age 10, but younger children can be taught to do it.	Luis recalls the animals he saw in the zoo by thinking first of the mammals, then the reptiles, then the amphibians, then the fish, and then the birds.
Elaboration	Associating items to be remembered with something else, such as a phrase, scene, or story	Older children are more likely to do this spontaneously and remember better if they make up their own elaboration; younger children remember better if someone else makes it up.	Yolanda remembers the lines of the musical staff (E, G, B, D, F) by associating them with the phrase *"Every good boy does fine."*

elaboration Mnemonic strategy of making mental associations involving items to be remembered

clothing) to make it easier to recall. In **elaboration,** children associate items with something else, such as an imagined scene or story. To remember to buy lemons, ketchup, and napkins, for example, a child might imagine a ketchup bottle balanced on a lemon, with a pile of napkins handy to wipe up spilled ketchup.

As children get older, they develop better strategies, use them more effectively, and tailor them to meet specific needs (Bjorklund, 1997). Even kindergartners recognize the value of *external aids,* and as children mature, they use them more (Kreutzer et al., 1975). Children usually do not use *rehearsal* spontaneously until after Grade 1; and if taught to do so in one situation, they seldom apply it to another (Flavell, Beach, & Chinsky, 1966; Flavell et al., 1993; Keeney, Canizzo, & Flavell, 1967). The picture is similar for the other two types of mnemonic strategies, though there is some evidence that even preschoolers, when taught to use *organization,* can generalize this learning to other situations. Again, older children are more likely than younger ones to use *elaboration* spontaneously and to transfer it to other tasks (Flavell et al., 1993). Children often use more than one strategy for a task and choose different kinds of strategies for different problems (Coyle & Bjorklund, 1997).

Selective Attention

School-age children can concentrate longer than younger children and can focus on the information they need and want while screening out irrelevant information. For example, they can summon up the appropriate meaning of a word they read and suppress other meanings that do not fit the context (Simpson & Foster, 1986; Simpson & Lorsbach, 1983). Students in Grade 5 are better able than those in Grade 1 to keep discarded information from re-entering working memory and vying with other material for attention (Harnishfeger & Pope, 1996). This growing ability to control the intrusion of older thoughts and associations and redirect attention to current, relevant ones is believed to be due to neurological maturation. It is one of the reasons memory functioning improves during middle childhood (Bjorklund & Harnishfeger, 1990; Harnishfeger & Bjorklund, 1993).

The ability to consciously direct attention may help explain why older children make fewer mistakes in recall than younger ones. It may enable them to select what they want to remember and what they can forget (Lorsbach & Reimer, 1997).

Information Processing and Piagetian Tasks

Improvements in information processing may help explain the advances Piaget described. For example, 9-year-olds may be better able than 5-year-olds to find their way to and from school because they can scan a scene, take in its important features, and remember objects in context, in the order in which the children encountered them (Allen & Ondracek, 1995).

Improvements in memory may contribute to the mastery of conservation tasks. Young children's working memory is so limited that, even if they are able to master the concept of conservation, they may not be able to remember all the relevant information (Siegler & Richards, 1982). They may forget that two differently shaped pieces of clay were originally identical. Gains in short-term memory may contribute to the ability to solve problems like this in middle childhood.

Robbie Case (1985, 1992), a neo-Piagetian theorist (refer back to chapter 2), suggests that as a child's application of a concept or scheme becomes more automatic, it frees space in working memory to deal with new information. This may help explain horizontal décalage: Children may need to become comfortable enough with one kind of conservation to use it without conscious thought before they can extend and adapt that scheme to other kinds of conservation.

Checkpoint ✔

Can you . . .

✔ Identify ways in which mental processes improve during middle childhood?

✔ Describe the three steps in memory?

✔ Name four common mnemonic aids and cite age differences in their use?

✔ Explain the importance of metamemory and selective attention?

✔ Tell how improved information processing may help explain cognitive advances?

Psychometric Approach: Assessment of Intelligence

Guidepost 3

How accurately can schoolchildren's intelligence be measured?

Intelligence tests (or IQ tests) are called **aptitude tests:** they claim to measure the capacity to learn, as contrasted with **achievement tests,** which assess how much children have already learned in various subject areas. However, as we'll see, it is virtually impossible to design a test that requires no prior knowledge. In addition, intelligence tests are validated against measures of achievement, such as school performance, and such measures are affected by factors beyond innate intelligence. For this and other reasons, there is strong disagreement over how accurately IQ tests assess differences among children.

aptitude tests Tests that measure children's general intelligence, or capacity to learn

achievement tests Tests that assess how much children know in various subject areas

Otis-Lennon School Ability Test Group intelligence test for kindergarten through Grade 12

Wechsler Intelligence Scale for Children (WISC–III) Individual intelligence test for schoolchildren, which yields verbal and performance scores as well as a combined score

Traditional Group and Individual Tests

The original IQ tests, such as those of Alfred Binet and Theodore Simon (see chapter 7), were designed to be given to individuals, and their modern versions still are used that way. The first group tests, developed during World War I to screen army recruits for appropriate assignments, became models for the group tests now given in schools. As both individual and group tests have been refined, their developers have turned from the original emphasis on general intelligence to more sophisticated distinctions among various kinds of abilities and have sought to adapt the tests to special needs (Anastasi & Urbina, 1997; Daniel, 1997).

One popular group test, the **Otis-Lennon School Ability Test,** has levels for kindergarten through Grade 12. Children are asked to classify items, to show an understanding of verbal and numerical concepts, to display general information, and to follow directions. Separate scores for verbal comprehension, verbal reasoning, pictorial reasoning, figural reasoning, and quantitative reasoning can identify strengths and weaknesses.

The most widely used individual test is the **Wechsler Intelligence Scale for Children (WISC–III).** This test for ages 6 through 16 measures verbal and performance abilities, yielding separate scores for each, as well as a total score. With separate subtest scores, it is easier to pinpoint a child's strengths and to diagnose specific problems. For example, if a child does well on verbal tests (such as general information and basic arithmetic operations) but

An individual intelligence test can help determine whether a child needs special help.

poorly on performance tests (such as doing a puzzle or drawing the missing part of a picture), the child may be slow in perceptual or motor development. A child who does well on performance tests but poorly on verbal tests may have a language problem. Another commonly used individual test is the Stanford-Binet Intelligence Scale (see chapter 10).

The most commonly used intelligence tests in Canada are produced in the United States. This can be a problem because many items may not be appropriate measures of intelligence of Canadian children (for example, using imperial measures instead of metric for arithmetic problems, or items requiring knowledge of U.S. culture and history, rather than Canadian). In addition, developers of American tests use American representative samples of children as the basis for developing norms against which individual children's scores are compared. The characteristics of the U.S. samples are different enough from the Canadian population to raise concerns about the appropriateness of using American norms for Canadian children. Canadian children score differently from American children (Weiss, Saklofske, Prifitera, Chen, & Hildebrand, 1999); for example, Aboriginal children might be at a disadvantage on tests that rely heavily on verbal abilities (Scaldwell, Frame, & Cookson, 1985). Canadian norms have been developed for the WISC–III (Wechsler, 1996), as have ways of using the test, appropriate for Canadian children, to look at different aspects of intelligence (Saklofske, Caravan, & Schwartz, 2000; Weiss et al., 1999).

The IQ Controversy

The use of psychometric intelligence tests is controversial. On the positive side, because IQ tests have been standardized and widely used, there is extensive information about their norms, validity, and reliability (see chapters 2 and 7). IQ scores during middle childhood are fairly good predictors of school achievement, especially for highly verbal children, and scores are more reliable than during the preschool years. IQ scores are the single best predictor of how long a child will stay in school (Neisser et al., 1996). They can help in selecting students for advanced or slow-paced classes and can aid in decision making about college applications and admissions.

But are IQ tests fair? Critics claim that the tests underestimate the intelligence of children who, for one reason or another, do not do well on tests (Anastasi, 1988; Ceci, 1991). Because the tests are timed, they equate intelligence with speed and penalize a child who works slowly and deliberately. A more fundamental criticism is that IQ tests infer intelligence from what children already know; and much of this knowledge is derived from schooling or culture, and thus cannot measure native ability.

Influence of Schooling

Schooling does seem to increase tested intelligence (Ceci & Williams, 1997; Neisser et al., 1996). In one study, differences in IQ between identical twins raised in different homes were directly related to the amount of education each twin had had (Bronfenbrenner, 1979). Children whose school entrance was significantly delayed (as happened, for example, in South Africa due to a teacher shortage and in the Netherlands during the Nazi occupation) lost as many as 5 IQ points per year, and some of these losses were never recovered (Ceci & Williams, 1997).

IQ scores also drop during summer vacation (Ceci & Williams, 1997). Among a national sample of 1,500 children, language, spatial, and conceptual scores improved much more between October and April, the bulk of the school year, than between April and October, which includes summer vacation and the beginning and end of the school year (Huttenlocher, Levine, & Vevea, 1998).

Influence of Ethnicity

Ethnicity also affects test scores, inspiring claims that the tests are unfair to minorities. Although there is a great deal of individual diversity, Aboriginal children tend to score lower than non-Aboriginal children on standardized measures of IQ, particularly on tests involving verbal intelligence (Beiser & Gotowiec, 2000). On the other hand, Inuit children in Arctic Quebec have been found to score higher than U.S. norms on a non-verbal intelligence test (the Raven's Coloured Progressive Matrices, measuring analytic intelligence), and similar to their non-Inuit counterparts in southern Quebec (Wright, Taylor, & Ruggiero, 1996). In the United States, African-Americans on average score about 15 points lower than white children and show a comparable lag on school achievement tests. However, Asian-Americans, who typically do better than other groups on academic achievement, do not seem to have a significant edge in IQ—a reminder of the limited predictive power of intelligence testing (Neisser et al., 1996).

What accounts for ethnic differences in IQ? Some writers have argued that part of the cause is genetic (Herrnstein & Murray, 1994; Jensen, 1969). However, while there is strong evidence of a genetic influence on *individual* differences in intelligence, there is *no* direct evidence that differences among ethnic, cultural, or racial groups are hereditary (Neisser et al., 1996).

Many scholars attribute such differences to inequalities in environment—in income, in nutrition, in living conditions, in intellectual stimulation, in schooling, in culture, or in other circumstances such as the effects of oppression and discrimination, which can affect self-esteem, motivation, and academic performance (Beiser et al., 2000; Kamin, 1974, 1981; Kottak, 1994; Miller-Jones, 1989). The IQ and achievement test gaps between white and black Americans appear to be narrowing (Neisser et al., 1996) as the life circumstances and educational opportunities of many African-American children improve. With improvements in educational opportunities in Canada, such as those offered by the Aboriginal Head Start program, it is likely that the gaps reported between Aboriginal and non-Aboriginal children will similarly diminish.

In the study of Aboriginal children, when IQ scores were adjusted for differences between Aboriginal and non-Aboriginal children in prenatal maternal health, English-language skills, socio-economic status, and parental attitudes towards school and cultural separation, the differences were virtually eliminated (Beiser et al., 2000). With better health care, socio-economic status, and educational opportunities for Aboriginal groups, the disparity in IQ scores will probably diminish. Generally, however, while prenatal health care, language skills, socio-economic status, and parental attitudes are correlated with IQ, these factors to not explain the entire inter-group variance in IQ (Beiser et al., 2000; Neisser et al., 1996; Suzuki & Valencia, 1997).

Cultural Bias

Some critics attribute ethnic differences in IQ to **cultural bias:** a tendency to include questions that use vocabulary or call for information or skills more familiar or meaningful to some cultural groups than to others (Sternberg, 1985a, 1987), particularly in established market economies in the industrialized world (Sternberg, Grigorenko, & Bundy, 2001). These critics argue that intelligence tests are built around the dominant thinking style and language of white people of European ancestry, putting minority children at a disadvantage (Heath, 1989; Helms, 1992).

Culture, language, and socio-economic status differences (Beiser et al., 2000) may well explain the lower IQs of First Nations children, who tend to do better on performance tasks than on verbal tasks (Neisser et al., 1996). Language may play a part in the black–white differential in the United States as well; some test items may be confusing to children who hear black English rather than standard English at home. Cultural bias also may affect the testing situation. For example, a child from a culture that stresses sociability and cooperation may be handicapped taking a test alone (Kottak, 1994). Still, while cultural bias may play a part in some children's performance, controlled studies have failed to show that it contributes substantially to overall group differences in IQ (Neisser et al., 1996).

Test developers have tried to design **culture-free** tests—tests with no culture-linked content—by posing tasks that do not require language, such as tracing mazes, putting the right shapes in the right holes, and completing pictures. But they have been unable to eliminate all cultural influences. Test designers also have found it virtually impossible to produce **culture-fair** tests consisting only of experiences common to people in various cultures. On a simple sorting task, for example, a child in a Western culture will categorize things by what they *are* (say, putting *bird* and *fish* in the category *animal*). Kpelle tribes-

cultural bias Tendency of intelligence tests to include items calling for knowledge or skills more familiar or meaningful to some cultural groups than to others

culture-free Describing an intelligence test that, if it were possible to design, would have no culturally linked content

culture-fair Describing an intelligence test that deals with experiences common to various cultures, in an attempt to avoid cultural bias

Checkpoint ✔

Can you . . .

✔ Name and describe two traditional intelligence tests for schoolchildren?

✔ Give arguments for and against IQ tests?

✔ Assess explanations that have been advanced for differences in the performance of children of various ethnic groups on intelligence tests?

Table 13-4	Eight Intelligences, According to Gardner	
Intelligence	**Definition**	**Fields or Occupations Where Used**
Linguistic	Ability to use and understand words and nuances of meaning	Writing, editing, translating
Logical-mathematical	Ability to manipulate numbers and solve logical problems	Science, business, medicine
Musical	Ability to perceive and create patterns of pitch and rhythm	Musical composition, conducting
Spatial	Ability to find one's way around in an environment and judge relationships between objects in space	Architecture, carpentry, city planning
Bodily-kinesthetic	Ability to move with precision	Dancing, athletics, surgery
Interpersonal	Ability to understand and communicate with others	Teaching, acting, politics
Intrapersonal	Ability to understand the self	Counselling, psychiatry, spiritual leadership
Naturalist	Ability to distinguish species	Hunting, fishing, farming, gardening, cooking

Source: Based on Gardner, 1993, 1998.

people in Nigeria consider it more intelligent to sort things by what they *do* (say, grouping *fish* with *swim*) (Sternberg, in Quinby, 1985; Sternberg, 1985a, 1986).

Is There More than One Intelligence?

Another serious criticism of IQ tests is that they focus almost entirely on abilities that are useful in school. They do *not* cover other important aspects of intelligent behaviour, such as common sense, social skills, creative insight, and self-knowledge. Yet these abilities, in which some children with modest academic skills excel, may become equally or more important in later life (Gardner, 1993; Sternberg, 1985a, 1987) and may even be considered separate forms of intelligence. Two of the chief advocates of this position are Howard Gardner and Robert Sternberg.

Gardner's Theory of Multiple Intelligences

In his **theory of multiple intelligences,** Howard Gardner (1993) defines *intelligence* as the ability to solve problems or create culturally valued products. He maintains that people have at least eight separate kinds of intelligence. Conventional intelligence tests tap only three of these "intelligences": *linguistic, logical-mathematical,* and, to some extent, *spatial.* The other four, which are not reflected in IQ scores, are *musical, bodily-kinesthetic, interpersonal,* and *intrapersonal.* Gardner (1998; 1999) recently added an eighth intelligence, *naturalist intelligence*, to his original list. (See Table 13-4 for definitions and examples of fields in which each "intelligence" is useful.)

High intelligence in one area is not necessarily accompanied by high intelligence in any of the others. A person may be extremely gifted in art (a spatial ability), precision of movement (bodily-kinesthetic), social relations (interpersonal), or self-understanding (intrapersonal), but not have a high IQ. The various intelligences also develop at different rates. For example, logical-mathematical ability tends to develop earlier and to decline more quickly in late life than interpersonal ability.

Gardner would assess each intelligence directly by observing its products—how well a child can tell a story, remember a melody, or get around in a strange area. Extended observation could reveal strengths and weaknesses so as to help children realize their potential, rather than to compare individuals (Gardner, 1995; Scherer, 1985). Of course, such assessments would be far more time-consuming and more open to observer bias than paper and pencil tests.

Sternberg's Triarchic Theory of Intelligence

Robert Sternberg (1997) defines *intelligence* as a group of mental abilities necessary for children or adults to adapt to any environment, and also to select and shape the contexts in which they live and act. Intelligent behaviour may differ from one culture to another—in England it is intelligent to drive on the left side of the road, in Canada on the right—but the mental processes that produce such behaviour are the same.

Sternberg's (1985a) **triarchic theory of intelligence** embraces three elements, or aspects, of intelligence: *componential, experiential,* and *contextual.* A person may be strong in one, two, or all three.

- The **componential element** is the *analytic* aspect of intelligence; it determines how efficiently people process information. It tells people how to solve problems, how to monitor solutions, and how to evaluate the results.
- The **experiential element** is *insightful;* it determines how people approach novel or familiar tasks. It allows people to compare new information with what they already know and to come up with new ways of putting facts together—in other words, to think originally.
- The **contextual element** is *practical;* it determines how people deal with their environment. It is the ability to size up a situation and decide what to do: adapt to it, change it, or get out of it.

Conventional IQ tests measure mainly componential ability; and since this ability is the kind most school tasks require, it's not surprising that the tests are fairly good predictors of school performance. Their failure to measure experiential (insightful) or contextual (practical) intelligence, says Sternberg, may explain why they are less useful in predicting success in the outside world, and contribute to the validity problems in applying currently used tests, or translations of those tests, in multicultural settings (Sternberg, 1999).

Alternative Directions in Intelligence Testing

Ever since intelligence tests were born, researchers have been trying to improve them. A diagnostic and predictive tool based on neurological research and information-processing theory is the **Kaufman Assessment Battery for Children (K-ABC)** (A. S. Kaufman & Kaufman, 1983).

This individual test for children 2½ to 12½ years old has separate scales for aptitude (processing abilities) and achievement. It also has a non-verbal scale for children with hearing impairments or speech or language disorders and for those whose primary language is not English. The K-ABC incorporates the concept of scaffolding: If a child fails any of the first three items on a subtest, the examiner can use different words or gestures or a different language to encourage a correct response.

Other new tests are based on Vygotsky's zone of proximal development (ZPD). These tests, which seek to capture the dynamic nature of intelligence formation, offer an alternative to traditional "static" tests that measure a child's abilities at a given moment. The dynamic cognitive assessment approach focuses on children working cooperatively with adults, measuring differences in the child's performance with and without adult assistance as a measure of the ZPD (Brown & Ferrara, 1999; Kozulin & Falik, 1995). Interaction is recognized as an important part of learning, and the assessment approach involves producing changes in the child as a way to understand learning potential and learning processes (Lidz, 1995; Tzuriel, 2001). Using this technique, assessment involves a pre-test, followed by an assisted learning phase, and finally a post-test (Kozulin & Garb, 2002).

Sternberg has developed tests consistent with his theory of intelligence. The **Sternberg Triarchic Abilities Test (STAT)** (Sternberg, 1993) seeks to measure each of the three components of intelligence—*analytic, creative,* and *practical*—through multiple-choice and essay questions in three domains: *verbal, quantitative,* and *figural* (or spatial). For example, a test of practical-quantitative intelligence might be to solve an everyday math problem having to do with buying tickets to a ball game. A creative-verbal item might ask a child to

triarchic theory of intelligence Sternberg's theory describing three types of intelligence: componential (analytical ability), experiential (insight and originality), and contextual (practical thinking)

componential element Sternberg's term for the analytic aspect of intelligence

experiential element Sternberg's term for the insightful aspect of intelligence

contextual element Sternberg's term for the practical aspect of intelligence

Kaufman Assessment Battery for Children (K-ABC) Non-traditional individual intelligence test designed to provide fair assessments of minority children and children with disabilities

Sternberg Triarchic Abilities Test (STAT) Test to measure componential, experiential, and contextual intelligence

Checkpoint

Can you . . .

✔ Compare Gardner's and Sternberg's theories, and name and describe specific abilities each proposed?

✔ Describe several new types of intelligence tests?

solve deductive reasoning problems that start with factually false premises (such as, "Money falls off trees"). An analytical-figural item might ask a child to identify the missing piece of a figure. Preliminary validation has found correlations with several other tests of critical thinking, creativity, and practical problem solving (Sternberg, 1997; Sternberg & Clinkenbeard, 1995).

Despite such innovations, it seems likely that conventional psychometric intelligence tests will continue to dominate the field for some time to come (Daniel, 1997). They are widely entrenched, heavily researched, and readily available, and their developers continue to respond to criticisms with each new revision. With or without intelligence tests, decisions will be made about children's abilities and educational placement. Even though current tests are far from perfect, if they are well designed, carefully administered, and wisely interpreted in the light of other relevant information, they can benefit children and society.

Language and Literacy

Language abilities continue to grow during middle childhood. Children are now better able to understand and interpret oral and written communication and to make themselves understood.

Vocabulary, Grammar, and Syntax

Guidepost 4

How do communicative abilities expand during middle childhood?

As vocabulary grows during the school years, children use increasingly precise verbs to describe an action *(hitting, slapping, striking, pounding).* They learn that a word like *run* can have more than one meaning, and they can tell from the context which meaning is intended. They learn, not only to use many more words, but to select the right word for a particular use. *Simile* and *metaphor,* figures of speech in which a word or phrase that usually designates one thing is compared or applied to another, become increasingly common (Owens, 1996; Vosniadou, 1987). Although grammar is quite complex by age 6, children during the early school years rarely use the passive voice (as in "The sidewalk is being shovelled"), verb tenses that include the auxiliary *have* ("I have already shovelled the sidewalk"), and conditional sentences ("If Barbara were home, she would help shovel the sidewalk") (C. S. Chomsky, 1969).

Up to and possibly after age 9, children's understanding of rules of *syntax* (how words are organized into phrases and sentences) becomes more sophisticated. Carol S. Chomsky (1969) found considerable variation in the ages at which children grasp certain syntactic structures. For example, most children under 5 or 6 years old think the sentences "John promised Bill to go shopping" and "John told Bill to go shopping" both mean that Bill is the one to go to the store. Their confusion is understandable, since almost all English verbs other than *promised* that might be used in such a sentence (such as *ordered, wanted,* and *expected*) would have that meaning. Many 6-year-olds have not yet learned how to deal with constructions such as the one in the first sentence, even though they know what a promise is and can use and understand the word correctly in other sentences. By age 8, most children can interpret the first sentence correctly, and by age 9 virtually all children can.

Sentence structure continues to become more elaborate. Older children use more subordinate clauses ("The boy *who delivers the newspapers* rang the doorbell"), and they now look at the semantic effect of a sentence as a whole, rather than focusing on word order as a signal of meaning. Still, some constructions, such as clauses beginning with *however* and *although,* do not become common until early adolescence (Owens, 1996).

Pragmatics: Knowledge about Communication

The major area of linguistic growth for school-age children is pragmatics, the use of language to communicate. These girlfriends are better able to carry on a conversation or recount happenings than when they were younger.

By the school years, most children have mastered the basic rules of form and meaning. They are better able to take the viewpoint of another person and to engage in social give-and-take. Their major area of linguistic growth is in *pragmatics:* the practical use of language to communicate.* This includes both conversational and narrative skills.

---

*This section is largely indebted to Owens (1996).

Good conversationalists probe by asking questions before introducing a topic with which the other person may not be familiar. They quickly recognize a breakdown in communication and do something to repair it. There are wide individual differences in such conversational skills; some 7-year-olds are better conversationalists than some adults (Anderson, Clark, & Mullin, 1994).

Schoolchildren are highly conscious of adults' power and authority. Grade 1 students respond to adults' questions with simpler, shorter answers than they give their peers. They tend to speak to parents in ways different from the ways they speak to other adults, issuing more demands and engaging in less extended conversation.

When children this age tell stories, they seldom make them up; they are more likely to relate a personal experience. Most 6-year-olds can retell the plot of a short book, movie, or television show. They are beginning to describe motives and causal links.

By Grade 2, children's stories become longer and more complex. Fictional tales often have conventional beginnings and endings ("Once upon a time…" and "They lived happily ever after," or simply "The end"). Word use is more varied than before, but characters do not show growth or change, and plots are not fully developed.

Older children usually "set the stage" with introductory information about the setting and characters, and they clearly indicate changes of time and place during the story. They construct more complex episodes than younger children do, but with less unnecessary detail. They focus more on the characters' motives and thoughts, and they think through how to resolve problems in the plot.

Literacy

Learning to read and write frees children from the constraints of face-to-face communication. Now they have access to the ideas and imagination of people in faraway lands and long-ago times.

Reading

Reading involves different levels of skills. Once children can translate the marks on a page into patterns of sound and meaning, they can develop increasingly sophisticated strategies to understand what they read.

Mechanics of Reading Traditionally, most children learned to read by mastering a phonetic code that matches the printed alphabet to spoken sounds that can be combined into words. A child who knows this code can "sound out," and thus "decode," unfamiliar words. Teaching methods that stress phonics take a *code emphasis* approach.

The *whole-language* approach (sometimes called *literature-based* or *process-oriented*), is based on very different principles. Whole-language advocates believe that children can learn to read and write naturally, through discovery, much as they learn to understand and use speech. They claim that phonetic instruction hampers this natural process by obscuring the purpose of written language—to communicate meaning—and produces readers who can decode but cannot comprehend.

The whole-language method emphasizes *visually based retrieval.* The child looks at a whole word and then retrieves it from memory, with the help of contextual cues if necessary. Whole-language programs are built around real literature and open-ended, student-initiated activities, in contrast with the more rigorous, teacher-directed tasks involved in phonics instruction. Proponents argue that children learn to read better—and enjoy it more—if they see written language as a way to gain information and express ideas and feelings, not as a system of isolated sounds and syllables that must be learned by memorization and drill.

Despite the popularity of the whole-language approach, reviews of the literature have found little support for its claims (Stahl, McKenna, & Pagnucco, 1994; Stahl & Miller, 1989). Critics hold it largely responsible for the failure of many schoolchildren to learn to read well—or even to want to read. A survey of 18,185 students in Grades 1 to 6 found that attitudes toward reading—both recreational and academic—worsen from Grade 1 on, especially among boys, who may prefer sports or other activities (McKenna, Kear, & Ellsworth, 1995).

Critics claim that whole-language teaching encourages children to skim through a text, guessing at words and their meaning, without trying to correct reading or spelling errors as long as the results "make sense." They say that reading, unlike talking, is a skill that must be taught; the brain is not programmed to acquire it. A long line of research supports the importance of phonemic awareness (the ability to analyze and manipulate sounds in words) and early phonics training as keys to reading proficiency (Hatcher, Hulme, & Ellis, 1994; Liberman & Liberman, 1990; National Reading Panel, 2000). In a comparison of whole language and an instructional approach that uses more direct instruction (the "Bridge" program, which uses icons to facilitate word identification), in inner-city children in Toronto who where at risk of reading failure, the Bridge group showed better reading scores at the end of Grade 1 and Grade 2 (Biemiller & Siegel, 1997).

The most effective way to teach reading—according to a comprehensive research review by the National Reading Panel, a U.S. congressionally mandated independent panel of experts—is by developing strong phonetic skills (phonetic awareness and phonics) along with methods to improve fluency and comprehension. The panel highlighted the value of *systematic* phonics instruction—teaching a planned sequence of phonics elements rather than merely pointing them out as they appear in a text. Children can become fluent by reading aloud frequently with guidance and feedback (Ehri et al., 2001; National Reading Panel, 2000).

How do students gain in comprehension—the goal of reading?

Comprehension The developmental processes that improve reading comprehension during the school years are similar to those that improve memory. As word recognition becomes faster and more automatic, children can focus on the meaning of what they read and look for inferences and connections. **Metacognition**—awareness of what is going on in their own minds—helps children monitor their understanding of what they read. It also helps them develop strategies to clear up any problems—such strategies as rereading difficult passages, reading more slowly, trying to visualize what is being described, and thinking of examples. Children learn to adjust their reading speed and attention to the importance and difficulty of the material. As their store of knowledge grows, they can more readily check new information against what they already know (Siegler, 1998).

Like the mechanics of reading, comprehension may best be taught through a variety of approaches. The National Reading Panel suggests that vocabulary be learned both directly and indirectly, as children encounter words in text. Repeated exposure to the same words helps; so may computerized programs that link words with their definitions. Using word processors for writing may improve children's reading: reading instruction is most effective when combined with writing (National Reading Panel, 2000).

Techniques to help students recall, summarize, and ask questions about what they read can enhance comprehension (National Reading Panel, 2000). Some school programs help children develop interpretive strategies through literary discussion. Teachers model effective strategies (such as making associations with prior knowledge, summarizing, visualizing relationships, and making predictions) and coach students on how to select and use them (R. Brown & Pressley, 1994; R. Brown, Pressley, Schuder, & Van Meter, 1994).

A balanced literacy approach used by effective teachers (Pressley, Wharton-McDonald, Mistretta-Hampston, & Echevarria, 1998) combines in about equal measure instruction in word reading and comprehension with literature-rich activities. These include extensive reading, writing about what was read, and the opportunity for students to select their own reading material from a variety of types and difficulty levels that are matched to the students' own ability (Guthrie, Schafer, & Huang, 2001; Pressley, 1998). This approach results in superior outcomes in reading achievement, in both advantaged and disadvantaged groups, and engages children in reading (Guthrie et al., 2001; Pressley, 1998), and it is advocated by the Canadian Psychological Association (Simner, 1993; 1998).

Efforts to improve the teaching of reading seem to be paying off. The 1998 National Assessment of Educational Progress showed significant increases in average reading scores

metacognition Awareness of a person's own mental processes

in Grades 4, 8, and 12 since 1994—the first time all three grades' averages have risen since the nationwide testing program began in 1971.

An assessment of reading abilities of 46,000 13- and 16-year-old students in all provinces and territories of Canada was carried out in 1994 and 1998 by the School Achievement Indicators Program (Council of Ministers of Education, Canada [CMEC], 1999). Results showed that 13- and 16-year-olds in 1994 and 1998 maintained expected reading levels between the two testing periods. However, writing scores improved significantly between the two measurement periods for both age groups (CMEC, 1999).

Writing

The acquisition of writing skill goes hand in hand with the development of reading. Writing is difficult for young children, and early compositions are usually quite short. Unlike conversation, which offers constant feedback, writing provides no immediate sign of how well the child has met his or her communicative goals (Siegler, 1998).

Young children, whose thinking is still somewhat egocentric, have difficulty separating what they know about a topic from what they can expect their readers to know, and they have trouble finding errors in their own work. As children get older and can take more than one perspective, they spend more time planning their writing so as to present it in a way that their audience will understand (Siegler, 1998).

In the typical classroom, children are discouraged from discussing their work with other children. This practice is based on the belief that children, especially friends, will distract one another. Research based on Vygotsky's social interaction model of language development suggests that this is not so.

In one study, Grade 4 students progressed more when they wrote with other children, especially friends. Children working in pairs wrote stories with more solutions to problems, more explanations and goals, and fewer errors in syntax and word use than did children working alone. Friends, working as a team, elaborated on each other's ideas and posed alternative ones (Daiute, Hartup, Sholl, & Zajac, 1993).

What makes collaboration between friends so fruitful? Friends understand each other's needs, abilities, and likely behaviours. They can expect reciprocal commitment, and they are more comfortable and trusting; thus they may be more willing to take intellectual risks (Hartup, 1996a, 1996b).

The Child in School

"What will the teacher be like?" 6-year-old Julia wonders as she walks up the steps to her new school, wearing her new backpack. "Will the work be too hard? Will the kids like me? What games will we play at recess?"

Even today, when many children go to preschool and most go to kindergarten, children often approach the start of Grade 1 with a mixture of eagerness and anxiety. The first day of "regular" school is a milestone—a sign of the developmental advances that make this new status possible.

Entering Grade 1

The first-grade experience lays the foundation for a child's entire school career. Just as the curriculum in each grade builds on what went before, so does the file that follows the child from year to year. This "paper trail" helps shape each new teacher's perceptions and expectations—expectations that can affect a student's achievement in the middle grades and even in high school. The Grade 1 report card is a forecast of what is to come—a more accurate predictor than initial test scores (Entwisle & Alexander, 1998).

Small differences in Grade 1 achievement tend to enlarge. In the Beginning School Study (BSS) which has followed 790 randomly selected African-American and white Baltimore children since 1982, when they entered Grade 1, first-graders from high-income families scored 20 points higher on a standardized reading test than classmates from low-income families, and 5 years later the gap had widened to more than 60 points (Entwisle, Alexander, & Olson, 1997).

Checkpoint ✔

Can you . . .

✔ Summarize improvements in language skills during middle childhood?

✔ Compare and evaluate the whole-language and code-emphasis (phonetic) methods of teaching reading?

✔ Tell how reading can best be taught and how comprehension can be improved?

✔ Explain why writing is harder for younger children than for older ones and why social interaction may improve children's writing?

Guidepost 5

What influences school achievement?

The BSS identified factors that can ease the Grade 1 transition (Entwisle & Alexander, 1998). One is the amount of kindergarten a child has had. Children who had attended full-day kindergarten did better on achievement tests and got higher marks in reading and math early in Grade 1 than those who had attended kindergarten half days or not at all. The age at which children enter kindergarten is related to later achievement; younger children in an Alberta study were more likely to be held back a year or need remedial help, but were more likely to have higher IQ scores than older children (Wilgosh et al., 1996; see chapter 10).

As in many other studies, children in two-parent families did better than children in single-parent families, apparently because of economic disparities. However, children who lived with a mother and grandmother had better work habits and gained more in reading skills than other children of single parents, even though their economic situation was similar.

To make the most academic progress, a child needs to be involved in what is going on in class. Interest, attention, and active participation were associated with achievement test scores and, even more so, with teachers' marks from Grade 1 through at least Grade 4 (K. L. Alexander, Entwisle, & Dauber, 1993). Since patterns of classroom behaviour seem to be established in Grade 1, this crucial year offers a "window of opportunity" for parents and teachers to help a child form good learning habits.

Checkpoint ✓

Can you . . .

✔ Explain the impact of the Grade 1 experience on a child's school career, and identify factors that affect success in Grade 1?

Environmental Influences on School Achievement

In addition to children's own characteristics, each level of the context of their lives, from the immediate family to what goes on in the classroom to the messages they receive from the larger culture (such as "It's not cool to be smart"), influences how well they do in school. Let's look at this "nest" of environmental influences.

The Family

Parents of achieving children provide a place to study and to keep books and supplies; they set times for meals, sleep, and homework; they monitor how much television their children watch and what their children do after school; and they show interest in their children's lives by talking with them about school and being involved in school activities. Parents' attitudes about homework directly affect their children's willingness to do it. As children get older, the responsibility for seeing that schoolwork gets done shifts from parent to child (Cooper, Lindsay, Nye, & Greathouse, 1998).

How do parents motivate children to do well? Some use *extrinsic* (external) means—giving children money or treats for good grades or punishing them for bad ones. Others encourage children to develop *intrinsic* (internal) motivation by praising them for ability and hard work. Intrinsic motivation seems more effective. In fact, some educators claim that even praise should be used sparingly, as it shifts the focus from the child's own motivation to the need to please others (Aldort, 1994). In a study of 77 students in Grades 3 and 4, those who were interested in the work itself did better in school than those who mainly sought grades or parents' approval (Miserandino, 1996).

Parenting styles (refer back to chapter 11) may affect motivation. In one study, the highest achieving students in Grade 5 had *authoritative* parents. These children were curious and interested in learning; they liked challenging tasks and enjoyed solving problems by themselves. *Authoritarian* parents, who kept after children to do their homework, supervised closely, and relied on extrinsic motivation, tended to have lower-achieving children. So did children of *permissive* parents, who were uninvolved and did not seem to care how the children did in school (G. S. Ginsburg & Bronstein, 1993). Quality of attachment is also related to academic achievement. In a longitudinal study of 108 French-Canadian school-age children, Moss and St-Laurent (2001) found that children who were securely attached to their mothers at 6 years of age tended to have higher scores than their insecurely attached peers on measures of school achievement at 8 years of age.

Socio-economic status can have long-lasting effects on school achievement. When researchers followed 1,253 students in Grades 2 to 4 for 2 to 4 years, those from low-income families tended to have lower reading and math achievement test scores, and the income gap in math achievement widened as time went on (Pungello, Kupersmidt, Burchinal, & Patterson, 1996).

The family is an important influence on school achievement. A child who takes the major responsibility for doing homework can benefit from a parent's active interest—and an occasional helping hand.

SES can affect parents' ability to provide an environment that enhances learning. Among 229 two-parent and single-parent families with school-age children, parents who reported adequate financial resources were more likely to have confidence in their effectiveness as parents, to set positive goals for their children, and to use parenting practices that promote children's competence. They set consistent routines, had harmonious family relationships, and were actively involved at school (G. H. Brody, Flor, & Gibson, 1999; G. H. Brody, Stoneman, & Flor, 1995).

Socio-economic status, then, does not itself determine school achievement. The Alberta study of age of kindergarten entry found no relationship between SES and later school achievement (Wilgosh et al., 1996). The difference comes from its effects on family life. In one longitudinal study, 8-year-olds whose home environment was cognitively stimulating had higher intrinsic motivation for academic learning at ages 9, 10, and 13 than children who lived in less stimulating homes. This was true over and above effects of SES (Gottfried, Fleming, & Gottfried, 1998).

Teacher Expectations

According to the principle of the **self-fulfilling prophecy,** children live up—or down—to other people's expectations for them. In the "Oak School" experiment, teachers were falsely told at the beginning of the term that some students had shown unusual potential for cognitive growth, when these children actually had been chosen at random. Yet several months later, many of them showed unusual gains in IQ (R. Rosenthal & Jacobson, 1968).

Later analyses cast doubt on the power of the self-fulfilling prophecy: its effects, on average, are small. Still, under certain conditions teachers' expectations do seem to function as self-fulfilling prophecies (Jussim, Eccles, & Madon, 1996), both predicting and influencing students' learning. In a multi-year study of long-term effects of expectancies on academic performance, Smith, Jussim, and Eccles (1999) found that expectancy effects generally diminish as children grow older, but in cases in which there is much contact between the teacher and student, they are maintained for up to 6 years. However, there was no evidence of expectancy effects accumulating over time. Teacher expectations seem to magnify performance differences in children in the early grades, and sustain those differences in later grades (Kuklinski & Weinstein, 2001).

A study of 147 student teachers at Queen's University examined the effects of expectations and disconfirming information on evaluations of a fictitious student's growth and achievement. Results showed that expectations can have a powerful influence on novice teachers' judgments. Teachers who were informed that the student was from a high SES level tended to maintain their original judgments despite evidence indicating poorer performance (Wilson & Martinussen, 1999).

In a longitudinal study of 110 four-year-olds, preschool teachers' over- and underestimates of children's intelligence (as compared with actual IQ) predicted grade-point averages and Scholastic Aptitude Test (SAT) scores 14 years later, even after controlling for individual differences in IQ, SES, and behavioural characteristics. The effect on grades was especially evident among children whose preschool teachers *under*estimated their ability. Teachers tended to have lower expectations for poor children. They also seemed to judge children on the basis of personality. Teachers tended to overestimate the intelligence of children they saw as competent, independent, assertive, and interesting and to underestimate the intelligence of children they saw as immature and insecure (Alvidrez & Weinstein, 1999).

If self-fulfilling prophecies are at work, early entries in a student's cumulative file can be vitally important. Performance can become self-perpetuating by fuelling teacher expectations, which, in turn, influence student achievement as a child passes from class to class (Entwisle & Alexander, 1998).

The Educational System

How can school best enhance children's development? Throughout the 20th century, conflicting educational philosophies, along with historical events, brought great swings in educational theory and practice—from the "three R's" (reading, 'riting, and 'rithmetic), to

self-fulfilling prophecy False expectation or prediction of behaviour that tends to come true because it leads people to act as if it already were true

"child-centred" methods that focused on children's interests, and then, when competition from Russia and then from Japan loomed and test scores plummeted, back to the "basics." In the 1980s, a series of governmental and educational commissions in the U.S. proposed plans for improvement, ranging from more homework (see Box 13-1) to a longer school day and school year to a total reorganization of schools and curricula.

Today, many educators recommend teaching children in the primary grades by integrating subject matter fields and building on children's natural interests and talents: teaching reading and writing, for example, in the context of a social studies project or teaching math concepts through the study of music. They favour cooperative projects, hands-on problem solving, and close parent–teacher cooperation (Rescorla, 1991). (Box 13-2 discusses the current controversy over the best way to teach math.)

Many contemporary educators also emphasize a "fourth R": reasoning. Children who are taught thinking skills in the context of academic subject matter perform better on intelligence tests and in school (R. D. Feldman, 1986; Sternberg, 1984, 1985a, 1985b). Everyday activities can also be routes to enhancing thinking skills (see Table 13-5). Research on Sternberg's triarchic theory suggests that students learn better when taught in a variety of ways, emphasizing creative and practical skills as well as memorization and critical thinking (Sternberg, Torff, & Grigorenko, 1998).

When the Chicago public schools in 1996 ended **social promotion,** the practice of promoting children who do not meet academic standards, many observers hailed the change. However, some educators maintain that the alternative—forcing failing students to go to summer school before they can graduate, or to repeat a grade—is shortsighted (Bronner, 1999). Although retention in some cases can be a "wake-up call," more often it is the first step on a remedial track that leads to lowered expectations, poor performance, and ultimately dropping out of school (J. M. Fields & Smith, 1998; McLeskey, Lancaster, & Grizzle, 1995). A number of countries with well-regarded educational systems, such as Denmark, Sweden, Norway, Japan, and South Korea, have automatic promotion policies.

Many educators say the only real solution to a high failure rate is to identify at-risk students early and intervene *before* they fail (Bronner, 1999). In a longitudinal study of students in kindergarten through to Grade 8 in the Chicago schools, retained students did more poorly on math and reading-achievement tests than peers who had been promoted, and also did more poorly in math than their new, younger classmates (McCoy & Reynolds, 1999).

What's your view ?

- Which approach to education do you favour for children in the primary grades: instruction in the "basics," a more flexible, child-centred curriculum, or a combination of the two?

social promotion Policy in which children are automatically promoted from one grade to another even if they do not meet academic standards for the grade they are completing

Table 13-5	Everyday Ways to Enhance Children's Thinking Skills

- When reading to children, ask open-ended questions (beginning with what, why, and how).
- Help children find the most important points in what they read, see, or hear.
- Ask children to compare new information with what they already know. Identifying commonalities and differences can help children organize information, which helps them think as well as remember.
- Teach children not to accept a statement that contradicts common knowledge without reliable proof.
- Encourage children to write. Putting thoughts on paper forces them to organize their thoughts. Projects may include keeping a journal, writing a letter to a famous person, and presenting an argument to parents (say, for an increase in allowance or a special purchase or privilege).
- Encourage children to think imaginatively about what they have learned. ("How do you think the soldiers in the First World War felt at the Battle of Vimy Ridge? What do you suppose they wore?")
- When writing a poem or drawing a picture, encourage children to produce a first version and then to polish or revise it.
- Show children how to approach a problem by identifying what they do and don't know about it, by designing a plan to solve it, by carrying out the plan, and then by deciding whether it has worked.
- Ask children to invent a new product, such as a gadget to ease a household chore.
- Teach children such skills as reading a map and using a microscope, and provide opportunities to practise them.

Sources: Marzano & Hutchins, 1987; Maxwell, 1987.

The homework debate is far from new. In the United States, historical swings in homework use have reflected shifts in educational philosophy (Cooper, 1989; Gill & Schlossman, 1996).

During the 19th century, the mind was considered a muscle, and homework a means of exercising it. But anti-homework crusaders argued that assignments lasting far into the evening endangered children's physical and emotional health and interfered with family life. By the 1940s, "progressive," child-centred education held sway, and homework had lost favour (Gill & Schlossman, 1996).

In the 1950s, when the Soviet Union's Sputnik launch brought calls for more rigorous science and math education, "More homework!" became a battle cry in campaigns to upgrade educational standards (Cooper, 1989).

By 1997, according to one survey, students in Grades 1 through 3 were spending about 2 hours a week on homework, three times as much as in 1981 (Hofferth & Sandberg, 1998). Child psychologists report an increase in homework-related anxieties (Winerip, 1999). A survey of Canadian adolescents showed that teenagers in homes with Internet access spend 8 hours a week on average on homework (Canadian Council on Social Development [CCSD], 2001). This is an increase by about an hour in comparison with 1998, and represents more time spent using computers. The average time spent researching on the Internet in order to complete school assignments is 2 hours each week. The majority of parents see this as beneficial to their children, with about 90 per cent reporting that Internet access has had a positive impact on their children. However, because Internet access at home is more likely for high-SES children, the benefits of Internet access are more likely to be available to children in higher-income families (CCSD, 2001).

Homework advocates claim that it disciplines the mind, develops good work habits, improves retention, and lets students cover more ground than they could in the classroom alone. Homework is a bridge between home and school, increasing parental involvement. Opponents claim that too much homework leads to boredom, anxiety, or frustration, puts unnecessary pressure on children, discourages intrinsic motivation, and usurps time from other worthwhile activities. They say that parental "help" can be counterproductive if parents become overly intrusive or use teaching methods that conflict with those taught at school (Cooper, 1989). Once again, some critics (Kralovec & Buell, 2000) want to ban homework, at least for young children.

Research supports a balanced view, recognizing that homework can improve achievement and long-term success, but also has costs (Larson & Verma, 1999). A comprehensive review of nearly 120 studies found that the value of homework depends on many factors, including the age, ability, and motivation of the child; the amount and purpose of homework; the home situation; and classroom follow-up. The older the child, the more effective homework can be. While it has strong benefits for high school students, it has only moderate benefits for junior high school students (and then only if limited to 2 hours a night), and virtually no benefits for elementary school students as compared with in-class study. Homework seems to work best when assignments are not overly complicated or completely unfamiliar, when material is spread out over several assignments, and when the need for parental involvement (which varies in effectiveness and can create tension at home) is kept to a minimum (Cooper, 1989).

Junior high and high school students who spend more time on homework tend to get better grades (Cooper et al., 1998; Cooper, Valentine, Nye, & Lindsay, 1999), but this is less true at the elementary level. The more homework younger children get, the more negatively they feel toward it. In a survey of 709 students in Grades 2 to 12, about one-third of lower-grade students said they typically did not finish their homework. Even in the upper grades, students who received lengthy assignments tended not to complete them (Cooper et al., 1998).

Homework, then, has value—but only in moderation and when geared to students' developmental levels. Homework serves different purposes at different ages. For young children, it can develop good study habits and an understanding that learning can take place at home as well as in school. In junior high, a mix of mandatory and voluntary homework can promote academic goals and motivate children to pursue studies that interest them. In high school, homework can provide opportunities for practice, review, and integration of what is being learned at school (Cooper, 1989).

Assignments in the elementary grades should be short and easy enough for children to succeed. Research-based recommendations range from one to three 15-minute assignments a week in the primary grades to four or five assignments a week, each lasting 75 to 120 minutes, in Grades 10 to 12. Instead of grading homework, teachers should use it to diagnose learning problems (Cooper, 1989).

What's your view

How much homework do you think is appropriate for children of various ages?

Check it out

For more information on this topic, go to **www.mcgrawhill.ca/college/papalia.**

In a second study of the same sample, those who had been in a high-quality early childhood education program were less likely to be held back in school or to drop out of high school (Temple, Reynolds, & Miedel, 2000).

Summer school may be helpful as an early intervention. Disadvantaged children, during the summer months, tend to fall behind their more advantaged peers, who have more opportunities for summer reading and other learning experiences (Harris, Kelly, Valentine, & Muhlenbruck, 2000). A projected 3-year study is following about 450 low-income Baltimore elementary school students randomly assigned to summer instruction in reading and

Should children learn math by rules and formulas, or by manipulating coloured blocks or pie-shaped segments to illustrate mathematical concepts? By memorizing and drilling in the multiplication tables, or by using computer simulations and relating math problems to real life?

These questions have spurred heated argument between proponents of traditional "skill-and-drill" math teaching and advocates of the newer *constructivist math* (or *whole math*), in which children actively construct their own mathematical concepts. This approach came into nationwide use after 1989, when the National Council of Teachers of Mathematics (NCTM) issued new standards of instruction based on constructivist principles.

The new standards de-emphasized basic skills. Instead, they stressed understanding how mathematics works. Rather than passively absorb rules from a teacher or textbook, children were to discover mathematical concepts for themselves, often on the basis of intuitive learning gleaned from telling time, playing board games, dealing with money, and other everyday experiences. Instead of arriving at precise answers to a problem such as 19×6, children were encouraged to make rough estimates from more familiar relationships, such as 20×5.

Much like older arguments about reading instruction, the math wars split educators into opposing camps. Many parents called the new curriculum "dumbed down" or "fuzzy math." They complained that their children could not add, subtract, multiply, divide, or do simple algebra. They questioned how well teachers could handle the new materials and methods—indeed, how well the teachers themselves understood the principles their students were groping to discover (Jackson, 1997a, 1997b).

The reforms were widely pronounced a failure. And then, the first scientific studies on their effectiveness proved generally favourable. A study of 2,369 big-city algebra students found that following the NCTM standards did not hurt students' performance on traditional tests and improved the performance of middle school students (Mayer, 1998). A study of elementary school students bore out the constructivist belief that children learn best by analyzing problems, figuring out *why* an answer is right or wrong (Siegler, 1995). And while the constructivist approach has been criticized as inappropriate for diverse school populations, a randomized study of 104 low-achieving, mostly poor and minority students in Grades 3 and 4 found otherwise. Students taught by problem-solving and/or peer collaboration outperformed students taught by more traditional methods on computation and word problems (Ginsburg-Block & Fantuzzo, 1998).

In the Third International Mathematics and Science Study (TIMSS) in 1998, Canadian Grade 12 students scored higher than the average of 21 competing nations on math literacy and higher than any of the other G-8 countries (McConaghy, 1998). However, immigrant children tend to score lower than native-born children in Canada. One explanation is that the poorer English language skills of first-generation immigrant children are contributing to difficulties in learning mathematics in English-language classrooms (Huang, 2000). The 2002 report of mathematics achievement by the CMEC showed mathematics scores, particularly in problem solving, improved between 1997 and 2001, and that children are performing at higher than expected levels (CMEC, 2002).

As in the reading wars, both sides of the math wars may have merit, and the best approach may be a combination of old and new approaches. That is what the NCTM (2000) now advocates with the issuance of its latest revised standards. The revision strives for a balance between conceptual understanding and mathematical procedures and re-emphasizes accuracy, efficiency, and fluency in basic computational skills.

What's your view?

Based on your own experience, which method of teaching math do you think would be more effective, or would you advocate a combination of both?

Check it out!

For more information on this topic, go to **www.mcgrawhill.ca/college/papalia**.

writing. In the first year of the study, kindergartners who attended at least 75 per cent of the time outscored 81 per cent of their peers who did not participate, and Grade 1 students outscored 64 per cent (Borman, Boulay, Kaplan, Rachuba, & Hewes, 1999).

Computer literacy and the ability to navigate the Web are opening new possibilities for individualized instruction, global communication, and early training in independent research skills. Under the Telecommunications Act of 1997, the U.S. Federal Communications Commission allotted $2.25 billion to help schools acquire the equipment necessary to make universal classroom Internet service a reality.

However, this tool poses dangers. Beyond the risk of exposure to harmful or inappropriate material, students need to learn to critically evaluate information they find in cyberspace and to separate facts from opinion and advertising (J. Lee, 1998). A focus on "visual literacy" may divert financial resources from other areas of the curriculum. Nor does computer use necessarily improve basic skills. In a major international math and science examination, Grade 4 students from 7 other countries out of 26 significantly outperformed Canadian and U.S. Grade 4 math students, and teachers in 5 of these countries reported that students never or almost never used computers in class (Mullis et al., 1997).

The Culture

Why do so many students of East Asian extraction do so well in school? Cultural influences in these children's countries of origin may hold the key.

Educational practices in East Asian societies differ markedly from those in Canada and the United States (Song & Ginsburg, 1987; H. W. Stevenson, 1995; Stigler, Lee, & Stevenson, 1987). The school day and year are longer, and the curriculum is set centrally. Classes are larger (about 40 to 50), and teachers spend more time teaching the whole class, whereas Canadian children spend more time working alone or in small groups and thus receive more individual attention but less total instruction.

East Asian cultures share values that foster educational success, such as obedience, responsibility, and respect for elders (Chao, 1994). In Japan, a child's entrance into school is a major occasion for celebration. Japanese and Korean parents spend a great deal of time helping children with schoolwork. Japanese children who fall behind are tutored or go to *jukus,* private remedial and enrichment schools (McKinney, 1987; Song & Ginsburg, 1987).

Chinese and Japanese mothers view academic achievement as a child's most important pursuit (H. W. Stevenson, 1995; H. W. Stevenson, Chen, & Lee, 1993; H. W. Stevenson, Lee, Chen, & Lummis, 1990; H. W. Stevenson, Lee, Chen, Stigler, et al., 1990). Their children spend more time on homework, like it better, and get more parental help than U.S. children (C. Chen & Stevenson, 1989). Whereas U.S. students socialize after school and engage in sports and other activities, Asian students devote themselves almost entirely to study (Fuligni & Stevenson, 1995; H. W. Stevenson, 1995; H. W. Stevenson et al., 1993).

East Asians carry over these values and practices to their new land. Many Asian-American families see education as the best route to upward mobility (Chao, 1996; Sue & Okazaki, 1990). The child's school success is a prime goal of parenting (Chao, 1994, 1996; Huntsinger & Jose, 1995). Nor is this academic success at the price of social skills. In a study of 36 students in Grades 1 and 2 children of Chinese immigrants, the Chinese-American children were equally well adjusted as a control group of European-American children and had more advanced academic skills (Huntsinger, Jose, & Larson, 1998).

Of course, as Asian-Canadian children grow up in Canadian culture and absorb its values, their attitudes toward learning may change (C. Chen & Stevenson, 1995; Huntsinger et al., 1998). Research on second-, third-, and fourth-generation Asian Canadians may help sort out cultural influences on educational achievement. In a comparison of Canadian and Hong Kong–Chinese children, Kwok & Lytton (1996) found that although Hong Kong–Chinese children outperformed Canadian-Chinese children in mathematical abilities, the Canadian children's ratings of their own abilities, along with those of their parents, were higher than ratings by Hong Kong respondents. The higher opinions of the Canadians might contribute to a sense of complacency that could account for their lower mathematics performance (Kwok et al., 1996).

Unlike Asian Canadians, some minority children whose cultures value behaviour different from that of the dominant culture are at a disadvantage in school (Helms, 1992; Tharp, 1989). The Kamehameha Early Education Program (KEEP) has produced dramatic improvements in primary-grade Hawaiian children's cognitive performance by designing educational programs to fit cultural patterns. Whereas children in non-KEEP classes score very low on standard achievement tests, children in KEEP classes approach national norms. A KEEP program also was established on the Navajo reservation in northern Arizona. Among the issues KEEP addresses are the following (Tharp, 1989):

- *Organization of the classroom:* Since Hawaiian culture values collaboration, cooperation, and assisted performance, children work in small groups of four to five students, who continually teach and learn from one another. For Navajo children, who are trained in self-sufficiency and are separated by sex from about age 8, the most effective groupings are limited to two or three children of the same sex.
- *Accommodation for language styles:* Hawaiians typically overlap one another's speech, a style of social involvement often interpreted by non-Hawaiian teachers as rude. By contrast, Navajos speak slowly, with frequent silent pauses. Non-Navajo teachers often interrupt, misinterpreting such pauses as signalling the end of a

Checkpoint ✔

Can you . . .

✔ Tell how parental beliefs and practices can influence school success?

✔ Discuss the impact of socio-economic status on school achievement?

✔ Evaluate the effects of teachers' perceptions and expectations?

✔ Trace major changes in educational philosophy and practice during the 20th century, including views about homework and teaching of math?

response. When teachers adjust their styles of speaking to their students', children participate more freely.

- *Adjustment for learning styles:* Whereas in most industrialized societies teaching stresses verbal and analytic thought, Aboriginal teaching stresses thinking in visual, holistic patterns and learning by imitation, with little verbal instruction. Parents in Aboriginal communities expect children to listen to an entire story without interruption before discussing it. Teachers can help children by acknowledging culturally different learning styles and helping children adjust to an unfamiliar style.

These themes are echoed in current initiatives for Aboriginal children in Canada. Although the proportion of Aboriginal students attending band-operated schools has risen dramatically (Frideres, 1998), more needs to be done to improve academic achievement and self-image of Aboriginal children. The number of Aboriginal children completing elementary school has risen from 63 to 76 per cent between 1981 and 1991. During this same time, the percentage completing high school has risen from 29 to 43 per cent (Frideres, 1998). The gaps between Aboriginal and non-Aboriginal completion rates are narrowing. However, self-perceived competence in the classroom is low, and contributes to difficulties that Aboriginal children experience when they attend majority-culture schools (Beiser, Sack Manson, Redshirt, & Dion, 1998).

Second-Language Education

Canada is an officially bilingual, French and English, multicultural nation, which celebrates its ethnic diversity as a cultural mosaic. Educating students to ensure proficiency in both official languages is encouraged in schools. Outside of Quebec, over 50 per cent of public school students in Canada are enrolled in either French immersion or regular French-language programs (Canadian Council on Social Development, 2001). With rising immigration, the proportion of schoolchildren who speak languages other than English or French at home has risen from 13 per cent in 1991 to 16 per cent in 1996 (CICH, 2000), with Ontario and British Columbia experiencing the greatest increases. Use of Aboriginal languages is also increasing (CICH, 2000). Similar trends exist in the United States and Western European countries, and schools there are also under pressure to meet the special needs of immigrant children. Whereas a main goal of most U.S. programs is to help non-English-speaking students learn English well enough to compete academically with native English speakers (NCES, 1996), the aim of Canadian and European programs is to help preserve students' cultural identity. The federal policy on multiculturalism was designed to ensure that every ethno-cultural group in Canada is able to maintain and enhance its cultural identity and values within the broader Canadian society (Friesen, 1995).

Some schools use an **English-immersion** approach, in which immigrant children are immersed in English from the beginning, in special classes. Other schools have adopted programs of **bilingual education,** in which children are taught in two languages, first learning in their native language with others who also speak it, and then switching to regular classes in English when they become more proficient in it. These programs can encourage children to become **bilingual** (fluent in two languages) and to feel pride in their cultural identity. **Heritage Language Programs** provide language and culture classes as a way for children to maintain and improve their native language abilities, and by doing so demonstrate that children's native languages are valued. When a child's first language is used and valued in schools, learning of a second language and academic achievement are enhanced (Swain & Lapkin, 1991; Genesee, 1987; Hakuta, 1986).

Advocates of early English-immersion claim that the sooner children are exposed to English and the more time they spend speaking it, the better they learn it (Rossel & Ross, 1986). Support for this view comes from findings that the effectiveness of second-language learning declines from early childhood through late adolescence (Newport, 1991). On the other hand, proponents of bilingual programs claim that children progress faster academically in their native language and later make a smoother transition to all-English classrooms (Padilla et al., 1991). Some educators maintain that the English-only approach stunts children's cognitive growth; because foreign-speaking children can understand only simple

Checkpoint ✓

Can you . . .

✔ Identify some ways of addressing cultural differences in the classroom?

Guidepost 6

How do schools meet the needs of non-English-speaking children and those with learning problems?

English immersion Approach to teaching English as a second language in which instruction is presented only in English

bilingual education System of teaching non-English-speaking children in their native language while they learn English, and later switching to all-English instruction

bilingual Fluent in two languages

Heritage Language Program Language classes given in the regular school day for children of immigrant background, designed to promote the home language and culture

English at first, the curriculum must be watered down, and children are less prepared to handle complex material later (Collier, 1995).

One of Canada's success stories is **French immersion**, which began in Montreal in the 1960s (Lambert & Tucker, 1972) and has spread across the country since. The program uses French as the language of instruction to English-speaking students living in English communities. Many studies have shown that French immersion is an effective way of teaching second-language skills to children. What is its effect on English-language skills? Research on French immersion has shown no negative effects on native language proficiency and academic achievement (Genesee, 1991), and longitudinal studies have demonstrated that, relative to those of non-immersion children, first-language skills seem to be enhanced by Grade 3 when basic proficiency in French is attained (Swain & Lapkin, 1991).

A study of 70,000 non-English-speaking students in high-quality second-language programs in five districts across the United States offers strong support for a bilingual approach (Collier, 1995; W. P. Thomas & Collier, 1997). The study compared not only English proficiency but also long-term academic achievement. In the primary grades, the type of language teaching made little difference; but from Grade 6 on, children who had remained in bilingual programs at least through Grade 6 caught up with or even surpassed their native English-speaking peers. At the same time, the relative performance of children who had been in traditional immersion programs began to decline. By the end of high school, those in part-time ESL (English language) programs trailed 80 per cent of native English speakers their age.

Most successful was a third, less common approach: **two-way, or dual-language learning,** in which English-speaking and foreign-speaking children learn together in their own and each other's languages. This approach avoids any need to place minority children in separate classes. By valuing both languages equally, it helps build self-esteem and thus improve school performance. An added advantage is that English speakers learn a foreign language at an early age, when they can acquire it most easily (Collier, 1995; W. P. Thomas & Collier, 1997, 1998). These findings echo earlier ones: The more bilingually proficient children are, the higher their cognitive and linguistic achievement—as long as school personnel value bilingualism and the second language is added at no sacrifice to the first (Diaz, 1983; Padilla et al., 1991).

A study of minority-language students in French-immersion programs in Ontario examined how well these children, who were also fluent in English, learned French in comparison with children whose first language was English. On all measures of grammar and oral language performance, minority-language students were superior to students of English background, while English-background students did better on measures of lexical (vocabulary) knowledge (Bild & Swain, 1989). The results indicate that learning a third language might be facilitated by other language learning—in this case, first learning of English by minority-language students. In a later study, students with a minority language and who read and write in their minority language were found to do better than English-background and non-literate minority-language students on most measures of French proficiency (Swain & Lapkin, 1991). Literacy, rather than oral language proficiency, in a minority language seemed to have a positive impact in learning a third language.

When bilingualism rises to the level of *biliteracy* (proficiency in reading and writing two languages), which makes possible full participation in both cultures, we see the most positive effects (Huang, 1995).

Children with Learning Problems

Some children, like Akira Kurosawa, are late bloomers when it comes to schoolwork. An unfortunate minority have serious learning problems.

Mental Retardation

Mental retardation is a clinical term for significantly subnormal cognitive functioning. In some fields like early childhood education and social work, the preferred term is *mentally challenged.* It is indicated by an IQ of about 70 or less, coupled with a deficiency in age-appropriate adaptive behaviour (such as communication, social skills, and self-care), appear-

French immersion Approach to teaching French as a second language in which English-speaking children are given instruction in French only

two-way (dual-language) learning Approach to second-language education in which English speakers and non-English speakers learn together in their own and each other's languages

Checkpoint

Can you . . .

✔ Describe and evaluate various types of second-language education?

mental retardation Significantly subnormal cognitive functioning

ing before age 18. Both IQ and behaviour are considered in making a diagnosis. About 1 per cent of the U.S. population are mentally retarded, about three boys for every two girls (American Psychiatric Association [APA], 1994).

In about 30 to 40 per cent of cases, the cause of mental retardation is unknown. Known causes (in declining order) include problems in embryonic development, such as those caused by a mother's alcohol or drug use; mental disorders, such as autism; environmental influences, such as lack of nurturance; problems in pregnancy and childbirth, such as fetal malnutrition or birth trauma; hereditary conditions, such as Tay-Sachs disease; and medical problems in childhood, such as trauma or lead poisoning (APA, 1994). Many cases of retardation may be preventable through genetic counselling, prenatal care, amniocentesis, routine screening and health care for newborns, and nutritional services for pregnant women and infants.

With a supportive and stimulating early environment and continued help and guidance, many mentally retarded children can expect a reasonably good outcome. Most retarded children can benefit from schooling. Intervention programs have helped many mildly or moderately retarded adults and those considered "borderline" (with IQs ranging from 70 up to about 85) to hold jobs, live in the community, and function fairly well in society. The profoundly retarded need constant care and supervision, usually in institutions. For some, daycare centres, hostels for retarded adults, and homemaking services for caregivers can be less costly and more humane alternatives.

Learning Disabilities

Nelson Rockefeller, former vice-president of the United States, had so much trouble reading that he ad libbed speeches instead of using a script. Rockefeller is one of many eminent persons, including the World War II hero General George Patton, the inventor Thomas Edison, the actor Whoopi Goldberg, the sculptor Auguste Rodin, and Leonardo da Vinci (Aaron & Guillemard, 1993) who reportedly have suffered from **dyslexia,** a developmental reading disorder in which reading achievement is substantially below the level predicted by IQ or age.

Dyslexia is the most commonly diagnosed of a large number of **learning disabilities (LDs),** disorders that interfere with specific aspects of school achievement, resulting in performance substantially lower than would be expected given a child's age, intelligence, and amount of schooling (APA, 1994). A growing number of children are classified as learning disabled (LD) (T. D. Snyder, Hoffman, & Geddes, 1997).

dyslexia Developmental disorder in which reading achievement is substantially lower than predicted by IQ or age

learning disabilities (LDs) Disorders that interfere with specific aspects of learning and school achievement

Children with dyslexia have trouble reading and writing, often demonstrating a more general language impairment.

Children with LDs often have near-average to higher-than-average intelligence and normal vision and hearing, but they seem to have trouble processing sensory information. They tend to be less task oriented and more easily distracted than other children; they are less well organized as learners and less likely to use memory strategies (Feagans, 1983). Learning disabilities can have devastating effects on self-esteem as well as on the report card.

Four out of five children with LDs have dyslexia. Estimates of its prevalence range from 5 to 17.5 per cent of the school population; it seems to affect boys and girls equally. It is generally considered to be a chronic, persistent medical condition. It is heritable and runs in families (S. E. Shaywitz, 1998).

The term *dyslexia* used to mean "mirror-reading" (saying "was" for "saw"), but now refers to any type of reading problem. Most cases are believed to result from a neurological defect in processing speech sounds: an inability to recognize that words consist of smaller units of sound, which are represented by printed letters. This defect in phonological processing makes it hard to decode words. Dyslexic children may also be weak in short-term verbal memory and other linguistic and cognitive skills (Morris et al., 1998; S. E. Shaywitz, 1998).

Brain imaging has revealed differences in the regions of the brain activated during phonological tasks in dyslexic as compared with normal readers (Horwitz, Rumsey, & Donohue, 1998; Shaywitz et al., 1998). In one such study, dyslexic boys used five times as much brain area to do oral language tasks as non-dyslexic boys. The researchers also found chemical differences in brain functioning (T. L. Richards et al., 1999).

Dyslexia does not go away. Although dyslexic children can be taught to read through systematic phonological training, the process never becomes automatic, as it does with most readers (S. E. Shaywitz, 1998).

Mathematical disabilities include difficulty in counting, comparing numbers, calculating, and remembering basic arithmetic facts. Each of these may involve distinct disabilities. One cause may be a neurological deficit.

Of course, not all children who have trouble with reading or arithmetic are learning disabled. Some haven't been taught properly, are anxious, have trouble reading or hearing directions, lack motivation to learn math, or have a developmental delay, which eventually disappears (Geary, 1993; Ginsburg, 1997; Roush, 1995).

Hyperactivity and Attention Deficits

Attention-deficit/hyperactivity disorder (ADHD) affects an estimated 2 to 11 per cent or more of school-age children worldwide (Zametkin & Ernst, 1999c). It is marked by persistent inattention, distractibility, impulsivity, low tolerance for frustration, and a great deal of activity at the wrong time and the wrong place, such as the classroom (APA, 1994). Boys are three to four times as likely to be diagnosed as girls (Barkley, 1998b; USDHHS, 1999c; Zametkin & Ernst, 1999). More than 1 in 4 children with learning disabilities has ADHD (Roush, 1995; Zametkin, 1995).

The disorder has two different sets of symptoms. Some children are inattentive but not hyperactive; others show the reverse pattern (USDHHS, 1999c). However, in 85 per cent of cases, the two kinds of behaviour go together (Barkley, 1998a). These characteristics appear to some degree in most children; there is cause for concern when they are unusually frequent and so severe that they interfere with the child's functioning in school and in daily life (AAP Committee on Children with Disabilities and Committee on Drugs, 1996; Barkley, 1998b; USDHHS, 1999c).

ADHD has a substantial genetic basis, with heritability approaching 80 per cent (APA, 1994; Barkley, 1998b; Elia, Ambrosini, & Rapoport, 1999; USDHHS, 1999c; Zametkin, 1995; Zametkin & Ernst, 1999). Perinatal complications that may play a part include premature birth, a prospective mother's alcohol or tobacco use, exposure to high levels of lead, and oxygen deprivation, which may lead to inadequate availability of the neurotransmitter dopamine (Barkley, 1998b; USDHHS, 1999c). However, the belief that ADHD children are brain-damaged has been discredited by brain-imaging studies (USDHHS, 1999c). Research has failed to substantiate any link between ADHD and food additives, such as artificial colourings and flavourings and the sugar substitute aspartame—or, for that matter, sugar itself (Barkley, 1998b; B. A. Shaywitz et al., 1994; Zametkin, 1995).

attention-deficit/hyperactivity disorder (ADHD) Syndrome characterized by persistent inattention and distractibility, impulsivity, low tolerance for frustration, and inappropriate overactivity

Imaging studies do suggest that children with ADHD have unusually small brain structures in the prefrontal cortex and basal ganglia, the regions that inhibit impulses and regulate attention and self-control. Children with ADHD tend to forget responsibilities, to speak aloud rather than giving themselves silent directions, to be easily frustrated or angered, and to give up when they don't see how to solve a problem. Parents and teachers may be able to help these children by giving them a structured environment: breaking down tasks into small "chunks," providing frequent prompts about rules and time, and giving frequent, immediate rewards for small accomplishments (Barkley, 1998b).

Although symptoms tend to decline with age, ADHD often persists into adolescence and adulthood and, if untreated, can lead to excessive injuries, academic problems, antisocial behaviour, risky driving, substance abuse, and anxiety or depression (Barkley, 1998b; Barkley, Murphy, & Kwasnik, 1996; Elia et al., 1999; McGee, Partridge, Williams, & Silva, 1991; USDHHS, 1999c; Wender, 1995; Zametkin, 1995).

ADHD is generally treated with drugs, sometimes combined with behavioural therapy, counselling, training in social skills, and special classroom placement. Psychotropic stimulants such as Ritalin, used in proper doses, appear to be safe and effective in the short run, but long-term effects are unknown (AAP Committee on Children with Disabilities and Committee on Drugs, 1996; Elia et al., 1999; NIH, 1998; Rodrigues, 1999; USDHHS, 1999c; Zametkin, 1995; Zametkin & Ernst, 1999). A 14-month randomized study of 579 children with ADHD found a carefully monitored program of Ritalin treatment, alone or in combination with behaviour modification, more effective than the behavioural therapy alone or standard community care (MTA Cooperative Group, 1999).

A disturbing trend is the increasing use of drugs such as Ritalin on preschoolers, even though their effectiveness on children that young has not been shown, and despite concerns about effects on the developing brain. The number of Ritalin pills dispensed in Canada has increased dramatically, more than doubling between 1994 and 1998 (CICH, 2000). A B.C. study found that there were significant disparities in the prevalence of Ritalin prescriptions across the regions of the province, and that children from lower-SES families were more likely to be prescribed Ritalin than children from more prosperous families (Miller, 2001).

Educating Children with Disabilities

Unlike the United States, which has national legislation ensuring appropriate education for all children with disabilities, Canada has no such national legislation. Education for children with disabilities is administered by the province or territory. In general, where there are provisions for providing appropriate services, an individual education plan is designed for each child, with parental involvement. Children are educated in the "least restrictive environment" appropriate to their needs: that means, whenever possible, the regular classroom. Many of these students can be served by "inclusion" programs, in which they are integrated with non-disabled children for all or part of the day. Inclusion can help children with disabilities learn to get along in society and can let non-disabled children know and understand people with disabilities. About 16 per cent of all school-age children in Canada have a disability (Winzer, 1996), 25 per cent of whom are educated outside of the regular school system (Wizner, 1997). Although most educators favour integrating children with disabilities into regular classrooms, two general approaches have emerged. The first is mainstreaming integration, which involves providing complete services to meet the needs of children with disabilities in the least restrictive environment possible. The second approach is inclusive integration in regular classrooms in children's neighbourhood schools, which would eliminate any segregation of children with disabilities from the regular classroom, and would involve altering the physical structure of schools to accommodate children with disabilites. Most provinces and territories currently favour implementing the mainstreaming integration approach (Doré, Wagner, Brunet, & Bélanger, 1999).

A potential problem with inclusion is that children with learning disabilities may be evaluated by unrealistic standards, resulting in their being held back and made to repeat grades. This has already happened on a large scale in some schools, despite evidence that retention is ineffective even with children of normal abilities (McLeskey et al., 1995).

Checkpoint

Can you . . .

✔ Describe the causes and prognoses for three common types of conditions that interfere with learning?

Checkpoint

Can you . . .

✔ Discuss the impact of provincial and territorial requirements for the education of children with disabilities?

Gifted Children

Giftedness, like intelligence, is hard to define and measure. Educators disagree on who qualifies as gifted and on what basis, and what kinds of educational programs these children need. Another source of confusion is that creativity and artistic talent are sometimes viewed as aspects or types of giftedness and sometimes as independent of it (Gardner, 2000; Hunsaker & Callahan, 1995).

Identifying Gifted Children

The traditional criterion of giftedness is high general intelligence, as shown by an IQ score of 130 or higher. This definition tends to exclude highly creative children (whose unusual answers often lower their test scores), children from minority groups (whose abilities may not be well developed, though the potential is there), and children with specific aptitudes (who may be only average or even show learning problems in other areas). Most provinces and school boards have therefore adopted a broader definition, which includes children who have shown high *potential* or *achievement* in one or more of the following: general intellect, specific aptitude (such as in mathematics or science), creative or productive thinking, leadership, talent in the arts (such as painting, writing, music, or acting), and psychomotor ability (Cassidy & Hossler, 1992). Many school districts now use multiple criteria for admission to programs for the gifted, including achievement test scores, grades, classroom performance, creative production, parent and teacher nominations, and student interviews; but IQ remains an important, and sometimes the determining, factor (Reis, 1989).

The Lives of Gifted Children

A classic longitudinal study of gifted children began in 1921, when Lewis M. Terman (who brought the Binet intelligence test to the United States) identified more than 1,500 California children with IQs of 135 or higher. The study demolished the widespread stereotype of the bright child as a puny, pasty-faced bookworm. These children were taller, healthier, better coordinated, better adjusted, and more popular than the average child (Wallach & Kogan, 1965), and their cognitive, scholastic, and vocational superiority has held up for nearly 80 years (Terman & Oden, 1959).

On the other hand, none of Terman's sample grew up to be Einsteins or Kurosawas, and those with the highest IQs became no more illustrious than those who were only moderately gifted. This lack of a close correlation between childhood giftedness and adult eminence has been supported by later research (Winner, 1997).

Mahito Takahashi of New Jersey made a perfect score in a worldwide mathematics Olympiad and has won close to 200 other awards. A well-rounded youngster, he sings in a chamber choir and acted in a school product on of Shakespeare's *Romeo and Juliet.* The key to helping such children achieve lies in recognizing and nurturing their natural gifts.

Guidepost 7

How is giftedness assessed and nurtured?

Checkpoint ✓

Can you . . .

✔ Tell how gifted children are identified?

Defining and Measuring Creativity

In Kurosawa's directorial debut in *Sanshiro Saguto* in 1943, he surprised audiences and critics by combining traditional Japanese samurai themes with tension-building techniques from American action movies. Throughout his career, innovation was his hallmark.

One definition of *creativity* is the ability to see things in a new light—to produce something never seen before or to discern problems others fail to recognize and find new and unusual solutions. High creativity and high academic intelligence (or IQ) do not necessarily go hand in hand. Classic research found only modest correlations (Anastasi & Schaefer, 1971; Getzels, 1964, 1984; Getzels & Jackson, 1962, 1963).

J. P. Guilford (1956, 1959, 1960, 1967, 1986) distinguished between two kinds of thinking: *convergent* and *divergent*. **Convergent thinking**—the kind IQ tests measure—seeks a single correct answer; **divergent thinking** comes up with a wide array of fresh possibilities. Tests of creativity call for divergent thinking. The Torrance Tests of Creative Thinking (Torrance, 1966, 1974; Torrance & Ball, 1984), among the most widely known tests of creativity, include such tasks as listing unusual uses for a paper clip, completing a figure, and writing down what a sound brings to mind.

One problem with many of these tests is that the score depends partly on speed, which is not a hallmark of creativity. Moreover, although the tests yield fairly reliable results, there is dispute over whether they are valid—whether they identify children who are creative in everyday life (Anastasi, 1988; Mansfield & Busse, 1981; Simonton, 1990). As Guilford recognized, divergent thinking may not be the only, or even the most important, factor in creative performance.

Educating Gifted, Creative, and Talented Children

Most provinces have special programs for the gifted; about 6 per cent of public school children participate (Winzer, 1996). They generally follow one of two approaches: *enrichment* or *acceleration*. **Enrichment** broadens and deepens knowledge and skills through extra classroom activities, research projects, field trips, or coaching by experts. **Acceleration,** often recommended for highly gifted children, speeds up their education by early school entrance, by grade skipping, by placement in fast-paced classes, or by advanced courses in specific subjects. Moderate acceleration does not seem to harm social adjustment, at least in the long run (Winner, 1997).

Children in gifted programs not only make academic gains but also tend to improve in self-concept and social adjustment (Ford & Harris, 1996). However, competition for funding and opposition to "elitism" threatens the continuation of these programs (Purcell, 1995; Winner, 1997). Some educators advocate moving away from an all-or-nothing definition of giftedness and including a wider range of students in more flexible programs (J. Cox, Daniel, & Boston, 1985; Feldhusen, 1992; R. D. Feldman, 1985). Some say that if the level of education were significantly improved for all children, only the most exceptional would need special classes (Winner, 1997).

There is no firm dividing line between being gifted and not being gifted, creative and not creative. All children benefit from being encouraged in their areas of interest and ability. What we learn about fostering intelligence, creativity, and talent in the most able children may help all children make the most of their potential. The degree to which they do this will affect their self-concept and other aspects of personality, as we discuss in chapter 14.

convergent thinking Thinking aimed at finding the one "right" answer to a problem

divergent thinking Thinking that produces a variety of fresh, diverse possibilities

enrichment Approach to educating the gifted, which broadens and deepens knowledge and skills through extra activities, projects, field trips, or mentoring

acceleration Approach to educating the gifted, which moves them through a curriculum at an unusually rapid pace

Checkpoint ✔

Can you . . .

✔ Discuss the relationships between giftedness and life achievements, and between IQ and creativity?

✔ Describe two approaches to education of gifted children?

What's your view ?

• Would you favour strengthening, cutting back, or eliminating special educational programs for gifted students?

Summary and Key Terms

Piagetian Approach: The Concrete Operational Child

Guidepost 1 How do school-age children's thinking and moral reasoning differ from those of younger children?

- A child from about age 7 to age 12 is in the stage of concrete operations. Children are less egocentric than before and are more proficient at tasks requiring logical reasoning, such as spatial thinking, understanding of causality, categorization, inductive and deductive reasoning, conservation, and working with numbers. However, their reasoning is largely limited to the here and now.

- Cultural experience, as well as neurological development, seems to contribute to the rate of development of conservation and other Piagetian skills.

- According to Piaget, moral development is linked with cognitive maturation and occurs in two stages: morality of constraint and morality of cooperation.

  concrete operations (315)   **seriation (316)**
  transitive inference (316)   **class inclusion (316)**
  inductive reasoning (316)   **deductive reasoning (317)**
  horizontal décalage (317)   **morality of constraint (319)**
  morality of cooperation (319)

Information-Processing Approach: Memory and Other Processing Skills

Guidepost 2 What advances in memory and other information-processing skills occur during middle childhood?

- Information-processing models describe three steps in memory: encoding, storage, and retrieval.

- Although sensory memory shows little change with age, the capacity of working memory increases greatly during middle childhood. The central executive, which controls the flow of information to and from long-term memory, seems to mature between ages 8 and 10. Reaction time, processing speed, selective attention, and concentration also increase. These gains in information-processing abilities may help explain the advances Piaget described.

- Metamemory, selective attention, and use of mnemonic strategies improve during these years.

  encoding (320)   **storage (320)**   **retrieval (320)**
  sensory memory (320)   **working memory (320)**
  central executive (320)   **long-term memory (321)**
  metamemory (321)   **mnemonic strategies (321)**
  external memory aids (321)   **rehearsal (321)**
  organization (321)   **elaboration (322)**

Psychometric Approach: Assessment Of Intelligence

Guidepost 3 How accurately can schoolchildren's intelligence be measured?

- The intelligence of school-age children is assessed by group or individual tests. Although intended as aptitude tests, they are validated against measures of achievement.

- IQ tests are fairly good predictors of school success but may be unfair to some children.

- Differences in IQ among ethnic groups appear to result to a considerable degree from socio-economic and other environmental differences. Schooling seems to increase measured intelligence.

- Attempts to devise culture-free or culture-fair tests have been unsuccessful.

- IQ tests tap only three of the "intelligences" in Howard Gardner's theory of multiple intelligences. According to Robert Sternberg's triarchic theory, IQ tests mainly measure the componential element of intelligence, not the experiential and contextual elements.

- New directions in intelligence testing include the Kaufman Assessment Battery for Children (K-ABC) and the Sternberg Triarchic Abilities Tests (STAT).

  aptitude tests (323)   **achievement tests (323)**
  Otis-Lennon School Ability Test (323)
  Wechsler Intelligence Scale for Children (WISC–III) (323)
  cultural bias (325)   **culture-free (325)**   **culture-fair (325)**
  theory of multiple intelligences (326)
  triarchic theory of intelligence (327)   **componential element (327)**
  experiential element (327)   **contextual element (327)**
  Kaufman Assessment Battery for Children (K-ABC) (327)
  Sternberg Triarchic Abilities Test (STAT) (327)

Language and Literacy

Guidepost 4 How do communicative abilities expand during middle childhood?

- Use of vocabulary, grammar, and syntax become increasingly sophisticated, but the major area of linguistic growth is in pragmatics.

- Metacognition contributes to progress in reading.

- Despite the popularity of whole-language programs, early phonics training is a key to reading proficiency.

- Interaction with peers fosters development of writing skills.

  metacognition (330)

The Child in School

Guidepost 5 What influences school achievement?

- Because schooling is cumulative, the foundation laid in Grade 1 is very important.

- Parents influence children's learning by becoming involved in their schooling, motivating them to achieve, and transmitting attitudes about learning. Socio-economic status can influence parental beliefs and practices that, in turn, influence achievement.

- Although the power of the self-fulfilling prophecy may not be as great as was once thought, teachers' perceptions and expectations can have a strong influence.

- Historical philosophical shifts affect such issues as amount of homework assigned, methods of teaching math, social promotion, and computer literacy.

- The superior achievement of children of East Asian extraction seems to stem from cultural factors. Minority children may benefit from educational programs adapted to their cultural styles.

self-fulfilling prophecy (333) social promotion (334)

Guidepost 6 How do schools meet the needs of non-English-speaking children and those with learning problems?

- Methods of second-language education are controversial. Issues include speed and facility with English, long-term achievement in academic subjects, and pride in cultural identity.

- French immersion, a Canadian innovation, is effective in teaching French in English-language communities, while at the same time not adversely affecting English-language proficiency or academic achievement.

- Three frequent sources of learning problems are mental retardation, learning disabilities (LDs), and attention-deficit/hyperactivity disorder (ADHD). Dyslexia is the most common learning disability.

- In Canada, all children with disabilities are entitled to a free, appropriate education. However, because there is no national legislation, the specific provisions for educating children with disabilities vary from province to province.

English-immersion (338)   bilingual education (338)
bilingual (338)   Heritage Language Program (338)
French immersion (339) two-way (dual-language) learning (339)
mental retardation (339)   dyslexia (340)
learning disabilities (LDs) (340)
attention-deficit/hyperactivity disorder (ADHD) (341)

Guidepost 7 How is giftedness assessed and nurtured?

- An IQ of 130 or higher is a common standard for identifying gifted children. Broader definitions include creativity, artistic talent, and other attributes and rely on multiple criteria for identification. Minorities are under-represented in programs for the gifted.

- In Terman's classic longitudinal study of gifted children, most turned out to be well adjusted and successful, but not outstandingly so.

- Creativity and IQ are *not* closely linked. Tests of creativity seek to measure divergent thinking, but their validity has been questioned.

- Special educational programs for gifted, creative, and talented children stress enrichment or acceleration.

convergent thinking (344)   divergent thinking (344)
enrichment (344)   acceleration (344)

OLC Preview

Supplementing the boxed material in this chapter, the official website for *A Child's World*, First Canadian Edition, offers additional information and links to recommended websites on topics such as "The Homework Debate" and "The Math Wars." Check out **www.mcgrawhill.ca/college/papalia**.

Psychosocial Development in Middle Childhood

Have you ever felt like nobody?
Just a tiny speck of air.
When everyone's around you,
And you are just not there.

—Karen Crawford, age 9

Focus *Marian Anderson, Operatic Trailblazer**

Marian Anderson

The African-American contralto Marian Anderson (1902–1993) had—in the words of the great Italian conductor Arturo Toscanini—a voice heard "once in a hundred years." She was also a pioneer in breaking racial barriers. Turned away by a music school in her hometown of Philadelphia, she studied voice privately and in 1925 won a national competition to sing with the New York Philharmonic. When she was refused the use of a concert hall in Washington, D.C., First Lady Eleanor Roosevelt arranged for her to sing on the steps of the Lincoln Memorial. The unprecedented performance on Easter Sunday, 1939, drew 75,000 people and was broadcast to millions. Several weeks later, Marian Anderson was the first black singer to perform at the White House. But not until 1955 did Anderson, at age 57, become the first person of her race to sing with New York's Metropolitan Opera.

A remarkable story lies behind this woman's "journey from a single rented room in South Philadelphia" (McKay, 1992, p. xxx). It is a story of nurturing family ties—bonds of mutual support, care, and concern that extended from generation to generation.

Marian Anderson was the eldest of three children of John and Annie Anderson. Two years after her birth, the family left their one-room apartment to move in with her father's parents and then into a small rented house nearby.

At the age of 6, Marian joined the junior choir at church. There she made a friend, Viola Johnson, who lived across the street from the Andersons. Within a year or two, they sang a duet together—Marian's first public performance.

When Marian was 10, her beloved father died, and the family again moved in with his parents, his sister, and her two daughters. Marian's grandfather had a steady job. Her grandmother took care of all the children, her aunt ran the house, and her mother contributed by cooking dinners, working as a cleaning woman, and taking in laundry, which Marian and her sister Alyce delivered.

The most important influence in Marian Anderson's life was the counsel, example, and spiritual guidance of her hardworking, unfailingly supportive mother. Annie Anderson placed great importance on her children's schooling and saw to it that they didn't skimp on homework. Even when she was working full time, she cooked their dinner every night, and she taught Marian to sew her own clothes. "Not once can I recall . . . hearing Mother lift her voice

*The chief source of biographical material about Marian Anderson and her family was Anderson (1992). Some details come from Kernan (1993) and from obituaries published in *Time* (April 19, 1993), *People Weekly*, *The New Yorker*, and *Jet* (April 26, 1993).

to us in anger . . . ," Marian wrote. "She could be firm, and we learned to respect her wishes" (Anderson, 1992, p. 92).

When Marian Anderson became a world-renowned concert artist, she often returned to her old neighbourhood in Philadelphia. Her mother and sister Alyce shared a modest house, and the other sister, Ethel, lived next door with her son.

"It is the pleasantest thing in the world to go into that home and feel its happiness, . . . " the singer wrote. "They are all comfortable, and they cherish and protect one another. . . . I know that it warms [Mother] to have her grandson near her as he grows up, just as I think that when he gets to be a man, making his own life, he will have pleasant memories of his home and family" (1992, p. 93). In 1992, Marian Anderson—widowed, childless, and frail at age 95—went to live with that nephew, James DePriest, then music director of the Oregon Symphony. She died of a stroke at his home the following year.

• • •

Marian Anderson experienced significant cultural changes, but one thing that never changed was the strong, supportive network of relationships that sustained her and her family. The kind of household a child lives in, and the relationships within the household, can have profound effects on psychosocial development in middle childhood, when children are developing a stronger sense of what it means to be responsible, contributing members, first of a family, and then of society. The family is part of a web of contextual influences, including the peer group, the school, and the neighbourhood in which the family lives. Marian Anderson's first friend, her church choir, and the neighbours for whom she did odd jobs to earn the price of a violin all played parts in her development.

In this chapter, we trace the rich and varied emotional and social lives of school-age children. We see how children develop a more realistic concept of themselves and how they become more independent, self-reliant, and in control of their emotions. Through being with peers they make discoveries about their own attitudes, values, and skills. Still, as Anderson's story shows, the family remains a vital influence. Children's lives are affected, not only by the way parents approach the task of child raising, but by whether and how they are employed, by the family's economic circumstances, and by its structure, or composition—whether the child lives with one parent or two; whether or not the child has siblings, and how many; and whether or not the household includes other relatives, such as Anderson's grandparents, aunt, and cousins. Although most children are emotionally healthy, some have mental health problems; we look at several of these. We also describe resilient children, who emerge from the stresses of childhood healthier and stronger.

After you have read and studied this chapter, you should be able to answer each of the Guidepost questions that appear at the top of the next page. Look for them again in the margins, where they point to important concepts throughout the chapter. To check your understanding of these Guideposts, review the end-of-chapter summary. Checkpoints throughout the chapter will help you verify your understanding of what you have read.

Guideposts for Study

1. How do school-age children develop a realistic self-concept, and what contributes to self-esteem?

2. How do school-age children show emotional growth?

3. How do parent–child relationships change in middle childhood?

4. What are the effects of parents' work and of poverty on family atmosphere?

5. What impact does family structure have on children's development?

6. How do siblings influence and get along with one another?

7. How do relationships with peers change in middle childhood, and what influences popularity and choice of friends?

8. What are the most common forms of aggressive behaviour in middle childhood, and what influences contribute to it?

9. What are some common emotional disturbances, and how are they treated?

10. How do the stresses of modern life affect children, and what enables "resilient" children to withstand them?

The Developing Self

Guidepost 1

How do school-age children develop a realistic self-concept, and what contributes to self-esteem?

The cognitive growth that takes place during middle childhood enables children to develop more complex concepts of themselves and to grow in emotional understanding and control.

Representational Systems: A Neo-Piagetian View

Judgments about the self become more realistic, more balanced, more comprehensive, and more consciously expressed in middle childhood (Harter, 1996, 1998). Around age 7 or 8, children reach the third of the neo-Piagetian stages of self-concept development described in chapter 11. Children now have the cognitive ability to form **representational systems:** broad, inclusive self-concepts that integrate different aspects of the self (Harter, 1993, 1996, 1998).

representational systems In neo-Piagetian terminology, the third stage in development of self-definition, characterized by breadth, balance, and the integration and assessment of aspects of the self

"At school I'm feeling pretty smart in certain subjects, Language Arts and Social Studies," says 8-year-old Lisa. "I got A's in these subjects on my last report card and was really proud of myself. But I'm feeling really dumb in Arithmetic and Science, particularly when I see how well the other kids are doing. . . . I still like myself as a person, because Arithmetic and Science just aren't that important to me. How I look and how popular I am are more important" (Harter, 1996, p. 208).

Lisa's self-description shows that she can focus on more than one dimension of herself. She has outgrown an all-or-nothing, black-or-white self-definition; she recognizes that she can be "smart" in certain subjects and "dumb" in others. Her self-descriptions are more balanced; she can verbalize her self-concept better, and she can weigh different aspects of it ("How I look and how popular I am are more important"). She can compare her *real self* with her *ideal self* and can judge how well she measures up to social standards in comparison with others. All of these changes contribute to the development of self-esteem, her assessment of her *global self-worth* ("I like myself as a person").

Self-esteem

According to Erikson (1982), a major determinant of self-esteem is children's view of their capacity for productive work. The issue to be resolved in the crisis of middle

Middle childhood, according to Erikson, is a time for learning the skills one's culture considers important. In driving geese to market, this Vietnamese girl is developing a sense of competence and gaining self-esteem.

industry versus inferiority
Erikson's fourth critical alternative of psychosocial development, in which children must learn the productive skills their culture requires or else face feelings of inferiority

childhood is **industry versus inferiority.** The "virtue" that develops with successful resolution of this crisis is *competence,* a view of the self as able to master skills and complete tasks.

Children have to learn skills valued in their society. Arapesh boys in New Guinea learn to make bows and arrows and to lay traps for rats; Arapesh girls learn to plant, weed, and harvest. Inuit children learn to hunt and fish. Children in industrialized countries learn to read, write, count, and use computers. Like Marian Anderson, many children learn household skills and help out with odd jobs. Children compare their abilities with those of their peers; if they feel inadequate, they may retreat to the protective embrace of the family. If, on the other hand, they become too industrious, they may neglect social relationships and turn into "workaholics."

A different view of the sources of self-worth comes from research by Susan Harter (1985, 1990, 1993). Harter (1985) asked 8- to 12-year olds to rate their appearance, behaviour, school performance, athletic ability, and acceptance by other children and to assess how much each of these areas affected their opinion of themselves. The children rated physical appearance most important. Social acceptance came next. Less critical were schoolwork, conduct, and athletics. In contrast, then, to the high value Erikson placed on mastery of skills, Harter suggests that today's school-age children, at least in North America, judge themselves more by good looks and popularity.

A major contributor to self-esteem is social support—first, from parents and classmates, then from friends and teachers. Do they like and care about the child? Do they treat the child as a person who matters and has valuable things to say? Even if Mike thinks it's important to be handsome and smart and considers himself both, his self-esteem will suffer if he does not feel valued by the important people in his life. Still, social support generally will not compensate for a low self-evaluation. If Anne-Marie thinks sports are important but that she is not athletic, she will lose self-esteem no matter how much praise she gets from others.

Children who are socially withdrawn or isolated may be overly concerned about their performance in social situations. They may attribute rejection to their own personality deficiencies, which they believe they are helpless to change. Rather than trying new ways to gain approval, they repeat unsuccessful strategies or just give up. (This is similar to the "helpless pattern" in younger children, described in chapter 11.) Children with high self-esteem, by contrast, tend to attribute failure to factors outside themselves or to the need to try harder. If initially unsuccessful, they persevere, trying new strategies until they find one that works (Erdley, Cain, Loomis, Dumas-Hines, & Dweck, 1997).

Checkpoint ✔

Can you . . .

✔ From a neo-Piagetian perspective, tell how the self-concept develops in middle childhood as compared with early childhood?

✔ Compare Erikson's and Harter's views about sources of self-esteem?

✔ Describe how the "helpless pattern" can affect children's reactions to social rejection?

Emotional Growth

Guidepost 2

How do school-age children show emotional growth?

As children grow older, they are more aware of their own and other people's feelings. They can better regulate their emotional expression in social situations, and they can respond to others' emotional distress (Saarni et al., 1998).

By age 7 or 8, children typically feel shame and pride (refer back to chapter 11). These emotions, which depend on awareness of the implications of their actions and on what kind of socialization children have received, affect their opinion of themselves (Harter, 1993, 1996). Children can also verbalize conflicting emotions. As Lisa says, "Most of the boys at school are pretty yukky. I don't feel that way about my little brother Jason, although he does get on my nerves. I love him but at the same time, he also does things that make me mad. But I control my temper. I'd be ashamed of myself if I didn't" (Harter, 1996, p. 208).

Children become more empathic and more inclined to pro-social behaviour in middle childhood. Pro-social behaviour is a sign of positive adjustment. Pro-social children tend to act appropriately in social situations, to be relatively free from negative emotion, and to cope with problems constructively (Eisenberg, Fabes, & Murphy, 1996).

Control of negative emotions is an aspect of emotional growth. Children learn what makes them angry, fearful, or sad and how other people react to a display of these emotions, and they learn to adapt their behaviour accordingly. They also learn the difference between having an emotion and expressing it. Kindergartners believe that a parent can make a child less sad by telling the child to stop crying, or can make a child less afraid of a dog by telling the child there is nothing to be afraid of. Students in Grade 6 know that an emotion may be suppressed, but it still exists (Rotenberg & Eisenberg, 1997).

Parents' reactions to children's displays of feelings affect emotional development. The quality of the child's relationship with the parents can have a profound effect on the development of pro-social behaviours: empathy and altruism. Parents who nurture a secure attachment and demonstrate empathy in the home tend to promote those qualities in their children (Eisenberg, 2002; Mussen & Eisenberg, 2001). Children whose mothers encourage them to express feelings constructively and help them focus on solving the root problem tend to cope more effectively and have better social skills than children whose mothers devalue their feelings by minimizing the seriousness of the situation (Eisenberg et al., 1996). Parents who acknowledge and legitimize children's own feelings of distress encourage empathy and pro-social development (Bryant, 1987). Children whose parents show disapproval of, or punish, negative emotions learn to hide such emotions—but may become anxious in situations that evoke them.

As children approach early adolescence, parents' intolerance of negative emotion may heighten parent–child conflict (Eisenberg, Fabes, et al., 1999). As we'll see in the next section, this is one of many ways in which the family environment affects children's development.

Checkpoint ✓

Can you . . .

✔ Identify some aspects of emotional growth in middle childhood and tell how parental treatment may affect children's handling of negative emotions?

The Child in the Family

Guidepost 3

How do parent–child relationships change in middle childhood?

School-age children spend more time away from home than when they were younger and become less close to their parents (Hofferth, 1998). With the upsurge in dual-earner and single-parent families, greater emphasis on education, and the faster pace of family life, children spend more time at school or in child care and in organized activities than a generation ago. They have less free time for unstructured play, outdoor activities, and leisurely family dinners. Much of the time parents and children spend together is task-centred: shopping, preparing meals, cleaning house, and doing homework (Hofferth & Sandberg, 1998; 2001). Still, home and the people who live there remain an important part of a child's life.

To understand the child in the family we need to look at the family environment—its atmosphere and structure. These in turn are affected by what goes on beyond the walls of the home. As Bronfenbrenner's theory describes (refer back to chapter 2), additional layers of influence—including parents' work and socio-economic status and societal trends such as urbanization, changes in family size, divorce, and remarriage—help shape the family environment and, thus, children's development.

One of the most important influences on a child's development is the atmosphere in the home. Loving, supportive parents who enjoy being with their children, like this mother, are likely to raise children who feel good about themselves—and about their parents.

Beyond these influences are cultural experiences and values that define rhythms of family life and roles of family members. Children generally are socialized differently in ethnic minority families and in white families. For example, although there are more similarities than differences, Aboriginal parents tend to have a more liberal approach to child rearing than do non-Aboriginal parents (Gfellner, 1990). In addition, the way in which children are brought up in immigrant families might be reflected in values that children express, in comparison with their non-immigrant peers. In an Ottawa-Hull study of children from different ethnic groups, differences in values were found. Although English, French, and Italian 10- to 12-year-olds demonstrated similar perspectives on self-esteem, children of English background had an individualist orientation, children of French background had a family orientation, and children of Italian background were most peer-oriented (Lortie-Lussier, & Fellers, 1991). The experience that children of Italian background have of assimilating into mainstream culture may be reflected in these outcomes (Lortie-Lussier et al., 1991).

As we look at the child in the family, then, we need to be aware of outside influences that impinge upon it.

Family Atmosphere

The most important influences of the family environment on children's development come from the atmosphere within the home. Is it supportive and loving, or conflict-ridden? Does the family have enough money to provide for basic needs? Often these two facets of family atmosphere are related.

Parenting Issues: Co-regulation and Discipline

As children's lives change, so do the issues between them and their parents, and the ways in which issues are resolved. During the course of childhood, control of behaviour gradually shifts from parents to child.

co-regulation Transitional stage in the control of behaviour in which parents exercise general supervision and children exercise moment-to-moment self-regulation

Middle childhood is the transitional stage of **co-regulation,** in which parent and child share power: Parents oversee, but children exercise moment-to-moment self-regulation (Maccoby, 1984). In problems with peers, for example, parents now rely less on direct management or supervision and more on consultation and discussion with their own child (Parke & Buriel, 1998). Children are more apt to follow their parents' wishes or advice when they recognize that the parents are fair and are concerned about the child's welfare and that they may "know better" because of experience. It also helps if parents try to defer to children's maturing judgment and take strong stands only on important issues (Maccoby, 1984).

The way parents and children resolve conflicts may be more important than the specific outcomes. If family conflict is constructive, it can help children see the need for rules and standards of behaviour. They also learn what kinds of issues are worth arguing about and what strategies can be effective (A. R. Eisenberg, 1996). If, however, parents use verbal aggression with their children, the children tend to have lower self-esteem and lower school grades (Solomon & Serres, 1999).

As children become preadolescents, and their striving for autonomy becomes more insistent, the quality of family problem-solving and negotiation often deteriorates. In one study, 63 two-parent families with Grade 4 children videotaped home discussions of two problems (for example, over allowance, bedtime, or chores) that had come up within the past month—one topic of the child's choosing and one of the parents' choosing. The families repeated the procedure two years later. Between the ages of 9 and 11, the children's participation became more negative, especially when discussing topics the parents had chosen. It made no difference what the topic was; the basic issue, apparently, was "who is in charge" (Vuchinich, Angelelli, & Gatherum, 1996).

The shift to co-regulation affects how parents handle discipline (Maccoby, 1984; Roberts, Block, & Block, 1984). Parents of school-age children are more likely to use inductive techniques that include reasoning. For example, 8-year-old Jared's father points out how his actions affect others: "Hitting Jermaine hurts him and makes him feel bad." In other situations, Jared's parents may appeal to his self-esteem ("What happened to the helpful boy who was here yesterday?"), sense of humour ("If you go one more day without a bath, we'll know when you're coming without looking!"), moral values ("A big, strong boy like you shouldn't sit on the train and let an old person stand"), or appreciation ("Aren't you glad that your father cares enough to remind you to wear boots so that you won't catch a cold?"). Above all, Jared's parents let him know he must bear the consequences of his behaviour ("No wonder you missed the school bus today—you stayed up too late last night! Now you'll have to walk to school").

Effects of Parents' Work

With more than 60 per cent of all Canadian women with children 3 years of age or over employed (Statistics Canada, 2002a), many children are unlikely to have any memory of a time when their mothers were *not* working for pay. By the time children reach school age, almost 80 per cent of Canadian mothers are working outside of the home (Canadian Council on Social Development, 2001).

The impact of a mother's work outside the home depends on many factors, including the child's age, sex, temperament, and personality; whether the mother works full- or part-time; why she is working, and how she feels about her work; whether she has a supportive or unsupportive mate, or none; the family's socio-economic status; and the kind of care the child receives before and/or after school (Parke & Buriel, 1998).

Some children are supervised after school by babysitters or relatives; some go to structured programs, either at school or in child-care settings. Like good child care for preschoolers, good after-school programs have relatively low enrolment, low child–staff ratios, and well-educated staff (Rosenthal & Vandell, 1996). Children, especially boys, in organized after-school programs marked by flexible programming and a positive emotional climate tended to adjust better in Grade 1 (Pierce, Hamm, & Vandell, 1999).

Eight per cent of 8- to 10-year-olds and 23 per cent of 11- and 12-year-olds in a nationally representative sample of 1,500 U.S. children regularly care for themselves at home without adult supervision. However, each child spends an average of only 1 hour alone each day (Hofferth & Jankuniene, 2000). This arrangement is advisable only for older children who are mature, responsible, and resourceful and know how to get help in an emergency, and if a parent stays in touch by telephone.

Often a single mother like Marian Anderson's must work to stave off economic disaster. How her working affects her children may hinge on how much time and energy she has left over to spend with them and what sort of role model she provides (B. L. Barber & Eccles, 1992)—clearly, a positive one in Annie Anderson's case.

The more satisfied a mother is with her employment status, the more effective she is likely to be as a parent (Parke & Buriel, 1998). School-age children of employed mothers tend to live in more structured homes than children of full-time homemakers, with clear-cut rules giving them more household responsibilities. They are also encouraged to be more independent (Bronfenbrenner & Crouter, 1982), and they have more egalitarian attitudes about gender roles (Parke & Buriel, 1998).

How does maternal employment affect school achievement? Both boys and girls in low-income families seem to benefit academically from the more favourable environment a working mother's income can provide (Goldberg, Greenberger, & Nagel, 1996; Vandell & Ramanan, 1992). In middle-class families, however, sons of working mothers tend to do less well in school than sons of homemakers, whereas daughters usually do as well or better when mothers work (Goldberg et al., 1996; Heyns & Catsambis, 1986). These gender differences in middle-class families may have to do with boys' greater need for supervision and guidance (Goldberg et al., 1996). Independence seems to help girls to become more competent, to achieve more in school, and to have higher self-esteem (Bronfenbrenner & Crouter, 1982).

Checkpoint

Can you . . .

✔ Describe how co-regulation works and how discipline and the handling of family conflict change during middle childhood?

Guidepost 4

What are the effects of parents' work and of poverty on family atmosphere?

"Latchkey" children who care for themselves after school while parents work, like this brother and sister, should be mature, responsible, and resourceful and should know how to get help in an emergency.

Children whose mothers entered the workforce in their first year tended to have negative performance academically, and some behavioural problems at ages 3 and 4, which persisted into the school years at ages 7 and 8, but this relationship was found with only white children (Han, Waldfogel, & Brooks-Gunn, 2001). Although these results were based on children studied in the 1980s, they support the argument that parents should have some paid leave to care for their children during the first year after birth, as practised in Canada. Although mothers continue to shoulder the bulk of parenting responsibilities, the role of fathers in parenting seems to be increasing (Yeung, Sandberg, Davis-Kean, & Hofferth, 2001).

As children approach adolescence, how well parents keep track of them may be more important than whether the mother works for pay. In one study, 9- to 12-year-old boys whose parents closely monitored their activities made better grades than less closely monitored children (Crouter, MacDermid, McHale, & Perry-Jenkins, 1990).

Poverty and Parenting

Twenty-one per cent of children lived in poverty (below the Statistics Canada low-income cut-off for their communities) in 1996, an increase from 15 per cent in 1989 (CICH, 2000). The experience of poverty is more frequent for children younger than 7 years (25 per cent) compared to children between 7 and 17 years (19 per cent) (CICH, 2000). The rate of poverty is dramatically higher for lone-mother families, consistent at about 60 per cent from 1981 to 1997 (CICH, 2000). However, the depth of poverty, how far below the low-income cut-off (LICO), is currently greater for two-parent families than for lone-mother families.

Poverty can harm children's development through its impact on parents' emotional state and parenting practices and on the home environment they create (Brooks-Gunn & Duncan, 1997; Brooks-Gunn et al., 1998). Vonnie McLoyd's (1990, 1998) ecological analysis of the effects of poverty traces a route that leads to adult psychological distress, to effects on child rearing, and finally to emotional, behavioural, and academic problems in children. Parents who live in poor housing (or have none), who have lost their jobs, who are worried about their next meal, and who feel a lack of control over their lives are likely to become anxious, depressed, or irritable. They may become less affectionate with, and less responsive to, their children. They may discipline inconsistently, harshly, and arbitrarily. They may ignore good behaviour and pay attention only to misbehaviour. The children, in turn, tend to become depressed themselves, to have trouble getting along with peers, to lack self-confidence, and to engage in anti-social acts (Brooks-Gunn, Britto, & Brady, in press; McLoyd, 1990, 1998).

Families under economic stress are less likely to monitor their children's activities, and lack of monitoring is associated with poorer school performance and social adjustment (Bolger, Patterson, Thompson, & Kupersmidt, 1995).

A father's involvement with his children tends to be related to his economic success; when a father feels like a failure as a breadwinner, his demoralization is likely to carry over to his fathering role and to negatively affect his relationships with his children. Thus fathering is especially vulnerable to economic and social forces that affect occupational opportunities (Doherty et al., 1998).

Poverty can sap parents' confidence in their ability to affect their children's development. Lack of financial resources also can make it harder for mothers and fathers to support each other in parenting. Lone-parent families working for minimum wage in 1996 had to work between a low of 61 hours, in British Columbia, and high of 80 hours per week, in Manitoba, to reach the LICO (CICH, 2000). For two-parent families with two children, the number of hours of work per week ranged from 89 to 118 hours, to reach the LICO. Families working under these conditions experience great stress, which can create difficulties for healthy family functioning. A solution to this problem would be to raise the minimum wage in order to allow parents better opportunities to maintain work and family responsibilities (CICH, 2000).

However, this bleak picture is not etched in stone. Parents who can turn to relatives (as Annie Anderson did) or to community representatives for emotional support, help with child care, and child-rearing information often can parent their children more effectively. These positive factors work to counteract the negative effects of poverty in Canada, and add to a child's resiliency in the face of the risks to healthy development, as found in the National Longitudinal Survey of Children and Youth. In fact, multiple risk factors are more

What's your view ?

- If finances permit, should either the mother or the father stay home to take care of the children?

Checkpoint ✔

Can you . . .

✔ Identify ways in which parents' work can affect children?

✔ Discuss effects of poverty on child raising?

likely to have a negative effect on development than a single risk factor like poverty (Landy & Tam, 1998). Also, some children are more adaptable than others; their temperament enables them to cope more successfully with a stressful environment (Ackerman, Kogos, Youngstrom, Schoff, & Izard, 1999).

Family Structure

Guidepost 5

What impact does family structure have on children's development?

Families in Canada have changed dramatically in recent decades. In earlier generations, the vast majority of children grew up in traditional families, with two biological parents or two parents who had adopted one or more children in infancy. Today, although most school-age children live with two parents, the proportion has decreased (see Figure 14-1). Furthermore, more traditional families are adoptive, and many two-parent families are stepfamilies, resulting from divorce and remarriage. There are also a growing number of other non-traditional families, including single-parent families or blended families, common-law families, gay and lesbian families, and grandparent-headed families (discussed in chapter 8). How do these various family structures affect children?

Traditional and Non-traditional Families: An Overview

As we will see in the following sections, much research has found that, other things being equal, children tend to do better in traditional (intact) families (Bray & Hetherington, 1993; Bronstein, Clauson, Stoll, & Abrams, 1993; D. A. Dawson, 1991; Hetherington, Bridges, & Insabella, 1998). For example, in a study of 136 Grade 5 students and their families, traditional parents did more with their children, talked with them more, disciplined them more appropriately, and were likely to share parenting responsibilities more cooperatively than non-traditional parents. The children in traditional families in the study were better adjusted (Bronstein et al., 1993).

However, other things are not always equal. Some traditional families are conflict-ridden, and many non-traditional families are harmonious. Thus the structure of the family is less important than its effect on family atmosphere.

Traditional families have not had to deal with the stress and disruption caused by divorce or the death of a parent; with the financial, psychological, and time pressures on single parents; or with the possible need to adjust to a new household or to remarriage. Not only objective changes in family life, but parents' emotional responses to those changes, can be stressful for children. What may affect children most is how these stresses influence the way the family functions day by day, bringing about changes in roles, relationships, and parenting practices (Hetherington et al., 1998).

Adoptive Families

Adoptive families are traditional families of a special kind. Adoption, the oldest solution to infertility, is found in all cultures throughout history. It is not only for infertile people; single people, older people, gay and lesbian couples, and people who already have children have become adoptive parents.

About 60 per cent of legal adoptions are by relatives, usually stepparents or grandparents (Goodman, Emery, & Haugaard, 1998; Haugaard, 1998). An increasing percentage of children available for adoption by *non*-relatives are beyond infancy, of foreign birth, or disabled. This is because ad-

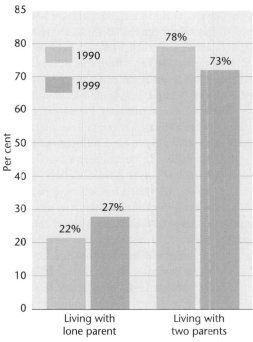

Figure 14-1

Living arrangements of school-age children, 1990–1999. Most children between 5 and 14 years in Canada live with two parents, but this proportion dropped during the past decade. Many of these two-parent families are stepfamilies.

Source: Canadian Council on Social Development, 2001.

Figure 14-2

Family structure in Canada in 2001. The types of Canadian families with children of all ages living in the household include not only traditional intact families, with children living with two married parents, but also a variety of non-traditional forms. *Note:* Percentages do not add up to 100 due to rounding.

Source: Adapted from Statistics Canada, 2002b.

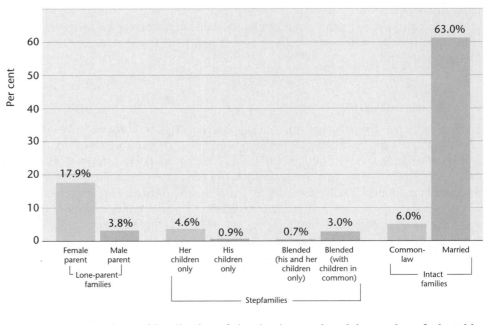

vances in contraception and legalization of abortion have reduced the number of adoptable Canadian babies.

Adopting a child carries special joys and privileges, especially for people who never thought they could be parents, or who find deep satisfaction in providing a home for a child who needs one. Adoption also carries special challenges. Adoptive parents need to deal with integrating the adopted child into the family, explaining the adoption to the child, and helping the child develop a healthy sense of self and perhaps resolve feelings about his or her biological parents. Eventually some adoptive parents help the child to find and contact the birth parents.

Traditionally, adoptions made through public or private agencies were confidential, with no contact between the birth mother and the adoptive parents, and the identity of the birth mother was kept secret. In recent years independent adoptions, made by agreement between birth parents and adoptive parents, have become increasingly common. Often these are *open adoptions,* in which the parties share information or have direct contact (Goodman et al., 1998).

Although some couples decide against open adoption for fear that the birth mother will try to reclaim the child, one study found that with direct contact the adoptive parents tend to feel more confidence in the permanence of the arrangement. At the same time, they are more likely to recognize the child's interest in knowing about her or his origins (Grotevant, McRoy, Elde, & Fravel, 1994). In a survey of 1,059 California families who had adopted children 3 years earlier, whether or not an adoption was open seemed to bear no relation to the children's adjustment or to the parents' satisfaction with the adoption, both of which were very high (Berry, Dylla, Barth, & Needell, 1998).

There are few significant differences in adjustment between adopted and non-adopted children, according to a review of the literature (Haugaard, 1998). Children adopted in infancy are least likely to have adjustment problems (Sharma, McGue, & Benson, 1996b). Any problems that do occur seem to surface around the time of sexual maturation (Goodman et al., 1998). This was true in a large-scale study of children in Grades 6 through 12 in 35 U.S. states. Adopted adolescents, especially boys, were slightly more likely than non-adopted peers to feel anxious, sad, or stressed, to have school problems, to use drugs, or to engage in anti-social behaviour, but these differences tended to level off by late adolescence. Interestingly, adoptees also were significantly more likely to show pro-social behaviour, perhaps because their own adoption represents an example of such behaviour on their adoptive parents' part (Sharma, McGue, & Benson, 1996a).

A more recent large-scale study found similar results with young adolescents, but found older adolescents had difficulties on measures of future hope, physical problems, and lying to parents (Miller, Fan, Christensen, Grotevant, & van Dulmen, 2000).

What's your view

• If you were infertile, do you think you would try to adopt? If so, would you want the adoption to be open? Why or why not?

Checkpoint

Can you . . .

✔ Discuss trends in adoption and the adjustment of adopted children?

When Parents Divorce

No matter how unhappy a marriage has been, its breakup usually comes as a shock to a child. Children may feel afraid of the future, guilty about their own (usually imaginary) role in causing the divorce, hurt by the parent who moves out, and angry at both parents.

The annual number of divorces has increased fivefold in the past 3 decades, with 30 per cent of Canadian marriages ending in divorce (Health Canada, 1999). How do children in these families adjust?

Adjusting to Divorce Although different children react differently, adjustment to divorce generally involves six "tasks" (Wallerstein, 1983; Wallerstein & Kelly, 1980): (1) acknowledging the reality of the marital rupture; (2) disengaging from parental conflict and distress and resuming customary pursuits; (3) resolving loss—of the parent they are not living with, of security in feeling loved and cared for by both parents, of familiar daily routines and family traditions; (4) resolving anger and self-blame; (5) accepting the permanence of the divorce; and (6) achieving realistic hope for their own intimate relationships.

What influences a child's adjustment? The child's age or maturity, gender, temperament, and psychological and social adjustment are important. So is the way parents handle such issues as custody and visitation arrangements, finances, reorganization of household duties, contact with the non-custodial parent, remarriage, and the child's relationship with a stepparent.

Younger children are more anxious about divorce, have less realistic perceptions of what caused it, and are more likely to blame themselves; but they may adapt more quickly than older children, who better understand what is going on. School-age children are sensitive to parental pressures and loyalty conflicts; like younger children, they may fear abandonment and rejection. Boys generally find it harder to adjust than girls do. However, this difference may be less significant than was once thought and may depend largely on how involved the father remains (Bray, 1991; Hetherington, Stanley-Hagan, & Anderson, 1989; Hetherington et al., 1998; Hines, 1997; Masten, Best, & Garmezy, 1990; Parke & Buriel, 1998).

In most divorce cases the mother gets custody, but paternal custody is a growing trend (Meyer & Garasky, 1993). The more recent the separation, the closer the father lives to his children, and the higher his socio-economic status, the more involved he is likely to be (Amato & Keith, 1991; Parke & Buriel, 1998). Non-custodial fathers are more likely to lose contact if they have biological children from a new marriage (Cooksey & Craig, 1998). Non-custodial mothers keep up twice as much contact with their children as non-custodial fathers and are less likely to break contact after remarriage (Hetherington et al., 1998).

Children do better when the custodial parent creates a stable, structured, nurturing environment and does not expect the children to take on more responsibility than they are ready for (Hetherington et al., 1989). According to an analysis of 63 studies, children living with divorced mothers do better when the father pays child support, which may be a barometer of the tie between father and child and also of relative lack of rancor between the ex-spouses. Frequency of contact with the father in itself is not as important as the quality of the father–child relationship. Children who are close to their non-resident fathers, and whose fathers use authoritative parenting, tend to do better in school; children who do not enjoy such relationships with their fathers are likely to have behaviour problems (Amato & Gilbreth, 1999). Children also perform better academically if their non-resident fathers are involved in their schools (National [U.S.] Center for Education Statistics [NCES], 1998b) and if their custodial mothers use effective parenting practices and provide skill-building activities at home (DeGarmo, Forgatch, & Martinez, 1999).

Emotional or behavioural problems may stem from parental conflict, both before and after divorce, as well as from the separation itself (Amato, Kurdek, Demo, & Allen, 1993; E. M. Cummings, 1994; Parke & Buriel, 1998; see Box 14-1). If parents can control their anger, cooperate in parenting, and avoid exposing the children to quarrelling, the children are less likely to have problems (Bray & Hetherington, 1993; Hetherington et al., 1989). Unfortunately, the strains of divorce make it harder for a couple to be effective parents (Hines, 1997).

Most research has found few advantages of *joint custody,* custody shared by both parents (Hetherington et al., 1998). When parents have joint *legal* custody, they share the right

Children of divorce tend to be better adjusted if they have reliable, frequent contact with the non-custodial parent, usually the father.

Box 14-1 *Should Parents Stay Together for the Sake of the Children?*

A generation ago, when divorce was far less common than it is today, it was widely believed that parents in troubled marriages should stay together for the sake of the children. More recent research has found that marital strife harms children more than divorce does—that children are better adjusted if they grow up in a harmonious single-parent household than in a two-parent home marked by discord and discontent (Hetherington et al., 1998; Hetherington & Stanley-Hagan, 1999). However, that finding may need some qualification.

Clearly, watching parents' spats can be hard on children. Aside from the distress, worry, or fear children may feel, marital dissension may diminish parents' responsiveness to children's needs. Young boys growing up in an atmosphere of parental anger and discord tend to become aggressive, girls to become withdrawn and anxious. Children do not become accustomed to marital conflict; the more they are exposed to it, the more sensitive they become (E. M. Cummings, 1994). Children see destructive parental quarrels as threatening their own security and that of the family (Davies & Cummings, 1998). Violent clashes, conflicts about a child to which the child is directly exposed, and those in which a child feels caught in the middle are the most damaging (Hetherington & Stanley-Hagan, 1999).

The *amount* of conflict in a marriage may make a difference. A 15-year longitudinal study, which followed a nationwide sample originally consisting of 2,033 married people (Amato & Booth, 1997), suggests that in only about 30 per cent of divorces involving children is there so much discord that the children are better off if the marriage ends. About 70 per cent of cases, according to this research, involve low-conflict marriages, in which children would benefit "if parents remained together until children are grown" (p. 238).

In as many as 1 in 5 divorced families, parental conflict continues or escalates. Two years after a divorce, children suffer more from dissension in a divorced family than do children in a non-divorced family. Thus, if conflict is going to *continue*, children

may be better off in an acrimonious two-parent household than if the parents divorce. On the other hand, if conflict *lessens* after a divorce, the children may be better off than they were before. Unfortunately, the amount of bickering after a divorce is not always easy to anticipate (Hetherington & Stanley-Hagan, 1999).

A longitudinal study of British children found that on most measures of long-term welfare, there were few differences between individuals whose parents divorced while they were children and those whose parents waited to divorce until after the children were grown (Furstenberg & Kiernan, 2001).

In evaluating the effects of divorce, then, we need to look at particular circumstances. Sometimes divorce may improve a child's situation by reducing the amount of conflict within the family, and sometimes not. Children's personal characteristics make a difference; intelligent, socially competent children without serious behaviour problems, who have a sense of control over their own lives, can cope better with both parental conflict and divorce (Hetherington & Stanley-Hagan, 1999). And, while the immediate effects of a marital breakup may be traumatic, in the long run some children may benefit from having learned new coping skills that make them more competent and independent (B. L. Barber & Eccles, 1992).

What's your view?

Would you advise parents who want a divorce to stay married until their children have grown up? Why or why not? What factors might you consider in giving your advice?

Check it out

For more information on this topic, go to **www.mcgrawhill.ca/college/papalia** which provides a link to a website that includes information on a wide range of relevant issues on children and divorce.

and responsibility to make decisions about the child's welfare. When parents have joint *physical* custody (which is less common), the child is supposed to live part time with each of them. The main determinant of the success of joint custody is the amount of conflict between the parents (Parke & Buriel, 1998). On the other hand, joint legal custody does seem to motivate non-resident fathers to visit their children more often (Seltzer, 1998), suggesting that "policies that encourage non-resident fathers to maintain the parental role after divorce can positively influence men's behaviour" (Amato & Gilbreth, 1999, p. 569).

The increasingly responsible behaviour of non-custodial fathers in recent years suggests that a policy shift away from traditional notions of custody and toward the adoption of mediated co-parenting plans might have beneficial effects on fathers' positive involvement in their children's lives (Amato & Gilbreth, 1999; U.S. Commission on Child and Family Welfare, 1996). Research-based parent education programs that teach separated or divorced couples how to prevent or deal with conflict, keep lines of communication open, develop an effective co-parenting relationship, and help children adjust to divorce have been introduced in many courts, with measurable success (Amato & Gilbreth, 1999; Shifflet & Cummings, 1999).

Long-term Effects of Divorce Most children of divorce eventually adjust reasonably well. In a nationally representative British study based on data gathered on children from birth on, the vast majority of those whose parents divorced came through well by their early 20s (Chase-Lansdale, Cherlin, & Kiernan, 1995).

Still, children who experience parental divorce are more than twice as likely to drop out of high school as children in intact families (McLanahan & Sandefur, 1994), and dropping out of school negatively affects future socio-economic status. Children of divorce also are more likely than children in intact families to marry young and to form unstable, unsatisfying relationships (Ross & Mirowsky, 1999). On the bright side, between 1973 and 1996 the chances of children of divorce ending their own marriages declined by almost 50 per cent, from 2.5 to 1.4 times as likely as for children of intact families (Wolfinger, 1999), perhaps because divorce is a more normative event than it used to be.

Of course, since all research on effects of divorce is correlational, we cannot be sure that a parental divorce caused children's later problems. Children may still be reacting to conflict preceding or surrounding the dissolution of the marriage.

Living in a One-Parent Family

One-parent families result from divorce or separation, unwed parenthood, or death. The number of lone-parent families in Canada almost doubled between 1961 and 1991, from 11 per cent to 20 per cent (Health Canada, 1999). Today a child has at least a 50 per cent chance of living with only one parent at some point (Bianchi, 1995; Hines, 1997; NCES, 1998b).

Although the growth of one-parent families is slowing, in 2001 they comprised 21.7 per cent of Canadian families, one-third less than the U.S. rate (Statistics Canada, 2002b; U.S. Bureau of the Census, 1998).

In 1998, about more than 5 out of 6 Canadian children who lived with a single parent lived with their mothers, but about 1 in 6 single-parent families was headed by the father (Lapierre-Adamcyk, 1999). The number of father-only families increased by over 40 per cent between 1986 and 1996 (CICH, 2000), apparently due largely to an increase in the number of fathers having custody after divorce (Garasky & Meyer, 1996; U.S. Bureau of the Census, 1998).

Compared with children in intact families, children in one-parent families have more behavioural and academic problems, especially when the absence of a parent is due to divorce (Hetherington et al., 1998; Walker & Hennig, 1997). Children in one-parent families are more on their own. They tend to have more household responsibility, more conflict with siblings, less family cohesion, and less support, control, or discipline from fathers, if it is the father who is absent from the household (Amato, 1987; Coley, 1998; Walker & Hennig, 1997). Single fathers tend to be more satisfied with parenting and to report fewer behaviour problems with their children than single mothers do (Walker & Hennig, 1997). Divorced mothers particularly tend to have trouble with school-age sons. In one experiment, a 12-month intervention consisting of group and individual treatment produced less coercive behaviour on the part of the mothers than shown by a control group who did not receive the intervention; and the more the mothers changed, the more their sons' behaviour improved (Forgatch & DeGarmo, 1999).

In one study, deficiencies in family relationships in single-mother households were almost entirely linked to socio-economic status (Bronstein et al., 1993). In other studies, however, even when income was controlled, children in *divorced* single-parent families had more problems than those in intact families (Hetherington et al., 1998).

Although it is widely believed that most mother-only families suffer from the mother's greatly reduced income after divorce and the father's failure to pay child support, a study of a random sample of 378 couples who divorced in Maricopa County, Arizona, in 1986 suggests that the data supporting this belief may be methodologically flawed (Braver & O'Connell, 1998). For one thing, the U.S. Census Bureau's statistics on child support are based on mothers' reports. Not surprisingly, the researchers in Maricopa County found a wide disparity between what fathers say they have paid and what custodial mothers say the fathers have paid. The findings suggest that employed fathers pay more than is generally assumed.

On average, men and women in Maricopa County fared about the same economically after divorce. This conclusion took into consideration such factors as tax advantages to the custodial mother, costs of establishing a new household and other "hidden" costs to the non-custodial father, and the difficulty of establishing equivalent poverty levels for households of different sizes. The analysis showed that families of *never-married* single mothers—many of whom are teenagers from low socio-economic backgrounds—but *not* divorced mothers tend to be below the poverty level (Braver & O'Connell, 1998).

This baby has two mothers—and both obviously dote on the child. Contrary to popular stereotypes, children living with gay or lesbian parents are no more likely than other children to have social or psychological problems or to turn out to be gay or lesbian themselves.

Living in a Stepfamily

Children in divorced families typically spend 5 years in a single-parent home, usually the mother's, before she remarries. Since about 75 per cent of divorced mothers and 80 per cent of divorced fathers remarry, families made up of "yours, mine, and ours" are common. Eighty-two per cent of children in remarriages live with their biological mother and a stepfather (CICH, 2000). About half of the 503,000 stepfamilies in Canada involve parents in common-law relationships, with the proportion of common-law stepfamilies in Quebec being particularly high (Statistics Canada, 2002b).

The stepfamily is different from the "natural" family. It has a larger cast, which may include the relatives of up to four adults (the remarried pair, plus one or two former spouses); and it has many stressors. A child's loyalties to an absent or dead parent may interfere with forming ties to a stepparent. Adjustment is harder when there are many children, including those from both the man's and the woman's previous marriages, or when a new child is born (Hetherington et al., 1989). Furthermore, because the increase in stepfamilies is fairly recent, social expectations for such families have not caught up. In combining two family units, each with its own web of customs and relationships, remarried families must invent their own ways of doing things (Hines, 1997). For these reasons, among others, remarriages are more likely to fail than first marriages, especially during the first 5 years (Parke & Buriel, 1998).

Findings on the impact of remarriage on children are mixed (Parke & Buriel, 1998). Some studies have found that boys, who often have more trouble than girls in adjusting to divorce and single-parent living (usually with the mother), benefit from a stepfather. A girl, on the other hand, may find the new man in the house a threat to her independence and to her close relationship with her mother and may be less likely to accept him (Bray & Hetherington, 1993; Hetherington, 1987; Hetherington et al., 1989; Hetherington et al., 1998; Hines, 1997).

Stepparents often assume a "hands-off" attitude toward children of the custodial parent, though stepmothers may take—or be expected to take—a more active role than stepfathers (Hetherington et al., 1989; Hetherington et al., 1998; Parke & Buriel, 1998; Santrock, Sitterle, & Warshak, 1988). Still, a stepchild's most enduring ties are with the custodial parent. Life generally goes more smoothly when stepparents support the natural parent and do not try to step in themselves (Hetherington et al., 1998).

Living with Gay or Lesbian Parents

The number of children of gay and lesbian parents in Canada is unknown (Dundas & Kaufman, 2000), although conservative estimates from the U.S. range from 6 to 14 million (C. J. Patterson, 1992; C. J. Patterson & Redding, 1996, 2000). There are an estimated 1 to 5 million lesbian mothers, and 1 to 3 million gay fathers (Gottman, 1990). These numbers are probably low because many gay and lesbian parents do not openly acknowledge their sexual orientation. Some are raising children born of previous heterosexual relationships. Others conceive by artificial means, become foster parents, or adopt children (C. J. Patterson, 1997).

Several studies have focused on the development of children of gays and lesbians, including sense of self, moral judgment, intelligence, and social relationships. Although research is still sparse and studies vary in adequacy of methodology, none has indicated psychological concerns (C. J. Patterson, 1992, 1995a, 1995b, 1997, 2000). A study of 27 lesbian mothers and their families in Toronto showed that children were content and did not feel any stigma about having two mothers (Dundas & Kaufman, 2000). Openly gay or lesbian parents usually have positive relationships with their children (P. H. Turner et al., 1985), and the children are no more likely than children raised by heterosexual parents to have social or psychological problems (Chan, Raboy, & Patterson, 1998; C. J. Patterson, 1992, 1995a, 1997, 2000). Abuse by gay or lesbian parents is rare (R. L. Barrett & Robinson, 1990; Cramer, 1986).

Children of gays and lesbians are *no* more likely to be homosexual themselves, or to be confused about their gender, than are children of heterosexuals (B. M. King, 1996; C. J. Patterson, 1997, 2000). In one study, the vast majority of adult sons of gay fathers were het-

Checkpoint ✔

Can you . . .

✔ List the psychological "tasks" children face in adjusting to divorce, and identify factors that affect adjustment?

✔ Assess the impact of parental divorce on children?

✔ Tell three ways in which a one-parent family can be formed, and how living in such a household can affect children's well-being?

✔ Discuss how parents and stepparents handle the issues and challenges of a stepfamily?

✔ Discuss the outcomes of child raising by gay and lesbian parents?

erosexual (Bailey, Bobrow, Wolfe, & Mikach, 1995). Likewise, in a longitudinal study of adult children of lesbians, a large majority identified themselves as heterosexual (Golombok & Tasker, 1996).

Such findings can have social policy implications for legal decisions on custody and visitation disputes, foster care, and adoptions.

Sibling Relationships

In remote rural areas or villages of Asia, Africa, Oceania, and Central and South America, it is common to see older girls caring for three or four younger siblings: feeding, comforting, and toilet-training them; disciplining them; assigning chores; and generally keeping an eye on them. In a poor agricultural or pastoral community, older siblings have an important, culturally defined role. Parents train children early to teach younger sisters and brothers how to gather firewood, carry water, tend animals, and grow food. Younger siblings absorb intangible values, such as respecting elders and placing the welfare of the group above that of the individual. Siblings may fight and compete, but they do so within societal rules and roles (Cicirelli, 1994a).

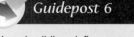

Guidepost 6

How do siblings influence and get along with one another?

In industrialized societies such as Canada, parents generally try not to "burden" older children with the care of younger ones (Weisner, 1993). Although some caretaking takes place, it is generally sporadic. Older siblings do teach younger ones, but this usually happens informally, by chance, and not as an established part of the social system (Cicirelli, 1994a).

The number of siblings in a family and their spacing, birth order, and gender often determine roles and relationships. The larger number of siblings in non-industrialized societies helps the family carry on its work and provide for aging members. In industrialized societies, siblings tend to be fewer and farther apart in age, making it easier for parents to pursue careers or other interests and to focus more resources and attention on each child (Cicirelli, 1994a).

Two longitudinal studies, one in England and one in Pennsylvania, based on naturalistic observation of siblings and mothers and interviews with the mothers, found that changes in sibling relationships were most likely to occur when one sibling was between ages 7 and 9. Both mothers and children often attributed these changes to outside friendships, which led to jealousy and competitiveness or loss of interest in, and intimacy with, the sibling. Sometimes the younger sibling's growing assertiveness played a part (Dunn, 1996). Nevertheless, a study of 40 children in Grades 5 to 6 in Quebec found important links between the quality of relationships with siblings and the children's own social and emotional development. The presence of a warm relationship with a sibling was associated with high levels of emotional understanding and self-disclosure. On the other hand, children who reported not trusting or not getting emotional support from a sibling were less likely to confide with the sibling (Howe, Aquan-Asee, Bukowski, Lehoux, & Rinaldi, 2001). This may lead to a pattern of interaction that provides few opportunities to build warmth and trust with a sibling (Howe et al., 2001).

These Inuit boys in a northern Canadian fishing camp enjoy caring for a baby brother. Children in many societies tend to have regular responsibility for siblings.

Sibling relations are a laboratory for conflict resolution. Siblings are impelled to make up after quarrels, since they know they will see each other every day. They learn that expressing anger does not end a relationship. Children are more apt to squabble with same-sex siblings; two brothers quarrel more than any other combination (Cicirelli, 1976, 1995).

Siblings influence each other, not only *directly,* through their own interactions, but *indirectly* through their impact on each other's relationship with the parents. Conversely, behaviour patterns established with parents tend to "spill over" into behaviour with siblings. An older child's positive relationship with the mother or father can mitigate the effects of that child's "difficult" temperament on sibling interactions (Brody, Stoneman, & Gauger, 1996).

Checkpoint ✔

Can you . . .

✔ Compare the roles and responsibilities of siblings in industrialized and non-industrialized countries?

✔ Discuss how siblings affect each other's development?

Guidepost 7

How do relationships with peers change in middle childhood, and what influences popularity and choice of friends?

The Child in the Peer Group

It is in middle childhood that the peer group comes into its own. Groups form naturally among children who live near one another or go to school together; thus peer groups often consist of children of the same racial or ethnic origin and similar socio-economic status. Children who play together are usually close in age, though a neighbourhood play group may include mixed ages. Too wide an age range brings differences, not only in size, but in interests and ability levels. Groups are usually all girls or all boys (Hartup, 1992). Children of the same sex have common interests; girls are generally more mature than boys, and girls and boys play and talk to one another differently. Same-sex groups help children to learn gender-appropriate behaviours and to incorporate gender roles into their self-concept (Hibbard & Buhrmester, 1998).

Today we are seeing new social patterns as technology changes the tools and habits of leisure. Television, DVDs and videocassettes turn some children into "couch potatoes." Computer games demand few social skills. Organized sports have adult rules and adult referees to settle disputes so that children do not need to find ways to resolve matters among themselves. Still, children spend more time with others their own age than they did in early childhood.

How does the peer group influence children? What determines their acceptance by peers and their ability to make friends? Why do some children become bullies and others, victims?

Positive and Negative Effects of Peer Relations

Children benefit from doing things with peers. They develop skills needed for sociability and intimacy, they enhance relationships, and they gain a sense of belonging. They are motivated to achieve, and they attain a sense of identity. They learn leadership and communication skills, cooperation, roles, and rules (Zarbatany, Hartmann, & Rankin, 1990).

As children begin to move away from parental influence, the peer group opens new perspectives and frees them to make independent judgments. Testing values they previously accepted unquestioningly against those of their peers helps them decide which to keep and which to discard. In comparing themselves with others their age, children can gauge their abilities more realistically and gain a clearer sense of self-efficacy (Bandura, 1994; refer back to chapter 11). The peer group helps children learn how to get along in society—how to adjust their needs and desires to those of others, when to yield, and when to stand firm. The peer group also offers emotional security. It is reassuring for children to find out that they are not alone in harbouring thoughts that might offend an adult.

The peer group can also have negative effects. To be part of a peer group, a child is expected to accept its values and behavioural norms, and even though these may be undesirable, children may not have the strength to resist. It is usually in the company of peers that children shoplift, begin to use drugs, and act in other anti-social ways. Preadolescent children are especially susceptible to pressure to conform, and this pressure may change a troublesome child into a delinquent one (Hartup, 1992). Of course, some degree of conformity to group standards is healthy. It is unhealthy when it becomes destructive or prompts people to act against their own better judgment.

Another negative influence of the peer group may be a tendency to reinforce **prejudice:** unfavourable attitudes toward "outsiders," especially members of certain racial or ethnic groups. A study done in Montreal, where tensions exist between some French-speaking and English-speaking citizens, found signs of prejudice in a sample of 254 English-speaking boys and girls in kindergarten through Grade 6 (Powlishta, Serbin, Doyle, & White, 1994). The children were given brief descriptions of positive and negative traits (such as *helpful, smart, mean,* and *naughty*) and were asked whether one or both of two cartoon children—one English-speaking and the other French-speaking—would be likely to possess each trait. A similar procedure was followed with male and female figures (using gender stereotypes such as *ambitious* and *gentle*) and figures of overweight and normal-weight children. The researchers also asked the children which of two pictured children they would like to play with.

prejudice Unfavorable attitude toward members of certain groups outside one's own, especially racial or ethnic groups

What's your view ?

- How can parents and schools reduce racial, religious, and ethnic prejudice?

In general, children showed biases in favour of children like themselves, but these biases (except for a preference for children of the same sex) diminished with age and cognitive development. Girls were more biased with regard to gender, and boys with regard to ethnicity. However, individual differences were significant, and a child who was highly prejudiced in one respect was not necessarily prejudiced in another. Similarly, a study conducted with Aboriginal and non-Aboriginal children in Northern Ontario showed that children tended to maintain same-race trust expectancies. Both Aboriginal and non-Aboriginal children expected children in the other group to be less likely to be trustworthy or to keep secrets and promises. This pattern tended to break down in children who attended schools that were mixed-race (Rotenberg & Cerda, 1995).

Broadening children's experience may lessen or eliminate prejudice. The most effective programs get children from different groups to work together toward a common goal, as on athletic teams (Gaertner, Mann, Murrell, & Dovidio, 1989).

Popularity

Popularity becomes more important in middle childhood. Children spend more time with other children, and peers' opinions greatly affect their self-esteem. Peer relationships in middle childhood are strong predictors of later adjustment (Masten & Coatsworth, 1998). Schoolchildren whose peers like them are likely to be well adjusted as adolescents. Those who have trouble getting along with peers are more likely to develop psychological problems, drop out of school, or become delinquent (Hartup, 1992; Kupersmidt & Coie, 1990; Morison & Masten, 1991; Newcomb, Bukowski, & Pattee, 1993; Parker & Asher, 1987).

Popular children typically have good cognitive abilities, are high achievers, are good at solving social problems, help other children, and are assertive without being disruptive or aggressive. They are trustworthy, loyal, and self-disclosing and provide emotional support. Their superior social skills make others enjoy being with them (Masten & Coatsworth, 1998; Newcomb et al., 1993). However, this picture is not universally true. Some aggressive or anti-social boys are among the most popular in the classroom, suggesting that criteria for popularity vary (Rodkin, Farmer, Pearl, & Van Acker, 2000). In a study of "rejected" Grade 4 students, aggressive boys tended to gain in status by the end of Grade 5, suggesting that behaviour shunned by younger children may be seen as "cool" or glamourous by preadolescents (Sandstrom & Coie, 1999).

Children can be unpopular for many reasons, some of which may not be fully within their control. While some unpopular children are aggressive, some are hyperactive and inattentive, and some are withdrawn (Dodge, Coie, Pettit, & Price, 1990; Masten & Coatsworth, 1998; Newcomb et al., 1993; A. W. Pope, Bierman, & Mumma, 1991). Others act silly and immature or anxious and uncertain. They are often insensitive to other children's feelings and do not adapt well to new situations (Bierman, Smoot, & Aumiller, 1993). Some show undue interest in being with groups of the other sex (Sroufe, Bennett, Englund, Urban, & Shulman, 1993). Some unpopular children *expect* not to be liked, and this becomes a self-fulfilling prophecy (Rabiner & Coie, 1989).

It is often in the family that children acquire behaviours that affect popularity (Masten & Coatsworth, 1998). Authoritative parents tend to have more popular children than authoritarian parents (Dekovic & Janssens, 1992). Children of authoritarian parents who punish and threaten are likely to threaten or act mean with other children; they are less popular than children whose authoritative parents reason with them and try to help them understand how another person might feel (C. H. Hart, Ladd, & Burleson, 1990).

In both North American and Chinese cultures, there is a bi-directional link between academic achievement and social competence. High achievers tend to be popular and socially skilled; and well-adjusted, well-liked children tend to do well in school (X. Chen, Rubin, & Li, 1997). One difference is that shyness and sensitivity are valued in China, but not in industrialized cultures. Thus, children who show these traits are more likely to be popular in China—at least in middle childhood (see Box 14-2).

How can unpopular children be helped? For some children extracurricular activities, such as team sports, can be a route to social acceptance. Children who realize how their own attitudes and behaviour may contribute to their social difficulties are more likely to improve their situation than those who blame all their problems on others. Parents who

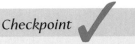

Checkpoint

Can you . . .

✔ Tell some ways in which members of a peer group tend to be alike?

✔ Identify positive and negative effects of the peer group?

Checkpoint

Can you . . .

✔ Describe characteristics of popular and unpopular children, and tell how they may vary?

✔ Identify family and cultural influences on popularity?

✔ Discuss ways of helping unpopular children?

Box 14-2 *Popularity: A Cross-cultural View*

How does culture affect popularity? Would a child who is popular in one culture be equally popular in another? Researchers compared 480 students in Grades 2 and 4 in Shanghai, with 296 children the same ages in Ontario (X. Chen, Rubin, & Sun, 1992). Although the two samples were quite different—for example, none of the Canadian children came from peasant families, but many of the Chinese children did—both samples were representative of school-age children in the two countries.

The researchers assessed the children's popularity by two kinds of peer perceptions. The children filled out a sociometric rating telling which three classmates they most and least liked to be with and which three classmates were their best friends. The results showed that certain traits are valued similarly in both cultures. A sociable, cooperative child is likely to be popular in both China and Canada, and an aggressive child is likely to be rejected in both countries. However, one important difference emerged: shy, sensitive children are well liked in China, but not in Canada. This is not surprising. Chinese children are encouraged to be cautious, to restrain themselves, and to inhibit their urges; thus a quiet, shy youngster is considered well behaved. In a North American culture, by contrast, such a child is likely to be seen as socially immature, fearful, and lacking in self-confidence. A related study of Grade 3 and 4 children in Toronto and Taipei, Taiwan, showed that children reported both closeness and conflict in their friendships in both cultures. However, there was less reported conflict among friends in Taiwan than in Canada. This may reflect negative attitudes towards the expression of conflict in Chinese culture (Benjamin, Schneider, Greenman, & Hum, 2001).

A follow-up study to the Shanghai study at ages 8 and 10 (X. Chen, Rubin, & Li, 1995) again found that shy, sensitive Chinese children were popular with peers. They also were rated by teachers as socially competent, as leaders, and as academic achievers. However, by age 12, an interesting twist had occurred: Shy, sensitive Chinese children were no longer popular. They tended to be rejected by their peers, just as in North American cultures.

It may be, then, that shyness and sensitivity take on different social meanings in China as children enter adolescence, when peer relationships become more important and adult approval becomes less so. As in Canada, a shy early adolescent may lack the assertiveness and communication skills needed to establish and maintain strong peer relationships.

This research suggests that the influence of culture may be tempered by developmental processes that are more or less universal. Even in China, with its strong tradition of obedience to authority, the influence of adult social standards may wane as children's urge to make their own independent judgments of their peers asserts itself.

During middle childhood, shy, sensitive children are better liked in China than in European and North American cultures, because they are considered well behaved. Children this age tend to accept adult standards of behaviour.

What's your view?

How would you advise parents of a shy, sensitive child who complains of being rejected by other children?

Check it out!

For more information on this topic, go to **www.mcgrawhill.ca/college/papalia** which will direct you to relevant links.

keep an eye on their children's friendships may be in a better position to help them deal with peer problems—though direct advice may be less effective than more subtle strategies, such as modelling and reinforcing social skills and finding ways to put their children in contact with peers (Sandstrom & Coie, 1999).

Friendship

Children may spend much of their free time in groups, but only as individuals do they form friendships. Popularity is the peer group's opinion of a child, but friendship is a two-way street.

Children look for friends who are like them: of the same age, sex, and ethnic group and with common interests. A friend is someone a child feels affection for, is comfortable with, likes to do things with, and can share feelings and secrets with. Friends know each other well, trust each other, feel a sense of commitment to one another, and treat each other as equals. The strongest friendships involve equal commitment and mutual give-and-take. Even unpopular children can make friends; but they have fewer friends than popular children and tend to find friends among younger children, other unpopular children, or children in a different class or a different school (George & Hartmann, 1996; Hartup, 1992, 1996a, 1996b; Newcomb & Bagwell, 1995). The friends of unpopular children often have more negative attitudes towards the friendship than the unpopular children do themselves (Brendgen, Little, & Krappmann, 2000).

Table 14-1	Selman's Stages of Friendship	
Stage	**Description**	**Example**
Stage 0: Momentary playmateship (ages 3 to 7)	On this *undifferentiated* level of friendship, children are egocentric and have trouble considering another person's point of view; they tend to think only about what they want from a relationship. Most very young children define their friends in terms of physical closeness and value them for material or physical attributes.	"She lives on my street," or "He has the Power Rangers."
Stage 1: One-way assistance (ages 4 to 9)	On this *unilateral* level, a "good friend" does what the child wants the friend to do.	"She's not my friend anymore, because she wouldn't go with me when I wanted her to," or 'He's my friend because he always says yes when I want to borrow his eraser."
Stage 2: Two-way fair-weather cooperation (ages 6 to 12)	This *reciprocal* level overlaps stage 1. It involves give-and-take but still serves many separate self-interests, rather than the common interests of the two friends.	"We are friends; we do things for each other," or "A friend is someone who plays with you when you don't have anybody else to play with."
Stage 3: Intimate, mutually shared relationships (ages 9 to 15)	On this *mutual* level, children view a friendship as having a life of its own. It is an ongoing, systematic, committed relationship that incorporates more than doing things for each other. Friends become possessive and demand exclusivity.	"It takes a long time to make a close friend, so you really feel bad if you find out that your friend is trying to make other friends too."
Stage 4: Autonomous interdependence (beginning at age 12)	In this *interdependent* stage, children respect friends' needs for both dependency and autonomy.	"A good friendship is a real commitment, a risk you have to take; you have to support and trust and give, but you have to be able to let go too."

Source: Selman, 1980; Selman & Selman, 1979.

Why is friendship important? With their friends, children learn to communicate and co-operate. They learn about themselves and others. They can help each other get through stressful transitions, such as starting a new school or adjusting to parents' divorce. The inevitable quarrels help children learn to resolve conflicts (Furman, 1982; Hartup, 1992, 1996a, 1996b; Hartup & Stevens, 1999; Newcomb & Bagwell, 1995).

Friendship seems to help children to feel good about themselves, though it's also likely that children who feel good about themselves have an easier time making friends. Peer rejection and friendlessness in middle childhood may have long-term effects. In one longitudinal study, Grade 5 students who had no friends were more likely than their classmates to show symptoms of depression in young adulthood. Young adults who had had friends in childhood had higher self-esteem (Bagwell, Newcomb, & Bukowski, 1998).

Children's concepts of friendship, and the ways they act with their friends, change with age, reflecting cognitive and emotional growth. Preschool friends play together, but friendship among school-age children is deeper and more stable. Children cannot be or have true friends until they achieve the cognitive maturity to consider other people's views and needs as well as their own (Hartup, 1992; Hartup & Stevens, 1999; Newcomb & Bagwell, 1995).

On the basis of interviews with more than 250 people between ages 3 and 45, Robert Selman (1980; Selman & Selman, 1979) traced changing conceptions of friendship through five overlapping stages (see Table 14-1). He found that most school-age children are in stage 2 (reciprocal friendship based on self-interest). Older children, from about age 9 up, may be in stage 3 (intimate, mutually shared relationships).

School-age children distinguish "best friends," "good friends," and "casual friends" on the basis of how intimate they are and how much time they spend together (Hartup & Stevens, 1999). Children this age typically have three to five "best" friends with whom they spend most of their free time, but they usually play with only one or two at a time (Hartup, 1992; Hartup & Stevens, 1999). Twelve per cent of children this age have only one friend or none (Hofferth, 1998).

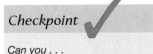

Checkpoint ✔

Can you . . .

✔ Distinguish between popularity and friendship?

✔ List characteristics children look for in friends?

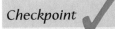

Checkpoint ✔

Can you . . .

✔ Tell how age and gender affect friendship?

School-age friends often share secrets—and laughs—as Anna and her friend Christina are doing.

School-age girls care less about having many friends than about having a few close friends they can rely on; boys have more friendships, but they tend to be less intimate and affectionate (Furman, 1982; Furman & Buhrmester, 1985; Hartup & Stevens, 1999).

Aggression and Bullying

During the school years, aggression declines and changes in form (Coie & Dodge, 1998). *Hostile* aggression (aggression aimed at hurting its target) becomes more common than *instrumental aggression* (aggression aimed at achieving an objective), the hallmark of the preschool period (Coie & Dodge, 1998). The National Longitudinal Survey of Children and Youth found that 3.5 per cent of Canadian children aged 2 to 4 years are physically aggressive, as indicated in a survey of the person most knowledgeable about the child (PMK). By the time they reach the ages of 5 to 11 years, 3.3 per cent of boys and only 0.6 per cent of girls are identified as physically aggressive by the PMK (Baillargeon, Tremblay, & Willms, 1999). Especially among girls, *overt* aggression (physical force or verbal threats) largely gives way to *relational,* or social, aggression ("putting down" or spreading rumours about another person, teasing, manipulating, and bidding for control; refer back to chapter 8). Nine-year-olds and older children recognize such behaviour as aggressive; they realize that it stems from anger and is aimed at hurting others (Crick, Bigbee, & Howes, 1996; Galen & Underwood, 1997).

Aggressors tend to be unpopular and to have social and psychological problems, but it is not clear whether aggression causes these problems or is a reaction to them (Crick & Grotpeter, 1995). Highly aggressive children tend to seek out friends like themselves and to egg each other on to anti-social acts (Hartup, 1989, 1992, 1996a; Hartup & Stevens, 1999; Masten & Coatsworth, 1998).

Aggression and Social-Information Processing

What makes children act aggressively? One answer may lie in the way they process social information: what features of the social environment they pay attention to, and how they interpret what they perceive (Crick & Dodge, 1994, 1996).

A child who is accidentally bumped in line may push back hard, assuming that the other child bumped her on purpose. This child may be a hostile (also called *reactive*) aggressor. These children often have a *hostile bias;* they see other children as trying to hurt them, and they strike out angrily in retaliation or self-defence (Crick & Dodge, 1996; Waldman, 1996). Children who seek dominance and control may be especially sensitive to slights, provocations, or other threats to their status. They may attribute such behaviour to hostility and react aggressively (Erdley et al., 1997). Rejected children also tend to have a hostile bias (Coie & Dodge, 1998; Masten & Coatsworth, 1998). Since people often *do* become hostile toward someone who acts aggressively toward them, a hostile bias may become a self-fulfilling prophecy, setting in motion a cycle of aggression.

Instrumental (or *proactive*) aggressors view force and coercion as effective ways to get what they want. They act deliberately, not out of anger. In social learning terms, they are aggressive because they expect to be rewarded for it; and when they *are* rewarded, their belief in the effectiveness of aggression is reinforced (Crick & Dodge, 1996).

Both types of aggressors need help in altering the way they process social information, so that they do not interpret aggression as either justified or useful. Adults can help children curb *hostile* aggression by teaching them how to recognize when they are getting angry and how to control their anger. *Instrumental* aggression tends to stop if it is not rewarded (Crick & Dodge, 1996).

Guidepost 8

What are the most common forms of aggressive behaviour in middle childhood, and what influences contribute to it?

Does Televised Violence Lead to Aggression?

Children see an enormous amount of violence on television. Canadian and U.S. children watch television between 12 and 25 hours a week (Hofferth, 1998; Sege & Dietz, 1994; Statistics Canada, 1997), averaging 23 hours per week (CPS, 1999). In the United States, about 6 out of 10 programs contain violence, and few show alternatives to violence. The worst culprits are movies, including those on premium cable channels, which show violence 85 per cent of the time (National [U.S.] Television Violence Study [NTVS], 1995) while over half of music videos depict violence against women (CPS, 1999). Thirty-nine per cent of children's programs on British television contain violence, mostly shootings or other physical assaults (Gunter & Harrison, 1997).

Correlational studies since the 1960s agree that children who see televised violence behave more aggressively (Coie & Dodge, 1998; National [U.S.] Institutes of Mental Health [NIMH], 1982; Strasburger & Donnerstein, 1999). This is true across geographic locations and socio-economic levels, for both boys and girls, and for normal children as well as for those with emotional problems. Now evidence from a wide range of other research, including experimental and longitudinal studies, supports a causal relationship between watching televised violence and acting aggressively (Coie & Dodge, 1998; Geen, 1994; Huston et al., 1992; Strasburger & Donnerstein, 1999).

Children, especially those whose parents use harsh discipline, are more vulnerable than adults to the influence of televised violence (Coie & Dodge, 1998). Classic social-learning research suggests that children imitate filmed models even more than live ones (Bandura, Ross, & Ross, 1963). The influence is stronger if the child believes the violence on the screen is real, identifies with the violent character, and watches without parental supervision (Coie & Dodge, 1998; Huesmann & Eron, 1986). Other groups of children showing higher susceptibility to the effects of TV violence include immigrant children, children with emotional problems, those with learning disabilities, victims of abuse by parents, and children in distressed families (CPS, 1999).

When children see televised violence, they may absorb the values depicted and come to view aggression as acceptable behaviour. Most programs glorify and glamourize violence. In 73 per cent of violent scenes, perpetrators go unpunished; in 47 per cent, victims go unharmed, suggesting that violence has no unpleasant consequences (NTVS, 1995). Children who see both heroes and villains on television getting what they want through violence are likely to conclude that violence is an effective way to resolve conflicts. They may become less sensitive to the pain it causes. They may learn to take violence for granted and may be less likely to intervene when they see it (Gunter & Harrison, 1997; NTVS, 1995, 1996; NIMH, 1982; Sege & Dietz, 1994; Singer, Slovak, Frierson, & York, 1998; M. E. Smith, 1993). Of course, some children are more impressionable, more impulsive, and more easily influenced than others (M. O. Johnson, 1996).

The larger the dose of television, the more harmful its apparent effects. In a survey of students in grades 3 through 8 in 11 Ohio public schools, the more television children said they watched each day, especially among those who preferred action programs, the more trauma symptoms (such as anxiety, depression, stress, and anger) and violent behaviour they reported. Children with psychological and behaviour problems may watch more television than children without such problems, and a heavy diet of television may well worsen such problems. Thus heavy television viewing may indicate problems that may need treatment (Singer et al., 1998).

The long-term influence of televised violence is greater in middle childhood than at earlier ages; 8- to 12-year-olds seem particularly susceptible (Eron & Huesmann, 1986). Among 427 young adults whose viewing habits had been studied at age 8, the best predictor of aggressiveness in 19-year-old men and women was the degree of violence in the shows they had watched as children (Eron, 1980, 1982). In a follow-up study, the amount of television viewed at age 8, and the preference among boys for violent shows, predicted the severity of criminal offences at age 30 (Huesmann, 1986; Huesmann & Eron, 1984).

The Canadian Paediatric Society (1999) and the American Psychological Association (1993) have called for a major effort to reduce violence on television. In 1996, the U.S. Congress enacted a law requiring all new television sets to be equipped with an electronic blocking device, the "V" chip, developed in Canada, that parents can use to screen out

Checkpoint ✓

Can you . . .

✔ Tell how aggression changes in form during middle childhood and how social information processing and televised violence can contribute to it?

What's your view ?

• What can and should be done about children's exposure to violent television programs?

bullying Aggression deliberately and persistently directed against a particular target, or victim, typically one who is weak, vulnerable, and defenceless

objectionable programs. The law also prods the networks to devise a violence rating system (Mifflin, 1996). Canadian television is encoded for the "V" chip. Although electronic blocking devices are useful in filtering out unwanted programming, they can create a false sense of security in parents who might believe that all violent programs are being eliminated. As a result, the CPS encourages parents to monitor their children's television viewing (CPS, 1999).

Bullies and Victims

Aggression becomes **bullying** when it is deliberately, persistently directed against a particular target: a victim who, typically, is weak, vulnerable, and defenceless. Male bullies tend to use physical force (overt aggression) and to select either boys or girls as victims. Female bullies use verbal or psychological means (relational aggression) and are more likely to victimize other girls (Boulton, 1995; CICH, 2000).

A study of Canadian children in Grades 4 to 6 showed boys to be more likely to report using physical aggression than girls to resolve conflicts. Although no gender differences were found in children's reports of using relational aggression, those children who did report using this form of aggression were more likely to indicate that they were concerned about avoiding trouble and maintaining relationships with their peer group than did children who reported using physical aggression in conflict resolution (Delveaux & Daniels, 2000).

Patterns of bullying and victimization may become established as early as kindergarten. As tentative peer groups form, children initially direct aggression at various targets. Aggressors soon get to know which children make the easiest "marks" and focus their aggression on them.

Victims tend to be anxious and submissive and to cry easily, or to be argumentative and provocative (Hodges, Boivin, Vitaro, & Bukowski, 1999; Olweus, 1995). They are apt to have low self-esteem—though it is not clear whether low self-esteem leads to or follows from victimization. Male victims tend to be physically weak (Boulton & Smith, 1994; Olweus, 1995). Children who are bullied may develop such behaviour problems as hyperactivity and overdependence, and they may become more aggressive themselves (Schwartz, McFadyen-Ketchum, Dodge, Pettit, & Bates, 1998). Having a best friend seems to provide some protection against victimization (Hodges et al., 1999).

A longitudinal study using naturalistic observation of bullying in Toronto schools showed that although peers were present most of the time, they intervened in only 19 per cent of bullying incidents. When they did intervene, the intervention was usually effective in stopping the bullying. The interventions tended to involve aggression when they were directed towards the bully, and non-aggressive when directed to the victim, or the victim–bully pair. Children were more likely to intervene when the victim and bully were the same sex as the child who was intervening (Hawkins, Pepler, & Craig, 2001).

Middle childhood is a prime time for bullying (Boulton & Smith, 1994). However, the likelihood of *being* bullied seems to decrease steadily throughout middle childhood and adolescence. As children get older, most of them may learn how to discourage bullying, leaving a smaller "pool" of available victims (P. K. Smith & Levan, 1995).

Bullying can be stopped or prevented. One intervention program in Grades 4 through 7 in Norwegian schools cut bullying in half and also reduced other anti-social behaviour. This was accomplished by creating an authoritative atmosphere marked by warmth, interest, and involvement combined with firm limits and consistent, non-physical punishment. Better supervision and monitoring at recess and lunchtime, class rules against bullying, and serious talks with bullies, victims, and parents were part of the program (Olweus, 1995).

Checkpoint ✔

Can you . . .

✔ Describe how patterns of bullying and victimization become established and change?

Guidepost 9

What are some common emotional disturbances, and how are they treated?

Mental Health

Although most children have a fairly high level of emotional adjustment, an estimated 1 in 10 children between the ages of 4 and 11 years shows evidence of hyperactivity, conduct disorder, or emotional disorders, according to parent reports (CICH, 2000). More boys than girls experience such disorders, with about one in four boys and less than one in five girls being identified with one or more mental health problems (CICH, 2000). About 3 per cent of children in this age group experienced social impairment as a result of their problems (Offord & Lipman, 1996). Most common are *anxiety* or *mood disorders* (feeling sad, depressed, unloved, nervous, fearful, or lonely); *disruptive conduct disorders* (aggression, defiance, or anti-social behaviour); and hyperactivity. Some problems seem to be associated with a particular phase of a child's life and will go away on their own, but others need to be treated to prevent future trouble (Achenbach & Howell, 1993; USDHHS, 1999c). A study of parent-reported mental health problems of more than 13,000 children in Australia, Belgium, China, Germany, Greece, Israel, Jamaica, the Netherlands, Puerto Rico, Sweden, Thailand, and the United States found remarkably similar complaints across cultures (Crijnen, Achenbach, & Verhulst, 1999).

Common Emotional Disturbances

It is during elementary school that children increasingly are referred for mental health treatment. Let's look at three common types of disturbances: disruptive behaviour disorders, anxiety disorders, and depression.

Disruptive Behaviour Disorders

Temper tantrums and defiant, argumentative, hostile, deliberately annoying behaviour—common among 4- and 5-year-olds—typically are outgrown by middle childhood. When such a pattern of behaviour persists until age 8, children (usually boys) may be diagnosed with **oppositional defiant disorder (ODD),** a pattern of defiance, disobedience, and hostility toward adult authority figures. Children with ODD constantly fight, argue, lose their temper, snatch things, blame others, are angry and resentful, and generally test the limits of adults' patience (APA, 1994; USDHHS, 1999c).

Some children with ODD move on to a repetitive, persistent pattern of aggressive, anti-social acts, such as truancy, setting fires, habitual lying, fighting, vandalism, rape or prostitution, and use of guns. This is called **conduct disorder (CD)** (APA, 1994). About 11 per cent of boys and 8 per cent of girls aged 4 to 11 years in Canada demonstrate symptoms of conduct disorder, according to parents' reports (Offord & Lipman, 1996). Many children with conduct disorder also have attention-deficit hyperactivity disorder (ADHD; refer back to Chapter 13). Although children with ADHD find it difficult to inhibit ongoing actions, children with CD or co-occurring CD and ADHD do not have trouble inhibiting ongoing activity (Schachar, Mota, Logan, Tannock, & Klim, 2000). Some 11- to 13-year-olds progress from conduct disorder to criminal violence—mugging, rape, and break-ins—and by age 17 may be frequent, serious offenders (Coie & Dodge, 1998; see the discussion of juvenile delinquency in chapter 17). Between 25 and 50 per cent of these highly anti-social children become anti-social adults (USDHHS, 1999c).

School Phobia and Other Anxiety Disorders

Nicole wakes up on a school morning complaining of nausea, stomach ache, or headache. Soon after she receives permission to stay home, the symptoms clear up. This goes on day after day, and the longer she is out of school, the harder it is to get her back.

Nicole's behaviour is typical of children with **school phobia,** an unrealistic fear of going to school. Some children have realistic reasons to avoid going to school: a sarcastic teacher, overly demanding work, or a bully in the schoolyard (Kochenderfer & Ladd, 1996). In such instances, the environment may need changing, not the child.

True school phobia may be a type of **separation anxiety disorder,** a condition involving excessive anxiety for at least 4 weeks about separation from home or from people to whom the child is attached. Separation anxiety disorder affects some 4 per cent of children and young adolescents and may persist through the college and university years. These children often come from close-knit, caring families. They may develop the disorder after the death of a pet, an illness, or a move to a new school (APA, 1994). Many children with separation anxiety also show symptoms of depression: sadness, withdrawal, apathy, or difficulty in concentrating (USDHHS, 1999c).

oppositional defiant disorder (ODD) Pattern of behaviour, persisting into middle childhood, marked by negativity, hostility, and defiance

conduct disorder (CD) Repetitive, persistent pattern of aggressive, anti-social behaviour violating societal norms or the rights of others

school phobia Unrealistic fear of going to school, may be a form of *separation anxiety disorder* or *social phobia*

separation anxiety disorder Condition involving excessive, prolonged anxiety about separation from home or from people to whom a child is attached

School-phobic children tend to be average or good students. They tend to be timid and inhibited away from home, but wilful, stubborn, and demanding with their parents (G. A. Bernstein & Garfinkel, 1988). The most important element in treatment is an early, gradual return to school. Usually children go back without too much trouble once treatment is begun.

School phobia also may be a form of **social phobia:** extreme fear and/or avoidance of social situations. Social-phobic children may be so afraid of embarrassment that they break into blushes, sweats, or palpitations when asked to speak in class or when meeting an acquaintance on the street (USDHHS, 1999c). Social phobia is much more common than was once believed, affecting about 5 per cent of children and 8 per cent of adults. Social phobias run in families, so there may be a genetic component. Often these phobias are triggered by traumatic experiences, such as a child's mind going blank when the child is called on in class. Children can also can develop social phobias by observing how their parents respond to social situations (Beidel & Turner, 1998; Stein, Chavira, & Jang, 2001).

Some children have a **generalized anxiety disorder**, which is not focused on one specific part of their lives, such as school or social relationships. These children worry about just about everything: school grades, being on time, wars, or earthquakes. Their worry seems independent of their performance or how they are regarded by others. They tend to be perfectionists, conformists, and self-doubters. They seek approval and need constant reassurance (APA, 1994; USDHHS, 1999c). Far less common is **obsessive-compulsive disorder**; sufferers are obsessed by repetitive, intrusive thoughts, images, or impulses and often show compulsive behaviours, such as constant handwashing, in an attempt to get rid of these obsessions (APA, 1994; USDHHS, 1999c).

Anxiety disorders of these types are among the most prevalent mental health problems in Canada for children and adolescents (Antony & Swinson, 1996). They are twice as common among girls as among boys. The heightened female vulnerability to anxiety begins as early as age 6. Females are also more susceptible to depression, which is similar to anxiety in some ways and often goes hand-in-hand with it (Lewinsohn, Gotlib, Lewinsohn, Seeley, & Allen, 1998). Both anxiety and depression may involve a neurologically based *behaviour inhibition system:* apprehensiveness, diminished motor activity, and watchful waiting for anticipated danger. A tendency to anxiety and depression may stem from early experiences that make children feel a lack of control over what happens around them (Chorpita & Barlow, 1998).

Childhood Depression

"Nobody likes me" is a common complaint among school-age children, who tend to be popularity-conscious; but a prolonged sense of friendlessness may be one sign of **childhood depression:** a disorder of mood that goes beyond normal, temporary sadness. At any given time, between 14 and 38 per cent of 4- to 11-year-old children have symptoms of depression, as reported by parents (CICH, 2000), such as inability to have fun or concentrate, fatigue, extreme activity or apathy, crying, sleep problems, feelings of worthlessness, weight change, physical complaints, or frequent thoughts about death or suicide. Any five of these symptoms, lasting at least 2 weeks, may point to depression (APA, 1994). If symptoms persist, the child should be given psychological help. Depression may lead to an attempted suicide and often signals the beginning of a recurrent problem that, if present during adolescence, is likely to persist into adulthood (Birmaher, 1998; Birmaher et al., 1996; Cicchetti & Toth, 1998; Kye & Ryan, 1995; USDHHS, 1999c; Weissman et al., 1999).

The exact causes of childhood depression are not known. Twin studies have found the heritability of childhood depression to be only modest, though 20 to 50 per cent of depressed children and adolescents have a family history of it. Depressed children tend to come from dysfunctional families, with high levels of parental depression, anxiety, substance abuse, or anti-social behaviour; and the atmosphere in such families may increase children's risk of depression. Early interactions with caregivers may lay the groundwork for the emergence of childhood depression (Cicchetti & Toth, 1998; USDHHS, 1999c; refer back to chapter 8).

Depression often emerges during the transition to middle school and may be related to academic pressures (Cicchetti & Toth, 1998). The prevalence of depression increases during adolescence. Three per cent of 12- to 14-year olds in Canada experience a major depression episode, and this number grows to 6 per cent for boys and 12 per cent for girls between 15 and 19 years of age (CICH, 2000). Adolescent girls, like adult women, are especially subject to depression (Birmaher et al., 1996; Cicchetti & Toth, 1998). This gender difference may be related to biological changes connected with puberty or to the way girls are socialized (Birmaher et al., 1996) and their greater vulnerability to stress in social relationships (USDHHS, 1999c).

First Nations children show a pattern of depression different from that of non–First Nations children, as demonstrated in the Flower of Two Soils study (Beiser, Sack, Manson, Redshirt, & Dion, 1998). In Grade 2, non–First Nations children report higher levels of depression compared to First Nations children, and this difference gradually decreases in magnitude until Grade 4, when the difference disappears. However, there is a high rate of depression among First Nations adolescents (Sack, Beiser, Baker-Brown, & Redshirt, 1994).

Treatment Techniques

Psychological treatment for emotional disturbances can take several forms. In **individual psychotherapy,** a therapist sees a child one-on-one, to help the child gain insights into his or her personality and relationships and to interpret feelings and behaviour. Such treatment may be helpful at a time of stress, such as the death of a parent or parental divorce, even when a child has not shown signs of disturbance. Child psychotherapy is usually more effective when combined with counselling for the parents.

In **family therapy,** the therapist sees the family together, observes how members interact, and points out both growth-producing and growth-inhibiting or destructive patterns of family functioning. Sometimes the child whose problem brings the family into therapy is, ironically, the healthiest member, responding openly to a troubled family situation. Therapy can help parents confront their own conflicts and begin to resolve them. This is often the first step toward resolving the child's problems as well.

When children have limited verbal and conceptual skills, or have suffered emotional trauma, *art therapy* can help them express or describe what is troubling them without having to put their feelings into words (Kozlowska & Hanney, 1999). The child may express deep emotions through choice of colours and subjects to depict (Garbarino, Dubrow, Kostelny, & Pardo, 1992). In family therapy, observing how a family plans, carries out, and then discusses an art project can reveal patterns of family interactions. Family members often "speak" more freely through such a shared activity (Kozlowska & Hanney, 1999).

Behaviour therapy, or *behaviour modification* (refer back to chapter 2), is a form of psychotherapy that uses principles of learning theory to eliminate undesirable behaviours (such as temper tantrums) or to develop desirable ones (such as putting away toys after play). In the latter example, every time the child puts toys away, she or he gets a reward, such as praise, a treat, or a token to be exchanged for a new toy.

A statistical analysis of many studies found that, in general, psychotherapy is effective with children and adolescents, especially with adolescent girls. Behaviour therapy was more effective than non-behavioural methods. Results were best when treatment was targeted to specific problems and desired outcomes (Weisz, Weiss, Han, Granger, & Morton, 1995).

The use of **drug therapy** to treat childhood emotional disorders greatly increased during the 1990s, often in combination with one or more forms of psychotherapy. However, sufficient research on its effectiveness and safety for children and adolescents is generally lacking (USDHHS, 1999c), and developmental scientists generally decry its use. Antidepressants are commonly prescribed for depression, and anti-psychotics for severe psychological problems. Yet many studies have found antidepressants no more effective than *placebos* (substances with no active ingredients) in treating depression in children and adolescents (Fisher & Fisher, 1996; Sommers-Flanagan & Sommers-Flanagan, 1996).

Two exceptions are the use of stimulants such as Ritalin to treat attention deficit/ hyperactivity disorder (refer back to chapter 13) and the use of *serotonin selective reuptake inhibitors (SSRIs)* to treat obsessive-compulsive and depressive disorders (Rodrigues, 1999; USDHHS, 1999c). A randomly controlled trial found fluoxetine (Prozac), the most popular of the SSRIs, superior to placebos. It is safer and has more tolerable side effects than other classes of drugs (Birmaher, 1998). However, Prozac can produce sleep

Everyone feels "blue" at times, but a child's chronic depression can be a danger signal and should be taken seriously, especially when it represents a marked change from the child's usual behaviour

individual psychotherapy Psychological treatment in which a therapist sees a troubled person one-on-one

family therapy Psychological treatment in which a therapist sees the whole family together to analyze patterns of family functioning

behaviour therapy Therapeutic approach using principles of learning theory to encourage desired behaviours or eliminate undesired ones; also called *behaviour modification*

drug therapy Administration of drugs to treat emotional disorders

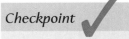

Checkpoint

Can you . . .

✔ Identify causes and symptoms of disruptive behaviour disorders, anxiety disorders, and childhood depression?

✔ Describe and evaluate five common types of therapy for emotional disorders?

disturbances and behavioural changes, and its long-term effects are unknown. There also is concern that SSRIs may be used instead of psychological therapies, rather than along with them (Rushton, Clark, & Freed, 1999).

Stress and Resilience

Guidepost 10

How do the stresses of modern life affect children, and what enables "resilient" children to withstand them?

Stressful events are part of childhood, and most children learn to cope. Stress that becomes overwhelming, however, can lead to psychological problems. Severe stressors, such as kidnapping or child abuse, may have long-term effects on physical and psychological well-being. Yet some children show remarkable resilience in surmounting such ordeals.

Stresses of Modern Life

The child psychologist David Elkind (1981, 1984, 1986, 1997) has called today's child the "hurried child." He warns that the pressures of modern life are forcing children to grow up too soon and are making their childhood too stressful. Today's children are expected to succeed in school, to compete in sports, and to meet parents' emotional needs. Children are exposed to many adult problems on television and in real life before they have mastered the problems of childhood. They know about sex and violence, and they often must shoulder adult responsibilities. Many children move frequently and have to change schools and leave old friends (Fowler, Simpson, & Schoendorf, 1993; G. A. Simpson & Fowler, 1994). The tightly scheduled pace of life also can be stressful (Hofferth & Sandberg, 1998). Yet children are not small adults. They feel and think like children, and they need the years of childhood for healthy development.

Given how much stress children are exposed to, it should not be surprising that they worry a lot. In a survey and interviews of 272 ethnically diverse students in Grades 2 through 6 in a large U.S. metropolitan area (Silverman, La Greca, & Wasserstein, 1995), school emerged as one of the children's chief concerns. So did health—their own or someone else's. However, the worry reported by the largest number of children (56 per cent of the sample) was personal harm from others: being robbed, stabbed, or shot.

These children were not in a high-crime area, nor had they personally experienced many attacks. Their intense anxiety about their safety seemed to reflect the high rates of crime and violence in the larger society—even including killings in schools. How much more stressful life must be, then, for children who are in real, constant danger—such as a 6-year-old in Washington, D.C., who saw her mother punched in the face by a drug addict, or a 10-year-old who ran away in terror after seeing a man shot in the back on the street! These inner-city children are typical of many who live in the midst of violence and are fearful, anxious, distressed, or depressed (Garbarino, Dubrow, Kostelny, & Pardo, 1992, 1998).

Children who grow up surrounded by violence often have trouble concentrating and sleeping. They may be afraid that their mothers will abandon them. Some become aggressive, and some come to take brutality for granted. Many do not allow themselves to become attached to other people, for fear of more hurt and loss (Garbarino et al., 1992, 1998). Children with multiple risks—those who live in violent communities, who are poor, and who receive inadequate parenting, education, and health care—are the most likely to suffer permanent developmental damage (Rutter, 1987).

To reduce violence, the Canadian Paediatric Society (1996) recommends regulating and restricting ownership of handguns and ammunition; supporting gun-registration legislation; enforcing strict standards for storing firearms; and teaching gun-owners the risks of having a gun in the home, particularly when there are children or adolescents in the home.

School-based programs designed to prevent violent behaviour by promoting social competence have been modestly successful. One such program, Providing Alternative Thinking Strategies (PATH), presumes that thoughts and behaviour are based on emotional awareness and control. Emotional and cognitive development are guided through carefully sequenced lessons that include instruction, worksheets, discussion, role playing, and modelling and reinforcement by teachers and peers. Experience with such programs suggests the desirability of school reforms aimed at integrating social-emotional and academic development, since children who are socially competent and have little conflict with classmates may be able to better concentrate on schoolwork (Henrich, Brown, & Aber, 1999).

Coping with Stress: The Resilient Child

Resilient children are those who weather circumstances that would blight most others, who maintain their composure and competence under challenge or threat, or who bounce back from traumatic events. These children do not possess mysterious qualities. They simply have managed, despite adverse circumstances, to hold onto the basic systems and resources that promote positive development in normal children (see Table 14-2). The two most important **protective factors,** which seem to help children overcome stress and contribute to resilience, are good *family relationships* and *cognitive functioning* (Masten & Coatsworth, 1998).

Resilient children are likely to have good relationships and strong bonds with at least one supportive parent (Pettit et al., 1997) or caregiver. If not, the child may be close to at least one other caring, competent adult (Masten & Coatsworth, 1998).

Resilient children tend to have high IQs and to be good problem solvers. Their superior information-processing skills may help them cope with adversity, protect themselves, regulate their behaviour, and learn from experience. They may attract the interest of teachers, who can act as guides, confidants, or mentors (Masten & Coatsworth, 1998).

Other frequently cited protective factors (Eisenberg et al., 1997; Masten et al., 1990; Masten & Coatsworth, 1998; E. E. Werner, 1993) include:

- *The child's personality:* Resilient children are adaptable, friendly, well liked, independent, and sensitive to others. They are competent and have high self-esteem. They are creative, resourceful, independent, and pleasant to be with.
- *Reduced risk:* Children who have been exposed to only one of a number of factors strongly related to psychiatric disorder (such as parental discord, low social status, a disturbed mother, a criminal father, and experience in foster care or an institution) are often better able to overcome stress than children who have been exposed to more than one risk factor.
- *Compensating experiences:* A supportive school environment or successful experiences in studies, in sports, in music, or with other children or adults can help make up for a destructive home life. In adulthood, a good marriage can compensate for poor relationships earlier in life.

All this does not mean that bad things that happen in a child's life do not matter. In general, children with unfavourable backgrounds have more problems in adjustment than children with more favourable backgrounds. Some outwardly resilient children may suffer internal distress that may have long-term consequences (Masten & Coatsworth, 1998). Still, what is heartening about these findings is that negative childhood experiences do not necessarily determine the outcome of a person's life and that many children have the strength to rise above the most difficult circumstances (Jenkins and Keating, 1998). In an interesting reversal of expected trends, immigrant children to Canada experience better

resilient children Children who weather adverse circumstances, function well despite challenges or threats, or bounce back from traumatic events

protective factors Influences that reduce the impact of early stress and tend to predict positive outcomes

What's your view **?**

- How can adults contribute to children's resilience? Give examples.

Table 14-2	Characteristics of Resilient Children and Adolescents
Source	**Characteristic**
Individual	Good intellectual functioning
	Appealing, sociable, easygoing disposition
	Self-efficacy, self-confidence, high self-esteem
	Talents
	Faith
Family	Close relationship to caring parent figure
	Authoritative parenting: warmth, structure, high expectations
	Socio-economic advantages
	Connections to extended supportive family networks
Extra-familial context	Bonds to pro-social adults outside the family
	Connections to pro-social organizations
	Attending effective schools

Source: Masten & Coatsworth, 1998, p. 212.

Figure 14-3

Prevalence of Mental Health Outcomes in New Immigrant and National Populations.

Source: Adapted from Beiser, Hou, et al., 1998.

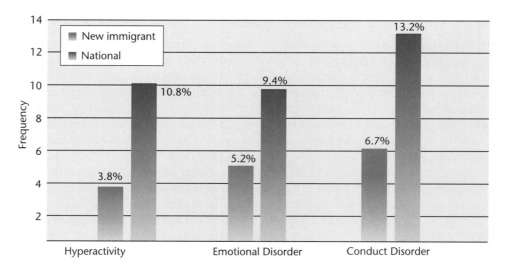

Checkpoint ✔

Can you . . .

✔ Explain Elkind's concept of the "hurried child"?

✔ Name the most common source of fear and anxiety in urban children and tell how fears change with age?

✔ Identify protective factors that contribute to resilience?

mental health than Canadian children, despite the fact that a larger proportion of immigrant children live in poverty, as shown in Figure 14-3. It seems that immigrant families provide adequate emotional support and stability to children, despite low income levels in the first years after immigration to Canada (Beiser, Hou, Hyman, & Tousignant, 1998; Human Resources Development Canada, 2002).

The findings on resilience also point to potential pathways to promote more positive development. This might be done by eliminating or reducing the impact of risk factors such as low birth weight and homelessness, adding compensating resources, or bolstering adaptational processes by improving parent–child relationships and designing experiences that build self-efficacy (Masten & Coatsworth, 1998).

Adolescence, too, is a stressful, risk-filled time—more so than middle childhood. Yet most adolescents develop the skills and competence to deal with the challenges they face, as we'll see in Part 6.

Summary and Key Terms

The Developing Self

Guidepost 1 How do school-age children develop a realistic self-concept, and what contributes to self-esteem?

- The self-concept becomes more realistic during middle childhood, when, according to neo-Piagetian theory, children form representational systems.

- According to Erikson, the chief source of self-esteem is children's view of their productive competence. This "virtue" develops through resolution of the crisis of industry versus inferiority. According to Susan Harter's research, however, self-esteem arises primarily from social support and self-evaluation.

  representational systems (351) industry versus inferiority (352)

Guidepost 2 How do school-age children show emotional growth?

- School-age children have internalized shame and pride and can better understand and control negative emotions.

- Empathy and pro-social behaviour increase.

- Emotional growth is affected by parents' reactions to displays of negative emotions.

The Child in the Family

Guidepost 3 How do parent–child relationships change in middle childhood?

- School-age children spend less time with, and are less close to, parents than before; but relationships with parents continue to be important. Culture influences family relationships and roles.

- Development of co-regulation may affect the way a family handles conflicts and discipline.

  co-regulation (354)

Guidepost 4 What are the effects of parents' work and of poverty on family atmosphere?

- The family environment has two major components: family structure and family atmosphere. Family atmosphere includes both emotional tone and economic well-being.

- The impact of mothers' employment depends on many factors concerning the child, the mother's work, and her feelings about it; whether she has a supportive mate; the family's socio-economic status; and the kind of care the child receives. Homes with employed mothers tend to be more structured and more egalitarian than homes with at-home mothers. Maternal employment has a positive influence on school achievement in low-income families, but boys in middle-class families tend to do less well.

- Parents living in persistent poverty may have trouble providing effective discipline and monitoring and emotional support.

Guidepost 5 What impact does family structure have on children's development?

- Many children today grow up in non-traditional family structures. Children tend to do better in traditional (intact) families. The structure of the family, however, is less important than its effects on family atmosphere.

- Adopted children are generally well adjusted, though they face special challenges.

- Children's adjustment to divorce depends on factors concerning the child; the parents' handling of the situation; custody and visitation arrangements; financial circumstances; contact with the non-custodial parent (usually the father); and a parent's remarriage.

- The amount of conflict in a marriage and the likelihood of its continuing after divorce may influence whether or not children are better off if the parents stay together.

- Children living with only one parent are at heightened risk of behavioural and academic problems, in part related to socio-economic status.

- Remarriages are more likely to fail than first marriages. Boys tend to have more trouble than girls in adjusting to divorce and single-parent living but tend to adjust better to the mother's remarriage.

- Stepmothers are usually more involved with stepchildren than stepfathers are.

- Studies have found no ill effects on children living with gay and lesbian parents.

Guidepost 6 How do siblings influence and get along with one another?

- The roles and responsibilities of siblings in non-industrialized societies are more structured than in industrialized societies.

- Siblings learn about conflict resolution from their relationships with each other. Relationships with parents affect sibling relationships.

The Child in the Peer Group

Guidepost 7 How do relationships with peers change in middle childhood, and what influences popularity and choice of friends?

- The peer group becomes more important in middle childhood. Peer groups generally consist of children who are similar in age, sex, ethnicity, and socio-economic status, and who live near one another or go to school together.

- The peer group helps children develop social skills, allows them to test and adopt values independent of parents, gives them a sense of belonging, and helps develop the self-concept. It also may encourage conformity and prejudice.

- Popularity influences self-esteem and future adjustment. Popular children tend to have good cognitive abilities and social skills. Behaviours that affect popularity may be derived from family relationships and cultural values.

- Intimacy and stability of friendships increase during middle childhood. Boys tend to have more friends, whereas girls have closer friends.

prejudice (364)

Guidepost 8 What are the most common forms of aggressive behaviour in middle childhood, and what influences contribute to it?

- During middle childhood, aggression typically declines. Relational aggression becomes more common than overt aggression, especially among girls. Also, instrumental aggression gives way to hostile aggression, often with a hostile bias. Highly aggressive children tend to be unpopular and maladjusted.

- Aggressiveness promoted by exposure to televised violence can extend into adult life.

- Middle childhood is a prime time for bullying; patterns may be established in kindergarten. Victims tend to be weak and submissive, or argumentative and provocative, and to have low self-esteem.

bullying (370)

Mental Health

Guidepost 9 What are some common emotional disturbances, and how are they treated?

- Common emotional and behavioural disorders among school-age children include disruptive behavioural disorders, anxiety disorders, and childhood depression.

- Treatment techniques include individual psychotherapy or family therapy (sometimes using art therapy), behaviour therapy, and drug therapy. Often therapies are used in combination.

oppositional defiant disorder (ODD) (371)
conduct disorder (CD) (371)   school phobia (371)
separation anxiety disorder (371)   social phobia (372)
generalized anxiety disorder (372)
obsessive-compulsive disorder (372)   childhood depression (372)
individual psychotherapy (373)   family therapy (373)
behaviour therapy (373)   drug therapy (373)

Guidepost 10 How do the stresses of modern life affect children, and what enables "resilient" children to withstand them?

- As a result of the pressures of modern life, many children experience stress. Children tend to worry about school, health, and personal safety.

- Resilient children are better able than others to withstand stress. Protective factors involve cognitive ability, family relationships, personality, degree of risk, and compensating experiences.

resilient children (375)   protective factors (375)

OLC Preview

The official website for *A Child's World,* First Canadian Edition, supplements the boxed material in this chapter focusing on children and divorce and on popularity, and offers links to recommended websites. Check out **www.mcgrawhill.ca/college/papalia**.

Physical Development and Health in Adolescence

What I like in my adolescents is that they have not yet hardened. We all confuse hardening and strength. Strength we must achieve, but not callousness.

—Anaïs Nin, *The Diaries of Anaïs Nin,* Vol. IV, 1971

Focus *Anne Frank, Diarist of the Holocaust**

Anne Frank

For her 13th birthday on June 12, 1942, Anne Frank's parents gave her a diary. This small, cloth-covered volume was the first of several notebooks in which Anne recorded her experiences and reflections during the next 2 years. Little did she dream that her jottings would become one of the most famous published accounts by victims of the Holocaust during World War II.

Anne Frank (1929–1945), her parents, Otto and Edith Frank, and her older sister, Margot, were German Jews who fled to Amsterdam after Hitler came to power in 1933, only to see the Netherlands fall to Nazi conquest 7 years later. In the summer of 1942, when the Nazis began rounding up Dutch Jews for deportation to concentration camps, the family went into hiding on the upper floors of the building occupied by Otto Frank's pharmaceutical firm. Behind a door concealed by a movable cupboard, a steep stairway led to the four rooms Anne called the "Secret Annexe." For 2 years, they stayed in those confined quarters with a couple named "Van Daan," their 15-year-old son, "Peter," and a middle-aged dentist, "Albert Dussel,"** who shared Anne's room. Then, on August 4, 1944, German and Dutch security police raided the "Secret Annexe" and sent its occupants to concentration camps, where all but Anne's father died.

Anne's writings, published by Otto Frank after the war, describe the life the fugitives led. During the day they had to be completely quiet so as not to alert people in the offices below. They saw no one except a few trusted Christian helpers who risked their lives to bring food, books, newspapers, and essential supplies. To venture outside—which would have been necessary to replace Anne's quickly outgrown clothes or to correct her worsening nearsightedness—was unthinkable.

The diary reveals the thoughts, feelings, daydreams, and mood swings of a high-spirited, introspective adolescent coming to maturity under traumatic conditions. Anne wrote of her concern about her "ugly" appearance, of her wish for "a real mother who understands me," and of her adoration for her father (Frank, 1958, pp. 36, 110). She expressed despair at the adults' constant criticism of her failings and at her parents' apparent favouritism toward her sister. She wrote about her fears, her urge for independence, her hopes for a return to her old life, and her aspirations for a writing career.

As tensions rose in the "Secret Annexe," Anne lost her appetite and began taking antidepressant medication. But as time went on, she became less self-pitying and more serious-minded. When she thought back to her previous carefree existence, she felt like a different person from the Anne who had "grown wise within these walls" (p. 149).

*Sources of biographical information about Anne Frank were Bloom (1999); Frank (1958, 1995), Lindwer (1991), Müller (1998), and Netherlands State Institute for War Documentation (1989). Page references are to the 1958 paperback version of the diary.
**Fictional names Anne invented for use in her diary.

She was deeply conscious of her sexual awakening: "I think what is happening to me is so wonderful, and not only what can be seen on my body, but all that is taking place inside. . . . Each time I have a period . . . I have the feeling that . . . I have a sweet secret, and . . . I always long for the time that I shall feel that secret within me again" (pp. 115–116).

Anne originally had regarded Peter as shy and gawky—a not-very-promising companion; but eventually she began visiting his attic room for long, intimate talks and finally, her first kiss. Her diary records the conflict between her stirring sexual passion and her strict moral upbringing.

One of the last diary entries is dated July 15, 1944, less than 3 weeks before the raid and 8 months before Anne's death in the concentration camp at Bergen-Belsen: ". . . in spite of everything, I still believe that people are really good at heart. . . . I hear the ever approaching thunder, which will destroy us too, I can feel the suffering of millions and yet, if I look up into the heavens, I think that it will all come right, that this cruelty too will end, and that peace and tranquillity will return again" (p. 233).

● ● ●

The moving story of Anne Frank's tragically abbreviated adolescence points up the insistent role of biology and its interrelationships with inner and outer experience. Anne's "coming of age" occurred under highly unusual conditions. Yet her normal physical maturation went on, along with a host of cognitive and psychosocial changes heightened by her stressful circumstances.

In this chapter, we describe the physical transformations of adolescence and how they affect young people's feelings. We consider the impact of early and late maturation. We discuss health issues associated with this time of life, and we examine two serious problems: maltreatment and teenage suicide.

After you have read and studied this chapter, you should be able to answer each of the Guidepost questions that appear at the top of the next page. Look for them again in the margins, where they point to important concepts throughout the chapter. To check your understanding of these Guideposts, review the end-of-chapter summary. Checkpoints located throughout the chapter will help you verify your understanding of what you have read.

Guideposts for Study

1. What is adolescence, and when does it begin and end?

2. What opportunities and risks does adolescence entail?

3. What physical changes do adolescents experience, and how do these changes affect them psychologically?

4. What are some common health problems in adolescence, and how can they be prevented?

Adolescence: A Developmental Transition

Guidepost 1

What is adolescence, and when does it begin and end?

Rituals to mark a child's "coming of age" are common in many societies. Rites of passage may include religious blessings, separation from the family, severe tests of strength and endurance, marking the body in some way, or acts of magic. The ritual may be held at a certain age; for example, bar mitzvah or bat mitzvah ceremonies mark a 13-year-old Jewish boy's or girl's assumption of responsibility for following traditional religious observance. Or a ritual may be tied to a specific event, such as a girl's first menstruation, which Apache tribes celebrate with a 4-day ritual of sunrise-to-sunset chanting.

In industrial societies, the passage to adulthood is generally less abrupt and less clearly marked. Instead, these societies recognize a long transitional period known as **adolescence,** a developmental transition between childhood and adulthood that entails major, interrelated physical, cognitive, and psychosocial changes. Thus adolescence is a social construction (refer back to chapter 1), a concept whose meaning depends on how a culture defines it.

adolescence Developmental transition between childhood and adulthood entailing major physical, cognitive, and psychosocial changes

Markers of Adolescence

Adolescence lasts about a decade, from about age 11 or 12 until the late teens or early 20s. Neither its beginning nor its end is clearly marked. Adolescence is generally considered to begin with **puberty,** the process that leads to sexual maturity, or fertility—the ability to reproduce.* Before the 20th century, children in Europe and North America entered the adult world when they matured physically or when they began a vocational apprenticeship. Today entry into adulthood takes longer and is less clear-cut. Puberty begins earlier than it used to; and entrance into a vocation tends to occur later, since complex societies require longer periods of education or vocational training before a young person can take on adult responsibilities.

puberty Process by which a person attains sexual maturity and the ability to reproduce

Contemporary Canadian society has a variety of markers of entrance into adulthood. There are *legal* definitions: At 17, young people may enlist in the armed forces; at age 18, in most provinces, they may marry without their parents' permission; at 18, they may vote in municipal, provincial, and federal elections. Using *sociological* definitions, people may call themselves adults when they are self-supporting or have chosen a career, have married or formed a significant relationship, or have started a family. There also are *psychological* definitions. Cognitive maturity is often considered to coincide with the capacity for abstract thought. Emotional maturity may depend on such achievements as discovering one's identity, becoming independent of parents, developing a system of values, and forming relationships. Some people never leave adolescence, no matter what their chronological age.

*Some people use the term *puberty* to mean the end of sexual maturation and refer to the process as *pubescence,* but our usage conforms to that of most psychologists today.

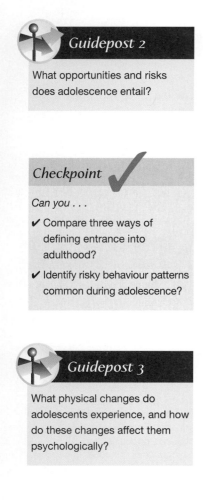

Guidepost 2

What opportunities and risks does adolescence entail?

Checkpoint ✔

Can you . . .

✔ Compare three ways of defining entrance into adulthood?

✔ Identify risky behaviour patterns common during adolescence?

Guidepost 3

What physical changes do adolescents experience, and how do these changes affect them psychologically?

Opportunities and Risks of Adolescence

Early adolescence (approximately ages 11 or 12 to 14), the transition out of childhood, offers opportunities for growth—not only in physical dimensions, but also in cognitive and social competence, autonomy, self-esteem, and intimacy. This period also carries great risks. Some young people have trouble handling so many changes at once and may need help in overcoming dangers along the way. Adolescence is a time of increasing divergence between the majority of young people, who are headed for a fulfilling and productive adulthood, and a sizable minority (about 1 out of 5) who will be dealing with major problems (Offer, 1987; Offer & Schonert-Reichl, 1992).

Canadian adolescents today face greater hazards to their physical and mental well-being than did their counterparts in earlier years (Petersen, 1993; Takanishi, 1993). Among these hazards are early pregnancy and child-bearing (see chapter 17) and high death rates from accidents, homicide, and suicide (CICH, 2000; National Center for Health Statistics [NCHS], 1998a). Behaviour patterns that contribute to these risks, such as heavy drinking, drug abuse, sexual and gang activity, motorcycling without helmets, and use of firearms, are established early in adolescence (Petersen, 1993; Rivara & Grossman, 1996). Yet, despite the risks of this period, most young people come through the teenage years in good physical and mental health.

Puberty: The End of Childhood

The biological changes of puberty, which signal the end of childhood, result in rapid growth in height and weight, changes in body proportions and form, and attainment of sexual maturity. These dramatic physical changes are part of a long, complex process of maturation that begins even before birth, and their psychological ramifications continue into adulthood.

How Puberty Begins

Puberty begins with a sharp increase in production of sex hormones. First, sometime between ages 5 and 9, the adrenal glands begin secreting larger amounts of androgens, which will play a part in the growth of pubic, axillary (armpit), and facial hair. A few years later, in girls, the ovaries step up their output of estrogen, which stimulates growth of female genitals and development of breasts. In boys, the testes increase the manufacture of androgens, particularly testosterone, which stimulate growth of male genitals, muscle mass, and body hair. Boys and girls have both types of hormones, but girls have higher levels of estrogen and boys have higher levels of androgens; in girls, testosterone influences growth of the clitoris, as well as of the bones and of pubic and axillary hair.

The precise time when this burst of hormonal activity begins seems to depend on reaching a critical weight level. Studies of mice and humans show that leptin, a protein hormone secreted by fatty tissue and identified as having a role in obesity (refer back to Chapter 12), is needed to trigger the onset of puberty (Chehab, Mounzih, Lu, & Lim, 1997; Clément et al., 1998; O'Rahilly, 1998; Strobel, Camoin, Ozata, & Strosberg, 1998). An accumulation of leptin in the bloodstream may stimulate the hypothalamus, a structure at the base of the brain, to send pulsating signals to the nearby pituitary gland, which in turn may signal the sex glands to increase their secretion of hormones. This may explain why overweight girls tend to enter puberty earlier than thin girls.

Some research attributes the heightened emotionality and moodiness of early adolescence—so apparent in Anne Frank's diary—to hormonal changes. Hormones are associated with aggression in boys and with both aggression and depression in girls (Brooks-Gunn, 1988; Buchanan, Eccles, & Becker, 1992). However, other influences, such as sex, age, temperament, and the timing of puberty, may moderate or even override hormonal ones. Hormones seem more strongly related to moods in boys than in girls, and especially in early adolescents, who are still adjusting to pubertal changes. Environmental factors also make a difference (Buchanan et al., 1992). Although there is a relationship

The Apache Indians of the southwestern United States celebrate a girl's entrance into puberty with a 4-day ritual that includes special clothing, a symbolic blanket, and singing from sunrise to sunset

between hormone production and sexuality, adolescents tend to begin sexual activity more in accord with what their friends do than with what their glands secrete (Brooks-Gunn & Reiter, 1990).

Timing, Sequence, and Signs of Maturation

Any Grade 8 or Grade 9 class photo reveals startling contrasts. Flat-chested little girls stand next to full-bosomed, full-grown young women. Skinny little boys are next to broad-shouldered, muscular young men.

There is about a 7-year range for the onset of puberty in both boys and girls. The process typically takes about 4 years for both sexes and begins about 2 or 3 years earlier in girls than in boys.

Physical changes in both boys and girls during puberty include the adolescent growth spurt, the development of pubic hair, a deeper voice, and muscular growth. The maturation of reproductive organs brings the beginning of menstruation in girls and the production of sperm in boys. These changes unfold in a sequence that is much more consistent than their timing (see Table 15-1), though it does vary somewhat. One girl, for example, may be developing breasts and body hair at about the same rate; in another, body hair may grow so fast that it shows an adult pattern a year or so before her breasts develop. Similar variations occur among boys.

On the basis of historical sources, developmentalists have found a **secular trend** (a trend that spans several generations) in the onset of puberty: a lowering of the age when puberty begins and when young people reach adult height and sexual maturity. The trend, which also involves increases in adult height and weight, began about 100 years ago and has occurred in Canada and the United States, Western Europe, and Japan. The most likely explanation seems to be a higher standard of living. Children who are healthier, better nourished, and better cared for mature earlier and grow bigger. Thus, the average age of sexual maturity is later in less developed countries than in more industrialized ones. Although the secular trend was believed to have ended in the United States, it now appears that girls—but not boys—are maturing 1 to 2 years earlier than previous studies showed (Herman-Giddens et al., 1997; Kaplowitz et al., 1999). Not only do they begin to menstruate earlier, but frequency of menstruation and other signs of reproductive maturity develop more

secular trend Trend that can be seen only by observing several generations, such as the trend toward earlier attainment of adult height and sexual maturity, which began a century ago

Table 15-1	Usual Sequence of Physiological Changes in Adolescence
Female Characteristics	**Age of First Appearance**
Growth of breasts	7–13
Growth of pubic hair	7–14
Body growth	9.5–14.5
Menarche	10–16.5
Underarm hair	About 2 years after appearance of pubic hair
Increased output of oil- and sweat-producing glands (which may lead to acne)	About the same time as appearance of underarm hair
Male Characteristics	**Age of First Appearance**
Growth of testes, scrotal sac	10–13.5
Growth of pubic hair	12–16
Body growth	10.5–16
Growth of penis, prostate gland, seminal vesicles	11–14.5
Change in voice	About the same time as growth of penis
First ejaculation of semen	About 1 year after beginning of growth of penis
Facial and underarm hair	About 2 years after appearance of pubic hair
Increased output of oil- and sweat-producing glands (which may lead to acne)	About the same time as appearance of underarm hair

rapidly than previously thought, suggesting a need for early education about pregnancy prevention (Legro, Lin, Demers, & Lloyd, 2000).

The average age for boys' entry into puberty is 12, but boys may begin to show changes any time between 9 and 16. Girls, on average, begin to show pubertal changes at 8 to 10 years of age. However, some controversial research suggests that it may be normal for girls to show breast budding and pubic hair as early as age 7 and as late as 14. (Chumlea, 1982; Ellis et al., 1997; Herman-Giddens et al., 1997; Kaplowitz et al., 1999).

The Adolescent Growth Spurt

adolescent growth spurt Sharp increase in height and weight that precedes sexual maturity

In Anne Frank's diary, she made rueful references to her physical growth—to shoes she could no longer get into and vests "so small that they don't even reach my tummy" (p. 71). Anne apparently was in the **adolescent growth spurt**—a rapid increase in height and weight, which generally begins in girls between ages 9½ and 14½ (usually at about 10) and in boys, between 10½ and 16 (usually at 12 or 13). The growth spurt typically lasts about 2 years; soon after it ends, the young person reaches sexual maturity. Since girls' growth spurt usually occurs earlier than that of boys, girls between ages 11 and 13 are taller, heavier, and stronger than boys the same age. After their growth spurt, boys are again larger, as before. Both boys and girls reach virtually their full height by age 18.

Boys and girls grow differently, of course. A boy becomes larger overall: his shoulders wider, his legs longer relative to his trunk, and his forearms longer relative to his upper arms and his height. A girl's pelvis widens to make child-bearing easier, and layers of fat are deposited under the skin, giving her a more rounded appearance.

The adolescent growth spurt affects practically all skeletal and muscular dimensions; muscular growth peaks at age 12½ for girls and 14½ for boys. Even the eye grows faster, causing (as in Anne Frank's case) an increase in nearsightedness, a problem that affects about one-fourth of 12- to 17-year-olds (Gans, 1990). The lower jaw becomes longer and thicker, the jaw and nose project more, and the incisor teeth become more upright. Because each of these changes follows its own timetable, parts of the body may be out of proportion for a while. The result is the familiar teenage gawkiness Anne noticed in Peter Van Daan, which accompanies unbalanced, accelerated growth.

These dramatic physical changes have psychological ramifications. Most young teenagers are more concerned about their looks than about any other aspect of themselves, and many do not like what they see in the mirror. Girls tend to be unhappier about their looks than boys, reflecting the greater cultural emphasis on women's physical attributes (Rosenblum & Lewis, 1999). Girls, especially those who are advanced in pubertal development, tend to think they are too fat (Richards, Boxer, Petersen, & Albrecht, 1990; Swarr & Richards, 1996), and this negative body image can lead to eating problems. Concern with body image may be related to the stirring of sexual attraction, which, as we shall see, has been found to begin as early as age 9 or 10.

Primary and Secondary Sex Characteristics

The **primary sex characteristics** are the organs necessary for reproduction. In the female, the sex organs are the ovaries, Fallopian tubes, uterus, and vagina; in the male, the testes, penis, scrotum, seminal vesicles, and prostate gland. During puberty, these organs enlarge and mature. In boys, the first sign of puberty is the growth of the testes and scrotum. In girls, the growth of the primary sex characteristics is not readily apparent because these organs are internal.

During the years from ages 11 to 13, girls are, on the average, taller, heavier, and stronger than boys, who reach their adolescent growth spurt later than girls do.

The **secondary sex characteristics** (see Table 15-2) are physiological signs of sexual maturation that do not directly involve the sex organs: for example, the breasts of females and the broad shoulders of males. Other secondary sex characteristics are changes in the voice and skin texture, muscular development, and the growth of pubic, facial, axillary, and body hair.

The first reliable sign of puberty in girls is the growth of the breasts. The nipples enlarge and protrude, the *areolae* (the pigmented areas surrounding the nipples) enlarge, and the breasts assume first a conical and then a rounded shape. Some adolescent boys, much to their distress, experience temporary breast enlargement; this is normal and may last up to 18 months.

The voice deepens, partly in response to the growth of the larynx and partly, especially in boys, in response to the production of male hormones. The skin becomes coarser and oilier. Increased activity of the sebaceous glands (which secrete a fatty substance) may give rise to pimples and blackheads. Acne is more common in boys and seems related to increased amounts of testosterone.

Pubic hair, which at first is straight and silky and eventually becomes coarse, dark, and curly, appears in different patterns in males and females. Adolescent boys are usually happy to see hair on the face and chest; but girls are usually dismayed at the appearance of even a slight amount of hair on the face or around the nipples, though this is normal.

Signs of Sexual Maturity: Sperm Production and Menstruation

In males, the principal sign of sexual maturity is the production of sperm. A boy may wake up to find a wet spot or a hardened, dried spot on the sheets—the result of a *nocturnal emission,* an involuntary ejaculation of semen (commonly referred to as a *wet dream*). Most adolescent boys have these emissions, sometimes in connection with an erotic dream. There is little research on boys' feelings about the first ejaculation (**spermarche**), which occurs at an average age of 13; most boys in one study reported positive reactions, though about two-thirds were somewhat frightened (Gaddis & Brooks-Gunn, 1985).

The principal sign of sexual maturity in girls is *menstruation,* a monthly shedding of tissue from the lining of the womb—what Anne Frank called her "sweet secret." The first menstruation, called **menarche,** occurs fairly late in the sequence of female development (refer back to Table 15-1). On average, girls in Canada first menstruate shortly before their 13th birthday. However, the normal timing of menarche can vary from ages 10 to 16½.

A combination of genetic, physical, emotional, and environmental influences may affect the timing of menarche. Age of first menstruation tends to be similar to that of the mother. Bigger girls and those whose breasts are more developed tend to menstruate ear-

primary sex characteristics
Organs directly related to reproduction, which enlarge and mature during adolescence

secondary sex characteristics
Physiological signs of sexual maturation (such as breast development and growth of body hair) that do not involve the sex organs

spermarche Boy's first ejaculation

menarche Girl's first menstruation

Table 15-2	Secondary Sex Characteristics	
Girls	**Boys**
Breasts	Pubic hair
Pubic hair	Axillary (underarm) hair
Axillary (underarm) hair	Muscular development
Changes in voice	Facial hair
Changes in skin	Changes in voice
Increased width and depth of pelvis	Changes in skin
Muscular development	Broadening of shoulders

lier. Strenuous exercise, as in competitive athletics, can delay menarche. Nutrition is also a factor. Even when these factors are controlled, girls with early menarche tend to be aggressive or depressed or to have poor family relationships—conflict with parents, lack of parental approval and warmth, or negative feelings about the home environment—which may be traced in part to a mother's depression (Ellis & Garber, 2000; Graber, Brooks-Gunn, & Warren, 1995; Moffitt, Caspi, Belsky, & Silva, 1992; Steinberg, 1988).

One longitudinal study suggests that the relationship with the father may be a key to pubertal timing. Among 173 randomly selected girls in Tennessee and Indiana, those who, as preschoolers, had close, supportive relationships with their parents—especially with an affectionate, involved father—showed later pubertal development than girls whose parental relationships had been cold or distant. Also, girls raised by single mothers tended to reach puberty earlier than girls from two-parent homes (Ellis, McFadyen-Ketchum, Dodge, Pettit, & Bates, 1999).

The mechanism by which family relationships may affect pubertal development is not clear. One suggestion is that human males, like some animals, may give off *pheromones,* odourous chemicals that attract mates. As a natural incest-prevention mechanism, sexual development may be inhibited in girls who are heavily exposed to their fathers' pheromones, as would happen in a close father–daughter relationship. On the other hand, frequent exposure to the pheromones of unrelated adult males, such as stepfathers or a single mother's boyfriends, may speed up pubertal development (Ellis & Garber, 2000). Since both the father's absence and early pubertal timing have been identified as risk factors for sexual promiscuity and teenage pregnancy, these findings suggest that the father's early presence and active involvement may be important to girls' healthy sexual development (Ellis et al., 1999).

Sexual Attraction

Do you remember the first time you were sexually attracted to someone? If so, how old were you?

It is commonly believed that the first stirrings of sexual attraction follow **gonadarche,** maturation of the testes and ovaries, which steps up hormone production. Yet in several studies, adolescent boys and girls—whether homosexual or heterosexual—recalled their earliest sexual attraction as having taken place at about age 10, about 2 to 4 years before sexual maturation (McClintock & Herdt, 1996).

What could prompt this early attraction? The answer may lie in **adrenarche,** the maturation of the adrenal glands, which occurs several years before gonadarche. Between ages 6 and 11, these glands, located above the kidneys, secrete gradually increasing levels of androgens, principally *dehydroepiandrosterone* (DHEA). DHEA is present in high levels at birth and then declines sharply, only to rise again when the adrenal glands mature. By age 10, levels of DHEA are ten times what they were between ages 1 and 4. The maturing of the sex organs triggers a second burst of DHEA production, which then rises to adult levels. DHEA is responsible for the initial sprouting of pubic hair and also for faster growth, oilier skin, and the development of body odour.

gonadarche Maturation of testes or ovaries

adrenarche Maturation of adrenal glands

These findings suggest that the transition to puberty may begin earlier and may be more gradual than is generally recognized. Puberty may consist of two stages: the maturing of the adrenal glands, followed a few years later by the maturing of the sex organs and the more obvious pubertal changes.

Psychological Effects of Early and Late Maturation

The effects of early and late maturing are not clear-cut and differ in boys and girls.

Some research done during the past several decades has found early-maturing boys to be more poised, relaxed, good-natured, popular with peers, likely to be leaders, and less impulsive than late maturers. Other studies have found them to be more worried about being liked, more cautious, more reliant on others, and more bound by rules and routines. Some studies suggest that early maturers retain a head start in cognitive performance into late adolescence and adulthood (Graber, Lewinsohn, Seeley, & Brooks-Gunn, 1997; R. T. Gross & Duke, 1980; M. C. Jones, 1957; Tanner, 1978). Late maturers have been found to feel more inadequate, self-conscious, rejected, and dominated; to be more dependent, aggressive, insecure, or depressed; to have more conflict with parents and more trouble in school; to have poorer social and coping skills; and to think less of themselves (Graber et al., 1997; Mussen & Jones, 1957; Peskin, 1967, 1973; Siegel, 1982).

Apparently there are pluses and minuses in both situations. Boys like to mature early, and those who do so seem to gain in self-esteem (Alsaker, 1992; Clausen, 1975). Being more muscular than late maturers, they are stronger and better in sports and have a more favourable body image. They also have an edge in dating (Blyth et al., 1981). However, an early maturer sometimes has trouble living up to expectations that he should act as mature as he looks. Negative effects of early maturation can persist in boys. Boys who were more developed in Grade 7 were found to be more likely to experience greater levels of hostility and internal distress than early maturers throughout Grades 8 to 10 (Ge, Conger, & Elder, 2001).

Unlike most boys, girls tend *not* to like maturing early; they are generally happier if their timing is about the same as that of their peers. Early-maturing girls tend to be less sociable, less expressive, and less poised; more introverted and shy; and more negative about menarche than later-maturing girls (M. C. Jones, 1958; Livson & Peskin, 1980; Ruble & Brooks-Gunn, 1982; Stubbs, Rierdan, & Koff, 1989). Perhaps because they feel rushed into confronting the pressures of adolescence before they are ready, they are more vulnerable to psychological distress and remain so at least through the mid-teens (ages 15 to 16). They are more likely to associate with anti-social peers (Ge, Conger, & Elder, 1996) They may have a poor body image and lower self-esteem than later-maturing girls (Alsaker, 1992; Graber et al., 1997; Simmons, Blyth, Van Cleave, & Bush, 1979). Early-maturing girls are at increased risk of various behavioural and mental health problems, including anxiety and depression, disruptive behaviour, eating disorders, early smoking and drinking, precocious sexual activity, substance abuse, and attempted suicide (Dick, Rose, Viken, & Kaprio, 2000; Graber et al., 1997). Early maturation is associated with a tendency toward risky behaviour in boys as well as girls (D. P. Orr & Ingersoll, 1995).

It is hard to generalize about the psychological effects of pubertal timing because they depend on how the adolescent and other people in his or her world interpret the accompanying changes. Effects of early or late maturation are most likely to be negative when adolescents are much more or less developed than their peers; when they do not see the changes as advantageous; and when several stressful events occur at about the same time (Petersen, 1993; Simmons, Blyth, & McKinney, 1983). Adults need to be sensitive to the potential impact of pubertal changes in order to help young people experience these changes as positively as possible.

Physical and Mental Health

These years are generally healthy, as most adolescents recognize. Nine out of 10 (91.8 per cent) of early and mid-adolescents consider themselves healthy, according to an

What's your view

- Did you mature early, late, or "on time"? How did the timing of your maturation affect you psychologically?

Checkpoint ✓

Can you . . .

✔ Tell how puberty begins and how its timing and length vary?

✔ Describe typical pubertal changes in boys and girls, and identify factors that affect psychological reactions to these changes?

✔ Identify the age of first sexual attraction and discuss its implications for the timing of puberty?

Guidepost 4

What are some common health problems in adolescence, and how can they be prevented?

Figure 15-1

Age-specific rates for prevalence of some high-risk behaviours, averaged out over 3 years.

Source: Adapted from Elliott, 1993.

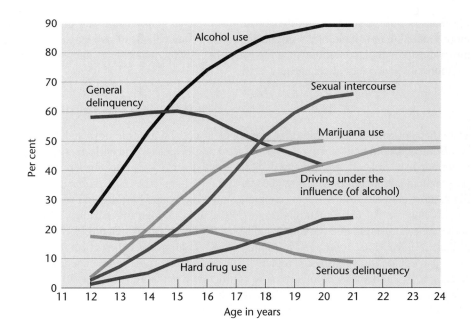

international school-based survey of more than 120,000 11, 13, and 15-year-olds in Canada and 27 other industrialized countries under auspices of the World Health Organization (WHO) (Scheidt, Overpeck, Wyatt, & Aszmann, 2000).*

Despite their general good health, many younger adolescents—especially girls—report frequent health problems and symptoms, such as headache, stomach ache, backache, nervousness, and feeling tired, lonely, or "low." Such reports are most common in Canada and the United States, perhaps because life in those cultures tends to be fast-paced and stressful (King, Boyce, & King, 1999; Scheidt et al., 2000).

Most adolescents have low rates of disability and chronic disease, and dental health has improved among both children and adolescents. Still, about 7 per cent of males and 8 per cent of females between the ages of 10 and 19 in Canada experience disabilities that result in a limitation in their daily activities (CICH, 2000), and one-fifth of 10- to 18-year-olds in the United States have at least one serious physical or mental health problem, and many more need counselling or other health services (Dougherty, 1993).

Many health problems are preventable, stemming from lifestyle or poverty. In industrialized countries, according to the WHO survey, adolescents from less affluent families tend to report poorer health and more frequent symptoms. More well-off adolescents, who are likely to be better educated, tend to have healthier diets and to be more physically active. On the other hand, socio-economic status seems to have no effect on smoking and drinking among 15-year-olds (Mullan & Currie, 2000).

In Canada and the United States, across ethnic and social-class lines, many early adolescents use drugs, drive while intoxicated, and become sexually active, and these behaviours increase throughout the teenage years (see Figure 15-1) (CICH, 2000; Health Canada, 1999a; King et al., 1999). Adolescents whose families have been disrupted by parental separation or death are more likely to start these activities early and to engage in them more frequently during the next few years (Millstein et al., 1992). Boys and girls who enter puberty early or whose cognitive maturation comes late are especially prone to risky behaviour (Orr & Ingersoll, 1995). So are gay, lesbian, and bisexual young people (Garofalo, Wolf, Kessel, Palfrey, & DuRant, 1998). These populations of Canadian adolescents typically do not acknowledge their sexuality, as they risk facing rejection or possible abuse (CICH, 2000).

Adolescents are less likely than younger children to see a physician regularly; they more frequently go to school-based health centres (CICH, 2000; Health Canada, 1999a; King et al., 1999). Young people who do not receive needed care are at increased risk of

*The other countries were Belgium, Czech Republic, Denmark, England, Estonia, Finland, France, Germany, Greece, Greenland, Hungary, Republic of Ireland, Israel, Latvia, Lithuania, Northern Ireland, Norway, Poland, Portugal, Russian Federation, Scotland, Slovak Republic, Spain, Sweden, Switzerland, the United States, and Wales.

physical and mental health problems, including frequent smoking and drinking (Ford, Bearman, & Moody, 1999). Although all Canadian youth have health services universally available to them, accessibility may vary, depending on level of awareness of health services, or on ability to reach those services, which is especially serious to those living in remote locations (Health Canada, 1999a). Adolescents with mental health problems are more likely to turn to family or friends (if anyone) than to professionals (Offer & Schonert-Reichl, 1992).

Let's look at several specific health concerns: physical fitness, sleep needs, eating disorders, drug abuse, and causes of death in adolescence. (Anxiety and depression were discussed in chapter 14.)

Physical Activity

Exercise—or lack of it—affects both physical and mental health. It improves strength and endurance, helps build healthy bones and muscles, helps control weight, reduces anxiety and stress, and increases self-confidence. Even moderate physical activity has health benefits if done regularly for at least 30 minutes on most, and preferably all, days of the week. A sedentary lifestyle that carries over into adulthood may result in increased risk of obesity, diabetes, heart disease, and cancer (Canadian Paediatric Society [CPS] Advisory Committee on Healthy Active Living for Children and Youth, 2002; Centers for Disease Control and Prevention [CDC], 2000a; National [U.S.] Institutes of Health [NIH] Consensus Development Panel on Physical Activity and Cardiovascular Health, 1996).

Many boys and, especially, girls become less active during adolescence. Adolescents in Canada rank in the mid-range, compared to other industrialized countries, on exercise duration, but Canada ranks highest, next to Denmark, in proportion of males who play computer games for 4 or more hours a week—an indicator that although many Canadian adolescents are spending a great deal of time in physical activity, the frequency is dropping and the proportion of adolescents engaged in sedentary activities is rising (King et al., 1999). Only 33 per cent of Canadian schools had physical education classes in 2001, with formal classes being optional after Grade 9 (CPS, 2002). The proportion of Canadian Grade 10 students who report exercising two or more times a week outside of school hours dropped from 83 to 75 per cent for males and from 59 to 54 per cent for females between 1990 and 1998 (King et al., 1999). However, only about a third of Canadian youth are active enough for optimal health (Health Canada, 1999a).

Young people who exercise generally feel better than those who do not. They tend to be more confident and spend more time with friends, suggesting that they may use sports as a means of socializing (Hickman et al., 2000). On the other hand, many high school students are injured in sports (CICH, 2000). Some of these injuries could be avoided by grouping players by size, skill, and maturational level instead of by age; by improved equipment design; by educating coaches, parents, and adolescents about sports safety; and by better supervision and enforcement of safety rules (AAP Committee on Sports Medicine and Committee on School Health, 1989; Cheng et al., 2000; CICH, 2000).

After puberty, girls should not play heavy-collision sports with boys because their lighter, smaller frames make them too subject to injury (AAP Committee on Pediatric Aspects of Physical Fitness, Recreation, and Sports, 1981). Post-pubertal girls still need to be physically active, however, for general fitness and for the benefit that weight-bearing exercise offers in the prevention of *osteoporosis,* a thinning of the bones that occurs mostly among middle-aged and older women. Engaging in athletics or other exercise, besides being emotionally satisfying in itself, also helps keep the body fit, reduces stress, gives girls a sense of mastery and competence, and makes them feel better about their appearance (Richards et al., 1990).

Sleep Needs

Many adolescents do not get enough sleep. Many report having difficulties falling asleep. About 25 per cent of Canadian adolescents report having trouble getting to sleep more than once a week, and girls tend to have more difficulties in falling asleep than boys (King et al., 1999). Many youth go to bed later than younger children and, on school days, get up as early or earlier. Yet adolescents need just as much sleep as before—about 9 hours per night. Nor does "sleeping in" on weekends make up for the loss. Adolescents or preadolescents who have irregular sleep schedules tend to be chronically sleep-deprived and to be sleepy in the daytime (Sadeh, Raviv, & Gruber, 2000; Wolfson & Carskadon, 1998). According to a study in Israel, this pattern is more likely to occur in families with older, less educated parents and more family stress (Sadeh et al., 2000). An average of 40 per cent of adolescents (mostly boys) in 28 industrialized countries report morning sleepiness at least once a week, and 22 per cent are sleepy most days. Norway and Finland have the highest proportions of morning tiredness, with the United States coming in third (Scheidt et al., 2000).

Sleep-deprived adolescents tend to show symptoms of depression, have sleep problems, and do poorly in school. In a survey of 3,120 Rhode Island high school students, total sleep time (on school nights and weekends) diminished by 40 to 50 minutes between ages 13 and 19, and students who got the least sleep got the worst grades (Wolfson & Carskadon, 1998).

Why do teenagers stay up late? In part it may be because they need to do homework, like to talk on the phone with friends or surf the Web, or want to act "grown up." However, physiological changes may also be involved (Sadeh et al., 2000). Adolescents undergo a shift in the brain's natural sleep cycle, or *circadian timing system.* The timing of secretion of *melatonin,* a hormone detectable in saliva, is a gauge of when the brain is ready for sleep. After puberty, this secretion takes place later at night (Carskadon, Acebo, Richardson, Tate, & Seifer, 1997). Thus adolescents need to go to bed later and get up later than younger children. Yet most secondary schools start earlier than elementary schools. Their schedules are out of sync with students' biological rhythms.

These findings fit in with adolescents' daily mood cycles, which also may be hormonally related. Teenagers tend to be least alert and most stressed early in the morning. Starting school later, or at least offering difficult courses later in the day, would maximize students' ability to concentrate (Crouter & Larson, 1998).

Nutrition and Eating Disorders

Canadian adolescents have less healthy diets than those in most other industrialized countries. They eat fewer fruits and vegetables and more sweets, chocolate, soft drinks, and other "junk" foods, which are high in cholesterol, fat, and calories, and low in nutrients (CICH, 2000; King et al., 1999; Vereecken & Maes, 2000) Adolescents who regularly watch television consume the most junk food (Hickman et al., 2000). Deficiencies of calcium, zinc, and iron are common at this age (Bruner, Joffe, Duggan, Casella, & Brandt, 1996; Lloyd et al., 1993). Adolescents in families with higher socio-economic status tend to have the healthiest diets (Vereecken & Maes, 2000).

Although poor nutrition is most common in economically depressed or isolated populations, it also may result from concern with body image and weight control (Vereecken & Maes, 2000). Eating disorders—both extreme overeating and extreme undereating—are most prevalent in industrialized societies, where food is abundant and attractiveness is equated with slimness (APA, 1994; Becker, Grinspoon, Klibanski, & Herzog, 1999).

Obesity

The average teenage girl needs about 2,200 calories per day; the average teenage boy needs about 2,800. Many adolescents eat more calories than they expend and thus accumulate excess body fat. Obesity is the most common outcome of eating difficulties in Canada. The prevalence of obesity in Canadians between 7 and 13 years has more than doubled between 1981 and 1996, and 70 per cent of obese adolescents become obese adults (CPS, 2002); 13.5 per cent of boys and 11.8 per cent of girls in this age range are in the 95th percentiles of body mass, based on age- and sex-norm data from 1981 (Tremblay & Willms, 2000).

Some causes of obesity—too little physical activity and poor eating habits—are within a person's control. Although about 64 per cent of Canadian Grade 10 students report eating fruit and vegetables at least once a day, about 10 percent eat french fries or potato chips daily, and 23 per cent eat candy or chocolate bars daily (King et al., 1998). About 28 per cent of 12- to-14-year olds, and 66 per cent of 15- to 19-year-olds in Canada are considered physically inactive (CPS, 2002). Given the choice that adolescents have over physical activity and eating habits, weight-loss programs that use behavioural modification techniques to help adolescents make changes in diet and exercise have had some success. However,

Checkpoint ✔

Can you . . .

✔ Summarize the status of adolescents' health and health care?

✔ Explain why physical activity is important in adolescence, and discuss risks and benefits of athletic activity for adolescent girls?

✔ Explain why adolescents often get too little sleep and how sleep deprivation can affect them?

genetic and other factors having nothing to do with willpower or lifestyle choices seem to make some people susceptible to obesity (refer back to chapter 12; Katzmarzyk, Pérusse, Rao, & Bouchard, 1999). Among these factors are faulty regulation of metabolism, inability to recognize body cues about hunger and satiation, and development of an abnormally large number of fat cells. Family functioning seems to be related to obesity in Canadian girls: Obese girls tend to rate their families as having lower levels of cohesion, expressiveness, and democratic style than non-obese girls, while obese boys did not differ from normal-weight boys on ratings of family style (Mendelson, White, & Schliecker, 1995).

Obese teenagers tend to become obese adults, subject to physical, social, and psychological risks (Gortmaker, Must, Perrin, Sobol, & Dietz, 1993). Being overweight in adolescence can lead to life-threatening chronic conditions in adulthood, even if the excess weight is lost (Must et al., 1992).

Body Image

Sometimes a determination *not* to become obese can result in graver problems than obesity itself. Girls' normal increase in body fat at puberty leads to more dissatisfaction with their bodies over the course of adolescence, while boys, who are becoming more muscular, become more satisfied with theirs (Rosenblum & Lewis, 1999; Swarr & Richards, 1996). These trends are increasing, according to an analysis of 222 studies from the past 50 years. Gender differences in body image increase from early to mid-adolescence and then begin to diminish (Feingold & Mazella, 1998).

Fashion magazines, which promote unrealistic ideals of thinness, influence girls' displeasure with their bodies (A.E. Field et al., 1999). By age 15, more than half the girls in 16 countries are dieting or think they should be. As adolescents progress through high school, a greater proportion of them express dissatisfaction with their bodies, with over half of Canadian boys and three-quarters of girls in Grade 10 indicating that they would like to change something about their bodies (King et al., 1999). More females than males express dissatisfaction with their body size, and more females than males are on a diet or feel the need to lose weight (King et al., 1999). Relationships with parents may be a factor in adolescents' concerns over body weight. In a study of 240 suburban white girls in Grades 5 through 9, girls who had positive relationships with their parents had fewer weight and eating concerns (Swarr & Richards, 1996).

Excessive concern with weight control and body image may be signs of **anorexia nervosa** or **bulimia nervosa**, which involve abnormal patterns of food intake. As chronic disorders, anorexia affects an estimated 1 to 2 per cent of females in Canada, and bulimia affects 3 to 5 per cent (CICH, 2000). Although most victims are adolescent girls and young women, about 5 to 15 per cent are male (Andersen, 1995). Anorexia and bulimia tend to run in families, suggesting a possible genetic basis. Other apparent causes are neurochemical, developmental, and social-cultural (Becker et al., 1999; "Eating Disorders–Part I, Part II," 1997; Kendler et al., 1991). These disorders are especially common among girls driven to excel in ballet, competitive swimming, long-distance running, figure skating, and gymnastics ("Eating Disorders–Part II," 1997; Skolnick, 1993). Body-esteem, which reflects self-satisfaction and self-evaluations of body weight, physical appearance, and perceptions of others' evaluations of one's body and appearance (Mendelson, Mendelson, & White, 2001), has been found to be positively related to global self-worth in Canadian children between 8 and 12 years of age (Mendelson, White, & Mendelson, 1996), as well as in adolescents (Mendelson, Mendelson, & Andrews, 2000). Males tend to have higher body-esteem than females (Medelson et al., 1996; Mendelson et al., 2000).

anorexia nervosa Eating disorder characterized by self-starvation

Anorexics have an unrealistic body image. Despite the evidence of their mirrors, they think they are too fat.

Anorexia Nervosa

Susanna, 14, diets obsessively. She is preoccupied with food—cooking it, talking about it, and urging others to eat—but she eats very little herself. Yet she has a distorted body image: She thinks she is too fat. Her weight becomes less than 85 per cent of what is considered normal for her height and age (APA, 1994). Meanwhile, she stops menstruating, and thick soft hair spreads over her body. To hide what she is doing to herself, she may wear baggy clothes or quietly pocket food and later throw it away; yet she denies that her behaviour is abnormal or dangerous. She is a good student, is described by her parents as a "model" child, is compulsive about exercising, and participates in gymnastics. She is also withdrawn and depressed and engages in repetitive, perfectionist behaviour ("Eating Disorders–Part I," 1997; Garner, 1993).

This is a typical scenario for **anorexia nervosa,** or self-starvation. This potentially life-threatening eating disorder occurs mostly in young women, typically beginning during adolescence.

Anorexia may be due to a combination of genetic and environmental factors. Some authorities point to a deficiency of a crucial chemical in the brain, a disturbance of the hypothalamus, or high levels of opiate-like substances in the spinal fluid ("Eating Disorders—Part I," 1997). Researchers in England, Sweden, and Germany have found reduced blood flow to certain parts of the brain, including an area thought to control visual self-perception and appetite (Gordon, Lask, Bryantwaugh, Christie, & Timini, 1997). Others see anorexia as a psychological disturbance related to fear of growing up or fear of sexuality or to a malfunctioning family that seems harmonious while members are actually overdependent, overly involved in each other's lives, and unable to deal with conflict ("Eating Disorders–Part I," 1997; Garner, 1993). As discussed earlier, anorexia may also in part be a reaction to societal pressure to be slender.

Early warning signs include determined, secret dieting; dissatisfaction after losing weight; setting new, lower weight goals after reaching an initial desired weight; excessive exercising; and interruption of regular menstruation.

Bulimia Nervosa

bulimia nervosa Eating disorder in which a person regularly eats huge quantities of food and then purges the body by laxatives, induced vomiting, fasting, or excessive exercise

In **bulimia nervosa**, a person—usually an adolescent girl or a young woman—regularly goes on huge eating binges within a short time, usually 2 hours or less, and then tries to undo the high caloric intake by self-induced vomiting, strict dieting or fasting, engaging in excessively vigorous exercise, or taking laxatives, enemas, or diuretics to purge the body. These episodes occur at least twice a week for at least 3 months (APA, 1994). (Binge eating without purging is a separate disorder associated with obesity.)

Bulimia is at least two or three times as common as anorexia, and, as with anorexia, most sufferers are females. Between 4 and 10 per cent of women may become bulimic at some time in their lives (APA, 1994; "Eating Disorders–Part I," 1997; Kendler et al., 1991). There is some overlap between anorexia and bulimia; some victims of anorexia have bulimic episodes, and some people with bulimia lose weight ("Eating Disorders–Part I," 1997; Edwards, 1993; Kendler et al., 1991). Nevertheless, the two are separate disorders.

Bulimia may have a biological basis; it seems to be related to low levels of the brain chemical serotonin ("Eating Disorders–Part I," 1997; K. A. Smith, Fairburn, & Cowen, 1999). However, this association does not necessarily mean that low serotonin levels *cause* bulimia. Then there is a psychoanalytic explanation: People with bulimia use food to satisfy their hunger for love and attention. This interpretation rests on reports by some bulimic patients that they felt abused, neglected, and deprived of parental nurturing ("Eating Disorders–Part I," 1997; Humphrey, 1986).

People with bulimia are obsessed with their weight and shape. They do not become abnormally thin, but they become overwhelmed with shame, self-contempt, and depression over their eating habits. They have low self-esteem, a slim ideal body image, and a history of wide weight fluctuation, dieting, or frequent exercise (Kendler et al., 1991). Many people with bulimia are also alcoholics or substance abusers or have other mental health problems, which may arise from the physical effects of the disorder ("Eating Disorders–Part I," 1997; Edwards, 1993; Kendler et al. 1991).

Treatment and Outcomes for Anorexia and Bulimia

What's your view ?

- Can you suggest ways to reduce the prevalence of eating disorders?

Anorexia can be treated, but the relapse rate is high. Up to 25 per cent of patients with anorexia progress to chronic invalidism, and between 2 and 10 per cent die prematurely (APA, 1994; Beumont, Russell, & Touyz, 1993; "Eating Disorders–Part I," 1997; Herzog, Keller, & Lavori, 1988). The immediate goal of treatment for anorexia is to get patients to eat and gain weight. They are likely to be admitted to a hospital, where they may be given

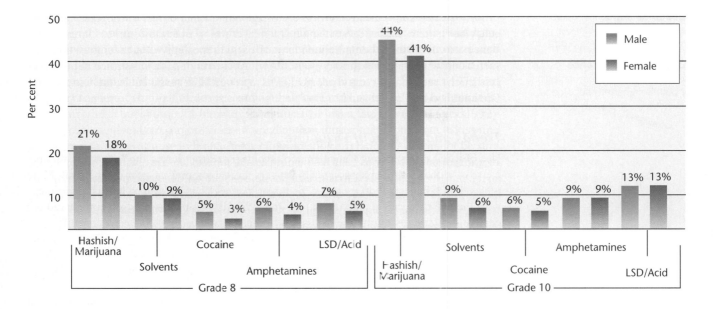

Figure 15-2

Trends in use of drugs by Grade 8 and 10 males and females in Canada in 1998. A sharp increase in marijuana use during the 1990s accounts for most of the increase in use of illicit drugs. The rise in use of marijuana accompanied an increase in ease of availability and a decrease in young people's perception of risk of harm from using the drug. Marijuana can be a "gateway" to use of harder drugs.

Source: Adapted from King et al., 1999, p. 98.

24-hour nursing, drugs to encourage eating and inhibit vomiting, and behaviour therapy, which rewards eating with such privileges as being allowed to get out of bed and leave the room (Beumont et al., 1993). Lack of access to interdisciplinary health teams, and limits in funding for supports by some provincial health plans can make treatment more difficult (Adolescent Medicine Committee, Canadian Paediatric Society, 1998).

Bulimia also may be treated with behaviour therapy. Patients keep daily diaries of their eating patterns and are taught ways to avoid the temptation to binge. Individual, group, or family psychotherapy can help both anorexics and bulimics, usually after initial behaviour therapy has brought symptoms under control. Since these patients are at risk for depression and suicide, antidepressant drugs can be helpful in treating bulimia and in stabilizing recovery from anorexia (Becker et al., 1999; Edwards, 1993; Fluoxetine-Bulimia Collaborative Study Group, 1992; Hudson & Pope, 1990; Kaye, Weltzin, Hsu, & Bulik, 1991).

The outlook for people with bulimia is better than for those with anorexia, because the patients generally want treatment. But even without treatment, symptoms often disappear by age 40 ("Eating Disorders–Part II," 1997; Herzog et al., 1999; Keel & Mitchell, 1997). People with anorexia, on the other hand, often have long-term psychological problems even after they have stopped starving themselves and have gained some weight. As much as 12 years after recovery, many continue to have an unrealistic body image, to be unusually thin, and to remain preoccupied with weight and eating. They tend to show perfectionist tendencies and to suffer from depression, anxiety disorders, or alcohol dependence (Sullivan, Bulik, Fear, & Pickering, 1998).

Use and Abuse of Drugs

Although the great majority of adolescents do not abuse drugs, a significant minority do (see Figure 15-2). They turn to drugs out of curiosity or a desire for sensation, because of peer pressure, or as an escape from overwhelming problems, and thereby endanger their present and future physical and psychological health.

Checkpoint ✔

Can you . . .

✔ Summarize the normal nutritional needs and typical dietary deficiencies of adolescent boys and girls?

✔ Discuss risk factors, effects, treatment, and prognosis for obesity, anorexia, and bulimia?

substance abuse Repeated, harmful use of a substance, usually alcohol or other drugs

substance dependence Addiction (physical, psychological, or both) to a harmful substance

Substance abuse means harmful use of alcohol or other drugs. It is a poorly adaptive behaviour pattern, lasting more than one month, in which a person continues to use a substance after knowingly being harmed by it or uses it repeatedly in a hazardous situation, such as driving while intoxicated (APA, 1994). Abuse can lead to **substance dependence** (addiction), which may be physiological or psychological, or both, and is likely to continue into adulthood.

Trends and Factors in Drug Use

Use of illicit drugs among Canadian adolescents increased during the 1990s possibly because of a decline in perception of its dangers and a softening of peer disapproval. More males than females are drug users. The major increase is in the use of hashish/marijuana, with the use of cocaine, amphetamines, and LSD slowly increasing. Solvent use did not change substantially during the 1990s. The trends in drug use have been accompanied by a decrease in the use of beer, wine, and liquor. This suggests a changing trend from alcohol to drug use, although by Grade 10 over 90 per cent of adolescents had tried alcohol (King et al., 1999) despite being younger than the legal drinking age (King et al., 1999; Mathias, 1999).

These findings come from a series of surveys of over 6,000 students in all regions of Canada, which represents the Canadian component of a World Health Organization cross-national study, called Health Behaviour in School-Aged Children. Ten other countries—Denmark, England, France, Germany, Greece, Norway, Poland, Sweden, Switzerland, and the United States—participated in the study (King et al., 1999). These surveys probably underestimate adolescent drug use since they do not reach high school dropouts, who are likely to have higher rates.

As indicated in a 1998 survey, about 4 per cent of Canadian adolescents have used MDMA ("ecstasy") (King et al., 1999). Ecstasy is a hallucinatory, amphetamine-like drug, one of several relatively low-cost "club drugs" popular at nightclubs, bars, and night-long "raves" or "trances." It can cause long-term brain damage and other physical and psychological problems. Short-term problems—rapid heart rate, sweating, muscle spasms, and high fever—are complicated by the factors associated with raves, including high temperatures, vigourous activity, and dehydration; six deaths have been associated with the use of ecstasy in Canada in the past 8 years (Rieder, 2002). Roypnol, GHB, and Ketamine are depressants; they are called "date rape drugs" because they are often colourless, odourless, and tasteless and thus can be slipped into someone's drink and swallowed unknowingly.

What makes it likely that a particular young person will abuse drugs? Research has pinpointed a number of risk factors: (1) poor impulse control and a tendency to seek out sensation (which may have a biochemical basis), (2) family influences (such as a genetic predisposition to alcoholism, parental use or acceptance of drugs, poor or inconsistent parenting practices, family conflict, and troubled or distant family relationships), (3) "difficult" temperament, (4) early and persistent behaviour problems, particularly aggression, (5) academic failure and lack of commitment to education, (6) peer rejection, (7) association with drug users, (8) alienation and rebelliousness, (9) favourable attitudes toward drug use, and (10) early initiation into drug use. The earlier young people start using a drug, the more frequently they are likely to use it and the greater the tendency to abuse it. Contrary to popular belief, poverty is not linked with drug abuse unless deprivation is extreme (Hawkins, Catalano, & Miller, 1992; Johnson, Hoffmann, & Gerstein, 1996; Masse & Tremblay, 1997; USDHHS, 1996b). The more risk factors that are present, the greater the chance that an adolescent or young adult will abuse drugs.

Drug use often begins as children move from elementary school to middle school, where they meet new friends and become more vulnerable to peer pressure. Students in Grades 4 to 6 may start using cigarettes, beer, and inhalants and, as they get older, move on to marijuana or harder drugs (National [U.S.] Parents' Resource Institute for Drug Education, 1999).

Inhalants are chemical vapours that adolescents sniff to get high, often from common household products such as glues, solvents, gasoline, butane, and aerosols. Because they are inexpensive and easy to obtain, they are most often used by younger students. Sniffing can damage hearing, brain, bone marrow, liver, and kidneys and also can cause oxygen depletion, heart failure, and death. Inhalant use has been on the decline, along with growing peer disapproval of its use (L. D. Johnston et al., 2000). However, for some Canadian populations, including Aboriginal youth, inhalant use is a serious problem (Coleman, Charles, & Collins, 2001). A retrospective study of 78 Aboriginal youth, who had received treatment for inhalant abuse in the National Breakthrough Inhalant Abuse Program, tailored for Aboriginal youth, at a treatment centre in western Canada, showed that many came from isolated and low-income families that experienced violence and histories of substance abuse. The average age of solvent use was 9.7 years, and typically gasoline was the most common inhalant, often accompanied by alcohol and other drugs. The likelihood of relapse after treatment seemed to be associated with abuse of inhalants immediately before admission to a treatment program, lack of motivation during treatment, and hospitalization during treatment (Coleman et al., 2001). Although Aboriginal adolescents show higher rates of use of inhalants, marijuana, and tobacco than non-Aboriginal matched adolescents, there are no differences in rates of alcohol use between these groups (Gfellner, 1994). Family background factors involving parents' drug-use attitudes and behaviours, and peer attitudes toward substance abuse predicted the likelihood that Aboriginal teenagers used inhalants, marijuana, and tobacco. Aboriginal teenagers who abuse drugs may be bypassing the use of alcohol in favour of other drugs (Gfellner, 1994).

Early smoking is a danger signal: adolescents who begin smoking by age 11 are twice as likely as other young people to engage in risky behaviours, such as riding in a car with a drinking driver; carrying knives or guns to school; using inhalants, marijuana, or cocaine; and making suicide plans. Early use of alcohol and marijuana is associated with multiple risk behaviours (DuRant, Smith, Kreiter, & Krowchuk, 1999).

An important early influence may be the omnipresence of substance use in the media. According to one study, alcohol, tobacco, or illicit drugs are shown in 70 per cent of prime-time network television dramas, 38 out of 40 top-grossing movies, and half of all music videos (Gerbner & Ozyegin, 1997). Among 50 children's animated feature films available on videotape from five major Hollywood studios, more than two-thirds show characters smoking or drinking, with no indication or warning of negative health effects (Goldstein, Sobel, & Newman, 1999). Although the tobacco industry has claimed that it does not target adolescents, cigarette brands popular with 10- to 15-year-olds are widely advertised in U.S. magazines popular with young readers (King, Siegel, Celebucki, & Connolly, 1998).

Gateway Drugs: Alcohol, Marijuana, and Tobacco

Alcohol, marijuana, and tobacco, the three drugs most popular with adolescents, are sometimes called **gateway drugs,** because their use can lead to use of more addictive substances, such as cocaine and heroin (Gerstein & Green, 1993; Kelley, Denny, & Young, 1999; Lindsay & Rainey, 1997). Young people who smoke or drink often associate with peers who introduce them to harder drugs as they grow older. Frequency of alcohol and tobacco use is high in many industrialized countries and is starting earlier than in the past (Gabhainn & François, 2000).

gateway drugs Drugs such as alcohol, tobacco, and marijuana, the use of which tends to lead to use of more addictive drugs

Despite the efforts to curb smoking among youth, there was an increase in the prevalence of smoking among adolescents during the 1990s. By Grade 10, 23 per cent of girls and 17 per cent of boys reported smoking daily (King et al., 1999). The most common reasons that female adolescents begin to smoke include weight control, stress management, and a perception that smoking is fashionable and symbolizes independence (B.C. Doctors' Stop-Smoking Program, 2002).

Alcohol is a potent, mind-altering drug with major effects on physical, emotional, and social well-being; it is a very serious problem in many countries (Gabhainn & François, 2000). Alcohol use among Canadian teenagers has begun to decline along with illicit drug use. Still, over 90 per cent of teenagers have consumed more than a few sips of alcohol by the end of high school, and 16 per cent of Grade 8 students and 43 per cent of those in Grade 10 admit to having been drunk two or more times (King et al., 1999). This is worrisome because young people who begin drinking before age 15 are four times as likely to become alcohol-dependent as those who do not start drinking until age 20 or later (Grant & Dawson, 1998).

Marijuana is the most widely used illicit drug in Canada; almost half of Grade 10 students say they have tried it. Aside from its own ill effects, marijuana use may lead to addiction to hard drugs.

Checkpoint ✔

Can you . . .

✔ Summarize recent trends in drug use among adolescents?

✔ Discuss factors and risks connected with use of drugs, specifically alcohol, marijuana, and tobacco?

sexually transmitted diseases (STDs) Diseases spread by sexual contact

Adolescents try marijuana for many of the same reasons they try alcohol: They are curious, they want to do what their friends do, and they want to be like adults. Despite a decline in marijuana use since 1979, it is still by far the most widely used illicit drug in Canada, and there is a trend for adolescents to begin using marijuana at an earlier age (Tonkin, 2002). In 1998, about 20 per cent of Grade 8 students and 43 per cent of those in Grade 10 admitted to having used it in the past year (King et al. 1999).

Marijuana smoke typically contains more than 400 carcinogens. Heavy use can damage the brain, heart, lungs, and immune system and cause nutritional deficiencies, respiratory infections, and other physical problems. Marijuana use can also impede memory and learning. It may lessen motivation, interfere with schoolwork and other activities, and cause family problems. It can cut down perception, alertness, attention span, judgment, and the motor skills needed to drive a vehicle, and thus can contribute to traffic accidents (AAP Committee on Drugs, 1980; Farrow, Rees, & Worthington-Roberts, 1987; National [U.S.] Institute on Drug Abuse [NIDA], 1996; Tonkin, 2002).

Contrary to a common belief, marijuana may be addictive. Injecting rats with marijuana initially produces a "high" by increasing levels of a brain chemical called *dopamine*. As with heroin, cocaine, and other addictive drugs, the brain's ability to produce dopamine gradually diminishes, creating a greater craving for the drug (Tanda, Pontieri, & DiChiara, 1997).

Adolescent tobacco use, in Canada as in most other industrialized countries, is a serious problem, with more girls than boys admitting to smoking daily (King et al., 1999). After the release of a U.S. Surgeon General's report in 1964, which linked cigarette smoking to lung cancer, heart disease, emphysema, and several other illnesses, smoking among high school students dropped sharply. As with other drugs, an upturn in usage occurred during the 1990s. It is hoped that, as a result of government initiatives to educate young smokers about the health hazards of smoking—including legislated changes to health warnings on cigarette packages, and an increase in government taxes on cigarette purchases—the trend will begin to reverse itself. Still, cigarette use begins early and remains high. Nearly one in ten Grade 8 students and one in three high school students are current smokers (King et al. 1999).

Peer influence on smoking has been documented extensively (Center on Addiction and Substance Abuse at Columbia University [CASA], 1996). Other research points to the family. A survey of 9,225 adults found a strong relationship between smoking and several adverse childhood experiences: emotional, physical, or sexual abuse; parental separation or divorce; and growing up with a battered mother or a substance-abusing, mentally ill, or incarcerated household member. The more such experiences a person had had, the earlier the initiation into smoking (Anda et al., 1999). The prevalence of early smoking is especially serious in light of findings that smoking during childhood or adolescence may damage the DNA in the lungs; this increases the danger of lung cancer even in people who later stop smoking (Wiencke et al., 1999).

Sexually Transmitted Diseases (STDs)

Sexually transmitted diseases (STDs) are diseases spread by sexual contact. Rates in Canada are typical of those in most Western countries, with the exception of the United States, which has among the highest rates of STDs in the industrialized world (Maticka-Tyndale, 2001).

Although the rates for some STDs had fallen over the 10 years ending in the late 1990s, there has been a slight increase in incidence since that time (King et al., 1999; Maticka-Tyndale, 2001). The chief reasons for the spread of STDs among adolescents are early sexual activity, which increases the likelihood of having multiple high-risk partners, and failure to use condoms or to use them regularly and correctly.

Young women show a higher prevalence of chlamydia, gonorrhea, and syphilis than young men (CICH, 2000; King et al., 1999; Maticka-Tyndale, 2001). Chlamydia is the most common SDT among young people in Canada, with a prevalence of slightly over 1000 cases per 100,000 for women, and about 200 for young men, and the incidence has been rising since 1997 (Maticka-Tyndale, 2001). Chlamydia is a *curable* STD that causes infections of the urinary tract, rectum, and cervix and can lead, in women, to pelvic inflammatory disease (PID), a serious abdominal infection. Although the prevalence of syphilis in Canada has dropped to the point of near-elimination (CICH, 2000; Maticka-

Table 15-3   Common Sexually Transmitted Diseases

Disease	Cause	Symptoms: Male	Symptoms: Female	Treatment	Consequences if Untreated
Chlamydia	Bacterial infection	Pain during urination, discharge from penis	Vaginal discharge, abdominal discomfort†	Tetracycline or erythromycin	Can cause pelvic inflammatory disease or eventual sterility
Trichomoniasis	Parasitic infection, sometimes passed on in moist objects such as towels and bathing suits	Often absent	May be absent, or may include vaginal discharge, discomfort during intercourse, odour, painful urination	Oral antibiotic	May lead to abnormal growth of cervical cells
Gonorrhea	Bacterial infection	Discharge from penis, pain during urination*	Discomfort when urinating, vaginal discharge, abnormal menses†	Penicillin or other antibiotics	Can cause pelvic inflammatory disease or eventual sterility; can also cause arthritis, dermatitis, and meningitis
HPV (genital warts)	Human papiloma virus	Painless growths that usually appear on penis, but may also appear on urethra or in rectal area*	Small, painless growths on genitals and anus; may also occur inside the vagina without external symptoms*	Removal of warts; but infection often reappears	May be associated with cervical cancer. In pregnancy, warts enlarge and may obstruct birth canal.
Herpes	Herpes simplex virus	Painful blisters anywhere on the genitalia, usually on the penis*	Painful blisters on the genitalia, sometimes with fever and aching muscles; women with sores on cervix may be unaware of outbreaks*	No known cure, but controlled with antiviral drug acyclovir	Possible increased risk of cervical cancer
Hepatitis B	Hepatitis B virus	Skin and eyes become yellow	Same as in men	No specific treatment; no alcohol	Can cause liver damage, chronic hepatitis
Syphilis	Bacterial infection	In first stage, reddish-brown sores on the mouth or genitalia, or both, which may disappear, though the bacteria remain; in the second, more infectious stage, a widespread skin rash*	Same as in men	Penicillin or other antibiotics	Paralysis, convulsions, brain damage, and sometimes death
AIDS (acquired immune deficiency syndrome)	Human immunodeficiency virus (HIV)	Extreme fatigue, fever, swollen lymph nodes, weight loss, diarrhea, night sweats, susceptibility to other diseases*	Same as in men	No known cure; protease inhibitors and other drugs appear to extend life	Death, usually due to other diseases, such as cancer

*May be asymptomatic

†Often asymptomatic

Tyndale, 2001), the incidence of new cases of gonorrhea is increasing, with almost 100 cases per 100,000 young women, and 40 young men per 100,000 in 2000 (Maticka-Tyndale, 2001). Table 15-3 summarizes some common STDs: their causes, most frequent symptoms, treatment, and consequences.

AIDS results from the human immunodeficiency virus (HIV), which is transmitted through bodily fluids (mainly blood and semen), usually by sharing of intravenous drug needles or by sexual contact with an infected partner. The virus attacks the body's immune system, leaving a person vulnerable to a variety of fatal diseases. HIV is believed to stay in the body for life, even though the person carrying it may show no signs of illness. Symptoms of AIDS—which include extreme fatigue, fever, swollen lymph nodes, weight loss, diarrhea, and night sweats—may not appear until 6 months to 10 or more years after initial infection. AIDS is incurable, but increasingly, the related infections that kill people are being stopped with antiviral therapy, including protease inhibitors (Palella et al., 1998). Many HIV-infected people lead active lives for years.

The most common route for HIV infection among young people between 15 and 19 years of age is heterosexual contact, which accounts for 32 per cent of HIV cases, followed by male homosexual activity, accounting for 29 per cent of cases, and intravenous drug use, accounting for 22 per cent of cases (CICH, 2000). Although the prevalence of HIV and AIDS in Canadian adolescents is small compared with adults, it is a cause for concern as many individuals with undetected HIV go unreported (CICH, 2000). AIDS is becoming a concern among Aboriginal communities. The annual proportion of AIDS cases in Aboriginal people rose from 1 per cent before 1990 to 15 per cent in 1999 (Health Canada, 1999b). It is also afflicting a greater proportion of Aboriginal youth: 26 per cent of Aboriginal people who are infected are under 30 years of age, whereas 17.6 per cent of non-Aboriginal people who are infected are under 30 years of age (Canadian Aboriginal AIDS Network, 1999). These numbers are underestimated because ethnicity is often not reported in many cases (Health Canada, 1999b).

STDs are more likely to develop undetected in women than in men, and in adolescents than in adults. In a single unprotected sexual encounter with an infected partner, a teenage girl runs a 1 per cent risk of acquiring HIV, a 30 per cent risk of genital herpes, and a 50 per cent risk of gonorrhea (AGI, 1999a). The World Health Organization (1997) estimates that half of the 30 million HIV infections worldwide are in young people ages 15 to 24.

As symptoms may not appear until a disease has progressed to the point of causing serious long-term complications, early detection is important. Regular, school-based screening and treatment, together with programs that promote abstention from or postponement of sexual activity, responsible decision making, and ready availability of condoms for those who are sexually active may have some effect in controlling the spread of STDs (AAP Committee on Adolescence, 1994; AGI, 1994; Cohen, Nsuami, Martin, & Farley, 1999; Ku, Sonenstein, & Pleck, 1992; Rotheram-Borus & Futterman, 2000). Studies suggest that most young people who find out they have HIV change their sexual behaviour, and half stop injecting drugs (Rotheram-Borus & Futterman, 2000). Box 15-1 lists steps people can take to protect themselves from STDs.

Checkpoint ✔

Can you . . .

✔ Identify and describe the most common sexually transmitted diseases?

✔ List risk factors for developing an STD during adolescence, and state effective prevention methods?

What's your view ❓

• Should marijuana be legal, like alcohol? Why or why not?

• Should there be tighter restrictions on cigarette advertising? If so, what kinds of restrictions?

• How can adolescents be helped to avoid or change risky behaviours?

Abuse and Neglect

Maltreatment of adolescents is much less widely discussed than maltreatment of younger children, but it does exist. Of the almost 136,000 children found by agencies to be victims of substantiated or indicated abuse or neglect in 1998, 18.5 children per 1,000 were boys between the ages of 12 and 15 years, and 25.1 per 1,000 were girls in the same age range, according to the Canadian Incidence Study of Reported Child Abuse and Neglect (Trocmé et al., 2001).

A longitudinal study in Calgary tracked 290 females on a variety of psychological and social factors from age 3 to age 13, and measured the incidence of maltreatment up to the age of 16. Results showed that early neurological problems, difficult temperament, mothers' stress, low income, poor attachment, and disrupted family were associated with higher likelihood of maltreatment (Bagley & Mallick, 2000).

Unlike younger children who are abused, teenagers are more likely to fight back or run away (Sedlak & Broadhurst, 1996). Physically abused teenagers are often perceived as

How can people protect themselves against sexually transmitted diseases (STDs)? Abstinence is safest, of course. For those who are sexually active, the following guidelines minimize the possibility of acquiring an STD and maximize the chances of getting good treatment if one is acquired.

- Have regular medical checkups. All sexually active persons should request tests specifically aimed at diagnosing STDs.
- Know your partner. The more discriminating you are, the less likely you are to be exposed to STDs. Partners with whom you develop a relationship are more likely than partners you do not know well to inform you of any medical problems they have.
- Avoid having sexual intercourse with many partners, promiscuous persons, and drug abusers.
- Practice "safer sex": avoid sexual activity involving exchange of bodily fluids. Use a latex condom during intercourse and oral sex. Avoid anal intercourse.
- Use a contraceptive foam, cream, or jelly; it will kill many germs and help to prevent certain STDs.
- Learn the symptoms of STDs: vaginal or penile discharge; inflammation, itching, or pain in the genital or anal area; burning during urination; pain during intercourse; genital, body, or mouth sores, blisters, bumps, or rashes; pain in the lower abdomen or in the testicles; discharge from or itching of eyes; and fever or swollen glands.
- Inspect your partner for any visible symptoms.
- If you develop any symptoms yourself, get immediate medical attention.
- Just before and just after sexual contact, wash genital and rectal areas with soap and water; males should urinate after washing.

- Do not have any sexual contact if you suspect that you or your partner may be infected. Abstinence is the most reliable preventive measure.
- Avoid exposing any cut or break in the skin to anyone else's blood (including menstrual blood), body fluids, or secretions.
- Practise good hygiene routinely: frequent, thorough handwashing and daily brushing under fingernails.
- Make sure needles used for ear piercing, tattooing, acupuncture, or any kind of injection are either sterile or disposable. Never share a needle.
- If you contract any STD, notify all recent sexual partners immediately so that they can obtain treatment and avoid passing the infection back to you or on to someone else. Inform your doctor or dentist of your condition so that precautions can be taken to prevent transmission. Do not donate blood, plasma, sperm, body organs, or other body tissue.

Source: Adapted from American Foundation for the Prevention of Venereal Disease (AFPVD), 1988; Upjohn Company, 1984.

What's your view?

As far as you know, do adolescents seem to be taking more precautions against STDs than in the past? If you were trying to persuade a friend to do so, on which of the guidelines listed here would you place the most emphasis?

Check it out

For more information on this topic, go to **www.mcgrawhill.ca/college/papalia** which has links to relative websites.

---

bearing at least part of the blame for provoking parents; they are more likely than other adolescents to use violence against parents and siblings.

Although abuse of teenagers is less likely to result in death or severe injury than abuse of younger children, it can have serious long-term results. Sexually abused teenagers are more likely than their peers to engage in early or heavy sexual activity; to become pregnant or delinquent; to abuse alcohol or other drugs; to be confused about their sexual identity; to be depressed or anxious; and to attempt suicide. Physically abused teenagers also tend to be anxious and depressed. They may show severe behavioural, academic, and sleeping problems; self-destructive or reckless actions; involvement in prostitution or heavy drug use; or suicidal tendencies (Council on Scientific Affairs of the American Medical Association, 1993; Schissel & Fedec, 1999).

Death in Adolescence

Death is not something adolescents normally think much about. Many adolescents take heedless risks. They hitchhike, drive recklessly, and experiment with drugs and sex—often with tragic results. Still, in many communities in which adolescents (and even younger children) live, violence and the threat of death are inescapable facts of daily life.

Not every death in adolescence is as poignant as Anne Frank's. Still, death this early in life is always tragic, and (unlike Anne's) usually accidental (CICH, 2000; USDHHS, 1999b)—but not entirely so. The frequency of car crashes, handgun deaths, and suicide in this age group reflects a violent culture, as well as adolescents' inexperience and immaturity, which often lead to risk taking and carelessness.

Deaths from Vehicle Accidents and Firearms

Motor vehicle collisions are the leading cause of death among Canadian teenagers; they account for more than half of all deaths of 10- to 14-year-olds (Canadian Council on Social Development, 2001). Collisions are more likely to be fatal when a 16- or 17-year-old driver carries passengers, perhaps because adolescents tend to drive more recklessly in the presence of peers (Chen, Baker, & Braver, & Li, 2000).

Death rates for this age group have dropped 52 per cent between 1975 and 1995, despite the high percentage of youth in Canada (12 per cent) who report drinking and driving at least once in the previous year. This percentage is higher than any other age group, excepting the 20- to 24-year-old group (CICH, 2000). Although the death rate for males is higher than for females, the gap is narrowing (CICH, 2000). Some provinces have adopted graduated licensing systems, which allow beginning drivers to drive only with supervision at first, and lift the restrictions gradually.

Firearm-related deaths of 15- to 19-year-olds (including homicide, suicide, and accidental deaths) are far more common in the United States than in other industrialized countries, comprising about one-third of all injury deaths and more than 85 percent of all homicides. The prevalence of deaths as a result of firearm injury in the United States is 1.7 children under the age of 15 per 100,000, whereas in Canada the rate is about 0.5 per 100,000 ([U.S.] Centers for Disease Control and Prevention, 1997). Contrary to the claims of gun-rights defenders, guns in the home are 43 times more likely to kill a family member or acquaintance than to be used in self-defence (AAP Committee on Injury and Poison Prevention, 2000).

Suicide

Although the frequency of suicide is low for Canadian youth, the rate has increased dramatically for males over several decades (CICH, 2000; Task Force on Suicide in Canada, 1994), and the rate is higher in Canada than in the United States (Leenaars & Lester, 1990; 1995). Currently, the rate of completed suicides for youth between 15 and 19 years is 19 per 100,000 males and 4 per 100,000 females (CICH, 2000). However, women tended to attempt suicide more frequently than males, with 265 women and 98 men per 100,000 being hospitalized for suicide attempts in 1996 to 1997, and street youth are more likely to attempt suicide than youth in school (CICH, 2000).

Although suicide affects all ethnic groups, the suicide death rate for Aboriginal males between 15 and 24 years of age is about five times higher, at 126 per 100,000, than it is for non-Aboriginal males of the same age range, and the rate is 35 per 100,000 Aboriginal females (CICH, 2000). One possible explanation for the higher prevalence may be related to the link between cultural continuity and Aboriginal suicide rates; as the number of protective cultural factors in a community—like self-governance, land claims negotiations, and local control over educational and health services—increase, rates of youth suicide decrease (CICH, 2000). Other factors that have been associated with suicide attempts among Inuit youth in particular are substance abuse, recent alcohol abuse, life event stressors, and the presence of a psychiatric problem (Kirmayer, Boothroyd, & Hodgins, 1998). The increased likelihood of suicide for individuals whose identity has been undermined by radical cultural change is particularly relevant for Aboriginal youth in Canada (Chandler & Lalonde, 1998; 1995). Given the wide variations of experience among Aboriginal communities, some bands show higher suicide rates than others, with some communities showing rates that are 800 times the national average, while other bands have virtually no suicide (Chandler et al., 1998). One possible explanation for these differences is cultural rehabilitation and preservation: Aboriginal communities that have taken steps to preserve and rehabilitate their own cultures have dramatically lower suicide rates (Chandler et al., 1998).

Gay and lesbian youth, who have high rates of depression, also have high rates of suicide and attempted suicide (AAP Committee on Adolescence, 2000; Remafedi, French, Story, Resnick, & Blum, 1998).

In a U.S. survey of students in Grades 7 to 12, almost one-fourth of the students reported that they had seriously considered suicide during the past year (AAP Committee on Adolescence, 2000). Young people who attempt suicide tend to have histories of emotional illness: commonly depression, substance abuse, anti-social or aggressive behaviour, negative social comparison, or unstable personality. They also tend to have attempted suicide

Box 15-2 *Preventing Teenage Suicide*

What can be done to stem the alarming rise in suicide among young people? Many people intent on killing themselves keep their plans secret, but others send out signals well in advance. An attempt at suicide is sometimes a call for help, and some people die because they are more successful than they intended to be.

Warning signs include withdrawal from relationships; talking about death, the hereafter, or suicide; giving away prized possessions; drug or alcohol abuse; personality changes, such as a rise in anger, boredom, or apathy; unusual neglect of appearance; difficulty concentrating at work or in school; staying away from work, school, or other usual activities; complaints of physical problems when nothing is organically wrong; and eating or sleeping much more or much less than usual. Friends or family may be able to help by talking to a young person about his or her suicidal thoughts to bring them out in the open; telling others who are in a position to do something—the person's parents or spouse, other family members, a close friend, a therapist, or a counsellor; and showing the person that she or he has other options besides death, even though none of them may be ideal.

Telephone hotlines are the most prevalent type of suicide intervention for adolescents, but their effectiveness appears to be minimal. In fact, some of these programs may do harm by exaggerating the extent of teenage suicide and painting it as a reaction to normal stresses of adolescence rather than a pathological act. Instead, programs should identify and treat young people at particular risk of suicide, including those who have already attempted it. Equally important is the need to attack the risk factors—for example, through programs to reduce substance abuse and strengthen families (Garland & Zigler, 1993). Programs to enhance self-esteem and build problem-solving and coping abilities can be directed toward young children and continued throughout the school years (Meehan, 1990).

Suicide intentions are sometimes accompanied by warning signs, such as withdrawal, as ways of calling out for help.

What's your view?

Have you ever experienced any of the warning signs described in this box? What would you do if a close friend or family member showed one or more of these signs?

Check it out!

For more information on this topic, go to **www.mcgrawhill.ca/college/papalia** which will direct you to links to statistics about suicide and to prevention materials.

---

before, or to have friends or family members who did (Barber, 2000; Garland & Zigler, 1993; NIMH, 1999a, 1999b; Slap, Vorters, Chaudhuri, & Centor, 1989; "Suicide–Part I," 1996). Alcohol plays a part in fully half of all teenage suicides (AAP Committee on Adolescence, 2000). Parents often underestimate the extent of depression and alcohol abuse in suicidal adolescents (Velting et al., 1998).

Suicidal teenagers tend to think poorly of themselves, to feel hopeless, and to have poor impulse control and low tolerance for frustration and stress. Feelings of depression may be masked as boredom, apathy, hyperactivity, or physical problems. These young people are often alienated from their parents and have no one outside the family to turn to. Many come from troubled families, often with a history of unemployment, imprisonment, or suicidal behaviour, and a high proportion of these young people have been abused or neglected (Deykin, Alpert, & McNamara, 1985; Garland & Zigler, 1993; Slap et al., 1989; "Suicide–Part I," 1996; Swedo et al., 1991). School problems—academic or behavioural—are common among would-be suicides (National [U.S.] Committee for Citizens in Education [NCCE], 1986).

Box 15-2 discusses ways of preventing suicide.

Checkpoint ✔

Can you . . .

✔ Tell how maltreatment of adolescents differs from maltreatment of younger children?

✔ Name the leading causes of death among adolescents.

✔ Assess risk factors and prevention programs for teenage suicide?

Checkpoint ✔

Can you . . .

✔ Identify factors that tend to protect adolescents from health risks?

Protective Factors: Health in Context

Adolescents' physical development, like that of younger children, does not occur in a vacuum. Young people live and grow in a social world. As we have pointed out throughout this book, the influences of the family and school environments, particularly, play an important part in physical and mental health.

A study of 12,118 students in Grades 7 through 12 in a random sample of 134 schools across the United States (Resnick et al., 1997) took a broad overview of risk factors and protective factors affecting four major aspects of adolescent health and well-being: emotional distress and suicidal behaviour; involvement in violence (fighting or threats or use of weapons); use of cigarettes, alcohol, and marijuana; and sexuality (including age of sexual initiation and any history of pregnancy). The students completed questionnaires and had 90-minute home interviews; during the sensitive portions of the interview, the young people listened to the questions through earphones and entered their answers on laptop computers. The adolescents' school administrators also filled out questionnaires.

The findings emphasize the interconnectedness of physical, cognitive, emotional, and social development. Perceptions of connectedness to others, both at home and at school, consistently affect young people's health and well-being in all domains. The findings underline the importance of parents' spending time with, and being available to, their children. Even more important, however, is an adolescent's sense that parents and teachers are warm and caring and that they have high expectations for the adolescent's achievement. The data also support the advisability of restrictions on adolescents' access to tobacco, alcohol, and guns.

These findings are clear and consistent with other research: Adolescents who are getting emotional support at home and are doing well in school have the best chance of avoiding the health hazards of adolescence.

Despite the perils of adolescence, most young people emerge from these years with a mature, healthy body and a zest for life. While their bodies have been developing, their minds have continued to develop too, as we will see in chapter 16.

Summary and Key Terms

Adolescence: A Developmental Transition

Guidepost 1 What is adolescence, and when does it begin and end?

- Adolescence is the transition from childhood to adulthood. Neither its beginning nor its end is clearly marked in industrialized societies; it lasts about a decade, between ages 11 or 12 and the late teens or early twenties.

- Legal, sociological, and psychological definitions of entrance into adulthood vary. In some non-industrialized cultures, "coming of age" is signified by special rites.

   adolescence (381)   puberty (381)

Guidepost 2 What opportunities and risks does adolescence entail?

- Adolescence is full of opportunities for physical, cognitive, and psychosocial growth, but also of risks to healthy development. Risky behaviour patterns, such as drinking alcohol, drug abuse, sexual and gang activity, and use of firearms tend to be established early in adolescence. About four out of five young people experience no major problems.

Puberty: The End of Childhood

Guidepost 3 What physical changes do adolescents experience, and how do these changes affect them psychologically?

- Puberty is triggered by hormonal changes, which may affect moods and behaviour. Puberty takes about 4 years, typically begins earlier in girls than in boys, and ends when a person can reproduce.

- During puberty, both boys and girls undergo an adolescent growth spurt. A secular trend toward earlier attainment of adult height and sexual maturity began about 100 years ago, probably because of improvements in living standards.

- Primary sex characteristics (the reproductive organs) enlarge and mature during puberty. Secondary sex characteristics also appear.

- The principal signs of sexual maturity are production of sperm (for males) and menstruation (for females). Spermarche typically occurs at age 13. Menarche occurs, on average, between the ages of 12 and 13 in Canada.

- Sexual attraction seems to begin at about age 10, when the adrenal glands increase their hormonal output.

- Teenagers, especially girls, tend to be sensitive about their physical appearance. Girls who mature early tend to adjust less easily than early maturing boys.

  secular trend (383)   adolescent growth spurt (384)   primary sex characteristics (385)   secondary sex characteristics (385) spermarche (385)   menarche (385)   gonadarche (386) adrenarche (386)

Physical and Mental Health

Guidepost 4   What are some common health problems in adolescence, and how can they be prevented?

- For the most part, the adolescent years are relatively healthy. Health problems are often are associated with poverty or a risk-taking lifestyle. Adolescents are less likely than younger children to get regular medical care.

- Many adolescents, especially girls, do not engage in regular vigorous physical activity.

- Many adolescents do not get enough sleep because the high school schedule is out of sync with their natural body rhythms.

- Three common eating disorders in adolescence are obesity, anorexia nervosa, and bulimia nervosa. All can have serious long-term effects. Anorexia and bulimia affect mostly girls. Outcomes for bulimia tend to be better than for anorexia.

- Adolescent substance abuse and dependence have lessened in recent years; still, drug use often begins as children move into middle school.

- Marijuana, alcohol, and tobacco are the most popular drugs with adolescents. All involve serious risks and can be gateways to the use of hard drugs.

- Rates of sexually transmitted diseases (STDs) in Canada are increasing. STDs are more likely to develop undetected in girls than in boys.

- Maltreatment of adolescents can lead to serious behaviour problems.

- Leading causes of death among adolescents include motor vehicle accidents and suicide.

  anorexia nervosa (391)   bulimia nervosa (392)   substance abuse (394)   substance dependence (394)   gateway drugs (395) sexually transmitted diseases (STDs) (396)

OLC Preview

The official website for *A Child's World*, First Canadian edition, provides information on topics such as sexually transmitted disease and teenage suicide with links to such recommended websites as the Centers for Disease Control and Prevention, and the Canadian Paediatric Society. Check out **www.mcgrawhill.ca/college/papalia.**

Cognitive Development in Adolescence

I should place [the prime of a man's life] at between fifteen and sixteen. It is then, it always seems to me, that his vitality is at its highest; he has greatest sense of the ludicrous and least sense of dignity. After that time, decay begins to set in.

—Evelyn Waugh, age 16, in a school debate, 1920

Focus *Nelson Mandela, Freedom Fighter**

Nelson Mandela

Rolihlahla, the name Nelson Mandela's father gave him at his birth in 1918, means "stirring up trouble." And that is exactly what Mandela did throughout his long and finally successful struggle to topple apartheid, South Africa's rigid system of racial separation and subjugation.

Mandela's election as his country's first black president in April 1994—only 4 years after his emergence from 28 years behind bars for conspiring to overthrow the white-dominated government—was the realization of a dream formed in his youth. It was a dream kindled as Mandela sat quietly listening to his tribal elders reminisce about a bygone era of self-government more than a century earlier, before the coming of white people—an era of peace, freedom, and equality.

"The land . . . belonged to the whole tribe and there was no individual ownership whatsoever," Mandela told the court that sentenced him to prison in 1962. "There were no classes, no rich or poor and no exploitation of man by man. . . . The council was so completely democratic that all members of the tribe could participate in its deliberations. Chief and subject, warrior and medicine man, all took part" (Meer, 1988, p. 12). Mandela recognized that his forebears' way of life would not be viable in the modern world. But the vision of a society "in which none will be held in slavery or servitude, and in which poverty, want and insecurity shall be no more" served as a lifelong inspiration.

Mandela has royal blood: One of his ancestors ruled his Thembu tribe, and his father was chief of Mvezo, a small, isolated village in Transkei where Mandela was born. Mandela seems to have inherited his "proud rebelliousness" and "stubborn sense of fairness" (Mandela, 1994, p. 6): Not long after his birth, his father, a counsellor to tribal kings, was deposed for refusing to honour a summons to appear before the local British magistrate. For standing on his traditional prerogatives and defying the magistrate's authority, Mandela's father paid with his lands and fortune.

Mandela's mother, his father's third of four wives, moved with her baby and his three sisters to the nearby village of Qunu, where they grew up in a compound of mud huts. The family raised all their own food—cows and goats for milk, and mealies (a form of corn), which his mother ground between two stones to make bread or boiled over an open fire. At 5, Mandela became a herd boy, driving sheep and cattle through the fertile grasslands. His was a simple life, governed for the most part by the time-honoured rules of his tribe. But his mother, who had become a Christian, had him baptized in the Methodist church; and at 7, he became the first member of his family to go to school. It was his first teacher who gave him his English name, Nelson.

*The main sources of biographical information about Nelson Mandela's youth are Benson (1986), Hargrove (1989), Harwood (1987), Mandela (1994), and Meer (1988).

When Mandela was 9, his father died, and his life changed completely. His mother sent him to live at the tribal headquarters at Mqhekezweni. The acting regent, who owed his position to Mandela's father, had offered to become his guardian and raise him as his own son.

As Mandela grew into adolescence, he observed tribal meetings, where any member could speak and the regent listened quietly before summing up the consensus. This style of leadership deeply impressed Mandela and influenced his own demeanour as a leader in later years. He also watched his guardian preside over council meetings to which minor chiefs brought disputes to be tried. His fascination with the presentation of cases and the cross-examination of witnesses planted the seeds of an ambition to be a lawyer—an ambition he eventually fulfilled. From the visiting chiefs and headmen, he heard tales about early African warriors who had fought against European domination. These stories stirred his interest in his people's history and laid the groundwork for his political activism.

At the age of 16, Mandela underwent circumcision, the traditional ritual by which a boy becomes recognized as a man and a participant in tribal councils. At the concluding ceremony, the main speaker, Chief Meligqili, struck a discordant note. The promise of manhood, he said, was an empty one in a land where Africans were a conquered people. "Among these young men," he said, "are chiefs who will never rule because we have no power to govern ourselves; soldiers who will never fight for we have no weapons to fight with; scholars who will never teach because we have no place for them to study. The abilities, the intelligence, the promise of these young men will be squandered in their attempt to eke out a living doing the simplest, most mindless chores for the white man. These gifts [we give them] today are naught, for we cannot give them the greatest gift of all, which is freedom and independence." Although Mandela did not appreciate it at the time, that speech sparked his political awakening.

• • •

The formative influences of Mandela's adolescent years helped shape his moral and political thinking and his life's work. The lessons he had learned about leadership and about his people's past glory stood him in good stead as he directed the resistance to an increasingly repressive regime, first in the streets and then from his island prison. Those lessons remained with him as he eventually managed to negotiate a new nonracial constitution and free elections—accomplishments for which he received a Nobel Peace Prize in 1993.

In this chapter, we first examine the Piagetian stage of formal operations, which makes it possible for a young person like Nelson Mandela to visualize an ideal world. We also look at what David Elkind has identified as some immature aspects of adolescents' thought and at their moral development. Finally, we explore practical aspects of cognitive growth—issues of school and vocational choice.

After you have read and studied this chapter, you should be able to answer each of the Guidepost questions that appear at the top of the next page. Look for them again in the margins, where they point to important concepts throughout the chapter. To check your understanding of these Guideposts, review the end-of-chapter summary. Checkpoints located throughout the chapter will help you verify your understanding of what you have read.

1. How do adolescents' thinking and use of language differ from younger children's?

2. On what basis do adolescents make moral judgments?

3. What influences affect success in secondary school, and why do some students drop out?

4. What factors affect educational and vocational planning and preparation?

Aspects of Cognitive Maturation

Adolescents not only look different from younger children; they also think differently. Their speed of information processing continues to increase, though not as dramatically as in middle childhood (Kail, 1991, 1997). Although their thinking may remain immature in some ways, they are capable of abstract reasoning and sophisticated moral judgments, and they can plan more realistically for the future.

Guidepost 1

How do adolescents' thinking and use of language differ from younger children's?

Piaget's Stage of Formal Operations

According to Piaget, adolescents enter the highest level of cognitive development—**formal operations**—when they develop the capacity for abstract thought. This development, usually around age 11, gives them a new, more flexible way to manipulate information. No longer limited to the here and now, they can understand historical time and extraterrestrial space. They can use symbols for symbols (for example, letting the letter *X* stand for an unknown numeral) and thus can learn algebra and calculus. They can better appreciate metaphor and allegory and thus can find richer meanings in literature. They can think in terms of what *might* be, not just what *is*. They can imagine possibilities and can form and test hypotheses.

As Nelson Mandela did during his adolescence, people in the stage of formal operations can integrate what they have learned in the past with the challenges of the present and make plans for the future. Thought at this stage has a flexibility not possible in the stage of concrete operations. The ability to think abstractly has emotional implications, too. Earlier, a child could love a parent or hate a classmate. Now "the adolescent can love freedom or hate exploitation. . . . The possible and the ideal captivate both mind and feeling" (H. Ginsburg & Opper, 1979, p. 201).

formal operations In Piaget's theory, the final stage of cognitive development, characterized by the ability to think abstractly

Hypothetical-Deductive Reasoning

To appreciate the difference formal reasoning makes, let's follow the progress of a typical child in dealing with a classic Piagetian problem, the pendulum problem.* The child, Adam, is shown the pendulum—an object hanging from a string. He is then shown how he can change any of four factors: the length of the string, the weight of the object, the height from which the object is released, and the amount of force he may use to push the object. He is asked to figure out which factor or combination of factors determines how fast the pendulum swings. (This and other Piagetian tasks for assessing the achievement of formal operations are pictured in Figure 16-1.)

When Adam first sees the pendulum, he is not yet 7 years old and is in the pre-operational stage. Unable to formulate a plan for attacking the problem, he tries one thing after another

---

*This description of age-related differences in the approach to the pendulum problem is adapted from H. Ginsburg and Opper (1979).

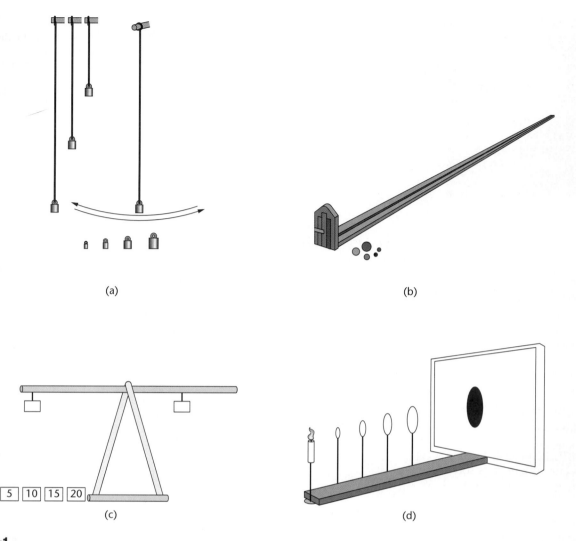

Figure 16-1

Piagetian tasks for measuring attainment of formal operations. *(a)* Pendulum. The pendulum's string can be shortened or lengthened, and weights of varying sizes can be attached to it. The student must determine what variables affect the speed of the pendulum's swing. *(b)* Motion in a horizontal plane. A spring device launches balls of varying sizes, which roll in a horizontal plane. The student must predict their stopping points. *(c)* Balance beam. A balance scale comes with weights of varying sizes, which can be hung at different points along the crossbar. The student must determine what factors affect whether or not the scale will balance. *(d)* Shadows. A board containing a row of peg holes is attached to a screen. A light source and rings of varying diameters can be placed in the holes, at varying distances from the screen. The student must produce two shadows of the same size, using different-sized rings.

Source: Adapted from Small, 1990, Fig. 8-12.

in a hit-or-miss manner. First he puts a light weight on a long string and pushes it; then he tries swinging a heavy weight on a short string; then he removes the weight entirely. Not only is his method random; he also cannot understand or report what has happened.

Adam next encounters the pendulum at age 10, when he is in the stage of concrete operations. This time, he discovers that varying the length of the string and the weight of the object affects the speed of the swing. However, because he varies both factors at the same time, he cannot tell which is critical or whether both are.

Adam is confronted with the pendulum for a third time at age 15, and this time he goes at the problem systematically. He designs an experiment to test all the possible hypotheses, varying one factor at a time—first, the length of the string; next, the weight of the object; then the height from which it is released; and finally, the amount of force used—each time holding the other three factors constant. In this way, he is able to determine that only one factor—the length of the string—determines how fast the pendulum swings.

Adam's solution of the pendulum problem shows that he has arrived at the stage of formal operations. He is now capable of **hypothetical-deductive reasoning.** He can develop a hypothesis and can design an experiment to test it. He considers all the relationships he can imagine and goes through them systematically, one by one, to eliminate the false and arrive at the true. Hypothetical-deductive reasoning gives him a tool to solve problems, from fixing the family car to constructing a political theory.

Microgenetic studies of problem-solving behaviour support Piaget's analysis of how concrete operations differ from formal operations. In one such study, students from Grades 5 and 6 and non-college-educated adults were asked to design experiments to understand physical phenomena (Schauble, 1996). For example, they were to vary the depth of water in a model canal and the size, shape, and weight of boats travelling through it, so as to maximize the speed of the vessels. Preadolescents were less systematic than adults in exploring such problems, typically varying more than one factor at the same time, as Adam did with the pendulum at that age.

To solve such problems, people need to think like scientists. They need theories and hypotheses to guide their problem-solving strategies, and they need to modify or abandon a hypothesis when the evidence does not fit. On the other hand, they should not rule out a hypothesis before testing it, just because it seems unlikely to be true—a common mistake among children (DeLoache, Miller, & Pierroutsakos, 1998). Above all, they need to know what theories and strategies they are following. Many preadolescents do not have coherent theories and strategies or do not consciously think about them (Kuhn, Garcia-Mila, Zohar, & Andersen, 1995).

What brings about the shift to formal reasoning? Piaget attributed it to a combination of brain maturation and expanding environmental opportunities. Both are essential: Even if young people's neurological development has advanced enough to permit formal reasoning, they can attain it only with appropriate environmental stimulation. One way this happens is through cooperative effort. When university students (average age, 18½) were given a chemistry problem and told to set up their own experiments to solve it, students randomly assigned to work in pairs solved more problems than those who worked alone. The more the partners challenged each other's reasoning, the greater were the advances in thinking (Dimant & Bearison, 1991).

As with the development of concrete operations, schooling and culture seem to play a role in addition to bio-neurological maturation—as Piaget (1972) ultimately recognized. French 10- to 15-year-olds in the 1990s did better on Piagetian tests of formal operations than their counterparts two to three decades earlier, at a time when fewer French adolescents (or their parents) had secondary school educations (Flieller, 1999). When adolescents in New Guinea and Rwanda were tested on the pendulum problem, none were able to solve it. On the other hand, Chinese children in Hong Kong, who had been to British schools, did at least as well as North American or European children. Schoolchildren in Central Java and New South Wales also showed some formal operational abilities (Gardiner et al., 1998). Apparently, this kind of thinking is a learned ability that is not equally necessary or equally valued in all cultures.

Evaluating Piaget's Theory

Piaget's analysis of the development of formal reasoning seems fairly accurate, as far as it goes. However, there are several advances, both in middle childhood and in adolescence, that it does not adequately take into account. Among them are the gradual accumulation of knowledge and expertise in specific fields; the gain in information-processing capacity; and the growth in *metacognition*, awareness and monitoring of one's own mental processes and strategies (Flavell et al., 1993).

Research has questioned Piaget's assertion of definite stages of development. For example, the distinction between the stages of concrete and formal operations may be less clear-cut than Piaget's theory suggests. His own writings provide many examples of children displaying aspects of scientific thinking well before adolescence. At the same time, Piaget seems to have *over*estimated older children's abilities. Many late adolescents and adults—perhaps one-third to one-half—seem incapable of abstract thought as Piaget defined it (Gardiner et al., 1998; Kohlberg & Gilligan, 1971; Papalia, 1972), and those who are capable do not always use it.

hypothetical-deductive reasoning Ability, believed by Piaget to accompany the state of formal operations, to develop, consider, and test hypotheses

Let's look at the game Twenty Questions, the object of which is to ask as few yes-or-no questions as necessary to discover the identity of a person, place, or thing. The efficiency with which young people can do this, by systematically narrowing down the categories within which the answer might fall, generally improves between middle childhood and late adolescence. However, in one study (Drumm & Jackson, 1996), high school students, especially boys, showed a greater tendency than either early adolescents or university students to jump to guessing the answer. This pattern of guesswork may have important practical implications: it may reflect a penchant for impulsive, risky behaviour—whether in driving, drug use, or sexual activity—at a time when young people have more autonomy than before and more choices to make.

Brain research suggests a possible reason for adolescents' rash judgments. In one study, 16 adolescents (ages 10 to 18) and 18 young adults were asked to look at pictures of people with fearful expressions, while researchers used magnetic resonance imaging (MRI) to examine their brains. Adults tended to process the pictures with the frontal lobes, which are involved in rational thinking. In adolescents, whose frontal lobes are not yet fully developed, the pictures aroused more activity in the amygdala, a small, almond-shaped structure deep in the temporal lobe that is heavily involved in emotional and instinctual reactions (refer back to Figure 6-4 in chapter 6). This was especially true of the younger adolescents, suggesting that immature brain development may permit feelings to override reason (Baird et al., 1999).

The familiarity of a situation and how much a child knows about it can greatly influence the sophistication of the child's reasoning. Yet Piaget, in most of his writings, paid little attention to individual differences, to variations in a child's performance of different kinds of tasks, or to social and cultural influences (Flavell et al., 1993). In his later years, Piaget himself "came to view his earlier model of the development of children's thinking, particularly formal operations, as flawed because it failed to capture the essential *role of the situation* in influencing and constraining . . . children's thinking" (Brown, Metz, & Campione, 1996, pp. 152–153).

Language Development

Although school-age children are quite proficient in use of language, adolescence brings further refinements. Vocabulary continues to grow as reading matter becomes more adult. Although individual differences are great, by ages 16 to 18 the average young person knows approximately 80,000 words (Owens, 1996).

With the advent of formal thought, adolescents can define and discuss such abstractions as *love, justice,* and *freedom.* They more frequently use such terms as *however, otherwise, anyway, therefore, really,* and *probably* to express logical relations between clauses or sentences. They become more conscious of words as symbols that can have multiple meanings; they take pleasure in using irony, puns, and metaphors (Owens, 1996).

Adolescents also become more skilled in *social perspective-taking,* the ability to understand another person's point of view and level of knowledge and to tailor their own speech accordingly. This ability is essential in order to persuade or just to engage in polite conversation. Conscious of their audience, adolescents speak a different language with peers and with adults (Owens, 1996; see Box 16-1). Teenage slang is part of the process of developing an independent identity separate from parents and the adult world (see chapter 17). In creating such expressions as "awesome" and "geek," young people use their newfound ability to play with words "to define their generation's unique take on values, tastes, and preferences" (Elkind, 1998, p. 29).

Elkind: Immature Characteristics of Adolescent Thought

We have seen how children develop from egocentric beings whose interest extends not much farther than the nipple to persons capable of solving abstract problems and imagining ideal societies. Yet in some ways adolescents' thinking seems strangely immature. They may be rude to adults, they have trouble making up their minds what to wear each day, and they often act as if the whole world revolved around them.

What's your view ?

• How can parents and teachers help adolescents improve their reasoning ability?

Checkpoint ✔

Can you . . .

✔ Explain the difference between formal operational and concrete operational thinking, as exemplified by the pendulum problem?

✔ Cite factors influencing adolescents' development of formal reasoning?

✔ Evaluate strengths and weaknesses of Piaget's theory of formal operations?

✔ Identify several characteristics of adolescents' language development that reflect cognitive advances?

Box 16-1 *"Pubilect": The Dialect of Adolescence*

"That guy's hot!"
"He's a hunk!"
"That's fab!"

Adolescents' conversation is mainly about the people and events in their everyday world (Labov, 1992). They use slang (non-standard speech) to label people ("nerd" or "dork"), to pronounce positive or negative judgments ("That's cool!" or "What a loser!"), and to describe alcohol or drug-related activity ("He's messed up").

The Canadian linguist Marcel Danesi (1994),* argues that adolescent speech is more than just slang (which, of course, adults can use, too). Instead, it constitutes a dialect of its own: *pubilect,* "the social dialect of puberty" (p. 97).

Pubilect is more than an occasional colourful expression. It is the primary mode of verbal communication among teenagers, by which they differentiate themselves from adults. As they approach puberty, youngsters absorb this dialect from slightly older peers. Like any other linguistic code, pubilect serves to strengthen group identity and to shut outsiders (adults) out. Teenage vocabulary is characterized by rapid change. Although some of its terms have entered common discourse, adolescents keep inventing new ones all the time.

Analysis of recorded samples of adolescent conversation reveals several key features of pubilect. First, it is an *emotive* code. Through exaggerated tone, slow and deliberate delivery, prolonged stress, accompanying gestures, and vulgar interjections, it draws attention to feelings and attitudes ("Yeah, riiight!" "Well, duuuh!"). Such emotive utterances seem to constitute about 65 per cent of adolescent speech. The use of fillers, such as the word *like,* as well as the typical pattern of narrative intonation, in which each phrase or sentence seems to end with a question mark, reflects unconscious uncertainty and serves to draw the listener into the speaker's state of mind.

A second feature of pubilect is its *connotative* function. Teenagers coin descriptive words (or extend the meaning of existing words) to convey their view of their world and the people in it—often, in highly metaphorical ways. A person does not need a dictionary to figure out the meanings of such expressions as "space cadet" and "ditz." Such terms provide a ready lexicon for quick, automatic value judgments about others.

In Canada, there is not just a single youth culture, but many subcultures. Vocabulary may differ by gender, ethnicity, age, geographical region, neighbourhood (city, suburban, or rural) and type of school (public or private) (Labov, 1992). Also, pubilect is *clique-coded:* It varies from one clique to another. "Druggies" and "jocks" engage in different kinds of activities, which form the main subjects of their conversation. This talk, in turn, cements bonds within the clique. Males use verbal duelling to assert power. Contenders for leadership trade insults and clever retorts in an effort to symbolically gain the upper hand in front of the group.

A study of teenage speech patterns in Naples, Italy, suggests that similar features may emerge "in any culture where teenagerhood constitutes a distinct social category" (Danesi, 1994, p. 123). Neapolitan teenagers use "mmmm" much as U.S. teenagers use "like": "Devo, mmmm, dire che, mmmm, non capisco, mmmm, . . ." ("I have, mmmm, to say that, mmmm, I don't understand, mmmm, . . ."). Exaggerated tone and rising intonation at the ends of phrases are also common. The Italian young people have terms roughly equivalent to the English "cool" (*togo*), "loser" (*grasta*), and "dork" or "nerd" (*secchione*). Other investigators report that adolescents in Milan, Bologna, and other northern Italian cities speak "the language of rock and roll." This cultural borrowing—the result of wide dissemination of English-language television channels, such as MTV—may well be creating a "symbolic universe" for teenagers around the world (Danesi, 1994, p. 123).

What's your view?

What are the implications of calling teenage slang a dialect? How does it reflect the culture of adolescence? In what ways is it similar to or different from other dialects?

Check it out!

For more information on this topic, go to **www.mcgrawhill.ca/college/papalia.**

*Unless otherwise referenced, the source of this discussion is Danesi, 1994.

According to the psychologist David Elkind (1984, 1998), such behaviour stems from adolescents' inexperienced ventures into formal operational thought. This new way of thinking, which fundamentally transforms the way they look at themselves and their world, is as unfamiliar to them as their reshaped bodies, and they sometimes feel just as awkward in its use. As they try out their new powers, they may sometimes stumble, like an infant learning to walk.

This immaturity of thinking manifests itself in at least six characteristic ways, according to Elkind:

1. *Idealism and criticalness:* As adolescents envision an ideal world, they realize how far the real world, for which they hold adults responsible, falls short by comparison. They become super-conscious of hypocrisy in public life; and, with their sharpened verbal reasoning, they relish magazines and entertainers that attack public figures with satire and parody. They are convinced that they know better than adults how to run the world; and they frequently find fault with their parents.

Argumentativeness—usually with parents—is a typical characteristic of adolescent thought, according to David Elkind.

2. *Argumentativeness:* Adolescents are constantly looking for opportunities to try out—and show off—their newfound formal reasoning abilities. They often become argumentative as they marshal facts and logic to build a case for, say, staying out later than their parents think they should.

3. *Indecisiveness:* Unlike younger children, adolescents can keep many alternatives in mind at the same time. Yet because of their inexperience, they lack effective strategies for choosing among them. Thus they may have trouble making up their minds even about such simple things as what to wear and whether to go to the mall with a friend or to the computer to work on a school assignment. One reason they like fast-food restaurants is that the choices are limited.

4. *Apparent hypocrisy:* Young adolescents often do not recognize the difference between expressing an ideal and making the sacrifices necessary to live up to it. In one example Elkind (1998) gives, teenagers concerned about animal welfare demonstrated in front of a furrier's shop but waited until a warm spring day to do it—thus avoiding having to stand outside in cloth coats in wintry weather. To an adult observer, this behaviour might seem hypocritical; but actually, these earnest young people did not realize the connection between their behaviour and the ideal they were advocating.

5. *Self-consciousness:* Once they are in the stage of formal operations, adolescents can think about thinking—their own and other people's. However, in their preoccupation with their own mental state, adolescents often assume that everyone else is thinking about the same thing they are thinking about: themselves. A teenage girl may be mortified if she wears "the wrong thing" to a party, thinking that everyone else must be looking askance at her. Elkind refers to this self-consciousness as the **imaginary audience,** a conceptualized "observer" who is as concerned with a young person's thoughts and behaviour as he or she is. The imaginary audience fantasy is especially strong in the early teens but persists to a lesser degree into adult life. It may surface when, for example, a person drops a fork on the tile floor of a noisy restaurant and imagines that everyone in the room is watching.

6. *Specialness and invulnerability:* Elkind uses the term **personal fable** to denote a belief by adolescents that they are special, that their experience is unique, and that they are not subject to the rules that govern the rest of the world ("Other people get hooked from taking drugs, not me," or, "No one has ever been as deeply in love as I am"). According to Elkind, this special form of egocentrism underlies much risky, self-destructive behaviour. Like the imaginary audience, the personal fable continues in adulthood. Without such a belief, people would become hermits, constantly shielding themselves from the very real dangers of contemporary life. It is the personal fable, says Elkind, that persuades people to take such everyday risks as driving a car despite statistics on highway deaths. Perhaps Elkind would say that it was in part the personal fable that led Nelson Mandela to engage in dangerous insurrection against a brutal dictatorship.

imaginary audience Elkind's term for an observer who exists only in an adolescent's mind and is as concerned with the adolescent's thoughts and actions as the adolescent is

personal fable Elkind's term for conviction that one is special, unique, and not subject to the rules that govern the rest of the world

The concepts of the imaginary audience and the personal fable have been widely accepted, but their validity as distinct earmarks of adolescence has little independent research support. In some studies of the personal fable, adolescents were *more* likely than university students or adults to see themselves as vulnerable to certain risks, such as alcohol and other drug problems, rather than *less* likely, as the personal fable would predict (Quadrel, Fischoff, & Davis, 1993). Rather than universal features of adolescents' cognitive development, it has been suggested that the imaginary audience and personal fable may be related to specific social experiences. And, since these concepts grew out of Elkind's clinical observations, they may be more characteristic of youngsters who are experiencing difficulties in adjustment (Vartanian & Powlishta, 1996). Social experiences can have an impact on other areas of cognitive development, such as moral reasoning.

Checkpoint ✔

Can you . . .

✔ Describe Elkind's six proposed aspects of immature adolescent thought, and explain how they may grow out of the transition to formal operational thought?

Moral Reasoning: Kohlberg's Theory

Guidepost 2

On what basis do adolescents make moral judgments?

A woman is near death from cancer. A druggist has discovered a drug that doctors believe might save her. The druggist is charging $2,000 for a small dose—ten times what the drug costs him to make. The sick woman's husband, Heinz, borrows from everyone he knows but can scrape together only $1,000. He begs the druggist to sell him the drug for $1,000 or let him pay the rest later. The druggist refuses, saying, "I discovered the drug and I'm going to make money from it." Heinz, desperate, breaks into the man's store and steals the drug. Should Heinz have done that? Why or why not? (Kohlberg, 1969).

Heinz's problem is the most famous example of Lawrence Kohlberg's approach to studying moral development. Starting in the 1950s, Kohlberg and his colleagues posed hypothetical dilemmas like this one to 75 boys ages 10, 13, and 16, and continued to question them periodically for more than 30 years. At the heart of each dilemma was the concept of justice. By asking respondents how they arrived at their answers, Kohlberg, like Piaget (refer back to chapter 13), concluded that the way people look at moral issues reflects cognitive development.

Contrary to socialization theory, which attributes moral behaviour to early upbringing and internalization of societal standards, the cognitive-developmental approach holds that people gradually develop their own moral code as they reach higher and higher levels of thinking. Both Piaget and Kohlberg described moral growth as progressing from externally imposed rules governed by the physical consequences of an act to more flexible, internal judgments that take circumstances into account. This development is made possible by the shift from egocentrism to decentration—the ability to look at things from more than one point of view.

Piaget believed that children develop concepts of fairness or justice through interaction with peers—competing, cooperating, and sharing. Kohlberg saw peer interaction as only one form of relevant social experience. All social relationships, according to Kohlberg, offer opportunities for social role-taking—taking the perspective of others—and thus stimulate moral development. Whereas peer relationships may be the most important avenue during childhood, the expanding environments of adolescence and adulthood broaden opportunities for moral growth (Gibbs, 1995).

Kohlberg's Levels and Stages

On the basis of thought processes shown by responses to his dilemmas (and, later, in response to real situations), Kohlberg (1969) described three levels of moral reasoning, each divided into two stages (see Table 16-1). (Kohlberg's early stages correspond roughly to Piaget's stages of moral development in childhood, but his most advanced stages do not occur until adulthood.)

- *Level I:* **Preconventional morality.** People act under external controls. They obey rules to avoid punishment or reap rewards, or act out of self-interest. This level, said Kohlberg, is typical of children ages 4 to 10.
- *Level II:* **Conventional morality (or morality of conventional role conformity).** People have internalized the standards of authority figures. They are concerned about being "good," pleasing others, and maintaining the social order. This level is typically reached after age 10; many people never move beyond it, even in adulthood.
- *Level III:* **Postconventional morality (or morality of autonomous moral principles).** People now recognize conflicts between moral standards and make their own judgments on the basis of principles of right, fairness, and justice. People generally do not reach this level of moral reasoning until at least early adolescence, or more commonly in young adulthood, if ever.

Kohlberg later added a transitional level between levels II and III, when people no longer feel bound by society's moral standards but have not yet developed rationally derived principles of justice. Instead, they base their moral decisions on personal feelings.

preconventional morality First level of Kohlberg's theory of moral reasoning, in which control is external and rules are obeyed in order to gain rewards or avoid punishment, or out of self-interest

conventional morality (or morality of conventional role conformity) Second level in Kohlberg's theory of moral reasoning, in which the standards of authority figures are internalized

postconventional morality (or morality of autonomous moral principles) Third level in Kohlberg's theory of moral reasoning, in which people follow internally held moral principles and can decide among conflicting moral standards

| Table 16-1 | Kohlberg's Six Stages of Moral Reasoning |

Levels	Stages of Reasoning	Typical Answers to Heinz's Dilemma
Level I: Preconventional morality (ages 4 to 10)	*Stage 1: Orientation toward punishment and obedience.* "What will happen to me?" Children obey rules to avoid punishment. They ignore the motives of an act and focus on its physical form (such as the size of a lie) or its consequences (for example, the amount of physical damage).	*Pro:* "He should steal the drug. It isn't really bad to take it. It isn't as if he hadn't asked to pay for it first. The drug he'd take is worth only $200; he's not really taking a $2,000 drug." *Con:* "He shouldn't steal the drug. It's a big crime. He didn't get permission; he used force and broke and entered. He did a lot of damage and stole a very expensive drug."
	Stage 2: Instrumental purpose and exchange. "You scratch my back, I'll scratch yours." Children conform to rules out of self-interest and consideration for what others can do for them. They look at an act in terms of the human needs it meets and differentiate this value from the act's physical form and consequences.	*Pro:* "It's all right to steal the drug, because his wife needs it and he wants her to live. It isn't that he wants to steal, but that's what he has to do to save her." *Con:* "He shouldn't steal it. The druggist isn't wrong or bad; he just wants to make a profit. That's what you're in business for—to make money."
Level II: Conventional morality (ages 10 to 13 or beyond)	*Stage 3: Maintaining mutual relations, approval of others, the golden rule.* "Am I a good boy or girl?" Children want to please and help others, can judge the intentions of others, and develop their own ideas of what a good person is. They evaluate an act according to the motive behind it or the person performing it, and they take circumstances into account.	*Pro:* "He should steal the drug. He is only doing something that is natural for a good husband to do. You can't blame him for doing something out of love for his wife. You'd blame him if he didn't love his wife enough to save her." *Con:* "He shouldn't steal. If his wife dies, he can't be blamed. It isn't because he's heartless or that he doesn't love her enough to do everything that he legally can. The druggist is the selfish or heartless one."

(Continued)

In Kohlberg's theory, it is the reasoning underlying a person's response to a moral dilemma, not the answer itself, that indicates the stage of moral development. As illustrated in Table 16-1, two people who give opposite answers may be at the same stage if their reasoning is based on similar factors.

Some adolescents, and even some adults, remain at Kohlberg's level I. Like young children, they seek to avoid punishment or satisfy their own needs. Most adolescents, and most adults, seem to be at level II. They conform to social conventions, support the status quo, and do the "right" thing to please others or to obey the law. (For Nelson Mandela, the event that triggered his emergence from this stage was his circumcision ceremony at age 16, when he listened to the shocking speech that challenged the morality of the system into which he was being initiated.)

Very few people reach level III, when they can choose between two socially accepted standards. In fact, at one point Kohlberg questioned the validity of stage 6, since so few people seem to attain it. Later, however, he proposed a seventh, "cosmic" stage, in which people consider the effect of their actions not only on other people but on the universe as a whole (Kohlberg, 1981; Kohlberg & Ryncarz, 1990).

Evaluating Kohlberg's Theory

Kohlberg and Piaget brought about a profound shift in the way we look at moral development. Instead of viewing morality solely as the attainment of control over self-gratifying impulses, investigators now look at how children make moral judgments based on their growing understanding of the social world.

Research has supported some aspects of Kohlberg's theory but has left others in question. The American boys whom Kohlberg and his colleagues followed through adulthood

Table 16-1   (*continued*)

Levels	Stages of Reasoning	Typical Answers to Heinz's Dilemma
	Stage 4: Social concern and conscience. "What if everybody did it?" People are concerned with doing their duty, showing respect for higher authority, and maintaining the social order. They consider an act always wrong, regardless of motive or circumstances, if it violates a rule and harms others.	*Pro:* "You should steal it. If you did nothing, you'd be letting your wife die. It's your responsibility if she dies. You have to take it with the idea of paying the druggist." *Con:* "It is a natural thing for Heinz to want to save his wife, but it's still always wrong to steal. He knows he's taking a valuable drug from the man who made it."
Level III: Postconventional morality (early adolescence, or not until young adulthood, or never)	*Stage 5: Morality of contract, of individual rights, and of democratically accepted law.* People think in rational terms, valuing the will of the majority and the welfare of society. They generally see these values as best supported by adherence to the law. While they recognize that there are times when human need and the law conflict, they believe it is better for society in the long run if they obey the law.	*Pro:* "The law wasn't set up for these circumstances. Taking the drug in this situation isn't really right, but it's justified." *Con:* "You can't completely blame someone for stealing, but extreme circumstances don't really justify taking the law into your own hands. You can't have people stealing whenever they are desperate. The end may be good, but the ends don't justify the means."
	Stage 6: Morality of universal ethical principles. People do what they as individuals think is right, regardless of legal restrictions or the opinions of others. They act in accordance with internalized standards, knowing that they would condemn themselves if they did not.	*Pro:* "This is a situation that forces him to choose between stealing and letting his wife die. In a situation where the choice must be made, it is morally right to steal. He has to act in terms of the principle of preserving and respecting life." *Con:* "Heinz is faced with the decision of whether to consider the other people who need the drug just as badly as his wife. Heinz ought to act not according to his feelings for his wife, but considering the value of all the lives involved."

Source: Adapted from Kohlberg, 1969; Lickona, 1976.

progressed through Kohlberg's stages in sequence, and none skipped a stage. Their moral judgments correlated positively with age, education, IQ, and socio-economic status (Colby, Kohlberg, Gibbs, & Lieberman, 1983).

However, research has generally noted the lack of a clear relationship between moral reasoning and moral behaviour. People at postconventional levels of reasoning do not necessarily act more morally than those at lower levels (Colby & Damon, 1992; Kupfersmid & Wonderly, 1980). Perhaps one problem is the remoteness from young people's experience of such dilemmas as the "Heinz" situation. (Box 16-2 describes adolescents' moral judgments on everyday issues.) On the other hand, juvenile delinquents (particularly boys) consistently show developmental delays in Kohlbergian tests of moral reasoning (Gregg, Gibbs, & Basinger, 1994).

Critics claim that a cognitive approach to moral development gives insufficient attention to the importance of emotion. Moral activity, they say, is motivated not only by abstract considerations of justice, but by such emotions as empathy, guilt, and distress and the internalization of pro-social norms (Gibbs, 1991, 1995; Gibbs & Schnell, 1985).

Some theorists today seek to synthesize the cognitive-developmental approach with the role of emotion and the insights of socialization theory (Gibbs, 1991, 1995; Gibbs & Schnell, 1985). Kohlberg himself did recognize that non-cognitive factors such as emotional development and life experience affect moral judgments. One reason the ages attached to Kohlberg's levels are so variable is that people who have achieved a high level of cognitive development do not always reach a comparably high level of moral development. A certain level of cognitive development is *necessary* but not *sufficient* for a comparable level of moral development. Thus other processes besides cognition must be at work.

What's your view

- Kohlberg's method of assessing moral development by evaluating participants' reactions to moral dilemmas is widely used. Does this seem like the most appropriate method? Why or why not? Can you suggest an alternative measure?

- Can you think of a time when you, or someone you know, acted contrary to his or her own moral judgment? Why do you think this happened?

Box 16-2 *How Do Psychosocial Issues Affect Adolescents' Moral Judgments?*

How many adolescents face the problem of having to get a rare and expensive medicine for a mortally ill spouse? Not many do. And yet, Kohlberg's theory of moral development is based on responses to dilemmas like this. Today some researchers are instead interviewing adolescents about moral issues they are likely to confront in everyday life, such as whether and how a bystander should respond to aggression, under what circumstances it might be all right to break a school rule, and whether to admit someone from a minority group to an exclusive club. The findings suggest that psychosocial issues, such as the needs for peer acceptance and personal autonomy, may be important factors in adolescents' moral choices.

In one study (Tisak & Tisak, 1996), interviewers asked 111 working-class and middle-class 10-, 12-, and 14-year-olds in rural Ohio what a person their age *would* do and *should* do, and why, when witnessing a good friend or a younger sibling hit or push someone, tear a book, or break a game. The answers fell into five main categories: (1) *looking out for others' welfare* ("He [the victim] will get hurt if she [the bystander] doesn't do something to stop it"), (2) *helping the aggressor avoid punishment* ("She will get in trouble if she continues to hit"), (3) *family responsibility* ("He is supposed to make sure his brother doesn't do that"), (4) *maintaining solidarity with friends* ("She will lose her as a friend [if she intervenes]"), and (5) *importance of the consequences* ("Why should she do anything, it's not important").

Older participants were less concerned about the welfare of the victim than about maintaining solidarity with the aggressor or helping him or her avoid punishment, perhaps reflecting adolescents' growing need for peer acceptance. However, they were less inclined to expect or favour *any* intervention, perhaps because they felt that the aggressor and the victim should be able to resolve the dispute themselves. Respondents of all ages thought a bystander would be more likely to stop a sibling's aggression than a friend's and had a greater obligation to do so. Girls were more apt to expect a bystander to intervene, though boys were just as likely to think it would be wrong not to. This finding may reflect girls' greater confidence in their ability to influence a peer's behaviour.

In another study, 120 students from Grades 5, 7, 9, and 11 were asked about the legitimacy of school rules (Smetana & Bitz, 1996). Both preadolescents and adolescents agreed that three kinds of conduct should be regulated: (1) *immoral* behaviour violating the rights and welfare of others, such as stealing, fighting, or failing to return textbooks; (2) *unconventional* behaviour violating customary standards, such as acting up in class, swearing, coming late, or talking back to the teacher; and (3) *imprudent* behaviour, such as smoking, drinking, taking drugs, and eating junk food for lunch. The young people viewed *personal* behaviour, such as whom to sit next to and talk to, choice of clothing or hairstyle, and eating or reading comics in class, as matters to decide for themselves.

The respondents were almost evenly split in their judgments about behaviour that is customarily regulated in school but not in other contexts, such as kissing a boyfriend or girlfriend in the hall, leaving class without permission, keeping forbidden items in a school locker, and passing notes to friends in class. As com-

pared with Grade 5 students, older participants were more likely to view this kind of behaviour as a matter of personal discretion rather than a proper subject for regulation. Adolescents' views about the legitimacy of rules were important predictors of how often they broke the rules, according to their own and teachers' reports.

In a third study (Phinney & Cobb, 1996), 120 European-American and Hispanic-American students in Grades 5, 8, and 11 were asked how they would respond to a Hispanic or European-American student's request to join an exclusive school club in which all the members were of the other ethnic group. In half of the cases, the hypothetical applicant was of the same ethnic group as the respondent; in the other half, of the other ethnic group.

About three-quarters of the students favoured accepting the applicant, mainly out of *fairness* ("Everybody should be treated the same") or *concern with individual welfare* ("So they won't hurt her feelings"). Other reasons were *upholding social principles* ("If they choose their own people, then they're never going to get along with each other") and the benefits of *cultural diversity* ("They can get to meet new people . . . learn about different cultures"). Less than 10 per cent favoured excluding the outsider, citing the *right of club members* to select their associates ("They're the ones who started this club and . . . they should have the right . . . to choose who they want") or *cultural barriers* ("If they start speaking Spanish, she's going to feel left out").

In contrast to these two groups, who strongly held to their views when challenged, about 12 per cent of the respondents (mostly students in Grades 5 and 8) originally favoured admission but switched when the interviewer suggested that "some people" would consider exclusion appropriate. The original reasons given by those who switched were largely pragmatic rather than principled ("Let him in, otherwise it'll cause a lot of tension").

Ethnicity did not affect the decisions but did seem to influence the reasons. European-American students tended to appeal to rights of free choice and rules ("The school says they could choose their own members") as reasons for exclusion, Hispanics to cultural barriers. Girls also tended to refer to rules. In line with Kohlberg's theory, older adolescents who favoured inclusion were more likely than younger ones to show awareness of the impact on the social order ("If you start getting your own little groups . . . that hurts the country").

What's your view?

What would be your answers to the three issues presented here, and why?

Check it out!

For more information on this topic, go to **www.mcgrawhill.ca/ college/papalia,** which will direct you to a website with links to a character education reading list and many projects and reports about character education.

A practical problem in using Kohlberg's system is its time-consuming testing procedures. The standard dilemmas need to be presented to each person individually and then scored by trained judges. One alternative is the Defining Issues Test (DIT), which can be given quickly to a group and scored objectively (Rest, 1975). Its results correlate moderately well with scores on Kohlberg's traditional tasks.

Family Influences

Neither Piaget nor Kohlberg considered parents important to children's moral development. More recent research, however, emphasizes parents' contribution in both the cognitive and the emotional realms.

In one study, parents of 63 students in Grades 1, 4, 7, and 10 were asked to talk with their children about two dilemmas: a hypothetical one and an actual one that the child described (L. J. Walker & Taylor, 1991). The children and adolescents who, during the next 2 years, showed the greatest progress through Kohlberg's stages were those whose parents had used humour and praise, listened to them, and asked their opinions. These parents had asked clarifying questions, reworded answers, and checked to be sure the children understood the issues. They reasoned with their children at a slightly higher level than the children were currently at, much as in the method of scaffolding. The children who advanced the least were those whose parents had lectured them or challenged or contradicted their opinions.

Adolescents are more likely to adopt their parents' perspectives if the parenting style is authoritative (Mackey, Arnold, & Pratt, 2001). Responsive parenting is also important to promoting acquisition of values in children (Grusec, Goodnow, & Kuczynski, 2000). Cultural differences are also important to development of moral judgment. Children 7, 9, and 11 years, in Taiwan, mainland China, and Canada were read stories about child characters telling lies. In Taiwan and mainland China, older children expressed positive opinions about lying about good deeds, whereas children at all ages in Canada had negative attitudes about lying. These results demonstrate an emphasis on modesty and self-effacing behaviour in Chinese traditional values (Lee, Xu, Fu, Cameron, & Chen, 2001).

Validity for Women and Girls

On the basis of research on women, Carol Gilligan (1982) argued that Kohlberg's theory is oriented toward values more important to men than to women. According to Gilligan, women see morality not so much in terms of justice and fairness as of responsibility to show care and avoid harm.

Research has not supported Gilligan's claim of a male bias in Kohlberg's stages, and she has since modified her position. However, some research has found gender differences in moral judgments in early adolescence, with girls scoring *higher* than boys (Garmon, Basinger, Gregg, & Gibbs, 1996; Skoe & Gooden, 1993). This may be because girls generally mature earlier and have more intimate social relationships (Garmon et al., 1996; Skoe & Diessner, 1994). Early adolescent girls do tend to emphasize care-related concerns more than boys do, especially when tested with open-ended questions ("How important is it to keep promises to a friend?") or self-chosen moral dilemmas related to their own experience (Garmon et al., 1996).

Cross-cultural Validity

Cross-cultural studies support Kohlberg's sequence of stages—despite the fact that his research was carried out with children in the United States—up to a point. Older people from countries other than the United States do tend to score at higher stages than younger people. However, people in non-industrialized cultures rarely score above stage 4 (Edwards, 1981; Nisan & Kohlberg, 1982; Snarey, 1985). It is possible that these cultures do not foster higher moral development, but it seems more likely that some aspects of Kohlberg's definition of morality may not fit the cultural values of some societies. When Kohlberg's dilemmas were tested in India, Buddhist monks from Ladakh, a Tibetan enclave, scored lower than laypeople. Apparently Kohlberg's model, while capturing the preconventional and conventional elements of Buddhist thinking, was inadequate for understanding postconventional Buddhist principles of cooperation and non-violence (Gielen & Kelly, 1983).

Checkpoint ✔

Can you . . .

✔ List Kohlberg's levels and stages, and discuss factors that influence how rapidly children and adolescents progress through them?

✔ Evaluate Kohlberg's theory with regard to the role of emotion and socialization, family influences, gender, and cultural validity?

It also has been argued that stages 5 and 6 cannot fairly be called the most mature stages of moral development, since they restrict "maturity" to a select group of people who are given to philosophical reflection (J. C. Gibbs, 1995).

Kohlberg's own view was that before people can develop a fully principled morality, they must recognize the relativity of moral standards. Adolescents may begin to understand that every society evolves its own definitions of right and wrong; in some cases, the values of one culture may even seem shocking to members of another. For example, the practice of circumcising girls before puberty, or *female genital mutilation*—widely practised in some parts of the non-industrialized world as a way of preserving virginity before marriage, reducing sexual appetite, enhancing beauty, and affirming femininity—has been condemned as harmful and abusive by the Canadian health authorities and World Health Organization but continues to be practised in many cultures (Council on Scientific Affairs, 1995; Federal Interdepartmental Working Group on Female Genital Mutilation, 2000; Samad, 1996). In industrialized countries, many young people question their earlier views about morality when they enter high school or college or the world of work and encounter people whose values, culture, and ethnic background are different from their own.

Educational and Vocational Issues

School is a central organizing experience in most adolescents' lives. It offers opportunities to learn information, master new skills, and sharpen old ones; to participate in sports, the arts, and other activities; to explore vocational choices; and to be with friends. It widens intellectual and social horizons. Some adolescents, however, experience school not as an opportunity but as one more hindrance on the road to adulthood. The school experience can have profound effects, not only on cognitive development, but on psychosocial adjustment and even on physical health.

Let's examine influences on school achievement. Then we'll look at why some young people drop out of school, and what penalties they pay. Finally, we'll consider planning for higher education and vocations.

Influences on School Achievement

Guidepost 3

What influences affect success in secondary school, and why do some students drop out?

The proportion of adolescents staying in school is rising: In 1980–81, 68 per cent of young people were students, and by 1995–96 the number rose to 84 per cent (CICH, 2000). By 1998, of those aged 25 to 29, 88 per cent of women, and 86 per cent of men completed high school (Council of Ministers of Education, Canada [CMEC] and Statistics Canada, 1999).

Historically in Canada, education has been the ticket to economic and social advancement and to a successful adult life. However, for some students, school does not serve this vital purpose. What makes one student strive for good grades while another fails?

As in the elementary grades, such factors as socio-economic status, the quality of the home environment, and parental involvement continue to influence the course of school achievement; in a longitudinal study of 174 disadvantaged children, these factors, as measured in Grade 1, closely predicted improvement or deterioration in academic performance by age 16 (Jimerson, Egeland, & Teo, 1999). Other factors include peer influence, quality of schooling, and (perhaps most important) students' (and parents') belief in their ability to succeed.

Self-Efficacy Beliefs and Academic Motivation

According to Albert Bandura (Bandura, Barbaranelli, Caprara, & Pastorelli, 1996; Zimmerman, Bandura, & Martinez-Pons, 1992), whose social-cognitive theory we discussed in chapters 2 and 11, students who are high in *self-efficacy*—who believe that they can master academic material and regulate their own learning—are more likely to try to achieve and more likely to succeed than students who do not believe in their own abilities.

Self-regulated learners are interested in learning. They set challenging goals and use appropriate strategies to achieve them. They try hard, persist in the face of difficulties, and seek help when necessary. Students who do not believe in their ability to succeed tend to become frustrated and depressed—feelings that make success harder to attain.

Table 16-2	Self-Efficacy Questionnaire for High School Students

Self-efficacy for self-regulated learning

How well can you:

1. finish homework assignments by deadlines?
2. study when there are other interesting things to do?
3. concentrate on school subjects?
4. take class notes of class instruction?
5. use the library to get information for class assignments?
6. plan your schoolwork?
7. organize your schoolwork?
8. remember information presented in class and textbooks?
9. arrange a place to study without distractions?
10. motivate yourself to do schoolwork?
11. participate in class discussions?

Self-efficacy for academic achievement

How well can you:

1. learn general mathematics?
2. learn algebra?
3. learn science?
4. learn biology?
5. learn reading and writing language skills?
6. learn to use computers?
7. learn foreign languages?
8. learn social studies?
9. learn English grammar?

Source: Adapted from Zimmerman et al., 1992, Table 1, p. 668.

In one study that found a link between self-efficacy beliefs and academic achievement, 116 students in Grades 9 and 10 of various ethnic backgrounds in two eastern U.S. high schools answered a questionnaire about their ability to learn and to regulate their own learning (Zimmerman et al., 1992; see Table 16-2). The students' perceived self-efficacy predicted the social studies grades they hoped for, expected, and actually achieved. Students' goals were influenced by their parents' goals for them, but that influence was tempered by the students' beliefs about their own abilities. The message is clear: If parents want their children to do well in school, they must do more than set high expectations. They must also see that children have learning experiences that build a belief in their ability to succeed.

Several factors, including parental beliefs and practices, socio-economic status, and peer influence, affect parents' power to strengthen children's achievement. As with other aspects of development, parents' own perceived self-efficacy—their belief in their ability to promote their children's academic growth—affects their success in doing so. Parents who are economically secure and who have high aspirations for their children and a strong sense of parental efficacy tend to have children with high academic goals and achievement (Bandura et al., 1996).

Socio-economic Status and the Family Environment

Socio-economic status can be a powerful factor in educational achievement—not in itself, but through its influence on family atmosphere, on choice of neighbourhood, and on parents' way of rearing children (National [U.S.] Research Council [NRC], 1993a). Children of poor, uneducated parents are more likely to experience negative family and school atmospheres and stressful events (Felner et al., 1995). The neighbourhood a family can afford generally determines the quality of schooling available, as well as opportunities for higher education; and the availability of such opportunities, together with attitudes in the neighbourhood peer group, affects motivation. In Canada, almost 84 per cent of children live with parents who have at least finished high school (Health Canada, 1999). According to the National

Longitudinal Survey of Children and Youth (NLSCY), the educational level of the person most knowledgeable about the child predicted how children did on verbal ability at 4 and 5 years of age, and how children did in mathematics in Grades 2 and 4 (Willms, 1996). Parents' attitudes towards education are also positively correlated with their own educational achievement; the parent with higher levels of educational achievement tended to spend more time reading to children and helping with homework (Ross, Scott, & Kelly, 1996).

When a school has a predominance of low-income children, negative effects of low socio-economic status tend to spread through the school population, affecting student achievement (Pong, 1997). Still, many young people from disadvantaged neighbourhoods do well in school and improve their condition in life. What may make the difference is **social capital:** the family and community resources children can draw upon. Parents who invest time and effort in their children and who have a strong network of community support build the family's social capital (J. S. Coleman, 1988).

social capital Family and community resources upon which a person can draw

In a 20-year study of 252 children born to mostly poor and African-American teenage mothers in Baltimore, those who—regardless of parents' income, education, and employment—had more social capital were more likely by the end of adolescence to have completed high school and in some cases to have gone to university, or to have entered the labour force and to be enjoying stable incomes (Furstenberg & Hughes, 1995).

Parental Involvement and Parenting Styles

Parents can affect their children's educational achievement by becoming involved in their children's schooling: acting as advocates for their children and impressing teachers with the seriousness of the family's educational goals (Bandura et al., 1996). Students whose parents are closely involved in their school lives and monitor their progress fare best in high school (National [U.S.] Center for Education Statistics [NCES], 1985). A study of 525 adolescents in Quebec found that parenting practices and involvement were more strongly related to school grades than were family characteristics (Deslandes, Potvin, & Leclerc, 1999).

Parenting style can make a difference. Research has consistently found that the benefits of authoritative parenting continue during adolescence. *Authoritative parents* urge adolescents to look at both sides of issues, admit that children sometimes know more than parents, and welcome their participation in family decisions. These parents strike a balance between making demands and being responsive. Their children receive praise and privileges for good grades; poor grades bring encouragement to try harder and offers of help.

Authoritarian parents, by contrast, tell adolescents not to argue with or question adults and tell them they will "know better when they are grown up." Good grades bring admonitions to do even better; poor grades upset the parents, who may punish by reducing allowances or "grounding." *Permissive parents* seem not to care about grades, make no rules about watching television, do not attend school functions, and neither help with nor check their children's homework. These parents may not be neglectful or uncaring, but simply convinced that teenagers should be responsible for their own lives.

Among about 6,400 California high school students, children of authoritative parents tended to do better in school than children of authoritarian and permissive parents (Dornbusch, Ritter, Leiderman, Roberts, & Fraleigh, 1987; Steinberg & Darling, 1994; Steinberg, Lamborn, Dornbusch, & Darling, 1992). Adolescents raised authoritatively not only achieve better academically but are more socially competent, are more emotionally healthy, and show fewer behaviour problems than children raised in an authoritarian or permissive manner (Glasgow, Dornbusch, Troyer, Steinberg, & Ritter, 1997).

Even though adolescents are more independent than younger children, the home atmosphere continues to influence school achievement. Parents help not only by monitoring homework but by taking an active interest in other aspects of teenagers' lives. Children of authoritative parents who discuss issues openly and offer praise and encouragement tend to do best in school.

What accounts for the academic success of authoritatively raised adolescents? Authoritative parents' greater involvement in schooling may be a factor, as well as their encouragement of positive attitudes toward work. A more subtle mechanism, consistent with Bandura's findings on self-efficacy, may be parents' influence on how children explain success or failure. In a study of 2,353 students at six high schools in California and three high schools in Wisconsin, youngsters who saw their parents as non-authoritative were more likely than their peers to attribute poor grades to external causes or to low ability—forces beyond their control—rather than to their own efforts. A year later, such students tended to pay less attention in class and to spend less time on homework (Glasgow et al., 1997). Thus a sense of helplessness associated with non-authoritative parenting may become a self-fulfilling prophecy, discouraging students from trying to succeed.

Recent Immigration

A large proportion of the school population in Canada comprises children of immigrants. According to information collected from the National Longitudinal Survey of Children and Youth, these students do as well as their non-immigrant schoolmates on a variety of educational measures including reading, writing, mathematics, and overall academic aptitude, particularly if the parents' first language is either English or French. For those whose parents' first language is not one of Canada's official languages, the children do as well as non-immigrant children on all measures except reading, on which they tend to perform lower. However, on average, these students catch up to their peers on reading by the time they turn 13 (Worswick, 2001). These results indicate that children of recent immigrants are adapting well to the Canadian school system, despite the economic difficulties that immigrant families often face when they arrive in Canada.

Quality of Schooling

The quality of a school strongly influences student achievement. A good high school has an orderly, unoppressive atmosphere; an active, energetic principal; and teachers who take part in making decisions. The principal and teachers have high expectations for students, emphasize academics more than extracurricular activities, and closely monitor student performance (Linney & Seidman, 1989).

Students who like their school do better academically and also are healthier. Adolescents, particularly boys, in most industrialized countries like school less than younger children. Adolescents are more satisfied with school if they are allowed to participate in making rules and feel support from teachers and other students (Samdal & Dür, 2000). Compared with students in other countries, Canadian students report being relatively satisfied with school, although the number claiming to enjoy school drops as they progress through higher grades. Good relations with parents, and good general health are linked with positive feelings towards school. On the other hand, more students are skipping classes, and bullying by boys and girls is a common occurrence in Canadian schools, making school a place where a small but significant number of students feel unsafe (King, Boyce, & King, 1999).

Schools that tailor teaching to students' abilities get better results than schools that try to teach all students in the same way. Research on Sternberg's triarchic theory of intelligence (refer back to chapter 13) found that students high in practical or creative intelligence do better when taught in a way that allows them to capitalize on those strengths and compensate for their weaknesses (Sternberg, 1997). Indeed, a combination of teaching styles may be most effective for all students. In an experiment in teaching psychology to gifted Grade 8 students, groups whose teachers used methods that tap creative and practical abilities as well as analysis and memory did better, even on multiple-choice tests, than groups taught by traditional memory-based or critical-thinking approaches alone (Sternberg, Torff, & Grigorenko, 1998).

For high school students who are falling behind—or who want to move ahead more rapidly—summer school can help. While all students benefit from summer school, students from middle-class homes gain the most. Remedial programs work best when classes are small and instruction is individualized and when parental involvement is required (Cooper, Charlton, Valentine, & Muhlenbruck, 2000).

These high school graduates are taking an important step toward their future careers. Today, more young people in Canada than ever before graduate from high school.

Dropping Out of High School

Society suffers when young people do not finish school. Canadian dropouts are more likely to be unemployed or to have low incomes, to end up on welfare, and to become involved with drugs, crime, and delinquency. In addition, the loss of taxable income burdens the public treasury (Clark, 1997; NCES, 1987, 1999).

Fewer students are dropping out these days, and some eventually go back to school to earn a high school equivalency certificate. The proportion of 20-year-olds who have not completed high school and are not currently enrolled in school dropped from 18 per cent in 1991 (Clark, 1997) to 12 per cent in 1999 (Bowlby & McMullen, 2002). The rate fell in every province in the country. In addition, the proportion of Aboriginal students living on reserves who remain in school until Grade 12 rose from 37 per cent in 1987–88 to 71 per cent in 1996–97 (CICH, 2000). Although this indicates a profound improvement, the higher school-leaving rate among Aboriginal students compared to non-Aboriginal students might be a reflection of the failings of the public school system to be sensitive to Aboriginal values and needs (Rabson, 2001). The differences continue through to higher education: 4 per cent of the Aboriginal population have university education, compared to 19 per cent of non-Aboriginal people (Canadian Education Statistics Council, 2000).

Having low grades did not seem to be the only reason for students to drop out of high school: 47 per cent of all school leavers had an average of B or more in the 1999 Youth in Transition Survey of Canadian adolescents (Bowlby et al., 2002). Low-income students are much more likely to drop out than middle- or high-income students (NCES, 1999). The higher dropout rates among groups living in poverty may stem in part from the poor quality of their schools as compared with those attended by more advantaged children.

Although the majority of Canadian dropouts lived in two-parent families during high school, students in single-parent and remarried households—even relatively affluent ones—are more likely to drop out than students living with both parents (Bowlby et al., 2002; Finn & Rock, 1997; Zimiles & Lee, 1991). Frequent moves may contribute to the effects of family instability, and changing schools may reduce a family's social capital. Families that move a lot generally have weaker social connections, know less about the children's school, and are less able to make wise decisions about schooling (Teachman, Paasch, & Carver, 1996).

Perhaps the most important factor in whether or not a student will finish school is *active engagement:* the extent to which the student is actively involved in schooling. On the most basic level, active engagement means coming to class on time, being prepared, listening and responding to the teacher, and obeying school rules. A second level of engagement consists of getting involved with the coursework—asking questions, taking the initiative to seek help when needed, or doing extra projects. Both levels of active engagement tend to pay off in positive school performance by at-risk students. In a nationwide U.S. sample of 1,803 low-income African-American and Hispanic students, active engagement was the chief distinction between those who graduated from high school on time, got reasonably good grades, and did fairly well on achievement tests and those who did not (Finn & Rock, 1997). Students who participate in extracurricular activities also are less likely to drop out (Mahoney, 2000). According to the Youth in Transition Survey, Canadian high school leavers were less likely to have friends who went on to post-secondary education, and were more likely to skip classes, drink alcohol regularly, and abuse drugs (Bowlby et al., 2002).

What factors promote active engagement? Family encouragement is undoubtedly one. Others may be small class size and a warm, supportive school environment. Since engaged or alienated behaviour patterns tend to be set early in a child's school career, dropout prevention should start early, too (Finn & Rock, 1997).

Educational and Vocational Preparation

How do young people develop career goals? How do they decide whether or not to go to college and, if not, how to enter the world of work? Many factors enter in, including individual ability and personality, education, socio-economic and ethnic background, the ad-

Checkpoint ✔

Can you . . .

✔ Explain how self-efficacy beliefs can contribute to adolescents' motivation to learn?

✔ Assess the influences of parents and peers on academic achievement?

✔ Discuss ethnic differences in attitudes toward school?

✔ Give examples of educational practices that can help high school students do better?

✔ Give reasons why some students drop out of school?

What's your view ?

• How can parents, educators, and societal institutions encourage young people to finish high school?

Guidepost 4

What factors affect educational and vocational planning and preparation?

vice of school counsellors, life experiences, and societal values. Let's look at some influences on educational and vocational aspirations. Then we'll look at what provisions exist for young people who do not plan to go to college or university. And we'll discuss the pros and cons of outside work for high school students.

Influences on Students' Aspirations

Students' self-efficacy beliefs—their confidence in their educational and vocational prospects—shape the occupational options they consider and the way they prepare for careers (Bandura et al., 1996). Parental aspirations and financial support often influence youngsters' plans. In fact, parental encouragement predicts high ambition better than social class does (T. E. Smith, 1981). The adjustment from school to work can be particularly stressful for some young people. Among Canadian adolescents, the difficulties that are often experienced in making the transition from school to work may be rooted in negative attitudes about themselves, the work they do, and poor social and decision-making skills (Sankey, 1995).

Despite the greater flexibility in career goals today, gender—and gender-stereotyping—often influence vocational choice. Interviews with students up to age 18 in a coeducational urban private school in Australia found that, except among the youngest children, boys had more restrictive ideas than girls about proper occupations for each sex. Boys knew more about the requirements for traditionally male occupations and girls about traditionally female ones. Older adolescent boys generally found school career programs helpful, while girls did not (McMahon & Patton, 1997).

A 1992 report by the American Association of University Women [AAUW] Educational Foundation claimed that schools shortchange girls by steering them away from science and math and into gender-typed pursuits. Even girls who did well in science and math were less likely than boys to choose careers in those fields. Six years later, a follow-up study (AAUW Educational Foundation, 1998a, 1998b) reported that girls were taking more science and math than before and doing better in those subjects.

According to the National [U.S.] Center for Education Statistics (1997), male and female high school seniors are equally likely to plan careers in math or science, but boys are much more likely to expect to go into engineering. Fewer girls than boys take physics and computer science, but more girls take chemistry. In vocational education and career exploration programs, girls cluster in traditionally female occupations. Boys take fewer

Is this career counsellor influenced by the student's gender in advising him about possible career choices? Even though there is little or no overall difference between boys and girls in mathematical or verbal ability, many school counsellors still steer young people into gender-typed careers.

English classes and lag in communications skills (AAUW Educational Foundation, 1998b; Weinman, 1998).

The educational system itself may act as a subtle brake on some students' vocational aspirations. The relatively narrow range of abilities valued and cultivated in many schools gives certain students the inside track. Students who can memorize and analyze tend to do well on intelligence tests that hinge on those abilities and in classrooms where teaching is geared to those abilities. Thus, as predicted by the tests, these students are achievers in a system that stresses the abilities in which they happen to excel.

Meanwhile, students whose strength is in creative or practical thinking—areas critical to success in certain fields—often do not get a chance to show what they can do. These young people may be frozen out of career paths or forced into less challenging and rewarding ones because of test scores and grades too low to put them on track to success (Sternberg, 1997). Recognition of a broader range of "intelligences" (see chapter 13), combined with more flexible teaching and career counselling at all levels, could allow more students to get the education and enter the occupations they desire and to make the contributions of which they are capable.

Conventional approaches to career counselling are sometimes inappropriate, particularly for Aboriginal youth for whom goals and values may be incompatible with those of mainstream counselling techniques (Neumann, McCormick, Amundson, & McLean, 2000). One attempt at a solution to the need for a culturally sensitive career-counselling approach is the First Nations Career-Life Planning Model, which is designed to integrate traditional values of connection with family, community, and culture within the process of guiding an individual's career decision-making. By involving family and community members in career counselling, and offering the option of including traditional practices of prayer, smudge ceremony, use of talking stick or eagle feather, the process has been found to be effective and meaningful to the young people involved (Neumann et al., 2000).

Guiding Students Not Bound for University

About 39 per cent of Canadian women and 45 per cent of Canadian men between the ages of 25 and 29 did not complete a post-secondary education before entering the workforce (CMEC and Statistics Canada, 1999). However, many Canadians return to school to complete their post-secondary education after having spent some time working (Council of Ontario Universities, 2000). Yet most vocational counselling in high schools is oriented toward college-bound youth.

Most industrialized countries offer some kind of structured guidance to non-university-bound students. Germany, for example, has an apprenticeship system, in which high school students go to school part time and spend the rest of the week in paid on-the-job training supervised by an employer-mentor (Hopfensperger, 1996).

In Canada and the United States, whatever vocational training programs do exist are less comprehensive and less closely tied to the needs of businesses and industries. Most young people get necessary training on the job or in community college courses. Many, ignorant about the job market, do not obtain the skills they need. Others take jobs beneath their abilities. Some do not find work at all (NRC, 1993a).

In some communities, demonstration programs help in the school-to-work transition. The most successful ones offer instruction in basic skills, counselling, peer support, mentoring, apprenticeship, and job placement (NRC, 1993a). In 1996, the federal government established the Department of Human Resources and Development, with the aim of improving the employment prospects of Canadians by developing initiatives like vocational training programs, in co-operation with provincial authorities.

Should High School Students Work Part Time?

Many high school students hold part-time jobs. This may be financially necessary in many families, and it fits in with a belief in the benefits of work. Paid work may teach young people to handle money, develop good work habits, and assume responsibility. It can help a student learn workplace skills, such as how to find a job. It may give young people a greater sense of competence, independence, and status with peers. By helping them learn more about a particular field of work, it may guide them in choosing careers (Elder & Caspi, 1990; Mortimer & Shanahan, 1991; National [U.S.] Commission on Youth, 1980; Phillips & Sandstrom, 1990; Steel, 1991). Also, by showing adolescents how demanding and difficult the world of work is and how unprepared they are for it, part-time jobs sometimes motivate young people to continue their education.

On the other hand, most Canadian high school students who work part time have low-level, repetitive jobs in which they do not learn skills useful later in life (Health Canada 1999). According to some research, teenagers who work are no more independent in making financial decisions and are unlikely to earn any more money as adults than those who do not hold jobs during high school. By assuming adult burdens they are not yet ready to deal with, young people may miss out on the opportunity to explore their interests and to develop close relationships. Outside work may require a stressful juggling of other commitments and cut down on active involvement in school (Greenberger & Steinberg, 1986). Long hours of work may undermine school performance and increase the likelihood of dropping out (Larson & Verma, 1999; NCES, 1987). Among Canadian youth, dropout rates are lowest (7 per cent) for those who work a moderate number of hours per week (10 to 19), while the highest dropout rate (21 per cent) is found among those who work the equivalent of a full-time job (30 hours or more). A surprising finding is that there is a substantial dropout rate (14 per cent) for those who do not work at all (Bowlby et al., 2002).

Paid work can have other hidden costs. Young people who work long hours are less likely to eat breakfast, exercise, get enough sleep, or have enough leisure time (Bachman & Schulenberg, 1993). They spend less time with their families and may feel less close to them. Some teenagers take jobs because they are uninterested in school or feel alienated from their families. Some spend their earnings on alcohol or drugs (Greenberger & Steinberg, 1986; Steinberg, Fegley, & Dornbusch, 1993).

Some of the alleged harmful effects of work may be overstated. One questionnaire study followed 1,000 randomly selected Grade 9 students in St. Paul, Minnesota, through 4 years of high school (Mortimer, Finch, Ryu, Shanahan, & Call, 1996). According to these self-reports, the number of hours an adolescent worked did not seem to reduce self-esteem, mental health, or mastery motivation. Working had no effect on homework time or grades until Grade 12, when students who worked more than 20 hours a week tended to do less homework than other students. Even so, their grades and achievement motivation did not suffer. And students who worked *fewer* hours had *higher* grades than those who did not work at all. Working was not related to smoking or behavioural problems at school. However, working more than 20 hours a week was associated with increased alcohol use. Another study of more than 12,000 randomly selected U.S. students in Grades 7 through 12 nationwide (also based largely on self-reports) found that teenagers who work 20 or more hours a week are more likely to feel stress, to smoke, drink, or use marijuana, and to begin sexual activity early (Resnick et al., 1997).

This research does not give a definitive answer on whether outside work is good or bad for adolescents. For one thing, the data come entirely from self-reports, which are always subjective. Furthermore, these studies addressed only how *much* young people work, and not the quality of their work experience. Other studies suggest that such factors as advancement opportunity, the chance to learn useful skills, and the kinds of responsibilities adolescents have at work may determine whether the experience is positive or negative (Call, Mortimer, & Shanahan, 1995; Finch, Shanahan, Mortimer, & Ryu, 1991; Shanahan, Finch, Mortimer, & Ryu, 1991).

Vocational planning is one aspect of an adolescent's search for identity. The question "What shall I do?" is very close to "Who shall I be?" People who feel they are doing something worthwhile, and doing it well, feel good about themselves. Those who feel that their work does not matter—or that they are not good at it—may wonder about the meaning of their lives. A prime personality issue in adolescence, which we discuss in chapter 17, is the effort to define the self.

What's your view

- Would you favour an apprenticeship program like Germany's in the United States? How successful do you think it would be in helping young people make realistic career plans? What negative effects, if any, might it have?

Checkpoint ✓

Can you . . .

✔ Discuss influences on educational and vocational planning?

✔ Give evidence as to the value of part-time work for high school students?

Summary and Key Terms

Aspects of Cognitive Maturation

Guidepost 1 How do adolescents' thinking and use of language differ from younger children's?

- People in Piaget's stage of formal operations can engage in hypothetical-deductive reasoning. They can think in terms of possibilities, deal flexibly with problems, and test hypotheses.

- Since environmental stimulation plays an important part in attaining this stage, not all people become capable of formal operations; and those who are capable do not always use it. Adolescents' immature brain development may permit emotions to interfere with rational thinking.

- Piaget's proposed stage of formal operations does not take into account such developments as accumulation of knowledge and expertise, gains in information-processing capacity, and the growth of metacognition. Piaget also paid little attention to individual differences, between-task variations, and the role of the situation.

- Vocabulary and other aspects of language development, especially those related to abstract thought, such as social perspective-taking, improve in adolescence. Adolescents enjoy wordplay and create their own "dialect."

- According to Elkind, immature thought patterns can result from adolescents' inexperience with formal thinking. These thought patterns include idealism and criticalness, argumentativeness, indecisiveness, apparent hypocrisy, self-consciousness, and an assumption of specialness and invulnerability. Research has cast doubt on the special prevalence of the latter two patterns during adolescence.

formal operations (407)   hypothetical-deductive reasoning (409) imaginary audience (412)   personal fable (412)

Moral Reasoning: Kohlberg's Theory

Guidepost 2 On what basis do adolescents make moral judgments?

- According to Kohlberg, moral reasoning is based on a developing sense of justice and growing cognitive abilities. Kohlberg proposed that moral development progresses from external control to internalized societal standards to personal, principled moral codes.

- Kohlberg's theory has been criticized on several grounds, including failure to credit the roles of emotion, socialization, and parental guidance. The applicability of Kohlberg's system to women and girls and to people in non-industrialized cultures has been questioned.

preconventional morality (413)   conventional morality (or morality of conventional role conformity) (413) postconventional morality (or morality of autonomous moral principles) (413)

Educational and Vocational Issues

Guidepost 3 What influences affect success in secondary school, and why do some students drop out?

- Academic motivation, socio-economic status, parental involvement, parenting styles, cultural and peer influences, and quality of schooling affect educational achievement. Self-efficacy beliefs and parental and peer attitudes can influence motivation to achieve. Poor families whose children do well in school tend to have more social capital than poor families whose children do not do well.

- Although most Canadians graduate from high school, the dropout rate is higher among poor and Aboriginal students and among those not living with both parents. Active engagement in studies is an important factor in keeping adolescents in school.

social capital (420)

Guidepost 4 What factors affect educational and vocational planning and preparation?

- Educational and vocational aspirations are influenced by several factors, including parental encouragement and gender stereotypes. About 33 per cent of high school graduates do not immediately go on to university. These students can benefit from vocational training.

- Part-time work seems to have both positive and negative effects on educational, social, and occupational development.

OLC Preview

The official website for *A Child's World,* First Canadian Edition, supplements the chapter's boxed material on "Pubilect: The Dialect of Adolescence" and "How Do Psychosocial Issues Affect Moral Judgments?" by providing hot links to recommended websites. Check out **www.mcgrawhill.ca/college/papalia.**

Psychosocial Development in Adolescence

This face in the mirror
stares at me
demanding Who are you? What will you become?
And taunting. You don't even know.
Chastened. I cringe and agree
and then
because I'm still young,
I stick out my tongue.

—Eve Merriam, "Conversation with Myself," 1964

Focus *David Suzuki, Naturalist*

David Suzuki

David Suzuki is one of Canada's best-known scientists. A spokesperson for ecology, he speaks out about the impact of science and industry on the environment. He and his twin sister were born in Vancouver just before the Second World War. His first memory is of his father planning a camping trip with him and taking him out to buy a pup tent; his father setting up the tent on the floor of the store to make sure it was just right for the two of them. The trip was the start of Suzuki's life-long love of nature, and what helped commit him to become a naturalist.

His ethnic background combined with the political events of his childhood later led to early experience with family displacement and injustice. His carefree childhood in B.C. came to a sudden halt when he and his family were forced to stay in an internment camp during the Second World War, a product of mass hysteria following the bombing of Pearl Harbor and the invoking of the War Measures Act in 1941. During that time in Canada, all people of Japanese descent were considered enemies of Canada, and all their property was confiscated. The years he spent with his family in a camp in the interior of B.C. helped to foster his love of and fascination with nature.

After the war, Suzuki's family moved to Ontario, where his parents worked as farm labourers. He excelled in high school, but felt like an outsider. His competitiveness in trying to be better than his classmates, a result of wishing to free his family from poverty, contributed to his feeling like an outsider: He was non-white in a white-dominated school environment, non-athletic, and intelligent. However, in his family he was lavished a great deal of attention, being the only male in a traditional Japanese family. His father urged him to excel, and to develop public speaking skills. He won a speaking contest in Grade 9, and competed in high school debating. He would fill his room with insect and fish specimens in his growing interest in biology. His success in high school led to a scholarship at Amherst College in Massachusetts, where he rose to the challenges of high expectations not only in educational but also in cultural and athletic pursuits. There a mentor who supervised his initial work introduced him to genetics.

*Sources of biographical information about David Suzuki were Knowles, 1995; Suzuki, 2000, Webb, 1991, and Wideman, 1990.

He went on to earn a Ph.D. in biology at the University of Chicago, and returned to Canada to work as a geneticist at U.B.C. This work became a passion to him, which resulted in significant contributions to science, substantial research support, and the leadership of a 20-person research team. He received many awards for his outstanding work as a scientist and came to the attention of the national media. Bringing science to Canadians in television programs such as *The Nature of Things*, he has become a spokesperson for and interpreter of science, speaking out against the misuses of science and urging the nation to focus on the responsibilities and ethics of genetic research. He promotes the importance and relevance of the balanced perspectives of Aboriginal values, manifested in the relationships that Aboriginal communities across Canada maintain with the natural world, seeing the earth not as a resource to be exploited but rather as an integral part of their identities. Suzuki urges all Canadians to adopt these values, as the only way to survive in a healthy and sustainable world.

David Suzuki remains committed to hard work and the power of human reason to change our culture and behaviour. His commitment to social justice and ecology was spurred on by his father's conviction to be a good Canadian citizen despite poor treatment by the Canadian government during World War II. This conveyed to David the same strong conviction to stand up for what he believes in.

● ● ●

Adolescence is a time of both opportunities and risks. Teenagers are on the threshold of love, of life's work, and of participation in adult society. Yet adolescence is also a time when some young people engage in behaviour that closes off their options and limits their possibilities. Today, research is increasingly focusing on how to help young people avoid hazards that can keep them from fulfilling their potential. What helped David Suzuki—in addition to the influence of his hardworking father's love of nature, his mother, sisters, and adult mentors—were his talent and his passion for preserving nature, which ultimately enabled him to channel his drive, energy, audacity, and intelligence in a positive direction.

In chapter 16 we looked at some physical and cognitive factors that contribute to an adolescent's sense of self, such as appearance and school achievement. In this chapter, we turn to psychosocial aspects of the quest for identity. We discuss how adolescents come to terms with their sexuality. We consider how teenagers' burgeoning individuality expresses itself in relationships with parents, siblings, and peers. We examine sources of anti-social behaviour and ways of reducing the risks of adolescence to make it a time of positive growth and expanding possibilities. Finally, we compare adolescents' views of themselves and their lives around the world.

After you have read and studied this chapter, you should be able to answer each of the Guidepost questions that appear at the top of the next page. Look for them again in the margins, where they point to important concepts throughout the chapter. To check your understanding of these Guideposts, review the end-of-chapter summary. Checkpoints located throughout the chapter will help you verify your understanding of what you have read.

Guideposts for Study

1. How do adolescents form an identity?

2. What determines sexual orientation?

3. What sexual practices are common among adolescents, and what leads some to engage in risky sexual behaviour?

4. How common is teenage pregnancy, and what are its usual outcomes?

5. How typical is "adolescent rebellion"?

6. How do adolescents relate to parents, siblings, and peers?

7. What are the root causes of anti-social behaviour and juvenile delinquency, and what can be done to reduce these and other risks of adolescence?

8. How does adolescence vary across cultures, and what are some common psychosocial features of the period?

The Search for Identity

Guidepost 1

How do adolescents form an identity?

The search for identity, which Erikson defined as confidence in one's inner continuity amid change, comes into focus during the teenage years. Adolescents' cognitive development now enables them to construct a "theory of the self" (Elkind, 1998). As Erikson (1950) emphasized, a teenager's effort to make sense of the self is not "a kind of maturational malaise." It is part of a healthy, vital process that builds on the achievements of earlier stages—on trust, autonomy, initiative, and industry—and lays the groundwork for coping with the crises of adult life.

Erikson: Identity versus Identity Confusion

The chief task of adolescence, said Erikson (1968), is to confront the crisis of **identity versus identity confusion** (or *identity versus role confusion*), to become a unique adult with a coherent sense of self and a valued role in society. The identity crisis is seldom fully resolved in adolescence; issues concerning identity crop up again and again throughout adult life.

Erikson's concept of the identity crisis was based on his own life and his research on adolescents in various societies. Growing up in Germany as the son of a Danish mother and a Jewish adoptive father, Erikson had felt confusion about his identity. He never knew his biological father; he floundered before settling on a vocation; and when he came to the United States, he needed to redefine his identity as an immigrant. All these issues found echoes in the identity crises he observed among disturbed adolescents, soldiers in combat, and members of minority groups (Erikson, 1968, 1973; L. J. Friedman, 1999).

According to Erikson, adolescents form their identity not by modelling themselves after other people, as younger children do, but by modifying and synthesizing earlier identifications into "a new psychological structure, greater than the sum of its parts" (Kroger, 1993, p. 3). To form an identity, adolescents must ascertain and organize their abilities, needs, interests, and desires so they can be expressed in a social context.

Erikson saw the prime danger of this stage as identity (or role) confusion, which can greatly delay reaching psychological adulthood. (He himself did not resolve his own identity crisis until his mid-twenties.) Some degree of identity confusion is normal. It accounts for both the seemingly chaotic nature of much adolescent behaviour and teenagers' painful self-consciousness. Cliquishness and intolerance of differences—both hallmarks of the adolescent social scene—are defences against identity confusion. Adolescents may also

identity versus identity confusion Erikson's fifth crisis of psychosocial development, in which an adolescent seeks to develop a coherent sense of self, including the role she or he is to play in society; also called *identity versus role confusion*.

Mastering the challenge of rappelling may help this adolescent girl assess her abilities, interests, and desires. According to Erikson, this process of self-assessment helps adolescents resolve the crisis of identity versus identity confusion.

show confusion by regressing into childishness to avoid resolving conflicts or by committing themselves impulsively to poorly thought-out courses of action.

Identity forms as young people resolve three major issues: the choice of an occupation, the adoption of values to believe in and live by, and the development of a satisfying sexual identity. During the crisis of middle childhood, that of *industry versus inferiority,* children acquire skills needed for success in their culture. Now, as adolescents, they need to find ways to use these skills. When young people have trouble settling on an occupational identity—or when their opportunities are artificially limited—they are at risk of behaviour with serious negative consequences, such as criminal activity or early pregnancy.

During the *psychosocial moratorium*—the "time out" period that adolescence provides—many young people search for commitments to which they can be faithful. These youthful commitments may shape a person's life for years to come. David Suzuki's commitments were to develop his abilities as a scientist and to help improve the natural world by promoting values that would ensure the survival of the earth. The extent to which young people remain faithful to commitments, as Suzuki did, influences their ability to resolve the identity crisis. Adolescents who satisfactorily resolve that crisis develop the "virtue" of *fidelity:* sustained loyalty, faith, or a sense of belonging to a loved one or to friends and companions. Fidelity also can mean identification with a set of values, an ideology, a religion, a political movement, a creative pursuit, or an ethnic group (Erikson, 1982). Self-identification emerges when young people choose values and people to be loyal to, rather than simply accepting their parents' choices.

Fidelity is an extension of trust. In infancy, it is important for trust of parents to outweigh mistrust; in adolescence, it becomes important to be trustworthy oneself. In addition, adolescents now extend their trust to mentors or loved ones. In sharing thoughts and feelings, an adolescent clarifies a tentative identity by seeing it reflected in the eyes of the beloved. However, these adolescent "intimacies" differ from mature intimacy, which involves greater commitment, sacrifice, and compromise.

Erikson's theory describes male identity development as the norm. According to Erikson, a man is not capable of real intimacy until after he has achieved a stable identity, whereas women define themselves through marriage and motherhood (something that may have been truer when Erikson developed his theory than it is today). Thus, said Erikson, women (unlike men) develop identity *through* intimacy, not before it. As we'll see, this male orientation of Erikson's theory has prompted criticism. Still, Erikson's concept of the identity crisis has inspired much valuable research.

Marcia: Identity Status—Crisis and Commitment

Kate, Andrea, Nick, and Mark are all about to graduate from high school. Kate has considered her interests and her talents and plans to become an engineer. She has narrowed her choices to three universities that offer good programs in this field.

Andrea knows exactly what she is going to do with her life. Her mother, a union leader at a plastics factory, has arranged for Andrea to enter an apprenticeship program there. Andrea has never considered doing anything else.

Nick, on the other hand, is agonizing over his future. Should he attend a community college or join the armed forces? He cannot decide what to do now or what he wants to do eventually.

Mark still has no idea of what he wants to do, but he is not worried. He figures he can get some sort of a job and make up his mind about the future when he is ready.

These four young people are involved in identity formation. What accounts for the differences in the way they go about it, and how will these differences affect the outcome? According to research by the psychologist James E. Marcia (1966, 1980), these students are in four different states of ego (self) development, or **identity statuses,** which seem to be related to certain aspects of personality.

Through 30-minute, semi-structured *identity-status interviews* (see Table 17-1), Marcia found four types of identity status: *identity achievement, foreclosure, moratorium,* and *identity diffusion.* The four categories differ according to the presence or absence of **crisis** and **commitment,** the two elements Erikson saw as crucial to forming identity (see Table 17-2).

identity statuses Marcia's term for states of ego development that depend on the presence or absence of crisis and commitment

crisis Marcia's term for period of conscious decision making related to identity formation

commitment Marcia's term for personal investment in an occupation or system of beliefs

Table 17-1   Identity-Status Interview

Sample Questions	Typical Answers for the Four Statuses
About occupational commitment: "How willing do you think you'd be to give up going into _____ if something better came along?"	*Identity achievement.* "Well, I might, but I doubt it. I can't see what 'something better' would be for me."
	Foreclosure. "Not very willing. It's what I've always wanted to do. The folks are happy with it and so am I."
	Moratorium. "I guess if I knew for sure, I could answer that better. It would have to be something in the general area—something related . . ."
	Identity diffusion. "Oh, sure. If something better came along, I'd change just like that."
About ideological commitment: "Have you ever had any doubts about your religious beliefs?"	*Identity achievement.* "Yes, I started wondering whether there is a God. I've pretty much resolved that now. The way it seems to me is . . ."
	Foreclosure. "No, not really; our family is pretty much in agreement on these things."
	Moratorium. "Yes, I guess I'm going through that now. I just don't see how there can be a God and still so much evil in the world . . ."
	Identity diffusion. "Oh, I don't know. I guess so. Everyone goes through some sort of stage like that. But it really doesn't bother me much. I figure that one religion is about as good as another!"

Source: Adapted from Marcia, 1966.

Table 17-2   Criteria for Identity Statuses

Identity Status	Crisis (Period of Considering Alternatives)	Commitment (Adherence to a Path of Action)
Identity achievement	Resolved	Present
Foreclosure	Absent	Present
Moratorium	In crisis	Absent
Identity diffusion	Absent	Absent

Source: Adapted from Marcia, 1980.

Marcia defines *crisis* as a period of conscious decision making, and *commitment* as a personal investment in an occupation or system of beliefs (ideology). He found relationships between identity status and such characteristics as anxiety, self-esteem, moral reasoning, and patterns of behaviour. Building on Marcia's theory, other researchers have identified other personality and family variables related to identity status (see Table 17-3). Here is a thumbnail sketch of people in each of the four identity statuses:

1. **Identity achievement** *(crisis leading to commitment).* Kate has resolved her identity crisis. During the crisis period, she devoted much thought and some emotional struggle to major issues in her life. She has made choices and expresses strong commitment to them. Her parents have encouraged her to make her own decisions; they have listened to her ideas and given their opinions without pressuring her to adopt them. Kate is thoughtful but not so introspective as to be unable to act. She has a sense of humour, functions well under stress, is capable of intimate relationships, and holds to her standards while being open to new ideas. Research in a number of cultures has found people in this category to be more mature and more competent in relationships than people in the other three (Marcia, 1993).

identity achievement Identity status, described by Marcia, which is characterized by commitment to choices made following a crisis, a period spent in exploring alternatives

Table 17-3	Family and Personality Factors Associated with Adolescents in Four Identity Statuses*			
Factor	Identity Achievement	Foreclosure	Moratorium	Identity Diffusion
Family	Parents encourage autonomy and connection with teachers; differences are explored within a context of mutuality.	Parents are overly involved with their children; families avoid expressing differences.	Adolescents are often involved in an ambivalent struggle with parental authority.	Parents are laissez-faire in child-rearing attitudes; are rejecting or not available to children.
Personality	High levels of ego development, moral reasoning, self-certainty, self-esteem, performance under stress, and intimacy.	Highest levels of authoritarianism and stereotypical thinking, obedience to authority, dependent relationships, low level of anxiety.	Most anxious and fearful of success; high levels of ego development, moral reasoning, and self-esteem.	Mixed results, with low levels of ego development, moral reasoning, cognitive complexity, and self-certainty; poor cooperative abilities.

*These associations have emerged from a number of separate studies. Since the studies have all been correlational, rather than longitudinal, it is impossible to say that any factor caused placement in any identity status.

Source: Kroger, 1993.

foreclosure Identity status, described by Marcia, in which a person who has not spent time considering alternatives (that is, has not been in crisis) is committed to other people's plans for his or her life

moratorium Identity status, described by Marcia, in which a person is currently considering alternatives (in crisis) and seems headed for commitment

identity diffusion Identity status, described by Marcia, which is characterized by absence of commitment and lack of serious consideration of alternatives

What's your view ?

- Which of Marcia's identity statuses do you think you fitted into as an adolescent? Has your identity status changed since then? If so, how?

2. **Foreclosure** *(commitment without crisis).* Andrea has made commitments, not as a result of a crisis, which would involve questioning and exploring possible choices, but by accepting someone else's plans for her life. She is happy and self-assured, perhaps even smug and self-satisfied, and she becomes dogmatic when her opinions are questioned. She has close family ties, is obedient, and tends to follow a powerful leader (like her mother), who accepts no disagreement.

3. **Moratorium** *(crisis with no commitment yet).* Nick is in crisis, struggling with decisions. He is lively, talkative, self-confident, and scrupulous, but also anxious and fearful. He is close to his mother but also resists her authority. He wants to have a girlfriend but has not yet developed a close relationship. He will probably come out of his crisis eventually with the ability to make commitments and achieve identity.

4. **Identity diffusion** *(no commitment, no crisis).* Mark has not seriously considered options and has avoided commitments. He is unsure of himself and tends to be uncooperative. His parents do not discuss his future with him; they say it's up to him. People in this category tend to be unhappy. They are often lonely because they have only superficial relationships.

These categories are not permanent, of course; they may change as people continue to develop (Marcia, 1979). From late adolescence on, more and more people are in moratorium or achievement: seeking or finding their own identity. Still, many people, even as young adults, remain in foreclosure or diffusion (Kroger, 1993). Although people in foreclosure seem to have made final decisions, that is often not so; when adults in mid-life look back on their lives, they most commonly trace a path from foreclosure to moratorium to identity achievement (Kroger & Haslett, 1991).

Gender Differences in Identity Formation

Much research supports Erikson's view that, for women, identity and intimacy develop together. Indeed, intimacy matters more to girls than to boys even in grade school friendships (Blyth & Foster-Clark, 1987). Rather than view this pattern as a departure from a male norm, however, some researchers see it as pointing to a weakness in Erikson's theory, which, they claim, is based on male-centred Western concepts of individuality, autonomy, and competitiveness. According to Carol Gilligan (1982, 1987a, 1987b; L. M. Brown & Gilligan, 1990), the female sense of self develops not so much through achieving a separate identity as through establishing relationships. Girls and women, says Gilligan, judge themselves on their handling of their responsibilities and on their ability to care for others as well as for themselves.

Some developmental scientists, however, have begun to question how different the male and female paths to identity really are—especially today—and to suggest that individual differences may be more important than gender differences (Archer, 1993; Marcia, 1993). Indeed, Marcia (1993) argues that relationships and an ongoing tension between independence and connectedness are at the heart of all of Erikson's psychosocial stages for *both* men and women.

Self-esteem, during adolescence, develops largely within relationships with peers, particularly those of the same sex. In line with Gilligan's view, male self-esteem seems to be linked with striving for individual achievement, whereas female self-esteem depends more on connections with others. In one longitudinal study, 84 mostly white, socio-economically diverse young adults, whose self-esteem had been measured at ages 14 and 18, described memories about important experiences with others. Men who had had high self-esteem during adolescence tended to recall wanting to assert themselves with male friends, whereas women who had had high self-esteem recalled efforts to help female friends—efforts that involved asserting themselves in a collaborative rather than a competitive way (Thorne & Michaelieu, 1996).

Some research suggests that adolescent girls have lower self-esteem than adolescent boys (Chubb, Fertman, & Ross, 1997). Highly publicized studies during the early 1990s found that girls' self-confidence and self-esteem stay fairly high until age 11 or 12 and then tend to falter (American Association of University Women [AAUW] Educational Foundation, 1992; L. M. Brown & Gilligan, 1990). A recent analysis of hundreds of studies involving nearly 150,000 respondents concluded that boys and men do have higher self-esteem than girls and women, especially in late adolescence, but the difference is small. Contrary to the earlier finding, both males and females seem to gain self-esteem with age (Kling, Hyde, Showers, & Buswell, 1999).

Ethnic Factors in Identity Formation

In 1971, the federal government announced a policy of multiculturalism, which was designed to safeguard the right of every ethnic group in Canada to maintain and develop its own values and culture (Freisen, 1995). Despite official policy supporting the growth of cultural diversity in Canada, the process of forming an identity for adolescent immigrants and members of some ethnic minorities can be difficult. This is particularly relevant when the values of the ethnic group, such as the case of a culture that emphasizes the community, are different from those of mainstream Canadian society, which emphasizes the individual. What happens to young people's identity when the values of their ethnic community conflict with those of the larger society—for example, when Aboriginal adolescents are expected to participate in a ceremony on a day when they are also supposed to be in school? Or when young people face and perhaps internalize (take into their own value system) prejudice against their own ethnic group? Or when discrimination limits their occupational choices, as it did for David Suzuki's father during World War II? All these situations can lead to identity confusion.

Identity formation is especially complicated for young people in minority groups. In fact, for some adolescents ethnicity may be central to identity formation. As Erikson (1968) pointed out, an "oppressed and exploited minority" may come to see themselves in the negative way the majority see them (p. 303). This is called *self-hatred*. Even in a more tolerant society in which ethnic minorities have become more assertive, skin colour and other physical features, language differences, and stereotyped social standing can be extremely influential in moulding minority adolescents' self-concept. At a time when adolescents want to fit in—when they are painfully self-conscious about physical differences—minority adolescents cannot help but stand out (Spencer & Dornbusch, 1998). With nearly double the number of immigrant young people between the ages of 6 and 15 arriving in Canada in 1997, compared to 1987 (Canadian Council on Social Development, 2001), the process of forming an identity can be difficult for many Canadian youth.

Teenagers have wider social networks and more mobility than younger children, and greater cognitive awareness of cultural attitudes and distinctions. Caught between two

Identity development can be especially complicated for young people from minority groups. Ethnicity—and the conflicts with the dominant culture it entails—may play a central part in their self-concept.

cultures, many minority youth are keenly conscious of conflicts between the values stressed at home and those dominant in the wider society. Despite positive appraisals by parents, teachers, community, and peers, minority adolescents' self-perceptions may, as Erikson noted, reflect negative views of their group by the majority culture. With the scale of diversity among Aboriginal cultures in Canada (see chapter 1), it is difficult to draw general conclusions about identity formation among young Aboriginal people in Canada. However, the shared history of these groups may be related to some of the difficulties many young Aboriginal people face in identity formation. Disruption of traditional ways of life through a history of colonization, relocation to reserves, separation from families and abuse in residential schools, and efforts at assimilation have dealt a severe blow to the maintenance of strong cultural identities in many communities. More recent introduction of mass media and other economic and political changes has introduced additional challenges to the development of an Aboriginal identity for young people, who are exposed to a large variety of influences and rapid cultural changes (Kirmayer et al., 2000).

A study of Chinese immigrant youth in Toronto showed that higher levels of social support and the presence of both parents in the life of the adolescent predicted more successful adaptation to Canadian culture, as indicated by good academic achievement, and low levels of conflict with parents (Leung, 2001).

Research dating back to the late 1970s and early 1980s has identified four stages of ethnic identity based on Marcia's identity statuses (Phinney, 1998):

1. *Diffuse:* Anastasia has done little or no exploration of her ethnicity and does not clearly understand the issues involved.
2. *Foreclosed:* Kwame had done little or no exploration of his identity but has clear feelings about it. These feelings may be positive or negative, depending on the attitudes he absorbed at home.
3. *Moratorium:* Cho-san has begun to explore her ethnicity but is confused about what it means to her.
4. *Achieved:* Mario has explored his identity and understands and accepts his ethnicity.

In a recent study of 64 U.S.-born Grade 10 students of various ethnicities (Phinney, 1998), researchers who coded the adolescents' responses to interviews and questionnaires were able to reliably assign all but four young people to three categories. About half of the sample (33) were *diffuse/foreclosed.* (The researchers combined these two categories—both involving lack of exploration of ethnicity—because they could not clearly distinguish between them on the basis of the young people's responses.) The other half were either in *moratorium* (14) or had apparently *achieved* identity (13).

About one-fifth of the participants (some at each stage) had negative attitudes toward their own ethnic group. However, those in the achieved stage showed better overall adjustment than those in the other groups. They thought more highly of themselves, had a greater sense of mastery, and reported more positive family relationships and social and peer interactions.

Place of birth of adolescent members of minority groups can have an influence on identity and self-esteem, likely based on differences in life experience (Lay & Verkuyten, 1999). A study of 31 Chinese adolescents who were Canadian-born, and 31 Chinese adolescents who immigrated to Canada, all living in Toronto, found that the foreign-born adolescents tended to identify themselves as Chinese, rather than Chinese-Canadian. The foreign-born adolescents tended to perceive themselves as being separate from the larger Canadian culture, regarded their ethnicity as more important, and were more likely to relate the collectivist values of their ethnic identities to their own self-identities than did the Canadian-born adolescents (Lay et al., 1999).

Particularly vulnerable to difficulties in forming healthy identity are child refugees, many of whom have settled in Canada. Particular problems they face, in addition to adapting to life in a new and often unfamiliar culture, include dealing with the trauma of war, persecution, dangerous escapes, and prolonged periods of settlement in refugee camps, many having witnessed killings, torture, and other atrocities (Fantino & Colak, 2001).

Elkind: The Patchwork Self

As Erikson and Marcia observed, not everyone achieves a strong sense of identity, during or after adolescence. Why is this so?

According to Elkind (1998), there are two paths to identity. The first, and healthiest, is a process of *differentiation* and *integration:* becoming aware of the many ways in which one differs from others, and then integrating these distinctive parts of oneself into a unified, unique whole. This inner-directed process requires much time and reflection; but when a person has achieved a sense of identity in this way, it is almost impossible to break down.

The second, initially easier, path is that of *substitution:* replacing one, childlike, set of ideas and feelings about the self with another by simply adopting other people's attitudes, beliefs, and commitments as one's own. A sense of self built mainly by substitution is what Elkind calls a **patchwork self**—a self put together from borrowed, often conflicting, bits and pieces. Young people with patchwork selves tend to have low self-esteem. They find it hard to handle freedom, loss, or failure. They may be anxious, conforming, angry, frightened, or self-punishing. They are highly susceptible to outside influence and highly vulnerable to stress because they have no inner compass, no distinctive sense of direction to guide them.

Elkind attributes increases in drug abuse, gun violence, risky sexual behaviour, and teenage suicide to the growing number of young people who have elements of the patchwork self. Today, says Elkind, many adolescents "have a premature adulthood thrust upon them" (1998, p. 7). They lack the time or opportunity for the psychosocial moratorium Erikson described—the protected "time out" period necessary to build a stable, inner-directed self.

Authoritative parenting can help. If young people see their parents acting according to firm, deeply held principles, they are more likely to develop firm, deeply held principles of their own. If parents show adolescents effective ways of dealing with stress, youngsters will be less likely to succumb to the pressures that threaten the patchwork self.

> **patchwork self** Elkind's term for a sense of identity constructed by substituting other people's attitudes, beliefs, and commitments for one's own

Checkpoint

Can you . . .

✔ List the three major issues involved in identity formation, according to Erikson?

✔ Describe four types of identity status found by Marcia?

✔ Discuss how gender and ethnicity can affect identity formation?

✔ Distinguish the two paths of identity development described by Elkind, and explain how he links risky behaviour with the patchwork self?

Sexuality

Seeing oneself as a sexual being, recognizing one's sexual orientation, coming to terms with sexual stirrings, and forming romantic or sexual attachments are all parts of achieving sexual identity. This urgent awareness of sexuality is an important aspect of identity formation, profoundly affecting self-image and relationships. Although this process is biologically driven, its expression is in part culturally defined.

Guidepost 2

What determines sexual orientation?

Sexual Orientation

Although present in younger children, it is in adolescence that a person's **sexual orientation** generally becomes a pressing issue: whether that person will consistently be sexually, romantically, and affectionately attracted to persons of the other sex *(heterosexual)* or of the same sex *(homosexual)* or of both sexes *(bisexual)*.

The incidence of homosexuality—gay and lesbian—among adolescents is hard to pinpoint. In one study of 38,000 Canadian youth ages 11 to 21, up to 98 per cent of high school leavers and university and college students described themselves as predominantly heterosexual and only 1 percent as predominantly homosexual or bisexual. (King, Beazley, Warren et al., 1988).

Although homosexuality was once considered a mental illness, several decades of research have found no association between sexual orientation and emotional or social problems (American Psychological Association, undated; C. J. Patterson, 1992, 1995a, 1995b). These findings eventually led the psychiatric profession to stop classifying homosexuality as a mental disorder. The current edition of the American Psychiatric

> **sexual orientation** Focus of consistent sexual, romantic, and affectionate interest, either heterosexual, homosexual (gay and lesbian), or bisexual

Association's *Diagnostic and Statistical Manual of Mental Disorders* contains no references to it at all.

Other common explanations for homosexuality—all scientifically discredited—point to disturbed relationships with parents; parental encouragement of unconventional, cross-gender behaviour; imitation of homosexual parents; or chance learning through seduction by a homosexual. Many young people have one or more homosexual experiences as they are growing up, usually before age 15. However, isolated experiences, or even homosexual attractions or fantasies, do not determine sexual orientation.

According to one theory, sexual orientation may be influenced by a complex prenatal process involving both hormonal and neurological factors (Ellis & Ames, 1987). If the levels of sex hormones in a fetus of either sex between the second and fifth months of gestation are in the typical female range, the person is likely to be attracted to males after puberty. If the hormone levels are in the male range, the person is likely to be attracted to females. Whether and how hormonal activity may affect brain development, and whether and how differences in brain structure may affect sexual orientation have not been established (Golombok & Tasker, 1996), but an anatomical difference between homosexual and heterosexual men in an area of the brain that governs sexual behaviour has been reported (LeVay, 1991).

There is also evidence that sexual orientation may be at least partly genetic. An identical twin of a homosexual has about a 50 per cent probability of being homosexual himself or herself, while a fraternal twin has only about a 20 per cent likelihood and an adopted sibling 10 per cent or less (Gladue, 1994). One series of studies linked male homosexuality to a small region of the X chromosome inherited from the mother (Hamer, Hu, Magnuson, Hu, & Pattatucci, 1993, Hu et al., 1995). However, later research failed to replicate this finding (G. Rice, Anderson, Risch, & Ebers, 1999).

Controversy remains as to whether or not sexual orientation is decisively shaped either before birth or at an early age. There is also dispute about the relative contributions of biological, psychological, and social influences (Baumrind, 1995; C. J. Patterson, 1995b). These influences may well be "impossible to untangle," and their relative strength may differ among individuals (Baumrind, 1995, p. 132).

Checkpoint ✔

Can you . . .

✔ Discuss theories and research about origins of sexual orientation?

Guidepost 3

What sexual practices are common among adolescents, and what leads some to engage in risky sexual behaviour?

Sexual Behaviour

It is difficult to do research on sexual expression. People willing to answer questions about sex tend to be sexually active and liberal in their attitudes toward sex and thus are not representative of the population. Also, there is often a discrepancy between what people say about sex and what they do, and there is no way to corroborate what people say. Some may conceal sexual activity, others may exaggerate. Problems multiply in surveying young people. For one thing, parental consent is often required, and parents who grant permission may not be typical. Methodology can make a difference: Adolescent boys are more open in reporting certain types of sexual activity when surveys are self-administered by computer (C. F. Turner et al., 1998). Still, even if we cannot generalize findings to the population as a whole, within the groups that take part in surveys we can see trends that reveal changes in sexual mores.

How has adolescent sexual behaviour changed in recent decades, and how does it vary across cultures?

The Sexual Evolution

In Canada and the United States, the early 1920s through the late 1970s witnessed an evolution in sexual behaviour. Premarital sexual activity has become more common, especially among girls. In the mid-1950s, one out of four girls had sexual experience by age 18. Today over 60 per cent of both girls and boys have had intercourse by that age. The average Canadian now has his or her sexual initiation at 17 (American Academy of Pediatrics [AAP] Committee on Adolescence, 1999; Singh, Wulf, Samara, & Cuca, 2000; Statistics

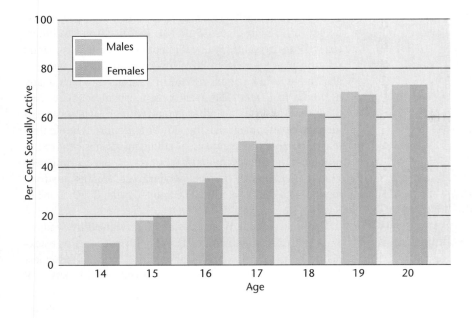

Figure 17-1

Cumulative percentage of Canadian men and women aged 20–24 in 1996 who report having sexual intercourse at each age. More than half of Canadian teenagers become sexually active by age 17.

Source: Adapted from Maticka-Tyndale et al., 2001, p. 12.

Canada, 1998). Still, about one young person in four does not have intercourse during the teens (Maticka-Tyndale, McKay, & Barrett, 2001, see Figure 17-1).

The wave of sexual liberation in Canada appears to be ebbing. After a steady rise since the 1970s, the median age of first intercourse has been constant at age 17 for men and women (Maticka-Tyndale et al., 2001). Among U.S. girls, from 1990 to 1995 the percentage who had had intercourse dropped from 55 to 50 per cent (Abma, Chandra, Mosher, Peterson, & Piccinino, 1997), and among never-married boys, from 60 to 55 per cent ("Teen Sex Down," 1997). A 1995 survey of more than 240,000 entering first-year students at colleges and universities in the United States found 43 per cent approving of casual sex, down from 52 per cent in 1987 (Sax, Astin, Korn, & Mahoney, 1996).

Internationally, there are wide variations in timing of sexual initiation, according to a survey sponsored by the World Health Organization (WHO), and another by the Canadian National Population Health Survey (Statistics Canada, 1998; Maticka-Tyndale, 2001; Maticka-Tyndale et al., 2001; Ross & Wyatt, 2000) The percentage of 15-year-old women who report having first intercourse is greater in Canada (about 25 per cent) than in France (20 per cent), Israel (11 per cent), and Poland (14 per cent), but it is less than the rate in the United States (38 per cent). On the other hand, fewer 15-year-old Canadian men (about 20 per cent) report having had sexual intercourse than 15-year-old men in the nine countries studied by the WHO (Finland, France, Hungary, Israel, Latvia, Northern Ireland, Poland, Scotland, and the United States). Although earlier male initiation is the norm in most cultures, in Canada more women than men report having had sexual intercourse by age 15 (Maticka-Tyndale et al., 2001)

Gay and Lesbian Identity and Behaviour

The sexual evolution in Canada has brought more general acceptance of homosexuality. In 1988, 31 per cent of college and university students agreed that homosexuality is acceptable, while 39 per cent said homosexuality is wrong. Forty per cent claimed that they would be comfortable talking with a gay or lesbian person, and 51 per cent agreed that homosexuals should be allowed to be teachers (King et al., 1988). Still, teenagers who openly identify as gay or lesbian often feel isolated in a hostile environment and may be subject to prejudice and even violence (CICH, 2000; C. J. Patterson, 1995b).

A widely proposed model for the development of gay or lesbian sexual identity goes something like this: (1) awareness of same-sex attraction (beginning at ages 8 to 11); (2)

Although sexual orientation may well be shaped before birth or very early in life, it is in adolescence that it becomes a pressing issue. In 2002, Marc Hall, an Ontario high school student, challenged his school's decision to prevent him from attending his end-of-year formal with his boyfriend.

same-sex sexual behaviours (ages 12 to 15); (3) identification as gay or lesbian (ages 15 to 18); (4) disclosure to others (ages 17 to 19); and (5) development of same-sex romantic relationships (ages 18 to 20). However, this model may not accurately reflect the experience of younger gay men, many of whom feel freer than in the past to openly declare their identities; of lesbian and bisexual women, whose sexual identity development may be slower and more flexible than that of homosexual men; and of ethnic minorities, whose traditional communities and cultures may espouse strong religious beliefs or stereotypical gender roles, leading to strong internal and family conflict (Diamond, 1998, 2000; Dubé & Savin-Williams, 1999).

In one U.S. study, researchers interviewed 89 women, ages 16 to 23. All called themselves either lesbian or bisexual or did not label their sexual identity. The results suggest that, in women, sexual identity is *not* firmly established at an early age. Few of the women reported exclusively same-sex attractions, and three out of four failed to recall either childhood indicators of sexual orientation, stability of same-sex attractions, or awareness of same-sex attractions before beginning to consciously question their sexual identity (Diamond, 1998). Furthermore, when 80 of the women were interviewed again 2 years later, half reported having changed sexual identities more than once, one-third since the previous interview. One out of four lesbians had had sexual contact with men during that time (Diamond, 2000).

In interviews and questionnaires, 139 young males ages 16 to 26—white, African-American, Latino, and Asian-American—explored what it meant to them to grow up gay or bisexual (Dubé & Savin-Williams, 1999). About half felt that they had fully accepted their sexual identities, and most had become sexually and romantically involved with other men—not necessarily at the same time. In contrast with their counterparts in earlier generations, who generally did not have same-sex relationships until (sometimes well into) adulthood, most of these youths had developed such relationships during high school or university.

Sexual Risk Taking

Two major concerns about adolescent sexual activity are the risks of contracting sexually transmitted diseases (refer back to chapter 15) and of pregnancy. Most in danger are young people who start sexual activity early, who have multiple partners, who do not use contraceptives, and who have inadequate information—or misinformation—about sex.

Early Sexual Activity

Why do some adolescents become sexually active at an early age? Various factors—including early entrance into puberty, poverty, poor school performance, lack of academic and career goals, a history of sexual abuse or parental neglect, and cultural or family patterns of early sexual experience—may play a part (AAP Committee on Adolescence, 1999; CICH, 2000; see Table 17-4). For example, a survey of British Columbia girls in Grades 7 to 12 showed that those who thought they looked older than their peers were more likely to report having sexual intercourse then those who thought they looked the same age as their peers (CICH, 2000).

One of the most powerful influences is perception of peer group norms. Among 1,389 Philadelphia students in Grade 6, the strongest predictor of which students would begin sexual activity by the end of the school year was the intention to do so, and that intention was most strongly influenced by the belief that most of their friends had already done so (Kinsman, Romer, Furstenberg, & Schwarz, 1998).

Table 17-4	Some Factors Associated with Timing of First Intercourse	
	Factors Associated with Early Age	**Factors Associated with Later Age**
Timing of puberty	Early	Late
Personality style and behaviour	Risk taking, impulsive	Traditional values, religious orientation
	Depressive symptoms Anti-social or delinquent	Prosocial or conventional behaviour
Substance use	Use of drugs, alcohol, tobacco	Non-use
Education	Fewer years of schooling	More years of schooling; valuing academic achievement
Family structure	Single-parent family	Two-parent family
Socio-economic status	Disadvantaged	Advantaged

Source: Dubé & Savin-Williams, 1999; B. C. Miller & Moore, 1990; Sonenstein, Pleck, & Ku, 1991.

Girls (and, to a lesser extent, boys) often feel under pressure to engage in activities they do not feel ready for. Although 93 per cent of teenage girls in the United States say their first intercourse was voluntary, about one-fourth of these girls say they did not want it (AGI, 1999a). Often girls who begin having sexual relations early are coerced into it by older men (AGI, 1994, 1999a; Children's Defense Fund, 1998). Seven out of 10 women whose first intercourse took place before age 13 report that it was unwanted or not voluntary (AGI, 1999a).

Use of Contraceptives

Nine out of 10 sexually active teenage girls and their partners use contraception, though not always correctly or consistently. A sexually active girl who does not use contraceptives has a 90 per cent chance of becoming pregnant within a year (AGI, 1999a).

The best safeguard for sexually active teens is the birth control pill, although regular use of condoms gives some protection against STDs as well as against pregnancy. Condom use has increased dramatically in recent years, probably due to educational campaigns aimed at preventing AIDS. By 1995, about three-fourths of girls and women who began premarital sexual activity reported using some kind of protection the first time they engaged in sex, and about two-thirds of these reported that their partners used condoms (Abma et al., 1997; AGI, 1999a). However, teenagers still tend to prefer the pill; 44 per cent of girls who use contraception choose it, as compared with 38 per cent for condoms and 17 per cent for other methods (AGI, 1999a).

Teenagers, especially young teens, are more likely than adult women to use contraception sporadically or not at all (AGI, 1999a). The younger a girl is when becoming sexually active, the less likely she is to use contraception at first intercourse (Abma et al., 1997). Many teenagers with multiple sex partners do not use reliable protection. Almost one-quarter of sexually active high school women and about one-third of sexually active high school men report two or more sex partners in a year (Maticka-Tyndale, 2001). About 13 per cent of female 15- to 19-year-olds and 19 per cent of males in the same age range who had two or more sex partners did not use condoms—an activity that places them at risk of developing sexually transmitted diseases (CICH, 2000). Studies of Canadian adolescent compliance in contraceptive use show that of those women who begin using oral contraceptives, only 49 per cent continue to use them after 12 months. The factors that predicted compliance were being in a higher grade at school, being a non-smoker, and having the father's support for using birth control (Kalagian, Delmore, Loewen, & Busca, 1998). In a study of Canadian adolescent use of condoms, although 75 per cent indicated at the outset that they would always use condoms, only 42 per cent reported using condoms in their last three experiences of intercourse. The factors that predicted having sex without a condom were being a female, having a negative attitude towards condoms, and having a weaker intention to use condoms (Richardson, Beazley, Delaney, & Langille, 1997).

Where Do Teenagers Get Information about Sex?

Today's teenagers tend to know more about sex than their predecessors did. In 1995, about 96 per cent of 18- to 19-year-olds (as compared with only 80 per cent of 25- to 29-year-olds and 65 per cent of 35- to 39-year-olds) reported having had formal sex instruction. This instruction typically covered birth control methods, sexually transmitted diseases, safe sex to prevent HIV infection, and how to say no to sex (Abma et al., 1997).

This is important because teenagers who are knowledgeable about sex are more likely to use contraceptives and to use them consistently (Ku, Sonenstein, & Pleck, 1992; Louis Harris & Associates, 1986; Luster & Small, 1994). They are also more likely to postpone sexual intimacy—the most effective means of birth control (Conger, 1988; Jaslow, 1982). Teenagers who can go to their parents or other adults with questions about sex and those who get sex education from school or community programs have a better chance of avoiding pregnancy and other risks connected with sexual activity (see Box 17-1).

Unfortunately, nearly 4 out of 10 teenagers get their sex education from the media (Princeton Survey Research Associates, 1996), which present a distorted view of sexual activity, associating it with fun, excitement, competition, danger, or violence, and rarely showing the risks of unprotected sexual relations (AAP Committee on Communications, 1995).

Several studies suggest a link between media influence and early sexual activity (Strasburger & Donnerstein, 1999). For example, the National Surveys of Children found that boys who watched more television (especially those who watched television without their families) were more likely to have early sexual relations (Peterson, Moore, & Furstenberg, 1991).

The amount of time young people spend watching television may be less important than their involvement with what they see. Among a multi-ethnic sample of 314 U.S. university undergraduates, students who said they identified strongly with the characters in situation comedies dealing with sexual issues, or who judged the portrayals as very realistic, tended to endorse recreational attitudes toward sex. They also tended to be more sexually experienced and to expect more sexual activity among peers than students who were less involved with what they saw on screen (Ward & Rivadeneyra, 1999). Thus television, at least for some young people, seems to help shape views of what is normative and expected.

In ironic contrast to the irresponsible portrayals of sexuality in television programming, network executives have almost universally refused to show contraceptive advertisements, claiming that they would be controversial and offensive and might encourage sexual activity. However, there is no evidence for the latter claim, and trial advertisements in limited markets have brought mostly commendations instead of complaints (AAP Committee on Communications, 1995).

Teenage Pregnancy and Childbearing

In Canada in 1997, the pregnancy rate for teenagers was 42.7 pregnancies for every 1,000 women between the ages of 15 and 19 (Statistics Canada, 2000), which had declined over the previous 3 years. This represents about 42,000 pregnancies. The U.S. rate, although also declining, is about double the Canadian rate. The Canadian pregnancy rate was higher for older adolescents (about 69 per 1,000 women between ages 18 and 19), reflecting their higher likelihood of being sexually active than younger women.

Many pregnant girls are inexperienced: 50 per cent had their first intercourse within the past six months (AGI, 1994; Children's Defense Fund, 1998; Ventura, Mathews, & Curtin, 1999). Some were coerced or sexually abused: About 1 in 5 infants born to unmarried minors are fathered by men at least 5 years older than the mother (AGI, 1999a).

The proportion of adolescents giving birth has fallen although the number of abortions has been constant over the past several years prior to 1997. In that year, the number of teenage pregnancies that were aborted (50.3 per cent) surpassed the number of live births (46.8 per cent). The remaining pregnancies ended in miscarriage (Statistics Canada, 2000).

During the 1990s, teenage pregnancy and birthrates fell to below 1970s levels, reflecting the trends toward decreased sexual activity and, more so, toward increased use of contraceptives. The regions of Canada that had the highest teenage pregnancy rates were the

Checkpoint ✓

Can you . . .

✔ Describe trends in sexual attitudes and activity among adolescents?

✔ Discuss factors in homosexual identity and relationship formation?

✔ Identify and discuss factors that increase the risks of sexual activity?

✔ Identify ways to prevent teenage pregnancy?

Guidepost 4

How common is teenage pregnancy, and what are its usual outcomes?

Box 17-1 *Preventing Teenage Pregnancy*

Teenage pregnancy rates in Canada dropped during the 1990s, and they are lower than in many other industrialized countries, where adolescents begin sexual activity just as early or earlier—half as high as in the United States, and equal to England (Maticka-Tyndale, 2001).

Experts disagree about the causes of teenage pregnancy. Some observers point to such factors as the reduced stigma on unwed motherhood, media glorification of sex, the lack of a clear message that sex and parenthood are for adults, the influence of childhood sexual abuse, and failure of parents to communicate with children. The European experience suggests the importance of two other factors: sex education and access to birth control (AAP Committee on Adolescence, 1999).

Europe's industrialized countries have long provided universal, comprehensive sex education—as has Canada. Canadian programs, following the Canadian Guidelines for Sexual Health Education (Health Canada, 1994), encourage young teenagers to delay intercourse but also aim to improve contraceptive use among adolescents who are sexually active. Such programs include education about sexuality and acquisition of skills for making responsible sexual decisions and communicating with partners. They provide information about risks and consequences of teenage pregnancy, about birth control methods, and about where to get medical and contraceptive help (Health Canada, 1994; McKay & Barrett, 1999; Sieccan [Sex Information and Education Council of Canada], 2000). Programs aimed at adolescent boys emphasize the wisdom of delaying fatherhood and the need to take responsibility when it occurs (Children's Defense Fund, 1998).

Of course, parents are young people's first and often best teachers. Teenagers whose parents have talked with them about sex from an early age, have communicated healthy attitudes, and have been available to answer questions tend to wait longer for sexual activity (J. J. Conger, 1988; Jaslow, 1982). However, many adolescents are uncomfortable talking about sex with parents. Peer counselling can be effective; teenagers often heed peers when they might not pay attention to the same advice from an older person (Jay, DuRant, Shoffitt, Linder, & Litt, 1984).

An important component of pregnancy prevention in European countries is access to reproductive services. Contraceptives are provided free to adolescents in Britain, France, Sweden, and, in many cases, the Netherlands. Sweden showed a fivefold reduction in the teenage birth rate following introduction of birth control education, free access to contraceptives, and free abortion on demand (Bracher & Santow, 1999).

In Canada, although sex education is widely available in public schools, students have complained that not enough information is provided on sexual feelings, alternatives and choices in sexuality, and ways to obtain confidential information and contraception (Maticka-Tyndale, 2001).

The problem of teenage pregnancy requires a multi-faceted solution. It must include programs and policies to encourage postponing or refraining from sexual activity. But it must also recognize that many young people do become sexually active and need education and information to prevent pregnancy and infection (AGI, 1999b). Ultimately, it requires attention to underlying factors that put teenagers and families at risk: reducing poverty, school failure, behavioural and family problems, and expanding employment, skills training, and family life education (AGI, 1994; Children's Defense Fund, 1998; Health Canada, 1994; Kirby, 1997). Programs for preschoolers and elementary school students have shown that comprehensive early intervention can reduce teenage pregnancy (Hawkins, Catalano, Kosterman, Abbott, & Hill, 1999; Schweinhart et al., 1993).

Since adolescents who have high aspirations are less likely to become pregnant, programs that focus on motivating young people to achieve and raising their self-esteem—not merely on the mechanics of contraception—have achieved some success.

What's your view?

If you were designing a school-based or community-based sexuality education program, what would you include? Do you favour programs that provide contraceptives to teenagers?

Check it out!

For more information on this topic, go to **www.mcgrawhill.ca/college/papalia** which provides links to relevant websites concerning teen pregnancy.

northern regions and prairie provinces. In the Northwest Territories (including Nunavut) the rate was 123 pregnancies per 1,000 teenage women, and over 60 per 1,000 in the Yukon and in Manitoba. The highest rates of abortion were in the northern regions and in Ontario, while the lowest rates were in Prince Edward Island and New Brunswick (Statistics Canada, 2000).

Nearly 8 in 10 teenage births in the United States are to unmarried girls (Curtin & Martin, 2000). The rate in Canada is lower than that in the United States. While past teenage pregnancies typically resulted in marriage or putting the child up for adoption, today most pregnant teenagers choose abortion or single parenthood (Daly & Sobol, 1993).

Teenage pregnancies often have poor outcomes. Many of the mothers are impoverished and poorly educated, and risk poor health. Many do not eat properly or do not gain enough weight. Their babies are likely to be premature or dangerously small and are at heightened risk of neonatal death, disability, or health problems (AAP Committee on Adolescence, 1999; AGI, 1999a; Children's Defense Fund, 1998; Maticka-Tyndale, 2001).

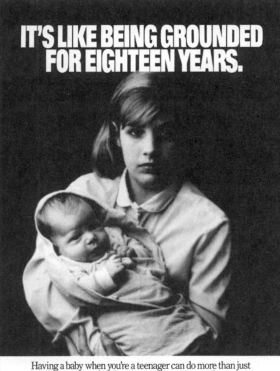

IT'S LIKE BEING GROUNDED
FOR EIGHTEEN YEARS.

Having a baby when you're a teenager can do more than just
take away your freedom, it can take away your dreams.
THE CHILDREN'S DEFENSE FUND

To teenagers, one of the most persuasive arguments against sexual risk-taking is the danger that pregnancy will ruin their lives. Teenage girls respond better when the advice comes from other girls close to their own age.

Checkpoint

Can you . . .

✔ Summarize trends in teenage pregnancy and birthrates?

✔ Discuss problems and outcomes of teenage pregnancy?

Guidepost 5

How typical is "adolescent rebellion"?

adolescent rebellion Pattern of emotional turmoil, characteristic of a minority of adolescents, which may involve conflict with family, alienation from adult society, reckless behaviour, and rejection of adult values

Babies of more affluent teenage mothers are also at risk. Among more than 134,000 U.S. white, largely middle-class girls and women, 13- to 19-year-olds were more likely than 20- to 24-year-olds to have low–birth weight babies, even when the mothers were married and well educated and had adequate prenatal care. Good prenatal care apparently cannot always overcome the biological disadvantage inherent in being born to a still-growing girl whose own body may be competing with the developing fetus for vital nutrients (Fraser et al., 1995).

Teenage unwed mothers and their families are likely to suffer financial hardship. Child support laws are spottily enforced, court-ordered payments are often inadequate, and many young fathers cannot afford them. Adolescent fathers often have poor school records, high dropout rates, and limited financial resources and income potential. Even if they want to be involved in their children's lives, they may not know how (AAP Committee on Adolescence, 1999).

About 7 out of 10 teenage mothers in the United States eventually finish high school (AGI, 1999a) and many obtain employment, but their immaturity and lack of parenting skills can take a toll on their children. During the preschool years, children born to teenage mothers are more likely than children born to older mothers to show cognitive delays, high levels of aggression, and impulsive behaviour. As adolescents, they are more likely to fail in school, to be delinquent, to be incarcerated, to abuse drugs, and to become pregnant (AAP Committee on Adolescence, 1999; Children's Defense Fund, 1998). However, these outcomes are far from universal. A 20-year study of more than 400 teenage mothers in Baltimore found that two-thirds of their daughters did not become teenage mothers themselves, and most graduated from high school (Furstenberg, Levine, & Brooks-Gunn, 1990).

In addition, more recent evidence from Canada shows that although children from single-parent families have difficulties as infants, by the time they begin school, any differences that might have existed in social, emotional, or cognitive development between children of teenage mothers and those of older mothers disappear (Maticka-Tyndale, 2001).

Relationships with Family, Peers, and Adult Society

Age becomes a powerful bonding agent in adolescence. Adolescents spend more time with peers and less with family. However, most teenagers' fundamental values (like David Suzuki's) remain closer to their parents' than is generally realized (Offer & Church, 1991). Even as adolescents turn to peers for companionship and intimacy, they look to parents for a "secure base" from which they can try their wings (Laursen, 1996).

Is Adolescent Rebellion a Myth?

The teenage years have been called a time of **adolescent rebellion,** involving emotional turmoil, conflict within the family, alienation from adult society, reckless behaviour, and rejection of adults' values. Yet school-based research on adolescents the world over suggests that only about 1 in 5 teenagers fits this pattern (Offer & Schonert-Reichl, 1992).

The idea of adolescent rebellion may have been born in the first formal theory of adolescence, that of the psychologist G. Stanley Hall. Hall (1904/1916) believed that young people's efforts to adjust to their changing bodies and to the imminent demands of adulthood usher in a period of "storm and stress," which produces conflict between the generations. Sigmund Freud (1935/1953) and his daughter, Anna Freud (1946), described "storm and stress" as universal and inevitable, growing out of a resurgence of early sexual drives toward the parents.

However, the anthropologist Margaret Mead (1928, 1935; see chapter 2: Focus), who studied adolescence in Samoa and other South Pacific islands, concluded that when a culture provides a gradual, serene transition from childhood to adulthood, "storm and stress" is not typical. Although her research in Samoa was later challenged (Freeman, 1983), her observation was eventually supported by research in 186 pre-industrial societies (Schlegel & Barry, 1991).

Full-fledged rebellion now appears to be uncommon even in industrialized countries, at least among middle-class youngsters who are in school. Only 15 to 25 per cent of families with adolescents report significant conflict, and many of those families had problems before the children reached their teens (W. A. Collins, 1990; J. P. Hill, 1987; Offer, 1969; Offer & Offer, 1974; Offer, Ostrov, & Howard, 1989). Although adolescents may defy parental authority with some regularity, the emotions attending this transition do not normally lead to family conflict of major proportions or to a sharp break with parental or societal standards (Arnett, 1999; Offer & Church, 1991; Offer et al. 1989). Most young people feel close to and positive about their parents, share similar opinions on major issues, and value their parents' approval (J. P. Hill, 1987; King et al., 1999; Offer et al., 1989; Offer, Ostrov, Howard, & Atkinson, 1988).

As Canadian youth get older, their relationships with parents, particularly in trust and expectations, worsens. About half of Grade 10 girls and one-third of Grade 10 boys agree that there are times when they would like to leave home. Most value their parents' opinions of them, but parents' expectations of school performance were felt to be too high by about a third of adolescents in Grade 10. Young people tend to find it easier to communicate with their mothers rather than their fathers. Canadian parents are slightly more distanced from their children than parents in many European countries (King et al., 1999). These results reflect similar ones from a study of "connectedness" between adolescents and their families in British Columbia (CICH, 2000). Feeling that the relationship is close, is caring, and fosters a sense of belonging indicates a high level of connectedness. The highest level of connectedness in young people is reported by 12-year-olds. Connectedness drops off steeply as young people progress through adolescence, until 17 years of age, when only 9 per cent of young people report high levels of connectedness (CICH, 2000). This can have serious consequences, because high levels of connectedness are correlated with low levels of risk behaviours such as early sexual activity, and alcohol and drug abuse.

Recognizing that adolescence may be a difficult time can help parents and teachers put troubling behaviour in perspective. But adults who assume that adolescent turmoil is normal and necessary may fail to heed the signals of the occasional young person who needs special help.

How Adolescents Spend Their Time—and with Whom

Young people who grow up in tribal or peasant societies, who must focus on production of the bare necessities of life, live lives very different from those of adolescents in technologically advanced societies (Larson & Verma, 1999). By comparison even with some societies in Asia, where schoolwork and family obligations are strongly stressed, Canadian, European, and U.S. adolescents have a great deal of discretionary time. As youngsters move through adolescence, much of this time is spent talking and "hanging out" with peers, and increasingly with peers of the other sex (King et al., 1999; Larson & Verma, 1999).

The amount of time spent with families declines dramatically between ages 10 and 18, from 35 per cent to 14 per cent of waking hours (Larson, Richards, Moneta, Holmbeck, & Duckett, 1996). This disengagement is not a rejection of the family, but a response to developmental needs. Early adolescents often retreat to their rooms; they seem to need time alone to step back from the demands of social relationships, regain emotional stability, and reflect on identity issues (Larson, 1997). High schoolers spend more of their free time with peers, with whom they identify and feel comfortable (Larson & Richards, 1991, 1998).

The character of family interactions changes during these years. Adolescents and their parents may spend less time than before watching television together, but just as much—

What's your view ?

- Can you think of values you hold that are different from those of your parents? How did you come to develop these values?

Checkpoint ✓

Can you . . .

✔ Assess the extent of adolescent rebellion and of storm and stress during the teenage years?

and among girls, more—in one-on-one conversations. As adolescents grow older, they increasingly see themselves as taking the lead in these discussions, and their feelings about contact with parents become more positive (Larson et al., 1996).

As adolescents get older, they find it progressively difficult to talk to their parents, with more difficulty communicating with fathers than with mothers. About two-thirds of Grade 10 students find it easy or very easy to talk with their mothers, while 55 per cent of boys, and only 33 per cent of girls, find it easy or very easy to talk with their fathers. Mothers appear to be more approachable than fathers for Canadian adolescents (King et al., 1999). In addition, about half of Grade 10 students feel that their parents understand them, with more boys than girls feeling this way (King et al., 1999).

Ethnic and cultural variations in time use tell us much about how culture affects psychosocial development. Interviews with 377 adolescents in Canada, Belgium, and Italy showed that Italian teenagers tended to maintain closer ties with their families, whereas friends occupied a more central position for Canadian adolescents. Belgian teenagers tended to maintain close ties with both family members and friends (Claes, 1998). It is likely that differences in cultural contexts and practices account for these differences: Parents seem to play a larger role in organizing daily life and behaving in ways that foster closeness in Italy, compared to Canada and Belgium. Despite these differences, there were similarities in relations. Friends emerged as important aspects of the social life of teens in all cultures, and the participants tended to have closer relations with their mothers than with their fathers (Claes, 1998).

With such variations in mind, let's look more closely at relationships with parents, and then with siblings and peers.

Checkpoint ✓

Can you . . .

✔ Identify age and cultural differences in how young people spend their time, and discuss their significance?

Guidepost 6

How do adolescents relate to parents, siblings, and peers?

Adolescents and Parents

Just as adolescents feel tension between dependency on their parents and the need to break away, parents often have mixed feelings, too. They want their children to be independent, yet they find it hard to let go. Parents have to walk a fine line between giving adolescents enough independence and protecting them from immature lapses in judgment. These tensions often lead to family conflict, and parenting styles can influence its shape and outcome. Also, as with younger children, parents' life situation—their work and marital and socio-economic status—affects their relationships with teenage children.

Family Conflict

Much family conflict is over the pace of adolescents' growth toward independence (Arnett, 1999). Arguments between teenagers and their parents often focus on "how much" or "how soon": how much freedom teenagers should have to plan their own activities or how soon they can take the family car. Most arguments concern day-to-day matters—chores, schoolwork, dress, money, curfews, dating, and friends—rather than fundamental values (B. K. Barber, 1994). However, some of these minor issues are proxies for more serious ones, such as substance use, safe driving, and sex. Furthermore, an accumulation of frequent "hassles" can add up to a stressful family atmosphere (Arnett, 1999).

Family conflict is most frequent during early adolescence but most intense in mid-adolescence (Laursen, Coy, & Collins, 1998). By Grade 10, 29 per cent of males and 36 per cent of females in Canada feel that they have a lot of arguments with their parents (King et al., 1999). The frequency of strife in early adolescence may be related to the strains of puberty and the need to assert autonomy. The more highly charged arguments in mid-adolescence and, to a lesser extent, in late adolescence may reflect the emotional strains that occur as adolescents try their wings. The reduced frequency of conflict in late adolescence may signify adjustment to the momentous changes of the teenage years and a renegotiation of the balance of power between parent and child. Or older adolescents may argue less with parents simply because they spend less time with them (Fuligni & Eccles, 1993; Laursen et al., 1998; Molina & Chassin, 1996; Steinberg, 1988). A study of Canadian adolescents showed that the nature of the conflict changes as teenagers develop. Arguments about chores, appearance, and politeness typically decrease between Grades 6 and 8, while conflict over finances increase (Galambos & Almeida, 1992).

Although *subjects* of conflict are similar across ethnic lines, *frequency* of conflict shows ethnic variations. In the United States, white parents report more frequent clashes with teenagers than black or Hispanic parents, who tend to enforce higher behavioural expectations (B. K. Barber, 1994). In African-American families in the rural South, highly religious parents tend to get along better with each other and with their pre-adolescent and early adolescent children (Brody, Stoneman, & Flor, 1996).

Working-class Chinese adolescents in Hong Kong report fewer conflicts with parents than European-American adolescents (Yau & Smetana, 1996), probably because Asian cultures stress control of emotions and expectations for respect, harmony, and obedience. However, by late adolescence Asian-American youngsters experience more family conflict, and their perceptions of their parents' warmth and understanding do not seem to improve as much as in European-American families. By college age, when many European-American young people have already renegotiated their relationships with parents, Asian-American parents and adolescents often are struggling over control of the young person's friends, activities, and private life (Greenberger & Chen, 1996). Conflict in both cultures is more likely with mothers than with fathers (Greenberger & Chen, 1996; Laursen et al., 1998; Steinberg, 1981, 1987), perhaps because most mothers are more closely involved with their children in the day-to-day issues that may excite conflict.

Regardless of ethnicity, the level of family discord seems to hinge primarily on adolescents' personalities and on their parents' treatment of them. These factors may explain why disagreements in some families tend to blow over, whereas in other families they escalate into major confrontations. Dissension is most likely when parents see a teenager as having negative personality characteristics (such as a hot temper, meanness, or anxiety) and a history of problem behaviour, or when parents use coercive discipline (B. K. Barber, 1994). In a U.S. study of 335 two-parent rural midwestern families with teenagers, conflict declined in warm, supportive families during early to middle adolescence but worsened in a hostile, coercive, or critical family atmosphere (Rueter & Conger, 1995).

What's your view ?

• What kinds of issues caused the most conflict in your family when you were a teenager, and how were they resolved? If you lived with both parents, were your conflicts more with one parent than with the other? Did your mother and father handle such issues similarly or differently?

Parenting Styles

Most adolescents (like David Suzuki) "excel in most areas of their lives when they simply feel that they come from a loving home with responsive parents" (Gray & Steinberg, 1999, p. 584). Still, although adolescents are different from younger children, authoritative parenting seems to work best (Baumrind, 1991). Overly strict, authoritarian parenting may be especially counterproductive as children enter adolescence and want to be treated more as adults. When parents do not adjust, an adolescent may reject parental influence and seek peer support and approval at all costs (Fuligni & Eccles, 1993).

Authoritative parents insist on important rules, norms, and values but are willing to listen, explain, and negotiate (Lamborn, Mounts, Steinberg, & Dornbusch, 1991). They exercise appropriate control over a child's conduct but not the child's sense of self (Steinberg & Darling, 1994). Parents who show disappointment in teenagers' misbehaviour are more effective in motivating them to behave responsibly than parents who punish them harshly (Krevans & Gibbs, 1996).

Authoritative parenting may bolster an adolescent's self-image. A questionnaire survey of 8,700 students in Grades 9 to 12 in Wisconsin and California concluded that "the more involvement, autonomy granting, and structure that adolescents perceive from their parents, the more positively teens evaluate their own general conduct, psychosocial development, and mental health" (Gray & Steinberg, 1999, p. 584). When adolescents thought their parents were trying to dominate their psychological experience, their emotional health suffered more than when parents tried to control their behaviour.

At the same time, teens whose parents were strict in enforcing behavioural rules had fewer behaviour problems (susceptibility to peer pressure and deviant

The warmth and acceptance this mother shows to her son are characteristic of an authoritative parenting style. Authoritative parents set reasonable rules about, for example, what time a child must come home, but are willing to listen to and respect the child's point of view. Authoritative parenting may be especially effective as children enter adolescence and want to be treated more like adults.

or anti-social behaviour, such as drug use) than those with more lenient parents. Adolescents with strict parents tended to develop self-control, self-discipline, and good study and personal habits; those whose parents gave them psychological autonomy tended to become self-confident and competent in both academic and social realms. They wanted to achieve and believed they could do what they set out to do.

Family Structure and Mothers' Employment

Many adolescents today live in families that are very different from families of a few decades ago. Many mothers are single; some are remarried. Many work outside the home. How do these family situations affect adolescents?

Contrary to some research, which found a greater tendency toward risky behaviour in adolescents in non-traditional homes (R. A. Johnson et al., 1996), divorce and single parenting do not necessarily produce problem adolescents. A review of the literature (B. L. Barber & Eccles, 1992) suggests that the detrimental effects of single-parent living have been overstated. By adolescence, differences in school achievement, self-esteem, and attitudes toward gender roles among children in such families may be minor or non-existent when other factors, such as socio-economic status and parental conflict, are held constant. In other words, it is the atmosphere in the home that makes the difference. As in any family, parental support may be more important than family structure (Landing and Tam, 1998).

The impact of a mother's work outside the home may depend on whether there are two parents or only one in the household. Often a single mother must work to stave off economic disaster; how her working affects her teenage children may hinge on how much time and energy she has left over to spend with them, how well she keeps track of their whereabouts, and what kind of role model she provides (B. L. Barber & Eccles, 1992).

Without close, consistent supervision, adolescents are more susceptible to peer pressure. High school students who are unsupervised after school tend to smoke, drink, use marijuana, or engage in other risky behaviour; to be depressed; and to have low grades. However, as long as parents know where their son or daughter is, their physical absence does not significantly increase the risk of problems (Richardson, Radziszewska, Dent, & Flay, 1993).

Studies of Canadian families show that when parents feel overworked, parent–child conflict tends to rise. Mothers who feel overloaded tend to become less caring and accepting, and their children often show behaviour problems (Galambos, Sears, Almeida, & Kolaric, 1995). When mothers are stressed, tensions between adolescents and fathers increase as well (Almeida & McDonald, 1998).

A mother's work status helps shape adolescents' attitudes toward women's roles (Galambos, Petersen, & Lenerz, 1988). In a study of adolescents' attitudes towards work, 14-year-olds in dual-earner families tended to have higher levels of respect towards their mothers' and fathers' work, when the work was seen as resulting in less strain and depersonalization along with more satisfaction for the parents (Galambos & Sears, 1998). Teenage sons of working mothers tend to have more flexible attitudes toward gender roles when they have warm relationships with their mothers, and teenage daughters show non-stereotypical attitudes when their mothers are happy with their dual roles (Galambos et al., 1988). Surprisingly, some of the strongest gender-typing occurs in families with full-time employed mothers. Gender divisions may be more egalitarian during the week, when everyone is occupied with work or school. On weekends, however, girls—like their mothers—do a larger share of the housework and of care of younger siblings (Crouter & Maguire, 1998).

Economic Stress

A major problem in many single-parent families is lack of money. Poverty can complicate family relationships—and also harm adolescents' development—through its impact on parents' emotional state (refer back to chapter 14).

Unemployed mothers, especially those without outside help and support, tend to become depressed; and depressed mothers tend to perceive their maternal role negatively and punish their children harshly. Young people who see their relationships with their mothers deteriorate tend to become depressed themselves and to have trouble in school (McLoyd, Jayaratne, Ceballo, & Borquez, 1994).

Of course, economic stress strikes two-parent families as well. Among 378 intact white families in an economically declining area of rural Iowa, parental depression and marital conflict worsened financial conflicts between parents and adolescents. Parents who fought with each other and with their children over money tended to be hostile and coercive, increasing the risk of teenage behaviour problems (R. C. Conger et al., 1994).

Many adolescents in economically distressed families benefit from accumulated social capital (refer back to chapter 16)—the support of kin and community. In 51 poor, urban African-American families in which teenagers were living with their mothers, grandmothers, or aunts, women who had strong kinship networks tended to be psychologically healthy, and so were the youngsters. The more social support the women received, the greater their self-esteem and acceptance of their children. Women with stronger support exercised firmer control and closer monitoring while granting appropriate autonomy, and their teenage charges were more self-reliant and had fewer behaviour problems (R. D. Taylor & Roberts, 1995).

Adolescents and Siblings

As adolescents begin to separate from their families and spend more time with peers, they have less time and less need for the emotional gratification they used to get from the sibling bond. Adolescents are less close to siblings than to either parents or friends, are less influenced by them, and become even more distant as they move through adolescence (Laursen, 1996).

Changes in sibling relationships may well precede similar changes in the relationship between adolescents and parents: more independence on the part of the younger person and less authority exerted by the older person. As children reach high school, their relationships with their siblings become progressively equal. Older siblings exercise less power over younger ones and fight with them less (Buhrmester & Furman, 1990). Adolescents still show intimacy, affection, and admiration for their brothers and sisters (Raffaelli & Larson, 1987), but their relationships are less intense (Buhrmester & Furman, 1990).

These changes seem to be fairly complete by the time the younger sibling is about 12 years old (Buhrmester & Furman, 1990). By this time, the younger child no longer needs as much supervision, and differences in competence and independence between older and younger siblings are shrinking. (A 6-year-old is vastly more competent than a 3-year-old, but a 15-year-old and a 12-year-old are more nearly equal.)

Older and younger siblings tend to have different feelings about their changing relationship. As the younger sibling grows, the older one has to give up some of his or her accustomed power and status and may look on a newly assertive younger brother or sister as a pesky annoyance. On the other hand, younger siblings still tend to look up to older ones and try to feel more "grown up" by identifying with and emulating them (Buhrmester & Furman, 1990). Even by age 17, younger siblings are more likely to get advice about plans and problems from older siblings, to be influenced by them, and to be satisfied with the support they receive from them than the other way around (Tucker, Barber, & Eccles, 1997).

Peers and Friends

An important source of emotional support during the complex transition of adolescence, as well as a source of pressure for behaviour that parents may deplore, is a young person's growing involvement with peers.

Adolescents going through rapid physical changes take comfort from being with others going through like changes. Teenagers challenging adult standards and parental authority find it reassuring to turn for advice to friends who are in the same position themselves. Adolescents questioning their parents' adequacy as

Checkpoint ✔

Can you . . .

✔ Identify factors that affect conflict with parents?

✔ Discuss the impact on adolescents of parenting styles and of marital status, mothers' employment, and socio-economic status?

What's your view ?

• If you have one or more brothers or sisters, did your relationships with them change during adolescence?

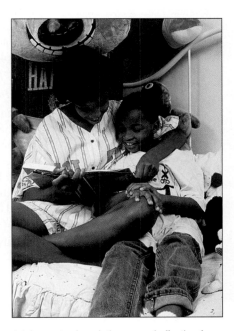

Adolescents show intimacy and affection for younger siblings, even though they spend less time together than before. Although differences in power and status lessen, younger siblings still look up to older ones.

models of behaviour, but not yet sure enough of themselves to stand alone, look to peers to show them what's "in" and what's "out." The peer group is a source of affection, sympathy, understanding, and moral guidance; a place for experimentation; and a setting for achieving autonomy and independence from parents. It is a place to form intimate relationships that serve as "rehearsals" for adult intimacy (Buhrmester, 1996; Gecas & Seff, 1990; Laursen, 1996).

Popularity

In sociometric studies, children are generally asked to name the classmates they like most and those they like least. Such studies have identified five *peer status groups: popular* (youngsters who receive many positive nominations), *rejected* (those who receive many negative nominations), *neglected* (those who receive few nominations of either kind), *controversial* (those who receive many positive and many negative nominations), and *average* (those who do not receive an unusual number of nominations of either kind).

A study of 1,903 preteens and teenagers (ages 10 to 16) in northern Greece used this technique along with teacher ratings and self-ratings (Hatzichristou & Hopf, 1996). The young people were also asked to name two classmates who best fit certain behavioural descriptions (for example, "quarrels often with other students," "liked by everybody and helps everybody," or "gets into trouble with the teacher"). By combining and comparing evaluations, the researchers filled out a portrait of rejected, neglected, and controversial adolescents.

The *rejected* group had the greatest adjustment problems. They also had academic difficulties and low achievement test scores. Rejected boys, particularly younger ones, tended to be aggressive and anti-social; rejected girls (and older boys) were more likely to be shy, isolated, and unhappy, and to have a negative self-image.

The *neglected* group—which, by high school age, included more boys than girls—were less pro-social and had more learning difficulties than average, which contributed to a poor self-image. The transitions from elementary to junior high school and from junior high to high school seem to be particularly hard for both the rejected and neglected groups.

The *controversial* group were viewed one way by teachers and another way by peers. Perhaps because this group tended to do well in school, teachers did not see them as having behavioural problems. Peers, on the other hand, saw the boys as aggressive and anti-social—but also as leaders, perhaps because peers expect and accept aggressiveness in boys. Particularly in elementary school, peers often rated the girls in this category as snobbish and arrogant, perhaps reflecting girls' tendency to form cliques at this age. By high school, these girls were better liked than before and also were seen as leaders.

Friendships

Friendships are fundamentally different from family relationships. They are more egalitarian than relationships with parents or siblings. Friendships are based on choice and commitment. By the same token, they are more unstable than family relationships. Awareness of the distinctive character of friendships, and of what it takes to maintain them, emerges in adolescence. Adolescents quarrel less angrily and resolve conflicts more equitably with friends than with family members, perhaps because they realize that too much conflict could cost them a friendship (Laursen, 1996).

Adolescents, like younger children, tend to choose friends who are like them, and friends influence each other to become even more alike (Berndt, 1982; Berndt & Perry, 1990). Friends are not necessarily of the same race: A study of inter-ethnic friendships of young adolescents in Toronto showed that most friends of students belong to other ethnic groups (Smith & Schneider, 2000). Although East-Asian students rated their same-ethnicity friendships as being of higher quality than their friendships with members of other ethnic groups, students of European, West-Indian, and East-Indian backgrounds indicated no differences in ratings of quality of friendships with members of different ethnic backgrounds. Friends do tend to have similar academic attitudes and performance and, especially, similar levels of drug use (Hamm, 2000) and to have similar status within the peer group (Berndt & Perry, 1990).

What's your view

- On the basis of the specific characteristics of rejected and neglected children, what do you think can be done to help such children?

The intensity and importance of friendships, as well as time spent with friends, are probably greater in adolescence than at any other time in life. Friendships become more reciprocal. Early adolescents begin to rely more on friends than on parents for intimacy and support, and they share confidences more than younger friends do (King et al., 1999). A stress on intimacy, loyalty, and sharing marks a transition to adultlike friendships (Berndt & Perry, 1990; Buhrmester, 1990, 1996; Hartup & Stevens, 1999; Laursen, 1996). Intimacy with same-sex friends increases during early to mid-adolescence, after which it typically declines as intimacy with the other sex grows (Laursen, 1996).

The increased intimacy of adolescent friendship reflects cognitive, as well as emotional, development. Adolescents are now better able to express their private thoughts and feelings. They can also more readily consider another person's point of view, and so it is easier for them to understand a friend's thoughts and feelings. Increased intimacy also reflects early adolescents' concern with getting to know themselves. Confiding in a friend helps young people explore their own feelings, define their identity, and validate their self-worth. Friendship provides a safe place to venture opinions, admit weaknesses, and get help with problems (Buhrmester, 1996).

The capacity for intimacy is related to psychological adjustment and social competence. Adolescents who have close, stable, supportive friendships generally have a high opinion of themselves, do well in school, are sociable, and are unlikely to be hostile, anxious, or depressed (Berndt & Perry, 1990; Buhrmester, 1990; Hartup & Stevens, 1999). A bi-directional process seems to be at work: Good friendships foster adjustment, which in turn fosters good friendships.

Friendship in adolescence requires an array of social skills. Because friends do more talking, they need to be able to start and sustain conversations. They need to know how to seek out friends, call them up, and make plans; how to handle conflicts and disagreements; how and when to share confidences; and how and when to offer emotional support. Friendships help adolescents develop these skills by offering opportunities to use them and to get feedback on their effectiveness (Buhrmester, 1996).

Sharing confidences and emotional support seem to be more vital to female friendships than to male friendships now and throughout life. Boys' friendships focus less on conversation than on shared activity, usually sports and competitive games (Blyth & Foster-Clark, 1987; Buhrmester, 1996; Bukowski & Kramer, 1986). Girls feel better after telling a friend about an upsetting experience than boys do; boys may express support by just spending time doing things together (Denton & Zarbatany, 1996). Boys tend to gain self-esteem from competition with friends, girls from helping them. However, both boys and girls rate their friendships with girls as more positive than their friendships with boys (Smith & Schneider, 2000). Loneliness is a common experience in adolescence, particularly in the absence of intimate friendships. There seem to be cultural differences in how loneliness is experienced by adolescents. In a survey of how adolescents experience loneliness, differences were found in comparisons between 100 Canadian and 206 Portuguese teenagers. In response to questions on experiences of loneliness, Canadian youth report more extreme feelings of emotional distress, social inadequacy and alienation, and interpersonal isolation than Portuguese youth (Rokach & Neto, 2001). These differences may reflect differences in how the individual and community interact in the two cultures. In Portuguese society the community provides support and a sense of belonging for the individual, whereas Canadian society emphasizes individual resources in finding support and a sense of belonging, with loneliness perceived as an example of individual failure (Rokach et al., 2001).

Anti-social Behaviour and Juvenile Delinquency

What influences young people to engage in—or refrain from—violence (see Box 17-2) or other anti-social acts? What determines whether or not a juvenile delinquent will grow up to be a hardened criminal?

As we examine the roots of delinquency, we need to keep in mind an important distinction. Some adolescents occasionally commit an anti-social act. A smaller group of chronic (repeat) offenders habitually commit a variety of serious anti-social acts, such as stealing, setting fires, breaking into houses or cars, destroying property, committing acts of

Checkpoint ✔

Can you . . .

✔ Describe typical changes in sibling relationships during adolescence?

✔ Describe characteristics that affect adolescents' popularity?

✔ Discuss important features of adolescent friendships?

Guidepost 7

What are the root causes of antisocial behaviour and juvenile delinquency, and what can be done to reduce these and other risks of adolescence?

On April 20, 1999, 18-year-old Eric Harris and 17-year-old Dylan Klebold entered Columbine High School in Littleton, Colorado, wearing black trench coats and carrying a rifle, a semi-automatic pistol, two sawed-off shotguns, and more than 30 homemade bombs. Laughing and taunting, they began spraying bullets at fellow students, killing 12 classmates and one teacher before fatally shooting themselves.

The massacre in Littleton was one of a string of incidents that add up to what has been called an epidemic of youth violence. Eight days after the Columbine massacre, a 14-year-old former student at W. R. Myers High School in Taber, Alberta, entered the school with a sawed-off rifle hidden under a parka, killing one student and seriously wounding another. The former student was a victim of bullying and was unpopular with his schoolmates. Victims of bullying in Canada have taken their own lives, as was the case of Hamed Sastoh, in Surrey, B.C., in March 2000, and Dawn-Marie Wesley, in Mission, B.C., in November 2000. Both were 14 years old, and both left suicide notes referring to their despair at being victims of bullying.

Psychologists point to potential warning signs that might avert future tragedies. Adolescents who are likely to commit violence often refuse to listen to authority figures, such as parents and teachers; ignore the feelings and rights of others; mistreat people; rely on violence or threatened violence to solve problems; and believe that life has treated them unfairly. They often look older than their peers. They tend to do poorly in school; cut classes or play truant; be held back or suspended or drop out; use alcohol, inhalants, and/or drugs; join gangs; and fight, steal, or destroy property (Resnick et al., 1997). Harris and Klebold showed some of these characteristics.

In three out of four assaults or murders by young people, the perpetrators are members of gangs (American Psychological Association, undated). The brutal murder of Reena Virk, in Victoria, B.C., on November 14, 1997, is a horrific example of the brutality of gang violence, in which six teenage girls and a teenage boy beat their victim unconscious and left her to drown. For many adolescents, gangs satisfy unfulfilled needs for identity, connection, and a sense of power and control. For youngsters who lack positive family relationships, a gang can become a substitute family. Gangs promote a sense of "us-versus-them"; violence against outsiders is accompanied by bonds of loyalty and support within the gang (Staub, 1996).

Teenage violence and anti-social behaviour have roots in childhood. Kindergarten girls in Montreal who showed patterns of highly disruptive behaviours during childhood had a higher likelihood of being diagnosed with conduct disorder as adolescents than those who showed little evidence of disruptive behaviours in childhood (Coté, Zoccolillo, Tremblay, Nagin, & Vitaro, 2001). Although fewer girls than boys report engaging in violent acts, as found in a survey of 962 Calgary high school students (Paetsch & Bertrand, 1999), the characteristics of female perpetrators of violence may be different from those of males. Case studies of six female offenders showed that they had negative opinions of themselves, had life experiences in which women were devalued, and in which violence was considered justified because victims provoke the assailants, particularly in cases of victims perceived to be threatening assailants' relationships with males (Artz, 1998). Children raised in a rejecting or coercive atmosphere, or in an overly permissive or chaotic one, tend to show aggressive behaviour; and the hostility they evoke in others increases their own aggression. Their negative self-image prevents them from succeeding at school or developing other constructive interests, and they generally associate with peers who reinforce their anti-social attitudes and behaviour (Staub, 1996). Young people who are impulsive or fearless, or who have low IQs or learning difficulties, also may be violence-prone. Boys in poor, unstable neighbourhoods are most likely to become involved in violence—one reason that the incident at Taber, in a middle-class suburban school, was so shocking (American Psychological Association, undated).

Of course, not all youngsters who grow up in difficult circumstances become violent. Factors that contribute to resilience (refer back to chapter 14) include positive role models; a close, trusting bond with a parent or other adult; supportive relationships with teachers and peers; development of self-esteem and self-efficacy; strong social skills; ability to take refuge in hobbies, work, or creative pursuits; and a sense of control over one's life (American Psychological Association, undated; Jenkins & Keating, 1998).

Adolescents are more likely to turn violent if they have witnessed or have been victims of violence, such as physical abuse or neighbourhood fights. Heavy exposure to media violence has a significant impact by desensitizing viewers to violence and depicting situations in which aggression is rewarded or justified (American Psychological Association, undated; Strasburger & Donnerstein, 1999; refer back to chapter 14). One in 5 rock music videos portrays overt violence, and 1 in 4 shows weapon carrying (DuRant et al., 1997). The media's contribution to real-life violence has been estimated at 5 to 15 per cent (Strasburger & Donnerstein, 1999).

Fortunately, despite occasional widely publicized tragedies such as the ones in Littleton and Taber, there are signs that the epidemic of youth violence is abating. Incidents of self-reported physical fighting and injury are dropping (Brener, Simon, Krug, & Lowry, 1999). Recent statistics show that youth crime in general, and youth violence in particular, is decreasing in Canada (The John Howard Society of Newfoundland, 1998).

Successful preventive programs have given parents help in reducing the stress of child raising (American Psychological Association, undated) and training in socialization skills. Cooperative learning practices in schools and multicultural education can create a sense of community and reduce the us-versus-them mentality. Giving young people substantial responsibilities and the opportunity to participate in making rules can help them understand how the individual's behaviour affects the group (Staub, 1996). There is evidence that social-skills training for young offenders in Canada may reduce the likelihood of repeated violent behaviour (Cunliffe, 1992).

Suggestions for parents include: limiting and monitoring television viewing; encouraging participation in sports and other supervised after-school activities; using non-physical methods of discipline, such as grounding; storing firearms unloaded and locked; and teaching young people to stand up against violence when they see it (American Psychological Association and AAP, 1996).

What's your view ?

How can the epidemic of youth violence best be stopped?

Check it out !

For more information and links to relevant websites on this topic, go to **www.mcgrawhill.ca/college/papalia**.

cruelty, fighting frequently, and rape. Chronic offenders are responsible for most juvenile crime and are most likely to continue their criminal activity in adulthood (Yoshikawa, 1994). Adolescents who were aggressive or got in trouble when they were younger—lying, being truant, stealing, or doing poorly in school—are more likely than other youngsters to become chronic delinquents (Loeber & Dishion, 1983; Yoshikawa, 1994).

How do "problem behaviours" escalate into chronic delinquency? Early and continuing patterns of parent–child interaction pave the way for negative peer influence, which reinforces and promotes anti-social behaviour.

Becoming a Delinquent: How Parental and Peer Influences Interact

Parents often worry about a teenager's "falling in with the wrong crowd"; but actually, parental upbringing influences the choice of peer groups and friends. Young people gravitate to others brought up like themselves, who are similar in school achievement, adjustment, and pro-social or anti-social tendencies (Collins et al., 2000; B. B. Brown, Mounts, Lamborn, & Steinberg, 1993).

Young people with anti-social tendencies tend to gravitate to others like themselves and reinforce each other's anti-social behaviour.

Parents of chronic delinquents often failed to reinforce good behaviour in early childhood and were harsh or inconsistent, or both, in punishing misbehaviour. Through the years, these parents have not been closely and positively involved in their children's lives (G. R. Patterson, DeBaryshe, & Ramsey, 1989). The children may get payoffs for anti-social behaviour: When they act up, they may gain attention or get their own way.

In the early years, parents begin to shape pro-social or anti-social behaviour by whether they meet children's basic emotional needs (Krevans & Gibbs, 1996; Staub, 1996). Children with behaviour problems tend to do poorly in school and do not get along with well-behaved classmates. Unpopular and low-achieving children and adolescents gravitate toward each other and egg each another on to further misconduct (G. R. Patterson, Reid, & Dishion, 1992).

Ineffective parenting tends to continue in adolescence. Anti-social behaviour at this age is closely related to parents' leniency, poor maternal communication and problem-solving skills, and failure to keep track of their children's activities (Klein, Forehand, Armistead, & Long, 1997; G. R. Patterson & Stouthamer-Loeber, 1984).

As in childhood, anti-social adolescents tend to have anti-social friends, and their anti-social behaviour increases when they associate with each other (Dishion, McCord, & Poulin, 1999; Hartup & Stevens, 1999). A young person with moderately deviant tendencies can be pushed further in that direction by associating with deviant peers (Vitaro, Tremblay, Kerr, Pagani, & Bukowski, 1997). The way anti-social teenagers talk among themselves constitutes a sort of "deviancy training." By laughing, nodding, or otherwise showing approval of talk about rule breaking, they reinforce each other in anti-social behaviour; youngsters without anti-social tendencies ignore such talk. When researchers videotaped 25-minute discussions among 206 thirteen- and fourteen-year-old Oregon boys and their friends, conversations showing deviancy training predicted an increased probability of delinquency, drug use, and violent behaviour at 15 and 16 (Dishion et al., 1999).

Authoritative parenting can help young people internalize standards that may insulate them against negative peer influences and open them to positive ones (Collins et al., 2000). In a study of 500 students in Grades 9 through 11, students whose close friends were drug users were less likely to increase their own self-reported drug use if they saw their parents as highly authoritative (Mounts & Steinberg, 1995).

Long-term Prospects

Few juvenile delinquents become adult criminals; many who are not hard-core offenders simply outgrow their behaviour (L. W. Shannon, 1982). Delinquency peaks at about age 15 and then declines, unlike alcohol use and sexual activity, which become more prevalent with age (refer back to Figure 15-1). Since alcohol and sexual activity are accepted parts of adult life, it is not surprising that as teenagers grow older they increasingly want to engage in them (Petersen, 1993). Anti-social behaviour that is not accepted in adulthood may diminish as most adolescents and their families come to terms with young people's need to assert independence.

Middle- and high-income adolescents may experiment with problem behaviours and then drop them, but low-income teenagers who do not see positive alternatives are more likely to adopt a permanently anti-social lifestyle (Elliott, 1993). A youth who sees that the only rich people in the neighbourhood are drug dealers may be seduced into a life of crime.

Preventing and Treating Delinquency

Since juvenile delinquency has roots early in childhood, so must preventive efforts. Young people who suffer from poor parenting are at less risk if their parents get community support. Effective programs attack the multiple risk factors that can lead to delinquency (National Crime Prevention Council, 1997; Yoshikawa, 1994; Zigler, Taussig, & Black, 1992).

Adolescents who took part in certain early childhood intervention programs were less likely to get in trouble (Yoshikawa, 1994; Zigler et al., 1992). Programs that have achieved impressive long-term results in preventing anti-social behaviour and delinquency include the Perry Preschool Project (refer back to chapter 10), the Syracuse Family Development Research Project, the Yale Child Welfare Project, and the Houston Parent Child Development Center. Each of these programs targeted high-risk urban children and lasted at least 2 years during the child's first 5 years of life. All influenced children directly, through high-quality daycare or education, and at the same time indirectly, by offering families assistance and support geared to their needs (Berrueta-Clement et al., 1985; Berrueta-Clement, Schweinhart, Barnett, & Weikart, 1987; Schweinhart et al., 1993; Seitz, 1990; Yoshikawa, 1994; Zigler et al., 1992).

These programs operated on Bronfenbrenner's mesosystem (refer back to chapter 2) by affecting interactions between the home and the school or child-care centre. The programs also went one step further to the exosystem, by creating supportive parent networks and linking parents with community services, including prenatal and postnatal health care and educational and vocational counselling (Yoshikawa, 1994; Zigler et al., 1992). Through their multi-pronged approach, these interventions had an impact on several early risk factors for delinquency.

Interventions need to target older students as well. In addition to spotting characteristics of troubled adolescents, it is important to find ways to reduce young people's exposure to high-risk settings that encourage anti-social behaviour. One way is to monitor adolescents' activities, especially after school, on weekend evenings, and in summer, when they are most likely to be idle and get into trouble. As David Suzuki's experience shows, getting teenagers involved in constructive activities like camping during their free time can pay long-range dividends (Larson, 1998). Participation in extracurricular school activities tends to cut down on dropout and criminal arrest rates among high-risk boys and girls (Mahoney, 2000).

Delinquent and pre-delinquent teenagers tend to be "stuck" in Kohlberg's stage 2: Like preschoolers, they are deterred from misconduct only by the threat of punishment and fear of getting caught. By moving to stage 3, where they are more concerned with meeting social norms and expectations, they may develop a "cognitive buffer" against temptation (Gibbs, Arnold, Ahlborn, & Cheesman, 1984). This may happen through interaction with a partner who is of higher peer status and at a higher level of moral reasoning—as was found when 40 institutionalized young male offenders were paired off with peers for face-to-face discussion of moral issues (Taylor & Walker, 1997).) Thus peer interaction can stimulate moral growth—if the peer climate is positive and does not offer opportunities for deviancy training (Dishion et al., 1999).

One multi-faceted intervention, called Equipping Youth to Help One Another (EQUIP), uses daily, adult-guided mutual peer support groups to teach each other how to manage anger, make moral decisions, and learn social skills (Gibbs, Potter, Barriga, & Liau, 1996; Gibbs, Potter, Goldstein, & Brendtro, 1998). Among 57 male juvenile offenders in a medium-security correctional facility, EQUIP participants improved significantly in conduct within the institution and had lower repeat offence rates during the first year after release than control groups that did not have the training (Leeman, Gibbs, & Fuller, 1993).

Another program, developed in Edmonton, called the High Risk Recognition Program, aims to reduce the likelihood of repetition of delinquent behaviours by adolescents (Howell & Enns, 1995). The program is based on the notion that risk factors, like social pressure, feelings of retaliation or revenge, self-gratification or pleasure seeking, lead to reoffending. Teaching young offenders about those risk factors, showing them how to monitor their daily activities for the presence of the risk factors, and helping them to develop coping strategies for those factors, equips young offenders to avoid repeating delinquent behaviours.

Fortunately, the great majority of adolescents do not get into serious trouble. Those who do show disturbed behaviour can—and should—be helped. With love, guidance, and support, adolescents can avoid risks, build on their strengths, and explore their possibilities as they approach adult life.

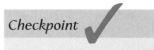

Checkpoint

Can you . . .

✔ Explain why parental and peer influences on anti-social behaviour interact to promote delinquency?

✔ Give examples of programs that have been successful in preventing or stopping delinquency and other risky behaviour?

Is There a "Universal Adolescent"?

How much does the psychosocial world of adolescence vary in cultures as diverse as those of Australia and Bangladesh? Is the communication revolution making the world a "global village" and breaking down cultural differences among the young people who inhabit it?

To answer questions like these, Daniel Offer and his colleagues (Offer et al., 1988) administered the Offer Self-Image Questionnaire to 5,938 adolescents in 10 countries: Australia, Bangladesh, Hungary, Israel, Italy, Japan, Taiwan, Turkey, the United States, and West Germany. The young people answered questions about five aspects of themselves: (1) the *psychological self:* impulse control, fluctuations in mood and emotions, and feelings about their bodies, (2) the *social self:* peer relations, moral attitudes, and educational and vocational goals, (3) the *sexual self:* attitudes toward sexuality and sexual behaviour, (4) the *familial self:* feelings about parents and the atmosphere in the home, and (5) the *coping self:* ability to deal with the world.

The researchers found cross-cultural commonalities in each of the five "selves," particularly familial, social, and coping. About 9 out of 10 adolescents in each country had positive feelings toward their parents, valued work and friendship, and tried to learn from failure. There was less consistency in the psychological and sexual areas; here socio-economic circumstances and local customs were more crucial. In general, however, these "universal adolescents" described themselves as happy; felt able to cope with life, make decisions, and use self-control; cared about others and liked being with and learning from them; enjoyed a job well done; were confident about their sexuality; did not harbour grudges against their parents; saw their mothers and fathers as getting along well most of the time; and expected to be able to take responsibility for themselves as they grew older. All in all, the researchers judged at least 73 per cent of the total sample to have "a healthy adolescent self-image" (p. 124).

In each country, teenagers showed characteristic strengths and weaknesses; in no country were adolescents better or worse adjusted in all respects. In Bangladesh, one of the world's poorest countries, even middle-class teenagers were low in impulse control; felt lonely, sad, and vulnerable; and had a poor body image. They also reported the most problems with peers and the highest rate of depression (48 per cent). In Taiwan, where traditional sexual taboos still operate, large numbers of young people seemed to be afraid of sex or inhibited about it. On the other hand, Bengali and Taiwanese youths seemed superior in their enjoyment of solving difficult problems and in their willingness to find out how to deal with new situations. The lower a country's economic output and the higher the proportion of adolescents who had to compete for places in school and for jobs, the less positive were the teenagers' emotional tone and peer relationships.

Guidepost 8

How does adolescence vary across cultures, and what are some common psychosocial features of the period?

These Israeli adolescents, growing up in a small nation wracked by internal tensions and surrounded by hostile neighbours, have had experiences very different from those of teenagers in Canada. Yet Daniel Offer and his colleagues found underlying similarities in self-image among adolescents in these and other countries the world over.

Some consistent age and gender differences emerged across cultures. Older adolescents were less self-conscious than younger ones, more willing to learn from others, and better able to take criticism without resentment. Older adolescents were also more comfortable with their sexuality and more realistic in their view of family relationships.

Boys felt surer of themselves than girls, less afraid of competition, more in control of their emotions, prouder of their bodies, and more interested in sex. Girls were more empathic, caring, and socially responsible, and more committed to work and study. Similarly, in questionnaires completed by 154 high school boys and 119 high school girls in Turkey, the boys tended to evaluate themselves in physical attributes and cognitive abilities, whereas girls stressed altruism and social and communication skills (Yildirim, 1997).

Offer and his colleagues attributed the "surprising unity of adolescent experience" across cultures largely to the media, which give young people a "collective consciousness" of what is going on in one another's lives all over the world (Offer et al., 1988, p. 114). Through the eye of television, adolescents see themselves as part of a world culture. Today that role is being taken over by the Internet.

We need to be careful about drawing overly broad generalizations from these findings. The samples included only young people in school, mostly urban or suburban and middle class. Also, some of the questionnaire items may have taken on different meanings in translation. Nevertheless, this research draws a fascinating picture of the universal and not-so-universal aspects of adolescence.

The normal developmental changes in the early years of life are obvious and dramatic signs of growth. The infant lying in the crib becomes an active, exploring toddler. The young child enters and embraces the worlds of school and society. The adolescent, with a new body and new awareness, prepares to step into adulthood.

Growth and development do not screech to a stop after adolescence. People change in many ways throughout adulthood. Human beings continue to shape their own development, as they have been doing since birth. What occurs in a child's world is significant, but it is not the whole story. We each continue to write our own story of human development for as long as we live.

Checkpoint ✔

Can you . . .

✔ Identify cross-cultural commonalities and differences in adolescents' self-image, attitudes, and personalities?

Summary and Key Terms

The Search for Identity

Guidepost 1 How do adolescents form an identity?

- A central concern during adolescence is the search for identity, which has occupational, sexual, and values components. Erik Erikson described the psychosocial crisis of adolescence as the conflict of identity versus identity confusion. The "virtue" that should arise from this crisis is *fidelity*.

- James Marcia, in research based on Erikson's theory, described four identity statuses with differing combinations of crisis and commitment: identity achievement, foreclosure, moratorium, and identity diffusion.

- Researchers differ on whether girls and boys take different paths to identity formation. Although some research suggests that girls' self-esteem tends to fall at adolescence, later research does not support that finding.

- Ethnicity is an important part of identity. Minority adolescents seem to go through stages of ethnic identity development much like Marcia's identity statuses.

- According to David Elkind, healthy, stable identity development is achieved by a slow process of differentiation and integration. Today many young people instead develop a "patchwork self," highly vulnerable to stress and outside influence.

identity versus identity confusion (431)
identity statuses (432)   crisis (432)   commitment (432)
identity achievement (433)   foreclosure (434)   moratorium (434)
identity diffusion (434)   patchwork self (437)

Sexuality

Guidepost 2 What determines sexual orientation?

- Sexual orientation appears to be influenced by an interaction of biological and environmental factors and may be at least partly genetic.

sexual orientation (437)

Guidepost 3 What sexual practices are common among adolescents, and what leads some to engage in risky sexual behaviour?

- Sexual behaviours are more liberal than in the past. Teenage sexual activity involves risks of pregnancy and sexually transmitted disease. Adolescents at greatest risk are those who begin sexual activity early, have multiple partners, do not use contraceptives, and are ill-informed about sex.

- The course of gay and lesbian identity and relationship development may vary with cohort, gender, and ethnicity.

Guidepost 4 How common is teenage pregnancy, and what are its usual outcomes?

- Teenage pregnancy and birthrates in Canada have declined. Most of these births are to unmarried mothers.
- Teenage pregnancy and child-bearing often have negative outcomes. Teenage mothers and their families tend to suffer ill health and financial hardship, and the children often suffer from ineffective parenting.

Relationships with Family, Peers, and Adult Society

Guidepost 5 How typical is "adolescent rebellion"?

- Although relationships between adolescents and their parents are not always smooth, full-scale adolescent rebellion is unusual.

  adolescent rebellion (444)

Guidepost 6 How do adolescents relate to parents, siblings, and peers?

- Adolescents spend an increasing amount of time with peers, but relationships with parents continue to be close and influential.
- Conflict with parents tends to be most frequent during early adolescence and most intense during middle adolescence. Authoritative parenting is associated with the most positive outcomes.

- Effects of divorce and single parenting on adolescents' development depend on the way they affect family atmosphere. Effects of maternal employment depend on such factors as how closely parents monitor adolescents' activity and the mother's workload. A mother's working may help shape attitudes toward gender roles.
- Economic stress affects relationships in both single-parent and two-parent families.
- Relationships with siblings tend to become more equal and more distant during adolescence.
- The peer group can have both positive and negative influences. Adolescents who are rejected by peers tend to have the greatest adjustment problems.
- Friendships, especially among girls, become more intimate and supportive in adolescence.

Guidepost 7 What are the root causes of anti-social behaviour and juvenile delinquency, and what can be done to reduce these and other risks of adolescence?

- Chronic delinquency is associated with multiple interacting risk factors, including ineffective parenting, school failure, peer influence, and low socio-economic status. Programs that attack such risk factors from an early age have had success.

Is There a Universal Adolescent?

Guidepost 8 How does adolescence vary across cultures, and what are some common psychosocial features of the period?

- Cross-cultural research has found striking commonalities in adolescents' self-image, attitudes, and coping ability. There is less consistency in the psychological and sexual areas. Age and gender differences exist across cultures.

OLC Preview

The official website for *A Child's World,* First Canadian edition, offers hot links to recommended websites on teenage pregnancy, contraception, and the epidemic of youth violence. Check out **www.mcgrawhill.ca/college/papalia.**

Glossary

A

A, not-B error Tendency, noted by Piaget, for 8- to 12-month-old infants to search for a hidden object in a place where they previously found it, rather than in the place they most recently saw it being hidden

acceleration Approach to educating the gifted, which moves them through a curriculum at an unusually rapid pace

accommodation Piaget's term for changes in a cognitive structure to include new information

achievement tests Tests that assess how much children know in various subject areas

activity limitations Chronic conditions that continually restrict everyday behaviours

acquired immune deficiency syndrome (AIDS) Viral disease that undermines effective functioning of the immune system

acute medical conditions Illnesses that last a short time

adaptation Piaget's term for adjustment to new information about the environment

adolescence Developmental transition between childhood and adulthood entailing major physical, cognitive, and psychosocial changes

adolescent growth spurt Sharp increase in height and weight that precedes sexual maturity

adolescent rebellion Pattern of emotional turmoil, characteristic of a minority of adolescents, which may involve conflict with family, alienation from adult society, reckless behaviour, and rejection of adult values

adrenarche Maturation of adrenal glands

alleles Paired genes (alike or different) that affect a trait

altruism Behaviour intended to help others out of inner concern and without expectation of external reward

ambivalent (resistant) attachment Pattern in which an infant becomes anxious before the primary caregiver leaves, is extremely upset during his or her absence, and both seeks and resists contact on his or her return

animism Tendency to attribute life to objects that are not alive

anorexia nervosa Eating disorder characterized by self-starvation

anoxia Lack of oxygen, which may cause brain damage

Apgar scale Standard measurement of a newborn's condition; it assesses *a*ppearance, *p*ulse, *g*rimace, *a*ctivity, and *r*espiration

aptitude tests Tests that measure children's general intelligence, or capacity to learn

assimilation Piaget's term for incorporation of new information into an existing cognitive structure

asthma A chronic respiratory disease characterized by sudden attacks of coughing, wheezing, and difficulty in breathing

attachment Reciprocal, enduring tie between infant and caregiver, each of whom contributes to the quality of the relationship

attention-deficit/hyperactivity disorder (ADHD) Syndrome characterized by persistent inattention and distractibility, impulsivity, low tolerance for frustration, and inappropriate overactivity

authoritarian Baumrind's term for parenting style emphasizing control and obedience

authoritative Baumrind's term for parenting style blending respect for a child's individuality with an effort to instill social values

autism Pervasive developmental disorder of the brain, characterized by lack of normal social interaction, impaired communication and imagination, and repetitive, obsessive behaviours

autobiographical memory Memory of specific events in one's own life

autonomy versus shame and doubt Erikson's second crisis in psychosocial development, in which children achieve a balance between self-determination and control by others

autosomes The 22 pairs of chromosomes not related to sexual expression

avoidant attachment Pattern in which an infant rarely cries when separated from the primary caregiver and avoids contact upon his or her return

B

basic trust versus basic mistrust Erikson's first crisis in psychosocial development, in which infants develop a sense of the reliability of people and objects in their world

Bayley Scales of Infant Development Standardized test of infants' mental and motor development

behaviour therapy Therapeutic approach using principles of learning theory to encourage desired behaviours or eliminate undesired ones; also called *behaviour modification*

behavioural genetics Quantitative study of relative hereditary and environmental influences

behaviourism Learning theory that emphasizes the predictable role of environment in causing observable behaviour

behaviourist approach Approach to the study of cognitive development that is concerned with basic mechanics of learning

bilingual Fluent in two languages

bilingual education System of teaching non-English-speaking children in their native language while they learn English, and later switching to all-English instruction

bioecological theory Bronfenbrenner's approach to understanding processes and contexts of development

birth trauma Injury sustained at the time of birth

body image Descriptive and evaluative beliefs about one's appearance

brain growth spurts Periods of rapid brain growth and development

Brazelton Neonatal Behavioural Assessment Scale (NBAS) Neurological and behavioural test to measure neonate's responses to the environment

bulimia nervosa Eating disorder in which a person regularly eats huge quantities of food and then purges the body by laxatives, induced vomiting, fasting, or excessive exercise

bullying Aggression deliberately and persistently directed against a particular target, or victim, typically one who is weak, vulnerable, and defenceless

C

Caesarean delivery Delivery of a baby by surgical removal from the uterus

canalization Limitation on variance of expression of certain inherited characteristics

caregiver–infant bond The caregiver's feeling of close, caring connection with his or her newborn

case study Study covering a single case or life

cell death Elimination of excess brain cells to achieve more efficient functioning

central executive In Baddeley's model, element of working memory that controls the processing of information

central nervous system Brain and spinal cord

centration In Piaget's theory, tendency of pre-operational children to focus on one aspect of a situation and neglect others

cephalocaudal principle Principle that development proceeds in a head-to-tail direction; that is, upper parts of the body develop before lower parts

child development Scientific study of processes of change and stability from conception through adolescence

child-directed speech (CDS) Form of speech often used in talking to babies or toddlers; includes slow, simplified speech, a high-pitched tone, exaggerated vowel sounds, short words and sentences, and much repetition; also called *parentese*

childhood depression Mood disorder characterized by such symptoms as a prolonged sense of friendlessness, inability to have fun or concentrate, fatigue, extreme activity or apathy, feelings of worthlessness, weight change, physical complaints, and thoughts of death or suicide

chromosomes Coils of DNA that carry the genes

chronic medical conditions Illnesses or impairments that persist for at least 3 months

chronosystem Bronfenbrenner's term for effects of time on other developmental systems

circular reactions Piaget's term for processes by which an infant learns to reproduce desired occurrences originally discovered by chance

class inclusion Understanding of the relationship between a whole and its parts

classical conditioning Learning based on associating a stimulus that does not ordinarily elicit a particular response with another stimulus that ordinarily does elicit the response

clone *(verb)* To make a genetic copy of an individual; *(noun)* a genetic copy of an individual

code mixing Use of elements of two languages, sometimes in the same utterance, by young children in households where both languages are spoken

code switching Process of changing one's speech to match the situation, as in people who are bilingual

cognitive neuroscience approach Approach to the study of cognitive development that links brain processes with cognitive ones

cognitive perspective View that thought processes are central to development

cohort Group of people who share a similar experience, such as growing up at the same time and in the same place

commitment Marcia's term for personal investment in an occupation or system of beliefs

committed compliance Wholehearted obedience to a parent's orders without reminders or lapses

componential element Sternberg's term for the analytic aspect of intelligence

concordant Term describing twins who share the same trait or disorder

concrete operations Third stage of Piagetian cognitive development (approximately from ages 7 to 12), during which children develop logical but not abstract thinking

conduct disorder (CD) Repetitive, persistent pattern of aggressive, anti-social behaviour violating societal norms or the rights of others

conscience Internal standards of behaviour, which usually control one's conduct and produce emotional discomfort when violated

conservation Piaget's term for awareness that two objects that are equal according to a certain measure remain equal in the face of perceptual alteration so long as nothing has been added to or taken away from either object

constructive play In Piaget's and Smilansky's terminology, the second cognitive level of play, involving use of objects or materials to make something

contextual element Sternberg's term for the practical aspect of intelligence

contextual perspective View of development that sees the individual as inseparable from the social context

control group In an experiment, a group of people similar to the people in the experimental group who do not receive the treatment whose effects are to be measured

conventional morality (*or* morality of conventional role conformity) Second level in Kohlberg's theory of moral reasoning, in which the standards of authority figures are internalized

convergent thinking Thinking aimed at finding the one "right" answer to a problem

co-regulation Transitional stage in the control of behaviour in which parents exercise general supervision and children exercise moment-to-moment self-regulation

corporal punishment Use of physical force with the intention of causing pain, but not injury, to correct or control behaviour

correlational study Research design intended to discover whether a statistical relationship between variables exists

crisis Marcia's term for period of conscious decision making related to identity formation

critical period Specific time when a given event, or its absence, has the greatest impact on development

cross-modal transfer Ability to use information gained by one sense to guide another

cross-sectional study Study design in which people of different ages are assessed on one occasion

cultural bias Tendency of intelligence tests to include items calling for knowledge or skills more familiar or meaningful to some cultural groups than to others

culture A society's or group's total way of life, including customs, traditions, beliefs, values, language, and physical products—all learned behaviour passed on from parents to children

culture-fair Describing an intelligence test that deals with experiences common to various cultures, in an attempt to avoid cultural bias

culture-free Describing an intelligence test that, if it were possible to design, would have no culturally linked content

D

decentre In Piaget's terminology, to think simultaneously about several aspects of a situation

deductive reasoning Type of logical reasoning that moves from a general premise about a class to a conclusion about a particular member or members of the class

deferred imitation Piaget's term for reproduction of an observed behaviour after the passage of time by calling up a stored symbol of it

Denver Developmental Screening Test Screening test given to children 1 month to 6 years old to determine whether they are developing normally

deoxyribonucleic acid (DNA) Chemical that carries inherited instructions for the formation and function of body cells

dependent variable In an experiment, the condition that may or may not change as a result of changes in the independent variable

depth perception Ability to perceive objects and surfaces three-dimensionally

developmental priming mechanisms Aspects of the home environment that seem necessary for normal cognitive and psychosocial development

differentiation Process by which neurons acquire specialized structure and function

"difficult" children Children with irritable temperament, irregular biological rhythms, and intense emotional responses

discipline Methods of moulding children's character and of teaching them self-control and acceptable behaviour

dishabituation Increase in responsiveness after presentation of a new stimulus; compare *habituation*

disorganized-disoriented attachment Pattern in which an infant, after being separated from the primary caregiver, shows contradictory behaviours upon his or her return

divergent thinking Thinking that produces a variety of fresh, diverse possibilities

dizygotic (two-egg) twins Twins conceived by the union of two different ova (or a single ovum that has split) with two different sperm cells; also called *fraternal twins*

dominant inheritance Pattern of inheritance in which, when a child receives contradictory alleles, only the dominant one is expressed

Down syndrome Chromosomal disorder characterized by moderate-to-severe mental retardation

drug therapy Administration of drugs to treat emotional disorders

dual representation hypothesis Proposal that children under the age of 3 have difficulty grasping spatial relationships because of the need to keep more than one mental representation in mind at the same time

dyslexia Developmental disorder in which reading achievement is substantially lower than predicted by IQ or age

E

early intervention Systematic provision of therapeutic and educational services to families to help meet young children's developmental needs

"easy" children Children with a generally happy temperament, regular biological rhythms, and a readiness to accept new experiences

egocentrism Piaget's term for inability to consider another person's point of view

elaboration Mnemonic strategy of making mental associations involving items to be remembered

electronic fetal monitoring Mechanical monitoring of fetal heartbeat during labour and delivery

embryonic stage Second stage of gestation (2 to 8 weeks), characterized by rapid growth and development of major body systems and organs

emergent literacy Preschoolers' development of skills, knowledge, and attitudes that underlie reading and writing

emotional maltreatment Action or inaction that may cause behavioural, cognitive, emotional, or mental disorders

emotions Subjective reactions to experience that are associated with physiological and behavioural changes

empathy Ability to put oneself in another person's place and feel what that person feels

encoding Process by which information is prepared for long-term storage and later retrieval

English immersion Approach to teaching English as a second language in which instruction is presented only in English

enrichment Approach to educating the gifted, which broadens and deepens knowledge and skills through extra activities, projects, field trips, or mentoring

enuresis Repeated urination in clothing or in bed

environment Totality of nonhereditary, or experiential, influences on development

episodic memory Long-term memory of specific experiences or events, linked to time and place

equilibration Piaget's term for the tendency to seek a stable balance among cognitive elements

ethnic group Group united by ancestry, race, religion, language, and/or national origins, which contribute to a sense of shared identity

ethnographic study In-depth study of a culture, which uses a combination of methods including participant observation

ethological perspective View of development that focuses on biological and evolutionary bases of behaviour

exosystem Bronfenbrenner's term for linkages between two or more settings, one of which does not contain the child

experiential element Sternberg's term for the insightful aspect of intelligence

experiment Rigorously controlled, replicable procedure in which the researcher manipulates variables to assess the effect of one on the other

experimental group In an experiment, the group receiving the treatment under study

explicit memory Memory that is intentional and conscious

extended family Kinship network of parents, children, and other relatives, sometimes living together in an *extended-family household*

external memory aids Mnemonic strategies using something outside the person

F

family therapy Psychological treatment in which a therapist sees the whole family together to analyze patterns of family functioning

fast mapping Process by which a child absorbs the meaning of a new word after hearing it once or twice in conversation

fertilization Union of sperm and ovum fuse to produce a zygote; also called *conception*

fetal alcohol syndrome (FAS) Combination of mental, motor, and developmental abnormalities affecting the offspring of some women who drink heavily during pregnancy

fetal stage Final stage of gestation (from 8 weeks to birth), characterized by increased detail of body parts and greatly enlarged body size

fine motor skills Physical skills that involve the small muscles and eye–hand coordination

fontanels Soft spots on head of young infant

foreclosure Identity status, described by Marcia, in which a person who has not spent time considering alternatives (that is, has not been in crisis) is committed to other people's plans for his or her life

formal operations In Piaget's theory, the final stage of cognitive development, characterized by the ability to think abstractly

French immersion Approach to teaching French as a second language in which English-speaking children are given instruction in French only

functional play In Piaget's and Smilansky's terminology, the lowest cognitive level of play, involving repetitive muscular movements

G

gateway drugs Drugs such as alcohol, tobacco, and marijuana, the use of which tends to lead to use of more addictive drugs

gender Significance of being male or female

gender constancy Awareness that one will always be male or female; also called *sex-category constancy*

gender identity Awareness, developed in early childhood, that one is male or female

gender roles Behaviours, interests, attitudes, skills, and traits that a culture considers appropriate for males or for females

gender-schema theory Theory, proposed by Bem, that children socialize themselves in their gender roles by developing a mentally organized network of information about what it means to be male or female in a particular culture

gender stereotypes Preconceived generalizations about male or female role behaviour

gender-typing Socialization process by which children learn appropriate gender roles

generalized anxiety disorder Anxiety not focused on any single target

generic memory Memory that produces scripts of familiar routines to guide behaviour

genes Small segments of DNA located in definite positions on particular chromosomes

genetic code Sequence of base pairs within DNA, which determine inherited characteristics

genetic counselling Clinical service that advises couples of their probable risk of having children with hereditary defects

genetic testing Procedure for ascertaining genetic makeup to identify predispositions to hereditary diseases or disorders

genotype Genetic makeup of a person, containing both expressed and unexpressed characteristics

genotype–environment correlation Tendency of certain genetic and environmental influences to reinforce each other; may be passive, reactive (evocative), or active; also called *genotype–environment covariance*

genotype–environment interaction The portion of phenotypic variation that results from the reactions of genetically different individuals to similar environmental conditions

germinal stage First 2 weeks of prenatal development, characterized by rapid cell division, increasing complexity and differentiation, and implantation in the wall of the uterus

gonadarche Maturation of testes or ovaries

goodness of fit Appropriateness of environmental demands and constraints to a child's temperament

gross motor skills Physical skills that involve the large muscles

guided participation Participation of an adult in a child's activity in a manner that helps to structure the activity and to bring the child's understanding of it closer to that of the adult

habituation Simple type of learning in which familiarity with a stimulus reduces, slows, or stops a response Compare *dishabituation*

handedness Preference for using a particular hand

heredity Inborn influences or traits inherited from biological parents

heritability Statistical estimate of contribution of heredity to individual differences in a specific trait within a given population

Heritage Language Program Language classes given in the regular school day for children of immigrant background, designed to promote the home language and culture

heterozygous Possessing differing alleles for a trait

holophrase Single word that conveys a complete thought

Home Observation for Measurement of the Environment (HOME) Instrument to measure the influence of the home environment on children's cognitive growth

homozygous Possessing two identical alleles for a trait

horizontal décalage Piaget's term for inability to transfer learning about one type of conservation to other types, which causes a child to master different types of conservation tasks at different ages

hostile aggression Aggressive behaviour intended to hurt another person

human genome Complete sequence or mapping of genes in the human body and their locations

hypotheses Possible explanations for phenomena, used to predict the outcome of research

hypothetical-deductive reasoning Ability, believed by Piaget to accompany the state of formal operations, to develop, consider, and test hypotheses

ideal self The self one would like to be

identification In Freudian theory, the process by which a young child adopts characteristics, beliefs, attitudes, values, and behaviours of the parent of the same sex

identity achievement Identity status, described by Marcia, which is characterized by commitment to choices made following a crisis, a period spent in exploring alternatives

identity diffusion Identity status, described by Marcia, which is characterized by absence of commitment and lack of serious consideration of alternatives

identity statuses Marcia's term for states of ego development that depend on the presence or absence of crisis and commitment

identity versus identity confusion Erikson's fifth crisis of psychosocial development, in which an adolescent seeks to develop a coherent sense of self, including the role she or he is to play in society; also called *identity versus role confusion*

imaginary audience Elkind's term for an observer who exists only in an adolescent's mind and is as concerned with the adolescent's thoughts and actions as the adolescent is

implicit memory Unconscious recall, generally of habits and skills; sometimes called *procedural memory*

imprinting Instinctive form of learning in which, during a critical period in early development, a young animal forms an attachment to the first moving object it sees, usually the mother

independent variable In an experiment, the condition over which the experimenter has direct control

individual differences Differences among children in characteristics, influences, or developmental outcomes

individual psychotherapy Psychological treatment in which a therapist sees a troubled person one-on-one

inductive reasoning Type of logical reasoning that moves from particular observations about members of a class to a general conclusion about that class

inductive techniques Disciplinary techniques designed to induce desirable behaviour by appealing to a child's sense of reason and fairness

industry versus inferiority Erikson's fourth critical alternative of psychosocial development, in which children must learn the productive skills their culture requires or else face feelings of inferiority

infant mortality rate Proportion of babies born alive who die within the first year

infertility Inability to conceive after 12 to 18 months of trying

information-processing approach Approach to the study of cognitive development by observing and analyzing the mental processes involved in perceiving and handling information

initiative versus guilt Erikson's third crisis in psychosocial development, in which children balance the urge to pursue goals with moral reservations that may prevent carrying them out

instrumental aggression Aggressive behaviour used as a means of achieving a goal

integration Process by which neurons coordinate the activities of muscle groups

intelligent behaviour Behaviour that is goal-oriented and adaptive to circumstances and conditions of life

internalization Process by which children accept societal standards of conduct as their own; fundamental to socialization

invisible imitation Imitation with parts of one's body that one cannot see

IQ (intelligence quotient) tests Psychometric tests that seek to measure intelligence by comparing a test-taker's performance with standardized norms

irreversibility Piaget's term for a preoperational child's failure to understand that an operation can go in two or more directions

K

Kaufman Assessment Battery for Children (K-ABC) Non-traditional individual intelligence test designed to provide fair assessments of minority children and children with disabilities

L

laboratory observation Research method in which all participants are observed in the same situation, under controlled conditions

language Communication system based on words and grammar

language acquisition device (LAD) In Chomsky's terminology, an inborn mechanism that enables children to infer linguistic rules from the language they hear

lanugo Fuzzy prenatal body hair, which drops off within a few days after birth

lateralization Tendency of each of the brain's hemispheres to have specialized functions

learning disabilities (LDs) Disorders that interfere with specific aspects of learning and school achievement

learning perspective View of development that holds that changes in behaviour result from experience, or adaptation to the environment

linguistic speech Verbal expression designed to convey meaning

literacy Ability to read and write

longitudinal study Study design to assess changes in a sample over time

long-term memory Storage of virtually unlimited capacity, which holds information for very long periods

low birth weight Weight of less than 2,500 g at birth because of prematurity or being small for date

M

macrosystem Bronfenbrenner's term for overall cultural patterns

maturation Unfolding of a natural sequence of physical and behavioural changes, including readiness to master new abilities

mechanistic model Model that views development as a passive, predictable response to stimuli

meconium Fetal waste matter, excreted during the first few days after birth

menarche Girl's first menstruation

mental retardation Significantly subnormal cognitive functioning

mesosystem Bronfenbrenner's term for linkages of two or more microsystems

metacognition Awareness of a person's own mental processes

metamemory Understanding of processes of memory

microgenetic study Study design that allows researchers to directly observe change by repeated testing over a short time

microsystem Bronfenbrenner's term for a setting in which a child interacts with others every day, face to face

mnemonic strategies Techniques to aid memory

monozygotic (one-egg) twins Twins resulting from the division of a single zygote after fertilization; also called *identical twins*

morality of constraint First of Piaget's two stages of moral development, characterized by rigid, egocentric judgments

morality of cooperation Second of Piaget's two stages of moral development, characterized by flexible judgments and formation of one's own moral code

moratorium Identity status, described by Marcia, in which a person is currently considering alternatives (in crisis) and seems headed for commitment

multifactorial transmission Combination of genetic and environmental factors to produce certain complex traits

mutations Permanent alterations in genes or chromosomes that may produce harmful characteristics

mutual regulation Process by which infant and caregiver communicate emotional states to each other and respond appropriately

myelination Process of coating neurons with a fatty substance (myelin) that enables faster communication between cells

N

nativism Theory that human beings have an inborn capacity for language acquisition

natural childbirth Method of childbirth that seeks to prevent pain by eliminating the mother's fear through education about the physiology of reproduction and training in breathing and relaxation during delivery

natural selection According to Darwin's theory of evolution, process by which characteristics that promote survival of a species are reproduced in successive generations, and characteristics that do not promote survival die out

naturalistic observation Research method in which behaviour is studied in natural settings without intervention or manipulation

neglect Failure to meet a child's basic needs

neglectful/uninvolved Maccoby and Martin's term for parents who focus on their own needs rather than on those of the child

neonatal jaundice Condition, in many newborn babies, caused by immaturity of liver and evidenced by yellowish appearance; can cause brain damage if not treated promptly

neonatal period First 4 weeks of life, a time of transition from intrauterine dependency to independent existence

neonate Newborn baby, up to 4 weeks old

neurons Nerve cells

niche-picking Tendency of a person, especially after early childhood, to seek out environments compatible with his or her genotype

non-normative Characteristic of an unusual event that happens to a particular person, or a typical event that happens at an unusual time of life

non-shared environmental effects The unique environment in which each child grows up, consisting of distinctive influences or influences that affect one child differently from another

normative Characteristic of an event that occurs in a similar way for most people in a group

nuclear family Kinship and household unit made up of parents and their natural or adopted children

O

obesity Extreme overweight in relation to age, sex, height, and body type; sometimes defined as having a body mass index (weight-for-height) at or above the 85th or 95th percentile of growth curves for children of the same age and sex

object permanence Piaget's term for the understanding that a person or object still exists when out of sight

observational learning Learning through watching the behaviour of others

obsessive-compulsive disorder Anxiety aroused by repetitive, intrusive thoughts, images, or impulses, often leading to compulsive ritual behaviours

operant conditioning Learning based on reinforcement or punishment

operational definitions Definitions stated in terms of operations or procedures used to produce or measure a phenomenon

oppositional defiant disorder (ODD) Pattern of behaviour, persisting into middle childhood, marked by negativity, hostility, and defiance

organismic model Model that views development as internally initiated by an active organism and as occurring in a sequence of qualitatively different stages

organization Mnemonic strategy of categorizing material to be remembered

organization Piaget's term for integration of knowledge into systems

Otis-Lennon School Ability Test Group intelligence test for kindergarten through Grade 12

overt aggression Aggression openly directed at its target

P

participant observation Research method in which the observer lives with the people or participates in the activity being observed

parturition Process of uterine, cervical, and other changes, usually lasting about 2 weeks, preceding childbirth

patchwork self Elkind's term for a sense of identity constructed by substituting other people's attitudes, beliefs, and commitments for one's own

perinatal Period from 28 weeks' gestation to 7 days after birth

permissive Baumrind's term for parenting style emphasizing self-expression and self-regulation

personal fable Elkind's term for conviction that one is special, unique, and not subject to the rules that govern the rest of the world

phenotype Observable characteristics of a person

physical abuse Action taken to endanger a child involving potential bodily injury

Piagetian approach Approach to the study of cognitive development that describes qualitative stages in cognitive functioning

plasticity Modifiability, or "moulding," of the brain through experience

postconventional morality (*or* morality of autonomous moral principles) Third level in Kohlberg's theory of moral reasoning, in which people follow internally held moral principles and can decide among conflicting moral standards

postmature Referring to a fetus not yet born as of 2 weeks after the due date or 42 weeks after the mother's last menstrual period

power assertion Disciplinary strategy to discourage undesirable behaviour through physical or verbal enforcement of parental control

pragmatics The practical knowledge needed to use language for communication

preconventional morality First level of Kohlberg's theory of moral reasoning, in which control is external and rules are obeyed in order to gain rewards or avoid punishment, or out of self-interest

prejudice Unfavourable attitude toward members of certain groups outside one's own, especially racial or ethnic groups

prelinguistic speech Forerunner of linguistic speech; utterance of sounds that are not words; includes crying, cooing, babbling, and accidental and deliberate imitation of sounds without understanding their meaning

pre-operational stage In Piaget's theory, the second major stage of cognitive development, in which children become more sophisticated in their use of symbolic thought but are not yet able to use logic

prepared childbirth Method of childbirth that uses instruction, breathing exercises, and social support to induce controlled physical responses to uterine contractions and reduce fear and pain

pretend play In Piaget's and Smilansky's terminology, the third cognitive level of play, involving imaginary people or situations; also called *fantasy play, dramatic play,* or *imaginative play*

preterm (premature) infants Infants born before completing the 37th week of gestation

primary sex characteristics Organs directly related to reproduction, which enlarge and mature during adolescence

private speech Talking aloud to oneself with no intent to communicate

pro-social behaviour Any voluntary behaviour intended to help others

protective factors Influences that reduce the impact of early stress and tend to predict positive outcomes

proximodistal principle Principle that development proceeds from within to

without; that is, parts of the body near the centre develop before the extremities

psychoanalytic perspective View of development as shaped by unconscious forces

psychometric approach Approach to the study of cognitive development that seeks to measure the quantity of intelligence a person possesses

psychosexual development In Freudian theory, an unvarying sequence of stages of personality development during infancy, childhood, and adolescence, in which gratification shifts from the mouth to the anus and then to the genitals

psychosocial development In Erikson's eight-stage theory, the socially and culturally influenced process of development of the ego, or self

puberty Process by which a person attains sexual maturity and the ability to reproduce

punishment In operant conditioning, a stimulus that discourages repetition of a behaviour

Q

qualitative change Change in kind, structure, or organization, such as the change from nonverbal to verbal communication

quantitative change Change in number or amount, such as in height, weight, or size of vocabulary

quantitative trait loci (QTL) Interaction of multiple genes, each with effects of varying size, to produce a complex trait

R

reaction range Potential variability, depending on environmental conditions, in the expression of a hereditary trait

real self The self one actually is

recall Ability to reproduce material from memory

recessive inheritance Pattern of inheritance in which a child receives identical recessive alleles, resulting in expression of a nondominant trait

reciprocity System of mutually binding, mutually responsive relationships into which a child is socialized

recognition Ability to identify a previously encountered stimulus

reflex behaviours Automatic, involuntary, innate responses to stimulation

rehearsal Mnemonic strategy to keep an item in working memory through conscious repetition

reinforcement In operant conditioning, a stimulus that encourages repetition of a desired behaviour

relational aggression Aggression aimed at damaging or interfering with another person's relationships, reputation, or psychological well-being; also called *covert, indirect,* or *psychological aggression*

representational ability Piaget's term for capacity to mentally represent objects and experiences, largely through the use of symbols

representational mappings In neo-Piagetian terminology, the second stage in development of self-definition, in which a child makes logical connections between aspects of the self but still sees these characteristics in all-or-nothing terms

representational systems In neo-Piagetian terminology, the third stage in development of self-definition, characterized by breadth, balance, and the integration and assessment of various aspects of the self

resilient children Children who weather adverse circumstances, function well despite challenges or threats, or bounce back from traumatic events

retrieval Process by which information is accessed or recalled from memory storage

risk factors Conditions that increase the likelihood of a negative developmental outcome

rough-and-tumble play Vigorous play involving wrestling, hitting, and chasing, often accompanied by laughing and screaming

S

sample Group of participants chosen to represent the entire population under study

scaffolding Temporary support to help a child master a task

schemes Piaget's term for organized patterns of behaviour used in different situations

schizophrenia Mental disorder marked by loss of contact with reality; symptoms include hallucinations and delusions

school phobia Unrealistic fear of going to school, may be a form of *separation anxiety disorder* or *social phobia*

scientific method System of established principles and processes of scientific inquiry

script General remembered outline of a familiar, repeated event, used to guide behaviour

secondary sex characteristics Physiological signs of sexual maturation (such as breast development and growth of body hair) that do not involve the sex organs

secular trend Trend that can be seen only by observing several generations, such as the trend toward earlier attainment of adult height and sexual maturity, which began a century ago

secure attachment Pattern in which an infant cries or protests when the primary caregiver leaves and actively seeks out the caregiver upon his or her return

self-awareness Realization that one's existence and functioning are separate from those of other people and things

self-concept Sense of self; descriptive and evaluative mental picture of one's abilities and traits

self-definition Cluster of characteristics used to describe oneself

self-efficacy Sense of capability to master challenges and achieve goals

self-esteem The judgment a person makes about his or her self-worth

self-fulfilling prophecy False expectation or prediction of behaviour that tends to come true because it leads people to act as if it already were true

self-regulation Child's independent control of behaviour to conform to understood social expectations

sensorimotor stage In Piaget's theory, the first stage in cognitive development, during which infants learn through sensory and motor activity

sensory memory Initial, brief, temporary storage of sensory information

separation anxiety Distress shown by an infant when a familiar caregiver leaves

separation anxiety disorder Condition involving excessive, prolonged anxiety about separation from home or from people to whom a child is attached

sequential study Study design that combines cross-sectional and longitudinal techniques

seriation Ability to order items along a dimension

sex chromosomes Pair of chromosomes that determines sex: XX in the normal female, XY in the normal male

sex-linked inheritance Pattern of inheritance in which certain characteristics carried on the X chromosome inherited from the mother are transmitted differently to her male and female offspring

sexual abuse Sexual activity involving a child and an older person

sexual orientation Focus of consistent sexual, romantic, and affectionate interest, either heterosexual, homosexual (gay and lesbian), or bisexual

sexually transmitted diseases (STDs) Diseases spread by sexual contact

single representations In neo-Piagetian terminology, first stage in development of self-definition, in which children describe themselves in terms of individual, unconnected characteristics and in all-or-nothing terms

situational compliance Obedience to parent's orders only in the presence of prompting or other signs of ongoing parental control

"slow-to-warm-up" children Children whose temperament is generally mild but who are hesitant about accepting new experiences

small-for-gestational age infants Infants whose birth weight is less than that of 90 per cent of babies of the same gestational age, as a result of slow fetal growth

social capital Family and community resources upon which a person can draw

social cognition Ability to understand that others have mental states and to judge their feelings and intentions

social cognitive theory Albert Bandura's expansion of social learning theory; holds that children learn gender roles through socialization

social construction Concept about the nature of reality, based on societally shared perceptions or assumptions

social-contextual approach Approach to the study of cognitive development focusing on environmental influences, particularly of parents and other caregivers

social interaction model Model, based on Vygotsky's socio-cultural theory, which proposes that children construct autobiographical memories through conversation with adults about shared events

social learning theory Theory that behaviours are learned by observing and imitating models; also called *social cognitive theory*

social phobia Extreme fear and/or avoidance of social situations

social promotion Policy in which children are automatically promoted from one grade to another even if they do not meet academic standards for the grade they are completing

social referencing Understanding an ambiguous situation by seeking out another person's perception of it

social speech Speech intended to be understood by a listener

socialization Development of habits, skills, values, and motives shared by responsible, productive members of a society

socio-cultural theory Vygotsky's theory of how contextual factors affect children's development

socio-economic status (SES) Combination of economic and social factors describing an individual or family, including income, education, and occupation

spermarche Boy's first ejaculation

spontaneous abortion Natural expulsion from the uterus of an embryo or fetus that cannot survive outside the womb; also called *miscarriage*

Stanford-Binet Intelligence Scale Individual intelligence test used to measure memory, spatial orientation, and practical judgment

state of arousal An infant's physiological and behavioural status at a given moment in the periodic daily cycle of wakefulness, sleep, and activity

Sternberg Triarchic Abilities Test (STAT) Test to measure componential, experiential, and contextual intelligence

"still-face" paradigm Research method used to measure mutual regulation in infants 2 to 9 months old

storage Retention of memories for future use

Strange Situation Laboratory technique used to study attachment

stranger anxiety Wariness of strange people and places, shown by some infants during the second half of the first year

stuttering Involuntary, frequent repetition or prolongation of sounds or syllables

substance abuse Repeated, harmful use of a substance, usually alcohol or other drugs

substance dependence Addiction (physical, psychological, or both) to a harmful substance

sudden infant death syndrome Sudden and unexplained death of an apparently healthy infant

symbolic function In Piaget's terminology, ability to use mental representations (words, numbers, or images) to which a child has attached meaning

syntax Rules for forming sentences in a particular language

systems of action Increasingly complex combinations of skills, which permit a wider or more precise range of movement and more control of the environment

T

telegraphic speech Early form of sentence consisting of only a few essential words

temperament Characteristic disposition or style of approaching and reacting to situations

teratogenic Capable of causing birth defects

theory Coherent set of logically related concepts that seeks to organize, explain, and predict data

theory of mind Awareness and understanding of mental processes

theory of multiple intelligences Gardner's theory that each person has several distinct forms of intelligence

transduction Piaget's term for a pre-operational child's tendency to mentally link particular experiences, whether or not there is logically a causal relationship

transitive inference Understanding of the relationship between two objects by knowing the relationship of each to a third object

triarchic theory of intelligence Sternberg's theory describing three types of intelligence: componential (analytical ability), experiential (insight and originality), and contextual (practical thinking)

two-way (dual-language) learning Approach to second-language education in which English speakers and non-English speakers learn together in their own and each other's languages

U

ultrasound Prenatal medical procedure using high-frequency sound waves to detect the outline of a fetus and its movements, in order to determine whether a pregnancy is progressing normally

V

vernix caseosa Oily substance on a neonate's skin that protects against infection

violation-of-expectations Research method in which dishabituation to a stimulus that conflicts with previous experience is taken as evidence that an infant recognizes the new stimulus as surprising

visible imitation Imitation with parts of one's body that one can see

visual cliff Apparatus designed to give an illusion of depth and used to assess depth perception in infants

visual preference Tendency of infants to spend more time looking at one sight than another

visual-recognition memory Ability to distinguish a familiar visual stimulus from an unfamiliar one when shown both at the same time

Wechsler Intelligence Scale for Children (WISC–III) Individual intelligence test for schoolchildren, which yields verbal and performance scores as well as a combined score

Wechsler Preschool and Primary Scale of Intelligence (WPPSI–III) Individual intelligence test for children ages 3 to 7, which yields verbal and performance scores as well as a combined score

withdrawal of love Disciplinary strategy that may involve ignoring, isolating, or showing dislike for a child

working memory Short-term storage of information being actively processed

Z

zone of proximal development (ZPD) Vygotsky's term for the difference between what a child can do alone and with help

zygote One-celled organism resulting from fertilization

Bibliography

Aaron, P. G., & Guillemard, J.-C. (1993). Artists as dyslexics. In D. M. Willows, R. S. Kruk, & E. Corcos (Eds.), *Visual processes in reading and reading disabilities* (pp. 393–415). Hillsdale, NJ: Lawrence Erlbaum Associates.

Abbey, A., Andrews, F. M., & Halman, J. (1992). Infertility and subjective well-being: The mediating roles of self-esteem, internal control, and interpersonal conflict. *Journal of Marriage and the Family, 54,* 408–417.

Abma, J. C., Chandra, A., Mosher, W. D., Peterson, L., & Piccinino, L. (1997). Fertility, family planning, and women's health: New data from the 1995 National Survey of Family Growth. *Vital Health Statistics, 23*(19). Washington, DC: National Center for Health Statistics.

Abramovitch, R., Corter, C., & Lando, B. (1979). Sibling interaction in the home. *Child Development, 50,* 997–1003.

Abramovitch, R., Corter, C., Pepler, D., & Stanhope, L. (1986). Sibling and peer interactions: A final follow-up and comparison. *Child Development, 57,* 217–229.

Abramovitch, R., Pepler, D., & Corter, C. (1982). Patterns of sibling interaction among preschool-age children. In M. E. Lamb (Ed.), *Sibling relationships: Their nature and significance across the lifespan.* Hillsdale, NJ: Erlbaum.

Abrams, B., & Parker, J. D. (1990). Maternal weight gain in women with good pregnancy outcome. *Obstetrics and Gynecology, 76*(1), 1–7.

Achenbach, T. M., & Howell, C. T. (1993). Are American children's problems getting worse? A 13-year comparison. *Journal of the American Academy of Child and Adolescent Psychiatry, 32,* 1145–1154.

Ackerman, B. P., Kogos, J., Youngstrom, E., Schoff, K., & Izard, C. (1999). Family instability and the problem behaviors of children from economically disadvantaged families. *Developmental Psychology, 35*(1), 258–268.

Acs, G., Shulman, R., Ng, M. W., & Chussid, S. (1999). Tooth decay may slow child's growth. *Pediatric Dentistry, 21,* 109–113.

Adair, J. (2001). Ethics of psychological research: New policies; continuing issues; new concerns. *Canadian Psychology, 42,* 25–37.

Adams, L. A., & Rickert, V. I. (1989). Reducing bedtime tantrums: Comparison between positive routines and graduated extinction. *Pediatrics, 84,* 756–761.

Addisa, A., Morettib, M. E., Syedb, F. A., Einarsonc, T. R., Korenb, G. (2001). Fetal effects of cocaine: An updated meta-analysis. *Reproductive Toxicology, 15,* 341–369.

Adolescent Medicine Committee, Canadian Paediatric Society. (1998). Eating disorders in adolescents: Principles of diagnosis and treatment. *Paediatrics and Child Health, 3,* 189–192.

Adolph, K. E. (1997). Learning in the development of infant locomotion. *Monographs of the Society for Research in Child Development, 62*(3, Serial No. 251).

Ainsworth, M. D. S. (1967). *Infancy in Uganda: Infant care and the growth of love.* Baltimore: Johns Hopkins University Press.

Ainsworth, M. D. S. (1969). Object relations, dependency, and attachment: A theoretical review of the infant–mother relationship. *Child Development, 40,* 969–1025.

Ainsworth, M. D. S., Blehar, M. C., Waters, E., & Wall, S. (1978). Patterns of attachment: A psychological study of the strange situation. Hillsdale, NJ: Erlbaum.

Alan Guttmacher Institute (AGI). (1994). *Sex & America's teenagers.* New York: Author.

Alan Guttmacher Institute (AGI). (1999a). *Facts in brief: Teen sex and pregnancy.* Retrieved January 31, 2000, from http://www.agi_usa.org/pubs/fb_teen_sex.html#sfd

Alan Guttmacher Institute (AGI). (1999b). *Occasional report: Why is teenage pregnancy declining? The roles of abstinence, sexual activity and contraceptive use.* Retrieved January 31, 2000, from http://www.agi-usa.org/pubs/or_teen_preg_decline.html

Albanese, A., & Stanhope, R. (1993). Growth and metabolic data following growth hormone treatment of children with intrauterine growth retardation. *Hormone Research, 39,* 8–12.

Aldort, N. (1994, summer). Getting out of the way. *Mothering,* 38–43.

Alessandri, S. M., Bendersky, M., & Lewis, M. (1998). Cognitive functioning in 8- to 18-month-old drug-exposed infants. *Developmental Psychology, 34,* 565–573.

Alessandri, S. M., Sullivan, M. W., Bendersky, M., & Lewis, M. (1995). Temperament in cocaine-exposed infants. In M. Lewis & M. Bendersky (Eds.), *Mothers, babies, and cocaine: The role of toxins in development* (pp. 273–286). Hillsdale, NJ: Erlbaum.

Alessandri, S. M., Sullivan, M. W., Imaizumi, S., & Lewis, M. (1993). Learning and emotional responsivity in cocaine-exposed infants. *Developmental Psychology, 29,* 989–997.

Alexander, G. R., Tompkins, M. E., Allen, M. C., & Hulsey, T. C. (2000). Trends and racial differences in birth weight and related survival. *Maternal and Child Health Journal, 3,* 71–79.

Alexander, K. L., Entwisle, D. R., & Dauber, S. L. (1993). First-grade classroom behavior: Its short- and long-term consequences for school performance. **Child Development, 64,** 801–814.

Aligne, C. A., & Stoddard, J. J. (1997). Tobacco and children: An economic evaluation of the medical effects of parental smoking. *Archives of Pediatric and Adolescent Medicine, 151,* 648–653.

Allen, G. L., & Ondracek, P. J. (1995). Age-sensitive cognitive abilities related to children's acquisition of spatial knowledge. *Developmental Psychology, 31,* 934–945.

Allen, J. P., Philliber, S., Herrling, S., & Kuperminc, G. P. (1997). Preventing teen pregnancy and academic failure: Experimental evaluation of a developmentally based approach. *Child Development, 64,* 729–742.

Allergy Section, Canadian Paediatric Society [CPS]. (1986). Secondhand cigarette smoke worsens symptoms in children with asthma. *Canadian Medical Association Journal, 135,* 321–323.

Almeida, D. M., & McDonald, D. (1998). Weekly rhythms of parents' work stress, home stress, and parent–adolescent tension. In A. Crouter & R. Larson (Eds.), *Temporal rhythms in adolescence: Clocks, calendars, and the coordination of daily life* (pp. 69–82). *[New Directions in Child and Adolescent Development, 82].* San Francisco: Jossey-Bass.

Alsaker, F. D. (1992). Pubertal timing, overweight, and psychological adjustment. *Journal of Early Adolescence, 12*(4), 396–419.

Alvidrez J., & Weinstein, R. S. (1999). Early teacher perceptions and later student academic achievement. *Journal of Educational Psychology, 91,* 731–746.

Amato, P. R. (1987). Family processes in one-parent, stepparent, and intact families: The child's point of view. *Journal of Marriage and the Family, 49,* 327–337.

Amato, P. R., & Booth, A. (1997). *A generation at risk: Growing up in an era of family upheaval.* Cambridge, MA: Harvard University Press.

Amato, P. R., & Gilbreth, J. G. (1999). Nonresident fathers and children's well-being: A meta-analysis. *Journal of Marriage and the Family, 61,* 557–573.

Amato, P. R., & Keith, B. (1991). Parental divorce and adult well-being: A meta-analysis. *Journal of Marriage and the Family, 53,* 43–58.

Amato, P. R., Kurdek, L. A., Demo, D. H., & Allen, K. R. (1993). Children's adjustment to divorce: Theories, hypotheses, and empirical support. *Journal of Marriage and the Family, 55,* 23–54.

American Academy of Child and Adolescent Psychiatry (AACAP). (1997). Children's sleep problems. [Fact sheet] No. 34. (Available from the AACAP, 3615 Wisconsin Ave., N.W., Washington, DC, 20016-3007.)

American Academy of Pediatrics (AAP) and Canadian Paediatric Society. (2000). Prevention and management of pain and stress in the neonate. *Pediatrics, 105*(2), 454–461.

American Academy of Pediatrics (AAP) and Center to Prevent Handgun Violence. (1994). *Keep your family safe from firearm injury.* Washington, DC: Center to Prevent Handgun Violence.

American Academy of Pediatrics (AAP) Committee on Accident and Poison Prevention. (1988). Snowmobile statement. *Pediatrics, 82,* 798–799.

American Academy of Pediatrics (AAP) Committee on Adolescence. (1994). Sexually transmitted diseases. *Pediatrics, 94,* 568–572.

American Academy of Pediatrics (AAP) Committee on Adolescence. (1999). Adolescent pregnancy—Current trends and issues: 1998. *Pediatrics, 103,* 516–520.

American Academy of Pediatrics (AAP) Committee on Adolescence. (2000). Suicide and suicide attempts in adolescents. *Pediatrics, 105*(4), 871–874.

American Academy of Pediatrics (AAP) Committee on Bioethics. (1992). Infants with anencephaly as organ sources: Ethical considerations. *Pediatrics, 89,* 1116–1119.

American Academy of Pediatrics (AAP) Committee on Child Abuse and Neglect. (1999). Guidelines for the evaluation of sexual abuse in children: Subject review. *Pediatrics, 103,* 186–191.

American Academy of Pediatrics (AAP) Committee on Children with Disabilities and Committee on Drugs. (1996). Medication for children with attentional disorders. *Pediatrics, 98,* 301–304.

American Academy of Pediatrics (AAP) Committee on Children with Disabilities and Committee on Psychosocial Aspects of Child and Family Health. (1993). Psychosocial risks of chronic health conditions in childhood and adolescence. *Pediatrics, 92,* 876–877.

American Academy of Pediatrics (AAP) Committee on Communications. (1995). Sexuality, contraception, and the media. *Pediatrics, 95,* 298–300.

American Academy of Pediatrics (AAP) Committee on Community Health Services. (1996). Health needs of homeless children and families. *Pediatrics, 88,* 789–791.

American Academy of Pediatrics (AAP) Committee on Drugs and Committee on Bioethics. (1997). Considerations related to the use of recombinant human growth hormone in children. *Pediatrics, 99,* 122–128.

American Academy of Pediatrics (AAP) Committee on Drugs. (1980). Marijuana. *Pediatrics, 65,* 652–656.

American Academy of Pediatrics (AAP) Committee on Drugs. (1994). The transfer of drugs and other chemicals into human milk. *Pediatrics, 93,* 137–150.

American Academy of Pediatrics (AAP) Committee on Environmental Health. (1993). Lead poisoning: From screening to primary prevention. *Pediatrics, 92,* 176–183.

American Academy of Pediatrics (AAP) Committee on Environmental Health. (1997). Environmental tobacco smoke: A hazard to children. *Pediatrics, 99,* 639–642.

American Academy of Pediatrics (AAP) Committee on Environmental Health. (1998). Screening for elevated blood lead levels. *Pediatrics, 101,* 1072–1078.

American Academy of Pediatrics (AAP) Committee on Fetus and Newborn and American College of Obstetricians and Gynecologists (ACOG) Committee on Obstetric Practice. (1996). Use and abuse of the Apgar score. *Pediatrics, 98,* 141–142.

American Academy of Pediatrics (AAP) Committee on Genetics. (1996). Newborn screening fact sheet. *Pediatrics, 98,* 1–29.

American Academy of Pediatrics (AAP) Committee on Genetics. (1999). Folic acid for the prevention of neural tube defects. *Pediatrics, 104,* 325–327.

American Academy of Pediatrics (AAP) Committee on Infectious Diseases. (1994). *Red book* (23rd ed.). Elk Grove Village, IL: Author.

American Academy of Pediatrics (AAP) Committee on Infectious Diseases. (2000). Recommended childhood immunization schedule—United States, 2002. Retrieved September 25, 2002, from http://www.aap.org/family/parents/im02.pdf

American Academy of Pediatrics (AAP) Committee on Injury and Poison Prevention. (1995a). Bicycle helmets. *Pediatrics, 95,* 609–610.

American Academy of Pediatrics (AAP) Committee on Injury and Poison Prevention. (1995b). Injuries associated with infant walkers. *Pediatrics, 95,* 778–780.

American Academy of Pediatrics (AAP) Committee on Injury and Poison Prevention. (2000). Firearm-related injuries affecting the pediatric population. *Pediatrics, 105*(4), 888–895.

American Academy of Pediatrics (AAP) Committee on Injury and Poison Prevention and Committee on Sports Medicine and Fitness. (1999). Policy statement: Trampolines at home, school, and recreational centers. *Pediatrics, 103,* 1053–1056.

American Academy of Pediatrics (AAP) Committee on Nutrition. (1992). Statement on cholesterol. *Pediatrics, 90,* 469–473.

American Academy of Pediatrics (AAP) Committee on Nutrition. (1992b). The use of whole cow's milk in infancy. *Pediatrics, 89,* 1105–1109.

American Academy of Pediatrics (AAP) Committee on Pediatric AIDS and Committee on Infectious Diseases. (1999). Issues related to human immunodeficiency virus transmission in schools, child care, medical settings, the home, and community. *Pediatrics, 104,* 318–324.

American Academy of Pediatrics (AAP) Committee on Pediatric AIDS. (2000). Education of children with human immunodeficiency virus infection. *Pediatrics, 105,* 1358–1360.

American Academy of Pediatrics (AAP) Committee on Pediatric Aspects of Physical Fitness, Recreation, and Sports. (1981). Competitive athletics for children of elementary school age. *Pediatrics, 67,* 927–928.

American Academy of Pediatrics (AAP) Committee on Psychosocial Aspects of Child and Family Health. (1998). Guidance for effective discipline. *Pediatrics, 101,* 723–728.

American Academy of Pediatrics (AAP) Committee on Sports Medicine and Committee on School Health. (1989). Organized athletics for preadolescent children. *Pediatrics, 84,* 583–584.

American Academy of Pediatrics (AAP) Committee on Sports Medicine and Fitness. (1992). Fitness, activity, and sports participation in the preschool child. *Pediatrics, 90,* 1002–1004.

American Academy of Pediatrics (AAP) Committee on Sports Medicine and Fitness. (1997). Participation in boxing by children, adolescents, and young adults. *Pediatrics, 99,* 134–135.

American Academy of Pediatrics (AAP) Committee on Sports Medicine and Fitness. (1999). Human immunodeficiency virus and other blood-borne viral pathogens in the athletic setting. *Pediatrics, 104*(6), 1400–1403.

American Academy of Pediatrics (AAP) Committee on Sports Medicine and Fitness. (2000). Injuries in youth soccer: A subject review. *Pediatrics, 105*(3), 659–660.

American Academy of Pediatrics (AAP) Committee on Substance Abuse and Committee on Children with Disabilities. (1993). Fetal alcohol syndrome and fetal alcohol effects. *Pediatrics, 91,* 1004–1006.

American Academy of Pediatrics (AAP) Newborn Screening Task Force (2000). Serving the family from birth to the medical home: A report from the Newborn Screening Task Force convened in Washington, DC, May 10–11, 1999. *Pediatrics, 106*(2), Part 2 of 3.

American Academy of Pediatrics (AAP) Task Force on Infant Positioning and SIDS. (1997). Does bed sharing affect the risk of SIDS? *Pediatrics, 100,* 272.

American Academy of Pediatrics (AAP) Task Force on Infant Sleep Position and Sudden Infant Death Syndrome. (2000). Changing concepts of sudden infant death syndrome: Implications for infant sleeping environment and sleep position. *Pediatrics, 105*(3), 650–656.

American Academy of Pediatrics (AAP) Work Group on Breastfeeding. (1997). Breastfeeding and the use of human milk. *Pediatrics, 100,* 1035–1039.

American Academy of Pediatrics (AAP). (1986). *Positive approaches to day care dilemmas: How to make it work.* Elk Grove Village, IL: Author.

American Academy of Pediatrics (AAP). (1989a, November). The facts on breast feeding [Fact sheet]. (Available from AAP, 141 Northwest Point Blvd., Elk Grove Village, IL, 60007-1098.)

American Academy of Pediatrics (AAP). (1989b). Follow-up on weaning formulas. *Pediatrics, 83,* 1067.

American Academy of Pediatrics (AAP). (1992a, January 15). AAP proposes handgun ban, other measures to curb firearm deaths, injuries [News release]. Elk Grove Village, IL: Author.

American Academy of Pediatrics (AAP). (1992b, spring). Bedtime doesn't have to be a struggle. Healthy Kids, pp. 4–10.

American Academy of Pediatrics (AAP). (1998). Policy statement on female genital mutilation. *Pediatrics, 102,* 153–156.

American Association of University Women (AAUW) Educational Foundation. (1992). *The AAUW report: How schools shortchange girls.* Washington, DC: Author.

American Association of University Women (AAUW) Educational Foundation. (1998a, October 14). Gender gaps fact sheets. Retrieved September 25, 2002, from http://www.aauw.org/2000/ggfs.html

American Association of University Women (AAUW) Educational Foundation. (1998b, October 14). Technology gender gap develops while gaps in math and science narrow, AAUW Foundation report shows. [Press release]. Retrieved September 23, 2002, from http://www.aauw.org/2000/ggpr.html

American College of Obstetrics and Gynecology (ACOG). (1994). *Exercise during pregnancy and the postpartum pregnancy* (Technical Bulletin No. 189). Washington, DC: Author.

American Foundation for the Prevention of Venereal Disease (AFPVD). (1988). *Sexually transmitted disease [venereal disease]: Prevention for everyone* (16th rev. ed.). New York: Author.

American Psychiatric Association (APA). (1994). *Diagnostic and statistical manual of mental disorders* (4th ed.). Washington, DC: Author.

American Psychological Association and American Academy of Pediatrics (AAP). (1996). Raising children to resist violence: What you can do? Retrieved September 23, 2002, from www.apa.org/pi/pii/raisingchildren.html.

American Psychological Association Commission on Violence and Youth. (1994). *Reason to hope.* Washington, DC: Author.

American Psychological Association. (1992). Ethical principles of psychologists and code of conduct. *American Psychologist, 47,* 1597–1611.

American Psychological Association. (1993). *Violence and youth: Psychology's response* (Vol. 1). Summary report of the American Psychological Association Commission on Violence and Youth. Washington, DC: Author.

American Psychological Association. (n.d.). *Answers to your questions about sexual orientation and homosexuality* [Brochure]. Washington, DC: Author.

Ames, E. W. (1997). *The development of Romanian orphanage children adopted to Canada: Final report* (National Welfare Grants Program, Human Resources Development, Canada). Burnaby, BC: Simon Fraser University, Psychology Department.

Ammenheuser, M. M., Berenson, A. B., Babiak, A. E., Singleton, C. R., & Whorton, E. B. (1998). Frequencies of hprt mutant lymphocytes in marijuana-smoking. *Mutation Research, 403,* 55–64.

Amsel, E., Goodman, G., Savoie, D., & Clark, M. (1996). The development of reasoning about causal and noncausal influences on levers. *Child Development, 67,* 1624–1646.

Anastasi, A. (1988). *Psychological testing* (6th ed.). New York: Macmillan.

Anastasi, A., & Schaefer, C. E. (1971). Note on concepts of creativity and intelligence. *Journal of Creative Behavior, 3,* 113–116.

Anastasi, A., & Urbina, S. (1997). *Psychological testing* (7th ed.). Upper Saddle River, NJ: Prentice-Hall.

Anda, R. F., Croft, J. B., Felitti, V. J., Nordenberg, D., Giles, W. H., Williamson, D. F., & Giovina, G. A. (1999). Adverse childhood experiences and smoking during adolescence and adulthood. *Journal of the American Medical Association, 282*(17), 1652–1658.

Andersen, A. E. (1995). Eating disorders in males. In K. D. Brownell & C. G. Fairburn (Eds.), *Eating disorders and obesity: A comprehensive handbook* (pp. 177–187). New York: Guilford.

Andersen, R. E., Crespo, C. J., Bartlett, S. J., Cheskin, L. J., & Pratt, M. (1998). Relationship of physical activity and television watching with body weight and level of fatness among children: Results from the Third National Health and Nutrition Examination Survey. *Journal of the American Medical Association, 279,* 938–942.

Anderson, A. H., Clark, A., & Mullin, J. (1994). Interactive communication between children: Learning how to make language work in dialog. *Journal of Child Language, 21,* 439–463.

Anderson, D., & Anderson, R. (1999). The cost-effectiveness of home birth. *Journal of Nurse-Midwifery, 44*(1), 30–35.

Anderson, M. (1992). *My Lord, what a morning.* Madison: University of Wisconsin Press.

Anderson, W. F. (1998). Human gene therapy. *Nature, 392*(Suppl.), 25–30.

Anisfeld, M. (1996). Only tongue protrusion modeling is matched by neonates. *Developmental Review, 16,* 149–161.

Annitto, W. J. (2000). Detoxification with buprenorphine of a pregnant heroin addict. *The American Journal on Addictions: American Academy of Psychiatrists in Alcoholism and Addictions, 9,* 92–93.

Antonarakis, S. E., & Down Syndrome Collaborative Group. (1991). Parental origin of the extra chromosome in trisomy 21 as indicated by analysis of DNA polymorphisms. *New England Journal of Medicine, 324,* 872–876.

Antony, M. M., & Swinson, R. P. (1996). *Anxiety disorders and their treatment: A critical review of the evidence-based literature.* Ottawa: Health Canada.

Anyaegbunam, A., Tran, T., Jadali, D., Randolph, G., & Mikhail, M. S. (1997). Assessment of fetal well-being in methadone-maintained pregnancies: Abnormal nonstress tests. *Gynecologic and Obstetric Investigation, 43,* 25–28.

Apgar, V. (1953). A proposal for a new method of evaluation of the newborn infant. *Current Research in Anesthesia and Analgesia, 32,* 260–267.

Arbuckle, T. E., Savitz, D. A., Mery, L. S., & Curtis, K. M. (1999). Exposure to phenoxy herbicides and the risk of spontaneous abortion. *Epidemiology, 10,* 752–760.

Arbuckle, T. E., Schrader, S. M., Cole, D., Hall, J. C., Bancej, C. M., Turner L. A., & Claman P. (1999). 2,4-Doichlorophenoxyacetic acid residues in semen of Ontario farmers. *Reproductive Toxicology, 13,* 421–429.

Arbuckle, T. E., Wilkins, R., Sherman, G. J. (1993). Birth weight percentiles by gestational age in Canada. *Obstetrics and Gynecology, 81,* 39–48.

Archer, S. L. (1993). Identity in relational contexts: A methodological proposal. In J. Kroger (Ed.), *Discussions on ego identity* (pp. 75–99). Hillsdale, NJ: Erlbaum.

Arcus, D., & Kagan, J. (1995). Temperament and craniofacial variation in the first two years. *Child Development, 66,* 1529–1540.

Arend, R., Gove, F., & Sroufe, L. A. (1979). Continuity of individual adaptation from infancy to kindergarten: A predictive study of ego-resiliency and curiosity in preschoolers. *Child Development, 50,* 950–959.

Arendt, R., Angelopoulos, J., Salvator, A., & Singer, L. (1999). Motor development of cocaine-exposed children at age two years. *Pediatrics, 103,* 86–92.

Armistead, L., Summers, P., Forehand, R., Morse, P. S., Morse, E., & Clark, L. (1999). Understanding of HIV/AIDS among children of HIV-infected mothers: Implications for prevention, disclosure, and bereavement. *Children's Health Care, 28,* 277–295.

Arnett, J. J. (1999). Adolescent storm and stress, reconsidered. *American Psychologist, 54,* 317–326.

Arnold, D. H., McWilliams, L., & Arnold, A. H. (1998). Teacher discipline and child misbehavior in day care: Untangling causality with correlational data. *Developmental Psychology, 34*(2), 276–287.

Arnold, D. S., & Whitehurst, G. J. (1994). Accelerating language development through picture book reading: A summary of dialogic reading and its effects. In D. K. Dickinson (Ed.), *Bridges to literacy: Children, families, and schools* (pp. 103–128). Oxford: Blackwell.

Arnup, K. (1994). *Education for motherhood: Advice for mothers in twentieth-century Canada.* Toronto: University of Toronto Press.

Artz, S. (1998). Where have all the school girls gone? Violent girls in the school yard. *Child and Youth Care Forum, 27,* 77–109.

Aslin, R. N. (1987). Visual and auditory development in infancy. In J. D. Osofsky (Ed.), *Handbook of infant development* (2nd ed., pp. 5–97). New York: Wiley.

Astington, J. W. (1993). *The child's discovery of the mind.* Cambridge, MA: Harvard University Press.

Astington, J. W., & Jenkins, J. M. (1999). A longitudinal study of the relation between language and theory-of-mind development. *Developmental Psychology, 35,* 1311–1320.

Atkinson, J. (1995). Through the eyes of an infant. In R. L. Gregory, J. Harris, P. Heard, & D. Rose (Eds.), *The artful eye.* Oxford: Oxford University Press.

Autism—Part II. (1997, April). *The Harvard Mental Health Letter,* 1–4.

Aylward, G. P., Pfeiffer, S. I., Wright, A., & Verhulst, S. J. (1989). Outcome studies of low birth weight infants published in the last decade: A meta-analysis. *Journal of Pediatrics, 115,* 515–520.

Azar, B. (1997, December). Researchers debunk myth of the "crack baby." *APA Monitor,* 14.

Azuma, H. (1994). Two modes of cognitive socialization in Japan and the United States. In P. M. Greenfield & R. R. Cocking (Eds.), *Cross-cultural roots of minority child development* (pp. 275–284). Hillsdale, NJ: Erlbaum.

B.C. Doctors' Stop-Smoking Program. (2002). *BC doctors' stop-smoking program: A program of the Society for Clinical Preventative Health Care.* Retrieved August 9, 2002, from

http://www.bcdssp.com/
female_teen_smokers.htm

Babu, A., & Hirschhorn, K. (1992). *A guide to human chromosome defects (Birth Defects: Original Article Series, 28*[2]). White Plains, NY: March of Dimes Birth Defects Foundation.

Bachman, J. G., & Schulenberg, J. (1993). How part-time work intensity relates to drug use, problem behavior, time use, and satisfaction among high school seniors: Are these consequences or merely correlates? *Developmental Psychology, 29,* 220–235.

Bachu, A. (1993). *Fertility of American women: June 1992* (Current Population Report No. P24-470). Washington, DC: U.S. Government Printing Office.

Baddeley, A. D. (1981). The concept of working memory: A view of its current state and probable future development. *Cognition, 10,* 17–23.

Baddeley, A. D. (1986). *Working memory.* London: Oxford University Press.

Bagley, C., & Mallick, K. (2000). Prediction of sexual, emotional, and physical maltreatment and mental health outcomes in a longitudinal cohort of 290 adolescent women. *Child Maltreatment, 5,* 218–227.

Bagwell, C. L., Newcomb, A. F., & Bukowski, W. M. (1998). Preadolescent friendship and peer rejection as predictors of adult adjustment. *Child Development, 69,* 140–153.

Bailey, A., Le Couteur, A., Gottesman, I., & Bolton, P. (1995). Autism as a strongly genetic disorder: Evidence from a British twin study. *Psychological Medicine, 25,* 63–77.

Bailey, J. M., Bobrow, D., Wolfe, M., & Mikach, S. (1995). Sexual orientation of adult sons of gay fathers. *Developmental Psychology, 31,* 124–129.

Baillargeon, R. (1994). How do infants learn about the physical world? *Current Directions in Psychological Science, 3,* 133–140.

Baillargeon, R. (1999). Young infants' expectations about hidden objects. *Developmental Science, 2,* 115–132.

Baillargeon, R., & DeVos, J. (1991). Object permanence in young infants: Further evidence. *Child Development, 62,* 1227–1246.

Baillargeon, R., Tremblay, R. E., & Willms, J. D. (1999). *The prevalence of physical aggression in Canadian children: A multi-group latent class analysis of data from the first collection cycle (1994–1995) of the NLSCY.*

Catalogue No. MP32-30/00-2E. Ottawa: Applied Research Branch, Strategic Policy, Human Resources Development Canada.

Baird, A. A., Gruber, S. A., Fein, D. A., Maas, L. C., Steingard, R. J., Renshaw, P. F., Cohen, B. M., & Yurgelon-Todd, D. A. (1999). Functional magnetic resonance imaging of facial affect recognition in children and adolescents. *Journal of the American Academy of Child and Adolescent Psychiatry, 38,* 195–199.

Baker, M. (2001). Families: Changing trends in Canada. *Toronto: McGraw-Hill Ryerson.*

Baldwin, D. A., & Moses, L. J. (1996). The ontogeny of social information gathering. *Child Development, 67,* 1915–1939.

Ball, T. M., Castro-Rodriguez, J. A., Griffith, K. A., Holberg, C. J., Martinez, F. D., & Wright, A. L. (2000). Siblings, day-care attendance, and the risk of asthma and wheezing during childhood. *New England Journal of Medicine, 343,* 538–543.

Baltes, P. B., Reese, H. W., & Lipsitt, L. (1980). Life-span developmental psychology. *Annual Review of Psychology, 31,* 65–110.

Bandura, A. (1977). *Social learning theory.* Englewood Cliffs, NJ: Prentice-Hall.

Bandura, A. (1986). *Social foundations of thought and action: A social cognitive theory.* Englewood Cliffs, NJ: Prentice-Hall.

Bandura, A. (1989). Social cognitive theory. In R. Vasta (Ed.), *Annals of child development.* Greenwich, CT: JAI.

Bandura, A. (1994). Self-efficacy. In V. S. Ramachaudran (Ed.), *Encyclopedia of Human Behavior* (Vol. 4, pp. 71–81). New York: Academic Press.

Bandura, A., Barbaranelli, C., Caprara, G. V., & Pastorelli, C. (1996). Multifaceted impact of self-efficacy beliefs on academic functioning. *Child Development, 67,* 1206–1222.

Bandura, A., Ross, D., & Ross, S. A. (1961). Transmission of aggression through imitation of aggressive models. *Journal of Abnormal and Social Psychology, 63,* 575–582.

Bandura, A., Ross, D., & Ross, S. A. (1963). Imitation of film-mediated aggressive models. *Journal of Abnormal and Social Psychology, 66,* 3–11.

Banks, E. (1989). Temperament and individuality: A study of Malay children. *American Journal of Orthopsychiatry, 59,* 390–397.

Barager, J. R. (Ed.). (1968). *Why Perón came to power: The background to Peronism in Argentina.* New York: Knopf.

Barber, B. K. (1994). Cultural, family, and personal contexts of parent–adolescent conflict. *Journal of Marriage and the Family, 56,* 375–386.

Barber, B. L., & Eccles, J. S. (1992). Long-term influence of divorce and single parenting on adolescent family- and work-related values, behaviors, and aspirations. *Psychological Bulletin, 111*(1), 108–126.

Barber, J. G. (2000). Relative misery and youth suicide. *Australian & New Zealand Journal of Psychiatry, 35,* 49–57.

Barkley, R. A. (1998a, February). How should attention deficit disorder be described? *Harvard Mental Health Letter,* 8.

Barkley, R. A. (1998b, September). Attention-deficit hyperactivity disorder. *Scientific American,* 66–71.

Barkley, R. A., Murphy, K. R., & Kwasnik, D. (1996). Motor vehicle competencies and risks in teens and young adults with attention deficit hyperactivity disorder. *Pediatrics, 98,* 1089–1095.

Barlow, S. E., & Dietz, W. H. (1998). Obesity evaluation and treatment: Expert committee recommendations. *Pediatrics, 102*(3), e29. Retrieved September 24, 2002, from http://www.pediatrics.org/cgi/content/full/102/3/e29

Barnat, S. B., Klein, P. J., & Meltzoff, A. N. (1996). Deferred imitation across changes in context and object: Memory and generalization in 14-month-old infants. *Infant Behavior and Development, 19,* 241–251.

Barnes, A., Colton, T., Gunderson, J., Noller, K., Tilley, B., Strama, T., Townsend, D., Hatab, P., & O'Brien, P. (1980). Fertility and outcome of pregnancy in women exposed in utero to diethylstilbestrol. *New England Journal of Medicine, 302*(11), 609–613.

Barnes, J. (1978). *Evita, first lady: A biography of Eva Perón.* New York: Grove.

Barr, R. G., Hopkins, B., & Green, J. A. (2000). Crying as a sign, a symptom and a signal: Evolving concepts of crying behavior. In R. G. Barr, B. Hopkins, & J. A. Green (Eds.), *Crying as a sign, a symptom, and a signal: Clinical, emotional and developmental aspects of infant and toddler crying* (pp. 1–7). London: MacKeith Press.

Barr, R., Dowden, A., & Hayne, H. (1996). Developmental changes in deferred imitation by 6- to 24-month-old infants. *Infant Behavior and Development, 19,* 159–170.

Barrett, R. L., & Robinson, B. E. (1990). *Gay fathers.* Lexington, MA: Lexington.

Barthel, J. (1982, May). Just a normal, naughty three-year-old. *McCall's,* pp. 78, 136–144.

Bartoshuk, L. M., & Beauchamp, G. K. (1994). Chemical senses. *Annual Review of Psychology, 45,* 419–449.

Bassuk, E. L. (1991). Homeless families. *Scientific American, 265*(6), 66–74.

Bassuk, E. L., Weinreb, L. F., Dawson, R., Perloff, J. N., & Buckner, J. C. (1997). Determinants of behavior in homeless and low-income housed preschooler children. *Pediatrics, 100,* 92–100.

Bates, E., Bretherton, I., & Snyder, L. (1988). *From first words to grammar: Individual differences and dissociable mechanisms.* New York: Cambridge University Press.

Bates, E., O'Connell, B., & Shore, C. (1987). Language and communication in infancy. In J. D. Osofsky (Ed.), *Handbook of infant development* (2nd ed.). New York: Wiley.

Bateson, M. C. (1984). *With a daughter's eye: A memoir of Margaret Mead and Gregory Bateson.* New York: William Morrow & Co.

Baumrind, D. (1971). Harmonious parents and their preschool children. *Developmental Psychology, 41,* 92–102.

Baumrind, D. (1989). Rearing competent children. In W. Damon (Ed.), *Child development today and tomorrow* (pp. 349–378). San Francisco: Jossey-Bass.

Baumrind, D. (1991). Parenting styles and adolescent development. In J. Brooks-Gunn, R. Lerner, & A. C. Peterson (Eds.), *The encyclopedia of adolescence* (pp. 746–758). New York: Garland.

Baumrind, D. (1995). Commentary on sexual orientation: Research and social policy implications. *Developmental Psychology, 31,* 130–136.

Baumrind, D. (1996a). A blanket injunction against disciplinary use of spanking is not warranted by the data. *Pediatrics, 88,* 828–831.

Baumrind, D. (1996b). The discipline controversy revisited. *Family Relations, 45,* 405–414.

Baumrind, D., & Black, A. E. (1967). Socialization practices associated with

dimensions of competence in preschool boys and girls. *Child Development, 38,* 291–327.

Baumwell, L., Tamis-LeMonda, C. S., & Bornstein, M. H. (1997). Maternal verbal sensitivity and child language comprehension. *Infant Behavior and Development, 20,* 247–258.

Baydar, N., Greek, A., & Brooks-Gunn, J. (1997). A longitudinal study of the effects of the birth of a sibling during the first 6 years of life. *Journal of Marriage and the Family, 59,* 939–956.

Baydar, N., Hyle, P., & Brooks-Gunn, J. (1997). A longitudinal study of the effects of the birth of a sibling during preschool and early grade school years. *Journal of Marriage and the Family, 59,* 957–965.

Bayley, N. (1993). *Bayley scales of infant development: II.* New York: Psychological Corporation.

Beal, C. R. (1994). *Boys and girls: The development of gender roles.* New York: McGraw-Hill.

Becker, A. E., Grinspoon, S. K., Klibanski, A., & Herzog, D. B. (1999). Eating disorders. *New England Journal of Medicine, 340,* 1092–1098.

Beckwith, L., Cohen, S. E., & Hamilton, C. E. (1999). Maternal sensitivity during infancy and subsequent life events relate to attachment representation at early adulthood. *Developmental Psychology, 35,* 693–700.

Behrman, R. E. (1992). *Nelson textbook of pediatrics* (13th ed.). Philadelphia: Saunders.

Beidel, D. C., & Turner, S. M. (1998). *Shy children, phobic adults: Nature and treatment of social phobia.* Washington, DC: American Psychological Association.

Beiser, M., & Gotowiec, A. (2000). Accounting for native/non-native differences in IQ scores. *Psychology in the Schools, 37,* 237–252.

Beiser, M., Dion, R., Gotowiec, A., Hyman, I., & Nhi, V. (1995). Immigrant and refugee children in Canada. *Canadian Journal of Psychiatry, 40,* 67–72.

Beiser, M., Hou, F., Hyman, I., & Tousignant, M. (1998). *Growing up Canadian: A study of new immigrant children.* Report No. W-98-24E. Ottawa: Applied Research Branch, Strategic Policy, Human Resources Development Canada.

Beiser, M., Hou, F., Hyman, I., & Tousignant, M. (2002). Poverty, family process, and the mental health of

immigrant children in Canada. *American Journal of Public Health, 92,* 220–227.

Beiser, M., Sack, W., Manson, S. M., Redshirt, R., & Dion, R. (1998). Mental health and the academic performance of First Nations and majority-culture children. *American Journal of Orthopsychiatry, 68,* 455–467.

Bell, M. A., & Fox, N. A. (1992). The relations between frontal brain electrical activity and cognitive development during infancy. *Child Development, 63,* 1142–1163.

Bellinger, D., Leviton, A., Watermaux, C., Needleman, H., & Rabinowitz, M. (1987). Longitudinal analyses of prenatal and postnatal lead exposure and early cognitive development. *New England Journal of Medicine, 316*(17), 1037–1043.

Belsky, J. (1984). Two waves of day care research: Developmental effects and conditions of quality. In R. Ainslie (Ed.), *The child and the day care setting.* New York: Praeger.

Belsky, J. (1993). Etiology of child maltreatment: A developmental-ecological analysis. *Psychological Bulletin, 114,* 413–434.

Belsky, J., & Rovine, M. (1990). Patterns of marital change across the transition to parenthood: Pregnancy to three years postpartum. *Journal of Marriage and the Family, 52,* 5–19.

Belsky, J., Fish, M., & Isabella, R. (1991). Continuity and discontinuity in infant negative and positive emotionality: Family antecedents and attachment consequences. *Developmental Psychology, 27,* 421–431.

Belsky, J., Lang, M., & Huston, T. L. (1986). Sex typing and division of labor as determinants of marital change across the transition to parenthood. *Journal of Personality and Social Psychology, 50,* 517–522.

Beltramini, A. U., & Hertzig, M. E. (1983). Sleep and bedtime behavior in preschool-aged children. *Pediatrics, 71,* 153–158.

Bem, S. L. (1983). Gender schema theory and its implications for child development: Raising gender-aschematic children in a gender-schematic society. *Signs, 8,* 598–616.

Bem, S. L. (1985). Androgyny and gender schema theory: A conceptual and empirical integration. In T. B. Sondregger (Ed.), *Nebraska Symposium on Motivation, 1984: Psychology and gender.* Lincoln: University of Nebraska Press.

Bem, S. L. (1993). *The lenses of gender: Transforming the debate on sexual inequality.* New Haven, CT: Yale University Press.

Bendersky, M., & Lewis, M. (1998). Arousal modulation in cocaine-exposed infants. *Developmental Psychology, 34,* 555–564.

Bendersky, M., Alessandri, S. M., & Lewis, M. (1996). Emotions in cocaine-exposed infants. In M. Lewis & M. W. Sullivan (Eds.), *Emotional development in atypical children* (pp. 89–108). Mahwah, NJ: Erlbaum.

Benenson, J. F. (1993). Greater preference among females than males for dyadic interaction in early childhood. *Child Development, 64,* 544–555.

Benes, F. M., Turtle, M., Khan, Y., & Farol, P. (1994). Myelination of a key relay zone in the hippocampal formation occurs in the human brain during childhood, adolescence, and adulthood. *Archives of General Psychiatry, 51,* 447–484.

Benjamin, W. J., Schneider, B. H., Greenman, P. S., & Hum, M. (2001). Conflict and childhood friendship in Taiwan and Canada. *Canadian Journal of Behavioural Science, 33,* 203–211.

Benson, J. B., & Uzgiris, I. C. (1985). Effect of self-inflicted locomotion on infant search activity. *Developmental Psychology, 21,* 923–931.

Benson, M. (1986). *Nelson Mandela: The man and the movement.* New York: Norton.

Berenbaum, S. A., & Snyder, E. (1995). Early hormonal influences on childhood sex-typed activity and playmate preferences: Implications for the development of sexual orientation. *Developmental Psychology, 31,* 31–42.

Bergeman, C. S., & Plomin, R. (1989). Genotype-environment interaction. In M. Bornstein & J. Bruner (Eds.), *Interaction in human development* (pp. 157–171). Hillsdale, NJ: Erlbaum.

Berk, L. E. (1986a). Development of private speech among preschool children. *Early Child Development and Care, 24,* 113–136.

Berk, L. E. (1986b). Private speech: Learning out loud. *Psychology Today, 20*(5), 34–42.

Berk, L. E. (1992). Children's private speech: An overview of theory and the status of research. In R. M. Diaz & L. E. Berk (Eds.), *Private speech: From social interaction to self-regulation* (pp. 17–53). Hillsdale, NJ: Erlbaum.

Berk, L. E., & Garvin, R. A. (1984). Development of private speech among low-income Appalachian children. *Developmental Psychology, 20,* 271–286.

Berkowitz, G. S., Skovron, M. L., Lapinski, R. H., & Berkowitz, R. L. (1990). Delayed childbearing and the outcome of pregnancy. *New England Journal of Medicine, 322,* 659–664.

Berndt, T. J. (1982). The features and effects of friendship in early adolescence. *Child Development, 53,* 1447–1460.

Berndt, T. J., & Perry, T. B. (1990). Distinctive features and effects of early adolescent friendships. In R. Montemayor, G. R. Adams, & T. P. Gullotta (Eds.), *From childhood to adolescence: A transitional period?* (Vol. 2, pp. 269–287). Newbury Park, CA: Sage.

Bernhardt, P. C. (1997). Influences of serotonin and testosterone in aggression and dominance: Convergence with social psychology. *Current Directions in Psychological Science, 6,* 44–48.

Bernstein, G. A., & Garfinkel, B. D. (1988). Pedigrees, functioning, and psychopathology in families of school phobic children. *American Journal of Psychiatry, 145,* 70–74.

Bernstein, J. (1973). *Einstein.* New York: Viking.

Berrick, J. D. (1998). When children cannot remain home: Foster family care and kinship care. *The Future of Children, 8,* 72–87.

Berrueta-Clement, J. R., Schweinhart, L. J., Barnett, W. S., & Weikart, D. P. (1987). The effects of early educational intervention on crime and delinquency in adolescence and early adulthood. In J. D. Burchard & S. N. Burchard (Eds.), *Primary prevention of psychopathology: Vol. 10. Prevention of delinquent behavior* (pp. 220–240). Newbury Park, CA: Sage.

Berrueta-Clement, J. R., Schweinhart, L. J., Barnett, W. S., Epstein, A. S., & Weikart, D. P. (1985). *Changed lives: The effects of the Perry Preschool Program on youths through age 19.* Ypsilanti, MI: High/Scope.

Berry, M., Dylla, D. J., Barth, R. P., & Needell, B. (1998). The role of open adoption in the adjustment of adopted children and their families. *Children and Youth Services Review, 20,* 151–171.

Berry, R. J., Li, Z., Erickson, J. D., Li, S., Moore, C. A., Wang, H., Mulinare, J., Zhao, P., Wong, L.-Y. C., Gindler, J., Hong, S.-X., & Correa, A. for the China–U.S. Collaborative Project for Neural Tube Defect Prevention. (1999). Prevention of neural-tube defects with folic acid in China. *New England Journal of Medicine, 341,* 1485–1490.

Bertenthal, B. I., & Campos, J. J. (1987). New directions in the study of early experience. *Child Development, 58,* 560–567.

Bertenthal, B. I., Campos, J. J., & Barrett, K. C. (1984). Self-produced locomotion: An organizer of emotional, cognitive, and social development in infancy. In R. N. Emde & R. J. Harmon (Eds.), *Continuities and discontinuities in development.* New York: Plenum.

Bertenthal, B. I., Campos, J. J., & Kermoian, R. (1994). An epigenetic perspective on the development of self-produced locomotion and its consequences. *Current Directions in Psychological Science, 3*(5), 140–145.

Beumont, P. J. V., Russell, J. D., & Touyz, S. W. (1993). Treatment of anorexia nervosa. *Lancet, 341,* 1635–1640.

Bianchi, S. M. (1995). The changing demographic and socioeconomic characteristics of single parent families. *Marriage and Family Review, 20*(1–2), 71–97.

Biemiller, A., & Siegel, L. S. (1997). A longitudinal study of the effects of the Bridge reading program for children at risk for reading failure. *Learning Disability Quarterly, 20,* 83–92.

Bierman, K. L., Smoot, D. L., & Aumiller, K. (1993). Characteristics of aggressive-rejected, aggressive (non-rejected), and rejected (non-aggressive) boys. *Child Development, 64,* 139–151.

Bigelow, A. E., & Birch, S. A. J. (2000). The effects of contingency in previous interactions on infants' preference for social partners. *Infant Behavior & Development, 22,* 367–382.

Bild, E.-R., & Swain, M. (1989). Minority language students in a French immersion programme: Their French proficiency. *Journal of Multilingual and Multicultural Development, 10,* 255–274.

Birch, L. L., Johnson, S. L., Andersen, G., Peters, J. C., & Schulte, M. C. (1991). The variability of young children's energy intake. *New England Journal of Medicine, 324,* 232–235.

Birch, S. H., & Ladd, G. W. (1997). The teacher–child relationship and children's early school adjustment. *Journal of School Psychology, 35,* 61–79.

Birmaher, B. (1998). Should we use antidepressant medications for children and adolescents with depressive disorders? *Psychopharmacology Bulletin, 34,* 35–39.

Birmaher, B., Ryan, N. D., Williamson, D. E., Brent, D. A., Kaufman, J., Dahl, R. E., Perel, J., & Nelson, B. (1996). Childhood and adolescent depression: A review of the past 10 years. *Journal of the American Academy of Child, 35,* 1427–1440.

Bivens, J. A., & Berk, L. E. (1988, April). *A longitudinal study of the development of elementary school children's private speech.* Paper presented at the meeting of the American Educational Research Association, New Orleans, LA.

Bjorklund, D. F. (1997). The role of immaturity in human development. *Psychological Bulletin, 122,* 153–169.

Bjorklund, D. F., & Harnishfeger, K. K. (1990). The resources construct in cognitive development: Diverse sources of evidence and a theory of inefficient inhibition. *Developmental Review, 10,* 48–71.

Black, J. E. (1998). How a child builds its brain: Some lessons from animal studies of neural plasticity. *Preventive Medicine, 27,* 168–171.

Black, M. M., & Krishnakumar, A. (1998). Children in low-income, urban settings: Interventions to promote mental health and well-being. *American Psychologist, 53,* 636–646.

Black, M. M., Dubowitz, H., and Starr, R. H. (1999). African American fathers in low income, urban families: Development, behavior, and home environment of their three-year-old children. *Child Development, 70,* 967–978.

Blakeslee, S. (1997, April 17). Studies show talking with infants shapes basis of ability to think. *New York Times,* p. D21.

Blanksten, G. I. (1953). *Perón's Argentina.* Chicago: University of Chicago Press.

Bloch, H., & Carchon, I. (1992). On the onset of eye–head coordination in infants. *Behavioural Brain Research, 49,* 85–90.

Bloom, H. (Ed.). (1999). *A scholarly look at* The Diary of Anne Frank. Philadelphia: Chelsea.

Blyth, D. A., & Foster-Clark, F. S. (1987). Gender differences in perceived intimacy with different members of adolescents' social networks. *Sex Roles, 17,* 689–718.

Blyth, D. A., Simmons, R. G., Bulcroft, R., Felt, D., Van Cleave, E. F., & Bush, D. M. (1981). The effects of physical development on self-image and satisfaction with body-image for early adolescent males. In R. G. Simmons (Ed.), *Research on community and mental health* (Vol. 2, pp. 43–73). Greenwich, CT: JAI.

Bodrova, E., & Leong, D. J. (1998). Adult influences on play: The Vygotskian approach. In D. P. Fromberg & D. Bergen (Eds.), *Play from birth to twelve and beyond: Contexts, perspectives, and meanings* (pp. 277–282). New York: Garland.

Bolger, K. E., Patterson, C. J., Thompson, W. W., & Kupersmidt, J. B. (1995). Psychosocial adjustment among children experiencing persistent and intermittent family economic hardship. *Child Development, 66,* 1107–1129.

Bond, C. A. (1989, September). A child prodigy from China wields a magical brush. *Smithsonian, 20,* pp. 70–79.

Borman G., Boulay, M., Kaplan, J., Rachuba, L., & Hewes, G. (1999, December 13). Evaluating the long-term impact of multiple summer interventions on the reading skills of low-income, early-elementary students. Preliminary report, Year 1. Baltimore, MD: Johns Hopkins University.

Bornstein, M. H., & Sigman, M. D. (1986). Continuity in mental development from infancy. *Child Development, 57,* 251–274.

Bornstein, M. H., & Tamis-LeMonda, C. S. (1994). Antecedents of information processing skills in infants: Habituation, novelty responsiveness, and cross-modal transfer. *Infant Behavior and Development, 17,* 371–380.

Bornstein, M. H., Tamis-LeMonda, C. S., & Haynes, O. M. (1999). First words in the second year: Continuity, stability, and models of concurrent and predictive correspondence in vocabulary and verbal responsiveness across age and context. *Infant Behavior and Development, 22,* 65–85.

Bornstein, M., Kessen, W., & Weiskopf, S. (1976). The categories of hue in infancy. *Science, 191,* 201–202.

Botto, L. D., Moore, C. A., Khoury, M. J., & Erickson, J. D. (1999). Neural-tube defects. *New England Journal of Medicine, 341,* 1509–1519.

Bouchard, T. J. (1994). Genes, environment, and personality. *Science, 264,* 1700–1701.

Boulton, M. J. (1995). Playground behaviour and peer interaction patterns of primary school boys classified as bullies, victims and not involved. *British Journal of Educational Psychology, 65,* 165–177.

Boulton, M. J., & Smith, P. K. (1994). Bully/victim problems in middle-school children: Stability, self-perceived competence, peer perception, and peer acceptance. *British Journal of Developmental Psychology, 12,* 315–329.

Bouza, A. V. (1990). *The police mystique: An insider's look at cops, crime, and the criminal justice system.* New York: Plenum.

Bower, B. (1993). A child's theory of mind. *Science News, 144,* 40–42.

Bowlby, J. (1951). Maternal care and mental health. *Bulletin of the World Health Organization, 3,* 355–534.

Bowlby, J. W., & McMullen, K. (2002). *At a crossroads: First results for the 18- to 20-year-old cohort of the Youth in Transition Survey.* Catalogue No. 81-591-XIE. Ottawa: Human Resources Development Canada and Statistics Canada.

Boyle, M. H., & Lipman, E. L. (1998). *Do places matter? A multilevel analysis of geographic variations in child behaviour in Canada.* Catalogue No. W-98-16E. Ottawa: Applied Research Branch, Strategic Policy, Human Resources Development Canada.

Boyum, L. A., & Parke, R. D. (1995). The role of family emotional expressiveness in the development of children's social competence. *Journal of Marriage and the Family, 57,* 593–608.

Bracher, G., & Santow, M. (1999). Explaining trends in teenage childbearing in Sweden. *Studies in Family Planning, 30,* 169–182.

Brackbill, Y., & Broman, S. H. (1979). *Obstetrical medication and development in the first year of life.* Unpublished manuscript.

Bradley, R. H. (1989). Home measurement of maternal responsiveness. In M. H. Bornstein (Ed.), *Maternal responsiveness: Characteristics and consequences (New Directions for Child Development 43).* San Francisco: Jossey-Bass.

Bradley, R. H., Caldwell, B. M., Rock, S. L., Ramey, C. T., Barnard, K. E., Gray, C., Hammond, M. A., Mitchell, S., Gottfried, A. W., Siegel, L., & Johnson, D. L. (1989). Home environment and cognitive development in the first 3 years of life: A collaborative study involving six sites and three ethnic groups in North America. *Developmental Psychology, 25*, 217–235.

Bradley, R., & Caldwell, B. (1982). The consistency of the home environment and its relation to child development. *International Journal of Behavioral Development, 5*, 445–465.

Bradley, R., Caldwell, B., & Rock, S. (1988). Home environment and school performance: A ten-year follow-up and examination of three models of environmental action. *Child Development, 59*, 852–867.

Braine, M. (1976). Children's first word combinations. *Monographs of the Society for Research in Child Development, 41*(1, Serial No. 164).

Brass, L. M., Isaacsohn, J. L., Merikangas, K. R., & Robinette, C. D. (1992). A study of twins and stroke. *Stroke, 23*(2), 221–223.

Braungart, J. M., Fulker, D. W., & Plomin, R. (1992). Genetic mediation of the home environment during infancy: A sibling adoption study of the HOME. *Developmental Psychology, 28*, 1048–1055.

Braungart, J. M., Plomin, R., DeFries, J. C., & Fulker, D. W. (1992). Genetic influence on tester-rated infant temperament as assessed by Bayley's Infant Behavior Record: Nonadoptive and adoptive siblings and twins. *Developmental Psychology, 28*, 40–47.

Braungart-Rieker, J., Garwood, M. M., Powers, B. P., & Notaro, P. C. (1998). Infant affect and affect regulation during the still-face paradigm with mothers and fathers: The role of infant characteristics and parental sensitivity. *Developmental Psychology, 34*(6), 1428–1437.

Braver, S. L., & O'Connell, D. (1998). *Divorced dads: Shattering the myths.* New York: Tarcher/Putnam.

Bray, J. H. (1991). Psychosocial factors affecting custodial and visitation arrangements. *Behavioral Sciences and the Law, 9*, 419–437.

Bray, J. H., & Hetherington, E. M. (1993). Families in transition: Introduction and overview. *Journal of Family Psychology, 7*, 3–8.

Brazelton, T. B. (1973). *Neonatal Behavioral Assessment scale.* Philadelphia: Lippincott.

Brazelton, T. B. (1984). *Neonatal Behavioral Assessment Scale.* Philadelphia: Lippincott.

Brazelton, T. B., & Nugent, J. K. (1995). *Neonatal Behavioral Assessment Scale* (3rd ed.). Cambridge, England: Cambridge University Press.

Brendgen, M., Little, T. D., & Krappmann, L. (2000). Rejected children and their friends: A shared evaluation of friendship quality? *Merrill-Palmer Quarterly, 46*, 45–70.

Brener, N. D., Simon, T. R., Krug, E. G., & Lowry, R. (1999). Recent trends in violence-related behaviors among high school students in the United States. *Journal of the American Medical Association, 282*, 440–446.

Brenneman, K., Massey, C., Machado, S. F., & Gelman, R. (1996). Young children's plans differ for writing and drawing. *Cognitive Development, 11*, 397–419.

Brenner, R. A., Overpeck, M. D., Trumble, A. C., DerSimonian, R., & Berendes, H. (1999). Deaths attributable to injuries in infants, United States, 1983–1991. *Pediatrics, 103*, 968–974.

Bretherton, I. (1990). Communication patterns, internal working models, and the intergenerational transmission of attachment relationships. *Infant Mental Health Journal, 11*(3), 237–252.

Bretherton, I. (1994). The origins of attachment theory: John Bowlby and Mary Ainsworth. In R. D. Parke, P. A. Ornstein, J. J. Rieser, & C. Zahn-Waxler (Eds.), *A century of developmental psychology* (pp. 431–471). Washington, DC: American Psychological Association.

Bretherton, I. (1997). Bowlby's legacy to developmental psychology. *Child Psychiatry and Human Development, 28*, 33–43.

Bretherton, I. (Ed.). (1984). *Symbolic play: The development of social understanding.* Orlando, FL: Academic.

Brezina, T. (1999). Teenage violence toward parents as an adaptation to family strain: Evidence from a national survey of male adolescents. *Youth & Society, 30*, 416–444.

Brian, D. (1996). *Einstein: A life.* New York: Wiley.

Briss, P. A., Sacks, J. J., Addiss, D. G., Kresnow, M., & O'Neil, J. (1994). A nationwide study of the risk of injury associated with day care center attendance. *Pediatrics, 93*, 364–368.

Brody, G. H., & Flor, D. L. (1998). Maternal resources, parenting practices, and child competence in rural, single-parent African American families. *Child Development, 69*, 803–816.

Brody, G. H., Flor, D. L., & Gibson, N. M. (1999). Linking maternal efficacy beliefs, developmental goals, parenting practices, and child competence in rural single-parent African American families. *Child Development, 70*(5), 1197–1208.

Brody, G. H., Stoneman, Z., & Flor, D. (1995). Linking family processes and academic competence among rural African American youths. *Journal of Marriage and the Family, 57*, 567–579.

Brody, G. H., Stoneman, Z., & Flor, D. (1996). Parental religiosity, family processes, and youth competence in rural, two-parent African American families. *Developmental Psychology, 32*, 696–706.

Brody, G. H., Stoneman, Z., & Gauger, K. (1996). Parent–child relationships, family problem-solving behavior, and sibling relationship quality: The moderating role of sibling temperaments. *Child Development, 67*, 1289–1300.

Brody, G. H., Stoneman, Z., Flor, D., McCrary, C., Hastings, L., & Conyers, O. (1994). Financial resources, parent psychological functioning, parent co-caregiving, and early adolescent competence in rural two-parent African-American families. *Child Development, 65*, 590–605.

Brody, J. E. (1995, June 28). Preventing birth defects even before pregnancy. *New York Times*, p. C10.

Brody, L. R., Zelazo, P. R., & Chaika, H. (1984). Habituation-dishabituation to speech in the neonate. *Developmental Psychology, 20*, 114–119.

Brodzinsky, D. (1997). Infertility and adoption adjustment: Considerations and clinical issues. In S. R. Leiblum (Ed.), *Infertility: Psychological issues and counseling strategies* (pp. 246–262). New York: Wiley.

Bronfenbrenner, U. (1979). *The ecology of human development.* Cambridge, MA: Harvard University Press.

Bronfenbrenner, U. (1986). Ecology of the family as a context for human development: Research perspectives. *Developmental Psychology, 22*, 723–742.

Bronfenbrenner, U. (1994). Ecological models of human development. In T. Husen & T. N. Postlethwaite (Eds.),

International encyclopedia of education (2nd ed., Vol. 3, pp. 1643–1647). Oxford: Pergamon Press/Elsevier Science.

Bronfenbrenner, U., & Crouter, A. (1982). Work and family through time and space. In S. B. Kamerman & C. D. Hayes (Eds.), *Families that work: Children in a changing world* (pp. 39–83). Washington, DC: National Academy of Science.

Bronfenbrenner, U., & Morris, P. A. (1998). The ecology of developmental processes. In W. Damon (Series Ed.) & R. Lerner (Vol. Ed.), *Handbook of child psychology: Vol. 1. Theoretical models of human development* (5th ed., pp. 993–1028). New York: Wiley.

Bronfenbrenner, U., Belsky, J., & Steinberg, L. (1977). *Daycare in context: An ecological perspective on research and public policy.* Review prepared for Office of the Assistant Secretary for Planning and Evaluation, U.S. Department of Health, Education, and Welfare.

Bronner, E. (1999, January 22). Plans to ask schools to deny promotion rekindles debate. New York Times. Retrieved September 24, 2002, from http://query.nytimes.com/search/abstract?res=F00D17F935540C718ED DA80894D1494D81

Bronstein, P. (1988). Father–child interaction: Implications for gender role socialization. In P. Bronstein & C. P. Cowan (Eds.), *Fatherhood today: Men's changing role in the family.* New York: Wiley.

Bronstein, P., Clauson, J., Stoll, M. F., & Abrams, C. L. (1993). Parenting behavior and children's social, psychological, and academic adjustment in diverse family structures. *Family Relations, 42,* 268–276.

Brooks, A. A. (1982). Family, youth, and leaving home in late-nineteenth-century rural Nova Scotia: Canning and the exodus, 1868–1893. In J. Parr (Ed.), *Childhood and family in Canadian history* (pp. 93–128). Toronto: McClelland and Stewart Limited.

Brooks, P. J., Tomasello, M., Dodson, K., and Lewis, L. B. (1999). Young children's overgeneralizations with fixed transitivity verbs. *Child Development, 70,* 1325–1337.

Brooks-Gunn, J. (1988). Pubertal processes and the early adolescent transition. In W. Damon (Ed.), *Child development today and tomorrow.* San Francisco: Jossey-Bass.

Brooks-Gunn, J., & Duncan, G. J. (1997). The effects of poverty on children. *The Future of Children, 7,* 55–71.

Brooks-Gunn, J., & Reiter, E. O. (1990). The role of pubertal processes. In S. S. Feldman & G. R. Elliott (Eds.), *At the threshold: The developing adolescent* (pp. 16–53). Cambridge, MA: Harvard University Press.

Brooks-Gunn, J., Britto, P. R., & Brady, C. (1998). Struggling to make ends meet: Poverty and child development. In M. E. Lamb (Ed.), *Parenting and child development in "non-traditional" families* (pp. 279–304). Mahwah, NJ: Erlbaum.

Brooks-Gunn, J., Duncan, G. J., Leventhal, T., & Aber, J. L. (1997). Lessons learned and future directions for research on the neighborhoods in which children live. In J. Brooks-Gunn, G. J. Duncan, & J. L. Aber (Eds.), *Neighborhood poverty: Context and consequences for children* (Vol. 1, pp. 279–297). New York: Russell Sage Foundation.

Brooks-Gunn, J., Klebanov, P. K., & Duncan, G. J. (1996). Ethnic differences in children's intelligence test scores: Role of economic deprivation, home environment, and maternal characteristics. *Child Development, 67,* 396–408.

Brooks-Gunn, J., Klebanov, P. K., Liaw, F., & Spiker, D. (1993). Enhancing the development of low-birthweight, premature infants: Changes in cognition and behavior over the first three years. *Child Development, 64,* 736–753.

Brooks-Gunn, J., McCarton, C. M., Casey, P. H., et al. (1994). Early intervention in low-birthweight premature infants: Results through age 5 years from the Infant Health Development Program. *Journal of the American Medical Association, 272,* 1257–1262.

Brosco, J. P. (1999). The early history of infant mortality rate in America: "A reflection upon the past and a prophecy of the future." *Pediatrics, 103,* 478–485.

Broude, G. J. (1995). *Growing up: A cross-cultural encyclopedia.* Santa Barbara, CA: ABC-CLIO.

Brousseau, L., Malcuit, G., Pomerleau, A., & Feider, H. (1996). Relations between lexical-temporal features in mothers' speech and infants' interactive behaviours. *First Language, 16,* 41–59.

Brown, A. L., & Ferrara, R. A. (1999). Diagnosing zones of proximal development. In P. Lloyd & C.

Fernyhough (Eds.), *Lev Bygotsky: Critical assessments: The zone of proximal development* (Vol. 3, pp. 225–256). New York: Routledge.

Brown, A. L., Metz, K. E., & Campione, J. C. (1996). Social interaction and individual understanding in a community of learners: The influence of Piaget and Vygotsky. In A. Tryphon & J. Voneche (Eds), *Piaget-Vygotsky: The social genesis of thought* (pp. 145–170). Hove, England: Psychology/Erlbaum (UK) Taylor & Francis.

Brown, B. (1999). Optimizing expression of the common human genome for child development. *Current Directions in Psychological Science, 8*(2), 37–41.

Brown, B. B., Mounts, N., Lamborn, S. D., & Steinberg, L. (1993). Parenting practices and peer group affiliation in adolescence. *Child Development, 64,* 467–482.

Brown, J. L. (1987). Hunger in the U.S. *Scientific American, 256*(2), 37–41.

Brown, J. R., & Dunn, J. (1996). Continuities in emotion understanding from three to six years. *Child Development, 67,* 789–802.

Brown, J., & Harvey, G. (1980). *Terry Fox: A pictorial tribute to the Marathon of Hope.* Don Mills, ON: General Publishing Co. Limited.

Brown, L. J., Kaste, L. M., Selwitz, R. H., & Furman, L. J. (1996). Dental caries and sealant usage in U.S. children, 1988–1991. *Journal of the American Dental Association, 127,* 335–343.

Brown, L. J., Wall, T. P., & Lazar, V. (1999). Trends in untreated caries in permanent teeth of children 6 to 18 years old. *Journal of the American Dental Association, 130,* 1637–1644.

Brown, L. J., Wall, T. P., & Lazar, V. (2000). Trends in untreated caries in primary teeth of children 2 to 10 years old. *Journal of the American Dental Association, 131,* 93–100.

Brown, L. M., & Gilligan, C. (1990, April). *The psychology of women and the development of girls.* Paper presented at the Laurel-Harvard Conference on the Psychology of Women and the Education of Girls, Cleveland, OH.

Brown, N. M. (1990). Age and children in the Kalahari. *Health and Human Development Research, 1,* 26–30.

Brown, P. (1993, April 17). Motherhood past midnight. *New Scientist,* pp. 4–8.

Brown, R., & Pressley, M. (1994). Self-regulated reading and getting meaning from text: The transactional strategies instruction model and its ongoing validation. In D. Schunk & B. Zimmerman (Eds.), *Self-regulation of learning and performance: Issues and educational applications* (pp. 155–179). Hillsdale, NJ: Erlbaum.

Brown, R., Pressley, M., Schuder, T., & Van Meter, P. (1994). *A quasi-experimental validation of transactional strategies instruction with previously low-achieving grade-2 readers.* Buffalo and Albany: State University of New York.

Brown, S. S. (1985). Can low birth weight be prevented? *Family Planning Perspectives, 17*(3), 112–118.

Browne, A., & Finkelhor, D. (1986). Impact of child sexual abuse: A review of research. *Psychological Bulletin, 99*(1), 66–77.

Bruce, J., Lloyd, C. B., & Leonard, A. (1995). *Families in focus: New perspectives on mothers, fathers, and children.* New York: Population Council.

Bruck, M., & Ceci, S. J. (1997). The suggestibility of young children. *Current Directions in Psychological Science, 6,* 75–79.

Bruck, M., Ceci, S. J., & Hembrooke, H. (1998). Reliability and credibility of young children's reports: From research to policy and practice. *American Psychologist, 53,* 136–151.

Bruner, A. B., Joffe, A., Duggan, A. K., Casella, J. F., & Brandt, J. (1996). Randomised study of cognitive effects of iron supplementation in non-anaemic iron-deficient adolescent girls. *Lancet, 348,* 992–996.

Bryant, B. K. (1987). Mental health, temperament, family, and friends: Perspectives on children's empathy and social perspective taking. In N. Eisenberg & J. Strayer (Eds.), *Empathy and its development* (pp. 245–270). Cambridge, UK: Cambridge University Press.

Bryson, K. (1996, October). *Household and family characteristics: March 1995* (Current Population Report No. P20-488; PPL-46). Washington, DC: U.S. Bureau of the Census.

Buchanan, C. M., Eccles, J. S., & Becker, J. B. (1992). Are adolescents the victims of raging hormones: Evidence for activational effects of hormones on moods and behavior at adolescence. *Psychological Bulletin, 111,* 62–107.

Buckner, J. C., Bassuk, E. L., Weinreb, L. F., & Brooks, M. G. (1999). Homelessness and its relation to the mental health and behavior of low-income school-age children. *Developmental Psychology, 35*(1), 246–257.

Buhrmester, D. (1990). Intimacy of friendship, interpersonal competence, and adjustment during preadolescence and adolescence. *Child Development, 61,* 1101–1111.

Buhrmester, D. (1996). Need fulfillment, interpersonal competence, and the developmental contexts of early adolescent friendship. In W. M. Bukowski, A. F. Newcomb, & W. W. Hartup (Eds.), *The company they keep: Friendship in childhood and adolescence* (pp. 158–185). New York: Cambridge University Press.

Buhrmester, D., & Furman, W. (1990). Perceptions of sibling relationships during middle childhood and adolescence. *Child Development, 61,* 138–139.

Bukowski, W. M., & Kramer, T. L. (1986). Judgments of the features of friendship among early adolescent boys and girls. *Journal of Early Adolescence, 6,* 331–338.

Bullock, M., Gelman, R., & Baillargeon, R. (1982). The development of causal reasoning. In W. J. Friedman (Ed.), *The developmental psychology of time* (pp. 209–254). New York: Academic.

Bunikowski, R., Grimmer, I., Heiser, A., Metze, B., Schafer, A., & Obladen, M. (1998). Neurodevelopmental outcome after prenatal exposure to opiates. *European Journal of Pediatrics, 157,* 724–730.

Burchinal, M. R., Campbell, F. A., Bryant, D. M., Wasik, B. H., & Ramey, C. T. (1997). Early intervention and mediating processes in cognitive performance of children of low-income African American families. *Child Development, 68,* 935–954.

Burchinal, M. R., Roberts, J. E., Nabors, L. A., & Bryant, D. M. (1996). Quality of center child care and infant cognitive and language development. *Child Development, 67,* 606–620.

Bureau of HIV/AIDS, STD and TB, Centre for Infectious Disease Prevention and Control. (2001). *Perinatal transmission of HIV.* Ottawa: Health Canada.

Bureau of Labor Statistics. (2000, June 23). *Employment characteristics of families in 1999* [news release] USDL 00-172. Washington, DC: U.S. Department of Labor.

Burhans, K. K., & Dweck, C. S. (1995). Helplessness in early childhood: The role of contingent worth. *Child Development, 66,* 1719–1738.

Burns, J. F. (1994, August 27). India fights abortion of female fetuses. *New York Times,* p. A5.

Burt, R. D., Vaughan, T. L., & Daling, J. R. (1988). Evaluating the risks of cesarean section: Low Apgar score in repeat C-section and vaginal deliveries. *American Journal of Public Health, 78,* 1312–1314.

Bushnell, E. W., & Boudreau, J. P. (1993). Motor development and the mind: The potential role of motor abilities as a determinant of aspects of perceptual development. *Child Development, 64,* 1005–1021.

Bussey, K., & Bandura, A. (1992). Self-regulatory mechanisms governing gender development. *Child Development, 63,* 1236–1250.

Bussey, K., & Bandura, A. (1999). Social cognitive theory of gender development and differentiation. *Psychological Review, 106,* 676–713.

Butterfield, S. A., & Loovis, E. M. (1993). Influence of age, sex, balance, and sport participation on development of throwing by children in grades K–8. *Perceptual and Motor Skills, 76,* 459–464.

Byrnes, J. P., & Fox, N. A. (1998). The educational relevance of research in cognitive neuroscience. *Educational Psychology Review, 10,* 297–342.

Caldwell, B. M., & Bradley, R. H. (1984). *Home observation for measurement of the environment.* Unpublished manuscript, University of Arkansas at Little Rock.

Calkins, S. D., & Fox, N. A. (1992). The relations among infant temperament, security of attachment, and behavioral inhibition at twenty-four months. *Child Development, 63,* 1456–1472.

Call, K. T., Mortimer, J. T., & Shanahan, M. (1995). Helpfulness and the development of competence in adolescence. *Child Development, 66,* 129–138.

Campbell, S. B., Cohn, J. F., & Meyers, T. (1995). Depression in first-time mothers: Mother–infant interaction and depression chronicity. *Developmental Psychology, 31,* 349–357.

Campfield, L. A., Smith, F. J., Guisez, Y., Devos, R., & Burn, P. (1995). Recombinant mouse OB protein: Evidence for a peripheral signal linking adiposity and central neural networks. *Science, 269,* 546–549.

Campos, J. J., Langer, A., & Krowitz, A. (1970). Cardiac responses on the visual cliff in prelocomotor human infants. *Science, 170,* 196–197.

Campos, J., Bertenthal, B., & Benson, N. (1980, April). *Self-produced locomotion and the extraction of form invariance.* Paper presented at the meeting of the International Conference on Infant Studies, New Haven, CT.

Camras, L. A., Oster, H., Campos, J., Campos, R., Vjiie, T., Miyake, K., Wang, L., & Meng, Z. (1998). Production of emotional facial expressions in European American, Japanese, and Chinese infants. *Developmental Psychology, 34*(4), 616–628.

Canadian Aboriginal AIDS Network. (1999). *AIDS & Aboriginal youth.* Retrieved August 19, 2002, from http://caan.ca/Epi/Dev/Design/factSheet8YouthAboriginal.pdf

Canadian Council on Social Development (2001). *The progress of Canada's children.* Ottawa: Author.

Canadian Dental Association (2002). *Early childhood tooth decay.* Retrieved July 27, 2002, from www.cda-adc.ca

Canadian Education Statistics Council. (2000). *Education indicators in Canada: Report of the Pan-Canadian education indicators program 1999.* Toronto: Author.

Canadian Foundation for the Study of Infant Deaths, the Canadian Institute of Child Health, the Canadian Paediatric Society and Health Canada. (1999, reaffirmed 2000). Reducing the risk of sudden infant death syndrome in Canada. *Paediatrics & Child Health, 4,* 223–224.

Canadian Health Network. (2001). *What can I do to ensure clean smoke-free air for my family and myself?* Retrieved September 20, 2002, from http://canadian-health-network.ca/faq-faq/tobacco-tabagisme/9e.html

Canadian Hospitals Injury Reporting and Prevention Program. (1999). *Injuries associated with shopping carts.* Retrieved September 20, 2002, from http://www.hc-sc.gc.ca/pphb-dgspsp/injury-bles/chirpp/injrep-rapbles/shpcrt_e.html

Canadian Institute for Health Information and Statistics Canada. (2000). *Health care in Canada 2000: A first annual report.* Catalogue No. 82-222-XIE. Ottawa: Author.

Canadian Institute of Child Health [CICH]. (2000). *The health of Canada's children: A CICH profile* (3rd ed.). Ottawa: Author.

Canadian Institute of Child Health. (2000). *The health of Canada's children* (3rd ed.). Ottawa: Author.

Canadian Paediatric Society Advisory Committee on Healthy Active Living for Children and Youth. (2002). Healthy active living for children and youth. *Paediatrics and Child Health, 7,* 339–345.

Canadian Paediatric Society and Health Canada (1994/2001). *Nutrition recommendations update: Dietary fat and children.* Ottawa: Canadian Paediatric Society.

Canadian Paediatric Society Injury Prevention Committee. (1985; reaffirmed 2000). *Baby walkers.* Ottawa: Author.

Canadian Paediatric Society Psychosocial Paediatrics Committee. (2001, February). Smoking and your child: What parents should know. *Paediatrics & Child Health, 6* (2). Retrieved September 20, 2002, from http://www.pulsus.com/Paeds/06_02/contents.htm

Canadian Paediatric Society, Dietitians of Canada and Health Canada. (1998). *Nutrition for healthy term infants.* Ottawa: Minister of Public Works and Government Services.

Canadian Paediatric Society. (1996). Prevention of firearm deaths in Canadian children and adolescents. *Paediatrics & Child Health, 1,* 231–233.

Canadian Paediatric Society. (1997). Canadian Paediatric Society practice guideline (ID MS 97-01). *Paediatrics & Child Health, 2*(6).

Canadian Paediatric Society. (1997). Enuresis. *Paediatrics & Child Health, 2,* 419–421.

Canadian Paediatric Society. (1999a). *Being well.* Ottawa: Author.

Canadian Paediatric Society. (1999b). Children and the media *Paediatrics & Child Health, 4,* 350–354.

Canadian Paediatric Society. (1999c). *Well beings: A guide to promote the physical health, safety and emotional well being of children in child care centres and family day care homes* (2nd ed.). Ottawa, ON: Author.

Canadian Paediatric Society. (2001). *Nutrition Recommendations Update . . . Dietary Fat and Children: Report of the Joint Working Group of the Canadian Paediatric Society (CPS) and Health Canada,* Reference No. N94-01. Ottawa: Author.

Canadian Perinatal Surveillance System. (2000). *Canadian perinatal health report, 2000.* Ottawa: Health Canada.

Canadian Task Force on the Periodic Health Examination. (1994). Periodic health examination, 1994 update: 1. Obesity in childhood. *Canadian Medical Association Journal, 150,* 871–879.

Canadian Working Group on Childhood Hearing. (2001). *Notice from the Canadian Working Group on Childhood Hearing to interested consumer groups.* Ottawa: Health Canada. Retrieved July 16, 2002, from http://www.hc-sc.gc.ca/pphb-dgspsp/rhs-ssg/index.html

Cantor, J. (1994). Confronting children's fright responses to mass media. In D. Zillman, J. Bryant, & A. C. Huston (Eds.), *Media, children, and the family: Social scientific, psychoanalytic, and clinical perspectives* (pp. 139–150). Hillsdale, NJ: Erlbaum.

Cao, A., Saba, L., Galanello, R., & Rosatelli, M. C. (1997). Molecular diagnosis and carrier screening for thalassemia. *Journal of the American Medical Association, 278,* 1273–1277.

Cao, X.-Y., Jiang, X.-M., Dou, Z.-H., Rakeman, M. A., Zhang, M.-L., O'Donnell, K., Ma, T., Amette, K., DeLong, N., & DeLong, G. R. (1994). Timing of vulnerability of the brain to iodine deficiency in endemic cretinism. *New England Journal of Medicine, 331,* 1739–1744.

Caplan, D. (1992). Neural structures. In W. Bright (Ed.), *International encyclopedia of linguistics* (Vol. 3, pp. 79–84). New York: Oxford University Press.

Caplan, M., Vespo, J., Pedersen, J., & Hay, D. F. (1991). Conflict and its resolution in small groups of one- and two-year olds. *Child Development, 62,* 1513–1524.

Capute, A. J., Shapiro, B. K., & Palmer, F. B. (1987). Marking the milestones of language development. *Contemporary Pediatrics, 4*(4), 24.

Carlson, E. A. (1998). A prospective longitudinal study of attachment disorganization/disorientation. *Child Development, 69*(4), 1107–1128.

Carlson, S. M., Moses, L. J., & Hix, H. R. (1998). The role of inhibitory processes in young children's difficulties with deception and false belief. *Child Development, 69*(3), 672–691.

Carpenter, M. W., Sady, S. P., Hoegsberg, B., Sady, M. A., Haydon, B., Cullinane, E. M., Coustan, D. R., & Thompson, P. D. (1988). Fetal heart rate response to maternal exertion. *Journal of the American Medical Association, 259*(20), 3006–3009.

Carpenter, M., Akhtar, N., & Tomasello, M. (1998). Fourteen- through 18-month-old infants differentially imitate intentional and accidental actions. *Infant Behavior and Development, 21,* 315–330.

Carraher, T. N., Schliemann, A. D., & Carraher, D. W. (1988). Mathematical concepts in everyday life. In G. B. Saxe & M. Gearhart (Eds.), Children's mathematics. *New Directions in Child Development, 41,* 71–87.

Carroll, D., & Benoit, C. (spring, 2001). Aboriginal midwifery in Canada: Blending traditional and modern forms. *Network Magazine, 4*(3). Retrieved July 14, 2002, from http://www.cwhn.ca/network-reseau/4-3/4-3pg2.html

Carskadon, M. A., Acebo, C., Richardson, G. S., Tate, B. A., & Seifer, R. (1997). Long nights protocol: Access to circadian parameters in adolescents. *Journal of Biological Rhythms, 12,* 278–289.

Carson, J. L., & Parke, R. D. (1996). Reciprocal negative affect in parent–child interactions and children's peer competency. *Child Development, 67,* 2217–2226.

Casaer, P. (1993). Old and new facts about perinatal brain development. *Journal of Child Psychology and Psychiatry, 34*(1), 101–109.

Case, R. (1985). *Intellectual development: Birth to adulthood.* Orlando, FL: Academic Press.

Case, R. (1992). Neo-Piagetian theories of child development. In R. Sternberg & C. Berg (Eds.), *Intellectual development* (pp. 161–196). New York: Cambridge University Press.

Case, R., & Okamoto, Y. (1996). The role of central conceptual structures in the development of children's thought. *Monographs of the Society for Research in Child Development, 61*(1–2, Serial No. 246).

Casper, L. M. (1996). Who's minding our preschoolers? *Current Population Reports* (P-70-53). Washington, DC: U.S. Bureau of the Census.

Casper, L. M. (1997). My daddy takes care of me: Fathers as care providers. *Current Population Reports* (P70-59). Washington, DC: U.S. Bureau of the Census.

Casper, L. M., & Bryson, K. R. (1998). *Co-resident grandparents and their grandchildren: Grandparent maintained families* (Population Division Working Paper No. 26). Washington, DC: U.S. Bureau of the Census.

Caspi, A. (2000). The child is father of the man: Personality continuity from childhood to adulthood. *Journal of Personality and Social Psychology, 78,* 158–172.

Caspi, A., & Silva, P. (1995). Temperamental qualities at age 3 predict personality traits in young adulthood: Longitudinal evidence from a birth cohort. *Child Development, 66,* 486–498.

Cassidy, J., & Hossler, A. (1992). State and federal definitions of the gifted: An update. *Gifted Child Quarterly, 15,* 46–53.

Cavazanna-Calvo, M., Hacein-Bey, S., de Saint Basile, G., Gross, F., Yvon, E., Nusbaum, P., Selz, F., Hue, C., Certain, S., Casanova, J. L., Bousso, P., Deist, F. L., & Fischer, A. (2000). Gene therapy of human severe combined immunodeficiency (SCID)-X1 disease. *Science, 288,* 669–672.

Ceci, S. J. (1991). How much does schooling influence general intelligence and its cognitive components? A reassessment of the evidence. *Developmental Psychology, 27,* 703–722.

Ceci, S. J., & Bruck, M. (1993). Child witnesses: Translating research into policy. *Social Policy Report of the Society for Research in Child Development, 7*(3).

Ceci, S. J., & Williams, W. M. (1997). Schooling, intelligence, and income. *American Psychologist, 52*(10), 1105–1058.

Celis, W. (1990, Aug. 16). More states are laying school paddle to rest. *New York Times,* pp. A1, B12.

Center on Addiction and Substance Abuse at Columbia University (CASA). (1996, June). *Substance abuse and the American woman.* New York: Author.

Centers for Disease Contol and Prevention. (1997). *Rates of homicide, suicide, and firearm-related death among industrialized countries.* Retrieved August 8, 2002, from http://www.cdc.gov/mmwr/preview/mmwrhtml/00046149.htm

Centers for Disease Control and Prevention (CDC). (1993). Rates of cesarean delivery—United States, 1991. *Morbidity and Mortality Weekly Report, 42,* 285–289.

Centers for Disease Control and Prevention (CDC). (1994). Homicides among 15- to 19-year-old males—United States, 1963–1991. *Morbidity and Mortality Weekly Report, 43,* 725–727.

Centers for Disease Control and Prevention (CDC). (1997). *Screening young children for lead poisoning: Guidance for state and local public health officials.* Atlanta, GA: U.S. Department of Health and Human Services, Public Health Service.

Centers for Disease Control and Prevention (CDC). (1999a). Impact of vaccines universally recommended for children—United States, 1900–1998. *Morbidity and Mortality Weekly Report, 48,* 243–248.

Centers for Disease Control and Prevention (CDC). (1999b). Knowledge and use of folic acid by women of childbearing age—United States, 1995 and 1998. *Morbidity and Mortality Weekly Report, 48,* 325–327.

Centers for Disease Control and Prevention (CDC). (1999c). Motor vehicle safety—A 20th century public health achievement. *Morbidity and Mortality Weekly Report, 48,* 369–374.

Centers for Disease Control and Prevention (CDC). (2000a). *CDC's guidelines for school and community programs: Promoting lifelong physical activity.* Retrieved May 26, 2000, from http://www.cdc.gov/nccdphp/dash/phactaag.htm

Centers for Disease Control and Prevention (CDC). (2000b). National, state, and urban area vaccination coverage levels among children aged 19–35 months—United States, 1999. *49*(26), 585–589.

Cernoch, J. M., & Porter, R. H. (1985). Recognition of maternal axillary odors by infants. *Child Development, 56,* 1593–1598.

Chalfie, D. (1994). *Going it alone: A closer look at grandparents parenting grandchildren.* Washington, DC: AARP Women's Initiative.

Chan, R. W., Raboy, B., & Patterson, C. J. (1998). Psychosocial adjustment among children conceived via donor insemination by lesbian and heterosexual mothers. *Child Development, 69,* 443–457.

Chandler, M. J., & Lalonde, C. (1995). The problem of self-continuity in the context of rapid personal and cultural change. In A. Oosterwegel & R. A. Wcklund (Eds.), *The self in European and North American culture: Development and processes.* NATO advanced science institutes series (pp. 45–63). Dordrecht, The Netherlands: Kluwer Academic Publishers.

Chandler, M. J., & Lalonde, C. (1998). Cultural continuity as a hedge against suicide in Canada's First Nations. *Transcultural Psychiatry, 35,* 191–219.

Chandra, A., Abma, J., Maza, P., & Bachrach, C. (1999). *Adoption, adoption seeking, and relinquishment for adoption in the United States* (Advance Data from Vital and Health Statistics No. 306). Hyattsville, MD: National Center for Health Statistics.

Channel 3000 News. (1998). *First test tube baby turns 20: Louise Brown 'no different' from peers.* Retrieved September 23, 2002, from http://www.channel3000.com/news/stories/news-980725-121445.html

Chao, R. (1996). Chinese and European American mothers' beliefs about the role of parenting in children's school success. *Journal of Cross-Cultural Psychology, 27,* 403–423.

Chao, R. K. (1994). Beyond parental control and authoritarian parenting style: Understanding Chinese parenting through the cultural notion of training. *Child Development, 65,* 1111–1119.

Chapman, A. R., & Frankel, M. S. (2000). Human inheritable genetic modifications: Assessing scientific, ethical, religious, and policy issues. *American Association for the Advancement of Science.* Retrieved September 25, 2000, from http://www.aaas.org/spp/dspp/sfri/germline/main.htm

Chapman, M., & Lindenberger, U. (1988). Functions, operations, and décalage in the development of transitivity. *Developmental Psychology, 24,* 542–551.

Chase-Lansdale, P. L., Cherlin, A. J., & Kiernan, K. E. (1995). The long-term effects of parental divorce on the mental health of young adults: A developmental perspective. *Child Development, 66,* 1614–1634.

Cheah, C. S. L., Nelson, L. J., & Rubin, K. H. (2001). Nonsocial play as a risk factor in social and emotional development. In A. Goencue & E. L. Klein (Eds.), *Children in play, story, and school* (pp. 39–71). New York: The Guildford Press.

Chehab, F. F., Mounzih, K., Lu, R., & Lim, M. E. (1997, January 3). Early onset of reproductive function in

normal female mice treated with leptin. *Science, 275,* 88–90.

Chen, C., & Stevenson, H. W. (1989). Homework: A cross-cultural examination. *Child Development, 60,* 551–561.

Chen, L., Baker S. P., Braver, E. R., & Li, G. (2000). Carrying passengers as a risk factor for crashes fatal to 16- and 17-year-old drivers. *Journal of the American Medical Association, 283*(12), 1578–1582.

Chen, X., Dong, Q., & Zhou, H. (1997). Authoritarian and authoritative parenting practices and social and school performance in Chinese children. *International Journal of Behavioral Development, 21,* 855–873.

Chen, X., Hastings, P. D., Rubin, K. H., Chen, H., Cen, G., & Stewart, S. L. (1998). Child-rearing attitudes and behavioral inhibition in Chinese and Canadian toddlers: A cross-cultural study. *Developmental Psychology, 34*(4), 677–686.

Chen, X., Rubin, K. H., & Li, D. (1997). Relation between academic achievement and social adjustment: Evidence from Chinese children. *Developmental Psychology, 33,* 518–525.

Chen, X., Rubin, K. H., & Li, Z. (1995). Social functioning and adjustment in Chinese children: A longitudinal study. *Developmental Psychology, 31,* 531–539.

Chen, X., Rubin, K. H., & Sun, Y. (1992). Social reputation and peer relationships in Chinese and Canadian children: A cross-cultural study. *Child Development, 63,* 1336–1343.

Cheng, T. L., Fields, C. B., Brenner, R. A., Wright, J. L., Lomax, T., Scheidt, P.C., & the District of Columbia Child/Adolescent Injury Research Network. (2000). Sports injuries: An important cause of morbidity in urban youth. *Pediatrics, 105*(3). Abstract retrieved September 23, 2002, from http://www.pediatrics.org/cgi/content/full/105/3/e32

Cherlin, A., & Furstenberg, F. F. (1986a). Grandparents and family crisis. *Generations, 10*(4), 26–28.

Cherlin, A., & Furstenberg, F. F. (1986b). *The new American grandparent.* New York: Basic Books.

Chervenak, F. A., Isaacson, G., & Mahoney, M. J. (1986). Advances in the diagnosis of fetal defects. *New England Journal of Medicine, 315*(5), 305–307.

Chess, S., & Thomas, A. (1982). Infant bonding: Mystique and reality. *American Journal of Orthopsychiatry, 52*(2), 213–222.

Cheung, M. C., Goldberg, J. D., & Kan, Y. W. (1996). Prenatal diagnosis of sickle cell anaemia and thalassaemia by analysis of fetal cells in maternal blood. *Nature Genetics, 14,* 264–268.

Children's Defense Fund. (1997, October). U.S. teen birth rate drops for fourth year in a row. *CDF Reports, 18*(11), 1–2.

Children's Defense Fund. (1998). *The state of America's children yearbook, 1998.* Washington, DC: Author.

Children's Defense Fund. (2000). *The state of America's children yearbook, 2000.* Washington, DC: Author.

Chiriboga, C. A., Brust, J. C. M., Bateman, D., & Hauser, W. A. (1999). Dose-response effect of fetal cocaine exposure on newborn neurologic function. *Pediatrics, 103,* 79–85.

Chomitz, V. R., Cheung, L. W. Y., & Lieberman, E. (1995). The role of lifestyle in preventing low birth weight. *The Future of Children, 5*(1), 121–138.

Chomsky, C. S. (1969). *The acquisition of syntax in children from five to ten.* Cambridge, MA: MIT Press.

Chomsky, N. (1957). *Syntactic structures.* The Hague: Mouton.

Chomsky, N. (1972). *Language and mind* (2nd ed.). New York: Harcourt Brace Jovanovich.

Chomsky, N. (1995). *The minimalist program.* Cambridge, MA: MIT Press.

Chorpita, B. P., & Barlow, D. H. (1998). The development of anxiety: The role of control in the early environment. *Psychological Bulletin, 124,* 3–21.

Christie, J. F. (1991). *Psychological research on play: Connections with early literacy development.* Albany: State University of New York Press.

Christie, J. F. (1998). Play as a medium for literacy development. In D. P. Fromberg & D. Bergen (Eds.), *Play from birth to twelve and beyond: Contexts, perspectives, and meanings* (pp. 50–55). New York: Garland.

Chubb, N. H., Fertman, C. I., & Ross, J. L. (1997). Adolescent self-esteem and locus of control: A longitudinal study of gender and age differences. *Adolescence, 32,* 113–129.

Chugani, H. T. (1998). A critical period of brain development: Studies of cerebral glucose utilization with PET. *Preventive Medicine, 27,* 184–187.

Chumlea, W. C. (1982). Physical growth in adolescence. In B. B. Wolman (Ed.), *Handbook of developmental psychology*. Englewood Cliffs, NJ: Prentice-Hall.

Cicchetti, D., & Toth, S. L. (1998). The development of depression in children and adolescents. *American Psychologist, 53*, 221–241.

Cicirelli, V. G. (1994). Sibling relationships in cross-cultural perspective. *Journal of Marriage and the Family, 56*, 7–20.

Cicirelli, V. G. (1994, November). *Sibling relationships over the life course*. Paper presented at the 49th Annual Scientific Meeting of the Gerontological Society of America, Atlanta, GA.

Cicirelli, V. G. (1995). *Sibling relationships across the life span*. New York: Plenum Press.

Claes, M. (1998). Adolescents' closeness with parents, siblings, and friends in three countries: Canada, Belgium, and Italy. *Journal of Youth and Adolescence, 27*, 165–184.

Clark, W. (spring, 1997). School leavers revisited. *Canadian Social Trends*. Catalogue No. 11-008-XPE (pp. 10–12). Ottawa: Statistics Canada.

Clarke-Stewart, K. A. (1987). Predicting child development from day care forms and features: The Chicago study. In D. A. Phillips (Ed.), *Quality in child care: What does the research tell us?* (Research Monographs of the National Association for the Education of Young Children). Washington, DC: National Association for the Education of Young Children.

Clausen, J. A. (1975). The social meaning of differential physical and sexual maturation. In S. E. Dragastin & G. H. Elder, Jr. (Eds.), *Adolescence in the life cycle*. New York: Halsted.

Clausen, J. A. (1993). *American lives*. New York: Free Press.

Clayton, R., & Heard, D. (Eds.). (1994). *Elvis up close: In the words of those who knew him best*. Atlanta, GA: Turner.

Clearfield, M. W., & Mix, K. S. (1999). Number versus contour length in infants' discrimination of small visual sets. *Current Directions in Psychological Science, 10*, 408–411.

Clément, K., Vaisse, C., Lahlou, N., Cabrol, S., Pelloux, V., Cassuto, D., Gourmelen, M., Dina, C., Chambaz, J., Lacorte, J.-M., Basdevant, A., Bougnères, P., Lebouc, Y., Froguel, P., & Guy-Grand, B. (1998). A mutation in the human leptin receptor gene causes obesity and pituitary dysfunction. *Nature, 392*, 398–401.

Cloutier, E. & Albert, T. (2001). *Economic burden of unintentional injury in British Columbia*. Vancouver: BC Injury Research and Prevention Unit.

Cnattingius, S., Bergstrom, R., Lipworth, L., & Kramer, M.S. (1998). Prepregnancy weight and the risk of adverse pregnancy outcomes. *New England Journal of Medicine, 338*, 147–152.

Cnattingius, S., Signorello, L. B., Anneren, G., Clausson, B., Ekbom, A., Ljunger, E., Blot, W. J., McLaughlin, J. K., Petersson, G., Rane, A., & Granath, F. (2000). Caffeine intake and the risk of first-trimester spontaneous abortion. *The New England Journal of Medicine, 343*, 1839–1845.

Cobrinick, P., Hood, R., & Chused, E. (1959). Effects of maternal narcotic addiction on the newborn infant. *Pediatrics, 24*, 288–290.

Cohen, D. A., Nsuami, M., Martin, D. H., & Farley, T. A. (1999). Repeated school-based screening for sexually transmitted diseases: A feasible strategy for reaching adolescents. *Pediatrics, 104*(6), 1281–1285.

Cohen, L. B., & Amsel, L. B. (1998). Precursors to infants' perception of the causality of a simple event. *Infant Behavior and Development, 21*, 713–732.

Cohen, L. B., & Oakes, L. M. (1993). How infants perceive a simple causal event. *Developmental Psychology, 29*, 421–433.

Cohen, L. B., Rundell, L. J., Spellman, B. A., & Cashon, C. H. (1999). Infants' perception of causal chains. *Current Directions in Psychological Science, 10*, 412–418.

Cohn, J. F., & Tronick, E. Z. (1983). Three-month-old infants' reaction to simulated maternal depression. *Child Development, 54*, 185–193.

Coie, J. D., & Dodge, K. A. (1998). Aggression and antisocial behavior. In W. Damon (Series Ed.) & N. Eisenberg (Vol. Ed.), *Handbook of child psychology: Vol. 3. Social, emotional, and personality development* (5th ed., pp. 780–862). New York: Wiley.

Colby, A., & Damon, W. (1992). *Some do care: Contemporary lives of moral commitment*. New York: Free Press.

Colby, A., Kohlberg, L., Gibbs, J., & Lieberman, M. (1983). A longitudinal study of moral development. *Monographs of the Society for Research in Child Development, 48*(1–2, Serial No. 200).

Cole, P. M., Barrett, K. C., & Zahn-Waxler, C. (1992). Emotion displays in two-year-olds during mishaps. *Child Development, 63*, 314–324.

Cole, T. B. (1999). Ebbing epidemic: Youth homicide rate at a 14-year low. *Journal of the American Medical Association, 281*, 25–26.

Coleman, H., Charles, G., & Collins, J. (2001). Inhalant use by Canadian Aboriginal youth. *Journal of Child & Adolescent Substance Abuse, 10*(3), 1–20.

Coleman, J. S. (1988). Social capital in the creation of human capital. *American Journal of Sociology, 94*(Suppl. 95), S95–S120.

Coley, R. L. (1998). Children's socialization experiences and functioning in single-mother households: The importance of fathers and other men. *Child Development, 69*, 219–230.

Collier, V. P. (1995). Acquiring a second language for school. *Directions in Language and Education, 1*(4), 1–11.

Collins, J. G., & LeClere, F. B. (1997). *Health and selected socioeconomic characteristics of the family: United States, 1988–90* (DHHS No. PHS 97–1523). Washington, DC: U.S. Government Printing Office.

Collins, R. C., & Deloria, D. (1983). Head Start research: A new chapter. *Children Today, 12*(4), 15–19.

Collins, W. A. (1990). Parent–child relationships in transition to adolescence: Continuity and change in interaction, affect, and cognition. In R. Montemayor, G. R. Adams, & T. P. Gullotta (Eds.), *From childhood to adolescence: A transitional period?* (Vol. 2, pp. 85–106). Newbury Park, CA: Sage.

Collins, W. A., Maccoby, E. E., Steinberg, L., Hetherington, E. M., & Bornstein, M. H. (2000). Contemporary research in parenting: The case for nature and nurture. *American Psychologist, 55*, 218–232.

Colombo, J. (1993). *Infant cognition: Predicting later intellectual functioning*. Thousand Oaks, CA: Sage.

Colombo, J., & Janowsky, J. S. (1998). A cognitive neuroscience approach to individual differences in infant cognition. In J. E. Richards (Ed.), *Cognitive neuroscience of attention* (pp. 363–391). Mahwah, NJ: Erlbaum.

Coltrane, S., & Adams, M. (1997). Work–family imagery and gender stereotypes: Television and the reproduction of difference. *Journal of Vocational Behavior, 50,* 323–347.

Conel, J. L. (1959). *The postnatal development of the human cerebral cortex.* Cambridge, MA: Harvard University Press.

Conger, J. J. (1988). Hostages to fortune: Youth, values, and the public interest. *American Psychologist, 43*(4), 291–300.

Conger, R. C., Ge, X., Elder, G. H., Lorenz, F. O., & Simons, R. L. (1994). Economic stress, coercive family processes, and developmental problems of adolescents. *Child Development, 65,* 541–561.

Conger, R. D., & Elder, G. H. (1994). *Families in troubled times: Adapting to change in America.* New York: Aldine de Gruyter.

Conger, R. D., Conger, K. J., Elder, G. H., Jr., Lorenz, F. O., Simons, R. L., & Whitbeck, L. B. (1993). Family economic stress and adjustment of early adolescent girls. *Developmental Psychology, 29,* 206–219.

Connor, S., & Brink, S. (1999). *The impacts of non-parental care on child development.* Ottawa: Applied Research Branch, Strategic Policy, Human Resources Development Canada.

Cook, E. H., Courchesne, R., Lord, C., Cox, N. J., Yan, S., Lincoln, A., Haas, R., Courchesne, E., & Leventhal, B. L. (1997). Evidence of linkage between the serotonin transporter and autistic disorder. *Molecular Psychiatry, 2,* 247–250.

Cooksey, E., & Craig, P. (1998). First children crowded out when divorced fathers have new kids. *Demography, 35,* 187–200.

Coon, H., Fulker, D. W., DeFries, J. C., & Plomin, R. (1990). Home environment and cognitive ability of 7-year-old children in the Colorado Adoption Project: Genetic and environmental etiologies. *Developmental Psychology, 26,* 459–468.

Coons, S., & Guilleminault, C. (1982). Development of sleep–wake patterns and non-rapid eye movement sleep stages during the first six months of life in normal infants. *Pediatrics, 69,* 793–798.

Cooper, H. (1989, November). Synthesis of research on homework. *Educational Leadership,* 85–91.

Cooper, H., Charlton, K., Valentine, J. C., & Muhlenbruck, L. (2000). Making the most of summer school: A meta-analytic and narrative review. *Monographs of the Society for Research in Child Development, 65*(1).

Cooper, H., Lindsay, J. J., Nye, B., & Greathouse, S. (1998). Relationships among attitudes about homework, amount of homework assigned and completed, and student achievement. *Journal of Educational Psychology, 90,* 70–83.

Cooper, H., Valentine, J. C., Nye, B., & Lindsay, J. J. (1999). Relationships between five after-school activities and academic achievement. *Journal of Educational Psychology, 91*(2), 369–378.

Cooper, R. P., & Aslin, R. N. (1990). Preference for infant-directed speech in the first month after birth. *Child Development, 61,* 1584–1595.

Coplan, R. J., & Rubin, K. H. (1998). Social play. In D. P. Fromberg & D. Bergen (Eds.), *Play from birth to twelve and beyond: Contexts, perspectives, and meanings* (pp. 368–377). New York: Garland.

Corbet, A., Long, W., Schumacher, R., Gerdes, J., Cotton, R., & the American Exosurf Neonatal Study Group 1. (1995). Double-blind developmental evaluation at 1-year corrected age of 597 premature infants with birth weights from 500 to 1350 grams enrolled in three placebo-controlled trials of prophylactic synthetic surfactant. *Journal of Pediatrics, 126,* S5–S12.

Corbin, C. (1973). *A textbook of motor development.* Dubuque, IA: Wm. C. Brown Publishers.

Cornelius, M. D., & Day, N. L. (2000). The effects of tobacco use during and after pregnancy on exposed children. *Alcohol Research and Health, 24,* 242–249.

Costello, S. (1990, December). Yani's monkeys: Lessons in form and freedom. *School Arts,* pp. 10–11.

Coster, W. J., Gersten, M. S., Beeghly, M., & Cicchetti, D. (1989). Communicative functioning in maltreated toddlers. *Developmental Psychology, 25,* 1020–1029.

Coté, S, Zoccolillo, M., Tremblay, R. E., Nagin, D., & Vitaro, F. (2001). Predicting girls' conduct disorder in

adolescence from childhood trajectories of disruptive behaviors. *Journal of the American Academy of Child and Adolescent Psychiatry, 40,* 678–684.

Council of Ministers of Education, Canada and Statistics Canada. (1999). *Education indicators in Canada: Report of the pan-Canadian education indicators program 1999.* Ottawa: Author.

Council of Ministers of Education, Canada. (1999). *School achievement indicators program: 1998 report on reading and writing assessment.* Toronto: Author.

Council of Ministers of Education, Canada. (2002). *School achievement indicators program: Mathematics III.* Toronto: Author.

Council of Ontario Universities. (2000). *Facts and figures 2000.* Retrieved August 9, 2000, from http://www.cou.on.ca/publications/briefs_reports/facts_and_figures_2000/factsfigs2000.htm

Council on Scientific Affairs of the American Medical Association. (1993). Adolescents as victims of family violence. *Journal of the American Medical Association, 276,* 1850–1856.

Cowan, N., Nugent, L. D., Elliott, E. M., Ponomarev, I., & Saults, J. S. (1999). The role of attention in the development of short-term memory: Age differences in the verbal span of apprehension. *Child Development, 70,* 1082–1097.

Cowan, P. A., Cowan, C. P., Schulz, M. S., & Heming, G. (1994). Prebirth to preschool family factors in children's adaptation to kindergarten. In R. D. Parke & S. G. Kellam (Eds.), *Exploring family relationships with other social contexts. Family research consortium: Advances in family research* (pp. 75–114). Hillsdale, NJ: Erlbaum.

Cox, J., Daniel, N., & Boston, B. O. (1985). *Educating able learners: Programs and promising practices.* Austin: University of Texas Press.

Coyle, J. T. (2000). Psychotropic drug use in very young children. *Journal of the American Medical Association, 283*(8), 1059–1060.

Coyle, T. R., & Bjorklund, D. F. (1997). Age differences in, and consequences of, multiple- and variable-strategy use on a multitrial sort-recall task. *Developmental Psychology, 33,* 372–380.

[CPS Joint Statement] Joint Statement: Canadian Foundation for the Study of

Infant Deaths, the Canadian Institute of Child Health, the Canadian Paediatric Society and Health Canada (1999). Reducing the risk of sudden infant death syndrome in Canada. *Paediatrics & Child Health, 4,* 223–224.

Craig, C. L., Cameron, C., Russell, S. J., & Beaulieu, A. (2001). *Increasing physical activity: Supporting children's participation.* Ottawa, ON: Canadian Fitness and Lifestyle Research Institute.

Craig, K. D., Gilbert-MacLeod, C. A., & Lilley, C. M. (2000). Crying as an indicator of pain in infants. In R. G. Barr, B. Hopkins, & J. A. Green (Eds.), *Crying as a sign, a symptom, and a signal: Clinical, emotional and developmental aspects of infant and toddler crying* (pp. 23–40). London: MacKeith Press.

Crain-Thoreson, C., & Dale, P. S. (1992). Do early talkers become early readers? Linguistic precocity, preschool language, and emergent literacy. *Developmental Psychology, 28,* 421–429.

Cramer, D. (1986). Gay parents and their children: A review of research and practical implications. *Journal of Counseling and Development, 64,* 504–507.

Cratty, B. J. (1986). *Perceptual and motor development in infants and children* (3rd ed.). Englewood Cliffs, NJ: Prentice-Hall.

Crick, N. R., & Dodge, K. A. (1994). A review and reformulation of social information-processing mechanisms in children's social adjustment. *Psychological Bulletin, 115,* 74–101.

Crick, N. R., & Dodge, K. A. (1996). Social information-processing mechanisms in reactive and proactive aggression. *Child Development, 67,* 993–1002.

Crick, N. R., & Grotpeter, J. K. (1995). Relational aggression, gender, and social-psychological adjustment. *Child Development, 66,* 710–722.

Crick, N. R., Bigbee, M. A., & Howes, C. (1996). Gender differences in children's normative beliefs about aggression: How do I hurt thee? Let me count the ways. *Child Development, 67,* 1003–1014.

Crijnen, A. A. M., Achenbach, T. M., & Verhulst, F. C. (1999). Problems reported by parents of children in multiple cultures: The Child Behavior Checklist syndrome constructs. *American Journal of Psychiatry, 156,* 569–574.

Crittenden, P. M. (1993). Comparison of two systems for assessing quality of attachment in the preschool years. In P. M. Crittenden (Chair), *Quality of attachment in the preschool years.* Symposium conducted at the Ninth Biennial Meeting of the International Conference on Infant Studies, Paris.

Crockenberg, S., & Lourie, A. (1996). Parents' conflict strategies with children and children's conflict strategies with peers. *Merrill-Palmer Quarterly, 42,* 495–518.

Crouter, A. C., & Maguire, M. C. (1998). Seasonal and weekly rhythms: Windows into variability in family socialization experiences in early adolescence. In A. C. Crouter & R. Larson (Eds.), *Temporal rhythms in adolescence: Clocks, calendars, and the coordination of daily life (New Directions for Child and Adolescent Development, 82).* San Francisco: Jossey-Bass.

Crouter, A. C., MacDermid, S. M., McHale, S. M., & Perry-Jenkins, M. (1990). Parental monitoring and perception of children's school performance and conduct in dual- and single-earner families. *Developmental Psychology, 26,* 649–657.

Crouter, A., & Larson, R. (Eds.). (1998). *Temporal rhythms in adolescence: Clocks, calendars, and the coordination of daily life (New Directions in Child and Adolescent Development, 82).* San Francisco: Jossey-Bass.

Crow, J. F. (1993). How much do we know about spontaneous human mutation rates? *Environmental and Molecular Mutagenesis, 21,* 122–129.

Crow, J. F. (1995). Spontaneous mutation as a risk factor. *Experimental and Clinical Immunogenetics, 12*(3), 121–128.

Crow, J. F. (1999). The odds of losing at genetic roulette. *Nature, 397,* 293–294.

Cummings, E. A., Reid, G. J., Finley, G. A., McGrath, P. J., et al. (1996). Prevalence and source of pain in pediatric inpatients. *Pain, 68,* 25–31.

Cummings, E. M. (1994). Marital conflict and children's functioning. *Social Development, 3,* 16–36.

Cummings, E. M., Iannotti, R. J., & Zahn-Waxler, C. (1989). Aggression between peers in early childhood: Individual continuity and developmental change. *Child Development, 60,* 887–895.

Cummings, P., Grossman, D. C., Rivara, F. P., & Koepsell, T. D. (1997). State gun safe storage laws and child

mortality due to firearms. *Journal of the American Medical Association, 278,* 1084–1086.

Cunliffe, T. (1992). Arresting youth crime: A review of social skills training with young offenders. *Adolescence, 27,* 891–900.

Cunningham, A. S., Jelliffe, D. B., & Jelliffe, E. F. P. (1991). Breastfeeding and health in the 1980s: A global epidemiological review. *Journal of Pediatrics, 118,* 659–666.

Cunningham, F. G., & Leveno, K. J. (1995). Childbearing among older women: The message is cautiously optimistic. *New England Journal of Medicine, 333,* 1002–1004.

Curtin, S. C., & Martin, J. A. (2000). Births: Preliminary data for 1999. *National Vital Statistics Reports, 48*(14). Hyattsville, MD: National Center for Health Statistics.

Curtin, S. C., & Park, M. M. (1999). *Trends in the attendant, place, and timing of births, and in the use of obstetric interventions: United States, 1989–97 (National Vital Statistics Reports, 47[27]).* Hyattsville, MD: National Center for Health Statistics.

Curtiss, S. (1977). *Genie.* New York: Academic Press.

Cutting, A. L., & Dunn, J. (1999). Theory of mind, emotion understanding, language, and family background: Individual differences and interrelations. *Child Development, 70,* 853–865.

Cutz, E., Perrin, D. G., Hackman, R., & Czegledy-Nagy, E. N. (1996). Maternal smoking and pulmonary neuroendocrine cells in sudden infant death syndrome. *Pediatrics, 88,* 668–672.

D'Alton, M. E., & DeCherney, A. H. (1993). Prenatal diagnosis. *New England Journal of Medicine, 32*(2), 114–120.

Daiute, C., Hartup, W. W., Sholl, W., & Zajac, R. (1993, March). *Peer collaboration and written language development: A study of friends and acquaintances.* Paper presented at the meeting of the Society for Research in Child Development, New Orleans.

Dale, P. S., Crain-Thoreson, C., Notari-Syverson, A., & Cole, K. (1996). Parent–child book reading as an intervention technique for young children with language delays. *Topics in Early Childhood Special Education, 16,* 213–235.

Daly, L. E., Kirke, P. N., Molloy, A., Weir, D. G., & Scott, J. M. (1995). Folate levels and neural tube defects: Implications for prevention. *Journal of the American Medical Association, 274,* 1698–1702.

Danesi, M. (1994). *Cool: The signs and meanings of adolescence.* Toronto: University of Toronto Press.

Daniel, M. H. (1997). Intelligence testing: Status and trends. *American Psychologist, 52,* 1038–1045.

Darling, N., & Steinberg, L. (1993). Parenting style as context: An integrative model. *Psychological Bulletin, 113,* 487–496.

Darlington, R. B. (1991). The long-term effects of model preschool programs. In L. Okagaki & R. J. Sternberg (Eds.), *Directors of development: Influences on the development of children's thinking.* Hillsdale, NJ: Erlbaum.

David, R. J., & Collins, J. W., Jr. (1997). Differing birth weight among infants of U.S.-born blacks, African-born blacks, and U.S.-born whites. *New England Journal of Medicine, 337,* 1209–1214.

Davidson, J. I. F. (1998). Language and play: Natural partners. In D. P. Fromberg & D. Bergen (Eds.), *Play from birth to twelve and beyond: Contexts, perspectives, and meanings* (pp. 175–183). New York: Garland.

Davidson, R. J., & Fox, N. A. (1989). Frontal brain asymmetry predicts infants' response to maternal separation. *Journal of Abnormal Psychology, 948*(2), 58–64.

Davies, P. T., & Cummings, E. M. (1998). Exploring children's emotional security as a mediator of the link between marital relations and child adjustment. *Child Development, 69,* 124–139.

Davis, B. E., Moon, R. Y., Sachs, H. C., & Ottolini, M. C. (1998). Effects of sleep position on infant motor development. *Pediatrics, 102,* 1135–1140.

Davis, D. L., Gottlieb, M. B., & Stampnitzky, J. R. (1998). Reduced ratio of male to female births in several industrial countries. *Journal of the American Medical Association, 279,* 1018–1023.

Davis, M., & Emory, E. (1995). Sex differences in neonatal stress reactivity. *Child Development, 66,* 14–27.

Dawson, D. A. (1991). Family structure and children's health and well-being: Data from the 1988 National Health Interview Survey on child health. *Journal of Marriage and the Family, 53,* 573–584.

Dawson, G., Frey, K., Panagiotides, H., Osterling, J., & Hessl, D. (1997). Infants of depressed mothers exhibit atypical frontal brain activity: A replication and extension of previous findings. *Journal of Child Psychology & Allied Disciplines, 38,* 179–186.

Dawson, G., Frey, K., Panagiotides, H., Yamada, E., Hessl, D. and Osterling, J. (1999). Infants of depressed mothers exhibit atypical frontal electrical brain activity during interactions with mother and with a familiar nondepressed adult. *Child Development, 70,* 1058–1066.

Dawson, G., Klinger, L. G., Panagiotides, H., Hill, D., & Spieker, S. (1992). Frontal lobe activity and affective behavior of infants of mothers with depressive symptoms. *Child Development, 63,* 725–737.

De Wolff, M. S., & van IJzendoorn, M. H. (1997). Sensitivity and attachment: A meta-analysis on parental antecedents of infant attachment. *Child Development, 68,* 571–591.

Dean, H. J., Mundy, R. L., & Moffatt, M. (1992). Non-insulin-dependent diabetes mellitus in Indian children in Manitoba. *Canadian Medical Association Journal, 148,* 147.

DeCasper, A. J., & Fifer, W. P. (1980). Of human bonding: Newborns prefer their mothers' voices. *Science, 208,* 1174–1176.

DeCasper, A. J., & Spence, M. J. (1986). Prenatal maternal speech influences newborns' perceptions of speech sounds. *Infant Behavior and Development, 9,* 133–150.

DeCasper, A. J., Lecanuet, J. P., Busnel, M. C., Granier-Deferre, C., & Maugeais, R. (1994). Fetal reactions to recurrent maternal speech. *Infant Behavior and Development, 17,* 159–164.

DeGarmo, D. S., Forgatch, M. S., & Martinez, C. R. (1999). Parenting of divorced mothers as a link between social status and boys' academic outcomes: Unpacking the effects of socioeconomic status. *Child Development, 70*(5), 1231–1245.

Dekovic, M., & Janssens, J. M. A. M. (1992). Parents' child-rearing style and child's sociometric status. *Developmental Psychology, 28,* 925–932.

Del Carmen, R. D., Pedersen, F. A., Huffman, L. C., & Bryan, Y. E. (1993). Dyadic distress management predicts subsequent security of attachment. *Infant Behavior and Development, 16,* 131–147.

DeLoache, J. (1995). The use of dolls in interviewing young children. In M. S. Zaragoza, J. R. Graham, G. C. N. Hall, & Y. S. Ben-Porath, (Eds.), *Memory and testimony in the child witness* (Vol. 1, pp. 160–178). Thousand Oaks, CA: Sage.

DeLoache, J. S., Miller, K. F., & Pierroutsakos, S. L. (1998). Reasoning and problem solving. In D. Kuhn & R. S. Siegler (Eds.), *Handbook of child psychology: Vol. 2. Cognition, perception, and language* (5th ed., pp. 801–850). New York: Wiley.

DeLoache, J. S., Miller, K. F., & Rosengren, K. S. (1997). The credible shrinking room: Very young children's performance with symbolic and nonsymbolic relations. *Psychological Science, 8,* 308–313.

DeLoache, J. S., Pierroutsakos, S. L., Uttal, D. H., Rosengren, K. S., & Gottlieb, A. (1998). Grasping the nature of pictures. *Psychological Science, 9,* 205–210.

Delveaux, K. D., & Daniels, T. (2000). Children's social cognitions: Physically and relationally aggressive strategies and children's goals in peer conflict situations. *Merrill-Palmer Quarterly, 46,* 672–691.

Dennis, W. (1936). A bibliography of baby biographies. *Child Development, 7,* 71–73.

Denny, F. W., & Clyde, W. A. (1983). Acute respiratory tract infections: An overview [Monograph]. *Pediatric Research, 17,* 1026–1029.

Denton, K., & Zarbatany, L. (1996). Age differences in support in conversations between friends. *Child Development, 67,* 1360–1373.

Deslandes, R., Potvin, P., & Leclerc, D. (1999). Family characteristics as predictors of school achievement: Parental involvement as a mediator. *McGill Journal of Education, 34,* 135–153.

Desrochers, S., Ricard, M., Decarie, T.-G., & Allard, L. (1994). Developmental synchrony between social referencing and Piagetian sensorimotor causality. *Infant Behavior and Development, 17,* 303–309.

Devlin, B., Daniels, M., & Roeder, K. (1997). The heritability of IQ. *Nature, 388,* 468–471.

deVries, A. P. J., Kassam-Adams, N., Cnaan, A., Sherman-Slate, E., Gallagher, P. R., & Winston, F. K.

(1999). Looking beyond the physical injury: Posttraumatic stress disorder in children and parents after pediatric traffic injury. *Pediatrics, 104,* 1293–1299.

DeVries, R. (1998). Games with rules. In D. P. Fromberg & D. Bergen (Eds.), *Play from birth to twelve and beyond: Contexts, perspectives, and meanings* (pp. 409–415). New York: Garland.

DeVries, R., Hildebrandt, C., & Zan, B. (2000). Constructivist early education for moral development. *Early Education & Development, 11,* 9–35.

Dewey, K. G., Heinig, M. J., & Nommsen-Rivers, L. A. (1995). Differences in morbidity between breast-fed and formula-fed infants. *Journal of Pediatrics, 126,* 696–702.

Deykin, E. Y., Alpert, J. J., & McNamara, J. J. (1985). A pilot study of the effect of exposure to child abuse or neglect on adolescent suicidal behavior. *American Journal of Psychiatry, 142*(11), 1299–1303.

Diamond, A. (1991). Neuropsychological insights into the meaning of object concept development. In S. Carey & R. Gelman (Eds.), *Epigenesis of mind* (pp. 67–110). Hillsdale, NJ: Erlbaum.

Diamond, A., Cruttenden, L., & Neiderman, D. (1994). AB with multiple wells: 1. Why are multiple wells sometimes easier than two wells? 2. Memory or memory P inhibition? *Developmental Psychology, 30,* 192–205.

Diamond, L. M. (1998). Development of sexual orientation among adolescent and young adult women. *Developmental Psychology, 34*(5), 1085–1095.

Diamond, L. M. (2000). Sexual identity, attractions, and behavior among young sexual-minority women over a 2-year period. *Developmental Psychology, 36,* 241–250.

Diamond, M. C. (1988). *Enriching heredity.* New York: Free Press.

Diaz, R. M. (1983). Thought and two languages: The impact of bilingualism on cognitive development. *Review of Research in Education, 10,* 23–54.

Dick, D. M., Rose, R. J., Viken, R. J., & Kaprio, J. (2000). Pubertal timing and substance use: Association between and within families across late adolescence. *Developmental Psychology, 36*(2), 180–189.

DiFranza, J. R., & Lew, R. A. (1995, April). Effect of maternal cigarette smoking on pregnancy complications and sudden infant death syndrome.

Journal of Family Practice, 40, 385–394.

Dimant, R. J., & Bearison, D. J. (1991). Development of formal reasoning during successive peer interactions. *Developmental Psychology, 27,* 277–284.

DiPietro, J. A., Hodgson, D. M., Costigan, K. A., & Johnson, T. R. B. (1996). Fetal antecedents of infant temperament. *Child Development, 67,* 2568–2583.

DiPietro, J. A., Hodgson, D. M., Costigan, K. A., Hilton, S. C., & Johnson, T. R. B. (1996). Fetal neurobehavioral development. *Child Development, 67,* 2553–2567.

Dishion, T. J., McCord, J., & Poulin, F. (1999). When intervention harms. *American Psychologist, 54,* 755–764.

Dixon, W. E., & Shore, C. (1997). Temperamental predictors of linguistic style during multiword acquisition. *Infant Behavior and Development, 20*(1), 99–103.

Dlugosz, L., Belanger, K., Helienbrand, K., Holfard, T. R., Leaderer, B., & Bracken, M. B. (1996). Maternal caffeine consumption and spontaneous abortion: A prospective cohort study. *Epidemiology, 7,* 250–255.

Dodge, K. A., Bates, J. E., & Pettit, S. G. (1990). Mechanisms in the cycle of violence. *Science, 250,* 1678–1683.

Dodge, K. A., Coie, J. D., Pettit, G. S., & Price, J. M. (1990). Peer status and aggression in boys' groups: Developmental and contextual analysis. *Child Development, 61,* 1289–1309.

Doherty, G. (1997). *Zero to six: The basics for school readiness.* Report No. R-97-8E. Ottawa: Applied Research Branch, Strategic Policy, Human Resources Development Canada.

Doherty, W. J., Kouneski, E. F., & Erickson, M. F. (1998). Responsible fathering: An overview and conceptual framework. *Journal of Marriage and the Family, 60,* 277–292.

Dolan, B. (1999). From the field: Cognitive profiles of First Nations and Caucasian children referred for psychoeducational assessment. *Canadian Journal of School Psychology, 15,* 63–71.

Donovan, W. L., Leavitt, L. A., & Walsh, R. O. (1998). Conflict and depression predict maternal sensitivity to infant cries. *Infant Behavior and Development, 21,* 505–517.

Doré, R., Wagner, S., Brunet, J.-P., & Bélanger, N. (1999). *School integration*

of children with a disability in provinces and territories in Canada. Commissioned paper submitted for the February 1999 PCERA Symposium. Retrieved September 20, 2002, from http://www.cmec.ca/stats/pcera/compaper/98-52en.pdf

Dornbusch, S. M., Ritter, P. L., Leiderman, P. H., Roberts, D. F., & Fraleigh, M. J. (1987). The relation of parenting style to adolescent school performance. *Child Development, 58,* 1244–1257.

Dorris, M. (1989). *The broken cord.* New York: Harper & Row.

Dougherty, D. M. (1993). Adolescent health. *American Psychologist, 48*(2), 193–201.

Dougherty, T. M., & Haith, M. M. (1997). Infant expectations and reaction time as predictors of childhood speed of processing and IQ. *Developmental Psychology, 33,* 146–155.

Dreher, M. C., Nugent, K., & Hudgins, R. (1994). Prenatal marijuana exposure and neonatal outcomes in Jamaica: An ethnographic study. *Pediatrics, 93,* 254–260.

Driedger, L. (2000). *Mennonites in the global village.* Toronto: University of Toronto Press.

Drumm, P., & Jackson, D. W. (1996). Developmental changes in questioning strategies during adolescence. *Journal of Adolescent Research, 11,* 285–305.

Dubé, E. M., & Savin-Williamn, R. C. (1999). Sexual identity development among ethnic sexual-minority youths. *Developmental Psychology, 35*(6), 1389–1398.

Duncan, G. J., & Brooks-Gunn, J. (1997). Income effects across the life span: Integration and interpretation. In G. J. Duncan & J. Brooks-Gunn (Eds.), *Consequences of growing up poor* (pp. 596–610). New York: Russell Sage Foundation.

Dundas, S., & Kaufman, M. (2000). The Toronto lesbian family study. *Journal of Homosexuality, 40,* 65–79.

Dundy, E. (1985). *Elvis and Gladys.* New York: Dell.

Dunham, P. J., Dunham, F., & Curwin, A. (1993). Joint-attentional states and lexical acquisition at 18 months. *Developmental Psychology, 29,* 827–831.

Dunn, J. (1985). *Sisters and brothers.* Cambridge, MA: Harvard University Press.

Dunn, J. (1991). Young children's understanding of other people:

Evidence from observations within the family. In D. Frye & C. Moore (Eds.), *Children's theories of mind: Mental states and social understanding.* Hillsdale, NJ: Erlbaum.

Dunn, J. (1996). Sibling relationships and perceived self-competence: Patterns of stability between childhood and early adolescence. In A. J. Sameroff & M. M. Haith (Eds.), *The five to seven year shift: The age of reason and responsibility* (pp. 253–269). Chicago: University of Chicago Press.

Dunn, J., & Kendrick, C. (1982). *Siblings: Love, envy and understanding.* Cambridge, MA: Harvard University Press.

Dunn, J., & Munn, P. (1985). Becoming a family member: Family conflict and the development of social understanding in the second year. *Child Development, 56*, 480–492.

Dunn, J., Brown, J., Slomkowski, C., Tesla, C., & Youngblade, L. (1991). Young children's understanding of other people's feelings and beliefs: Individual differences and antecedents. *Child Development, 62*, 1352–1366.

Dunne, R. G., Asher, K. N., & Rivara, F. P. (1992). Behavior and parental expectations of child pedestrians. *Pediatrics, 89*, 486–490.

Dunning, P. (2000). Aboriginal head start. *Education Canada, 39*(4), 38–39.

DuPont, R. L. (1983). Phobias in children. *Journal of Pediatrics, 102*, 999–1002.

Durand, A. M. (1992). The safety of home birth: The Farm study. *American Journal of Public Health, 82*, 450–452.

DuRant, R. H., Rich, M., Emans, S. J., Rome, E. S., Allred, E., & Woods, E. R. (1997). Violence and weapon carrying in music videos: A content analysis. *Archives of Pediatric and Adolescent Medicine, 151*, 443–448.

DuRant, R. H., Smith, J. A., Kreiter, S. R., & Krowchuk, D. P. (1999). The relationship between early age of onset of initial substance use and engaging in multiple health risk behaviors among young adolescents. *Archives of Pediatrics & Adolescent Medicine, 153*, 286–291.

Durrant, J. E. (1995). Culture, corporal punishment, and child abuse. In K. Covell (Ed.), *Readings in child development: A Canadian perspective.* (pp. 28–48). Toronto: Nelson.

Durrant, J. E., Broberg, A. G., & Rose-Krasnor, L. (1999). Predicting mother's use of physical punishment during mother–child conflicts in Sweden and Canada. In C. C. Piotrowski & P. D. Hastings (eds.), *Conflict as a context for understanding maternal beliefs about child rearing and children's misbehaviour. (New Directions for Child and Adolescent Development, 86).* San Francisco: Jossey-Bass Publishers.

Dwyer, T., Ponsonby, A. L., Blizzard, L., Newman, N. M., & Cochrane, J. A. (1995). The contribution of changes in the prevalence of prone sleeping position to the decline in sudden infant death syndrome in Tasmania. *Journal of the American Medical Association, 273*, 783–789.

Dzakpasu, S., Joseph, K. S., Kramer, M. S., & Allen, A. C. (2000). The Matthew Effect: Infant mortality in Canada and internationally. *Pediatrics, 106*, 1–5.

Eating disorders—Part I. (1997, October). *The Harvard Mental Health Letter,* pp. 1–5.

Eating disorders—Part II. (1997, November). *The Harvard Mental Health Letter,* pp. 1–5.

Eaton, W. O., & Enns, L. R. (1986). Sex differences in human motor activity level. *Psychological Bulletin, 100*, 19–28.

Eccles, A. (1982). *Obstetrics and gynaecology in Tudor and Stuart England.* Kent, OH: Kent State University Press.

Echeland, Y., Epstein, D. J., St-Jacques, B., Shen, L., Mohler, J., McMahon, J. A., & McMahon, A. P. (1993). Sonic hedgehog, a member of a family of putative signality molecules, is implicated in the regulation of CNS polarity. *Cell, 75*, 1417–1430.

Eckenrode, J., Laird, M., & Doris, J. (1993). School performance and disciplinary problems among abused and neglected children. *Developmental Psychology, 29*, 53–62.

Eckerman, C. O., & Didow, S. M. (1996). Nonverbal imitation and toddlers' mastery of verbal means of achieving coordinated action. *Developmental Psychology, 32*, 141–152.

Eckerman, C. O., & Stein, M. R. (1982). The toddler's emerging interactive skills. In K. H. Rubin & H. S. Ross (Eds.), *Peer relationships and social skills in childhood.* New York: Springer-Verlag.

Eckerman, C. O., Davis, C. C., & Didow, S. M. (1989). Toddlers' emerging ways of achieving social coordination with a peer. *Child Development, 60*, 440–453.

Edler, G. H., Jr. (1998). The life course and human development. In W. Damon (Series Ed.) & R. M. Lerner (Vol. Ed.), *Handbook of child psychology: Vol. 1. Theoretical models of human development* (5th ed., pp. 939–992). New York: Wiley.

Edwards, C. P. (1981). The comparative study of the development of moral judgment and reasoning. In R. Monroe, R. Monroe, & B. B. Whiting (Eds.), *Handbook of cross-cultural human development.* New York: Garland.

Edwards, K. I. (1993). Obesity, anorexia, and bulimia. *Clinical Nutrition, 77*, 899–909.

Egbuono, L., & Starfield, B. (1982). Child health and social status. *Pediatrics, 69*, 550–557.

Egeland, B., & Sroufe, L. A. (1981). Attachment and early maltreatment. *Child Development, 52*, 44–52.

Egeland, B., Jacobvitz, D., & Sroufe, L. A. (1988). Breaking the cycle of abuse. *Child Development, 59*, 1080–1088.

Ehri, L. C., Nunes, S. R., Willows, D. M., Schuster, B. V., Zoreh, Y. Z., & Shanahan, T. (2001). Phonemic awareness instruction helps children learn to read: Evidence from the National Reading Panel's meta-analysis. *Reading Research Quarterly, 36*, 250–287.

Eiberg, H. (1995). Nocturnal enuresis is linked to a specific gene. *Scandinavian Journal of Urology and Nephrology, 173*(Supplement), 15–17.

Eiberg, H., Berendt, I., & Mohr, J. (1995). Assignment of dominant inherited nocturnal enuresis (ENUR1) to chromosome 13q. *Nature Genetics, 10*, 354–356.

Eiger, M. S., & Olds, S. W. (1999). *The complete book of breastfeeding* (3rd ed.). New York: Workman.

Eimas, P. (1985). The perception of speech in early infancy. *Scientific American, 252*(1), 46–52.

Eimas, P. D., Siqueland, E. R., Jusczyk, P., & Vigorito, J. (1971). Speech perception in infants. *Science, 171*, 303–306.

Eimas, P., Siqueland, E., Jusczyk, P., & Vigorito, J. (1971). Speech perception in infants. *Science, 171*, 303–306.

Eisen, M., & Zellman, G. L. (1987). Changes in incidence of sexual intercourse of unmarried teenagers following a community-based sex education program. *Journal of Sex Research, 23*(4), 527–544.

Eisenberg, A. R. (1996). The conflict talk of mothers and children: Patterns related to culture, SES, and gender of child. *Merrill-Palmer Quarterly, 42,* 438–452.

Eisenberg, N. (1992). *The caring child.* Cambridge, MA: Harvard University Press.

Eisenberg, N. (2002). Empathy-related emotional responses, altruism, and their socialization. In R. J. Davidson & A. Harrington (Eds.), *Visions of compassion.* New York: Oxford University Press.

Eisenberg, N., & Fabes, R. A. (1998). Prosocial development. In W. Damon (Series Ed.) & N. Eisenberg (Vol. Ed.), *Handbook of child psychology: Vol. 3. Social, emotional, and personality development* (5th ed., pp. 701–778). New York: Wiley.

Eisenberg, N., & Mussen, P. (2001). Prosocial development in context. In A. C. Bohart & D. J. Stipek (Eds.), *Constructive and destructive behavior: Implications for family, school, and society.* Washington, DC: APA.

Eisenberg, N., Fabes, R. A., & Murphy, B. C. (1996). Parents' reactions to children's negative emotions: Relations to children's social competence and comforting behavior. C*hild Development, 67,* 2227–2247.

Eisenberg, N., Fabes, R. A., Guthrie, I. K., & Reiser, M. (2000). Dispositional emotionality and regulation: Their role in predicting quality of social functioning. *Journal of Personality and Social Psychology, 78,* 136–157.

Eisenberg, N., Fabes, R. A., Nyman, M., Bernzweig, J., & Pinuelas, A. (1994). The relations of emotionality and regulation to children's anger-related reactions. *Child Development, 65,* 109–128.

Eisenberg, N., Fabes, R. A., Schaller, M., & Miller, P. A. (1989). Sympathy and personal distress: Development, gender differences, and interrelations of indexes. In N. Eisenberg (Ed.), *Empathy and related emotional responses (New Directions for Child Development, 44).* San Francisco: Jossey-Bass.

Eisenberg, N., Fabes, R. A., Shepard, S. A., Guthrie, I. K., Murphy, B. C., & Reiser, M. (1999). Parental reactions to children's negative emotions: Longitudinal relations to quality of children's social functioning. *Child Development, 70*(2), 513–534

Eisenberg, N., Guthrie, I. K., Fabes, R. A., Reiser, M., Murphy, B. C.,

Holgren, R., Maszk, P., & Losoya, S. (1997). The relations of regulation and emotionality to resiliency and competent social functioning in elementary school children. *Child Development, 68,* 295–311.

Eisenberg, N., Guthrie, I. K., Murphy, B. C., Shepard, S. A., Cumberland, A., & Carlo, G. (1999). Consistency and development of prosocial dispositions: A longitudinal study. *Child Development, 70*(6), 1360–1372.

Elder, G. H., Jr. (1974). *Children of the Great Depression: Social change in life experience.* Chicago: University of Chicago Press.

Elder, G. H., Jr. (1998). The life course and human development. In W. Damon (Series Ed.) & R. M. Lerner (Vol. Ed.), *Handbook of child psychology: Vol. 1. Theoretical models of human development* (5th ed., pp. 939–992). New York: Wiley.

Elder, G. H., Jr., & Caspi, A. (1990). Studying lives in a changing society: Sociological and personological explorations. In A. I. Rabin, R. A. Zucker, R. Emmons, & S. Franks (Eds.), *Studying persons and lives.* New York: Springer.

Elia, J., Ambrosini, P. J., & Rapoport, J. L. (1999). Treatment of Attention-Deficit-Hyperactivity Disorder. *New England Journal of Medicine, 340,* 780–788.

Elicker, J., Englund, M., & Sroufe, L. A. (1992). Predicting peer competence and peer relationships in childhood from early parent–child relationships. In R. Parke & G. Ladd (Eds.), *Family–peer relationships: Modes of linkage* (pp. 77–106). Hillsdale, NJ: Erlbaum.

Elkind, D. (1981). *The hurried child.* Reading, MA: Addison-Wesley.

Elkind, D. (1984). *All grown up and no place to go.* Reading, MA: Addison-Wesley.

Elkind, D. (1986). *The miseducation of children: Superkids at risk.* New York: Knopf.

Elkind, D. (1997). *Reinventing childhood: Raising and educating children in a changing world.* Rosemont, NJ: Modern Learning Press.

Elkind, D. (1998). *All grown up and no place to go.*Reading, MA: Addison-Wesley.

Elliott, D. S. (1993). Health enhancing and health compromising lifestyles. In S. G. Millstein, A. C. Petersen, & E. O. Nightingale (Eds.), *Promoting the health of adolescents: New directions*

for the twenty-first century (pp. 119–145). New York: Oxford University Press.

Ellis, B. J., & Garber, J. (2000). Psychosocial antecedents of variation in girls' pubertal timing: Maternal depression, stepfather presence, and marital family stress. *Child Development, 71*(2), 485–501

Ellis, B. J., McFadyen-Ketchum, S., Dodge, K. A., Pettit, G. S., & Bates, J. E. (1999). Quality of early family relationships and individual differences in the timing of pubertal maturation in girls: A longitudinal test of an evolutionary model. *Journal of Personality and Social Psychology, 77,* 387–401.

Ellis, K. J., Abrams, S. A., & Wong, W. W. (1997). Body composition of a young, multiethnic female population. *American Journal of Clinical Nutrition, 65,* 724–731.

Ellis, L., & Ames, M. A. (1987). Neuro-hormonal functioning and sexual orientation: A theory of homosexuality–heterosexuality. *Psychological Bulletin, 101*(2), 233–258.

Emde, R. N. (1992). Individual meaning and increasing complexity: Contributions of Sigmund Freud and René Spitz to developmental psychology. *Developmental Psychology, 28,* 347–359.

Emde, R. N., Plomin, R., Robinson, J., Corley, R., DeFries, J., Fulker, D. W., Reznick, J. S., Campos, J., Kagan, J., & Zahn-Waxler, C. (1992). Temperament, emotion, and cognition at 14 months: The MacArthur longitudinal twin study. *Child Development, 63,* 1437–1455.

Engle, P. L., & Breaux, C. (1998). Fathers' involvement with children: Perspectives from developing countries. *Social Policy Report, 12*(1), 1–21.

Enloe, C. F. (1980). How alcohol affects the developing fetus. *Nutrition Today, 15*(5), 12–15.

Ennouri, K., & Bloch, H. (1996). Visual control of hand approach movements in new-borns. *British Journal of Developmental Psychology, 14,* 327–338.

Entwisle, D. R., & Alexander, K. L. (1998). Facilitating the transition to first grade: The nature of transition and research on factors affecting it. *The Elementary School Journal, 98,* 351–364.

Entwisle, D. R., Alexander, K. L., & Olson, L. S. (1997). *Children, schools, and inequality.* Boulder, CO: Westview.

Eppler, M. A., Adolph, K. E., & Weiner, T. (1996). The developmental relationship between infants' exploration and action on sloping surfaces. *Infant Behavior and Development, 19,* 259–264.

Erdley, C. A., Cain, K. M., Loomis, C. C., Dumas-Hines, F., & Dweck, C. S. (1997). Relations among children's social goals, implicit personality theories, and responses to social failure. *Developmental Psychology, 33,* 263–272.

Erikson, E. H. (1950). *Childhood and society.* New York: Norton.

Erikson, E. H. (1968). *Identity: Youth and crisis.* New York: Norton.

Erikson, E. H. (1973). The wider identity. In K. Erikson (Ed.), *In search of common ground: Conversations with Erik H. Erikson and Huey P. Newton.* New York: Norton.

Erikson, E. H. (1982). *The life cycle completed.* New York: Norton.

Erikson, E. H., Erikson, J. M., & Kivnick, H. Q. (1986). *Vital involvement in old age: The experience of old age in our time.* New York: Norton.

Eriksson, P. S., Perfilieva, E., Björk-Eriksson, T., Alborn, A., Nordborg, C., Peterson, D. A., & Gage, F. H. (1998). Neurogenesis in the adult human hippocampus. *Nature Medicine, 4,* 1313–1317.

Eron, L. D. (1980). Prescription for reduction of aggression. *American Psychologist, 35,* 244–252.

Eron, L. D. (1982). Parent–child interaction, television violence, and aggression in children. *American Psychologist, 37,* 197–211.

Eron, L. D., & Huesmann, L. R. (1986). The role of television in the development of prosocial and antisocial behavior. In D. Olweus, J. Block, & M. Radke-Yarrow (Eds.), *The development of antisocial and prosocial behavior: Research, theories, and issues.* New York: Academic.

European Collaborative Study. (1994). Natural history of vertically acquired human immunodeficiency virus-1 infection. *Pediatrics, 94,* 815–819.

Evans, G. (1976). The older the sperm . . . *Ms., 4*(7), 48–49.

Evans, G. W., Maxwell, L. E., & Hart, B. (1999). Parental language and verbal responsiveness to children in crowded homes. *Developmental Psychology, 35,* 1020–1023.

Evans, J. (1998, November). "Princesses are not into war 'n things, they always scream and run off": Exploring gender stereotypes in picture books. *Reading,* pp. 5–11.

Evans, M. A. (1998). Parental involvement in beginning reading: Preliminary report from a three-year longitudinal study. *Canadian Journal of School Psychology, 14,* 11–20.

Evans, M. A., Shaw, D., & Bell, M. (2000). Home literacy activities and their influence on early literacy skills. *Canadian Journal of Experimental Psychology, 54,* 65–75.

Evers, S. (1987). The prevalence of diabetes in Indians and Caucasians living in Southwestern Ontario. *Canadian Journal of Public Health, 78,* 240–243.

Eyre-Walker, A., & Keightley, P. D. (1999). High genomic deleterious rates in hominids. *Nature, 397,* 344–347.

Fabes, R. A., & Eisenberg, N. (1992). Young children's coping with interpersonal anger. *Child Development, 63,* 116–128.

Fabes, R. A., & Eisenberg, N. (1996). *An examination of age and sex differences in prosocial behavior and empathy.* Unpublished data, Arizona State University.

Fabes, R. A., Eisenberg, N., Smith, M. C., & Murphy, B. C. (1996). Getting angry at peers: Associations with liking of the provocateur. *Child Development, 67,* 942–956.

Fagot, B. I. (1997). Attachment, parenting, and peer interactions of toddler children. *Developmental Psychology, 33,* 489–499.

Fagot, B. I., & Gauvain, M. (1997). Mother–child problem solving: Continuity through the early childhood years. *Developmental Psychology, 33,* 480–488.

Fagot, B. I., & Hagan, R. (1991). Observations of parent reaction to sex-stereotyped behaviors: Age and sex effects. *Child Development, 62,* 617–628.

Fagot, B. I., & Leinbach, M. D. (1995). Gender knowledge in egalitarian and traditional families. *Sex Roles, 32,* 513–526.

Fagot, B. I., & Leve, L. (1998). Gender identity and play. In D. P. Fromberg & D. Bergen (Eds.), *Play from birth to twelve and beyond: Contexts, perspectives, and meanings* (pp. 187–192). New York: Garland.

Faison, S. (1997, August 17). Chinese happily break the "one child" rule. *New York Times,* pp. 1, 10.

Falbo, T., & Polit, D. F. (1986). Quantitative review of the only child literature: Research evidence and theory development. *Psychological Bulletin, 100*(2), 176–189.

Falbo, T., & Poston, D. L. (1993). The academic, personality, and physical outcomes of only children in China. *Child Development, 64,* 18–35.

Faltermayer, C., Horowitz, J. M., Jackson, D., Lofaro, L., Maroney, T., Morse, J., Ramirez, A., & Rubin, J. C. (1996, August 5). Where are they now? *Time,* p. 18.

Fantino, A. M., & Colak, A. (2001). Refugee children in Canada: Searching for identity. *Child Welfare, 80,* 587–596.

Fantz, R. L. (1963). Pattern vision in newborn infants. *Science, 140,* 296–297.

Fantz, R. L. (1964). Visual experience in infants: Decreased attention to familiar patterns relative to novel ones. *Science, 146,* 668–670.

Fantz, R. L. (1965). Visual perception from birth as shown by pattern selectivity. In H. E. Whipple (Ed.), New issues in infant development. *Annals of the New York Academy of Science, 118,* 793–814.

Fantz, R. L., & Nevis, S. (1967). Pattern preferences and perceptual-cognitive development in early infancy. *Merrill-Palmer Quarterly, 13,* 77–108.

Fantz, R. L., Fagen, J., & Miranda, S. B. (1975). Early visual selectivity. In L. Cohen & P. Salapatek (Eds.), *Infant perception: From sensation to cognition: Vol. 1. Basic visual processes* (pp. 249–341). New York: Academic Press.

Farrow, J. A., Rees, J. M., & Worthington-Roberts, B. S. (1987). Health, developmental, and nutritional status of adolescent alcohol and marijuana abusers. *Pediatrics, 79,* 218–223.

Farver, J. A. M., Kim, Y. K., & Lee, Y. (1995). Cultural differences in Korean- and Anglo-American preschoolers' social interaction and play behavior. *Child Development, 66,* 1088–1099.

Feagans, L. (1983). A current view of learning disabilities. *Journal of Pediatrics, 102*(4), 487–493.

Federal Bureau of Investigation. (1995, December). *Juveniles and violence* (updated). Washington, DC: Author.

Feightner, J. W. (1994). Routine preschool screening for visual and hearing problems. In Canadian Task Force on the Periodic Health Examination. *Canadian guide to clinical preventative health care* (pp. 298–304). Ottawa: Health Canada.

Feingold, A., & Mazzella, R. (1998). Gender differences in body image are increasing. *Psychological Science, 9*(3), 190–195.

Feinman, S., & Lewis, M. (1983). Social referencing at ten months: A second-order effect on infants' responses. *Child Development, 54,* 878–887.

Feldhusen, J. F. (1992). *Talent identification and development in education (TIDE).* Sarasota, FL: Center for Creative Learning.

Feldman, R. D. (1985, August 6). Libraries open the books on local adult illiteracy. *Chicago Sun-Times School Guide,* pp. 10–11.

Feldman, R. D. (1986, April). What are thinking skills? *Instructor,* pp. 62–71.

Feldman, R., Greenbaum, C. W., & Yirmiya, N. (1999). Mother–infant affect synchrony as an antecedent of the emergence of self-control. *Developmental Psychology, 35*(5), 223–231.

Felner, R. D., Brand, S., DuBois, D. L., Adan, A. M., Mulhall, P. F., & Evans, E. G. (1995). Socioeconomic disadvantage, proximal environmental experiences, and socioemotional and academic adjustment in early adolescence: Investigation of a mediated effect. *Child Development, 66,* 774–792.

Ferber, R. (1985). *Solve your child's sleep problems.* New York: Simon & Schuster.

Fergusson, D. M., Horwood, L. J., & Shannon, F. T. (1986). Factors related to the age of attainment of nocturnal bladder control: An 8-year longitudinal study. *Pediatrics, 78,* 884–890.

Fernald, A. (1984). The perceptual and affective salience of mothers' speech to infants. In L. Feagans, C. Garvey, & R. Golinkoff (Eds.), *The origins and growth of communication* (pp. 5–29). Norwood, NJ: Ablex.

Fernald, A., & O'Neill, D. K. (1993). Peekaboo across cultures: How mothers and infants play with voices, faces, and expectations. In K. MacDonald (Ed.), *Parent–child play* (pp. 259–285). Albany: State University of New York Press.

Fernald, A., & Simon, T. (1984). Expanded intonation contours in mothers' speech to newborns. *Developmental Psychology, 20,* 104–113.

Fernald, A., Pinto, J. P., Swingley, D., Weinberg, A., & McRoberts, G. W. (1998). Rapid gains in speed of verbal processing by infants in the 2nd year. *Psychological Science, 9*(3), 228–231.

Fernandez, C. V., & Rees, E. P. (1994). Pain management in Canadian level 3 neonatal intensive care units. *Canadian Medical Association Journal, 150,* 499–504.

Fetters, L., & Tronick, E. Z. (1996). Neuromotor development of cocaine-exposed and control infants from birth through 15 months: Poor and poorer performance. *Pediatrics, 98,* 1–6.

Field, A. E., Cheung, L., Wolf, A. M., Herzog, D. B., Gortmaker, S. L., & Colditz, G. A. (1999). Exposure to the mass media and weight concern among girls. *Pediatrics, 103,* e36. Retrieved September 23, 2002, from http://www.pediatrics.org/cgi/content/full/103/3/e36

Field, T. (1995). Infants of depressed mothers. *Infant Behavior and Development, 18,* 1–13.

Field, T. (1998a). Emotional care of the at-risk infant: Early interventions for infants of depressed mothers. *Pediatrics, 102,* 1305–1310.

Field, T. (1998b). Massage therapy effects. *American Psychologist, 53,* 1270–1281.

Field, T. (1998c). Maternal depression effects on infants and early intervention. *Preventive Medicine, 27,* 200–203.

Field, T. M. (1978). Interaction behaviors of primary versus secondary caretaker fathers. *Developmental Psychology, 14,* 183–184.

Field, T. M. (1986). Interventions for premature infants. *Journal of Pediatrics, 109*(1), 183–190.

Field, T. M. (1987). Interaction and attachment in normal and atypical infants. *Journal of Consulting and Clinical Psychology, 55*(6), 853–859.

Field, T. M., & Roopnarine, J. L. (1982). Infant–peer interaction. In T. M. Field, A. Huston, H. C. Quay, L. Troll, & G. Finley (Eds.), *Review of human development.* New York: Wiley.

Field, T. M., Sandberg, D., Garcia, R., Vega-Lahr, N., Goldstein, S., & Guy, L. (1985). Pregnancy problems, postpartum depression, and early infant–mother interactions. *Developmental Psychology, 21,* 1152–1156.

Field, T., Fox, N. A., Pickens, J., Nawrocki, T., & Soutollo, D. (1995). Right frontal EEG activation in 3- to 6-month-old infants of depressed mothers. *Developmental Psychology, 31,* 358–363.

Field, T., Grizzle, N., Scafidi, F., Abrams, S., Richardson, S., Kuhn, C., & Schanberg, S. (1996). Massage therapy for infants of depressed mothers. *Infant Behavior and Development, 19,* 107–112.

Fields, J. M., & Smith, K. E. (1998, April). *Poverty, family structure, and child well-being: Indicators from the SIPP* (Population Division Working Paper No. 23, U.S. Bureau of the Census). Paper presented at the Annual Meeting of the Population Association of America, Chicago.

Fifer, W. P., & Moon, C. M. (1995). The effects of fetal experience with sound. In J. P. Lecanuet, W. P. Fifer, N. A. Krasnegor, & W. P. Smotherman (Eds.), *Fetal development: A psychobiological perspective* (pp. 351–366). Hillsdale, NJ: Erlbaum.

Finch, M. D., Shanahan, M. J., Mortimer, J. T., & Ryu, S. (1991). Work experience and control orientation in adolescence. *American Sociological Review, 56,* 597–611.

Finn, J. D., & Rock, D. A. (1997). Academic success among students at risk for dropout. *Journal of Applied Psychology, 82,* 221–234.

Fiscella, K., Kitzman, H. J., Cole, R. E., Sidora, K. J., & Olds, D. (1998). Does child abuse predict adolescent pregnancy? *Pediatrics, 101,* 620–624.

Fischer, K. (1980). A theory of cognitive development: The control and construction of hierarchies of skills. *Psychological Review, 87,* 477–531.

Fischer, K. W., & Rose, S. P. (1994). Dynamic development of coordination of components in brain and behavior: A framework for theory and research. In G. Dawson & K. W. Fischer (Eds.), *Human behavior and the developing brain* (pp. 3–66). New York: Guilford.

Fischer, K. W., & Rose, S. P. (1995, fall). Concurrent cycles in the dynamic development of brain and behavior. *SRCD Newsletter,* pp. 3–4, 15–16.

Fisher, R. L., & Fisher, S. (1996). Antidepressants for children: Is scientific support necessary? *Journal of Nervous Mental Disorders (United States), 184,* 99–102.

Fivush, R., & Schwarzmueller, A. (1998). Children remember childhood: Implications for childhood amnesia. *Applied Cognitive Psychology, 12,* 455–473.

Fivush, R., Hudson, J., & Nelson, K. (1983). Children's long-term memory for a novel event: An exploratory study. *Merrill-Palmer Quarterly, 30,* 303–316.

Flake, A. W., Roncarolo, M. G., Puck, J. M., Almeida-Porada, G., Evans, M. I., Johnson, M. P., Abella, E. M., Harrison, D. D., & Zanjani, E. D. (1996). Treatment of X-linked severe combined immunodeficiency by in utero transplantation of paternal bone marrow. *New England Journal of Medicine, 335,* 1806–1810.

Flavell, J. (1963). *The developmental psychology of Jean Piaget.* New York: Van Nostrand.

Flavell, J. H. (1992). Cognitive development: Past, present, and future. *Developmental Psychology, 28,* 998–1005.

Flavell, J. H. (1993). Young children's understanding of thinking and consciousness. *Current Directions in Psychological Science, 2,* 40–43.

Flavell, J. H., Beach, D., & Chinsky, J. (1966). Spontaneous verbal rehearsal in a memory task as a function of age. *Child Development, 37,* 283–299.

Flavell, J. H., Flavell, E. R., Green, F. L., & Korfmacher, J. E. (1990). Do young children think of television images as pictures, or as real objects? *Journal of Broadcasting and Electronic Media, 34,* 399–419.

Flavell, J. H., Green, F. L., & Flavell, E. R. (1986). Development of knowledge about the appearance–reality distinction. *Monographs of the Society for Research in Child Development, 51* (1, Serial No. 212).

Flavell, J. H., Green, F. L., & Flavell, E. R. (1995). Young children's knowledge about thinking. *Monographs of the Society for Research in Child Development, 60*(1, Serial No. 243).

Flavell, J. H., Green, F. L., Flavell, E. R., & Grossman, J. B. (1997). The development of children's knowledge about inner speech. *Child Development, 68,* 39–47.

Flavell, J. H., Green, F. L., Flavell, E. R., & Lin, N. T. (1999). Development of children's knowledge about unconsciousness. *Child Development, 70,* 396–412.

Flavell, J. H., Miller, P. H., & Miller, S. A. (1993). *Cognitive development.* Englewood Cliffs, NJ: Prentice-Hall.

Flieller, A. (1999). Comparison of the development of formal thought in adolescent cohorts aged 10 to 15 years (1967–1996 and 1972–1993).

Developmental Psychology, 35, 1048–1058.

Flores, J. (1952). *The woman with the whip: Eva Perón.* Garden City, NY: Doubleday.

Fluoxetine-Bulimia Collaborative Study Group. (1992). Fluoxetine in the treatment of bulimia nervosa: A multicenter placebo-controlled, double-blind trial. *Archives of General Psychiatry, 49,* 139–147.

Flynn, J. R. (1984). The mean IQ of Americans: Massive gains 1932 to 1978. *Psychological Bulletin, 95,* 29–51.

Flynn, J. R. (1987). Massive IQ gains in 14 nations: What IQ tests really measure. *Psychological Bulletin, 101,* 171–191.

Fontanel, B., & d'Harcourt, C. (1997). *Babies, history, art, and folklore.* New York: Abrams.

Ford, C. A., Bearman, P. S., & Moody, J. (1999). Foregone health care among adolescents. *Journal of the American Medical Association, 282*(23), 2227–2234.

Ford, D. Y., & Harris, J. J., III. (1996). Perceptions and attitudes of black students toward school, achievement, and other educational variables. *Child Development, 67,* 1141–1152.

Ford, R. P., Schluter, P. J., Mitchell, E. A., Taylor, B. J., Scragg, R., & Stewart, A. W. (1998). Heavy caffeine intake in pregnancy and sudden infant death syndrome (New Zealand Cot Death Study Group). *Archives of Disease in Childhood, 78*(1), 9–13.

Forgatch, M. S., & DeGarmo, D. S. (1999). Parenting through change: An effective prevention program for single mothers. *Journal of Consulting and Clinical Psychology, 67,* 711–724.

Forman, B. M., Thotonoz, P., Chen, J., Brun, R. P., Spiegelman, B. M., & Evans, R. M. (1995). 15-deoxy-delta 12, 14-prostaglandin J2 is a ligand for the adopocyte determination factor PPAR gamma. *Cell, 83,* 803–812.

Fowler, M. G., Simpson, G. A., & Schoendorf, K. C. (1993). Families on the move and children's health care. *Pediatrics, 91,* 934–940.

Fox, N. A., Kimmerly, N. L., & Schafer, W. D. (1991). Attachment to mother/attachment to father: A meta-analysis. *Child Development, 62,* 210–225.

Fraga, C. G., Motchnik, P. A., Shigenaga, M. K., Helbock, H. J., Jacob, R. A., & Ames, B. N. (1991).

Ascorbic acid protects against endogenous oxidative DNA damage in human sperm. *Proceedings of the National Academy of Sciences of the United States, 88,* 11003–11006.

Frank, A. (1958). *The diary of a young girl* (B. M. Mooyaart-Doubleday, Trans.). New York: Pocket.

Frank, A. (1995). *The diary of a young girl: The definitive edition* (O. H. Frank & M. Pressler, Eds.; S. Massotty, Trans.). New York: Doubleday.

Frankenburg, W. K., Dodds, J. B., Fandal, A. W., Kazuk, E., & Cohrs, M. (1975). *The Denver Developmental Screening Test: Reference manual.* Denver: University of Colorado Medical Center.

Frankenburg, W. K., Dodds, J., Archer, P., Bresnick, B., Maschka, P., Edelman, N., & Shapiro, H. (1992). *Denver II training manual.* Denver: Denver Developmental Materials.

Fraser, A. M., Brockert, J. F., & Ward, R. H. (1995). Association of young maternal age with adverse reproductive outcomes. *New England Journal of Medicine, 332*(17), 1113–1117.

Fraser, N., & Navarro, M. (1996). *Evita: The real life of Eva Perón.* New York: Norton.

Frazier, J. A., & Morrison, F. J. (1998). The influence of extended-year schooling on growth of achievement and perceived competence in early elementary school. *Child Development, 69,* 495–517.

Freedman, D. G. (1979, January). Ethnic differences in babies. *Human Nature,* pp. 15–20.

Freedman, D. S., Dietz, W. H., Srinivasan, S. R., & Berenson, G. S. (1999). The relation of overweight in cardiovascular risk factors among children and adolescents: The Bogalusa Heart Study. *Pediatrics, 103,* 1175–1182.

Freedman, D. S., Srinivasan, S. R., Valdez, R. A., Williamson, D. F., & Berenson, G. S. (1997). Secular increases in relative weight and adiposity among children over two decades: The Bogalusa Heart Study. *Pediatrics, 88,* 420–426.

Freeman, D. (1983). *Margaret Mead and Samoa: The making and unmaking of an anthropological myth.* Cambridge, MA: Harvard University Press.

French, A. P. (Ed.). (1979). *Einstein: A centenary volume.* Cambridge, MA: Harvard University Press.

French, C. D., French, F., & Rutherford, P. J. (1999). Applications of the WPPSI–R with a Canadian sample. *Canadian Journal of School Psychology, 15,* 1–10.

French, J., & Pena, S. (1991). Children's hero play of the 20th century: Changes resulting from television's influence. *Child Study Journal, 21,* 79–94.

Freud, A. (1946). *The ego and the mechanisms of defense.* New York: International Universities Press.

Freud, S. (1953). *A general introduction to psychoanalysis* (J. Riviere, Trans.). New York: Perma-books. (Original work published 1935)

Freud, S. (1964a). New introductory lectures on psycho-analysis. In J. Strachey (Ed. & Trans.), *The standard edition of the complete psychological works of Sigmund Freud* (Vol. 22). London: Hogarth. (Original work published 1933)

Freud, S. (1964b). An outline of psycho-analysis. In J. Strachey (Ed. & Trans.), *The standard edition of the complete psychological works of Sigmund Freud* (Vol. 23). London: Hogarth. (Original work published 1940)

Frideres, J. S. (1998). *Aboriginal peoples in Canada: Contemporary conflicts.* Scarborough, ON: Prentice Hall Allyn and Bacon Canada.

Fried, P. A., & Watkinson, B. (2001). Differential effects on facets of attention in adolescents prenatally exposed to cigarettes and marihuana. *Neurotoxicology and Teratology, 23,* 421–430.

Fried, P. A., James, D. S., & Watkinson, B. (2001). Growth and pubertal milestones during adolescence in offspring prenatally exposed to cigarettes and marihuana. *Neurotoxicology and Teratology, 23,* 431–436.

Fried, P. A., Watkinson, B., & Willan, A. (1984). Marijuana use during pregnancy and decreased length of gestation. *American Journal of Obstetrics and Gynecology, 150,* 23–27.

Friedman, J. M., & Halaas, J. L. (1998). Leptin and the regulation of body weight in mammals. *Nature, 395,* 763–770.

Friedman, L. J. (1999). *Identity's architect.* New York: Scribner.

Friend, M., & Davis, T. L. (1993). Appearance–reality distinction: Children's understanding of the physical and affective domains. *Developmental Psychology, 29,* 907–914.

Friesen, J. W. (1995). Multicultural education as a component of formal socialization. In K. Covell (Ed.), *Readings in child development: A Canadian perspective* (pp. 172–184). Toronto: Nelson Canada.

Frith, U. (1989). *Autism: Explaining the enigma.* Oxford: Basil Blackwell.

Fromkin, V., Krashen, S., Curtiss, S., Rigler, D., & Rigler, M. (1974). The development of language in Genie: Acquisition beyond the "critical period." *Brain and Language, 15*(9), 28–34.

Frydman, O., & Bryant, P. (1988). Sharing and the understanding of number equivalence by young children. *Cognitive Development, 3,* 323–339.

Fuligni, A. J., & Eccles, J. S. (1993). Perceived parent–child relationships and early adolescents' orientation toward peers. *Developmental Psychology, 29,* 622–632.

Fuligni, A. J., & Stevenson, H. W. (1995). Time use and mathematics achievement among American, Chinese, and Japanese high school students. *Child Development, 66,* 830–842.

Furman, W. (1982). Children's friendships. In T. M. Field, A. Huston, H. C. Quay, L. Troll, & G. E. Finley (Eds.), *Review of human development.* New York: Wiley.

Furman, W., & Bierman, K. L. (1983). Developmental changes in young children's conception of friendship. *Child Development, 54,* 549–556.

Furman, W., & Buhrmester, D. (1985). Children's perceptions of the personal relationships in their social networks. *Developmental Psychology, 21,* 1016–1024.

Furnival, R. A., Street, K. A., & Schunk, J. E. (1999). Trampoline injuries triple among children. *Pediatrics, 103,* e57. Retrieved May 21, 1999, from http://www.pediatrics.org/egi/content/full/103/5/e57

Furrow, D. (1984). Social and private speech at two years. *Child Development, 55,* 355–362.

Furstenberg, F. F., & Hughes, M. E. (1995). Social capital in successful development. *Journal of Marriage and the Family, 57,* 580–592.

Furstenberg, F. F., & Kiernan, K. E. (2001). Delayed parental divorce: How much do children benefit? *Journal of Marriage and Family, 63,* 446–457.

Furstenberg, F. F., Levine, J. A., & Brooks-Gunn, J. (1990). The children of teenage mothers: Patterns of early child bearing in two generations. *Family Planning Perspectives, 22*(2), 54–61.

Furth, H. G., & Kane, S. R. (1992). Children constructing society: A new perspective on children at play. In H. McGurk (Ed.), *Childhood social development: Contemporary perspectives* (pp. 149–173). Hove: Erlbaum.

Gabbard, C. P. (1996). *Lifelong motor development* (2nd ed.). Madison, WI: Brown and Benchmark.

Gabhainn, S., & François, Y. (2000). Substance use. In C. Currie, K. Hurrelmann, W. Settertobulte, R. Smith, & J. Todd (Eds.), *Health behaviour in school-aged children: A WHO cross-national study (HBSC) international report* (pp. 97–114). WHO Policy Series: Healthy Policy for Children and Adolescents, Series No. 1.

Gabriel, T. (1996, January 7). High-tech pregnancies test hope's limit. *New York Times,* pp. 1, 18–19.

Gaddis, A., & Brooks-Gunn, J. (1985). The male experience of pubertal change. *Journal of Youth and Adolescence, 14,* 61–69.

Gaertner, S. L., Mann, J., Murrell, A., & Dovidio, J. F. (1989). Reducing inter-group bias: The benefits of recategorization. *Journal of Personality and Social Psychology, 57,* 239–249.

Galambos, N. L., & Almeida, D. M. (1992). Does parent–adolescent conflict increase in early adolescence? *Journal of Marriage and the Family, 54,* 737–747.

Galambos, N. L., & Sears, H. A. (1998). Adolescents' perceptions of parents' work and adolescents' work values in two-earner families. *Journal of Early Adolescence, 18,* 397–420.

Galambos, N. L., Petersen, A. C., & Lenerz, K. (1988). Maternal employment and sex typing in early adolescence: Contemporaneous and longitudinal relations. In A. D. Gottfried & A. W. Gottfried (Eds.), *Maternal employment and children's development: Longitudinal research.* New York: Plenum.

Galambos, N. L., Sears, H. A., Almeida, D. M., & Kolaric, G. C. (1995). Parents' work overload and problem behavior in young adolescents. *Journal of Research on Adolescence, 5*(2), 201–223.

Gale, J. L., Thapa, P. B., Wassilak, S. G., Bobo, J. K., Mendelman, P. M., & Foy, H. M. (1994). Risk of serious acute neurological illness after immunization with diptheria-tetanus-pertussis vaccine: A population-based case-control study. *Journal of the American Medical Association, 271*, 37–41.

Galen, B. R., & Underwood, M. K. (1997). A developmental investigation of social aggression among children. *Developmental Psychology, 33*, 589–600.

Galotti, K. M., Komatsu, L. K., & Voelz, S. (1997). Children's differential performance on deductive and inductive syllogisms. *Developmental Psychology, 33*, 70–78.

Gannon, P. J., Holloway, R. L., Broadfield, D. C., & Braun, A. R. (1998). Asymmetry of chimpanzee planum temporale: Humanlike pattern of Wernicke's brain language homolog. *Science, 279*, 22–222.

Gans, J. E. (1990). *America's adolescents: How healthy are they?* Chicago: American Medical Association.

Garasky, S., & Meyer, D. R. (1996). Reconsidering the increase in father-only families. *Demography, 33*, 385–393.

Garbarino, J., & Kostelny, K. (1993). Neighborhood and community influences on parenting. In T. Luster & L. Okagaki (Eds.), *Parenting: An ecological perspective* (pp. 203–226). Hillsdale, NJ: Erlbaum.

Garbarino, J., Dubrow, N., Kostelny, K., & Pardo, C. (1992). *Children in danger: Coping with the consequences of community violence.* San Francisco: Jossey-Bass.

Garbarino, J., Dubrow, N., Kostelny, K., & Pardo, C. (1998). *Children in danger: Coping with the consequences of community violence.* San Francisco: Jossey-Bass.

Garcia, M. M., Shaw, D. S., Winslow, E. B., & Yaggi, K. E. (2000). Destructive sibling conflict and the development of conduct problems in young boys. *Developmental Psychology, 36*(1), 44–53.

Gardiner, H. W., Mutter, J. D., & Kosmitzki, C. (1998). *Lives across cultures: Cross-cultural human development.* Boston: Allyn and Bacon.

Gardner, H. (1993). *Frames of mind: The theory of multiple intelligences.* New York: Basic. (Original work published 1983)

Gardner, H. (1995). Reflections on multiple intelligences: Myths and messages. *Phi Delta Kappan*, pp. 200–209.

Gardner, H. (1998). Are there additional intelligences? In J. Kane (Ed.), *Education, information, and transformation: Essays on learning and thinking.* Englewood Cliffs, NJ: Prentice-Hall.

Gardner, H. (1999). *Intelligence reframed: Multiple intelligences for the 21st century.* New York: Basic Books.

Gardner, H. (2000). The giftedness matrix: A developmental perspective. In R. C. Friedman & B. M. Shore (Eds.), *Talents unfolding: Cognition and development.* Washington, DC: APA.

Garland, A. F., & Zigler, E. (1993). Adolescent suicide prevention: Current research and social policy implications. *American Psychologist, 48*(2), 169–182.

Garland, J. B. (1982, March). *Social referencing and self-produced locomotion.* Paper presented at the meeting of the International Conference on International Studies, Austin.

Garmezy, N., Masten, A., & Tellegen, A. (1984). The study of stress and competence in children: A building block for developmental psychopathology. *Child Development, 55*, 97–111.

Garmon, L. C., Basinger, K. S., Gregg, V. R., & Gibbs, J. C. (1996). Gender differences in stage and expression of moral judgment. *Merrill-Palmer Quarterly, 42*, 418–437.

Garner, B. P. (1998). Play development from birth to age four. In D. P. Fromberg & D. Bergen (Eds.), *Play from birth to twelve and beyond: Contexts, perspectives, and meanings* (pp. 137–145). New York: Garland.

Garner, D. M. (1993). Pathogenesis of anorexia nervosa. *Lancet, 341*, 1631–1635.

Garner, P. W., & Power, T. G. (1996). Preschoolers' emotional control in the disappointment paradigm and its relation to temperament, emotional knowledge, and family expressiveness. *Child Development, 67*, 1406–1419.

Garofalo, R., Wolf, R. C., Kessel, S., Palfrey, J., & DuRant, R. H. (1998). The association between health risk behaviors and sexual orientation among a school-based sample of adolescents. *Pediatrics, 101*, 895–902.

Gauvain, M. (1993). The development of spatial thinking in everyday activity. *Developmental Review, 13*, 92–121.

Ge, X., Conger, R. D., & Elder, G. H. (2001). The relation between puberty and psychological distress in adolescent boys *Journal of Research on Adolescence, 11*, 49–70.

Ge, X., Conger, R. D., & Elder, G. H., Jr. (1996). Coming of age too early: Pubertal influences on girls' vulnerability to psychological distress. *Child Development, 67*, 3386–3400.

Geary, D. C. (1993). Mathematical disabilities: Cognitive, neuropsychological, and genetic components. *Psychological Bulletin, 114*, 345–362.

Geary, D. C. (1999). Evolution and developmental sex differences. *Current Directions in Psychological Science, 8*(4), 115–120.

Gecas, V., & Seff, M. A. (1990). Families and adolescents: A review of the 1980s. *Journal of Marriage and the Family, 52*, 941–958.

Geen, R. G. (1994). Television and aggression: Recent developments in research and theory. In D. Zillman, J. Bryant, & A. C. Huston (Eds.), *Media, children, and the family: Social scientific, psychoanalytic, and clinical perspectives* (pp. 151–162). Hillsdale, NJ: Erlbaum.

Gelfand, D. M., & Teti, D. M. (1995, November). How does maternal depression affect children? *The Harvard Mental Health Letter*, p. 8.

Gelis, J. (1991). *History of childbirth: Fertility, pregnancy, and birth in early modern Europe.* Boston: Northeastern University Press.

Gelman, R., & Gallistel, C. R. (1978). *The child's understanding of number.* Cambridge, MA: Harvard University Press.

Gelman, R., Spelke, E. S., & Meck, E. (1983). What preschoolers know about animate and inanimate objects. In D. R. Rogers & J. S. Sloboda (Eds.), *The acquisition of symbolic skills* (pp. 297–326). New York: Plenum.

Genesee, F. (1987). *Learning through two languages: Studies of immersion and bilingual education.* Cambridge, MA: Newbury House.

Genesee, F. (1991). Second language learning in school settings: Lessons from immersion. In A. G. Reynolds (Ed.), *Bilingualism, multiculturalism, and second language learning: The McGill conference in honour of Wallace E. Lambert* (pp. 183–201). Hillsdale, NJ: Lawrence Erlbaum Associates.

Genesee, F., Nicoladis, E., & Paradis, J. (1995). Language differentiation in early bilingual development. *Journal of Child Language, 22*, 611–631.

George, C., Kaplan, N., & Main, M. (1985). *The Berkeley Adult Attachment*

Interview. Unpublished protocol, Department of Psychology, University of California, Berkeley, CA.

George, T. P., & Hartmann, D. P. (1996). Friendship networks of unpopular, average, and popular children. *Child Development, 67,* 2301–2316.

Gerbner, G., & Ozyegin, N. (1997, March 20). *Alcohol, tobacco, and illicit drugs in entertainment television, commercials, news, "reality shows," movies, and music channels.* Report from the Robert Wood Johnson Foundation. Princeton, NJ.

Gerstein, D. R., & Green, L. W. (1993). *Preventing drug abuse.* Washington, DC: National Academy of Science.

Gertner, B. L., Rice, M. L., & Hadley, P. A. (1994). Influence of communicative competence on peer preferences in a preschool classroom. *Journal of Speech and Hearing Research, 37,* 913–923.

Gesell, A. (1929). Maturation and infant behavior patterns. *Psychological Review, 36,* 307–319.

Getzels, J. W. (1964). Creative thinking, problem-solving, and instruction. In *Yearbook of the National Society for the Study of Education* (Pt. 1, pp. 240–267). Chicago: University of Chicago Press.

Getzels, J. W. (1984, March). *Problem-finding in creativity in higher education.* The Fifth Rev. Charles F. Donovan, S.J., Lecture. Boston College, School of Education, Boston.

Getzels, J. W., & Jackson, P. W. (1962). *Creativity and intelligence: Explorations with gifted students.* New York: Wiley.

Getzels, J. W., & Jackson, P. W. (1963). The highly intelligent and the highly creative adolescent: A summary of some research findings. In C. W. Taylor & F. Baron (Eds.), *Scientific creativity: Its recognition and development* (pp. 161–172). New York: Wiley.

Gfellner, B. M. (1990). Culture and consistency in ideal and actual child-rearing practices: A study of Canadian Indian and white parents. *Journal of Comparative Family Studies, 21,* 413–423.

Gibbs, J. C. (1991). Toward an integration of Kohlberg's and Hoffman's theories of moral development. In W. M. Kurtines & J. L. Gewirtz (Eds.), *Handbook of moral behavior and development: Advances in theory, research, and application* (Vol. 1). Hillsdale, N.J.: Erlbaum.

Gibbs, J. C. (1995). The cognitive developmental perspective. In W. M. Kurtines & J. L. Gewirtz (Eds.), *Moral development: An introduction.* Boston: Allyn & Bacon.

Gibbs, J. C., & Schnell, S. V. (1985). Moral development "versus" socialization. *American Psychologist, 40*(10), 1071–1080.

Gibbs, J. C., Arnold, K. O., Ahlborn, H. H., & Cheesman, F. L. (1984). Facilitation of sociomoral reasoning in adolescents. *Journal of Clinical and Consulting Psychology, 52,* 37–45.

Gibbs, J. C., Potter, G. B., Barriga, A. Q., & Liau, A. K. (1996). Developing the helping skills and prosocial motivation of aggressive adolescents in peer group programs. *Aggression and Violent Behavior, 1*(3), 283–305.

Gibbs, J. C., Potter, G. C., Goldstein, A. P., & Brendtro, L. K. (1998). How EQUIP programs help youth change. *Reclaiming Children and Youth, 7*(2), 117–122.

Gibbs, N. (1995, October 2). The EQ factor. *Time,* pp. 60–68.

Gibson, E. J., & Walker, A. S. (1984). Development of knowledge of visual–tactual affordances of substance. *Child Development, 55,* 453–460.

Gibson, J. J. (1979). *The ecological approach to visual perception.* Boston: Houghton-Mifflin.

Gibson, R. S., MacDonald, C. A., & Smit Vanderkooy, P. D. (1993). Dietary fat patterns of some Canadian preschool children in relation to indices of growth, iron, zinc and dietary status. *Journal of the Canadian Dietary Association, 54,* 33–37.

Gielen, U., & Kelly, D. (1983, February). *Buddhist Ladakh: Psychological portrait of a nonviolent culture.* Paper presented at the Annual Meeting of the Society for Cross-Cultural Research: Washington, DC.

Gilbert, S. (1998, May 19). Benefits of assistant for childbirth go far beyond the birthing room. *New York Times,* p. F7.

Gilbert, W. M., Nesbitt, T. S., & Danielsen, B. (1999). Childbearing beyond age 40: Pregnancy outcome in 24,032 cases. *Obstetrics and Gynecology, 93,* 9–14.

Gill, B., & Schlossman, S. (1996). "A sin against childhood": Progressive education and the crusade to abolish homework, 1897–1941. *American Journal of Education, 105,* 27–66.

Gilligan, C. (1982). *In a different voice: Psychological theory and women's development.* Cambridge, MA: Harvard University Press.

Gilligan, C. (1987a). Adolescent development reconsidered. In E. E. Irwin (Ed.), *Adolescent social behavior and health.* San Francisco: Jossey-Bass.

Gilligan, C. (1987b). Moral orientation and moral development. In E. F. Kittay & D. T. Meyers (Eds.), *Women and moral theory* (pp. 19–33). Totowa, NJ: Rowman & Littlefield.

Gillis, J. (1992). Views of Native parents about early childhood education. *Canadian Journal of Native Education, 19,* 73–81.

Ginsburg, G. S., & Bronstein, P. (1993). Family factors related to children's intrinsic/extrinsic motivational orientation and academic performance. *Child Development, 64,* 1461–1474.

Ginsburg, H. P. (1997). Mathematics learning disabilities: A view from developmental psychology. *Journal of Learning Disabilities, 30,* 20–33.

Ginsburg, H., & Opper, S. (1979). *Piaget's theory of intellectual development* (2nd ed.). Englewood Cliffs, NJ: Prentice-Hall.

Ginsburg-Block, M. D., & Fantuzzo, J. W. (1998). An evaluation of the relative effectiveness of NCTM standards-based interventions for low-achieving urban elementary students. *Journal of Educational Psychology, 90,* 560–569.

Giordano, P. C., Cernkovich, S. A., & DeMaris, A. (1993). The family and peer relations of black adolescents. *Journal of Marriage and the Family, 55,* 277–287.

Gladue, B. A. (1994). The biopsychology of sexual orientation. *Current Directions in Psychological Science, 3,* 150–154.

Glasgow, K. L., Dornbusch, S. M., Troyer, L., Steinberg, L., & Ritter, P. L. (1997). Parenting styles, adolescents' attributions, and educational outcomes in nine heterogeneous high schools. *Child Development, 68,* 507–529.

Glaxo Wellcome Inc. (2000). *Asthma in Canada: A landmark survey.* Mississauga, ON: Author.

Gleason, T. R., Sebanc, A. M., & Hartup, W. W. (2000). Imaginary companions of preschool children. *Developmental Psychology, 36,* 419–428.

Gleitman, L. R., Newport, E. L., & Gleitman, H. (1984). The current status of the motherese hypothesis. *Journal of Child Language, 11,* 43–79.

Goldberg, W. A., Greenberger, E., & Nagel, S. K. (1996). Employment and achievement: Mothers' work involvement in relation to children's achievement behaviors and mothers' parenting behaviors. *Child Development, 67*, 1512–1527.

Golden, A., Currie, W. H., Greaves, E., & Latimer, E. J. (1999). *Taking responsibility for homelessness: An action plan for Toronto—Report of the mayor's homelessness action task force.* Toronto: Access Toronto.

Goldenberg, R. L., & Rouse, D. J. (1998). Prevention of premature labor. *New England Journal of Medicine, 339*, 313–320.

Goldenberg, R. L., & Tamura, T. (1996). Prepregnancy weight and pregnancy outcome. *Journal of the American Medical Association, 275*, 1127–1128.

Goldenberg, R. L., Tamura, T., Neggers, Y., Copper, R. L., Johnston, K. E., DuBard, M. B., & Hauth, J. C. (1995). The effect of zinc supplementation on pregnancy outcome. *Journal of the American Medical Association, 274*, 463–468.

Goldin-Meadow, S., & Mylander, C. (1998). Spontaneous sign systems created by deaf children in two cultures. *Nature, 391*, 279–281.

Goldman, A. (1981). *Elvis.* New York: McGraw-Hill.

Goldsmith, M., Mackay, A., & Woudhuysen, J. S. (Eds.). (1980). *Einstein: The first hundred years.* Oxford: Pergamon.

Goldstein, A. O., Sobel, R. A., & Newman, G. R. (1999). Tobacco and alcohol use in G-rated children's animated films. *Journal of the American Medical Association, 281*, 1131–1136.

Goleman, D. (1993, June 11). Studies reveal suggestibility of very young as witnesses. *New York Times*, pp. A1, A23.

Goleman, D. (1995). *Emotional intelligence: Why it can matter more than IQ.* New York: Bantam.

Golinkoff, R. M., Jacquet, R. C., Hirsh-Pasek, K., & Nandakumar, R. (1996). Lexical principles may underlie the learning of verbs. *Child Development, 67*, 3101–3119.

Golomb, C., & Galasso, L. (1995). Make believe and reality: Explorations of the imaginary realm. *Developmental Psychology, 31*, 800–810.

Golombok, S., & Tasker, F. (1996). Do parents influence the sexual orientation of their children? Findings from a longitudinal study of lesbian families. *Developmental Psychology, 32*, 3–11.

Goodman, G. S., Emery, R. E., & Haugaard, J. J. (1998). Developmental psychology and law: Divorce, child maltreatment, foster care, and adoption. In W. Damon (Series Ed.), I. E. Sigel & K. A. Renninger (Vol. Eds.), *Handbook of child psychology* (Vol. 4, pp. 775–874). New York: Wiley.

Goodwin, J. (1994). *Akira Kurosawa and intertextual cinema.* Baltimore: Johns Hopkins University Press.

Goodwyn, S. W., & Acredolo, L. P. (1998). Encouraging symbolic gestures: A new perspective on the relationship between gesture and speech. In J. M. Iverson & S. Goldin-Meadow (Eds.), *The nature and functions of gesture in children's communication* (pp. 61–73). San Francisco: Jossey-Bass.

Gordon, I., Lask, B., Bryantwaugh, R., Christie, D., & Timini, S. (1997). Childhood onset anorexia nervosa: Towards identifying a biological substrate. *International Journal of Eating Disorders, 22*(2), 159–165.

Gorman, K. S., & Pollitt, E. (1996). Does schooling buffer the effects of early risk? *Child Development, 67*, 314–326.

Gorman, M. (1993). Help and self-help for older adults in developing countries. *Generations, 17*(4), 73–76.

Gortmaker, S. L., Must, A., Perrin, J. M., Sobol, A. M., & Dietz, W. H. (1993). Social and economic consequences of overweight in adolescence and young adulthood. *New England Journal of Medicine, 329*, 1008–1012.

Goswami, U., & Brown, A. L. (1989). Melting chocolate and melting snowmen: Analogical reasoning and causal relations. *Cognition, 35*, 69–95.

Gottfried, A. E., Fleming, J. S., & Gottfried, A. W. (1998). Role of cognitively stimulating home environment in children's academic intrinsic motivation: A longitudinal study. *Child Development, 69*, 1448–1460.

Gottlieb, G. (1991). Experiential canalization of behavioral development theory. *Developmental Psychology, 27*(1), 4–13.

Gottlieb, L. N., & Mendelson, M. J. (1990). Parental support and firstborn girls' adaptation to the birth of a sibling. *Journal of Applied Developmental Psychology, 11*, 29–48.

Gottman, J. S. (1990). Children of gay and lesbian parents. In F. W. Bozett & M. B. Sussman (Eds.), *Homosexuality and family relations* (pp. 177–196). New York: Harrington Park Press.

Goubet, N., & Clifton, R. K. (1998). Object and event representation in 6 1/2-month-old infants. *Developmental Psychology, 34*, 63–76.

Gould, E., Reeves, A. J., Graziano, M. S. A., & Gross, C. G. (1999). Neurogenesis in the neocortex of adult primates. *Science, 286*, 548–552.

Government of Saskatchewan. (2000). *Secondhand tobacco smoke health risks: Infants and children at home.* Retrieved September 20, 2002, from http://www.health.gov.sk.ca/rr_2ndhandsmoke_ic.html

Graber, J. A., Brooks-Gunn, J., & Warren, M. P. (1995). The antecedents of menarcheal age: Heredity, family environment, and stressful life events. *Child Development, 66*, 346–359.

Graber, J. A., Lewinsohn, P. M., Seeley, J. R., & Brooks-Gunn, J. (1997). Is psychopathology associated with the timing of pubertal development? *Journal of the American Academy of Child and Adolescent Psychiatry, 36*, 1768–1776.

Grant, A. (1996). *No end of grief: Indian residential schools in Canada.* Winnipeg, MB: Pemmican Publications, Inc.

Grant, B. F., & Dawson, D. A. (1998). Age of onset of alcohol use and its association with *DSM–IV* alcohol abuse and dependence: Results from the National Longitudinal Alcohol Epidemiological Survey. *Journal of Substance Abuse, 9*, 103–110.

Grantham-McGregor, S., Powell, C., Walker, S., Chang, S., & Fletcher, P. (1994). The long-term follow-up of severely malnourished children who participated in an intervention program. *Child Development, 65*, 428–439.

Gray, M. R., & Steinberg, L. (1999). Unpacking authoritative parenting: Reassessing a multidimensional construct. *Journal of Marriage and the Family, 61*, 574–587.

Graziano, A. M., & Mooney, K. C. (1982). Behavioral treatment of "nightfears" in children: Maintenance and improvement at 2 1/2 to 3-year follow-up. *Journal of Counseling and Clinical Psychology, 50*, 598–599.

Greenberger, E., & Chen, C. (1996). Perceived family relationships and depressed mood in early and late adolescence: A comparison of European and Asian Americans. *Developmental Psychology, 32*, 707–716.

Greenberger, E., & Steinberg, L. (1986). *When teenagers work.* New York: Basic Books.

Greenhouse, L. (2000a, February 29). Program of drug-testing pregnant women draws review by the Supreme Court. *New York Times*, p. A12.

Greenhouse, L. (2000b, September 9). Should a fetus's well-being override a mother's rights? *New York Times*, pp. B9, B11.

Greenough, W. T., Black, J. E., & Wallace, C. S. (1987). Experience and brain development. *Child Development, 58*, 539–559.

Gregg, V., Gibbs, J. C., & Basinger, K. S. (1994). Patterns of developmental delay in moral judgment by male and female delinquents. *Merrill-Palmer Quarterly, 40*, 538–553.

Groce, N. E., & Zola, I. K. (1993). Multiculturalism, chronic illness, and disability. *Pediatrics, 91*, 1048–1055.

Gross, R. T., & Duke, P. (1980). The effect of early versus late physical maturation on adolescent behavior. [Special issue: I. Litt (Ed.), Symposium on adolescent medicine.] *Pediatric Clinics of North America, 27*, 71–78.

Grotevant, H. D., McRoy, R. G., Elde, C. L., & Fravel, D. L. (1994). Adoptive family system dynamics: Variations by level of openness in the adoption. *Family Process, 33*(2), 125–146.

Grubman, S., Gross, E., Lerner-Weiss, N., Hernandez, M., McSherry, G. D., Hoyt, L. G., Boland, M., & Oleske, J. M. (1995). Older children and adolescents living with perinatally acquired human immunodeficiency virus. *Pediatrics, 95*, 657–663.

Grunau, R. E., Whitfield, M. F., & Petrie, J. (1994). Pain sensitivity and temperament in extremely low-birth-weight premature toddlers and preterm and full-term controls. *Pain, 58*, 341–346.

Grunau, R. V., Kearney, S. M., & Whitfield, M. F. (1990). Language development at 3 years in pre-term children of birth weight below 1000 g. *British Journal of Disorders of Communication, 25*, 173–182.

Grusec, J. E., & Goodnow, J. J. (1994). Impact of parental discipline methods on the child's internalization of values: A reconceptualization of current points of view. *Developmental Psychology, 30*, 4–19.

Grusec, J. E., Goodnow, J. J., & Kuczynski, L. (2000). New directions in analyses of parenting contributions to children's acquisition of values. *Child Development, 71*, 205–211.

Grych, J. H., & Clark, R. (1999). Maternal employment and development of the father–infant relationship in the first year. *Developmental Psychology, 35*, 893–903.

Guberman, S. R. (1996). The development of everyday mathematics in Brazilian children with limited formal education. *Child Development, 67*, 1609–1623.

Guilford, J. P. (1956). Structure of intellect. *Psychological Bulletin, 53*, 267–293.

Guilford, J. P. (1959). Three faces of intellect. *American Psychologist, 14*, 469–479.

Guilford, J. P. (1960). Basic conceptual problems of the psychology of thinking. *Proceedings of the New York Academy of Sciences, 91*, 6–21.

Guilford, J. P. (1967). *The nature of human intelligence.* New York: McGraw-Hill.

Guilford, J. P. (1986). *Creative talents: Their nature, uses and development.* Buffalo, NY: Bearly.

Guillermoprieto, A. (1996, December 2). Little Eva. *The New Yorker*, pp. 98–106.

Gunnar, M. R., Larson, M. C., Hertsgaard, L., Harris, M. L., & Brodersen, L. (1992). The stressfulness of separation among nine-month-old infants: Effects of social context variables and infant temperament. *Child Development, 63*, 290–303.

Gunnoe, M. L., & Mariner, C. L. (1997). Toward a developmental-contextual model of the effects of parental spanking on children's aggression. *Archives of Pediatric and Adolescent Medicine, 151*, 768–775.

Gunter, B., & Harrison, J. (1997). Violence in children's programmes on British television. *Children & Society, 11*, 143–156.

Guralnick, P. (1994). *Last train to Memphis: The rise of Elvis Presley.* Boston: Little, Brown.

Guthrie, J. T., Schafer, W. D., & Huang, C.-W. (2001). Benefits of opportunity to read and balanced instruction on the NAEP. *The Journal of Educational Research, 94*, 145–162.

Guyer, B., Hoyert, D. L., Martin, J. A., Ventura, S. J., MacDorman, M. F., & Strobino, D. M. (1999). Annual summary of vital statistics—1998. *Pediatrics, 104*, 1229–1246.

Guyer, B., Strobino, D. M., Ventura, S. J., & Singh, G. K. (1995). Annual summary of vital statistics—1994. *Pediatrics, 96*, 1029–1039.

Guzick, D. S., Carson, S. A., Coutifaris, C., Overstreet, J. W., Factor-Litvak, P., Steinkampf, M. P., Hill, J. A., Mastroianni, L., Buster, J. E., Nakajima, S. T., Vogel, D. L., & Canfield, R. E. (1999). Efficacy of superovulation and intrauterine insemination in the treatment of infertility. *New England Journal of Medicine, 340*, 177–183.

Gwiazda, J. & Birch, E. E. (2001). Perceptual development: Vision. In B. E. Goldstein (Ed.), *Blackwell handbook of perception.* (pp. 636–668). Oxford: Blackwell Publishers.

Habbick, B. F., Pizzichini, M. M. M., Taylor, B., Rennie, D., Senthilselvan, A., & Sears, M. R. (1999). Prevalence of asthma, rhinitis and eczema among children in 2 Canadian cities: The international study of asthma and allergies in childhood. *Canadian Medical Association Journal, 160*, 1824–1828.

Hack, M., Friedman, H., & Fanaroff, A. A. (1996). Outcomes of extremely low birth weight infants. *Pediatrics, 98*, 931–937.

Haddow, J. E., Palomaki, G. E., Allan, W. C., Williams, J. R., Knight, G. J., Gagnon, J., O'Heir, C. E., Mitchell, M. L., Hermos, R. J., Waisbren, S. E., Faix, J. D., & Klein, R. Z. (1999). Maternal thyroid deficiency during pregnancy and subsequent neuropsychological development of the child. *New England Journal of Medicine, 341*, 549–555.

Haddow, J. E., Palomaki, G. E., Knight, G. J., Williams, J., Polkkiner, A., Canick, J. A., Saller, D. N., & Bowers, G. B. (1992). Prenatal screening for Down's syndrome with use of maternal serum markers. *New England Journal of Medicine, 327*, 588–593.

Haden, C. A., & Fivush, F. (1996). Contextual variation in maternal conversational styles. *Merrill-Palmer Quarterly, 42*, 200–227.

Haden, C. A., Haine, R. A., & Fivush, R. (1997). Developing narrative structure in parent–child reminiscing across the preschool years. *Developmental Psychology, 33*, 295–307.

Haight, W. L., Wang, X., Fung, H. H., Williams, K., & Mintz, J. (1999). Universal, developmental, and variable aspects of young children's play: A cross-cultural comparison of pretending at home. *Child Development, 70*(6), 1477–1488.

Haith, M. M. (1986). Sensory and perceptual processes in early infancy. *Journal of Pediatrics, 109*(1), 158–171.

Haith, M. M. (1998). Who put the cog in infant cognition? Is rich interpretation too costly? *Infant Behavior and Development, 21*(2), 167–179.

Haith, M. M., & Benson, J. B. (1998). Infant cognition. In D. Kuhn & R. S. Siegler (Eds.), *Handbook of Child Psychology: Vol. 2. Cognition, perception, and language* (5th ed., pp. 199–254). New York: Wiley.

Hakuta, K. (1986). *The mirror of language: The debate on bilingualism.* New York: Basic Books.

Hala, S., & Chandler, M. (1996). The role of strategic planning in accessing false-belief understanding. *Child Development, 67,* 2948–2966.

Halaas, J. L., Gajiwala, K. S., Maffei, M., Cohen, S. L., Chait, B. T., Rabinowitz, D., Lallone, R. L., Burley, S. K., & Friedman, J. M. (1995). Weight reducing effects of the plasma protein encoded by the obese gene. *Science, 269,* 543–546.

Hale, S., Bronik, M. D., & Fry, A. F. (1997). Verbal and spatial working memory in school-age children: Developmental differences in susceptibility to interference. *Developmental Psychology, 33,* 364–371.

Hall, D. G., & Graham, S. A. (1999). Lexical form class information guides word-to-object mapping in preschoolers. *Child Development, 70,* 78–91.

Hall, G. S. (1916). *Adolescence.* New York: Appleton. (Original work published 1904)

Halpern, D. F. (1997). Sex differences in intelligence: Implications for education. *American Psychologist, 52*(10), 1091–1102.

Halpern, S. H., Leighton, B. L., Ohlsson, A., Barrett, J. F. R., & Rice, A. (1998). Effect of epidural vs. parenteral opioid analgesia on the progress of labor. *Journal of the American Medical Association, 280,* 2105–2110.

Halterman, J. S., Aligne, A., Auinger, P., McBride, J. T., & Szilagyi, P. G. (2000). Inadequate therapy for asthma among children in the United States. *Pediatrics, 105*(1), 272–276.

Haltiwanger, J., & Harter, S. (1988). *A behavioral measure of young children's presented self-esteem.* Unpublished manuscript, University of Denver, Denver, CO.

Hamer, D. H., Hu, S., Magnuson, V. L., Hu, N., & Pattatucci, A. M. L. (1993). A linkage between DNA markers on the X chromosome and male sexual orientation. *Science, 261,* 321–327.

Hamm, J. V. (2000). Do birds of a feather flock together? The variable bases for African American, Asian American and European American adolescents' selection of similar friends. *Developmental Psychology, 36*(2), 209–219.

Han, W.-J., Waldfogel, J., & Brooks-Gunn, J. (2001). The effects of early maternal employment on later cognitive and behavioral outcomes. *Journal of Marriage and Family, 63,* 336–354

Hanna, E., & Meltzoff, A. N. (1993). Peer imitation by toddlers in laboratory, home, and day care contexts: Implications for social learning and memory. *Developmental Psychology, 29,* 701–710.

Hansen, M., Kurinczuk, J. J., Bower, C., & Webb, S. (2002). The risk of major birth defects after intracytoplasmic sperm injection and in vitro fertilization. *The New England Journal of Medicine, 346,* 725–730.

Hardy-Brown, K., & Plomin, R. (1985). Infant communicative development: Evidence from adoptive and biological families for genetic and environmental influences on rate differences. *Developmental Psychology, 21,* 378–385.

Hardy-Brown, K., Plomin, R., & DeFries, J. C. (1981). Genetic and environmental influences on rate of communicative development in the first year of life. *Developmental Psychology, 17,* 704–717.

Hardyck, C., & Petrinovich, L. F. (1977). Left-handedness. *Psychological Bulletin, 84,* 385–404.

Hareven, T. (1986). Historical changes in the family and the life course: Implications for child development. In A. M. Smuts & J. W. Hagen (Eds.), History and research in child development: *Monographs of the Society for Research in Child Development, 50,* (4–5, Serial No. 211), 8–23.

Hargrove, J. (1989). *Nelson Mandela. South Africa's silent voice of protest.* Chicago: Children's Press.

Harley, K. and Reese, E. (1999). Origins of autobiographical memory. *Developmental Psychology, 35,* 1338–1348.

Harlow, H. F., & Harlow, M. K. (1962). The effect of rearing conditions on behavior. *Bulletin of the Menninger Clinic, 26,* 213–224.

Harlow, H. F., & Zimmerman, R. R. (1959). Affectional responses in the infant monkey. *Science, 130,* 421–432.

Harnishfeger, K. K., & Bjorklund, D. F. (1993). The ontogeny of inhibition mechanisms: A renewed approach to cognitive development. In M. L. Howe & R. P. Pasnak (Eds.), *Emerging themes in cognitive development* (Vol. 1, pp. 28–49). New York: Springer-Verlag.

Harnishfeger, K. K., & Pope, R. S. (1996). Intending to forget: The development of cognitive inhibition in directed forgetting. *Journal of Experimental Psychology, 62,* 292–315.

Harrell, J. S., Gansky, S. A., Bradley, C. B., & McMurray, R. G. (1997). Leisure time activities of elementary school children. *Nursing Research, 46,* 246–253.

Harris, C., Kelly, C., Valentine, J. C., & Muhlenbruck, L. (2000). Making the most of summer school: A meta-analytic and narrative review. *Monographs of the Society for Research in Child Development, 65*(1), v–118.

Harris, P. L., Brown, E., Marriott, C., Whittall, S., & Harmer, S. (1991). Monsters, ghosts, and witches: Testing the limits of the fantasy–reality distinction in young children. In G. E. Butterworth, P. L. Harris, A. M. Leslie, & H. M. Wellman (Eds.), *Perspective on the child's theory of mind.* Oxford: Oxford University Press.

Harrison, A. O., Wilson, M. N., Pine, C. J., Chan, S. Q., & Buriel, R. (1990). Family ecologies of ethnic minority children. *Child Development, 61,* 347–362.

Harrist, A. W., Zain, A. F., Bates, J. E., Dodge, K. A., & Pettit, G. S. (1997). Subtypes of social withdrawal in early childhood: Sociometric status and social-cognitive differences across four years. *Child Development, 68,* 278–294.

Hart, B., & Risley, T. R. (1989). The longitudinal study of interactive systems. *Education and Treatment of Children, 12,* 347–358.

Hart, B., & Risley, T. R. (1992). American parenting of language-learning children: Persisting differences in family–child interactions observed in natural home environments. *Developmental Psychology, 28,* 1096–1105.

Hart, B., & Risley, T. R. (1996, August). *Individual differences in early intellectual experience of typical American children: Beyond SES, race, and IQ.* Address at the annual convention of the American Psychological Association, Toronto.

Hart, C. H., DeWolf, M., Wozniak, P., & Burts, D. C. (1992). Maternal and paternal disciplinary styles: Relations with preschoolers' playground behavioral orientation and peer status. *Child Development, 63,* 879–892.

Hart, C. H., Ladd, G. W., & Burleson, B. R. (1990). Children's expectations of the outcome of social strategies: Relations with sociometric status and maternal disciplinary style. *Child Development, 61,* 127–137.

Hart, C. H., Nelson, D. A., Robinson, C. C., Olsen, S. F., & McNeilly-Choque, M. K. (1998). Overt and relational aggression in Russian nursery-school-age children: Parenting style and marital linkages. *Developmental Psychology, 34,* 687–697.

Hart, S. N., & Brassard, M. R. (1987). A major threat to children's mental health: Psychological maltreatment. *American Psychologist, 42*(2), 160–165.

Hart, S., Field, T., del Valle, C., & Pelaez-Nogueras, M. (1998). Depressed mothers' interactions with their one-year-old infants. *Infant Behavior and Development, 21,* 519–525.

Harter, S. (1985). Competence as a dimension of self-worth. In R. Leahy (Ed.), *The development of the self.* New York: Academic Press.

Harter, S. (1990). Causes, correlates, and the functional role of global self-worth: A life-span perspective. In J. Kolligan & R. Sternberg (Eds.), *Competence considered: Perceptions of competence and incompetence across the life-span* (pp. 67–97). New Haven: Yale University Press.

Harter, S. (1993). Developmental changes in self-understanding across the 5 to 7 shift. In A. Sameroff & M. Haith (Eds.), *Reason and responsibility: The passage through childhood.* Chicago: University of Chicago Press.

Harter, S. (1996). Developmental changes in self-understanding across the 5 to 7 shift. In A. J. Sameroff & M. M. Haith (Eds.), *The five to seven year shift: The age of reason and responsibility* (pp. 207–235). Chicago: University of Chicago Press.

Harter, S. (1998). The development of self-representations. In W. Damon (Series Ed.) & N. Eisenberg (Vol. Ed.), *Handbook of child psychology: Vol. 3. Social, emotional, and personality development* (5th ed., pp. 553–617). New York: Wiley.

Hartshorn, K., Rovee-Collier, C., Gerhardstein, P., Bhatt, R. S., Wondoloski, R. L., Klein, P., Gilch, J., Wurtzel, N., & Campos-de-Carvalho, M. (1998). The ontogeny of long-term memory over the first year-and-a-half of life. *Developmental Psychobiology, 32,* 69–89.

Hartup, W. W. (1989). Social relationships and their developmental significance. *American Psychologist, 44,* 120–126.

Hartup, W. W. (1992). Peer relations in early and middle childhood. In V. B. Van Hasselt & M. Hersen (Eds.), *Handbook of social development: A lifespan perspective* (pp. 257–281). New York: Plenum.

Hartup, W. W. (1996a). The company they keep: Friendships and their developmental significance. *Child Development, 67,* 1–13.

Hartup, W. W. (1996b). Cooperation, close relationships, and cognitive development. In W. M. Bukowski, A. F. Newcomb, & W. W. Hartup (Eds.), *The company they keep: Friendship in childhood and adolescence* (pp. 213–237). New York: Cambridge University Press.

Hartup, W. W., & Stevens, N. (1999). Friendships and adaptation across the life span. *Current Directions in Psychological Science, 8,* 76–79.

Harvey, E. (1999). Short-term and long-term effects of early parental employment on children of the National Longitudinal Survey of Youth. *Developmental Psychology, 35*(2), 445–459.

Harvey, J. H., & Pauwels, B. G. (1999). Recent developments in close-relationships theory. *Current Directions in Psychological Science, 8*(3), 93–95.

Harwood, R. (1987). *Mandela.* New York: New American Library.

Harwood, R. L., Schoelmerich, A., Ventura-Cook, E., Schulze, P. A., & Wilson, S. P. (1996). Culture and class influences on Anglo and Puerto Rican mothers' beliefs regarding long-term socialization goals and child behavior. *Child Development, 67,* 2446–2461.

Haskett, M. E., & Kistner, J. A. (1991). Social interaction and peer perceptions of young physically abused children. *Child Development, 62,* 979–990.

Haskins, R. (1989). Beyond metaphor: The efficacy of early childhood education. *American Psychologist, 44*(2), 274–282.

Haswell, K., Hock, E., & Wenar, C. (1981). Oppositional behavior of preschool children: Theory and prevention. *Family Relations, 30,* 440–446.

Hatano, G., Siegler, R. S., Richards, D. D., Inagaki, K., Stavy, R., & Wax, N. (1993). The development of biological knowledge: A multi-national study. *Cognitive Development, 8,* 47–62.

Hatch, E. E., Palmer, J. R., Titus-Ernstoff, L., Nolton, K. L., Kaufman, R. H., Mittendorf, R., Robboy, S. J., Hyer, M., Cowan, C. M., Adam, E., Coloton, T., Harter, P. S., & Hoover, R. N. (1998). Cancer risk in women exposed to diethylstilbestrol in utero. *Journal of the American Medical Association, 280,* 630–634.

Hatcher, P. J., Hulme, C., & Ellis, A. W. (1994). Ameliorating early reading failure by integrating the teaching of reading and phonological skills: The phonological linkage hypothesis. *Child Development, 65,* 41–57.

Hatzichristou, C., & Hopf, D. (1996). A multiperspective comparison of peer sociometric status groups in childhood and adolescence. *Child Development, 67,* 1085–1102.

Haugaard, J. J. (1998). Is adoption a risk factor for the development of adjustment problems? *Clinical Psychology Review, 18,* 47–69.

Haugh, S., Hoffman, C., & Cowan, G. (1980). The eye of the very young beholder: Sex typing of infants by young children. *Child Development, 51,* 598–600.

Hausfather, A., Toharia, A., LaRoche, C., & Engelsmann, F. (1997). Effects of age of entry, daycare quality, and family characteristics on preschool behavior. *Journal of Child Psychology and Psychiatry, 38,* 441–448.

Hawkins, D. L., Pepler, D. J., & Craig, W. M. (2001). Naturalistic observations of peer interventions in bullying. *Social Development, 10,* 512–527.

Hawkins, J. (1999). Trends in anesthesiology during childbirth. *Anesthesiology, 91,* A1060.

Hawkins, J. D., Catalano, R. F., & Miller, J. Y. (1992). Risk and protective factors for alcohol and other drug problems in adolescence and early adulthood: Implications for substance abuse programs. *Psychological Bulletin, 112*(1), 64–105.

Hawkins, J. D., Catalano, R. F., Kosterman, R., Abbott, R., & Hill, K. G. (1999). Preventing adolescent health-risk behaviors by strengthening protection during childhood. *Archives of Pediatrics and Adolescent Medicine, 153,* 226–234.

Hay, D. F., Pedersen, J., & Nash, A. (1982). Dyadic interaction in the first year of life. In K. H. Rubin & H. S. Ross (Eds.), *Peer relationships and social skills in children.* New York: Springer.

Hayes, A., & Batshaw, M. L. (1993). Down syndrome. *Pediatric Clinics of North America, 40,* 523–535.

Hayne, H., MacDonald, S., & Barr, R. (1997). Developmental changes in the specificity of memory over the second year of life. *Infant Behavior and Development, 20,* 233–245.

Health Canada. (1994). *Canadian guidelines for sexual health education.* Ottawa: Minister of Supply and Services.

Health Canada. (1998a). *Canadian immunization guide* (5th ed.). Ottawa: Author.

Health Canada. (1998b). *For the Safety of Canadian Children and Youth.* Ottawa: Author.

Health Canada. (1999a). *Healthy development of children and youth: The role of the determinants of health.* Catalogue No. H39-501/1999E. Ottawa: Author.

Health Canada. (1999b). *Aboriginal peoples and the AIDS epidemic in Canada.* Ottawa: Health Canada Laboratory Centre for Disease Control. Retrieved August 10, 2002, from http://caan.ca/Epi/Dev/Design/Epi-Update.pdf

Health Canada. (2000a). *Crib safety.* Ottawa: Author.

Health Canada. (2000b). *Family-centred maternity and newborn care: National guidelines* (4th ed.). Ottawa: Minister of Public Works and Government Services.

Health Canada. (2000c). *Perinatal health indicators for Canada: A resource manual.* Ottawa: Minister of Public Works and Government Services Canada.

Health Canada. (2000d). *Rural health.* Retrieved September 20, 2002, from http://www.hc-sc.gc.ca/english/media/releases/2000/2000_61ebk2.htm

Health Canada. (2001a). *A conceptual and epidemiological framework for child maltreatment surveillance.* Ottawa: Minister of Public Works and Government Services Canada.

Health Canada. (2001b). *Respiratory disease in Canada.* Ottawa: Author.

Healthy Active Living Committee, Canadian Paediatric Society. (2002). Healthy active living for children and youth. *Paediatrics & Child Health, 7* 339–345.

Heath, S. B. (1989). Oral and literate tradition among black Americans living in poverty. *American Psychologist, 44,* 367–373.

Helgason, A., & Lund, K. E. (2001). Environmental tobacco smoke exposure of young children: Attitudes and health-risk awareness in the Nordic countries. *Nicotine and Tobacco Research, 3,* 341–345.

Helms, J. E. (1992). Why is there no study of cultural equivalence in standardized cognitive ability testing? *American Psychologist, 47,* 1083–1101.

Helwig, C. C., & Jasiobedzka, U. (2001). The relation between law and morality: Children's reasoning about socially beneficial and unjust laws. *Child Development, 72,* 1382–1393.

Helwig, C. C., Zelazo, P. D., & Wilson, M. (2001). Children's judgments of psychological harm in normal and noncanonical situations. *Child Development, 72,* 66–81.

Henly, W. L., & Fitch, B. R. (1966). Newborn narcotic withdrawal associated with regional enteritis in pregnancy. *New York Journal of Medicine, 66,* 2565–2567.

Henrich, C. C., Brown, J. L., & Aber, J. L. (1999). Evaluating the effectiveness of school-based violence prevention: Developmental approaches. *Social Policy Report, SRCD, 13*(3), 1–16.

Herman-Giddens, M. E., Brown, G., Verbiest, S., Carlson, P. J., Hooten, E. G., Howell, E., & Butts, J. D. (1999). Underascertainment of child abuse mortality in the United States. *Journal of the American Medical Association, 282,* 463–467.

Herman-Giddens, M. E., Slora, E. J., Wasserman, R. C., Bourdony, C. J., Bhapkar, M. V., Koch, G. G., & Hasemeier, C. M. (1997). Secondary sexual characteristics and menses in young girls seen in office practice: A study from the Pediatric Research in Office Settings network. *Pediatrics, 99,* 505–512.

Herrmann, H. J., & Roberts, M. W. (1987). Preventive dental care: The role of the pediatrician. *Pediatrics, 80,* 107–110.

Herrnstein, R. J., & Murray, C. (1994). *The bell curve: Intelligence and class structure in American life.* New York: Free Press.

Hertzman, C. (2002). *Leave no child behind! Social exclusion and child development.* Toronto: The Laidlaw Foundation.

Herzog, D. B., Dorer, D. J., Keel, P. K., Selwyn, S. E., Ekeblad, E. R., Flores, A. T., Greenwood, D. N., Burwell, R. A., & Keller, M. B. (1999). Recovery and relapse in anorexia and bulimia nervosa: A 7.5-year follow-up study. *Journal of the American Academy of Child and Adolescent Psychiatry, 38,* 829–837.

Herzog, D. B., Keller, M. B., & Lavori, P. W. (1988). Outcome in anorexia nervosa and bulimia. *Journal of Nervous and Mental Disease, 176,* 131–143.

Hetherington, E. M. (1987). Family relations six years after divorce. In K. Pasley & M. Ihinger-Tallman (Eds.), *Remarriage and parenting today: Research and theory.* New York: Guilford.

Hetherington, E. M., & Stanley-Hagan, M. (1999). The adjustment of children with divorced parents: A risk and resiliency perspective. *Journal of Child Psychology and Psychiatry, 40,* 129–140.

Hetherington, E. M., Bridges, M., & Insabella, G. M. (1998). What matters? What does not? Five perspectives on the association between marital transitions and children's adjustment. *American Psychologist, 53,* 167–184.

Hetherington, E. M., Stanley-Hagan, M., & Anderson, E. (1989). Marital transitions: A child's perspective. *American Psychologist, 44,* 303–312.

Hetzel, B. S. (1994). Iodine deficiency and fetal brain damage. *New England Journal of Medicine, 331,* 1770–1771.

Hewlett, B. S. (1987). Intimate fathers: Patterns of paternal holding among Aka pygmies. In M. E. Lamb (Ed.), *The father's role: Cross-cultural perspectives* (pp. 295–330). Hillsdale, NJ: Erlbaum.

Hewlett, B. S. (1992). Husband–wife reciprocity and the father–infant relationship among Aka pygmies. In B. S. Hewlett (Ed.), *Father–child relations: Cultural and biosocial contexts* (pp. 153–176). New York: de Gruyter.

Hewlett, B. S., Lamb, M. E., Shannon, D., Leyendecker, B., & Schölmerich, A. (1998). Culture and early infancy among central African foragers and farmers. *Developmental Psychology, 34*(4), 653–661.

Heyns, B., & Catsambis, S. (1986). Mother's employment and children's achievement: A critique. *Sociology of Education, 59,* 140–151.

Hibbard, D. R., & Buhrmester, D. (1998). The role of peers in the socialization of gender-related social interaction styles. *Sex Roles, 39,* 185–202.

Hickman, M., Roberts, C., & de Matos, M. G. (2000). Exercise and leisure time activities. In C. Currie, K. Hurrelmann, W. Settertobulte, R. Smith, & J. Todd (Eds.), *Health and health behaviour among young people.* WHO Policy Series: Healthy Policy for Children and Adolescents, Series No. 1. (pp. 73–82).

Hill, J. P. (1987). Research on adolescents and their families: Past and prospect. In E. E. Irwin (Ed.), *Adolescent social behavior and health.* San Francisco: Jossey-Bass.

Hinds, T. S., West, W. L., Knight, E. M., & Harland, B. F. (1996). The effect of caffeine on pregnancy outcome variables. *Nutrition Reviews, 54,* 203–207.

Hines, A. M. (1997). Divorce-related transitions, adolescent development, and the role of the parent–child relationship: A review of the literature. *Journal of Marriage and the Family, 59,* 375–388.

Hines, M., Chiu, L., McAdams, L. A., Bentler, M. P., & Lipcamon, J. (1992). Cognition and the corpus callosum: Verbal fluency, visual spatial ability, language lateralization related to midsagittal surface areas of the corpus callosum. *Behavioral Neuroscience, 106,* 3–14.

Hintz, R. L., Attie, K. M., Baptista, J., & Roche, A., for the Genentech Collaborative Group. (1999). Effect of growth hormone treatment on adult height of children with idiopathic short stature. *New England Journal of Medicine, 340*(7), 502–507.

Hirsch, H. V., & Spinelli, D. N. (1970). Visual experience modifies distribution of horizontally and vertically oriented receptive fields in cats. *Science, 168,* 869–871.

Ho, C. S. -H., & Fuson, K. C. (1998). Children's knowledge of teen quantities as tens and ones: Comparisons of Chinese, British, and American kindergartners. *Journal of Educational Psychology, 90,* 536–544.

Ho, W. C. (1989). *Yani: The brush of innocence.* New York: Hudson Hills.

Hobson, J. A., & Silvestri, L. (1999, February). Parasomnias. *Harvard Mental Health Letter,* pp. 3–5.

Hodges, E. V. E., Boivin, M., Vitaro, F., & Bukowski, W. M. (1999). The power of friendship: Protection against an escalating cycle of peer victimization. *Developmental Psychology, 35,* 94–101.

Hofferth, S. (1996). Child care in the United States today. *The Future of Children, 6*(2), 41–61.

Hofferth, S. L. (1998). *Healthy environments, healthy children: Children in families* (Report of the 1997 Panel Study of Income Dynamics, Child Development Supplement). Ann Arbor: University of Michigan Institute for Social Research.

Hofferth, S. L., & Jankuniene, Z. (2000, April 2). *Children's after-school activities.* Paper presented at biennial meeting of the Society for Research on Adolescence, Chicago.

Hofferth, S. L., & Sandberg, J. (1998). *Changes in American children's time, 1981–1997* (Report of the 1997 Panel Study of Income Dynamics, Child Development Supplement). Ann Arbor: University of Michigan Institute for Social Research.

Hofferth, S. L., & Sandberg, J. F. (2001). How American children spend their time. *Journal of Marriage and Family, 63,* 295–308.

Hoffman, H. J., & Hillman, L. S. (1992). Epidemiology of the sudden infant death syndrome: Maternal, neonatal, and postneonatal risk factors. *Clinics in Perinatology, 19,* 717–737.

Hoffman, M. L. (1970a). Conscience, personality, and socialization techniques. *Human Development, 13,* 90–126.

Hoffman, M. L. (1970b). Moral development. In P. H. Mussen (Ed.), *Carmichael's manual of child psychology* (Vol. 2, 3rd ed., pp. 261–360). New York: Wiley.

Hoffman, M. L. (1977). Sex differences in empathy and related behaviors. *Psychological Bulletin, 84,* 712–722.

Hoffman, M. L., & Hoffman, L. W. (Eds.). (1964). *Review of child development research.* New York: Russell Sage Foundation.

Holden, G. W., & Miller, P. C. (1999). Enduring and different: A meta-analysis of the similarity in parents' child rearing. *Psychological Bulletin, 125,* 223–254.

Holloway, L. (2000, October 17). Immersion promoted as alternative to bilingual instruction. *New York Times,* p. B1.

Holloway, S. D. (1999). Divergent cultural models of child rearing and pedagogy in Japanese preschools. *New Directions for Child and Adolescent Development, 83,* 61–75.

Holmes, L. D. (1987). *Quest for the real Samoa: The Mead–Freeman controversy and beyond.* South Hadley, MA: Bergin & Garvey.

Holsti, L., Grunau, R. V. E., & Whitfield, M. F. (2002). Developmental coordination disorder in extremely low birth weight children at nine years. *Journal of Developmental and Behavioral Pediatrics, 23,* 9–15.

Holtzman, N. A., Murphy, P. D., Watson, M. S., & Barr, P. A. (1997). Predictive genetic testing: From basic research to clinical practice. *Science, 278,* 602–605.

Hopfensperger, J. (1996, April 15). Germany's fast track to a career. *Minneapolis Star-Tribune,* pp. A1, A6.

Hopkins, B., & Westra, T. (1988). Maternal handling and motor development: An intracultural study. *Genetic, Social and General Psychology Monographs, 14,* 377–420.

Hopkins, B., & Westra, T. (1990). Motor development, maternal expectations and the role of handling. *Infant Behavior and Development, 13,* 117–122.

Horbar, J. D., Wright, E. C., Onstad, L., & the Members of the National Institute of Child Health and Human Development Neonatal Research Network. (1993). Decreasing mortality associated with the introduction of surfactant therapy: An observational study of neonates weighing 601 to 1300 grams at birth. *Pediatrics, 92,* 191–196.

Horowitz, F. D. (2000). Child development and the PITS: Simple questions, complex answers, and developmental theory. *Child Development, 71*(1) 1–10.

Horwitz, B., Rumsey, J. M., & Donohue, B. C. (1998). Functional connectivity of the angular gyrus in normal reading and dyslexia. *Proceedings of the National Academy of Sciences USA, 95,* 8939–8944.

Horwood, L. J., & Fergusson, D. M. (1998). Breastfeeding and child achievement. [Electronic version]. *Pediatrics, 101*(1). Retrieved January 5, 1998, from http://www.pediatrics.org/cgi/content/full/101/1/e9

Householder, J., Hatcher, R., Burns, W., & Chasnoff, I. (1982). Infants born to narcotics-addicted mothers. *Psychological Bulletin, 92*, 453–468.

Howe, M. L., & Courage, M. L. (1993). On resolving the enigma of infantile amnesia. *Psychological Bulletin, 113*, 305–326.

Howe, M. L., & Courage, M. L. (1997). The emergence and early development of autobiographical memory. *Psychological Review, 104*, 499–523.

Howe, N., Aquan-Assee, J., Bukowski, W. M., Lehoux, P. M., & Rinaldi, C. M. (2001). Siblings as confidants: Emotional understanding, relationship warmth, and sibling self-disclosure. *Social Development, 10*, 439–454.

Howe, R. B. (1995). Evolving policy on children's rights in Canada. In K. Covell (Ed.), *Readings in child development* (pp. 3–27). Toronto: Nelson.

Howell, A. J., & Enns, R. A. (1995). A high risk recognition program for adolescents in conflict with the law. *Canadian Psychology, 36*, 149–161.

Howell, N. (1996). Families and ethnicity. In M. Baker, M. Luxton et al. (Eds.), *Families: Changing trends in Canada*, 3rd ed. (pp.119–139). Toronto: McGraw-Hill Ryerson.

Howes, C. (1997). Teacher-sensitivity, children's attachment and play with peers. *Early Education and Development, 8*, 41–49.

Howes, C., & Matheson, C. C. (1992). Sequences in the development of competent play with peers: Social and social pretend play. *Developmental Psychology, 28*, 961–974.

Howes, C., Matheson, C. C., & Hamilton, C. E. (1994). Maternal, teacher, and child care history correlates of children's relationships with peers. *Child Development, 65*, 264–273.

Hoyert, D. L., Kochanek, K. D., & Murphy, S. L. (1999). *Deaths: Final data for 1997 (National Vital Statistics Reports, 47*[19]). Hyattsville, MD: National Center for Health Statistics.

Hu, S., Pattatucci, A. M. L., Patterson, C., Li, L., Fulker, D. W., Cherny, S. S., Kruglyak, L., & Hamer, D. H. (1995). Linkage between sexual orientation and chromosome Xq28 in males but not in females. *Nature Genetics, 11*, 248–256.

Huang, G. G. (1995). Self-reported biliteracy and self-esteem: A study of Mexican American 8th graders. *Applied Psycholinguistics, 16*, 271–291.

Huang, G. G. (2000). Mathematics achievement by immigrant children: A comparison of five English-speaking countries. *Education Policy Analysis Archives, 8*(25). Retrieved May 3, 2002, from http://epaa.asu.edu/epaa

Hubbard, F. O. A., & van IJzendoorn, M. H. (1991). Maternal unresponsiveness and infant crying across the first 9 months: A naturalistic longitudinal study. *Infant Behavior and Development, 14*, 299–312.

Hudson, J. I., & Pope, H. G. (1990). Affective spectrum disorder: Does antidepressant response identify a family of disorders with a common pathophysiology? *American Journal of Psychiatry, 147*(5), 552–564.

Huesmann, L. R. (1986). Psychological processes promoting the relation between exposure to media violence and aggressive behavior by the viewer. *Journal of Social Issues, 42*, 125–139.

Huesmann, L. R., & Eron, L. D. (1984). Cognitive processes and the persistence of aggressive behavior *Aggressive Behavior, 10*, 243–251.

Huesmann, L. R., & Eron, L. D. (1986). *Television and the aggressive child: A cross-national perspective*. Hillsdale, NJ: Erlbaum.

Hughes, C. and Cutting, A. L. (1999). Nature, nurture, and individual differences in early understanding of mind. *Psychological Science, 10*, 429–432.

Hughes, M. (1975). *Egocentrism in preschool children*. Unpublished doctoral dissertation, Edinburgh University, Edinburgh.

Hulse, G. K., & O'Neill, G. (2001). Methadone and the pregnant user: A matter for careful clinical consideration. *The Australian and New Zealand Journal of Obstetrics and Gynaecology, 41*, 329–332.

Hulse, G. K., Milne, E., English, D. R., & Holman, C. D. (1997). The relationship between maternal use of heroin and methadone and infant birth weight. *Addiction, 92*, 1571–1579.

Hulse, G. K., O'Neill, G., Pereira, C., & Brewer, C. (2001). Obstetric and neonatal outcomes associated with maternal naltrexone exposure. *The Australian and New Zealand Journal of Obstetrics and Gynaecology, 41*, 424–428.

Human Resources Development Canada. (1996). *Growing up in Canada. National longitudinal survey of children and youth*. Ottawa: HRDC.

Human Resources Development Canada. (2002). More immigrant children enjoy good mental health than Canadian children. Bulletin: Special edition on child development. Retrieved September 20, 2002, from http://www.hrdc-drhc.gc.ca/sp-ps/arb-dgra/publications/bulletin/child_dev/chi_dev13.shtml

Humphrey, L. L. (1986). Structural analysis of parent–child relationships in eating disorders. *Journal of Abnormal Psychology, 95*(4), 395–402.

Humphreys, A. P., & Smith, P. K. (1984). Rough-and-tumble in preschool and playground. In P. K. Smith (Ed.), *Play in animals and humans*. Oxford: Blackwell.

Hunsaker, S. L., & Callahan, C. M. (1995). Creativity and giftedness: Published instrument uses and abuses. *Gifted Child Quarterly, 39*(2), 110–114.

Hunt, C. E. (1996). Prone sleeping in healthy infants and victims of sudden infant death syndrome. *Journal of Pediatrics, 128*, 594–596.

Hunter, S. (1999). *Visual and performing artists: Women in profile*. New York: Crabtree Publishing Company.

Huntsinger, C. S., & Jose, P. E. (1995). Chinese American and Caucasian American family interaction patterns in spatial rotation puzzle solutions. *Merrill-Palmer Quarterly, 41*, 471–496.

Huntsinger, C. S., Jose, P. E., & Larson, S. L. (1998). Do parent practices to encourage academic competence influence the social adjustment of young European American and Chinese American children? *Developmental Psychology, 34*(4), 747–756.

Huston, A., Donnerstein, E., Fairchild, H., Feshbach, N. D., Katz, P. A., Murray, J. P., Rubenstein, E. A., Wilcox, B. L., & Zuckerman, D. (1992). *Big world, small screen: The role of television in American society*. Lincoln: University of Nebraska Press.

Huttenlocher, J. (1998). Language input and language growth. *Preventive Medicine, 27*, 195–199.

Huttenlocher, J., Haight, W., Bryk, A., Seltzer, M., & Lyons, T. (1991). Early vocabulary growth: Relation to language input and gender. *Developmental Psychology, 27*, 236–248.

Huttenlocher, J., Levine, S., & Vevea, J. (1998). Environmental input and cognitive growth: A study using time-period comparisons. *Child Development, 69*, 1012–1029.

Huttenlocher, J., Newcombe, N., & Vasilyeva, M. (1999). Spatial scaling in young children. *Psychological Science, 10,* 393–398.

Huttenlocher, J., Vasilyeva, M., Cymerman, E., & Levine, S. (in preparation). *Language input and child language.* Unpublished manuscript.

Hwang, S. J., Beaty, T. H., Panny, S. R., Street, N. A., Joseph, J. M., Gordon, S., McIntosh, I., & Francomano, C. A. (1995). Association study of transforming growth factor alpha (TGFa) TaqI polymorphism and oral clefts: Indication of gene-environment interaction in a population-based sample of infants with birth defects. *American Journal of Epidemiology, 141,* 629–636.

Hyde, M. L., & Riko, K. (2000). Design and evaluation issues in Universal Newborn Hearing Screening Programs. *Journal of Speech Language Pathology and Audiology, 24,* 102–118.

Ikonomidou, C., Bittigau, P., Ishimaru, M. J., Wozniak, D. F., Koch, C., Genz, K., Price, M. T., Stefovska, V., Horster, F., Tenkova, T., Dikranian, K., & Olney, J. W. (2000). Ethanol-induced apoptotic neurodegeneration and fetal alcohol syndrome. *Science, 287,* 1056–1060.

Impagnatiello, F. Guidotti, A. R., Pesold, C. Dwivedi, Y., Caruncho, H., Pisu, M. G., Uzonov, D. P., Smalheiser, N. R., Davis, J. M., Pandey, G. N., Pappas, G. D., Tueting, P., Sharma, R. P., & Costa, E. (1998). A decrease of reelin expression as a putative vulnerability factor in schizophrenia. *Proceedings of the National Academy of Science, 95,* 15718–15723.

Indian and Inuit Health Committee, Canadian Paediatric Society. (1987). Growth charts for Indian and Inuit children. *Canadian Medical Association Journal, 136,* 118–119.

Indian and Inuit Health Committee, Canadian Paediatric Society. (1994). Diabetes and the First Nations. *The Canadian Journal of Paediatrics, 1,* 222–224.

Infant Health and Development Program (IHDP). (1990). Enhancing the outcomes of low-birth-weight, premature infants. *Journal of the American Medical Association, 263*(22), 3035–3042.

Infante-Rivard, C., Fernández, A., Gauthier, R., David, M., & Rivard, G. E. (1993). Fetal loss associated with caffeine intake before and during pregnancy. *Journal of the American Medical Association, 270,* 2940–2943.

Infectious Diseases and Immunization Committee, Canadian Paediatric Society. (2000). Care of the infant born to an HIV-positive mother. *Paediatrics & Child Health, 5,* 161–164.

Infectious Diseases and Immunization Committee, Canadian Paediatric Society. (2001). Measles-mumps-rubella vaccine and autistic spectrum disorder: A hypothesis only. *Paediatrics & Child Health, 6,* 387–389.

Ingersoll, E. W., & Thoman, E. B. (1999). Sleep/wake states of preterm infants: Stability, developmental change, diurnal variation, and relation with caregiving activity. *Child Development, 70,* 1–10.

Institute of Medicine (IOM) National Academy of Sciences. (1993, November). *Assessing genetic risks: Implications for health and social policy.* Washington, DC: National Academy of Sciences.

Interdepartmental Working Group on Female Genital Mutilation. (2000). *Female genital mutilation and health care: Current situation and legal status.* Ottawa: Health Canada.

International Perinatal HIV Group. (1999). The mode of delivery and the risk of vertical transmission of human immunodeficiency virus type 1: A meta-analysis of 15 prospective cohort studies. *New England Journal of Medicine, 340,* 977–987.

Irwin, S. H., & Lero, D. S. (1997). *In our way: Child care barriers to full workforce participation experience by parents of young children with special needs and potential remedies.* Cape Breton: Breton Books.

Isabella, R. A. (1993). Origins of attachment: Maternal interactive behavior across the first year. *Child Development, 64,* 605–621.

ISLAT Working Group (1998, July 31). ART into science: Regulation of fertility techniques. *Science, 281,* 651–652.

Isley, S., O'Neil, R., & Parke, R. (1996). The relation of parental affect and control behaviors to children's classroom acceptance: A concurrent and predictive analysis. *Early Education and Development, 7,* 7–23.

Izard, C. E., Huebner, R. R., Resser, D., McGinness, G. C., & Dougherty, L. M. (1980). The young infant's ability to produce discrete emotional expressions. *Developmental Psychology, 16,* 132–140.

Izard, C. E., Porges, S. W., Simons, R. F., Haynes, O. M., & Cohen, B. (1991). Infant cardiac activity: Developmental changes and relations with attachment. *Developmental Psychology, 27,* 432–439.

Jackson, A. (1997a). The math wars: California battles it out over mathematics Education Reform (Part I). *Notices of the AMS.* Retrieved January 22, 1999, from http://www.ams.org/notices/199706/comm-calif.html

Jackson, A. (1997b). The math wars: California battles it out over mathematics Education Reform (Part II). *Notices of the AMS.* Retrieved January 22, 1999, from http://www.ams.org/notices/199708/comm-calif2.html

Jackson, R. S., Creemers, J. W. M., Ohagi, S., Raffin-Sanson, M. L., Sanders, L., Montague, C. T., Hutton, J. C., & O'Rahilly, S. (1997). Obesity and impaired prohormone processing associated with mutations in the human prohormone convertase 1 gene. *Nature Genetics, 16,* 303–306.

Jacobsen, T., & Hofmann, V. (1997). Children's attachment representations: Longitudinal relations to school behavior and academic competency in middle childhood and adolescence. *Developmental Psychology, 33,* 703–710.

Jacobson, J. L., & Wille, D. E. (1986). The influence of attachment pattern on developmental changes in peer interaction from the toddler to the preschool period. *Child Development, 57,* 338–347.

Jacobson, S. W., Chiodo, L. M., & Jacobson, J. L. (1999). Breast-feeding effects on intelligence quotient in 4- and 11-year-old children. *Pediatrics 103*(5). Retrieved September 23, 2002, from http://www.pediatrics.org/cgi/content/full/103/5/e71

Jagers, R. J., Bingham, K., & Hans, S. L. (1996). Socialization and social judgments among inner-city African-American kindergartners. *Child Development, 67,* 140–150.

Jakobson, L. S., Frisk, V., Knight, R. M., Downie, A. L. S., & Whyte, H. (2001). The relationship between periventricular brain injury and deficits in visual processing among extremely-low-birthweight (<1000 g) children. *Journal of Pediatric Psychology, 26,* 503–512.

Jamieson, C. E. (2001). *Genetic testing for late onset diseases: Current research practices and analysis of* policy development. Working Paper 01–02. Ottawa: Health Canada Policy Research Communications Unit.

Jankowiak, W. (1992). Father–child relations in urban China. *Father–child relations: Cultural and bisocial contexts* (pp. 345–363). New York: de Gruyter.

Janowsky, J. S., & Carper, R. (1996). Is there a neural basis for cognitive transitions in school-age children? In A. J. Sameroff & M. M. Haith (Eds.), *The five to seven year shift: The age of reason and responsibility* (pp. 33–56). Chicago: University of Chicago Press.

Jarrell, R. H. (1998). Play and its influence on the development of young children's mathematical thinking. In D. P. Fromberg & D. Bergen (Eds.), *Play from birth to twelve and beyond: Contexts, perspectives, and meanings* (pp. 56–67). New York: Garland.

Jaslow, C. K. (1982). *Teenage pregnancy* (ERIC/CAPS Fact Sheet). Ann Arbor, MI: Counseling and Personnel Services Clearing House.

Jay, M. S., DuRant, R. H., Shoffitt, T., Linder, C. W., & Litt, I. F. (1984). Effect of peer counselors on adolescent compliance in use of oral contraceptives. *Pediatrics, 73,* 126–131.

Jefferson, T. (1999). Pediatricians alerted to five new vaccines. *Journal of the American Medical Association, 281,* 1973–1975.

Jeffery, H. E., Megevand, M., & Page, M. (1999). Why the prone position is a risk factor for sudden infant death syndrome. *Pediatrics, 104,* 263–269.

Jenkins, J. J. & Astington, J. W. (1996). Cognitive factors and family structure associated with theory of mind development in young children. *Developmental Psychology, 32,* 70–78.

Jenkins, J., & Keating, D. (1998). *Risk and resilience in six- and ten-year-old children.* Catalogue No. W-98-23E. Ottawa: Applied Research Branch, Strategic Policy, Human Resources Development Canada.

Jenkins, J., & Keating, D. (1999). *Risk and resilience in six- and ten-year-old children.* Retrieved September 23, 2002, from http://www.hrdc-drhc.gc.ca/sp-ps/arb-dgra/publications/research/1999docs/w-98-23e.pdf

Jensen, A. R. (1969). How much can we boost IQ and scholastic achievement? *Harvard Educational Review, 39,* 1–123.

Ji, B. T., Shu, X. O., Linet, M. S., Zheng, W., Wacholder, S., Gao, Y. T., Ying, D. M., & Jin, F. (1997). Paternal cigarette smoking and the risk of childhood cancer among offspring of nonsmoking mothers. *Journal of the National Cancer Institute, 89,* 238–244.

Jiao, S., Ji, G., & Jing, Q. (1996). Cognitive development of Chinese urban only children and children with siblings. *Child Development, 67,* 387–395.

Jimerson, S., Egeland, B., & Teo, A. (1999). A longitudinal study of achievement trajectories: Factors associated with change. *Journal of Educational Psychology, 91*(1), 116–126

Johnson, E. (1997). Children's understanding of epistemic conduct in self-deception and other false belief stories. *Child Development, 68,* 1117–1132.

Johnson, J. E. (1998). Play development from ages four to eight. In D. P. Fromberg & D. Bergen (Eds.), *Play from birth to twelve and beyond: Contexts, perspectives, and meanings* (pp. 145–153). New York: Garland.

Johnson, K. L., Lero, D. S., & Rooney, J. A. (2001). *Work–life compendium 2001: 150 Canadian statistics on work, family, & well-being.* Guelph, ON: Centre for Families, Work and Well-Being.

Johnson, M. H. (1998). The neural basis of cognitive development. In D. Kuhn & R. S. Siegler (Eds.), *Handbook of Child Psychology: Vol. 2. Cognition, perception, and language* (5th ed., pp. 1–49). New York: Wiley.

Johnson, M. O. (1996). Television violence and its effect on children. *Journal of Pediatric Nursing, 11,* 94–98.

Johnson, N., & Cremo, E. (1995). Socialization and the Native family. In K. Covell (Ed.), *Readings in child development: A Canadian perspective* (pp. 159–171). Toronto: Nelson.

Johnson, R. A., Hoffmann, J. P., & Gerstein, D. R. (1996). *The relationship between family structure and adolescent substance use* (DHHS Publication No. SMA 96–3086). Washington, DC: U.S. Department of Health and Human Services.

Johnson, S. L., & Birch, L. L. (1994). Parents' and children's adiposity and eating styles. *Pediatrics, 94,* 653–661.

Johnston, B. D., Grossman, D. C., Connell, F. A., & Koepsell, T. D. (2000). High-risk periods for childhood injury among siblings. *Pediatrics, 105*(3), 562–568.

Johnston, J., & Ettema, J. S. (1982). *Positive images: Breaking stereotypes with children's television.* Newbury Park, CA: Sage.

Johnston, L. D., O'Malley, P. M., & Bachman, J. G. (2000). *The Monitoring the Future results on adolescent drug use. Overview of key findings 1999.* USDHSS, PHS, NIDA, NIH Publication number 00-490. Bethesda, MD: National Institute on Drug Abuse.

Joint Working Group of the Canadian Paediatric Society and Health Canada. (1994, reaffirmed 2001). *Nutrition recommendations update: Dietary fat and children.* Ottawa: Author.

Jones, H. W., & Toner, J. P. (1993). The infertile couple. *New England Journal of Medicine, 329,* 1710–1715.

Jones, M. C. (1957). The late careers of boys who were early- or late-maturing. *Child Development, 28,* 115–128.

Jones, M. C. (1958). The study of socialization patterns at the high school level. *Journal of Genetic Psychology, 93,* 87–111.

Jones, N. A., Field, T., Fox, N. A., Davalos, M., Lundy, B., & Hart, S. (1998). Newborns of mothers with depressive symptoms are physiologically less developed. *Infant Behavior & Development, 21*(3), 537–541.

Jones, N. A., Field, T., Fox, N. A., Lundy, B., & Davalos, M. (1997). EEG activation in one-month-old infants of depressed mothers. *Development and Psychopathology, 9,* 491–505..

Jones, S. S. (1996). Imitation or exploration? Young infants' matching of adults' oral gestures. *Child Development, 67,* 1952–1969.

Jordan, B. (1993). Birth in four cultures: *A crosscultural investigation of childbirth in Yucatan, Holland, Sweden, and the United States* (4th ed.). Prospect Heights, IL: Waveland Press. (Original work published 1978)

Joseph, K. S., Marcoux, S., Ohlsson, A., Liu, S., Allen, A. C., Kramer, M. S., & Wen, S. W. (2001). Changes in stillbirth and infant mortality associated with increases in preterm birth among twins. *Pediatrics, 108,* 1055–1061.

Jusczyk, P. W. (in press). The role of speech perception capacities in early language acquisition. In M. T. Banich & M. Mack (Eds.), *Mind, brain, and language: Multidisciplinary perspectives.* Mahwah, NJ: Erlbaum.

Jusczyk, P. W., & Hohne, E. A. (1997). Infants' memory for spoken words. *Science, 277,* 1984–1986.

Jussim, L., Eccles, J., & Madon, S. (1996). Social perception, social stereotypes, and teacher expectations: Accuracy and the quest for the powerful self-fulfilling prophecy. In M. P. Zanna (Ed.), *Advances in experimental social psychology* (Vol. 28, pp. 281–388). San Diego: Academic.

Kaback, M., Lim-Steele, J., Dabholkar, D., Brown, D., Levy, N., & Zeiger, K., for the International TSD Data Collection Network. (1993). Tay-Sachs disease: Carrier screening, prenatal diagnosis, and the molecular era. *Journal of the American Medical Association, 270,* 2307–2315.

Kagan, J. (1997). Temperament and the reactions to unfamiliarity. *Child Development, 68,* 139–143.

Kagan, J., & Snidman, N. (1991a). Infant predictors of inhibited and uninhibited behavioral profiles. *Psychological Science, 2,* 40–44.

Kagan, J., & Snidman, N. (1991b). Temperamental factors in human development. *American Psychologist, 46,* 856–862.

Kail, R. (1991). Processing time declines exponentially during childhood and adolescence. *Developmental Psychology, 27,* 259–266.

Kail, R. (1997). Processing time, imagery, and spatial memory. *Journal of Experimental Child Psychology, 64,* 67–78.

Kail, R., & Park, Y. (1994). Processing time, articulation time, and memory span. *Journal of Experimental Child Psychology, 57,* 281–291.

Kalagian, W., Delmore, T., Loewen, I., & Busca, C. (1998). Adolescent oral contraceptive use: Factors predicting compliance at 3 and 12 months. *The Canadian Journal of Human Sexuality, 7,* 1–8.

Kalish, C. W. (1998). Young children's predictions of illness: Failure to recognize probabilistic cause. *Developmental Psychology, 34*(5), 1046–1058.

Kamin, L. J. (1974). *The science and politics of IQ.* Potomac, MD: Erlbaum.

Kamin, L. J. (1981). Commentary. In S. Scarr (Ed.), *Race, social class, and individual differences in I.Q.* Hillsdale, NJ: Erlbaum.

Kandall, S. R., Doberczak, T. M., Jantunen, M., & Stein, J. (1999). The methadone-maintained pregnancy. *Clinics in Perinatology, 26,* 173–183.

Kaplan, H., & Dove, H. (1987). Infant development among the Ache of East Paraguay. *Developmental Psychology, 23,* 190–198.

Kaplowitz, P. B. , Oberfield, S. E., & the Drug and Therapeutics and Executive Committees of the Lawson Wilkins Pediatric Endocrine Society. (1999). Reexamination of the age limit for defining when puberty is precocious in girls in the United States: Implications for evaluation and treatment. *Pediatrics, 104,* 936–941.

Katzman, R. (1993). Education and prevalence of Alzheimer's disease. *Neurology, 43,* 13–20.

Katzmarzyk, P. T., Pérusse, L., Rao, D. C., & Bouchard, C. (1999). Familial risk of obesity and central adipose tissue distribution in the general Canadian population. *American Journal of Epidemiology, 149,* 933–942.

Kaufman, A. S., & Kaufman, N. L. (1983). *Kaufman assessment battery for children: Administration and scoring manual.* Circle Pines, MN: American Guidance Service.

Kaufman, J., & Zigler, E. (1987). Do abused children become abusive parents? *American Journal of Orthopsychiatry, 57*(2), 186–192.

Kaye, W. H., Weltzin, T. E., Hsu, L. K. G., & Bulik, C. M. (1991). An open trial of fluoxetine in patients with anorexia nervosa. *Journal of Clinical Psychiatry, 52,* 464–471.

Keegan, R. T., & Gruber, H. E. (1985). Charles Darwin's unpublished "Diary of an Infant": An early phase in his psychological work. In G. Eckardt, W. G. Bringmann, & L. Sprung (Eds.), *Contributions to a history of developmental psychology: International William T. Preyer Symposium* (pp. 127–145). Berlin: Walter de Gruyter.

Keel, P. K., & Mitchell, J. E. (1997). Outcome in bulimia nervosa. *American Journal of Psychiatry, 154,* 313–321.

Keenan, K., & Shaw, D. (1997). Developmental and social influences on young girls' early problem behavior. *Psychological Bulletin, 121*(1), 95–113.

Keeney, T. J., Canizzo, S. R., & Flavell, J. H. (1967). Spontaneous and induced verbal rehearsal in a recall task. *Child Development, 38,* 953–966.

Kelleher, K. J., Casey, P. H., Bradley, R. H., Pope, S. K., Whiteside, L., Barrett, K. W., Swanson, M. E., & Kirby, R. S. (1993). Risk factors and outcomes for failure to thrive in low birth weight preterm infants. *Pediatrics, 91,* 941–948.

Keller, H. (1905). *The story of my life.* New York: Grosset & Dunlap.

Keller, H. (1920). *The world I live in.* New York: Century. (Original work published 1908)

Keller, H. (1929). *The bereaved.* New York: Leslie Fulenwider, Inc.

Kelley, M. L., Smith, T. S., Green, A. P., Berndt, A. E., & Rogers, M. C. (1998). Importance of fathers' parenting to African-American toddler's social and cognitive development. *Infant Behavior & Development, 21,* 733–744.

Kelley, R. M., Denny, G., & Young, M. (1999). Modified stages of acquisition of gateway drug use: A primary prevention application of the stages of change model. *Journal of Drug Education, 29,* 189–203.

Kellogg, R. (1970). Understanding children's art. In P. Cramer (Ed.), *Readings in developmental psychology today.* Delmar, CA: CRM.

Kemp. J. S., Unger, B., Wilkins, D., Psara, R. M., Ledbetter, T. L., Graham, M. A., Case, M., and Thach, B. T. (2000). Unsafe sleep practices and an analysis of bedsharing among infants dying suddenly and unexpectedly: Results of a four-year, population-based, death-scene investigation study of sudden infant death and related syndromes. *Pediatrics, 106*(3), e41.

Kendall-Tackett, K. A. (1997, July 7). *Postpartum depression and the breastfeeding mother.* Paper presented to the 25th Annual Seminar for Physicians on Breastfeeding, sponsored by La Leche League International, the American Academy of Pediatrics, and the American College of Obstetricians and Gynecologists, Washington, DC.

Kendall-Tackett, K. A., Williams, L. M., & Finkelhor, D. (1993). Impact of sexual abuse on children: A review and synthesis of recent empirical studies. *Psychological Bulletin, 113*(1), 164–180.

Kendler, K. S., MacLean, C., Neale, M., Kessler, R., Heath, A., & Eaves, L. (1991). The genetic epidemiology of bulimia nervosa. *American Journal of Psychiatry, 148,* 1627–1637.

Kernan, M. (1993, June). The object at hand. *Smithsonian,* pp. 14–16.

Kerns, K. A., Don, A., Mateer, C. A., & Streissguth, A. P. (1997). Cognitive deficits in nonretarded adults with fetal alcohol syndrome. *Journal of Learning Disabilities, 30,* 685–693.

Kestenbaum, R., & Gelman, S. A. (1995). Preschool children's identification and understanding of mixed emotions. *Cognitive Development, 10*, 443–458.

Kier, C., & Lewis, C. (1998). Preschool sibling interaction in separated and married families: Are same-sex pairs or older sisters more sociable? *Journal of Child Psychology and Psychiatry, 39*, 191–201.

Kimball, M. M. (1986). Television and sex-role attitudes. In T. M. Williams (Ed.), *The impact of television: A natural experiment in three communities* (pp. 265–301). Orlando, FL: Academic Press.

Kimbrough, R. D., LeVois, M., & Webb, D. R. (1994). Management of children with slightly elevated blood lead levels. *Pediatrics, 93*, 188–191.

King, A. J. C., Boyce, W. F., & King, M. A. (1999). *Trends in the health of Canadian youth.* Ottawa: Health Canada.

King, A., Beazley, R., Warren, W., Hankins, C., Robertson, A., Radford, J. (1988). *Canada youth and AIDS study.* Kingston, ON: Social Program Evaluation Group, Queen's University.

King, B. M. (1996). *Human sexuality today.* Englewood Cliffs, NJ: Prentice-Hall.

King, C. (2000). From cradleboard to motherboard: Buffy Sainte-Marie's interactive multimedia curriculum transforms Native American studies. *Teaching Tolerance, 17*, 10–13.

King, C., Siegel, M., Celebucki, C., & Connolly, G. N. (1998). Adolescent exposure to cigarette advertising in magazines. *Journal of the American Medical Association, 279*, 1–520.

Kinney, H. C., Filiano, J. J., Sleeper, L. A., Mandell, F., Valdes-Dapena, M., & White, W. F. (1995). Decreased muscarinic receptor binding in the arcuate nucleus in Sudden Infant Death Syndrome. *Science, 269*, 1446–1450.

Kinsbourne, M. (1994). Sugar and the hyperactive child. *New England Journal of Medicine, 330*, 355–356.

Kinsman, S., Romer, D., Furstenberg, F. F., & Schwarz, D. F. (1998). Early sexual initiation: The role of peer norms. *Pediatrics, 102*, 1185–1192.

Kirby, D. (1997). *No easy answers: Research findings on programs to reduce teen pregnancy.* Washington, DC: National Campaign to Prevent Teen Pregnancy.

Kirmayer, L. J., Boothroyd, L. J., & Hodgins, S. (1998). Attempted suicide among Inuit youth: Psychosocial correlates and implications for prevention. *Canadian Journal of Psychiatry, 43*, 816–822.

Kirmayer, L. J., Brass, G. M., & Tait, C. L. (2000). The mental health of Aboriginal peoples: Transformations of identity and community. *Canadian Journal of Psychiatry, 45*, 607–616.

Kisilevsky, B. S., Hains, S. M. J., Lee, K., Muir, D. W., Xu, F., Fu, G., Zhao, Z. Y., & Yang, R. L. (1998). The still-face effect in Chinese and Canadian 3- to 6-month-old infants. *Developmental Psychology, 34*(4), 629–639.

Kisilevsky, B. S., Muir, D. W., & Low, J. A. (1992). Maturation of human fetal responses to vibroacoustic stimulation. *Child Development, 63*, 1497–1508.

Kistner, J., Eberstein, I. W., Quadagno, D., Sly, D., Sittig, L., Foster, K., Balthazor, M., Castro, R., & Osborne, M. (1997). Children's AIDS-related knowledge and attitudes: Variations by grade, race, gender, socioeconomic status, and size of community. *AIDS Education and Prevention, 9*, 285–298.

Kjos, S. L., & Buchanan, T. A. (1999). Gestational diabetes mellitus. *New England Journal of Medicine, 341*(23), 1749-1756.

Klar, A. J. S. (1996). A single locus, RGHT, specifies preference for hand utilization in humans. In *Cold Spring Harbor Symposia on Quantitative Biology* (Vol. 61, pp. 59–65). Cold Spring Harbor, NY: Cold Spring Harbor Laboratory Press.

Klaus, M. H., & Kennell, J. H. (1982). *Parent–infant bonding* (2nd ed.). St. Louis, MO: Mosby.

Klaus, M. H., & Kennell, J. H. (1997). The doula: An essential ingredient of childbirth rediscovered. *Acta Paediatrica, 86*, 1034–1036.

Klebanoff, M. A., Levine, R. J., DerSimonian, R., Clemens, J. D., & Wilkins, D. G. (1999). Maternal serum paraxanthine, a caffeine metabolite, and the risk of spontaneous abortion. *New England Journal of Medicine, 341*, 1639–1644.

Klebanov, P. K., Brooks-Gunn, J., & McCormick, M. C. (1994). Classroom behavior of very low birth weight elementary school children. *Pediatrics, 94*, 700–708.

Klebanov, P. K., Brooks-Gunn, J., McCarton, C., & McCormick, M. C. (1998). The contribution of neighborhood and family income to developmental test scores over the first three years of life. *Child Development, 69*(5), 1420–1436.

Klein, K., Forehand, R., Armistead, L., & Long, P. (1997). Delinquency during the transition to early adulthood: Family and parenting predictors from early adolescence. *Adolescence, 32*, 61–80.

Kleinman, R. E., Murphy, J. M., Little, M., Pagano, M., Wehler, C. A., Regal, K., & Jellinek, M. S. (1998). Hunger in children in the United States: Potential behavioral and emotional correlates. *Pediatrics, 101*(1), e3.

Klesges, R. C., Klesges, L. M., Eck, L. H., & Shelton, M. L. (1995). A longitudinal analysis of accelerated weight gain in preschool children. *Pediatrics, 95*, 126–130.

Kliegman, R., Madura, D., Kiwi, R., Eisenberg, I., & Yamashita, T. (1994). Relation of maternal cocaine use to the risk of prematurity and low birth weight. *Journal of Pediatrics, 124*, 751–756.

Kliewer, S. A., Lenhard, J. M., Willson, T. M., Patel, I., Morris, D. C., & Lehmann, J. M. (1995). A prostaglandin JZ metabolite binds peroxisome proliferator-activated receptor gamma and promotes adipocyte differentiation. *Cell, 83*, 813–819.

Kling, K. C., Hyde, J. S., Showers, C. J., & Buswell, B. N. (1999). Gender differences in self-esteem: A meta-analysis. *Psychological Bulletin, 125*, 470–500.

Knoblock, H., Stevens, F., & Malone, A. F. (1980). *Manual of developmental diagnosis: The administration and interpretation of the revised Gesell and Amatruda developmental and neurologic examination.* New York: Harper & Row.

Knowles, D. W. (1995). The development of giftedness. In K. Covell (Ed.), *Readings in child development: A Canadian perspective* (pp. 237–261). Toronto: Nelson Canada.

Kochanska, G. (1992). Children's interpersonal influence with mothers and peers. *Developmental Psychology, 28*, 491–499.

Kochanska, G. (1993). Toward a synthesis of parental socialization and child temperament in early development of conscience. *Child Development, 64*, 325–437.

Kochanska, G. (1995). Children's temperament, mothers' discipline, and security of attachment: Multiple pathways to emerging internalization. *Child Development, 66*, 597–615.

Kochanska, G. (1997a). Multiple pathways to conscience for children with different temperaments: From toddlerhood to age 5. *Developmental Psychology, 33,* 228–240.

Kochanska, G. (1997b). Mutually responsive orientation between mothers and their young children: Implications for early socialization. *Child Development, 68,* 94–112.

Kochanska, G. Tjebkes, T. L., & Forman, D. R. (1998). Children's emerging regulation of conduct: Restraint, compliance, and internalization from infancy to the second year. *Child Development, 69*(5), 1378–1389.

Kochanska, G., & Aksan, N. (1995). Mother–child positive affect, the quality of child compliance to requests and prohibitions, and maternal control as correlates of early internalization. *Child Development, 66,* 236–254.

Kochanska, G., Murray, K., & Coy, K. C. (1997). Inhibitory control as a contributor to conscience in childhood: From toddler to early school age. *Child Development, 68,* 263–277.

Kochenderfer, B. H., & Ladd, G. W. (1996). Peer victimization: Cause or consequence of school maladjustment? *Child Development, 67,* 1305–1317.

Kogan, M. D., Alexander, G. R., Kotelchuck, M., MacDorman, M. F., Buekens, P., Martin, J. A., & Papiernik, E. (2000). Trends in twin birth outcomes and prenatal care utilization in the United States, 1981–1997. *Journal of the American Medical Association, 284,* 335–341.

Kogan, M. D., Martin, J. A., Alexander, G. R., Kotelchuck, M., Ventura, S. J., & Frigoletto, F. D. (1998). The changing pattern of prenatal care utilization in the United States, 1981–1995, using different prenatal care indices. *Journal of the American Medical Association, 279,* 1623–1628.

Kohen, D. E., Hertzman, C., & Brooks-Gunn, J. (1998). *Neighbourhood influences on children's school readiness.* Catalogue No. W-98-15E. Ottawa: Applied Research Branch, Strategic Policy, Human Resources Development Canada.

Kohen, D. E., Soubhi, H., & Raina, P. (1999). *A Canadian picture of maternal reports of childhood injuries.* Vancouver: BC Injury Research and Prevention Unit.

Kohen, D., Hertzman, C., & Wiens, M. (1998). *Environmental changes and children's competencies.* Working Paper W-98-25E. Ottawa: Applied Research Branch, Human Resources Development Canada.

Kohlberg, L. (1966). A cognitive-developmental analysis of children's sex-role concepts and attitudes. In E. E. Maccoby (Ed.), *The development of sex differences.* Stanford, CA: Stanford University Press.

Kohlberg, L. (1969). Stage and sequence: The cognitive-developmental approach to socialization. In D. A. Goslin (Ed.), *Handbook of socialization theory and research.* Chicago: Rand McNally.

Kohlberg, L. (1981). *Essays on moral development.* San Francisco: Harper & Row.

Kohlberg, L., & Gilligan, C. (1971, fall). The adolescent as a philosopher: The discovery of the self in a postconventional world. *Daedalus,* pp. 1051–1086.

Kohlberg, L., & Ryncarz, R. A. (1990). Beyond justice reasoning: Moral development and consideration of a seventh stage. In C. N. Alexander & E. J. Langer (Eds.), *Higher stages of human development* (pp. 191–207). New York: Oxford University Press.

Kohlberg, L., Yaeger, J., & Hjertholm, E. (1968). Private speech: Four studies and a review of theories. *Child Development, 39,* 691–736.

Kolata, G. (1988, March 29). Fetuses treated through umbilical cords. *New York Times,* p. C3.

Kolbert, E. (1994, January 11). Canadians curbing TV violence. *New York Times,* pp. C15, C19.

Kolder, V. E., Gallagher, J., & Parsons, M. T. (1987). Court-ordered obstetrical interventions. *New England Journal of Medicine, 316,* 1192–1196.

Kopp, C. B. (1982). Antecedents of self-regulation. *Developmental Psychology, 18,* 199–214.

Kopp, C. B., & Kaler, S. R. (1989). Risk in infancy: Origins and implications. *American Psychologist, 44*(2), 224–230.

Kopp, C. B., & McCall, R. B. (1982). Predicting later mental performance for normal, at-risk, and handicapped infants. In P. B. Baltes & O. G. Brim (Eds.), *Life-span development and behavior* (Vol. 4). New York: Academic Press.

Koren, G., Pastuszak, A., & Ito, S. (1998). Drugs in pregnancy. *New England Journal of Medicine, 338,* 1128–1137.

Korner, A. (1996). Reliable individual differences in preterm infants' excitation management. *Child Development, 67,* 1793–1805.

Korner, A. F., Zeanah, C. H., Linden, J., Berkowitz, R. I., Kraemer, H. C., & Agras, W. S. (1985). The relationship between neonatal and later activity and temperament. *Child Development, 56,* 38–42.

Korte, D., & Scaer, R. (1984). *A good birth, a safe birth.* New York: Bantam.

Kottak, C. P. (1994). *Cultural anthropology.* New York: McGraw-Hill.

Kozlowska, K., & Hanney, L. (1999). Family assessment and intervention using an interactive art exercise. *Australia and New Zealand Journal of Family Therapy, 20*(2), 61–69.

Kozulin, A., & Falik, L. (1995). Dynamic cognitive assessment of the child. *Current Directions in Psychological Science, 4,* 192–196.

Kozulin, A., & Garb, E. (2002). Dynamic assessment of EFL text comprehension. *School Psychology International, 23,* 112–127.

Kraemer, H. C., Korner, A., Anders, T., Jacklin, C. N., & Dimiceli, S. (1985). Obstetric drugs and infant behavior: A reevaluation. *Journal of Pediatric Psychology, 10,* 345–353.

Kralovec, E., & Buell, J. (2000). *The end of homework.* Boston: Beacon.

Kramer, L., Perozynski, L. A., & Chung, T. (1999). Parental responses to sibling conflict: The effects of development and parent gender. *Child Development, 70*(6), 1401–1414.

Kramer, M. S., Platt, R., Yang, H., Joseph, K. S., Wen, S. W., Morin, L., & Usher, R. H. (1998). Secular trends in preterm birth: A hospital-based cohort study. *Journal of the American Medical Association, 280,* 1849–1854.

Krauss, S., Concordet, J. P., & Ingham, P. W. (1993). A functionally conserved homolog of the Drosophila segment polarity gene hh is expressed in tissues with polarizing activity in zebrafish embryos. *Cell, 75,* 1431–1444.

Kreutzer, M., Leonard, C., & Flavell, J. (1975). An interview study of children's knowledge about memory. *Monographs of the Society for Research in Child Development, 40*(1, Serial No. 159).

Krevans, J., & Gibbs, J. C. (1996). Parents' use of inductive discipline: Relations to children's empathy and prosocial behavior. *Child Development, 67,* 3263–3277.

Kristensen, P., Judge, M. E., Thim, L., Ribel, U., Christjansen, K. N., Wulff, B. S., Clausen, J. T., Jensen, P. B.,

Madsen, O. D., Vrang, N., Larsen, P. J., & Hastrup, S. (1998). Hypothalamic CART is a new anorectic peptide regulated by leptin. *Nature, 393,* 72–76.

Kristof, N. D. (1991, June 17). A mystery from China's census: Where have young girls gone? *New York Times,* pp. A1, A8.

Kristof, N. D. (1993, July 21). Peasants of China discover new way to weed out girls. *New York Times,* pp. A1, A6.

Kroger, J. (1993). Ego identity: An overview. In J. Kroger (Ed.), *Discussions on ego identity* (pp. 1–20). Hillsdale, NJ: Erlbaum.

Kroger, J., & Haslett, S. J. (1991). A comparison of ego identity status transition pathways and change rates across five identity domains. *International Journal of Aging and Human Development, 32,* 303–330.

Ku, L. C., Sonenstein, F. L., & Pleck, J. H. (1992). The association of AIDS education and sex education with sexual behavior and condom use among teenage men. *Family Planning Perspectives, 24,* 100–106.

Kuczmarski, R. J., Ogden, C. L., Grummer-Strawn, L. M., Flegal, K. M., Guo, S. S., Wei, R., Mei, Z., Curtin, L. R., Roche, A. F., & Johnson, C. L. (2000). CDC growth charts: United States. *Advance Data,* No. 314. Centers for Disease Control and Prevention, U.S. Department of Health and Human Services.

Kuczynski, L., & Kochanska, G. (1995). Function and content of maternal demands: Developmental significance of early demands for competent action. *Child Development, 66,* 616–628.

Kuhl, P. K., Andruski, J. E., Chistovich, I. A., Chistovich, L. A., Kozhevnikova, E. V., Ryskina, V. L., Stolyarova, E. I., Sundberg, U., & Lacerda, F. (1997). Cross-language analysis of phonetic units in language addressed to infants. *Science, 277,* 684–686.

Kuhl, P. K., Williams, K. A., Lacerda, F., Stevens, K. N., & Lindblom, B. (1992). Linguistic experience alters phonetic perception in infants by 6 months of age. *Science, 255,* 606–608.

Kuhn, D., Garcia-Mila, M., Zohar, A., & Andersen, C. (1995). Strategies of knowledge acquisition. *Monographs of the Society for Research in Child Development, 60*(4, Serial No. 245).

Kuklinski, M. R., & Weinstein, R. S. (2001). Classroom and developmental differences in a path model of teacher expectancy effects. *Child Development, 72,* 1554–1578.

Kupersmidt, J. B., & Coie, J. D. (1990). Preadolescent peer status, aggression, and school adjustment as predictors of externalizing problems in adolescence. *Child Development, 61,* 1350–1362

Kupfersmid, J., & Wonderly, D. (1980). Moral maturity and behavior: Failure to find a link. *Journal of Youth and Adolescence, 9*(3), 249–261.

Kurdek, L. A. (1999). The nature and predictors of the trajectory of change in marital quality for husbands and wives over the first 10 years of marriage. *Developmental Psychology, 35,* 1283–1296.

Kurjak, A., Kupesic, S., Matijevic, R., Kos, M., & Marton, U. (1999). First trimester malformation screening. *European Journal of Obstetrics, Gynecology, and Reproductive Biology (E4L), 85,* 93–96.

Kurosawa, A. (1983). *Something like an autobiography* (A. E. Bock, Trans.). New York: Vintage.

Kuxhaus, D. (November 1, 1997). Sniffing mother came out of fog, took back her life. *Winnipeg Free Press,* A12.

Kwok, D. C., & Lytton, H. (1996). Perceptions of mathematics ability versus actual mathematics performance: Canadian and Hong Kong Chinese children. *British Journal of Educational Psychology, 66,* 209–222.

Kye, C., & Ryan, N. (1995). Pharmacologic treatment of child and adolescent depression. *Child and Adolescent Psychiatric Clinics of North America, 4,* 261–281.

Labov, T. (1992). Social and language boundaries among adolescents. *American Speech, 67,* 339–366.

Lackmann, G. M., Salzberger, U., Tollner, U., Chen, M., Carmella, S. G., & Hecht, S. S. (1999). Metabolites of a tobacco-specific carcinogen in the urine of newborns. *Journal of the National Cancer Institute, 91,* 459–465.

Ladd, G. W. (1996). Shifting ecologies during the 5 to 7 year period: Predicting children's adjustment during the transition to grade school. In A. J. Sameroff & M. M. Haith (Eds.), *The five to seven year shift: The age of reason and responsibility* (pp. 363–386). Chicago: University of Chicago Press

Ladd, G. W., & Colter, B. S. (1988). Parents' management of preschoolers' peer relations: Is it related to children's social competence? *Developmental Psychology, 24,* 109–117.

Ladd, G. W., & Hart, C. H. (1992). Creating informal play opportunities: Are parents' and preschoolers' initiations related to children's competence with peers? *Developmental Psychology, 28,* 1179–1187.

Ladd, G. W., Birch, S. H., and Buhs, E. S. (1999). Children's social and scholastic lives in kindergarten: Related spheres of influence? *Child Development, 70,* 1373–1400.

Ladd, G. W., Kochenderfer, B. J., & Coleman, C. C. (1996). Friendship quality as a predictor of young children's early school adjustment. *Child Development, 67,* 1103–1118.

Lagercrantz, H., & Slotkin, T. A. (1986). The "stress" of being born. *Scientific American, 254*(4), 100–107.

Laible, D. J., & Thompson, R. A. (1998). Attachment and emotional understanding in preschool children. *Developmental Psychology, 34*(5), 1038–1045.

Lalonde, C. E., & Werker, J. F. (1995). Cognitive influences on cross-language speech perception in infancy. *Infant Behavior and Development, 18,* 459–475.

Lamb, M. E. (1981). The development of father–infant relationships. In M. E. Lamb (Ed.), *The role of the father in child development* (2nd ed.). New York: Wiley.

Lamb, M. E. (1982a). The bonding phenomenon: Misinterpretations and their implications. *Journal of Pediatrics, 101*(4), 555–557.

Lamb, M. E. (1982b). Early contact and maternal–infant bonding: One decade later. *Pediatrics, 70,* 763–768.

Lamb, M. E. (1983). Early mother–neonate contact and the mother–child relationship. *Journal of Child Psychology & Psychiatry & Allied Disciplines, 24,* 487–494.

Lamb, M. E. (1987). Predictive implications of individual differences in attachment. *Journal of Consulting and Clinical Psychology, 55*(6), 817–824.

Lamb, M. E., Frodi, A. M., Frodi, M., & Hwang, C. P. (1982). Characteristics of maternal and paternal behavior in traditional and non-traditional Swedish families. *International Journal of Behavior Development, 5,* 131–151.

Lamb, M. E., Pleck., J., Charnov, E. L., & Levine, J. A. (1985). Paternal behavior in humans. *American Zoologist, 25,* 883–894.

Lambert, W. E., & Tucker, G. R. (1972). *The bilingual education of children:*

The St. Lambert experiment. Rowley, MA: Newbury House.

Lamborn, S. D., Mounts, N. S., Steinberg, L., & Dornbusch, S. M. (1991). Patterns of competence and adjustment among adolescents from authoritative, authoritarian, indulgent, and neglectful families. *Child Development, 62,* 1049–1065.

Landesman-Dwyer, S., & Emanuel, I. (1979). Smoking during pregnancy. *Teratology, 19,* 119–126.

Landry, D. J., Kaeser, L., & Richards, C. L. (1999). Abstinence promotion and the provision of information about contraception in public school district sexuality education policies. *Family Planning Perspectives, 31,* 280–286.

Landy, S., & Tam, K. K. (1996). Yes, parenting does make a difference to the development of children in Canada. In Human Resources Development Canada & Statistics Canada, *Growing up in Canada. National Longitudinal Survey of Children and Youth.* Ottawa: Author.

Landy, S., & Tam, K. K. (1998). *Understanding the contribution of multiple risk factors on child development at various ages.* Catalogue No. W-98-22E. Ottawa: Applied Research Branch, Strategic Policy, Human Resources Development Canada.

Lane, H. (1976). *The wild boy of Aveyron.* Cambridge, MA: Harvard University Press.

Lange, G., MacKinnon, C. E., & Nida, R. E. (1989). Knowledge, strategy, and motivational contributions to preschool children's object recall. *Developmental Psychology, 25,* 772–779.

Lansford, J. E., & Parker, J. G. (1999). Children's interactions in triads: Behavioral profiles and effects of gender and patterns of friendships among members. *Developmental Psychology, 35,* 80–93.

Lanting, C. I., Fidler, V., Huisman, M., Touwen, B. C. L., & Boersma, E. R. (1994). Neurological differences between 9-year-old children fed breast-milk or formula-milk as babies. *Lancet, 334,* 1319–1322.

Lapham, E. V., Kozma, C., & Weiss, J. O. (1996). Genetic discrimination: Perspectives of consumers. *Science, 274,* 621–624.

Lapierre-Adamcyk, E. (1999). *Family status from the children's perspective. Canadian families at the approach of the year 2000.* Ottawa: Statistics Canada.

Larivée, S., Normandeau, S., & Parent, S. (2000). The French connection: Some contributions of French-language research in the post-Piagetian era. *Child Development, 71,* 823–839.

Larner, M. B., Stevenson, C. S., & Behrman, R. E. (1998). Protecting children from abuse and neglect: Analysis and recommendations. *The Future of Children, 8,* 4–22.

Larson, R. (1998). Implications for policy and practice: Getting adolescents, families, and communities in sync. In A. Crouter & R. Larson (Eds.), *Temporal rhythms in adolescence: Clocks, calendars, and the coordination of daily life (New Directions in Child and Adolescent Development, 82,* pp. 83–88). San Francisco: Jossey-Bass.

Larson, R. W. (1997). The emergence of solitude as a constructive domain of experience in early adolescence. *Child Development, 68,* 80–93.

Larson, R. W., & Verma, S. (1999). How children and adolescents spend time across the world: Work, play, and developmental opportunities. *Psychological Bulletin, 125,* 701–736.

Larson, R. W., Richards, M. H., Moneta, G., Holmbeck, G., & Duckett, E. (1996). Changes in adolescents' daily interactions with their families from ages 10 to 18: Disengagement and transformation. *Developmental Psychology, 32,* 744–754.

Larson, R., & Richards, M. (1998). Waiting for the weekend: Friday and Saturday nights as the emotional climax of the week. In A. Crouter & R. Larson (Eds.), *Temporal rhythms in adolescence: Clocks, calendars, and the coordination of daily life (New Directions in Child and Adolescent Development, 82,* pp. 37–51). San Francisco: Jossey-Bass.

Larson, R., & Richards, M. H. (1991). Daily companionship in late childhood and early adolescence: Changing developmental contexts. *Child Development, 62,* 284–300.

Larson, R., & Richards, M. H. (1994). *Divergent realities: The emotional lives of mothers, fathers, and adolescents.* New York: Basic Books.

Lash, J. P. (1980). *Helen and teacher: The story of Helen Keller and Anne Sullivan Macy.* New York: Delacorte.

Laucht, M., Esser, G., & Schmidt, M. H. (1994). Contrasting infant predictors of later cognitive functioning. *Journal of Child Psychology and Psychiatry, 35,* 649–652.

Laursen, B. (1996). Closeness and conflict in adolescent peer relationships: Interdependence with friends and romantic partners. In W. M. Bukowski, A. F. Newcomb, & W. W. Hartup (Eds.), *The company they keep: Friendship in childhood and adolescence* (pp. 186–210). New York: Cambridge University Press.

Laursen, B., Coy, K. C., & Collins, W. A. (1998). Reconsidering changes in parent–child conflict across adolescence: A meta-analysis. *Child Development, 69,* 817–832.

Lawson, C. (1993, October 4). Celebrated birth aside, teen-ager is typical now. *New York Times,* p. A18.

Lay, C., & Verkuyten, M. (1999). Ethnic identity and its relation to personal self-esteem: A comparison of Canadian-born and foreign-born Chinese adolescents. *Journal of Social Psychology, 139,* 288–299.

Leacy, F. H. (Ed.) (1983). *Historical statistics of Canada* (2nd ed.). Ottawa: Statistics Canada.

Leaper, C., Anderson, K. J., & Sanders, P. (1998). Moderators of gender effects on parents' talk to their children: A meta-analysis. *Developmental Psychology, 34*(1), 3–27.

Leavitt, L. A. (1998). Research perspectives: Mothers' sensitivity to infant signals. *Pediatrics, 102,* 1247–1249.

Lecanuet, J. P., Granier-Deferre, C., & Busnel, M.-C. (1995). Human fetal auditory perception. In J. P. Lecanuet, W. P. Fifer, N. A. Krasnegor, & W. P. Smotherman (Eds.), *Fetal development: A psychobiological perspective* (pp. 239–262). Hillsdale, NJ: Erlbaum.

LeDoux, J. (1989). Cognitive and emotional interactions in the brain. *Cognition and Emotion, 3,* 265–289.

Lee, J. (1998). Children, teachers, and the internet. *Delta Kappa Gamma Bulletin, 64*(2), 5–9.

Lee, K., Eskritt, M., Symons, L. A., & Muir, D. (1998). Children's use of triadic eye gaze information for "mind reading." *Developmental Psychology, 34,* 525–539.

Lee, K., Xu, F., Cameron, C. A., & Chen, S. (2001). Taiwan and Mainland Chinese and Canadian children's categorization and evaluation of lie- and truth-telling: A modesty effect. *British Journal of Developmental Psychology, 19,* 525–542.

Leeman, L. W., Gibbs, J. C., & Fuller, D. (1993). Evaluation of a multicomponent group treatment program for juvenile delinquents. *Aggressive Behavior, 19,* 281–292.

Leenaars, A. A., & Lester, D. (1990). Suicide in adolescents: A comparison of Canada and the United States. *Psychological Reports, 67,* 867–873.

Leenaars, A. A., & Lester, D. (1995). The changing suicide pattern in Canadian adolescents and youth, compared to their American counterparts. *Adolescence, 30,* 539–548.

Lefebvre, P., & Merrigan, P. (1998). *Family background, family income, maternal work and child development.* Catalogue No. W-98-12E. Ottawa: Applied Research Branch, Strategic Policy, Human Resources Development Canada.

Legro, R. S., Lin, H. M., Demers, L. M., & Lloyd, T. (2000). Rapid maturation of the reproductive axis during perimenarche independent of body composition. *Journal of Clinical Endocrinology and Metabolism, 85,* 1021–1025.

Leibel, R. L. (1997). And finally, genes for human obesity. *Nature Genetics, 16,* 218–220.

Leichtman, M. D., & Ceci, S. J. (1995). The effects of stereotypes and suggestions on preschoolers' reports. *Developmental Psychology, 31,* 568–578.

Lelwica, M., & Haviland, J. (1983). *Ten-week-old infants' reactions to mothers' emotional expressions.* Paper presented at the biennial meeting of the Society for Research in Child Development, Detroit, MI.

Lenneberg, E. H. (1967). *Biological functions of language.* New York: Wiley.

Lenneberg, E. H. (1969). On explaining language. *Science, 164*(3880), 635–643.

Lerner, J. V., & Galambos, N. L. (1985). Maternal role satisfaction, mother–child interaction, and child temperament: A process model. *Child Development, 21,* 1157–1164.

Lesch, K. P., Bengel, D., Heils, A., Sabol, S. Z., Greenberg, B. D., Petri, S., Benjamin, J., Müller, C. R., Hamer, D. H., & Murphy, D. L. (1996). Association of anxiety-related traits with a polymorphism in the serotonin transporter gene regulatory region. *Science, 274,* 1527–1531.

Leslie, A. M. (1982). The perception of causality in infants. *Perception, 11,* 173–186.

Leslie, A. M. (1984). Spatiotemporal continuity and the perception of causality in infants. *Perception, 13,* 287–305.

Leslie, A. M. (1988). The necessity of illusion: Perception and thought in infancy. In L. Weiskrantz (Ed.), *Thought without language* (pp. 185–210). Oxford: Oxford Science.

Leslie, A. M. (1994). ToMM, ToBy, and Agency: Core architecture and domain specificity. In S. A. Gelman & L. A. Hirschfeld (Eds.), *Mapping the mind: Domain specificity in cognition and culture* (pp. 119–148). New York: Cambridge University Press.

Leslie, A. M., & Keeble, S. (1987). Do six-month-old infants perceive causality? *Cognition, 25,* 265–288.

Lester, B. M., & Boukydis, C. F. Z. (1985). *Infant crying: Theoretical and research perspectives.* New York: Plenum.

Lester, B. M., & Dreher, M. (1989). Effects of marijuana use during pregnancy on newborn cry. *Child Development, 60,* 765–771.

Leung, C. (2001). The sociocultural and psychological adaptation of Chinese migrant adolescents in Australia and Canada. *International Journal of Psychology, 36,* 8–19.

LeVay, S. (1991). A difference in hypothalamic structure between heterosexual and homosexual men. *Science, 253,* 1034–1037.

Leve, L. D., & Fagot, B. I. (1997). Gender-role socialization and discipline processes in one- and two-parent families. *Sex Roles, 36,* 1–21.

Leventhal, T., & Brooks-Gunn, J. (2000). The neighborhoods they live in: The effects of neighborhood residence on child and adolescent outcomes. *Psychological Bulletin, 126*(2), 309–337.

LeVine, R. A. (1974). Parental goals: A cross-cultural view. *Teacher College Record, 76,* 226–239.

LeVine, R. A. (1989). Human parental care: Universal goals, cultural strategies, individual behavior. In R. A. LeVine, P. M. Miller, & M. M. West (Eds.), *Parental behavior in diverse societies* (pp. 3–12). San Francisco: Jossey-Bass.

LeVine, R. A. (1994). *Child care and culture: Lessons from Africa.* Cambridge, England: Cambridge University Press.

LeVine, R. A., Dixon, S., LeVine, S., Richman, A., Leiderman, P. H.,

Keefer, C. H., & Brazelton, T. B. (1994). *Child care and culture: Lessons from Africa.* New York: Cambridge University Press.

Levine, S. C., Huttenlocher, J., Taylor, A., & Langrock, A. (1999). Early sex differences in spatial skill. *Developmental Psychology, 35*(4), 940–949.

Levitt, C. A., Kaczorowski, J., Hanvey, L., Avard, D., & Chance, G. W. (1996). Breast-feeding policies and practices in Canadian hospitals providing maternity care. *Canadian Medical Association Journal, 155,* 181–188.

Levitt, M. J., Guacci-Franco, N., & Levitt, J. L. (1993). Convoys of social support in childhood and early adolescence: Structure and function. *Developmental Psychology, 29,* 811–818.

Levron, J., Aviram, A., Madgar, I., Livshits, A., Raviv, G., Bider, D., Hourwitz, A., Barkai, G., Goldman, B., & Mashiach, S. (1998, October). *High rate of chromosomal aneupoloidies in testicular spermatozoa retrieved from azoospermic patients undergoing testicular sperm extraction for in vitro fertilization.* Paper presented at the 16th World Congress on Fertility and Sterility and the 54th annual meeting of the American Society for Reproductive Medicine, San Francisco.

Levy, G. D., & Carter, D. B. (1989). Gender schema, gender constancy, and gender-role knowledge: The roles of cognitive factors in preschoolers' gender-role stereotype attributions. *Developmental Psychology, 25,* 444–449.

Levy-Shiff, R. (1994). Individual and contextual correlates of marital change across the transition to parenthood. *Developmental Psychology, 30,* 591–601.

Levy-Shiff, R., Goldschmidt, I., & Har-Even, D. (1991). Transition to parenthood in adoptive families. *Developmental Psychology, 27,* 131–140.

Lewin, T. (1997, April 23). Detention of pregnant women for drug use is struck down. *New York Times,* p. A-16.

Lewinsohn, P. M., Gotlib, I. H., Lewinsohn, M., Seeley, J. R., & Allen, N. B. (1998). Gender differences in anxiety disorders and anxiety symptoms in adolescents. *Journal of Abnormal Psychology, 107,* 109–117.

Lewis, M. (1995). Self-conscious emotions. *American Scientist, 83,* 68–78.

Lewis, M. (1997). The self in self-conscious emotions. In S. G. Snodgrass & R. L. Thompson (Eds.), *The self across psychology: Self-recognition, self-awareness, and the self-concept* (Vol. 818, pp. 118–142). New York: The New York Academy of Sciences, Annals of the New York Academy of Sciences.

Lewis, M. (1998). Emotional competence and development. In D. Pushkar, W. Bukowski, A. E. Schwartzman, D. M. Stack, & D. R. White (Eds.), *Improving competence across the lifespan* (pp. 27–36). New York: Plenum.

Lewis, M. D., Koroshegyi, C., Douglas, L., & Kampe, K. (1997). Age-specific associations between emotional responses to separation and cognitive performance in infancy. *Developmental Psychology, 33,* 32–42.

Lewis, M., & Brooks, J. (1974). Self, other, and fear: Infants' reaction to people. In H. Lewis & L. Rosenblum (Eds.), *The origins of fear: The origins of behavior* (Vol. 2). New York: Wiley.

Lewis, M., Worobey, J., Ramsay, D. S., & McCormack, M. K. (1992). Prenatal exposure to heavy metals: Effect on childhood cognitive skills and health status. *Pediatrics, 89,* 1010–1015.

Lewit, E., & Kerrebrock, N. (1997). Population-based growth stunting. *The Future of Children, 7*(2), 149–156.

Liaw, F., & Brooks-Gunn, J. (1993). Patterns of low-birth-weight children's cognitive development. *Developmental Psychology, 29,* 1024–1035.

Liberman, I. Y., & Liberman, A. M. (1990). Whole language vs. code emphasis: Underlying assumptions and their implications for reading instruction. *Annals of Dyslexia, 40,* 51–76.

Lickona, T. (Ed.). (1976). *Moral development and behavior.* New York: Holt.

Lidz, C. S. (1995). Dynamic assessment and the legacy of L. S. Vygotsky. *School Psychology International, 16,* 143–153.

Lie, E., & Newcombe, N. S. (1999). Elementary school children's explicit and implicit memory for faces of preschool classmates. *Developmental Psychology, 35,* 102–112.

Lightwood, J. M., Phibbs, C. S., & Glantz, S. A. (1999). Short-term health and economic benefits of smoking cessation: Low birth weight. *Pediatrics, 104,* 1312–1320.

Lillard, A. S. (1998). Ethnopsychologies: Cultural variations in theory of mind. *Psychological Bulletin, 123,* 3–33.

Lillard, A., & Curenton, S. (1999). Do young children understand what others feel, want, and know? *Young Children, 54*(5), 52–57.

Lindegren, M. L., Byers, R. H., Jr., Thomas, P., Davis, S. F., Caldwell, B., Rogers, M., Gwinn, M., Ward, J. W., & Fleming, P. L. (1999). Trends in perinatal transmission of HIV/AIDS in the United States. *Journal of the American Medical Association, 282,* 531–538.

Lindsay, G. B., & Rainey, J. (1997). Psychosocial and pharmacologic explanations of nicotine's "gateway drug" function. *Journal of School Health, 67,* 123–126.

Lindwer, W. (1991). *The last seven months of Anne Frank* (A. Meersschaert, Trans.). New York: Pantheon.

Linney, J. A., & Seidman, E. (1989). The future of schooling. *American Psychologist, 44*(2), 336–340.

Lipman, E. L., Boyle, M. H., Dooley, M. D., & Offord, D. R. (1998). *Children and lone-mother families: An investigation of factors influencing child well-being.* Report No. W-98-11E. Ottawa: Applied Research Branch, Strategic Policy, Human Resources Development Canada.

Litovitz, T. L., Klein-Schwartz, W., Caravati, E. M., Youniss, J., Crouch, B., & Lee, S. (1999). Annual report of the American Association of Poison Control Centers Toxic Exposure Surveillance System. *American Journal of Emergency Medicine, 17,* 435–487.

Liu, J. (1996). Down syndrome birth rates surprising. *CDSS Quarterly, 9,* 8.

Livson, N., & Peskin, H. (1980). Perspectives on adolescence from longitudinal research. In J. Adelson (Ed.), *Handbook of adolescent psychology.* New York: Wiley.

Lloyd, T., Andon, M. B., Rollings, N., Martel, J. K., Landis, J. R., Demers, L. M., Eggli, D. F., Kieselhorst, K., & Kulin, H. E. (1993). Calcium supplementation and bone mineral density in adolescent girls. *Journal of the American Medical Association, 270,* 841–844.

Lock, A., Young, A., Service, V., & Chandler, P. (1990). Some observations on the origin of the pointing gesture. In V. Volterra & C. J. Erting (Eds.), *From gesture to language in hearing and deaf children.* New York: Springer.

Loeber, R., & Dishion, T. (1983). Early predictors of male delinquency: A review. *Psychological Bulletin, 94,* 68–99.

Lonigan, C. J., Fischel, J. E., Whitehurst, G. J., Arnold, D. S., & Valdez-Menchaca, M. C. (1992). The role of otitis media in the development of expressive language disorder. *Developmental Psychology, 28,* 430–440.

Looft, W. R. (1973). Socialization and personality: Contemporary psychological approaches. In P. B. Baltes & K. W. Schaie (Eds.), *Life-span developmental psychology.* New York: Academic Press.

Lorenz, K. (1957). Comparative study of behavior. In C. H. Schiller (Ed.), *Instinctive behavior.* New York: International Universities Press.

Lorsbach, T. C., & Reimer, J. F. (1997). Developmental changes in the inhibition of previously relevant information. *Journal of Experimental Child Psychology, 64,* 317–342.

Lortie-Lussier, M. & Feller, G. L. (1991). Self–ingroup relationships: Their variations among Canadian pre-adolescents of English, French, and Italian origin. *Journal of Cross-Cultural Psychology, 22,* 458–471.

Louis Harris & Associates. (1986). *American teens speak: Sex, myths, TV and birth control: The Planned Parenthood poll.* New York: Planned Parenthood Federation of America.

Louise Brown: From miracle baby to regular teen. (1994, February 7). *People Weekly,* p. 12.

Louise Brown: The world's first "test-tube baby" ushered in a revolution in fertility. (1984, March). *People Weekly,* p. 82.

Lozoff, B., Klein, N. K., Nelson, E. C., McClish, D. K., Manuel, M., & Chacon, M. E. (1998). Behavior of infants with iron-deficiency anemia. *Child Development, 69*(1), 24–36.

Lozoff, B., Wolf, A., & Davis, N. S. (1985). Sleep problems seen in pediatric practice. *Pediatrics, 75,* 477–483.

Luecke-Aleksa, D., Anderson, D. R., Collins, P. A., & Schmitt, K. L. (1995). Gender constancy and television viewing. *Developmental Psychology, 31,* 773–780.

Lugaila, T. A. (1998). *Marital status and living arrangements: March 1998* (update) (Current Population Reports,

P20-514). Washington, DC: U.S. Bureau of the Census.

Luke, B., Mamelle, N., Keith, L., Munoz, F., Minogue, J., Papiernik, E., Johnson, T. R., & Timothy, R. B. (1995). The association between occupational factors and preterm birth: A United States nurses' study. *American Journal of Obstetrics and Gynecology, 173*, 849–862.

Lundy, B. L., Jones, N. A., Field, T., Nearing, G., Davalos, M., Pietro, P. A., Schanberg, S., & Kuhn, C. (1999). Prenatal depression effects on neonates. *Infant Behavior and Development, 22*, 119–129.

Lundy, B., Field, T., & Pickens, J. (1996). Newborns of mothers with depressive symptoms are less expressive. *Infant Behavior and Development, 19*, 419–424.

Luster, T., & Small, S. A. (1994). Factors associated with sexual risk-taking among adolescents. *Journal of Marriage and the Family, 56*, 622–632.

Lutke, J. (2000). Works in progress: The meaning of success for individuals with FAS/E. In J. Kleinfeld, B. Morse, & S. Wescott (Eds.), *Fanastic Antone grows up: Adolescents and adults with fetal alcohol syndrome.* Fairbanks, AK: University of Alaska Press.

Lyman, R. (1997, April 15). Michael Dorris dies at 52: Wrote of his son's suffering. *New York Times*, p. C24.

Lyon, T. D., & Saywitz, K. J. (1999). Young maltreated children's competence to take the oath. *Applied Developmental Science, 3*(1), 16–27.

Lyons-Ruth, K., Alpern, L., & Repacholi, B. (1993). Disorganized infant attachment classification and maternal psychosocial problems as predictors of hostile-aggressive behavior in the preschool classroom. *Child Development, 64*, 572–585.

Lytton, H., & Romney, D. M. (1991). Parents' differential socialization of boys and girls: A meta-analysis. *Psychological Bulletin, 109*(2), 267–296.

Maccoby, E. (1980). *Social development.* New York: Harcourt Brace Jovanovich.

Maccoby, E. E. (1984). Middle childhood in the context of the family. In W. A. Collins (Ed.), *Development during middle childhood.* Washington, DC: National Academy.

Maccoby, E. E. (1988). Gender as a social category. *Developmental Psychology, 24*, 755–765.

Maccoby, E. E. (1990). Gender and relationships: A developmental

account. *American Psychologist, 45*(11), 513–520.

Maccoby, E. E. (1992). The role of parents in the socialization of children: An historical overview. *Developmental Psychology, 28*, 1006–1017.

Maccoby, E. E. (1994). Commentary: Gender segregation in childhood. In C. Leaper (Ed.), *Childhood gender segregation: Causes and consequences (New Directions for Child Development, 65*, pp. 87–97). San Francisco: Jossey-Bass.

Maccoby, E. E., & Martin, J. A. (1983). Socialization in the context of the family: Parent–child interaction. In P H. Mussen (Series Ed.) & E. M. Hetherington (Vol. Ed.), *Handbook of child psychology: Vol. 4. Socialization, personality, and social development* (pp. 1–101). New York: Wiley.

Maccoby, E., & Jacklin, C. (1974). *The psychology of sex differences.* Stanford, CA: Stanford University Press.

Macfarlane, A. (1975). Olfaction in the development of social preferences in the human neonate. In *Parent–infant interaction* (CIBA Foundation Symposium No. 33). Amsterdam: Elsevier.

Mackey, K., Arnold, M. L., & Pratt, M. W. (2001). Adolescents' stories of decision making in more and less authoritative families: Representing the voices of parents in narrative. *Journal of Adolescent Research, 16*, 243–268.

MacMillan, H. L., Fleming, J. E., Trocmé, N., Boyle, M. H., Wong, M., Racine, Y. A., Beardslee, W. R., & Offord, D. R. (1997). Prevalence of child physical and sexual abuse in the community: Results from the Ontario health supplement. *Journal of the American Medical Association, 278*(2), 131–135.

MacMillan, H. M., Boyle, M. H., Wong, M. Y.-Y., Duku, E. K., Fleming, J. E., & Walsh, C. A. (1999). Slapping and spanking in childhood and its association with lifetime prevalence of psychiatric disorders in a general population sample. *Canadian Medical Association Journal, 161*, 805–809.

Mahoney, J. L. (2000). School extracurricular activity participation as a moderator in the development of antisocial patterns. *Child Development, 71*(2), 502–516.

Main, M. (1983). Exploration, play, and cognitive functioning related to infant–mother attachment. *Infant Behavior and Development, 6*, 167–174.

Main, M. (1995). Recent studies in attachment: Overview, with selected implications for clinical work. In S. Goldberg, R. Muir, & J. Kerr (Eds.), *Attachment theory: Social, developmental, and clinical perspectives* (pp. 407–470). Hillsdale, NJ: Analytic Press.

Main, M., & Solomon, J. (1986). Discovery of an insecure, disorganized/disoriented attachment pattern: Procedures, findings, and implications for the classification of behavior. In M. Yogman & T. B. Brazelton (Eds.), *Affective development in infancy.* Norwood, NJ: Ablex.

Main, M., Kaplan, N., & Cassidy, J. (1985). Security in infancy, childhood and adulthood: A move to the level of representation. In I. Bretherton & E. Waters (Eds.), Growing points in attachment. *Monographs of the Society for Research in Child Development, 50*(1–20), 66–104.

Makrides, M., Neumann, M., Simmer, K., Pater, J., & Gibson, R. (1995). Are long-chain polyunsaturated fatty acids essential nutrients in infancy? *Lancet, 345*, 1463–1468.

Mandel, D. R., Jusczyk, P. W., & Pisoni, D. B. (1995). Infants' recognition of the sound patterns of their own names. *Psychological Science, 6*(5), 314–317.

Mandela, N. (1994). *Long walk to freedom: The autobiography of Nelson Mandela.* Boston: Little, Brown.

Mandler, J. (1998). The rise and fall of semantic memory. In M. A. Conway, S. E. Gathercole, & C. Cornoldi (Eds.), *Theories of memory* (Vol. 2). East Sussex, England: Psychology Press.

Mangan, P. A., Franklin, A., Tignor, T., Bolling, L., & Nadel, L. (1994). Development of spatial memory abilities in young children. *Society for Neuroscience Abstracts, 20*, 363.

Mansfield, R. S., & Busse, T. V. (1981). *The psychology of creativity and discovery: Scientists and their work.* Chicago: Nelson-Hall.

March of Dimes Birth Defects Foundation. (1987). *Genetic counseling: A public health information booklet* (Rev. ed.). White Plains, NY: Author.

Marcia, J. E. (1966). Development and validation of ego identity status. *Journal of Personality and Social Psychology, 3*(5), 551–558.

Marcia, J. E. (1979, June). *Identity status in late adolescence: Description and some clinical implications.* Address given at symposium on identity development, Rijksuniversitat Groningen, Netherlands.

Marcia, J. E. (1980). Identity in adolescence. In J. Adelson (Ed.), *Handbook of adolescent psychology.* New York: Wiley.

Marcia, J. E. (1993). The relational roots of identity. In J. Kroger (Ed.), *Discussions on ego identity* (pp. 101–120). Hillsdale, NJ: Erlbaum.

Marcon, R. A. (1999). Differential impact of preschool models on development and early learning of inner-city children: A three-cohort study. *Developmental Psychology, 35*(2), 358–375.

Marcovitch, S., & Zelazo, P. D. (1999). The A-Not-B error: Results from a logistic meta-analysis. *Child Development, 70,* 1297–1313.

Marcus, G. F., Vijayan, S., Rao, S. B., & Vishton, P. M. (1999). Rule learning by seven-month-old infants. *Science, 283,* 77–80.

Margolis, L. H., Foss, R. D., & Tolbert, W. G. (2000). Alcohol and motor vehicle-related deaths of children as passengers, pedestrians, and bicyclists. *Journal of the American Medical Association, 283*(17), 2245–2248.

Markoff, J. (1992, October 12). Miscarriages tied to chip factories. *New York Times,* pp. A1, D2.

Marling, K. A. (1996). *Graceland: Going home with Elvis.* Cambridge, MA: Harvard University Press.

Marquet, P., Chevrel, J., Lavignasse, P., Merle, L., & Lachatre, G. (1997). Buprenorphine withdrawal syndrome in a newborn. *Clinical Pharmacology and Therapeutics, 62,* 569–571.

Martens, P. J., Phillips, S. J., Cheang, M. S., Rosolowich, V., & Breastfeeding Promotion Steering Committee of Manitoba. (2000). How baby-friendly are Manitoba hospitals? The provincial infant feeding study. *Canadian Journal of Public Health, 91,* 51–57.

Martin, C. L., & Halverson, C. F. (1981). A schematic processing model of sex typing and stereotyping in children. *Child Development, 52,* 1119–1134.

Martin, C. L., Eisenbud, L., & Rose, H. (1995). Children's gender-based reasoning about toys. *Child Development, 66,* 1453–1471.

Martin, J. A., & Park, M. M. (1999). *Trends in twin and triplet births: 1980–97* (National Vital Statistics Reports, 47[24], DHHS Publication No. [PHS] 99-1120). Hyattsville, MD: National Center for Health Statistics.

Marwick, C. (1997). Health care leaders from drug policy group. *Journal of the American Medical Association, 278,* 378.

Marwick, C. (1998). Physician leadership on national drug policy finds addiction treatment works. *Journal of the American Medical Association, 279,* 1149–1150.

Marzano, R. J., & Hutchins, C. L. (1987). *Thinking skills: A conceptual framework* (ERIC Document Reproduction Service No. ED 266436).

Masataka, N. (1996). Perception of motherese in a signed language by 6-month-old deaf infants. *Developmental Psychology, 32,* 874–879.

Masataka, N. (1998). Perception of motherese in Japanese sign language by 6-month-old hearing infants. *Developmental Psychology, 34*(2), 241–246.

Masataka, N. (1999). Preference for infant-directed signing in 2-day-old hearing infants of deaf parents. *Developmental Psychology, 35,* 1001–1005.

Mason, J. A., & Herrmann, K. R. (1998). Universal infant hearing screening by automated auditory brainstem response measurement. *Pediatrics, 101,* 221–228.

Masse, L. C., & Tremblay, R. E. (1997). Behavior of boys in kindergarten and the onset of substance use during adolescence. *Archives of General Psychiatry, 54,* 62–68.

Masten, A. S., & Coatsworth, J. D. (1998). The development of competence in favorable and unfavorable environments: Lessons from research on successful children. *American Psychologist, 53,* 205–220.

Masten, A., Best, K., & Garmezy, N. (1990). Resilience and development: Contributions from the study of children who overcome adversity. *Development and Psychopathology, 2,* 425–444.

Mathews, T. J., & Ventura, S. J. (1997). *Birth and fertility rates by educational attainment: United States, 1994* (Monthly Vital Statistics Report, 45[10, Suppl.], DHHS Publication No. PHS 97-1120). Hyattsville, MD: National Center for Health Statistics.

Mathews, T. J., Curtin, S. C., & MacDorman, M. F. (2000). Infant mortality statistics from the 1998 period linked birth/infant death data set. *National Vital Statistics Reports, 48*(12). Hyattsville, MD: National Center for Health Statistics.

Mathias, R. (1999). Tracking trends in teen drug abuse over the years. *NIDA Notes (National Institute on Drug Abuse), 14*(1), p. S8.

Maticka-Tyndale, E. (2001). Sexual health and Canadian youth: How do we measure up? *The Canadian Journal of Human Sexuality, 10,* 1–16.

Maticka-Tyndale, E., McKay, A., & Barrett, M. (2001). Teenage sexual and reproductive behavior in developed countries: Country report for Canada. Occasional Report No. 4. New York: The Alan Guttmacher Institute.

Maurer, D., Stager, C. L., & Mondloch, C. J. (1999). Cross-modal transfer of shape is difficult to demonstrate in one-month-olds. *Child Development, 70,* 1047–1057.

Maxwell, L. (1987, January). *Eight pointers on teaching children to think* (Research in Brief No. IS 87-104 RIB). Washington, DC: U.S. Department of Education, Office of Educational Research and Improvement.

May, K. A., & Perrin, S. P. (1985). Prelude: Pregnancy and birth. In S. M. H. Hanson & F. W. Bozett (Eds.), *Dimensions of fatherhood.* Beverly Hills, CA: Sage.

Mayer, D. P. (1998). Do new teaching standards undermine performance on old tests? *Educational Evaluation and Policy Analysis, 20,* 53–73.

Mayes, L. C., Granger, R. H., Frank, M. A., Schottenfeld, R., & Bornstein, M. H. (1993). Neurobehavioral profiles of neonates exposed to cocaine prenatally. *Pediatrics, 91,* 778–783.

McCain, M., & Mustard, J. F. (1999). *The early years: Reversing the real brain drain.* Toronto: Ontario Children's Secretariat.

McCall, R. B., & Carriger, M. S. (1993). A meta-analysis of infant habituation and recognition memory performance as predictors of later IQ. *Child Development, 64,* 57–79.

McCarton, C. M., Brooks-Gunn, J., Wallace, I. F., Bauer, C. R., Bennett, F. C., Bernbaum, J. C., Broyles, S., Casey, P. H., McCormick, M. C., Scott, D. T., Tyson, J., Tonascia, J., & Meinert, C. L., for the Infant Health and Development Program Research Group. (1997). Results at age 8 years of early intervention for low-birth-weight premature infants. *Journal of the American Medical Association, 277,* 126–132.

McCarton, C. M., Wallace, I. F., Divon, M., & Vaughan, H. G. (1996).

Cognitive and neurologic development of the preterm, small for gestational age infant through age 6: Comparison by birth weight and gestational age. *Pediatrics, 98,* 1167–1178.

McClearn, G. E., Johansson, B., Berg, S., Pedersen, N. L., Ahern, F., Petrill, S. A., & Plomin, R. (1997). Substantial genetic influence on cognitive abilities in twins 80 or more years old. *Science, 276,* 1560–1563.

McClintock, M. K., & Herdt, G. (1996). Rethinking puberty: The development of sexual attraction. *Current Directions in Psychological Science, 5*(6), 178–183.

McConaghy, T. (1998). Canada's participation in TIMSS. *Phi Delta Kappan, 79,* 793–800.

McCord, J. (1996). Unintended consequences of punishment. *Pediatrics, 88,* 832–834.

McCormick, M. C., McCarton, C., Brooks-Gunn, J., Belt, P., & Gross, R. T. (1998). The infant health and development program: Interim summary. *Journal of Developmental and Behavioral Pediatrics, 19,* 359–371.

McCoy, A. R., & Reynolds, A. J. (1999). Grade retention and school performance: An extended investigation. *Journal of School Psychology, 37,* 273–298.

McGauhey, P. J., Starfield, B., Alexander, C., & Ensminger, M. E. (1991). Social environment and vulnerability of low birth weight children: A social-epidemiological perspective. *Pediatrics, 88,* 943–953.

McGee, R., Partridge, F., Williams, S., & Silva, P. A. (1991). A twelve-year follow-up of preschool hyperactive children. *Journal of the American Academy of Child and Adolescent Psychiatry, 30,* 224–232.

McGrath, P. J. (1996). There is more to pain measurement in children than "ouch." *Canadian Psychology, 37,* 63–75.

McGreal, D., Evans, B. J., & Burrows, G. D. (1997). Gender differences in coping following loss of a child through miscarriage or stillbirth: A pilot study. *Stress Medicine, 13*(3), 159–165.

McGue, M. (1997). The democracy of the genes. *Nature, 388,* 417–418.

McGue, M., Bouchard, T. J., Jr., Iacono, W. G., & Lykken, D. T. (1993). Behavioral genetics of cognitive ability: A life-span perspective. In R. Plomin & G. E. McClearn (Eds.), *Nature, nurture and psychology* (pp. 59–76).

Washington, DC: American Psychological Association.

McGuffin, P., Owen, M. J., & Farmer, A. E. (1995). Genetic basis of schizophrenia. *Lancet, 346,* 678–682.

McIntire, D. D., Bloom, S. L., Casey, B. M., & Leveno, K. J. (1999). Birth weight in relation to morbidity and mortality among newborn infants. *New England Journal of Medicine, 340,* 1234–1238.

McIntyre, L., Connor, S., & Warren, J. (1998). *A glimpse of child hunger in Canada.* Report No. W-98-26E. Ottawa: Applied Research Branch, Strategic Policy, Human Resources Development Canada.

McKay, A., & Barrett, M. (1999). Preservice sexual health education training of elementary, secondary, and physical health education teachers in Canadian faculties of education. *Canadian Journal of Human Sexuality, 8,* 91–101.

McKay, N. Y. (1992). Introduction. In M. Anderson, *My Lord, what a morning* (pp. ix–xxxiii). Madison: University of Wisconsin Press.

McKenna, J. J., & Mosko, S. (1993). Evolution and infant sleep: An experimental study of infant–parent co-sleeping and its implications for SIDS. *Acta Paediatrica, 389*(Suppl.), 31–36.

McKenna, J. J., Mosko, S. S., & Richard, C. A. (1997). Bedsharing promotes breastfeeding. *Pediatrics, 100,* 214–219.

McKenna, M. C., Kear, D. J., & Ellsworth, R. A. (1995). Children's attitudes toward reading: A national survey. *Reading Research Quarterly, 30,* 934–956.

McKim, M. K., Cramer, K. M., Stuart, B., & O'Connor, D. L. (1999). Infant care decisions and attachment security: The Canadian Transition to Child Care Study. *Canadian Journal of Behavioural Science, 31,* 92–106.

McKinney, K. (1987, March). *A look at Japanese education today* (Research in Brief No. IS 87-107 RIB). Washington, DC: U.S. Department of Education, Office of Educational Research and Improvement.

McLanahan, S., & Sandefur, G. (1994). *Growing up with a single parent.* Cambridge, MA: Harvard University Press.

McLeod, P. J., & Watt, M. (1995). Speaking to infants: How and why we modify our voices. In K. Covell (Ed.), *Readings in child development* (pp. 72–88). Toronto: Nelson.

McLeskey, J., Lancaster, M., & Grizzle, K. L. (1995). Learning disabilities and grade retention: A review of issues with recommendations for practice. *Learning Disabilities Research & Practice, 10,* 120–128.

McLoyd, V. C. (1990). The impact of economic hardship on black families and children: Psychological distress, parenting, and socioemotional development. *Child Development, 61,* 311–346.

McLoyd, V. C. (1998). Socioeconomic disadvantage and child development. *American Psychologist, 53,* 185–204.

McLoyd, V. C., Jayaratne, T. E., Ceballo, R., & Borquez, J. (1994). Unemployment and work interruption among African American single mothers: Effects on parenting and adolescent socioemotional functioning. *Child Development, 65,* 562–589.

McMahon, M. J., Luther, E. R., Bowes, W. A., & Olshan, A. F. (1996). Comparison of a trial of labor with an elective second cesarean section. *New England Journal of Medicine, 335,* 689–695.

McMahon, M., & Patton, W. (1997). Gender differences in children and adolescents' perceptions of influences on their career development. *The School Counselor, 44,* 368–376.

McNeilly-Choque, M. K., Hart, C. H., Robinson, C. C., Nelson, L. J., & Olsen, S. F. (1996). Overt and relational aggression on the playground: Correspondence among different informants. *Journal of Research in Childhood Education, 11,* 47–67.

Mead, M. (1928). *Coming of age in Samoa.* New York: Morrow.

Mead, M. (1930). *Growing up in New Guinea.* New York: Blue Ribbon.

Mead, M. (1935). *Sex and temperament in three primitive societies.* New York: Morrow.

Mead, M. (1972). *Blackberry winter: My earlier years.* New York: Morrow.

Meehan, P. J. (1990). Prevention: The endpoint of suicidology. *Mayo Clinic Proceedings, 65,* 115–118.

Meer, F. (1988). *Higher than hope: The authorized biography of Nelson Mandela.* New York: Harper & Row.

Meier, R. (1991, January–February). Language acquisition by deaf children. *American Scientist, 79,* 60–70.

Meier, R. P., & Willerman, R. (1995). Prelinguistic gesture in deaf and hearing infants. In K. Emmorey & J. S. Reilly (Eds.), *Language, gesture, and* space (pp. 391–409). Hillsdale, NJ: Lawrence Erlbaum Associates.

Meins, E. (1998). The effects of security of attachment and maternal attribution of meaning on children's linguistic acquisitional style. *Infant Behavior and Development, 21,* 237–252.

Melnick, S., Cole, P., Anderson, B. A., & Herbst, A. (1987). Rates and risks of diethylstilbestrol-related clear-cell adenocarcinoma of the vagina and cervix. *New England Journal of Medicine, 316,* 514–516.

Meltzoff, A. N., & Moore, M. K. (1983). Newborn infants imitate adult facial gestures. *Child Development, 54,* 702–709.

Meltzoff, A. N., & Moore, M. K. (1989). Imitation in newborn infants: Exploring the range of gestures imitated and the underlying mechanisms. *Developmental Psychology, 25,* 954–962.

Meltzoff, A. N., & Moore, M. K. (1994). Imitation, memory, and the representation of persons. *Infant Behavior and Development, 17,* 83–99.

Meltzoff, A. N., & Moore, M. K. (1998). Object representation, identity, and the paradox of early permanence: Steps toward a new framework. *Infant Behavior & Development, 21,* 201–235.

Mendelsohn, A. L., Dreyer, B. P., Fierman, A. H., Rosen, C. M., Legano, L. A., Kruger, H. A., Lim, S. W., & Courtlandt., C. D. (1998). Low-level lead exposure and behavior in early childhood. *Pediatrics, 101*(3), e10. Retrieved September 24, 2002, from http://www.pediatrics.org/cgi/content/full/101/3/e10

Mendelson, B. K., Mendelson, M. J., & White, D. R. (2001). Body-esteem scale for adolescents and adults. *Journal of Personality Assessment, 76,* 90–106.

Mendelson, B. K., White, D. R., & Mendelson, M. J. (1996). Self-esteem and body esteem: Effects of gender, age, and weight. *Journal of Applied Developmental Psychology, 17,* 321–346.

Mendelson, B. K., White, D. R., & Schliecker, E. (1995). Adolescents' weight, sex, and family functioning. *International Journal of Eating Disorders, 17,* 73–79.

Mendelson, M. J., Mendelson, B. K., & Andrews, J. (2000). Self-esteem, body esteem, and body-mass in late adolescence: Is a competence x importance model needed? *Journal of*

Applied Developmental Psychology, 21, 249–266.

Mennella, J. A., & Beauchamp, G. K. (1996a). The early development of human flavor preferences. In E. D. Capaldi (Ed.), *Why we eat what we eat: The psychology of eating* (pp. 83–112). Washington, DC: American Psychological Association.

Mennella, J. A., & Beauchamp, G. K. (1996b). The human infants' response to vanilla flavors in mother's milk and formula. *Infant Behavior and Development, 19,* 13–19.

Meyer, D. R., & Garasky, S. (1993). Custodial fathers: Myths, realities, and child support policy. *Journal of Marriage and the Family, 55,* 73–89.

Meyers, A. F., Sampson, A. E., Weitzman, M., Rogers, B. L., & Kayne, H. (1989). School breakfast program and school performance. *American Journal of Diseases of Children, 143,* 1234–1239.

Michelmore, P. (1962). *Einstein: Profile of the man.* London: Frederick Muller, Ltd.

Miedzian, M. (1991). *Boys will be boys: Breaking the link between masculinity and violence.* New York: Doubleday.

Mifflin, L. (1996, February 15). 4 networks plan a ratings system for their shows. *New York Times,* pp. A1, C24.

Milberger, S., Biederman, J., Faraone, S. V., Chen, L., & Jones, J. (1996). Is maternal smoking during pregnancy a risk factor for attention hyperactivity disorder in children? *American Journal of Psychiatry, 153,* 1138–1142.

Millar, W. J., Wadhera S., & Nimrod C. (1992). Multiple births: Trends and patterns in Canada, 1974–1990. *Health Reports, 4,* 223–250.

Miller, A. (2001). Prescription of methylphenidate to children and youth, 1990–1996. *Canadian Medical Association Journal, 165,* 1489–1494.

Miller, B. C., & Moore, K. A. (1990). Adolescent sexual behavior, pregnancy, and parenting: Research through the 1980s. *Journal of Marriage and the Family, 52,* 1025–1044.

Miller, B. C., Fan, X., Christensen, M., Grotevant, H. D., & van Dulmen, M. (2000). Comparisons of adopted and nonadopted adolescents in a large, nationally representative sample. *Child Development, 71,* 1458–1473.

Miller, C., Degenhart, K., & Sassoon, D. A. (1998). Fetal exposure to DES results in de-regulation of Wnt7a

during uterine morphogenesis. *Nature Genetics, 20,* 229–230.

Miller, J. B., & Stiver, I. P. (1997). *The healing connection: How women form relationships in therapy and in life.* Boston: Beacon Press, Inc.

Miller, J. R. (1996). *Singwauk's vision: A history of Native residential schools.* Toronto: University of Toronto Press.

Miller, K. F., Smith, C. M., Zhu, J., & Zhang, H. (1995). Preschool origins of cross-national differences in mathematical competence: The role of number-naming systems. *Psychological Science, 6,* 56–60.

Miller, M. W., Astley, S. J., & Clarren, S. K. (1999). Number of axons in the corpus callosum of the mature macaca nemestrina: Increases caused by prenatal exposure to ethanol. *Journal of Comparative Neurology, 412,* 123–131.

Miller, P. H. (1993). *Theories of personality development* (3rd ed.). New York: Freeman.

Miller, P. H. (2002). *Theories of developmental psychology* (4th ed.). New York: Freeman.

Miller, V., Onotera, R. T., & Deinard, A. S. (1984). Denver Developmental Screening Test: Cultural variations in Southeast Asian children. *Journal of Pediatrics, 104*(3), 481–482.

Miller-Jones, D. (1989). Culture and testing. *American Psychologist, 44*(2), 360–366.

Mills, D. L., Cofley-Corina, S. A., & Neville, H. J. (1997). Language comprehension and cerebral specialization from 13 to 20 months. *Developmental Neuropsychology, 13,* 397–445.

Mills, J. L., Holmes, L. B., Aarons, J. H., Simpson, J. L., Brown, Z. A., Jovanovic-Peterson, L. G., Conley, M. R., Graubard, B. I., Knopp, R. H., & Metzger, B. E. (1993). Moderate caffeine use and the risk of spontaneous abortion and intrauterine growth retardation. *Journal of the American Medical Association, 269,* 593–597.

Millstein, S. G., Irwin, C. E., Adler, N. E., Cohn, L. D., Kegeles, S. M., & Dolcini, M. M. (1992). Health-risk behaviors and health concerns among young adolescents. *Pediatrics, 89,* 422–428.

Milunsky, A. (1992). *Heredity and your family's health.* Baltimore: Johns Hopkins University Press.

Minister of Public Works and Government Services Canada. (2001). *Federal/provincial/territorial early childhood development agreement: Report on Government of Canada activities and expenditures 2000–2001*. Ottawa: Author.

Ministry of Community, Family and Children's Services. (2002). *Early years challenge fund*. Toronto: Queen's Printer for Ontario.

Ministry of Health (1996). *New reproductive and genetic technologies: Setting boundaries, enhancing health*. Retrieved September 20, 2002, from http://www.hc-sc.gc.ca/english/protection/biologics_genetics/reproduction/nrgt/index.htm

Minkler, M., & Roe, K. M. (1996). Grandparents as surrogate parents. *Generations, 20*(1), 34–38.

Miotti, P. G., Taha, T. E. T., Kumwenda, N. I., Broadhead, R., Mtimavalye, L. A. R., Van der Hoeven, L., Chiphangwi, J. D., Liomba, G., & Biggar, R. J. (1999). HIV transmission through breastfeeding: A study in Malawi. *Journal of the American Medical Association, 282*, 744–749.

Miserandino, M. (1996). Children who do well in school: Individual differences in perceived competence and autonomy in above-average children. *Journal of Educational Psychology, 88*(2), 203–214.

Misra, D. P., & Guyer, B. (1998). Benefits and limitations of prenatal care: From counting visits to measuring content. *Journal of the American Medical Association, 279*, 1661–1662.

Mitchell, A. A. (2002). Infertility treatment: More risks and challenges. *The New England Journal of Medicine, 346*, 769–770.

Mitchell, D., Brynelsen, D., & Holm, M. (1988). Evaluating the process of early intervention programmes. *Irish Journal of Psychology, 9*, 235–248.

Mix, K. S., Levine, S. C., & Huttenlocher, J. (1999). Early fraction calculation ability. *Developmental Psychology, 35*, 164–174.

Miyake, K., Chen, S., & Campos, J. (1985). Infants' temperament, mothers' mode of interaction and attachment in Japan: An interim report. In I. Bretherton & E. Waters (Eds.), Growing points of attachment theory and research. *Monographs of the Society for Research in Child Development, 50*(1–2, Serial No. 109), 276–297.

Mlot, C. (1998). Probing the biology of emotion. *Science, 280*, 1005–1007.

Modell, J. (1989). *Into one's own: From youth to adulthood in the United States, 1920–1975*. Berkeley: University of California Press.

Moffitt, T. E., Caspi, A., Belsky, J., & Silva, P. A. (1992). Childhood experience and the onset of menarche: A test of a sociobiological model. *Child Development, 63*, 47–58.

Molina, B. S. G., & Chassin, L. (1996). The parent–adolescent relationship at puberty: Hispanic ethnicity and parent alcoholism as moderators. *Developmental Psychology, 32*, 675–686.

Montague, C. T., Farooqi, I. S., Whitehead, J. P., Soos, M. A., Rau, H., Wareham, N. J., Sewter, C. P., Digby, J. E., Mohammed, S. N., Hurst, J. A., Cheetham, C. H., Earley, A. R., Barnett, A. H., Prins, J. B., & Orahilly, S. (1997). Congenital leptin deficiency is associated with severe early onset obesity in humans. *Nature, 387*, 903–908.

Montgomery, L. E., Kiely, J. L., & Pappas, G. (1996). The effects of poverty, race, and family structure on U.S. children's health: Data from the NHIS, 1978 through 1980 and 1989 through 1991. *American Journal of Public Health, 86*, 1401–1405.

Montour, L. T., MacAulay, A. C., & Adelson, N. (1989). Diabetes mellitas in Mohawks of Kahnawake, PQ: A clinical and epidemiological description. *Canadian Medical Association Journal, 141*, 549–552.

Moon, C., & Fifer, W. P. (1990, April). *Newborns prefer a prenatal version of mother's voice*. Paper presented at the biannual meeting of the International Society of Infant Studies, Montreal.

Moon, C., Cooper, R. P., & Fifer, W. P. (1993). Two-day-olds prefer their native language. *Infant Behavior and Development, 16*, 495–500.

Moon, R. Y., Patel, K. M., & Shaefer, S. J. McD. (2000). Sudden infant death syndrome in child care settings. *Pediatrics, 106*, 295–300.

Moore, C., Barresi, J., & Thompson, C. (1998). The cognitive basis of future-oriented prosocial behavior. *Social Development, 7*, 198–218.

Moore, S. E., Cole, T. J., Poskitt, E. M. E., Sonko, B. J., Whitehead, R. G., McGregor, I. A., & Prentice, A. M. (1997). Season of birth predicts mortality in rural Gambia. *Nature, 388*, 434.

Morange, F., & Bloch, H. (1996). Lateralization of the approach movement and the prehension movement in infants from 4 to 7 months. *Early Development and Parenting, 5*, 81–92.

Morelli, G. A., Rogoff, B., Oppenheim, D., & Goldsmith, D. (1992). Cultural variation in infants' sleeping arrangements: Questions of independence. *Developmental Psychology, 28*, 604–613.

Moretti, M. E., Lee, A., Ito, S. (2000). Which drugs are contraindicated during breastfeeding? Practice guidelines. *Canadian Family Physician, 46*, 1753–1757.

Morison, P., & Masten, A. S. (1991). Peer reputation in middle childhood as a predictor of adaptation in adolescence: A seven-year follow-up. *Child Development, 62*, 991–1007.

Morison, S. J., & Ellwood, A.-L. (2000). Resiliency in the aftermath of deprivation: A second look at the development of Romanian orphanage children. *Merrill-Palmer Quarterly, 46*, 717–737.

Morison, S. J., Ames, E. W., & Chisholm, K. (1995). The development of children adopted from Romanian orphanages. *Merrill-Palmer Quarterly Journal of Developmental Psychology, 41*, 411–430.

Morris, R. D., Stuebing, K. K., Fletcher, J. M., Shaywitz, S. E., Lyon, G. R., Shankweiler, D. P., Katz, L., Francis, D. J., & Shaywitz, B. A. (1998). Subtypes of reading disability: Variability around a phonological core. *Journal of Educational Psychology, 90*, 347–373.

Morris, R., & Kratochwill, T. (1983). *Treating children's fears and phobias: A behavioral approach*. Elmsford, NY: Pergamon.

Mortensen, P. B., Pedersen, C. B., Westergaard, T., Wohlfahrt, J., Ewald, H., Mors, O., Andersen, P. K., & Melbye, M. (1999). Effects of family history and place and season of birth on the risk of schizophrenia. *New England Journal of Medicine, 340*, 603–608.

Mortimer, J. T., & Shanahan, M. J. (1991). *Adolescent work experience and relations with peers*. Paper presented at the American Sociological Association Annual Meeting, Cincinnati, OH.

Mortimer, J. T., Finch, M. D., Ryu, S., Shanahan, M. J., & Call, K. T. (1996). The effects of work intensity on adolescent mental health, achievement, and behavioral adjustment: New evidence from a prospective study. *Child Development, 67,* 1243–1261.

Mosher, W. D., & Pratt, W. F. (1991). Fecundity and infertility in the United States: Incidence and trends. *Fertility and Sterility, 56,* 192–193.

Moss, E., & St-Laurent, D. (2001). Attachment at school age and academic performance. *Developmental Psychology, 37,* 863–874.

Mossberg, H. O. (1989, August 26). 40-year follow-up of overweight children. *Lancet,* pp. 491–493.

Mounts, N. S., & Steinberg, L. (1995). An ecological analysis of peer influence on adolescent grade point average and drug use. *Developmental Psychology, 31,* 915–922.

MTA Cooperative Group. (1999). A 14-month randomized clinical trial of treatment strategies for attention-deficit/hyperactivity disorder. *Archives of General Psychiatry, 56,* 1073–1986.

Mullan, D., & Currie, C. (2000). Socioeconomic equalities in adolescent health. In C. Currie, K. Hurrelmann, W. Settertobulte, R. Smith, & J. Todd (Eds.), *Health and health behaviour among young people: A WHO cross-national study (HBSC) international report* (pp. 65–72). WHO Policy Series: Healthy Policy for Children and Adolescents, Series No. 1.

Müller, M. (1998). *Anne Frank: The biography.* New York: Holt.

Mullis, I. V. S., Martin, M. O., Beaton, A. E., Gonzalez, E. J., Kelly, D. L., & Smith, T. A. (1997). *Mathematics achievement in the primary school years: IEA's Third International Mathematics and Science Study (TIMSS).* Chestnut Hill, MA: TIMSS International Study Center, Boston College.

Munakata, Y. (2001). Task-dependency in infant behavior: Toward an understanding of the processes underlying cognitive development. In F. Lacerda, C. von Hofsten, & M. Heimann (Eds.), *Emerging cognitive abilities in early infancy.* Hillsdale, NJ: Erlbaum.

Munakata, Y., McClelland, J. L., Johnson, M. J., & Siegler, R. S. (1997). Rethinking infant knowledge: Toward an adaptive process account of successes and failures in object permanence tasks. *Psychological Review, 104,* 686–714.

Muñoz, K. A., Krebs-Smith, S. M., Ballard-Barbash, R., & Cleveland, L. E. (1997). Food intakes of U.S.

children and adolescents compared with recommendations. *Pediatrics, 100,* 323–329.

Murachver, T., Pipe, M., Gordon, R., Owens, J. L., & Fivush, R. (1996). Do, show, and tell: Children's event memories acquired through direct experience, observation, and stories. *Child Development, 67,* 3029–3044.

Murchison, C., & Langer, S. (1927). Tiedemann's observations on the development of the mental facilities of children. *Journal of Genetic Psychology, 34,* 205–230.

Muris, P., Merckelbach, H., & Collaris, R. (1997). Common childhood fears and their origins. *Behaviour Research and Therapy, 35,* 929–937.

Murphy, C. C., Schei, B., Myhr, T. L., & Du Mont, J. (2001). Abuse: A risk factor for low birth weight? A systematic review and meta-analysis. *Canadian Medical Association Journal, 164,* 1567–72.

Murphy, C. M., & Bootzin, R. R. (1973). Active and passive participation in the contact desensitization of snake fear in children. *Behavior Therapy, 4,* 203–211.

Murray, A. D., Dolby, R. M., Nation, R. L., & Thomas, D. B. (1981). Effects of epidural anesthesia on newborns and their mothers. *Child Development, 52,* 71–82.

Murray, B. (1998, June). Dipping math scores heat up debate over math teaching: Psychologists differ over the merits of teaching children "whole math." *APA Monitor, 29*(6), 34–35.

Murray, J. A., & Terry, D. J. (1999). Parental reactions to infant death: The effects of resources and coping strategies. *Journal of Social & Clinical Psychology, 18,* 341–369.

Mussen, P. H., & Jones, M. C. (1957). Self-conceptions, motivations, and interpersonal attitudes of late- and early-maturing boys. *Child Development, 28,* 243–256.

Must, A., Jacques, P. F., Dallal, G. E., Bajema, C. J., & Dietz, W. H. (1992). Long-term morbidity and mortality of overweight adolescents: A follow-up of the Harvard Growth Study of 1922 to 1935. *New England Journal of Medicine, 327*(19), 1350–1355.

Myers, J. E., & Perrin, N. (1993). Grandparents affected by parental divorce: A population at risk? *Journal of Counseling and Development, 72,* 62–66.

Myers, N., & Perlmutter, M. (1978). Memory in the years from 2 to 5. In P.

Ornstein (Ed.), *Memory development in children.* Hillsdale, NJ: Erlbaum.

Naeye, R. L., & Peters, E. C. (1984). Mental development of children whose mothers smoked during pregnancy. *Obstetrics and Gynecology, 64,* 601.

Nafstad, P., Hagen, J. A., Oie, L., Magnus, P., & Jaakkola, J. J. K. (1999). Day care and respiratory health. *Pediatrics, 103,* 753–758.

Nakajima, H., & Mayor, F. (1996). Culture and health. *World Health, 49*(2), 13–15.

Napiorkowski, B., Lester, B. M., Freier, C., Brunner, S., Dietz, L., Nadra, A., & Oh, W. (1996). Effects of in utero substance exposure on infant neurobehavior. *Pediatrics, 98,* 71–75.

Nash, J. M. (1997, February 3). Fertile minds. *Time,* pp. 49–56.

Nathanielsz, P. W. (1995). The role of basic science in preventing low birth weight. *The Future of Our Children, 5*(1), 57–70.

National Advisory Committee on Immunization. (1997). Guidelines for childhood immunization practices. *Canada Communicable Disease Report, 23,* 1–5.

National Center for Education Statistics (NCES). (1985). *The relationship of parental involvement to high school grades* (Publication No. NCES-85-205b). Washington, DC: U.S. Government Printing Office.

National Center for Education Statistics (NCES). (1987). *Who drops out of high school? From high school and beyond.* Washington, DC: U.S. Department of Education, Office of Educational Research and Improvement.

National Center for Education Statistics (NCES). (1996). *Education indicators: An international perspective* (NCES 96-003). Washington, DC: U.S. Department of Education.

National Center for Education Statistics (NCES). (1997). *The condition of education 1997: Women in mathematics and science* (NCES 97-982). Washington, DC: Author.

National Center for Education Statistics (NCES). (1998a). *Violence and discipline problems in U.S. public schools: 1996–97: Executive summary.* Retrieved September 24, 2002, from http://www.nces.ed.gov/pubs98/violence/98030001.html

National Center for Education Statistics (NCES). (1998b, June). *Nonresident fathers can make a difference in children's school performance* (Issue

Brief, NCES 98-117). Washington, DC: U.S. Department of Education, Office of Educational Research and Improvement.

National Center for Education Statistics (NCES). (1999). *The condition of education, 1999* (NCES 1999-022). Washington, DC: U.S. Government Printing Office.

National Center for Health Statistics (NCHS). (1993). *Health, United States, 1992 and prevention profile.* Washington, DC: U.S. Public Health Service.

National Center for Health Statistics (NCHS). (1994a). *Advance report of final natality statistics, 1992* (*Monthly Vital Statistics Report, 43*[5, Suppl.]). Hyattsville, MD: U.S. Public Health Service.

National Center for Health Statistics (NCHS). (1994b). *Health, United States, 1993.* Hyattsville, MD: U.S. Public Health Service.

National Center for Health Statistics (NCHS). (1997). *Health United States, 1996–97 and injury chartbook* (DHHS Publication No., PHS 97–1232). Hyattsville, MD: U.S. Department of Health and Human Services.

National Center for Health Statistics (NCHS). (1998). *Health, United States, 1998 with socioeconomic status and health chartbook.* Hyattsville, MD: Author.

National Center for Health Statistics (NCHS). (1999). *Health, United States, 1999* (DHS Publication No. PHS 99–1232). Hyattsville, MD: Author.

National Center for Health Statistics (NCHS). (2000a). *2 to 20 years: Boys stature-for-age and weight-for-age percentiles.* Retrieved December 4, 2002, from http://www.cdc.gov/growthcharts

National Center for Health Statistics (NCHS). (2000b). *2 to 20 years: Girls stature-for-age and weight-for-age percentiles.* Retrieved December 4, 2002, from http://www.cdc.gov/growthcharts

National Commission for the Protection of Human Subjects of Biomedical and Behavioral Research. (1978). *Report.* Washington, DC: Author.

National Commission on Youth. (1980). *The transition to adulthood: A bridge too long.* New York: Westview.

National Committee for Citizens in Education (NCCE). (1986, winter holiday). Don't be afraid to start a suicide prevention program in your school. *Network for Public Schools* pp. 1, 4.

National Council of Teachers of Mathematics. (2000). *Principles and standards for school mathematics.* Reston, VA: National Council of Teachers of Mathematics.

National Crime Prevention Council. (1997). *Preventing crime by investing in families and communities: Promoting positive outcomes in youth—twelve to eighteen years old.* Ottawa: Author.

National Enuresis Society. (1995). *Enuresis.* [Fact sheet].

National Institute of Child Health and Development (NICHD). (1997; updated 1/12/00). [Fact sheet] Sudden Infant Death Syndrome. Retrieved January 30, 2001, from http://www.nichd.nih.gov/sids/sids_fact.htm

National Institute of Mental Health (NIMH). (1982). *Television and behavior: Ten years of scientific progress and implications for the eighties: Vol. 1. Summary report* (DHHS Publication No. ADM 82-1195). Washington, DC: U.S. Government Printing Office.

National Institute of Mental Health (NIMH). (1999a, April). Suicide facts. Washington, DC: Author. Retrieved September 24, 2002, from http://www.nimh.nih.gov/research/suifact.htm

National Institute of Mental Health (NIMH). (1999b, June 1). Older adults: Depression and suicide facts. Washington, DC: Author. Retrieved September 24, 2002, from http://www.nimh.nih.gov/publicat/elderlydepsuicide.cfm

National Institute of Neurological Disorders and Stroke. (1999, November 10). *Autism* [Fact sheet]. (NIH Publication No. 96-1877.) Bethesda, MD: National Institutes of Health.

National Institute on Drug Abuse (NIDA). (1996). *Monitoring the future.* Washington, DC: National Institutes of Health.

National Institutes of Health (NIH) Consensus Development Panel on Physical Activity and Cardiovascular Health. (1996). Physical activity and cardiovascular health. *Journal of the American Medical Association, 276,* 241–246.

National Institutes of Health (NIH). (1993). Early identification of hearing impairment in infants and young children. *NIH Consensus Statement, 11*(1), 1–24.

National Institutes of Health (NIH). (1998). Diagnosis and treatment of attention deficit hyperactivity disorder (ADHD). *NIH Consensus Statement, 16*(2), 1–37.

National Parents' Resource Institute for Drug Education. (1999, September 8). *PRIDE surveys, 1998–99 national summary: Grades 6–12.* Bowling Green, KY: Author.

National Reading Panel. (2000). *Report of the National Reading Panel: Teaching children to read: An evidence-based assessment of the scientific research literature on reading and its implications for reading instruction: Reports of the subgroups.* Washington, DC: National Institute of Child Health and Human Development.

National Research Council (NRC). (1993a). *Losing generations: Adolescents in high-risk settings.* Washington, DC: National Academy Press.

National Research Council (NRC). (1993b). *Understanding child abuse and neglect.* Washington, DC: National Academy Press.

National Television Violence Study. (1995). *Scientific Papers: 1994–1995.* Studio City, CA: Mediascope.

National Television Violence Study: Key findings and recommendations. (1996, March). *Young Children, 51*(3), 54–55.

Natural Science and Engineering Research Council. (2000). *Tri-Council policy statement: Ethical conduct for research involving humans.* Retrieved September 20, 2002, from http://www.nserc.ca/programs/ethics/english/policy.htm

Nduati, R., John, G., Mbori-Ngacha, D., Richardson, B., Overbaugh, J., Mwatha, A., Ndinya-Achola, J., Bwayo, J., Onyango, F. E., Hughes, J., & Kreiss, J. (2000). Effect of breastfeeding and formula feeding on transmission of HIV-i. A randomized clinical trial. *Journal of the American Medical Association, 283*(9), 1167–1174.

Needleman, H. L., & Gatsonis, C. A. (1990). Low-level lead exposure and the IQ of children: A meta-analysis of modern studies. *Journal of the American Medical Association, 263,* 673–678.

Needleman, H. L., Riess, J. A., Tobin, M. J., Biesecker, G. E., & Greenhouse, J.

B. (1996). Bone lead levels and delinquent behavior. *Journal of the American Medical Association, 275,* 363–369.

Neisser, U., Boodoo, G., Bouchard, T. J., Jr., Boykin, A. W., Brody, N., Ceci, S. J., Halpern, D. F., Loehlin, J. C., Perloff, R., Sternberg, R. J., & Urbina, S. (1996). Intelligence: Knowns and unknowns. *American Psychologist, 51*(2), 77–101.

Nelson, C. A. (1995). The ontogeny of human memory: A cognitive neuroscience perspective. *Developmental Psychology, 31,* 723–738.

Nelson, K. (1973). Structure and strategy in learning to talk. *Monographs of the Society for Research in Child Development, 38*(1–2).

Nelson, K. (1981). Individual differences in language development: Implications for development and language. *Developmental Psychology, 17,* 170–187.

Nelson, K. (1992). Emergence of autobiographical memory at age 4. *Human Development, 35,* 172–177.

Nelson, K. (1993a). Events, narrative, memory: What develops? In C. Nelson (Ed.), *Memory and affect in development: The Minnesota Symposia on Child Psychology* (Vol. 26, pp. 1–24). Hillsdale, NJ: Erlbaum.

Nelson, K. (1993b). The psychological and social origins of autobiographical memory. *Psychological Science, 47,* 7–14.

Nelson, K. B., Dambrosia, J. M., Ting, T. Y., & Grether, J. K. (1996). Uncertain value of electronic fetal monitoring in predicting cerebral palsy. *New England Journal of Medicine, 334,* 613–618.

Nelson, L. J., & Marshall, M. F. (1998). *Ethical and legal analyses of three coercive policies aimed at substance abuse by pregnant women.* Report published by the Robert Wood Johnson Substance Abuse Policy Research Foundation.

Neppl, T. K., & Murray, A. D. (1997). Social dominance and play patterns among preschoolers: Gender comparisons. *Sex Roles, 36,* 381–393.

Ness, R. B., Grisso, J. A., Hirschinger, N., Markovic, N., Shaw, L. M., Day, N. L., & Kline, J. (1999). Cocaine and tobacco use and the risk of spontaneous abortion. *New England Journal of Medicine, 340,* 333–339.

Netherlands State Institute for War Documentation. (1989). *The diary of Anne Frank: The critical edition* (D. Barnouw & G. van der Stroom, Eds.; A. J. Pomerans & B. M. Mooyaart-Doubleday, Trans.). New York: Doubleday.

Neugebauer, R., Hoek, H. W., & Susser, E. (1999). Prenatal exposure to wartime famine and development of antisocial personality disorder in early adulthood. *Journal of the American Medical Association, 282,* 455–462.

Neumann, H., McCormick, R. M., Amundson, N. E., & McLean, H. B. (2000). Career counselling First Nations youth: Applying the First Nations Career-Life Planning Model. *Canadian Journal of Counselling, 34,* 172–185.

Newacheck, P. W., & Halfon, N. (2000). Prevalence, impact, and trends in childhood disability due to asthma. *Archives of Pediatrics and Adolescent Medicine, 154,* 287–293.

Newacheck, P. W., Stoddard, J. J., & McManus, M. (1993). Ethnocultural variations in the prevalence and impact of childhood chronic conditions. *Pediatrics, 91,* 1031–1047.

Newacheck, P. W., Strickland, B., Shonkoff, J. P., Perrin, J. M., McPherson, M., McManus, M., Lauver, C., Fox, H., & Arango, P. (1998). An epidemiologic profile of children with special health care needs. *Pediatrics, 102,* 117–123.

Newcomb, A. F., & Bagwell, C. L. (1995). Children's friendship relations: A meta-analytic review. *Psychological Bulletin, 117*(2), 306–347.

Newcomb, A. F., Bukowski, W. M., & Pattee, L. (1993). Children's peer relations: A meta-analytic review of popular, rejected, neglected, controversial, and average sociometric status. *Psychological Bulletin, 113,* 99–128.

Newcombe, N., & Fox, N. A. (1994). Infantile amnesia: Through a glass darkly. *Child Development, 65,* 31–40.

Newcombe, N., Huttenlocher, J., Drummey, A. B., & Wiley, J. G. (1998). The development of spatial location coding: Place learning and dead reckoning in the second and third years. *Cognitive Development, 13,* 185–201.

Newman, D. L., Caspi, A., Moffitt, T. E., & Silva, P. A. (1997). Antecedents of adult interpersonal functioning: Effects of individual differences in age 3 temperament. *Developmental Psychology, 33,* 206–217.

Newman, J. (1995). How breast milk protects newborns. *Scientific American, 273,* 76–79.

Newport, E. L. (1991). Contrasting conceptions of the critical period for language. In S. Carey & R. Gelman (Eds.), *The epigenesis of mind: Essays on biology and cognition.* Hillsdale, NJ: Erlbaum.

Newport, E., & Meier, R. (1985). The acquisition of American Sign Language. In D. Slobin (Ed.), *The crosslinguistic study of language acquisition* (Vol. 1, pp. 881–938). Hillsdale, NJ: Erlbaum.

Newson, J., Newson, E., & Mahalski, P. A. (1982). Persistent infant comfort habits and their sequelae at 11 and 16 years. *Journal of Child Psychology and Psychiatry, 23,* 421–436.

NICHD Early Child Care Research Network. (1996). Characteristics of infant child care: Factors contributing to positive caregiving. *Early Childhood Research Quarterly, 11,* 269–306.

NICHD Early Child Care Research Network. (1997a). The effects of infant child care on infant–mother attachment security: Results of the NICHD study of early child care. *Child Development, 68,* 860–879.

NICHD Early Child Care Research Network. (1997b). Familial factors associated with the characteristics of nonmaternal care for infants. *Journal of Marriage and the Family, 59,* 389–408.

NICHD Early Child Care Research Network. (1997b, April). *The relationship of child care to cognitive and language development.* Paper presented at the meeting of the Society for Research in Child Development, Washington, DC.

NICHD Early Child Care Research Network. (1998a). Early child care and self-control, compliance and problem behavior at twenty-four and thirty-six months. *Child Development, 69,* 1145–1170.

NICHD Early Child Care Research Network. (1998b). Relations between family predictors and child outcomes: Are they weaker for children in child care? *Developmental Psychology, 34,* 1119–1127.

NICHD Early Child Care Research Network. (1998c, November). *When child-care classrooms meet recommended guidelines for quality.* Paper presented at the meeting of the National Association for the Education of Young People.

NICHD Early Child Care Research Network. (1999a). Child outcomes when child care center classes meet recommended standards for quality. *American Journal of Public Health, 89,* 1072–1077.

NICHD Early Child Care Research Network. (1999b). Chronicity of maternal depressive symptoms, maternal sensitivity, and child functioning at 36 months. *Developmental Psychology, 35,* 1297–1310.

NICHD Early Child Care Research Network. (2000). The relation of child care to cognitive and language development. *Child Development, 71,* 960–980.

Nielsen, K., McSherry, G., Petru, A., Frederick, T., Wara, D., Bryson, Y., Martin, N., Hutto, C., Ammann, A. J., Grubman, S., Oleske, J., & Scott, G. B. (1997). A descriptive survey of pediatric human immunodeficiency virus-infected long-term survivors. *Pediatrics, 99.* Retrieved September 24, 2002, from http://www.pediatrics.org/cgi/content/full/99/4/e4

Nisan, M., & Kohlberg, L. (1982). Universality and variation in moral judgment: A longitudinal and cross-sectional study in Turkey. *Child Development, 53,* 865–876.

Nishimura, H., Hashikawa, K., Doi, K., Iwaki, T., Watanabe, Y., Kusuoka, H., Nishimura, T., & Kubo, T. (1999). Sign language "heard" in the auditory cortex. *Nature, 397,* 116.

Niskar, A. S., Kieszak, S. M., Holmes, A., Esteban, E., Rubin, C., & Brody D. J. (1998). Prevalence of hearing loss among children 6 to 19 years of age: The third National Health and Nutrition Examination Survey. *Journal of the American Medical Association, 279,* 1071–1075.

Nix, R. L., Pinderhughes, E. E., Dodge, K. A., Bates, J. E., Pettit, G. S., & McFadyen-Ketchum, S. A. (1999). The relation between mothers' hostile attribution tendencies and children's externalizing behavior problems: The mediating role of mothers' harsh discipline practices. *Child Development, 70*(4), 896–909.

Nobre, A. C., & Plunkett, K. (1997). The neural system of language: Structure and development. *Current Opinion in Neurobiology, 7,* 262–268.

Noirot, E., & Algeria, J. (1983). Neonate orientation towards human voice differs with type of feeding. *Behavioral Processes, 8,* 65–71.

Norris, C., Brink, S., & Mosher, P. (1999). *Measuring non-parental care in the NLSCY: Content and process issues.* Technical Paper T-00-1E. Ottawa: Applied Research Branch, Strategic Policy, Human Resources Development Canada.

Notzon, F. C. (1990). International differences in the use of obstetric interventions. *Journal of the American Medical Association, 263*(24), 3286–3291.

Nourot, P. M. (1998). Sociodramatic play: Pretending together. In D. P. Fromberg & D. Bergen (Eds.), *Play from birth to twelve and beyond: Contexts, perspectives, and meanings* (pp. 378–391). New York: Garland.

Nozyce, M., Hittelman, J., Muenz, L., Durako, S. J., Fischer, M. L., & Willoughby, A. (1994). Effect of perinatally acquired human immunodeficiency virus infection on neurodevelopment in children during the first two years of life. *Pediatrics 94,* 883–891.

Nsamenang, A. B. (1987). A West African perspective. In M. E. Lamb (Ed.), *The father's role: Cross-cultural perspectives* (pp. 273–293). Hillsdale, NJ: Erlbaum.

Nsamenang, A. B. (1992a). *Human development in a third world context.* Newbury Park: Sage.

Nsamenang, A. B. (1992b). Perceptions of parenting among the Nso of Cameroon. In B. S. Hewlett (Ed.), *Father–child relations: Cultural and biosocial contexts* (pp. 321–344). New York: de Gruyter.

Nucci, L., & Smetana, J. G. (1996). Mothers' concepts of young children's areas of personal freedom. *Child Development, 67,* 1870–1886.

Nugent, J. K., Lester, B. M., Greene, S. M., Wieczorek-Deering, D., & O'Mahony, P. (1996). The effects of maternal alcohol consumption and cigarette smoking during pregnancy on acoustic cry analysis. *Child Development, 67,* 1806–1815.

Nugent, T. (1999, September). At risk: 4 million students with asthma: Quick access to rescue inhalers critical for schoolchildren. *AAP News,* pp. 1, 10.

Nutrition Committee, Canadian Paediatric Society. (1991). Meeting the iron needs of infants and young children: An update. *Canadian Medical Association Journal, 144,* 1451–1454.

Nutrition Committee, Canadian Paediatric Society. (1995). Nutrient needs and feeding of premature infants. *Canadian Medical Association Journal, 152,* 1765–1785.

Nutrition Committee, Canadian Paediatric Society. (1996). The use of fluoride in infants and children. *Paediatrics & Child Health, 1,* 131–134.

O'Rahilly, S. (1998). Life without leptin. *Nature, 392,* 330–331.

O'Sullivan, J. T., Howe, M. L., & Marche, T. A. (1996). Children's beliefs about long-term retention. *Child Development, 67,* 2989–3009.

Oakes, L. M. (1994). Development of infants' use of continuity cues in their perception of causality. *Developmental Psychology, 30,* 869–879.

Offer, D. (1987). In defense of adolescents. *Journal of the American Medical Association, 257,* 3407–3408.

Offer, D., & Church, R. B. (1991). Generation gap. In R. M. Lerner, A. C. Petersen, & J. Brooks-Gunn (Eds.), *Encyclopedia of adolescence* (pp. 397–399). New York: Garland.

Offer, D., & Offer, J. B. (1974). Normal adolescent males: The high school and college years. *Journal of the American College Health Association, 22,* 209–215.

Offer, D., & Schonert-Reichl, K. A. (1992). Debunking the myths of adolescence: Findings from recent research. *Journal of the American Academy of Child and Adolescent Psychiatry, 31,* 1003–1014.

Offer, D., Ostrov, E., & Howard, K. I. (1989). Adolescence: What is normal? *American Journal of Diseases of Children, 143,* 731–736.

Offer, D., Ostrov, E., Howard, K. I., & Atkinson, R. (1988). *The teenage world: Adolescents' self-image in ten countries.* New York: Plenum.

Offord, D. R., & Lipman, E. L. (1996). Emotional and behavioural problems. In Human Resources Development Canada and Statistics Canada. *Growing up in Canada: National Longitudinal Survey of Children and Youth.* Ottawa: Author.

Offord, D. R., Lipman, E. L., & Duku, E. K. (1998). *Sports, the arts and community programs: Rates and correlates of participation.* Working Paper W-98-18E. Ottawa: Applied Research Branch, Strategic Policy, Human Resources Development Canada.

Ogden, C. L., Troiano, R. P., Briefel, R. R., Kuczmarski, R. J., Flegal, K. M., & Johnson, C. L. (1997). Prevalence of overweight among preschool children in the United States, 1971 through 1994. *Pediatrics, 99.* Retrieved September 24, 2002, from http://www.pediatrics.org/cgi/content/full/99/4/e1

Olds, D. L., Eckenrode, J., Henderson, C. R., Jr., Kitzman, H., Powers, J., Cole, R., Sidora, K., Morris, P., Pettitt, L. M., & Luckey, D. (1997). Long-term effects of home visitation on maternal life course and child abuse and neglect: Fifteen-year follow-up of a randomized trial. *Journal of the American Medical Association, 278,* 637–643.

Olds, D. L., Henderson, C. R., & Tatelbaum, R. (1994a). Intellectual impairment in children of women who smoke cigarettes during pregnancy. *Pediatrics, 93,* 221–227.

Olds, D. L., Henderson, C. R., & Tatelbaum, R. (1994b). Prevention of intellectual impairment in children of women who smoke cigarettes during pregnancy. *Pediatrics, 93,* 228–233.

Olds, D. L., Henderson, C. R., Klitzman, H. J., Eckenrode, J. J., Cole, R. E., & Tatelbaum, R. C. (1999). Prenatal and infancy home visitation by nurses: Recent findings. *The Future of Children, 9,* 44–65.

Olds, S. (in press). *That is our way.* Kathmandu, Nepal: Mandala Book Point.

Olds, S. W. (1989). *The working parents' survival guide.* Rocklin, CA: Prima.

Olweus, D. (1995). Bullying or peer abuse at school: Facts and intervention. *Current Directions in Psychological Science, 4,* 196–200.

Orr, D. P., & Ingersoll, G. M. (1995). The contribution of level of cognitive complexity and pubertal timing to behavioral risk in young adolescents. *Pediatrics, 95*(4), 528–533.

Ortiz, A. D. (1996). *Eva Perón* (S. Fields, Trans.). New York: St. Martin's.

Oshima-Takane, Y., Goodz, E., & Derevensky, J. L. (1996). Birth order effects on early language development: Do secondborn children learn from overheard speech? *Child Development, 67,* 621–634.

Ostrea, E. M., & Chavez, C. J. (1979). Perinatal problems (excluding neonatal withdrawal) in maternal drug addiction: A study of 830 cases. *Journal of Pediatrics, 94*(2), 292–295.

Owens, J., Maxim, R., McGuinn, M., Nobile, C., Msall, M., & Alario, A. (1999). Television-viewing habits and sleep disturbances in school children. *Pediatrics, 104*(3), e27.

Owens, R. E. (1996). *Language development* (4th ed.). Boston: Allyn and Bacon.

Padden, C. A. (1996). Early bilingual lives of deaf children. In I. Parasnis (Ed.), *Cultural and language diversity and the deaf experience* (pp. 99–116). New York: Cambridge University Press.

Padilla, A. M., Lindholm, K. J., Chen, A., Durán, R., Hakuta, K., Lambert, W., & Tucker, G. R. (1991). The English-only movement: Myths, reality, and implications for psychology. *American Psychologist, 46*(2), 120–130.

Paetsch, J. J., & Bertrand, L. D. (1999). Victimization and delinquency among Canadian youth. *Adolescence, 34,* 351–367.

Palella, F. J., Delaney, K. M., Moorman, A. C., Loveless, M. O., Fuhrer, J., Satten, G. A., Aschman, D. J., Holmberg, S. D., & the HIV Outpatient Study investigators. (1998). Declining morbidity and mortality among patients with advanced human immunodeficiency virus infection. *New England Journal of Medicine, 358,* 853–860.

Palkovitz, R. (1985). Fathers' birth attendance, early contact, and extended contact with their newborns: A critical review. *Child Development, 56,* 392–406.

Pally, R. (1997). How brain development is shaped by genetic and environmental factors. *International Journal of Psycho-Analysis, 78,* 587–593.

Panigrahy, A., Filiano, J., Sleeper, L. A., Mandell, F., Valdes-Dapena, M., Krous, H. F., Rava, L. A., Foley, E., White, W. F., & Kinney, H. C. (2000). Decreased serotonergic receptor binding in rhombic lip-derived regions of the medulla oblongata in the sudden infant death syndrome. *Journal of Neuropathology and Experimental Neurology, 59,* 377–384.

Papalia, D. (1972). The status of several conservation abilities across the life-span. *Human Development, 15,* 229–243.

Park, S., Belsky, J., Putnam, S., & Crnic, K. (1997). Infant emotionality, parenting, and 3-year inhibition: Exploring stability and lawful discontinuity in a male sample. *Developmental Psychology, 33,* 218–227.

Parke, R. D., & Buriel, R. (1998). Socialization in the family: Ethnic and ecological perspectives. In W. Damon (Series Ed.) & N. Eisenberg (Vol. Ed.), *Handbook of child psychology: Vol. 3. Social, emotional, and personality development* (5th ed., pp. 463–552). New York: Wiley.

Parke, R. D., Grossman, K., & Tinsley, R. (1981). Father–mother–infant interaction in the newborn period: A German–American comparison. In T. M. Field, A. M. Sostek, P. Viete, & P. H. Leideman (Eds.), *Culture and early interaction.* Hillsdale, NJ: Erlbaum.

Parke, R. D., Ornstein, P. A., Rieser, J. J., & Zahn-Waxler, C. (1994). The past as prologue: An overview of a century of developmental psychology. In R. D. Parke, P. A. Ornstein, J. J. Rieser, & C. Zahn-Waxler (Eds.), *A century of developmental psychology* (pp. 1–70). Washington, DC: American Psychological Association.

Parker, J. G., & Asher, S. R. (1987). Peer relations and later personal adjustment: Are low-accepted children at risk? *Psychological Bulletin, 102,* 357–389.

Parker, L., Pearce, M. S., Dickinson, H. O., Aitkin, M., & Craft, A. W. (1999). Stillbirths among offspring of male radiation workers at Sellafield nuclear reprocessing plant. *Lancet, 354,* 1407–1414.

Parler, B. D. (2001). Raising a child: The traditional way. In *Aboriginal Head Start (Urban and Northern Communities) National Newsletter.* Spring/summer 2001 (p. 6). Ottawa: Health Canada.

Parmelee, A. H. (1986). Children's illnesses: Their beneficial effects on behavioral development. *Child Development, 57,* 1–10.

Parmelee, A. H., Wenner, W. H., & Schulz, H. R. (1964). Infant sleep patterns: From birth to 16 weeks of age. *Journal of Pediatrics, 65,* 576.

Parr, J. (1982). Introduction. In J. Parr (Ed.), *Childhood and family in Canadian history* (pp. 7–16). Toronto: McClelland and Stewart Limited.

Parrish, K. M., Holt, V. L., Easterling, T. R., Connell, F. A., & LeGerfo, J. P. (1994). Effect of changes in maternal age, parity, and birth weight distribution on primary cesarean delivery rates. *Journal of the American Medical Association, 271,* 443–447.

Parten, M. B. (1932). Social play among preschool children. *Journal of Abnormal and Social Psychology, 27,* 243–269.

Pascalis, O., & de Schonen, S. (1994). Recognition memory in 3- to 4-day-old human neonates. *Neuroreport, 5,* 1721–1724.

Patterson, C. J. (1992). Children of lesbian and gay parents. *Child Development, 63,* 1025–1042.

Patterson, C. J. (1995a). Lesbian mothers, gay fathers, and their children. In A. R. D'Augelli & C. J. Patterson (Eds.), *Lesbian, gay, and bisexual identities over the lifespan: Psychological perspectives* (pp. 293–320). New York: Oxford University Press.

Patterson, C. J. (1995b). Sexual orientation and human development: An overview. *Developmental Psychology, 31,* 3–11.

Patterson, C. J. (1997). Children of gay and lesbian parents. In T. H. Ollendick & R. J. Prinz (Eds.), *Advances in clinical child psychology* (Vol. 19, pp. 235–282). New York: Plenum.

Patterson, C. J. (2000). Family relationships of lesbians and gay men. *Journal of Marriage and Family, 62,* 1052–1070.

Patterson, C. J., & Redding, R. E. (1996). Lesbian and gay families with children: Implications of social science research for policy. *Journal of Social Issues, 52*(3), 29–50.

Patterson, G. R. (1984). Siblings: Fellow travelers in coercive family processes. In R. J. Blanchard (Ed.), *Advances in the study of aggression* (pp. 174–213). New York: Academic.

Patterson, G. R. (1995). Coercion: A basis for early age of onset for arrest. In J. McCord (Ed.), *Coercion and punishment in long-term perspective* (pp. 81–105). New York: Cambridge University Press.

Patterson, G. R., & Stouthamer-Loeber, M. (1984). The correlation of family management practices and delinquency. *Child Development, 55,* 1299–1307.

Patterson, G. R., DeBaryshe, B. D., & Ramsey, E. (1989). A developmental perspective on antisocial behavior. *American Psychologist, 44*(2), 329–335.

Patterson, G. R., Reid, J. B., & Dishion, T. J. (1992). *Antisocial boys.* Eugene, OR: Castalia.

Pear, R. (2000, March 20). White House seeks to curb pills used to calm the young: Risks would be outlined: National study is planned to look at effect of psychiatric drugs on preschoolers. *New York Times,* p. A1.

Pederson, D. R., Gleason, K. E., Moran, G., & Bento, S. (1998). Maternal attachment representations, maternal sensitivity, and the infant–mother attachment relationship. *Developmental Psychology, 34,* 925–933.

Pellegrini, A. D. (1998). Rough-and-tumble play from childhood through adolescence. In D. P. Fromberg & D Bergen (Eds.), *Play from birth to twelve and beyond: Contexts, perspectives, and meanings* (pp. 401–408). New York: Garland.

Pellegrini, A. D., & Smith, P. K. (1998). Physical activity play: The nature and function of a neglected aspect of play. *Child Development, 69,* 577–598.

Pelletier, A. R., Quinlan, K. P., Sacks, J. J., Van Gilder, T. J., Gilchrist, J., & Ahluwalia, H. K. (2000). Injury prevention practices as depicted in G-rated and PG-rated movies. *Archives of Pediatrics and Adolescent Medicine, 154,* 283–286.

Pelleymounter, N. A., Cullen, M. J., Baker, M. B., Hecht, R., Winters, D., Boone, T., & Collins, F. (1995). Effects of the obese gene product on body regulation in ob/ob mice. *Science, 269,* 540–543.

Pennisi, E. (2000). And the gene number is . . .? *Science, 288,* 1146–1147.

Pepler, D. J., & Sedighdeilami, F. (1998). *Aggressive girls in Canada.* Report No. W-98-30E. Ottawa: Applied Research Branch, Strategic Policy, Human Resources Development Canada.

Pepper, S. C. (1942). *World hypotheses.* Berkeley: University of California Press.

Perlman, M., & Ross, H. S. (1997). The benefits of parent intervention in children's disputes: An examination of concurrent changes in children's fighting styles. *Child Development, 64,* 690–700.

Perozynski, L., & Kramer, L. (1999). Parental beliefs about managing sibling conflict. *Developmental Psychology, 35,* 489–499.

Pérusse, L., Chagnon, Y. C., Weisnagel, J., & Bouchard, C. (1999). The human obesity gene map: The 1998 update. *Obesity Research, 7,* 111–129.

Peskin, H. (1967). Pubertal onset and ego functioning. *Journal of Abnormal Psychology, 72,* 1–15.

Peskin, H. (1973). Influence of the developmental schedule of puberty on learning and ego functioning. *Journal of Youth and Adolescence, 2,* 273–290.

Peskin, J. (1996). Guise and guile: Children's understanding of narratives in which the purpose of pretence is deception. *Child Development, 67,* 1735–1751.

Peter, K. A. (1983). The certainty of salvation: Ritualization of religion and economic rationality among Hutterites. *Comparative Studies in Society and History, 25,* 222–240.

Petersen, A. C. (1993). Presidential address: Creating adolescents: The role of context and process in developmental transitions. *Journal of Research on Adolescents, 3*(1), 1–18.

Petersen, A. C., Compas, B. E., Brooks-Gunn, J., Stemmler, M., Ey, S., & Grant, K. E. (1993). Depression in adolescence. *American Psychologist, 48*(2), 155–168.

Peterson, C. C. (1999). Children's memory for medical emergencies: 2 years later. *Developmental Psychology, 35,* 1493–1506.

Peterson, C., & McCabe, A. (1994). A social interactionist account of developing decontextualized narrative skill. *Developmental Psychology, 30,* 937–948.

Peterson, J. L., Moore, K. A., & Furstenberg, F. F., Jr. (1991). Television viewing and early initiation of sexual intercourse: Is there a link? *Journal of Homosexuality, 21,* 93–118.

Peth-Pierce, R. (1998). *The NICHD study of early child care.* Retrieved September 24, 2002, from http://www.nichd.nih.gov/publications/pubs/early_child_care.htm

Petitto, L. A., & Marentette, P. F. (1991). Babbling in the manual mode: Evidence for the ontogeny of language. *Science, 251,* 1493–1495.

Pettit, G. S., Bates, J. E., & Dodge, K. A. (1997). Supportive parenting, ecological context, and children's adjustment: A seven-year longitudinal study. *Child Development, 68,* 908–923.

Phelps, J. A., Davis, J. O., & Schartz, K. M. (1997). Nature, nurture, and twin research strategies. *Current Directions in Psychological Science, 6*(5), 117–121.

Phillips, D. F. (1998). Reproductive medicine experts till an increasingly fertile field. *Journal of the American Medical Association, 280,* 1893–1895.

Phillips, R. B., Sharma, R., Premachandra, B. R., Vaughn, A. I., & Reyes-Lee, M. (1996). Intrauterine exposure to cocaine: Effect on neurobehavior of neonates. *Infant Behavior and Development, 19,* 71–81.

Phillips, S., & Sandstrom, K. L. (1990). Parental attitudes towards youth work. *Youth and Society, 22,* 160–183.

Phinney, J. S. (1998). Stages of ethnic identity development in minority group adolescents. In R. E. Muuss & H. D. Porton (Eds.), *Adolescent behavior and society: A book of readings* (pp. 271–280). Boston: McGraw-Hill.

Phinney, J. S., & Cobb, N. J. (1996). Reasoning about intergroup relations among Hispanic and Euro-American adolescents. *Journal of Adolescent Research, 11,* 306–324.

Piaget, J. (1929). *The child's conception of the world.* New York: Harcourt Brace.

Piaget, J. (1932). *The moral judgment of the child.* New York: Harcourt Brace.

Piaget, J. (1951). *Play, dreams, and imitation* (C. Gattegno & F. M. Hodgson, Trans.). New York: Norton.

Piaget, J. (1952). *The origins of intelligence in children.* New York: International Universities Press. (Original work published 1936)

Piaget, J. (1954). *The construction of reality in the child.* New York: Basic.

Piaget, J. (1962). *The language and thought of the child* (M. Gabain, Trans.). Cleveland, OH: Meridian. (Original work published 1923)

Piaget, J. (1969). *The child's conception of time* (A. J. Pomerans, Trans.). London: Routledge & Kegan Paul.

Piaget, J. (1972). Intellectual evolution from adolescence to adulthood. *Human Development, 15,* 1–12.

Piaget, J., & Inhelder, B. (1967). *The child's conception of space.* New York: Norton.

Pickering, L. K., Granoff, D. M., Erickson, J. R., Mason, M. L., Cordle, C. T., Schaller, J. P., Winship, T. R., Paule, C. L., & Hilty, M. D. (1998). Modulation of the immune system by human milk and infant formula containing nucleotides. *Pediatrics, 101,* 242–249.

Pierce, K. M., Hamm, J. V., & Vandell, D. L. (1999). Experiences in after-school programs and children's adjustment in first-grade classrooms. *Child Development, 70*(3), 756–767

Pillow, B. H., & Henrichon, A. J. (1996). There's more to the picture than meets the eye: Young children's difficulty understanding biased interpretation. *Child Development, 67,* 803–819.

Pines, M. (1981). The civilizing of Genie. *Psychology Today, 15*(9), 28–34.

Pirkle, J. L., Brody, D. J., Gunter, E. W., Kramer, R. A., Raschal, D. C., Flegal, K. M., & Matte, T. D. (1994). The decline in blood lead levels in the United States. *Journal of the American Medical Association, 272,* 284–291.

Pirkle, J. L., Flegal, K. M., Bernert, J. T., Brody, D. J., Etzel, R. A., & Maurer, K. R. (1996). Exposure of the U.S. population to environmental tobacco smoke: The Third National Health and Nutrition Examination Survey, 1988–1991. *Journal of the American Medical Association, 275,* 1233–1240.

Pleck, J. H. (1997). Paternal involvement: Levels, sources, and consequences. In M. E. Lamb et al. (Eds.), *The role of the father in child development* (3rd ed., pp. 66–103). New York: Wiley.

Plomin, R. (1989). Environment and genes: Determinants of behavior. *American Psychologist, 44*(2), 105–111.

Plomin, R. (1990). The role of inheritance in behavior. *Science, 248,* 183–188.

Plomin, R. (1995). Molecular genetics and psychology. *Current Directions in Psychological Science, 4*(4), 114–117.

Plomin, R. (1996). Nature and nurture. In M. R. Merrens & G. G. Brannigan (Eds.), *The developmental psychologist: Research adventures across the life span* (pp. 3–19). New York: McGraw-Hill.

Plomin, R., & Daniels, D. (1987). Why are children in the same family so different from one another? *Behavioral and Brain Sciences, 10,* 1–16.

Plomin, R., & DeFries, J. C. (1999). The genetics of cognitive abilities and disabilities. In S. J. Ceci & W. M. Williams (Eds.), *The nature nurture debate: The essential readings* (pp. 178–195). Malden, MA: Blackwell.

Plomin, R., & Rutter, M. (1998). Child development, molecular genetics, and what to do with genes once they are found. *Child Development, 69*(4), 1223–1242.

Plomin, R., Dale, P., Simonoff, E., Eley, T., Oliver, B., Price, T., Purcell, S., Bishop, D., & Stevenson, J. (1998). Genetic influence on language delay in two-year-old children. *Nature Neuroscience, 1,* 324–328.

Plomin, R., Owen, M. J., & McGuffin, P. (1994). The genetic bases of behavior. *Science, 264,* 1733–1739.

Plotkin, S. A., Katz, M., & Cordero, J. F. (1999). The eradication of rubella. *Journal of the American Medical Association, 281,* 561–562.

Plumert, J. M. (1995). Relations between children's overestimation of their physical abilities and accident proneness. *Developmental Psychology, 31,* 866–876.

Plumert, J. M., Pick, H. L., Jr., Marks, R. A., Kintsch, A. S., & Wegesin, D. (1994). Locating objects and communicating about locations: Organizational differences in children's searching and direction-giving. *Developmental Psychology, 30,* 443–453.

Plumert, J., & Nichols-Whitehead, P. (1996). Parental scaffolding of young children's spatial communication. *Developmental Psychology, 32,* 523–532.

Polit, D. F., & Falbo, T. (1987). Only children and personality development: A quantitative review. *Journal of Marriage and the Family, 49,* 309–325.

Pollock, L. A. (1983). *Forgotten children.* Cambridge, England: Cambridge University Press.

Pong, S. L. (1997). Family structure, school context, and eighth-grade math and reading achievement. *Journal of Marriage and the Family, 59,* 734–746.

Poole, D. A., & Lindsay, D. S. (2002). Reducing child witnesses' false reports of misinformation from parents. *Journal of Experimental Child Psychology, 81,* 117–140.

Pope, A. W., Bierman, K. L., & Mumma, G. H. (1991). Aggression, hyperactivity, and inattention-immaturity: Behavior dimensions associated with peer rejection in elementary school boys. *Developmental Psychology, 27,* 663–671.

Portwood, S. G., & Repucci, N. D. (1996). Adults' impact on the suggestibility of preschoolers' recollections. *Journal of Applied Developmental Psychology, 17,* 175–198.

Posada, G., Gao, Y., Wu, F., Posada, R., Tascon, M., Schoelmerich, A., Sagi, A., Kondo-Ikemura, K., Haaland, W., & Synnevaag, B. (1995). The secure-base phenomenon across cultures: Children's behavior, mothers' preferences, and experts' concepts. In E. Waters, B. E. Vaughn, G. Posada, & K. Kondo-Ikemura (Eds.), Caregiving, cultural, and cognitive perspectives on secure-base behavior and working models: New growing points of attachment theory and research (pp. 27–48). *Monographs of the Society for Research in Child Development, 60*(2–3, Serial No. 244).

Posner, J. K., & Vandell, D. L. (1999). After-school activities and the development of low-income urban children: A longitudinal study. *Developmental Psychology, 35*(3), 868–879.

Post, S. G. (1994). Ethical commentary: Genetic testing for Alzheimer's disease. *Alzheimer Disease and Associated Disorders, 8,* 66–67.

Povinelli, D. J., Landau, K. R., & Perilloux, H. K. (1996). Self-recognition in young children using delayed versus live feedback: Evidence of a developmental asynchrony. *Child Development, 67,* 1540–1554.

Powell, M. B., & Thomson, D. M. (1996). Children's memory of an occurrence of a repeated event: Effects of age, repetition, and retention interval across three question types. *Child Development, 67,* 1988–2004.

Power, T. G., & Chapieski, M. L. (1986). Childrearing and impulse control in toddlers: A naturalistic investigation. *Developmental Psychology, 22,* 271–275.

Powlishta, K. K., Serbin, L. A., Doyle, A. B., & White, D. R. (1994). Gender, ethnic, and body type biases: The generality of prejudice in childhood. *Developmental Psychology, 30,* 526–536.

Pratt, M. W., & Savoy-Levine, K. M. (1998). Contingent tutoring of long-division skills in fourth and fifth graders: Experimental tests of some hypotheses about scaffolding. *Journal of Applied Developmental Psychology, 19,* 287–304.

Prechtl, H. F. R., & Beintema, D. J. (1964). The neurological examination of the full-term newborn infant. *Clinics in Developmental Medicine, 12.* London: Heinemann.

Pressley, M. (1998). *Reading instruction that works: The case for balanced teaching.* New York: The Guilford Press.

Pressley, M., Wharton-McDonald, R., Mistretta-Hampston, J., & Echevarria, M. (1998). Literacy instruction in 10 fourth- and fifth-grade classrooms in upstate New York. *Scientific Studies of Reading, 2,* 159–194.

Price, J. M. (1996). Friendships of maltreated children and adolescents: Contexts for expressing and modifying relationship history. In W. M. Bukowski, A. F. Newcomb, & W. W. Hartup (Eds.), *The company they keep: Friendship in childhood and adolescence* (pp. 262–285). New York: Cambridge University Press.

Price-Williams, D. R., Gordon, W., & Ramirez, M., III. (1969). Skills and conservation: A study of pottery-making children. *Developmental Psychology, 1,* 769.

Princeton Survey Research Associates. (1996). *The 1996 Kaiser Family Foundation Survey on Teens and Sex: What they say teens today need to know, and who they listen to.* Menlo Park, CA: Kaiser Family Foundation.

Project 2061. (1999). *Few middle school math textbooks will help students learn, says AAAS' Project 2061 evaluation.* News release. Retrieved February 2, 1999, from http://project2061.aaas.org/newsinfo/press/rl012299.htm

Pruett, K. D. (1998). Research perspectives: Role of the father. *Pediatrics, 102* (Suppl.), 1253–1261.

Psychosocial Paediatrics Committee, Canadian Paediatric Society. (1997). Effective discipline for children. *Paediatrics & Child Health, 2*(1), 29–33.

Pungello, E. P., Kupersmidt, J. B., Burchinal, M. R., & Patterson, C. J. (1996). Environmental risk factors and children's achievement from middle childhood to early adolescence. *Developmental Psychology, 32,* 755–767.

Purcell, J. H. (1995). Gifted education at a crossroads: The program status study. *Gifted Child Quarterly, 39*(2), 57–65.

Quadrel, M. J., Fischoff, B., & Davis, W. (1993). Adolescent (in)vulnerability. *American Psychologist, 48,* 102–116.

Quasha, S. (1980). *Albert Einstein: An intimate portrait.* Larchmont, NY: Forest.

Quinby, N. (1985, October). On testing and teaching intelligence: A conversation with Robert Sternberg. *Educational Leadership,* pp. 50–53.

Quinlan, K. P., Brewer, R. D., Sleet, D. A., & Dellinger, A. M. (2000). Characteristics of child passenger deaths and injuries involving drinking drivers. *Journal of the American Medical Association, 283,* 2249–2252.

Quinn, P. C., Eimas, P. D., & Rosenkrantz, S. L. (1993). Evidence for representations of perceptually similar natural categories by 3-month-old and 4-month-old infants. *Perception, 22,* 463–475.

Quintero, R. A., Abuhamad, A., Hobbins, J. C., & Mahoney, M. J. (1993). Transabdominal thin-gauge embryofetoscopy: A technique for early prenatal diagnosis and its use in the diagnosis of a case of Meckel-Gruber syndrome. *American Journal of Obstetrics and Gynecology, 168,* 1552–1557.

Rabiner, D., & Coie, J. (1989). Effect of expectancy induction on rejected peers' acceptance by unfamiliar peers. *Developmental Psychology, 25,* 450–457.

Rabson, M. (August 30, 2001). School system fails aboriginals: Lewis. *Winnipeg Free Press,* A9.

Racine, A., Joyce, T., & Anderson, R. (1993). The association between prenatal care and birth weight among women exposed to cocaine in New York City. *Journal of the American Medical Association, 270,* 1581–1586.

Raffaelli, M., & Larson, R. W. (1987). *Sibling interactions in late childhood and early adolescence.* Paper presented at the biennial meeting of the Society for Research in Child Development, Baltimore, MD.

Rafferty, Y., & Shinn, M. (1991). Impact of homelessness on children. *American Psychologist, 46*(11), 1170–1179.

Ramey, C. T., & Campbell, F. A. (1991). Poverty, early childhood education, and academic competence. In A. Huston (Ed.), *Children reared in poverty* (pp. 190–221). Cambridge, England: Cambridge University Press.

Ramey, C. T., & Ramey, S. L. (1996). Early intervention: Optimizing development for children with disabilities and risk conditions. In M. Wolraich (Ed.), *Disorders of development and learning: A practical guide to assessment and management* (2nd ed., pp. 141–158). Philadelphia: Mosby.

Ramey, C. T., & Ramey, S. L. (1998a). Early intervention and early experience. *American Psychologist, 53,* 109–120.

Ramey, C. T., & Ramey, S. L. (1998b). Prevention of intellectual disabilities: Early interventions to improve cognitive development. *Preventive Medicine, 21,* 224–232.

Ramey, C. T., Campbell, F. A., Burchinal, M., Skinner, M. L., Gardner, D. M., & Ramey, S. L. (2000). Persistent effects of early childhood education on high-risk children and their mothers. *Applied Developmental Science, 4*(1), 2–14.

Ramey, S. L. (1999). Head Start and preschool education: Toward continued improvement. *American Psychologist, 54,* 344–346.

Ramey, S. L., & Ramey, C. T. (1992). Early educational intervention with disadvantaged children: To what effect?

Applied and Preventive Psychology, 1, 131–140.

Ramsey, P. G., & Lasquade, C. (1996). Preschool children's entry attempts. *Journal of Applied Developmental Psychology, 17,* 135–150.

Rank, M. R., & Hirschl, T. A. (1999). The economic risk of childhood in America: Estimating the probability of poverty across the formative years. *Journal of Marriage and the Family, 61,* 1058–1067.

Rapin, I. (1997). Autism. *New England Journal of Medicine, 337,* 97–104.

Rappaport, L. (1993). The treatment of nocturnal enuresis: Where are we now? *Pediatrics, 92,* 465–466.

Rask-Nissilä, L., Jokinen, E., Terho, P., Tammi, A., Lapinleimu, H., Ronnemaa, T., Viikari, J., Seppanen, R., Korhonen, T., Tuominen, J., Valimaki, I., & Simell, O. (2000). Neurological development of 5-year-old children receiving a low-saturated fat, low-cholesterol diet since infancy. *Journal of the American Medical Association, 284*(8), 993–1000.

Raymond, J. M. (1991). *The nursery world of Dr. Blatz.* Toronto: University of Toronto Press.

Redding, R. E., Harmon, R. J., & Morgan, G. A. (1990). Maternal depression and infants' mastery behaviors. *Infant Behavior and Development, 113,* 391–396.

Reese, E. (1995). Predicting children's literacy from mother–child conversations. *Cognitive Development, 10,* 381–405.

Reese, E., & Fivush, R. (1993). Parental styles of talking about the past. *Developmental Psychology, 29,* 596–606.

Reese, E., Haden, C., & Fivush, R. (1993). Mother–child conversations about the past: Relationships of style and memory over time. *Cognitive Development, 8,* 403–430.

Reid, J. R., Patterson, G. R., & Loeber, R. (1982). The abused child: Victim, instigator, or innocent bystander? In D. J. Berstein (Ed.), *Response structure and organization.* Lincoln: University of Nebraska Press.

Reijo, R., Alagappan, R. K., Patrizio, P., & Page, D. C. (1996). Severe oligozoospermia resulting from deletions of azoospermia factor gene on Y chromosome. *Lancet, 347,* 1290–1293.

Reinisch, J. M., Sanders, S. A., Mortensen, E. L., Psych, C., &

Rubin, D. B. (1995). In utero exposure to phenobarbital and intelligence deficits in adult men. *Journal of the American Medical Association, 274,* 1518–1525.

Reis, S. M. (1989). Reflections on policy affecting the education of gifted and talented students: Past and future perspectives. *American Psychologist, 44,* 399–408.

Reiss, A. L., Abrams, M. T., Singer, H. S., Ross, J. L., & Denckla, M. B. (1996). Brain development, gender and IQ in children: A volumetric imaging study. *Brain, 119,* 1763–1774.

Remafedi, G., French, S., Story, M., Resnick, M. D., & Blum, R. (1998). The relationship between suicide risk and sexual orientation: Results of a population-based study. *American Journal of Public Health, 88,* 57–60.

Remafedi, G., Resnick, M., Blum, R., & Harris, L. (1992). Demography of sexual orientation in adolescents. *Pediatrics, 89,* 714–721.

Rennie, J. (1994, June). Grading the gene tests. *Scientific American,* pp. 86–97.

Repacholi, B. M., & Gopnik, A. (1997). Early reasoning about desires: Evidence from 14- and 18-month-olds. *Developmental Psychology, 33,* 12–21.

Rescorla, L. (1991). Early academics: Introduction to the debate. In L. Rescorla, M. C. Hyson, & K. Hirsh-Pasek (Eds.), *Academic instruction in early childhood: Challenge or pressure? (New Directions for Child Development, 53,* pp. 5–11). San Francisco: Jossey-Bass.

Resnick, L. B. (1989). Developing mathematical knowledge. *American Psychologist, 44,* 162–169.

Resnick, M. B., Gomatam, S. V., Carter, R. L., Ariet, M., Roth, J., Kilgore, K. L., Bucciarelli, R. L., Mahan, C. S., Curran, J. S., & Eitzman, D. V. (1998). Educational disabilities of neonatal intensive care graduates. *Pediatrics, 102,* 308–314.

Resnick, M. D., Bearman, P. S., Blum, R. W., Bauman, K. E., Harris, K. M., Jones, J., Tabor, J., Beuhring, T., Sieving, R. E., Shew, M., Ireland, M., Bearinger, L. H., & Udry, J. R. (1997). Protecting adolescents from harm: Findings from the National Longitudinal Study on Adolescent Health. *Journal of the American Medical Association, 278,* 823–832.

Rest, J. R. (1975). Longitudinal study of the Defining Issues Test of moral judgment: A strategy for analyzing

developmental change. *Developmental Psychology, 11,* 738–748.

Restak, R. (1984). *The brain.* New York: Bantam.

Revised Regulations of Ontario. (1990). Day Nurseries Act. Regulation 262. Toronto: Printer of Ontario.

Revised Statutes of British Columbia. (1996). Health professions act: Midwives regulation. Victoria, BC: Queen's Printer.

Reynolds, A. J. (1994). Effects of a preschool plus follow-on intervention for children at risk. *Developmental Psychology, 30,* 787–804.

Reynolds, A. J. and Temple, J. A. (1998). Extended early childhood intervention and school achievement: Age thirteen findings from the Chicago Longitudinal Study. *Child Development, 69,* 231–246.

Reynolds, G. (1998). Welcoming place: An urban community of Inuit families. *Canadian Children, 23*(1), 5–11.

Rheingold, H. L. (1985). Development as the acquisition of familiarity. *Annual Review of Psychology, 36,* 1–17.

Rice, C., Koinis, D., Sullivan, K., Tager-Flusberg, H., & Winner, E. (1997). When 3-year-olds pass the appearance–reality test. *Developmental Psychology, 33,* 54–61.

Rice, G., Anderson, C., Risch, N., & Ebers, G. (1999). Male homosexuality: Absence of linkage to microsatellite markers at Xq28. *Science, 284,* 665–667.

Rice, M. L. (1982). Child language: What children know and how. In T. M. Field, A. Huston, H. C. Quay, L. Troll, & G. E. Finley (Eds.), *Review of human development research.* New York: Wiley.

Rice, M. L. (1989). Children's language acquisition. *American Psychologist, 44*(2), 149–156.

Rice, M. L., Hadley, P. A., & Alexander, A. L. (1993). Social biases toward children with speech and language impairments: A correlative causal model of language limitations. *Applied Psycholinguistics, 14,* 445–471.

Rice, M. L., Huston, A. C., Truglio, R., & Wright, J. (1990). Words from "Sesame Street": Learning vocabulary while viewing. *Developmental Psychology, 26,* 421–428.

Rice, M. R., Alvanos, L., & Kenney, B. (2000). Snowmobile injuries and deaths in children: A review of national injury data and state legislation. *Pediatrics, 105*(3), 615–619.

Rice, M., Oetting, J. B., Marquis, J., Bode, J., & Pae, S. (1994). Frequency of input effects on SLI children's word comprehension. *Journal of Speech and Hearing Research, 37,* 106–122.

Richards, M. H., Boxer, A. M., Petersen, A. C., & Albrecht, R. (1990). Relation of weight to body image in pubertal girls and boys from two communities. *Developmental Psychology, 26,* 313–321.

Richards, T. L., Dager, S. R., Corina, D., Serafini, S., Heide, A. C., Steury, K., Strauss, W., Hayes, C. E., Abbott, R. D., Craft, S., Shaw, D., Posse, S., & Berninger, V. W. (1999). Dyslexic children have abnormal brain lactate response to reading-related language tasks. *American Journal of Neuroradiology, 20,* 1393–1398.

Richardson, H. R. L., Beazley, R. P., Delaney, M. E., & Langille, D. B. (1997). Factors influencing condom use among students attending high school in Nova Scotia. *The Canadian Journal of Human Sexuality, 6,* 185–196.

Richardson, J. (1995). *Achieving gender equality in families: The role of males* (Innocenti Global Seminar, Summary Report). Florence, Italy: UNICEF International Child Development Centre, Spedale degli Innocenti.

Richardson, J. L., Radziszewska, B., Dent, C. W., & Flay, B. R. (1993). Relationship between after-school care of adolescents and substance use, risk-taking, depressed mood, and academic achievement. *Pediatrics, 92,* 32–38.

Richie, D. (1984). *The films of Akira Kurosawa.* Berkeley: University of California Press.

Riddle, R. D., Johnson, R. L., Laufer, E., & Tabin, C. (1993). Sonic hedgehog mediates the polarizing activity of the ZPA. *Cell, 75,* 1401–1416.

Rieder, M. J. (2002). Ecstasy. *Paediatrics and Child Health, 7,* 71–72.

Rifkin, J. (1998, May 5). Creating the "perfect" human. *Chicago Sun-Times,* p. 29.

Ripple, C. H., Gilliam, W. S., Chanana, N., and Zigler, E. (1999). Will fifty cooks spoil the broth? The debate over entrusting Head Start to the states. *American Psychologist, 54,* 327–343.

Ristow, M., Muller-Wieland, D., Pfeiffer, A., Krone, W., & Kahn, R. (1998). Obesity associated with a mutation in genetic regulator of adiposity differentiation. *New England Journal of Medicine, 339,* 953–959.

Ritter, J. (1999, November 23). Scientists close in on DNA code. *Chicago Sun-Times,* p. 7.

Rivara, F. P. (1999). Pediatric injury control in 1999: Where do we go from here? *Pediatrics, 103*(4), 883–888.

Rivara, F. P., & Grossman, D. C. (1996). Prevention of traumatic deaths to children in the United States: How far have we come and where do we need to go? *Pediatrics, 97,* 791–798.

Rivara, F. P., Bergman, A. B., & Drake, C. (1989). Parental attitudes and practices toward children as pedestrians. *Pediatrics, 84,* 1017–1021.

Rivera, S. M., Wakely, A., & Langer, J. (1999). The drawbridge phenomenon: Representational reasoning or perceptual preference? *Developmental Psychology, 35*(2), 427–435.

Rizzo, T. A., Metzger, B. E., Dooley, S. L., & Cho, N. H. (1997). Early malnutrition and child neurobehavioral development: Insights from the study of children of diabetic mothers. *Child Development, 68,* 26–38.

Roberts, G. C., Block, J. H., & Block, J. (1984). Continuity and change in parents' child-rearing practices. *Child Development, 55,* 586–597.

Roberts, I., Kramer, M., & Suissa, S. (1996). Does home visiting prevent childhood injury? A systematic review of randomized controlled trials. *British Medical Journal, 312,* 29–33.

Rochat, P. Querido, J. G., & Striano, T. (1999). Emerging sensitivity to the timing and structure of proto conversations in early infancy. *Developmental Psychology, 35,* 950–957.

Rock, A. M. L., Trainor, L. J., & Addison, T. L. (1999). Distinctive messages in infant-directed lullabies and play songs. *Developmental Psychology, 35,* 527–534.

Rodier, P. M. (2000, February). The early origins of autism. *Scientific American,* pp. 56–63.

Rodkin, P. C., Farmer, T. W., Pearl, R., & Van Acker, R. (2000). Heterogeneity of popular boys: Antisocial and prosocial configurations. *Developmental Psychology, 36*(1), 14–24.

Rodrigues, D. (1999, April 26). *Ensuring safe and effective psychotropic medications for children* [News release]. Washington, DC: National Institute of Mental Health.

Rogoff, B. (1990). *Apprenticeship in thinking: Cognitive development in social context.* New York: Oxford University Press.

Rogoff, B. (1998). Cognition as a collaborative process. In W. Damon (Ed.), D. Kuhn, & R. S. Siegler (Vol. Eds.), *Handbook of child psychology: Vol. 2. Cognition, perception, and language* (5th ed., pp. 679–744). New York: Wiley.

Rogoff, B., & Morelli, G. (1989). Perspectives on children's development from cultural psychology. *American Psychologist, 44,* 343–348.

Rogoff, B., Mistry, J., Göncü, A., & Mosier, C. (1993). Guided participation in cultural activity by toddlers and caregivers. *Monographs of the Society for Research in Child Development, 58*(8, Serial No. 236).

Rokach, A., & Neto, F. (2001). The experience of loneliness in adolescence: A cross cultural comparison. *International Journal of Adolescence and Youth, 9,* 159–173.

Rolls, B. J., Engell, D., & Birch, L. L. (2000). Serving portion size influences 5-year-old but not 3-year-old children's food intake. *Journal of the American Dietetic Association, 100,* 232–234.

Rome-Flanders, T., Cronk, C., & Gourde, C. (1995). Maternal scaffolding in mother–infant games and its relationship to language development: A longitudinal study. *First Language, 15,* 339–355.

Ronca, A. E., & Alberts, J. R. (1995). Maternal contributions to fetal experience and the transition from prenatal to postnatal life. In J. P. Lecanuet, W. P. Fifer, N. A. Krasnegor, & W. P. Smotherman (Eds.), *Fetal development: A psychobiological perspective* (pp. 331–350). Hillsdale, NJ: Erlbaum.

Roopnarine, J. L., Hooper, F. H., Ahmeduzzaman, M., & Pollack, B. (1993). Gentle play partners: Mother–child and father–child play in New Delhi, India. In K. MacDonald (Ed.), *Parent–child play* (pp. 287–304). Albany: State University of New York Press.

Roopnarine, J. L., Talokder, E., Jain, D., Josh, P., & Srivastav, P. (1992). Personal well-being, kinship ties, and mother–infant and father–infant interactions in single-wage and dual-wage families in New Delhi, India. *Journal of Marriage and the Family, 54,* 293–301.

Roopnarine, J., & Honig, A. S. (1985, September). The unpopular child. *Young Children*, pp. 59–64.

Rose, S. A. (1994). Relation between physical growth and information processing in infants born in India. *Child Development, 65*, 889–902.

Rose, S. A., & Feldman, J. F. (1995). Prediction of IQ and specific cognitive abilities at 11 years from infancy measures. *Developmental Psychology, 31*, 685–696.

Rose, S. A., & Feldman, J. F. (1997). Memory and speed: Their role in the relation of infant information processing to later IQ. *Child Development, 68*, 630–641.

Rosenberg, H. M., Ventura, S. J., Maurer, J. D., Heuser, R. L., & Freedman, M. A. (1996). *Births and deaths: United States, 1995 (Monthly Vital Statistics Report, 45*[3, Suppl. 2], DHHS Publication No. 96-1120). Hyattsville, MD: National Center for Health Statistics.

Rosenblatt, R. A., Dobie, S. A., Hart, L. G., Schneeweiss, R., Gould, D., Raine, T. R., Benedetti, T. J., Pirani, M. J., & Perrin, E. B. (1997). Interspeciality differences in the obstetric care of low risk women. *American Journal of Public Health, 87*, 344–351.

Rosenblum, G. D., & Lewis, M. (1999). The relations among body image, physical attractiveness, and body mass in adolescence. *Child Development, 70*, 50–64.

Rosengren, K. S., Gelman, S. A., Kalish, C. W., & McCormick, M. (1991). As time goes by: Children's early understanding of growth in animals. *Child Development, 62*, 1302–1320.

Rosenthal, C., & Gladstone, J. (2000). *Grandparenthood in Canada.* Ottawa: The Vanier Institute of the Family.

Rosenthal, E. (1998, November 1). For one-child policy, China rethinks iron hand. *New York Times*, pp. 1, 20.

Rosenthal, R., & Jacobson, L. (1968). *Pygmalion in the classroom.* New York: Holt.

Rosenthal, R., & Vandell, D. L. (1996). Quality of care at school-aged child-care programs: Regulatable features, observed experiences, child perspectives, and parent perspectives. *Child Development, 67*, 2434–2445.

Rosenzweig, M. R. (1984). Experience, memory, and the brain. *American Psychologist, 39*, 365–376.

Rosenzweig, M. R., & Bennett, E. L. (Eds.). (1976). *Neural mechanisms of learning and memory.* Cambridge, MA: MIT Press.

Roskinski, R. R. (1977). *The development of visual perception.* Santa Monica, CA: Goodyear.

Ross, C. E., & Mirowsky, J. (1999). Parental divorce, life-course disruption and adult depression. *Journal of Marriage and the Family, 61*, 1034–1045.

Ross, D. P., Roberts, P. A., & Scott, K. (1998). *Mediating factors in child development outcomes: Children in lone-parent families.* Catalogue No. W-98-8E. Ottawa: Applied Research Branch, Strategic Policy, Human Resources Development Canada.

Ross, D. P., Scott, K., & Kelly, M. A. (1996). Overview: children in Canada in the 1990s. In Human Resources Development Canada and Statistics Canada, *Growing up in Canada: National Longitudinal Survey of Children and Youth.* Catalogue No. 89-550-MPE, No. 1. (pp. 15–45). Ottawa: Author.

Ross, G., Lipper, E. G., & Auld, P. A. M. (1991). Educational status and school-related abilities of very low birth weight premature children. *Pediatrics, 8*, 1125–1134.

Ross, H. S. (1996). Negotiating principles of entitlement in sibling property disputes. *Developmental Psychology, 32*, 90–101.

Ross, J., & Wyat, W. (2000). Sexual behaviour. In C. Currie, K. Jurrelman, W. Settertobulte, R. Smith, & J. Todd (Eds.), *Health and health behaviour among young people* (pp. 115–120). WHO Policy Series: Health policy for children and adolescents. Issue 1. International Report. Copenhagen, Denmark: WHO European Region. Retrieved September 20, 2002, from http://www.ruhbc.ed.ac.uk/hbsc/download/hbsc.pdf

Ross, J., & Wyatt, W. (2000). Sexual behaviour. *WHO Policy Series: Healthy Policy for Children and Adolescents,* Series No. 1. pp. 115–120.

Rossel, C., & Ross, J. M. (1986). *The social science evidence on bilingual education.* Boston: Boston University Press.

Rotenberg, K. J., & Cerda, C. (1995). Racially based trust expectancies of Native American and Caucasian children. *The Journal of Social Psychology, 134*, 621–631.

Rotenberg, K. J., & Eisenberg, N. (1997). Developmental differences in the understanding of and reaction to others' inhibition of emotional expression. *Developmental Psychology, 33*, 526–537.

Rothbart, M. K., Ahadi, S. A., & Evans, D. E. (2000). Temperament and personality: Origins and outcomes. *Journal of Personality and Social Psychology, 78*, 122–135.

Rotheram-Borus, M. J., & Futterman, D. (2000). Promoting early detection of human immunodeficiency virus infection among adolescents. *Archives of Pediatric and Adolescent Medicine, 154*, 435–439.

Roush, W. (1995). Arguing over why Johnny can't read. *Science, 267*, 1896–1898.

Rovee-Collier, C. (1996). Shifting the focus from what to why. *Infant Behavior and Development, 19*, 385–400.

Rovee-Collier, C. (1999). The development of infant memory. *Current Directions in Psychological Science, 8*, 80–85.

Rovee-Collier, C., & Boller, K. (1995). Current theory and research on infant learning and memory: Application to early intervention. *Infants and Young Children, 7*(3), 1–12.

Royal Commission on New Reproductive Technologies. (1993). *Proceed with care: Final report of the Royal Commission on New Reproductive Technologies.* Ottawa: Canadian Government Publishing

Rubenstein, C. (1993, November 18). Child's play, or nightmare on the field? *New York Times*, pp. C1, C10.

Rubin, D. H., Erickson, C. J., San Agustin, M., Cleary, S. D., Allen, J. K., & Cohen, P. (1996). Cognitive and academic functioning of homeless children compared with housed children. *Pediatrics, 97*, 289–294.

Rubin, D. H., Krasilnikoff, P. A., Leventhal, J. M., Weile, B., & Berget, A. (1986, August 23). Effect of passive smoking on birth-weight. *Lancet*, pp. 415–417.

Rubin, K. (1982). Nonsocial play in preschoolers: Necessary evil? *Child Development, 53*, 651–657.

Rubin, K. H., Bukowski, W., & Parker, J. G. (1998). Peer interactions, relationships, and groups. In W. Damon (Series Ed.) & N. Eisenberg (Vol. Ed.), *Handbook of child psychology: Vol. 3. Social, emotional, and personality development* (5th ed., pp. 619–700). New York: Wiley.

Rubin, K. H., Fein, G. G., & Vandenberg, B. (1983). Play. In P. H.

Mussen (Series Ed.) & E. M. Hetherington (Vol. Ed.), *Handbook of child psychology: Vol. 4. Socialization, personality, and social development* (pp. 694–774). New York: Wiley.

Ruble, D. M., & Brooks-Gunn, J. (1982). The experience of menarche. *Child Development, 53,* 1557–1566.

Ruble, D. N., & Dweck, C. S. (1995). Self-conceptions, person conceptions, and their development. In N. Eisenberg, (Ed.), *Social development: Review of personality and social psychology* (pp. 109–139). Thousand Oaks, CA: Sage.

Ruble, D. N., & Martin, C. L. (1998). Gender development. In W. Damon (Series Ed.) & N. Eisenberg (Vol. Ed.), *Handbook of child psychology: Vol. 3. Social, emotional, and personality development* (5th ed., pp. 933–1016). New York: Wiley.

Rudy, D., & Grusec, J. (2001). Correlates of authoritarian parenting in individualist and collectivist cultures and implications for understanding the transmission of values. *Journal of Cross Cultural Psychology, 32,* 202–212.

Rueter, M. A., & Conger, R. D. (1995). Antecedents of parent–adolescent disagreements. *Journal of Marriage and the Family, 57,* 435–448.

Ruff, H. A., Bijur, P. E., Markowitz, M., Ma, Y. C., & Rosen, J. F. (1993). Declining blood lead levels and cognitive changes in moderately lead-poisoned children. *Journal of the American Medical Association, 269,* 1641–1646.

Rushton, J. L., Clark, S. J., & Freed, G. L. (May 1999). *Newest depression medications widely prescribed for children.* Paper presented at the Pediatric Academic Societies Annual Meeting, San Francisco, CA.

Rutter, M. (1987). Continuities and discontinuities from infancy. In J. Osofsky (Ed.), *Handbook of infant development.* New York: Wiley.

Rutter, M., & the English and Romanian Adoptees (ERA) Study Team. (1998). Developmental catch-up, and deficit, following adoption after severe global early privation. *Journal of Child Psychology and Psychiatry, 39,* 465–476.

Ryan, A. S. (2000). *Ross Mothers Survey.* Abbott Park, IL: Ross Products Division, Abbott Laboratories.

Ryan, B. A., & Adams, G. R. (1998). *Family relationships and children's school achievement: Data from the National Longitudinal Survey of Children and Youth.* Catalogue No. W-98-13E. Ottawa: Applied Research Branch, Strategic Policy, Human Resources Development Canada.

Rymer, R. (1993). *An abused child: Flight from silence.* New York: HarperCollins.

Saarni, C., Mumme, D. L., & Campos, J. J. (1998). Emotional development: Action, communication, and understanding. In W. Damon (Series Ed.) & N. Eisenberg (Vol. Ed.), *Handbook of child psychology: Vol. 3. Social, emotional, and personality development* (5th ed., pp. 237–309). New York: Wiley.

Sabbagh, M. A., & Taylor, M. (2000). Neural correlates of theory-of-mind reasoning: An event-related potential study. *Psychological Science, 11*(1), 46–50.

Sachs, B. P., Kobelin, C., Castro, M. A., & Frigoletto, F. (1999). The risks of lowering the cesarean-delivery rate. *New England Journal of Medicine, 340,* 54–57.

Sack, W. H., Beiser, M., Baker-Brown, G., & Redshirt, R. (1994). Depressive and suicidal symptoms in Indian school children: Findings from the Flower of Two Soils. *American Indian & Alaska Native Mental Health Research, 4,* 81–96.

Sadeh, A., Raviv, A., & Gruber, R. (2000). Sleep patterns and sleep disruptions in school age children. *Developmental Psychology, 36*(3), 291–301.

Saigal, S., Hoult, L. A., Streiner, D. L., Stoskopf, B. L., & Rosenbaum, P. L. (2000). School difficulties at adolescence in a regional cohort of children who were extremely low birth weight. *Pediatrics, 105,* 325–331.

Sainte-Marie, B. (1996). *Biography.* Retrieved August 1, 2002, from http://creative-native.com/biograp.htm

Saklofske, D. H., & Schwean, V. L. (1995). Psychological and educational assessment of children. In K. Covell (Ed.), *Readings in child development* (pp. 185–208). Toronto: Nelson.

Salzinger, S., Feldman, R. S., Hammer, M., & Rosario, M. (1993). Effects of physical abuse on children's social relations. *Child Development, 64,* 169–187.

Samad, A. (1996, August). Understanding a controversial rite of passage: Afterword. *Natural History,* p. 52.

Samdal, O., & Dür, W. (2000). The school environment and the health of adolescents. In C. Currie, K. Hurrelmann, W. Settertobulte, R. Smith, & J. Todd (Eds.), *Health and health behaviour among young people: A WHO cross-national Study (HBSC) international report* (pp. 49–64). WHO Policy Series: Healthy Policy for Children and Adolescents, Series No. 1.

Sameroff, A. J., Seifer, R., Baldwin, A., & Baldwin, C. (1993). Stability of intelligence from preschool to adolescence: The influence of social and family risk factors. *Child Development, 64,* 80–97.

Sandler, D. P., Everson, R. B., Wilcox, A. J., & Browder, J. P. (1985). Cancer risk in adulthood from early life exposure to parents' smoking. *American Journal of Public Health, 75,* 487–492.

Sandstrom, M. J., & Coie, J. D. (1999). A developmental perspective on peer rejection: Mechanisms of stability and change. *Child Development, 70*(4), 955–966.

Sankey, G. R. (1995). Transition to work: A concern for many Canadian youth. *Counseling, 10,* 5–10.

Santer, L. J., & Stocking, C. B. (1991). Safety practices and living conditions of low-income urban families. *Pediatrics, 88,* 111–118.

Santos, I. S., Victora, C. G., Huttly, S., & Carvalhal, J. B. (1998). Caffeine intake and low birthweight: A population-based case-control study. *American Journal of Epidemiology, 147,* 620–627.

Santrock, J. W., Sitterle, K. A., & Warshak, R. A. (1988). Parent–child relationships in stepfather families. In P. Bronstein & C. P. Cowan (Eds.), *Fatherhood today: Men's changing role in the family.* New York: Wiley.

Sapp, F., Lee, K., & Muir, D. (2000). Three-year-olds' difficulty with the appearance–reality distinction: Is it real or apparent? *Developmental Psychology, 36,* 547–560.

Saunders, N. (1997, March). Pregnancy in the 21st century: Back to nature with a little assistance. *Lancet, 349,* s17–s19.

Savage, S. L., & Au, T. K. (1996). What word learners do when input contradicts the mutual exclusivity assumption. *Child Development, 67,* 3120–3134.

Sax, L. J., Astin, L. W., Korn, W. F., & Mahoney, K. M. (1996). *The American freshman: Norms for fall, 1995.* Los Angeles: UCLA Higher Education Institute.

Saxe, G. B., Guberman, S. R., & Gearhart, M. (1987). Social processes in early number development. *Monographs of the Society for Research in Child Development, 52*(216).

Scaldwell, W., Frame, J., & Cookson, D. (1985). Individual assessment of Chippewa, Muncey and Oneida children using the WISC–R. *Canadian Journal of School Psychology, 1*, 15–21.

Scarborough, H. S. (1990). Very early language deficits in dyslexic children. *Child Development, 61*, 1728–1743.

Scariati, P. D., Grummer-Strawn, L. M., & Fein, S. B. (1997a). A longitudinal analysis of infant morbidity and the extent of breastfeeding in the United States. *Pediatrics, 99*(6), e5. Retrieved September 24, 2002, from http://www.pediatrics.org/cgi/content/full/99/6/e5

Scarr, S. (1992). Developmental theories for the 1990s: Development and individual differences. *Child Development, 63*, 1–19.

Scarr, S. (1993). Biological and cultural diversity: The legacy of Darwin for development. *Child Development, 64*, 1333–1353.

Scarr, S. (1997a). Behavior-genetics and socialization theories of intelligence: Truce and reconciliation. In R. J. Sternberg & E. Grigorenko (Eds.), *Intelligence, heredity, and environment* (pp. 3–41). Cambridge, England: Cambridge University Press.

Scarr, S. (1997b). Why child care has little impact on most children's development. *Current Directions in Psychological Science, 6*(5), 143–148.

Scarr, S. (1998). American child care today. *American Psychologist, 53*, 95–108.

Scarr, S., & McCartney, K. (1983). How people make their own environments: A theory of genotype-environment effects. *Child Development, 54*, 424–435.

Schachar, R., Mota, V. L., Logan, G. D., Tannock, R., & Klim, P. (2000). Confirmation of an inhibitory control deficit in attention-deficit/hyperactivity disorder. *Journal of Abnormal Child Psychology, 20*, 227–235.

Schanberg, S. M., & Field, T. M. (1987). Sensory deprivation illness and supplemental stimulation in the rat pup and preterm human neonate. *Child Development, 58*, 1431–1447.

Schauble, L. (1996). The development of scientific reasoning in knowledge-rich contexts. *Developmental Psychology, 32*, 102–119.

Scheidt, P., Overpeck, M. D., Wyatt, W., & Aszmann, A. (2000). In C. Currie, K. Hurrelmann, W. Settertobulte, R. Smith, & J. Todd (Eds.), *Health and health behaviour among young people: A WHO cross-national study (HBSC) international report* (pp. 24–38). WHO Policy Series: Healthy Policy for Children and Adolescents, Series No. 1.

Scher, M. S., Richardson, G. A., & Day, N. L. (2000). Effects of prenatal crack/cocaine and other drug exposure on electroencephalographic sleep studies at birth and one year. *Pediatrics, 105*, 39–48.

Scherer, M. (1985, January). How many ways is a child intelligent? *Instructor*, pp. 32–35.

Schilpp, P. A. (1970). *Albert Einstein: Philosopher-scientist* (3rd ed.). La Salle, IL: Open Court. (Original work published 1949)

Schissel, B., & Fedec, K. (1999). The selling of innocence: The gestalt of danger in the lives of youth prostitutes. *Canadian Journal of Criminology, 41*, 33–57.

Schlegel, A., & Barry, H. (1991). *Adolescence: An anthropological inquiry.* New York: Free Press.

Schmitt, B. D. (1997). Nocturnal enuresis. *Pediatrics in Review, 18*, 183–190.

Schmitt, B. D., & Kempe, C. H. (1983). Abused and neglected children. In R. E. Behrman & V. C. Vaughn (Eds.), *Nelson textbook of pediatrics* (12th ed.). Philadelphia: Saunders.

Schmitz, S., Saudino, K. J., Plomin, R., Fulker, D. W., & DeFries, J. C. (1996). Genetic and environmental influences on temperament in middle childhood: Analyses of teacher and tester ratings. *Child Development, 67*, 409–422.

Schoendorf, K. C., Hogue, C. J. R., Kleinman, J. C., & Rowley, D. (1992). Mortality among infants of black as compared with white college-educated parents. *New England Journal of Medicine, 326*, 1522–1526.

Scholer, S. J., Mitchel, E. F., & Ray, W. A. (1997). Predictors of injury mortality in early childhood. *Pediatrics, 100*, 342–347.

Scholten, C. M. (1985). *Childbearing in American society: 1650–1850.* New York: New York University Press.

Schonfeld, D. J., Johnson, S. R., Perrin, E. C., O'Hare, L. L., & Cicchetti, D. V. (1993). Understanding of acquired immunodeficiency syndrome by elementary school children: A developmental survey. *Pediatrics, 92*, 389–395.

Schore, A. N. (1994). *Affect regulation and the origin of the self: The neurobiology of emotional development.* Hillsdale, NJ: Erlbaum.

Schreiber, J. B., Robins, M., Striegel-Moore, R., Obarzanek, E., Morrison, J. A., & Wright, D. J. (1996). Weight modification efforts reported by preadolescent girls. *Pediatrics, 96*, 63–70.

Schupf N., Kapell, D., Nightingale, B., Rodriguez, A., Tycko, B., & Mayeux, R. (1998). Earlier onset of Alzheimer's disease in men with Down syndrome. *Neurology, 50*, 991–995

Schwartz, D., McFadyen-Ketchum, S. A., Dodge, K. A., Pettit, G. S., & Bates, J. E. (1998). Peer group victimization as a predictor of children's behavior problems at home and in school. *Development and Psychopathology, 10*, 87–99.

Schwartz, P. J., Priori, S. G., Dumaine, R., Napolitano, C., Antzelevitch, C., Stramba-Badiale, M., Richard, T. A., Berti, M. R., & Bloise, R. (2000). A molecular link between the sudden infant death syndrome and the long-QT syndrome. *New England Journal of Medicine, 343*(4), 262–267.

Schwartz, P. J., Stramba-Badiale, M., Segantini, A., Austoni, P., Bosi, G., Giorgetti, R., Grancini, F., Marni, E. D., Perticone, F., Rosti, D., & Salice, P. (1998). Prolongation of the QT interval and the sudden infant death syndrome. *New England Journal of Medicine, 338*, 1709–1714.

Schwebel, D. C., & Plumert, J. M. (1999). Longitudinal and concurrent relations among temperament, ability estimation, and injury proneness. *Child Development, 70*, 700–712.

Schweinhart, L. J., Barnes, H. V., & Weikart, D. P. (1993). Significant benefits: The High/Scope Perry Preschool Study through age 27. *Monographs of the High/Scope Educational Research Foundation, 10.* Ypsilanti, MI: High/Scope.

Scrivener, L. (2000). *Terry Fox: His story.* Toronto: McClelland & Steward Ltd.

Sedlak, A. J., & Broadhurst, D. D. (1996). *Executive summary of the third national incidence study of child abuse and neglect (NIS-3).* Washington, DC: U.S. Department of Health and Human Services.

Segalowitz, S. J. (1995). Brain growth and the child's mental development. In K.

Covell (Ed.), *Readings in child development* (pp. 51–71). Toronto: Nelson.

Sege, R., & Dietz, W. (1994). Television viewing and violence in children: The pediatrician as agent for change. *Pediatrics, 94,* 600–607.

Seifer, R., Schiller, M., Sameroff, A. J., Resnick, S., & Riordan, K. (1996). Attachment, maternal sensitivity, and infant temperament during the first year of life. *Developmental Psychology, 32,* 12–25.

Seiner, S. H., & Gelfand, D. M. (1995). Effects of mother's simulated withdrawal and depressed affect on mother–toddler interactions. *Child Development, 60,* 1519–1528.

Seitz, V. (1990). Intervention programs for impoverished children: A comparison of educational and family support models. *Annals of Child Development, 7,* 73–103.

Selman, R. L. (1980). *The growth of interpersonal understanding: Developmental and clinical analyses.* New York: Academic.

Selman, R. L., & Selman, A. P. (1979, April). Children's ideas about friendship: A new theory. *Psychology Today,* pp. 71–80.

Seltzer, J. A. (1998). Father by law: Effects of joint legal custody on nonresident fathers' involvement with children. *Demography, 35,* 135–146.

Serbin, L. A., Moller, L. C., Gulko, J., Powlishta, K. K., & Colburne, K. A. (1994). The emergence of gender segregation in toddler playgroups. In C. Leaper (Ed.), *Childhood gender segregation: Causes and consequences (New Directions for Child Development, 65,* pp. 7–17). San Francisco: Jossey-Bass.

Shanahan, M. J., Finch, M. D., Mortimer, J. T., & Ryu, S. (1991). Adolescent work experience and depressive affect. *Social Psychology Quarterly, 54,* 299–317.

Shannon, L. W. (1982). *Assessing the relationship of adult criminal careers to juvenile careers.* Iowa City: University of Iowa, Iowa Urban Community Research Center.

Shannon, M. (2000). Ingestion of toxic substances by children. *New England Journal of Medicine, 342,* 186–191.

Sharma, A. R., McGue, M. K., & Benson, P. L. (1996a). The emotional and behavioral adjustment of United States adopted adolescents, Part I: An overview. *Children and Youth Services Review, 18,* 83–100.

Sharma, A. R., McGue, M. K., & Benson, P. L. (1996b). The emotional and behavioral adjustment of United States adopted adolescents, Part II: Age at adoption. *Children and Youth Services Review, 18,* 101–114.

Shatz, M., & Gelman, R. (1973). The development of communication skills: Modifications in the speech of young children as a function of listener. *Monographs of the Society for Research in Child Development, 38*(5, Serial No. 152).

Shaw, G. M., Velie, E. M., & Schaffer, D. (1996). Risk of neural tube defect–affected pregnancies among obese women. *Journal of the American Medical Association, 275,* 1093–1096.

Shaw, G. M., Wasserman, C. R., Lammer, E. J., O'Malley, C. D., Murray, J. C., Basart, A. M., & Tolarova, M. M. (1996). Orofacial clefts, parental cigarette smoking, and transforming growth factor–alpha gene variants. *American Journal of Human Genetics, 58,* 551–561.

Shaywitz, B. A., Sullivan, C. M., Anderson, G. M., Gillespie, S. M., Sullivan, B., & Shaywitz, S. E. (1994). Aspartame, behavior, and cognitive function in children with attention deficit disorder. *Pediatrics, 93,* 70–75.

Shaywitz, S. E. (1998). Current concepts: Dyslexia. *New England Journal of Medicine, 338,* 307–312.

Shaywitz, S. E., Shaywitz, B. A., Pugh, K. R., Fulbright, R. K., Constable, R. Y., Mend, W. E., Shankweiler, D. P., Liberman, A. M., Skudlarski, P., Fletcher, J. M., Katz, L., Marchione, K. E., Lacadie, C., Gratenby, C., & Gore, J. C. (1998). Functional disruption in the organization of the brain for reading in dyslexia. *Proceedings of the National Academy of Science, USA, 95,* 2626–2641.

Shaywitz, S. E., Shaywitz, B. A., Pugh, K. R., Fulbright, R. K., Skudlarski, P., Mencl, W. E., Constable, R. T., Naftolin, F., Palter, S. F., Marchione, K. E., Katz, L., Shankweiler, D. P., Fletcher, J. M., Lacadie, C., Keltz, M., & Gore, J. C. (1998). Effects of estrogen on brain activation patterns in postmenopausal women during working memory tasks. *Journal of the American Medical Association, 281,* 1197–1202.

Shea, K. M., Little, R. E., & the ALSPAC Study Team (1997). Is there an association between preconceptual paternal x-ray exposure and birth outcome? *American Journal of Epidemiology, 145,* 546–551.

Shea, S., Basch, C. E., Stein, A. D., Contento, I. R., Irigoyen, M., & Zybert, P. (1993). Is there a relationship between dietary fat and stature or growth in children three to five years of age? *Pediatrics, 92,* 579–586.

Sherer Smith, M. (1991). An evolutionary perspective on grandparent–grandchild relationships. In P. K. Smith (Ed.), *The psychology of grandparenthood: An international perspective.* London: Routledge.

Sherman, A. (1997). *Poverty matters: The cost of child poverty in America.* Washington, DC: Children's Defense Fund.

Sherman, L. W., & Berk, R. A. (1984, April). The Minneapolis domestic violence experiment. *Police Foundation Reports,* pp. 1–8.

Shifflett, K., & Cummings, M. (1999). A program for educating parents about the effects of divorce and conflict on children: An initial evaluation. *Family Relations, 48*(1), 79–89.

Shiono, P. H., & Behrman, R. E. (1995). Low birth weight: Analysis and recommendations. *The Future of Children, 5*(1), 4–18.

Shrecker, T., Somerville, M. A., Hoffmaster, B., & Wellington, A. (1998). *Biotechnology, ethics and government: Report to the interdepartmental working group on ethics.* Ottawa: Canadian Biotechnology Strategy Task Force.

Shwe, H. I., & Markman, E. M. (1997). Young children's appreciation of the mental impact of their communicative signals. *Developmental Psychology, 33*(4), 630–636.

Sieccan [Sex Information and Education Council of Canada]. (2000). Common questions about sexual health education. *Canadian Journal of Human Sexuality, 9,* 129–137.

Siegal, M., & Peterson, C. C. (1998). Preschoolers' understanding of lies and innocent and negligent mistakes. *Developmental Psychology, 34*(2), 332–341.

Siegel, A. C., & Burton, R. V. (1999). Effects of baby walkers on motor and mental development in human infants. *Journal of Developmental and Behavioral Pediatrics, 20,* 355–361.

Siegel, O. (1982). Personality development in adolescence. In B. B. Wolman (Ed.),

Handbook of developmental psychology. Englewood Cliffs, NJ: Prentice-Hall.

Siegler, R. S. (1995). How does change occur: A microgenetic study of number conservation. *Cognitive Psychology, 28,* 225–273.

Siegler, R. S. (1998). *Children's thinking* (3rd ed.). Upper Saddle River, NJ: Prentice-Hall.

Siegler, R. S., & Richards, D. (1982). The development of intelligence. In R. Sternberg (Ed.), *Handbook of human intelligence.* London: Cambridge University Press.

Sigelman, C., Alfeld-Liro, C., Derenowski, E., Durazo, O., Woods, T., Maddock, A., & Mukai, T. (1996). Mexican-American and Anglo-American children's responsiveness to a theory-centered AIDS education program. *Child Development, 67,* 253–266.

Sigman, M. D., Kasari, C., Kwon, J. H., & Yirmiya, N. (1992). Responses to the negative emotions of others by autistic, mentally retarded, and normal children. *Child Development, 63,* 796–807.

Sigman, M., Cohen, S. E., & Beckwith, L. (1997). Why does infant attention predict adolescent intelligence? *Infant Behavior and Development, 20,* 133–140.

Silver, C. (summer, 2000). Being there: The time dual-earner couples spend with their children. *Canadian Social Trends.* Catalogue No. 11-008. Ottawa: Statistics Canada.

Silverman, W. K., La Greca, A. M., & Wasserstein, S. (1995). What do children worry about? Worries and their relation to anxiety. *Child Development, 66,* 671–686.

Silvern, S. B. (1998). Educational implications of play with computers. In D. P. Fromberg & D. Bergen (Eds.), *Play from birth to twelve and beyond: Contexts, perspectives, and meanings* (pp. 530–536). New York: Garland.

Simmons, R. G., Blyth, D. A., & McKinney, K. L. (1983). The social and psychological effect of puberty on white females. In J. Brooks-Gunn & A. C. Petersen (Eds.), *Girls at puberty: Biological and psychological perspectives.* New York: Plenum.

Simmons, R. G., Blyth, D. A., Van Cleave, E. F., & Bush, D. M. (1979). Entry into early adolescence: The impact of school structure, puberty, and

early dating on self-esteem. *American Sociological Review, 44*(6), 948–967.

Simner, M. L. (1993). Beginning reading instruction: A position paper on beginning reading instruction in Canadian schools. *Canadian Journal of School Psychology, 9,* 96–99.

Simner, M. L. (1998). The Canadian Psychological Association's stand on beginning reading instruction. *Canadian Journal of Research in Early Childhood Education, 7,* 157–158.

Simon, T. J., Hespos, S. J., & Rochat, P. (1995). Do infants understand simple arithmetic: A replication of Wynn (1992). *Cognitive Development, 10,* 253–269.

Simons, R. L., Lin, K.-H., & Gordon, L. C. (1998). Socialization in the family of origin and male dating violence: A prospective study. *Journal of Marriage and the Family, 60,* 467–478.

Simons-Morton, B. G., McKenzie, T. J., Stone, E., Mitchell, P., Osganian, V., Strikmiller, P. K., Ehlinger, S., Cribb, P., & Nader, P. R. (1997). Physical activity in a multiethnic population of third graders in four states. *American Journal of Public Health, 87,* 45–50.

Simonton, D. K. (1990). Creativity and wisdom in aging. In J. E. Birren & K. W. Schaie (Eds.), *Handbook of the psychology of aging* (pp. 320–329). New York: Academic Press.

Simpson, G. A., & Fowler, M. G. (1994). Geographic mobility and children's emotional/behavioral adjustment and school functioning. *Pediatrics, 93,* 303–309.

Simpson, G. B., & Foster, M. R. (1986). Lexical ambiguity and children's word recognition. *Developmental Psychology, 22,* 147–154.

Simpson, G. B., & Lorsbach, T. C. (1983). The development of automatic and conscious components of contextual facilitation. *Child Development, 54,* 760–772.

Simpson, J. L., & Elias, S. (1993). Isolating fetal cells from maternal blood: Advances in prenatal diagnosis through molecular technology. *Journal of the American Medical Association, 270,* 2357–2361.

Sinclair, Judge M., Phillips, D., & Bala, N. (1991). Aboriginal child welfare in Canada. In N. Bala, J. Rornick, & R. Vogl (Eds.), *Canadian child welfare law.* Toronto: Thompson Publishing.

Singer, D. G., & Singer, J. L. (1990). *The house of make-believe: Play and the*

developing imagination. Cambridge, MA: Harvard University Press.

Singer, J. L., & Singer, D. G. (1981). *Television, imagination, and aggression: A study of preschoolers.* Hillsdale, NJ: Erlbaum.

Singer, J. L., & Singer, D. G. (1998). Barney & Friends as entertainment and education: Evaluating the quality and effectiveness of a television series for preschool children. In J. K. Asamen & G. L. Berry (Eds.), *Research paradigms, television, and social behavior* (pp. 305–367). Thousand Oaks, CA: Sage.

Singer, L. T., Salvator, A., Guo, S., Collin, M., Lilien, L., & Baley, J. (1999). Maternal psychological distress and parenting stress after the birth of a very low-birth-weight infant. *Journal of the American Medical Association, 281,* 799–805.

Singer, L. T., Yamashita, T. S., Hawkins, S., Cairns, D., Baley, J., & Kliegman, R. (1994). Increased incidence of intraventricular hemorrhage and developmental delay in cocaine-exposed, very low birth weight infants. *Journal of Pediatrics, 124,* 765–771.

Singer, M. I., Slovak, K., Frierson, T., & York, P. (1998). Viewing preferences, symptoms of psychological trauma, and violent behaviors among children who watch television. *Journal of the American Academy of Child and Adolescent Psychiatry, 37*(10), 1041–1048.

Singh, S., Forrest, J. D., & Torres, A. (1989). *Prenatal care in the United States: A state and country inventory.* New York: Alan Guttmacher Institute.

Singh, S., Wulf, D., Samara, R., & Cuca, Y. P. (2000). Gender differences in the timing of first intercourse: Data from 14 countries. *International Family Planning Perspectives, Part 1, 26,* 21–28.

Sit, C., Yeung, D. L., He, M., & Anderson, G. H. (2001). The growth and feeding patterns of 9- to 12-month-old Chinese Canadian infants. *Nutrition Research, 21,* 505–516.

Skadberg, B. T., Morild, I., & Markestad, T. (1998). Abandoning prone sleeping: Effects on the risk of sudden infant death syndrome. *Journal of Pediatrics, 132,* 234–239.

Skinner, B. F. (1938). *The behavior of organisms: An experimental approach.* New York: Appleton-Century.

Skinner, B. F. (1957). *Verbal behavior.* New York: Appleton-Century-Crofts.

Skinner, D. (1989). The socialization of gender identity: Observations from Nepal. In J. Valsiner (Ed.), *Child development in cultural context* (pp. 181–192). Toronto: Hogrefe & Huber.

Skinner, J. D., Carruth, B. R., Moran, J., III, Houck, K., & Coletta, F. (1999). Fruit juice intake is not related to children's growth. *Pediatrics, 103,* 58–64.

Skjaerven, R., Wilcox, A. J., & Lie, R. T. (1999). A population-based study of survival and childbearing among female subjects with birth defects and the risk of recurrence in their children. *New England Journal of Medicine, 340,* 1057–1062.

Skoe, E. E., & Diessner, R. E. (1994). Ethics of care, justice, identity, and gender: An extension and replication. *Merrill-Palmer Quarterly, 40,* 272–289.

Skoe, E. E., & Gooden, A. (1993). Ethics of care and real-life moral dilemma content in male and female early adolescents. *Journal of Early Adolescence, 13*(2), 154–167.

Skolnick, A. A. (1993). "Female athlete triad" risk for women. *Journal of the American Medical Association, 270,* 921–923.

Skuse, D. H., James, R. S., Bishop, D. V. M., Coppin, B., Dalton, P., Aamodt-Leeper, G., Bacarese-Hamilton, M., Creswell, C., McGurk, R., & Jacobs, P. A. (1997). Evidence from Turner's syndrome of an imprinted X-linked locus affecting cognitive function. *Nature, 387,* 705–708.

Slade, A., Belsky, J., Aber, J. L., & Phelps, J. L. (1999). Mothers' representation of their relationships with their toddlers: Links to adult attachment and observed mothering. *Developmental Psychology, 35,* 611–619.

Slap, G. B., Vorters, D. F., Chaudhuri, S., & Centor, R. M. (1989). Risk factors for attempted suicide during adolescence. *Pediatrics, 84,* 762–772.

Slater, A. (2000). Visual perception in the young infant: Early organization and rapid learning. In D. Muir & A. Slater (Eds.), *Infant development: The essential readings* (pp. 95–116). Oxford: Blackwell Publishers.

Slobin, D. (1971). Universals of grammatical development in children. In W. Levett & G. B. Flores d'Arcais (Eds.), *Advances in psycholinguistic research.* Amsterdam: New Holland.

Slobin, D. (1973). Cognitive prerequisites for the acquisition of language. In C.

Ferguson & D. Slobin (Eds.), *Studies of child language development.* New York: Holt, Rinehart, & Winston.

Slobin, D. (1983). Universal and particular in the acquisition of grammar. In E. Wanner & L. Gleitman (Eds.), *Language acquisition: The state of the art.* Cambridge, England: Cambridge University Press.

Sly, R. M. (2000). Decreases in asthma mortality in the United States. *Annals of Allergy, Asthma, and Immunology, 85,* 121–127.

Small, M. Y. (1990). *Cognitive development.* New York: Harcourt Brace.

Smetana, J. G., & Bitz, B. (1996). Adolescents' conception of teachers' authority and their relations to rule violations in school. *Child Development, 67,* 1153–1172.

Smilansky, S. (1968). *The effects of sociodramatic play on disadvantaged preschool children.* New York: Wiley.

Smith, A. E., Jussim, L., & Eccles, J. (1999). Do self-fulfilling prophecies accumulate, dissipate, or remain stable over time? *Journal of Personality and Social Psychology, 77,* 548–565.

Smith, A., & Schneider, B. H. (2000). The inter-ethnic friendships of adolescent students: A Canadian study. *International Journal of Intercultural Relations, 24,* 247–258.

Smith, B. A., & Blass, E. M. (1996). Taste-mediated calming in premature, preterm, and full-term human infants. *Developmental Psychology, 32,* 1084–1089.

Smith, E., & Jackson, A. (2002). *Does a rising tide lift all boats? The labour market experiences and incomes of recent immigrants, 1995 to 1998.* Ottawa: Canadian Council on Social Development.

Smith, G. A., & Shields, B. J. (1998). Trampoline-related injuries to children. *Archives of Pediatrics and Adolescent Medicine, 152,* 694–699.

Smith, K. A., Fairburn, C. G., & Cowen, P. J. (1999). Symptomatic release in bulimia nervosa following acute tryptophan depletion. *Archives of General Psychiatry (72C), 56*(2), 171–176.

Smith, M. (1998, February 25). U.S. 12th-graders trail students of other nations in math, science. *Minneapolis Star-Tribune,* p. A5.

Smith, M. E. (1993). *Television violence and behavior: A research summary.* ERIC/IT Digest (ED366 329).

Retrieved September 24, 2002, from http://npin.org/library/pre1998/n00155/n00155.html

Smith, M. M., & Lifshitz, F. (1994). Excess fruit juice consumption as a contributing factor in nonorganic failure to thrive. *Pediatrics, 93,* 438–443.

Smith, P. K., & Levan, S. (1995). Perceptions and experiences of bullying in younger pupils. *British Journal of Educational Psychology, 65,* 489–500.

Smith, R. (1999, March). The timing of birth. *Scientific American,* pp. 68–75.

Smith, T. E. (1981). Adolescent agreement with perceived maternal and paternal educational goals. *Journal of Marriage and the Family, 43,* 85–93.

Smotherman, W. P., & Robinson, S. R. (1995). Tracing developmental trajectories into the prenatal period. In J. P. Lecanuet, W. P. Fifer, N. A. Krasnegor, & W. P. Smotherman (Eds.), *Fetal development: A psychobiological perspective* (pp. 15–32). Hillsdale, NJ: Erlbaum.

Smotherman, W. P., & Robinson, S. R. (1996). The development of behavior before birth. *Developmental Psychology, 32,* 425–434.

Snarey, J. R. (1985). Cross-cultural universality of social-moral development: A critical review of Kohlbergian research. *Psychological Bulletin, 97,* 202–232.

Snow, C. E. (1990). The development of definitional skill. *Journal of Child Language, 17,* 697–710.

Snow, C. E. (1993). Families as social contexts for literacy development. In C. Daiute (Ed.), *The development of literacy through social interaction (New Directions for Child Development, 61,* pp. 11–24). San Francisco: Jossey-Bass.

Snow, M. E., Jacklin, C. N., & Maccoby, E. E. (1983). Sex-of-child differences in father–child interaction at one year of age. *Child Development, 54,* 227–232.

Snyder, J., West, L., Stockemer, V., Gibbons, S., & Almquist-Parks, L. (1996). A social learning model of peer choice in the natural environment. *Journal of Applied Developmental Psychology, 17,* 215–237.

Snyder, T. D., Hoffman, C. M., & Geddes, C. M. (1997). *Digest of education statistics 1997* (NCES 98-015). Washington, DC: U.S. Department of Education, National Center for Education Statistics.

Sobsey, D. (2002). Exceptionality, education, and maltreatment. *Exceptionality, 10,* 29–46.

Society for Assisted Reproductive Technology, The American Fertility Society. (1993). Assisted reproductive technology in the United States and Canada: 1991 results from the Society for Assisted Reproductive Technology generated from The American Fertility Society Registry. *Fertility and Sterility, 59,* 956–962.

Society for Research in Child Development. (1996). Ethical standards for research with children. In *Directory of members* (pp. 337–339). Ann Arbor, MI: Author.

Society of Obstetricians and Gynaecologists of Canada. (1993, March). *The use of folic acid for the prevention of neural tube defects.* SOGC Policy Statement no. 19. Ottawa: Health Canada.

Society of Obstetricians and Gynaecologists of Canada. (1996a). *Fetal health surveillance in labour.* Policy Statement No. 45. Ottawa: Author.

Society of Obstetricians and Gynaecologists of Canada. (1996b). *Early discharge and length of stay for term birth.* Policy Statement No. 56. Ottawa: Author.

Society of Obstetricians and Gynaecologists of Canada. (1998). *Healthy beginnings: Guidelines for care during pregnancy and childbirth.* Policy Statement No. 71. Ottawa: Author

Society of Obstetricians and Gynaecologists of Canada. (2000a). *Be careful what you wish for . . .* [Press Release, June 27, 2000].

Society of Obstetricians and Gynaecologists of Canada. (2000b). *Healthy beginnings: The complete get-ready-for-baby guide.* Ottawa: Author.

Solderstrom, B., Stewart, P. J., Kaitell, C., & Chamberlain, M. (1990). Interest in alternative birthplaces among women in Ottawa-Carleton. *Canadian Medical Association Journal, 142,* 963–969.

Solomon, C. R., & Serres, F. (1999). Effects of parental verbal aggression on children's self-esteem and school marks. *Child Abuse & Neglect, 23,* 339–351.

Sommers-Flanagan, J., & Sommers-Flanagan, R. (1996). Efficacy of antidepressant medication with depressed youth: What psychologists should know. *Professional Psychology: Research & Practice, 27,* 145–153.

Sonenstein, F. L., Pleck, J. H., & Ku, L. C. (1991). Levels of sexual activity among adolescent males in the United States. *Family Planning Perspectives, 23*(4), 162–167.

Song, M., & Ginsburg, H. P. (1987). The development of informal and formal mathematical thinking in Korean and U.S. children. *Child Development, 58,* 1286–1296.

Sophian, C. (1988). Early developments in children's understanding of number: Inferences about numerosity and one-to-one correspondence. *Child Development, 59,* 1397–1414.

Sophian, C. (2000). From objects to quantities: Developments in preschool children's judgments about aggregate amount. *Developmental Psychology, 36,* 724–730.

Sophian, C., & Wood, A. (1997). Proportional reasoning in young children: The parts and the whole of it. *Journal of Educational Psychology, 89,* 309–317.

Sophian, C., Garyantes, D., & Chang, C. (1997). When three is less than two: Early developments in children's understanding of fractional quantities. *Developmental Psychology, 33,* 731–744.

Sorce, J. F., Emde, R. N., Campos, J., & Klinnert, M. D. (1985). Maternal emotional signalling: Its effect on the visual cliff behavior of 1-year-olds. *Developmental Psychology, 21,* 195–200.

Sorensen, T., Nielsen, G., Andersen, P., & Teasdale, T. (1988). Genetic and environmental influence of premature death in adult adoptees. *New England Journal of Medicine, 318,* 727–732.

Sorrentino, C. (1990). The changing family in international perspective. *Monthly Labor Review, 113*(3), 41–58.

Sosin, D. M., Sacks, J. J., & Webb, K. W. (1996). Pediatric head injuries and death from bicycling, United States. *Pediatrics, 98,* 868–870.

Soubhi, H., Raina, P., & Kohen, D. (2001). *Effects of neighbourhood, family, and child behaviour on childhood injury in Canada.* Report No. W-01-6E. Ottawa: Applied Research Branch, Strategic Policy, Human Resources Development Canada.

South Carolina Attorney General's Office (1997, October 27). Condon pleased that crack baby decision is reaffirmed. Retrieved June 26, 1998, from http://scattorneygeneral.org.

South Carolina Attorney General's Office. (1998, May 26). Supreme Court ruling a victory for South Carolina's children. Retrieved June 26, 1998, from http://scattorneygeneral.org/

Spelke, E. (1994). Initial knowledge: Six suggestions. *Cognition, 50,* 431–445.

Spelke, E. S. (1998). Nativism, empiricism, and the origins of knowledge. *Infant Behavior and Development, 21*(2), 181–200.

Spencer, M. B., & Dornbusch, S. M. (1998). Challenges in studying minority youth. In R. E. Muuss & H. D. Porton (Eds.), *Adolescent behavior and society: A book of readings* (pp. 316–330). Boston: McGraw-Hill.

Spitz, R. A. (1945). Hospitalism: An inquiry into the genesis of psychiatric conditioning in early childhood. In D. Fenschel et al. (Eds.), *Psychoanalytic studies of the child* (Vol. 1, pp. 53–74). New York: International Universities Press.

Spitz, R. A. (1946). Hospitalism: A follow-up report. In D. Fenschel et al. (Eds.), *Psychoanalytic studies of the child* (Vol. 1, pp. 113–117). New York: International Universities Press.

Spohr, H. L., Willms, J., & Steinhausen, H.-C. (1993). Prenatal alcohol exposure and long-term developmental consequences. *Lancet, 341,* 907–910.

Squire, L. R. (1992). Memory and the hippocampus: A synthesis of findings with rats, monkeys, and humans. *Psychological Review, 99,* 195–231.

Srinivasan, S. R., Meyers, L., & Berenson, G. S. (2001). Rate of change in adiposity and its relationship to concomitant changes in cardiovascular risk variables among biracial (black-white) children and adults: The Bogalusa heart study. *Metabolism, 50,* 299–305.

Sroufe, L. A. (1979). Socioemotional development. In J. Osofsky (Ed.), *Handbook of infant development.* New York: Wiley.

Sroufe, L. A. (1997). *Emotional development.* Cambridge, England: Cambridge University Press.

Sroufe, L. A., Bennett, C., Englund, M., Urban, J., & Shulman, S. (1993). The significance of gender boundaries in preadolescence: Contemporary correlates and antecedents of boundary violation and maintenance. *Child Development, 64,* 455–466.

Sroufe, L. A., Carlson, E., & Shulman, S. (1993). Individuals in relationships: Development from infancy through adolescence. In D. C. Funder, R. D. Parke, C. Tomlinson-Keasey, & K. Widaman (Eds.), *Studying lives through time: Personality and development* (pp. 315–342). Washington, DC: American Psychological Association.

Stahl, S. A., & Miller, P. D. (1989). Whole language and language experience approaches for beginning reading: A quantitative research synthesis. *Review of Educational Research, 59,* 87–116.

Stahl, S. A., McKenna, M. C., & Pagnucco, J. R. (1994). The effects of whole-language instruction: An update and a reappraisal. *Educational Psychologist, 29,* 175–185.

Standley, J. M. (1998). Strategies to improve outcomes in critical care: The effect of music and multimodal stimulation on responses of premature infants in neonatal intensive care. *Pediatric Nursing, 24,* 532–538.

Starfield, B. (1991). Childhood morbidity: Comparisons, clusters, and trends. *Pediatrics, 88,* 519–526.

Starfield, B., Katz, H., Gabriel, A., Livingston, G., Benson, P., Hankin, J., Horn, S., & Steinwachs, D. (1984). Morbidity in childhood: A longitudinal view. *New England Journal of Medicine, 310,* 824–829.

States look to detention for pregnant drug users. (1998, May 2). *Minneapolis Star-Tribune,* p. A15.

Statistics Canada. (1994). *Low income cut-offs* (Catalogue No. 13-551-XPB). Ottawa: Author.

Statistics Canada. (1996). *1996 Census Nation tables.* Retrieved September 24, 2002, from http://www.statcan.ca/english/census96/nation.htm

Statistics Canada. (1998). *National Population Health Survey, 1996–97.* Ottawa: Author.

Statistics Canada. (1999). *Leading causes of death at different ages, 1997.* Ottawa: Author.

Statistics Canada. (2000). *Average hours per week of television viewing, fall 2000* (Catalogue no. 87F0006XPB). Retrieved September 24, 2002, from http://www.statcan.ca/english/Pgdb/People/Culture/arts23.htm

Statistics Canada. (2000, October 20). Teenage pregnancy. *The Daily.* Retrieved September 20, 2002, from http://www.statcan.ca/Daily/English/001020/d001020b.htm

Statistics Canada. (2002a). *Women in Canada: Work chapter updates.* Catalogue No. 89F0133XIE. Ottawa: Minister of Industry.

Statistics Canada. (2002b). *Changing conjugal life in Canada.* Catalogue No. 89-576-XIE. Ottawa: Minister of Industry.

Statistics Canada. (2002c). *General social survey—Cycle 15: Family history.* Catalogue No. 89-575-X1E. Ottawa: Minister of Industry.

Staub, E. (1996). Cultural-societal roots of violence: The examples of genocidal violence and of contemporary youth violence in the United States. *American Psychologist, 51,* 117–132.

Stauder, J. E. A., Molenaar, P. C. M., & Van der Molen, M. W. (1993). Scalp topography of event-related brain potentials and cognitive transition during childhood. *Child Development, 64,* 769–788.

Steel, L. (1991). Early work experience among white and non-white youths: Implications for subsequent enrollment and employment. *Youth and Society, 22,* 419–447.

Stein, M. B., Chavira, D. A., & Jang, K. L. (2001). Bringing up bashful baby: Developmental pathways to social phobia. In F. R. Schneier (Ed.), *The Psychiatric Clinics of North America, 24,* 661–675.

Steinberg, L. (1981). Transformations in family relations at puberty. *Developmental Psychology, 17,* 833–840.

Steinberg, L. (1987). Impact of puberty on family relations: Effect of pubertal status and pubertal timing. *Developmental Psychology, 23,* 451–460.

Steinberg, L. (1988). Reciprocal relation between parent–child distance and pubertal maturation. *Developmental Psychology, 24,* 122–128.

Steinberg, L., & Darling, N. (1994). The broader context of social influence in adolescence. In R. Silberstein & E. Todt (Eds.), *Adolescence in context.* New York: Springer.

Steinberg, L., Fegley, S., & Dornbusch, S. M. (1993). Negative impact of part-time work on adolescent adjustment: Evidence from a longitudinal study. *Developmental Psychology, 29,* 171–180.

Steinberg, L., Lamborn, S. D., Dornbusch, S. M., & Darling, N. (1992). Impact of parenting practices on adolescent achievement: Parenting, school involvement, and

encouragement to succeed. *Child Development, 47,* 723–729.

Stennies, G., Ikeda, R., Leadbetter, S., Houston, B., & Sacks, J. (1999). Firearm storage practices and children in the home, United States, 1994. *Archives of Pediatrics and Adolescent Medicine, 153,* 586–590.

Sternberg, R. J. (1984, September). How can we teach intelligence? *Educational Leadership,* pp. 38–50.

Sternberg, R. J. (1985a). *Beyond IQ: A triarchic theory of human intelligence.* New York: Cambridge University Press.

Sternberg, R. J. (1985b, November). Teaching critical thinking, Part I: Are we making critical mistakes? *Phi Delta Kappan,* pp. 194–198.

Sternberg, R. J. (1986). *Intelligence applied: Understanding and increasing your intellectual skills.* San Diego: Harcourt Brace.

Sternberg, R. J. (1987, September 23). The use and misuse of intelligence testing: Misunderstanding meaning, users over-rely on scores. *Education Week,* pp. 22, 28.

Sternberg, R. J. (1993). *Sternberg Triarchic Abilities Test.* Unpublished manuscript.

Sternberg, R. J. (1997). The concept of intelligence and its role in lifelong learning and success. *American Psychologist, 52,* 1030–1037.

Sternberg, R. J. (1999). A triarchic approach to the understanding and assessment of intelligence in multicultural populations. *Journal of School Psychology, 37,* 145–159.

Sternberg, R. J., & Clinkenbeard, P. (1995). A triarchic view of identifying, teaching, and assessing gifted children. *Roeper Review, 17,* 255–260.

Sternberg, R. J., Grigorenko, E. L., & Bundy, D. A. (2001). The predictive value of IQ. *Merrill-Palmer Quarterly, 47,* 1–41.

Sternberg, R. J., Torff, B., & Grigorenko, E. L. (1998). Teaching triarchically improves school achievement. *Journal of Educational Psychology, 90*(3), 374–384.

Stevens, J. H., & Bakeman, R. (1985). A factor analytic study of the HOME scale for infants. *Developmental Psychology, 21,* 1106–1203.

Stevenson, H. W. (1995). Mathematics achievement of American students: First in the world by the year 2000? In C. A. Nelson (Ed.), *The Minnesota Symposia on Child Psychology: Vol. 28. Basic and applied perspectives on learning, cognition, and development* (pp. 131–149). Mahwah, NJ: Erlbaum.

Stevenson, H. W., Chen, C., & Lee, S. Y. (1993). Mathematics achievement of Chinese, Japanese, and American children: Ten years later. *Science, 258* (5081), 53–58.

Stevenson, H. W., Lee, S. Y., Chen, C., Stigler, J. W., Hsu, C. C., & Kitamura, S. (1990). Contexts of achievement: A study of American, Chinese, and Japanese children. *Monographs of the Society for Research in Child Development, 55*(1–2, Serial No. 221).

Stevenson, H. W., Lee, S., Chen, C., & Lummis, M. (1990). Mathematics achievement of children in China and the United States. *Child Development, 61,* 1053–1066.

Stevenson-Hinde, J., & Shouldice, A. (1996). Fearfulness: Developmental consistency. In A. J. Sameroff & M. M. Haith (Eds.), *The five to seven year shift: The age of reason and responsibility* (pp. 237–252). Chicago: University of Chicago Press.

Steward, M. S., & Steward, D. S. (1996). Interviewing young children about body touch and handling. *Monographs of the Society for Research in Child Development, 61*(4–5, Serial No. 248).

Stewart, I. C. (1994, January 29). Two-part message [Letter to the editor]. *New York Times,* p. A18.

Stick, S. M., Burton, P. R., Gurrin, L., Sly, P. D., & LeSouëf, P. N. (1996). Effects of maternal smoking during pregnancy and a family history of asthma on respiratory function in newborn infants. *Lancet, 348,* 1060–1064.

Stifter, C. A., Coulehan, C. M., & Fish, M. (1993). Linking employment to attachment: The mediating effects of maternal separation anxiety and interactive behavior. *Child Development, 64,* 1451–1460.

Stigler, J. W., & Fernandez, C. (1995). Learning mathematics from classroom instruction: Cross-cultural and experimental perspectives. In C. A. Nelson et al. (Eds.), *Basic and applied perspectives on learning cognition, and development* (pp. 103–130). *Minnesota Symposia on Child Psychology,* Vol. 28. Mahwah, NJ: Erlbaum.

Stigler, J. W., Lee, S., & Stevenson, H. W. (1987). Mathematics classrooms in Japan, Taiwan, and the United States. *Child Development, 58,* 1272–1285.

Stipek, D. J., & Ryan, R. H. (1997). Economically disadvantaged preschoolers: Ready to learn but further to go. *Developmental Psychology, 33,* 711–723.

Stipek, D. J., Gralinski, H., & Kopp, C. B. (1990). Self-concept development in the toddler years. *Developmental Psychology, 26,* 972–977.

Stolberg, S. G. (1997, May 16). Senate tries to define fetal viability: Murky concepts still clouding the debate over abortion laws. *New York Times,* p. A18.

Stolberg, S. G. (2000, January 27). Teenager's death is shaking up field of human gene-therapy experiments. *New York Times,* p. A20.

Strasburger, V. C., & Donnerstein, E. (1999). Children, adolescents, and the media: Issues and solutions. *Pediatrics, 103,* 129–139.

Strassberg, Z., Dodge, K. A., Pettit, G. S., & Bates, J. E. (1994). Spanking in the home and children's subsequent aggression toward kindergarten peers. *Development and Psychopathology, 6,* 445–461.

Straus, M. A. (1994a). *Beating the devil out of them: Corporal punishment in American families.* San Francisco, CA: Jossey-Bass.

Straus, M. A. (1994b). Should the use of corporal punishment by parents be considered child abuse? In M. A. Mason & E. Gambrill (Eds.), *Debating children's lives: Current controversies on children and adolescents* (pp. 196–222). Newbury Park, CA: Sage.

Straus, M. A., & Paschall, M. J. (1999, July). *Corporal punishment by mothers and children's cognitive development: A longitudinal study of two age cohorts.* Paper presented at the Sixth International Family Violence Research Conference, University of New Hampshire, Durham, NH.

Straus, M. A., & Stewart, J. H. (1999). Corporal punishment by American parents: National data on prevalence, chronicity, severity, and duration, in relation to child and family characteristics. *Clinical Child and Family Psychology Review, 2*(2), 55–70.

Straus, M. A., Sugarman, D. B., & Giles-Sims, J. (1997). Spanking by parents and subsequent antisocial behavior of children. *Archives of Pediatric and Adolescent Medicine, 151,* 761–767.

Strauss, M., Lessen-Firestone, J., Starr, R., & Ostrea, E. (1975). Behavior of narcotics-addicted newborns. *Child Development, 46,* 887–893.

Strauss, R. S. (2000). Adult functional outcome of those born small for gestational age: Twenty-six-year follow-up of the 1970 British Birth Cohort. *Journal of the American Medical Association, 283,* 625–632.

Streissguth, A. P., Aase, J. M., Clarren, S. K., Randels, S. P., LaDue, R. A., & Smith, D. F. (1991). Fetal alcohol syndrome in adolescents and adults. *Journal of the American Medical Association, 265,* 1961–1967.

Streissguth, A. P., Martin, D. C., Barr, H. M., Sandman, B. M., Kirchner, G. L., & Darby, B. L. (1984). Intrauterine alcohol and nicotine exposure: Attention and reaction time in 4-year-old children. *Developmental Psychology, 20,* 533–541.

Strobel, A., Camoin, T. I. L., Ozata, M., & Strosberg, A. D. (1998). A leptin missense mutation associated with hypogonadism and morbid obesity. *Nature Genetics, 18,* 213–215.

Strömland, K., & Hellström, A. (1996). Fetal alcohol syndrome: An ophthalmological and socioeducational prospective study. *Pediatrics, 97,* 845–850.

Strong-Boag, V. (1982). Intruders in the nursery: Childcare professionals reshape the years one to five, 1920–1940. In J. Parr (Ed.), *Childhood and family in Canadian history* (pp.160–178). Toronto: McClelland and Stewart Limited.

Stuart, J. (1991). Introduction. In Z. Zhensun & A. Low, *A young painter: The life and paintings of Wang Yani—China's extraordinary young artist* (pp. 6–7). New York: Scholastic.

Stubbs, M. L., Rierdan, J., & Koff, E. (1989). Developmental differences in menstrual attitudes. *Journal of Early Adolescence, 9*(4), 480–498.

Sturges, J. W., & Sturges, L. V. (1998). In vivo systematic desensitization in a single-session treatment of an 11-year-old girl's elevator phobia. *Child & Family Behavior Therapy, 20,* 55–62.

Subar, A. F., Krebs-Smith, S. M., Cook, A., & Kahle, L. L. (1998). Dietary sources of nutrients among U.S. children, 1989–1991. *Pediatrics, 102,* 913–923.

Sue, S., & Okazaki, S. (1990). Asian-American educational achievements: A phenomenon in search of an explanation. *American Psychologist, 45*(8), 913–920.

Sugarman, J. (1999). Ethical considerations in leaping from bench to bedside. *Science, 285,* 2071–2072.

Suicide: Part I. (1996, November). *The Harvard Mental Health Letter,* pp. 1–5.

Sullivan, P. (1994). Growth in membership of phys-ed lobby group sign of growing concern about children's fitness. *Canadian Medical Association Journal, 151,* 634–635.

Sullivan, P. F., Bulik, C. M., Fear, J. L., & Pickering, A. (1998). Outcome of anorexia nervosa: A case-control study. *American Journal of Psychiatry, 155,* 939–946.

Sullivan-Bolyai, J., Hull, H. F., Wilson, C., & Corey, L. (1983). Neonatal herpes simplex virus infection in King County, Washington. *Journal of the American Medical Association, 250,* 3059–3062.

Suomi, S., & Harlow, H. (1972). Social rehabilitation of isolate-reared monkeys. *Developmental Psychology, 6,* 487–496.

Supreme Court ruling a victory for South Carolina's children. (1998, May 26). South Carolina Attorney General's Office. Retrieved June 26, 1998, from http://scattorneygeneral.org

Susman-Stillman, A., Kalkoske, M., Egeland, B., & Waldman, I. (1996). Infant temperament and maternal sensitivity as predictors of attachment security. *Infant Behavior and Development, 19,* 33–47.

Sutherland, N. (2000). *Children in English-Canadian society: Framing the twentieth-century consensus.* Waterloo, ON: Wilfrid Laurier University Press.

Suzuki, D. (2001). The nature of things. In H. Newbold (Ed.), *Life stories: World renowned scientists reflect on their lives and the future of life on earth* (pp. 55–73). Berkeley, CA: University of California Press.

Suzuki, L. A., & Valencia, R. R. (1997). Race-ethnicity and measured intelligence: Educational implications. *American Psychologist, 52,* 1103–1114.

Swain, I. U., Zelazo, P. R., & Clifton, R. K. (1993). Newborn infants' memory for speech sounds retained over 24 hours. *Developmental Psychology, 29,* 312–323.

Swain, M., & Lapkin, S. (1991). Additive bilingualism and French immersion education: The roles of language proficiency and literacy. In A. G. Reynolds (Ed.), *Bilingualism, multiculturalism, and second language learning: The McGill conference in honour of Wallace E. Lambert* (pp. 203–216). Hillsdale, NJ: Lawrence Erlbaum Associates.

Swanston, H. Y., Tebbutt, J. S., O'Toole, B. I., & Oates, R. K. (1997). Sexually abused children 5 years after presentation: A case-control study. *Pediatrics, 100,* 600–608.

Swarr, A. E., & Richards, M. H. (1996). Longitudinal effects of adolescent girls' pubertal development, perceptions of pubertal timing, and parental relations on eating problems. *Developmental Psychology, 32,* 636–646.

Swedo, S., Rettew, D. C., Kuppenheimer, M., Lum, D., Dolan, S., & Goldberger, E. (1991). Can adolescent suicide attemptors be distinguished from at-risk adolescents? *Pediatrics, 88*(3), 620–629.

Symons, D. (1978). *Play and aggression: A study of rhesus monkeys.* New York: Columbia University Press.

Symons, D. K. & Clark, S. E. (2000). A longitudinal study of mother–child relationships and theory of mind in the preschool period. *Social Development, 9,* 3–23.

Symons, D. K. (1998). Post-partum employment patterns, family-based care arrangements, and the mother–infant relationship at age two. *Canadian Journal of Behavioural Science, 30,* 121–131.

Symons, D., & Carr, T. (1995). Maternal employment and early infant social development: Process and policy. In K. Covell (Ed.), *Readings in child development: A Canadian perspective.* Toronto: Nelson Canada.

Szatmari, P. (1999). Heterogeneity and the genetics of autism. *Journal of Psychiatry and Neuroscience, 24,* 159–165.

Szkrybalo, J., & Ruble, D. N. (1999). "God made me a girl": Sex category constancy judgments and explanations revisited. *Developmental Psychology, 35,* 392–403.

Taddio, A., Katz, J., Ilersich, A. L., & Koren, G. (1997). Effect of neonatal circumcision on pain response during subsequent routine vaccination. *Lancet, 349,* 599–603.

Taddio, A., Nulman, L., Goldbach, M., Ipp, M., & Koren, G. (1994). Use of lidocain-prilocain cream for vaccination pain in infants. *Journal of Pediatrics, 124,* 643–648.

Takanishi, R. (1993). The opportunities of adolescence: Research, interventions, and policy. *American Psychologist, 48,* 85–87.

Tanda, G., Pontieri, F. E., & DiChiara, G. (1997). Cannabinoid and heroin activation of mesolimbic dopamine transmission by a common N1 opiod receptor mechanism. *Science, 276,* 2048–2050.

Tanner, J. M. (1978). *Fetus into man: Physical growth from conception to maturity.* Cambridge, MA: Harvard University Press.

Tao, K.-T. (1998). An overview of only child family mental health in China. *Psychiatry and Clinical Neurosciences, 52*(Suppl.), S206–S211.

Tardif, T. (1996). Nouns are not always learned before verbs: Evidence from Mandarin speakers' early vocabularies. *Developmental Psychology, 32,* 492–504.

Taylor, H. S., Arici, A., Olive, D., & Igarashi, P. (1998). HOXA10 is expressed in response to sex steroids at the time of implantation in the human endometrium. *Journal of Clinical Investigation, 101,* 1379–1384.

Taylor, J. A., Krieger, J. W., Reay, D. T., Davis, R. L., Harruff, R., & Cheney, L. K. (1996). Prone sleep position and the sudden infant death syndrome in King's County, Washington: A case-control study. *Journal of Pediatrics, 128,* 626–630.

Taylor, J. H., & Walker, L. J. (1997). Moral climate and the development of moral reasoning: The effects of dyadic discussions between young offenders. *Journal of Moral Education, 26*(1), 21–43.

Taylor, M. (1997). The role of creative control and culture in children's fantasy/reality judgments. *Child Development, 68,* 1015–1017.

Taylor, M. G. (1996). The development of children's beliefs about social and biological aspects of gender differences. *Child Development, 67,* 1555–1571.

Taylor, M., & Carlson, S. M. (1997). The relation between individual differences in fantasy and theory of mind. *Child Development, 68,* 436–455.

Taylor, M., Cartwright, B. S., & Carlson, S. M. (1993). A developmental investigation of children's imaginary companions. *Developmental Psychology, 28,* 276–285.

Taylor, R. D., & Roberts, D. (1995). Kinship support in maternal and adolescent well-being in economically disadvantaged African-American families. *Child Development, 66,* 1585–1597.

Teachman, J. D., Paasch, K., & Carver, K. (1996). Social capital and dropping out of school early. *Journal of Marriage and the Family, 58,* 773–783.

Teen sex down, new study shows: Secretary Shalala announces new teen pregnancy prevention grant programs

[Press release]. (1997, May 1). Washington, DC: National Center for Health Statistics.

Teller, D. Y., & Bornstein, M. H. (1987). Infant color vision and color perception. In P. Salapatek & L. B. Cohen (Eds.), *Handbook of infant perception: Vol. 1. From sensation to perception* (pp. 185–236). Orlando, FL: Academic Press.

Temple, J. A., Reynolds, A. J., & Miedel, W. T. (2000). Can early intervention prevent high school dropout? Evidence from the Chicago Child–Parent Centers. *Urban Education, 35*(1), 31–57.

Terman, L. M., & Oden, M. H. (1959). *Genetic studies of genius: Vol. 5. The gifted group at mid-life.* Stanford, CA: Stanford University Press.

Termine, N. T., & Izard, C. E. (1988). Infants' responses to their mothers' expressions of joy and sadness. *Developmental Psychology, 24,* 223–229.

Terry, D. (1996, August 17). In Wisconsin, a rarity of a fetal-harm case: Attempted-murder charges for alcoholic. *New York Times,* p. 6.

Tesman, J. R., & Hills, A. (1994). Developmental effects of lead exposure in children. *Social Policy Report of the Society for Research in Child Development, 8*(3), 1–16.

Test-tube baby: It's a girl. (1978, August 7). *Time,* p. 68.

Teti, D. M., & Ablard, K. E. (1989). Security of attachment and infant–sibling relationships: A laboratory study. *Child Development, 60,* 1519–1528.

Teti, D. M., Gelfand, D. M., Messinger, D. S., & Isabella, R. (1995). Maternal depression and the quality of early attachment: An examination of infants, preschoolers, and their mothers. *Developmental Psychology, 31,* 364–376.

Teti, D. M., Sakin, J. W., Kucera, E., Corns, K. M., & Eiden, R. D. (1996). And baby makes four: Predictors of attachment security among preschool-age firstborns during the transition to siblinghood. *Child Development, 67,* 579–596.

Thacker, S. B., Addiss, D. G., Goodman, R. A., Holloway, B. R., & Spencer, H. C. (1992). Infectious diseases and injuries in child day care: Opportunities for healthier children. *Journal of the American Medical Association, 268,* 1720–1726.

Thal, D., Tobias, S., & Morrison, D. (1991). Language and gesture in late talkers: A one-year follow-up. *Journal of Speech and Hearing Research, 34,* 604–612.

Tharp, R. G. (1989). Psychocultural variables and constants: Effects on teaching and learning in schools. *American Psychologist, 44,* 349–359.

The Canadian Early and Mid-Trimester Amniocentesis Trial (CEMAT) Group. (1998). Randomized trial to assess safety and fetal outcome of early and midtrimester amniocentesis. *Lancet, 351,* 242–247.

The first test-tube baby. (1978, July 31). *Time,* pp. 58–70.

The John Howard Society of Newfoundland. (1998). *Youth and the criminal justice system: Some highlights of youth crime and the treatment of young offenders in Canada.* St. John's, NF: Author.

Thelen, E. (1994). Three-month-old infants can learn task-specific patterns of interlimb coordination. *Psychological Science, 5,* 280–285.

Thelen, E. (1995). Motor development: A new synthesis. *American Psychologist, 50*(2), 79–95.

Thelen, E., & Fisher, D. M. (1982). Newborn stepping: An explanation for a "disappearing" reflex. *Developmental Psychology, 18,* 760–775.

Thelen, E., & Fisher, D. M. (1983). The organization of spontaneous leg movements in newborn infants. *Journal of Motor Behavior, 15,* 353–377.

Thomas, A., & Chess, S. (1977). *Temperament and development.* New York: Brunner/Mazel.

Thomas, A., & Chess, S. (1984). Genesis and evolution of behavioral disorders: From infancy to early adult life. *American Journal of Orthopsychiatry, 141*(1), 1–9.

Thomas, A., Chess, S., & Birch, H. G. (1968). *Temperament and behavior disorders in children.* New York: New York University Press.

Thomas, R. M. (1996). *Comparing theories of child development* (4th ed.). Pacific Grove, CA: Brooks-Cole.

Thomas, W. P., & Collier, V. P. (1997). *School effectiveness for language minority students.* Washington, DC: National Clearinghouse for Bilingual Education.

Thomas, W. P., & Collier, V. P. (1998). Two languages are better than one. *Educational Leadership, 55*(4), 23–28.

Thompson, D. C., Rivara, F. P., & Thompson, R. S. (1996). Effectiveness of bicycle safety helmets in preventing head injuries: A case-control study. *Journal of the American Medical Association, 276,* 1968–1973.

Thompson, L. A., Goodman, D. C., & Little, G. A. (2002). Is more neonatal intensive care always better? Insights from a cross-national comparison of reproductive care. *Pediatrics, 109,* 1036–1043.

Thompson, R. A. (1990). Vulnerability in research: A developmental perspective on research risk. *Child Development, 61,* 1–16.

Thompson, R. A. (1991). Emotional regulation and emotional development. *Educational Psychology Review, 3,* 269–307.

Thompson, R. A. (1998). Early sociopersonality development. In W. Damon (Series Ed.) & N. Eisenberg (Vol. Ed.), *Handbook of child psychology: Vol. 3. Social, emotional, and personality development* (4th ed., pp. 25–104). New York: Wiley.

Thomson M. (1990). Heavy birthweight in native Indians of British Columbia. *Canadian Journal of Public Health, 81,* 443–6.

Thorne, A., & Michaelieu, Q. (1996). Situating adolescent gender and self-esteem with personal memories. *Child Development, 67,* 1374–1390.

Tiedemann, D. (1897). *Beobachtungen über die entwickelung der seelenfähigkeiten bei kindern* [Record of an infant's life]. Altenburg, Germany: Oscar Bonde. (Original work published 1787)

Timiras, P. S. (1972). *Developmental psychology and aging.* New York: Macmillan.

TIMSS International Study Center. (1998). *Mathematics and achievement in the final year of secondary school: IEA's Third International Mathematics and Science Report.* Chestnut Hill, MA: Author.

Tincoff, R., & Jusczyk, P. W. (1999). Some beginnings of word comprehension in 6-month-olds. *Psychological Science, 10,* 172–177.

Tisak, M. S., & Tisak, J. (1996). My sibling's but not my friend's keeper: Reasoning about responses to aggressive acts. *Journal of Early Adolescence, 16,* 324–329.

Tisdale, S. (1988). The mother. *Hippocrates, 2*(3), 64–72.

Tong, S., Baghurst, P. A., Sawyer, M. G., Burns, J., & McMichael, A. J. (1998). Declining blood lead levels and changes in cognitive function during childhood: The Port Pirie Cohort Study. *Journal of the American Medical Association, 280,* 1915–1919.

Tonkin, R. S. (2002). Marijuana use in adolescence. *Paediatrics and Child Health, 7,* 73–75.

Torrance, E. P. (1966). *The Torrance Tests of Creative Thinking: Technical-norms* manual (Research ed.). Princeton, NJ: Personnel Press.

Torrance, E. P. (1974). *The Torrance Tests of Creative Thinking: Technical-norms manual.* Bensonville, IL: Scholastic Testing Service.

Torrance, E. P., & Ball, O. E. (1984). *Torrance Tests of Creative Thinking: Streamlined (revised) manual, Figural A and B.* Bensonville, IL: Scholastic Testing Service.

Towner, D., Castro, M. A., Eby-Wilkens, E., & Gilbert, W. M. (1999). Effect of mode of delivery in nulliparous women on neonatal intracranial injury. *New England Journal of Medicine, 341,* 1709–1714.

Townsend, N. W. (1997). Men, migration, and households in Botswana: An exploration of connections over time and space. *Journal of Southern African Studies, 23,* 405–420.

Trainor, C., & Mihorean, K. (Eds.). (2001). *Family violence in Canada: A statistical profile.* Ottawa: Canadian Centre for Justice Statistics and Statistics Canada.

Tramontana, M. G., Hooper, S. R., & Selzer, S. C. (1988). Research on the preschool prediction of later academic achievement: A review. *Developmental Review, 8,* 89–146.

Tremblay, M. S., & Willms, J. D. (2000). Secular trends in the body mass index of Canadian children. *Canadian Medical Association Journal, 163,* 1429–1433.

Tremblay, R. E., Boulerice, B., Harden, P. W., McDuff, P., Perusse, D., Pihl, R. O., & Zoccolillo, M. (1996). Do children in Canada become more aggressive as they approach adolescence? In Human Resources Development Canada & Statistics Canada, *Growing up in Canada: National Longitudinal Survey of Children and Youth.* Ottawa: Author.

Trocmé, N., & Wolfe, D. (2001). *Child maltreatment in Canada: Selected results from the Canadian Incidence Study of Reported Child Abuse and Neglect.* Ottawa: Minister of Public Works and Government Services Canada.

Trocmé, N., MacLaurin, B., Fallon, B., Daciuk, J., Billingsley, D., Tourigny, M., Mayer, M., Wright, J., Barter, K., Burford, G., Hornick, J., Sullivan, R., & McKenzie, B. (2001). *Canadian incidence study of reported child abuse and neglect: Final report.* Ottawa: Health Canada.

Tronick, E. (1972). Stimulus control and the growth of the infant's visual field. *Perception and Psychophysics, 11,* 373–375.

Tronick, E. Z. (1980). On the primacy of social skills. In D. B. Sawin, L. O. Walker, & J. H. Penticuff (Eds.), *The exceptional infant: Psychosocial risk in infant environment transactions.* New York: Brunner/Mazel.

Tronick, E. Z. (1989). Emotions and emotional communication in infants. *American Psychologist, 44*(2), 112–119.

Tronick, E. Z., Frank, D. A., Cabral, H., Mirochnick, M., & Zuckerman, B. (1996). Late dose-response effects of prenatal cocaine exposure on newborn neurobehavioral performance. *Pediatrics, 98,* 76–83.

Tronick, E. Z., Morelli, G. A., & Ivey, P. (1992). The Efe forager infant and toddler's pattern of social relationships: Multiple and simultaneous. *Developmental Psychology, 28,* 568–577.

Troseth, G. L., & DeLoache, J. S. (1998). The medium can obscure the message: Young children's understanding of video. *Child Development, 69,* 950–965.

Trost, S. G., Pate, R. R., Dowda, M., Saunders, R., Ward, D. S., & Felton, G. (1996). Gender differences in physical activity and determinants of physical activity in rural fifth grade children. *Journal of School Health, 66,* 145–150.

Trottier, G., Srivastava, L., & Walker, C. (1999). Etiology of infantile autism: A review of recent advances in genetic and neurobiological research. *Journal of Psychiatry and Neuroscience, 24,* 103–115.

Tucker, C. J., Barber, B. L., & Eccles, J. S. (1997). Advice about life plans and personal problems in late adolescent sibling relationships. *Journal of Youth and Adolescence, 26,* 63–76.

Turner, C. F., Ku, L., Rogers, S. M., Lindberg, L. D., Pleck, J. H., & Sonenstein, F. L. (1998). Adolescent sexual behavior, drug use, and violence: Increased reporting with computer survey technology. *Science, 280,* 867–873.

Turner, P. H., Scadden, L., & Harris, M. B. (1990). Parenting in gay and lesbian families. *Journal of Gay and Lesbian Psychotherapy, 1,* 55-66.

Turner, P. J., & Gervai, J. (1995). A multidimensional study of gender typing in preschool children and their parents: Personality, attitudes, preferences, behavior, and cultural differences. *Developmental Psychology, 31,* 759–772.

Tyson, H. (1991). Outcomes of 1001 midwife-attended home births in Toronto, 1983–1988. *Birth, 18,* 14–19.

Tzuriel, D. (2001). *Dynamic assessment of young children.* New York: Kluwer Academic/Plenum.

U.S. Bureau of the Census. (1993). *Statistics on characteristics of single-parent households.* Washington, DC: Author.

U.S. Bureau of the Census. (1995). *Statistical Abstract of the United States* (155th ed.). Washington, DC: U.S. Government Printing Office.

U.S. Bureau of the Census. (1998). *Household and family characteristics: March 1998* (Update) (Current Population Reports, P20-514). Washington, DC: U.S. Government Printing Office.

U.S. Bureau of the Census. (1999). World population profile: 1998—Highlights. Retrieved September 24, 2002, from http://www.census.gov/ipc/www/wp98001.html

U.S. Commission on Child and Family Welfare. (1996). *Parenting our children: In the best interest of the nation.* Washington, DC: U.S. Government Printing Office.

U.S. Consumer Product Safety Commission. (1991). *Statistics on shopping cart safety.* Washington, DC: Author.

U.S. Department of Commerce. (1996). *Statistical abstract of the United States, 1996.* Washington, DC: U.S. Government Printing Office.

U.S. Department of Education. (1992). *Dropout rates in the U.S., 1991* (Publication No. NCES 92–129). Washington, DC: U.S. Government Printing Office.

U.S. Department of Education. (1996). *National Center for Education Statistics: Schools and staffing in the United States: A statistical profile, 1993–94* (NCES 96–124). Washington, DC: Author.

U.S. Department of Health and Human Services (USDHHS). (1990). *Health, United States, 1989* (DHHS Publication

No. PHS 90–1232). Washington, DC: U.S. Government Printing Office.

U.S. Department of Health and Human Services (USDHHS). (1996a). *Health, United States, 1995* (DHHS Publication No. PHS 96–1232). Washington, DC: U.S. Government Printing Office.

U.S. Department of Health and Human Services (USDHHS). (1996). *HHS releases study of relationship between family structure and adolescent substance abuse* [Press release]. Retrieved September 24, 2002, from http://www.hhs.gov/news/press/1996pres/960906b.html

U.S. Department of Health and Human Services (USDHHS). (1999a). *Blending perspectives and building common ground: A report to Congress on substance abuse and child protection.* Washington, DC: U.S. Government Printing Office.

U.S. Department of Health and Human Services (USDHHS). (1999b). *Healthy People 2000 Review* (PHS 99–1256). Washington, DC: Author.

U.S. Department of Health and Human Services (USDHHS). (1999b). *Mental health: A report of the surgeon general.* Rockville, MD: U.S. Department of HHS, Substance Abuse and Mental Health Services Administration, NIH, NIMH.

U.S. Department of Health and Human Services (USDHHS). (2000, April 10). HHS reports new child abuse and neglect statistics. HHS NEWS. Retrieved April 13, 2000, from http://www.hhs.gov/news/press/2000pres/20000410.html

U.S. Environmental Protection Agency. (1994). *Setting the record straight: Secondhand smoke is a preventable health risk* (EPA Publication No. 402-F-94-005). Washington, DC: U.S. Government Printing Office.

Umberger, F. G., & Van Reenen, J. S. (1995). Thumb sucking management: A review. *International Journal of Orofacial Myology, 21,* 41–47.

UNICEF. (1992). *State of the world's children.* New York: Oxford University Press.

UNICEF. (1996). *State of the world's children.* New York: Oxford University Press.

Upjohn Company. (1984). *Writer's guide to sex and health.* Kalamazoo, MI: Author.

Vainio, S., Heikkiia, M., Kispert, A., Chin, N., & McMahon, A. P. (1999). Female development in mammals is regulated by Wnt-4 signalling. *Nature, 397,* 405–409.

Van den Boom, D. C. (1989). Neonatal irritability and the development of attachment. In G. A. Kohnstamm, J. E. Bates, & M. K. Rothbart (Eds.), *Temperament in childhood* (pp. 299–318). Chichester, England: Wiley.

Van den Boom, D. C. (1994). The influence of temperament and mothering on attachment and exploration: An experimental manipulation of sensitive responsiveness among lower-class mothers with irritable infants. *Child Development, 65,* 1457–1477.

Van Dyck, J. (1995). *Manufacturing babies and public consent: Debating the new reproductive technologies.* New York: New York University Press.

van IJzendoorn, M. H. (1995). Adult attachment representations, parental responsiveness, and infant attachment: A meta-analysis on the predictive validity of the Adult Attachment Interview. *Psychological Bulletin, 117*(3), 387–403.

van IJzendoorn, M. H., & Kroonenberg, P. M. (1988). Cross-cultural patterns of attachment: A meta-analysis of the strange situation. *Child Development, 59,* 147–156.

van IJzendoorn, M. H., & Sagi, A. (1997). Cross-cultural patterns of attachment: Universal and contextual dimensions. In J. Cassidy & P. Shaver (Eds.), *Handbook on attachment theory and research.* New York: Guilford Press.

van IJzendoorn, M. H., & Sagi, A. (1999). Cross-cultural patterns of attachment: Universal and contextual dimensions. In J. Cassidy & P. R. Shaver (Eds.), *Handbook of attachment: Theory, research, and clinical applications* (pp. 713–734). New York: Guilford.

Vance, M. L., & Mauras, N. (1999). Growth hormone therapy in adults and children. *New England Journal of Medicine, 341*(16), 1206–1216.

Vandell, D. L., & Bailey, M. D. (1992). Conflicts between siblings. In C. U. Shantz & W. W. Hartup (Eds.), *Conflict in child and adolescent development* (pp. 242–269). New York: Cambridge University Press.

Vandell, D. L., & Ramanan, J. (1992). Effects of early and recent maternal employment on children from low-income families. *Child Development, 63,* 938–949.

Vargha-Khadem, F., Gadian, D. G., Watkins, K. E., Connelly, A., Van Paesschen, W., & Mishkin, M. (1997). Differential effects of early hippocampal pathology on episodic and semantic memory. *Science, 277,* 376–380.

Vartanian, L. R., & Powlishta, K. K. (1996). A longitudinal examination of the social-cognitive foundations of adolescent egocentrism. *Journal of Early Adolescence, 16,* 157–178.

Vaughn, B. E., Stevenson-Hinde, J., Waters, E., Kotsaftis, A., Lefever, G. B., Shouldice, A., Trudel, M., & Belsky, J. (1992). Attachment security and temperament in infancy and early childhood: Some conceptual clarifications. *Developmental Psychology, 28,* 463–473.

Velting, D. M., Shaffer, D., Gould, M. S., Garfinkel, R., Fisher, P., & Davies, M. (1998). Parent–victim agreement in adolescent suicide research. *Journal of the American Academy of Child & Adolescent Psychiatry, 37,* 1161–1166.

Venter, J. C., Adams, M. D., Myers, E. W., Li, P. W., Mural, R. J., Sutton, G. G., Smith, H. O., Yandall, M., Evans, C. A., & Holt, R. A. (2001). The sequence of the human genome. *Science, 291,* 1304–1351.

Ventura, S. J., & Bachrach, C. A. (2000). Nonmarital childbearing in the United States, 1940–99. *National Vital Statistics Reports, 48*(16). Hyattsville, MD: National Center for Health Statistics.

Ventura, S. J., Curtin, S. C., & Mathews, T. J. (2000). Variations in teenage birth rates, 1991–1998: National and state trends. *National Vital Statistics Reports, 48*(6). Hyattsville, MD: National Center for Health Statistics.

Ventura, S. J., Martin, J. A., Curtin, S. C., & Mathews, T. J. (1998). *Report of final natality statistics, 1996 (Monthly Vital Statistics Report, 46*[11, Suppl.]). Hyattsville, MD: National Center for Health Statistics.

Ventura, S. J., Martin, J. A., Curtin, S. C., & Mathews, T. J. (1999). *Births: Final data for 1997 (National Vital Statistics Reports, 47*[18]). Hyattsville, MD: National Center for Health Statistics.

Ventura, S. J., Matthews, T. J., & Curtin, S. C. (1999). Declines in teenage birth rates 1991–1998: Update of national and state trends. *National Vital Statistics Reports, 47*(6). Hyattsville, MD: National Center for Health Statistics.

Vereecken, C., & Maes, L. (2000). Eating habits, dental care and dieting. In C. Currie, K. Hurrelmann, W.

Settertobulte, R. Smith, & J. Todd (Eds.), *Health and health behaviour among young people: A WHO cross-national Study (HBSC) international report* (pp. 83–96). WHO Policy Series: Healthy Policy for Children and Adolescents, Series No. 1.

Verloove-Vanhorick, S. P., Veen, S., Ens-Dokkum, M. H., Schreuder, A. M., Brand, R., & Ruys, R. H. (1994). Sex differences in disability and handicap at five years of age in children born at very short gestation. *Pediatrics, 93,* 576–579.

Verschueren, K., Marcoen, A., & Schoefs, V. (1996). The internal working model of the self, attachment, and competence in five-year-olds. *Child Development, 67,* 2493–2511.

Vgontzas, A. N., & Kales, A. (1999). Sleep and its disorders. *Annual Review of Medicine, 50,* 387–400.

Vitaro, F., Tremblay, R. E., Kerr, M., Pagani, L., & Bukowski, W. M. (1997). Disruptiveness, friends' characteristics, and delinquency in early adolescence: A test of two competing models of development. *Child Development, 68,* 676–689.

von Kries, R., Koletzko, B., Sauerwald, T., von Mutius, E., Barnert, T., Grunert, V., & von Voss, H. (1999). Breast feeding and obesity: Cross-sectional study. *British Medical Journal, 319,* 147–150.

Vosniadou, S. (1987). Children and metaphors. *Child Development, 58,* 870–885.

Vuchinich, S., Angelelli, J., & Gatherum, A. (1996). Context and development in family problem solving with preadolescent children. *Child Development, 67,* 1276–1288.

Vuori, L., Christiansen, N., Clement, J., Mora, J., Wagner, M., & Herrera, M. (1979). Nutritional supplementation and the outcome of pregnancy: 2. Visual habitation at 15 days. *Journal of Clinical Nutrition, 32,* 463–469.

Vygotsky, L. S. (1956). *Selected psychological investigations.* Moscow: Izdstel'sto Akademii Pedagogicheskikh Nauk USSR.

Vygotsky, L. S. (1962). *Thought and language.* Cambridge, MA: MIT Press. (Original work published 1934)

Vygotsky, L. S. (1978). *Mind in society: The development of higher psychological processes.* Cambridge, MA: Harvard University Press.

Wagner, C. L., Katikaneni, L. D., Cox, T. H., & Ryan, R. M. (1998). The impact of prenatal drug exposure on the neonate. *Obstetrics and Gynecology Clinics of North America, 25,* 169–194.

Wakefield, M., Reid, Y., Roberts, L., Mullins, R., & Gillies, P. (1998). Smoking and smoking cessation among men whose partners are pregnant: A qualitative study. *Social Science and Medicine, 47,* 657–664.

Wakschlag, L. S., Lahey, B. B., Loeber, R., Green, S. M., Gordon, R. A., & Leventhal, B. L. (1997). Maternal smoking during pregnancy and the risk of conduct disorder in boys. *Archives of General Psychiatry, 54,* 670–676.

Waldman, I. D. (1996). Aggressive boys' hostile perceptual and response biases: The role of attention and impulsivity. *Child Development, 67,* 1015–1033.

Walk, R. D., & Gibson, E. J. (1961). A comparative and analytical study of visual depth perception. *Psychological Monographs, 75*(15), 44.

Walker, D., Greenwood, C., Hart, B., & Carta, J. (1994). Prediction of school outcomes based on early language production and socioeconomic factors. *Child Development, 65,* 606–621.

Walker, L. J., & Hennig, K. H. (1997). Parent/child relationships in single-parent families. *Canadian Journal of Behavioural Science, 29,* 63–75.

Walker, L. J., & Taylor, J. H. (1991). Family interactions and the development of moral reasoning. *Child Development, 62,* 264–283.

Wallach, M. A., & Kogan, M. (1965). *Modes of thinking in young children: A study of the creativity-intelligence distinction.* New York: Holt.

Wallerstein, J. S. (1983). Children of divorce: The psychological tasks of the child. *American Journal of Orthopsychiatry, 53,* 230–243.

Wallerstein, J. S., & Kelly, J. B. (1980). *Surviving the break-up: How children actually cope with divorce.* New York: Basic Books.

Ward, L. M., & Rivadeneyra, R. (1999). Contributions of entertainment television to adolescents' sexual attitudes and expectations: The roles of viewing amount versus viewer involvement. *Journal of Sex Research, 36,* 237–249.

Ward, M. (1998). *The family dynamic: A Canadian perspective* (2nd ed.). Toronto: ITP Nelson.

Wasik, B. H., Ramey, C. T., Bryant, D. M., & Sparling, J. J. (1990). A longitudinal study of two early intervention strategies: Project CARE *Child Development, 61,* 1682–1696.

Waters, E., & Deane, K. E. (1985). Defining and assessing individual differences in attachment relationships: Q-methodology and the organization of behavior in infancy and early childhood. *Monographs of the Society for Research in Child Development, 50,* 41–65.

Waters, E., Wippman, J., & Sroufe, L. A. (1979). Attachment, positive affect, and competence in the peer group: Two studies in construct validation. *Child Development, 50,* 821–829.

Waters, K. A., Gonzalez, A., Jean, C., Morielli, A., & Brouillette, R. T. (1996). Face-straight-down and face-near-straight-down positions in healthy prone-sleeping infants. *Journal of Pediatrics, 128,* 616–625.

Watson, A. C., Nixon, C. L., Wilson, A., & Capage, L. (1999). Social interaction skills and theory of mind in young children. *Developmental Psychology, 35*(2), 386–391.

Watson, J. B., & Rayner, R. (1920). Conditioned emotional reactions. *Journal of Experimental Psychology, 3,* 1–14.

Weathers, W. T., Crane, M. M., Sauvain, K. J., & Blackhurst, D. W. (1993). Cocaine use in women from defined populations: Prevalence at delivery and effects on growth in infants. *Pediatrics, 91,* 350–354.

Webb, M. (1991). *David Suzuki: Superstar of science.* Mississauga, ON: Copp Clark Pitman.

Wechsler, D. (1996). *Wechsler Intelligence Scale for Children–III. Canadian manual supplement.* Toronto: The Psychological Corporation.

Wegman, M. E. (1992). Annual summary of vital statistics: 1991. *Pediatrics, 90,* 835–845.

Wegman, M. E. (1994). Annual summary of vital statistics: 1993. *Pediatrics, 94,* 792–803.

Wegman, M. E. (1999). Foreign aid, international organizations, and the world's children. *Pediatrics, 103*(3), 646–654.

Weinberg, M. K., & Tronick, E. Z. (1996). Infant affective reactions to the resumption of maternal interaction after still face. *Child Development, 67,* 905–914.

Weinberg, M. K., Tronick, E. Z., Cohn, J. F., & Olson, K. L. (1999). Gender differences in emotional expressivity and self-regulation during early infancy. *Developmental Psychology, 35*(1), 175–188.

Weinberg, R. A. (1989). Intelligence and IQ: Landmark issues and great debates. *American Psychologist, 44*(2), 98–104.

Weinberger, B., Anwar, M., Hegyi, T., Hiatt, M., Koons, A., & Paneth, N. (2000). Antecedents and neonatal consequences of low Apgar scores in preterm newborns. *Archives of Pediatric and Adolescent Medicine, 154*, 294–300.

Weinman, J. (1998). Do public schools shortchange girls on educational opportunities? *Insight, 14*(46), 24–26.

Weisner, T. S. (1993). Ethnographic and ecocultural perspectives on sibling relationships. In Z. Stoneman & P. W. Berman (Eds.), *The effects of mental retardation, visibility, and illness on sibling relationships* (pp. 51–83). Baltimore, MD: Brooks.

Weiss, B., Dodge, K. A., Bates, J. E., & Pettit, G. S. (1992). Some consequences of early harsh discipline: Child aggression and a maladaptive social information processing style. *Child Development, 63*, 1321–1335.

Weiss, L. G., Saklofske, D. H., Prifitera, A., Chen, H.-Y., & Hildebrand, D. (1999). The calculation of the WISC–III general ability index using Canadian norms. *Canadian Journal of School Psychology, 14*, 1–9.

Weissman, M. M., Warner, V., Wickramaratne, P. J., & Kandel, D. B. (1999). Maternal smoking during pregnancy and psychopathology in offspring followed to adulthood. *Journal of the American Academy of Child and Adolescent Psychiatry, 38*, 892–899.

Weisz, J. R., Weiss, B., Han, S. S., Granger, D. A., & Morton, T. (1995). Effects of psychotherapy with children and adolescents revisited: A meta-analysis of treatment outcome studies. *Psychological Bulletin, 117*(3), 450–468.

Weitzman, M., Gortmaker, S., & Sobol, A. (1992). Maternal smoking and behavior problems of children. *Pediatrics, 90*, 342–349.

Welch-Ross, M. K. (1997). Mother–child participation in conversation about the past: Relationships to preschoolers' theory of mind. *Developmental Psychology, 33*(4), 618–629.

Welch-Ross, M. K., & Schmidt, C. R. (1996). Gender-schema development and children's story memory: Evidence for a developmental model. *Child Development, 67*, 820–835.

Wellman, H. M., & Gelman, S. A. (1998). Knowledge acquisition in foundational domains. In W. Damon (Series Ed.), D. Kuhn, & R. S. Siegler (Vol. Eds.), *Handbook of child psychology: Vol. 2. Cognition, perception, and language* (5th ed., pp. 523–573). New York: Wiley.

Wellman, H. M., & Woolley, J. D. (1990). From simple desires to ordinary beliefs: The early development of everyday psychology. *Cognition, 35*, 245–275.

Wellman, H. M., Cross, D., & Bartsch, K. (1986). Infant search and object permanence: A meta-analysis of the A-not-B error. *Monographs of the Society for Research in Child Development, 51*(3, Serial No. 214).

Wells, G. (1985). Preschool literacy-related activities and success in school. In D. R. Olson, N. Torrence, & A. Hilyard (Eds.), *Literacy, language, and learning* (pp. 229–255). New York: Cambridge University Press.

Wen, S. W., Liu, S., Marcoux, S., & Fowler, D. (1998). Trends and variations in length of hospital stay for childbirth in Canada. *Canadian Medical Association Journal, 158*, 875–880.

Wen, S. W., Mery, L. S., Kramer, M. S., Jimenez, V., Trouton, K., Herbert, P., & Chalmers, B. (1999). Attitudes of Canadian women toward birthing centres and midwife care for childbirth. *Canadian Medical Association Journal, 161*, 708–709.

Wender, P. H. (1995). *Attention-deficit hyperactivity disorder in adults.* New York: Oxford University Press.

Werker, J. F. (1989). Becoming a native listener. *American Scientist, 77*, 54–59.

Werker, J. F., & Tees, R. C. (1999). Experiential influences on infant speech processing: Towards a new synthesis. In J. T. Spence, J. M. Darley, & D. J. Foss (Associate Eds.), *Annual Review of Psychology, 50* (pp. 509–535). Palo Alto, CA: Annual Reviews.

Werker, J. F., Cohen, L. B., Lloyd, V. L., Casasola, M., & Stager, C. L. (1998). Acquisition of word–object associations by 14-month-old infants. *Developmental Psychology, 34*, 1289–1309.

Werker, J. F., Pegg, J. E., & McLeod, P. J. (1994). A cross-language investigation of infant preference for infant-directed communication. *Infant Behavior and Development, 17*, 323–333.

Werler, M. M., Louik, C., Shapiro, S., & Mitchell, A. A. (1996). Prepregnant weight in relation to risk of neural tube defects. *Journal of the American Medical Association, 275*, 1089–1092.

Werner, E. E. (1985). Stress and protective factors in children's lives. In A. R. Nichol (Ed.), *Longitudinal studies in child psychology and psychiatry.* New York: Wiley.

Werner, E. E. (1987, July 15). *Vulnerability and resiliency: A longitudinal study of Asian Americans from birth to age 30.* Invited address at the Ninth Biennial Meeting of the International Society for the Study of Behavioral Development, Tokyo.

Werner, E. E. (1989). Children of the garden island. *Scientific American, 260*(4), 106–111.

Werner, E. E. (1993). Risk and resilience in individuals with learning disabilities: Lessons learned from the Kauai longitudinal study. *Learning Disabilities Research and Practice, 8*, 28–34.

Werner, E. E. (1995). Resilience in development. *Current Directions in Psychological Science, 4*(3), 81–85.

Werner, E., Bierman, L., French, F. E., Simonian, K., Conner, A., Smith, R., & Campbell, M. (1968). Reproductive and environmental casualties: A report on the 10-year follow-up of the children of the Kauai pregnancy study. *Pediatrics, 42*, 112–127.

West Berlin Human Genetics Institute. (1987). *Study on effects of nuclear radiation at Chernobyl on fetal development.* Berlin: Author.

Westen, D. (1998). The scientific legacy of Sigmund Freud: Toward a psychodynamically informed psychological science. *Psychological Bulletin, 124*, 333–371.

Whitaker, R. C., Wright, J. A., Pepe, M. S., Seidel, K. D., & Dietz, W. H. (1997). Predicting obesity in young adulthood from childhood and parental obesity. *New England Journal of Medicine, 337*, 869–873.

White, B. L. (1971, October). *Fundamental early environmental influences on the development of competence.* Paper presented at the Third Western Symposium on Learning: Cognitive Learning, Western Washington State College, Bellingham, WA.

White, B. L., Kaban, B., & Attanucci, J. (1979). *The origins of human competence.* Lexington, MA: Heath.

Whitehurst, G. J., & Lonigan, C. J. (1998). Child development and emergent literacy. *Child Development, 69*, 848–872.

Whitehurst, G. J., Falco, F. L., Lonigan, C. J., Fischel, J. E., DeBaryshe, B. D., Valdez-Menchaca, M. D., & Caufield,

M. (1988). Accelerating language development through picture book reading. *Developmental Psychology, 24,* 552–559.

Whitehurst, G. J., Zevenbergen, A. A., Crone, D. A., Schultz, M. D., Velting, O. N., and Fischel, J. E. (1999). Outcomes of an emergent literacy intervention from Head Start through second grade. *Journal of Educational Psychology, 91,* 261–272.

Whitrow, G. J. (1967). *Einstein: The man and his achievement.* New York: Dover.

WHO/UNICEF Constitution on HIV Transmission and Breastfeeding. (1992). Consensus statement from the WHO/UNICEF Constitution on HIV Transmission and Breastfeeding, Geneva. *Weekly Epidemiological Record, 67,* 177–184.

Wideman, R. (1990). *David Suzuki.* Markham, ON: Fitzhenry & Whiteside.

Widom, C. S. (1989). The cycle of violence. *Science, 244,* 160–166.

Wiencke, J. K., Thurston, S. W., Kelsey, K. T., Varkonyi, A., Wain, J. C., Mark, E. J., & Christiani, D. C. (1999). Early age at smoking initiation and tobacco carcinogen damage in the lung. *Journal of the National Cancer Institute, 91,* 614–619.

Wilcox, A. J., Baird, D. B., & Weinberg, C. R. (1999). Time of implantation of the conceptus and loss of pregnancy. *New England Journal of Medicine, 340,* 1796–1799.

Wilcox, A. J., Weinberg, C. R., & Baird, D. D. (1995). Timing of sexual intercourse in relation to ovulation: Effects on the probability of conception, survival of the pregnancy, and sex of the baby. *New England Journal of Medicine, 333,* 1563–1565.

Wilgosh, L., Meyer, M., & Mueller, H. H. (1996). Longitudinal study of effects on academic achievement for early and late age of school entry. *Canadian Journal of School Psychology, 11,* 43–51.

Williams, E. R., & Caliendo, M. A. (1984). *Nutrition: Principles, issues, and applications.* New York: McGraw-Hill.

Williams, J. E., & Best, D. L. (1982). *Measuring sex stereotypes: A thirty-nation study.* Beverly Hills, CA: Sage.

Williams, P. L., Innis, S. M., Vogel, A. M. P., & Stephen, L. J. (1999). Factors influencing infant feeding practices of mothers in Vancouver. *Canadian Journal of Public Health, 90,* 114–119.

Willinger, M., Hoffman, H. T., & Hartford, R. B. (1994). Infant sleep position and risk for sudden infant

death syndrome: Report of meeting held January 13 and 14, 1994. *Pediatrics, 93,* 814–819.

Willms, J. D. (1996). Indicators of mathematics achievement in Canadian elementary schools. In Human Resources Development Canada and Statistics Canada, *Growing up in Canada: National Longitudinal Survey of Children and Youth.* Catalogue No. 89-550-MPE, No. 1 (pp. 69-82). Ottawa: Author.

Wilson, A. (1996). *Heartbeat of the earth: A First Nations artist records injustice and resistance.* Gabriola Island, B.C.: New Society Publishers.

Wilson, B., & Steinman, C. (2000). *Hungercount 2000, a surplus of hunger: Canada's annual survey of emergency food programs.* Toronto: Canadian Association of Food Banks.

Wilson, B., & Tsoa, E. (2001). *Hungercount 2001, food bank lines in insecure times: Canada's annual survey of emergency food programs.* Toronto: Canadian Association of Food Banks.

Wilson, G., McCreary, R., Kean, J., & Baxter, J. (1979). The development of preschool children of heroin-addicted mothers: A controlled study. *Pediatrics, 63,* 135–141.

Wilson, R. J., & Martinussen, R. L. (1999). Factors affecting the assessment of student achievement. *The Alberta Journal of Educational Research, 45,* 267–277.

Winerip, M. (1999, January 3). Homework bound. *Education Life supplement to New York Times,* pp. 28–31, 40.

Winkleby, M. A., Robinson, T. N., Sundquist, J., & Kraemer, H. C. (1999). Ethnic variation in cardiovascular disease risk factors among children and young adults: Findings from the Third National Health and Nutrition Examination Survey, 1988–1994. *Journal of the American Medical Association, 281,* 1006–1013.

Winner, E. (1997). Exceptionally high intelligence and schooling. *American Psychologist, 52*(10), 1070–1081.

Winsler, A., Díaz, R. M., Espinosa, L., & Rodríguez, J. L. (1999). When learning a second language does not mean losing the first: Bilingual language development in low-income, Spanish-speaking children attending bilingual preschool. *Child Development, 70*(2), 349–362.

Winzer, M. A. (1996). *Children with exceptionalities in Canadian*

classrooms (4th ed.). Scarborough, ON: Allyn & Bacon.

Winzer, M. A. (1997). *Special education in early childhood: An inclusive approach.* Toronto: Allyn & Bacon.

Wittrock, M. C. (1980). Learning and the brain. In M. C. Wittrock (Ed.), *The brain and psychology.* New York: Academic Press.

Wolfe, D. A. (1985). Child-abusive parents: An empirical review and analysis. *Psychological Bulletin, 97*(3), 462–482.

Wolfe, D. A., Edwards, B., Manion, I., & Koverola, C. (1988). Early intervention for parents at risk of child abuse and neglect: A preliminary investigation. *Journal of Consulting and Clinical Psychology, 56,* 40–47.

Wolff, P. H. (1963). Observations on the early development of smiling. In B. M. Foss (Ed.), *Determinants of infant behavior* (Vol. 2). London: Methuen.

Wolff, P. H. (1966). The causes, controls, and organizations of behavior in the newborn. *Psychological Issues, 5* (1, Whole No. 17), 1–105.

Wolff, P. H. (1969). The natural history of crying and other vocalizations in early infancy. In B. M. Foss (Ed.), *Determinants of infant behavior* (Vol. 4). London: Methuen.

Wolff, R. (1993). *Good sports: The concerned parent's guide to Little League and other competitive youth sports.* New York: Dell.

Wolfinger, N. H. (1999, August 10). *Coupling and uncoupling: Changing marriage patterns and the intergenerational transmission of divorce.* Paper presented at the annual meeting of the American Sociological Association, Chicago.

Wolfson, A. R., & Carskadon, M. A. (1998). Sleep schedules and daytime functioning in adolescents. *Child Development, 69,* 875–887.

Wolraich, M. L., Lindgren, S. D., Stumbo, P. J., SteGink, L. D., Appelbaum, M. I., & Kiritsky, M. C. (1994). Effects of diets high in sucrose or aspartame on the behavior and cognitive performance of children. *New England Journal of Medicine, 330,* 301–307.

Wolraich, M. L., Wilson, D. B., & White, J. W. (1995). The effect of sugar on behavior or cognition in children: A meta-analysis. *Journal of the American Medical Association, 274*(20), 1617–1621.

Woman delivers a baby boy after refusing a caesarean. (1993, December 30). *New York Times*, p. A12.

Wood, D. (1980). Teaching the young child: Some relationships between social interaction, language, and thought. In D. Olson (Ed.), *The social foundations of language and thought*. New York: Norton.

Wood, D., Bruner, J., & Ross, G. (1976). The role of tutoring in problem solving. *Journal of Child Psychiatry and Psychology, 17,* 89–100.

Woodward, A. L., Markman, E. M., & Fitzsimmons, C. M. (1994). Rapid word learning in 13- and 18-month olds. *Developmental Psychology, 30,* 553–566.

Wooley, J. D., Phelps, K. E., Davis, D. L. and Mandell, D. J. (1999). Where theories of mind meet magic: The development of children's beliefs about wishing. *Child Development, 70,* 571–587.

Woolley, J. D. (1997). Thinking about fantasy: Are children fundamentally different thinkers and believers from adults? *Child Development, 68*(6), 991–1011.

Woolley, J. D., & Bruell, M. J. (1996). Young children's awareness of the origins of their mental representations. *Developmental Psychology, 32,* 335–346.

World Health Organization (WHO). (1996, May). *WHO Fact Sheet, 119,* pp. 1–3.

World Health Organization. (1997). Report on the global HIV/AIDS epidemic. Retrieved November 1997 from http://www.unaids.org/highband/document/epidemio/report97.html

Worswick, C. (2001). *School performance of the children of immigrants in Canada, 1994–1998*. Ottawa: Statistics Canada.

Wright, A. L., Holberg, C. J., Taussig, L. M., & Martinez, F. D. (1995). Relationship of infant feeding to recurrent wheezing at age 6 years. *Archives of Pediatric Adolescent Medicine, 149,* 758–763.

Wright, J. T., Waterson, E. J., Barrison, I. G., Toplis, P. J., Lewis, I. G., Gordon, M. G., MacRae, K. D., Morris, N. F., & Murray Lyon, I. M. (1983, March 26). Alcohol consumption, pregnancy, and low birth weight. *Lancet*, pp. 663–665.

Wright, M. J. (1999). The history of developmental psychology in Canada. *Canadian Journal of Research in Early Childhood Education, 8,* 31–36.

Wright, M. J. (2002). Flashbacks in the history of psychology in Canada: Some early "headline" makers. *Canadian Psychology, 43,* 21–34.

Wright, S. C., Taylor, D. M., & Ruggiero, K. M. (1996). Examining the potential for academic achievement among Inuit children: Comparisons on the Raven Coloured Progressive Matrices. *Journal of Cross-Cultural Psychology, 27,* 733–753.

WuDunn, S. (1996, March 23). Japan's single mothers face discrimination. *Cleveland Plain Dealer*, p. 5E.

WuDunn, S. (1997, January 14). Korean women still feel demands to bear a son. *New York Times (International Ed.)*, p. A3.

Wynn, K. (1992). Evidence against empiricist accounts of the origins of numerical knowledge. *Mind and Language, 7,* 315–332.

Yamazaki, J. N., & Schull, W. J. (1990). Perinatal loss and neurological abnormalities among children of the atomic bomb. *Journal of the American Medical Association, 264,* 605–609.

Yang, B., Ollendick, T. H., Dong, Q., Xia, Y., & Lin, L. (1995). Only children and children with siblings in the People's Republic of China: Levels of fear, anxiety, and depression. *Child Development, 66,* 1301–1311.

Yarrow, M. R. (1978, October). *Altruism in children.* Paper presented at program, Advances in Child Development Research, New York Academy of Sciences, New York, NY.

Yau, J., & Smetana, J. G. (1996). Adolescent–parent conflict among Chinese adolescents in Hong Kong. *Child Development, 67,* 1262–1275.

Yazigi, R. A., Odem, R. R., & Polakoski, K. L. (1991). Demonstration of specific binding of cocaine to human spermatozoa. *Journal of the American Medical Association, 266,* 1956–1959.

Yeung, W. J., Sandberg, J. F., Davis-Kean, P. E., & Hofferth, S. L. (2001). Children's time with fathers in intact families. *Journal of Marriage and Family, 63,* 136–154.

Yildirim, A. (1997). Gender role influences on Turkish adolescents' self-identity. *Adolescence, 32,* 217–231.

Yoshikawa, H. (1994). Prevention as cumulative protection: Effects of early family support and education on chronic delinquency and its risks. *Psychological Bulletin, 115*(1), 28–54.

Youngblade, L. M., & Belsky, J. (1992). Parent–child antecedents of 5-year-olds' close friendships: A longitudinal analysis. *Developmental Psychology, 28,* 700–713.

Youngstrom, N. (1992, January). Inner-city youth tell of life in "a war zone." *APA Monitor*, pp. 36–37.

Zabin, L. S., & Clark, S. D. (1983). Institutional factors affecting teenagers' choice and reasons for delay in attending a family planning clinic. *Family Planning Perspectives, 15,* 25–29.

Zahn-Waxler, C., Friedman, R. J., Cole, P. M., Mizuta, I., & Hiruma, N. (1996). Japanese and U.S. preschool children's responses to conflict and distress. *Child Development, 67,* 2462–2477.

Zahn-Waxler, C., Radke-Yarrow, M., Wagner, E., & Chapman, M. (1992). Development of concern for others. *Developmental Psychology, 28,* 126–136.

Zametkin, A. J. (1995). Attention-deficit disorder: Born to be hyperactive. *Journal of the American Medical Association, 273*(23), 1871–1874.

Zametkin, A. J., & Ernst, M. (1999). Problems in the management of Attention-Deficit-Hyperactivity Disorder. *New England Journal of Medicine, 340,* 40–46.

Zarbatany, L., Hartmann, D. P., & Rankin, D. B. (1990). The psychological functions of preadolescent peer activities. *Child Development, 61,* 1067–1080.

Zelazo, P. D., & Boseovski, J. J. (2001). Video reminders in a representational change task: Memory for cues but not beliefs or statements. *Journal of Experimental Child Psychology, 78,* 107–129.

Zelazo, P. D., Reznick, J. S., & Spinazzola, J. (1998). Representational flexibility and response control in a multistep, multilocation search task. *Developmental Psychology, 34,* 203–214.

Zelazo, P. R., Kearsley, R. B., & Stack, D. M. (1995). Mental representations for visual sequences: Increased speed of central processing from 22 to 32 months. *Intelligence, 20,* 41–63.

Zelazo, P. R., Zelazo, N. A., & Kolb, S. (1972). "Walking" in the newborn. *Science, 176,* 314–315.

Zhang, Y., Proenca, R., Maffei, M., Barone, M., Leopold, L., & Friedman, J. M. (1994). Positional cloning of the mouse obese gene in its human homologue. *Nature, 372,* 425–431.

Zhensun, Z., & Low, A. (1991). *A young painter: The life and paintings of Wang*

Yani: China's extraordinary young artist. New York: Scholastic.

Zhu, B.-P., Rolfs, R. T., Nangle, B. E., & Horan, J. M. (1999). Effect of the interval between pregnancies on perinatal outcomes. *New England Journal of Medicine, 340,* 589–594.

Zigler, E. (1998). School should begin at age 3 years for American children. *Journal of Developmental and Behavioral Pediatrics, 19,* 37–38.

Zigler, E. F. (1987). Formal schooling for four-year-olds? *North American Psychologist, 42*(3), 254–260.

Zigler, E., & Styfco, S. J. (1993). Using research and theory to justify and inform Head Start expansion. *Social Policy Report of the Society for Research in Child Development, 7*(2), 1-21.

Zigler, E., & Styfco, S. J. (1994). Head Start: Criticisms in a constructive context. *American Psychologist, 49*(2), 127–132.

Zigler, E., Taussig, C., & Black, K. (1992). Early childhood intervention: A promising preventative for juvenile delinquency. *American Psychologist, 47,* 997–1006.

Zimiles, H., & Lee, V. E. (1991). Adolescent family structure and educational progress. *Developmental Psychology, 27,* 314–320.

Zimmerman, B. J., Bandura, A., & Martinez-Pons, M. (1992). Self-motivation for academic attainment: The role of self-efficacy beliefs and personal goal setting. *American Educational Research Journal, 29,* 663–676.

Zimmerman, M. A., Salem, D. A., & Maton, K. I. (1995). Family structure and psychosocial correlates among urban African-American adolescent males. *Child Development, 66,* 1598–1613.

Zimrin, H. (1986). A profile of survival. *Child Abuse and Neglect, 10,* 339–349.

Zito, J. M., Safer D. J., dosReis, S., Gardner, J. F., Boles, M., & Lynch, F. (2000). Trends in the prescribing of psychotropic medications to preschoolers. *Journal of the American Medical Association, 283*(8), 1025–1030.

Zola, M. (1984). *Terry Fox.* Toronto: Grolier Limited.

Zucker, K. J., Wilson-Smith, D. N., Kurita, J. A., & Stern, A. (1995). Children's appraisals of sex-typed behavior in their peers. *Sex Roles, 33,* 703–725.

Zuckerman, B. S., & Beardslee, W. R. (1987). Maternal depression: A concern for pediatricians. *Pediatrics, 79,* 110–117.

Federal, Provincial, and Territorial Advisory Committee on Population Health. (1996). Report on the health of Canadians. Retrieved October 18, 2002, from http://www.hc-sc.gc.ca/hppb/nhrdp/healthofcanadians/v697.pdf

Learning Disabilities Association of Canada. (2001). *Environmental health: Watch out for lead!* Ottawa: Author. Retrieved September 8, 2002, from http://www.ldac-taac.ca/english/envirmnt/watchout.htm

Acknowledgments

The authors wish to thank the following copyright owners for permission to reprint the following copyrighted material.

Textual Credits

Chapter 2

Figure 2-2: Cole, M., and S.R. Cole (1989) From *The Development of Children* by Cole and Cole. Copyright © 1989 by Michael Cole, Sheila R. Cole, and Judith Boies. Used with permission of W.H. Freeman and Company.

Table 2-3: Papalia, D., S.W. Olds, and R.D. Feldman (2001) From *Human Development,* Eighth Edition. Copyright © 2001. Reprinted with the permission of The McGraw-Hill Companies.

Table 2-4: Papalia, D., S.W. Olds, and R.D. Feldman (2001) From *Human Development,* Eighth Edition. Copyright © 2001. Reprinted with the permission of The McGraw-Hill Companies.

Figure 2-3: Papalia, D. and S.W. Olds. (1997) From *Human Development,* Seventh Edition. Copyright © 1997. Reprinted with the permission of The McGraw-Hill Companies.

Figure 2-4: Papalia, D., S.W. Olds, and R.D. Feldman (2001) From *Human Development,* Eighth Edition. Copyright © 2001. Reprinted with the permission of The McGraw-Hill Companies.

Chapter 3

Figure 3-1: Papalia, D., S.W. Olds, and R.D. Feldman (2001) From *Human Development,* Eighth Edition. Copyright © 2001. Reprinted with the permission of The McGraw-Hill Companies.

Figure 3-2: Ritter, J. (1999, November 23) From "Scientists close in on DNA code," *Chicago Sun-Times,* p. 7. Reprinted with special permission from the Chicago Sun-Times, Inc. © 1991.

Figure 3-3: Papalia, D., S.W. Olds, and R.D. Feldman (2001) From *Human Development,* Eighth Edition. Copyright © 2001. Reprinted with the permission of The McGraw-Hill Companies.

Table 3-1: Adapted from AAP Committee on Genetics (1996) Copyright © by the American Academy of Pediatrics. Reprinted with permission.
Fahey, V. (1988). Adapted from "The Gene Screen: Looking in on baby," (in Tisdale, "The Mother"), *Hippocrates,* Vol. 2, No. 3, 1988, pp. 68–69. Reprinted with the permission of Time, Inc. Health.

Table 3-2: Milunsky, A. (1992) Adapted from *Heredity and Your Family's Health.* Copyright © 1992. Reprinted with the permission of Little, Brown and Company, Inc.

Figure 3-6: Babu, A. and K. Hirschhorn. (1992) From *A Guide to Human Chromosome Defects,* Third Edition [Birth Defects: Original Article Series, 28(2)].

Chapter 4

Opener: Sexton, A. (1966) Excerpt from "My Little Girl, My String Bean, My Lovely Woman," *Live or Die.* Copyright © 1966 by Anne Sexton. Reprinted with the permission of Houghton Mifflin Company and Sterling Lord Literistic, Inc. All rights reserved.

Figure 4-2: Brody J.E. (1995) From "Preventing birth defects even before pregnancy," *The New York Times,* June 28, 1995, p. C10. Copyright © 1995 by The New York Times Company. Reprinted with permission.

Figure 4.3: Fig. 1, Infant Mortality rates in Canadian provinces and the Yukon between 1961-1965 and 1991-1995 from Dzakpasu, s. et al, "The Matthew Effect: Infant Mortality in Canada and Internationally." Reproduced with permission from *Pediatrics,* Vol. 106, Page e5, Figure 1, Copyright 2000.

Chapter 5

Box 5-1: Olds, S.W. (1995) **Excerpts** [approximately 930 words] from *Having a Baby in the Himalayas.* Copyright © 1995 by Sally Wendkos Olds. Reprinted with permission.

Figure 5-1: Lagercrantz, H. and T.A. Slotkin. (1986) Adapted from "The 'stress' of being born," *Scientific American, 254*(4), 1986, 100–107. Reprinted with the permission of Patricia J. Wynne.

Table 5-1: Timiras, P.S. (1972) From *Developmental Physiology and Aging* by P.S. Timiras, Macmillan Publishing Co. Reprinted by permission of the author.

Table 5-2: Apgar, V. (1953) Adapted from "A proposal for a new method of evaluation of the newborn infant," *Current Research in Anesthesia & Analgesia, 32,* 1953, 260–267. Reprinted with the permission of Williams & Wilkins.

Table 5-3: Prechtl, H.F.R. and D.J. Beintema (1964) Adapted from "The neurological examination of the full-term newborn infant," *Clinics in Developmental Medicine,* No. 12. Reprinted with permission.
Wolff, P.H. (1966) Adapted from "The causes, controls, and organizations of behavior in the newborn," *Psychological Issues, 5* (1, Whole No. 17), 1–105. Copyright © 1966. Reprinted with the permission.

Chapter 6

Figure 6-3: Casaer, P. (1993) From "Old and new facts about perinatal brain development," *Journal of Child Psychology & Psychiatry,* Vol 34, 1993. Reprinted with the permission of Cambridge University Press.
Restak, R. (1984) From "Illustration," *The Brain.* Copyright © 1984 by Educational Broadcasting Corporation and Richard M. Restak, M.D. Reprinted with the permission of Bantam Books and Sterling Lord Literistic, Inc.

Figure 6-4: Lach, J. (1997) From "Cultivating the mind," *Newsweek,* Special Issue, Spring/Summer 1997, pp. 39–39. Copyright ©1997 by Newsweek, Inc. All rights reserved. Reprinted with permission.

Figure 6-5: Conel, J.L. (1939–1967) From *The Postnatal Development of the Cerebral Cortex.* Copyright © 1939–1967 by the President and Fellows of Harvard College. Reprinted with the permission of the publisher.

Figure 6-6: Nash, J.M. (1997) From "Fertile lands," *Time,* February 3, 1997, pp. 49–56. Copyright © 1997 by Time, Inc. Reprinted with permission.

Table 6-1: "Early human reflexes." Adapted in part from Gabbard, C. P.

(1996) From *Lifelong Motor Development*, Second Edition. Madison, WI: Brown and Benchmark.

Figure 6-7: Wegman, M.E. (1996) From "Infant mortality: Some international comparisons," *Pediatrics*, Vol 98, 1996, p. 1022. Reprinted with the permission of *Pediatrics*.

Chapter 7

Figure 7-2: Rovee-Collier-Collier, C. and K. Boller (1995) From "Current theory and research on infant learning and memory: Application to early intervention," *Infants and Young Children, 7*(3), 1–12. Copyright © 1995 by Aspen Publishers, Inc. Reprinted with the permission of the publishers.

Table 7-1: Bayley, N. (1993) From *Bayley Scales of Infant Development*, Second Edition. Copyright © 1993 by The Psychological Corporation. Reprinted with permission. All rights reserved. *Bayley Scales of Infant Development* is a registered trademark of The Psychological Corporation.

Figure 7-3: Adapted from "The Mismatch Between Opportunity and Investment" from *How Nurture Becomes Nature: The Influence of Social Structures on Brain Development* by B. Perry, 2002. http://www.ChildTrauma.org

Figure 7-5: Baillargeon, R. and J. DeVos. (1991) From "Object permanence in young infants: Further evidence," *Child Development*, Vol. 62, 1991, pp. 1227–1246. Copyright © by the Society for Research in Child Development, Inc.

Figure 7-6: Baillargeon, R. (1994) Adapted from "How do infants learn about the physical world?," *Current Directions in Psychological Science*, Vol. 3, No. 5, 1994, pp. 133–139. Reprinted with the permission of Blackwell.

Table 7-4: Papalia, D., S.W. Olds, and R.D. Feldman (2001) From *Human Development*, Eighth Edition. Copyright © 2001. Reprinted with the permission of The McGraw-Hill Companies.

Figure 7-7: Petitto, L.A. and P.F. Marentette. (1991) From "Babbling in the manual mode: Evidence for the ontogeny of language," *Science, 251*, 1991, pp. 1493–1495. Copyright © 1991 by the American Association for the Advancement of Science. Reprinted with permission.

Chapter 8

Opening Verse: Hartford, J. (1971) Excerpt from "Life Prayer," *Work Movies*. Copyright © 1968 by Ensign Music Corporation. Reprinted with permission.

Table 8-1: Sroufe, L.A. (1979) Adapted from "Socioemotional development." In J. Osofsky (ed.), *Handbook of Infant Development*. Copyright © 1979 by John Wiley & Sons. Adapted with permission.

Figure 8-1: Lewis, M. (1997) Adapted from "The self in self-conscious emotions." In S.G. Snodgrass and R.L. Thompson (eds.), "The self across psychology: Self-recognition, self-awareness, and the self-concept," *Annals of the New York Academy of Sciences*, Vol. 818. Reprinted with the permission of the New York Academy of Sciences and Professor Michael Lewis.

Table 8-2: Thomas, A. and S. Chess. (1984) Adapted from "Genesis and evolution of behavioral disorders: From infancy to early adult life," *American Journal of Psychiatry, 141* (1), 1984, pp. 1–9. Copyright © 1984 by the American Psychiatric Association. Adapted with permission.

Table 8-3: Thompson, R.A. (1998) Based on "Early sociopersonality development." In N. Eisenberg (ed.), *Handbook of Child Psychology, Volume 3*, pp. 37–39. Copyright © 1998. Reprinted with permission.

Chapter 9

Figure 9-1: Reproduced from *Canada's Food Guide to Healthy Eating*, Health Canada, 1992. © Minister of Public Works and Government Services Canada, 2002.

Figure 9-2: Ferber, R. (1985) From *Solve Your Child's Sleep Problems*. Copyright © 1985 by Richard Ferber, M.D. Reprinted with the permission of Simon & Schuster, Inc.

Table 9-2: Corbin, C.B. (1973) Adapted from *A Textbook of Motor Development*. Copyright © 1973. Reprinted with the permission of The McGraw-Hill Companies.

Figure 9-3: Kellogg, R. (1970) From *Analyzing Children's Art*. Copyright © 1969, 1970 by Rhoda Kellogg. Reprinted with the permission of Mayfield Publishing Company.

Figure 9-4: Adapted from the Statistics Canada publication "The Leading Causes of Death at Different Ages, Canada," Catalogue No. 84F0503, 1997.

Table 9-4: Kendall-Tackett, K.A., L.M. Williams, and D. Finkelhorn. (1993) Adapted from "Impact of sexual abuse on children: A review and synthesis of recent empirical studies," *Psychological Bulletin, 113*, 1993, pp. 164–180. Copyright © 1993 by the American Psychological Association. Reprinted with permission.

Chapter 10

Table 10-4: Berk, L. and R. Garvin. (1984) Adapted from "Development of private speech among low income Appalachian children," *Developmental Psychology, 202*(2), 1984, 271–284. Copyright © 1984 by the American Psychological Association. Adapted with permission.

Chapter 11

Table 11-3: Morris, R. J., and T. R. Kratochwill. (1983) Adapted from "Childhood fears," in *Treating Children's Fears and Phobias: A Behavioral Approach*, by R.J. Morris and T.R. Kratochwill, p.2. Copyright © 1983 by Allyn and Bacon. Reprinted by permission.

Stevenson-Hinde, J., & Shouldice, A. (1996). "Fearfulness: Developmental consistency." In A. J. Sameroff & M. M. Haith (Eds.), *The five to seven year shift: The age of reason and responsibility* (pp. 237–252). Reprinted with the permission of the University of Chicago Press.

Chapter 12

Opening Verse: Nash, O. (1984) **Excerpt** from "The absentees," *Verses from 1929 On*. Copyright © 1956 by Ogden Nash. Copyright © renewed 1984 by Frances Nash, Isabel Nash Eberstadt, and Linnel Nash Smith. Reprinted with the permission of Curtis Brown Ltd.

Table 12-2: Cratty, B.J. (1986) Adapted from *Perceptual and Motor Development in Infants and Children*, Third Edition. Copyright © 1986 by Allyn & Bacon. Adapted by permission.

Box 12-2: In part from Groce, N.E. and I.K. Zola (1993) "Multiculturalism, chronic illness, and disability," *Pediatrics*, Vol. 91, 1993, pp. 1048–1055. Copyright © 1993. Reprinted with permission.

Chapter 13

Table 13-2: Hoffman, M.L. (1970) From "Moral development," *Carmichael's Manual of Child Psychology, Volume 2*, edited by P.H. Mussen, pp. 261–360. Copyright © 1970. Reprinted with the permission of John Wiley & Sons, Inc. Kohlberg, L. (1964) From "The development of moral character and moral ideology," *Review of Child Development Research*, edited by M. Hoffman and L. Hoffman. Copyright © 1964 by the Russell Sage Foundation.

Table 13-4: Gardner, H. (1993, 1998). "Eight intelligences, according to Gardner." Based on *Frames of Mind: The Theory of Multiple Intelligences*. New York: Basic. Also based upon Gardner, H. (1998) "Are there additional intelligences?" In J. Kane (Ed.), *Education, Information, and Transformation: Essays on Learning and Thinking*. Englewood Cliffs, NJ: Prentice-Hall.

Chapter 14

Figure 14-1: Derived from the Statistics Canada General Social Survey-Cycle 15, "Family History," Catalogue No. 89-575, July 2002.

Table 14-1: Selman, R.L. (1980) From *The Growth of Interpersonal Understanding: Developmental and Clinical Analyses*. Reprinted with the permission of Academic Press, Inc. Selman, R.L. and A.P. Selman (1979) From "Children's ideas about friendship: A new theory," *Psychology Today*, April 1979, pp. 71–80. Copyright © 1979 by Sussex Publishers, Inc. Reprinted with the permission of *Psychology Today* magazine.

Table 14-2: Masten, A. S. & J. D. Coatsworth, (1998) "Characteristics of resilient children and adolescents." From The development of competence in favorable and unfavorable environments: Lessons from research on successful children. *American Psychologist, 53*, 205–220. Copyright © 1998 by the American Psychological Association. Reprinted with permission.

Figure 14-2: From "Work Life Balance in the New Millennium: Where are We? Where do We Need to Go?" by Linda Duxbury and Chris Higgins, 2001. The Work Network. Canadian Policy Research Networks. www.jobquality.ca/indicator_e/dem002.stm

Chapter 15

Figure 15-1: Elliott, D.S. and B.J. Morse (1993) Adapted from "Delinquency and drug use as risk factors in teenage sexual activity," *Youth and Society, 21*, 1989, p. 21–60. Reprinted with the permission of Sage Publications, Inc.

Chapter 16

Figure 16-1: Small, M.Y. and J. Kagan (1990) Adapted from *Cognitive Development*. Copyright © 1990 by Harcourt Brace & Company. Reprinted with the permission of the publisher.

Table 16-1: Kohlberg, L. (1969) Adapted from "Stage and Sequence: The cognitive-developmental approach to socialization," in *Handbook of Socialization Theory and Research*, by David A. Goslin. Reprinted with the permission of David A. Goslin.

Lickona, T.E. (1976) From *Moral Development and Behavior*. Reprinted with the permission of Thomas E. Lickona.

Table 16-2: "Self-Efficacy Questionnaire for High School Students." Zimmerman, B. J. et al. (1992) Adapted from Zimmerman, B. J., Bandura, A., & Martinez-Pons, M. (1992). Self-motivation for academic attainment: The role of self-efficacy beliefs and personal goal setting. *American Education Research Journal, 29*, 663–676. Copyright © 1992 by the American Educational Research Association. Adapted by permission of the publisher.

Chapter 17

Merriam, E. (1964) "Conversation with Myself," *A Sky Full of Poems*. Copyright © 1964, 1970, 1973 by Eve Merriam. All rights reserved. Used by permission of Marian Reiner.

Table 17-1: Marcia, J.E. (1966) Adapted from "Development and validation of ego identity status," *Journal of Personality and Social Psychology, 3*(5), 1966, pp. 551–558. Copyright © 1966 by the American Psychological Association. Adapted with permission.

Table 17-2: Marcia, J.E. (1980) From "Identity in Adolescence," in *Handbook of Adolescent Psychology*, edited by J. Adelson. Copyright © 1980 by John Wiley & Sons, Inc. Reprinted with the permission of John Wiley & Sons, Inc.

Table 17-3: Kroger, J. (1993) From "Ego Identity: An overview," in *Discussion of Ego Identity*, edited by J. Kroger. Reprinted with permission.

Photo Credits

Chapter 1

Opener: © Kenneth Gabrielsen/Liaison Agency; **p. 3:** Contemporary portrait of Victor of Aveyron from DE L'EDUCATION D'UN HOMME. Reproduced by kind permission of The British Library; **p. 15:** National Archives of Canada/PA-185530

Chapter 2

Opener: © Jon Feingersh/Corbis Stock Market; **p. 19:** Bettmann/Corbis; **p. 23:** National Library of Medicine; **p. 24:** UPI/Corbis-Bettmann; **p. 28:** © Joe McNally; **p. 29:** © Yves De Braine/Black Star; **p. 33:** A.R. Luria/Dr. Michael Cole, Laboratory of Human Cognition, University of California, San Diego; **p. 41:** © James Wilson/Woodfin Camp & Associates

Chapter 3

Opener: EyeWire Collection/Getty Images; **p. 47:** © Lester Sloan/Woodfin Camp & Associates; **p. 51:** © John Coletti/Index Stock Imagery

Chapter 4

Opener: © P. Wysocki/Explorer/Photo Researchers; **p. 76, 77:** [first page of 2 pages], top to bottom: © Petit Format/Nestle/Science Source/Photo Researchers; © Petit Format/Nestle/Science Source/Photo Researchers, © Lennart Nilsson, A CHILD IS BORN. English translation © 1966, 1977 by Dell Publishing Co. Inc.; © J.S. Allen/Daily Telegraph/International Stock; © James Stevenson/Photo Researchers; [second page of 2 pages], top to bottom: © Lennart Nilsson, BEING BORN; © Petit Format/Nestle/Science Source/Photo Researchers; © Petit Format/Nestle/Science Source/Photo Researchers; © Ronn Maratea/

International Stock Photo;
p. 85: © Mugshots/Corbis Stock Market

Chapter 5
Opener: © Kindra Clineff/Index Stock Imagery; **p. 93:** Bettmann/Corbis; **p. 100:** © J.T. Miller; **p. 108:** © Mike Teruya/Free Spirit Photography

Chapter 6
Opener: © PhotoDisc/Volume 2, People and Lifestyles; **p. 115:** Library of Congress; **p. 119:** © Myrleen Ferguson Cate/PhotoEdit; **p. 127:** top row, left to right: © Mimi Forsyth/Monkmeyer; © Lew Merrim/Monkmeyer; © Laura Dwight/Black Star; bottom row, left to right: © Mimi Forsyth/Monkmeyer; © Elizabeth Crews; © Elizabeth Crews; **p. 129:** Courtesy Children's Hospital of Michigan; **p. 134:** © Innervisions; **p. 139:** © Keren Su/Corbis

Chapter 7
Opener: © Laura Dwight/PhotoEdit; **p. 143:** Neg. No. 326799 Courtesy Department Library Services/American Museum of Natural History; **p. 147:** Courtesy of Carolyn Rovee-Collier; **p. 155:** © Laura Dwight; **p. 159:** © James Kilkelly; **p. 170:** © José Pelaez/Corbis Stock Market; **p. 174:** © Anthony Wood/Stock, Boston

Chapter 8
Opener: © Jim Erickson/Corbis Stock; **p. 177:** © Ken Heyman/Woodfin Camp & Associates; **p. 186:** © Ruth Duskin Feldman; **p. 188:** Harlow Primate Laboratory/University of Wisconsin; **p. 190:** © Cameramann/The Image Works; **p. 191:** Jonathan Finley; **p. 194:** © David Young-Wolff/PhotoEdit; **p. 203:** © Eastcott/The Image Workks; **p. 205:** © Joseph Schuyler/Stock, Boston

Chapter 9
Opener: Doug Menuez/PhotoDisc/Getty Images; **p. 211:** © Cynthia Johnson/Liaison Agency; **p. 226** © Tony Freeman/PhotoEdit

Chapter 10
Opener: © Laura Dwight; **p. 235:** Bettmann/Corbis; **p. 245:** © Shelia Sherican/Monkmeyer; **p. 249:** Ryan McVay/© PhotoDisc, Volume 66; **p. 257:** © Erika Stone/Photo Researchers; **p. 259:** CP Picture Archive/Cathie Coward

Chapter 11
Opener: © Joan Teasdale/Corbis Stock Market; **p. 265:** CP Picture Archive; **p. 275:** © Erika Stone/Photo Researchers; **p. 290:** © Owen Franken/Stock, Boston

Chapter 12
Opener: © Robert Finken/Index Stock Imagery; **p. 297:** CP Picture Archive/Jacques Nadeau; **p. 301:** © Mary Kate Denny/PhotoEdit; **p. 302:** © Van Bucher/Photo Researchers; **p. 307:** © Martin Rogers/Stock, Boston; **p. 310:** © Lawrence Megdale/Stock, Boston

Chapter 13
Opener: © Erika Stone; **p. 313:** © René Burri/Magnum Photos; **p. 317:** © Laura Dwight; **p. 321:** CP Picture Archive/Clifford Skarstedt; **p. 323:** © Laura Dwight/PhotoEdit; **p. 328:** © Jon Feingersh/Corbis Stock Market; **p. 332:** Education/Corbis Royalty-Free; **p. 340:** © Richard S. Orton; **p. 343:** © Ken Kerbs/Monkmeyer

Chapter 14
Opener: © Tom McCarthy/Corbis Stock; **p. 349:** Bettmann/Corbis; **p. 352:** © M. Justice/The Image Works; **p. 354:** Barbara Penoyar/PhotoDisc

Getty Images; **p. 355:** Geostock/PhotoDisc; **p. 359:** © Erika Stone; **p. 362:** © Deborah Davis/PhotoEdit; **p. 363:** Momatiuk/Eastcott/Woodfin Camp & Associates; **p. 366:** © Dallas & John Heaton/Stock, Boston; **p. 368:** © Erika Stone; **p. 373:** © Gabe Palmer Mugshots/Corbis Stock Market

Chapter 15
Opener: Ryan McVay/PhotoDisc/Getty Images; **p. 379:** Culver Pictures; **p. 383:** © Bill Gillette/Stock, Boston; **p. 385:** © Mary Kate Denny/PhotoEdit; **p. 391:** © Susan Rosenberg/Science Photo Library/Photo Researchers; **p. 396:** ©PhotoDisc/Volume 45 Lifestyles; **p. 401:** SW Productions/PhotoDisc/Getty Images

Chapter 16
Opener: © Doug Martin/Photo Researchers; **p. 405:** © Reuters/Corbis; **p. 412:** © Laura Dwight; **p. 420:** © Erika Stone; **p. 421:** © Spencer Grant/Photo Researchers; **p. 423:** © Richard Pasley/Stock, Boston

Chapter 17
Opener: © Paula Lerner/Index Stock Imagery; **p. 429:** CP Picture Archive/Rene Johnston; **p. 432:** © Grafton Marshall Smith/Corbis Stock Market; **p. 435:** © Bob Daemmrich/The Image Works; **p. 440:** CP Picture Archive/Kevin Frayer; **p. 444:** The Children's Defense Fund; **p. 447:** © David Young-Wolff/PhotoEdit; **p. 449:** © Steve Skjold/PhotoEdit; **p. 453:** © Richard Hutchings/PhotoEdit; **p. 455:** © A. Ramey/Stock, Boston

Index

Name Index

Clinkenbeard, P., 328
Cloutier, E., 223
Clyde, W.A., 222
CMEC, 336, 424
Cnattingius, S., 82, 85
Coatsworth, J.D., 365, 368, 375, 376
Cobb, N.J., 316
Cochrane, J.A., 139
Cofley-Corina, S.A., 172
Cohen, B., 194
Cohen, D.A., 398
Cohen, L.B., 162, 167
Cohen, S.E., 160, 195
Cohn, J.F., 197
Cohrs, M., 132
Coie, J., 365, 368, 369, 371
Coie, J.D., 230, 271, 286, 287, 365, 366
Colak, A., 436
Colburne, K.A., 279
Colby, A., 415
Cole, 32
Cole, D., 88
Cole, K., 252
Cole, P., 83
Cole, P.M., 198, 287
Coleman, C.C., 292
Coleman, H., 395
Coleman, J.S., 420
Coletta, F., 121
Coley, R.L., 361
Collier, V.P., 339
Collins, J., 395
Collins, J.G., 308
Collins, P.A., 275
Collins, R.C., 259
Collins, W.A., 64, 66, 67, 445, 446, 453
Colombo, J., 149, 158, 160
Colter, B.S., 292
Coltrane, S., 277
Committee on Children with Disabilities, 84
Concordet, J.P., 75
Conel, J.L., 124
Conger, J.J., 442, 443
Conger, R.C., 449
Conger, R.D., 387, 447
Connell, F.A., 98
Connolly, G.N., 395
Connor, S., 204, 206, 226, 301
Cook, A., 301
Cook, E.H., 70
Cooksey, E., 359
Cookson, D., 324
Coon, H., 150
Coons, S., 110
Cooper, H., 335, 421
Cooper, R.P., 80, 130, 173
Coplan, R.J., 279
Corbet, A., 106
Corbin, C., 220
Cordero, J.F., 87
Corey, L., 87
Cornelius, M.D, 85
Corns, K.M., 203
Corter, C., 289
Costello, S., 211
Coster, W.J., 230
Costigan, K.A., 79
Coté, S., 452
Coulehan, C.M., 194
Council of Ministers of Education, Canada, 331, 418
Council of Ontario Universities, 424
Council on Scientific Affairs of the American Medical Association, 399, 418
Courage, M.L., 254
Cowan, C.P., 260
Cowan, G., 272

Cowan, N., 320, 321
Cowan, P.A., 260
Cowen, P.J., 392
Cox, J., 344
Cox, T.H., 85
Coy, K.C., 201, 446
Coyle, T.R., 322
CPS Injury Prevention Committee, 136
CPS Joint Statement, 120
CPS Psychosocial Paediatrics Committee, 225
Craft, A.W., 88
Craig, C.L., 306
Craig, K.D., 181
Craig, P., 359
Craig, W.M., 370
Crain-Thoreson, C., 174, 252
Cramer, D., 362
Cramer, K.M., 205
Crane, M.M., 86
Cratty, B.J., 304
Cremo, E., 15, 285
Crespo, 303
Crick, N.R., 368
Crijnen, A.A., 371
Crittenden, P.M., 193
Crnic, K., 185
Crockenberg, S., 292
Cronk, C., 156
Crouter, A., 355, 390
Crouter, A.C., 356, 448
Crow, J.F., 57, 88
Cruttenden, L., 154
Cuca, 438
Cummings, E.M., 286, 359, 360
Cummings, M., 360
Cunliffe, T., 452
Cunningham, A.S., 120
Cunningham, F.G., 87
Curenton, S., 244, 245, 248
Currie, C., 388
Currie, W.H., 226
Curtin, S.C., 81, 89, 97, 99, 442, 443
Curtiss, S., 16
Curwin, A., 172
Cutting, A.L., 248
Cutz, E., 138
Cymerman, E., 249
Czegledy-Nagy, E.N., 138

Daiute, C., 331
Dale, P.S., 174, 252
Daling, J.R., 103
Dallel, G.E., 303
D'Alton, M.E., 89
Daly, 443
Daly, L.E., 82
Dambrosia, J.M., 98
Damon, W., 415
Danesi, M., 411
Daniel, M.H., 323
Daniel, N., 344
Daniels, D., 67
Daniels, M., 68
Daniels, T., 370
Danielsen, B., 87
Darling, N., 284, 420, 447
Darlington, R.B., 260
Darwin, C., 5, 143–144
Dauber, S.L., 332
Davalos, M., 198
David, M., 85
Davidson, J.I.F., 277
Davidson, R.J., 195
Davies, P.T., 360
Davis, B.E., 139
Davis, C.C., 204
Davis, D.L., 78, 247

Davis, J.O., 64
Davis, M., 190
Davis, N.S., 217
Davis, T.L., 246
Davis, W., 412
Davis-Kean, P.E., 356
Dawson, D.A., 395
Dawson, G., 128, 198
Day, N.L., 85, 86
De Wolff, M.S., 194
Dean, H.J., 309
Deane, K.E., 193
DeBaryshe, B.D., 453
Decarie, T.-G., 199
DeCasper, A.J., 80, 130, 166
DeCherney, A.H., 89
Deering, D., 84
DeFries, J.C., 56, 64, 67, 68, 69, 150, 172, 185
DeGarmo, D.S., 359, 361
Degenhart, K., 83
Dekovic, M., 365
Del Carmen, R.D., 194
del Valle, C., 198
Delaney, M.E., 441
Delmore, T., 441
DeLoache, J.S., 238, 239, 240, 409
Deloria, D., 259
Delveaux, K.D., 370
Demers, L.M., 384
Demo, D.H., 359
Denckla, M.B., 273
Dennis, W., 5
Denny, F.W., 222
Denny, G., 395
Dent, C.W., 448
Denton, K., 451
Derevensky, J.L., 173
DerSimonian, R., 85
deSchonen, S., 131
Deslandes, R., 420
Desrochers, S., 199
Devlin, B., 68
Devos, J., 161
Devos, R., 302
deVries, A.P.J., 223
DeVries, R., 319
Dewey, K.G., 120
DeWolf, M., 291
Deykin, E.Y., 401
d'Harcourt, C., 49, 50, 52, 95, 97, 99, 118, 119
Diamond, A., 154, 163
Diamond, L.M., 440
Diamond, M.C., 128
Diaz, R.M., 339
DiChiara, G., 396
Dick, D.M., 387
Dick-Read, G., 99
Dickinson, H.O., 88
Didow, S.M., 204
Diessner, R.E., 417
Dietitians of Canada, 119, 120, 121
Dietz, W., 369
Dietz, W.H., 121, 303, 391
DiFranza, J.R., 84
Dimant, R.J., 409
Dimiceli, S., 100
Dion, R., 13, 338, 373
DiPietro, J.A., 79
Dishion, T., 453, 454
Divon, M., 106
Dixon, W.E., 185
Dlugosz, L., 85
Doberczak, T.M., 85
Dodds, J.B., 132
Dodge, K.A., 230, 231, 271, 281, 282, 284, 286, 287, 291, 365, 368, 369, 370, 371, 386
Doherty, G., 226

Frank, A., 379–380
Frank, D.A., 86
Frank, M.A., 86
Frankel, M.S., 63
Frankenburg, W.K., 132
Franklin, A., 163
Fraser, A.M., 87, 444
Fravel, D.L., 358
Freed, G.L., 374
Freedman, D.G., 126
Freedman, D.S., 302, 303
Freeman, D., 38, 445
Freisen, 435
French, A.P., 235
French, C.D., 148
French, F., 148
French, J., 278
French, S., 400
Freud, A., 445
Freud, S., 23–25, 445
Frey, K., 128
Frideres, J.S., 338
Fried, P.A., 85
Friedman, H., 106
Friedman, J.M., 302
Friedman, L.J., 431
Friedman, R.J., 287
Friend, M., 246
Frierson, T., 369
Friesen, J.W., 338
Frigoletto, F., 98
Frisk, V., 106
Frith, U., 3
Frodi, A.M., 188
Frodi, M., 188
Fry, A.F., 321
Frydman, O., 318
Fu, 417
Fuligni, A.J., 446, 447
Fulker, D.W., 69, 185
Fuller, D., 455
Furman, L.J., 301, 449
Furman, W., 291, 367, 368
Furrow, D., 251
Furstenberg, F.F., 190, 360, 420, 440, 442, 444
Furth, H.G., 277
Fuson, K.C., 242
Futterman, 398

Gabbard, C.P., 121, 126, 127
Gabhainn, 395
Gaddis, A., 385
Gaertner, S.L., 365
Galambos, N.L., 184, 185, 447, 448
Galanello, R., 61
Galasso, L., 247
Gale, J.L., 139
Galen, B.R., 368
Gallagher, J., 81
Gallistel, C.R., 242
Galotti, K.M., 317
Gannon, P.J., 170
Gans, J.E., 384
Gansky, S.A., 303
Garasky, S., 359, 361
Garbarino, J., 230, 373, 374
Garber, J., 386
Garcia, M.M., 287
Garcia-Mila, M., 409
Gardiner, H.W., 100, 135, 136, 318, 409
Gardner, H., 326
Garfinkel, B.D., 372
Garland, A.F., 401
Garland, J.B., 133
Garmezy, N., 231, 359
Garmon, L.C., 417
Garner, 392

Garner, B.P., 278
Garner, P.W., 268
Garofalo, R., 388
Garvin, R.A., 251
Garwood, M.M., 197
Garyantes, D., 318
Gatherum, A., 354
Gatsonis, C.A., 88
Gauger, K., 363
Gauthier, R., 85
Gauvain, M., 256, 257, 315
Ge, X., 387
Gearhart, M., 241
Geary, D.C., 341
Gecas, V., 450
Geddes, C.M., 340
Geen, R.G., 369
Gelfand, D.M., 197, 198
Gélis, 49
Gelis, J., 95
Gelman, R., 239, 241, 242, 250, 253
Gelman, S.A., 239, 241, 269
Genentech Collaborative Group, 300
Genesee, F., 173, 338, 339
George, C., 195
George, T.P., 366
Gerbner, G., 395
Gerstein, D.R., 394, 395
Gersten, M.S., 230
Gertner, B.L., 252
Gervai, J., 271, 276
Gesell, A., 23, 135
Getzels, J.W., 344
Gfellner, B.M., 354, 395
Gibbons, S., 279
Gibbs, J., 415, 417
Gibbs, J.C., 413, 415, 418, 447, 453, 454, 455
Gibson, E., 134
Gibson, E.J., 159
Gibson, J.J., 134
Gibson, N.M., 333
Gibson, R., 120
Gibson, R.S., 215
Gielen, U., 417
Gilbert, S., 101
Gilbert, W.M., 87, 99
Gilbert-MacLeod, C.A., 181
Gilbreth, J.G., 359, 360
Giles-Sims, J., 282
Gill, B., 335
Gillies, P., 88
Gilligan, C., 409, 417, 434, 435
Gillis, J., 258
Ginsburg, G.S., 332
Ginsburg, H., 407
Ginsburg, H.P., 337, 341
Ginsburg-Block, M.D., 336
Gladstone, J., 190
Gladue, B.A., 438
Glasgow, K.L., 420, 421
Gleason, K.E., 194
Gleason, T.R., 247
Goldbach, M., 180
Goldberg, J.D., 89
Goldberg, W.A., 355
Golden, A., 226
Goldenberg, R.L., 82, 105, 106, 107
Goldin-Meadow, S., 171
Goldman, A., 93
Goldschmidt, I., 112
Goldsmith, M., 235
Goldstein, A.O., 395
Goldstein, A.P., 454
Goleman, D., 240
Golinkoff, R.M., 249
Golomb, C., 247
Golombok, S., 363, 438

Göncü, A., 164
Gonzalez, A., 138
Gooden, A., 417
Goodman, D.C., 107
Goodman, G., 316
Goodman, G.S., 357, 358
Goodman, R.A., 223
Goodnow, J.J., 200, 281, 283, 284, 417
Goodwin, J., 313
Goodwyn, S.W., 167
Goodz, E., 173
Gopnik, A., 169
Gordon, I., 392
Gordon, L.C., 282
Gordon, R., 255
Gordon, W., 318
Gorman, K.S., 302
Gorman, M., 10
Gortmaker, S., 84, 391
Goswami, U., 241
Gotlib, I.H., 372
Gotowiec, A., 13, 324
Gottesman, I., 70
Gottfried, A.E., 333
Gottfried, A.W., 333
Gottlieb, A., 238
Gottlieb, G., 64, 65, 66
Gottlieb, L.N., 203
Gottlieb, M.B., 78
Gottman, J.S., 362
Goubet, N., 155, 162
Gould, E., 125
Government of Saskatchewan, 225
Graber, J.A., 386, 387
Graham, S.A., 249
Gralinski, H., 199
Granger, D.A., 373
Granger, R.H., 86
Granier-Deferre, C., 80, 166
Grant, A., 15
Grant, B.F., 395
Grantham-McGregor, S., 302
Gray, M.R., 447
Graziano, A.M., 214
Graziano, M.S.A., 125
Greaves, E., 226
Greek, A., 203
Green, A.P., 189
Green, F.L., 42, 238, 244, 246
Green, J.A., 180
Green, L.W., 395
Greenbaum, C.W., 201
Greenberger, E., 355, 425, 447
Greene, S.M., 84
Greenhouse, J., 227
Greenhouse, L., 81
Greenman, P.S., 38, 366
Greenough, W.T., 128
Greenwood, C., 149
Gregg, V., 415, 417
Grether, J.K., 98
Grigorenko, E.L., 325, 334, 421
Grinspoon, 390
Grizzle, K.L., 334
Groce, N.E., 307
Gross, J.J., 108
Gross, R.T., 387
Gross, S.G., 125
Grossman, D.C., 382
Grossman, J.B., 244
Grossman, K., 188
Grotevand, H.D., 358
Grotevant, H.D., 358
Grotpeter, J.K., 368
Groude, C., 156
Gruber, H.E., 143, 144
Gruber, R., 390

Meltzoff, A.N., 156
Mendelsohn, A.L., 227
Mendelson, B.K., 391
Mendelson, M.J., 203, 391
Mennella, J.A., 80, 130
Merikangas, K.R., 68
Merle, L., 85
Merrigan, P., 205, 207
Messinger, D.S., 197
Metz, K.E., 410
Metzger, B.E., 87
Meyer, D.R., 359, 361
Meyer, M., 260
Meyers, A.F., 302
Meyers, L., 303
Meyers, T., 197
Michaelieu, Q., 435
Michelmore, P., 235, 236
Miedel, W.T., 335
Miedzian, M., 276
Mifflin, L., 370
Mihorean, K., 228, 229
Mikach, S., 363
Mikhail, M.S., 85
Milberger, S., 84
Millar, W.J., 51
Miller, A., 342
Miller, B.C., 358, 441
Miller, C., 83
Miller, J.B., 26
Miller, J.R., 15
Miller, J.Y., 394
Miller, K.F., 238, 239, 242, 409
Miller, M.W., 84
Miller, P.A., 271
Miller, P.C., 284
Miller, P.H., 15, 31, 170
Miller, S.A., 170
Miller-Jones, D., 325
Mills, D.L., 172
Mills, J.L., 85
Millstein, S.G., 388
Milne, E., 85
Milunsky, A., 59, 60
Minister of Public Works and Government
    Services Canada, 232
Ministry of Community, Family and Children's
    Services, 260
Minkler, M., 191
Miotti, P.G., 120
Miranda, S.B., 159
Mirochnick, M., 86
Mirowsky, J., 361
Miserandino, M., 332
Misra, D.P., 91
Mistretta-Hampston, J., 330
Mistry, J., 164
Mitchel, E.F., 224
Mitchell, A.A., 52, 82
Mitchell, D., 150
Mitchell, J.E., 393
Mix, K.S., 162, 318
Miyake, K., 193
Mizuta, I., 287
Mlot, C., 182, 183
Modell, J., 13
Moffatt, M., 309
Moffitt, T.E., 186, 386
Mohr, J., 219
Molenaar, P.C.M., 318
Molina, B.S.G., 446
Moller, L.C., 279
Molloy, A., 82
Mondloch, C.J., 159
Moneta, G., 445
Montague, C.T., 302
Montgomery, L.E., 225

Montour, L.T., 309
Moody, J., 389
Moon, C., 80, 130
Moon, R.Y., 139
Mooney, K.C., 214
Moore, C., 285
Moore, C.A., 57
Moore, K.A., 441, 442
Moore, M.K., 155, 161
Moore, S.E., 82
Moran, G., 194
Moran, J III, 121
Morange, F., 159
Morelli, G., 38, 187
Moretensen, E.L., 83
Moretti, M.E., 83
Morgan, G.A., 198
Morielli, A., 138
Morild, I., 138
Morison, P., 365
Morison, S.J., 129, 150
Morris, P.A., 31
Morris, R., 289
Morris, R.D., 341
Morrison, D., 252
Mortenson, 69
Mortimer, J.T., 425
Morton, T., 373
Moses, L.J., 199, 245
Mosher, P., 206
Mosher, W.D., 51, 439
Mosier, C., 164
Mosko, S., 140
Moss, E., 332
Mota, V.L., 371
Mounts, N., 453
Mounts, N.S., 447
Mounzih, K., 382
MTA Cooperative Group, 342
Mueller, H.H., 260
Muhlenbruck, L., 335, 421
Muir, D., 169, 246
Muir, D.W., 80
Mullan, D., 388
Müller, M., 379
Muller-Wieland, D., 302
Mullin, J., 329
Mullins, R., 88
Mullis, I.V.S., 336
Mumma, G.H., 365
Mumme, D.L., 269
Munakata, Y., 162
Mundy, R.L., 309
Munn, P., 203
Muñoz, K.A., 215, 301, 303
Murachver, T., 255
Murchison, C., 5
Murphy, B.C., 292, 353
Murphy, C.C., 105
Murphy, K.R., 342
Murphy, P.D., 63
Murray, A.D., 99, 279
Murray, J.A., 107
Murray, K., 201
Murrell, A., 365
Mussen, P., 353
Mussen, P.H., 387
Must, A., 303, 391
Mustard, J.F., 31, 128, 150, 207, 260
Mutter, J.D., 100
Myers, N., 253
Myhr, T.L., 105
Mylander, C., 171

Nabors, L.A., 206
Nadel, L., 163
Naeye, R.L., 84

Nafstad, P., 225
Nagel, S.K., 355
Nagin, D., 452
Nakajima, H., 140
Nandakumar, R., 249
Nangle, B.E., 105
Napiorkowski, B., 86
Nash, A., 204
Nash, J.M., 125
Nathanielsz, P.W., 105
Nationa, R.L., 99
National Advisory Committee on Immunization
    (NACI), 139
National Center for Chronic Disease Prevention
    and Health, 212, 215, 299, 300
National Center for Education Statistics (NCES)
    (US), 359, 361, 420, 422, 423, 425
National Center for Health Statistics, 212, 215,
    299, 300, 310, 382
National Commission on Youth, 425
National Committee for Citizens in Education
    (NCCE), 401
National Crime Prevention Council, 454
National Enuresis Society (U.S.), 219
National Institute of Child Health and Human
    Development (NICHD), 120
National Institute of Mental Health (NIMH) (US),
    369
National Institute of Neurological Disorders and
    Stroke (NINDS) (US), 70
National Institute on Drug Abuse (U.S.), 36, 396
National Institutes of Health Consensus
    Develpoment Panel on Physical Activity and
    Cardiovascular Health, 389
National Parents' Resource Institute for Drug
    Education, 394
National Reading Panel, 330
National Research Council, 229, 230, 231, 232,
    419, 424
National Television Violence Study (NTVS), 369
Nawrocki, T., 198
NCES, 338
Nduati, R., 120
Needell, B., 358
Needleman, H., 87–88
Needleman, H.L., 227
Neiderman, D., 154
Neisser, 149, 257, 259, 271, 272, 273, 324, 325
Neisser, U., 68
Nelson, C.A., 163
Nelson, K., 254, 255
Nelson, K.B., 98, 99
Nelson, L.J., 81, 279, 286
Neppl, T.K., 279
Nesbitt, T.S., 87
Ness, R.B., 86
Netherlands State Institute for War
    Documentation, 379
Neto, F., 451
Neugebauer, R., 82
Neumann, H., 424
Neumann, N., 120
Neville, H.J., 172
Nevis, S., 159
Newacheck, P.W., 308
Newcomb, A.F., 365, 366, 367
Newcombe, N., 163, 239
Newcombe, N.S., 255
Newman, D.L., 186
Newman, G.R., 395
Newman, J., 120
Newman, N.M., 139
Newport, 166
Newport, E., 171
Newport, E.L., 16, 338
Newson, E., 217
Newson, J., 217

Index

quantitative change, 8
timeline of pioneers in field, 6
child-directed speech, 173–174
childbirth
attendants, 100–101
and bonding, 109
Caesarean delivery, 98–99
changes in, 95–97
complications. *See* childbirth complications
delivery methods, 98–100
doula, 101
electronic fetal monitoring, 98
in the Himalayas, 96
humanization of, 97
Lamaze method, 99
medicated delivery, 99–100
midwives, 100
natural childbirth, 99
parturition, 97
prepared childbirth, 99
process, 97–101
safety of, 96–97
settings, 100–101
stages, 97–98
unmedicated delivery, 99–100
vaginal births, 98–99
walking epidurals, 100
childbirth complications
birth trauma, 104
low birth weight, 104–107
postmaturity, 107
stillbirth, 107
supportive environment and, 107–109
childhood depression, 372–373
children with disabilities
inclusion, 342
learning problems. *See* learning problems
Children's Behavior Questionnaire, 185
China, one-child policy in, 290
cholesterol, 121
chorion control studies, 64, 78
chorionic villus sampling, 89
chromosomal abnormalities
described, 60
Down syndrome, 60
mutations, 57
sex chromosome abnormalities, 61
trisomy-21, 60
chromosomes, 54
chronic medical conditions, 308
chronosystem, 33
circadian timing system, 390
circular reactions, 152
class inclusion, 316
classical conditioning, 27, 146
clone, 49
co-regulation, 354
co-twin control studies, 64
cocaine, and pregnancy, 85–86
code mixing, 173
code switching, 173
cognition, and environment, 66
cognitive development
in adolescence. *See* adolescent cognitive development
behaviourist approach, 145–147
classic approaches, 145–157
cognitive neuroscience approach, 163–164

critical periods, deprivation during, 15
described, 8
in early childhood. *See* early childhood cognitive development
and emotions, 180
in infancy. *See* infant and toddler cognitive development
information-processing approach, 158–163, 253–255, 320–323
language development. *See* language development
in middle childhood. *See* middle childhood cognitive development
newer approaches, 157–164
Piagetian approach, 152–157, 237–248, 407
psychometric approach, 147–152, 255–257
and self-concept, 267–268
social-contextual approach, 158, 164
cognitive neuroscience approach
defined, 31, 158
explicit memory, 163
implicit memory, 163
working memory, 163
cognitive perspective
accommodation, 29
adaptation, 29
assimilation, 29
cognitive neuroscience approach, 31
cognitive-stage theory, 29–30
defined, 29
equilibration, 29
gender development, 274–275
information-processing approach, 30
Jean Piaget, 29–30
neo-Piagetian theories, 30–31
organization, 29
schemes, 29
cognitive-stage theory, 29–30
cohort, 14
collaborative process of growth, 33
commitment, 432–434
committed compliance, 202
compensatory preschool programs, 259–260
componential element, 327
computational models, 30
conception
changing ideas about, 49–50
fertilization, 50–51
two-seed theory, 50
concordant, 64
concrete operations
class inclusion, 316
cognitive advances, 315–318
conservation, 317
culture, influence of, 318
deductive reasoning, 317
defined, 315
horizontal décalage, 317
inductive reasoning, 315–316
moral reasoning, 318–320
neurological development, influence of, 318
number, 317–318
seriation, 315
space, 315
transitive inference, 316
conduct disorder (CD), 371
confident children, 186
congenital adrenal hyperplasia, 273

conscience
committed compliance, 202
defined, 201
development of, 200–202
inhibitory control, 201
origins of, 201–202
consensus, 7–8, 23
conservation, 242, 317
constructive play, 278
contextual element, 327
contextual perspective
bioecological theory, 31–33
chronosystem, 33
defined, 31
exosystem, 33
Lev Vygotsky, 33–34
macrosystem, 33
mesosystem, 33
microsystem, 32–33
scaffolding, 34
social component, emphasis on, 34
socio-cultural theory, 33–34
Urie Bronfenbrenner, 31–33
zone of proximal development (ZPD), 33
continuous development, 22
continuous self, 267
contraceptive use, 441
control group, 40
conventional morality, 413
conventional social gestures, 167
convergent thinking, 344
corporal punishment, 281, 282
correlational studies, 39
correlations
active correlations, 66–67
described, 39
evocative correlations, 66
genotype-environment correlation, 66–67, 67
passive correlations, 66
reactive correlations, 66
corticotropin-releasing hormones (CRH), 97
cow's milk, 120–121
crawling, 133
creative children. *See* gifted children
creativity, 344
crisis, 432–434
critical periods, 14–15, 109
cross-cultural differences
see also culture
fatherhood, 189
parenting styles, 284–285
social interaction, 187
temperament, 186–187
cross-cultural research, 38
cross-modal transfer, 159
cross-sectional studies, 42–43
crying, 111, 165, 180–181
cultural bias, 325–326
culture
see also cross-cultural differences
aggression, influence on, 287–288
and attachment, 193, 194
code mixing, 173
code switching, 173
concrete operations, influence on, 318
education, influence on, 337–338
female genital mutilation, 418
gender development, influences on, 276–277

effectiveness of, 151
early sensory capacities, 129–131
"easy" children, 184
eating disorders
    anorexia nervosa, 391–393
    bulimia nervosa, 392, 393
    in middle childhood, 303
economic stress, 448–449
ectoderm, 75
education
    active engagement, 422
    in adolescence, 418–425
    Asian-Canadian children, 337
    bilingual education, 338
    cultural influences, 337–338
    dropping out of high school, 422
    dual-language learning, 339
    in early childhood. See early childhood
        education
    educational system, 333–336
    English-immersion approach, 338
    French immersion, 339
    gifted children, 343–344
    grade 1, 331–332
    Heritage Language Programs, 338
    homework debate, 335
    intelligence, influence on, 324
    learning problems. See learning problems
    in middle childhood, 331–344
    non-university bound students, 424
    quality of schooling, 421
    recent immigration, 421
    school achievement. See school achievement
    second-language, 338–339
    self-fulfilling prophecy, 333
    social promotion, 334
    summer school, 335–336
    two-way learning, 339
educational and vocational preparation,
    423–424
educational system, 333–336
ego, 24
egocentrism, 243
Einstein, Albert, 235–236, 252
elaboration, 322
elaborative style, 255
electronic fetal monitoring, 98
embryonic disk, 75
embryonic stage, 78
embryoscopy, 89
emergent literacy, 252–253
emotional maltreatment, 228, 231
emotions
    brain growth and, 182–183
    and cognitive development, 180
    crying, 180–181
    defined, 179
    directed toward the self, 269
    in early childhood, 268–270
    early signs of, 180–181
    emotional growth in middle childhood, 353
    ethological perspective, 180
    laughing, 181
    self-conscious, 182
    simultaneous, 269–270
    smiling, 181
    timing of development, 181–182
empathy, 244

encoding, 320
endoderm, 75
English-immersion approach, 338
enrichment, 344
enuresis, 219
environment
    characteristics influenced by, 68–70
    cognition and, 66
    defined, 10
    genotype-environment correlation, 66–67
    genotype-environment interaction, 66
    and health, 224–228
    vs. heredity, 21
    heredity, working with, 64–68
    home environment, impact of, 150
    illness, exposure to, 225
    intelligence, 68–69
    lead, exposure to, 227–228
    non-shared environmental effects, 67
    obesity, 68
    personality and, 66
    physical traits, 68
    physiological traits, 68
    poverty. See poverty
    prenatal development, influences on, 80–88
    prenatal environment, effects of, 64
    relative influences of, 61–64
    school achievement, 68–69, 332–338
    smoking, exposure to, 225
episodic memory, 163, 254
equilibration, 29
Equipping Youth To Help One Another
    (EQUIP), 454–455
Erikson, Erik, 25–26
Erikson's theory
    autonomy vs. shame and doubt, 200
    basic trust vs. basic mistrust, 26, 191
    described, 25–26
    identity vs. identity confusion, 431–432
    industry vs. inferiority, 352
    initiative vs. guilt, 270
estrogens, 273
ethics of research, 44, 128
ethnic group, 13
ethnicity
    identity formation, 435–436
    influence of, 13
    intelligence, influence on, 324–325
    self-hatred, 435
ethnographic studies, 38
ethological perspective, 31
ethology, 31
evocative correlations, 66
exosystem, 33
experience
    the brain, effect on, 128–129
    early emotional development, 128
experiential element, 327
experimental group, 39–40
experiments
    conduct of, 39
    confounding, 40
    control group, 40
    defined, 39
    degree of control, 41
    dependent variables, 40
    experimental group, 39–40
    field, 41

generalized results, 41
    independent variables, 40
    laboratory, 41
    natural, 41
    random assignment, 40
explicit memory, 163
extended family, 10–12
extended-family households, 10, 190
external memory aids, 321
extinguishment, 28
eyewitness testimony of children, 240

false beliefs, 245–246
family
    atmosphere, 354–357
    conflict, 446–447
    connectedness, feelings of, 445
    extended family, 10–12
    extended-family households, 190
    influence of, 10–12
    intelligence, influence on, 257
    interactions during adolescence, 445–446
    meanings of, 10
    middle childhood, effect on, 353–363
    moral development and, 417
    nuclear family, 10, 190
    school achievement, influence on, 332–333,
        419–420
    sibling relationships, 363
    social capital, 420
    structure of. See family structure
family structure
    and adolescence, 448
    adoptive families, 357–358
    divorce, 359–361
    extended-family households, 10, 190
    gay or lesbian parents, 362–363
    non-traditional, 357
    nuclear family, 10, 190
    one-parent families, 361
    overview, 357
    stepfamilies, 362
    traditional, 357
family studies, 62
family systems theory, 189
family therapy, 373
fantasy, vs. reality, 246–247
fantasy play. See pretend play
fast mapping, 249
fathers
    among the Aka, 189
    in Cameroon, 189
    cross-cultural differences in role, 189
    economic success, and involvement with
        children, 356
    in Inner Mongolia, 189
    paternal custody, 359
    psychosocial development, role in, 188–189
    puberty, effect on, 386
female genital mutilation, 418
fertilization, 50–51
fetal alcohol effects (FAS/E), 73
fetal alcohol syndrome (FAS), 73, 84
fetal blood sampling, 89
fetal stage, 78–79
fetal welfare, vs. mothers' rights, 81
fidelity, 432
field experiments, 41

reelin, 69
reflexes
    early, 126–127
    locomotor, 126
    postural, 126
    primitive, 126
    reflex behaviour, 126
regression, 25
rehearsal, 321
reinforcement, 28
relational aggression, 286
reliability, 36
repetitive style, 255
representational ability, 153
representational gestures, 167
representational mappings, 268
representational systems, 351
repression, 25
research
    applied research, 7
    basic research, 7
    correlations, 39
    cross-cultural, 38
    ethics of, 44, 128
    methods. See research methods
    operational definitions, 36
    principles, 44
    and theory, 34
    variables, 39
    violation-of-expectations. See violation-of-expectations
research designs
    basic, 37–42
    case studies, 37
    correlational studies, 39
    cross-sectional studies, 42–43
    developmental, 42–43
    ethnographic studies, 38
    experiments, 39–41
    longitudinal studies, 42
    microgenetic studies, 43
    sequential studies, 43
research methods
    basic research designs, 37–42
    data collection, 35–37
    developmental research designs, 42–43
    generalized results, 35
    population, 35
    sampling, 34–35
    scientific method, 34
    "still-face" paradigm, 197
reserved children, 186
residential schools, 15
resilience, 8
resilient children, 375–376
respiratory distress syndrome, 105
retrieval, 320
risk factors, 12
Rothbart Infant Behavior Questionnaire, 185
rough-and-tumble play, 304

Sainte-Marie, Buffy, 265–266
sample, 35
sampling, 34–35
scaffolding, 34, 257
schema, 275
schemes, 29, 152
schizophrenia, 69

school achievement
    see also education
    academic motivation, 418–419
    in adolescence, 418–421
    and attachment, 332
    culture, influence of, 337–338
    environmental influences, 68–69, 332–338
    family, influence of, 332–333, 419–420
    and heredity, 68–69
    maternal employment, effect of, 355–356
    and quality of schooling, 421
    reasoning skills and, 334
    self-efficacy beliefs, 418–419
    socio-economic status, 257, 332–333, 419–420
School Achievement Indicators Program, 331
school phobia, 371–372
schools. See education
scientific method, 34
script, 254
second-language education, 338–339
secondary sex characteristics, 385
secular trend, 383–384
secure attachment, 192
selective attention, 322
the self. See the developing self
self-awareness, 182
self-concept, 199–200, 267–268
self-definition, 268
self-efficacy beliefs, 418–419
self-esteem, 270–271, 351–352, 435
self-fulfilling prophecy, 333
self-hatred, 435
self-regulation, 200–201
self-reports, 35–36
semantic memory, 163
sensitive periods, 15
sensorimotor stage, 152–154
sensory memory, 320
separation anxiety, 195
separation anxiety disorder, 371
sequential studies, 43
seriation, 315
sex, determination of, 54–55
sex-category constancy, 274
sex chromosomes, 54
sex-linked inheritance, 57, 59
sexual abuse, 228, 231
sexual attraction, 386–387
sexual evolution, 438–439
sexual maturity, 385–386
sexual orientation, 437–438, 439–440
sexual risk taking, 440–442
sexuality
    contraceptive use, 441
    early sexual activity, 440–441
    gay identity and behaviour, 439–440
    information about sex, 442
    lesbian identity and behaviour, 439–440
    risk taking, 440–442
    sexual behaviour, 438–440
    sexual evolution, 438–439
    sexual orientation, 437–438
    teenage pregnancy, 442–444
sexually transmitted diseases (STDs)
    in adolescence, 396–398
    AIDS/HIV. See AIDS; HIV
    common, 397

    gender differences, 396, 398
    and pregnancy, 86–87
    protection against, 399
shyness, 185
siblings
    adolescents and, 449
    arrival of new baby, 203
    differences among, 67
    interaction, 203–204
    parenting, 289–291
    relationships, 363
    rivalry, 289–290
sickle-cell anemia, 57
simultaneous emotions, 269–270
single representations, 268
situational compliance, 202
sleep
    adolescents and, 389–390
    bedtime struggles, 217–218
    bedwetting, 219
    circadian timing system, 390
    customs, 140
    disturbances and disorders, 217–219
    in early childhood, 214, 217–219
    in infancy, 110
    nightmares, 218
    patterns, 110, 217–219
    problems, 217–219
    sleep terrors, 218–219
    sleepwalking, 218
    transitional objects, 217
"slow-to-warm-up" children, 184
small-for-gestational age infants, 104
smell, in infancy, 130
smiling, 181
smoking
    exposure to, 225
    peer influence, 396
    and pregnancy, 84–85
    and risky health behaviours, 395
social capital, 420
social cognition, 244–245
social cognitive theory, 275
    see also social learning theory
social construction
    defined, 9
    periods of development, 9
social-contextual approach
    defined, 158
    guided participation, 164
    zone of proximal development (ZPD), 164
social-information processing, and aggression, 368
social interaction
    child-directed speech, 173–174
    cross-cultural differences, 187
    in early childhood, 252–253
    and language development, 172–173
    model, 254
    prelinguistic period, 172
    Turner's syndrome and, 247–248
    vocabulary development, 172–173
social learning theory
    defined, 28
    gender development, 275–276
social phobia, 372
social promotion, 334
social referencing, 198–199

Multimedia Courseware for Child Development

Charlotte J. Patterson

Table of Contents